Criminal Law
IN SOUTH AFRICA

CRIMINAL JUSTICE

OXFORD
UNIVERSITY PRESS

Oxford University Press is a department of the University of Oxford. It furthers the University's objective of excellence in research, scholarship, and education by publishing worldwide. Oxford is a registered trade mark of Oxford University Press in the UK and in certain other countries.

Published in South Africa by
Oxford University Press Southern Africa (Pty) Limited

Vasco Boulevard, Goodwood, N1 City, Cape Town, South Africa, 7460
P O Box 12119, N1 City, Cape Town, South Africa, 7463

First published 2012
Third Edition published in 2018

Criminal Law in South Africa

ISBN 978 019 072362 0

Second impression 2014
Third impression 2015
Fourth impression 2015

Typeset in Utopia Std Regular 9.5pt on 12pt
Printed on [insert paper quality e.g. acid-free paper]

Acknowledgements
Publisher: Penny Lane
Project manager: Lindsay-Jane Lücks
Copy editor: Lee-Ann Ashcroft
Proofreader: Language Mechanics
Indexer: Language Mechanics
Typesetter: Barbara Hirsch
Cover designer: Judith Cross
Designers: Studio designers
Printed and bound by: Academic Press

The authors and publisher gratefully acknowledge permission to reproduce copyright material in this book. Every effort has been made to trace copyright holders, but if any copyright infringements have been made, the publisher would be grateful for information that would enable any omissions or errors to be corrected in subsequent impressions.

Contents in brief

Contents

Preface

This book, aimed primarily at students, law teachers and practitioners, sets out the general principles of criminal law in South Africa as well as the most important common law and statutory crimes that are criminalised under this country's law. The growing importance of international and transnational criminal law prompts the discussion of these topics from a South African perspective and is dealt with in Part Four of this book. South Africa's possible withdrawal from the Rome Statute of the International Criminal Court (ICC) receives specific attention.

South African criminal law is not codified. One of the aims of this book is therefore not only to set out the legal principles but also to illustrate the richness of sources and influences that have shaped and are still shaping South African criminal law. This is a dynamic subject and we have aimed to reflect that in our basic method and presentation. An additional critical aspect which is introduced in Chapter 1 is the debate on the decolonisation of the law. This important, yet contested, topic deserves serious attention. It is not something that will be fleshed out in this edition alone; rather it is expected that decolonisation as methodology will inform critical aspects of future editions of this book.

A brief overview of the most important features of criminal procedure in South Africa is included in Chapter 2. This book deals with substantive criminal law, but an outline of the criminal process can help to contextualise the substantive material, especially for the reader for whom this text is a first encounter with criminal justice.

We have aimed to set out the general principles and specific crimes as clearly as possible, without losing sight of the underlying historical, cultural and normative foundations. We have identified the impact of the Constitution and, in particular, the Bill of Rights on the development of South African criminal law. Important areas of law reform have been pointed out with reference to recent jurisprudence, for example sexual offences and the position of children, the decriminalisation of the private use of cannabis (dagga), the abolishment of the defence of reasonable disciplinary chastisement of children by parents/guardians, and the constitutional parameters of euthanasia/assisted suicide.

This book is not primarily a legal-comparative work, but we have highlighted (where appropriate) the value and impact of foreign law on the past and possible future development of South African criminal law.

The body of general principles of South African criminal law reflects the rich history of legal and cultural influences that have shaped, over many generations, modern criminal law doctrine. The first two parts of the book deal with these principles. The role of case law in the formation and expression of general principles cannot be overstated, and we have discussed the most important cases as well as relevant academic commentary.

It has been noted above that South African criminal law is not codified. It is therefore not always easy to discuss specific crimes within the confines of a book like this - there are simply too many. We have therefore opted for a systematic discussion of specific crimes (as one would normally find in textbooks on criminal law). The system of classification is fairly orthodox, but includes some critical reflection as to why the crimes have been categorised as such. The choices of specific crimes were informed, firstly, by the system of classification that reflects broad protected interests (crimes against the person, crimes against property, and so on) and, secondly, to illustrate the scope of human (and corporate) activities that are criminalised under modern South African criminal law (from crimes against morality, to organised crime, to commercial crime and many more).

An important aim of the book is to invite the reader to engage critically with the material. While this approach is reflected in the general tone and style of the book, we have also included 'Discussion boxes' to draw specific attention to areas of the law that perhaps deserve further debate, or areas that are subject to imminent law reform.

We want to thank Penny Lane, Lindsay-Jane Lücks and their colleagues at Oxford University Press for general and technical support, and Lee-Ann Ashcroft for her excellent work as copy editor.

Every effort was made to state the law as at August 2018.

Gerhard Kemp
Stellenbosch
September 2018

About the authors

Gerhard Kemp
BA LLB LLM LLD (Stellenbosch), ILSC (Antwerp)
Gerhard Kemp is professor in the Faculty of Law at Stellenbosch University, where he lectures in criminal law, criminal procedure and international criminal law. He is also a fellow of the Stellenbosch Institute for Advanced Studies (STIAS). Gerhard is regional editor of *Criminal Law Forum*, assistant editor of the *African Yearbook on International Humanitarian Law* and a member of the South African Academy of Science and Art. He is an advocate of the High Court of South Africa, and serves on the board of directors and executive committee of the Institute for Justice and Reconciliation, Cape Town. Gerhard is an NRF-rated, level B3 (internationally acclaimed) researcher, focusing his work in the fields of criminal law, criminal procedure, international criminal law and international humanitarian law. He is a senior research fellow of the Robert Bosch Academy in Berlin and a fellow of the Alexander von Humboldt Stiftung, affiliated with Humboldt University, Berlin.

Dumile Baqwa
BProc (Durban-Westville), LLM (Georgetown)
Dumila Baqwa is a lecturer in the School of Law at the University of KwaZulu-Natal, Howard College Campus. His teaching focuses on specific criminal offences, the foundations of South African law and legal studies. He publishes research in the fields of commercial law and criminal law.

Christopher Gevers
LLB (KwaZulu-Natal), LLM (London School of Economics)
Christopher Gevers is a lecturer in the School of Law at the University of KwaZulu-Natal, Howard College Campus, where his teaching focuses on human rights and international criminal law. He has acted as an adviser to litigants in cases concerning international law in South Africa and abroad, and as a consultant for various non-governmental organisations on issues relating to human rights and international law. His research focuses broadly on international law, with specific interest in international criminal law, international humanitarian law and international legal theory.

Brian Leslie
BA LLB (Cape Town), LLM (Rhodes)
Brian Leslie is a senior lecturer in the Department of Law at the University of Zululand where he currently lectures in tax law, labour law and administrative law, and chairs the university's legal committee. He is an advocate of the High Court of South Africa.

Robin Palmer
BA LLB (Witwatersrand), PG Dip Maritime Law, LLM (Natal)
Robin Palmer is professor of law at the University of Canterbury, New Zealand, and an honorary research fellow at the University of KwaZulu-Natal. He is an advocate of the High Court of South Africa, and practices as an associate member of the KwaZulu-Natal bar. Professor Palmer has been an instructor at the Law Society of South Africa (LSSA) School for Legal Practice in Durban for more than 20 years.

Anton Steynberg

BCom LLB (KwaZulu-Natal)

Anton Steynberg is a senior trial lawyer in the Office of the Prosecutor at the International Criminal Court, The Hague (ICC). He has practised as a prosecutor for the past 27 years, prosecuting a wide range of criminal cases in both the lower and superior courts of South Africa. In 2001, he joined the Directorate of Special Operations ('Scorpions') where he led the investigation and prosecution of many complex cases involving organised crime, corruption and economic crime. He was appointed Deputy Director of Public Prosecutions in 2002. Prior to 2010, he was a regular guest lecturer on criminal procedure and organised crime legislation at the Associated Law Society's School for Legal Practice, and also lectured in the University of KwaZulu-Natal's postgraduate diploma programme in forensic accounting. Since 2010, Anton has led investigation and prosecution teams at the ICC in the Democratic Republic of Congo, Mali and Kenya.

Shelley Walker

BA LLB (Natal), LLM (KwaZulu-Natal)

Shelley Walker is a lecturer in the School of Law on the Howard College campus of the University of KwaZulu-Natal, where she teaches criminal law. She is a former public prosecutor and an advocate of the High Court of South Africa, in which capacity she practised at the Durban bar from 1996 to 2002.

About the book

Criminal Law in South Africa is a pedagogically rich learning resource. This book is designed to form a strong foundation of understanding, to develop the skills to engage independently and judiciously with legal principles, and to create skilled and proficient lawyers.

Brief description of features:

Discussion boxes: This pedagogical feature considers the policy ramifications of the law; how the law works in practice; its logic and consistency with other principles; possible alternatives, and other key issues. This feature instils a broader and deeper understanding of the subject matter. It stimulates critical and reflective discussion, supports independent thinking, and develops the ability to engage meaningfully with relevant issues.

Diagrams: These provide overviews, and explain key concepts visually. This feature reinforces understanding, helps to clarify key concepts, and shows more clearly the interrelationship between distinct legal concepts and processes.

Tables: These are used to distinguish content, and to aid conceptualisation.

Chapter in essence: This section summarises the key areas and core topics covered in the chapter in a succinct list of essential points.

How to answer problem-type questions: Annexure 1 presents a seven-step methodology for answering problem-type questions in tests and examinations.

Bibliography: A list of reference works appears at the end of the book. The works cover the most important South African sources (including common law authorities) as well as relevant international and comparative sources.

Glossary: This contains explanations for the words and phrases that constitute the jargon, or terms of art, which are particular to the area of study covered in the book. Latin phrases and many others are explained and contextualised.

PART ONE

General introduction

Chapter 1

Introduction to criminal law

CHAPTER OBJECTIVES

The objectives of this chapter are to:
- introduce the concepts of crime and the criminal justice system
- explain the origins of criminal law
- describe the factors that influence the criminalisation of conduct
- explain the principal sources of modern South African criminal law
- introduce the debate on the decolonisation of criminal law
- describe some of the fundamental principles and values that underlie South African criminal law
- provide a brief overview of the principal elements of criminal liability and theories of punishment.

1.1 Criminal law and its place in the legal system

The criminal justice system is the part, or subsystem, of the national legal system that determines the circumstances and procedures according to which the state may punish people and legal entities for criminal conduct.

We usually draw a distinction between the so-called substantive aspects of the criminal justice system and its procedural aspects. The study of **criminal law** generally focuses on the substantive law, namely the principles of law according to which criminal liability (guilt or innocence) is determined, while the *law of criminal procedure*, together with the *law of evidence*, generally focuses on the procedures used to decide criminal liability and theories of punishment.

A study of the substantive criminal law, in turn, requires two things:
1. An examination of the general principles of liability (the principles applicable to all crimes generally)
2. An examination of the definitions and particular requirements of the various individual crimes (also called specific offences)[1]

We must also draw a distinction between *national criminal law* and **international criminal law**. National criminal law or criminal law usually refers to internal or domestic criminal law, which is governed by the legal system of the country concerned. International criminal law, a more recent branch of the law, is viewed by some as a branch of public international law. We suggest here that international criminal law is, at least in the material sense, and to a growing extent also in the institutional and procedural sense, a discipline in its own right. We discuss the aspects of international criminal law relevant to South African criminal law in Part 4 of this book.[2]

Another area of criminal law that has developed in more recent years is *transnational criminal law*. This branch of the law is concerned with cooperative arrangements between countries or nation states aimed at preventing and combating the type of crimes that are

1 Strictly speaking, the word 'offence' should only be used for statutory and not common law crimes. The term 'crime' is a generic term that can be used to refer to either common law crimes or statutory offences. In this book, however, as is general practice, the terms are used interchangeably.

2 For a general discussion, see Cassese A *International Criminal Law* (2003) 15–42, and earlier, Sunga LS *The Emerging System of International Criminal Law: Developments in Codification and Implementation* (1997) 7. Some prominent authors discuss international criminal law as a discipline equal to the other disciplines in the broader field of criminal justice, namely criminal law and criminal procedure. See, for instance, Van den Wyngaert C, Vandromme S and De Smet B *Strafrecht en Strafprocesrecht in Hoofdlijnen* 9 ed (2015).

commonly committed across national borders, such as terrorism, drug trafficking, money laundering and human trafficking. This area of the law also deals with matters such as extraditing suspected criminals and securing witnesses and evidence in foreign countries.[3]

Lastly, we need to distinguish between criminal law and **criminology**. In criminal law, we study crime purely from a legalistic and normative perspective: the legal elements that constitute a crime and the principles of law that apply to criminal liability. Criminology, however, is concerned with the study of crime and criminal behaviour from a sociological and psychological perspective, seeking to understand the underlying causes and effects of criminal behaviour in society, and methods of controlling and preventing crime.[4]

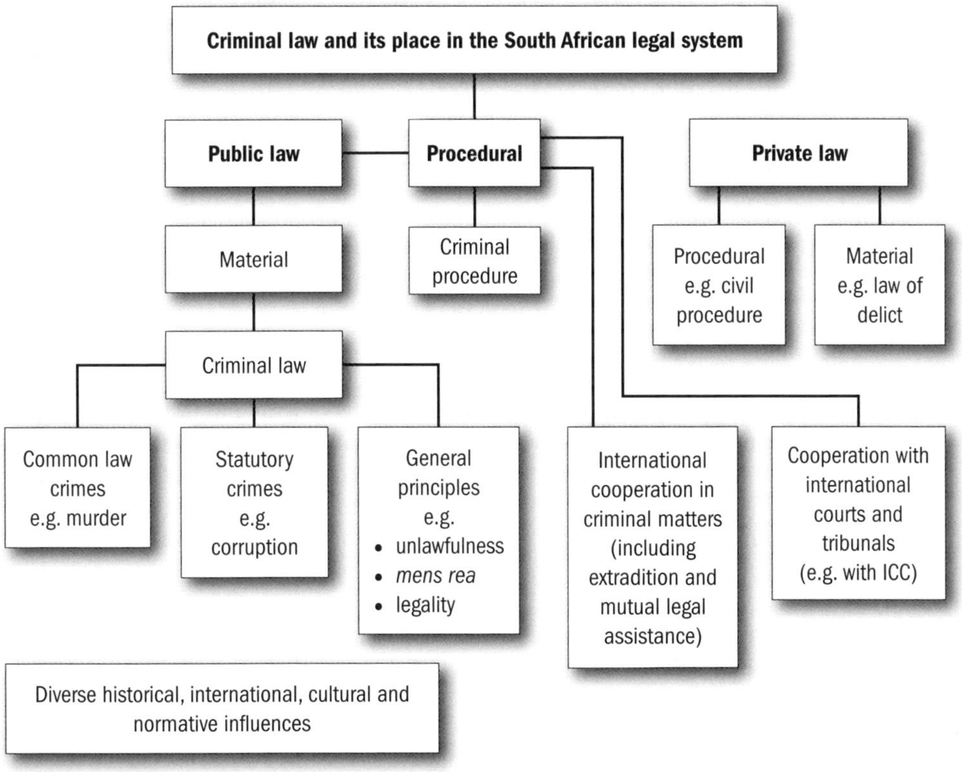

Figure 1.1 *Criminal law and its place in the legal system*

1.2 The concept of crime

The term 'crime' is a familiar word in common use among members of the public. Most people can readily name a range of common law crimes, such as murder, robbery, theft and housebreaking, as well as statutory offences such as reckless and negligent driving, unlawful possession of drugs, and the failure to submit income tax returns. However, most people would struggle to come up with a comprehensive definition of a crime. Some may suggest that a crime involves conduct that is bad, harmful or damaging to society, but if you were to

3 See, for example, the International Co-operation in Criminal Matters Act 75 of 1996 and the Extradition Act 67 of 1962. For a discussion, see Du Toit et al *Commentary on the Criminal Procedure Act* (1987) (revision service 59, 2017) Appendix B 'International and Transnational Criminal Procedure'.

4 See the glossary for definitions of the terms in bold.

respond by pointing out that adultery is also bad, harmful and damaging to society and yet it is not a crime in South Africa, they would be at a loss to explain why not. Nor would they be able to explain why it is a crime to travel in a vehicle without wearing a seatbelt, or to own a television set without possessing a valid television licence.

By defining what a crime is, we should be able to assess whether any given conduct will amount to a crime simply by comparing that conduct with the relevant definition. However, because criminal conduct and the definitions of individual crimes vary so widely, it is difficult to formulate a definition of a crime that has general application. Ultimately, most authors settle for a simple, positivist definition[5] along these lines: a crime is unlawful, blameworthy conduct punishable by the state.[6] Therefore, referring to certain conduct as a crime means that the conduct concerned fits the definition of a crime as established over time in the common law, or it fits the definition of an offence as contained in a national, provincial or municipal statute.[7]

The above definition, however, tells us little about what *type* of conduct is likely to be defined by law as a crime in any given society at any given time, or why that particular society may choose to punish persons who engage in those types of conduct.

For the answers to such questions, we need to consider how criminal law originated and how it developed its current shape and content. This, in turn, requires a proper understanding of relevant historical narratives. In the South African context, the current body of law known as 'criminal law', has its origins in the legal traditions of the European colonists who came to settle in what is now the Republic of South Africa. But the criminalisation of wrongful or harmful human conduct is obviously not a European invention. The origins of criminal law are embedded in universal human reactions to wrongful or harmful human conduct. For instance, homicide is a wrong against human life. We now define the crimes of 'murder' and 'culpable homicide' in South African common law, however it is clear that the unlawful killing of another human being was outlawed in the indigenous legal systems that existed in South Africa at the time of the arrival of the European colonists. While the elements of and the case law on the crimes of murder and culpable homicide in modern South African criminal law were shaped by Roman-Dutch and English common law, one can also point to the underlying protected interest of human life and the collective societal interests that formed the basis for the punishment of homicide in the various indigenous systems.[8]

1.3 The origins of criminal law

Criminal law developed because of two main factors: the desire for vengeance and the pervasive influence of religious beliefs and practices.

The first factor is the 'eye for an eye' approach: the instinctive human desire to seek revenge against those who harm us or cause us loss. In early societies, this desire was normally satisfied by a system of private vengeance, namely by allowing those individuals who had suffered harm or loss at the hands of another to settle the score directly by taking

5 A positivist approach to law is one that is concerned with describing what the law *is*, rather than explaining what it *ought* to be or *why* it is like it is.

6 Snyman CR *Criminal Law* 6 ed (2014) 4.

7 The term 'crime' is generic, encompassing both common law and statutory crimes. The term 'offence' is generally used only when referring to statutory crimes. South African law does not draw a terminological distinction between serious crimes (felonies) and less serious crimes (misdemeanours) as is done in some foreign jurisdictions.

8 See also section 27.1.

revenge on whoever was responsible.[9] Not only was this socially acceptable at the time, it was often considered to be a moral duty – a way of preserving the honour of a person's self, family and clan.[10]

However, a system of private vengeance has inherent flaws. For one thing, it means that redress is only available to those with the power to exact it. For another, it offers no guarantee that the vengeance will indeed settle the score; in other words, that it will be a fair response to the original offence and that it will be accepted as such by the offender. Throughout history, reliance on private vengeance has tended to result in an escalation of conflict, with entire families, clans or tribes waging private wars (feuds) with each other for generations, sometimes long after the original reason for the quarrel has been forgotten.

Gradually, as societies became more enlightened, they recognised that the system of private vengeance needed to be curtailed. They also realised, however, that this objective could not be achieved unless the natural desire for revenge could be satisfied in some other acceptable way. The solution was to introduce a system of publicly imposed punishment in which, by general consensus, a more centralised entity (the state, in a modern context) took on the role of avenger and acts of private revenge were eventually outlawed.[11] The evolution from private revenge to punishment by the state involved the two systems running parallel to each other for some time. Today, the emphasis is almost exclusively on punishment by the state. In many criminal justice systems (such as in South Africa), victims are removed from involvement determining guilt and punishment.[12]

Secondly, apart from the need to replace private vengeance with public punishment, the development of criminal law was also influenced to some extent by religious beliefs and practices, in particular the desire to avoid the wrath of potentially vengeful deities by observing certain forms and standards of behaviour.[13] Since the transgression of religious taboos could mean disaster for the entire community, members of the community would often join together on such occasions, usually at the instigation of their religious leaders, to punish the offender in the hope of appeasing the deity and averting its wrath. In some cases, the shedding of the offender's blood, or even the sacrifice of his life, would be seen as the only adequate way of atoning for the offence.[14] This explains why, even in those legal systems that generally practised private vengeance, there would invariably be a small handful of offences that were regarded as wrongs against the public interest and which were therefore dealt with by the whole community. Some of these crimes, such as blasphemy, still exist today.[15]

Both of the above factors explain why the element of punishment[16] is a distinctive feature of criminal law. From a practical perspective, it is both a way of making offenders atone for their transgressions, thereby restoring the moral order of society, and a way of appeasing the victims of the transgressions, thereby removing the temptation for them to take the law into their own hands.

---

9 Von Bar CL et al *A History of Continental Criminal Law* (1916) 4.

10 The practice of honour killings persists in tribal communities in many parts of the world to this day. See http://www.amnestyusa.org/violence/honor-killings.

11 In the historical development of criminal law in Europe, the centralisation of state power and the power to punish is illustrated by the adoption of the Constitutio Criminalis Carolina (1532) and the Criminal Ordinances of Philip II (1570). See further, Jörg N, Kelk C and Klip AH *Strafrecht Met Mate* (2012) 25–27.

12 For historical and moral perspectives, see Eisenstat, S 'Revenge, justice and law: Recognizing the victim's desire for vengeance as a justification for punishment' 50(4) *Wayne L. Rev* 1115 (2004).

13 Von Bar *A History of Continental Criminal Law* 4.

14 Von Bar *A History of Continental Criminal Law* 4.

15 See Burchell JM *Principles of Criminal Law* 5 ed (2016) 790–793.

16 Strictly speaking, the term 'punishment' should be used only to refer to one of the many objectives of imposing a *sentence* on a convicted accused. It is often, however, also used as a synonym for the sentence itself.

1.4 Why is a particular conduct defined as a crime?

There is no general rule that determines which type of conduct is defined as a crime, in other words, criminalised. Instead, this depends on **public policy**, which varies from society to society and even from time to time in the same society. Although it is therefore impossible to generalise, it is possible to gain an insight into the nature of criminal conduct by considering what prompts or motivates a given society to define certain forms of conduct as crimes.[17] Essentially, the criminalisation of conduct in modern societies arises in response to four main factors or pressures:

1. Protection of basic human interests
2. Public morality
3. Promotion of public welfare
4. Need to ensure the preservation of the state[18]

1.4.1 The protection of basic human interests

Human beings, by their very nature, are concerned with protecting certain basic interests such as life, physical integrity, sexual integrity, dignity, property and personal freedom. Indeed, in many modern legal systems, these interests are considered to be so important that they are elevated to the status of *human rights*. However, even where this is not the case, these interests are generally accorded a measure of protection by the state against infringement by other persons.

For this reason, most legal systems define acts such as homicide, assault, robbery, rape, *crimen iniuria*, theft, arson and kidnapping as crimes. The underlying rationale is not hard to find as the infringement of these interests will inevitably lead to a sense of grievance on the part of the victim which, if not avenged by the state, is likely to result in individuals taking the law into their own hands. As previously explained, this is one of the oldest reasons for criminalising conduct. It also explains why most legal systems have certain crimes in common, even though the terminology and definitions may vary.

1.4.2 Public morality

Every society has its own moral, religious and cultural values. It is not unusual for a society to enforce the values that it holds most dear by using criminal law to punish transgressors. This is possibly a remnant of the role played by early criminal law in enforcing certain minimum standards of conduct to avoid offending potentially wrathful deities.

Perhaps the most widespread and contentious example of these pressures at work is the criminalisation of conduct that offends against sexual morality.[19] At various times over the years, most legal systems have criminalised conduct such as adultery, fornication,[20]

---

17 Rabie, Strauss and Mare described the modern notion of crime as a 'socio-political artefact':

> **What a legislature will label as criminal, may differ from one period in history to another and from one society to another, since legislatures are influenced by ideals, needs and values governing a particular society at a given time. There may be various moral, social, economic and other considerations why certain conduct is made criminal; however, when conduct has once been criminalized, it will be criminal not because it is immoral or harmful to the community, but because it has been declared criminal by the legislature. Although social harmfulness may have been a consideration why certain conduct is criminally prohibited, this conduct, when it is declared criminal, will be criminal not because it is harmful to the community, but because the legislature deems it to be so harmful.**

See Rabie MA, Strauss SA and Mare MC *Punishment: An Introduction to Principles* 5 ed (1994) 5.

18 Gross H *A Theory of Criminal Justice* (1979) 119.

19 See also Chapter 28 of this book.

20 Sexual intercourse outside the bonds of marriage.

sodomy,[21] bigamy, prostitution, public indecency, the possession and sale of pornography, sexual acts with children and bestiality.[22] In fact, most of these forms of conduct are still regarded as crimes somewhere in the world. What are the possible explanations for this?

In some of the given examples, it is clear that the conduct involved is harmful to others. Examples are bigamy and crimes that relate to the sexual abuse or exploitation of children. There are, however, also examples, such as sodomy, where the law prohibits sexual conduct that takes place in private between consenting adults for no apparent reason other than because a sufficiently large or influential segment of society finds this behaviour morally offensive.[23]

The question that arises in the case of these and other victimless crimes is whether it is appropriate to use the criminal sanction to enforce pure morality. Most South Africans would probably argue that morality is a private matter and that it is not appropriate for the law to intrude into private matters. Nevertheless, we continue to use the criminal law to enforce certain moral values. For example, see the following case.

S v M

In *S v M*,[24] the accused was charged with the common law crime of bestiality. He challenged the constitutionality of this crime on the grounds that it infringed his right to freedom and security of his person, his right to privacy, and his right not to be discriminated against unfairly on the basis of his sexual orientation. The court, however, rejected his argument and held that certain prohibitions were reasonable and justifiable. In so doing, it relied, inter alia, on the following passage from *National Coalition for Gay and Lesbian Equality and another v Minister of Justice and others*:[25]

> There are undoubtedly some acts which are so repugnant to and in conflict with human dignity as to amount to perversion of the natural order ... Bestiality seems to me to be an obvious example of an independent unnatural offence which justifies this categorisation ... It seems to me that the state has (or can justify the existence of) a responsibility to its citizens to prevent any individual or group from descending to the level of the beast (literally or figuratively). Unrestrained licence has always been the mark of a society in decay.[26]

We can conclude from this that even in South Africa where personal liberty is highly prized, popular sentiment and popular conceptions of morality will continue to play a role in shaping criminal law.

---

21 Anal sex between men.

22 Sexual intercourse with an animal. See the discussion below on *S v M* 2004 (1) SACR 228 (O).

23 Because the Constitution of the Republic of South Africa, 1996 prohibits discrimination on the basis of sexual orientation, the court in *S v Kampher* 1997 (4) SA 460 (C) abolished the crime of sodomy. However, it still remains a crime in many countries, as well as on the African continent. Many laws in Africa that criminalise sodomy are based on British colonial era laws against sodomy. For a comparative overview, see http://www.consultancyafrica.com/index.php?option=com_content&view=article&id=472:colonial-sodomy-homophobic-threat-within-common-law&catid=91:rights-in-focus&Itemid=296; Morris HF 'A history of the adoption of codes of criminal law and procedure in British Colonial Africa, 1876–1935' (1974) 18(1) *J Afr L* 6–23.

24 *S v M* 2004 (1) SACR 228 (O).

25 *S v M* supra at 15.

26 *National Coalition for Gay and Lesbian Equality and another v Minister of Justice and others* 1998 (2) SACR 102 (W) at 127D–F.

DISCUSSION **Law and morality**

How should a court determine what the moral viewpoint of society is on an issue? Which society is the court's reference point? These questions are especially important in a multicultural, pluralistic society like South Africa. We could call these questions ones of macro-morality or public morality, which probe the broad societal views on a range of issues, for instance the meaning and criminality of indecency, pornography and blasphemy.

Morality is not a simple question of what is generally accepted. In other words, it is not about conducting an opinion poll on a matter. However, when many (or most) people share the same views on, for example, child pornography, this may serve as an indication of an offence, not because it has been so declared by the state, but as a moral offence. *Morality is a subjective condition of a person* who may or may not share the same moral convictions with many or most in society. *Law*, however, is objective – it *applies to all and is enforceable by the state*, regardless of its morality. Of course, *law and morality can overlap*: to tell lies is a moral offence. To commit fraud, an unlawful misrepresentation, is a crime.[27] Morality also plays a role at a micro-level, for example at the level of theories of punishment. One such theory is the *moral education theory* (the philosopher Plato was an early exponent of this theory). The key aspect of this theory is that 'punishment is permissible primarily because it is a desirable thing for the person punished, not (or only secondarily) because it is a benefit to the general public'.[28] In other words, the focus is on making the individual wrongdoer a better person. The focus is not on society, and by implication, society's views on the matter.

1.4.3 The promotion of public welfare

Modern societies expect the state to do more than merely maintain law and order and defend the country's borders. They also expect it to protect and promote the safety, health and welfare of its citizens in various spheres of life, such as education, health services, work safety, road safety, public works and environmental protection. To do this, the state needs to create administrative organs, maintain them and regulate their conduct. It also needs to regulate the conduct of individual citizens in dealing with these organs of state and, where necessary, with each other.

To these ends, modern states tend to evolve numerous rules, standards and procedures that are embodied in legislation and regulations. Compliance with these laws and regulations is generally enforced by invoking the criminal sanction. In this way, a host of statutory offences has arisen, commonly referred to as public welfare offences. Examples of public welfare offences are to be found in the legislation that governs the preparation, distribution and sale of medicines and foodstuffs, the safety of buildings, occupational health and safety, road transportation, the conduct of motorists on public roads (for example, common traffic offences), and the protection of the environment.

27 See Derrett JDM *Law and Morality* (1998) 15–18.

28 Roederer C and Moellendorf D *Jurisprudence* (2004) 561.

1.4.4 The preservation of the state

Each society has an interest in preserving the governmental structures and state institutions that serve its needs and enable it to function. Consequently, conduct that undermines the state and its institutions is often criminalised. This results in common law crimes such as treason, sedition, obstructing the course of justice, contempt of court, perjury and bribery, as well as statutory offences that relate to income tax and exchange control.

1.5 *Mala in se* and *mala prohibita*

Because there are various factors that may play a role in criminalising certain types of behaviour, the contemporary concept of crime spans a wide variety of conduct. In some cases, such as murder, assault, rape, theft and fraud, the conduct involved is considered inherently wrong and immoral, and is criminalised in virtually all societies worldwide. The term '***malum in se***' is sometimes used to describe a criminal act of this type.[29]

In other cases, the conduct is not inherently wrong and immoral, but is only wrong because it has been prohibited by law and because it is generally considered wrong to disobey the law. Failing to wear a seatbelt when travelling in a car or possessing a television set without the required licence would be examples of this type of conduct. The term '***malum prohibitum***' is sometimes used to describe this type of crime and distinguish it from crimes that are *mala in se*.[30] The vast majority of so-called public welfare offences are *mala prohibita*.

1.6 The sources of South African criminal law

South African criminal law, which is not codified, stems primarily from **Roman-Dutch law**, an amalgamation of the Germanic customary law of the Netherlands with Roman law, which was incorporated into the laws of the Netherlands from the 15th century to the early 19th century. **Canon law**, the law of the Roman Catholic Church, also played a significant role in shaping Roman-Dutch law, largely as a result of the considerable influence that the Church had over secular matters during the Holy Roman Empire. This legal system was brought to southern Africa by the Dutch East India Company when its representative, Jan van Riebeeck, established a refreshment station at the Cape of Good Hope in 1652.

This foundation of Roman-Dutch law was later substantially influenced by **English common law**. After Britain occupied the Cape in 1795 and again in 1806, it decided to retain Roman-Dutch law as the law of the Cape Colony. However, it was not long before English law began to exert its influence, initially in the fields of civil and criminal procedure and evidence, but ultimately on substantive law as well. As English law had not been subjected to the same influences as the continental legal systems, it differed from Roman-Dutch law in a number of respects.

Therefore, in some cases, crimes under Roman-Dutch law were redefined according to English law. Also, English case authority was used to decide difficult points of law. This was assisted by the adoption of the Native Territories' Penal Code[31] of 1886 (also known as the Transkei Penal Code). This code was an almost verbatim replica of an earlier attempt by Sir James Stephen, an English judge, to codify English criminal law. Thus, although the Native

29 *Malum in se* means 'wrong or evil in itself' (plural: *mala in se*).

30 *Malum prohibitum* means 'bad because it is prohibited' (plural: *mala prohibita*).

31 A code is a comprehensive collection of laws on a particular topic, in written form.

Territories' Penal Code officially applied only in the Transkei, it was often used as a convenient reference work on English criminal law generally.

English law continued to exert a steady influence on South African law until the trend was reversed by adherents of the purist movement, which gained impetus after the Nationalist government came to power in 1948, and which lasted well into the 1970s and 1980s. This movement had as its express objective the eradication of the influence of English law and a return to the so-called pure principles of Roman-Dutch law. In the process, a number of concepts and presumptions that had been inherited from English law were removed from South African law and replaced with their Roman-Dutch law counterparts. When it was necessary to consult foreign authority, adherents of the purist movement often looked to German law, rather than the law of the various British Commonwealth countries, as German law[32] was considered to bear a closer kinship with Roman-Dutch law.[33] However, the purist movement did not have much influence on the rules of criminal procedure and evidence, which remained largely replicas of English law of the time.

1.7 Criminal law, constitutionalism and decolonisation of the law

The most important development in South African criminal law in recent times has been the adoption of the Constitution in 1996.[34] In the aftermath of colonialism and apartheid, the Constitution of 1996 requires that all conduct and all law, whether statute or common law, now need to be constitutionally compliant.[35] The Constitution has already had a significant impact in the fields of criminal law and procedure. For example, the death penalty was declared unconstitutional in the case of *S v Makwanyane and another*[36] and sodomy (consensual sexual intercourse between adult males) was decriminalised in *S v Kampher*.[37] As time passes, other aspects of criminal law will no doubt also be tested for constitutional compliance. In this book, we consider, where appropriate, the impact of the Constitution on the development of general principles of criminal law, the content and scope of specific common law and statutory crimes, as well as aspects of punishment.

For some, *constitutionalisation* of the law in the post-apartheid era is not the same as *decolonisation* of the law. It is trite to note that modern South African law is to a large extent based on the legal culture of the colonisers, first the Dutch and thereafter and more significantly, the British. Roman-Dutch and English law thus form the bedrock of South African law, not only in the historical sense, but also in terms of a continuing Eurocentric orientation for purposes of learning and further development of the law. The post-apartheid Constitution did not cause a rupture with the past; it recognises common law (i.e. the common law as it developed from Roman-Dutch and English law), customary law (i.e. indigenous laws) and statutory law (whether adopted before or after the end of apartheid) as the law of South Africa, and all law must be consistent with the Constitution, which is the supreme law of the Republic.[38] The Constitution furthermore declares that customary

32 Another reason for the introduction of German criminal law theory is the systematic and scientific approach to the general principles of criminal liability. A prominent South African proponent is Prof CR Snyman. See Snyman *Criminal Law* 8–9.

33 For an example of a case where this was done, see *S v Goosen* 1989 (4) SA 1013 (A).

34 The 1996 Constitution replaced the Interim Constitution of the Republic of South Africa Act 200 of 1993.

35 This is due to s 2 of the Constitution, commonly known as the supremacy clause, which provides, in effect, that the Constitution is the highest authority in the land.

36 *S v Makwanyane and another* 1995 (3) SA 391 (CC).

37 *S v Kampher* 1997 (4) SA 460 (C).

38 S 2 Constitution of the Republic of South Africa, 1996.

international law is law in the Republic, unless it is inconsistent with the Constitution or an Act of Parliament.[39] In short, then, the Constitution of 1996 *transformed* South Africa into a rather typical constitutional democracy.

For Andile Mngxitama, the constitutionalisation of the colonial and apartheid legal systems has not resulted in decolonisation of the law, but has rather resulted in an embrace of colonialism. In a collection of essays marking the 21st anniversary of the entry into force of the Constitution, 1996,[40] Mngxitama argues for a rejection of the retention of Roman-Dutch and English common law in South Africa, together with the broader Western ideological context in which the Constitution and modern South African law is to be understood. Mngxitama groups the African native responses to colonialism in South Africa into two broad strands. He calls the first group *amaqaba*, namely those who (a) refuse to accept Western ideology, and (b) refuse to accept what he calls the 'terms of surrender after the great defeat by the settler colonial powers'.[41] The second group, *amagqobhoka*, are those who embrace colonialism. This latter group accepted the reality of colonial rule and the dominance of Western ideology.[42]

For *amaqaba* the Constitution stands in the way of true liberation of black South Africans. For *amagqobhoka* the Constitution is a document of liberation in the tradition of the Freedom Charter of 1955.[43] The Freedom Charter, it will be recalled, expressed the aspirational principle that South Africa should be a non-racial society, and that 'South Africa belongs to all who live in it, both black and white'.[44] The Freedom Charter thus reflected ANC policy that South Africa is the home not only of indigenous black Africans, but also the home of those who came as settlers or indentured labourers in past centuries.[45] This ethic of accommodation and non-racialism clearly informed the ANC's policy positions, later also articulated at the constitutional negotiations and are indeed reflected in the letter and spirit of the Constitution of 1996.[46]

Mngxitama views the ANC, currently the governing party of South Africa and the leading liberation movement at the time of the constitutional negotiations of the early 1990s, as part of the *amagqobhoka*.[47] For Mngxitama, true decolonisation means a rejection of the accommodationist Constitution of 1996. Mngxitama's radical view of decolonisation is primarily informed by the question of land reform, but his critique goes beyond that and includes the whole post-1994 constitutional project. Arguing for a rejection of the constitutional settlement of the 1990s, Mngxitama notes that South Africa's common law is still based on Roman-Dutch and English law. The Constitution did not repeal these 'colonial structures', and this, in turn, explains the 'growing movement questioning the very terms of the negotiated settlement'.[48]

Whether there is widespread support for Mngxitama's radical notion of decolonisation remains to be seen. There is, however, another, alternative and more organic view of decolonisation of the law which emphasises the decolonisation of the curriculum of legal education, but within a transformative constitutional paradigm. The premise of this

39 S 232 Constitution of the Republic of South Africa, 1996.
40 Meiring, J (ed) *South Africa's Constitution at Twenty-One* (2017) 150–159.
41 Mngxitama in Meiring *South Africa's Constitution at Twenty-One* 150.
42 Mngxitama in Meiring *South Africa's Constitution at Twenty-One* 150.
43 Mngxitama in Meiring *South Africa's Constitution at Twenty-One* 151, 153.
44 For a comprehensive historical and contextual analysis, see Vadi, I *The Congress of the People and Freedom Charter: A People's History* (2015).
45 Vadi *The Congress of the People and the Freedom Charter* 148.
46 Mngxitama in Meiring *South Africa's Constitution at Twenty-One* 153–154.
47 Mngxitama in Meiring *South Africa's Constitution at Twenty-One* 154.
48 Mngxitama in Meiring *South Africa's Constitution at Twenty-One* 159.

approach is that decolonisation of the law must start with the decolonisation of the LLB curriculum. This will require more than cosmetic gestures. It is imperative to develop a comprehensive rediscovery of African indigenous law,[49] resulting in a digest which can serve as the basis for an informed transformation of the law and legal processes in South Africa.[50]

South Africa is a pluralistic, multicultural country. The post-apartheid constitutional dispensation was not imposed on the country by external forces or international organisations; it resulted from a negotiated settlement between the major political and cultural formations in South Africa. As pointed out above, the current constitutional framework can be traced to the principles of non-racialism and unity expressed in the Freedom Charter of 1955. At the same time it must be acknowledged that the rich traditions of Roman-Dutch and English law were in fact imposed on the majority of South Africans against their will.[51] But these traditions, the foundations of modern South African law, are constitutionally recognised as part of the South African legal fabric, and can still play a role in a constitutional and postcolonial context. The challenge is to see the decolonisation project not only as a normative and political imperative, but as an opportunity to create, in a thoughtful and transformative way, a truly South African (criminal) law. A romantic but ultimately futile attempt to recreate a pre-colonial state of affairs is not only counterproductive, but may also lead to the kind of parochialism which a modern constitutional state should avoid. In a cosmopolitan, complex and globalising world the best way forward is to use the richness of the diverse legal traditions of South Africa to construct a criminal law for this country which is reflective of the cultural heritage of all and which shows commitment to the rediscovery and restoration of formerly oppressed legal cultures. All of this should occur within the paradigm of a supreme Constitution, because the norms and values expressed in that document and the safeguards against tyranny contained in the constitutional rule of law, should not be taken for granted.

In a practical sense, and as far as this book is concerned, it is clear that the project of decolonisation of the law, including criminal law, will not be achieved in the form of a quick fix.[52] This book is by its nature a book on South African criminal law (which includes international criminal law) *as it stands*. It is not primarily a book on law reform, or a book on what the law *should be*. Of course, we include critical reflections and suggestions for law reform where appropriate, and even in our discussions of the positive law we take a critical stance where appropriate. The task at hand is, however, to participate in a broad academic endeavour, and where possible, make suggestions for the way forward, not only in this edition of the book but certainly in editions to come. The academic discourse in the years to come will hopefully be characterised by academic rigour in the pursuit of the rediscovery and recovery of indigenous criminal law and principles and norms, which can help to construct a truly inclusive South African criminal law.[53]

49 For a useful bibliography on customary law sources in South Africa, see the list compiled by the Chair in Customary Law at the University of Cape Town, available at https://africanlii.org/content/customary-law-bibliography.

50 'NADEL discuss decolonisation of the law at AGM' *De Rebus*, 1 May 2017, available at http://www.derebus.org.za/nadel-discuss-decolonisation-law-agm/. Indeed, educationalists point out that the first phase in decolonisation is rediscovery and recovery, whereby colonised peoples rediscover and recover their history, culture, language, identity and, one may add, laws. See Le Grange, L 'Decolonising the university curriculum' 30(2) *SAJHE* (2016) 1, at 3, available at http://dx.doi.org/10.20853/30-2-709.

51 Schärf, W and Nina, D (eds) *The Other Law: Non-state ordering in South Africa* (2001) 14–24.

52 For more on this issue, see Roy, A 'Postcolonial theory and law: A critical introduction' 29(2) *Adel L Rev* (2008) 315.

53 For academics, who are for the most part still almost exclusively trained in Western legal traditions, it is often difficult to identify and recover indigenous law. See, for instance, Hoctor SV 'Comparing criminal law rules: A role for customary law concepts?' 12(1) *Fundamina* 168 (2006). On the disconnect between indigenous law in the 'official' sense, and the living indigenous law, see Schärf and Nina *The Other Law* 29–36.

1.8 Criminal law and the law of delict

A comparison of criminal law and the **law of delict** reveals numerous areas of similarity between these two branches of the law: both deal with wrongdoing by individuals, and both branches of the law offer redress for such wrongdoing, aimed at vindicating, satisfying and appeasing those affected.[54] There are also a number of similarities in the requirements for criminal and delictual liability, as well as in the defences that may be raised to exclude such liability. There are, however, a number of important differences between a crime and a delict. We discuss some of these below.

1.8.1 Public versus private wrongs

The most important distinction is that a crime is a *public* wrong – a wrong against society – while a delict is a *private* wrong – a wrong against a specific individual or a group of individuals. Because of this, alleged criminal offenders (accused persons) are normally prosecuted by and at the instance of the state.[55] Also, the state may decide to prosecute a particular accused even if the victim does not wish such a prosecution to proceed. A delict, by contrast, forms the basis for a civil action that is brought entirely at the discretion of the victim (the plaintiff). The state's only role is to provide the forum (the court and support staff) in which the matter is adjudicated.

1.8.2 Victimless crimes

Another important difference between a crime and a delict, which arises from the distinction between a crime as a public wrong and a delict as a private wrong, is that a delict requires an identifiable victim, that is, someone who has suffered some tangible form of harm or loss (damages) as a result of the defendant's wrongful conduct. There can be no such thing as a victimless delict. However, because crimes are regarded as wrongs against society in general, it is entirely possible for conduct to be defined as a crime without that conduct having caused any identifiable harm or prejudice to any individual or group of individuals. Many of the so-called public welfare offences fall into this category as do some of the crimes that offend against sexual morality.[56]

1.8.3 Punishment versus compensation

A third important distinction between a crime and a delict lies in the essential purpose of the remedies of criminal law and the law of delict. The essential purpose of the law of delict is to provide a mechanism for *compensating* the victim. The essential purpose of criminal law is to provide a mechanism for *punishing*[57] the offender.

Thus, although it would be incorrect to say that the prospect of an award of delictual damages may not have a deterrent effect on potential wrongdoers, or that such an award may not serve some of the same purposes as punishment, a delictual action is not primarily aimed at punishing the wrongdoer and punishment is not regarded as a legitimate goal when determining delictual damages, at least not in South African law.[58] Conversely, although the Criminal Procedure Act 51 of 1977 does make limited provision for a criminal court to order

---

54 Loubser M and Midgley R (eds) *The Law of Delict in South Africa* 2 ed (2012) 8–9. See also Snyman *Criminal Law* 3–5.

55 The Criminal Procedure Act 51 of 1977 does, however, permit the bringing of a private prosecution in certain circumstances. See ss 7 and 8 of the Act. See also *Phillips v Botha* 1999 (2) SA 555 (SCA); *National Society for the Prevention of Cruelty to Animals v Minister of Justice and Constitutional Development and others* 2017 (1) SACR 284 (CC).

56 See the discussion on public morality in section 1.4.2.

57 See the discussion on punishment in section 1.9.

58 Courts in the US, for example, can and do make awards of so-called punitive damages. For an overview, see Christie, GC 'Current trends in the American law of punitive damages' 20(3) *Anglo-Am L Rev* 349 (1991).

an accused to pay compensation to a person who has suffered loss or damage as a result of his crime,[59] a criminal prosecution is not primarily aimed at obtaining compensation for the victim. Also, the compensation of the victim is not regarded as a necessary, or even an important, objective when meting out sentence. Instead, the two branches of the law are intended to supplement one another so that if, for example, a person suffers harm as a result of an assault by another, the former would be entitled to lay a criminal charge against the latter for the assault while simultaneously instituting a delictual action for compensation for pain and suffering, medical costs, and so forth.

There are also other distinctions between a crime and a delict, but these distinctions are not of particular importance for present purposes and so do not need to be discussed here.

DISCUSSION **Deciding criminal and civil liability in one set of proceedings**

Is it necessary, or even desirable, to maintain the traditional distinction between criminal and civil matters? Considering the time and expense involved in trial proceedings, should we not avoid the need for the victims of crime to endure two separate sets of proceedings by having a single trial aimed at achieving both compensation for themselves and punishment of the offender?

The idea is not as novel as it may sound. On the one hand, there is increasing recognition of the need to make provision in the criminal justice system for what has been termed restorative justice - procedures aimed at, inter alia, restitution and reconciliation. On the other hand, the concept of punitive damages, also known as exemplary damages, although not part of South African law, is well established in countries like the US and Canada. At present, section 300 of the Criminal Procedure Act provides for the possibility that a court may award compensation where a crime caused damages to or loss of property. The rather restricted ambit of section 300 is not comparable to the possibility of punitive or exemplary damages referred to above.

1.9 Fundamental principles of South African criminal law

While a detailed discussion of the historical and philosophical foundations of the various principles underlying South African criminal law is beyond the scope of this work, it is nevertheless important to discuss some of these principles briefly.[60]

1.9.1 The principle of inaction

Part of the fundamental ethos underlying libertarian jurisprudence is that no person may be burdened with an *unchosen* obligation (duty) towards another. A considerable portion of our law is, in fact, directed towards determining just when a person will be regarded as having assumed an obligation, either expressly or as a result of his conduct.

Since criminal law does not wish to punish individuals for failing to comply with obligations they have not assumed, it is primarily directed towards prohibiting harmful acts. In other words, it is primarily *prohibitory* in nature. It takes the view that, as a general rule, an individual should not render himself liable to punishment by simply doing nothing.

59 See ss 300 and 301 of the Criminal Procedure Act 51 of 1977.

60 For a more detailed analysis, see Burchell JM *South African Criminal Law and Procedure Vol I: General Principles of Criminal Law* 4 ed (2011).

However, this rule is not inflexible so there will always be exceptions.[61] As may be expected, statute law, especially public welfare legislation, represents a major source of such exceptions. When it comes to common law exceptions, the law tends to take a more conservative view. Essentially, the law requires such exceptions to conform to the legal convictions of society, not only regarding the way in which we would like individuals to behave towards one another, but also concerning the extent to which we expect the state to preserve individual liberty and freedom of action.

1.9.2 Free will or self-determinism

An important area in which canon law influenced the development of criminal law during the Middle Ages may be found in the Judeo-Christian doctrine of *free will*, namely the idea that individuals are free to choose their actions. They are therefore free to choose, in spite of temptation, between doing right and doing wrong. This idea is an important foundation on which rests, in turn, the idea that individuals are personally responsible for their own wrongdoing.

The philosophical equivalent of the religious doctrine of free will is the theory of *self-determinism*.[62] This is the notion that individuals can direct their own actions and that their actions are therefore not merely determined by pre-existing factors or causes, such as fate, heredity or environment.[63] The doctrine of free will forms a vital cornerstone of our modern criminal law, in particular our concept of criminal responsibility, or *criminal capacity*, as it is more commonly known. Thus, although the law is not blind to the fact that nature and nurture may predispose people to act in certain ways, it takes the view that normal people are nevertheless capable of governing their own conduct and that, consequently, they can be held responsible for how they choose to act.

1.9.3 The concept of personal responsibility

Flowing from the doctrine of free will is the further idea, also originally derived from canon law and now fundamental to our criminal law, that because human beings have the freedom to choose how they act, they are personally responsible for their own misconduct.

There are two sides to this proposition. The first is the notion that each individual is responsible for his own wrongdoing and can therefore be held to account and punished for it. This is commonly referred to as the *principle of culpability*. In a society founded on liberal precepts and values, it is this principle which permits the state to condemn and punish offenders for breaking the law. According to this principle, holding a person responsible for his crime, and punishing the person accordingly, is not cruel, inhuman or degrading. In fact, it is an affirmation of his inherent status and dignity as a human being. By contrast, some have advocated that criminality should be regarded as an illness for which offenders should be pitied and treated rather than punished.[64] This reduces them to something less than fully

61 These exceptions are discussed fully in section 4.2 of this book on unlawful omissions.

62 Medieval theologian-philosopher, St Thomas Aquinas (1225–1274) was an early proponent of this theory, which he set out in his leading works, *The Treatise on Human Nature: Summa Theologiae*, Pars 1 (2002) and *Summa Contra Gentiles*, reprinted ed (1975).

63 This theory, therefore, stands in opposition to the theory of determinism (the idea that all events, including human actions, are caused by pre-existing factors) and indeterminism (the idea that events and even human actions occur randomly and have no cause at all).

64 For example, during the 1960s, the British sociologist and criminologist, Lady Barbara Wootton, advocated the abolition of the entire system of criminal justice based on concepts of crime and punishment in favour of a therapeutic, preventative approach to antisocial behaviour. For more detail on Lady Wootton's proposals, see Logan, A 'Women and the provision of criminal justice advice: Lessons from England and Wales 1944–1964' 50(6) *Brit J Crim* 1077 (2010).

human and is therefore an affront to their inherent human dignity.[65] It follows, however, that it is only acceptable to punish a person for conduct that was, in fact, a product of his own free will, conduct, in other words, for which he or she is *personally responsible* and therefore blameworthy. Thus, for example, individuals are not normally held responsible for their involuntary actions, nor if they genuinely lacked the capacity for rational choice and self-control, as in the case of young children and the mentally ill.

The other side of this same proposition is the notion that each person is accountable and punishable *only* for his own wrongdoing and not for anyone else's.[66] Thus, for example, parents are not normally responsible for crimes committed by their children and employers are similarly not responsible for crimes committed by their employees (although the legislature has seen fit to impose such liability in certain cases).[67]

An important exception to this principle applies in cases governed by the **common purpose rule**: where two or more persons associate together to commit a crime, they will each be liable for the conduct of the other to the extent that it falls within the scope of their common purpose.[68] The common purpose rule is therefore an important deviation from the normal principles that underlie our criminal law.

The doctrine of command or superior responsibility, which plays an important role in international criminal law, also seems to be in conflict with the notion of personal responsibility. In terms of this doctrine, superior officers or commanders are held liable for the criminal conduct of their subordinates, for instance war crimes, if they knew or had reason to know that there was wrongdoing, or that wrongdoing was about to be committed, and they failed to prevent or punish those responsible for the crimes. This doctrine casts the net of criminal liability widely, but it can be justified in terms of efforts to eradicate impunity for serious crimes under international law.[69]

1.9.4 The presumption of innocence

The presumption of innocence originated in English criminal law and was adopted into South African law along with the English rules of criminal procedure and evidence.[70] It is now entrenched in section 35 of the Constitution, which provides that one of the features of the right to a fair trial is the right 'to be presumed innocent, to remain silent, and not to testify during the proceedings'.[71]

What this presumption means is that, as a general rule, the state bears the onus (burden) of proof in criminal cases. The Appellate Division of the High Court (now the Supreme Court

65 See further, Hoctor S 'Dignity, criminal law and the Bill of Rights' (2004) 121(2) *SALJ* 304 at 308 and further authorities cited there.

66 The notion of criminal liability as a purely personal matter was at odds with early Germanic law, which regarded crime as a matter that concerned not only the offender and the victim, but also their extended families on both sides. Under the influence of Enlightenment philosophy, notably the work of the German philosopher, Immanuel Kant, criminal law became essentially individualised. Indeed, secularisation, individualisation, rationalisation and humanisation impacted greatly on modern criminal law theory and resulted in the fundamental concept of individual criminal responsibility – the bedrock of most modern criminal law systems. For more on the influence of the Enlightenment on European criminal law in general, and German criminal law theory in particular, see Vormbaum T and Bohlander M (eds) *A Modern History of German Criminal Law* (2014) 14–16, 19–32.

67 See section 22.3 for a discussion on vicarious liability.

68 The common purpose rule is discussed fully in section 25.3.2.

69 See Osiel MJ *Obeying Orders: Atrocity, Military Discipline and the Law of War* (1999) 192–193. See further, Part Four of this book for a more detailed discussion of general principles of, and specific crimes under, international criminal law from a South African perspective.

70 See section 1.6.

71 S 35(3)(*h*) of the Constitution.

of Appeal) explained its effect in *R v Ndhlovu* in the following terms:

> **In all criminal cases it is for the Crown [the state] to establish the guilt of the accused, not for the Accused to establish his innocence. The *onus* is on the Crown to prove all averments necessary to establish his guilt.**[72]

Not only is the state required to prove all the elements necessary to establish an accused's guilt, it must do so beyond a reasonable doubt. This requires a higher standard of proof than in civil cases. In civil cases, the onus of proof only needs to be discharged on a balance of probabilities. This means a court will weigh up the evidence on both sides and decide whether the version of the party who bears the onus (A) is more probable than the version of the other party (B). If so, the onus has been discharged and the court will find in favour of A. If both versions are equally probable or if B's version is the more probable one, the onus has not been discharged and the court will find in favour of B.

What is meant by proof beyond a reasonable doubt? It does not mean proof beyond any shadow of a doubt nor does it mean absolute certainty. Thus, a court is not required to entertain fanciful doubts and far-fetched possibilities.[73] Nor does it matter whether the presiding officer is personally convinced of the accused's guilt. A reasonable doubt means a doubt that would be entertained by a reasonable court. Therefore, for all practical purposes, proof beyond a reasonable doubt simply means a very high degree of probability that the accused is guilty.

If, however, there is a reasonable possibility that the accused may be innocent, then there is a reasonable doubt as to his guilt, and he must be given the benefit of that doubt and acquitted. If proof is by inference, then the inference that points to the accused's guilt must be the *only* reasonable inference that can be drawn from the proven facts.

Note, however, that there are various exceptions to the rule that the state bears the onus of proof. The most important exception is when an accused raises the defence of mental illness or intellectual disability. In such a case, the accused bears the onus of proving his or her defence.[74] This reversal of the onus of proof arises out of a long standing common law principle that all persons are presumed to be sane unless the contrary is proven.

There are also cases where the legislature has placed the onus on the accused to prove certain elements of his or her defence. However, a number of these provisions have been declared unconstitutional because they unreasonably and unjustifiably infringed on the presumption of innocence.[75] This does not mean, however, that every infringement on the presumption of innocence is necessarily unconstitutional. For example, the National Road Traffic Act 93 of 1996 contains a rebuttable presumption that, for purposes of any prosecution, the driver of a vehicle at any given time is its (registered) owner.[76] The predecessor of this presumption, contained in the former Road Traffic Act 29 of 1989,[77] was challenged for constitutionality, but was found to be justifiable in terms of section 36 of the Constitution (the limitations clause). The reason for this was that it would be impossible for the state to enforce the rules of the road if it was obliged to establish the actual identity of each and every driver before it could issue summons for a traffic offence.[78]

---

72 *R v Ndhlovu* 1945 AD 369 at 386.

73 See, for example, *S v Van Heerden and another* 2010 (1) SACR 529 (ECP).

74 See ss 78(1A) and (1B) of the Criminal Procedure Act.

75 See, for example, *S v Bhulwana; S v Gwadiso* [1996] 1 All SA 11 (CC); *S v Coetzee and others* 1997 (3) SA 527 (CC). For a discussion, see Kemp GP 'Die grondwetlikheid van statutêre vermoedens' (1998) 9(1) *Stell LR* 106.

76 S 73(1) of the National Road Traffic Act 93 of 1996.

77 S 130 of the Road Traffic Act 29 of 1989.

78 See *S v Meaker* 1998 (2) SACR 73 (W).

1.9.5 The principle of legality

The principle of legality holds, in essence, that no person should be subjected to punishment by the state except for conduct that is defined as a crime according to valid and applicable law. It is a corollary of the *Rule of Law*, which was an idea that was developed, mainly during the 17th and 18th centuries, by political philosophers such as Montesquieu and Beccaria, in reaction to the harshness and arbitrariness of the political systems of their day.

The doctrine of the Rule of Law holds that people should be governed by and according to law (a body of established and impartial rules) rather than according to the arbitrary whims of those in power, and that everyone, including those in power, should be subject to the law. In other words, no one should be above the law. As far as criminal law is concerned, the Rule of Law is expressed through the principle of legality and its corollaries.

The first formal statement of the principle of legality may be found in article 8 of the French Declaration of the Rights of Man (1791), which held that '[n]o one may be punished except by virtue of a law established and promulgated before the crime and legally applied.' The German jurist, Paul Johann Anselm Ritter von Feuerbach, further developed and introduced this principle into the Bavarian Penal Code of 1813.[79] He first coined the now well-known legal maxim, *Nulla poena sine lege, nulla poena sine crimine, nullum crimen sine poena legali.* This means, 'No punishment without law, no punishment without crime, no crime without lawful punishment'.

There are a number of corollaries to this principle, the most important for our purposes being the following:

- Punishment may only be imposed for conduct that is defined as a crime by law.[80] Since courts may not make new laws, they may therefore not create new crimes nor may they extend the definitions of existing crimes to embrace new forms of conduct. They are bound by existing law. This principle is known as the *ius acceptum.*
- Punishment may only be imposed for conduct that was defined as a crime by a law that was in force and applicable to the accused at the time when the conduct occurred. This is the rule against retrospective criminalisation, also known as the *ius praevium.*[81]
- No punishment may be imposed that is more severe than the punishment that was applicable to the crime at the time when it was committed. This is the rule against retrospectivity of punishment.
- People are entitled to know the law and, in particular, to know in advance what conduct will be regarded as criminal. Hence, laws may not take effect before they are promulgated (the principle of publicity) and people are entitled to reasonable notice before a new criminal law comes into effect (the principle of fair warning).
- The definitions of crimes should be reasonably precise and settled so that people need not live in fear of breaking the law inadvertently. This is the principle of certainty, also known as the *ius certum.*

---

79 See Ritter von Feuerbach PJA *Lehrbuch des Gemeinen in Deutschland Gültigen Peinlichen Rechts* (1805).

80 This is the *nulla poena sine lege* part of the legality principle. See *S v Malgas* 2001 (1) SACR 469 (SCA) at 472G–H and *S v Dodo* 2001 (1) SACR 594 (CC) at 604E–F.

81 For a case in which this rule was applied, see *Masiya v Director of Public Prosecutions, Pretoria and another* (*Centre for Applied Legal Studies and another, amici curiae*) 2007 (2) SACR 435 (CC). For a discussion of the academic debate on the judgment in *Masiya*, see Burchell *South African Criminal Law and Procedure Vol I* 39–40. For a critical assessment of the case, see in particular Snyman *Criminal Law* 45–48. For qualified support of the judgment, see Kemp G '*Nullum crimen sine lege*: "Hoe staan dit nou in ons reg?"' in Du Plessis J and Lubbe G (eds) *A Man of Principle: The Life and Legacy of JC de Wet* (2013) 376, 387–388.

- Where the law is ambiguous, it should be interpreted in favour of the accused. This is the principle of strict interpretation of penal statutes, also known as the *ius strictum*.[82]

The Rule of Law and the principle of legality are entrenched in the Constitution. Section 1(*c*) of the preamble to the Constitution states that the Republic of South Africa is founded on the supremacy of the Constitution and the Rule of Law. Section 35(3) of the Bill of Rights (which deals with the rights of arrested and detained persons) entrenches the principle of legality and, in particular, the rules against retrospectivity of offences and of punishment:

> **Everyone who is arrested for allegedly committing an offence has the right: ...**
> **(*l*) not to be convicted for an act or omission that was not an offence either under national or international law at the time it was committed or omitted: ...**
> **(*n*) to the benefit of the least severe of the prescribed punishments if the prescribed punishment for the offence has been changed between the time that the offence was committed and the time of sentencing.**

The corollaries to the principle of legality, as highlighted above, are clear in theory, but not always in practice, as illustrated by the example below.

In *Director of Public Prosecutions, Western Cape v Arnold Prins*,[83] the Western Cape High Court considered the legality principle with respect to certain offences created by the Criminal Law (Sexual Offences and Related Matters) Amendment Act 32 of 2007. While the Act provided for the elements of these statutory offences, it did not (either by design or by neglect) expressly provide for corresponding penalties in every instance. The High Court held that these 'crimes' were not in fact crimes at all because, without the necessary prescribed penalties, the *nulla poena sine lege* aspect of the legality principle was violated. In response to this judgment, the legislature subsequently adopted the Criminal Law (Sexual Offences and Related Matters) Amendment Amendment Act 6 of 2012 in an attempt to rectify the legality problem.[84] While Parliament was debating how best to deal with the lack of express penalty provisions in the 2007 Act, the Director of Public Prosecutions appealed to the Supreme Court of Appeal (SCA) against the Western Cape High Court's ruling in *Prins*. In a unanimous decision, the SCA upheld the appeal.[85] In so doing, it noted that there had been three other conflicting judgments on the same point where other provincial high courts had come to different conclusions than the Western Cape High Court.[86]

In the case of *common law crimes*, such as murder, theft and fraud, high courts in South Africa have traditionally had a fair degree of discretion to impose any sentence that was deemed appropriate.[87] Magistrates' courts are, of course, bound by the statutory limits on

---

82 Williams GL *Criminal Law: The General Part* 2 ed (1961) 575–608; Snyman *Criminal Law* 35–49.

83 *Director of Public Prosecutions, Western Cape v Prins* 2012 (2) SACR 67 (WCC).

84 Act 6 of 2012 inserts s 56A in the Criminal Law (Sexual Offences and Related Matters) Amendment Act 32 of 2007. S 56A(1) provides:

> **A court shall, if- (*a*) that or another court has convicted a person of an offence in terms of this Act; and (*b*) a penalty is not prescribed in respect of that offence in terms of this Act or by any other Act, *impose a sentence, as provided for in section 276 of the Criminal Procedure Act, 1977 (Act No 51 of 1977), which that court considers appropriate and which is within that court's penal jurisdiction.* (Emphasis added)**

85 *Director of Public Prosecutions, Western Cape v Prins and others* (369/12) [2012] ZASCA 106; 2012 (2) SACR 183 (SCA); 2012 (10) BCLR 1049 (SCA); [2012] 3 All SA 245 (SCA) (15 June 2012).

86 *DPP v Prins* at 5. In the Free State: *S v Booi* (14/2010) [2010] ZAFSHC 91 (12 August 2010); in Kwazulu-Natal: *S v Mchunu* (CC 168/2011) [2011] ZAKZDHC 89 (16 September 2011); and in Gauteng (South Gauteng High Court): *S v Rikhotso* (SS105/11) [2012] ZAGPJHC 106 (15 May 2012).

87 The power of courts generally to punish common law and statutory crimes can be found in s 276 of the Criminal Procedure Act.

sentencing jurisdiction laid down by their governing legislation. It is only fairly recently that various legislative regimes (notably on minimum sentencing)[88] have also circumscribed the sentencing discretion of the high courts in relation to common law crimes. However, by virtue of their status as crimes under common law, common law crimes are already effectively criminalised under South African law. The question as to whether courts have free or limited discretion to impose sentences does not affect the fact that the relevant conduct is a crime under common law and is punishable as such.

The position regarding *statutory crimes* is different: a statute cannot simply provide that conduct is an offence and then leave it at that. Thus, the SCA in *DPP v Prins* considered the effect of the absence of a penalty provision on the offences created in the Sexual Offences Act. The SCA opted to analyse the Act as a whole, to look at all the provisions (including those without specific penalties) contextually and held as follows:

> **The language of the sections is unequivocal and the context provided by the need to protect vulnerable people against sexual attacks in the light of the Constitution and South Africa's international obligations reinforces the construction that each of the relevant sections creates a criminal offence.**[89]

Moreover, the SCA linked the specific reading and interpretation of the Sexual Offences Act with the general empowering provision of section 276 of the Criminal Procedure Act, which provides for the punishment of common law and statutory crimes by the courts (magistrates' courts and high courts).[90] The SCA concluded that the absence of specific penalties for some of the offences created in the Sexual Offences Act did not violate the legality principle, including the *nulla poena sine lege* aspect of the principle.[91]

The SCA's application of the legality principle in *DPP v Prins* is, all aspects considered, probably correct as far as the provisions of the Sexual Offences Act are concerned. However, in terms of general criminal law theory, it is prudent to warn against using section 276 of the Criminal Procedure Act to fill the gaps where legislation, for whatever reason, is silent on specific penalties for crimes created. Some authors deem the SCA's approach in *DPP v Prins* to be a step in the right direction, but not necessarily enough from a constitutional point of view.[92] The legality principle, in our view, demands, in principle, adherence to both aspects: *nullum crimen sine lege* and *nulla poena sine lege.*[93]

Where legislation provides for the unlawfulness of certain conduct, but omits to expressly provide that the unlawful conduct in question constitutes a criminal offence, it will be improper for a court to fill the void and to create an offence where there is none.[94]

88 For the statutory regime on minimum sentences, see the Criminal Law Amendment Act 105 of 1997; *S v Dodo* supra.

89 *DPP v Prins* at 20.

90 *DPP v Prins* at 31.

91 *DPP v Prins* at 38.

92 Kemp G '*Nullum crimen sine lege*: "Hoe staan dit nou in ons reg?"' in Du Plessis J and Lubbe G (eds) *A Man of Principle: The Life and Legacy of JC de Wet* (2013) 376, 391–393; Burchell *Principles of Criminal Law* 41.

93 For a legal-historical analysis of the legality principle in South African law, see De Wet JC and Swanepoel HL *Strafreg* 4 ed (1985) 44–47. Professor de Wet, with reference to Roman-Dutch authorities, supported a strict application of the legality principle. The strict approach has now even stronger support in light of the constitutionalised legality principle (as per s 35 of the Constitution).

94 *S v Frederiksen* 2017 JDR 1654 (FB). In this case the court held that ss 55 and 58 of the National Health Act 61 of 2003 provide for the unlawfulness of certain conduct relating to the removal and transplantation of human tissue of living persons. However, the legislature failed to criminalise explicitly the conduct defined in the relevant sections. It was held that 'the court cannot venture into the arena of the legislature by creating criminal offences merely because it might be of the view that a casus omissus has occurred'. *S v Frederiksen* at 16.

1.9.6 The principle of fair labelling

A criminal conviction carries with it certain immediate implications for the accused, regardless of the severity or leniency of his sentence. Firstly, a guilty verdict is a formal, public condemnation (denunciation) of the accused and, as such, it is a direct affront (an *iniuria*) to his dignity.[95] Secondly, it determines the stigma that will attach to the accused in the eyes of the public and, hence, the extent to which his reputation stands to suffer as a result of his conviction. A criminal conviction therefore impairs the accused's rights of personality in two ways.

Although it is commonly accepted that these impairments are justified by the accused's wrongdoing against society,[96] it stands to reason that they are only justifiable as long as the court's verdict is a true reflection of the accused's guilt. This means that when an accused is pronounced guilty of a crime, the court's verdict should be couched in terms that fairly and accurately reflect the accused's actual wrongdoing. Thus, the verdict should convey the particular *type* of wrongdoing involved in the crime, its relative *gravity* compared with other crimes of the same type, and the extent of the accused's *legal and moral blameworthiness* (his culpability). This is commonly known as the *principle of fair labelling*.[97] Its primary concern is to ensure that the *stigma* (label) attaching to the accused by virtue of his conviction is a fair and accurate reflection of his guilt, and hence neither more nor less than he deserves.[98] It can be regarded as a further corollary of the principle of culpability.[99]

In many cases, the importance of fair labelling is self-evident. For example, no one would argue that it is acceptable to stigmatise a thief as a murderer or a robber as a rapist. However, questions of fair labelling often involve far more subtle distinctions than these and can lead to considerable debate. Thus, for example, when the common law crime of rape was statutorily redefined to include forms of penetration other than penile–vaginal penetration so as to make the offence non-gender specific, there was considerable debate regarding the merits of doing so.[100] Some objectors felt that other forms of sexual penetration could never be equated with the conduct involved in the original common law definition of rape[101] and that to do so would dilute and even trivialise the intrinsic gravity of the crime. The issue was largely one of fair labelling.

One particular area where questions of fair labelling arise is in relation to the doctrine of common purpose. We explained that the doctrine of common purpose represents a far-reaching exception to the principle of personal responsibility in that it allows a secondary participant to be convicted of a crime that he did not in fact commit, purely by virtue of his association with the actual perpetrator along with the necessary *mens rea*. It is not necessary to show that he contributed towards the commission of the crime in a physical or even

95 Dignity (*dignitas*) denotes a person's sense of personal pride and self-worth. Along with reputation (*fama*), body (*corpus*) and physical freedom (*libertas*), it makes up the bundle of physical and psychological interests that are recognised by law as the four constituents of human personality (Loubser and Midgley *The Law of Delict in South Africa* 321). While all four constituents confer justiciable rights on the individual, dignity is accorded special importance in South African law by virtue of ss 1 and 10 of the Constitution. See further, Lagodny O 'Human dignity and its impact on German substantive criminal law and criminal procedure' (1999) 33(3) *Is LR* 575 at 578.

96 Lagodny supra 578.

97 The original exponent of the principle of fair labelling (or representative labelling as he originally named it) was the noted British scholar and criminologist, Professor Andrew Ashworth. See Ashworth AJ 'The elasticity of *mens rea*' in Tapper CFH (ed) *Crime, Proof and Punishment: Essays in Memory of Sir Rupert Cross* (1981) 45, 53. He subsequently elucidated the principle in his standard textbooks on criminal law. See, for example, Ashworth A *Principles of Criminal Law* 6 ed (2009) 78.

98 In this sense, the principle of fair labelling serves the interests of society as much as it serves the interests of the offender.

99 See section 1.8.3.

100 For an account of this debate, see Burchell *Principles of Criminal Law* 41–44.

101 Snyman is one such objector. For his reasoning, see Snyman *Criminal Law* 45–48.

psychological sense. As a matter of policy, the conduct of the actual perpetrator is simply imputed to all his fellow participants. Consequently, liability for a serious crime such as murder can arise from a relatively trivial act of association, which in no way contributed to the death of the deceased, or encouraged or facilitated the commission of the crime. Some commentators regard this as a prime example of unfair labelling.[102] A better approach, they argue, would be to convict these lesser participants of being *accomplices* to the crime, rather than convicting them of the crime itself.[103]

Although it is only in relatively recent years that the principle of fair labelling has been elucidated, it has come to be accepted as an important foundational principle of international criminal law.[104] In South African law, the principle of fair labelling has yet to be accorded explicit recognition by the courts. However, it can be argued that it is a principle that ought to be accorded particular significance in our law because of the special importance accorded to the right to dignity in the Constitution.

1.10 Punishment, theories of punishment and sentencing

We noted above that the essential purpose of criminal law is to provide a mechanism for *punishing* the offender.[105] While punishment is indeed a primary function of criminal law, the term needs to be explored. However, it is first necessary to distinguish between the concepts 'sentence', 'sentencing' and 'punishment':

- *Sentence* refers to 'any measure applied by a court to the person convicted of a crime and which finalises the case', except where 'specific provision is made for reconsideration' of that measure.[106] While the conditions of a suspended sentence would normally not be regarded as part of the sentence, a caution does fall under the term 'sentence'.[107]
- *Sentencing* is simply the 'imposition of a sentence by the court, on a particular offender'.[108]
- *Punishment* (in the broadest sense) can be described as 'something which is unpleasant to experience' that is 'imposed by a court after conviction'.[109] In this sense, it is clear that not all sentences will constitute punishment, for instance, the majority of suspended sentences or a caution. However, from a procedural perspective, we can state that most forms of punishment are sentences.

Sentencing in the broad, procedural sense is often studied as a discipline in its own right alongside related fields such as criminal law, criminal procedure and criminology/penology. Since the focus of this book is criminal law (that is, the general principles of criminal liability and some of the important specific crimes), we will not deal here with all the complexities and nuances of sentencing. It is, however, important to acknowledge the interdisciplinary

102 See, for example, Burchell *Principles of Criminal Law* 491.

103 See further, Chapter 25.

104 For example, Robinson identifies the principle of fair labelling as one of three fundamental principles of criminal law, recognised by international criminal law, which distinguish a liberal system of criminal justice from an authoritarian system. See Robinson D 'The identity crisis of international criminal law' (2008) 21(4) *LJIL* 925 at 926. See also Robinson D 'The two liberalisms of international criminal law' in Stahn C and Van den Herik L (eds) *Future Perspectives on International Criminal Justice* (2010) 115, 119–120. The other two principles that he identifies are the principle of personal culpability and the principle of legality (discussed above).

105 See section 1.8.3.

106 Joubert JJ (ed) et al *Criminal Procedure Handbook* 12 ed (2017) 374.

107 Joubert (ed) et al *Criminal Procedure Handbook* 374.

108 Joubert (ed) et al *Criminal Procedure Handbook* 375.

109 Joubert (ed) et al *Criminal Procedure Handbook* 374–375.

nature of the study of criminal law, punishment, sentencing and criminal procedure, as well as the important contextual fields of criminology and penology. What we will highlight here is the role of punishment in criminal law and the most important theories underlying punishment.

One of the reasons why it is necessary to discuss briefly punishment and the theories of punishment in the context of criminal law, is because punishment (or the requirement of a criminal sanction) is also an element or expression of the principle of legality, discussed above. The legality principle involves the twin elements of the criminal norm (*nullum crimen sine lege*) and the punishment norm (*nulla poena sine lege*). The theories of punishment go further and ask the question: why does the criminal justice system punish individuals? In other words, *what is the purpose of punishment*?

A number of theories of punishment have been advanced over the years in an attempt to address these questions.[110] These theories are normally grouped or classified into three main categories: the absolute theory (retributive), relative theories (preventive, deterrent and reformative), and the combination theory (combination of absolute and relative theories).

The *absolute or retributive theory of punishment* is perhaps the best known theory and has ancient roots.[111] It is also known as 'just desert' or 'commensurate desert'. This theory is sometimes described as 'non-empirical, effect-independent norm-affirmation'.[112] In its purest form one can say that the absolute theory of punishment focuses on the categorical demand that individuals must comply with legal norms irrespective of any social purpose. A violation of the norm must be punished, irrespective of whether others will be deterred, or whether future norm violation by others will be prevented by punishing the individual wrongdoer.[113] Ancient notions of justice (including the idea of an eye for an eye)[114] clearly informed this theory of punishment. In modern criminal law, we should be careful not to confuse retribution with vengeance. The focus now is not on vengeance (private or otherwise), but on a more nuanced and enlightened attempt to restore the balance that was disturbed by the criminal conduct. An important premise to keep in mind when considering the retributive theory of punishment is the fundamental notion in criminal law that individuals are personally responsible for their own wrongdoing (the idea of free will or self-determinism).[115]

The *relative theories of punishment*, sometimes also known as *utilitarian theories*, concern three main approaches: prevention, deterrence and reform. Each is briefly considered. The *preventive theory*, in its most extreme form, means that the criminal offender is permanently incapacitated and can no longer pose a risk to society. Capital punishment is the obvious example of an extreme (absolute) form of the preventive theory. Of course, the death penalty can also be seen as the ultimate form of retribution so, in this sense, we can see that the various theories sometimes overlap. Less drastic examples of the preventive

---

110 For an overview, see Rabie A 'Die strafteorieë: 'n Oorsig' (1976) 5(2) *Crime, Punishment and Correction* 33–48; Van der Merwe DP 'Retribution in criminal law' (1980) *Obiter* 43–50; Snyman *Criminal Law* 10–20.

111 It is called the absolute theory because it regards punishment as an end in itself, rather than as the means to an end like the relative theories.

112 Simester AP, Du Bois-Pedain, A and Neumann, U (eds) *Liberal Criminal Theory: Essays for Andreas von Hirsch* (2014) 25.

113 The German philosopher Immanuel Kant (*The Metaphysics of Morals*, 1797) was perhaps the best-known exponent of this school of thought. See also Simester, Du Bois-Pedain and Neumann (eds) *Liberal Criminal Theory* 25–26.

114 The ancient *lex talionis*. For an historical discussion, see Van Drunen D 'Natural law, the *lex talionis*, and the power of the sword' 2(3) *Liberty U L Rev* 945 (2008).

115 See section 1.9.2.

approach to punishment include (preventive) imprisonment and the forfeiture of a driver's licence.[116]

Of all the relative theories, the theory that punishment serves (or should serve) as a *deterrent* to crime is arguably the most popular, but expectations should be managed. A distinction is drawn between *individual deterrence and general deterrence*.[117] The former tries to individualise the punishment in order to deter the particular offender from committing further crimes. General deterrence, however, means that the deterrent effect of the punishment is also aimed at a wider audience – society as a whole or at least a significant part of society. Thus, while the primary function of punishment in this context may be aimed at the individual offender, the particular punishment may also serve the secondary aim of deterring society in general from committing the type of crime in question. There is a problem here, however. If the punishment meted out to the individual offender is *disproportionately harsh* in order to serve as a warning to the rest of society, then the punishment can no longer be described as a just desert[118] (in terms of the retributive theory) and, in the South African context, there may also be a constitutional objection.[119] The general deterrent approach to punishment is thus less attractive (or at least not as attractive as the retributive theory, which holds out the possibility of better proportionality).

This brings us to the reform approach to punishment. This approach is, on the face of it, quite attractive since it purports to be sophisticated and aimed not at retribution, but at *reform*, which connotes positive impressions of the betterment of individuals and society. It also reminds us of the *moral education theory*, discussed above under section 1.4.2. There are, however, many practical and theoretical objections to the reform approach to punishment. Essentially, the verdict seems to be that this approach to punishment does not actually work in practice – the criminal justice system is simply not good at reforming people. There is also a theoretical and moral objection: if the focus is only on the individual offender who needs to be reformed, then there is no justice in terms of the victims or the broader society. This leaves the very real impression or perception that justice was not served.[120]

The various theories of punishment all contain positive and negative aspects. A well-balanced combination of the elements that are best suitable in terms of the interests of society, the individual offender and the nature of the crime that was committed, should go a long way towards the ideal of just and fair punishment. This balanced approach is also known as the *combination theory of punishment*. In the famous case of *S v Zinn*,[121] Rumpff JA identified the so-called *triad*, consisting of the crime, the offender and the interests of society, as the fundamental principles underlying sentencing, thus confirming the combination theory as the best approach.[122]

---

116 Snyman *Criminal Law* 15.

117 Snyman *Criminal Law* 15.

118 Indeed, deterrence and just desert (as composite justification for punishment) may sometimes pull in opposite directions if the right balance is not achieved. See Simester, Du Bois-Pedain and Neumann (eds) *Liberal Criminal Theory* 45.

119 See also *S v Dodo* supra at 38.

120 Snyman *Criminal Law* 18–19.

121 *S v Zinn* 1969 (2) SA 537 (A).

122 For a more recent judgment on the various factors to be considered when imposing an appropriate sentence (and the role that the theories of punishment might play), see *S v M (Centre for Child Law as amicus curiae)* 2007 (2) SACR 539 (CC).

DISCUSSION

A South African approach to punishment: *Ubuntu* and restorative justice

In *S v Makwanyane*, the Constitutional Court declared the death penalty to be unconstitutional.[123] The court furthermore accepted that retribution is a legitimate object of punishment, but this theory should not be given undue weight given South Africa's human rights ethos and the role that *ubuntu* (should) play in society.[124] Indeed, the Constitutional Court held that the primary object of punishment is prevention and rehabilitation, not revenge.[125]

Ubuntu, in the most general sense, is described as an African philosophy, an 'interactive ethic', which focuses on the developmental and aspirational aspects of an individual human being's life journey. It is about the interaction with other human beings. African values and philosophical traditions such as *ubuntu* are often (wrongly) projected as simplistically collectivist (in contradistinction with the individualistic Western values). Cornell and Van Marle have pointed out that *ubuntu* is not simply a 'privileging of the community over the individual'. *Ubuntu* rather concerns the 'process of becoming a person', or 'how one is given the chance to become a person at all'.[126]

The restorative aims of the Child Justice Act 75 of 2008 are often presented as an *ubuntu*-inspired regime for the reform of and reintegration into society and family life of children who have committed crimes. Indeed, the Act explicitly links the criminal responsibility of children who are perpetrators of crime to the restorative aims contained in the Act, notably diversion from the formal criminal justice system, an increased emphasis on rehabilitation and reintegration, and reconciliation with victims.[127]

The various theories of punishment and the sentencing practices of South African criminal courts are perhaps not yet truly reflective of *ubuntu* or, indeed, restorative justice in the broad sense. There will arguably always be a place for retribution, deterrence and the other approaches to punishment discussed in this chapter. None of these theories have developed in a value-neutral or ahistorical setting. For instance, it is safe to say that those approaches which emphasise the individual characteristics of the wrongdoer and the justification of punishment as 'just desert', were strongly influenced by liberal criminal theory (one can think of the work of theorists like the German academic Andreas von Hirsch).[128] The challenge for South African criminal courts is to develop a truly South African theory of punishment, and it is suggested that restorative justice should play a prominent role in this regard. In the words of Desmond Tutu, the former Archbishop of Cape Town and chairperson of South Africa's Truth and Reconciliation Commission:

> **I contend that there is another kind of justice, restorative justice, which was characteristic of traditional African jurisprudence. Here the central concern is not retribution or punishment but, in the spirit of *ubuntu*, the healing of breaches, the redressing of imbalances, the restoration of broken relationships. This kind of**

123 *S v Makwanyane and another* 1995 (3) SA 391 (CC).
124 *S v Makwanyane* supra; Chaskalson at 129.
125 *S v Makwanyane* supra; Chaskalson at 130–131.
126 Cornell D and Van Marle K 'Exploring ubuntu: Tentative reflections' 5(2) *Afr Hum Rts L J* (2005) 195 at 205–206.
127 See the Preamble of the Child Justice Act 75 of 2008. Academic commentators have argued that the Preamble should play a significant role in interpreting the restorative aims of the Child Justice Act. See Sloth-Nielsen J and Gallinetti, J '"Just say sorry?" *Ubuntu*, Africanisation and the child justice system in the Child Justice Act 75 of 2008' 14(4) *PER* (2011) 62 at 67.
128 See, in general, Simester, Du Bois-Pedain and Neumann (eds) *Liberal Criminal Theory*.

justice seeks to rehabilitate both the victim and the perpetrator, who should be given the opportunity to be reintegrated into the community he or she has injured by his or her offence. This is a far more personal approach, which sees the offence as something that has happened to people and whose consequence is a rupture in relationships. Thus we would claim that justice, restorative justice, is being served when efforts are being made to work for healing, for forgiveness and for reconciliation.[129]

1.11 Overview of the elements of criminal liability

We have shown that for a person to be found guilty of a crime, he must have engaged in conduct that was defined by law as a crime at the time it was committed. Depending on the definition of the relevant crime, this *unlawful conduct* may consist of a positive act (the most usual form of crime), an omission (less common), or even being in a prohibited situation or state of affairs (for example, being in unlawful possession of drugs or other prohibited items). In addition, some crimes, such as murder, require the state to prove that the accused person's conduct caused a particular consequence. In the case of murder, this would be the death of the deceased.

However, whatever form the unlawful conduct takes, it needs to meet two basic requirements: it must be the conduct of a person and it must be voluntary. Individuals are not, as a rule, liable for acts and omissions that are beyond their physical power to prevent or control. Therefore, the involuntariness of a particular act or omission is a *defence* that the accused could raise to escape liability.

An accused could also raise the defence that although his conduct apparently conformed to the definition of a crime, it was not in fact unlawful because he had a lawful justification for that conduct. For example, the accused may have been acting in self-defence, or in a situation of necessity, or under duress (compulsion) from another person. In other words, conduct that appears to be unlawful at first sight will not in fact be unlawful if the accused had a legally acceptable reason for acting as he did.

Unlawful conduct alone is normally insufficient for criminal liability. As in most modern legal systems, guilt in our law depends as much on an accused's guilty state of mind at the relevant time as on his outward conduct. Mental guilt,[130] broadly speaking, is in turn made up of two elements:

1. Having the power to recognise and avoid wrongdoing in the first instance (criminal capacity)
2. Consciously choosing to do what is wrong (fault or *mens rea*)

Both these elements of liability will generally involve an enquiry into the accused's subjective state of mind.[131]

129 Archbishop Desmond Tutu, quoted in Roche D 'Restorative justice and the Regulatory state in South African townships' 42(3) *Brit J Crim* (2002) 514 at 520.

130 The term 'culpability' is sometimes used to denote the mental elements of criminal liability and distinguish them from the element of conduct, although the term 'culpability' can also be used in a more general sense simply to denote blameworthiness.

131 The exception is where the relevant form of fault is *culpa* or negligence. This is an objective concept and is therefore not concerned with the accused's subjective state of mind.

Criminal capacity implies that at the time of the unlawful conduct, the individual must, firstly, be capable of appreciating that what he is contemplating doing is indeed wrong. Secondly, he must be capable of controlling his behaviour to avoid doing what he understands to be wrong. This is something that normal adults would generally be able to do, but young children and persons who are mentally ill or heavily intoxicated may not be able to do these things. If this is the case, they would not be criminally liable because they did not have criminal capacity. Lack of criminal capacity is therefore another possible defence that an accused could raise to escape liability.

Lastly, for criminal liability to arise, unlawful conduct and criminal capacity must be accompanied by **fault** (***mens rea***) in the form required by the definition of the crime concerned. Our law recognises two forms of fault, namely ***dolus*** (**criminal intent**) and ***culpa*** (**negligence**). The form of fault normally required for criminal liability is *dolus* or criminal intent. By criminal intent, we do not mean that the accused must necessarily have wanted, desired or meant to commit the crime in question. It will normally be sufficient if the accused was aware of the possibility that he might be conducting himself unlawfully, but nevertheless persisted in his intended course of conduct.[132]

Dolus does, however, imply conscious wrongdoing in the sense that the accused must have known that he was breaking the law, or must at least have foreseen the possibility that he might be doing so. Accordingly, where the accused made a material mistake of fact or law, which led him to believe that he was acting in a lawful manner when this was not in fact the case, the accused can raise this as a defence to escape liability.

Although *dolus* is the normal form of fault in criminal matters, there are cases where mere negligence will suffice. Originally, there was only one such crime at common law: culpable homicide.[133] In the case of statutory offences, especially so-called public welfare offences, where the object of the legislation is to protect or promote public safety by penalising careless or negligent behaviour, it is quite common for the legislature to provide that *culpa* will be a sufficient form of fault. *Culpa* is a fundamentally different concept from *dolus*. It is not judged subjectively, but objectively, that is, according to the standards of a reasonable person in the same position as the accused. Although a mistake of fact or law could conceivably be a defence in cases where *culpa* is the required form of fault, it will only exclude liability if a reasonable person in the same position as the accused would have made the same mistake.

Lastly, although all common law crimes require fault in some form, there may be statutory offences for which the legislature has dispensed with the need to prove fault at all. This is known as *strict* or *no-fault liability*. In such cases, it would not benefit the accused to argue that he had no intention of committing the offence concerned and/or that he was not negligent in this regard. Liability would be based on his unlawful conduct alone. An example is where a company director (representing a juristic person) is held liable for the unlawful conduct of the juristic person (the company). This type of liability is often employed by the legislature in the context of public interest offences or so-called regulatory offences. In terms of South African constitutional jurisprudence, this form of liability can generally be regarded as unacceptable.[134]

---

132 This form of intention is known as *dolus eventualis*. We discuss it fully in section 19.3.3.

133 It has been held, however, that in cases of contempt of court, when it is committed by a newspaper editor publishing comment on a matter that is **sub judice** (still under decision by the court), *culpa* will also be a sufficient form of fault – see *S v Harber and another: In re S v Baleka and others* 1986 (4) SA 214 (T). See also Burchell *Principles of Criminal Law* 874.

134 See also section 1.9.4.

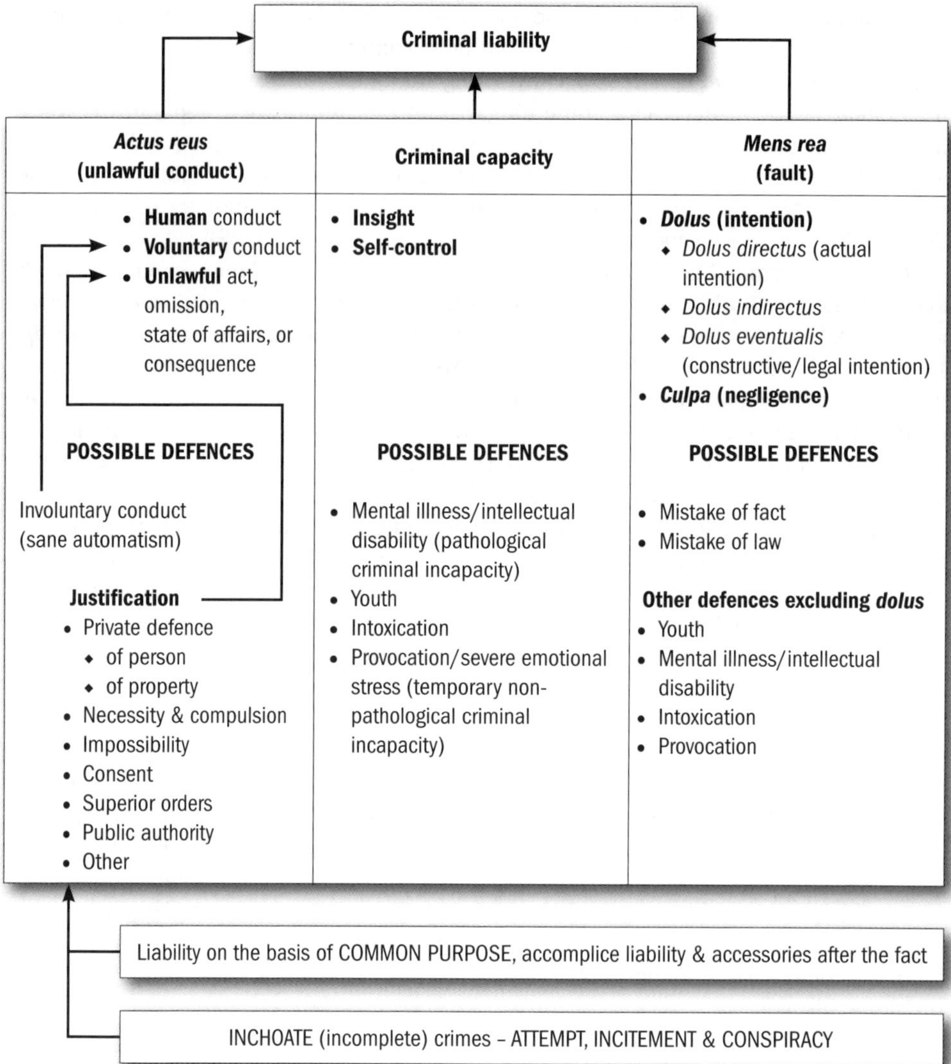

Figure 1.2 Criminal liability

We can see, therefore, that for an accused person to be liable for a crime, the state must prove three things, namely that:

1. the accused committed the unlawful conduct required by the definition of that particular crime
2. at the time that he committed the crime, the accused had the capacity (ability):
   a) to appreciate the wrongfulness of this conduct
   b) to act in accordance with that appreciation
3. at the same time, the accused intended to commit the crime in question (in the case of crimes that require criminal intention), or was negligent in that regard (in the case of crimes requiring negligence).

There are thus three principal elements of criminal liability:

1. Unlawful conduct
2. Criminal capacity
3. Fault (intention or negligence)

If any one of these elements is lacking or if the state is unable to prove it beyond reasonable doubt, then the accused cannot be held criminally liable. Figure 1.2 depicts the elements of criminal liability together with the applicable defences.

The next few chapters consist of a detailed examination of each of the three elements of criminal liability together with the possible defences that an accused person could raise to exclude (or negate) that particular element. Although we study the three elements separately for purposes of convenience, it is important to remember that, in practice, they are all interrelated and even overlap in places. In the end, they are all concerned with establishing one thing: the accused person's criminal liability, that is, whether the accused is guilty of the crime or not.

DISCUSSION

Determining criminal liability

Suppose that Abe is charged with the murder of Ben. Murder is defined as a crime in this country. It is the intentional unlawful killing of a person. Therefore, to prove that Abe is liable for murder, the state must first prove that Abe caused Ben's death and that he did so unlawfully. If Ben's death was not caused by Abe, or if Abe killed Ben involuntarily (for example, while sleepwalking), or if Abe killed Ben lawfully (for example, in self-defence), then Abe would not be liable for murder because there would be no unlawful conduct.

Once the state has established that Abe caused Ben's death unlawfully, it must prove that Abe had the necessary criminal capacity to commit murder. In other words, it must prove that at the time that he killed Ben, Abe was capable of appreciating that it was wrong to kill Ben and that he was capable of controlling his behaviour to avoid doing what he knew was wrong.[135] If Abe was a normal adult at the time of the killing, the state would normally have no difficulty in proving this. However, if Abe was a child, or mentally ill, or heavily intoxicated at the time, he may not have been capable of appreciating that it was wrong to kill Ben in the particular circumstances. Alternatively, he may have been capable of appreciating this, but may have been unable to control his behaviour to avoid doing what he knew was wrong. In cases such as these, Abe would not be liable for murder because he would have lacked criminal capacity.

If, however, the state can establish that Abe had the necessary criminal capacity, it must finally prove that Abe had the necessary form of fault for murder. Murder is a crime requiring criminal intent (*dolus*). *Dolus* must therefore be proved in relation to every element of the alleged crime. This means that the state must prove that at the time when Abe killed Ben, he was aware that his conduct may lead to Ben's death, that he was aware that Ben was a person and that he was aware that he had no lawful justification for killing Ben. If, however, Abe was not aware of these things, for example

135 Note that if Abe raises the defence of mental illness or intellectual disability, then the onus of proving criminal capacity is not on the state. Abe would have to prove this defence because our law presumes that all persons are sane until proven otherwise. This is an important exception to the normal rules relating to the onus of proof in criminal cases. The defence of mental illness or intellectual disability, is discussed fully in the section dealing with criminal capacity.

he may not have realised that he could actually cause Ben's death, he may have mistaken Ben for an animal, or he may have believed that Ben was about to attack him and that he needed to defend himself, then Abe would not be liable for murder because he would lack fault in the form of *dolus*. If the state can prove that Abe had the necessary intention to murder Ben, then the state will have proved its case and Abe will be found guilty of murder.

THIS CHAPTER IN ESSENCE

In this chapter key historical, normative and conceptual aspects of South African criminal law, as well as theories of punishment, were addressed. It also introduced the important debate on the decolonisation of the criminal law curriculum.

Chapter 2

The conduct of a criminal trial

CHAPTER OBJECTIVES

The objectives of this chapter are to:
- describe briefly the procedure normally followed at a criminal trial
- identify and distinguish between a charge, a conviction and a sentence
- identify and distinguish between direct and circumstantial evidence
- explain what is meant by a competent verdict and provide common examples.

2.1 Introductory remarks

The purpose of this chapter is to provide a brief and broad overview of the principal features of a criminal trial in order to provide a context for the material that follows. It is not intended to be a thorough treatment of the subject. The rules of criminal procedure and evidence warrant detailed attention in their own right and readers seeking more information on these subjects are advised to consult an appropriate work where the matters touched on here are dealt with in considerably more depth.[1] This work is on substantive South African criminal law. It is, however, helpful to have a basic understanding of procedural law to see how the rules of substantive law find application in the criminal process.

2.2 Pre-trial procedures

2.2.1 Securing the accused's presence in court

There are two main ways of ensuring that a person accused of a crime comes to court to stand trial: by way of a **summons** or a notice to the accused calling on him to appear in court on a particular date, or by way of arrest.[2]

2.2.2 Bail

If the accused is brought to court under arrest, he is entitled to apply to be released on bail.[3] **Bail** is an amount of money, determined by the court, which the accused must pay as security for his due appearance in court on the dates on which his case is due to proceed. Contrary to what many laypersons believe, bail is not a preliminary fine or other form of punishment imposed on the accused in advance. Its purpose is to minimise interference with the accused's liberty, while discouraging him from absconding.[4] Thus, if the accused duly appears in court and stands trial, he is entitled to the refund of his bail money at the end of the proceedings, regardless of the outcome. If the accused does not appear in court when he is required to, however, his bail money will be forfeited to the state and a warrant will be issued for his re-arrest.[5]

In addition to setting the amount of bail, the court can impose conditions on the accused when ordering his release on bail. For example, the court can order that the accused must surrender his passport, or must report to a certain police station at set intervals, or may not leave (or enter) a certain area without the court's permission, or may not approach or communicate with certain individuals. The purpose of the last-mentioned example is to prevent the accused from tampering with evidence or interfering with state witnesses. If the accused breaches these conditions, the state can apply for his bail to be cancelled.

Where the accused is charged with a less serious offence and there is little risk of absconsion, the court may release the accused on warning, that is, without having to pay bail. Children are commonly released into the custody of their parents.

2.2.3 Preparation for trial

An accused is entitled to be given sufficient information by the state to enable him to prepare properly for his trial. Thus, he is entitled to examine the **charge sheet**[6] and is also entitled

---

1 For commentary on South African criminal procedure, see Du Toit et al *Commentary on the Criminal Procedure Act* (1987) (revision service 59, 2017) and Hiemstra VG and Kruger A *Hiemstra's Criminal Procedure* 6 ed (2008) (regular updates). For evidence, see Zeffert DT and Paizes AP *The South African Law of Evidence* 3 ed (2017) and Schwikkard PJ and Van der Merwe SE *Principles of Evidence* 4 ed (2016). For sentencing, see Terblanche SS *A Guide to Sentencing in South Africa* 3 ed (2016).

2 Ss 39–56 of the Criminal Procedure Act 51 of 1977.

3 Ss 58–71 of the Criminal Procedure Act. For a detailed discussion, see Van der Berg J *Bail: A Practitioner's Guide* 3 ed (2012).

4 *Minister van Wet en Orde en andere v Dipper* 1993 (3) SA 591 (A); *S v Van Wyk* 2005 (1) SACR 41 (SCA).

5 S 67(1) of the Criminal Procedure Act.

6 S 80 of the Criminal Procedure Act. A charge sheet is a formal document indicating the crime(s) with which the accused is to be charged and setting out the essential allegations on which the state intends to rely for a conviction of that/those crime(s). In the High Court, this document is called an **indictment**.

to such additional particulars (details) as he needs for purposes of preparation.[7] The present practice is that the prosecuting authorities normally supply the accused's legal representative with a copy of the charge sheet, copies of witness statements and copies of any statement made by the accused as a matter of course. This usually obviates the need for the accused to request further particulars.

2.2.4 Legal representation

Sections 35(2)(*c*) and 35(3)(*g*) of the Constitution provide that the accused has a right to legal representation. If the accused cannot afford such representation, he has a right to be represented by a legal practitioner assigned and paid for by the state if substantial injustice would otherwise result.[8] There is no obligation on an accused to have legal representation, however. An accused is fully entitled to conduct his own defence if he wishes.

2.3 The trial

2.3.1 The parties in a criminal trial

The parties in a criminal trial are the state, represented by a public prosecutor (in the High Court this is a State Advocate), and the accused, represented by his legal practitioner if he has one. The complainant (the victim of the crime or other person who laid the charges against the accused) is not a party to the proceedings, but may be called as a witness.

Criminal trials in the lower courts are presided over by a magistrate or regional magistrate and in the High Court by a judge, sometimes sitting with one or two assessors whose function is to help the judge or magistrate make findings of fact on the evidence presented to the court. South Africa does not have a jury system.[9]

2.3.2 The charge

At the beginning of the trial, the state puts the charge(s) to the accused. The prosecutor normally reads out the charge sheet or indictment containing the state's allegations against the accused. Once this has been done, we say that the accused has been **charged with** the crime or crimes in question.[10]

Where the state alleges that the accused has committed more than one crime, whether on the same occasion or on different occasions, it may charge the accused with all these crimes simultaneously.[11] The purpose of this is to avoid the time and expense involved in conducting a series of separate trials, and to minimise interference with the accused's liberty. In this case, each crime is regarded as a separate **count**; the accused must plead to each count; the state must lead evidence to prove each count; and the court must ultimately pronounce a verdict on each count.

By the same token, where the state alleges that more than one person committed a particular crime or series of crimes, it may charge them all with those crimes

7 S 87 of the Criminal Procedure Act.

8 The Constitution of the Republic of South Africa, 1996.

9 In South Africa, the practice of having juries in criminal matters was abolished in 1969.

10 A charge means a burden. Once the accused has been charged, although he is still presumed to be innocent, he is nevertheless burdened with having to undergo a trial to establish his guilt or innocence. He is no longer a completely free agent.

11 S 81 of the Criminal Procedure Act.

simultaneously.[12] In these cases, for the sake of convenience and to avoid confusion, the various accused are traditionally numbered 'accused no 1', 'accused no 2', and so on, and are then referred to by those numbers during the trial. Each accused is, however, required to plead separately to each crime with which he is charged; the court must hear evidence with regard to the liability of each accused on each count; and it must ultimately pronounce a verdict in respect of each count with which each accused has been charged.

Where the state is uncertain as to which of a number of possible crimes it will be able to prove against the accused in court, it may charge him with all or any of these possible crimes, either together or in the alternative,[13] and leave it to the court to decide, after hearing evidence, what crime or crimes he has actually committed.

2.3.3 The plea

Once the charge has been put to the accused, the accused is required to respond to it by **pleading** to the charge.[14] The usual pleas are 'guilty' or 'not guilty'.

However, there are also certain technical pleas that an accused can raise, for example that he has already been tried for substantially the same crime and has either been acquitted of it or has been convicted of it as the case may be (the so-called double jeopardy pleas).[15] Also, the accused can plead that the court does not have the necessary jurisdiction to hear the matter or that the prosecutor does not have the necessary authority to prosecute.[16] There are other technical pleas as well, but they need not be mentioned here.

If the accused refuses to plead, the court must record a plea of 'not guilty'.[17]

2.3.3.1 Plea of guilty

Where the accused has pleaded guilty to the charge and where the offence is a relatively minor one – that is, an offence for which the court may not impose a sentence of imprisonment or a fine in excess of a specified amount (currently R5,000) – the court may convict the accused on the basis of his guilty plea alone and proceed to the sentencing stage.[18]

In all other cases, the court must first satisfy itself that the accused is indeed guilty of the crime charged, at least on his own version of the facts. For this purpose, the accused may hand in a written statement, in which he admits sufficient facts to show that he is indeed guilty. Where the accused is represented, his legal representative will prepare this statement.[19] Alternatively, if the accused does not hand in such a statement, the court must question the accused to establish his guilt.[20] If the accused admits sufficient facts to establish his guilt, the court will convict the accused of the crime charged and the trial may proceed to the sentencing phase. If the accused does not admit all the essential allegations, the court must record a plea of not guilty and the trial will proceed as though the accused had pleaded not guilty at the outset.[21]

Where a number of accused are charged with a particular crime and some of them plead guilty while others plead not guilty, their trials will be separated. Those who pleaded guilty

12 Ss 155 and 156 of the Criminal Procedure Act.
13 S 83 of the Criminal Procedure Act.
14 S 105 of the Criminal Procedure Act.
15 The pleas of *autrefois acquit* and *autrefois convict*.
16 Ss 106(1)(*c*)–(*h*) of the Criminal Procedure Act.
17 S 109 of the Criminal Procedure Act.
18 S 112(1)(*a*) of the Criminal Procedure Act.
19 S 112(2) of the Criminal Procedure Act.
20 S 112(1)(*b*) of the Criminal Procedure Act.
21 S 113 of the Criminal Procedure Act.

will then proceed directly to the sentencing stage, while a trial will be held in respect of those who pleaded not guilty.

2.3.3.2 Plea of not guilty

Where the accused pleads not guilty, the court will invite the accused to make a statement disclosing the basis of his defence. If the accused does not want to make such a statement, the court may put questions to the accused to ascertain the basis of his defence.[22] The purpose of this step is to define the issues in dispute between the parties and thus simplify and shorten the proceedings. Because an accused has the right to remain silent, however, he is not obliged to make such a statement nor is he obliged to answer the court's questions in this regard.

2.3.3.3 Formal admissions

If the accused wishes to do so, he may formally admit certain of the allegations against him, thereby making it unnecessary for the state to lead evidence to prove those particular allegations.[23] For example, where the accused's defence is that he acted in self-defence, he may well admit killing or injuring the victim, and simply place the unlawfulness of his conduct in dispute. Once again, an accused is under no obligation to make any such admission if he does not wish to do so.

2.3.4 The state's case

Once these preliminaries are over, the evidence stage begins. Because the state normally bears the onus of proof in a criminal trial, it always leads its evidence first. It will do this by calling witnesses to testify in court and it can also introduce documentary evidence and real evidence in the form of exhibits, recordings, photographs, plans and so forth. If the state considers it necessary, it can call experts to testify on its behalf and it can also call for an inspection *in loco* of the scene of the crime or any other place relevant to the proceedings. Where the accused has made a free and voluntary confession, the state can also prove this confession against the accused.[24] A discussion of the law of evidence is beyond the scope of this book, but a few words concerning direct and circumstantial evidence may be useful.

Essentially, the state can prove its case against the accused by means of direct evidence, or by means of circumstantial (indirect) evidence, or by means of a combination of the two. **Direct evidence** is the term used for evidence given by a witness who testifies as to the accused's guilt on the basis of what he personally saw, heard or otherwise perceived with his own senses. **Circumstantial evidence** is the term given to evidence of other facts from which the court is asked to infer (draw a conclusion as to) the accused's guilt. For example, if A saw B stabbing and killing C, and A testifies to this effect in court, this would be an example of direct evidence on a charge of murder. Similarly, if B told A that he had stabbed and killed C and A testifies to this effect in court, this would be another example of direct evidence. If, however, A did not witness the stabbing, but merely saw B running away from the scene of the crime shortly afterwards, brandishing a bloodstained knife, this would be an example of circumstantial evidence from which the state would ask the court to infer B's guilt. Fingerprint evidence, ballistics evidence and DNA evidence are all examples of circumstantial evidence.

---

22 S 115 of the Criminal Procedure Act.
23 S 220 of the Criminal Procedure Act.
24 S 217 of the Criminal Procedure Act.

The layperson often labours under the misapprehension that the state requires direct evidence to prove its case beyond a reasonable doubt, but this is not so. Nor is direct evidence necessarily stronger than circumstantial evidence. An eyewitness's account of a crime is necessarily subjective since it is filtered through the witness's own perceptions and memory. Its probative value depends on the reliability of the witness – as experience has taught us, human beings are notoriously fallible, susceptible to bias, whether conscious or unconscious, and sometimes just dishonest. In contrast, certain types of circumstantial evidence can be compelling. For example, where the accused's fingerprints are found on the murder weapon, or at the scene of the crime, in circumstances where the accused is unable to offer any innocent explanation as to how this may have occurred, the court may well be justified in drawing the inference that the accused is guilty. An important point to note with regard to the drawing of inferences, however, is that a court may only draw an inference of guilt against an accused if that is the *only* reasonably possible inference that can be drawn from all the proven facts. Where there is another reasonably possible inference which is consistent with the accused's innocence, then there is a reasonable doubt as to the accused's guilt and the accused is entitled to the benefit of that doubt.

After each state witness has given his evidence in chief, the defence is entitled to cross-examine the witness. Where there is more than one accused, each accused (through his legal representative) has the right to cross-examine the witness in turn. The purpose of such cross-examination is to elicit evidence favourable to the accused's case. This can be done in a variety of ways, for example by getting the witness to give information that he did not mention in his evidence in chief, or by showing that the witness is unreliable and not to be believed. After cross-examination is complete, the state has the right to re-examine the witness to clarify any matters arising from the cross-examination. The court is also entitled to put questions to the witness to obtain any further information that it considers relevant.

Once the state has led all its evidence, it will close its case.

2.3.5 Application for discharge after the state's case

An accused is not required to rebut the state's case if the state has not succeeded in presenting sufficient evidence to sustain a conviction. Accordingly, after the state has closed its case, the court may return a verdict of not guilty if it is of the opinion that there is no evidence that the accused committed the crime referred to in the charge or any crime of which he may be convicted on the charge. The state has the right to oppose and argue against the granting of the application. If, after hearing argument for both sides, the court agrees that the state has not presented evidence on which a reasonable person would convict the accused, it must grant the application and find the accused not guilty there and then.[25] If the application is rejected, the accused will be put on his defence. A trial court's decision on an application for discharge is not subject to appeal.

2.3.6 The defence case

Once the accused is put on his defence, he has a further choice. He may lead evidence to rebut the state case, or he can simply close his case without leading any evidence at all. Of course, if he chooses not to lead any evidence, he runs the risk of being convicted on the basis of the state's evidence. If, however, the state has made out a *prima facie* case, but its evidence is unable to withstand close scrutiny, then there could well be a reasonable doubt

25 S 174 of the Criminal Procedure Act. See also *S v Lubaxa* 2001 (2) SACR 703 (SCA); *S v Dewani* (CC 15/2014) [2014] ZAWCHC 188 (8 Dec 2014).

as to the accused's guilt and the court will acquit the accused despite the lack of evidence for the defence.

If the defence chooses to lead evidence, the accused may give evidence on his own behalf and the defence can also place evidence before the court by calling witnesses and introducing real evidence just as the state is entitled to do.

An accused is not obliged to testify in his own defence. One of the consequences of the right to remain silent and not to be convicted out of one's own mouth is that no one can be compelled to give evidence at his own trial. If the accused elects to testify, however, he will normally give his evidence first, before his witnesses, so that he cannot be accused of tailoring his evidence to correspond with that of his witnesses. Remember that, generally speaking, the accused has the right to be present at all stages of his trial, and will therefore also hear the testimony of all witnesses, including defence witnesses. A further consequence of electing to testify is that once the accused has given his evidence in chief, he is obliged to submit to cross-examination by the state. The court also has the right to put questions to the accused. The same applies to any witnesses called to testify for the defence. After cross-examination, the defence may re-examine the accused and his witnesses on matters arising from the cross-examination.

Once all the defence witnesses have completed their evidence, the defence will close its case and the trial will proceed to the argument stage.

2.3.7 Argument

At this stage, the state presents its argument as to why the accused should be convicted, followed by argument for the defence as to why the accused should not be convicted. The state has the right of reply to the defence argument.

2.3.8 Judgment and verdict

Once the court has heard argument for both sides, it will deliver its judgment, that is, its findings of fact and its decision on any points of law raised at the trial. At the end of its judgment, it will pronounce its **verdict** – it will pronounce the accused 'guilty' (convict the accused) or 'not guilty' (acquit the accused), as the case may be. Where the accused was charged with more than one crime, a verdict must be pronounced on each count.

Normally, where the accused is found not guilty of any crime, the court will discharge him, that is, tell him that he is free to leave. However, where the accused has successfully raised the defence of mental illness, the court must enter what is called a special verdict and must pronounce the accused 'not guilty by reason of mental illness'. Where a special verdict is pronounced, the accused is not discharged after the verdict as the court must direct what is to happen to the accused. Here the court has various options,[26] which may include making an order that the accused be detained indefinitely in a psychiatric institution or mental hospital.[27]

2.3.8.1 Competent verdicts

What happens where the state was unable to prove the accused guilty of the crime or crimes with which he was charged, but was able to prove that he is guilty of some other crime? The general rule is that a court may not convict a person of a crime with which he has not

26 S 78(6) of the Criminal Procedure Act.

27 The options available to the court are discussed more fully in Chapter 15, dealing with the defence of mental illness/intellectual disability (see section 15.5).

specifically been charged as this would be procedurally unfair. However, there is an important and far-reaching exception to this general rule. This is where a conviction of the crime in question is a **competent verdict** on the crime with which the accused was actually charged.

A competent verdict is a less serious offence, the essential elements of which are impliedly embraced by the essential elements of the crime with which the accused has actually been charged.[28] When the evidence presented in court does not prove the accused guilty of the crime with which he was charged, but it does prove the accused guilty of some other lesser offence, which is a competent verdict on that charge, then the court is empowered (competent) to convict the accused of that lesser offence instead of acquitting him outright. There is no need for the state to have charged him expressly with the lesser offence as an alternative to the original charge.[29]

It is important to note that a competent verdict is only permissible when the main charge has *not* been successfully proved against the accused, but all the essential elements of the lesser offence *have* been proved beyond a reasonable doubt.

The Criminal Procedure Act makes provision for a range of competent verdicts in respect of a variety of crimes, ranging from murder to rape and theft.[30] The competent verdicts on a charge of murder, for example, include culpable homicide, assault with intent to do grievous bodily harm, robbery, common assault, public violence and pointing a firearm.[31] In addition, sections 256 and 257 of the Act provide that a person accused of *any* crime can be convicted instead of an attempt to commit that crime or of being an accessory after the fact to that crime.[32]

It may happen that, at the commencement of the trial, an accused will plead not guilty to the crime with which he has actually been charged, but offer a plea of guilty to a lesser crime which is a competent verdict on that charge. It is then open to the state, if it wishes, to accept the accused's plea of guilty to the lesser charge and abandon the original charge. The state's decision in this regard is then binding on the court.

2.4 Sentence

Once the accused has been convicted of a crime, whether after trial or on a plea of guilty, the sentencing phase begins. The state normally begins by informing the court whether the accused has any previous convictions and, if so, what these convictions are.[33] For this purpose, the state will hand in a copy of the accused's criminal record if he has one (form SAP 69).[34]

It is then open to both parties to lead evidence in relation to the sentence if they wish. The court may also call for evidence on any matter that it considers necessary for purposes of passing an appropriate sentence. In the case of young offenders, the court will often ask

28 These are sometimes referred to as latent (hidden) offences. In American law, they are referred to as lesser included offences.

29 The purpose of competent verdicts is to make it unnecessary for the state to add a number of express alternative charges every time it charges an accused.

30 Ss 258–269A of the Criminal Procedure Act. S 270 deals with offences not expressly provided for in the Act.

31 S 258 of the Criminal Procedure Act.

32 See also Chapter 26 for a discussion of the principles regarding attempts and other incomplete forms of criminal conduct.

33 The court is not allowed to know of any previous convictions before it has determined the accused's guilt since this information may prejudice the court against the accused.

34 Form SAP 69 is a record extracted from the police service's criminal record system, detailing the accused's previous convictions, including the relevant offence, date of conviction and sentence.

for a probation officer to investigate the accused's personal circumstances and provide the court with a report. In many matters, however, the parties simply address the court from the bar. The defence informs the court of any factors relevant to mitigation of sentence, while the state deals with aggravating factors. Once the court has heard the addresses for both sides, it will determine an appropriate sentence and impose it on the accused.

In current South African law, a sentence may take a variety of forms, namely imprisonment, including life imprisonment and periodical imprisonment;[35] declaration as a habitual criminal or as a dangerous criminal;[36] committal to an institution or drug treatment centre;[37] a fine;[38] and correctional supervision.[39] In appropriate cases, a combination of different forms of sentence may be imposed. The court also has the power to order that the passing of sentence be postponed for a specific period, whether conditionally or unconditionally, or that the operation of all or any portion of the imposed sentence be suspended for a specific period on certain conditions.[40] The most usual condition is good conduct where the accused should not repeat his offence within the period of postponement or suspension, but more creative conditions, such as community service and/or the compensation of the victim, may also be imposed.

Young offenders (persons under 18) are generally dealt with in terms of Chapter 10 of the Child Justice Act 75 of 2008. This Act also provides for alternatives to traditional forms of punishment, notably the various diversion options (Chapter 6 of the Act) in the case of minor offences.

Once sentence has been passed, the case is then regarded as finalised and the accused, if he wishes, may have recourse to his rights of appeal and review.

---

35 S 276(1)(*b*)-(*c*) of the Criminal Procedure Act.

36 S 276(1)(*d*), read with s 286 and ss 286A and 286B of the Criminal Procedure Act. These provisions allow for the indefinite imprisonment, within certain limits, of habitual and dangerous criminals.

37 Ss 276(1)(*e*) and 296 of the Criminal Procedure Act.

38 S 276(1)(*f*) of the Criminal Procedure Act.

39 S 276(1)(*h*)-(*i*) of the Criminal Procedure Act.

40 S 297 of the Criminal Procedure Act.

PART TWO

General principles of criminal law

SECTION 1 UNLAWFUL CONDUCT

SECTION 2 CRIMINAL CAPACITY

SECTION 3 FAULT

SECTION 4 DEGREES OF PARTICIPATION IN CRIME

SECTION 5 INCOMPLETE CRIMES

Chapter 3

Unlawful conduct

CHAPTER OBJECTIVES

The objectives of this chapter are to:
- introduce the concept of unlawful conduct
- introduce the essential requirements for unlawful conduct
- define the term 'human conduct' and explain its relevance to criminal liability
- define the term 'voluntary conduct' and explain its relevance to criminal liability
- define the term 'automatism' and explain its relevance to criminal liability
- distinguish between sane and insane automatism
- identify and explain the circumstances in which culpable prior voluntary conduct will result in criminal liability for involuntary acts and omissions.

3.1 Introduction

At the end of Chapter 1, we explained that there are three essential elements of criminal liability:
1. Unlawful conduct
2. Criminal capacity
3. Fault (in the form of intention or negligence)

Although, in theory, we could begin studying the general principles of criminal liability with any one of these three elements, the usual starting point is to consider the accused's conduct. This is because if the state is unable to prove that there was unlawful conduct on the part of the accused (the legal term for this is the ***actus reus***),[1] then the accused cannot be criminally liable, and the enquiries into criminal capacity and fault become redundant. Furthermore, as we will explain at the appropriate points, criminal capacity and fault are never determined in isolation, but must be determined in relation to the relevant accused's particular unlawful conduct. For this reason, a trial court normally begins its judgment by considering whether the state has proved the *actus reus* before going on to consider the other two elements of liability.

Since each crime has its own definition, the *actus reus* will vary according to the crime concerned.[2] There are, however, three essential requirements that must invariably be met to satisfy the unlawful conduct part of the enquiry:

- The conduct in question must have been that of a *human being*.
- The conduct in question must have been *voluntary*.
- The conduct in question must also have been *unlawful* in that it must consist of conduct that was defined by law as a crime at the time that the conduct took place. This is to satisfy the principle of legality.

The law in question could be common law or it could be a statute (legislation). Where the conduct with which the accused is charged does not fit the definition of a crime, or if that crime did not exist at the time that the conduct occurred, the principle of legality has not been satisfied and the accused cannot be held liable. In such cases, the accused is entitled to object to the charge on the grounds that it does not disclose an offence.[3] Where the accused raises such an objection, he is entitled to have the point decided ***in limine***[4] before being required to plead.

Conduct that is defined by law as a crime may take various forms. Depending on the definition of the crime concerned, it may consist of:

1. committing an act that was prohibited by law; or
2. omitting to perform an act that was required by law; or
3. being in a state of affairs that is prohibited by law; or
4. causing a consequence prohibited by law.

We will consider each of the above requirements in turn.

3.2 Human conduct

In criminal law, we are concerned only with punishing the conduct of human beings. We do not use the criminal justice system to punish animals for their misconduct.[5] Therefore, the first requirement of unlawful conduct is that it must have been the conduct of a human

1 See the glossary for definitions of the terms in bold.

2 Murder and culpable homicide are notable exceptions. Murder is the *intentional* unlawful killing of a person, while culpable homicide is the *negligent* unlawful killing of a person. Therefore, the *actus reus* for murder and the *actus reus* for culpable homicide are identical: each consists of the unlawful killing of a person. The sole difference between the two crimes lies in the fault element: intention is required for murder, whereas negligence is sufficient for culpable homicide. See further, Chapter 27.

3 S 85 *et seq* of the Criminal Procedure Act 51 of 1977.

4 A preliminary point, usually of a technical nature.

5 However, this was a common practice in medieval times, and continued in some places into the 19th century. Indeed, the last recorded case of animal prosecution in Europe took place in Switzerland as recently as 1906 when two men and one dog were tried for murder. The men were given life imprisonment and the dog was sentenced to death. Edward Payson Evans provided a detailed account of animal prosecutions in his 1906 book *The Criminal Prosecution and Capital Punishment of Animals*, which formed the subject of an article by Paul Schiff Berman, entitled 'Rats, pigs, and statues on trial: The creation of cultural narratives in the prosecution of animals and inanimate objects' (1994) 69(2) *NYU L Rev* 288.

being. Note, however, that if someone uses an animal to carry out a criminal act, for example inciting a dog to bite a person, this does not exonerate the perpetrator. However, it is the *human act* (inciting the dog to bite) that is punishable.[6]

3.3 Voluntary conduct

In criminal law, we are concerned only with punishing conduct that the accused had the power to prevent or avoid if he had wanted to do so. Therefore, in the first instance, in order to attract criminal liability, the accused's unlawful conduct must have been voluntary.

The term 'voluntary', as it is used in this part of the enquiry, has a special and restricted meaning in our law. It has nothing to do with what the accused intended, desired or wanted to do (this is part of the fault enquiry). It is concerned merely with whether the accused's actions were controlled by his conscious will in the sense that the accused was physically able to direct his actions, prevent them or stop them if he had chosen to do so.[7]

Involuntary actions are not regarded as conduct for purposes of criminal liability. The same applies to involuntary omissions. These are cases where the accused failed to act as required by law because he lacked the physical ability to control his actions at the relevant time. The following examples will therefore usually not be regarded as voluntary conduct for the purposes of criminal law:

- *Actions that result from imposed physical force:* For example, if I grab A's hand and use it to slap B, A is not guilty of assault but I would be.
- *Uncontrollable muscular movements, such as those resulting from spasticity or pure muscular reflex:* An example here is if I happen to kick my doctor while he is testing my reflexes.
- *Acts and omissions that occur during sleep or unconsciousness:* Examples include taking my baby to sleep with me, rolling onto her in my sleep and suffocating her, or if I black out while driving my car, lose control of the vehicle and cause an accident.[8]
- *Acts and omissions that occur during a state of* ***automatism****:* An example is if I attack someone while I am sleepwalking.

This last example, automatism, requires further discussion.

3.3.1 Automatism

The term 'automatism' is derived from the word 'automaton', meaning 'robot': a mechanical device with no thought or will of its own. A person may perform what *appears* to be a conscious and goal-directed action, but he may actually not be in conscious control of that action or even be aware of what he is doing. In such cases, the person is said to be acting in a *state of automatism*, that is, acting mechanically, with no will or thought of his own, like a robot. In some cases, such a person commits an act, which if committed voluntarily, would amount to a crime. However, because his conduct is involuntary, he cannot be held criminally liable for that act or its consequences.

---

6 Burchell JM *Principles of Criminal Law* 5 ed (2016) 71.

7 Do not confuse involuntary conduct with conduct performed as a result of duress or coercion. Where a person uses violence or threats of violence to compel another to perform a criminal act against his wishes, the latter's conduct is still regarded as voluntary in our law, but he will escape criminal liability on the basis that his conduct was not unlawful in the circumstances (see further on the defence of compulsion, Chapter 8).

8 However, I may be criminally liable if my involuntary act/omission was the result of culpable prior voluntary conduct on my part – see section 3.3.2.

Cases of genuine automatism are not common and may be difficult to prove. Most people have heard of sleepwalking, but there are other manifestations of automatism as well.

DISCUSSION **When is conduct no longer wilful, but rather *mechanical*?**

There is no closed list of examples of mechanical behaviour. In this section, we discuss the most important examples, for instance sleepwalking or epilepsy. Authors have also identified other examples where a person may or may not act in a state of automatism. For instance, a driver of a motor vehicle is stung by a bee and pulls the steering wheel reflexively. Was the driver at that moment still in control of the vehicle, or did he act, even for a second, mechanically and more like a robot? What about sneezing?[9] Many drivers have experienced an uncontrollable sneezing fit and the resultant (and inadvertent) reflexive pull on the steering wheel or closing of the eyes. The essential question is whether the person concerned 'was capable of subjecting her bodily movements or her behaviour to the control of her will'.[10] From a policy point of view, a further question is whether any of these examples are intolerable categories of potential cases of automatism. More to the point, is it medico-legally and scientifically true that a sneeze can lead to a reflex movement, thus excluding voluntary conduct?

Automatism may be classified according to whether it is:
- *organic:* originating in the body, possibly as a result of physical illness or injury, such as epilepsy, concussion or brain tumour
- *toxic:* caused by the consumption of alcohol, drugs or some other intoxicating substance
- *psychogenic:* originating in the mind, due to psychological factors that may or may not result from a mental illness or intellectual disability.

The above classification is not of particular importance to the question of criminal liability, but it is important to distinguish between sane and insane automatism. Where the automatism is due to a mental illness or intellectual disability, whether organic or psychogenic in origin, it is termed *insane automatism*. In such cases, the accused must raise the defence of mental illness or intellectual disability. This is a defence that excludes criminal capacity (rather than unlawful conduct) and has two significant consequences for the accused:
1. He bears the burden of proving his defence on a balance of probabilities.
2. If the defence succeeds, the court is obliged to enter a special verdict[11] with the result that the accused may run the risk of being detained indefinitely in a mental institution.[12]

9 See Snyman CR *Criminal Law* 6 ed (2014) 55 where the author lists sneezing (and the resultant reflex movement) as an example of mechanical behaviour.

10 Snyman *Criminal Law* 55.

11 'Not guilty by reason of mental illness', or 'not guilty by reason of intellectual disability', as the case may be. See ss 78 and 79 of the Criminal Procedure Act. Following the decision by the Constitutional Court in *De Vos NO v Minister of Justice and Constitutional Development* 2015 (2) SACR 217 (CC), sections 77–79 of the Criminal Procedure Act were amended by the Criminal Procedure Amendment Act 4 of 2017. One of the changes brought about by the amendment to the Criminal Procedure Act, is the replacement of the outdated term 'mental defect' with the term 'intellectual disability'.

12 See further, s 78(6) of the Criminal Procedure Act.

We will discuss the defence of insane automatism (pathological automatism) in more detail in Chapter 15 when we deal with the defences that exclude criminal capacity. In this part of the book, we are concerned only with sane (non-pathological) automatism.[13] A case that illustrates the difference between sane and insane automatism is *S v Stellmacher*.[14]

S v Stellmacher

Stellmacher was an epileptic who shot and killed someone in a state of automatism. Before the incident, he had been on a severe diet for some weeks. On the day in question, he ate nothing and did hard physical labour. At about 18h00, he went to the bar of the local hotel and drank half a bottle of brandy. He had a gun with him. There in the bar, according to his evidence, he 'lapsed into a state of automatism, as a result of the strong reflection in his eyes of the setting sun through an empty bottle'.[15] He became involved in an altercation with someone in the bar, took out his gun and let off a few shots. Then, for no apparent reason, he shot the deceased who had just come into the bar and asked if he could order a drink.

At the trial, expert evidence was led that Stellmacher was suffering from 'amnesia and automatism' due to hypoglycaemia and/or epilepsy, possibly triggered by his fasting and drinking.[16] The central issue at the trial was not whether Stellmacher should be convicted of murder (it was accepted that he was not liable), but whether he had suffered from a temporary mental disorder, necessitating a special verdict. The court held that a mental disorder is 'a pathological disturbance of an accused's mental capacity and not a mere temporary mental confusion that is not attributable to a mental abnormality, but rather attributable to external stimuli such as alcohol, drugs or provocation'.[17] It held that Stellmacher's automatism, in this case, was due to physical factors and not to any mental abnormality, and thus a special verdict was not required. He was found not guilty and acquitted outright.

We now consider some of the more common forms and causes of sane automatism: sleepwalking,[18] epilepsy,[19] hypoglycaemia, blackouts, amnesia and intoxication. We will also consider the considerably less common phenomenon of psychogenic sane automatism.[20]

3.3.1.1 Somnambulism (sleepwalking)

When we are asleep, we do not lie perfectly still all the time - we turn over and move our limbs, often without being conscious of doing so. Some individuals also get up and walk around in their sleep, or perform other activities that are normally only performed when awake. Sleepwalkers' eyes are open and they are generally able to navigate their surroundings. In some cases, they may even perform fairly complicated tasks, such as getting into a car and switching on the engine. Some commit acts of violence while in this state, but a sleepwalker is not conscious of his actions and will not remember them when he wakes up.

---

13 'Pathological' means disease related. Thus, pathological criminal incapacity means lack of criminal capacity due to mental illness or intellectual disability. The term TNPCI is now generally used as a catch-all reference to all mental incapacity defences that are not classified as mental illnesses.

14 *S v Stellmacher* 1983 (2) SA 181 (SWA).

15 *S v Stellmacher* 181.

16 *S v Stellmacher* 184–185.

17 *S v Stellmacher* 187–188.

18 *S v Naidoo* 1971 (3) SA 605 (N).

19 Authors such as Burchell still regard the question of whether conduct during an epileptic fit would fall under pathological or non-pathological automatism as inconclusive. Burchell JM *South African Criminal Law and Procedure Vol I: General Principles of Criminal Law* 4 ed (2011) 69 fn 18.

20 The causes discussed here are not an exhaustive list.

The medical term for sleepwalking is *somnambulism*. It is commonly regarded as a sleep disorder. Its cause is unknown although some experts believe that it probably results from immaturity in the brain's regulation of sleep–wake cycles, which would explain why it is more common in children than in adults. Sleepwalking in adults tends to be associated with psychiatric problems, although it can also occur as a reaction to drugs or alcohol.[21] Since actions performed when sleepwalking are involuntary, the general rule is that they cannot give rise to criminal liability, as illustrated in the case of *R v Dhlamini*.[22]

R v Dhlamini

Dhlamini was spending the night in a room with the deceased and others. While Dhlamini was asleep, the deceased approached him and stooped to pick up a nearby sleeping mat. Dhlamini reacted by stabbing and killing the deceased. At his trial, Dhlamini testified that he had a vague recollection of seeing faces looking at him through a window and had dreamed that he was being attacked and was defending himself. There was no motive for the killing.

The court found it probable that Dhlamini had just awakened out of a nightmare and that he was 'acting mechanically, without intention, volition or motive'.[23] He was therefore acquitted. However, the court held, obiter, that according to Roman-Dutch law, a sleepwalker who killed another person in his sleep *could* be held criminally liable, albeit to a lesser extent,[24] if he had been *negligent*, that is, if he had known that he was prone to committing acts of violence in his sleep and had failed to take reasonable precautions for the safety of others before going to sleep (culpable prior voluntary conduct).[25]

3.3.1.2 Epilepsy

The main symptom of *epilepsy* is repeated seizures, usually with convulsions. The exact causes of epilepsy are not fully known or understood, but it is thought to be caused by a chemical imbalance in the brain that causes some of the nerve cells in the brain to become overactive and fire off random, uncontrolled signals. This results in a seizure.

There are different types of epileptic seizures. Seizures may be partial and affect only a particular part of the brain, or generalised and affect the whole brain. A person who suffers a simple partial seizure will remain conscious and will merely experience a strange sensation (commonly known as an aura). A person who suffers a complex partial seizure will experience a brief loss of consciousness, during which they may blink, twitch, chew or smack their lips. They may also throw things around and struggle if restrained. They may seem to be conscious, but will not, in fact, be aware of their actions or surroundings.

In the case of generalised seizures, a person may also suffer no more than a momentary loss of consciousness. This is also known as an absence seizure or a petit mal seizure. Alternatively, they may lose consciousness for a few minutes, fall to the floor and make involuntary jerking movements with their body and limbs. This is known as a grand mal seizure. In some cases, a grand mal seizure may be preceded by a simple partial seizure, which then spreads to the rest of the brain. In such cases, the aura (strange sensation, taste

---

21 Information on sleepwalking taken from health-cares.net, available at http://neurology.health-cares.net/sleepwalking-causes.php. On the legal and psychological issues, see also Cartwright R 'Sleepwalking violence: A sleep disorder, a legal dilemma, and a psychological challenge' (2004) 161(7) *Am J Psychiatry* 1149–1158.

22 *R v Dhlamini* 1955 (1) SA 120 (T).

23 *R v Dhlamini* 121–122.

24 That is, liable for culpable homicide rather than murder.

25 See section 3.3.2. For further cases involving sleepwalking, see *R v Nhete* 1941 SR 1 (referred to in the *Dhlamini* judgment) and *R v Ngang* 1960 (3) SA 363 (T).

or smell) accompanying the partial seizure can serve as a warning of the impending grand mal seizure. In other cases, however, there is no such warning.[26]

Movements performed during an epileptic seizure are involuntary and generally, therefore, cannot result in criminal liability. However, because the cause of epilepsy is centred in the brain, for some time there was doubt as to whether it should not perhaps be regarded as a mental illness or intellectual disability. If so, this would mean that the defence of insanity would have to be raised, relying on section 78 of the Criminal Procedure Act. It was ultimately settled that in South African law, epilepsy is not a mental illness or intellectual disability, and so a special verdict is not required.[27]

A case in which a defence relying on epilepsy succeeded was *R v Mkize*.[28]

R v Mkize

Mkize was an epileptic. One day while cutting meat with a sharp knife, he experienced an epileptic episode that the medical expert who testified at the trial described as an 'epileptic equivalent' – 'an attack where the ordinary fit is replaced by a period of confusion'.[29] During this episode, Mkize suddenly stabbed and killed his sister, who was standing next to him, for no apparent reason. His defence was that his conduct was involuntary. The court accepted that when he acted, Mkize had 'neither judgement, will, purpose, nor reasoning', and that the stabbing was the result of 'blind reflex activity'.[30] Accordingly, his actions could not constitute unlawful conduct for purposes of criminal liability and he was acquitted.

3.3.1.3 Hypoglycaemia (low blood sugar)

Hypoglycaemia is a condition where the level of glucose (natural sugar) in the blood drops below that required for the brain to function properly. Symptoms of mild hypoglycaemia include weakness, tiredness, shaking, sweating, dizziness, hunger, and anxiety or irritability. In more severe cases, the sufferer may become confused, disorientated, irrational, aggressive or violent, and in some cases, may engage in involuntary behaviour, exhibiting symptoms not unlike those of heavy intoxication and sometimes mistaken for it. If the blood glucose level drops far enough, it leads to loss of consciousness, a hypoglycaemic coma and even death.

It is possible for a person to suffer from hypoglycaemia as a medical condition on its own (non-diabetic hypoglycaemia). However, hypoglycaemic episodes, also known as hypos, which can be extremely serious, are also one of the risks commonly associated with sugar diabetes (high blood sugar). This can result from taking too much insulin or other diabetic medication, not eating enough, engaging in unusual physical exertion, experiencing unusual emotional stress, consuming alcohol, or a combination of any of these factors.

Although most diabetics have recognisable early warning signs when they are about to experience a hypo, thus enabling them to avoid it, long-time sufferers may become desensitised to these signs. This means that they may develop severe hypoglycaemia quite

26 Information on epilepsy taken from the ehealthMD.com website: http://www.ehealthmd.com/library/epilepsy/EPI_whatis.html. See also Joubert AF, Verschoor T and Van Rensburg PHJJ 'Epilepsy and the law' (1997) 16(4) *Med & L* 769.

27 See, for example, *S v Stellmacher*, discussed above; but see also the article by Blackbeard M 'Epilepsy and criminal liability' (1996) 9(2) *SACJ* 191. Snyman *Criminal Law* 55 fn 17 is of the view that the court in *Stellmacher* was correct to acquit the accused. However, the author is of the opinion that the court erred 'in regarding his [the accused's] hypoglycaemia and/or epileptic state as a factor excluding criminal capacity'.

28 *R v Mkize* 1959 (2) SA 260 (N).

29 *R v Mkize* 262–263. This seems to be an account of what today would be classed as a complex partial seizure, probably temporal lobe epilepsy.

30 *R v Mkize* 264.

suddenly and without sufficient opportunity to take avoidance action. Involuntary antisocial behaviour is not uncommon in such cases. However, because it is involuntary, it will not generally give rise to criminal liability. The case of *S v Viljoen*[31] illustrates this point.

S v Viljoen

Viljoen (V) was a type 1 diabetic. He had to inject himself with insulin. On the day in question, he injected himself in the morning and ate at 10h00, but then ate nothing more after that. Late in the afternoon, he became involved in an altercation with the deceased, who was molesting V's sister-in-law. V took a knife and stabbed the deceased to death. He was then charged with murder.

At his trial, V testified that he could remember taking out his knife, but nothing after that. Expert medical evidence was led to the effect that a person with V's condition should eat six times a day. Accordingly, at the time of the stabbing, V could have been suffering from hypoglycaemia. The court held that, in the circumstances, it was possible that V was acting in a state of sane automatism when he stabbed and killed the deceased and V was acquitted.

3.3.1.4 Blackouts and amnesia

Quite often, an accused will claim that he simply blacked out[32] when committing the alleged crime and/or that he cannot remember what happened. For purposes of criminal liability, it is important to distinguish between *amnesia* and a *blackout*: amnesia is a loss of memory, whereas a blackout is a temporary loss of consciousness.[33]

It stands to reason that it is impossible for a person to remember events that occurred during a period when he was unconscious. Since the conscious mind is not functioning when a person acts in a state of automatism, amnesia is an indication of automatism, but it is not the only one. Furthermore, the mere fact that the accused has no *memory* of committing a crime is not a defence in itself, nor is it likely to be accepted by a court[34] without additional supporting evidence (corroboration) as proof that the accused was acting in a state of automatism at the relevant time.[35]

In *S v Henry*, the court referred to what it called 'the relatively common occurrence of psychogenic amnesia',[36] namely the subconscious repression of an unacceptable memory, and stated as follows:

> **While it would appear from the evidence to be generally accepted that automatism results in amnesia it follows that the converse is not true. In other words, amnesia is not necessarily indicative of automatism. An accused person therefore may quite genuinely have no subsequent recollection of a voluntary act giving rise to criminal responsibility.**[37]

Suffering a blackout *is* a defence in our law, but naturally courts are sceptical of cases in which an accused claims that he simply blacked out for no apparent reason while the criminal act was being committed and that he is now suffering from amnesia.

---

31 *S v Viljoen* 1992 (1) SACR 601 (T).

32 See, for instance, *R v Du Plessis* 1950 (1) SA 297 (O); *S v Van Zyl* 1964 (2) SA 113 (A) at 118H; *S v Trickett* 1973 (3) SA 526 (T) at 528–529; *S v Evans* 1985 (2) SA 865 (ZS).

33 Le Roux J and Nel PW ''n Kritiese perspektief op die rol van amnesie by die vasstelling van strafregtelike aanspreeklikheid' (2010) 43(1) *De Jure* 20.

34 See *S v Piccione* 1967 (2) SA 334 (N); *R v Johnson* 1970 (2) SA 405 (R); *S v Majola* 2001 (1) SACR 337 (N). See further commentary by Hoctor S 'Amnesia and criminal responsibility' (2000) 13(3) *SACJ* 273.

35 In *S v Ramdass* 2017 (1) SACR 30 (KZD) at 7.

36 *S v Henry* 1999 (1) SACR 13 (SCA) 20G.

37 *S v Henry* supra 20H.

Bratty v Attorney-General for Northern Ireland

In the English case of *Bratty v Attorney-General for Northern Ireland*,[38] Bratty strangled a passenger in his car. His defence was that he had suffered a blackout and could not remember the critical events. He was convicted of murder and appealed. On appeal, Lord Denning dismissed Bratty's defence as 'the first refuge of a guilty conscience'.[39] He held further: 'An act is not involuntary merely because it is not remembered; amnesia does not equal automatism'.[40]

To raise the defence of blackout successfully, the accused must lay an evidentiary foundation for it – a court will not simply accept the accused's own word that he had blacked out. Also, if the blackout was the result of a mental illness, then this would be insane, not sane, automatism, which would necessitate a special verdict.

By contrast with *Bratty's* case, in *S v Evans*,[41] the accused satisfied the court that he had suffered a genuine blackout and the court held that this was a valid defence.

S v Evans

Evans was a train driver who had a blackout during which he ignored a red light and caused a collision with another train. Two people were killed. He was convicted of culpable homicide in the Magistrates' Court and appealed to the Zimbabwean Supreme Court. On appeal, the court referred to *Bratty's* case and held that:

- unlike Bratty, Evans had laid a sufficient evidential foundation for his defence;
- blackout is a defence in itself if a court is satisfied that it is genuine;
- Evans had blacked out and his conscious mind was cut off. Therefore, he was not driving the train at the time of the collision and so could not be said to have done so negligently;
- temporary loss of memory, consciousness or vision is not a mental disorder or intellectual disability necessitating a special verdict.

Evans's appeal was upheld.

3.3.1.5 Severe intoxication

When a person is extremely drunk or otherwise intoxicated, it can lead to temporary loss of consciousness and sometimes to automatic behaviour.[42] As a general principle of criminal liability, we do not distinguish between automatism as a result of intoxication and other forms of sane automatism, regardless of whether the intoxication was voluntary or involuntary (discussed further below).

In *S v Chretien*,[43] the leading authority on the defence of intoxication, the Appellate Division of the Supreme Court distinguished between three different stages of intoxication and their effect on criminal liability:

1. If the accused was so drunk that he was lying and performing involuntary movements with his arms and legs ('dead' drunk), he would not be criminally liable because such movements would not be regarded as conduct for purposes of criminal liability.

---

38 *Bratty v Attorney-General for Northern Ireland* [1963] AC 386; [1961] 3 All ER 523.
39 *Bratty v Attorney-General for Northern Ireland* 414.
40 *Bratty v Attorney-General for Northern Ireland* 409.
41 *S v Evans* 1985 (2) SA 865 (ZS).
42 See, for example, the case of *S v Johnson* 1969 (1) SA 201 (A), although, as subsequently pointed out in Chretien's case, on the facts this may not have been a genuine case of automatism since Johnson's recollection of the critical events was too clear.
43 *S v Chretien* 1981 (1) SA 1097 (A).

2. If he was less drunk, but drunk enough that he had lost his powers of insight and/or self-control, he would not be liable because he would lack criminal capacity.
3. If he was even less drunk, but merely drunk enough that he failed to foresee the unlawful consequences of his actions, he would lack fault in the form of intention and would therefore escape liability for a crime that required this form of fault. However, he could still be negligent and might therefore not escape liability for a crime that required this form of fault.

The case of *Chretien* explains why intoxication features as a defence under unlawful conduct, again under criminal capacity and again under fault. This defence will be discussed more fully under the heading of criminal capacity (Section 2 of Part 2). However, for present purposes, note that it is only extreme intoxication that leads to involuntary conduct.

The general principles that relate to voluntary intoxication have been modified, firstly by a long standing principle of Roman-Dutch law known as the ***actio libera in causa*** rule and, more recently, by the provisions of the Criminal Law Amendment Act 1 of 1988. We will discuss each briefly:

- *The actio libera in causa rule*:[44] If a person deliberately gets drunk in order to commit a crime that he may otherwise not have had the courage to commit, he will be guilty of that crime even if his conduct was not voluntary at the time of committing it. This is because the *original cause* of that conduct (getting drunk) was within his conscious control at the time that he did so (see section 3.3.2).
- *The Criminal Law Amendment Act 1 of 1988*: Chretien led to a public outcry, which resulted in Parliament intervening and passing the Criminal Law Amendment Act 1 of 1988. Section 1(1) of this Act makes it a criminal offence *in itself* for a person to commit a criminal act while his criminal capacity (insight and/or self-control) is impaired by the voluntary use of an intoxicating substance if he *knew* that the substance was one that tended to have an intoxicating effect, and if he is then found not liable for the crime in question due to his lack of criminal capacity. Note that in such a case, the accused is not found guilty of the crime itself. He commits another offence, namely a contravention of section 1(1) of the Act, but the Act provides that he can be subjected to the same punishment.[45] The provisions of the Act will be discussed more in section 17.3.

3.3.1.6 Psychogenic sane automatism

Up to now, we have considered cases that involve the defence of sane automatism due to organic or other physical factors such as somnambulism, epilepsy or intoxication. However, there have also been cases where the accused has claimed that he temporarily lost conscious control of his actions as a result of the combined effects of overwhelming psychological factors, such as severe provocation occurring at a time of extreme emotional stress/distress, or provocation resulting in extreme emotional distress. This form of automatism is distinguishable from temporary insanity in that it is not associated with any mental illness or intellectual disability, however temporary.[46] It is thus a form of sane automatism.

44 The rule in full reads '*actio non in se, sed tamen in sua causa libera*', meaning literally 'an act which was not in his power (at the time), but yet its (original) cause was in his power'. For cases where this rule was relied on, referred to or criticised, see *S v Chretien* supra 1105; *S v Kekala* 2009 JDR 0718 (NWM) 11; *S v Baartman* 1983 (4) SA 395 (NC) 400.

45 The tendency is, however, that courts often impose lower sentences for the statutory crime than if the accused had been convicted of the underlying offence. See *S v Maki* 1994 (2) SACR 414 (E); *S v Vika* 2010 (2) SACR 444 (ECG).

46 See the minimum requirements for a mental illness/intellectual disability (mental disorder) as stated in *Stellmacher*, discussed above.

This defence has sometimes also been referred to as **temporary non-pathological criminal incapacity** (TNPCI).[47] For some time, it was unclear whether there was a distinction between sane automatism and TNPCI in our law, and if so, what this distinction was. The question was finally resolved in *S v Eadie* (see below).

The defence of *psychogenic sane automatism* was first raised successfully in the Cape Provincial Division (now the Western Cape High Court) in *S v Arnold*.[48]

S v Arnold

Arnold shot and killed his wife, Tina, one day at their home. At his murder trial, it emerged that he had been under severe emotional stress at the time of the incident. Apart from long-standing financial and marital problems, he was deeply distressed at parting from his disabled son, whom he had just delivered to a children's home. He had placed the boy there at Tina's insistence. He had taken his gun with him for protection. On returning home, he went into the living room to put it away. Tina was in the living room and an argument broke out between them. At one point, Arnold banged his gun on the back of a sofa and it went off by accident, but no one was harmed (he was never asked to explain why he did not disable the gun after this happened). Tina told Arnold that she wanted to resume her previous occupation as a stripper and bared her breasts to him. At this, he fired at her and killed her. Later, he claimed that he had no recollection of aiming and pulling the trigger. The psychiatrist who gave evidence for the defence testified that at the time of the shooting, Arnold's consciousness had been 'so "flooded" by emotions'[49] that he may have lost the capacity to control his actions. In other words, he was saying that Arnold could have lacked criminal capacity.

The court, however, identified the legal issues in dispute as follows:

- Did Arnold perform an act in the legal sense (that is, was his conduct voluntary)?
- If so, did he have the necessary criminal capacity at the time?
- If so, did he have the required intention to commit murder?

In answer to these questions, the court held that it was not satisfied that the state had passed the first hurdle and that it had failed to prove beyond a reasonable doubt that Arnold's conduct was voluntary. However, even if it had, the court was not satisfied that the state had proved beyond a reasonable doubt that Arnold had criminal capacity at the relevant time. He was therefore acquitted.

After *Arnold*, there were a number of murder trials in which the accused claimed that they too had acted involuntarily and/or had lacked criminal capacity as a result of severe emotional stress, coupled with provocation. Although the defence enjoyed a measure of temporary success in the (then) Supreme Court (now called the High Court),[50] there has only been one case thus far in which it has succeeded in the Appellate Division (AD) or in the Supreme Court of Appeal (SCA), namely that of *S v Wiid*.[51]

---

47 See footnote 13.
48 *S v Arnold* 1985 (3) SA 256 (C).
49 *S v Arnold* 263C.
50 See cases like *S v Nursingh* 1995 (2) SACR 331 (D) and *S v Moses* 1996 (1) SACR 701 (C), discussed in section 18.2.
51 *S v Wiid* 1990 (1) SACR 561 (A).

S v Laubscher

In *S v Laubscher*,[52] Laubscher, a medical student, shot and killed his father-in-law, and also attempted to shoot his mother-in-law and his estranged wife one day at his in-laws' home. Like Arnold, he too had experienced a considerable amount of stress in the period leading up to the incident, including the fact that his wife had left him and returned to her parents, taking their baby with her. At his trial, he tried to raise the defence that his conduct was the result of a 'total psychological breakdown' or 'disintegration of his personality'[53] of a temporary nature, and therefore his conduct was not voluntary. This defence failed, however, because Laubscher's behaviour, according to his own version of events, did not support such a finding. His actions were goal directed and purposeful before, during and immediately after the shooting. Altogether, he fired 21 shots into various rooms of the house, requiring him to reload his gun at least twice. He also managed to drive away from the house immediately afterwards in an attempt to escape. The trial court found that this was not consistent with automatic behaviour and convicted him. Although he appealed, the AD upheld the trial court's decision.

It was in *Laubscher* that the court first adopted the term 'temporary non-pathological criminal incapacity' (TNPCI). The court used the term to distinguish between lack of criminal capacity due to mental illness or intellectual disability (pathological incapacity), and lack of criminal capacity due to other factors, such as intoxication, provocation and severe emotional stress.

For a long time, it was unclear whether the defence of TNPCI was at all different from the defence of sane automatism, and if so, what the difference was. This question was finally resolved in *S v Eadie*.[54]

S v Eadie

Eadie clubbed a fellow motorist to death with a broken hockey stick in a fit of road rage. He had been drinking heavily. He raised the defence of TNPCI. His defence was rejected and he was convicted. He appealed to the SCA. In a long and thorough judgment delivered by Navsa JA, the SCA considered the historical development of the defences of TNPCI and sane automatism, and ultimately concluded that they are one and the same thing.[55] He went on to hold that a normal person can only lack self-control (and hence lack criminal capacity) if he is acting in a state of automatism.

It will be seen that, at one end of the spectrum, the defence of involuntary conduct deals with acts that are no more than mere muscular reflexes, such as movements during sleep, while paralytically drunk or having a seizure. At the other end of the spectrum are acts that are more than mere muscular reflexes, but less than acts of conscious volition, such as those involved in cases of sane automatism (or TNPCI). At this end of the spectrum, the enquiry into voluntariness begins to overlap with the enquiry into criminal capacity. Thus, this issue may be considered to be an aspect of unlawful conduct, but actually results in a finding that affects criminal capacity.[56]

52 *S v Laubscher* 1988 (1) SA 163 (A).
53 *S v Laubscher* supra at 166E.
54 *S v Eadie* 2002 (3) SA 719 (SCA).
55 *S v Eadie* supra at 42–71.
56 See, in general, Chapter 14 and the subsequent discussions of various aspects of criminal capacity.

3.3.2 Culpable prior voluntary conduct

Although involuntary acts and omissions cannot in themselves give rise to criminal liability, the obiter dictum in *Dhlamini*[57] highlights a situation that requires special consideration. This is when the accused is liable, not on the basis of his final involuntary act or omission, but on the basis of some prior voluntary conduct, coupled with the required form of fault (usually negligence), where such conduct is causally linked to the later involuntary act or omission.[58]

To use the example that was given in *Dhlamini*, if a person is prone to committing acts of violence in his sleep and knows of this propensity, he must take reasonable steps to avoid putting himself in situations where he is a potential danger to other people. If he fails to do so and kills someone while sleepwalking, he will be negligent and will accordingly be guilty of culpable homicide.

This principle is an extension of the *actio libera in causa* rule of Roman-Dutch law, discussed above, which holds that where a person deliberately gets drunk in order to commit a crime, he will be liable for that crime even if his conduct at the time of the commission of the crime was involuntary, because the original cause of that conduct (getting drunk) was within his conscious control.

Thus, in such cases we do not consider only the final act of the accused in the sequence of events. Where the accused is not liable on the basis of his involuntary act or omission, we must then consider whether he is liable on the basis of some prior voluntary conduct, which was culpable, and which was causally linked to the later involuntary act or omission. Accordingly, for a person to be liable on the basis of his prior voluntary conduct, the following requirements must be met:

- The involuntary act or omission must have been preceded by some voluntary conduct on the part of the accused. This could be a positive act or an omission (usually a failure to take reasonable steps to prevent the later involuntary act or omission).
- The accused's prior voluntary conduct must be causally connected with his later involuntary conduct in the sense that the latter would not have occurred if it had not been for the prior voluntary conduct.[59]
- The prior voluntary conduct must have been culpable – it must have been accompanied by fault in the form required by the definition of the crime in question (whether intention or negligence). All the decided cases thus far have involved crimes that required fault in the form of *negligence*, but Burchell argues that there is no logical reason why an accused could not also be found liable for a crime that required *intention*.[60]

R v Victor

In *R v Victor*,[61] the accused was an epileptic who had experienced epileptic seizures since the age of 14 or 15, but still drove a car against medical advice. One day, he had a seizure while driving and had an accident in which someone was badly injured. He was charged with and convicted of reckless/negligent driving because the court held that he ought to have foreseen the possibility of just such a seizure and its consequences, and that he should not have driven at all in the circumstances. Thus, even though his conduct was not voluntary at the time of the accident, he could not use his disability to escape liability. He was convicted on the basis of his negligent prior voluntary conduct (driving on a public road when he was not medically fit to drive).

57 *R v Dhlamini* supra.
58 This form of liability is referred to as *antecedent liability*.
59 For a full discussion of the causation enquiry, see Chapter 6.
60 Burchell *Principles of Criminal Law* 74–75.
61 *R v Victor* 1943 TPD 77.

R v Schoonwinkel

In *R v Schoonwinkel*,[62] the accused, who was also an epileptic, suffered a seizure while driving and caused an accident in which the driver of the other vehicle was killed. He was charged with culpable homicide. However, unlike Victor, Schoonwinkel had only had two minor attacks previously, and the court accepted that such attacks could come without warning. Immediately before the collision, his mind had gone blank because of the seizure, giving him no time to take evasive action. In the circumstances, the court found that Schoonwinkel's prior conduct had not been negligent and acquitted him of culpable homicide.[63]

In the chapters that follow, we discuss the different forms that unlawful conduct may take, namely committing an unlawful act or an unlawful omission, being in an unlawful state of affairs, or causing a prohibited consequence.

THIS CHAPTER IN ESSENCE

1. To qualify as conduct for purposes of the requirement of unlawful conduct, the relevant act or omission must have been the conduct of a human being and it must have been voluntary. If the relevant act or omission was not voluntary, then the general rule is that the accused is not criminally liable.
2. The state (prosecution) bears the onus of proving that the accused's conduct was voluntary, but if the accused alleges he acted involuntarily, then he must lay an evidential foundation for that defence. It is not sufficient for the accused simply to place the issue in dispute and leave it at that.
3. Even where an accused's act or omission was involuntary, he may still be held criminally liable if the involuntary conduct was made possible by some culpable prior voluntary conduct on the part of the accused.

62 *R v Schoonwinkel* 1953 (3) SA 136 (C).

63 See also *R v Shevill* 1964 (4) SA 51 (SRA); *S v Trickett* supra, especially the passage at 531G–532D; *S v Grobler* 1974 (2) SA 663 (T); *S v Van Rensburg* 1987 (3) SA 35 (T).

Chapter 4

Acts and omissions

CHAPTER OBJECTIVES

The objectives of this chapter are to:

- introduce the four principal forms that unlawful conduct may take
- distinguish between crimes of commission and crimes of omission
- explain the general rule relating to liability for omissions
- explain the flexible test for liability in the case of omissions
- identify the established situations when such liability will arise
- explain the relevance of proof of causation to the enquiry into omissions liability
- distinguish briefly between liability for omissions in criminal law and liability for omissions in delictual law.

4.1 Unlawful acts

In many cases, the accused's conduct will take the form of actually committing an act that has been prohibited by law, in other words, *positive conduct*. This type of unlawful conduct probably corresponds most closely with the popular conception of a crime, and indeed, most common law crimes fall into this category.[1] For example, Abe punches Ben, thus assaulting him; Chris has sexual intercourse with Dora without her consent, thus raping her; Elvin breaks into Fred's house and steals his property, thus committing housebreaking and theft. This form of positive unlawful conduct is generally easy to identify and understand.

4.2 Unlawful omissions

Unlawful conduct may also take the form of an *omission* – a failure to act. The position relating to omissions is somewhat less straightforward.

It is easy enough to understand that where a particular law imposes a legal duty on a person to perform some particular act, for example to render one's tax return by a certain date, or to pay one's employees a stipulated minimum wage, then the failure to perform that act, as and when required by law, will be regarded as unlawful conduct. Offences of this type, where the mere failure to perform the required act constitutes the relevant offence, are commonly called *crimes of pure omission*.

More complex, however, are situations in which the failure to act is not unlawful in and of itself, but the omission leads to another person suffering financial or physical harm, or even death. It is always *prima facie* unlawful to inflict physical harm on another person, but when, if ever, is one legally obliged to prevent another person from suffering harm that has arisen from some other source? In short, when is there a legal duty to protect or rescue?

For example, suppose that I am walking next to a river one day and I see a man drowning. If I fail to rescue him, am I criminally liable for his death? Would it make any difference to my liability if I happened to be a strong swimmer? What if the drowning person was a child? What if it was *my* child? What if it was my child, but I was unable to swim?

The *general rule* in our law – and hence our basic point of departure – is that no one is obliged to act positively to prevent harm from coming to another even if he can easily and ought morally to do so.[2] This rule is based on the recognition that:

- the imposition of such an obligation must inevitably represent a serious invasion of personal liberty and freedom of action
- the law does not, as a general rule, seek to penalise a person for simply doing nothing
- it is not the proper role of the law to enforce pure morality.

There are, however, *exceptions* to the general rule, that is to say, situations in which there is a legal duty (an obligation) to act and where a person's failure to do so will accordingly be regarded as unlawful. We start by considering the general, overarching test for establishing civil and criminal liability for omissions.

4.2.1 The general test for liability for omissions

In *Minister van Polisie v Ewels*,[3] the Appellate Division (AD) formulated a broad, flexible test for delictual liability arising out of omissions. It held that in order for such liability to arise:

> **... the circumstances of the case must be of such a nature that the omission not only excites moral indignation, but also that the legal convictions of the community demand that it ought to be regarded as unlawful.**[4]

1 This is not mere coincidence, but a consequence of the fundamental principle of inactivity, referred to below in section 4.2.

2 *Minister van Polisie v Ewels* 1975 (3) SA 590 (A). This rule is commonly referred to as the *fundamental principle of inaction*. It holds good for both criminal law and for the law of delict.

3 *Minister van Polisie v Ewels* supra.

4 *Minister van Polisie v Ewels* supra 597A.

This flexible test was adopted into criminal law in *S v Gaba*[5] (discussed below). However, in *S v A*,[6] the AD pointed out that just because a particular omission may give rise to delictual liability, it does not necessarily follow that the same omission will also give rise to criminal liability because different policy considerations apply.[7]

DISCUSSION

Determining and tempering the 'legal convictions of the community'

Considering the reason for the decision or *ratio decidendi* in *Minister van Polisie v Ewels*, *S v Gaba* and *S v A*, what are the different policy considerations that apply to criminal matters and by which method are they determined? How is the Bill of Rights relevant to this method and what is the effect of section 39(2) of the Constitution?[8] How are the legal convictions of the community determined?

The premise seems to be that criminal law should reflect the values and consensus of society. The policy consideration in this context is that it is only when the criminal sanction reflects this consensus that there can be the type of respect for the law that leads to the concomitant stigma attaching to conviction under this law. However, Burchell warns that there is a risk here: 'the dangers of the legal convictions of the community becoming a weapon for imposing sectional interests are disturbing'.[9]

This is why the legal convictions of the community always need to be considered, but with due regard for the rights of individuals, the legality principle and the general ethos of the Rule of Law (not merely rule by law).

Furthermore, the notion of too flexible a test for unlawful conduct is in conflict with one of the fundamental tenets of our criminal law, namely the principle of legality, which requires, inter alia, that the definitions of crimes should be reasonably precise and settled (the *ius certum*), and that no one should be held criminally liable for conduct that was not defined as a crime at the time of its commission (the *ius praevium*). This is not to suggest that a criminal court may *never* use a flexible test for determining liability.[10] However, it is clear that such tests are to be used sparingly and with caution. Where possible, therefore, criminal liability for a particular omission should be established with reference to established law and precedent.

4.2.2 Crystallised categories of liability for omissions

In deference to the principle of legality, authors and commentators on criminal law usually rely on those established categories of liability that have emerged from case law over the years. These categories of liability may be regarded as the crystallised legal convictions of the community referred to in *Ewels*[11] and are for omissions where:

- the accused was under a statutory duty to perform the act in question

5 *S v Gaba* 1981 (3) SA 745 (O).

6 *S v A en 'n ander* 1993 (1) SACR 600 (A).

7 As to what these considerations are, see, for example, *Moses v Minister of Safety and Security* 2000 (3) SA 106 (C) at 114 B–D; see also Packer HL *The Limits of the Criminal Sanction* (1968) 296 on the appropriate use of the criminal sanction; and see further, Burchell JM *Principles of Criminal Law* 5 ed (2016) 86–93 on some of the policy considerations affecting the state's duty to protect individuals against violent crime.

8 S 39(2) of the Constitution of the Republic of South Africa, 1996 provides as follows:

> **When interpreting any legislation, and when developing the common law or customary law, every court, tribunal or forum must promote the spirit, purport and objects of the Bill of Rights.**

9 Burchell JM *South African Criminal Law and Procedure Vol I: General Principles of Criminal Law* 4 ed (2011) 115.

10 Consider, for example, the test for legal causation, discussed in Chapter 6.

11 Burchell *Principles of Criminal Law* 81; Snyman CR *Criminal Law* 6 ed (2014) 59–60.

- the risk of harm was created in the first instance by some prior positive conduct on the part of the accused
- the accused was in control of potentially dangerous property
- the accused had a protective relationship with the person concerned
- the accused held a public or quasi-public office that obliged him to perform the act in question as a consequence of his employment.

We will examine each of these categories in turn.

4.2.2.1 Statutory duty

A particular statute may impose a legal duty on a person to act positively in certain circumstances for the purpose of preventing or limiting harm to another. Thus, for example, the National Road Traffic Act imposes a duty on any motorist who is involved in a collision to ascertain injuries and render assistance to injured persons.[12]

Where such a duty is imposed, a person who fails to comply will not only be liable for committing the offence of failing to comply with the relevant statute, but can also be held liable for any harm that is suffered as a consequence of such failure.

Note that the Constitution entrenches[13] various fundamental human rights in the Bill of Rights,[14] and places a duty on the state, through its various organs and agencies, to respect and protect those rights. Thus, for example, it has been held that section 205(3) of the Constitution, together with the South African Police Service Act,[15] imposes a duty on the police to maintain law and order, and protect members of the public against crime.[16]

Statutory frameworks aimed at combating complex criminal phenomena, such as money laundering,[17] organised crime[18] and the financing of terrorism,[19] often provide for legal duties, coupled with the criminalisation of the failure to comply with such duties. The criminalisation of the failure to comply with the legal duty (the secondary crime) can thus be seen as a strategy to combat the primary crime such as terrorism, theft or fraud.

4.2.2.2 Prior positive conduct[20]

Where a person, through his positive conduct, creates a situation and sets in motion a chain of events that poses a potential danger to other persons, he attracts a legal duty to prevent that danger from materialising and causing harm to others. This is the so-called *omissio per commissionem* rule.[21]

---

12 S 61 of the National Road Traffic Act 93 of 1996. See Burchell *Principles of Criminal Law* 194–195 for further examples.

13 This means that by virtue of s 2 of the Constitution (the supremacy clause), the sections that contain the rights concerned prevail over any conflicting statute, regulation, common law principle or inconsistent conduct.

14 Ss 7–39 of the Constitution.

15 Act 68 of 1995.

16 See, for example, *Van Eeden v Minister of Safety and Security (Women's Legal Centre Trust as amicus curiae)* 2003 (1) SA 389 (SCA); *Minister of Safety and Security and another v Carmichele* 2004 (3) SA 305 (SCA); *Minister of Safety and Security v Van Duivenboden* 2002 (6) SA 431 (SCA).

17 See Chapter 44.

18 See Chapter 44.

19 See Chapter 49.

20 The phrase 'prior positive conduct' is used to distinguish it from prior conduct in the form of omissions.

21 This rule is a further example of antecedent liability (liability based on prior knowledge and conduct). For a brief discussion and an example, see Snyman CR *Strafreg* (1981) 60.

R v Miller[22]

In this English case, Miller was squatting in a certain house. He fell asleep on a mattress while smoking and woke up to find the mattress smouldering. He did nothing to put out the burning mattress, but merely went to sleep in another room. The house caught fire and Miller was subsequently convicted of recklessly causing damage to the house through his failure to prevent the fire.

A rather more contentious case is *S v Russell*.[23]

S v Russell

Russell was an employee of the Department of Water Affairs who, together with his supervisor and co-workers, was unloading pipes onto a lorry at a railway station. The workers were using an overhead crane, parked under the railway's electric power lines. Because of the danger, the power had been switched off. While Russell's supervisor and co-workers were away having lunch, the power was turned on again. A railway employee told Russell to warn the crane operator about this when the workers returned, and Russell accepted this instruction without pointing out that he was not the supervisor. He did not, however, pass on the warning when loading resumed. The crane touched the power line and the operator was electrocuted.

Russell was convicted of culpable homicide and appealed to the Supreme Court (now the High Court). On appeal, the Supreme Court held that the *way* in which Russell had (apparently) accepted the warning had created a potentially dangerous situation. This being the case, he had attracted a legal duty to pass on the warning. By failing culpably in this duty, he was clearly negligent. His conviction of culpable homicide was confirmed.

4.2.2.3 Control of a dangerous thing

A person who is in control of a dangerous thing, such as a vicious animal, arms and ammunition, or explosives, has a legal duty to prevent that property from causing harm to others.

In *S v Fernandez*,[24] for instance, the accused kept an aggressive baboon in a cage. He failed to keep the cage door in good repair with the result that the baboon escaped and killed a child. The accused was convicted of culpable homicide because the court found that he should have foreseen the possibility of such an event and should have taken steps to prevent it.

4.2.2.4 Protective relationship

When one person has a protective relationship with another, then the former attracts a legal duty to protect the latter from harm. Such a relationship may arise by virtue of family ties, contractual undertaking, law or some other conduct whereby the accused assumes such a duty, even if only on a temporary basis. For example, prison officers have a duty to safeguard prisoners in their custody, and an adult who babysits children has a legal obligation to protect the children for the duration of the babysitting session.[25]

22 *R v Miller* [1983] 1 All ER 978 (HL).
23 *S v Russell* 1967 (3) SA 739 (N).
24 *S v Fernandez* 1966 (2) SA 259 (A).
25 See examples in Snyman *Criminal Law* 60.

4.2.2.4.1 Natural relationships

At common law, it is well established that certain legal duties arise from the inherent nature of the family unit, for example the reciprocal duty of maintenance that exists between parent and child, between spouses, and even between grandparent and grandchild. Another duty that arises is the duty of protection against harm. However, the scope (ambit and extent) of this duty is not always clear.

It is clear that in South African law, a person has a legal duty to protect his own minor child from harm.[26] The duty to protect would appear to extend also to stepchildren and even the children of a so-called common law or life partner.[27]

The duty towards spouses and life partners is less clear. There is authority to suggest that a protective duty is owed to one's lawful husband or wife,[28] and also to one's life partner, but probably not to a casual sexual partner.[29]

There is also persuasive authority to suggest that a protective relationship is formed when a person takes in a sick, elderly and/or otherwise incapacitated relative to care for them. See, for example, the old English case of *R v Instan*,[30] as well as the more recent case of *R v Stone and Dobinson*.[31] Note that in the latter case, it was not the natural relationship that was found to be decisive by the court, but the deliberate (even if tacit) assumption of a duty to take care of the person concerned, similar to the principle that Briggs FJ referred to in *Chenjere*.[32]

---

26 For example, in *S v B en 'n ander* 1994 (2) SACR 237 (E), the second accused, who was B's partner, violently assaulted B's two-and-a-half-year-old son over a three-month period, with the result that the child eventually died. B was aware of the assaults and their severity, but did nothing to protect her child. The court found that in abandoning her parental duty of protection, B was guilty of assault with intent to do grievous bodily harm.

27 For example, in *R v Chenjere* 1960 (1) SA 473 (FC), Chenjere (C) struck up a relationship with a married woman (A) who had a young child. They ran away together, taking the child, but then decided they did not want it. C suggested they abandon the child. A said that she could not just abandon the child and leave him to die, and that it would be better to kill him. She then strangled the child. They were both charged with murder.

At the trial, there was a dispute as to whether C had actively helped A to kill the child or whether, as he claimed, he had merely stood by while she did so. The trial court did not believe him and convicted them both. C appealed to the Federal Court, but his conviction was confirmed although different judges gave different reasons for doing so. In his minority judgment, Briggs FJ held, obiter (at 482), that even if C had not actively assisted A in killing the child, he was still liable for murder because he had assumed a duty to protect it and his inaction thus amounted to an unlawful omission:

> **To cause death by inaction may be criminal if there is a positive duty to preserve the life of the person in question. The duty arises where the potential victim is helpless through infancy, senility or illness and the potential killer stands, either naturally or through a deliberate acceptance of responsibility, in a protective relationship to the victim. There was no natural relationship between [Chenjere] and the deceased, but I think that, by taking the mother and a child of that age (2–3) from the protection of the natural guardian, husband and father, with the apparent intention of forming a new 'family' relationship of a permanent, or at least prolonged, nature, [Chenjere] had deliberately assumed a protective relationship towards both of them.**

28 This duty has not always been universally recognised. See, for example, the Australian case of *R v Russell* 1933 VLR 59. Russell watched as his suicidal wife drowned herself and their two children in a public pool. He was subsequently convicted of manslaughter in respect of the children because the court held that as their father, he had a duty to protect them, but not in respect of his wife because the court held that she was capable of looking after herself and he was therefore under no duty to prevent her death.

29 *People v Beardsley* 150 Mich. 206, 113 NW 1128 (1907). In a more recent Canadian case, *R v Mallaley* C/C/7/2001 (Court of Queens Bench of New Brunswick), the accused (M) left his life partner to die in a fire that she had started in her apartment building. She had been drinking heavily and they had quarrelled. M knew that she had started the fire, and that she was incapacitated and unable to escape by herself, but he took no steps to rescue her, or even alert the firefighters to her presence in the building. He was charged with criminal negligence causing death. The court held that in the circumstances, M had been under a legal duty to take reasonable steps to obtain assistance for the deceased. Because he had taken no steps at all, he was accordingly convicted.

30 *R v Instan* [1893] 1 QB 450.

31 *R v Stone and Dobinson* [1977] 1 QB 354.

32 *R v Chenjere* supra.

4.2.2.4.2 Contractual relationships

Since it has been shown that a protective relationship can be deliberately assumed, it would be obvious that such a relationship can arise out of a contractual undertaking. Thus, for example, if A employs B as a bodyguard, B assumes a duty to protect A from unlawful attack by third parties. If he fails to do so, his omission will be unlawful. By the same token, if Dr X accepts Y as a patient, Dr X assumes a duty to render medical treatment and advice to Y when necessary. If he fails to do so, his omission will be unlawful.

Note that in such cases, the scope (ambit and extent) of B's and Dr X's duty is determined by the terms and conditions of their respective contracts. It is never an unlimited duty.

4.2.2.4.3 Other protective relationships

It would appear that in our law, when one person deprives another of the ability to protect and care for themselves, the former attracts a duty of protection and care towards the latter. The most obvious example of this can be seen in the duty owed by police officers and prison officials towards persons who are taken into or held in custody.[33] The duty of police officers (and, by logical extension, prison authorities) to protect detainees against assault was confirmed in the delictual case of *Ewels*,[34] as well as in the criminal cases of *S v Barnes*[35] and *S v Williams*[36] (discussed below).

Our courts have also held that the duty to protect detainees extends further than preventing them from being assaulted. Thus, for example, there is a duty to obtain medical treatment for them when necessary.[37] In addition, it has been held that a protective duty is owed to young children who are in the care of a person at the time that this person is arrested and detained.[38]

4.2.2.5 Public and quasi-public office

In some cases, public officials[39] have a duty to protect, assist and/or render services to members of the public by virtue of the very nature of their employment. We have already mentioned, for example, that police officers have a duty to maintain law and order, and protect members of the public against crime, and especially violent crime. By the same token, public health workers have a duty to provide medical assistance to patients at the

---

33 This duty was first highlighted in a delictual case, *Mtati v Minister of Justice* 1958 (1) SA 221 (A). Mtati was in custody on charges of assaulting a policeman. The officer who was in charge of the cells (A) gave the keys to another policeman (B) at B's request. B then entered Mtati's cell and assaulted him. Mtati subsequently sued the Minister of Justice, in his capacity as A's employer, for damages.

The trial court found against Mtati, holding that A had no duty to prevent the assault even though it was foreseeable in the circumstances. The AD reversed this decision on appeal, holding that a policeman in charge of prisoners, who are unable to protect themselves against attack by escaping, has a duty to see that no one enters their cells without good reason. A had failed culpably in this duty, thus permitting the assault on Mtati. Damages were accordingly awarded to Mtati.

34 *Minister van Polisie v Ewels* supra.

35 *S v Barnes and another* 1990 (2) SACR 485 (N).

36 *S v Williams and others* 1998 (2) SACR 191 (SCA).

37 See *Minister of Police v Skosana* 1977 (1) SA 31 (A).

38 *S v Van As en 'n ander* 1967 (4) SA 594 (A). Van As was a police officer. One night, he and other policemen arrested a man for drunken driving and took him into custody. During the arrest, five young children, who were in the care of the detainee, ran away and disappeared. The detainee begged the police to go and look for them and the police made a cursory search, but failed to find them. Three of the children found their way home, but the other two were found the next morning, dead from exposure.

Van As et al were convicted of culpable homicide and they appealed. On appeal, the AD reversed the trial court's decision, not because the police did not have a duty to search for the missing children, but because, despite the existence of such a duty, the state could not prove beyond a reasonable doubt that they would have found the children if they had searched more thoroughly. The state was therefore unable to prove that the deaths of the two children had been *caused by* the policemen's omission.

39 Employees of the state and state-controlled institutions.

facilities where they are employed. A failure to comply with such a duty, which results in another person suffering harm, will accordingly constitute unlawful conduct.

A similar duty exists in the case of privately employed individuals whose function it is to protect, rescue and/or render assistance, if not to the public generally, then to a particular sector of the public, for example their employer's clients, guests, tenants or patients. Typical examples are a lifeguard employed to protect swimmers at a private club or hotel's swimming pool, a security guard employed to protect particular premises and/or persons lawfully using such premises, and staff employed to provide medical treatment to patients at a private hospital. Such individuals are regarded as quasi-public officials.

Note that in all such cases, the scope of the duty owed by the official concerned is determined - and thus limited - by the terms and conditions of his employment contract. The rule is that no one owes an *unlimited* duty in our law. Accordingly, a public or quasi-public official's failure to render assistance in any particular case will only give rise to liability if such failure represented a breach of his contract with his employer.[40]

Therefore, in such cases, it is not sufficient merely to establish the existence of a duty. It is of vital importance to establish the scope of that duty and, in particular, whether it entailed the performance of the envisaged positive conduct.

4.2.2.5.1 Police officers

One particular category of public officials - police officers - is important enough to warrant special mention. In *Minister of Law and Order v Kadir*,[41] the Supreme Court of Appeal held that the principal duties of the police are to maintain law and order, and to prevent, detect and investigate crime.[42] The duty to detect and investigate crime clearly extends to reporting and divulging information that concerns the commission of crimes and the identity of the perpetrators of crimes.[43]

In a number of delictual cases, it has been held that police officers have a legal duty to protect members of the public from violent crime,[44] and that the state will be liable for damages if they fail culpably in this duty.[45] As previously explained, it does not necessarily follow that a breach of this duty will also give rise to criminal liability on the part of the offending officer. It therefore remains to be seen what view the criminal courts will take in respect of such omissions.[46]

It will be evident from the above that a particular individual's duty to prevent harm in a given situation could conceivably fall into more than one of the established categories. Thus,

---

40 See *Compass Motors Industries (Pty) Ltd v Callguard (Pty) Ltd* 1990 (2) SA 520 (W) at 526B.

41 *Minister of Law and Order v Kadir* 1995 (1) SA 303 (A).

42 Regrettably, the court then went on to hold that the police have no duty to assist a person who has been severely injured in a car accident by recording the details of the other driver, who may well have been at fault for the accident, for purposes of a potential civil claim, apparently forgetting that reckless and negligent driving are also criminal offences.

43 See, for example, *S v Gaba* supra. Gaba was a policeman at the time when the police detectives at his station were looking for a certain gangster who went by the name of Godfather. One day, two detectives brought in a suspect for questioning. Gaba came in while the suspect was being questioned and the detectives asked him if he knew who the suspect was. Gaba remained silent, whereas he knew full well that the suspect was in fact the very same Godfather who was being sought by his colleagues. Because of Gaba's silence, the suspect was released. When this came to light, Gaba was charged with and convicted of defeating the administration of justice because of his failure to divulge what he knew. See further, *S v Barnes* supra (discussed below); *S v Williams* supra.

44 This duty also extends to the prosecuting authorities. See *Carmichele v Minister of Safety and Security and another (Centre for Applied Legal Studies Intervening)* 2001 (4) SA 938 (CC); 2004 (3) SA 305 (SCA).

45 See, for example, *Van Eeden v Minister of Safety and Security* supra; *Minister of Safety and Security v Van Duivenboden* supra; *Minister of Safety and Security v Hamilton* 2004 (2) SA 216 (SCA); *Minister of Safety and Security v Venter and others* 2011 (2) SACR 67 (SCA).

46 See Burchell *Principles of Criminal Law* 86–93 for a discussion of the subject.

for example, if a police officer is present and on duty when a member of the public is being assaulted, that police officer has a duty to intervene, both as a statutory duty and as a consequence of the public office that he holds. If the victim also happens to be a detainee in the police officer's custody, then the latter's duty to intervene would be, in addition, a consequence of the protective relationship that exists between them. Accordingly, when attempting to ascertain the unlawfulness of a particular omission, it is advisable to consider possible alternative bases of liability.

4.2.3 Additional requirements

Even where a person has a legal duty to prevent harm, he will only be liable for his failure to do so if the state is able to prove beyond reasonable doubt that he had the necessary means and opportunity to prevent the harm in question, and that the harm that did occur is directly attributable to (was caused by) his unlawful omission.

4.2.3.1 Means and opportunity

A person can only be held liable for harm that he had the power to prevent had he chosen to do so. Thus, the state must prove that the accused not only had the necessary means, ability and resources to prevent the harm in question, but also that he had sufficient time and opportunity to do so.[47]

4.2.3.2 Causation

By the same token, an accused may only be held liable for the harm that he actually caused through his unlawful omission, and not for harm that may well have occurred in any event. Causation in such cases is established by notionally inserting the required positive conduct (what the accused had a legal duty to do) in place of the accused's inaction, and enquiring whether the harm would still have occurred if the accused had acted as required by law. If it is reasonably possible that the harm would have occurred in any event, then the accused's omission cannot be said to have caused the harm, and the accused will accordingly not be liable.[48]

---

47 See, for example, *S v Barnes* supra. Barnes and another police officer had custody of the deceased, whom they had arrested for the theft of a firearm. When the deceased would not take them to the place where he was keeping it, Barnes assaulted him. There were four separate assaults: the first three were relatively minor, but the last one was sudden and violent. The final assault proved fatal. While the assaults were taking place, the second accused stood by and did nothing to protect the deceased. Nor did he later report what Barnes had done.

Both of them were convicted of culpable homicide in the NPD and subsequently appealed to a full bench. On appeal, the court confirmed Barnes' conviction, but set aside the conviction of the second accused because there was no evidence that he knew, or had any reason to know, that Barnes was about to launch the fourth and fatal assault, or that he had had the time and opportunity to prevent it. Thus, there was no evidence that the second accused was negligent or that his omission was the cause of the deceased's death. The court held, however, that as a police officer, the second accused was under a duty to report Barnes' conduct after the event. Because he did not do so, the inescapable conclusion was that he was shielding Barnes. He was therefore found guilty of being an accessory after the fact to culpable homicide (competent verdict).

48 See *S v Van As* supra where the AD held that the state had failed to prove beyond a reasonable doubt that the accused would have succeeded in finding the missing children, even if they had conducted a more thorough search.

However, compare this with *S v Van Heerden and another* 2010 (1) SACR 529 (ECP). Van Heerden (Van H), a surgeon, was charged with culpable homicide after the death of one of his patients. Van H had performed a hysterectomy on the deceased and had then left the hospital to attend to other duties. The deceased's condition began to deteriorate and the nurse in charge telephoned Van H timeously to inform him, but he did not return to attend to the deceased until after a second telephone call, by which time it was too late. At his trial, Van H argued that even if he had responded immediately to the first call, there would still have been some risk of death. The court found, however, that the risk of death in that case was remote and speculative, and that if Van H had responded when he should have, the deceased would actually have survived. Van H's omission was thus found to have been the cause of death and he was convicted of culpable homicide.

The above enquiry is merely the test for factual causation. It must then be followed by a further enquiry into legal causation. The full enquiry into causation in our law is discussed in detail in Chapter 6.

PAUSE FOR REFLECTION

How to perform the enquiry for liability arising from an unlawful omission

- *Step 1*: First decide whether the accused falls into one of the established categories of liability. If the answer is 'no', then there can be no liability and the enquiry ends here. If the answer is 'yes', then continue to the next step.
- *Step 2*: Determine the *scope* of the accused's legal duty by asking questions such as: what exactly was the accused required to do? When was he required to do it? Where was he required to do it? For whose benefit was he required to do it? Then decide whether the accused *failed to perform* this duty *as and when required by law*. If the answer is 'no', then there can be no liability and the enquiry ends here. If the answer is 'yes', then continue to the next step.
- *Step 3*: Decide whether the accused had the necessary means and skill (if relevant) as well as sufficient opportunity to perform his legal duty if he had chosen to do so. If the answer is 'no', then there can be no liability and the enquiry ends here. If the answer is 'yes', then continue to the next step.
- *Step 4*: Lastly, decide whether the accused would have succeeded in *preventing* the harm that occurred if he *had* performed his legal duty, by applying the tests for factual and legal causation. If the answer is 'no', then there can be no liability and the enquiry ends here. If the answer is 'yes', you have succeeded in proving unlawful conduct on the part of the accused.[49]

THIS CHAPTER IN ESSENCE

1. Although unlawful conduct most often takes the form of an act (positive conduct), there are occasions when an omission will be regarded as unlawful and will thus give rise to criminal liability.
2. The general rule is that a person will not be criminally liable for failing to protect or rescue another person because there is no general duty on any person to prevent harm from coming to another even if it could be done easily and even if it would be the morally correct thing to do.
3. There are, however, certain situations where such a duty does exist because the legal convictions of the community demand that in these situations, the failure to protect or rescue should be regarded as unlawful conduct. These situations generally fall into the following broad categories:
   3.1 There was a statutory duty to perform the act in question.
   3.2 The accused created the dangerous situation through his own prior positive conduct.
   3.3 The accused was in control of dangerous property.
   3.4 The accused had a protective relationship with the victim, whether through natural relationship, contract or some other conduct whereby the accused deliberately, or even tacitly, assumed such a duty.
   3.5 The accused held a public office or quasi-public office, in which rendering the required assistance fell within the course and scope of his employment.

49 This, of course, is not the end of the entire matter since criminal capacity and the required form of fault would also need to be proved.

4. However, once it has been established that the accused had a legal duty to prevent the harm, he will only be liable for his failure to do so if he had the necessary means and opportunity to prevent it from occurring, and if the harm that did occur was directly attributable to his unlawful omission.

Chapter 5

Unlawful states of affairs

CHAPTER OBJECTIVES

The objectives of this chapter are to:
- explain the nature of state of affairs crimes
- identify the requirements for liability in the case of such crimes
- identify the requirements for the unlawful possession of contraband
- distinguish between the criminal law and civil law concepts of possession
- explain the legal position of the unwilling possessor of contraband.

5.1 Introduction

Having considered unlawful acts and omissions, we will now consider the third form of unlawful conduct: being in an unlawful state of affairs.

Although unlawful conduct most commonly takes the form of a positive act or an omission, there are instances in which it may consist of merely being in a prohibited situation or state of affairs, for example:
- occupying the driver's seat of a motor vehicle, with the engine running, while under the influence of drugs or alcohol[1]
- being in possession of prohibited goods (contraband), such as stolen property, housebreaking implements, drugs, unlicensed firearms or ammunition, uncut gemstones or unwrought gold, and banned publications.

1 See s 65(1)(*b*) of the National Road Traffic Act 93 of 1996.

Note that such offences are invariably statutory offences: the notion of criminal liability arising from an unlawful state of affairs does not form part of our common law. In many of these cases, although not all, the conduct in question has been criminalised because it is known to be a common precursor or accompaniment to the commission of some other, more serious crime, which may be far more difficult to intercept or detect.

An unlawful state of affairs may arise in one of two possible ways: as a result of prior conduct on the part of the accused or as a result of the accused's failure to terminate a prohibited state of affairs within a reasonable time.[2]

5.1.1 Prior conduct

The obvious form of transgression is when the accused entered into the unlawful state of affairs of his own accord. For example, X drinks too much, then gets into the driver's seat of his car and starts the engine; or X buys prohibited drugs from his drug dealer. In cases like these, the accused's liability is founded on his prior conduct, which must, of course, be voluntary, accompanied by the requisite form of fault (*dolus* or *culpa*, depending on the statute concerned). It follows that if the accused did not enter into the prohibited state of affairs through his own voluntary act, then as a general rule, he will not be liable.[3]

5.1.2 Failure to terminate within a reasonable time

The mere fact that the accused did not enter into the unlawful state of affairs through his own voluntary act will not always afford him a defence. Where a person finds himself in an unlawful state of affairs as a result of someone else's conduct or simply by chance, he acquires a duty to terminate that state of affairs. If he fails to do so within a reasonable time, he will become liable.[4] What is regarded as a reasonable time depends on the facts of the particular case. Clearly, however, a person is required to give some priority to the matter and not merely act at his personal convenience.[5] Furthermore, even if the accused had an innocent motive for unreasonably prolonging the unlawful state of affairs, for example to hand the prohibited item over to the authorities, this will not be a defence.[6]

5.2 Unlawful possession

The unlawful possession of prohibited items (contraband) is a state of affairs crime.[7] For a person to fulfil the requirements of unlawful conduct for such an offence, he must satisfy the two legal requirements for possession: *detentio* and *animus possidendi.*

5.2.1 *Detentio* – physical control

Detentio simply means that the item in question must be in the accused's physical control. It does not mean that the item must be on the accused's person or even in his immediate vicinity. It could, for example, be in the accused's house or in his car while he is elsewhere, as long as the accused has effective physical control of the item.

2 Whiting RC 'The unwilling possessor of pornography' (1971) 88(3) *SALJ* 296 at 300.
3 *R v Achterdam* 1911 EDL 336.
4 Whiting 'The unwilling possessor of pornography' at 300.
5 See, for example, *S v Brick* 1973 (2) SA 571 (A); *S v Collett* 1991 (2) SA 854 (A).
6 See *S v Brick* 1973 (2) SA 571 (A).
7 For a detailed discussion of possession as a constituting element of statutory offences, see Snyman CR *Criminal Law* 6 ed (2014) 62–70.

5.2.2 *Animus possidendi* – intention to possess

Animus possidendi is an essential requirement of the act of possession. Although it consists of a mental element, it nevertheless forms part of the *actus reus*. It must not, therefore, be confused with *dolus*, which remains part of the fault enquiry. *Animus possidendi* implies, at the very least, that the accused knew[8] that the item in question was in his physical control at the relevant time, even if he did not know that its possession was unlawful.[9] Positive knowledge does not require the possessor to have been consciously aware of his possession at all relevant times. If a person knows that he has contraband in his possession and then forgets about it, his subsequent forgetfulness is no defence.[10]

However, unlike its meaning in civil law, *animus possidendi* for purposes of criminal liability does not normally require the accused to have intended to keep the prohibited item for his own use or benefit (this type of possession is called *possessio civilis*). As a rule, it is sufficient if he knows that he has the item in his physical control and decides to keep it, even temporarily (this type of possession is called *possessio naturalis*), or, in the case of the unwilling possessor, if he keeps it for longer than is reasonably necessary to terminate the unlawful state of affairs.

Even though *possessio naturalis* will normally suffice for criminal liability, there may be cases where something more is required.[11] Ultimately, therefore, there is no hard and fast rule that can be applied in all cases. The decision as to what will constitute *animus possidendi* in any given case will ultimately depend on the intention of the legislature, as interpreted from the relevant statutory provisions.

---

8 In *S v Hanekom* 1979 (2) SA 1130 (C), a number of banned political pamphlets were found among other pamphlets in Hanekom's (H) study and he was charged with their unlawful possession. It emerged at his trial that he was involved in church work and had a vast quantity of publications in his study – there were piles and boxes full of them. He testified that people sent literature to him from all over the world and he did not even know that he had the publications in question. There were some that he knew were banned when he received them, but he thought that he had disposed of these or lost them. Others he did not know were banned when he received them. The state argued (on the basis of the decision in *R v African Canning Co (SWA) Ltd and others* 1954 (1) SA 197 (SWA)) that he *ought* to have known or foreseen that he had the literature. The court rejected this argument and acquitted H because it held that he had to have *positive* knowledge that he had the pamphlets in question and that what he should have known was consequently irrelevant. Hanekom was consequently acquitted.

9 He must therefore have known (1) what the item was, and (2) that it was in his physical control. Knowledge of the unlawfulness of the possession, however, forms part of the fault enquiry and is therefore irrelevant at this stage. See, for example, *R v Betelezie* 1941 TPD 191. Liquor had been illegally stored in Betelezie's house without his knowledge. He was charged with the illegal possession of the liquor, but he was acquitted because the court accepted that he did not know that it was there at all.

In *R v African Canning Co(SWA) Ltd* supra, the accused company was charged with being in unlawful possession of undersized crayfish. The crayfish had been caught in a trawling net and brought in, but the catch had not yet been unloaded. The company's explanation was they were still going to sift the catch and would then throw back any undersized crayfish. The court accepted the truth of this statement, but convicted the company anyway on the basis that their explanation showed they either knew there were undersized crayfish in the catch or were taking a calculated risk.

10 *S v Cleminshaw* 1981 (3) SA 685 (C); *S v Young* 1983 (4) SA 120 (ZS).

11 See, for example, *S v Cameron* 2005 (2) SACR 179 (SCA). Cameron was charged with possession of undersized crayfish that he had caught while diving off Salt Rock Beach. He had left the water with the crayfish in his bag and was apprehended at the foot of the stairs that led up to the road where his car was parked. His defence was that he lacked *animus possidendi* as he had no intention of keeping any undersized crayfish. He was going to measure his catch at the steps and would have then returned any crayfish that were undersized. The trial court rejected this defence and convicted him. On appeal, the SCA held that Cameron's version of events was reasonably possibly true. Furthermore, it held that *animus possidendi* for purposes of the relevant regulation required not only knowledge of control, but also the intention to exercise such control for personal gain or benefit. His appeal was upheld.

5.2.3 The defence of necessity

We have explained that the mere fact that the accused did not enter into the unlawful state of affairs through his own voluntary act is not a defence in itself. Furthermore, even if the accused's motive for unreasonably prolonging the unlawful state of affairs was to hand the prohibited item over to the authorities, this will also not be a defence. However, in appropriate circumstances, the unwilling possessor may be able to raise the defence of necessity, in that he may be able to claim that he was keeping the prohibited item temporarily to prevent its unlawful further distribution or abuse.[12]

5.3 The fault enquiry

Unless the legislature has provided for no-fault liability (an unlikely scenario, especially in light of constitutional considerations), knowledge of the unlawfulness of the state of affairs is required. Thus, in the case of offences that require *dolus*, genuine ignorance of the law would be a defence. In offences that require *culpa*, ignorance of the law would seldom offer a defence because whenever a person sets out on a particular course of action, he has a duty to take reasonable steps to ascertain the applicable law. If he does not, he will be negligent (see further, the defence of mistake or ignorance of the law).

DISCUSSION

Receiving prohibited articles – the requirement of voluntariness

A situation can arise where someone becomes the unwilling receiver of prohibited items. Professor CR Snyman describes the following hypothetical scenario: 'Assume that one day X walks to her post box, opens it, finds an envelope addressed to herself in it, opens the envelope, and discovers that it contains photos of child pornography, the possession of which is a crime. X did not order the photos from anyone. Some unknown person with a perverted sense of humour simply sent them to her. Sometime thereafter, the police visit her house and find the envelope containing the photos on her dining-room table. Is she guilty of the unlawful possession of the photos?'[13] In answering the question, Snyman proposes that the general requirement applicable to all acts and omissions[14] be applied, namely 'that only an act or an omission which is *voluntary* can lead to a conviction'. Furthermore, in 'factual situations such as these, the requirement of voluntariness means that the conduct of possessing the article begins only when the time during which X might reasonably be allowed to get rid of the article, or to inform the police about it, has elapsed'.[15]

THIS CHAPTER IN ESSENCE

1. In the case of certain statutory offences, unlawful conduct may take the form of being in a prohibited situation or state of affairs.
2. As a general rule, the accused must have come into the unlawful state of affairs by his own voluntary act. If he finds himself in an unlawful state of affairs through someone else's act or simply by accident, he must end the unlawful state of affairs within a reasonable time. Being an unwilling transgressor is

12 *S v Collett* supra. The requirements for the defence of necessity are discussed in Chapter 8.
13 Snyman *Criminal Law* 69.
14 See also Chapter 4.
15 Snyman *Criminal Law* 70. (Emphasis added)

therefore not a defence in itself. What is regarded as a reasonable time will depend on the facts of the case, but it essentially means that the accused must act at the first available opportunity and not merely at his own convenience.

3. Where a person is accused of being in possession of contraband, he will only be liable if he had *detentio* (physical control) of the item(s) in question, coupled with *animus possidendi* (intention to possess).
   3.1 If the accused did not know that the contraband was in his physical control, there can be no *animus possidendi*.
   3.2 If the accused knew that the item was in his physical control, but then forgot about it, it does not mean that he lacked *animus possidendi*.
   3.3 It is not normally necessary for the accused to have intended to use the item himself or to derive some personal benefit from it (although this may be required in some cases, depending on the intention of the legislature).
   3.4 An unwilling possessor of contraband may, in appropriate circumstances, be able to raise the defence of necessity.

Chapter 6

Causation

CHAPTER OBJECTIVES

The objectives of this chapter are to:
- introduce the concept of causation
- identify and give examples of consequence crimes
- explain the essential purpose and nature of the causation enquiry in our law
- explain and distinguish between the enquiries for factual causation and legal causation in our law
- explain the test for factual causation
- explain the most commonly used tests for legal causation
- explain the role of a *novus actus interveniens* in the enquiry for legal causation
- explain how the enquiry for legal causation has been approached in specific circumstances.

6.1 The concept of causation

In this chapter, we will consider the fourth and final form of unlawful conduct: causing an unlawful consequence. Certain crimes are defined not in terms of what the accused did or failed to do, but in terms of the consequences that resulted from the accused's conduct. These crimes are sometimes referred to as **consequence crimes** or as materially defined crimes. Murder and culpable homicide are perhaps the most notable examples:

- Murder is the intentional unlawful killing of a person.
- Culpable homicide is the negligent unlawful killing of a person.

To kill means to cause death. Thus, the crimes of murder and culpable homicide are only complete if and when the victim dies, and the accused will only be liable if his conduct was the cause of death.[1] It does not matter whether death was caused by a positive act or an omission, however. Nor, in the case of a positive act, does it necessarily matter whether that act was unlawful in itself: a neutral causal act may also give rise to liability if it was aimed at producing an unlawful consequence.[2] However, the same does not apply in the case of omissions since, as discussed previously, liability will only arise from an omission that was unlawful in itself.

Murder and culpable homicide are not the only consequence crimes. Abortion, arson, fraud, robbery and extortion are also examples of common law crimes for which the accused's liability depends on his having produced a particular unlawful result.[3]

6.2 Proving causation

In all consequence crimes, the state bears the onus of proving beyond a reasonable doubt that there is a sufficient causal link between the accused's initial conduct and the prohibited consequence.[4] If there is no causal link, or if the link is too tenuous, then the accused will not be guilty of the crime concerned although he may perhaps be guilty of an attempt to commit that crime or some other offence.

Although we all have an intuitive understanding of relationships of cause and effect, it is not always a simple task to establish **causation** with the degree of precision and certainty that we need in order to attribute liability in law.[5] For example, if A shoots B and B dies instantly from the gunshot wound, there is normally no difficulty in proving that A caused B's death. However, what is the position if A only wounds B and, while B is being rushed to hospital, the vehicle that he is in has an accident and B is killed in the accident? Can A still be said to have caused B's death in those circumstances? What if B arrives at the hospital, but the surgeon who operates on him is negligent and B dies as a result of the surgery? What if B refuses a blood transfusion and dies from loss of blood? What if it is found, when the

1 Since we must all die sooner or later, this must be taken to mean hastening or causing the *premature* death of the deceased in the sense that the deceased would not have died *when he did die* if it had not been for the accused's conduct. See *S v Hartmann* 1975 (3) SA 532 (C) (this case will be discussed in Chapter 12).

2 See, for example, *Ex parte Die Minister van Justisie: In re S v Grotjohn* 1970 (2) SA 355 (A), discussed in section 6.4.2.

3 See Part 3 for a description of these crimes.

4 An important exception to this rule is where the accused's liability is based on his criminal association with another person who caused the relevant consequence, in other words, when the *doctrine of common purpose* applies. This doctrine is discussed fully in section 25.3.

5 For an overview and critical review of the theories of causation in South African criminal law, see Burchell JM *South African Criminal Law and Procedure Vol I: General Principles of Criminal Law* 4 ed (2011) 95–98.

postmortem examination is done, that B actually died from heart failure because he had a weak heart, and not from the gunshot wound? Can A be said to have caused B's death in any of these circumstances?

Another factor to consider is the longer-term consequences of A's conduct. For example, what if B's wife, whom A knows to be emotionally unstable, commits suicide when she learns of B's death? Is A responsible for causing her death? What if B's children starve to death once both their parents are dead? Is A responsible for causing their deaths as well?

There are two points to be made here:

1. Each of our actions gives rise to a potentially endless train of consequences. The law is unwilling to hold a person responsible for consequences that are too far removed from his initial conduct, otherwise the scope of criminal liability would be spread too widely.
2. A particular consequence may have had more than one contributory cause. The law is unwilling to hold a person responsible for consequences that resulted primarily from factors over which he had no control or influence.

The law has attempted to address these challenges by developing a two-stage causation enquiry:

- *Step 1*: We must first establish whether there is a causal link (*nexus*) between the accused's initial conduct and the consequence in question. If there is no causal link, there can be no liability and that is the end of the matter. If there is a causal link, we proceed to the next step.
- *Step 2*: Having established that there is a causal link between the accused's initial conduct and the consequence, we must then consider whether that causal link is sufficiently close and strong that, as a matter of law and policy, the accused should be held liable for his role in producing that consequence.[6]

This two-stage enquiry can be broken down into two elements: a factual element (the first stage of the enquiry) and a legal (or policy) element (the second stage of the enquiry).

6.3 Factual causation: The *conditio sine qua non* test

The first stage of the enquiry aims to determine whether the accused's conduct was the actual or scientific cause of the consequence, in that the consequence would not have occurred, either at all or when it did, if it had not been for the accused's conduct.[7] To decide this, a court will apply the *conditio sine qua non* test (also known as the 'but for' test). *Conditio sine qua non*, literally translated, means 'the condition without which ... not'; in other words, the condition without which the consequence in question would not have occurred. 'But for' is simply an archaic way of saying 'if not for'.

The *conditio sine qua non* test is performed as follows:

- In the case of *positive acts*, courts will notionally (hypothetically) eliminate the accused's act from the sequence of events and then consider whether the consequence would have occurred when it did. If the accused's act cannot be eliminated from the sequence of events without the consequence also disappearing, then the accused's act is proved to have been the factual cause of that consequence. If, however, there is a reasonable

6 See Corbett JA's clear explanation of this two-stage enquiry in *Minister of Police v Skosana* 1977 (1) SA 31 (A) at 34.
7 For an overview of the scientific aspects, see Joyner K (ed) *Aspects of Forensic Medicine: An Introduction for Healthcare Professionals* (2010) 138–153.

possibility that the consequence would have occurred in any event,[8] then the accused cannot be held to have caused that consequence and he will not be liable.

- In the case of *omissions*, courts will notionally insert the required positive conduct[9] in place of the accused's inaction (failure to act) and then consider whether the consequence in question would have occurred when it did. If the consequence would not have occurred, then the accused's omission is proved to have been the factual cause of that consequence. If, however, there is a reasonable possibility that the consequence would have occurred in any event, then the accused cannot be held to have caused that consequence and he will not be liable.[10]

The *conditio sine qua non* test has also sometimes been described as the test for 'scientific' causation. This is because of its similarity to the type of scientific experiment in which a single factor (the variable) is introduced to prove that this factor, to the exclusion of other factors, is responsible for producing a particular result. In the *conditio sine qua non* test, the accused's conduct represents the variable in the experiment.

Although the *conditio sine qua non* test appears to be firmly entrenched in our law, it has not received unqualified approval from all the leading commentators. One fairly common criticism is that the test is useless as a device for detecting *what* (and therefore *who*) was the cause of a particular consequence.[11] Like the type of scientific experiment mentioned above, the test is only useful for establishing the validity of an existing hypothesis (assumption) regarding cause and effect. In other words, we must approach the test with some specific conduct, and thus a specific perpetrator, in mind. This does not mean, however, that we cannot apply the test to a series of acts and/or omissions on the part of one or more possible perpetrators to ascertain which of them caused or contributed towards causing the consequence in question. In this way, we can arrive at our answer by a process of elimination.

A further criticism is that the test is sometimes capable of producing unsatisfactory and even bizarre results, especially in cases of independent concurrent causation. Snyman gives the following example:[12] suppose that X and Y, acting independently,[13] simultaneously inflict

---

8 In other words, if there is reasonable doubt as to whether the consequence would have disappeared. Bear in mind that the state bears the onus of proving *beyond reasonable doubt* that the accused caused the consequence in question.

9 That is, whatever it was that the accused was under a legal duty to do.

10 *S v Van As en 'n ander* 1967 (4) SA 594 (A). See also the delictual case of *Moses v Minister of Safety and Security* 2000 (3) SA 106 (C) where the court held that the plaintiff had failed to prove that reasonable steps taken by the police would have been sufficient to prevent the fatal assault on the prisoner. However, compare *Van As* and *Moses* with that of *Minister of Police v Skosana* supra, which concerned the failure of the police to provide timeous medical treatment to a prisoner who had been injured in a car accident and was then arrested for drunken driving. He ultimately died of his injuries and his widow brought a claim for damages arising out of his wrongful death. Her claim was upheld because there was adequate proof that the deceased would probably have survived if he had received medical attention earlier. See also the case of *S v Van Heerden and another* 2010 (1) SACR 529 (ECP) (discussed previously in section 4.2.3.2 under 'Unlawful omissions'); and see further the majority approach in the delictual case of *Lee v Minister for Correctional Services* 2013 (2) SA 144 (CC), which suggests that the substitution test may not be the only permissible approach. For a critical assessment of the case, see Price, A 'Factual causation after Lee' (2014) 131(3) *SALJ* 491–500; Paizes, A 'Factual causation: Which "conditio" must be "sine qua non"? A critical discussion of the decision in *Lee v Minister for Correctional Services*' (2014) 131(3) *SALJ* 500–509.

11 See, for example, Van Rensburg ADJ *Juridiese Kousaliteit en Aspekte van Aanspreeklikheidsbeperking by die Onregmatige Daad* (LLD Thesis) (1971) 51–55 and 64–65; Carstens A and Grebe H (eds) *Taallandskap: Huldigingsbundel vir Christo van Rensburg Pont* (2001) 395–396. Objections are discussed in Snyman CR *Criminal Law* 6 ed (2014) 82 and Neethling J and Potgieter JM *Neethling-Potgieter-Visser Law of Delict* 6 ed (2010) 178–187.

12 Snyman CR *Strafreg* (1981) 50.

13 Note that these conundrums only arise in cases where the individuals concerned act independently. Where they act in concert, then, according to the common purpose rule, each is liable for the other's conduct as well as their own, so it will not matter which of them actually caused the death of the deceased. They will both be equally liable.

instantly fatal gunshot injuries on Z. According to the *conditio sine qua non* test, neither X nor Y would be liable for Z's death because eliminating the conduct of either one of them would make no difference to the end result, namely Z's death at the time that he died.

Van Rensburg gives an equally problematic example:[14] suppose that two grains of arsenic are needed to kill Z. Acting independently, but more or less simultaneously, X and Y each administer two grains (a fatal dose) to Z who dies. According to the *conditio sine qua non* test, neither of them would be liable for Z's death for the same reason given in Snyman's example. Suppose, however, that X and Y only administer one grain (a non-fatal dose) each so that Z dies from the combined effect of their actions. In this case, according to the *conditio sine qua non* test, both of them would then be liable for Z's death.

As both Snyman and Van Rensburg point out, the law could not possibly countenance such a nonsensical outcome. In real life, cases such as these, where two people acting simultaneously but independently, both contribute towards causing the death of a third person, will be rare. One that came close, however, was the case of *S v Mbambo and another*.[15]

S v Mbambo and another

Mbambo, the first accused, had chased the deceased with a knife, while the second accused had thrown stones at him. According to the post-mortem report, the cause of death was 'a penetrating stab wound and head injuries'.

The trial court found there was no proof that the two accused had acted in concert so each was liable only for his own conduct. The trial court convicted the first accused of murder and the second accused of culpable homicide. Both appealed.

On appeal, the Appellate Division (AD) held that in such a case it was vital to determine which of the injuries, that is, the stab wound or the head wounds (stones), was the actual cause of death. It reviewed all the medical evidence closely and concluded that it was the stab wound that was the actual cause of death rather than the head injuries, which were such that they might have caused death later. The AD, therefore, upheld the first accused's conviction for murder, but held that the second accused should have been convicted of assault with intent to do grievous bodily harm rather than culpable homicide, because he had played no part in causing the deceased's death.

The AD was again called on to wrestle with a complex set of facts that involved factual causation in *S v Daniels and another*.[16]

S v Daniels and another

The two accused (the Daniels brothers) and a third person (Muller) had gone to Grabouw to seek work. They found work, but no accommodation, so they decided to go home to Botrivier. According to Muller (who later gave evidence for the state), the first accused went off to organise a taxi and, in due course, returned in a taxi driven by the deceased. The second accused and Muller got in and the deceased drove off towards Botrivier. After the deceased had driven some distance, he was told to stop. The first accused and the deceased got out of the taxi and exchanged some words. The first accused produced a pistol and the deceased started to run away. The first accused pursued him, firing three shots at him in quick succession. The second accused then ran after

14 Carstens and Grebe *Taallandskap* 395–396, cited by Snyman in *Criminal Law* 82.
15 *S v Mbambo and another* 1965 (2) SA 845 (A).
16 *S v Daniels en 'n ander* 1983 (3) SA 275 (A).

them. The deceased fell down on the road. Then one more shot was heard. It was never established whether this shot had been fired by the first or second accused. The two of them went off together in the taxi, but had an accident and abandoned it. That evening, the first accused sold the deceased's watch in the bar of a hotel in Greyton. The deceased's body was found the next day, lying on the road, with two rear-entry bullet wounds in his back and a side-entry head wound, which was the immediate cause of death. Logically, this must have come from the fourth and final gunshot. The first and second accused were both convicted of murder and robbery (charges were withdrawn against Muller). They appealed.

On appeal, the AD held that it was clear that the first accused had formed a plan to rob the deceased. The unresolved question was whether the second accused had ever been party to this plan or had even known about it. It was also unclear who had fired the fourth gunshot. The state, in argument, conceded that it had been unable to prove any common purpose between the two accused. The bench could not agree on the solution: each of the five judges had his own view of the matter.

Jansen JA and Van Winsen AJA took the view that even if it was the second accused who had fired the fourth and fatal shot, it was because the gunshot wounds inflicted by the first accused had made the deceased a 'sitting duck' for the second accused to do this. Therefore, by applying the *conditio sine qua non* test to the conduct of the first accused, this conduct was held to have been the factual cause of death. Regarding legal causation, they held further that criminal liability is not necessarily based on proximate cause: the enquiry should rather be whether there are policy considerations that exonerate the accused from liability for the consequence that has occurred in accordance with his intention. They held that the second accused's intervention (if any) was not such a policy consideration. Thus, the first accused's conduct was also the legal cause of death. He was therefore rightly convicted of murder.

Nicholas AJA and Trengrove JA took the view that the 'sitting duck' approach was not sufficient to satisfy the test for legal causation and render the first accused liable for the deceased's death if the second accused had indeed fired the fatal shot. But Nicholas AJA held (despite the state's concession) that there was sufficient proof of common purpose between the two accused. Thus, it did not matter who fired the fatal shot – both were equally guilty of murder. Trengrove JA took the view that there was no proof of common purpose and, since the first accused had not caused the deceased's death, held that he should have been found guilty only of attempted murder. Botha JA concurred with Nicholas AJA's finding on the issue of common purpose and consequently declined to express a view on the issue of causation. The first accused's conviction of murder and robbery was consequently upheld on a majority of four to one.

As regards the second accused, Jansen JA, Trengrove JA and Van Winsen AJA found that it had not been proven beyond a reasonable doubt that he had been party to the first accused's plan to rob and kill the deceased, or that he had fired the shot that actually killed the deceased. Accordingly, he could not be held liable for either the murder or the robbery. Nicholas AJA and Botha AJA thought that there was sufficient proof of his complicity to render him liable for both crimes on the basis of common purpose. The second accused's appeal was consequently upheld on a majority of three to two and his convictions were set aside.

Daniels illustrates how even a seemingly simple and 'scientific' test like the *conditio sine qua non* test can be interpreted and applied in different ways. It may well be argued that it also illustrates how the judiciary will sometimes interpret legal principle in such a way as to satisfy what it regards as the broader demands of justice.

6.4 Legal causation

Factual causation is only the first part of the enquiry. Once factual causation has been established, a court also has to decide whether the accused should be held legally responsible for the consequence that he has caused, either alone or in combination with other causal factors.

On the one hand, the law does not want individuals to escape liability for the natural and probable consequences of their conduct. On the other hand, the law does not seek to hold individuals liable for consequences that are too remote from their original conduct, otherwise the net of criminal liability would be spread too widely.

6.4.1 Different approaches to establishing legal causation

Although most authorities agree that there needs to be a second stage to the enquiry, there is no unanimity on exactly what it should entail.[17] At different times, our courts have spoken of various possible approaches and criteria, such as sole cause, direct cause, proximate cause, dominant cause, operative cause, foreseeable cause and adequate cause. At the same time, they have been loath to reduce the enquiry to a simple, mechanistic one. Thus, for example, our courts have never adopted the sole cause approach, nor have they attached much weight to such simplistic factors as proximity in terms of time and space.[18] The most influential approaches are discussed below.

The *individualisation approaches* require us to choose, from all the various causal factors, the one single act or event that can be regarded as the *causa causans*[19] of the consequence (also sometimes described as the real, operative, effective, dominant or decisive cause). Various criteria have been proposed for this purpose, most notably the *direct or proximate cause tests*, which focus on the factor closest to the consequence in the chronological sequence of events. The difficulty with the individualisation approaches is that they tend to assume that there can be only *one* legal cause of a particular consequence whereas this is not necessarily the case.[20]

The *adequate cause approach*, also known as the *generalisation approach*, bases legal causation on the generalisations that can be made by ordinary persons about the relationships between certain types of events and certain types of consequences. According to this approach, an act is the legal cause of a situation if, according to human experience and in the normal course of events, the act has the general tendency to bring about that type of situation.[21] The difficulty with this approach is that it does not take account of intervening

---

17 See Burchell *South African Criminal Law and Procedure Vol I* 97–98.

18 Thus, for example, South African law has not adopted the 'year-and-a-day' rule of English law, according to which a person will not be liable for murder unless the victim died within a year and a day of the causal act or omission. This is not to say that a South African court will not take into account the length of time that elapsed between the causal act or omission and the death of the deceased in deciding whether the accused should be liable for murder or only for attempted murder. However, mere lapse of time is not decisive in itself.

19 Literally translated as 'the cause of causes'.

20 Consider, for example, the situation where X inflicts a life-threatening, but readily treatable, injury on Y. Y is admitted to hospital, but the hospital's medical personnel are negligent in their treatment of Y with the result that Y succumbs to the injury and dies. In this case, it would be fair to say that Y's death is attributable to the conduct of *both* X *and* the medical personnel, and that the liability of one should not serve to exonerate the other. Compare with *S v Tembani* 2007 (1) SACR 355 (SCA).

21 Snyman *Criminal Law* 85. The adequate cause approach derives from German law and is Snyman's preferred approach (see further, Snyman *Criminal Law* 85–86). The adequate cause approach has been applied by our courts in a few cases. See, for example, *R v De Bruyn and another* 1953 (4) SA 206 (SWA), *R v Loubser* 1953 (2) PH H190 (WPA) and the judgment of Jansen JA in *S v Daniels* supra. However, it is not the generally accepted approach in South Africa.

acts and events which, while they may not alter the final *outcome*, may nevertheless alter the course of events *leading* to that outcome to such an extent that it would be unreasonable to hold the initial actor responsible for it.[22]

According to the *novus actus interveniens* approach, the factual cause of a consequence will also be its legal cause as long as there is no new intervening act or event (*novus actus interveniens*) breaking the chain of causation. Note, however, that a *novus actus interveniens* is not really a test *for* legal causation, but rather a defence *excluding* legal causation. It has therefore been suggested that this approach is nothing more than a negative way of applying the direct or proximate cause test.[23] Unlike the individualisation approaches, however, this approach does not assume that there can be only one legal cause of a particular consequence, but allows for the recognition of contributory causes.

In *S v Mokgethi*,[24] Van Heerden JA discussed the various approaches to legal causation and concluded that none of them should be the sole criterion. However, they could all be used to assist with the main enquiry, which was simply whether there is 'a sufficiently close nexus' between the accused's initial conduct and the ensuing consequence, or whether the consequence is 'too remote' for purposes of founding criminal liability.[25]

This means that the test for legal causation is essentially a flexible one, in which a court is guided, to a large extent, by considerations of fairness, reasonableness and public policy. The problem with a flexible test, however (as previously explained in relation to omissions liability), is that it provides little guidance to a court. Thus, it does not help to create the reasonable certainty of outcome that we need in criminal law to satisfy the principle of legality. For practical reasons, therefore, and despite the dictum in *Mokgethi*, the courts in the majority of cases still tend to adopt the *direct or proximate cause approach*. However, this approach has been developed and modified to the point where it is indistinguishable from the *novus actus interveniens* approach, while also having much in common with the adequate cause approach.[26]

According to the direct or proximate cause approach, the accused's conduct will be regarded as the legal cause of a consequence if the consequence arose directly from the accused's conduct.[27] The conduct will not be regarded as such if there was some new act or event that intervened between the accused's conduct and the consequence in question that altered the natural and probable course of events in such a way that the accused's conduct, even though it may have been the original (and thus factual) cause of the consequence, can no longer be regarded as its direct or proximate (closest) cause. If this happens, we say that the chain of causation has been broken and the accused is accordingly absolved from liability. The legal term for an intervening act or event that breaks the chain of causation is a ***novus actus interveniens***.

---

22 For example, human experience tells us that a life-threatening injury always has the tendency to cause death, but merely because X inflicts a life-threatening injury on Y can surely not mean that X must *invariably* be regarded as the legal cause of Y's death if Y eventually dies, regardless of what happens in the intervening period. See further, Burchell *Principles of Criminal Law* 107.

23 This is because, once there is an intervening act or event that contributes to the result, the original factual cause can no longer be said to be the proximate (closest) or direct cause of that result. See, for example, Hunt PMA and Milton JRL *South African Criminal Law and Procedure Vol II: Common Law Crimes* 3 ed (1996) ch 19 IIIC.

24 *S v Mokgethi en andere* 1990 (1) SA 32 (A).

25 *S v Mokgethi* supra at 40.

26 See, for example, the approaches adopted by the SCA in *S v Lungile and another* 1999 (2) SACR 597 (SCA) and *S v Tembani* supra.

27 See *S v Van Heerden* supra.

6.4.2 The *novus actus interveniens* enquiry

In considering what will and what will not constitute a *novus actus interveniens* in any given situation, it is important to bear in mind that this stage of the enquiry involves strong policy considerations. It is thus not an enquiry into whether there was merely some kind of additional or external factor that contributed towards the consequence in question, but whether that factor is of such a nature and magnitude that it should exonerate the accused from liability for the actual consequences of his conduct.[28]

The most recent and authoritative definition of the term '*novus actus interveniens*' may be found in *S v Lungile*:[29] 'In our law, a *novus actus interveniens* is an event which is, in the context of the act that was committed, abnormal and completely independent of the acts of the accused'.[30] There are thus three principal requirements that must be met for a particular act or event to qualify as a *novus actus interveniens*:

1. It must be an *intervening* act or event, that is, something that occurs between the time of the accused's initial (causal) act or omission and the time that the consequence occurs.[31]
2. It must be an *abnormal* act or event, that is, something unusual, unexpected or unlikely according to the standards of normal human experience.[32]
3. It must have occurred *independently* of the accused's initial conduct, that is, it must not have been prompted, caused or brought about by the accused's conduct, nor may it be something that the accused had a legal duty to prevent.

Consequently, where the accused's causal act or omission gives rise to a sequence of events in which each step in the sequence is simply a natural progression from the one immediately before it, there is no *novus actus interveniens*. This is the case regardless of the number of steps in the sequence or the amount of time that elapses between the accused's initial conduct and the final consequence. Thus, for example, if A seriously wounds B and the wound becomes septic, and B then develops septicaemia and ultimately dies of it, the septicaemia would not normally be regarded as a *novus actus interveniens*. However, if B, while receiving treatment in hospital, contracts and dies from a totally unrelated illness, this would clearly be a *novus actus interveniens*.[33] Interventions that arise from unusual natural events, such as earthquakes, floods or lightning, would obviously rank as *novi acti intervenientes*.

There is one situation in which an intervening act or event that would ordinarily qualify as a *novus actus interveniens* will not be regarded as such. This occurs when the intervening act or event was actually planned, intended or foreseen by the accused, in the sense that it was a calculated part of the causal sequence. As some authorities put it, intended consequences can never be too remote to found liability.[34]

---

28 See the judgment of Jansen JA and Van Winsen AJA in *S v Daniels* supra, discussed above.

29 *S v Lungile* supra at 30.

30 This definition corresponds with the English and American definitions of the concept.

31 For this reason, a pre-existing situation or state of affairs, such as an existing injury or physical weakness, can never be a *novus actus interveniens*. See further the discussion on the thin skull rule in section 6.4.2.1.

32 Burchell JM *Principles of Criminal Law* 4 ed (2013) 100.

33 See, for example, *Bush v Commonwealth* 78 KY 268 (1880 Kentucky), where a shooting victim contracted scarlet fever from a doctor while in hospital and died from it.

34 Boberg PQR *The Law of Delict Vol 1: Aquilian Liability* (1984) 440.

The relevant principle was explained by the AD in *Ex parte Die Minister van Justisie: In re S v Grotjohn* in the following terms:

> **Where the act ... is a calculated part of the chain of causation which the perpetrator started, an eventuality which the perpetrator foresees as a possibility and which he desires to employ to attain his object, ... it would be contrary to accepted principles of law and to all sense of justice to allow him to take shelter behind the act as a *novus actus interveniens*.**[35]

DISCUSSION

Do we really need a second stage to the causation enquiry?

The usual answer to this question is that the enquiry for legal causation is necessary to limit the scope of liability.[36] It could be argued, however, that liability is in any event limited by the fault and criminal capacity enquiries. If a person cannot be held liable for a consequence that he did not intend and if intended consequences can never be too remote to found liability, why do we not simply establish factual causation and then proceed to ask whether the accused intended to cause the consequence that he did in fact cause? Does the legal causation enquiry really serve any purpose and, if so, what is it?[37]

One possible answer is that the enquiry into criminal liability must invariably begin with unlawful conduct. If unlawful conduct cannot be established, there can be no question of fault *in relation* to that conduct. To put it differently, the intention to commit a *lawful* act can never amount to fault. This would suggest that we need to complete the enquiry into unlawful conduct - including any policy considerations affecting such enquiry - before attempting to determine fault.

With these broad principles in mind, let us now consider some situations that require special comment.

6.4.2.1 The victim's pre-existing physical susceptibilities

What is the position in cases where the victim was suffering from a physical condition, such as a weak heart, haemophilia, a cerebral aneurism or an earlier injury, that rendered him particularly susceptible to harm and thereby contributed to his death? The maxim in our law is 'you take your victim as you find him', that is, with all his weaknesses and susceptibilities. This rule is commonly known as the *thin skull* or *eggshell skull rule* and comes from a number of early English cases in which the victims were found to have had abnormally thin skulls, which rendered them especially vulnerable to harm in cases of relatively minor injury.[38]

---

35 *Ex parte Die Minister van Justisie: In re S v Grotjohn* supra at 364B–C. This is an English translation from Burchell JM *Cases and Materials on Criminal Law* 3 ed (2007) 147. As authority for this proposition, the AD relied on Matthaeus A *De Criminibus* (1994) 48.5.1, where he cites, as an example of a murderer, a person who, with malicious intent, gives false evidence so that another will be convicted of a capital crime, and also a magistrate who knowingly sentences an innocent person to death.

36 Burchell *South African Criminal Law and Procedure Vol I* 46.

37 For a discussion on this point, see Neethling and Potgieter *Neethling-Potgieter-Visser Law of Delict* 187–191.

38 It appears to have originated in the delictual case of *Dulieu v White & Sons* [1901] 2 KB 669, in which the court held: 'If a man is negligently run over or otherwise negligently injured in his body, it is no answer to the sufferer's claim for damages that he would have suffered less injury, or no injury at all, if he had not had an unusually thin skull or an unusually weak heart'.

In dealing with these cases, English courts held that as a matter of policy, a victim's pre-existing physical susceptibilities can never rank as a *novus actus interveniens*. This policy also accords with principle, in that a pre-existing state of affairs cannot, by definition, be regarded as an intervening act or event. South African law has adopted the same approach.[39]

6.4.2.2 The victim's own conduct

What is the position in cases where the victim's own intervening conduct was a contributory cause, or even the immediate cause of the consequence, for example, where the victim died by his own hand? Or where the victim refused or failed to seek medical treatment, thus contributing towards his own death? One of the principal difficulties with this kind of situation (as well as the situations discussed below) is that, unlike natural phenomena, human beings have independent volition (will). Because of this, some authorities have argued that it can *never* be correct to speak of one person as having 'caused' another's voluntary act or omission. Consequently, *any* intervening human conduct, if voluntary, must *invariably* rank as a *novus actus interveniens*.[40]

Despite the unassailable logic behind this argument, however, it can lead to some highly inequitable results in practice. Thus, where the accused's conduct was clearly reprehensible, our courts have generally been reluctant to regard the victim's own conduct in the matter as a *novus actus interveniens*, even when such conduct was a contributory cause of the consequence in question, and even when such conduct may well appear foolish, at least in hindsight. The general approach to such cases appears to be that the victim's own conduct will be regarded as a *novus actus interveniens* only if:

- it was abnormal or unreasonable for a person in that particular position; and/or
- it was a truly independent and voluntary act or omission – the so-called 'conscious act of another volition' referred to in *S v De Bruyn* – and not merely a natural response to the accused's unlawful conduct or something that the accused had a duty to prevent.[41]

Against the above background, it is appropriate to consider the following specific situations.

---

39 *R v Makali* 1950 (1) SA 340 (N). Makali was a member of a mob that attacked the deceased's house. He slashed the deceased on his wrist with a cane knife, causing considerable bleeding. The deceased complained of chest pains and later died in hospital. He was found to have been suffering from angina (a heart condition). The cause of death was a heart attack, precipitated by the injury and consequent loss of blood which had aggravated his heart condition. Makali was convicted of murder and appealed to the Natal Provincial Division (NPD). The NPD held that the thin skull rule applied. Consequently, Makali was indeed both the factual and legal cause of the deceased's death. His conviction was, however, reduced to culpable homicide because he lacked the necessary intention to kill.

40 The principal exponents of this argument were the internationally acclaimed jurists, Hart and Honoré, in their influential treatise on causation, initially published in the late 1950s. See Hart HLA and Honoré T *Causation in the Law* (1959) 69.

41 *R v De Bruyn* supra at 215E. De Bruyn, who held a blasting certificate, was employed by a farmer to supervise certain blasting operations on a farm. Contrary to accepted practice, however, he failed to plug some holes where the charges had not fired, and then allowed the labourers to continue drilling without supervision and without warning them not to drill in the vicinity of the misfired holes. One of the labourers drilled into a misfired hole and was killed in the resulting explosion. De Bruyn was charged with culpable homicide, but claimed that he was not liable because the deceased had caused his own death through his own negligence. The court found that the deceased had not been negligent, merely ignorant. Furthermore, De Bruyn had been under a legal duty to guard against the very thing that the deceased had done. Consequently, the deceased's conduct was not a *novus actus interveniens*. De Bruyn was accordingly convicted of culpable homicide. See also in this regard, *R v John* 1969 (2) SA 560 (RA).

6.4.2.2.1 Refusal of medical treatment

What is the position in cases where the victim, perhaps unwisely, fails or refuses to obtain medical treatment, or neglects to follow medical advice?[42]

The AD was required to address this question in *S v Mokgethi*.[43]

S v Mokgethi

Mokgethi and others committed an armed robbery, in the course of which they shot the deceased, a bank employee, in the spine. The deceased survived the shooting, but his lower body was permanently paralysed and he was confined to a wheelchair. The doctors warned him that he had to move his position in the wheelchair otherwise he would develop pressure sores. He ignored the advice with the result that he developed pressure sores, which turned septic. He ultimately died from septicaemia some six months after the shooting.

Mokgethi et al were convicted of his murder, but appealed. On appeal, the AD ruled that a perpetrator is not responsible for causing a victim's death (that is, the consequence will be regarded as too remote) where:

- it was the victim's failure to obtain medical advice or treatment, or heed instructions that was the immediate (direct) cause of his death; and
- the original injury was not inherently mortal (life threatening), or it was no longer so at time of death; and
- the victim's failure was objectively unreasonable in light of his personal characteristics and/or principles.

It found that all three of these requirements applied to the deceased. Accordingly, his failure to follow the advice of his doctors ranked as a *novus actus interveniens*, and Mokgethi and others were consequently not the legal cause of his death. Their convictions for murder were set aside.

6.4.2.2.2 Suicide

Since we have already established that the mere fact that the victim was the immediate cause of his own death will not necessarily exonerate the accused, the question arises as to what the legal position is when one person encourages or assists another to commit suicide. Although such cases are hardly commonplace, the courts have occasionally been called on to consider this question with varying results. Two early (and apparently conflicting) cases

42 An early case that dealt with this question was *R v Loubser* 1953 (2) PH H190 (WPA): Loubser inflicted a head wound on the deceased, a man who lived in rural and primitive conditions. The deceased's employers advised him to go to hospital, but he did not. Instead, he bound his head up with some rags, contracted tetanus from the wound and died nine days later. The court held that it was not abnormal for people living in rural conditions to do as the deceased had done. The deceased's failure to get medical help was therefore not a *novus actus interveniens*. Loubser was accordingly found to be both the factual and legal cause of the deceased's death. An English case that dealt with the same question was *R v Blaue* 1975 (3) All ER 446 (CA): Blaue stabbed the deceased, who then needed a blood transfusion. She refused the transfusion because she was a Jehovah's Witness. She subsequently died. When Blaue was tried for her murder, he claimed that he was not the cause of her death, but rather it was her own unreasonable refusal of the transfusion. The court held that, as a matter of policy, Blaue could not escape liability for the consequences of his unlawful act on the basis he claimed. It suggested (without deciding the point) that an appropriate way of dealing with such cases was to extend the thin skull rule to include not only the victim's physical susceptibilities, but also his mental and psychological susceptibilities, in other words, 'the whole person'. This suggestion has since been followed by English courts, but South African courts have not chosen to extend the thin skull rule to include mental and psychological susceptibilities. They would probably take a somewhat different view of the matter, namely that in view of the importance that people commonly attribute to their religious beliefs, it is not unreasonable or abnormal for a person to refuse to abandon a firmly held religious belief.

43 *S v Mokgethi* supra.

were those of *R v Peverett*[44] and *R v Nbakwa*.[45] In *S v Gordon*,[46] the Natal Provincial Division of the Supreme Court attempted to reconcile the conflicting approaches in *R v Peverett* and *R v Nbakwa* by distinguishing between them on the facts.

S v Gordon

Gordon and the deceased were thwarted lovers who made a suicide pact. Gordon obtained some tranquillisers and sleeping pills, then drove them both to a scenic spot where they took the pills. The deceased ultimately died of the overdose, but Gordon survived and was charged with murder.

The court held that the mere fact that the deceased had committed suicide did not necessarily mean that Gordon had not killed her - he had supplied the pills knowing that she would take them and probably die. The court held, however, that the swallowing of the pills was the deceased's own voluntary and independent act and, as such, it constituted a *novus actus interveniens*. Gordon was consequently found not liable for her death.

In reaching this conclusion, the court distinguished between *Peverett* and *Nbakwa* on the basis that while Peverett himself had done everything necessary to cause Mrs S's death, including the final act of switching on the engine, Nbakwa had not committed the final act himself and the same accordingly applied to Gordon.

However, although the High Court's approach in *Gordon* may have been appealingly simple, it did not find favour with the AD in *Ex parte Minister van Justisie: In re S v Grotjohn*.[47]

Ex parte Die Minister van Justisie: In re S v Grotjohn

Grotjohn's wife was an invalid and a manic-depressive. One day, during an argument with Grotjohn, she told him to hand her the gun that he had with him as she wanted to shoot herself. He loaded the gun and handed it to her, telling her to shoot herself if she wanted because she was just a burden. She shot and killed herself. He was charged with murder. The trial court followed the *Gordon* case, that is, it held that as the deceased's act was her own voluntary, independent act, it was a *novus actus interveniens* and Grotjohn was acquitted of murder.

The Minister of Justice, however, put two questions of law to the AD for decision: does a person who instigates, assists or places another person in a position to commit suicide commit a crime? If so, what crime? In reply, the AD (without overruling or disapproving of the NPD's decision in *Gordon*) held that the causal chain will not necessarily be broken by the suicide victim's final act:

> **To have this effect, it would need to be a completely independent act, in the sense of being totally separate from and unconnected with the perpetrator's act or conduct; and this would not be the case where the [perpetrator's] act or conduct is in fact the cause that induces[48] the [other person's]**

---

44 *R v Peverett* 1940 AD 213: Peverett and Mrs S, his married lover, made a suicide pact. P rigged his car so that the fumes from the exhaust pipe would flow into the cabin. He and Mrs S then sat in the car with the doors and windows closed and P started the engine. Both lost consciousness, but were rescued before they could die. P was convicted of attempted murder, but appealed. On appeal, the AD held that, because P had done everything necessary to bring about Mrs S's death, he had been correctly convicted of attempted murder.

45 *R v Nbakwa* 1956 (2) SA 557 (SR): Nbakwa's mother was apparently responsible for causing the death of N's child. N insisted that his mother, who was ill in bed at the time, should kill herself. She agreed. He made a noose from a piece of rope, tied it to a rafter and, at her request, fetched a block of wood for her to stand on. She then stood on the block, put her head in the noose and hanged herself. N was charged with murder, but the defence took exception to the indictment on the grounds that it did not disclose an offence. In deciding the exception, the court agreed that, on the alleged facts, no murder had been committed, as N's conduct had not been the direct cause of death - the deceased's act of hanging herself was a *novus actus interveniens*. The exception was decided in N's favour and he was acquitted.

46 *S v Gordon* 1962 (4) SA 727 (N).

47 *Ex parte Die Minister van Justisie: In re S v Grotjohn* supra.

48 In the original Afrikaans judgment, the term *aanleidende oorsaak* is used. *Aanleidend* means 'inducing'.

> act, even though the [other person's] act is innocent in itself. Where the [other person's] act ... is a calculated part of the chain of events that [the perpetrator] has set in motion, an event which [the perpetrator] foresees as a possibility and wishes to use in order to achieve his goal, or as something upon which he can rely to bring about the desired result, intention would also not be lacking, and it would be contrary to accepted legal principles and all sense of justice to permit him to shelter behind the [other person's] act as a subsequent intervening act. That the [other person's] act is not a criminal act can make no difference. So, too, in the case of suicide I think it obvious that the deceased's final act, though it may be his own independent act and the immediate cause of his death, need not necessarily be a completely independent act in the above sense, and that its non-criminality is of little relevance to the question of the causative effect of the actions or conduct of the person who encouraged, helped or enabled the deceased to commit suicide. It is reasonably conceivable that [the perpetrator's] intentional acts or conduct may be an immediate cause that induces the final deed. Someone, for example, who provides another with the means whereby he wishes to commit an act, contributes to the act and its consequence, and the use of the means together with the resulting consequences may rightly be seen as the direct result of the provision of the means. The conclusion can hardly be avoided that he who provides the desired or necessary means for a proposed suicide, has a causal role therein if suicide is committed; and if he does it willingly and knowingly, with the necessary intention of putting an end to the life of the person who wishes to commit suicide, he is guilty of murder, even though the final act is performed by the non-criminal hand of the suicide, because he is then unlawfully and intentionally instrumental in ending the life of another. If the deed is not completed he could similarly be guilty of attempted murder ...[49]

> As will be evident from the aforegoing, the answers to the questions posed may be found in the applicable principles of our criminal law. The first question cannot be answered with a simple 'yes' or 'no'. Whether a person who encourages, assists or enables another to commit suicide commits a crime will depend on the facts of the particular case. With regard to the facts which gave rise to the questions, it is necessary to emphasise that the mere fact that the final act was the suicide victim's own, voluntary, non-criminal act does not without more mean that the said person cannot be found guilty of any crime. The answer to the second question likewise depends on the factual circumstances. As appropriate, the crime could be murder, attempted murder or culpable homicide.

The AD's ruling in *Grotjohn* has often been thought to mean that whenever one person intentionally supplies another with the means to commit suicide, the first must invariably be guilty of murder if death results,[50] but this is not an adequate statement of the law, as Wallis JA observed in *Minister of Justice and Correctional Services v Estate Stransham-Ford.*[51] Merely because there may be cases in which the final act of the deceased does not rank as a *novus actus interveniens* does not mean that there may not also be cases in which it does. Each case must therefore be judged on its own merits.

49 *Ex parte Die Minister van Justisie: In re S v Grotjohn* supra at 363H–364H (authors' translation).

50 Thus, for example, in *S v Hibbert* 1979 (4) SA 717 (D) (a case with facts similar to those of *Grotjohn*), the accused was convicted of murder, even though the court accepted that he had not contrived or even desired his wife's death. This interpretation of the law was also the High Court's point of departure in *Stransham-Ford v Minister of Justice and Correctional Services and Others* 2015 (4) SA 50 (GP). For a critique of the judgment in *Hibbert*, see Van Oosten FFW '*S v Hibbert* 1979 4 SA 717 (D) *Aandadigheid aan selfmoord*' 1980(1) *TSAR* 83.

51 *Minister of Justice and others v Estate Stransham-Ford* 2017 (3) SA 152 (SCA) at para 29 and see also paras 52 to 54.

DISCUSSION

In what circumstances should the final act of a person who causes his own death be regarded as a *novus actus interveniens*?

Consider the following scenario: X and Y, feeling reckless but not suicidal, agree to play Russian Roulette with X's revolver. X takes the first turn. He spins the barrel, places the gun to his head and pulls the trigger. The gun does not fire. Y then takes the gun from X and repeats the procedure. This time the gun fires. Y shoots himself in the head and dies. According to the common interpretation of *Grotjohn's* case, X would then be guilty of Y's murder. Despite Wallis JA's reservations about this interpretation (see above) it is difficult to see how the facts could be interpreted otherwise: X supplied the means (the gun) with which Y ended his own life, well knowing that this could happen. Y's act of placing the gun to his head and pulling the trigger was not abnormal or unexpected in the context of the game they were playing, nor was it completely unconnected with X's conduct, since they were both involved in playing the game together. But what, then, would the position be if X had shot and killed himself instead of Y? Would Y then escape liability, merely because it was not he who had supplied the fatal weapon? And what would the position be if the gun had not been supplied by either of them - for example, if they had found Z's gun and used that to play with? Or if they had each used their own guns?

In a case like this, where X and Y were both equal participants in the game, it seems illogical for their liability to turn on so arbitrary a factor as who supplied the fatal weapon. Furthermore, fairness would seem to demand that X and Y be treated the same - either both of them should be liable in the event of the other's death, or neither of them. But if the supply of the means is not the (or a) decisive factor, then what should that factor (or those factors) be?[52] Zimmermann suggests that, on a proper interpretation of *Grotjohn*, the decisive factor is whether the deceased's final act can be regarded as truly independent.[53] If this is correct, the immediate challenge lies in knowing what criteria would need to be satisfied before the deceased's act can be said to be a truly independent act, unrelated to the conduct of the person who supplied the means for the suicide. This is an important question in view of its implications for the

52 One of the difficulties with answering this question is that our courts have consistently refused to recognise the concept of 'psychological causation' - the idea that a consequence need not be the result of a physical act or event, but could also be caused *psychologically*. This concept is of particular relevance in the case of crimes committed in concert. Its arch-proponent was the late Professor JC De Wet (De Wet JC and Swanepoel HL *Die Suid-Afrikaanse Strafreg* 2 ed (1960) 169–170; and see also SA Strauss '*Oorsaaklikheidsverband en daderskap: Moord sonder veroorsaking*?' (1960) 23 *THRHR* 95, 101–102). However, in *S v Safatsa and others* 1988 (1) SA 868 (A) (which dealt with the doctrine of common purpose), Botha JA (at 901C–D) rejected the concept of psychological causation as 'stretching the concept of causation ... to such unrealistic limits as to border on absurdity'. As a result, our courts have limited themselves to determining causation on the basis of some *physical* conduct (act or omission) on the part of the accused, leaving psychological factors out of consideration. Liability for crimes committed in concert is discussed fully in Chapter 25.

53 Zimmermann H 'Self-determination, paternalism or human care? Suicide and criminal responsibility in South African and German law' (1979) (3) *TSAR* 183 at 189–190. See also the delictual case of *Road Accident Fund v Russell* 2001 (2) SA 34 (SCA), where the deceased's suicide was held not to be a *novus actus interveniens*, because it was not a truly voluntary and independent act, but was induced by depression, which was the direct result of the head injury and consequent brain damage sustained by the deceased in the motor vehicle accident caused by the negligence of the insured driver.

legality (or otherwise) of physician-assisted suicide (PAS),[54] a subject which has generated considerable public interest in the wake of the SCA's decision in the *Stransham-Ford* case.[55]

6.4.2.3 Conduct of a third person

The independent act of a third person, whether innocent or criminal, will normally be regarded as a *novus actus interveniens.*[56] However, this would not apply to an act that was occasioned by the accused's own (unlawful) conduct.[57]

6.4.2.3.1 Medical intervention

In line with the principles outlined above, where the deceased died as a result of (possibly risky) medical treatment, necessitated by the injury inflicted by the accused and administered in good faith, such treatment is not a *novus actus interveniens.* The same applies if the deceased died as a result of complications, such as an infection, that arose directly from such an injury.

It is also clear that a doctor's inability to save the life of a victim who is already moribund (dying) is not a *novus actus interveniens.* The same applies when medical

54 Physician-assisted suicide (PAS) describes the situation where a medical practitioner supplies a patient with the means to end his own life. It should be distinguished from physician-assisted euthanasia (PAE), where the medical practitioner himself applies those means so as to end the patient's life, as well as from so-called passive euthanasia, where medical personnel withhold life-prolonging medical treatment (usually at the patient's request), thus allowing death to occur in the natural course of events. For further discussion of these terms and the legal implications of each, see *Minister of Justice and others v Estate Stransham-Ford* (supra) at paras paras 28–56.

55 In *Stransham-Ford v Minister of Justice and Correctional Services and others* (supra) the applicant, who was dying of cancer, sought an urgent declaratory order in the Pretoria High Court to the effect that a medical practitioner could lawfully assist him to end his life by administering a lethal agent (PAE), or by supplying him with a lethal agent to administer himself (PAS), without incurring any civil or criminal liability or professional sanction. After some delay, the court granted such an order, however, unbeknown to it, the applicant had already died of natural causes. On appeal, the SCA set the order aside, chiefly because the applicant had died before the order had been made and the High Court was consequently not competent to grant it (see *Minister of Justice and others v Estate Stransham-Ford,* supra). In the course of its judgment, the SCA (per Wallis JA) considered the various avenues available to medical practitioners in dealing with terminally ill patients. It held that passive euthanasia (as described above) is lawful, even if accompanied by palliative treatment that has the secondary effect of hastening death (see paras 30–34). In contrast, PAE amounts to murder according to our current law. For such conduct to be legalised the law would require considerable development (see paras 36–40). PAS is a different matter, however. As our law stands, PAS is not necessarily unlawful, however the SCA left the question undecided, holding that it fell to be decided by the court when presented with such a case (see paras 55–56).

56 See the judgments of Nicholas AJA and Trengrove JA in *S v Daniels* supra.

57 *S v Lungile* supra. Lungile and his co-accused had staged an armed robbery at a Scotts store in Main Street, Port Elizabeth. A policeman, De Reuck, arrived on the scene and there was an exchange of gunfire, in the course of which an employee of Scotts was shot and killed. It was not established whether the shot had come from the second accused (who was the one with the gun) or from De Reuck.

Both accused were convicted of murder and robbery, and appealed to the SCA on various grounds. One of their grounds of appeal was that De Reuck's act in shooting was a *novus actus interveniens,* which the accused had not foreseen. The SCA rejected this argument, holding that in our law, a *novus actus interveniens* is 'an event which is, in the context of the act that was committed, abnormal, and completely independent of the acts of the accused' at para 30. Since the robbers had armed themselves, the death of the deceased, caused by a gunshot fired in the course of a gun battle between the second accused and De Reuck, was not abnormal, unforeseeable or independent of the acts of the accused. It was foreseeable that a policeman could enter the scene, that a gun battle could ensue and that an innocent party might be injured or killed in the crossfire, regardless of who fired the harmful shot or shots. The accused were found to have been both the factual and legal cause of the deceased's death.

personnel end a fruitless attempt to save a victim's life,[58] for example by turning off his life-support system.[59]

Even where medical personnel are negligent and thereby contribute towards the death of the deceased, it has been held that this will not necessarily rank as a *novus actus interveniens*.[60]

In such cases, much will depend on the nature of the initial injury:

- Where the original injury was inherently life-threatening, subsequent medical negligence will not constitute a *novus actus interveniens*.[61]
- Subsequent medical negligence will only constitute a *novus actus interveniens* if the original injury was not inherently life-threatening or it was no longer so at the time of such negligence.[62]
- It has yet to be decided whether the position would be different in a case of gross medical negligence or other improper conduct on the part of medical personnel.[63]

6.4.2.3.2 Criminal acts

We have explained that the independent criminal act of a third person will normally rank as a *novus actus interveniens*. However, this will probably not be the case if that act was one that the accused had a legal duty to prevent.

This has become an accepted principle of delictual liability.[64] Although it does not necessarily follow that criminal liability will also arise in such cases (see below), a person will be criminally liable for harm that the victim inflicts on himself if that harm was something that the accused had a legal duty to prevent.[65] There appears to be no reason *in principle* why the same reasoning should not apply to harm inflicted by third persons.

6.4.2.4 Conduct of the accused

In principle, there is no reason why an intervening act by the accused himself should not rank as a *novus actus interveniens*, but in order to do so, the act would need to be totally unrelated to the earlier causal act or omission. If the accused's intervening act was simply a

58 *S v Williams* 1986 (4) SA 1188 (A). Williams shot the deceased, who was taken to hospital and put on a respirator. After 48 hours, she was pronounced brain dead so the respirator was disconnected. When Williams was tried for her murder, he claimed that he had not been the cause of death, but rather it was the conduct of the doctors in disconnecting the respirator. He was convicted and appealed to the AD. On appeal, the court held that since the injury inflicted by Williams had been mortal (life threatening) and the deceased was merely being kept alive by artificial means, the doctors did not cause her death when they disconnected the respirator – they were merely ending a fruitless attempt to save her life. Williams' conviction was upheld.

59 The same is not necessarily true of active euthanasia, however. See also the article by McQuoid-Mason D 'Pacemakers and "living wills": Does turning down a pacemaker to allow death with dignity constitute murder?' (2005) 18(1) *SACJ* 24–40, where he considers the legal implications of switching off a patient's pacemaker after brain death. See also the discussion on euthanasia in Chapter 27.

60 *S v Counter* 2000 (2) SACR 241 (T); *S v Tembani* supra. Burchell points out that Cameron JA did not opt for a specific theory of causation in *Tembani*. However, the judge's awareness of the South African reality of different standards of medical care might support the view that disparities in medical care, as such, can be intervening events, thus compatible with the *novus actus* theory. See Burchell *South African Criminal Law and Procedure Vol I* 107.

61 *S v Tembani* supra.

62 *S v Tembani* supra. Compare with the AD's approach in *S v Mokgethi* supra, discussed above.

63 In *S v Counter supra*, it was held (obiter) that gross negligence or other improper conduct would be a *novus actus interveniens*, but in *S v Tembani* supra, it was held (also obiter) that even gross medical negligence would not be a *novus actus interveniens* where the accused had deliberately inflicted a life-threatening injury.

64 See, for example, *Minister of Safety and Security and another v Carmichele* 2004 (3) SA 305 (SCA); *Van Eeden v Minister of Safety and Security (Women's Legal Centre Trust, as Amicus Curiae)* 2003 (1) SA 389 (SCA); *Minister of Safety and Security v Van Duivenboden* 2002 (6) SA 431 (SCA).

65 See *R v De Bruyn* supra.

continuation of earlier conduct aimed at causing the death of the deceased, or was merely a direct and/or natural response thereto, then it will not rank as a *novus actus interveniens*.

Suppose, for example, that X inflicts a mortal injury on Y and, mistakenly believing that he has succeeded in killing Y, buries Y's supposed remains, thereby actually causing Y's death by asphyxiation. X's act of burying Y will not rank as a *novus actus interveniens* because it is not an abnormal act in the circumstances nor is it independent of X's earlier conduct.[66] Or suppose that X inflicts a mortal injury on Y, but actually causes Y's death in a well-meaning, but misguided attempt to save Y's life. Again, X's intervening conduct would not be regarded as a *novus actus interveniens* because it cannot be regarded as an abnormal or independent act.

However, the situation would probably be different in a case where the initial injury is not inherently life threatening. For example, X inflicts a minor injury on Y, but inadvertently causes Y's death through an incompetent attempt to treat that injury. X's intervention in this case would probably be regarded as a *novus actus interveniens*. Likewise, if X inflicts a mortal injury on Y, but actually causes Y's death through an accident that is in no way related to his earlier conduct (for example, he accidentally runs over Y while driving out of Y's yard), this too would rank as a *novus actus interveniens*.[67]

6.5 Causation in criminal law compared with causation in delict

As any study of the law of delict will show, a defendant to an **Aquilian action** will only be held liable for harm or damage that he has caused. Hence, proof of causation is essential for delictual liability. Just as in criminal law, causation for purposes of delictual liability is established by means of a two-stage enquiry: an enquiry into factual causation followed by an enquiry into legal causation. The tests used for these enquiries are framed in exactly the same terms as in criminal law.

However, it does not necessarily follow that what is regarded as adequate proof of legal causation for delictual liability will also be regarded as sufficient proof for criminal liability. This was pointed out by Van Heerden JA in *S v Mokgethi*, where he cited the following:[68]

> **[T]he legal cause may vary from one branch of the law to another. A [person] may be regarded as having caused a particular injury for the purposes of determining that he is liable to pay damages in delict to the injured person, but it does not follow that he would be regarded as having caused the injury for the purpose of determining whether he is liable to criminal punishment in respect of the occurrence.**[69]

Therefore, as in cases of omissions liability, delictual cases are a helpful aid to understanding causation in criminal law, but they need to be viewed with caution.

66 See *S v Mtombeni* 1993 (1) SACR 591 (ZS), discussed in more detail in Chapter 21.

67 This does not necessarily mean that X would escape liability altogether in these cases, but it would mean that his liability would be assessed on the basis of his fault (if any) at the time of his intervening act and not at the time of inflicting the initial injury. See further the discussion in Chapter 21.

68 Gordon GH *The Criminal Law of Scotland* 2 ed (1978) 104.

69 *S v Mokgethi* supra at 40.

PAUSE FOR REFLECTION

Guidelines for performing a causation enquiry

The enquiry *must* be performed in the given order – it is imperative to test for *factual causation first* using the *conditio sine qua non* test. Only if factual causation is established, is it then possible to apply the test for legal causation. If factual causation cannot be established, there can be no liability and that is the end of the matter.

In performing the test for factual causation, it is the accused's *conduct* that is the point of the enquiry. Identify and specify the propounded causal act or omission. This is important because:

- in certain cases it may be necessary to consider the accused's liability on the basis of more than one possible causal act or omission[70]
- it is only when the relevant causal act or omission has been established that it is possible to enquire whether it was accompanied by the requisite criminal capacity and fault.[71]

In performing the test for legal causation, it is best to apply the test for direct or proximate causation first to ascertain whether the causal link remains intact or whether it has been broken by a *novus actus interveniens*. When dealing with a situation which has previously been addressed by the courts, you can use the relevant case law to assist with this enquiry. When dealing with a situation which the courts have not yet addressed, apply the three general requirements for a *novus actus interveniens* (as derived from *S v Lungile*).

When establishing cause of death, bear in mind that as a general rule, a court will be less likely to regard an intervening act or event as a *novus actus interveniens* if the original injury was inherently life threatening and was still so at the time of the intervening act or event.

If there was an intervening act or event that would ordinarily amount to a *novus actus interveniens*, consider whether it was nevertheless a calculated part of the causal sequence. If so, it will not in fact be regarded as a *novus actus interveniens*.

If there was no *novus actus interveniens*, consider whether there are any additional facts or policy considerations that would prompt the court to decide that the consequence was nevertheless too remote from the causal act or omission to found liability. Bear in mind, however, that any such policy considerations would need to be extremely compelling (and probably unusual) for the court to decide that the accused should be absolved from the actual consequence of his conduct.

If it is necessary to determine the liability of more than one perpetrator, deal with each of them *in turn*, completing the enquiries for both factual and legal causation. Do not be distracted by the fact that other persons may also have contributed towards causing the unlawful consequence. It is entirely possible for more than one person to be criminally liable for causing a particular consequence. The liability of one perpetrator does not automatically exonerate the others. Contributory conduct will only exonerate the original perpetrator if it breaks the chain of causation and it will only do this if it amounts to a *novus actus interveniens*.

70 Consider, for example, cases of culpable prior voluntary conduct and prior positive conduct.

71 Consider, for example, the following scenario: X deliberately stabs Y. X is immediately sorry and rushes Y to hospital in his car. In his haste to reach the hospital, however, X negligently fails to stop at an intersection, causing a car accident in which Y is killed. In a case like this, it is not sufficient simply to say that X caused Y's death. We need to decide whether X caused Y's death by means of the *stabbing*, in which case he is guilty of murder, or by means of the *car accident*, in which case he is guilty only of culpable homicide.

THIS CHAPTER IN ESSENCE

1. Consequence crimes, such as murder and culpable homicide, require the state to prove that the accused caused a particular consequence, for example the death of the deceased.
2. Causation is established by a two-stage enquiry: an enquiry into factual causation, followed by an enquiry into legal causation.
3. The test for factual causation is the *conditio sine qua non* or 'but for' test. In this test, we ask whether the consequence in question would have occurred when it did or whether it would have occurred at all had it not been for the accused's conduct (either a positive act or an omission).
4. Having established factual causation, we must next establish whether the accused's conduct was also the legal cause of the consequence in question, namely whether the nexus (link) between the accused's conduct and the consequence was sufficiently close and strong so that, as a matter of law and policy, the accused ought to be held criminally liable for his role in producing that consequence.
5. In most cases, this requirement will be satisfied if the accused's conduct was the direct or proximate cause of the consequence.
   5.1 However, this is not the case if there was a *novus actus interveniens* (a new intervening act or event) that broke the chain of causation. This stage of the enquiry involves strong policy considerations.
   5.2 Hence, it is not an enquiry into whether there was merely some kind of intervening act or event that contributed towards the consequence in question, but whether that intervening act or event was of such a nature and magnitude that it should exonerate the accused from liability for the consequence that he did in fact produce.
   5.3 Normally, therefore, a particular intervening act or event will only be regarded as a *novus actus interveniens* if, when viewed in context, it was something abnormal and completely independent of the accused's conduct.
6. An intervening act or event is more likely to be regarded as a *novus actus interveniens* if the initial injury inflicted by the accused (if any) was not inherently life threatening or was no longer so at the time of the intervening act or event. Where, however, a person inflicts a life-threatening injury on another, then, for as long as the injury remains life threatening, the former will normally be held responsible for the ensuing death of the latter even if external factors, such as medical negligence, also play a role in causing that death.
7. An intervening act or event that would normally rank as a *novus actus interveniens* will not be regarded as such if it was a calculated part of the causal sequence, that is, something that the accused foresaw and meant to happen.
8. However, it may happen that conduct that outwardly meets all these requirements is not in fact unlawful because the accused had a lawful justification for acting as he did. We will therefore now consider the various defences that an accused may raise in order to claim justification for his apparently unlawful conduct.

Chapter 7

Private defence

CHAPTER OBJECTIVES

The objectives of this chapter are to:

- explain the concept of justification
- identify the various justification defences
- explain the requirements for the defence of private defence of person

- explain the requirements for the defence of private defence of property
- discuss the use of lethal force in private defence of person and property
- distinguish between the defence of private defence (proper) and the defence of putative private defence.

7.1 The concept of justification

In the previous chapters, we discussed the essential requirements for unlawful conduct, namely that the conduct must be human and voluntary, and it must conform to the definition of a crime. We have also considered the forms that unlawful conduct may take, namely committing an unlawful act or an unlawful omission, being in an unlawful state of affairs or causing an unlawful consequence.

However, it may happen that a person, whose conduct outwardly corresponds with the requirements for unlawful conduct, will not be criminally liable because his conduct was *justified* in the particular circumstances in which he acted. In other words, conduct that is *prima facie* unlawful will not in fact be unlawful if the perpetrator had a lawful reason for acting as he did.

For example, it is always *prima facie* unlawful for one person to kill or injure another.[1] However, if the person concerned had a lawful reason for doing so, for example he was acting in self-defence, his conduct will not in fact be unlawful. If he is then charged with having committed a crime, he can raise this as a defence at his trial to escape liability.

The broad term '**justification**' is used to describe a number of individual defences:

- Private defence of persons and property
- Necessity
- Compulsion
- Impossibility
- Consent
- Obedience to superior orders
- Public authority
- Moderate disciplinary chastisement

Notably missing from the above list is provocation. In modern criminal law, provocation is not regarded as a justification for contravening the law. The subject of provocation will be discussed in Chapter 14 on criminal capacity.

DISCUSSION

Should there be a general ground of justification?

Some authorities have argued that the list of justification defences is not a closed list, but merely examples of the crystallised legal convictions of the community.[2] According to this argument, an accused would not need to bring his defence within the ambit of one or other of the abovementioned defences – he could simply plead that his conduct was reasonable for any person in the same circumstances and that it was therefore justified. Burchell warns, however, that expanding the list of available defences is as much an infringement of the principle of legality – and thus potentially as dangerous

1 See, for example, *S v Manona* 2001 (1) SACR 426 (Tk).

2 See, for example, Snyman CR *Criminal Law* 6 ed (2014) 97–98.

– as expanding the list of available crimes because it creates uncertainty as to what conduct will and will not be considered criminal.[3]

The point was argued in *S v Engelbrecht*,[4] in which the *amicus curiae* (friend of the court) tried to persuade the court to apply *a general defence of reasonableness*. The court declined to do this without hearing further proposals and debate. It held further that the criteria laid down in terms of the recognised justification defences would in any event probably remain the most appropriate criteria for determining whether or not a particular accused's conduct was reasonable in any given circumstances. *The court did not, however, completely reject the notion of a general ground of justification, so the question is still open for debate.*

7.2 Private defence

The term '**private defence**'[5] covers a fairly broad category of defences: self-defence, defence of other persons and defence of property. It is called private defence because it refers to a situation in which an individual, acting in his personal capacity, uses force or violence to defend his legal interests, or those of another person, rather than relying on the police or other public authorities for protection.[6]

Traditionally, however, we generally distinguish between private defence of person (namely self-defence and defence of other persons) and private defence of property because the law pertaining to each defence differs slightly. Also, for obvious reasons,[7] the law generally permits a greater amount of force to be used to defend the interests of life, physical integrity, sexual integrity and dignity (that is, personal interests)[8] than to defend property and proprietary interests. We will begin with the defence of private defence of person and then move on to private defence of property.

7.2.1 Private defence of person

The general rule, and hence our basic point of departure, is that the law does not permit private individuals to use force against other persons to protect their legal interests. It prefers that, instead, they use the agencies of the state that exist for this purpose, namely the law enforcement agencies and the justice system. There are, however, instances where this is

3 Burchell JM *Principles of Criminal Law* 5 ed (2016) 116.

4 *S v Engelbrecht* 2005 (2) SACR 41 (W).

5 Authors, such as Burchell, prefer the term 'private defence'. This broader term is indeed 'wide enough to include legitimate defence of a third party'. See Burchell JM *South African Criminal Law and Procedure Vol I: General Principles of Criminal Law* 4 ed (2011) 47. We agree with this approach.

6 This does not mean, however, that this defence is not also available to a police officer who defends himself or some other person against an unlawful attack. Police officers have the same right of private defence as other individuals in addition to the special powers of search, seizure and arrest conferred on them by the state to enable them to carry out their functions.

7 Especially in the context of a constitutional dispensation like South Africa, which fosters a normative culture of respect for human life, dignity and freedom.

8 This is not always easy to determine or uncontroversial. See *Ntamo and others v Minister of Safety and Security* 2001 (1) SA 830 (TkH) at para 35 for the court's reasoning on the relevance of the legal convictions of the community for purposes of determining the scope of the common law of self-defence as seen in light of the Constitution of the Republic of South Africa, 1996. See also *S v Dougherty* 2003 (2) SACR 36 (W) for the impact of the Constitution on the private defence of self-defence. For a critical analysis of this case, see Snyman CR 'Private defence in criminal law: An unwarranted raising of the test of unreasonableness' (2004) 67 *THRHR* 325 at 330.

simply not realistic. Thus, for example, the law will allow a person to use force if it is necessary to defend himself or someone else against an unlawful attack by another person, but only in specific circumstances and only to a limited extent.[9]

Therefore, there are certain preconditions that must be met before an individual may resort to using force against another person, and there are also limits to how much force they are entitled to use and what they are entitled to do. We will begin by considering the various requirements for private defence of person.

7.2.1.1 Requirements for the attack or threat

7.2.1.1.1 There must be an unlawful attack or threat of attack

One requirement is that there must be an unlawful attack or a threat of such an attack.[10] A person may not defend himself against a lawful invasion of his interests, such as a lawful arrest or deprivation of liberty. This does not mean that the attack need be criminal per se. A person may lawfully defend himself against an unlawful attack by a child or insane person (someone who lacks criminal capacity). This would not prevent the attack from being unlawful. It must, however, be an attack by a person since only a person may act unlawfully. Thus, the use of force to defend oneself against a vicious animal is not private defence - it would fall under the defence of necessity.

It does not matter, however, who the initial aggressor was. For example, if A attacks B and B uses excessive force in defending himself, B acts unlawfully. Accordingly, at the point at which B began to use such excessive force, A would be entitled to defend himself against B even though A was the initial aggressor.[11]

7.2.1.1.2 The attack must threaten some legally protected interest

To be considered as private defence of person, the attack must threaten some personal (human) interest protected by law, which is recognised as being worthy of protection through the use of force. The interests of human life, physical integrity, sexual integrity and personal freedom have generally been considered worthy of such protection. However, not all legal interests will justify the use of force.

S v Kamffer

In *S v Kamffer*,[12] the accused wanted to take his child from his ex-wife for a weekend access visit. His ex-wife tried to prevent him and he struck her. When he was tried for assault, he tried to argue that he was defending his legal right of access to his child. The court held that the right in question was not something in respect of which a person was justified in using force. It convicted the accused of assault.

---

9 Le Roux J 'Private defence: Strict conditions to be satisfied – *Govender v Minister of Safety and Security* 2009 (2) SACR 87 (N)' (2010) 73(2) *THRHR* 328.

10 This means a *real* attack, actual or threatened. Do not confuse a *fear* of attack with a *threat* of attack. The mere fact that the threat was *conditional* does not make it any less real, however. Thus, the robber who says, 'Your money or your life', is uttering a real threat against his victim's life.

11 *R v N'Thauling and another* 1943 AD 649 at 654. See also Snyman CR *Strafreg* (1981) 106–107.

12 *S v Kamffer* 1965 (3) SA 96 (T).

Although the position is not entirely clear,[13] it has been held that it is justifiable to use moderate force to protect dignity unaccompanied by a threat to physical integrity.[14] However, if this is indeed the case, the injury to dignity would need to be extremely serious to warrant the use of any level of physical force in response.

A person may resort to force to defend a third person against an unlawful attack.[15] The person in question need not be someone whom one is under a legal duty to protect, but it must be a specific person. A person may not claim to be defending the community at large.[16]

DISCUSSION **Defence of third persons**

In the case of defence of third persons, the law balances two seemingly competing interests: on the one hand, *the law does not want to impose a general duty to protect and/or rescue* because, as has previously been explained, this would be a serious invasion of personal liberty and it is not regarded as the proper role of law to enforce pure morality. On the other hand, *the law does wish to encourage individuals to act morally and to rescue other persons who may be in danger.* In such cases, therefore, those individuals who do choose to intercede enjoy the protection of the law.

7.2.1.1.3 The attack must be in progress or imminent

Another requirement is that the attack must have already begun or be imminent (that is, about to begin immediately) and it must not yet be over. Although a person is not obliged to wait for his attacker to strike the first blow,[17] he is not entitled to use force to pre-empt an attack that is likely to happen only at some indefinite time in the future. Nor may he use force, or continue to do so, after the attack is over as this would amount to mere retaliation, which the law does not condone.

7.2.1.2 Requirements for the defender's response

7.2.1.2.1 The use of force must be necessary

The first requirement for the defender's response is that it must be necessary for the defender to avert the attack through the use of force, that is, there must be no other practical way of averting the attack. Thus, the law will generally expect a person to retreat or flee, if practically possible, rather than resorting to force – a person is always expected to choose the lesser of the two evils. However, a person is not expected to flee if it is not a practical solution, for example if doing so will expose him to greater danger.[18]

13 See *Burchell Principles of Criminal Law* 124 footnote 22 and further authorities cited there.

14 See *R v Van Vuuren and another* 1961 (3) SA 305 (E); *S v Ndlangisa* 1969 (4) SA 324 (E).

15 *R v Patel* 1959 (3) SA 121 (A). Patel shot and killed the deceased, who was attacking his brother with a hammer. The Appellate Division (AD) held at 123A that '[a] person has the same right to use force in defence of another from a threatened danger, as he would have to defend himself, if he were the person threatened'.

16 Burchell *Principles of Criminal Law* 124.

17 *R v Hope* (1917) 38 NPD 145 at 146.

18 See, for instance, *R v Zikalala* 1953 2 SA 568 (A). The accused stabbed and killed the deceased in a crowded beer hall. He claimed that the deceased had attacked him with a knife and that he was acting in self-defence. He was convicted of murder but appealed. On appeal, the AD held that no one is expected to flee if this does not offer a safe avenue of escape, for example if it will merely expose one to a stab in the back. In such circumstances, a person is entitled to stand his ground and defend himself. The AD referred to the fact that in Zikalala's case, the beer hall was packed with people and movement was difficult, thus he may not have been able to escape safely. His conviction was overturned and he was acquitted. For a more recent example, see *S v Steyn* 2010 (1) SACR 411 (SCA).

Snyman points out that there may also be other situations in which a person is not required to flee.[19] For example, if a police officer is threatened while performing an official duty, such as pursuing a suspect or making an arrest, we cannot expect him to flee and thereby abandon his duty.[20] Snyman also argues that we cannot expect a person to flee if threatened in his own home since a person's home is normally regarded as his last refuge.

7.2.1.2.2 The force used must be reasonable

The defender's response must be a reasonable (and proportionate)[21] response to the attack. The means and the amount of force used to avert the attack must be no more than is reasonably necessary, in the circumstances, for the defender to protect himself against the aggressor's unlawful attack.[22]

Older authorities used to require an equivalence (balancing) of force, means and interests, for example similar weapons, matching strength and equivalent interests.[23] On this basis, a person would not, for example, be allowed to use a knife to defend himself against a fist attack, or use a gun to defend himself against a knife attack. By the same token, a person would not be allowed to use lethal force unless his own life were in danger. These days, this approach is regarded as unduly artificial and unrealistic.

The current test is simply whether there was a *reasonable relationship* between the attack and the defensive act, taking into account factors such as:

- the relationship between the parties
- their respective ages, gender and physical strength
- the location of the incident
- the nature, severity and persistence of the attack
- the nature of any weapon used in the attack
- the nature and severity of any injury or harm likely to be sustained in the attack
- the means available to avert the attack
- the nature of the means used to offer defence
- the nature and extent of the harm likely to be caused by the defence.[24]

On this basis, a defender is entitled to use lethal force, even where his life is not necessarily in danger, as long as:

- the threat is sufficiently serious to warrant the use of such force; and
- such force is reasonably necessary in the circumstances to ward off the attack or threatened attack; and
- less drastic means are not available or would not prove effective.

Another important factor that courts will take into account when determining the reasonableness of a defender's response, is the speed with which the attack was taking place and the degree of imminence of the threatened harm. As the Appellate Division (AD) pointed out in *R v Patel*,[25] a person who is faced with a choice of alternatives in a moment of crisis

19 Snyman *Criminal Law* 106–108, 111.

20 The use of force in connection with arrests is discussed in Chapter 10 on public authority.

21 *S v Engelbrecht* supra at para 228.

22 *Grigor v The State* (unreported) (607/11) [2012] ZASCA 95 (1 June 2012) at para 5.

23 Burchell *Principles of Criminal Law* 128.

24 *S v Steyn* supra. See also *S v Trainor* 2003 (1) SACR 35 (SCA) and Walker S 'Determining reasonable force in cases of private defence: A comment on the approach in *S v Steyn* 2010 (1) SACR 411 (SCA)' (2012) 25(1) *SACJ* 84.

25 *R v Patel* supra.

should not be judged as though he had the time and opportunity to weigh up all the pros and cons. Allowance must be made for his circumstances.[26]

7.2.1.2.3 The use of excessive force

The question arises as to what the legal position is when a defender is justified in resorting to force, but uses more force than is reasonably necessary. This question was discussed in detail by the Appellate Division in *S v Ntuli*.[27]

S v Ntuli

Ntuli killed his mother-in-law, a frail old woman. She had attacked him first, but he used so much force against her that he cracked her skull and broke her jaw. He therefore exceeded the bounds of legitimate self-defence. He was convicted of culpable homicide and sentenced to three years' imprisonment. The AD was asked to decide whether this was an appropriate punishment. In considering this question, the AD considered the defence of private defence and what the position would be when a defender uses more force than necessary. It held the following:

- B may intentionally and lawfully use as much force as is reasonably necessary to protect himself against an unlawful threatened or actual attack at the hands of C. The test of whether B acts reasonably is an objective one.
- If B's response is reasonable, his use of force and his intention to use it are both lawful. B cannot then be said to have *dolus*. *Dolus* consists of an intention to commit an *unlawful* act.
- If the stage is reached at which B ought reasonably to realise that he is using more force than necessary to protect himself against C, and he ought reasonably to foresee the possibility that

26 See *S v Steyn* supra. Mrs Steyn (Mrs S) had shot and killed her ex-husband, a man who had abused her mentally and physically over the years of their relationship. She claimed self-defence. According to her evidence, the deceased had been drinking on the evening in question and was in a bad mood. At one point, he swore at Mrs S and assaulted her. She took refuge in her bedroom and the deceased told her to stay there. After a while, however, she took her gun and headed towards the kitchen to fetch some food. When the deceased saw her out of her room, he rushed at her with a steak knife, shouting that he would kill her. Mrs S shot him once in the chest, killing him. She was charged with murder.

The trial court held that knowing the deceased's condition and mood, Mrs S had acted unreasonably in placing herself in a position of danger where she may be required to defend herself with her firearm. It held that she could have avoided the entire incident by telephoning for help and waiting for assistance before leaving her room. It concluded that she had acted negligently and, although it acquitted her of murder, it convicted her of culpable homicide.

On appeal, Mrs S's counsel argued that the trial court had confused the question of unlawfulness with the question of negligence (fault). The Supreme Court of Appeal (SCA) found that this argument was not without substance, but declined to decide the point since it had sufficient evidence to make its own finding on the lawfulness of Mrs S's conduct. It held further that it is impossible to formulate a precise test for lawfulness in such cases and that each case must be determined according to its own circumstances. Nevertheless, the point of the enquiry was whether there was 'a reasonable balance between the attack and the defensive act ..., [or] whether, taking all the factors into account, the defender acted reasonably in the manner in which he defended himself or his property' at para 19.

The SCA then rejected the state's argument that Mrs S could have avoided harm by fleeing to her bedroom, holding that, given the deceased's proximity and the imminence of harm, retreat would not have offered her a safe avenue of escape. It also rejected the state's argument that, as a former police reservist, Mrs S ought to have been able to dissuade the deceased from attacking her or deter him by firing a warning shot. It held that her response was to be judged in light of the fact that she was a woman who had been unable to resist the deceased's physical abuse in the past, and who was both 'scared ... and thoroughly dominated by him' at para 23.

The SCA also rejected the trial court's conclusion that Mrs S had acted unreasonably, and therefore negligently, in leaving her bedroom and exposing herself to danger in the first place. It held that she had been lawfully entitled to leave her bedroom to fetch food in her own home and could not be expected to telephone for assistance every time she needed to do something.

Lastly, the SCA held that, in assessing Mrs S's conduct, it needed to be borne in mind that she had been acting in circumstances of stress and great personal danger, in which her life had been at stake. The SCA accordingly found that Mrs S's use of lethal force had been reasonable in the circumstances and her conduct was consequently lawful. Her conviction was set aside.

27 *S v Ntuli* 1975 (1) SA 429 (A) at 436H–437G.

C might die as a result, and C does die, then B will be guilty of culpable homicide. C's death has resulted from B's negligence (*culpa*) and not from any unlawful intention (*dolus*).
- If, in the above scenario, C's death is not reasonably foreseeable, or if C does not in fact die, then B will not be criminally liable. In our common law, there is no crime of negligently injuring another person. Assault requires *dolus*.
- If B subjectively realises that he is using more force than necessary to protect himself against C, B is both applying that force unlawfully and has the intention to do so (*dolus*). B is then guilty of assault. Whether B realised that he was using excessive force is a question of fact, involving an enquiry into his state of mind.
- If the stage is reached at which B realises that he is using more force than necessary to protect himself against C, and B foresees the possibility that C might die as a result, but persists regardless of whether death ensues or not, and C does die, then B will be guilty of murder. He would also be guilty of murder if he directly intended to cause C's death.
- Where the question of self-defence is raised or is suggested by the evidence, the onus remains on the state to prove beyond reasonable doubt that the accused acted unlawfully, and that he realised or reasonably ought to have realised that he was exceeding the bounds of self-defence, and that he foresaw or reasonably ought to have foreseen the possibility of resultant death.

7.2.1.2.4 The force used must be directed against the attacker

The defender's response must be directed against the unlawful attacker. Thus, it will not be private defence when a person intentionally or mistakenly harms an innocent third person. However, in appropriate circumstances, he may be able to raise the defence of necessity.[28] In the case of mistake, he may be able to raise putative private defence.[29]

7.2.2 Private defence of property

This defence is available when a person uses force to defend an interest in property, for example to:
- prevent a would-be thief or robber from taking his own or another's property
- prevent someone from damaging or destroying his own or another's property
- prevent an intruder from entering his own or another's property (this would include the use of preventative devices such as spiked fences and electrified fencing).

The requirements for private defence of property are similar in many respects to those for private defence of persons, but there are certain differences.

7.2.2.1 Requirements for the danger or threat

7.2.2.1.1 There must be an unlawful threat or danger

As with private defence of persons, there must be an unlawful threat or danger to property arising from some unlawful act or conduct on the part of a human aggressor. A person is not entitled to use force to prevent a lawful attachment, search, seizure or sale of his property.

28 See Chapter 8.
29 See section 7.3.

7.2.2.1.2 A legal interest in property must be threatened or endangered

The legal interest, threatened or endangered, must relate to property of some kind. This could be any kind of property, either movable or immovable, and theoretically could also be incorporeal property.[30] The property need not belong to the defender; a person may lawfully defend someone else's property if he chooses and he can also use force to defend a right that is less than ownership, such as a right of possession.

However, the property should not be of negligible value although a court will judge the value of the property according to the circumstances of the owner. What is of little value to a wealthy person may be of great value to a poorer person.[31]

7.2.2.1.3 The threat or danger must be serious

The danger or threat to the property must be a serious one, that is, a risk of loss, damage, destruction or other substantial interference with the right involved.

7.2.2.1.4 The threat or danger must be present

The threat or danger must be present at the time. Once the threat or danger is over, the defender may not use force to retaliate against the perpetrator, for example to assault a would-be thief who has already abandoned the stolen property.

The question arises of whether a person is justified in using force after the event to *recover* stolen property that is still in the possession of the thief. Burchell suggests that this would be permissible in view of the fact that theft is a continuing crime.[32]

Appealing though this argument may be, it is unlikely to find favour with the courts, given prevailing attitudes towards self-redress. It is more likely that criminal law will coincide with civil law on this point, namely that measures taken to recover stolen property will be regarded as lawful only if they occur soon enough after the original dispossession that they can be regarded as part of the same train of events.[33]

However, unlike private defence of person, the threat or danger need not have actually materialised or be imminent as long as it is present. It is thus permissible to use devices such as spiked fences, electric fences or even traps in anticipation of a future danger, provided that:

- the threat or danger is sufficiently serious to warrant the measures taken
- the public is given adequate warning[34]
- the device is designed to prevent or deter would-be thieves or intruders, and not merely to retaliate after the event.[35]

---

30 For example, intellectual property.

31 *S v Mogohlwane* 1982 (2) SA 587 (T). Mogohlwane (M) had been robbed by the deceased (armed with a tomahawk) of a bag containing M's clothing, shoes and food. M went to his home nearby, fetched a knife and then returned to recover his property. When M tried to take back his bag, the deceased resisted and again threatened M with the tomahawk. M then stabbed him with the knife. The deceased died and M was charged with murder. The court held that M had been justified in his conduct because his attempt to recover his property was close enough in time to the robbery to be part of the same train of events. The court also held that what is of little value to a wealthy man may be of great value to a poorer man. Given M's financial circumstances, the stolen items were of value to him. The court accordingly sanctioned his use of lethal force.

32 Burchell *Principles of Criminal Law* 136. See also section 31.1.4.

33 See *S v Mogohlwane* supra.

34 *Ex parte Die Minister van Justisie: In re S v Van Wyk* 1967 (1) SA 488 (A) at 509.

35 See Burchell *Principles of Criminal Law* 136.

7.2.2.2 Requirements for the defender's response

7.2.2.2.1 The use of force must be necessary

As with private defence of person, the use of force must have been the only practical means of averting the threat or danger. However, the question of retreating or fleeing does not always arise here. Thus, for example, a person who is being robbed of his property is not required to yield it up, nor is a person expected to flee his home rather than confront an intruder.[36] Conversely, in a case where the owner would easily have been able to recover his property without resorting to the use of force, this requirement would not be satisfied.[37]

7.2.2.2.2 The force used must be reasonable

As with private defence of persons, the means and the amount of force that are used must be no more than is reasonably necessary in the circumstances to avert the threat or danger.

The value of the property is an important consideration in assessing whether the amount of force and the means used were reasonable in the circumstances. A person is not entitled to inflict serious harm to protect some item of trifling value (but see *S v Mogohlwane*).[38]

The question arises as to whether it is permissible to use lethal force in defence of property. Early decisions on this point were contradictory.[39] Ultimately, the question was referred to the AD for decision in *Ex parte Minister van Justisie: In re S v Van Wyk*.[40]

Ex parte Minister van Justisie: In re S v Van Wyk

Van Wyk owned a shop that had been broken into on numerous occasions. He had called in the police and tried various ways of preventing the burglaries, but to no avail. In desperation, and after informing the police of his intentions, he rigged up a shotgun so that it would fire at any intruder who tried to enter through a certain window. He tried to rig it so that the intruder would be shot in the legs. He also posted a notice on the door, in English and Afrikaans, that he had done this and that persons entered at their own risk. A man later broke into the shop and sustained fatal injuries when he was shot. Van Wyk was charged with murder, but raised the defence of private defence and was acquitted.

The Minister of Justice then put two questions of law to the AD:

- Can a person rely on private defence when he kills or wounds another person in defence of property?
- If so, did Van Wyk exceed the bounds of private defence?

The AD considered the various authorities and concluded that a person is entitled to use whatever force is necessary to defend his property. If the circumstances are such that the use of lethal force is absolutely necessary, then this will be justified, but only then. It went on to say that the defender must issue a warning, if it is reasonably possible to do so, and must limit himself to the least dangerous response that would be effective. It held further that although the value of the property is relevant to the enquiry, proportionality is not a general requirement for the defence. It reasoned that a person who invades another's rights, defiantly ignoring the prohibition, warning and resistance of the right-holder, is the author of his own misfortune if extreme measures are used against him.

36 Given the levels of violent crime in South Africa, this would often be the prudent thing to do. However, there is no *legal obligation* on a person to do this.
37 *Ex parte Minister van Justisie: In re S v Van Wyk* supra at 498.
38 *S v Mogohlwane* supra.
39 See Milton JRL 'Killing in defence of property: An historical footnote' (1968) 85(3) *SALJ* 327.
40 *Ex parte Minister van Justisie: In re S v Van Wyk* supra.

Although *Van Wyk* has not been expressly overruled, it pre-dates the present Constitution,[41] section 11 of which guarantees the right to life, and the common law rules that relate to the use of lethal force must accordingly be viewed in light of this constitutional right. One cannot simply assume that the ruling in *Van Wyk* continues to apply. In *S v Makwanyane*,[42] the Constitutional Court, in dealing with the death penalty, held that 'greater restriction on the use of lethal force may be one of the consequences ... of a [Constitution] which respects every person's right to life'. Its subsequent decision in *S v Walters*[43] suggests that killing in defence of property may no longer pass the test of constitutionality. Many commentators consequently take the view that because the value of property can never outweigh the value of a human life, it is no longer justifiable to kill in defence of property in any circumstances.[44] Some authors thus suggest that the law as espoused in *Van Wyk* is ripe for consideration by the Constitutional Court and should be declared unconstitutional.[45]

However, it could equally be argued that even if a proportionality test must now be applied, as was suggested in *Walters*,[46] one must consider, when balancing the interests of the parties, that one of them is acting *lawfully*, while the other is acting *unlawfully*. Furthermore, although the right to life is highly prized[47] and unqualified,[48] it is not an absolute right; it is in principle subject to the limitation clause in the Constitution.[49] At the same time, cases can be envisaged in which particular property may be of life-sustaining importance to the right-holder. There is therefore still a possibility that when the question is finally decided, killing in defence of property might be permitted, albeit in *exceptional* circumstances only.

7.2.2.2.3 The force must be directed against the attacker or would-be attackers

As with private defence of person, the force used by the defender must be directed against the unlawful aggressor or would-be aggressors, not against innocent third persons.

DISCUSSION **Towards developing an argument in favour of permitting lethal force in defence of property**

One of the principal difficulties with the debate on the use of lethal force in defence of property is the overly simplistic view that is usually taken of the competing interests of life on the one hand and property on the other. Consider, however, the following scenario: X is in hospital and dependent on a respirator. Y is about to smash and

41 Constitution of the Republic of South Africa, 1996.

42 *S v Makwanyane and another* 1995 (2) SACR 1 (CC) at para 140.

43 *Ex parte Minister of Safety and Security and others: In re S v Walters* 2002 (2) SACR 105 (CC) at para 53.

44 See, for example, Ally D and Viljoen F 'Homicide in defence of property in an age of constitutionalism' (2003) 16(2) *SACJ* 121; Du Plessis A 'When can I fire? Use of lethal force to defend property' (2004) 8 *SACQ* 1, available at https://journals.assaf.org.za/sacq/article/view/1038.

45 For a critical reflection on this point, see Burchell *Principles of Criminal Law* 139–142. Burchell submits that the judgment in *Van Wyk* can no longer be supported. The author argues that the principles espoused in *Van Wyk* should be reconsidered by the Constitutional Court and should be regarded as 'an unreasonable and unjustifiable infringement on the right to life'. However, Burchell suggests that if the Constitutional Court would not find the law as stipulated in *Van Wyk* to be unconstitutional, then the type of conduct (as in *Van Wyk*) could, instead of being framed as justifiable, rather be presented as *excusable*. For more on the constitutional debate, see S Krause 'Killing in defence of property: A constitutional approach' (2012) 3 *TSAR* 469.

46 This is almost certainly the wrong approach, however. The correct approach is to apply the provisions of s 36 of the Constitution (the so-called limitations clause).

47 *S v Makwanyane* supra at paras 144 and 146.

48 Currie I and De Waal J *The Bill of Rights Handbook* 6 ed (2013) 259.

49 S 36 of the Constitution.

destroy the respirator when he is noticed by a hospital security guard. May the guard use lethal force if that is the only practical way to prevent Y from carrying out his plan? The obvious answer is 'yes'. The interest at stake here is X's *life*. The respirator is merely an instrument keeping X alive.

Bearing this in mind, consider the next scenario: Y has doused X's house with petrol and is standing outside with a lighter, about to set fire to the house. The house and its contents represent X's sole assets, his family home, which he has taken a lifetime to acquire. X is not a wealthy man and his property is not insured. The only remedy that X has at his disposal is a firearm. Should X be permitted to use lethal force, if necessary, to prevent Y from burning down his house? Most people would argue that he should. The reason for this is that the house is, at least arguably, as much an instrument of X's survival as the respirator in the previous scenario.

From this it is evident that it is not helpful to approach the issue by simply weighing the value of human life against the value of property in the pure economic sense. *Far greater consideration needs to be given to the content of the right to life and the implications of the right to property, as well as the normative impact of other constitutional rights and values, notably human dignity.*

7.3 Putative private defence

The requirements for all the justification defences, including private defence of person and property, are assessed objectively, from an external point of view, taking all relevant factors into account, including those that were unknown – and could not have been known – to the accused at the relevant time.[50] The requirements are not assessed according to the accused's subjective (personal) beliefs or perceptions. Thus, a person's genuine but mistaken belief that he was acting in private defence, whereas this was not in fact the case, for example because there was no actual attack or threat, will not render his conduct lawful. However, in such a case, the accused may nevertheless escape criminal liability on the basis that he lacked *dolus* in the form of the necessary intention to act unlawfully.[51] Where this belief is also reasonable, and provided that the accused acted reasonably in light of his belief, then he would escape liability for crimes based on negligence as well.[52] This defence is commonly called *putative private defence*.

7.4 The evidentiary burden

Because harming and killing people are always *prima facie* unlawful, the accused must lay a proper evidentiary foundation if he wishes to rely on the defence of private defence. Once the state has proved that the accused injured or killed another person, or once the accused has admitted this, he attracts an evidentiary burden, that is, he must place some evidence before the court to explain and justify his conduct. This does not mean that the accused acquires the onus of proof. In criminal cases, the onus is always on the state to prove beyond reasonable doubt the elements of criminal liability, including the unlawfulness of the

50 That is to say, it is an *ex post facto* enquiry.

51 See the definition of *dolus* in the extract from *S v Ntuli* supra.

52 See *S v De Oliveira* 1993 (2) SACR 59 (A). See also *S v Ntuli* supra and *S v Naidoo* 1997 (1) SACR 62 (T). Putative private defence is a form of the defence of mistake of fact. This defence will be discussed in more detail in section 24.4.

accused's conduct.[53] However, he cannot simply allege that he acted in private defence and leave it to the state to prove otherwise.[54] The principle is that the state must prove the absence of the defence properly raised by the accused. This principle applies to any defence (including self-defence or private defence) raised by the accused.[55]

In the following chapter, we will consider the next two justification defences: necessity and impossibility.

THIS CHAPTER IN ESSENCE

1. A person whose conduct was *prima facie* unlawful will not be criminally liable if his conduct, even though it outwardly met the requirements for unlawful conduct, was not in fact unlawful, because it was justified in the circumstances. One possible ground of justification is private defence.
2. The requirements for the defence of private defence of person (namely self-defence and defence of other persons) are that there must have been an unlawful attack, or threat of such attack, against a legally protected personal interest, such as life, limb, sexual integrity or personal liberty, and the attack must have already begun or be imminent.
   2.1 When these preconditions are met, the defender is permitted to use force to repel or prevent the attack, provided that the use of force is necessary for this purpose, the amount of force used is a reasonable response to the attack and such force is directed against the unlawful aggressor.
3. The requirements for private defence of property are that there must be a serious, unlawful and present threat or danger to property of some kind.
   3.1 Where these preconditions are met, the defender is permitted to use force to repel or prevent the attack, provided that the use of force is necessary for this purpose, the amount of force used is a reasonable response to the attack and that such force is directed against the unlawful aggressor or would-be aggressor.
4. The requirements for private defence of person and property are always judged objectively (from an external point of view) and not according to the defender's subjective beliefs and perceptions. Where a person believes that he is justified in using force to defend person or property, but is not in fact justified in doing so, he cannot rely on the defence of private defence. He may, however, be able to raise the defence of putative private defence, which is a defence excluding fault.

53 *R v Ndhlovu* 1945 AD 369; *S v Tembani* 1999 (1) SACR 192 (W).

54 See, for example, *S v Manona* supra.

55 *S v Ngomane* 1979 (3) SA 859 (A) (private defence). See further, Schwikkard PJ and Van der Merwe SE *Principles of Evidence* 4 ed (2016) 603–604.

Chapter 8

Necessity and impossibility

CHAPTER OBJECTIVES

The objectives of this chapter are to:
- explain the requirements for the defence of necessity
- explain the requirements for the defence of impossibility
- distinguish between situations calling for the defence of necessity and those calling for the defence of impossibility
- explain the principles that relate to killing under compulsion
- distinguish between proper necessity and impossibility, and putative necessity and impossibility.

8.1 The defence of necessity

The defence of **necessity** arises when a person is faced with a situation – usually some kind of emergency – in which he has a choice between two evils, namely to break the letter of the law, or to suffer some more serious fate. In such a case, a person is justified in breaking the law and his conduct in doing so will not be unlawful. The defence of necessity encompasses the defence of **compulsion**, that is, they are essentially the same defence and have the same requirements. However, compulsion describes a particular type of necessity where the accused broke the letter of the law because he was acting under duress from some other person (that is, a threat of harm from some human agency).

However, the defence of necessity extends more widely than this. Thus, the choice of two evils can arise out of some non-human agency, such as chance circumstances, a natural calamity or disaster, or some other type of emergency. Necessity, therefore, encompasses a wide variety of situations that are recognised by law, but do not fall within the ambit of private defence,[1] for example:

- when force or violence is used against an innocent third party
- when force is used against something other than a person, for example an animal or another person's property
- when no force or violence is involved at all, but merely the breaking of a law, for example breaking the speed limit to rush a seriously ill person to hospital.[2]

The defence of necessity applies only in cases where the accused in question has committed some positive act that is *prima facie* unlawful. In cases where he seeks to justify some apparently unlawful omission, the appropriate defence is not necessity, but impossibility.[3]

As in the case of private defence, the circumstances in which a person may break the letter of the law with impunity are strictly limited, and there are also limits on how a person may act when doing so.

8.1.1 Requirements for the threat or danger

8.1.1.1 A legal interest must be in danger

A legally protected interest, such as life, bodily integrity or property (one's own or another person's), must be threatened or in danger. A mere economic interest will not suffice – a person is never justified in breaking the law out of sheer economic necessity.[4] To put it more succinctly (and perhaps more accurately), not every case of *need* is a situation of *necessity*.

1 On the relationship between private defence and necessity, see *Maimela and another v Makhado Municipality and another* 2011 (2) SACR 339 (SCA).

2 *S v Pretorius* 1975 (2) SA 85 (SWA).

3 See *R v Canestra* 1951 (2) SA 317 (A) (summarised below); *S v Leeuw* 1975 (1) SA 439 (O).

4 *R v Canestra* supra. Canestra was charged with catching undersized fish in a net with others of proper size. He raised the defence of impossibility, saying it was impossible for him not to catch some undersized fish with this method of fishing. This defence was rejected. He was convicted and appealed to the Appellate Division (AD). The AD confirmed his conviction, holding that:

- the defence of impossibility only applies in the case of omissions – where the accused's defence is that it was 'impossible' for him not to have acted as he did, the proper defence is necessity and must be tested as such
- the law does not recognise economic necessity as a defence – Canestra was not obliged to catch fish for a living nor was he obliged to do so with a net. He could not justify catching undersized fish on the basis of needing to earn a living.

See also *S v Adams; S v Werner* 1981 (1) SA 187 (A). Adams, a non-white, raised the defence of necessity to justify his contravention of the apartheid-era Group Areas Act 36 of 1966, claiming that he had been obliged to reside in a white area because there was an acute shortage of housing in Johannesburg for his own racial group. The AD rejected this defence, likening Adams's situation to that of Canestra and holding that, in any event, there was no evidence of an absolute shortage of housing. Burchell, however, criticises the court's reasoning in both of these decisions (see Burchell JM *Principles of Criminal Law* 5 ed (2016) 168–169). Perhaps the real problem with economic necessity and comparable situations lies not so much in the nature of the *interest* threatened as in the difficulty of establishing the *imminence* of the threatened harm in such cases.

8.1.1.2 The danger must have commenced or be imminent

As with private defence, the threat or danger must have already begun or must be about to begin immediately. It is not sufficient that the threat or danger is anticipated at some time in the future. However, this does not mean that the accused needs to wait for the danger or threat to materialise before he takes steps to avert it.[5] For this defence to be applicable, the threat or danger must still be in existence and not yet over.[6]

In cases of compulsion, it is often assumed that the threat can only be imminent or real in the presence of the aggressor. However, some argue that the existence of aggressive and effective criminal networks, and organised criminality, may make threats from these faceless (and perhaps remote) groups just as real and imminent.[7]

8.1.1.3 The danger must not have arisen through the accused's own fault

It is a fundamental rule of our law that a person may not profit from his own wrongdoing. Accordingly, a person may not use his own prior negligence or misconduct to justify his later actions and thus escape liability. According to this rule, an accused would not be able to rely on the defence of necessity where he caused the threat or danger himself through his own culpable conduct. However, it is not clear to what extent this rule holds good, at least when expressed in absolutist terms. A qualified and more nuanced approach seems more appropriate.

Snyman accepts that the rule applies to cases such as *S v Bradbury*[8] and *S v Lungile and another*,[9] in which the accused voluntarily joined a criminal gang, knowing of the gang's disciplinary code, but argues that it should not apply to other cases. He cites the situation in which a parent negligently lets a young child play with a pill-box. The child takes the pills and the parent breaks the speed limit rushing the child to hospital. In such a case, Snyman argues, the parent should not be precluded from relying on the defence of necessity. He proposes that the creation of the danger and the act of rescue should be kept separate. If the act that created the danger constitutes a crime, then the accused should be held liable for that crime, but this should not preclude him from relying on the defence of necessity to justify the act of rescue.[10]

Burchell suggests that the rule should apply only to cases in which the threat or danger arose directly from the accused's misconduct, but not where it was merely the indirect result of such misconduct, as in *R v Mahomed*.[11] He argues further that the courts should not give too broad an interpretation to the meaning of fault – it should mean something more than mere foresight of the risk of creating the danger or, as in Snyman's example, mere negligence in that regard.[12]

5 *S v Moller* 1971 (4) SA 327 (T) at 329–330. See further, Burchell JM *South African Criminal Law and Procedure Vol I: General Principles of Criminal Law* 4 ed (2011) 151–152.
6 *R v Baxter* 1929 EDL 189; *S v Mtewtwa* 1977 (3) SA 628 (E) at 631.
7 See comments by Burchell *South African Criminal Law and Procedure Vol I* 152.
8 *S v Bradbury* 1967 (1) SA 387 (A).
9 *S v Lungile and another* 1999 (2) SACR 597 (SCA).
10 Snyman CR *Criminal Law 6 ed (2014) 118–119.*
11 *R v Mahomed and another* 1938 AD 30.
12 Burchell *Principles of Criminal Law* 171-172; Burchell *South African Criminal Law and Procedure Vol I* 153–154.

8.1.2 Requirements for the response

8.1.2.1 The act must be necessary

The course of action taken by the accused must have been necessary *and* reasonable in order to avert the threatened harm or danger.[13] This does not mean that there must literally have been no alternative,[14] but merely that there was no other practical way of averting the threatened harm or danger. Burchell suggests that the test should be whether the threatened harm would probably have followed had the accused not acted as he did.[15]

8.1.2.2 The act must be reasonable

The accused's actions and the means used, as pointed out above, must have been a reasonable response[16] to the threatened harm or danger. This means that:

- the accused must not have done more harm than was actually necessary to avert the harm or danger; and
- the harm done must not be greater than the harm avoided (the accused must literally have chosen the lesser of the two evils).

8.1.3 Special situations

There are two situations that require special comment with regard to the above: obligation to suffer or endure harm, and killing in the circumstances of necessity.

8.1.3.1 Obligation to suffer or endure harm

There are certain circumstances in which a person is legally obliged to suffer or endure harm, for example to submit to lawful arrest, search, seizure or punishment, or to tell the truth in court, regardless of possible reprisals. In such cases, a person who breaks the law will not be able to rely on the defence of necessity.[17]

8.1.3.2 Killing in circumstances of necessity

The old authorities took the view that a person was never justified in killing an innocent person to save his own life. It was thought that a person should rather submit to death although the threat to his own life might be regarded as a mitigating factor.[18] This approach survived for quite some time, as is illustrated in the old English case of *R v Dudley and Stephens*.[19]

R v Dudley and Stephens

Dudley and Stephens were involved in a shipwreck and cast adrift in an open boat with two other persons: a man called Brooks and a 17-year-old cabin boy called Parker. After 17 days at sea, eight of which were without food and six were without water, it became clear that they were unlikely

---

13 *S v Adams* 1979 (4) SA 793 (T).

14 There is no such thing as absolute necessity.

15 Burchell *Principles of Criminal Law* 173.

16 *R v Mahomed* supra; *R v Samuel and others* 1960 (4) SA 702 (SR). See further comments by Burchell *South African Criminal Law and Procedure Vol I* 155.

17 See, in general, Snyman *Criminal Law* 119; Burchell *South African Criminal Law and Procedure Vol I* 156.

18 Voet (4.2.1) states that fear of death induced by one person is not a defence but could be mitigatory. Matthaeus (*Proleg 1.13*) holds that a good man must be prepared to be crucified rather than commit a crime, but also holds that a person who committed a crime under duress was not liable to the normal penalty because he had acted partly voluntarily and partly involuntarily.

19 *R v Dudley and Stephens* (1884) 14 QBD 273 DC.

to survive much longer. Dudley and Stephens agreed that Dudley should kill Parker so they could eat him. They reasoned that, being younger and weaker, he would be the first to die anyway. Brooks did not agree to the plan. Dudley went ahead and killed Parker and all three of them ate his remains for the next four days. On the fifth day, they were rescued. Dudley and Stephens were charged with murder and raised the defence of necessity. The court rejected this defence and convicted them, holding that the law expects the average man to sacrifice his own life for that of an innocent victim. Although the court sympathised with their dreadful predicament, it held (per Lord Coleridge) that '[w]e are often compelled to set up standards we cannot reach ourselves, and to lay down rules which we could not ourselves satisfy. But a man has no right to declare temptation to be an excuse, though he might himself have yielded to it, nor allow compassion for the criminal to change or weaken in any manner the legal definition of the crime'.

In *R v Werner*[20] and *S v Bradbury*,[21] the Appellate Division (AD) (now the Supreme Court of Appeal (SCA)) essentially followed the same approach as in *R v Dudley and Stephens*, but in the more recent case of *S v Goliath*,[22] it took a different view.

S v Goliath

Goliath and another person (the first accused in the trial) came upon the deceased and the first accused began to rob him. The first accused produced a knife and told Goliath to tie up the deceased. Goliath objected and the first accused said he would stab Goliath if he did not obey. Goliath then tied up the deceased. The first accused then stabbed the deceased to death. The first accused told Goliath to take off the deceased's shoes and, when Goliath hesitated, again threatened to kill him. Goliath complied. They were both charged with murder, Goliath as an accomplice.

The trial court convicted the first accused, but acquitted Goliath on the basis that he had acted under compulsion. The state, however, reserved certain questions of law for decision by the AD, most pertinently whether the defence of compulsion could ever constitute a defence to murder. In reply, the AD held (in direct contradiction to Lord Coleridge's earlier dictum in *R v Dudley and Stephens*) that the law can demand no more from a person than what is reasonable and that 'reasonable' in this context means what can be expected from the ordinary, average person in the same circumstances. It is generally accepted that a person's own life is more important to him than the life of another and to expect the accused to sacrifice his own life for that of another, irrespective of the circumstances, would be to hold him to a standard of heroism that the average person does not possess. The AD thus accepted that necessity, in the form of compulsion, can be a complete defence to the killing of an innocent third person, provided that the level of compulsion was so strong that a reasonable person in the same circumstances would not have been able to resist it either. It is not a defence that will be accepted lightly, however; it will depend on all the surrounding circumstances. In Goliath's case, the decisive factor was that the first accused had the means and will to carry out his threat to kill Goliath *there and then* if Goliath did not comply with his demands. It also weighed heavily with the court that Goliath was not the instigator or the main perpetrator, merely a reluctant accomplice; nor did he profit in any way from the crime.[23]

Killing another human being out of necessity or compulsion is certainly legally and morally controversial. South African jurisprudence has moved away from the unrealistic view in English common law which perhaps places too much faith in human beings as heroic

20 *R v Werner and another* 1947 (2) SA 828 (A).
21 *S v Bradbury* supra.
22 *S v Goliath* 1972 (3) SA 1 (A).
23 See the commentary on *Goliath* in *S v Mandela* 2001 (1) SACR 156 (C) at 166 (citing Burchell).

creatures who would rather suffer harm themselves than kill a fellow human being. However, as Burchell points out,[24] the current position in South African law, where the defence of necessity or compulsion is still regarded as a general defence to all crimes, including murder, may offend against the right to life[25] and the right to equality[26] in the Constitution. Indeed, the implication of the defence as it stands at present is that on a charge of murder, a successful defence of necessity or compulsion might suggest that one life (that of the accused) is more valuable than that of the deceased. So, if the English law approach is too unrealistic and the South African law (as it stands) is constitutionally controversial, how then should the law develop in this regard?[27]

This debate is not only relevant for domestic South African criminal law, but also for international criminal law where necessity as a justification and duress as an excuse also complicate legal analysis. This resulted in a rather confusing provision in the Rome Statute of the International Criminal Court, 1998, which seems to combine the two defences.[28]

DISCUSSION **Killing out of necessity**

Can one innocent life have more value than another innocent life? In *Re A (Children)*,[29] the English Court of Appeals had to consider the matter of conjoined (Siamese) twins, Marie and Jodie. The background was as follows:

> They each had their own brain, heart, lungs and other vital organs, and they each had arms and legs; they were joined at the lower abdomen and could be separated. But the operation would kill the weaker twin, Mary. This was because her lungs and heart were too deficient to oxygenate and pump blood through her body. Had she been born a singleton, she would not have been viable and resuscitation would have been abandoned. She would have died shortly after her birth. She was alive only because a common artery enabled her sister, who was stronger, to circulate life-sustaining oxygenated blood for both of them. Separation would require the clamping and then the severing of that common artery. Within minutes of so doing, Mary would die. Yet if the operation did not take place, both would die within three to six months, or perhaps a little longer, because Jodie's heart would eventually fail.

---

24 Burchell *South African Criminal Law and Procedure Vol I* 169.

25 S 11 of the Constitution of the Republic of South Africa, 1996.

26 S 9 of the Constitution.

27 Burchell's suggestion is that the solution to this moral and legal difficulty may be found (at least in part) in German legal doctrine (Burchell *Principles of Criminal Law* 183–184). The German Criminal Code provides (in s 34) for necessity as a justificatory defence and (in s 35) for duress (or compulsion) as an excusatory defence. When a court is confronted with a situation like *Goliath*, we submit that it should be a question of excuse and not justification (affecting unlawfulness). The killing of another human being (under duress or compulsion) should be regarded as unlawful, but excusable, thus excluding culpability.

28 Article 31(1)(*d*) of the Rome Statute of the International Criminal Court, 1998, provides as follows:

> **In addition to other grounds for excluding criminal responsibility provided for in this Statute, a person shall not be criminally responsible if, at the time of that person's conduct: (*d*) The conduct which is alleged to constitute a crime within the jurisdiction of the Court has been caused by duress resulting from a threat of imminent death or of continuing or imminent serious bodily harm against that person or another person, and the person acts necessarily and reasonably to avoid this threat, provided that the person does not intend to cause a greater harm than the one sought to be avoided. Such a threat may either be: (i) Made by other persons; or (ii) Constituted by other circumstances beyond that person's control.**

For critical commentary on and analysis of this provision, see Knoops GJ *Defenses in Contemporary International Criminal Law* 2 ed (2001) 92–94.

29 *Re A (Children)* [2001] Fam 147.

The parents refused to consent to the operation. The twins were equal in their eyes and they could not agree to kill one, even to save the other. As devout Roman Catholics, they sincerely believed that it was God's will that their children were afflicted in this way and that they must be left in God's hands.

The doctors were convinced they could carry out the operation so as to give Jodie a life which, in most respects, would be relatively normal. Under the circumstances, the hospital sought a declaration that the operation may be lawfully carried out.

The High Court, as common law protector of the interests of children, granted the order. The parents appealed. The appeal was dismissed. The Court of Appeals considered and applied the following three requirements for the application of the doctrine of necessity:

- The act is needed to avoid inevitable and irreparable evil.
- No more should be done than is reasonably necessary for the purpose to be achieved.
- The evil inflicted must not be disproportionate to the evil avoided. The court was realistic about its role in this dilemma of law and morality. The court concluded:

Given that the principles of modern family law point irresistibly to the conclusion that the interests of Jodie must be preferred to the conflicting interests of Mary, I consider all three these requirements are satisfied in this case. Finally, the doctrine of the sanctity of life respects the integrity of the human body. The proposed operation would give these children's bodies the integrity which nature denied them.[30]

8.2 The defence of impossibility

Impossibility is the appropriate defence (excluding unlawfulness)[31] in cases where the law places a person under a legal duty to perform a positive act and the person is unable to comply with this duty. It is summed up in the maxim: 'The law does not demand the impossible (*lex non cogit ad impossibilia*)'. The policy rationale for this ground of justification is that it would be unfair to punish an individual who contravened the law under conditions where he could not act otherwise.[32] In this regard, impossibility could be regarded as the 'flip side' of necessity. However, it will be seen that the requirements of the two defences do not correspond exactly.

8.2.1 Requirements for the defence

8.2.1.1 The accused's conduct must take the form of an unlawful omission

In cases where the accused's conduct involves performing some prohibited act (positive conduct), then he cannot rely on the defence of impossibility. He must instead raise the

30 *Re A (Children)* [2001] Fam 147 at 240. For a summary of the case, see Arenson KJ, Bagaric M and Gillies P *Australian Criminal Law in the Common Law Jurisdictions: Cases and Materials* 3 ed (2011) 639–649.

31 There is academic disagreement on whether impossibility constitutes a ground of justification excluding unlawfulness, or whether it excludes the voluntary nature of an omission. The former position is supported by Burchell *South African Criminal Law and Procedure Vol I* 170, while the latter is supported by Snyman *Criminal Law* 60–62.

32 Burchell *South African Criminal Law and Procedure Vol I* 170.

defence of necessity and he will be judged accordingly.[33] Sometimes, however, even courts confuse the two defences.[34]

8.2.1.2 Compliance with the law must have been absolutely impossible

It must have been absolutely (physically) impossible for the accused to comply with the law, not merely difficult or inconvenient.[35]

8.2.1.3 The impossibility must not be due to the accused's own fault

As in the case of necessity, a person cannot rely on the defence of impossibility in situations where he created the impossibility himself through his own misconduct.[36] The comments offered above regarding applying this rule to the defence of necessity will probably apply equally to the defence of impossibility. In other words, the impossibility should have arisen as a direct (rather than indirect) result of the accused's misconduct and mere negligence would probably not be sufficient to constitute misconduct.

8.3 Putative necessity and putative impossibility

Just as with the defence of private defence, the defences of necessity and impossibility are judged objectively, that is, from an external point of view and not according to the accused's subjective beliefs or perceptions. Thus, a person's genuine but mistaken belief that he was acting in a situation of necessity, or that it was physically impossible for him to comply with a particular duty, when in fact this was not the case, will not render his conduct lawful.

However, in such a case, the accused may nevertheless escape criminal liability on the basis that he lacked fault in the form of the necessary intention to commit the relevant act or omission unlawfully (*dolus*). This would therefore be a defence in its own right. It is known as *putative* (supposed) *necessity* or *putative impossibility* (as the case may be). This defence will be discussed further in section 24.2.

THIS CHAPTER IN ESSENCE

1. The defence of necessity, which includes the defence of compulsion, may be invoked in cases where the accused acts contrary to law to avoid suffering some more serious fate.
2. The requirements for this defence are that there must be an imminent threat or danger to some legal interest that does not arise out of the accused's own misconduct.
   2.1 Where these preconditions are met, the accused will be justified in breaking the letter of the law if this is the only practical way of averting the harm or danger and provided that, in so doing, the accused does no more harm than is actually necessary and the harm that he does is no greater than the harm thereby avoided.

---

33 *R v Canestra* supra; *S v Leeuw* supra. Leeuw was charged with and convicted of driving without a licence. His defence was that it was impossible for him to obtain a driver's licence because he was subject to an order under the Suppression of Communism Act 44 of 1950, which restricted him to the district of Witsieshoek where there were no licensing facilities. On appeal, the OPD supported the view that the defence of impossibility is only available where the accused's conduct takes the form of an unlawful omission. It pointed out that there is no legal obligation on anyone to acquire a driver's licence – the law merely prohibits anyone who does not have a licence from driving. It held further that even if the defence of impossibility was available to Leeuw, he did not meet its requirements because it was not physically impossible for him to obtain a licence.

34 Compare, for instance, *S v Mafu* 1966 (2) SA 240 (E) with *S v Moeng* 1977 (3) SA 986 (O), the latter being the correct application of the legal principles.

35 *Jetha v R* (1929) 50 NPD 91; *R v Hoko* 1941 SR 211.

36 *R v Close Settlement Corp Ltd* 1922 AD 294 at 301.

3. The defence of impossibility may be invoked in cases where the accused was under a legal duty to perform some positive act, but found it physically impossible to comply with this duty for reasons that did not arise out of his own misconduct.
4. The requirements for the defences of necessity and impossibility are always judged from an external point of view and not according to what the accused thought or believed. Where a person believes that he is acting in a situation of necessity or impossibility, when this is not in fact the case, he cannot rely on the relevant defences. He may, however, be able to raise the defence of putative necessity or putative impossibility, which is a defence excluding fault.

Chapter 9

Obedience to superior orders

CHAPTER OBJECTIVES

The objectives of this chapter are to:

- explain the nature of the defence of obedience to superior orders
- explain the requirements for the defence
- explain the extent to which this defence applies in cases of obedience to an unlawful order.

9.1 Obedience to superior orders

The defence of *obedience to superior orders* usually applies to members of the military and paramilitary forces, but it also applies to some extent to police officers and members of the protection services.[1] This defence, which is available under South African criminal law to the above-mentioned categories of individuals,[2] has particular significance for international criminal law.[3] We deal with the application of some of the most important crimes under international law[4] in South African criminal law[5] in part four of this book.

Perhaps the most relevant crime under international law for purposes of this discussion is the group of crimes known as war crimes. The conduct of soldiers during armed conflicts (international or non-international) can lead to situations in which individual soldiers, acting within the chain of command, are charged with war crimes, and who then want to

1 *S v Mostert* 2006 (1) SACR 560 (N) on the applicability of the defence to orders by traffic officers.

2 It seems doubtful that the defence can apply outside the context of obedience to military and police commands. See Burchell JM *South African Criminal Law and Procedure Vol I: General Principles of Criminal Law* 4 ed (2011) 174 for references to South African case law. See also Burchell J *Principles of Criminal Law* 5 ed (2016) 190–196.

3 For a critical reflection, see Cassese A and Gaeta P *International Criminal Law* 3 ed (2013) 228–248.

4 Notably war crimes, crimes against humanity and genocide.

5 In terms of the Implementation of the Rome Statute of the International Criminal Court Act 27 of 2002.

rely on the defence that they were merely following the orders of their superior officers. The rationale for this defence[6] is that military discipline requires immediate and unquestioning obedience to orders, which is backed up by stern punishment for disobedience.[7]

In *S v Banda*, the court held that the defence of obedience to superior orders was a form of the defence of compulsion in that the subordinate was compelled to follow the orders of his superior officer.[8] It is thus considered unjust to hold a soldier criminally liable for merely following orders.

While it is certainly assumed that soldiers would normally act in compliance with a superior order because they have to, the defence of superior orders is not based on a fiction, namely that soldiers are automatons, but rather that subordinates are still reasoning agents.[9] This dilemma of the reasoning subordinate, acting under conditions of military discipline and in a hierarchical context, has been the subject of many arguments before national and international criminal courts and military tribunals. Not all legal systems, including international criminal tribunals, are willing to accept that obedience to superior orders is a complete defence comparable to compulsion or necessity.[10] Indeed, the position in South Africa is that obedience to superior orders should be accepted as a defence only when the orders in question were not manifestly and palpably unlawful.[11]

9.2 Requirements for the defence

9.2.1 The order must have come from someone in lawful authority over the accused

The order must have been issued by a person who was (1) lawfully authorised to issue the order, and (2) in lawful authority over the accused (not merely of a higher rank). Purely private allegiances are not protected by the defence.[12]

---

6 See Osiel MJ *Obeying Orders: Atrocity, Military Discipline and the Law of War* (1999) on the philosophical and military roots of this defence; Knoops GJ *Defenses in Contemporary International Criminal Law* 2 ed (2008) 162–166 on superior orders and moral choice; and Burchell *South African Criminal Law and Procedure Vol I* (2011) 174–175 on the nature and rationale of the defence of superior orders. See also Ambos K 'Defences in international criminal law' in Brown BS (ed) *Research Handbook on International Criminal Law* (2011) 299; Van Sliedregt E *Individual Criminal Responsibility in International Law* (2012) 213 *et seq*; and Werle G and Jessberger F *Principles of International Criminal Law* 3 ed (2014) 248–253.

7 Compare, for instance, the following provision in a United States Army manual:

> **The plea [of obedience to superior order] is valid if the accused does not and should not have known that the order was illegal. Many courts use the language 'illegal on its face' to express the proposition that the illegality of the order must be obvious before the accused should be held liable for an act committed pursuant to that order. The reasoning is justified on the grounds that *soldiers acting in wartime are trained to follow orders of their superiors relatively automatically, and would not normally be expected to question those orders except where their invalidity was fairly obvious.* (Emphasis added)**

See US Dept. of Army Pamphlet No. 27-161-2, II International Law 251 (1961), quoted in Bassiouni MC *International Criminal Law Vol I* 2 ed (1999) 224.

8 *S v Banda and others* 1990 (3) SA 466 (BG) at 479.

9 *United States v Kinder* 14 CMR 742 (ABR 1954); *United States v Calley* 483 F. 2d 1401 (4th Cir.1973). See further discussion in Bassiouni *International Criminal Law* 226–227.

10 See, for instance, the following paragraph from the Report of the Secretary-General Pursuant to Paragraph 2 of Security Council Resolution 808 (1993) UN SC Doc S/25704 (1993) 32 *International Legal Materials* 1163:

> **Acting upon an order of a Government or a superior cannot relieve the perpetrator of the crime or his criminal responsibility and should not be a defence. Obedience to superior orders may, however, be considered a mitigating factor, should the International Tribunal [for the Former Yugoslavia] determine that justice so requires. For example, the International tribunal may consider the factor of superior orders in connection with other defences such as coercion or lack of moral choice.**

11 Burchell *South African Criminal Law and Procedure Vol I* 178.

12 *R v Werner and another* 1947 (2) SA 828 (A); *S v Sixishe* 1992 (1) SACR 624 (CkA).

9.2.2 The accused must have been under a duty to obey the order

There is always a duty to obey a lawful order from a superior officer, but what is the position in a situation where a soldier is given an unlawful order and obeys it? Can he still rely on the defence of obedience to superior orders? This dilemma goes to the heart of the defence of superior orders.

The reality is that modern military training, in most jurisdictions, involves some kind of exposure to the rules and norms of international humanitarian law, the laws of war and, where relevant, criminal law and international criminal law. At the normative level, one can therefore accept that soldiers should have a general awareness that they must adhere to the rules and norms of international humanitarian law and, where relevant, criminal law and international criminal law. Of course, there is always the possibility that a soldier, in the heat of the moment, could make a *mistake of fact* (for instance, mistakenly identify someone as an active enemy combatant rather than a civilian). Given the level of training of modern soldiers and the changing normative context, it is clear that there should be little or no norm for *mistake of law* as a complete defence in the context of superior orders.[13]

South African courts are similarly reluctant to concede that simple obedience to any order will automatically be a complete defence, but at the same time, they are equally reluctant to punish a soldier for obeying an order that might have *appeared* to be lawful at the time. It is therefore necessary to strike a balance.[14] For many years, the leading case on this point was *R v Smith*.[15]

R v Smith

Smith was on patrol during the Anglo-Boer War (1899–1902) with one Captain Cox. They arrived at a certain farm where one of the employees – a civilian – was instructed to fetch a bridle. When he refused, Smith shot him on Cox's orders. When Smith was tried for murder, the court had to decide whether he had been under a duty to obey the order. The court outlined the two possible extremes: either absolute obedience is required and a soldier is always excused if he obeys, or a soldier is bound to obey only lawful orders and is thus liable if he obeys an unlawful order. The court adopted a middle course, namely that if the order is not manifestly (obviously) unlawful, a soldier will not be liable if he obeys it. However, if the order is manifestly unlawful, a soldier is justified in refusing to obey it, and a soldier who does obey it will be liable for the consequences.

The position was considered again at length in *S v Banda*, the treason trial that was held after the abortive military coup in Bophuthatswana in 1988. In his judgment, Friedman J amplified and clarified the rule as follows:

> **Where ... orders are manifestly beyond the scope of the authority of the officer issuing them, and are so manifestly and palpably ... illegal that a reasonable man in the circumstances of the soldier would know them to be manifestly and palpably illegal, he is justified in refusing to obey such orders. The defence of obedience to orders ... will not protect a soldier for acts committed pursuant to such manifestly and palpably illegal orders.**[16]

13 Cassese and Gaeta *International Criminal Law* 230.
14 Burchell *South African Criminal Law and Procedure Vol I* 178.
15 *R v Smith* (1900) 17 SC 561.
16 *S v Banda* supra at 496C–D.

Thus, if a soldier obeyed an order that was unlawful, but which was not 'manifestly and palpably illegal', he would still be able to rely on the defence of obedience to superior orders. However, if, for example, a soldier was ordered to massacre civilians, or to rape and loot, he would not be able to rely on this defence since conduct of this nature would be manifestly and palpably illegal.[17]

9.2.3 No more harm must be done than is necessary to carry out the order

If a soldier exceeds the limits of an order, he cannot claim that he was acting under the orders of a superior.[18] This requirement does not assume that subordinates always have the time or opportunity to analyse carefully the legality or legal limits of an order. The conduct of a subordinate must be analysed with due regard to the reality on the ground. This, in turn, must be balanced with the normative expectation that subordinates still need to appraise the legality or illegality of orders.[19]

9.3 Digression: An international criminal law perspective on the defence of superior orders and the implications for South African criminal law

South Africa is a state party to the Rome Statute of the International Criminal Court, 1998,[20] and has incorporated this multilateral treaty into domestic law via the Implementation of the Rome Statute of the International Criminal Court Act.[21] Neither the Rome Statute nor South Africa's implementation legislation can be regarded as comprehensive codifications of international criminal law. However, both instruments provide for the criminalisation of the most serious crimes under international law, namely war crimes, crimes against humanity and genocide. These instruments also provide for related matters such as general principles of criminal liability. For present purposes, two provisions from the Rome Statute and South Africa's implementation legislation will be highlighted.

Article 33 of the Rome Statute of the International Criminal Court provides as follows:

> **1. The fact that a crime within the jurisdiction of the Court has been committed by a person pursuant to an order of a Government or of a superior, whether military or civilian, shall not relieve that person of criminal responsibility unless:**
> **(*a*) The person was under a legal obligation to obey orders of the Government or the superior in question;**
> **(*b*) The person did not know that the order was unlawful; and**
> **(*c*) The order was not manifestly unlawful.**
>
> **2. For the purposes of this article, orders to commit genocide or crimes against humanity are manifestly unlawful.**

17 See also *R v Smith* supra; *R v Werner* supra; *S v Sixishe* supra.

18 See, for example, *R v Mayers* 1958 (3) SA 793 (SR); *S v Mostert* supra.

19 Cassese and Gaeta *International Criminal Law* 229–230.

20 United Nations: Rome Statute of the International Criminal Court [adopted July 17, 1998] UN Doc No/A/CONF 183/9 (July 17, 1998) *ILM* (1998) 37(5):999. South Africa's continued membership of the ICC, and related matters, are discussed in chapters 46 and 48 of this book.

21 Act 27 of 2002. We discuss in part four of this book the substantive provisions of this Act, which provides for the criminalisation of war crimes, crimes against humanity and genocide in South African law.

The relevant South African provision, namely section 4(2)(*b*) of the Implementation Act, provides as follows:

> **Despite any other law to the contrary, including customary and conventional international law, the fact that a person:**
>
> **(*b*) being a member of a security service or armed force, was under a legal obligation to obey a manifestly unlawful order of a government or superior, is neither:**
>
> **(i) a defence to a crime; nor**
>
> **(ii) a ground for any possible reduction of sentence once a person has been convicted of a crime.**

Burchell correctly observes that section 4(2)(*b*) of the Implementation Act is superfluous since it merely confirms the scope of the defence of superior orders under South African law and international law. The only reason for this provision's inclusion, according to Burchell, is the fact that an unsuccessful reliance on the defence of obedience to manifestly unlawful superior orders may not result in a mitigation of sentence, based on the same unlawful factual matrix.[22]

There is one further problem with the provision on the defence of superior orders under the Rome Statute to which we would like to draw attention. Article 33(2) provides that 'orders to commit genocide or crimes against humanity are always manifestly [unlawful]'. One can certainly agree with this, but what about superior orders to commit war crimes, the other category of serious crimes under international law provided for in the Rome Statute? Should such orders not also be regarded as 'manifestly unlawful'? This question is, of course, the essence of the problem with the defence of superior orders. However, the underlying assumption of article 33(2) seems to be that genocide and crimes against humanity are so clearly and palpably evil that no subordinate should be able to claim that he thought an order to commit these crimes was lawful. In practical terms, this comes close to the absolute liability principle under international criminal law.[23]

The implication of article 33(2) with respect to war crimes seems to be that war crimes are less clear and certain, and thus there may be more scope for uncertainty in the mind of a subordinate as to the lawfulness of an order to commit an act that turns out to be a war crime. In practical terms, this leaves open the possibility of the exclusion of responsibility in cases of obedience to superior orders to commit war crimes.[24] This inconsistency in the text of the Rome Statute was rightly criticised by some of the leading scholars of international criminal law.[25]

Section 4 of the South African Implementation Act does not draw any distinction between the different crimes with respect to the 'manifestly unlawful' nature of the crimes. It simply provides that a subordinate who obeys a manifestly unlawful order cannot raise this as a defence to a crime. This more general, elastic provision is perhaps more realistic, and more in line with the aim of international criminal law to fight impunity for the most serious crimes under international law, than article 33(2) of the Rome Statute. Nevertheless, Burchell criticises the reference in the text of article 4 to a '*legal* duty to obey a *manifestly unlawful* order' as 'inherently contradictory'.[26] We agree with this assessment. Section 4 is satisfactory in terms of the general reference to manifestly unlawful orders. It is less satisfactory in terms of the confusing reference to a 'legal' duty to obey such orders.

---

22 Burchell *South African Criminal Law and Procedure Vol I* 180.
23 Werle and Jessberger *Principles of International Criminal Law* 252.
24 Werle and Jessberger *Principles of International Criminal Law* 252.
25 See the discussion by Cassese and Gaeta *International Criminal Law* 231.
26 Burchell *South African Criminal Law and Procedure Vol I* 180.

DISCUSSION **A 'legal' duty to obey a 'manifestly unlawful order'?**

In *S v Banda*, the court held that the defence of obedience to superior orders was a form of the defence of compulsion in that the subordinate was compelled to follow the orders of his superior officer.[27] As previously discussed, compulsion is a form of necessity. South African courts have also held that the defence of *necessity* is available only where the accused has committed a positive act that is contrary to law. Where the accused's unlawful conduct took the form of an omission, the appropriate defence is *impossibility*.[28] *Does this then mean that the defence of obedience to superior orders is unavailable to a soldier or police officer who failed to perform a legal duty because his superior officer ordered him not to do so or ordered him to do something else instead?*

THIS CHAPTER IN ESSENCE

1. The defence of obedience to superior orders is available to military personnel, police officers and members of the protection services.
2. Where such a person carries out the lawful orders of his superior officer, his conduct will be regarded as lawful, provided that he does no more harm than was necessary to carry out the order.
3. This defence also applies to a subordinate who carried out an unlawful order from his superior officer as long as the order was not manifestly and palpably illegal. Under international criminal law (at least as we find it in the Rome Statute of the International Criminal Court, 1998), orders to commit genocide and crimes against humanity are regarded as manifestly unlawful and can therefore not serve as a basis for a defence of superior orders.
4. The position regarding war crimes seems to be more nuanced and therefore, in practical terms, one can argue that the defence of superior orders is still available for war crimes.
5. South African law does not distinguish between the different crimes, but provides for a general principle in terms of which the defence of superior orders will not be available for orders that were manifestly unlawful.

27 *S v Banda* supra at 479.

28 *R v Canestra* 1951 (2) SA 317 (A); *S v Leeuw* 1975 (1) SA 439 (O).

Chapter 10

Public authority

CHAPTER OBJECTIVES

The objectives of this chapter are to:
- explain the nature of the defence of public authority
- explain the requirements for the defence when force (including lethal force) is used to effect an arrest
- explain the circumstances in which this defence could be raised.

10.1 The defence of public authority

In certain circumstances, officers of court, the law and the state generally, acting in the performance of their duties, may commit acts that are *prima facie* unlawful, including acts of aggression on life, person and property, and they are immune from liability. The reason why their actions are not punishable is because they are acting under the lawful authority of the state and therefore their conduct is not in fact unlawful. The power to authorise public officials to engage in conduct that would otherwise be unlawful is a feature of the state's legitimate monopoly on the use of force.

Burchell points out that there are four main situations in which the defence of public authority may be raised.[1] These four situations are discussed below.

10.1.1 In terms of a statutory indemnity provision

State officials may be given *statutory indemnity*, that is, immunity from civil and/or criminal proceedings, for certain conduct. For example, the Indemnity Act 61 of 1961 indemnifies the president, members of the executive council, members of the South African National Defence Force (SANDF), the police force, employees of the railways and harbours, and public servants generally from liability for civil and criminal proceedings for acts conducted

1 Burchell JM *Principles of Criminal Law* 5 ed (2016) 143–146; see also Burchell *South African Criminal Law and Procedure Vol I: General Principles of Criminal Law* 4 ed (2011) 194–215.

in good faith for purposes of suppressing internal disorder, maintaining law and order, public safety and essential services, or preserving life or property.[2] An oppressive or authoritarian state, or indeed a corrupt state could, of course, abuse indemnity provisions as part of a strategy to undermine the rule of law and the rights of citizens. Therefore, indemnity provisions should generally be applied with restraint.[3]

10.1.2 Under the rules of consular or diplomatic immunity

According to standard international practice regulated in South Africa by the Diplomatic Immunities and Privileges Act 37 of 2001, foreign heads of state, diplomatic agents, special envoys and so on are immune from civil and criminal proceedings in South African courts.[4] Immunity can be waived, in which case a diplomat who has allegedly committed a criminal offence in South Africa can in principle be tried in South Africa.[5]

The Minister of International Relations and Cooperation, acting in accordance with s 7(2) of the Diplomatic Immunities and Privileges Act, may grant immunity to a foreign visitor if it is deemed to be in the national interest.[6]

10.1.3 Under the authority of a court

Sheriffs and messengers of court serving court documents, executing an order or judgment of the court, and so on, are entitled to do so, and their actions in doing so will not be unlawful. It is important to note, however, that this exemption does not apply to a situation in which a court has no jurisdiction.[7] If the official believed that he was acting within his powers (in other words, he thought the court had jurisdiction), his actions would still be unlawful, but he would not have acted with the necessary criminal intent. Therefore, he would be able to escape liability for a crime requiring *dolus* on the basis of the defence of *putative* public authority. Since a certain degree of knowledge can be expected from court officials, the actions of the official acting without criminal intent would nevertheless be regarded as negligent,[8] and such an official would therefore not escape liability if the crime required this form of fault.

10.1.4 To carry out a lawful arrest, search or seizure of property

10.1.4.1 Use of force to effect an arrest

Police officers are given powers of search, seizure and arrest in terms of the Criminal Procedure Act 51 of 1977 (the Act). It is obvious that they would be unable to perform these

---

2 S 1 of the Indemnity Act 61 of 1961, as amended by the Justice Laws Rationalisation Act 18 of 1996.

3 See Hoexter C 'The administration of justice defence indemnities and standing' (1989) 2(3) *SACJ* 346.

4 See, in general, Strydom H et al *International Law* (2016) 316–317.

5 For an overview of the content and practical implications of diplomatic privileges and immunity, see Bennett TW and Strug J *Introduction to International Law* (2013) 170–175.

6 See, for instance, immunity granted to Grace Mugabe in August 2017, during her visit to South Africa in a private capacity. At the time she was the First Lady of Zimbabwe. The immunity shielded her from any civil or criminal litigation in South Africa, flowing from an assault allegedly committed by her in Johannesburg in 2017. For the relevant Government Notice in which the minister announced the granting of the immunity, see *Government Gazette*, No 41056, GN850, 20 August 2017. For commentary, see Kemp G 'Grace Mugabe: Why diplomatic immunity isn't always an "out of jail" ticket' *The Conversation*, 21 August 2017, available at http://theconversation.com/grace-mugabe-why-diplomatic-immunity-isnt-always-an-out-of-jail-ticket-82721. In *Democratic Alliance v Minister of International Relations and Co-operation* [2018] ZAGPPHC 534 (30 July 2018), the court declared that the Minister's decision to recognise Grace Mugabe's immunities was inconsistent with the Constitution.

7 *S v Madihlaba* 1990 (1) SA 76 (T); Burchell *South African Criminal Law and Procedure Vol I* 196.

8 Burchell *Principles of Criminal Law* 145. See further, Chapter 24, which deals with the defence of mistake or ignorance of the law.

functions effectively if no force could lawfully be used for such purposes. A detailed discussion of the relevant provisions is beyond the scope of this work. However, it is appropriate to include a short discussion of the provisions that relate to the use of force in effecting an arrest.

The powers of public officials (and even private citizens) to carry out an arrest, with or without a warrant, are set out in the Act. Section 48 of the Act authorises the breaking open of premises for purposes of effecting an arrest, while section 49 authorises the use of force against the person, including deadly force in certain circumstances.[9] The present version of section 49 reads as follows:

> **(1) For the purposes of this section—**
> **(*a*) 'arrestor' means any person authorised under this Act to arrest or to assist in arresting a suspect;**
> **(*b*) 'suspect' means any person in respect of whom an arrestor has a reasonable suspicion that such person is committing or has committed an offence; and**
> **(*c*) 'deadly force' means force that is likely to cause serious bodily harm or death and includes, but is not limited to, shooting at a suspect with a firearm.**
>
> **(2) If any arrestor attempts to arrest a suspect and the suspect resists the attempt, or flees, or resists the attempt and flees, when it is clear that an attempt to arrest him or her is being made, and the suspect cannot be arrested without the use of force, the arrestor may, in order to effect the arrest, use such force as may be reasonably necessary and proportional in the circumstances to overcome the resistance or to prevent the suspect from fleeing, but, in addition to the requirement that the force must be reasonably necessary and proportional in the circumstances, the arrestor may use deadly force only if—**
> **(*a*) the suspect poses a threat of serious violence to the arrestor or any other person; or**
> **(*b*) the suspect is suspected on reasonable grounds of having committed a crime involving the infliction or threatened infliction of serious bodily harm and there are no other reasonable means of effecting the arrest, whether at that time or later.**[10]

If arrestors act within the limits of these provisions, their use of force will not be unlawful and, if charged with a criminal offence involving their use of such force, they can raise the defence of public authority.

In *Govender v Minister of Safety and Security*[11] and *Ex parte Minister of Safety and Security and others: In re S v Walters and another*,[12] the Supreme Court of Appeal (SCA) and the Constitutional Court respectively reinterpreted the original, pre-constitutional provisions

9 'Deadly force', for purposes of effecting an arrest, is currently defined as 'force that is likely to cause serious bodily harm or death and includes, but is not limited to, shooting at a suspect with a firearm' (s 49(1)(*c*) of the Act). It is therefore not limited to lethal force which is force that actually causes death.

10 S 49 of the Criminal Procedure Act 51 of 1977, as amended by s 1 of the Criminal Procedure Amendment Act 9 of 2012, which came into force on 25 September 2012. For a discussion of this section, as well as the predecessors of the current s 49, see Du Toit et al *Commentary on the Criminal Procedure Act* (1987) (revision service 59, 2017) 5-24–5-41.

11 *Govender v Minister of Safety and Security* 2001 (2) SACR 197 (SCA).

12 *Ex parte Minister of Safety and Security and others: In re S v Walters* 2002 (2) SACR 105 (CC).

of section 49 in accordance with the rights enshrined in the Constitution.[13] Kriegler J set out the relevant principles succinctly in *Walters*:[14]

> **The purpose of arrest is to bring before court for trial persons suspected of having committed offences.**
>
> **Arrest is not the only means of achieving this purpose, nor always the best.**
>
> **Arrest may never be used to punish a suspect.**
>
> **Where arrest is called for, force may be used only where it is necessary in order to carry out the arrest.**
>
> **Where force is necessary, only the least degree of force reasonably necessary to carry out the arrest may be used.**
>
> **In deciding what degree of force is both reasonable and necessary, all the circumstances must be taken into account, including the threat of violence the suspect poses to the arrester or others, and the nature and circumstances of the offence the suspect is suspected of having committed; the force being proportional in all these circumstances.**
>
> **Shooting a suspect solely in order to carry out an arrest is permitted in very limited circumstances only.**
>
> **Ordinarily such shooting is not permitted unless the suspect poses a threat of violence to the arrestor or others or is suspected on reasonable grounds of having committed a crime involving the infliction or threatened infliction of serious bodily harm and there are no other reasonable means of carrying out the arrest, whether at that time or later.**
>
> **These limitations in no way detract from the rights of an arrestor attempting to carry out an arrest to kill a suspect in self-defence or in defence of any other person.**

The above general guidelines, based as they are on the provisions of the Constitution, are still of application today, despite the subsequent amendment of section 49 of the Act, and should thus be read together with the provisions of that section.[15]

The current prerequisites relating to the use of force for purposes of effecting an arrest can therefore be summarised as follows:

- The person effecting the arrest (the arrestor) must be attempting to *arrest* the suspect and not, for example, merely searching or questioning him.
- This must have been made clear to the suspect at the time either by the arrestor or someone else, or be obvious from the surrounding facts and circumstances.

---

13 Constitution of the Republic of South Africa, 1996.

14 *Walters* supra at 54.

15 Burchell *Principles of Criminal Law* 161 suggests that the *Walters* checklist (the criteria laid down by the Constitutional Court in *Walters*) may be sufficiently detailed, making a statutory regime obsolete. According to Burchell, there is the added advantage that the Constitutional Court's own checklist for the use of lethal force in effecting arrests would not have to undergo 'further constitutional scrutiny' for the foreseeable future at least. While we agree with this sentiment expressed by Burchell, it does seem better to have a statutory framework on the use of force as part of the broader regime on arrests provided for in the Criminal Procedure Act. For more on the effect of s 49 as it currently reads, see Snyman CR *Criminal Law* 6 ed (2014) 130–134.

- The suspect *himself* must be deliberately trying to resist arrest, or flee, or both.[16]
- It must be impossible to arrest the suspect without the use of force.

Once these prerequisites have been met, then the arrestor is lawfully justified in using such force as is reasonably necessary and proportional in the circumstances to overcome the suspect's resistance or to prevent him from fleeing.

To meet the requirement that the force was *reasonably necessary*, it needs to be shown (in addition to showing that the arrest could not have been effected without the use of force) that the means and amount of force used by the arrestor were those that, objectively speaking, would have caused the least amount of injury. In so doing, regard must be had for the means and methods available to the arrestor at the relevant time, but alternative methods need be considered only if they would have proved reasonably practical and effective.[17] A court should avoid so-called armchair speculation.[18]

In determining *what degree of force is proportional*, regard must be had not only for the nature and seriousness of the offence that the suspect is suspected of having committed, but also the threat, if any, that he poses to the safety of the arrestor and other persons.[19] Thus, for example, it is not permissible to cause serious harm to a person suspected of even a serious offence if the suspect poses no real threat of physical harm to the arrestor, other persons or society at large.[20]

Keeping these general requirements in mind, it is now necessary to turn to the use of deadly force. Deadly force, in the present context, means not only *lethal* force (force that actually causes death), but also *potentially* lethal force, in particular, shooting at a suspect with a firearm.[21]

10.1.4.2 Use of deadly force to effect an arrest

The use of deadly force for purposes of arrest is possibly the most contentious of all the powers conferred on police officers. Arrest is essentially a *procedural* device that aims to secure the accused's presence in court so that his guilt or innocence can be established according to proper trial procedures. This being the case, the use of deadly force for such purposes may seem an anachronism, reminiscent of medieval outlawry, or the bounty hunters and 'Wanted Dead or Alive' posters of the old Wild West. However, it is recognised that police officers often have to arrest individuals who are not only uncooperative but extremely dangerous and that, in so doing, they may be exposed to life-threatening situations that call for split-second responses. Clearly, therefore, a balance needs to be struck between the interests of law and order on the one hand, and the interests of the individual suspect on the other. To achieve the right balance, section 49(2) of the Act, dealing with the use of deadly force, has undergone a number of amendments.

---

16 It is therefore not permissible to use force against a person who, for example, is merely a passenger in the rear of a vehicle driven by someone else, who is trying to evade his own arrest (*Msomi v Minister of Law and Order and others* 1992 (2) SACR 557 (W)).

17 Du Toit et al *Commentary on the Criminal Procedure Act* (revision service 59, 2017) 5-30.

18 *Dikane v Minister van Wet en Orde* 1992 (2) SACR 211 (W).

19 Du Toit et al *Commentary on the Criminal Procedure Act* (revision service 59, 2017) 5-40A.

20 *Govender v Minister of Safety and Security* supra at 204j–205a.

21 In *S v Kruger* (A347/2013) [2014] ZAWCHC 196 (17 December 2014), the court held that the state needed to prove beyond reasonable doubt that the force used by the appellant was deadly force, this being relevant to the nature of the resultant onus resting on the accused in terms of s 49(2). The court noted that the state could do so either by proving that the force was intended to cause death or grievous bodily harm regardless of whether or not the force was likely to have that effect, or that it was indeed likely to do so even though the accused did not intend the force to have that effect.

The original section 49(2) permitted the use of deadly force, if necessary, to arrest a person reasonably suspected of committing a Schedule 1 offence,[22] or to prevent that person from fleeing.[23] The Constitutional Court declared this provision unconstitutional in *Walters*,[24] holding that the circumstances in which lethal force was permitted by the wording of the section were so wide as to be constitutionally unjustifiable.

In 1998, section 49 was re-enacted in a form that still allowed for the use of deadly force, but in certain clearly defined circumstances only, consistent with the judgments in *Govender* and *Walters*.[25]

However, the amended version of section 49 attracted criticism in the ranks of the police force and associated authorities. The prevailing perception, whether right or wrong, was that its provisions were complex and ambiguous, hampered the police in the exercise of their duties and gave them insufficient powers to defend themselves in an age characterised by increasing levels of criminal violence. A decision was therefore taken that section 49 should be amended yet again. After extensive debate regarding the rewording of the relevant provisions, the section was eventually re-enacted in its present form in 2012.[26] The present version of section 49 allows for the use of deadly force in two situations only, namely:

1. where the suspect poses a threat of serious violence to the arrestor or some other person (section 49(2)(*a*)); or
2. where the suspect is reasonably suspected of having committed a crime involving the infliction or threatened infliction of serious bodily harm and there are no other reasonable means of effecting the arrest, whether at that time or later (section 49(2)(*b*)).

The question has arisen whether the provisions of section 49(2)(*a*), which must be read with the general proviso that *any* force used must be reasonably necessary and proportional in the circumstances, are anything more than a restatement of the well-established common law principles of private defence of person.[27] This being the case, it may be questioned

22 Schedule 1 offences are generally serious offences, such as murder, rape and robbery, but also include comparatively less serious offences such as theft (regardless of the value of the item stolen) and receiving stolen property (see Schedule 1 of the Criminal Procedure Act).

23 Le Roux-Kemp A and Horne CS 'An analysis of the wording, interpretation and development of the provisions dealing with the use of lethal force in effecting an arrest in South African criminal procedure' (2011) 24(3) *SACJ* 266.

24 Supra.

25 S 49(2) of the Criminal Procedure Act, as amended by s 7 of the Judicial Matters Second Amendment Act 122 of 1998, which came into force on 18 July 2003, reads as follows:

> **(2) If any arrestor attempts to arrest a suspect and the suspect resists the attempt, or flees, or resists the attempt and flees, when it is clear that an attempt to arrest him or her is being made, and the suspect cannot be arrested without the use of force, the arrestor may, in order to effect the arrest, use such force as may be reasonably necessary and proportional in the circumstances to overcome the resistance or to prevent the suspect from fleeing: Provided that the arrestor is justified in terms of this section in using deadly force that is intended or is likely to cause death or grievous bodily harm to a suspect, only if he or she believes on reasonable grounds:**
>
> **(*a*) that the force is immediately necessary for the purposes of protecting the arrestor, any person lawfully assisting the arrestor or any other person from imminent or future death or grievous bodily harm;**
>
> **(*b*) that there is a substantial risk that the suspect will cause imminent or future death or grievous bodily harm if the arrest is delayed; or**
>
> **(*c*) that the offence for which the arrest is sought is in progress and is of a forcible and serious nature and involves the use of life threatening violence or a strong likelihood that it will cause grievous bodily harm.**

26 Act 9 of 2012.

27 For the requirements of private defence of person, see Chapter 7. It has been observed that s 49(2)(*a*) does not specify that the threatened violence need be imminent, but that the word 'poses' makes this implicit (Burchell *Principles of Criminal Law* 161).

whether it was really necessary to include this subsection in the Act at all.[28] Although there may be some merit in this contention, the inclusion of the subsection serves to clarify the point that a police officer threatened with serious violence in the course of effecting an arrest is not obliged to take the line of least resistance, thereby abandoning or compromising his duty.[29] He is entitled to use sufficient force *to complete the arrest*,[30] including deadly force where the requirements of reasonableness, necessity and proportionality permit.

Section 49(2)(*b*) goes further than the above and allows for the use of deadly force for the *specific* purpose of overcoming a suspect's resistance, or preventing him from fleeing, even where there is no threat of serious violence to the arrestor or any other person. Apart from the general requirements that must be met before any degree of force can be used for purposes of arrest (see above), section 49(2)(*b*) adds three further requirements:

1. The suspect must be suspected of having committed a crime involving the infliction or threatened infliction of serious bodily harm; and
2. The suspicion must be a reasonable one; and
3. There must be no other reasonable means of arresting the suspect either then or at a later time.

It will be seen from the above requirements that the present section 49(2)(*b*), like its predecessor, combines both objective and subjective elements. This is unusual because the test for the various justification defences is normally strictly *objective*, that is, the accused's conduct is normally judged from an external point of view and not according to his subjective beliefs or perceptions.[31]

Because the arrestor's suspicion must be both genuine and reasonable, he will have to give evidence that he held the necessary suspicion and the reasons why he did so. A court will assess whether the given reasons were sufficient to justify the suspicion, objectively tested. If the reasons were not sufficient, then the arrestor's use of deadly force will be judged to have been unreasonable and thus unlawful, even if it subsequently emerged that the suspicion was correct.

However, where the arrestor genuinely suspected the suspect of having committed a crime involving the infliction or threatened infliction of serious bodily harm, where such suspicion was not a reasonable one, he would lack *dolus* in respect of the unlawfulness of his use of deadly force. He would therefore escape liability for a crime such as murder, attempted murder or assault with intent to do grievous bodily harm, all of which require *dolus* (and hence subjective knowledge of unlawfulness). The appropriate defence would then be *putative* (supposed) public authority. However, an arrestor who killed a suspect on the basis of an unreasonable suspicion would obviously be liable for culpable homicide because he could not claim that he had reasonable grounds for his mistaken belief in the lawfulness of his conduct. He would thus be adjudged negligent in respect of his use of deadly force. Where his suspicion was grossly unreasonable, a court may well reject his claim that it was even genuine.[32]

---

28 See, for example, Burchell *Principles of Criminal Law* 161.

29 Snyman's view is that this is in any event the existing common law position, but the question is by no means settled law (Snyman *Criminal Law* 132).

30 The requirements of private defence permit only the use of sufficient force as is reasonably necessary to ward off the threat.

31 See, for example, *S v De Oliveira* 1993 (2) SACR 59 (A), discussed in Chapter 7.

32 See *S v Nel and another* 1980 (4) SA 28 (E); *S v Reabow* 2007 (2) SACR 292 (E).

Bear in mind that even where the above preconditions have been satisfied, the amount of force used (in this case deadly force) must still have been both reasonably necessary and proportional. This means that deadly force must have been:

- the minimum amount of force necessary to effect the arrest; and
- a proportional (reasonable) response in all the circumstances, taking account of factors such as the danger posed by the suspect, the type of offence he is suspected of having committed, his ability to escape (for example, strength, speed and agility, and availability of back-up) and the likelihood of being able to trace, identify and arrest the suspect on some future occasion if he did manage to escape.[33]

In addition, deadly force should ideally be used as a last resort only after less dangerous means have been exhausted or would be impractical. Thus, the preferred sequence of events before shooting at a fleeing suspect is an oral warning, followed by a warning shot, then a shot at the legs and only then, as a final resort, a shot intended to kill.[34] It is recognised, however, that this sequence of events may not be possible or practical in all situations.[35] Allowance will therefore be made for the circumstances of each case.

Under the previous section 49(2), according to case law, the arrestor bore the onus of proving, on a balance of probabilities, that his conduct fell within the ambit of the subsection.[36] Because section 49 has been substantially revised, and because the presumption of innocence is now enshrined in the Constitution, these decisions probably no longer apply. However, an arrestor who uses lethal force will always attract an evidentiary burden since killing another person is always *prima facie* unlawful.[37] The Constitutional Court in *Walters* did not deal with the burden of proof as such. It is submitted that the seriousness of lethal force and the risk of abuse of power by state powers, justify, if not a full burden of proof, then at least an evidentiary burden.[38]

DISCUSSION

How much power should be granted to the police to use deadly force?

How much power should be granted to the police to use deadly force against private citizens in a constitutional democracy founded on respect for human life, liberty and dignity? Does the present section 49 strike a satisfactory balance between the interests of law and order, on the one hand, and the rights of the individual citizen, on the other? Is it an improvement on its predecessor?

Given the high levels of violent crime in South Africa and the dangers faced by police officers on a daily basis, is it sufficient that deadly force is authorised for purposes of *arrest* only or are there other circumstances in which the police may justifiably need to use deadly force in the performance of their duties? If so, are these situations adequately covered by the alternative defences of private defence and necessity, or is there a need for further legislative intervention?

33 Du Toit et al *Commentary on the Criminal Procedure Act* (revision service 59, 2017) 5-35–5-36.

34 *Matlou v Makhubedu* 1978 (1) SA 946 (A); *Minister van Wet en Order en 'n ander v Ntsane* 1993 (1) SACR 256 (A).

35 Thus, for example, a warning shot is not required if innocent bystanders may be injured by it, nor are warnings required where there is insufficient time or opportunity to give them (*Macu v Du Toit en 'n ander* 1983 (4) SA 629 (A)).

36 See the Appellate Division's decisions in *R v Britz* 1949 (3) SA 293 (A) and *S v Swanepoel* 1985 (1) SA 576 (A). See also *S v Janse van Rensburg and another* 2009 (2) SACR 216 (C) at 22.

37 For this reason, the onus does indeed fall on the arrestor in delictual proceedings arising from the death or injury of a suspect during an arrest.

38 See comments by Van der Walt T 'The use of force in effecting arrest in South Africa and the 2010 Bill: A step in the right direction?' (2011) 14(1) *PELJ* 137. See also Burchell *South African Criminal Law and Procedure Vol I* 209–211.

THIS CHAPTER IN ESSENCE

1. The defence of public authority may be invoked by a public official when his apparent unlawful conduct was in fact sanctioned by the state for some lawful purpose:
   1.1 in terms of a statutory indemnity provision
   1.2 under the rules of consular or diplomatic immunity
   1.3 under the authority of a court of law
   1.4 to carry out a lawful arrest, search or seizure of property.
2. Sections 48 and 49 of the Criminal Procedure Act deal with the use of force against property and person for purposes of effecting a lawful arrest.
3. Section 49 of the Act empowers the police and those assisting them to use deadly force for such purposes. The amended section 49, which came into force in September 2012, brings the statutory framework in line with the guidelines on the use of force as set out in the Constitutional Court case *Walters*.

Chapter 11

Lawful disciplinary chastisement

CHAPTER OBJECTIVES

The objectives of this chapter are to:

- explain the nature of the defence of lawful disciplinary chastisement
- set out and explain the requirements for this defence
- discuss recent developments concerning the continued validity of the defence.

11.1 The defence of lawful disciplinary chastisement

An old and well-established principle of Roman, Roman-Dutch and English law, that has been incorporated into South African law, is that parents have the power in law to discipline and chastise (punish) their children for purposes of correction. This power stems from their parental authority over the child.

The power of chastisement extends also to persons who are *in loco parentis* (teachers, guardians, step-parents, child-minders, and so on)[1] and to those to whom the power of chastisement has been specifically delegated by the parent.[2] It has been held that teachers have an inherent power of chastisement, which arises by virtue of their own position of authority,[3] and which therefore exists independently of whether such power is specifically conferred or withheld by the parent.[4]

The power to chastise has traditionally extended to the administration of moderate corporal (physical) punishment. However, the range of persons by whom and on whom any form of corporal punishment may lawfully be imposed has been narrowed down considerably

1 See, for example, *R v Scheepers* 1915 AD 337; *R v Schoombee* 1924 TPD 481; *R v Le Maitre and Avenant* 1947 (4) SA 616 (C); *Du Preez v Conradie and another* 1990 (4) SA 46 (BG).

2 *Du Preez v Conradie* supra.

3 *R v Muller* 1948 (4) SA 848 (O); *Du Preez v Conradie* supra.

4 Neethling J and Potgieter JM *Neethling-Potgieter-Visser Law of Delict* 6 ed (2010) 114.

over the years. The Constitutional Court in *S v Williams*[5] declared unconstitutional the imposition of corporal punishment on child offenders by the courts, because it was held to be cruel, inhuman and degrading. Section 10 of the South African Schools Act has outlawed the imposition of corporal punishment on learners in schools.[6]

It seems, therefore, that the only persons who have thus far retained the right to administer corporal punishment to children are parents and persons who are *in loco parentis*, but excluding teachers and other school authorities. However, this does not mean that the latter may not resort to other forms of punishment, for example detention, extra homework and removal of privileges.

11.2 Requirements for the defence

11.2.1 The punishment must have been administered for purposes of correction

The punishment must have been administered (1) in response to some misconduct and (2) in the realistic expectation that it will teach the child to modify his future behaviour.[7] Punishment that is inflicted purely out of malice, to assuage the parent's anger, or for retribution will not meet this requirement - see the following passage from the old English case of *R v Hopley*:

> **A parent ... may for the purposes of correcting what is evil in the child inflict moderate and reasonable corporal punishment always however with this condition that it is moderate and reasonable. If it be administered for the gratification of passion or of rage, or if it be immoderate and excessive in its nature or degree, or if it be protracted beyond the child's power of endurance or with an instrument unfitted for the purpose and calculated to produce danger to life and limb, in all such cases the punishment is excessive and the violence is unlawful.**[8]

By the same token, where punishment has failed to produce the desired change in behaviour, there is no justification for inflicting it repeatedly.[9]

11.2.2 The punishment must have been moderate and reasonable

Only moderate and reasonable forms of punishment are protected by the defence. Punishment that exceeds the bounds of moderation is unlawful and constitutes abuse. What constitutes moderate and reasonable punishment must be determined according to the facts of each case, taking account of factors such as the child's age, gender, physical and mental constitution, the means of correction, and the nature and seriousness of the transgression.[10]

South African courts have held that the power of lawful chastisement confers a discretion on the parent similar to the discretion that a trial court has in determining sentence.

5 *S v Williams and others* 1995 (2) SACR 251 (CC).

6 S 10 of the South African Schools Act 84 of 1996 provides that no person may administer corporal punishment on a learner at a school and makes it a criminal offence to do so. The constitutionality of this section was upheld in *Christian Education South Africa v Minister of Education* 2000 (4) SA 757 (CC).

7 *R v Janke and Janke* 1913 TPD 382.

8 *R v Hopley* (1860) 2 F and F 202, cited with approval in *R v Janke and Janke* supra at 385.

9 *R v Janke and Janke* supra at 388.

10 *R v Janke and Janke* supra; *Du Preez v Conradie* supra.

Consequently, a court will normally interfere with the exercise of this discretion only where the punishment is unduly severe or unreasonable,[11] or where the discretion is exercised in an arbitrary or capricious manner.[12]

11.3 Chastisement distinguished from force used for other purposes

Before considering the future of the defence of lawful disciplinary chastisement, it is necessary to distinguish between force used against a child for purposes of punishment and force used for other purposes, such as protecting the child from some immediate harm or danger. Parents have a duty to protect their children and this may require them to employ a measure of force in order to restrain the child and/or remove it from the path of danger. Force used for this purpose is not justified by the defence of lawful chastisement, but by the defence of necessity and must therefore comply with the requirements of that defence.[13] Equally, where a parent uses force against a child in order to protect himself or some other person against an unlawful attack by the child, the appropriate defence will be private defence, not lawful chastisement.[14]

11.4 The future of the defence of lawful disciplinary chastisement

Despite its ancient roots, the continued validity of the defence of lawful disciplinary chastisement has been vigorously debated in recent years.[15] Modern ideas of good parenting, coupled with the current emphasis on children's rights, have inevitably raised the question of whether it can ever be considered acceptable to discipline a child by means of corporal punishment, even if the amount of force used is moderate. Arguments in favour of maintaining corporal punishment in the home are generally based on the right to privacy and family life, as well as the right to religious freedom, since the administration of corporal punishment for disciplinary purposes is regarded as an important parental duty by certain religious groups. Sachs J left the question open in *Christian Education South Africa v Minister of Education*.[16] The clearly evident global trend has however been to abolish *all* forms of corporal punishment, irrespective of degree and context.[17]

The main impetus behind this trend has been the United Nations Convention on the Rights of the Child (CRC).[18] Article 19 of the CRC enjoins state parties to take appropriate measures to 'protect the child from all forms of physical or mental violence, injury or abuse, ... while in the care of parent(s), legal guardian(s) or any other person who has care of the child ...', while article 37 enjoins signatories to ensure that no child is 'subjected to torture, or other cruel, inhuman or degrading treatment or punishment'. Although initially open to some doubt, the United Nations Committee on the Rights of the Child (the CRC Committee)

11 *R v Schoombee* supra; *R v Le Maitre and Avenant* supra at 621–622.
12 *R v Theron and another* 1936 OPD 166.
13 These requirements are discussed in chapter 8.
14 The requirements of this defence are discussed in chapter 7.
15 For a critical and comparative perspective, see Saunders BJ 'Ending the physical punishment of children by parents in the English-speaking world: The impact of language, tradition and law' (2013) 21(2) *Int'l J Child Rts* 278–304.
16 *Christian Education South Africa v Minister of Education* supra at 48.
17 For further information, see Burchell JM *Principles of Criminal Law* 5 ed (2016) 199–203.
18 The United Nations Convention on the Rights of the Child (1989). South Africa signed this convention in 1993 and ratified it in 1995.

has since made it clear that the above measures extend to the total abolition of all forms of corporal punishment, including moderate disciplinary chastisement in the home.[19]

A further international instrument that touches on the subject is the African Charter on the Rights and Welfare of the Child (ACRWC).[20] Article 16 of the ACRWC contains a provision similar to article 19 of the CRC, while article 20 provides that parents and caregivers have the duty, inter alia, to 'ensure that domestic discipline is administered with humanity and in a manner consistent with the inherent dignity of the child'.[21] In 2011, the African Committee of Experts on the Rights and Welfare of the Child (ACERWC), which monitors the implementation of the ACRWC by state parties, issued a statement in which it called for the public condemnation and elimination of all notions which accepted, tolerated and encouraged violence against children, including corporal punishment.[22]

In addition to signing and ratifying the above instruments, South Africa has adopted a Constitution that expressly recognises and protects the rights and interests of children, including the right to be protected from maltreatment, neglect, abuse or degradation.[23] Its main legislative instrument for achieving this purpose is the Children's Act 38 of 2005.[24] When this Act was initially presented, there was considerable speculation and debate as to whether it would – or should – include a provision abolishing corporal punishment in the home. Public opinion on the subject was sharply divided and, ultimately, no such provision was adopted. As a consequence, however, South Africa's lack of progress in complying with its obligations under the CRC and the ACRWC has elicited concern.[25]

More recently, the Gauteng Local Division, Johannesburg, of the High Court had occasion to consider the constitutionality of the defence of lawful disciplinary chastisement, in the case of *S v YG*:[26]

S v YG

The appellant, YG, had been convicted of assaulting his wife and 13-year-old son (M) in two separate incidents on the same day. In answer to the charge of assaulting M, he had raised the defence of lawful disciplinary chastisement, but this defence failed because the trial court found that the degree of force used by the appellant exceeded that permissible in terms of the defence.

19 See UNCRC Committee's General Comment No 8, on the right of the child to protection from corporal punishment and other cruel or degrading forms of punishment, CRC/C/GC/8, 2 March 2007; see also General Comment No 13, on the right of the child to be free from all forms of violence, CRC/C/GC/13, 18 April 2011, especially para 17: 'The Committee has consistently maintained the position that all forms of violence against children, however light, are unacceptable. "All forms of physical or mental violence" does not leave room for any level of legalized violence against children. Frequency, severity of harm and intent to harm are not prerequisites for the definitions of violence. States parties may refer to such factors in intervention strategies in order to allow proportional responses in the best interests of the child, but definitions must in no way erode the child's absolute right to human dignity and physical and psychological integrity by describing some forms of violence as legally and/or socially acceptable'.

20 The African Charter on the Rights and Welfare of the Child (1990). South Africa signed this charter in 1997 and ratified it in 2000.

21 Article 20 of the African Charter on the Rights of the Child.

22 African Committee of Experts on the Rights and Welfare of the Child, *Statement on violence against children*, Addis Ababa, April 2011

23 S 28(1)(*d*) of the Constitution of the Republic of South Africa 1996. S 28(2) provides further that '[a] child's best interests are of paramount importance in every matter concerning the child'.

24 The Children's Act 38 of 2005.

25 See, for example, the UNCRC Committee's Concluding Observations on the Second Periodic Report of South Africa, CRC/C/ZAF/CO/2, 30 September 2016, para 33. See also the Concluding Recommendations by the ACERWC on the Republic of South Africa Initial Report on the Status of Implementation of the African Charter on the Rights and Welfare of the Child at para 35, available at http://www.acerwc.org/download/concluding_observations_south_africa/?wpdmdl=8754.

26 *S v YG* 2018 (1) SACR 64 (GJ).

Although the High Court ultimately agreed with this finding when the matter came before it on appeal, it considered it necessary to deal first with a more fundamental and far-reaching issue, namely the constitutional validity of the defence itself.[27]

In considering this question, the High Court referred to South Africa's obligations in terms of the CRC and took, as its fundamental point of departure, the Constitutional Court's recognition in *S v M* that children have a right to an independent identity, separate and distinct from that of their parents.[28] They do not derive their constitutional rights from their parents and their parents have a duty to respect and protect those rights. If they fail to do so, that duty then falls on the state. The court also held (citing the same case) that our Constitution requires a child-centred model of child justice, whereas the defence of lawful chastisement, derived as it is from archaic notions of parental power and parental rights, is essentially *parent*-centred and thus incompatible with the child-centred approach envisaged by the Constitution.

The court accepted that the defence is subject to limits that provide some measure of protection to the child, but rejected the argument that moderate and reasonable corporal punishment is ultimately in the child's best interests and that it is distinguishable from child abuse.[29] The court held that the rules of the defence allow a parent so much latitude to decide what is 'reasonable' in any given case that it introduces an element of arbitrariness. Furthermore, because corporal punishment inevitably involves some degree of violence, it violates the child's constitutional right to protection from *all* forms of violence *from both public and private sources*,[30] as well as the right to bodily and psychological integrity.[31] It is therefore of no consequence that the violence is inflicted by the child's own parent (a private source), nor does it matter whether it is the child's bodily or psychological integrity that is violated, so the degree of force used is irrelevant.[32] Additionally, the court held, corporal punishment must inevitably involve a measure of degradation or loss of dignity for the child, which is a further violation of the child's constitutional rights.

The court held that, by allowing a parent to infringe a child's constitutional rights with impunity, the law effectively treats children as second-class citizens, infringing their right to dignity and an independent identity and affording them less protection against assault than it affords to adults, which is unfairly discriminatory and antithetical to the priority accorded by the Constitution to the best interests of the child. The court held further that these infringements could not be justified under section 36 of the Constitution (the general limitations clause).

The court also rejected the argument that the abolition of the defence would have the unwanted effect of criminalising many well-meaning parents and rendering them liable to prosecution and even the possible loss of their children. It held that such fears were unwarranted, given that the objectives of the Children's Act are to promote and support positive parenting, not to criminalise errant parents. It pointed out that the necessary mechanisms for achieving these

27 For this purpose, the High Court invited submissions from the prosecution, the defence, the Minister of Justice and Correctional Services and the Minister of Social Development. The Minister of Justice and Correctional Services did not respond, but the Minister of Social Services made written submissions, supporting the view that the defence of disciplinary chastisement is constitutionally non-compliant. Four interested organisations were also admitted as *amici curiae* and made submissions to the court. They were the Children's Institute, the Quaker Peace Centre, Sonke Gender Justice and Freedom of Religion South Africa (FORSA). The first three submitted that the defence of disciplinary chastisement is incompatible with the Constitution. Only the fourth *amicus* argued that it is constitutionally compliant, being protected under the right to freedom of religion.

28 *S v YG* supra at 61, referring to *S v M (Centre for Child Law as Amicus Curiae)* 2008 (3) SA 232 (CC) at 19.

29 This was FORSA's contention. It also echoes Professor CR Snyman's views on the subject (Snyman *Criminal Law* 138).

30 S 12(1)(*c*).

31 S 12(2).

32 In the introductory portions of the judgment, the court expressly acknowledged South Africa's obligations under the CRC to protect children against all forms of violence, including corporal punishment in the home.

objectives are already in place and that there is thus no valid reason to anticipate a flood of prosecutions for relatively trivial transgressions.[33]

In response to the contention that the abolition of the defence would undermine freedom of religion and belief, as well as the right of religious communities to practice their religion,[34] the court accepted that such a ruling might well result in some limitation of these rights, but not in sufficient measure to warrant the retention of a defence that so fundamentally undermines the rights of children.

Ultimately, therefore, the court concluded that the defence of lawful disciplinary chastisement is unconstitutional and no longer applies in our law.[35]

Because a High Court ruling is binding only within the court's area of jurisdiction, it remains to be seen whether the decision in *S v YG* will be followed in the rest of South Africa and whether it will be upheld if taken on appeal.[36] However, even though it may not be the final word on the subject, it must be acknowledged that the judgment is thorough and well-reasoned, as well as being firmly grounded in current jurisprudence on the rights of the child. Furthermore, given the manner in which the court countered the various arguments in favour of retaining the defence, it is difficult to imagine any further basis on which its decision could be successfully challenged. It does therefore seem that the defence of lawful disciplinary chastisement is rapidly reaching the end of its days, if it has not already done so.

If this is so, it also remains to be seen how the law will deal in practice with parents who continue to employ corporal punishment despite the abolition of the defence, as they will undoubtedly do. Although the court correctly pointed out that there are mechanisms whereby offending parents can be counselled and corrected without subjecting them to conviction and punishment, it is doubtful whether South Africa has sufficient resources to respond to an increase in the demand for social services, given the well-publicised shortage of social workers in this country. Furthermore, there is nothing that restricts the prosecuting authorities to the mechanisms envisaged in the Children's Act. Straightforward prosecution and conviction still remain available options. Burchell has speculated that the abolition of the defence of lawful disciplinary chastisement could result in an increased reliance on prosecutorial discretion and the defence of *de minimis non curat lex* to avoid criminal liability in cases of minor and trivial assault and, in light of the circumstances, this might well prove to be the case.[37]

Lastly, it should be noted that the High Court's ruling in *S v YG* does not affect a parent's right to use force against a child for purposes of protection or self-defence, provided that the parent's conduct falls within the scope of the defences of necessity or private defence, respectively.

---

33 S 45 of the Children's Act envisages that cases of alleged maltreatment will be brought before a children's court, which has very wide remedial powers, including ordering the parent/caregiver and/or the child to undergo professional counselling, or to participate in mediation, a family group conference, or other appropriate problem-solving forum, or to undergo a specified skills development, training, treatment or rehabilitation programme (see further, s 46(1)(*h*) of the Act).

34 These rights are protected by ss 15 and 31 of the Constitution.

35 The court however emphasised, in accordance with the principle of legality, that this ruling is *prospective* only and therefore does not criminalise conduct falling within the scope of the defence which was committed before the date of the ruling.

36 FORSA has announced that it has applied for leave to appeal the High Court's ruling – see https://forsa.org.za/press-release-for-sa-appeals-spanking-judgement/. The outcome of this application is unknown at time of writing.

37 Burchell *Principles of Criminal Law* 203 and 247. The defence of *de minimis non curat lex* (meaning 'the law does not concern itself with trivia') is discussed fully in Chapter 13.

DISCUSSION

Was the High Court right to abolish corporal punishment in the home?

Do you agree with the High Court's ruling in *S v YG*? Are you satisfied that all the relevant issues were fully ventilated in court? If not, can you think of any further considerations or arguments, either for or against the ruling, that ought to have been taken into account? What do you think will be the practical effect of the ruling if it is upheld and followed in the rest of the country? What, in your opinion, would be the best way of ensuring that parents are not criminalised for minor and trivial transgressions?[38]

THIS CHAPTER IN ESSENCE

1. Parents have long had the lawful authority to inflict moderate and reasonable punishment, including corporal punishment, on their children for purposes of correction.
2. This authority has extended to persons who are *in loco parentis* and those to whom the parent has specifically delegated his authority.
3. However, school authorities are forbidden from administering corporal punishment in schools by virtue of section 10 of the South African Schools Act.
4. More recently, the Gauteng Local Division, Johannesburg, of the High Court ruled that the defence of lawful disciplinary chastisement is unconstitutional and is thus no longer available to a parent to justify the administration of corporal punishment in the home. It is therefore very likely that this defence has fallen away, or will do so very soon.

38 For further critical perspectives on this issue, see Naylor, B and Saunders, B 'Whose rights? Children, parents and discipline' (2009) 34(2) *Alt L J* 80–85; Kaime, T 'The African Children's Charter: Does it represent a relevant vision of childhood and children's rights?' (2009) 29 *CLRJ* 11–29.

Chapter 12

Consent

CHAPTER OBJECTIVES

The objectives of this chapter are to:

- distinguish between consent and agreement
- distinguish between consent to suffer actual harm and voluntary assumption of the risk of harm
- identify the situations where consent will be a valid defence to a criminal charge of inflicting physical harm on another person
- explain the requirements for valid consent
- distinguish between the defences of consent (proper) and putative consent.

12.1 The defence of consent

Certain crimes depend on the absence of consent as an essential or requisite element of the offence. For example, rape (now redefined in terms of the Criminal Law (Sexual Offences and Related Matters) Amendment Act 32 of 2007) is defined as unlawfully and intentionally committing an act of sexual penetration with a complainant without his or her consent. Thus, where the complainant concerned did in fact consent, or the state is unable to prove that he or she did not consent, one of the essential elements of the *actus reus* for rape is missing and there can be no liability.[1] However, what is the position in the case of other crimes? Can consent exclude the element of unlawfulness in the case of theft and indecent assault? What about common assault? What about assault with intent to do grievous bodily harm? And what about homicide, for example in cases of euthanasia (mercy killing)?

The state has an interest in the welfare of its citizens and thus it has an interest in promoting and preserving their lives, health and well-being. Because of this, the law takes the (rather paternalistic) view that a person can consent to *physical* harm within certain limits only.[2] Beyond those limits, the choice no longer lies with the individual: it becomes a question of public policy.[3] Thus, while the law will readily allow a person to waive his economic rights and his non-physical personality rights (dignity and reputation) without needing a good reason to do so, the law takes a more restrictive view when it comes to questions of life and bodily integrity.

The general rule is that a person cannot validly consent to actual bodily (physical) harm unless the harm is inflicted for some purpose that the law recognises as legitimate according to public policy. Because of this, consent is not a valid defence to all crimes or in all situations. When considering whether an accused can rely on the defence of consent in any given case, it is therefore necessary to begin by considering whether consent would constitute a legally valid defence to that particular crime.

Before considering the various situations in which consent is a valid defence for crimes involving infliction of bodily injury, it is important and helpful to distinguish between two different types of consent:

1. Consent to suffer actual injury
2. Acceptance of the mere risk of injury, more properly referred to as the voluntary assumption of the risk of harm

This distinction is important because, as you will see, the law takes a more restrictive approach in cases that involve consent to suffer actual bodily injury, and a more permissive approach in cases that involve the voluntary assumption of the mere risk of such injury.

12.2 Consent as a valid defence to physical injury[4]

12.2.1 Minor injuries that are merely 'transient and trifling'

A person may freely consent to physical injury in situations where the injury is not serious and does not produce actual bodily harm, because this does not violate the general rule

1 For more on the Criminal Law (Sexual Offences and Related Matters) Amendment Act 32 of 2007, see Chapter 28.
2 Strauss SA 'Bodily injury and the defence of consent' (1964) 81(2) *SALJ* 179.
3 See, for example, *S v Collett* 1978 (3) SA 206 (RA).
4 See, in general, Burchell JM *Principles of Criminal Law* 5 ed (2016) 209–226; Snyman CR *Criminal Law* 6 ed (2014) 122–128.

outlined above.[5] It follows that the consent can only be valid and lawful if the consenting person had full knowledge of the extent of his rights as well as the nature and scope of the harm.[6] In the English case of *R v Donovan*, the term 'bodily harm' was defined as: '... any hurt or injury calculated to interfere with the health or comfort of the complainant. It need not be permanent, but it must be more than merely transient and trifling'.[7]

Where the injury produces actual bodily harm, the accused's conduct is regarded as ***malum in se*** (inherently bad and immoral) and, in this case, the victim's consent cannot constitute a defence.[8]

12.2.2 Medical operations and treatments

A surgical operation and other medical procedures can involve actual bodily harm, but still be lawful.[9] Their lawfulness rests on two factors:

1. The patient's informed consent to the actual procedure as well as his voluntary assumption of the accompanying risks[10]
2. The therapeutic purpose of the procedure, which is recognised as a legitimate purpose according to public policy

The concept of 'therapeutic purpose' has been accepted as embracing not only surgery and treatment that is strictly necessary to prolong life and/or alleviate physical suffering, but also cosmetic surgery and treatments as long as the associated risks are relatively minor. It would not extend to highly risky procedures, mutilation or disfigurement for so-called cosmetic purposes. The requirements for consent for purposes of research and experimentation on human subjects, both for therapeutic purposes and otherwise, are now regulated by the National Health Act 61 of 2003.[11]

DISCUSSION

Circumcision of minors, parental consent and children's rights

The circumcision of young boys forms an integral part of many religious and cultural practices, including those of the Jewish and Muslim faiths, as well as traditional African communities. Some parents also circumcise their baby boys for medical reasons. Complex legal, constitutional and moral questions concerning freedom of religion, children's rights and cultural diversity inform the debate about this practice in the 21st century.

One pertinent legal question is whether the consent of the parent(s) is enough to justify the bodily harm caused by the circumcision. In May 2012, a court in Cologne, Germany, held that the circumcision of a Muslim boy (aged four) 'constituted an unlawful offence of causing actual bodily harm'. Furthermore, the court held that

5 See *R v McCoy* 1953 (2) SA 4 (SR).

6 *Esterhuizen v Administrator, Transvaal* 1957 (3) SA 710 (T).

7 *R v Donovan* [1934] All ER 207 (CCA). See also *R v McCoy* supra; *S v Collett* supra.

8 *S v D* 1963 (3) SA 263 (E).

9 Strauss '*Bodily injury and the defence of consent*' 179 *et seq*.

10 A number of statutes, as well as the Constitution of the Republic of South Africa, 1996, in particular ss 10 and 12, are relevant in this context. See further, Chapter 9 of the National Health Act 61 of 2003; Mental Health Care Act 17 of 2002; Children's Act 38 of 2005; Choice on Termination of Pregnancy Act 92 of 1996; Sterilisation Act 44 of 1998. For a discussion of the legal aspects of informed consent, see Le Roux-Kemp A *Law, Power and the Doctor-Patient Relationship: A Legal Perspective* (2011) 79–103. See also Landman AA and Landman WJ *A Practitioner's Guide to the Mental Health Care Act* (2014) 6, 12, 31, 36–37, 78, 85–89, 107–108, 132–134, 185.

11 S 71 of the National Health Act, which came into force on 1 March 2012.

'[c]onsent by the four-year-old was not given and could not be given due to a lack of intellectual maturity. The consent of the parents was given, but could not justify the infliction of bodily harm'.[12]

Do you think the German court's approach to parental consent is correct? How should a court in South Africa deal with this question, given the protection of children's rights as well as the protection of religious and other freedoms in the Constitution? What would be a balanced, principled and constitutionally sound approach to consent in criminal law in sensitive cases like this one?

12.2.3 Religious, customary and superstitious practices

A distinction is drawn between injuries inflicted for medical purposes and those inflicted for religious, customary and superstitious purposes. In the latter case, there is no departure from the general rule. Thus, where the practice concerned results or is likely to result in minor injury only, consent will negate the unlawfulness of the aggression. However, in cases where the injury produces actual bodily harm, then consent will be no defence. Compare, for example, the cases of *R v Njikelana and S v Sikunyana*.[13]

R v Njikelana and S v Sikunyana

Njikelana was a traditional healer who rubbed a powder, supposedly an aphrodisiac, onto the victim's private parts, with her consent, to cure her frigidity. The powder caused irritation and pain, but as her discomfort was transient, the court held that her consent to this procedure was a valid defence. Njikelana was acquitted of indecent assault.

Sikunyana and his co-accused were traditional herbalists who were consulted by the complainant, a young woman, who asked them to remove an evil spirit from her. To do this, they made her inhale fumes of a medicine sprinkled over live coals while they held her over the coals under a blanket. Her face and upper body were badly burnt. They were convicted of assault with intent to do grievous bodily harm in the Magistrates' Court and appealed to the Supreme Court, relying, inter alia, on *Njikelana*.

On appeal, the Supreme Court held that a highly dangerous practice, such as that which the four accused had perpetrated, could never be made lawful by the victim's consent. The court distinguished the facts from those in *Njikelana* where there was no evidence that the powder was really harmful. It held that the accused's conduct in the present case was *malum in se*. Their convictions were confirmed.

DISCUSSION **Where to draw the line?**

The question arises as to where, in a diverse society like South Africa, it is appropriate to draw the line between consent to medical treatment on the one hand, and consent to religious, customary and superstitious practices on the other. Will the law recognise consent to treatment according to mainstream medical practice only? If so, how then should we deal with consent to the treatments used in alternative forms of medicine,

12 Judgment by the Landgericht Cologne, 7 May 2012, Docket No 151 Ns 169/11 – final. For a translation of the judgment and additional notes by Alexander Aumüller and Michael Bohlander, see http://www.dur.ac.uk/ilm/news/itemno=14984.

13 *R v Njikelana* 1925 EDL 204; *S v Sikunyana and others* 1961 (3) SA 549 (E).

such as acupuncture, osteopathy and homeopathy, which are widely practised and highly regarded? Also, if we recognise these alternative forms of medicine, is there any justification for discriminating against traditional medicine and other traditional healing practices, which are undoubtedly also intended and believed to have therapeutic benefits?

However, if we do place these practices on a par with mainstream medicine, how do we then provide for the situation that arose in *Sikunyana*? Presumably, it could have been argued that the complainant had not been told of the material risks of harm that accompanied the procedure and that she had not accepted those risks. However, suppose that she had in fact been told and had in fact given her consent? Should that consent have been sufficient to remove the taint of unlawfulness from the conduct of the accused?

New Zealand law, unlike our own, does not apply a results-based approach, in which the level of injury is a decisive factor. In *R v Lee*,[14] the accused was convicted of manslaughter after he caused a woman's death by sitting on her chest and allegedly strangling her during the course of an exorcism. The trial court held that consent could not operate as a valid defence to such an act and directed the jury to disregard the issue of consent altogether.

On appeal, the Supreme Court held that consent could be a valid defence to the infliction of any injury short of death unless there are good public policy reasons to forbid it. These reasons must be sufficient to outweigh the social utility, if any, of the activity involved and the high value placed on personal autonomy. When considering whether such reasons exist, the judge is required to weigh up the degree of injury intended or risked, the degree of risk of such injury, the social utility (or otherwise) of the activity involved, the right to personal autonomy, the rationality of the consent and any other relevant factor. The Supreme Court held, therefore, that the jury had been wrongly directed and ordered a retrial.[15]

Given the importance of religious freedom and personal autonomy, should South Africa adopt a similarly flexible approach?

12.2.4 Sports and contests for entertainment

In modern times, certain sports or contests, such as duelling, prize-fighting (boxing without gloves) and games of Russian roulette, are illegal because of the risk of serious injury and even death.[16] In such cases, the consent of the participants will be no defence.[17] However, in the case of lawful sports and contests,[18] it is not the purpose of the sport or contest to inflict serious injury, and there are either rules designed to prevent and/or limit injuries, or serious injury is not contemplated by the participants. In this case, the participants are taken as having voluntarily assumed the risk of the type of injuries that are likely to occur during the game or contest while it is being played according to the rules. In such cases, the players do not consent to any actual bodily harm – they merely assume the risk of such harm. Assault or

14 *R v Lee* [2006] 3 NZLR 42.

15 For further discussion on the approach in *Lee*, see Burchell *Principles of Criminal Law* 219–222.

16 Burchell *Principles of Criminal Law* 224.

17 The position was different in the past when such contests were regarded as legitimate trials of prowess and/or ways of settling personal differences.

18 This is not limited to organised sports and contests, but also includes informal games and playful behaviour.

injuries caused by dangerous or reckless play that does not fall within the normal, anticipated range of injuries a person can expect in a contact sport such as rugby, will of course not be covered by the defence of consent and should be treated as criminal conduct and/or a possible delict.[19]

12.2.5 Infringements of sexual integrity

The distinction between a welcome act of sexual intimacy and crimes such as rape and sexual assault lies entirely in the consent of the parties. Valid consent is accordingly accepted as a complete defence to the crime of rape.[20] Consent will also exclude the element of unlawfulness required for sexual aggressions other than rape, such as sexual assault and *crimen iniuria* where the accused's conduct is of a sexual nature. However, in cases where actual bodily harm is inflicted for purposes of sexual gratification, the conduct of the accused will be regarded as inherently unlawful and the consent of the 'victim', however willing, will not be a defence.[21] The English case of *R v Brown and others* is illustrative in this regard.[22]

R v Brown and others

Brown and his co-accused were members of a group of sado-masochists who willingly inflicted and received physical injury in various ways. They were charged with contravening certain sections of the (English) Offences Against the Person Act 1861.[23] They raised the defence of consent. The trial court ruled that lack of consent was not an element of the offences in question. It convicted them and they appealed.

On appeal, the House of Lords held the following:

- It is not in the public interest that a person should wound or cause actual bodily harm to another person for no good reason and, in the absence of a good reason, the victim's consent is no defence to a charge under the Act.
- Satisfying sado-masochistic desires is not a valid reason for causing hurt or injury calculated to interfere with the health or comfort of another person. The injuries concerned were not transient or trifling, and therefore the consent of the 'victims' was irrelevant.

The convictions were upheld.[24]

12.3 Voluntary euthanasia (mercy killing)

The position in South Africa has always been that the consent of the deceased cannot make his killing by another person lawful.[25] This position was confirmed in the well-known case of *S v Hartmann*.[26]

---

19 For more on the limits of lawful injuries caused in a game of sport, see *Boshoff v Boshoff* 1987 (2) SA 694 (O); Burchell *Principles of Criminal Law* 224.

20 The question of what constitutes valid consent is discussed in section 12.4.

21 *R v Taylor* 1927 CPD 16; *R v P* 1960 (1) PH H 159 (OPA); *S v D* 1963 (3) SA 263 (E).

22 *R v Brown and others* [1993] 2 WLR 556 (HL).

23 In South Africa, they would have been charged with the crimes assault or assault with intent to do grievous bodily harm.

24 For a criticism of the approach applied by the House of Lords in *R v Brown*, see Tolmie J 'Consent to harmful assaults: The case for moving away from category based decision making' (2012) (9) *Crim LR* 656; Burchell *Principles of Criminal Law* 215–218. Compare also the House of Lords' approach in *R v Brown* with the New Zealand Supreme Court's approach in *R v Lee* supra, discussed above.

25 For background on the euthanasia debate, see Dörfling DF *'Genadedood' in die strafreg: 'n Regsfilosofiese en regsvergelykende perspektief* (LLM thesis, Rand Afrikaans University – now University of Johannesburg) (1991); Benatar SR 'Dying and "euthanasia"' (1992) 82(1) *S Afr Med J* 35.

26 *S v Hartmann* 1975 (3) SA 532 (C). See also *S v Mshumpa and another* 2008 (1) SACR 126 (E).

S v Hartmann

Hartmann was a doctor whose father was very old, terminally ill and in great pain. He hastened his father's death by administering a fatal injection of pentothal (an anaesthetic) and was charged with murder. At his trial, he gave evidence that he had asked his father if he wanted to 'sleep' and his father had vaguely nodded his head in approval.

The court held that according to our law, deliberately hastening a person's death, even by a few hours, is murder. Furthermore, even if the deceased had consented, this would not be a defence to the crime of murder. Hartmann was convicted of murder but received a wholly suspended sentence.

In considering South African law on the subject of voluntary euthanasia, it is necessary in the first instance to distinguish between euthanasia and the hastening of death by the provision of pain-relieving drugs that have the *secondary* effect of shortening the patient's life. This is not regarded as a form of euthanasia, but merely the exercise of a doctor's proper and normal duty to alleviate pain and suffering.[27] As such, it is lawful and the patient's consent will operate as a valid defence.[28]

The law further distinguishes between what may be termed 'active' and 'passive' euthanasia. Active euthanasia involves actively hastening another person's death.[29] Passive euthanasia is merely the ending of a fruitless attempt to save or prolong life in cases where the patient concerned has no reasonable prospect of recovery. Examples of passive euthanasia include disconnecting a life-support system, withholding naso-gastric feeding or declining to resuscitate a patient in crisis.[30]

As far as passive euthanasia is concerned, our law recognises that a person has the right to hasten his own death by refusing medical treatment.[31] Although medical personnel normally have a legal duty to provide treatment and nursing care to their patients, they are not entitled to do so if the patient has specifically refused such treatment or care, as this would amount to assault. Compliance with the patient's instructions is therefore lawful.[32] Here the law is straightforward, although practical complications may arise in cases where the patient is mentally or physically unable to make his own decision and convey it to his doctors.[33]

27 In other words, it falls within the ambit of normal therapeutic treatment, as previously discussed.

28 28 See *Clarke v Hurst NO* supra at 656H-I; see also *Minister of Justice and others v Estate Stransham-Ford* 2017 (3) SA 152 (SCA) at para 34 (facts discussed in Chapter 6, section 6.4.2.2.2).

29 As in the *Hartmann* case, supra

30 See, for example, *S v Williams* 1986 (4) SA 1188 (A) discussed previously in Chapter 6. See also *Clarke v Hurst NO and others* 1992 (4) SA 630 (D) on the termination of a life support system of a patient in a persistent vegetative state. For further commentary, see Lupton ML '*Clarke v Hurst NO, Brain NO and Attorney-General*, Natal (Unreported 1992 (N)): A living will, brain death and the best interests of a patient' (1992) 5 *SACJ* 342; Dörfling DF 'Eutanasie: Die reg van die curator personae om verdere behandeling van 'n pasient te verbied: 'n Nuwe regverdigingsgrond in die Suid-Afrikaanse reg' (1993) 2 *TSAR* 345; Boister N 'Causation at the death? *Clarke v Hurst* 1992 (2) SA 676 (D)' (1993) 56 *THRHR* 516; Strauss SA 'The right to die or passive euthanasia: Two important decisions: One American and the other South African' (1993) 6(2) *SACJ* 196; Taitz JL 'Euthanasia and the "legal convictions of society" in a South African context' (1993) 110(3) *SALJ* 440; Burchell *Principles of Criminal Law* 211–217.

31 *Minister of Justice and others v Estate Stransham-Ford* supra at para 31.

32 Ibid. See also McQuoid-Mason D 'Pacemakers and living wills: Does turning down a pacemaker to allow death with dignity constitute murder?' (2005) 18(1) *SACJ* 24–40.

33 In such cases, family members or medical personnel will often approach the courts for a ruling on the lawfulness of withholding treatment or care. See, for example, *Clarke v Hurst NO and others* 1992 (4) SA 630 (D). For similar cases in other jurisdictions, see *Cruzan v Director, Missouri Department of Health* 497 U.S. 261 (1990); 110 S Ct 2841 (1990); *In the Matter of In re Quinlan* (70 NJ 10, 355 A. 2d 647 (NJ 1976)); *Auckland Area Health Board v Attorney-General* [1993] 1 NZLR 235 (HC) (Auckland Area Health Board).

On the subject of active euthanasia, in *Minister of Justice and Correctional Services v Stransham-Ford* the SCA drew a further distinction between physician assisted *suicide* (PAS) and physician assisted *euthanasia* (PAE).[34] As South African law stands at present, PAE is unlawful and the consent of the patient, however willing and well-considered, cannot render it lawful. It will amount to murder. In the case of PAS, there may be scope for the common law to be developed so as to permit this, but if so the issue is more likely to turn on the question of causation,[35] rather than that of consent.[36]

The changing legal convictions of society, the developing ethics surrounding medical care and decision making, constitutional norms and values informed by fundamental considerations such as human dignity, privacy and personal autonomy, as well as (progressive) comparative perspectives, warrant further debate and law reform. The South African Law Reform Commission (SALRC) recognised this and, in 1999, produced its 'Report on euthanasia and the artificial preservation of life'. Legislation dealing with euthanasia is recommended by the Commission. The report contains some recommended principles for further discussion as well as a draft bill.[37] An ever-evolving South African society is in need of legislation to clarify the legal position, including the role of consent in this context. The broader question of the decriminalisation of euthanasia, raised by Labuschagne more than two decades ago and further prompted by decisions such as *Stransham-Ford*,[38] is more acute than ever. This is an area in need of urgent, but thoughtful and sensitive, legislative action.[39]

12.4 Requirements for valid consent

12.4.1 The meaning of consent

Consent does not mean agreement (consensus). Agreement requires a meeting of the minds between two or more people. It is a bilateral or multilateral act. Consent is a unilateral act.[40] Consent need not only be expressed in words, whether written or spoken, but can also be given tacitly by conduct. However, mere silence or submission does not amount to consent.[41]

In cases where consent is a valid defence to the crime concerned, the consent needs to meet the requirements for valid consent:

- The person giving it must have had the *legal capacity* to consent.
- It must be *genuine* consent.
- It must be operative *at the time* of the act in question.

34 Physician-assisted suicide (PAS) describes the situation where a medical practitioner supplies a patient with the means to end his own life. Physician-assisted euthanasia (PAE) describes the situation where the medical practitioner himself applies those means so as to end the patient's life (as in the *Hartmann* case, supra).

35 That is, the question of whether and in what circumstances the final act of the patient will rank as a *novus actus interveniens*.

36 See further the discussion in Chapter 6, section 6.4.2.2.2.

37 For brief comments, see Burchell *Principles of Criminal Law* 211–213

38 Labuschagne JMT 'Dekriminalisasie van eutanasie' (1988) 51 *THRHR* 167.

39 See also the discussion in Chapter 27.

40 For this reason, consent can be withdrawn unilaterally.

41 *Ex parte Minister of Justice: In re R v Gesa, R v De Jongh* 1959 (1) SA 234 (A). See also, for example, *R v McCoy* supra and *S v Volschenk* 1968 (2) PH H.283 (D).

12.4.2 Requirements

12.4.2.1 Capacity to consent

To be valid, the consent must have been given by a person who, at the relevant time, was mentally capable of forming and exercising his will. The generally accepted test is whether the person concerned was capable of understanding and appreciating the nature of the act or transaction to which he apparently consented.

The following persons lack the capacity to give valid consent in law:

- Persons who are too young to understand and appreciate the nature of the relevant act or transaction
- Persons who are mentally ill or intellectually disabled to the point where they are not able to understand and appreciate the nature of the relevant act or transaction
- Persons who are intoxicated (drunk or drugged) to the same extent
- Persons who are asleep or unconscious

As far as children are concerned, the general rule at common law can be stated as follows: children under seven years of age are always deemed incapable of consenting to any act or transaction. In the case of children aged seven years and older, the validity of the child's consent will depend on whether he was able to understand and appreciate the nature of the act to which he allegedly consented. Factors such as intelligence, education and background will be taken into account. Thus, a person need not be a legal major (18 years or over) to give valid consent.

The above general rule is, however, modified by various exceptions:

- The common law exception relates to the age of consent in respect of sexual acts in the case of girls only. There was an irrebuttable presumption that a girl under 12 years cannot validly consent to sexual intercourse. For this reason, sex with a girl under 12 would *always* amount to rape even if she did understand the nature of the sexual act and did give her consent.[42] This presumption was, however, eclipsed by the Sexual Offences Act, which replaced the common law definition of rape. This Act provides that *any child* under 12 years is incapable of appreciating the nature of an act of sexual penetration or violation, and is thus incapable of giving valid consent (section 1(3)).
- Sections 14 and 15 of the old Sexual Offences Act 23 of 1957 went further and made it a statutory offence for a male to have sex or attempt to have sex with a girl less than 16 years of age, or for a female to have sex or attempt to have sex with a boy less than 16 years of age.[43] Sections 15 and 16 of the 2007 Sexual Offences Act replaced these provisions by making it an offence for a person of *either* sex to perform an act of sexual penetration or violation with *any* child under 16 years of age.[44]
- In the case of medical operations and treatment, section 129 of the Children's Act makes provision for the age of consent to various medical procedures as well as for proxy consent to medical operations and treatment. The Choice on Termination of Pregnancy Act provides that any woman, regardless of age, can choose to terminate her pregnancy.[45]

In certain cases, where a person is unable to give consent, consent can be given on that person's behalf by someone else with the necessary authority to do so. This is known as

---

42 *R v Z* 1960 (1) SA 739 (A).

43 This offence was commonly referred to in popular parlance as statutory rape. In fact, it was not rape at all (and was thus not subject to the same penalties), but rather a separate and distinct statutory offence.

44 See further, Chapter 28.

45 S 5(2) of the Choice on Termination of Pregnancy Act.

consent by proxy. Thus, for example, parents, guardians and care-givers can consent to their underage children undergoing medical treatment or surgery, and such consent would be valid. Where such consent is unreasonably withheld, or the parent/guardian/care-giver is deceased, cannot be traced or is incapable of consenting, consent may be given by the Minister of Health, a children's court or the High Court and, in cases of extreme urgency, by the superintendent of the hospital.[46]

In the case of adult persons who are mentally ill or intellectually disabled, a *curator ad personam* can be appointed by the High Court on application by an interested party. The curator would then have the power to consent to medical treatment or operations on behalf of the person concerned. Note, however, that some acts are so personal in nature, for example sexual acts, that no one can validly consent to such an act on behalf of another. Thus, a parent cannot validly consent to an underage child having sexual intercourse.

DISCUSSION **Should there be further aspects to the test for consensual capacity?**

It is evident that the present test for consensual capacity focuses purely on the individual's cognitive (intellectual) capacity. However, the Sexual Offences Act provides that a mentally disabled person cannot validly consent to a sexual act if he is unable to appreciate the nature and reasonably foreseeable consequences of that act, *is unable to act in accordance with such appreciation (that is, lacks self-control), or is unable to communicate his unwillingness to participate*. This provision highlights the fact that a person's ability to form and express his will also relies on his conative (volitional) capacity together with his ability to communicate.[47] Logically, this must apply not only to mentally disabled persons in the case of sexual acts, but across the board. The question therefore arises as to whether the general test for consensual capacity should not be extended to include an enquiry into a person's conative capacity and ability to express/communicate.

12.4.2.2 Genuine consent

12.4.2.2.1 The consent must be given freely and voluntarily

Mere submission is not consent. Thus, compliance induced by duress by means of threats, force or intimidation is not genuine consent.[48] In this regard, one can consider *R v McCoy* and *S v Volschenk*.[49]

R v McCoy

McCoy, the general manager of an airline corporation, inflicted a caning on an air hostess for failing to comply with safety regulations. He was convicted of assault, but appealed on the grounds that the complainant had consented to the caning. It emerged, however, that she had agreed to the caning only as an alternative to being suspended or grounded, both of which would have had serious financial implications for her. The Appeal Court held that there had not been consent but only submission under duress. His conviction was upheld.

46 Ss 129(4), (5), (6), (7) and (9) of the Children's Act.

47 For an explanation of the meaning and relevance of the terms 'cognitive' and 'conative' faculties, see section 14.3.

48 *Ex parte Minister of Justice: In re R v Gesa, R v De Jongh* supra.

49 *R v McCoy* supra; *S v Volschenk* supra.

S v Volschenk

Volschenk, a policeman, raided the room where the complainant was illegally sleeping. He took her to an isolated spot and induced her to have sex with him because he threatened to lay a criminal charge against her if she did not comply with his wishes. The court held that consent obtained under duress was not true consent. Volschenk was convicted of rape.

The Sexual Offences Act provides that in the case of sexual acts, consent will not be valid where it was obtained through an abuse of power or authority over the complainant.[50]

12.4.2.2.2 The consent must be informed consent

The person giving the consent must be aware of the material facts concerning the act to which he is consenting. This is especially important in the case of medical procedures.[51] In such cases:

- the patient must have consented to the medical procedure or treatment in question and not to some other procedure or treatment
- the patient must also have been told of the material (important) risks of harm that accompany the operation or treatment.[52]

12.4.2.2.3 Consent may be vitiated (nullified) by fraud or deception

It follows from the previous point that where consent is obtained by means of fraud or deception, it is not genuine consent. Fraud or deception can take the form of actively misleading the other person as to the nature, circumstances and/or consequences of the act to which he is consenting, or intentionally withholding information that is material to the other person's decision.

However, not all forms of fraud or deception will necessarily vitiate consent. Essentially, fraud or deception will vitiate consent only if it is *material* in nature, in other words, if the complainant would not have consented at all if he had known the truth, or would only have consented on substantially different terms.

In the case of sexual acts, it has long been the accepted common law rule that consent will be vitiated only by fraud or deception that induces either *error in negotio* (error as to the nature of the act),[53] or *error in personae* (error as to the identity of the accused).[54] Other types of deception were not regarded as sufficiently important or serious to vitiate consent to

50 For a thoughtful analysis and critique of the consent-based sexual offences regime in the Sexual Offences Act, see Du Toit L 'From consent to coercive circumstances: Rape law reform on trial' (2012) 28(3) *SAJHR* 380–404. The author points out that the 2007 Sexual Offences Act retained consent as a key element in the definition of rape in contrast with the SALRC's evaluation and ultimate recommendation that the element of consent be replaced with a more complex and nuanced notion of 'coercive circumstances'. By evaluating the surrounding coercive circumstances, a determination of *prima facie* unlawfulness can be made according to this view. The author furthermore points out that there seems to be a discrepancy between the preamble to the Act's mention of 'vulnerable persons', and the operative part of the Act's retention of the element of consent, which seems to be premised on sexual autonomy that exists and is in place for all individuals regardless of their gender and circumstances. Thus, consent, as retained in the Sexual Offences Act, has meanings that 'are deeply embedded in modernity's contradictory view of women's sexual autonomy'. Of course, it should also be pointed out that the definition of rape under the Sexual Offences Act is gender neutral, a fact that Du Toit acknowledges. But the author's critique regarding the dangers of a too simplistic notion of consent that is still possible under the Sexual Offences Act seems to be a reasonable critique and worthy of further debate.

51 See Le Roux-Kemp A *Law, Power and the Doctor-Patient Relationship* (2011) 81–103.

52 See, in general, Van den Heever P 'The patient's right to know: Informed consent in South African medical law' (January 1995) *De Rebus* 53. See also the delictual cases of *Esterhuizen v Administrator, Transvaal* supra and *Castell v De Greef* 1994 (4) SA 408 (C).

53 For a full discussion of the law in this regard, see *S v Notito* (123/11) [2011] ZASCA 198 (23 November 2011).

54 *R v C* 1952 (4) SA 117 (O).

sexual acts, for example a sexual partner's deceptions regarding his age, pedigree, wealth, marital status, and willingness to marry the complainant or pay for his services.

However, one area of particular concern, in light of the HIV/AIDS pandemic, is the position where the partner is suffering from some serious sexually transmissible infection and fails to disclose this fact to the complainant. English law originally held that failure to disclose the fact that one had a venereal disease (an old term for a sexually transmissible infection) could vitiate consent to sexual intercourse - see *R v Bennett* and *R v Sinclair*.[55] Then came the civil case of *Hegarty v Shine*,[56] which was an action for damages arising from assault and breach of promise. The plaintiff had lived with the defendant for one year without being married to him, had had a baby by him, and then found out that she had contracted syphilis from him and had transmitted it to their baby. He had concealed his illness from her. The court dismissed her claim because it held that their extramarital cohabitation was immoral and illegal, and there was no duty of disclosure in such an immoral relationship.

Shortly afterwards, in *R v Clarence*,[57] clearly (and almost certainly wrongly) influenced by the decision in *Hegarty v Shine*, the majority of the court held that a husband's failure to disclose the fact that he had gonorrhoea did not vitiate his wife's consent to sexual intercourse. Despite its evident inequity, the ruling in *Clarence* has since been followed in England, as well as in various other countries, such as South Africa and Canada, that follow the English law.

However, a recent development has been the decision of the Canadian Supreme Court in *R v Cuerrier*.[58]

R v Cuerrier

The accused was charged with aggravated assault, under the Canadian Criminal Code, for having unprotected sex with two complainants without informing them of his HIV-positive status. He candidly admitted that he knew very well that they would not have consented to have sex with him if he had told them the truth. The lower courts applied the ruling in *Clarence* and acquitted Cuerrier, but on appeal, the Supreme Court held that he should have been convicted and ordered a new trial.

Seven judges heard the appeal and gave different reasons for coming to this conclusion. Two of the judges took the view that the English law had taken a wrong turn with the decision in *Clarence*. They recommended a return to the pre-*Clarence* approach to the non-disclosure of sexually transmissible infections, holding that this would be an incremental change to the common law, such as a court is entitled to make without usurping the functions of the legislature.

The Sexual Offences Act makes specific provision for consent to be vitiated by fraud or deception leading to an *error in negotio* or *error personae* (section 1(3)(*c*)), but makes it clear that the circumstances specified in section 1(3) are not a closed list.[59] There is thus no reason why the same reasoning as adopted in *Cuerrier* could not be followed in a South African court.[60]

---

55 *R v Bennett* (1866) 4 F & F 1105; *R v Sinclair* (1867) 13 Cox CC 28.

56 *Hegarty v Shine* (1878) 14 Cox CC 145.

57 *R v Clarence* (1888) 22 QBD 23.

58 *R v Cuerrier* [1998] 2 SCR 371.

59 S 1(3), read with s 1(2), of the Sexual Offences Act.

60 Our courts appear to have opted for a different approach, however, namely to regard the accused's conduct in such cases as attempted murder. See *S v Phiri* 2014 (1) SACR 211 (GNP), in which the North Gauteng Provincial Division of the High Court upheld the conviction for attempted murder of an HIV/AIDS counsellor, who was himself HIV-positive and who had unprotected sex with the complainant, whom he knew to be HIV-negative. See also *S v Nyalungu* 2013 (2) SACR 99 (T).

12.4.2.2.4 The consent must be operative at the time of the act

Subsequent condonation or ratification is not the same as consent. Consent will be valid only if it was given before the act or at the time that the act commenced. Also, it must still be operative when the act is carried out, in other words, it must not have been withdrawn.

In this last regard, note that because consent is a unilateral act, it can be withdrawn unilaterally, at least until such time as the act commences, although perhaps not after it has already commenced. A relevant, but dated, case in this regard is *R v Handcock*.[61]

> ***R v Handcock***
>
> Handcock had sexual intercourse with the complainant, initially with her consent. While they were so engaged, she heard her employer approaching and told Handcock to stop, but he refused and continued. She later charged him with rape. The court held that where a woman consents to have sex with a man and, after the commencement of the act, but before its completion, changes her mind and the man then refuses to desist and completes his purpose, he has not committed rape. Handcock was consequently acquitted.

The above decision can critically be compared with the New Zealand case of *R v Kaitamaki*,[62] in which the House of Lords held that sexual intercourse is a continuing act, which begins with penetration and ends only with withdrawal. Consequently, if consent is withdrawn at any time during the act, what follows will amount to rape. It remains to be seen what view a modern South African court would take of the question.

12.5 Putative consent

As in the case of the other justification defences, the requirements for the defence of consent are judged objectively, that is, according to the external facts and not according to what the accused thought or believed. Thus, where the accused genuinely but mistakenly believed that the complainant consented to an act in respect of which consent would have constituted a valid defence in law, the accused's conduct will still be unlawful. However, he will not be criminally liable because he lacked the intention to act unlawfully.[63] This can therefore be raised as a defence in its own right. This defence is known as *putative consent*.[64]

THIS CHAPTER IN ESSENCE

1. In some cases, apparently unlawful conduct can be justified on the basis that the conduct in question took place with the consent of the victim.
2. However, the victim's consent is not a valid defence to all acts.
3. As a general rule, consent is not a valid defence to the infliction of actual bodily harm (injuries that are more than merely transient and trifling), unless such harm was inflicted for some legitimate purpose according to considerations of public policy.

---

61 *R v Handcock* 1925 OPD 147.
62 *R v Kaitamaki* 1980 1 NZLR 59; [1985] AC 147 (HL).
63 *S v J* 1989 (1) SA 525 (A).
64 Putative consent is a form of mistake of fact and will be discussed further in Chapter 24 in section 24.4.

Chapter 13

De minimis non curat lex

CHAPTER OBJECTIVES

The objectives of this chapter are to:

- explain the nature of the defence of *de minimis non curat lex*
- set out and explain the requirements for this defence.

13.1 *De minimis non curat lex*

The maxim ***de minimis non curat lex***, commonly abbreviated to *de minimis*, means 'the law is not concerned with trivialities'. It is an ancient maxim, derived apparently from English law.[1] It means, in essence, that the law is not concerned with punishing trivial transgressions. Therefore, when the accused's conduct amounts to a trivial transgression, he would be entitled to raise the defence of *de minimis* to escape liability.

In terms of criminal law theory, *de minimis* should not be treated as a justification for the accused's conduct. This defence is therefore distinguishable from the defences that we have discussed in the preceding chapters.[2] In cases of *de minimis*, the accused's conduct remains unlawful, but on account of its triviality, goes unpunished. The rationale for the defence is well explained in the Canadian case of *Canadian Foundation for Children, Youth and The Law v Canada (Attorney General)*:

> **Generally, the justifications for a *de minimis* excuse are that: (1) it reserves the application of the criminal law to serious misconduct; (2) it protects an accused from the stigma of a criminal conviction and from the imposition of severe penalties for relatively trivial conduct; and (3) it saves courts from being swamped by an enormous number of trivial cases ... In part, the theory is based on a notion that the evil to be prevented by the offence section has not actually occurred. This is consistent with the dual fundamental principle of criminal justice that there is no culpability for harmless and blameless conduct.**[3]

Reported cases in which this defence has been raised are relatively few because the prosecuting authorities generally decline to prosecute in cases where the unlawful conduct

1 See Burchell JM *Principles of Criminal Law* 5 ed (2016) 245. There was no equivalent rule in Roman or Roman-Dutch law. However, the defence is also recognised in Canadian law and, in certain respects, in American law.

2 See comments by Snyman CR *Criminal Law* 6 ed (2014) 139–140; Burchell *Principles of Criminal Law* 245.

3 *Canadian Foundation for Children, Youth and the Law v Canada (Attorney General)*, [2004] 1 S.C.R. 76, 2004 SCC 4 at 204.

is extremely trivial. See, however, *R v Dane*,[4] in which the accused was charged with malicious injury to property because she had trimmed her neighbour's side of their common boundary hedge in addition to her own side. Although she was convicted in the Magistrates' Court, her conviction was set aside on appeal on the basis of *de minimis non curat lex*.

The defence was also upheld in *S v Kgogong* in respect of the theft of a simple piece of paper that was no longer of any use, but not in *S v Nedzamba* where the stolen pieces of paper happened to be two cheque forms.[5] The defence has also been successfully raised in cases of very minor assault in which no actual harm resulted.[6] However, as Burchell points out, resulting harm is not a requirement of the crime of assault, and thus the fact that the complainant suffered no harm will not automatically indicate that the case is one of *de minimis*.[7] Ultimately, therefore, it is for a court to decide, in all the circumstances of the case, whether the accused's conduct amounts to a trivial transgression or not.

In the case of statutory offences, the intention of the legislature is important when determining whether the accused's conduct constituted a trivial transgression or something more. Thus, for example, the defence of *de minimis* was not upheld in *S v Danster*[8] where the accused was found in possession of a small quantity of cannabis (dagga). Nor was it upheld in *Director for Public Prosecutions, Eastern Cape v Klue*[9] where the accused had driven on a public road with a blood-alcohol concentration that exceeded the legal limit by 0,02 grams per 100 millilitres of blood. Generally, therefore, where the legislature has seen fit to impose a specific limit on a certain type of conduct, it will not avail the accused to argue that he exceeded that limit by a minimal amount only.

DISCUSSION

A substantive rule in policy and procedural perspective

We have mentioned that there are relatively few reported cases dealing with the *de minimis* defence. In Chapter 11 we discussed the developments surrounding the abolishment of the defence of lawful chastisement in the context of corporal punishment of children at home. In future, and in the context of charges of assault against parents who have administered some level of physical chastisement of their children, it is conceivable that there will be an increase in reliance on *de minimis* to distinguish between those cases that are truly deserving of a criminal sanction and those that are not.[10]

The *de minimis* defence is furthermore a good illustration of a rule of substantive criminal law that could be of great help to prosecutors when exercising their prosecutorial discretions (whether to prosecute a case or not).

We have now completed our discussion of the first element of criminal liability - unlawful conduct - and the defences that may be raised to exclude that element. We will now proceed to the next element of liability, namely criminal capacity.

4 *R v Dane* 1957 (2) SA 472 (N).

5 *S v Kgogong* 1980 (3) SA 600 (A); *S v Nedzamba* 1993 (1) SACR 673 (V).

6 *R v MaGuire* 1969 (4) SA 191 (RA); *S v Bester* 1971 (4) SA 28 (T). But see also *S v Visagie* 2009 (2) SACR 70 (W), in which the complainant suffered a fractured wrist.

7 Burchell *Principles of Criminal Law* 246. See further, Burchell's criticism of the decision in *S v Visagie* supra at 245–246.

8 *S v Danster* 1976 (3) SA 668 (SWA).

9 *Director of Public Prosecutions, Eastern Cape v Klue* 2003 (1) SACR 389 (E).

10 See, for example, the discussion on the use of the *de minimis* defence in such cases in *Canadian Foundation for Children, Youth and the Law v Canada (Attorney General)* supra.

THIS CHAPTER IN ESSENCE

1. Apart from the justification defences, which are aimed at excluding the unlawfulness of the accused's conduct, it is also open to an accused to raise the defence that his conduct, although unlawful, is so trivial in nature that it should go unpunished.
2. As a matter of policy, the law is not concerned with punishing trivial transgressions.

Chapter 14

Criminal capacity

CHAPTER OBJECTIVES

The objectives of this chapter are to:
- introduce and explain the concept of criminal capacity
- explain the development of criminal capacity as a discrete element of liability in our law
- describe the current test for criminal capacity in our law
- distinguish between lack of criminal capacity and lack of fault
- distinguish between lack of criminal capacity and involuntary conduct
- identify the three categories of mental functions in human beings and explain how they relate to the capacity enquiry
- identify the four principal defences that may exclude criminal capacity.

14.1 Historical background

By the second century AD, Roman law took the view that criminal liability consisted of two elements: unlawful conduct (*actus reus*) accompanied by a guilty state of mind (*mens rea*). A person could not be punished either for his conduct alone or for his thoughts alone. Roman law also recognised that young children and insane persons should not be held responsible for their wrongful conduct. Thus, for example, Justinian's *Digest* records that mental illness was a complete defence in Roman law.[1]

---

1 D.1.18.14 declares that a person in a certain state of insanity, '*ut continua mentis alienatione omni intellectu careat*', should not be punished. According to De Wet JC and Swanepoel HL *Strafreg* 3 ed (1975) 105, the old authorities regarded the absence of *intellectus* (of the insane person or the very young person) to be the reason why their conduct was not punished. The authors further pointed out that there was an alternative basis for not holding an insane person criminally liable, namely that the person's insanity as such was regarded as his punishment (D1.18.14; D.48.9.9.).

The notion of a mental element as a prerequisite for liability was unknown in early Germanic law,[2] which based liability purely on the offender's conduct. Accordingly, when the law of the various Germanic tribes replaced Roman law as the primary law of most of Western Europe, the element of *mens rea* was largely forgotten. However, during the Frankish Empire (the fifth to the ninth centuries AD), the Christian Church grew more powerful and began to exert its influence on secular matters, including the development of criminal law. As a result of the Church's influence, the concepts of sin, guilt and immorality came to be inextricably intertwined.[3] The Church's view of sin as something based as much on wrongful thoughts as on wrongful acts, reintroduced the idea that *mens rea* was an essential prerequisite for criminal liability.

Another important area in which Christian thinking influenced the development of criminal law was through the doctrine of free will (self-determinism) and the concept of personal responsibility.[4] This was the idea that in spite of temptation and human frailty, individuals have the power to choose between doing right and doing wrong, and that each individual is accordingly responsible for his own wrongdoing.[5]

These ideas effectively laid the foundation for the modern view that criminal liability rests as much on the offender's mental guilt as on his outward conduct. They also laid the foundation for the modern view that there are, in turn, two elements to the concept of mental guilt:

1. Having the power to choose between doing right and doing wrong (criminal capacity)
2. Consciously doing wrong (fault or *mens rea*)

Although it is evident that these are two discrete (separate and distinct) enquiries, it is only in relatively recent years that they have been separated into two discrete elements of liability.[6] Until the 1980s, it was considered that there were only two principal elements of criminal liability: (1) unlawful conduct (*actus reus*), and (2) fault (*mens rea*). However, *lack* of criminal capacity was regarded as a *defence excluding fault*.[7] Furthermore, at that time, there were only two grounds on which an accused could claim to have lacked criminal capacity: (1) mental illness, or (2) youth.

However, the Appellate Division (AD) (now the Supreme Court of Appeal (SCA)) ruling on the defence of voluntary intoxication in *S v Chretien*[8] extended the range of defences that could be raised to exclude criminal capacity. The ruling also suggested that criminal capacity was a third, discrete element of criminal liability, which would normally need to be proven by the state beyond reasonable doubt. This idea rapidly gained currency. Thus, for example, by the time of *S v Arnold*, reported in 1985, we see the Cape Provincial Division (now the Western Cape High Court) identifying the legal issues in the trial in the following terms:

- Did the accused perform an act in the legal sense, that is, was his conduct voluntary?
- If so, did he have the necessary criminal capacity at the time?
- If so, did he have the requisite intention to commit murder?[9]

---

2 The position was somewhat more nuanced in the early Middle Ages. See Schmidt E *Einfuhrung in die Geschichte der Deutschen Strafrechtspflege* (1995) section 58. As a general proposition, however, it is safe to say that early Germanic law placed the emphasis on conduct (*actus reus*) and not the guilty mind (*mens rea*).

3 See Von Bar KL et al *A History of Continental Criminal Law* (1916) for general background.

4 See section 1.9.3.

5 See further, section 1.9.2.

6 Snyman still refers to them jointly with the term 'culpability'. See Snyman CR *Criminal Law* 6 ed (2014) 145.

7 For this reason, in some of the earlier cases, courts do not distinguish between lack of fault and lack of criminal capacity. See, for example, *S v Dyk and others* 1969 (1) SA 601 (C).

8 *S v Chretien* 1981 (1) SA 1097 (A). This case is discussed in section 3.3.1.5.

9 *S v Arnold* 1985 (3) SA 256 (C). This case is discussed in section 3.3.1.6.

This three-stage enquiry has now become the well-established approach in our criminal law. However, although the state normally bears the onus of proving all three elements of criminal liability, in practice it is normally only where the accused places his criminal capacity in dispute, or where it becomes apparent to a court that he may well have lacked criminal capacity, for example where the accused is a child, that it will be necessary for the state to place evidence before a court to prove that the accused did indeed have criminal capacity. Thus, despite the adoption of criminal capacity as a discrete element of criminal liability, it is still considered principally in terms of its defences.

14.2 The modern concept of criminal capacity

The enquiry into criminal capacity is essentially an enquiry into whether, at the time of his unlawful conduct, the accused was *psychologically responsible* for that conduct.[10] The Rumpff Commission explained that the psychological basis of criminal responsibility rests on two 'legs':[11]

> **Two psychological factors render a person responsible for his voluntary acts: First the free choice, decision and voluntary action of which he is capable, and secondly his capacity to distinguish between right and wrong, good and evil (insight) before committing the act.**

The current test for criminal capacity in South African law was derived from the wording of section 78(1) of the Criminal Procedure Act 51 of 1977, which was in turn based on the findings and recommendations of the Rumpff Commission.[12] This test is therefore concerned with establishing two things, namely whether at the time of his unlawful conduct, the accused in question was:

1. capable of appreciating the wrongfulness of that conduct[13]
2. capable of acting in accordance with that appreciation.[14]

---

10 The Afrikaans term for criminal responsibility (or capacity) is *toerekeningsvatbaarheid*. This term, which has its roots in the legal comparative work of Prof JC de Wet, was adopted and applied by the so-called Rumpff Commission: Kommissie van Ondersoek na die Toerekeningsvatbaarheid van Geestelik Versteurde Persone en Aanverwante Aangeleenthede RP 69/1967 (1967). The recommendations of the Rumpff Commission resulted in the adoption of ss 77 (capacity of accused to understand proceedings), 78 (mental illness or intellectual disability and criminal responsibility) and 79 (panel for purposes of enquiry and report under ss 77 and 78) of the Criminal Procedure Act 51 of 1977. See also Landman AA and Landman WJ *A Practitioner's Guide to the Mental Health Care Act* (2014) 145–146.

11 The Rumpff Report supra at para 9.30 (discussed further in Chapter 15).

12 S 78(1) of the Criminal Procedure Act provides that:

> **A person who commits an act or makes an omission which constitutes an offence and who at the time of such commission or omission suffers from a mental illness or intellectual disability which makes him or her incapable—**
> **(*a*) of appreciating the wrongfulness of his or her act or omission; or**
> **(*b*) of acting in accordance with an appreciation of the wrongfulness of his or her act or omission, shall not be criminally responsible for such act or omission.**

Although this provision was originally intended to apply only to the defence of mental illness or intellectual disability (pathological criminal incapacity), its formulation of the two elements of criminal capacity (the tests for *insight* and *self-control*) have since been adopted as the standard test for criminal capacity in South African law. For a detailed discussion of s 78(1) of the Criminal Procedure Act, as amended by Act 4 of 2017, see Du Toit et al *Commentary on the Criminal Procedure Act* (1987) (revision service 59, 2017) 13-22–13-35.

13 If this ability is present, we say that the individual had *insight* into the wrongfulness of his conduct. This part of the enquiry is therefore commonly referred to as the insight leg of the capacity enquiry.

14 If this ability is present, we say that the accused had *self-control*. This part of the enquiry is therefore commonly referred to as the self-control leg of the capacity enquiry.

For a person to have criminal capacity, both requirements must be satisfied. If either of them is lacking, then the person lacks criminal capacity as a whole and cannot be held criminally liable.

Section 78 of the Criminal Procedure Act must be read with section 48(5)(*b*) of the Child Justice Act 75 of 2008. The latter provides the situation where a child has been referred for a decision relating to mental illness or intellectual disability in terms of section 78 of the Criminal Procedure Act. The relevant proceedings under the Child Justice Act may then be postponed for a period determined by the inquiry magistrate.

14.2.1 The distinction between insight and fault

It is important to appreciate at the outset that the first part of the capacity enquiry is concerned with establishing whether the accused was *capable* of appreciating the wrongfulness of his conduct. It is thus *not* an enquiry into whether the accused did in fact appreciate that he was conducting himself unlawfully – this question forms part of the fault enquiry. It is an enquiry into whether he had the *ability* or *power* to do so if he had wanted to, in other words, whether he had the necessary *mental faculties* to equip himself for this purpose. It stands to reason that where a person lacks the ability to appreciate the wrongfulness of his conduct, then he will in fact not do so, and he will therefore, of necessity, also lack fault.[15]

14.2.2 The distinction between voluntary conduct and self-control

Equally, the second part of the capacity enquiry is not an enquiry into whether the accused's conduct was voluntary in the sense that he was able to control his bodily movements – this question forms part of the conduct enquiry. It is rather an enquiry into whether the accused had the ability to control his *behaviour*. Once again, this is an enquiry into whether the accused had the necessary *mental faculties* to equip himself for this purpose. It stands to reason that where a person's conduct is involuntary because his conscious mind has ceased to function altogether, for example in a state of automatism, he will not be capable of insight or self-control and thus he will also, of necessity, lack criminal capacity.

14.3 Which mental faculties are relevant to the capacity enquiry?

The Rumpff Commission identified and distinguished between three principal categories of mental functions (or faculties) in human beings: the cognitive, conative and affective functions.[16]

The **cognitive functions** are our *intellectual* functions, that is, our ability to assimilate information from the environment, remember it, organise and process it in a rational manner, draw rational conclusions, and make appropriate decisions. Thus, they include our functions of perception, thinking, reasoning, understanding, judgement and recall. A person's ability to distinguish between right and wrong; to know when certain conduct would be wrong according to the standards of law, society and/or morality; and to decide on an appropriate course of action, depends on that person's cognitive functions. Where the cognitive functions are impaired through mental illness or intellectual disability, intoxication or are not yet fully developed as in the case of children, the individual would be unable to do these things effectively, if at all.

15 It was for this reason that lack of criminal capacity was originally regarded as a defence excluding fault and, for the reasons given, it will still have this effect, despite the fact that it is now regarded as a third, discrete element of liability.

16 Rumpff Report supra at para 9.9.

The **conative functions** are our *volitional* functions, that is, our ability to control and direct our behaviour towards achieving a particular goal or object by exercising our power of will, rather than merely acting on impulse. A person's ability to govern his behaviour to avoid doing what he knows or believes to be wrong depends on the exercise of his conative functions. Where the conative functions are impaired through mental illness or intellectual disability, intoxication or are not yet fully developed as in the case of children (who are notoriously impulsive), the person would be unable to do this effectively, if at all.

The **affective functions** are our *emotions*, both pleasant and unpleasant, and simple and complex, such as love, hate, rage, fear, joy, anxiety, disappointment, jealousy, empathy and remorse. Emotions can be a powerful motivating force, causing us to want to act in a particular way. Intense emotions can even produce involuntary physiological changes, such as sweating, blushing or blanching, trembling and fist clenching, over which we have no control.[17] The way in which we feel in certain situations can also cause us to adopt unconsciously certain characteristic poses and gestures - so-called body language - which, because they are instinctive reactions, may be difficult to control or avoid. Despite these facts, a normal adult is capable of controlling the expression of his emotions to avoid committing antisocial acts.

We can conclude from the above that the criminal capacity enquiry is concerned with two of the three mental functions: the cognitive and the conative functions. The first part of the enquiry (whether the accused was able to appreciate the wrongfulness of his conduct) depends on the state of the accused's cognitive functions. The second part of the enquiry (whether the accused was able to act in accordance with that appreciation) depends on the state of the accused's conative functions.

We can also see that the affective functions do *not* play a direct role in the enquiry into criminal capacity. Although we know that emotions play a powerful role in motivating a person to act in certain ways, we do not accept that he should escape liability for his criminal acts purely because he had a strong motivation to act as he did.

14.4 Defences excluding criminal capacity

There are currently four defences in South African law that are accepted as excluding criminal capacity: mental illness or intellectual disability, youth, intoxication, and provocation or severe emotional stress or distress.[18] In the next chapters, we consider each of these defences, beginning with the defence of mental illness or intellectual disability (or, pathological criminal incapacity, to use the technically more correct term).

THIS CHAPTER IN ESSENCE

1. A person who engages in unlawful conduct will only be criminally liable - and therefore punishable - if he had criminal capacity at the relevant time.
2. The enquiry into criminal capacity is essentially an enquiry as to whether the accused was *psychologically* responsible for his unlawful conduct. This in turn depends on two things, namely whether at the time of his unlawful conduct, the accused was capable of:
   2.1 appreciating the wrongfulness of that conduct (commonly referred to as the insight leg of the enquiry), and

17 Louw R 'Principles of criminal law: Pathological and non-pathological criminal incapacity' in Kaliski S (ed) *Psycholegal Assessment in South Africa* (2006) 40.

18 When considering this defence, we will consider whether it remains a viable defence in South African law.

2.2 acting in accordance with that appreciation (commonly referred to as the self-control leg of the enquiry).

3. The insight leg of the capacity enquiry requires an investigation of the accused's cognitive (intellectual) faculties, while the self-control leg of the enquiry requires an investigation of the accused's conative (volitional) faculties.
4. Where one or both of these faculties are undeveloped, impaired or have disintegrated to such an extent that the accused lacked either insight or self-control, then the accused will have lacked criminal capacity as a whole and cannot be held criminally liable.
5. Four situations have commonly been accepted as having the potential to exclude criminal capacity:
   - 5.1 Mental illness or intellectual disability
   - 5.2 Youth
   - 5.3 Intoxication
   - 5.4 Severe emotional distress arising, inter alia, from provocation
6. Each of these constitutes a possible defence aimed at excluding criminal capacity.

Chapter 15

Pathological incapacity

CHAPTER OBJECTIVES

The objectives of this chapter are to:
- explain and distinguish between the concepts of mental illness and intellectual disability
- briefly explain how a mental illness or intellectual disability may cause an individual to lack criminal capacity
- distinguish between lack of criminal capacity due to mental illness or intellectual disability and:
  - diminished responsibility
  - unfitness to stand trial
- briefly explain the procedure for enquiring into an accused's criminal capacity at a trial
- explain the requirements for the defence of mental illness or intellectual disability as set out in section 78(1) of the Criminal Procedure Act
- explain the consequences of a successful defence of mental illness or intellectual disability
- briefly explain how our courts have dealt with the psychopathic offender.

15.1 Historical background

The defence of criminal incapacity due to mental illness or intellectual disability is also referred to as the defence of pathological criminal incapacity.[1] The defence of mental illness, or insanity as it was previously known, dates back to Roman law. In Roman law, mental illness was regarded as a misfortune and constituted a complete defence.[2] In medieval law, there was no consistent approach to mental illness. In some cases, mentally ill persons were regarded as comparable to children and were punished only if they were capable of distinguishing between right and wrong. In other cases, mental illness was regarded as the result of demonic influences or as a punishment for sin and was neither exculpatory nor mitigatory.[3]

In Roman-Dutch law, the approach appears to have been an objective one - liability is excluded, either partially or wholly, according to the type and the degree of mental abnormality suffered by the accused.[4] English law initially adopted a similar approach, although in later years, courts began to adopt a subjective test, namely whether the accused was able to distinguish between right and wrong. If he could, then he would be punishable despite having a mental illness.[5] In addition, some Roman-Dutch authorities appear to have accepted that a person whose conative functions were impaired by a mental illness should not be held criminally responsible.[6]

The present defence of mental illness in South African law developed from English law. Although English law had long recognised the defence of mental illness, it did not have a

1 Pathological means disease related. See Burchell JM *Principles of Criminal Law* 5 ed (2016) 280. The pathological part of the test for mental illness is sometimes also referred to as the biological aspect of the test. See Snyman CR *Criminal Law* 6 ed (2014) 165.

2 D.48.8.12. See also Kruger A *Mental Health Law in South Africa* (1980) 149–151.

3 Crotty HD 'The history of insanity as a defence to crime in English criminal law' (Jan 1924) 12(2) *California Law Review* 105; Hahlo HR and Kahn E *The South African Legal System and its Background* (1973) 472–473.

4 Moorman J and Van Hasselt JJ *Verhandelinge over de Misdaden en der Selver Straffen* 2 ed (1770) 2.15.

5 Crotty 'The history of insanity' supra 112–113.

6 Van Der Linden J and Morice GT *Koopmans Handboek* 2 ed (1922) 2.1.4; Kruger *Mental Health Law in South Africa* 149–151.

consistent set of rules for dealing with such cases until 1843 when the case of Daniel M'Naghten[7] obliged the English judiciary to formulate one.[8]

M'Naghten

M'Naghten suffered from persecution mania,[9] believing that he was being harassed and persecuted by Catholic spies with the support of the British ruling party. He decided that the only way to protect himself was to assassinate the British prime minister, Sir Robert Peel. By mistake, he shot and killed the prime minister's secretary, Mr Edward Drummond, instead.

Nine experts gave evidence at M'Naghten's trial to the effect that he was insane and unable to distinguish between right and wrong. The jury brought in a verdict of not guilty on the ground of insanity (the so-called 'special verdict') and M'Naghten was committed to a mental institution where he spent the rest of his life.

However, there was public consternation at this outcome because M'Naghten did not fit the popular notion of how an insane person ought to look and behave - he was clean, well dressed, spoke coherently and was apparently able to take care of himself. After a debate arose in Parliament, the House of Lords summoned the judiciary to provide it with an opinion on the law regarding the criminal responsibility of insane persons.

15.1.1 The M'Naghten rules

The principles laid down by the English judiciary in response to the House of Lords came to be known as the *M'Naghten rules*.[10] They were subsequently applied as law in England and Wales, and many other commonwealth countries, including South Africa, followed suit. The rules that are relevant for present purposes can be summarised as follows:

- Every person is presumed to be sane and to have sufficient powers of reason to be held responsible for his crimes until the contrary is proved.
- To establish a defence on the ground of insanity, it must be clearly proved that at the time of committing the act, the accused was labouring under such a defect of reason, from disease of the mind, as not to know the nature and quality of the act he was doing or, if he did know it, he did not know that what he was doing was wrong.[11]

We can see that the M'Naghten rules were concerned only with the state of an accused's *cognitive* functions. Thus, if the accused was able to know the nature and quality of his act, and that it was wrong, but was not capable of controlling his conduct to act in accordance with that knowledge, he would still be found criminally responsible. The M'Naghten rules therefore overlooked the fact that a mental illness may manifest itself not in an impairment of the cognitive functions, but in an impairment of the *conative* functions - in short, in an inability to control one's *behaviour*.

---

7 Sometimes the spelling 'M'Naughten' or 'McNaughten' is used instead.

8 See *M'Naghten*, House of Lords, 10 CL. & F. 200, 8 Eng. Rep. 718 (1843).

9 What we would today call paranoid schizophrenia.

10 See further, Burchell *Principles of Criminal Law* 276–277.

11 Two further rules, dealing with delusions, were added to the above: (1) persons acting under the influence of an insane delusion are punishable if they knew at the time of committing the crime that they were acting contrary to law, and (2) a person under a partial delusion is to be considered as if the facts, with respect to which the delusion exists, were real.

15.1.2 The irresistible impulse rule

South African courts did not take long to recognise and remedy this deficiency. Thus, in *R v Hay*,[12] influenced by American case law as well as by certain pre-*M'Naghten* English cases, De Villiers CJ accepted that in certain cases, mentally ill persons may be able to distinguish between right and wrong, but were nevertheless unable to resist their impulse to commit a criminal act. If so, they were entitled to rely on the defence of insanity.

Subsequently, in *R v Smit*, Innes CJ reformulated the rules for the defence of mental illness as follows:

> **The first rule is this – that every man is presumed to be sane, and able to control his actions, and to be responsible for the consequences of his actions until it is proved that he is not.**
>
> **The second rule is that if a man is proved to have committed an act which in ordinary circumstances would be criminal, but if owing to mental disease he did not know at the time what he was doing was wrong, then he is not criminally liable.**
>
> **[The third rule is] that though a man may have committed an act which, if an ordinary man had done it, would have entailed criminal consequences, yet if the jury are satisfied that by reason of mental disease he could not resist the impulse under which he acted, then he is not criminally liable.**[13]

This last addition to the rules came to be known as the *irresistible impulse rule*.[14] Although the irresistible impulse rule added a much-needed enquiry into an accused's conative faculties, it created its own difficulties, in particular the difficulty of establishing whether the impulse was truly irresistible. It was not sufficient for an accused to prove that he had merely failed to resist the impulse under which he acted; he had to prove that he had been overpowered by the impulse and was thus totally incapable of resisting it. The use of the word 'impulse' also suggested that an accused would escape liability only if his unlawful conduct was the result of a sudden impulse. He would not escape liability if his unlawful conduct was the result of an overwhelming compulsion which might have developed over a period of time, and which the accused might indeed have been able to resist successfully up to that point in time. Ultimately, however, there was no need to resolve these issues because historical events intervened.

15.1.3 The Rumpff Commission

In September 1966, the South African prime minister, Dr HF Verwoerd, was assassinated in the House of Assembly by a parliamentary messenger named Dimitrios Tsafendas. Tsafendas had a history of mental illness, in the form of paranoid schizophrenia, for which he had occasionally been institutionalised. In particular, he claimed to be plagued by a giant tapeworm that spoke to him and told him what to do. As a result of his mental illness, he was found unfit to stand trial,[15] and he was committed to prison as a so-called state president's patient without the benefit of trial.[16] He never had the opportunity, therefore, to raise the defence of mental illness, so we cannot know whether this defence would have succeeded.

---

12 *R v Hay* (1899) 9 CTR 292.

13 *R v Smit* 1906 TS 783 at 785–787.

14 English law eventually adopted the irresistible impulse rule in 1960 in *R v Byrne* [1960] 2 QB 396.

15 The concept of fitness to stand trial (triability) will be discussed in section 15.2.1.

16 Initially, he was detained in Pretoria Central Prison, but in 1989, he was transferred to Zonderwater Prison near Cullinan. He was eventually released in 1994 but had nowhere else to go. He died in prison in 1999.

However, as with the *M'Naghten* case, many people were deeply concerned that a person who outwardly appeared to be quite normal, who was able to secure and retain a position of considerable responsibility, and who was able to use that position to carry out a deliberate, planned assassination, could escape the normal penalties of the law on the basis that he was mentally ill. Because of the public's reaction to the case, the government established a commission of enquiry into the assassination. This commission recommended a further enquiry, which resulted in the establishment of the Commission of Inquiry into the Responsibility of Mentally Deranged Persons and Related Matters under the chairmanship of Judge Rumpff. It is hence now commonly known as the Rumpff Commission.[17]

The Rumpff Commission conducted an extensive investigation into the nature of mental illness and intellectual disability, and their effects on criminal responsibility. In so doing, it considered the evidence of numerous psychologists, psychiatrists and jurists. Among the conclusions that the Commission reached were certain findings about human personality.[18] It defined human personality as a dynamic integration of the cognitive, conative and affective functions (as previously described), with the ego (the conscious conception of self) as the pivot or unifying function. In the normal personality, these functions form an integrated whole. Under certain circumstances, however, one or more of them may break down to a greater or lesser extent.

15.1.3.1 Disintegration of the cognitive functions

When a person suffers from intellectual disability (extremely low IQ), he is likely to have inadequate insight into his behaviour and may act irresponsibly. A person's cognitive functions may also disintegrate due to a mental illness. If so, his thought processes are likely to be disjointed and disorganised; he will not be able to reason in a logical manner, draw appropriate conclusions and form rational judgements; and he may suffer from illusions, delusions, hallucinations and confabulations. Individuals who lack the normal cognitive functions may therefore be unable to appreciate the wrongfulness of their unlawful conduct - they lack the capacity for insight. If so, they are not criminally responsible.

15.1.3.2 Disintegration of the conative functions

When a person's conative functions have disintegrated, he is unable to exercise his willpower to control his behaviour. Normal individuals are capable of setting goals for themselves consciously and deliberately, and of controlling their behaviour accordingly. Because of this, they are also able to refrain from engaging in antisocial behaviour despite the temptation to do so. Individuals whose conative functions have disintegrated severely may, however, be unable to control their behaviour to avoid doing what they know to be wrong - they lack the capacity for self-control. If so, they are not criminally responsible.

15.1.3.3 Disintegration of the affective functions

Where there is a disintegration of the affective functions, a person may be incapable of experiencing appropriate emotional responses. His emotions may be blunted so that he feels very little, or he may not be able to experience complex emotions, such as loyalty, compassion, sympathy, sorrow, humour or seriousness, that would be appropriate in the circumstances. Conversely, he may suffer from abnormally intense emotions, or be completely dominated

---

17 The Commission's report was published in *Government Gazette* RP 69/1967 (1967).

18 The account that follows is based on the Commission's report at 9.10–9.33. For ease of reference, the relevant extract may be found in Burchell JM *Cases and Materials on Criminal Law* 3 ed (2007) 88.

by a particular emotion, which may make it very difficult for him to govern his behaviour. Sometimes, people give in to uncontrolled emotional outbursts and then try to escape liability by claiming that they were acting on an irresistible, uncontrollable impulse. There is, however, a difference between an *uncontrolled* impulse and an *uncontrollable* impulse. An impulse is only *uncontrollable* if a person lacks the normal conative functions. If the conative functions are intact, a person can control his behaviour despite the temptation not to do so. If he simply fails to control his behaviour, he is criminally responsible. In other words, a disintegration of the affective functions *alone* will not result in a lack of criminal capacity. To have this effect, it must be accompanied by a disintegration of the conative and/or cognitive functions.

15.1.3.4 Diminished capacity

There may be cases where a person's cognitive and/or conative functions are impaired although not to the point where he is completely incapable of insight or self-control.[19] This person *still* has criminal capacity, albeit in a reduced or diminished form, and will therefore be liable accordingly. His diminished capacity may, however, reduce his moral blameworthiness and, if this is the case, then it is a factor that may be considered during sentence. In other words, whereas lack of criminal capacity is exculpatory (results in an acquittal), diminished capacity is only mitigatory (results in a more lenient sentence).

15.2 Chapter 13 of the Criminal Procedure Act 51 of 1977

The provisions of Chapter 13 of the Criminal Procedure Act 51 of 1977 (the Act) were enacted in response to the findings and recommendations of the Rumpff Commission. It consists of three sections:

1. Section 77 deals with an accused's fitness to stand trial.
2. Section 78 deals with the defence of mental illness or intellectual disability, as well as with diminished responsibility.
3. Section 79 deals with the procedure for enquiring into an accused's mental state for purposes of both sections 77 and 78.

Although the principal focus of this book is on the substantive law and hence on the provisions of section 78(1) of the Act (the current requirements for the defence of mental illness or intellectual disability in South African law), a brief account of the procedural provisions of the Act will be given for the sake of completeness.[20]

15.2.1 Fitness to stand trial (section 77)

The modern notion of a fair trial requires that the accused be given an opportunity to defend himself in court. To do this, he needs to be able to understand the proceedings to make a proper defence. Even where the accused is represented, he must still be able to follow the proceedings so that he can give his legal representative appropriate instructions as the trial progresses. A person who cannot do this is considered unfit to stand trial.

Although the question of fitness to stand trial, or *triability* as it is sometimes called, is usually raised before a trial commences, it can be raised at any stage during the proceedings

---

19 Psychopaths would be a typical example.

20 For a comprehensive discussion, see Du Toit et al *Commentary on the Criminal Procedure Act* (revision service 59, 2017) Chapter 13. For a less detailed discussion, see Tredoux C et al *Psychology and Law* (2005) 384–410. For practical notes on the reception of medical and expert reports concerning the criminal responsibility of accused persons by criminal courts, see Landman AA and Landman WJ *A Practitioner's Guide to the Mental Health Care Act* (2014) 162–163.

until the time of sentence.[21] The question may be raised not only by the accused, but also by the state or even by a court itself. Section 77(1) of the Act provides that if at any stage in a criminal trial, it appears to a court that the accused has a mental illness or intellectual disability that makes him incapable of understanding the proceedings, or to make a proper defence, the court must order an enquiry into the matter.

The court can only make a finding on triability once it has received a report under section 79 of the Criminal Procedure Act.[22] A satisfactory factual or medical basis must be established for the court to be able to send the accused for observation under section 79.[23] It should be noted that the bar for referral for observation is not very high; judges and magistrates are lay persons in the field of psychiatry and psychology and should therefore rather defer to experts.[24]

Parts of section 77 were declared unconstitutional by the Constitutional Court. In *De Vos NO v Minister of Justice and Constitutional Development*[25] the Constitutional Court made the following order:

> **1. The declaration of invalidity made by the Western Cape Division of the High Court, Cape Town, on 5 September 2014 is not confirmed.**
>
> **2. Section 77(6)(*a*)(i) of the Criminal Procedure Act 51 of 1977 is declared to be inconsistent with the Constitution and invalid to the extent that it provides for:**
> **(*a*) compulsory imprisonment of an adult accused person; and**
> **(*b*) compulsory hospitalisation or imprisonment of children.**
>
> **3. The declaration of invalidity is suspended for a period of 24 months from the date of this judgment in order to allow Parliament to correct the defects in light of this judgment.**
>
> **4. Section 77(6)(*a*)(ii) of the Criminal Procedure Act 51 of 1977 is declared to be inconsistent with the Constitution and invalid. From the date of this order section 77(6)(*a*)(ii) is to be read as follows:**
> **"(ii) where the court finds that the accused has committed an offence other than one contemplated in subparagraph (i) or that he or she has not committed any offence—**
> **(*aa*) be admitted to and detained in an institution stated in the order as if he or she were an involuntary mental health care user contemplated in section 37 of the Mental Health Care Act 17 of 2002;**
> **(*bb*) be released subject to such conditions as the court considers appropriate; or**
> **(*cc*) be released unconditionally."**
>
> **5. The orders in paragraphs 2 and 4 are not retrospective.**

Section 77(6) of the Criminal Procedure Act was amended by the Criminal Procedure Amendment Act 4 of 2017. This was in response to the Constitutional Court's judgment in *De Vos*. One of the important consequences of the legislative reform is that in matters where

21 *S v M* 1989 (3) SA 887 (W); *S v April* 1985 (1) SA 639 (NC).

22 *S v Matjhesa* 1981 (3) SA 854 (O); *S v Pedro* 2015 (1) SACR 42 (WCC) at 68.

23 *S v Chauke* 2016 (1) SACR 408 (SCA) at 10; *In re JY* 2016 (1) SACR 399 (KZP) at 17; *S v Mabena and another* 2007 (1) SACR 482 (SCA) at 16.

24 Landman and Landman *A Practitioner's Guide to the Mental Health Care Act* at 145; Du Toit et al *Commentary on the Criminal Procedure Act* (revision service 59, 2017) 13-9.

25 *De Vos NO and others v Minister of Justice and Constitutional Development and others* 2015 (2) SACR 217 (CC).

the triability of accused persons is in question, a court now has a wide discretion. Most notably, it is no longer compulsory to order that an accused who was found to be unfit to stand trial, and who was to have probably committed the conduct in question, and in respect of offences of serious violence, be detained in a psychiatric hospital or a prison, pending the decision of a judge in chambers in terms of section 47 of the Mental Health Care Act.[26]

Commentators have noted that the amendment of section 77(6) appears to go beyond what the Constitutional Court had in mind with respect to the possibility of detention in prison for purposes of psychiatric observation. The amended section 77(6) excludes the option of committing an accused person to prison, even temporarily.[27] The only available option would be detention in a medical facility. The Constitutional Court in fact left open the possibility of detention in prison for purposes of psychiatric observation and where the patient 'is likely to cause serious harm to himself or others. These instances are permissible as they serve the constitutionally mandated purpose of protecting the public'.[28]

15.2.2 Procedural aspects (section 79)

This section deals with the procedure for enquiring into an accused's mental state, both for establishing his fitness to stand trial and for establishing whether he had criminal capacity at the time of the commission of the alleged offence.[29] A crucial part of this procedure is the compilation of and submission to court of a report by a panel of psychiatrists.[30]

The judgment by the High Court in *S v Pedro*[31] prompted the amendment to section 79(1)(*b*) of the Criminal Procedure Act, 1977.[32] This concerns the composition of the panel of experts that need to compile the report on the accused's mental state. It is now provided that:

> **[W]here the accused is charged with murder or culpable homicide or rape or compelled rape as provided for in sections 3 or 4 of the Criminal Law (Sexual Offences and Related Matters) Amendment Act, 2007, respectively, or another charge involving serious violence, or if the court considers it to be necessary in the public interest, or where the court in any particular case so directs—**
>
> **(i) by the head of the designated health establishment, or by another psychiatrist delegated by the head concerned;**
>
> **(ii) by a psychiatrist appointed by the court;**
>
> **(iii) by a psychiatrist appointed by the court, upon application and on good cause shown by the accused for such appointment; and**
>
> **(iv) by a clinical psychologist where the court so directs.**

Psychiatric reports on the mental state of the accused should be clear and aimed at assisting the court, which ultimately needs to make a finding on the mental condition of the accused. Contradicting or ambiguous opinions will not assist the court.[33] The need for clear and unambiguous psychiatric reports is imperative, given the fact that 'mental illness or intellectual disability' is not defined in the Criminal Procedure Act, thus depriving the court

26 Du Toit et al *Commentary on the Criminal Procedure Act* (revision service 59, 2017) 13-16.

27 Du Toit et al *Commentary on the Criminal Procedure Act* (revision service 59, 2017) 13-17.

28 *De Vos NO* supra at 47.

29 Du Toit et al *Commentary on the Criminal Procedure Act* (revision service 59, 2017) 13-49–13-57.

30 S 79(1)(*b*)(i) – (iii) Criminal Procedure Act, 1977; *S v Ramokoka* 2006 (2) SACR 57 (W); *S v Pedro* 2015 (1) SACR 42 (WCC).

31 *S v Pedro* 2015 (1) SACR 42 (WCC).

32 Criminal Procedure Amendment Act 4 of 2017.

33 Du Toit et al *Commentary on the Criminal Procedure Act* (revision service 59, 2017) 13-53; *S v Chauke* 2016 (1) SACR 408 (SCA) at 14.

of a tool to give meaning to the crucial terms at the foundation of the procedural and substantive enquiries into triability and criminal capacity.

15.2.3 The defence of mental illness or intellectual disability (section 78)

Section 78 of the Criminal Procedure Act[34] is the most important section for present purposes since it deals with the substantive requirements for the defence of mental illness or intellectual disability (section 78(1)). It also deals with diminished responsibility (section 78(7)).

Section 78(1) provides as follows:

> **A person who commits an act or makes an omission which constitutes an offence and who at the time of such commission or omission suffers from a mental illness or intellectual disability which makes him or her incapable—**
> **(*a*) of appreciating the wrongfulness of his or her act or omission; or**
> **(*b*) of acting in accordance with an appreciation of the wrongfulness of his or her act or omission,**
> **shall not be criminally responsible for such act or omission.**[35]

These provisions are discussed in detail below.

15.3 Requirements for the defence

The requirements for the defence of mental illness or intellectual disability in South African law now depend entirely on the provisions of section 78(1) of the Criminal Procedure Act. The M'Naghten and irresistible impulse rules are no longer applied since they have been eclipsed by the provisions of this subsection. From these provisions, one can formulate a three-stage enquiry for the defence of mental illness or intellectual disability:

1. Did the accused commit an unlawful act or omission?
2. If so, was the accused suffering from a mental illness or an intellectual disability at the time of that unlawful act or omission?
3. If so, was that mental illness or intellectual disability of such a nature and degree as to render the accused unable *either*:
   (a) to appreciate the wrongfulness of that unlawful act or omission, *or*
   (b) to act in accordance with that appreciation?

If so, the accused will succeed in his defence and cannot be found guilty. We will now consider the individual elements of the above test in more detail.

---

34 If the accused person is a child, s 78 of the Criminal Procedure Act must be read with s 48(5)(*b*) of the Child Justice Act 75 of 2008. If it is alleged that the accused is 'for any other reason' (that is, not by reason of mental illness or intellectual disability) not criminally responsible, s 78(2) of the Criminal Procedure Act provides that the court *may* direct that the matter be enquired into and reported on in accordance with the provisions of s 79 of the Act. On the importance of the distinction between the two sets of reasons for lack of criminal capacity (mental illness or intellectual disability versus 'any other reason'), the Court in *S v Volkman* 2005 (2) SACR 402 (C) at 8 observed as follows:

> **Clearly, the Legislature made a distinction between allegations of criminal incapacity based on mental illness or mental defect on the one hand, and such incapacity based on 'any other reason' on the other. Where there is an allegation or appearance of mental illness or mental defect, the court is obliged ('the court shall') to direct that the accused be referred for observation in terms of section 79 of the Act. If, however, there is an allegation of lack of criminal responsibility for any reason other than mental illness or mental defect, the court has a discretion whether to refer the accused for observation or not. Non-pathological incapacity falls within the latter category. Entrusting the court with discretion in cases of non-pathological incapacity is not surprising.**

35 S 78(1), as amended by Criminal Procedure Amendment Act 4 of 2017.

15.3.1 The accused must have committed an unlawful act or omission

For the defence of mental illness or intellectual disability to succeed, a court must find that the accused did in fact commit the unlawful conduct according to the definition of the crime with which he has been charged. This means that the accused must have been formally charged with the relevant crime, he must have pleaded to the charge and the court's finding must be based on admissible evidence, proving the unlawful conduct beyond a reasonable doubt.[36] Such a finding, of course, is not the same as a finding of criminal liability since a person cannot be criminally liable if he lacked criminal capacity. However, where a court cannot make a finding that the accused committed the unlawful conduct, he is entitled to an ordinary acquittal and discharge.

15.3.2 The accused must have suffered from a mental illness or intellectual disability

The terms 'mental illness' and 'intellectual disability' are not defined in the Criminal Procedure Act. They must therefore be given their ordinary meanings. The difficulty with this is that they are also somewhat nebulous terms and are thus difficult to define with the level of precision normally considered desirable in criminal matters.[37] Le Roux and Stevens noted as follows:

> **The test for pathological criminal incapacity or insanity does not define the terms "mental illness" or "mental defect" [intellectual disability] nor does it specify the particular mental disorders that constitute "mental illness" or "mental defect" [intellectual disability]. What becomes evident is that the test only identifies the effects which should result as a consequence of a particular "mental illness" or "mental defect" [intellectual disability].[38]**

Where then, is a court to turn for guidance? Below are some tools which a court can use to give meaning to the terms 'mental illness' and 'intellectual disability'.

15.3.2.1 Other legislation

Although the terms 'mental illness' and 'intellectual disability' (previously 'mental defect') are not defined in the Criminal Procedure Act, section 1 of the Mental Health Care Act does provide a definition of mental illness: 'A positive diagnosis of a mental health related illness in terms of accepted diagnostic criteria made by a mental health care practitioner authorised to make such diagnosis'.

Although a criminal court may look to this definition for guidance, it is not, however, binding on a criminal court. Furthermore, we need to bear in mind that the Mental Health Care Act was enacted for very different purposes than the Criminal Procedure Act. Consequently, the above definition is of limited assistance in criminal matters.

15.3.2.2 Expert evidence

The Criminal Procedure Act makes specific provision for mental health experts to play a role in the enquiry into the accused's mental state (section 79). Although a court will rely

---

36 *S v Luphuwana* 2014 (1) SACR 503 (GJ); see also *S v Dewhurst* 2012 (1) SACR 627 (ECP).

37 For an attempt to give meaning to the concepts 'mental illness' and 'mental defect' in s 78 of the Criminal Procedure Act, see *S v Stellmacher* 1983 (2) SA 181 (SWA) 187.

38 Le Roux J and Stevens GP 'Pathological criminal incapacity and the conceptual interface between law and medicine' (2012) 25(1) *SACJ* 44 at 48.

heavily[39] on the evidence of such experts when it comes to matters of abnormal psychology, and may not simply ignore their opinions and conclusions,[40] the court is never bound by the opinion of an expert witness. Ultimately, it is the court itself that must decide what weight to attach to the expert evidence and what conclusions to draw from it. Expert reports are also not always reliable because of vagueness or other defects.[41]

An additional complication is the fact that 'mental illness' and 'intellectual disability' are legal terms, not medical terms. Thus, although mental health experts commonly diagnose and attach labels to abnormal mental conditions for purposes of classification and treatment, their labels will not necessarily correspond to what a court would regard as a mental illness or intellectual disability for purposes of the Act.

A further difficulty with expert evidence is that an expert witness, no matter how well respected and well intentioned, is not trained to evaluate evidence and make findings of fact in quite the same way as a court of law.[42]

15.3.2.3 Judicial precedent

Judicial precedent is of a little more assistance in the matter although our courts have generally been reluctant to make pronouncements on what does and does not constitute a mental illness or intellectual disability. Indeed, in *S v Mahlinza*,[43] the Appellate Division (AD) held that it was not possible or even desirable to lay down any general symptom by which a mental illness or intellectual disability could be recognised, but that each case should be decided on its own merits. In *S v Stellmacher*, however, the court held that a mental illness is 'a pathological disturbance of the accused's mental capacity and not a mere temporary mental confusion which was attributable not to a mental abnormality but rather to external stimuli such as *inter alia* alcohol', drugs or provocation.[44]

A pathological mental disturbance refers to a disease of the mind, in other words, an identifiable mental disorder, and not a mere character defect or the result of poor upbringing. It does not matter, however, whether the illness is of short or long duration, treatable or

---

39 See *S v Mabena and another* 2007 (1) SACR 482 (SCA) at 16: '"Mental illness" and "mental defect" are morbid disorders that are not capable of being diagnosed by a lay court without the guidance of expert psychiatric evidence. An inquiry into the mental state of an accused person that is embarked upon without such guidance is bound to be directionless and futile'.

40 See *S v Mabena* supra; *S v Sikutu* 2012 (2) SACR 324 (ECB); *S v Zondi* 2012 (2) SACR 445 (KZP).

41 *S v Chauke* 2016 (1) SACR 408 (SCA) at 14.

42 This was illustrated in *S v Harris* 1965 (2) SA 340 (A). Harris was an anti-apartheid activist who placed a time-bomb at the Johannesburg railway station, killing a bystander. His defence was that he was suffering from a mental illness, at the time referred to as 'manic ecstasy', and that therefore he lacked criminal capacity. This defence was supported by the evidence of a psychiatrist, a widely recognised authority on mental disease, who had examined Harris on a number of occasions after the event.

The difficulty that the court had with accepting the psychiatrist's diagnosis of Harris' mental illness was that it was based exclusively on information provided by Harris himself after the event. The court held that evidence of mental illness should be approached with the greatest caution, particularly if that evidence derives exclusively from the accused. In such cases, a court has to make an assessment of the accused's credibility. In Harris' case, the court found that he had elaborated on his state of mind each time he recounted his version and that his lapses of memory were conveniently selective. It concluded that he was not being honest about his mental condition. It also alluded to the fact that Harris' mother, her sister and another relative on his father's side had suffered from mental disorders similar to that claimed by Harris, and that he would therefore be familiar with the relevant symptoms. It was therefore likely that he had misled his psychiatrist.

Ultimately, therefore, the court rejected the psychiatrist's evidence that Harris had been suffering from a mental illness at the time of the bombing. Harris was found guilty as charged and sentenced to death.

43 *S v Mahlinza* 1967 1 SA 408 (A).

44 *S v Stellmacher* supra at 187H (translated from the original Afrikaans).

untreatable, or likely to recur or not, although these are all factors that a court can consider in deciding whether the accused's mental condition amounts to a mental illness.[45]

It is also irrelevant whether the illness is organic or psychogenic in origin,[46] provided that the cause is internal to the accused. That means a (temporary) mental condition, resulting from external factors such as a head injury, or delirium as a result of drug or alcohol use, will not qualify as a 'mental illness'. The situation is different with respect to prolonged use of alcohol or drugs which may permanently affect an individual's mental health, thus impacting on responsibility just like any other mental illness.[47]

Even though the accused's mental condition may meet the requirements set out in *Stellmacher*, it does not necessarily mean that he will be found to have been suffering from a mental illness. As we have already seen, certain medical conditions, such as epilepsy and hypoglycaemia, which are both internal and pathological in nature, and which can affect the functioning of the brain causing the individual to lose conscious control of his actions, are not regarded as mental illnesses, but as physical illnesses.[48] Ultimately, therefore, the decision of whether the accused's mental condition amounts to a mental illness in any given case requires a court to make a judgment, in which it is guided as much by considerations of practical convenience and ordinary common sense as by law and medical opinion.[49]

A court's finding as to whether a mental condition amounts to a mental illness in a particular case is a finding of *fact* in each case and, as such, rules of judicial precedent do not apply. Each case must therefore be decided on its own merits and on the evidence placed before that court.

15.3.2.4 The meaning of the term 'mental defect' ('intellectual disability')

The term 'mental defect', now replaced with the term 'intellectual disability',[50] is perhaps somewhat easier to define. In common parlance, it refers to an abnormally low intellectual ability. The Rumpff Commission referred to the measurement of an individual's intelligence quotient (IQ) as a measure of cognitive ability. An intellectually disabled person is a person who has an IQ that is substantially below the norm, far more so than just a below average IQ.

The Rumpff Commission reported that such individuals are capable only of perceiving concrete things and have little or no ability to think in an abstract way. They therefore have inadequate insight into their behaviour and tend to do irresponsible things. They are also incapable of experiencing emotions that require abstract reasoning, such as patriotism or loyalty to an ideal. Their emotional life is thus limited. They experience only a few primary emotions over which they may have inadequate control. It is thus possible that such individuals may lack not only insight, but also self-control.

---

45 Burchell *Principles of Criminal Law* 280.

46 See the passage from the judgment of Lord Devlin in *R v Kemp* (1956) 3 All ER 249, cited with approval by the Appellate Division (AD) in *S v Mahlinza* supra at 418.

47 Slovenko R 'The meaning of mental illness in criminal responsibility' (1984) 5(1) *J Legal Med* 37.

48 See, however, Blackbeard M 'Epilepsy and criminal liability' (1996) 9(2) *SACJ* 191, in which she argues that epilepsy (or at least certain forms of epilepsy) should, by right, be regarded as a mental illness.

49 South Africa is not the only legal system which struggles to find an acceptable and coherent definition of 'mental illness', for purposes of a criminal trial. JH Hardisty pointed out that the term 'mental illness' has no defined meaning in law. Courts therefore rely on psychiatric expert witnesses to assist the court, even though 'mental illness' or 'mental disease' are undefined in psychiatry as well. See Hardisty JH 'Mental illness: A legal fiction' (1973) 48 *Wash L Rev* 735 at 739.

50 Criminal Procedure Amendment Act 4 of 2017.

15.3.3 The mental illness or intellectual disability must have existed at the time of the offence

The mental illness or intellectual disability must have been present and active at the time of the unlawful conduct.[51] It is thus irrelevant, for the present enquiry, whether the accused was mentally ill or intellectually disabled before or after the unlawful conduct. This requirement is linked to the next requirement, namely that the accused must have lacked the capacity for insight or for self-control *in respect of* his unlawful conduct *as a result of* his mental illness or intellectual disability. These causal connections cannot be present if the accused was mentally ill or intellectually disabled at some other time. Furthermore, a mentally ill person can sometimes experience a lucid (sane) interval. If he commits a crime during such an interval, then he will be criminally responsible.[52]

15.3.4 The accused must have lacked criminal capacity as a result of his mental illness or intellectual disability

The fact that the accused was suffering from a mental illness or intellectual disability at the time of the unlawful conduct does not necessarily mean that he lacked criminal capacity. We have already explained that a mental illness or intellectual disability that manifests purely as a disintegration of the accused's *affective* functions will not result in the accused lacking criminal capacity. The same applies to minor or partial impairments of the accused's cognitive or conative functions (diminished capacity).

An accused will only lack criminal capacity if his mental illness or intellectual disability was of such a nature and degree that it *either*:

- caused his *cognitive* functions to disintegrate to the point where he was incapable of appreciating the wrongfulness of his particular unlawful act or omission (lacked insight) *or*
- caused his *conative* functions to disintegrate to the point where he was incapable of acting in accordance with such appreciation (lacked self-control).

---

51 Burchell *Principles of Criminal Law* 279.

52 The problem raised by s 78(1) of the Criminal Procedure Act provision is how to treat an accused who was mentally ill at the time of the commission of the offence, but who has recovered by the time of the trial. This problem arose in *S v McBride* 1979 (4) SA 313 (W).

McBride was charged with murder after shooting and killing his wife, whom he dearly loved. He was diagnosed as having suffered from endogenous depression at the time of the shooting. The expert evidence was that because of his mental condition, he was incapable of exercising any rational control over his actions, that is, he lacked self-control. However, by the time the matter came to trial, McBride had received treatment for his condition and had begun to recover and rebuild his life. It was noted that if he were found not guilty by reason of his mental condition, then, in terms of the (then) provisions of the Act, the court would have no option but to commit him to a mental hospital.

The doctors who testified on McBride's behalf felt that this would be counterproductive and might cause his depression to re-emerge. They therefore asked the court to find, not that he had been mentally ill at the time of the shooting, but that he had suffered from diminished responsibility. This would then result in him being found guilty, but given a more lenient (probably non-custodial) sentence.

The court, therefore, had to consider whether endogenous depression was a mental illness as contemplated in the Act. The court pointed out that it was not bound by even a unanimous decision on the part of the psychiatrists who testified, but that it must make its own findings after considering all the evidence. The court acknowledged that it was not an expert in the field of psychiatry and that it would not lightly reject the opinions of the psychiatrists. In fact, it would do so only if their opinions were based on inadequate knowledge of any relevant facts or if they ignored such relevant facts. The court would also reject the psychiatrists' evidence if they had misunderstood the provisions of the Act and had thus come to a technically incorrect finding.

Ultimately, the court concluded that the description of endogenous depression given by the psychiatrists was one that complied with all the requirements of a mental illness as contemplated in the Act. Since the court was bound to apply the provisions of the Act, it could not make a finding of diminished capacity. The accused was thus found 'not guilty by reason of mental illness'.

In other words, a mental illness or intellectual disability that did not cause the accused to lack either insight or self-control in relation to his unlawful conduct will not serve to exonerate him. To use a rather simplistic example, where an accused suffers from kleptomania (an overwhelming compulsion to steal), this may afford a defence where he is charged with a crime such as shoplifting, but it will obviously not assist him if he is charged with a crime such as murder. By the same token, the accused's lack of insight and/or self-control must have been due to his mental illness or intellectual disability, and not to some other factor such as intoxication or provocation.

15.3.4.1 Capacity to appreciate the wrongfulness of the act (insight)

It is evident from the above that in modern South African law, the insight enquiry is not performed *in abstracto*. It is thus no longer an enquiry as to whether the accused could distinguish between right and wrong in a general or abstract sense, nor is it an enquiry as to whether he could appreciate that it is generally wrong to kill, harm, rape, steal, and so on. The enquiry is whether he was able to appreciate that his *particular* unlawful conduct was wrong at the time and in the context in which it occurred.

Note that the term 'appreciate' in the Criminal Procedure Act is broader than the term 'know' used in the original M'Naghten rules. For a person to appreciate the wrongfulness of his conduct, he must not only have knowledge of the nature of that conduct, but must also be able to evaluate it and understand its implications for himself and others.[53]

The term 'wrongfulness' in the Act is ambiguous – it could mean *legal* wrongfulness or it could mean *moral* wrongfulness. In other words, we could either ask whether the accused was able to appreciate that his conduct was *legally* wrong (unlawful), or we could ask whether he was able to appreciate that his conduct was *morally* wrong. Our courts have not yet been called on to decide this question. There are arguments for and against both interpretations.

The advantage of the legal wrongfulness interpretation is that because criminal law is reasonably precise and settled, it is relatively easy to establish whether the accused's conduct was in fact unlawful. Having done so, all we would then have to ask is whether he was capable of appreciating this fact. This interpretation also dovetails more neatly with the concept of fault as requiring knowledge of unlawfulness (as opposed to knowledge of immorality). Its disadvantage is that it does not allow for a situation in which the accused knew that his conduct was unlawful, but deludedly believed that it was morally right.

To illustrate this point, Burchell cites the pre-M'Naghten case of *Hadfield* who was tried for treason after attempting to assassinate King George III of England.[54] It emerged that Hadfield, a former soldier, had developed paranoid delusions after receiving head injuries in the war. Believing that his death would prompt the second coming of Christ, but fearful of damnation if he committed suicide, he launched the assassination attempt to orchestrate his own execution. If the legal wrongfulness interpretation were applied to Hadfield, he would be considered criminally responsible because his whole plan depended on his deliberate commission of what he knew very well to be a capital crime. However, he was certainly unable to appreciate the true moral nature of his act.[55]

Although this may suggest that the moral wrongfulness interpretation is preferable, the disadvantage of this approach is that morality is often a personal matter and moral

53 Burchell *Principles of Criminal Law* 287–288.

54 See the case of *Hadfield* (1800) 27 Howell's State Trials 1281, referred to in Burchell *Principles of Criminal Law* 287–288.

55 For a more recent example, see the Canadian case of *R v Chaulk* (1991) 1 CRR 1 (SCC) referred to in Burchell *Principles of Criminal Law* 289.

wrongfulness is more difficult to ascertain as an objective fact. For example, many normal people may think that what Tsafendas (see 15.1.3) did was morally defensible. Furthermore, not all crimes involve conduct that is *malum in se* (bad and immoral in itself). Ordinary sane people may therefore be unable to agree on the moral wrongfulness of a particular accused's unlawful conduct. This being the case, it seems illogical to base the test for the accused's criminal responsibility on his inability to appreciate something that even normal persons would have difficulty appreciating. Burchell, however, suggests that the real point of the moral wrongfulness enquiry is whether the accused was capable of appreciating that his conduct was wrong 'according to the ordinary standard adopted by reasonable men'.[56] It is thus not a question of personal morality. He points out further that this is the standard that has been adopted in Canadian law.[57]

Burchell's suggested solution, which we would support, is that wrongfulness probably means a combination of both legal *and* moral wrongfulness. Thus, an accused would be found to lack criminal capacity if he was incapable of appreciating that his conduct was unlawful, *or* if, while capable of appreciating its unlawfulness, he was incapable of appreciating that it was morally wrong according to the ordinary standards of his society.[58]

15.3.4.2 Capacity to act in accordance with the appreciation of wrongfulness (self-control)

Even though a person may have been able to appreciate the wrongfulness of his conduct, it is possible that due to the effect of a mental illness or defect on his conative functions, he was unable to control his behaviour to avoid doing what he knew to be wrong.

We have explained that prior to the present Criminal Procedure Act, the enquiry into the accused's conative capacity was governed by the irresistible impulse rule, but this rule introduced certain difficulties of its own. However, the ambit of section 78(1)(*b*) of the Act is wider than the old irresistible impulse rule and, therefore, caters for situations that were not previously covered by the rule.[59]

As a result, it is no longer necessary to consider whether the accused acted on a sudden impulse or how to ascertain whether the impulse was in fact irresistible. Nor is it necessary to establish that the accused's actions were involuntary in the sense that he was unable to control his bodily movements – this forms part of the *actus reus* enquiry. The present enquiry is simply whether, as a result of his mental illness, the accused had lost the power of exercising rational control over his behaviour so as to restrain himself from engaging in the unlawful conduct.[60] If so, he will have lacked criminal capacity.[61]

---

56 Burchell *Principles of Criminal Law* 288 (referring to *R v Codere* (1916) 12 Cr App Rep 21 at 27).

57 Burchell *Principles of Criminal Law* 289, referring to *R v Chaulk* supra.

58 Burchell *Principles of Criminal Law* 287–288.

59 *S v Kavin* 1978 (2) SA 731 (W). Kavin shot and killed his wife, one of his daughters and his son. He also shot his third child, but did not kill her. At the time he did this, he believed that if they all died together, they would be reunited in heaven, away from their earthly problems.

The psychiatrists who assessed Kavin were of the opinion that he was suffering from a severe reactive depression. This, superimposed on an existing personality disorder, had led to a mental illness and had caused him to act in a dissociative state. Consequently, although Kavin had been able to appreciate the wrongfulness of his conduct, and although he was not acting on an irresistible impulse per se, he had been unable to act in accordance with such appreciation.

The court held that in terms of the Act, the self-control leg of the capacity enquiry is wider than the old irresistible impulse rule. It accordingly accepted the expert's evidence that Kavin had lacked self-control and that this was due to his mental illness. He was accordingly found not guilty by reason of mental illness and was ordered to be detained in a prison or mental hospital.

60 See *S v McBride* supra.

61 See also Burchell *Principles of Criminal Law* 287.

DISCUSSION **The difficult case of amnesia**

Amnesia (partial or total loss of memory) poses difficulties for the courts when dealing with the question of criminal responsibility. Hoctor points out that the clinical (neuropsychological) insights into amnesia have not always translated easily into legal concepts of criminal responsibility.[62] Because of this difficulty, courts seem to be reluctant to accept defences based on amnesia. Part of the scepticism is apparently informed by the generally accepted idea that amnesia is easily faked. Is this a satisfactory situation? Judges, who are, of course, legally trained persons, are indeed not experts in the field of neuropsychology. This just strengthens Hoctor's submission that courts must provide an interpretative framework that will facilitate in the cogent and consistent evaluation of amnesia whenever it is raised as a defence in a criminal trial. In a broader sense, this problem also illustrates the difficult, but unavoidable, interaction between law and science.[63]

15.4 The onus of proof

The onus of proof when the defence of mental illness or intellectual disability is raised is dealt with in sections 78(1A) and (1B) of the Criminal Procedure Act.[64] As with the M'Naghten rules, the Act assumes that everyone is sane until proven otherwise. Accordingly, if either the state or the accused alleges that he is suffering from a mental illness or intellectual disability, then the party making the allegation bears the onus of proving it.[65] However, proof beyond reasonable doubt is not required; only proof on a balance of probabilities.[66]

The position regarding the criminal capacity of children (other than capacity in the context of youthfulness[67]) is also governed by sections 78(1A) and 78(1B) insofar as the child's incapacity is based on mental illness or intellectual disability.[68]

15.5 Verdict and consequence

If a court finds that the accused meets the requirements for the defence of mental illness or intellectual disability, he is not entitled to an ordinary verdict of 'not guilty'. Instead, the court must enter a special verdict, that is, it must find the accused 'not guilty by reason of mental illness or intellectual disability'. Section 78(6)(*b*)(i) and (ii), as amended by Act 4 of 2017, provides for a number of options available to a court after a verdict of not guilty by

62 Kidd M and Hoctor S (eds) *Stella Juris: Celebrating 100 Years of Teaching Law in Pietermaritzburg* (2012) 349.

63 For a helpful introduction, see Berger MA and Solan LM 'The uneasy relationship between science and law: An essay and introduction' (2008) 73(3) *Brook L R* 847–855.

64 Even before the adoption of ss 78(1A) and (1B) of the Criminal Procedure Act, the position in South African law was that the burden of proving lack of criminal responsibility due to mental illness was on the defence, who would normally raise it. See *S v Mahlinza* supra at 419A–B; *S v Steyn* 1963 (1) SA 797 (W) at 799C–H.

65 Although it is difficult to envisage situations where the state may wish to establish that an accused was mentally ill, this may happen, for example where the accused was seeking an ordinary acquittal on the basis of sane automatism. The state could then lead evidence to show that the automatism was actually insane automatism, thus leading to a special verdict and detention of the accused rather than an ordinary acquittal.

66 Du Toit et al *Commentary on the Criminal Procedure Act* (revision service 59, 2017) 13-35.

67 Criminal capacity and youthfulness is governed by ss 7(2) and 11(1) of the Child Justice Act 75 of 2008. S 7(2) provides for a rebuttable presumption that a child between the ages of 10 and 14 lacks criminal responsibility. The burden is on the state to prove the criminal responsibility of the child in question.

68 *S v TS* 2015 (1) SACR 489 (WCC) at 12.

reason of mental illness or intellectual disability. These options include: detention in a psychiatric hospital; temporary detention in a correctional health facility of a prison where a bed is not immediately available in a psychiatric hospital; admission to a designated health establishment; admission to a safe care facility in terms of the Children's Act, 2005; conditional release, and unconditional release.[69]

15.6 Diminished responsibility

In the previous chapter, we explained that diminished responsibility is not exculpatory, but only mitigatory.[70] Section 78(7) of the Criminal Procedure Act makes specific provision for a court to make a finding of diminished responsibility in cases where it finds that the accused had criminal capacity at the time of the crime, but that his criminal capacity was diminished by reason of mental illness or intellectual disability, and also for the court to take such finding into account in relation to the sentence.[71] Section 78(7) reads as follows:

> **If the court finds that the accused at the time of the commission of the act in question was criminally responsible for the act but that his capacity to appreciate the wrongfulness of the act or to act in accordance with an appreciation of the wrongfulness of the act was diminished by reason of mental illness or intellectual disability, the court may take the fact of such diminished responsibility into account when sentencing the accused.**

Originally, the main reason for including this provision in the Act was to cater for the problem of psychopathic offenders so that courts would not be obliged to impose the death penalty for murder in such cases.[72]

15.6.1 Psychopathy

One of the difficulties faced by courts over the years has been the problem of the psychopathic or sociopathic offender.[73] These terms are sometimes used interchangeably, but some mental health practitioners prefer to distinguish between them, regarding psychopathy as the more severe condition.[74]

Sociopaths are characterised by a lack of conscience, selfishness, egocentricity, deceitfulness, callousness, impulsiveness, exaggerated sexuality, excessive boasting, risk taking, inability to resist temptation, inability to love or be loved, aggressiveness and sadism. *Psychopaths* are characterised by glib and superficial charm, a grandiose sense of self-worth, the ability to con and manipulate, a lack of remorse or guilt, shallow emotions, callousness and a lack of empathy, a parasitic lifestyle, poor behavioural controls, promiscuity, fearlessness, early behavioural problems, lack of realistic long-term goals, impulsiveness, irresponsibility, a failure to accept responsibility for their own actions, juvenile delinquency and criminal versatility.[75]

---

69 For more detail, see Du Toit et al *Commentary on the Criminal Procedure Act* (revision service 59, 2017) 13-41-13-42.

70 See, in general, Van der Merwe DP 'Die begrip verminderde toerekeningsvatbaarheid en die implementering daarvan' (1983) 8(2) *Tydskrif vir Regswetenskap* 172; Burchell *Principles of Criminal Law* 304–306; Snyman *Criminal Law* 170–171.

71 See observations by Boruchowitz AJA in *S v Mnisi* 2009 (2) SACR 227 (SCA) at 4.

72 See Chapter 8 of the report of the Rumpff Commission, especially at 8.12 and 8.13.

73 For background, see Van Rooyen JH 'The psychopath in South African criminal and mental health law: Part I' (1976) 9(1) *CILSA* 1; Rumpff Commission Report Chapter 8 at 8.12–8.13.

74 Both of these conditions have much in common with a third condition known as *antisocial personality disorder* but are generally regarded as discrete conditions. For more detail, see Kaliski S (ed) *Psycholegal Assessment in South Africa* (2006) 247.

75 For a brief discussion and comparison of the terms, see 'Psychopaths versus sociopaths: what is the difference?', available at https://theconversation.com/psychopaths-versus-sociopaths-what-is-the-difference-45047.

It has commonly been believed that sociopaths are the product of poor child rearing and socialisation, most notably the absence of an authority figure in early life and the lack of any bonding with societal authority. In contrast, it is now thought that psychopathy cannot be understood in terms of antisocial rearing or development. Some recent studies have suggested that psychopathy may even be linked to abnormalities in the brain that prevent a person from developing the normal aversion to pain and fear of punishment, which is necessary for conditioning to conform to societal norms of behaviour. This is because psychopaths have been shown to have a very low response to situations that would normally produce fear and anxiety in a person.[76]

Both psychopaths and sociopaths can commit horrendous crimes without remorse. Their conduct can be so appalling, and they can be so incorrigible, that it is impossible to avoid the conclusion that they are mentally abnormal, in which case the question arises as to whether they should not perhaps be treated more leniently on that account. The difficulty with this suggestion is that the cognitive and conative functions of both psychopaths and sociopaths are relatively intact. Although their view of the world is probably not quite the same as that of a normal person, they are capable of perceiving reality as it is. They have a normal range of intelligence and they do not suffer from delusions or hallucinations. When they commit crimes, they are usually aware that what they are doing is wrong by societal standards. Their problem is that they simply do not care. Also, although they are undoubtedly impulsive, they are normally capable of controlling their behaviour when they choose to do so. Glanville Williams sums up the dilemma in the following terms:

> **The lawyer's objection to treating psychopathy as an excuse for crime rests chiefly on the difficulty of distinguishing psychopaths from habitual criminals ... Everyone knows that some persons ... [spend] their lives in and out of prison and hitherto they have been regarded merely as exceptionally troublesome or wicked people ... It would certainly be odd if a moderately wicked person were regarded as responsible and subject to punishment while a very wicked person were regarded for that reason as mentally sick and therefore exempt. There might be a ground for distinction if a recognised medical procedure existed for treating psychopathy, but it would be going too far to say that any exists ... But if the purpose of the definition is to distinguish between the wicked and the irresponsible, there is something logically wrong in inferring irresponsibility from acts that would otherwise be taken to be acts of [wrongfulness].[77]**

For these reasons, South African law has persistently declined to recognise sociopathy, or even psychopathy (the more severe condition), as causes of pathological criminal incapacity. Thus, for example, in *S v Mnyanda*,[78] the AD (per Rumpff CJ) held that in the absence of any exceptional symptoms, a complete psychopath knows what is and what is not lawful and has the capacity to exercise his will accordingly. He therefore has criminal capacity, albeit in a reduced or diminished form.

Since diminished capacity cannot result in a special verdict, it is at best only relevant in sentencing.[79] This does not imply that a court will always impose a more lenient sentence

76 See, for example, Sabbatini *The Psychopath's Brain*, available at http://www.cerebromente.org.br/n07/doencas/disease_i.htm.

77 Williams GL *Criminal Law: The General Part* 2 ed (1961) 535–536. Reproduced with permission of The Licensor through PLSclear.

78 *S v Mnyanda* 1976 (2) SA 751 (A).

79 See *S v Mnisi* supra.

in cases where it finds diminished capacity arising from sociopathy or psychopathy. In some cases, the courts have accepted such a personality disorder as a mitigating factor,[80] while in other cases they have not.[81] On the contrary, psychopathy may well provide a reason for a court to impose a heavier sentence or even to declare the accused a dangerous criminal in terms of sections 286A and 286B of the Criminal Procedure Act.[82]

15.6.2 More recent application of section 78(7)

With the abolition of the death penalty, the importance of section 78(7) declined. A court did not need to make a finding of diminished responsibility to impose a more lenient sentence if it thought it appropriate in the circumstances. However, with the introduction of mandatory minimum sentences by the Criminal Law Amendment Act 105 of 1997, section 78(7) has again received prominence. This Act provides a range of minimum sentences that a court must impose when certain crimes are committed under certain circumstances unless there are 'substantial and compelling' reasons not to do so. Clearly, a finding of diminished responsibility in terms of section 78(7) could well constitute such a reason.

S v Engelbrecht

In *S v Engelbrecht*,[83] the accused deliberately killed her abusive husband while he was asleep. It was a premeditated murder. In terms of the Criminal Law Amendment Act, the mandatory minimum sentence for premeditated murder is life imprisonment. The High Court found, however, that the accused's years of abuse at the hands of the deceased had caused her to suffer from a mental state that diminished her criminal capacity in that her power to resist the temptation to kill him on the night in question was greatly depleted. She was found guilty as charged but given a token sentence - detention until the rising of the court.

Having dealt with the defence of mental illness or intellectual disability, we will in the next chapter discuss the second defence that may exclude criminal capacity: youth.

THIS CHAPTER IN ESSENCE

1. The defence of criminal incapacity due to mental illness or Intellectual disability (pathological criminal incapacity) evolved from a combination of the M'Naghten rules and the irresistible impulse rule.
2. The present requirements for this defence are governed by section 78(1) of the Criminal Procedure Act. This section provides that a person who commits an act or makes an omission that constitutes an offence, and who at the time of such commission or omission suffers from a mental illness or intellectual disability that makes him incapable of appreciating the wrongfulness of his act or omission, or of acting in accordance with an appreciation of the wrongfulness of his act or omission, shall not be criminally responsible for such act or omission.

80 See, for example, *S v Lehnberg en 'n ander* 1975 (4) SA 553 (A), where the court held that the first accused's psychopathic tendencies, combined with her youth, should be regarded as extenuating circumstances, but that this was a matter to be approached with great caution. Equally, it found that the second accused's mental immaturity, coupled with the influence of the first accused's stronger personality, also constituted extenuating circumstances. Both accused consequently escaped the death penalty. See also *S v Radebe* 1973 (1) SA 796 (A); *S v J* 1975 (3) SA 146 (O).

81 See, for example, *R v Roberts* 1957 (4) SA 265 (A); *S v Mnyanda* supra; *S v Phillips and another* 1985 (2) SA 727 (N); *S v Eiman* 1989 (2) SA 863 (A).

82 In *S v Bull and another; S v Chavulla and others* 2001 (2) SACR 681 (SCA), the court held that these provisions, although potentially drastic in nature, are not unconstitutional. See further, Terblanche SS *Guide to Sentencing in South Africa* 2 ed (2007) 241-243.

83 *S v Engelbrecht* 2005 (2) SACR 41 (W) and 2005 (2) SACR 163 (W) (on sentence). For further examples, see *S v Mnisi* supra and *S v Mtshali* 2012 (2) SACR 255 (KZD).

3. The relevant enquiry is therefore:
   3.1 whether the accused committed an unlawful act or omission
   3.2 and if so, whether he suffered from a mental illness or intellectual disability at the time of such unlawful act or omission
   3.3 and if so, whether he was deprived by such mental illness or intellectual disability of the ability to:
      (a) appreciate the wrongfulness of his unlawful act or omission, and
      (b) act in accordance with such appreciation.

   If so, the accused will be found to lack criminal capacity.
4. As with the M'Naghten rules, the Criminal Procedure Act assumes that all persons are sane. If, however, either the state or the accused alleges that the accused is suffering from a mental illness or intellectual disability, then the onus lies on the party making the allegation to prove it on a balance of probabilities.
5. If a court finds that the accused was suffering from a mental illness or intellectual disability at the time of committing the crime, and that he consequently lacked criminal capacity, he is not entitled to an ordinary acquittal. Instead, the court must enter a special verdict, that is, it must find the accused 'not guilty by reason of mental illness' or 'intellectual disability' as the case may be.
6. A special verdict has certain consequences for the accused as the court must then direct what is to happen to him. The options are set out in section 78(6) of the Criminal Procedure Act, 1977.

Chapter 16

Youth

CHAPTER OBJECTIVES

The objectives of this chapter are to:
- identify the different categories of youthful offenders in our law, both at common law and in terms of the Child Justice Act 75 of 2008
- explain the presumptions that apply to certain categories of youthful offenders
- explain the test for criminal capacity in the case of youthful offenders
- explain the presumption of coercion.

16.1 Introduction

It is generally recognised that children lack both the intellectual maturity and the self-control necessary to be held criminally or delictually responsible for their wrongdoing.[1] Although legal systems vary in their ideas of the age at which criminal responsibility ought to begin, children are generally not punished to the full extent of the law until they have passed puberty. Indeed, most legal systems traditionally exempt very young children from

1 See, in general, De Villiers DS *Die strafregtelike verantwoordelikheid van kinders* (LLD thesis, University of Pretoria) (1988); Snyman CR *Criminal Law* 6 ed (2014) 173–175; Burchell JM *South African Criminal Law and Procedure Vol I: General Principles of Criminal Law* 4 ed (2011) 263–279.

punishment entirely. South African common law inherited a number of well-defined rules from Roman-Dutch and English law in this regard. These rules have been amended by the provisions of the Child Justice Act 75 of 2008,[2] which came into effect on 1 April 2010.

16.2 The relevant age categories

16.2.1 Children under 10 years of age

At common law, children who had not yet reached the age of seven years were irrebuttably presumed to lack criminal capacity.[3] They were regarded as being both *doli incapax* and *culpae incapax*, that is, incapable of having either *dolus* (criminal intent) or *culpa* (negligence). Because the presumption was irrebuttable, a court could not hear evidence to the contrary and come to its own conclusion regarding the child's criminal capacity. Therefore, to all intents and purposes, children under seven years of age were effectively immune from prosecution. In terms of the Child Justice Act, this age has now been raised to 10 years[4] to accord more closely with international norms and conventions.[5] Children under 10 are now explicitly immune from prosecution.[6]

One of the problems with the common law approach, however, was that it meant that very young child offenders were not only immune from prosecution, but were also effectively placed beyond the reach of the law at an age where they stood to benefit most from corrective intervention. The Act has remedied this deficiency by introducing a number of procedural steps and mechanisms for dealing with offenders in this age category, including referral for counselling and referral to a children's court.[7]

16.2.2 Children between 10 and 14 years of age

At common law, a child over the age of seven but under the age of 14 years was still presumed to lack criminal capacity, but the presumption became rebuttable.[8] It was therefore open to the state to lead evidence to prove that, despite the child's youth, he did in fact have criminal capacity and could thus be held responsible for his crime. Under the Child Justice Act, this

---

2 S 7 of the Child Justice Act 75 of 2008.

3 In English law, this was statutorily raised to eight years in 1933 and to 10 years in 1963 (s 50 of the Children and Young Persons Act, 1933, as amended).

4 Ten years has been the minimum age in English law since 1963 when the Children and Young Persons Act was amended to this effect. By comparison, s 19 of the German Criminal Code provides that persons under the age of 14 cannot be held liable for criminal conduct although they can still be held liable in terms of civil law. See further, Bohlander M *Principles of German Criminal Law* (2009) 22–23. In Belgium, the age of criminal liability is even higher. In terms of art 36.4 of the *Jeugdbeschermingswet* 1965, the age of criminal liability is set at 18 years of age. This has less to do with actual criminal capacity based on age and should be considered as a purely legislative intervention. The practical effect is that persons under the age of 18 years cannot be put on trial in a criminal court in Belgium. Minors are dealt with by specialised juvenile courts and the judges in these courts can impose 'sanctions' with an educational aim and objective only. There are thus no criminal sanctions. In exceptional cases, persons between the ages of 16 and 18 years can be referred to ordinary criminal courts. See Van den Wyngaert C *Strafrecht en Strafprocesrecht* 8 ed (2011) 289–291.

5 For further discussion on the background to the Child Justice Act and considerations affecting the choice of 10 years as the new minimum age for criminal capacity, see Skelton A and Badenhorst C *The Criminal Capacity of Children in South Africa: International Developments and Considerations for a Review* (2011) published by the Child Justice Alliance and available at http://www.childjustice.org.za/publications/criminalcapacity_SA.pdf.

6 S 7(1) of the Child Justice Act states, 'A child who commits an offence while under the age of ten years does not have criminal capacity and cannot be prosecuted for that offence ...'

7 See also Sloth-Nielsen J and Gallinetti J '"Just say sorry?" *Ubuntu*, Africanisation and the child justice system in the Child Justice Act 75 of 2008' (2011) 14(4) *PELJ* 62–90.

8 The ancient Romans considered the age of seven to be 'the age of reason'. It was thus considered that a child of seven or older may well have sufficient powers of reason to know that his conduct was wrong.

rebuttable presumption still applies to children who have reached the age at which they may be prosecuted (10 years), but who have not yet reached the age of 14 years.[9] Thus, the onus remains on the state, if it decides to prosecute a child in this age category, to prove that the child had criminal capacity in accordance with the provisions of the Act. The provisions of the Act that relate to proving criminal capacity in this age category will be discussed below.

The Act also provides, however, that a child in this age category may not be prosecuted merely as a matter of course. The prosecutor must make a formal decision on whether or not to prosecute, taking account of a number of factors, including the nature and seriousness of the offence, the child's age and maturity, and the prospects of being able to prove criminal capacity. Therefore, it is clear that the Act intends such prosecutions to be the exception rather than the rule. As an alternative to prosecution, the Act provides a number of procedural steps and mechanisms aimed at diverting child offenders away from the formal criminal justice system, which involves arrest, trial and punishment, to a less formal and more age-appropriate system of correction.[10]

16.2.3 Children of 14 years of age and older

At common law, once a child had reached the age of 14 years, there were no presumptions to assist him. The age of 14 was chosen because the ancient Romans considered this age to be the end of puberty in boys and hence the beginning of manhood.[11] Accordingly, if a child of 14 or older disputed his criminal capacity, the defence would have to lead sufficient evidence to create a reasonable doubt on the point, or the child would have to rely on one of the other established adult defences excluding criminal capacity. It was also open to the defence simply to place fault in dispute (see below).

The substantive law governing the criminal capacity of children aged 14 years and older has not been changed by the Child Justice Act. However, the Act also envisages diversion for such children as an alternative to prosecution. Diversionary mechanisms are in fact available to young offenders right up until the age of 21 although they will be used more sparingly in the case of persons over the age of 18.

16.3 Review of the minimum age for criminal capacity

Since its enactment, the Child Justice Act has provoked considerable discussion and a fair amount of criticism.[12] Much of this criticism has been aimed at the new age categories. Many child justice experts take the view that while the age of 10 is an improvement on the age of seven as a minimum age for criminal capacity, it is still too low and the age of 12 would have been more in keeping with current medical opinion and international law.[13] Although representations were made to Parliament in this regard while the Act was still in bill form, Parliament chose not to adopt the higher age of 12, fixing the minimum age at 10. However, it did provide, in section 8 of the Act, for the Minister of Justice and Constitutional Development to submit a report to Parliament, not later than five years after the commencement of the Act (by the end of March 2015), to determine whether to raise the

---

9 S 7(2) of the Child Justice Act.

10 For an account of these measures, see Burchell JM *Principles of Criminal Law* 5 ed (2016) 270–271.

11 Girls were generally considered to reach puberty earlier at the age of 12, but the age limit was not lowered for girls for purposes of the presumption of lack of capacity.

12 See Walker S 'The requirements for criminal capacity in section 11(1) of the new Child Justice Act, 2008: A step in the wrong direction?' (2011) 24(1) *SACJ* 33–41.

13 Skelton and Badenhorst *The Criminal Capacity of Children in South Africa* supra; Skelton A 'Proposals for the review of the minimum age of criminal responsibility' (2013) 26(3) *SACJ* 257.

minimum age for criminal capacity. The reason for the five-year delay was to allow for further research into the matter and, in particular, the collection of statistics relating to the prosecution of child offenders in the 10–13 year age category.[14] Although the five-year deadline has expired, no decision has as yet been taken on whether to amend the present minimum age for criminal capacity. The subject is still being debated.

DISCUSSION

Is the age of 10 years for criminal capacity rational and justifiable?

Should the age be 14 years as in German law? Should it return to the common law position? This question involves *constitutional* issues (the rights of children), psychological issues (at what age can children really make moral and legal choices and act on these choices?), and issues of criminal justice and policy in general (how should the criminal justice system deal with children accused of crimes?). It is, in other words, a multifaceted debate and not a simple matter of criminal capacity. If we want to analyse the issue purely from a doctrinal point of view, that is, from a general principles of criminal liability perspective, we should be careful not to confuse the issues: the general and correct inclination to regard children in the criminal justice system as vulnerable and worthy of a special dispensation, as is now the case in terms of the Child Justice Act, is not the same as to ask the question: *at what age can human beings draw moral distinctions and act accordingly*?

16.4 Proof of criminal capacity in children between 10 and 14 years of age

The position of children of 10 years and older, but under the age of 14, is dealt with in section 7(2) of the Act, which reads as follows:

> **A child who is 10 years or older but under the age of 14 years and who commits an offence is presumed to lack criminal capacity, unless the State proves that he or she has criminal capacity in accordance with section 11.**

Section 11(1) in turn provides that:

> **The State must prove beyond reasonable doubt the capacity of a child who is 10 years or older but under the age of 14 years to appreciate the difference between right and wrong at the time of the commission of an alleged offence and to act in accordance with that appreciation.**

16.4.1 The test for insight

We can see that the insight or cognitive leg of the test for criminal capacity in section 11(1) is not simply a restatement of the common law as it existed immediately prior to the Act, but harks back to an older test, which was found to be inadequate. As with the early tests for the defence of mental illness, early tests for criminal capacity in children in English and Roman-Dutch law tended to focus solely on the child's cognitive development, the usual test being whether the child was able to distinguish between right and wrong. Some rather bizarre procedural practices were sometimes adopted to assist in this enquiry. For example,

14 See further, Skelton 'Proposals for the review of the minimum age of criminal responsibility' supra.

in certain parts of Holland under Roman-Dutch law, the child would be offered a choice between a coin and an apple or a loaf of bread. If he chose the food, this was interpreted to mean that he lacked the intellectual sophistication to be able to distinguish between right and wrong. He would therefore be considered to lack criminal capacity. If, however, he chose the coin, this was interpreted to mean that he had developed sufficient powers of discrimination and was hence capable of distinguishing between right and wrong. He would therefore be considered to have criminal capacity.

The right and wrong test was, however, gradually discarded in favour of the more specific test for insight that currently applies in our law, namely whether the accused was able to appreciate the wrongfulness of his particular unlawful conduct.[15] Indeed, in *S v Pietersen*, Kannemeyer J held that '[t]he presumption [of lack of capacity] is not rebutted on mere proof that a child can distinguish between right and wrong ... "... his mind must be malicious in relation to the circumstances under which he committed the act complained of"'.[16] He went on to explain his reasoning as follows:

> **If a 13-year-old, who appears to be of normal intellectual development, pleads guilty to theft from a self-service shop, his statement that he appreciated that what he was doing was wrongful would surely be sufficient to rebut the presumption. The eighth commandment states, after all, a generally accepted norm of behaviour and a deliberate breach of it would, in the circumstances, carry with it an appreciation that the act in question was wrongful. On the other hand, while an eight-year-old may know, in general terms, that it is wrong to steal, he may well not consider taking a peach from his neighbour's garden as being theft or in any way morally reprehensible.**[17]

---

15 See, for example, the minority judgment of Joubert JA in *Weber v Santam Versekeringsmaatskappy Bpk* 1983 (1) SA 381 (A) at 403C. It will be evident that this test was derived from the provisions of s 78(1) of the Criminal Procedure Act 51 of 1977, which deals with the defence of mental illness or intellectual disability. Thus, although s 78(1) was originally enacted solely for the purpose of setting out the requirements for the defence of mental illness or intellectual disability, its provisions have had a wider and more profound influence in that they have since been extrapolated into our general test for criminal capacity.

16 *S v Pietersen and others* 1983 4 SA 904(E) at 907A–C.

17 *S v Pietersen and others* supra at 907A–C. See also *S v Dyk and others* 1969 (1) SA 601 (C) and *S v Ngobese and others* 2002 (1) SACR 562 (W). In *S v Dyk*, the third accused (Andries), a boy of 11, kept watch during a housebreaking committed by the other two accused, one of whom appeared to be his elder sister or aunt. All three were convicted of housebreaking. On review, the High Court decided that although Andries may have appreciated that it was wrong to break into the house, he may not have appreciated at the time that the peripheral role he played in the housebreaking was equally wrong. The High Court was therefore not satisfied that he had had the necessary criminal capacity and set his conviction aside. Note that no distinction was drawn between the fault and the capacity enquiries in this pre-*Chretien* case (see *S v Chretien* 1981 (1) SA 1097 (A)). Even in later cases, we can observe that the courts have an unfortunate tendency to conflate the capacity and fault enquiries. For example, in *S v Ngobese*, three accused were convicted of housebreaking and theft in the magistrates' court. On review, the High Court noticed that the second accused had been only 13 years old at the time of the offence and asked the magistrate to provide reasons for the conviction. The magistrate's response was that the presumption of lack of capacity had been rebutted by the accused's conduct in that he had run away from the scene of the crime when confronted by the complainant, showing that he knew his conduct was wrong. The state, however, had led no positive evidence to prove his criminal capacity. The High Court held that the facts relied on by the magistrate were no indication of the accused's state of mind or criminal capacity at the time of his unlawful conduct. It outlined the factors that a court must consider in assessing the capacity of an accused in this age group: (1) *the actual age of the accused*: the presumption of lack of capacity weakens as the accused's age approaches the age of 14, and (2) *the nature of the crime*: the presumption of lack of capacity weakens where the accused's conduct was *malum in se* (inherently bad and immoral). It held, however, that whatever these factors might indicate, the onus lies with the state to prove that the particular accused appreciated the distinction between right and wrong and knew that his act was wrong within the context of the facts of the particular case. Because the state had not discharged this onus, the second accused's conviction was set aside.

Other cases show that children may emulate behaviour that they have seen in others, but without being able to appreciate that what they are doing is wrong.[18]

It is unlikely that the legislature deliberately intended to amend the common law test for criminal capacity in children aged between 10 and 14 years of age when it passed the Child Justice Act. The reintroduction of the old right and wrong test for insight appears to have been no more than an unfortunate error. However, it is one that does not promote the best interests of the child since it represents an unwarranted lowering of the requirements of proof. It also creates an anomaly in that the test for criminal capacity for children of 14 years of age and older has not been amended by the Act and therefore remains the standard common law enquiry.[19] It is therefore noteworthy that in *S v TS*, the High Court did not apply the literal wording of section 11(1) of the Act,[20] but instead applied the ordinary common-law test for insight, explaining the proper enquiry as follows:[21]

> **The question is not whether the child had the capacity to distinguish between right and wrong in the abstract, and to act in accordance with that appreciation, but whether the child had the capacity to appreciate the wrongfulness of the particular act with which he or she is charged in the circumstances in which it occurred, and to act in accordance with that particular appreciation.**

16.4.2 The test for self-control

Older cases tended to focus almost exclusively on the child's cognitive faculties and capacity for insight. However, the second leg of the criminal capacity enquiry – the test for self-control – is also of great importance in cases involving children, because children are notoriously impulsive as well as being easily influenced. It is therefore important for the state to prove that the child had the necessary maturity to be able to control his impulses and resist temptation.[22] Where a child has committed a criminal act with other, older persons, the state must prove that the child was able to resist their influence.[23]

Where the older person is someone close to the child and someone whom the accused would be expected to obey, there is in fact a presumption that the child was **coerced** into

18 See, for example, *S v F* 1989 (1) SA 460 (ZH). F, a boy of 10, allegedly had sexual intercourse with an eight-year-old girl. He was charged with indecent assault, was convicted and received four cuts. On review, the Zimbabwean High Court saw a probation officer's report that had been obtained for sentencing purposes by the trial court, and which said that the accused was too young to appreciate the wrongfulness of his actions; he was merely mimicking the behaviour of adults. The High Court held that it was common knowledge that young children necessarily internalised the perceived behaviour of those around them and often proceeded to experiment without being aware of the wrongfulness of such behaviour. In so doing, they were not acting criminally. His conviction was accordingly set aside.

19 See further, Walker S 'The requirements for criminal capacity in section 11(1) of the new Child Justice Act' (2011) 24(1) *SACJ* 33.

20 *S v TS* 2015 (1) SACR 489 (WCC). In this case, the accused had been convicted of culpable homicide, following a plea of guilty in the regional magistrates' court, for killing her stepfather when she was 13 years old. According to her, the deceased had assaulted her earlier in the day and, when she went out later, she armed herself with a knife as a precaution in case she met him. She did meet him and he threatened to throw two half-bricks at her and to hit her. She responded by stabbing him in the chest, causing his death. On review, the Western Cape High Court raised a number of concerns regarding her conviction and sentence, in particular whether the court *a quo* had properly satisfied itself concerning her criminal capacity. After considering the magistrate's response to its queries, the court concluded that the accused's criminal capacity had not been properly established and set her conviction and sentence aside. See further, Walker S 'Determining the criminal capacity of children aged 10 to 14 years: A comment in light of *S v TS* 2015 (1) SACR 489 (WCC)' (2015) 28(3) *SACJ* 337.

21 *S v TS* supra at para 15.

22 Snyman CR *Criminal Law* 6 ed (2014) 175.

23 *S v Ngobese* supra at 565 F–H. See also Burchell *Principles of Criminal Law* 273 and older cases cited there.

committing the crime by the older person.[24] The state would therefore be required to rebut this presumption as well as the presumption of incapacity. Where there has been coercion, the child's conduct would not be unlawful, in other words, the appropriate defence would be one of compulsion and the enquiry into criminal capacity would become superfluous. Even where the child is found to have acted without coercion and with the necessary criminal capacity, the influence of an older person, a person in authority, or someone with a more forceful personality would be relevant to the question of sentence:[25]

> **Where a person is subject to a strong and over-riding pressure, either because of youth or sex or status the Courts will sometimes punish less severely. Thus a wife who acts under the influence of her husband may be treated more leniently ... as will also a person who comes under the influence of a forceful personality ...**

16.5 The fault enquiry

Even where the child is found to have had criminal capacity, the state still bears the onus of proving beyond a reasonable doubt that he had the necessary form of fault (*dolus* or *culpa*) for the commission of the crime in question. *Dolus* implies subjective awareness of the unlawfulness of the relevant conduct. It is therefore open to the defence to argue that although the child was able to appreciate the wrongfulness of his conduct, he was not in fact aware of its unlawfulness and/or did not subjectively foresee its possible unlawful consequences, in other words, that he simply lacked *dolus*.

16.6 Estimating the age of an accused

Section 337 of the Criminal Procedure Act provides as follows:

> **If in any criminal proceedings the age of any person is a relevant fact of which no or insufficient evidence is available at the proceedings, the presiding judge or judicial officer may, in addition to the provisions of sections 14 to 16 of the Child Justice Act, 2008, estimate the age of such person by his or her appearance or from any information which may be available, and the age so estimated shall be deemed to be the correct age of such person, unless—**
>
> **(*a*) it is subsequently proved that the said estimate was incorrect; and**
>
> **(*b*) the accused at such proceedings could not lawfully have been convicted of the offence with which he or she was charged if the correct age had been proved.**

In the absence of evidence regarding the age of a person including a child, or where the evidence is insufficient, the court may *estimate* the age of the person. There is no closed list of factors that a court will employ to estimate the age of a person. However, a number of typical factors have emerged. Mere observation of the physical appearance of a person is discouraged. It is submitted by Le Roux-Kemp that where age is significant for the outcome

24 See, for example, *S v Khubeka en andere* 1980 (4) SA 221 (O). A child of 11 was charged with stock theft along with his older brother (aged 22) and cousin, a man of 27. All pleaded guilty in the magistrates' court and, after questioning in terms of s 112 of the Criminal Procedure Act, all three were convicted. On review, the High Court noticed that in response to the questions put to him, the child had said that he knew it was wrong to take cattle, but his brother had threatened him with a hiding if he did not cooperate. The court held at 222H that '[w]here a young child commits a crime like theft, together with a person whom he would be expected to obey, such as an older brother, it can be presumed that he acted as a result of coercion'. The 11-year-old's conviction was accordingly set aside.

25 *S v Lehnberg en 'n ander* 1975 (4) SA 553 (A) at 563B–C, quoting from the judgment of the court *a quo*.

of the trial, a reliance on appearance alone should be discouraged. In such cases, the court should also rely on expert evidence and contextual factors in conjunction with its own observations about the physical appearance of a person.[26]

THIS CHAPTER IN ESSENCE

1. The legal position of child offenders is now regulated by the Child Justice Act.
2. This Act provides that children under 10 years of age are irrebuttably presumed to lack criminal capacity and are thus immune from prosecution. It provides further that children aged 10 years and over but under the age of 14 years are rebuttably presumed to lack criminal capacity.
3. Although the test laid down by the Act for proving the criminal capacity of such a child is somewhat different from the usual common law test, it appears that the courts are still applying the common law test.
4. The law that relates to the criminal capacity of children aged 14 years and older remains unchanged by the Act. Here, there are no presumptions to protect the child and his criminal capacity will be judged as though he were an adult.

26 See Le Roux-Kemp A 'Estimating the age of an accused' in Du Toit et al *Commentary on the Criminal Procedure Act* (1987) (revision service 59, 2017) at 33-15–33-16. See also *S v M* 1967 (1) SA 70 (N).

Chapter 17

Intoxication

CHAPTER OBJECTIVES

The objectives of this chapter are to:
- explain the effect of intoxication on a person's mental faculties
- explain the distinction between voluntary and involuntary intoxication
- explain briefly the historical development of the defence of voluntary intoxication in our common law
- explain the present common law with regard to the defence of voluntary intoxication
- explain the provisions of section 1(1) of the Criminal Law Amendment Act 1 of 1988
- critically discuss the provisions of this Act.

17.1 Introduction

Intoxication may be caused by ingesting drugs, alcohol or other substances with an intoxicating effect, not necessarily deliberately, for example by inadvertently breathing intoxicating paint or petrol fumes.[1] The following symptoms occur when a person becomes intoxicated:[2]

- *Intoxication leads to the impairment of the cognitive functions*: It can reduce a person's ability to think and reason clearly, to form rational judgements, to foresee the consequences or the unlawfulness of his conduct, or even his ability to appreciate that what he is doing is wrong. Severe intoxication may cause a person to lose consciousness altogether or to act in an automatic state.[3]
- *Intoxication may lead to the impairment of the conative functions*: It can reduce a person's ability to withstand temptation or provocation. In cases of more severe intoxication, it

1 See, in general, Burchell JM *Principles of Criminal Law* 5 ed (2016) 307–326; Snyman CR *Criminal Law* 6 ed (2014) 216–230.

2 For the clinical effects of alcohol specifically, see Le Roux A 'Medico-legal aspects regarding drunk driving' (2007) 20(2) *SACJ* 220 at 221–229.

3 See, for example, *S v Stellmacher* 1983 (2) SA 181 (SWA).

can relax a person's inhibitions to the point where he is no longer able to exercise any control over his behaviour.

- *Intoxication commonly also impacts the affective functions*: It can cause changes in mood and either dull or heighten a person's emotions, depending on the nature of the substance and the specific effect that it has on the individual. Where heightened emotions are coupled with loss of inhibitions, it is obvious that a person's propensity for antisocial conduct will increase. However, the same may occur in situations where a person's dulled emotions lead to a lack of empathy with others and/or a lack of concern for the implications and consequences of his conduct.

It stands to reason, therefore, that intoxication may increase a person's propensity for criminal conduct, and it is well known that many crimes are in fact committed under the influence of intoxicating substances.

Added to the above, severe long-term alcohol abuse can lead to permanent brain damage and other characteristic disorders, sometimes resulting in mental illness. In the case of long-term drug abuse, the consequences will depend on the specific effects of the particular drug. However, many long-term drug users undergo temporary or even permanent personality changes, develop personality disorders and may even become mentally ill or defective in the legal meaning of these terms.

17.2 Intoxication and criminal liability

In terms of the implications of intoxication for criminal liability, it is important first to distinguish between the following different situations:

- *Involuntary intoxication*: This occurs when the accused becomes intoxicated through no will or desire of his own,[4] resulting in involuntary conduct and lack of criminal capacity or fault. Such intoxication has always been recognised as a complete defence.
- *Deliberate intoxication*: This occurs when the accused purposefully becomes intoxicated in order to commit a crime that he would otherwise not have had the audacity to commit. In such cases, the *actio libera in causa* rule applies.[5] Such intoxication is no defence.
- *Chronic alcoholism or drug dependency*: This is now regarded as a disease. It is not a defence in itself where a crime has been committed under the influence of an intoxicating substance, but it may, in appropriate circumstances, be accepted as a mitigating factor. It may however lead to a mental illness or intellectual disability (see below).
- *Mental illness or intellectual disability from long-term alcohol or drug abuse*: In cases where long-term alcohol or drug abuse results in a mental illness or intellectual disability that impairs the cognitive or conative functions, it may exclude criminal capacity. In this case, the accused must raise the defence of mental illness or intellectual disability with the resulting implications and consequences.[6]
- *Voluntary intoxication*: Depending on the degree of intoxication and its effect on the accused's mental faculties, this may exclude fault, criminal capacity or voluntariness of conduct. That is, voluntary intoxication may be a complete defence, but then the provisions of the Criminal Law Amendment Act 1 of 1988 must be considered. These provisions are discussed further below.

---

4 For example, inadvertently breathing intoxicating paint or glue fumes, or drinking a drink that has been spiked with alcohol or drugs.

5 For an explanation of the *actio libera in causa* rule, see section 3.3 in Chapter 3.

6 See, for example, *R v Holliday* 1924 AD 250.

17.3 The defence of voluntary intoxication

Voluntary intoxication has not always been recognised as a defence in South African law. In Roman-Dutch law, which was first applied in South Africa, voluntary intoxication was no defence, but only a mitigating factor.[7] English law initially took the same approach as Roman-Dutch law. However, during the early 1900s, it was decided that voluntary intoxication could be a *partial* defence in that it could negate the specific intent required for the commission of certain crimes, such as murder, attempted murder and assault with intent to do grievous bodily harm. The result was that the accused would instead be convicted of a lesser crime, such as culpable homicide or common assault, which did not require specific intent.[8] South Africa followed suit, adopting the English law approach in *Fowlie v R*.[9]

The change in South African law came in 1981 with the case of *S v Chretien*.[10]

S v Chretien

On leaving a party that he had been attending, and somewhat intoxicated, Chretien drove his minibus into a crowd of departing party-goers, killing one and injuring five others. He was charged with one count of murder and five counts of attempted murder. His defence was that he did not intend to kill or even injure anyone - he thought that the people would move out of his way.

The trial court accepted this and acquitted Chretien of murder, convicting him instead of culpable homicide. Mindful of the criticisms levelled against earlier case law, the trial court declined to apply the specific intent rule to the five counts of attempted murder. It acquitted Chretien outright on these charges.

The Attorney-General therefore reserved a question of law for decision by the Appellate Division (AD), namely whether the trial court was correct in acquitting Chretien outright on the five attempted murder charges, or whether he should instead have been convicted of assault in accordance with the specific intent rule. The AD held that Chretien had been rightly acquitted of both murder and common assault because he lacked the necessary intention either to kill or to injure. In the process, it re-examined the defence of voluntary intoxication, in particular the approach applied earlier in *S v Johnson*.[11] It held the following:

- The specific intent rule, as applied in *Johnson*, was 'juridically impure' and did not belong in South African law.[12]
- Voluntary intoxication could therefore be a complete defence in South African law. Depending on the degree of intoxication, it could negate voluntary conduct, criminal capacity or *dolus*.

---

7 See, for example, Matthaeus A *De Criminibus, On Crimes: A Commentary on Books XLVII and XLVIII of the Digest* (1994) 33.

8 The specific intent rule is a rule of English law, which takes the view that certain crimes require the intention to produce a specific consequence or achieve a specific objective, while other crimes require only the intention to conduct oneself in a generally unlawful manner (general intent). Murder and attempted murder are typical examples of crimes that require specific intent (intention to kill), while common assault is regarded as a crime that requires general intent only. South African law does not draw such a distinction. In essence, all South African crimes require specific intent (see further, Chapter 24 on the need for fault to correspond with every element of the *actus reus*).

9 *Fowlie v R* 1906 TS 505. The rule was subsequently applied in *S v Johnson* 1969 (1) SA 201 (A). In this case, the accused, who had been arrested for being drunk in a public place, killed his cellmate by bashing him over the head with a bucket. He was charged with culpable homicide, but sought an outright acquittal on the basis that he was so drunk that he was acting in a state of (toxic) sane automatism at the time. The trial court accepted his version of the facts, but held that, even so, the law precluded it from acquitting him outright. Since culpable homicide was not a specific intent crime, he was convicted as charged. On appeal, the AD confirmed that voluntary intoxication could never be a complete defence and that Johnson had been correctly convicted. This judgment was criticised, however, because it did not accord with principle, in that Johnson had not satisfied any of the essential elements of criminal liability.

10 *S v Chretien* 1979 (4) SA 871 (D); *S v Chretien* 1981 (1) SA 1097 (A).

11 *S v Johnson* supra.

12 *S v Chretien* supra at 1103H–1104A.

Accordingly, the AD confirmed that Chretien had been rightly convicted of culpable homicide because of his *negligence* (not because of the specific intent rule) and that he had been rightly acquitted on the other five counts.[13]

Since *Chretien*, it has been accepted that voluntary intoxication can be a complete defence to any crime:

- In extreme cases, where a person is so intoxicated that he is unconscious of what he is doing ('dead drunk'), he is not criminally liable because an involuntary muscular movement performed in this condition does not constitute unlawful conduct. There is thus no *actus reus*.
- Where a person commits an unlawful act (more than an involuntary muscular movement), but is so intoxicated that he cannot appreciate the wrongfulness of that act, or cannot act in accordance with that appreciation, he is not criminally liable because he lacks criminal capacity.[14]
- Where a person commits an unlawful act with criminal capacity, but is sufficiently intoxicated that he fails to foresee the possible consequences of his conduct (as in *Chretien*) and/or fails to foresee its unlawfulness, he may escape liability on the basis that he lacks *dolus*. However, such a person may be adjudged negligent and would not escape liability if he was charged with a crime that required this form of fault, such as culpable homicide.

It follows logically that where a person is so intoxicated that he lacks criminal capacity, he will also necessarily lack *mens rea* because without criminal capacity, a person cannot form a criminal intention nor can he be negligent. It follows, too, that where a person is so intoxicated that he is totally unconscious of what he is doing, he will not only lack voluntary conduct, but will also necessarily lack criminal capacity and *mens rea* as well.

17.4 Criminal Law Amendment Act 1 of 1988

Although the decision in *Chretien* represented a return to strict legal principle,[15] it did not satisfy the community's attitude towards criminal acts committed under the influence of alcohol or drugs. Therefore, Parliament intervened by passing the Criminal Law Amendment Act 1 of 1988 (the Act).[16] Section 1(1) of the Act creates the following statutory offence:

> **Any person who consumes or uses any substance which impairs his or her faculties to appreciate the wrongfulness of his or her acts, or to act in accordance with that appreciation, while knowing that such substance has that effect, and who while such faculties are thus impaired commits any act prohibited by law under any penalty, but is not criminally liable because his or her faculties were impaired as aforesaid, shall be guilty of an offence and shall be liable on conviction to the penalty which may be imposed in respect of the commission of that act.**

13 There is no crime of negligent injury in our law and thus there was no offence that Chretien could be convicted of in respect of the five persons whom he unintentionally injured, but did not kill.

14 See, for example, *S v Ramdass* 2017 (1) SACR 30 (KZD).

15 The 'pure jurisprudential approach'. See in general comments by the South African Law Commission Project 49. This project led to the adoption of the Criminal Law Amendment Act 1 of 1988. See further, Paizes A 'Intoxication through the looking-glass' (1988) 105(4) *SALJ* 776.

16 See, in general, Burchell *Principles of Criminal Law* 313–319; Snyman *Criminal Law* 224–230. Also see *S v Hutchinson* 1990 (1) SACR 149 (D) for a critical discussion of the elements of the statutory crime in terms of s 1(1) of the Act, and *S v Lange* 1990 (1) SACR 199 (W).

A contravention of section 1(1) is a crime in its own right.[17] Section 1(2) provides that a contravention of section 1(1) is also a competent verdict on any charge where the accused is acquitted of some other crime (we will refer to this as the principal crime) on account of his faculties being impaired as contemplated in section 1(1), provided that the evidence before the court proves such a contravention.

The state, therefore, has a choice. If it believes that the accused is likely to be acquitted of the principal crime on account of his intoxication, it can charge him directly with contravening section 1(1) of the Act. If it is not sure, it can charge the accused with the principal crime, and then seek to rely on section 1(1) as a competent verdict in the event that it is unable to prove the accused's liability for the principal crime.

However, it does not follow that whenever a person is acquitted of an offence on account of his voluntary intoxication, he will automatically be found guilty of contravening section 1(1) of the Act. To secure such a conviction, the state must prove *all the elements* (requirements) of the offence created by section 1(1)[18] and must do so beyond a reasonable doubt.[19] The relevant requirements can be listed as follows:[20]

- The accused must have voluntarily consumed or used an intoxicating substance.
- The accused must have known that it was an intoxicating substance when consuming or using it.[21]
- The accused's faculties of insight and/or self-control must have been impaired by the intoxicating substance *to such an extent that he lacked criminal capacity.*
- The accused must have committed an unlawful act while lacking criminal capacity.
- The accused must be (or must have been) found not criminally liable for the said act *because of his lack of criminal capacity.*

It is important to appreciate that the term 'impaired' as it appears in section 1(1) means *absent* rather than merely diminished since it is only an absence of insight or self-control that will result in a lack of criminal capacity and will thus be exculpatory.[22] It is therefore evident that section 1(1) of the Act can apply only in cases where the accused was sufficiently intoxicated to lack criminal capacity. However, if, *like Chretien himself,* the accused had criminal capacity at the time of the unlawful act, but merely lacked intent then he cannot be convicted of contravening section 1(1) of the Act. He must be acquitted outright.

This leads to the anomalous situation where the state must prove beyond reasonable doubt that the accused *had* criminal capacity to secure a conviction of the principal crime. To secure a conviction of contravening section 1(1) of the Act, the state must prove beyond reasonable doubt that he *lacked* criminal capacity. The state's mere inability to prove the *presence* of criminal capacity does not constitute adequate proof of the *absence* of criminal capacity.[23] It is therefore insufficient for the state only to establish uncertainty as to whether the accused's faculties of insight and self-control were present or absent at the time of the

17 *S v Vika* 2010 (2) SACR 444 (ECG).

18 *S v Mphungatje* 1989 (4) SA 139 (O); *S v Lange* supra.

19 Although the Act makes no specific provision for the onus of proof, it has been held, in keeping with the normal rules of criminal procedure, that the onus is on the state to prove all the elements of the offence and that the applicable standard of proof is proof beyond a reasonable doubt. See *S v September* 1996 (1) SACR 325 (A) at 328A–B; *S v Ramdass* supra at para 33.

20 Adapted from *S v Lange* supra.

21 This does not mean that the accused must have known the exact extent to which the substance would impair his faculties, but merely that it was the type of substance that would have the general effect of impairing a person's faculties of insight and/or self-control. See *S v Ingram* 1999 (2) SACR 127 (W).

22 Diminished capacity is not exculpatory, merely mitigatory.

23 *S v September* supra at 328B–C; *S v Ramdass* supra at para 33

unlawful act. If there is reasonable doubt on this point, then the accused must be acquitted of both the principal crime and also of contravening section 1(1) of the Act.[24]

This problem does not arise in cases where the accused was so intoxicated that he acted involuntarily since he must also, of necessity, have lacked criminal capacity. In this case, the accused would be acquitted of the principal crime, but convicted instead of contravening section 1(1) of the Act. Because of the above anomalies, however, it is evident that the Act does not really achieve the objective for which it was originally enacted, namely to address the type of situation that arose in *Chretien*.[25]

DISCUSSION **Voluntary intoxication as a complete defence?**

Do you think that the AD was right in accepting voluntary intoxication as a complete defence? If not, what approach would you suggest instead and how would you reconcile this approach with accepted legal principle? Is the Criminal Law Amendment Act helpful in this regard?

When the legislature enacted this Act, it had a wide range of options open to it. For example, it could simply have overridden the common law and provided that voluntary intoxication would not constitute a defence to any crime, or it could have provided that it would be a partial defence to certain crimes. It could also have provided that a conviction of contravening section 1(1) would be an automatic consequence of an acquittal due to voluntary intoxication. Do you agree with the way in which the legislature chose to approach the matter? If not, what approach would you advocate instead? As a starting point, consider the options highlighted above.

THIS CHAPTER IN ESSENCE

1. Voluntary intoxication is now recognised as a complete defence in our law.
   1.1 In extreme cases, where a person is so intoxicated that he is unconscious of what he is doing (dead drunk), he is not criminally liable because an involuntary muscular movement performed in this condition does not constitute unlawful conduct. There is thus no *actus reus*.
   1.2 Where a person commits an unlawful act (more than an involuntary muscular movement), but is so intoxicated that he cannot appreciate the wrongfulness of that act, or cannot act in accordance with that appreciation, he is not criminally liable because he lacks criminal capacity.
   1.3 Where a person commits an unlawful act with criminal capacity, but is sufficiently intoxicated that he fails to foresee the possible consequences of his conduct and/or fails to foresee its unlawfulness, he may escape liability on the basis that he lacks *dolus*. Such a person could, however, have *culpa* and would not escape liability if he was charged with a crime that required this form of fault.
2. Where a person is not liable for a crime on account of his voluntary intoxication, he may instead be convicted of contravening section 1(1) of the Criminal Law Amendment Act.
3. The Act will only apply, however, where the state is able to prove beyond reasonable doubt that the accused was so intoxicated that he lacked criminal capacity or acted involuntarily. Where the accused merely lacked fault, or where there is merely doubt as to whether or not he had criminal capacity, the provisions of the Act will not apply and he will escape liability altogether.

24 See *S v Mbele* 1991 (1) SA 307 (W). See also Booysen J's comments on this point in *S v Hutchinson* supra at 154–155.

25 For a more detailed discussion and critique of the Act, see Burchell *Principles of Criminal Law* 313–319; Burchell JM *South African Criminal Law and Procedure Vol I: General Principles of Criminal Law* 4 ed (2011) 322–330. For a comparative perspective, see Burchell *South African Criminal Law and Procedure Vol I* 330–335.

Chapter 18

Non-pathological criminal incapacity

CHAPTER OBJECTIVES

The objectives of this chapter are to:

- explain briefly the historical approach that our courts have taken over the years in cases of provocation
- explain the origins and legal implications of the defence of temporary non-pathological criminal incapacity (TNPCI)
- explain the technical distinction between psychogenic sane automatism and TNPCI, and describe the relationship between the two
- discuss the impact of the SCA's decision in *S v Eadie* on this area of the law
- explain the present approach of our law to the defence of TNPCI/sane automatism.

18.1 The historical approach to provocation

The general approach, not only in South African law but in most legal systems, is that when a person simply loses his temper, this can never justify or be an excuse for killing or harming another person. Normal adults are expected to keep their emotions under control. At the same time, most legal systems agree that where an accused's loss of temper was provoked by the victim's own wrongful conduct, the accused is less morally blameworthy than a person who kills or harms another for no good reason, and hence deserves to be treated more leniently.[1]

The questions that then arise are how much leniency the accused should receive, and how and where such leniency should be built into the criminal justice process. Thus, for instance, in a case where the accused has killed under severe provocation, should he be acquitted outright? Or, should he be acquitted of murder, but convicted of some lesser offence, such as culpable homicide or assault? Or, should he be convicted of murder, but simply given a more lenient sentence?

1 See, for instance, art 411 of the *Strafwetboek* (Belgium) and commentary in Van den Wyngaert C and Vandromme S *Strafrecht en Strafprocesrecht in Hoofdlijnen: Boek 1: Strafrecht* 9 ed (2014) 274–276; s 21 of the German Criminal Code and commentary by Bohlander M *Principles of German Criminal Law* (2009) 135.

Roman and Roman-Dutch law took the latter approach, namely that provocation would never be exculpatory, but could be a mitigating factor. So, for example, where one person killed another under severe provocation, the former would normally escape the death penalty.[2]

English law took a different approach, namely that in cases of murder only, severe provocation on the part of the victim was regarded as a *partial defence* in that it excluded the element of malice aforethought (premeditation) required for murder in English law. The result was that the accused would then be convicted instead of the lesser crime of manslaughter.[3] However, provocation would be accepted as a partial defence only if it amounted to a sufficiently serious wrong done to the accused by the deceased. A wrong done by mere words would generally not suffice, but misconduct such as adultery and assault was generally recognised as sufficient provocation.[4] Note also that, unlike intoxication, the rule in this case applied only on a charge of murder and was not applicable to other crimes, such as assault or malicious injury to property, where these had been occasioned by provocation.

Prior to 1917, South Africa followed Roman-Dutch law, that is, provocation was not regarded as a defence, but merely a mitigating factor. Then in 1917, the Criminal Procedure and Evidence Act 31 of 1917 was passed, making it mandatory for courts to impose the death penalty in all cases where the accused was convicted of murder. Courts were left with no discretion as to sentence, even when they regarded the death penalty as unduly harsh in the circumstances. Accordingly, to avoid injustice in cases where an accused had killed under severe provocation, courts switched to the English law approach in terms of which provocation could constitute a partial defence. For assistance, with interpreting English law, they resorted to the Transkei Penal Code of 1886.[5] Section 141 of the Transkei Penal Code, which dealt with provocation, provided as follows:

> **Homicide which would otherwise be murder may be reduced to culpable homicide if the person who causes death does so in the heat of passion occasioned by sudden provocation.**
>
> **Any wrongful act or insult of such a nature as to be sufficient to deprive an ordinary person of the power of self-control may be sufficient provocation, if the offender acts upon it on the sudden, and before there has been time for his passion to cool.**
>
> **Whether any particular wrongful act or insult, whatever may be its nature, amounts to provocation, and whether the person provoked was actually deprived of the power of self-control by the provocation which he received, shall be questions of fact.**

2 See, in general, Hoctor S 'A peregrination through the law of provocation' in Joubert JJ (ed) *Essays in Honour of CR Snyman* (2008) 110–168; Burchell JM *South African Criminal Law and Procedure Vol I: General Principles of Criminal Law* 4 ed (2011) 338–340; Snyman CR *Criminal Law* 6 ed (2014) 230–235.

3 Ormerod DC *Smith and Hogan's Criminal Law* 13 ed (2011) 519–523.

4 See Ormerod's *Smith and Hogan's Criminal Law* 519–523 and authorities cited therein.

5 As its name suggests, the Transkei Penal Code was enacted for use in the area of the former Transkei. However, it was based almost verbatim on an earlier attempt to codify the English criminal law and, as such, it was regarded as a simple, accurate and easily accessible account of English criminal law. See Snyman *Criminal Law* 8. In *R v Butelezi* 1925 AD 160, the Appellate Division (AD) held that s 141 of the Transkei Penal Code was a correct reflection of South African law on the subject of provocation.

If we analyse the above provisions, it is clear that there were three basic requirements that had to be met for provocation to constitute a partial defence in any given case:

1. The accused actually had to have been deprived of his power of self-control.
2. The deprivation had to have occurred as a result of a wrongful act or insult on the part of the victim.
3. That wrongful act or insult had to have been of such a nature that it would have been sufficient to deprive an ordinary person of the power of self-control.

We can see, therefore, that the requirements contained both subjective and objective (normative) elements, and included an enquiry into the wrongfulness of the victim's conduct. It may thus be regarded as an unusual hybrid defence, based partly on lack of criminal capacity and partly on justification in the sense that the deceased had to have been, to some extent, the author of his own misfortune.

In 1935, the Criminal Procedure and Evidence Act 31 of 1917 was amended by the Criminal Procedure and Evidence Act 46 of 1935 to introduce the concept of extenuating circumstances in murder cases. The rule requiring that the death penalty be imposed for murder was therefore no longer inflexible. After this amendment, support for the English law approach, as encapsulated in section 141 of the Transkei Penal Code, began to wane and courts began to revert to the Roman-Dutch law approach. By 1949, the reversal was virtually complete. Thus, in *R v Thibani*, the Appellate Division (AD) held that provocation was not a defence in itself – not even a partial defence – but merely part of the evidence that a court had to take into account, along with all the other evidence, in determining whether the accused had acted voluntarily and had the necessary intention to kill.[6] Ultimately, in *S v Mokonto* in 1971, the AD confirmed that section 141 of the Transkei Penal Code applied only in the Transkei and was not a reflection of South African law generally.[7] The AD's decisions in *R v Thibani* and *S v Mokonto* effectively put an end to any possibility of provocation being regarded as a defence in its own right, or even as a partial defence. This remains the position today.

18.2 An alternative approach to provocation

Although it is clear that provocation per se will not be regarded as a defence, the AD's decision in *S v Chretien* opened up alternative possibilities.[8] *Chretien* represents a landmark case in South African law,[9] not only for the defence of voluntary intoxication, but also, and more importantly, because it led to criminal capacity being recognised as a third, discrete element of criminal liability, which normally had to be proved by the state beyond reasonable doubt.

As a result of the decision in *Chretien*, the question arose as to whether, apart from youth and voluntary intoxication, other forms of temporary *non-pathological* criminal incapacity would be recognised as defences. In particular, would the law recognise the possibility that severe mental and emotional stress, caused, for example, by extreme anger, fear or jealousy, might temporarily deprive a person of his criminal capacity?

6 *R v Thibani* 1949 (4) SA 720 (A). The relevant passage does not refer to criminal capacity because at that stage, criminal capacity was not regarded as a discrete element of criminal liability. The current version of the enquiry is that formulated in *S v Arnold* 1985 (3) SA 256 (C).

7 *S v Mokonto* 1971 (2) SA 319 (A).

8 *S v Chretien* 1981 (1) SA 1097 (A).

9 See also comments by Hoctor *A peregrination through the law of provocation* 121 fn 2.

In *S v Van Vuuren*,[10] the AD, in a judgment delivered by Diemont AJA, answered the question in the affirmative. It held that, in principle, there is no reason to limit the enquiry into criminal capacity to the case of a person who is too drunk to know what he is doing:

> **I am prepared to accept that an accused person should not be held criminally responsible for an unlawful act where his failure to comprehend what he is doing is attributable not to drink alone, but to a combination of drink and other facts such as provocation and severe mental or emotional stress. In principle there is no reason for limiting the enquiry to the case of the man too drunk to know what he is doing. Other factors which may contribute towards the conclusion that he failed to realise what was happening or to appreciate the unlawfulness of his act must obviously be taken into account in assessing his criminal liability.**[11]

The next development was the decision in *S v Arnold*.[12]

S v Arnold

In this case, the Supreme Court accepted that it is not only youth, mental illness or intellectual disability, and intoxication that can lead to lack of criminal capacity, but other factors as well, such as extreme emotional distress. The psychiatrist who gave expert evidence at Arnold's trial testified that Arnold's consciousness was so 'flooded with emotions' that he may have lost the capacity to control his conduct, that is, he temporarily lacked criminal capacity.[13] The court held, however, that there were three main issues to be decided:

- Did the accused perform an act in the legal sense? In other words, was his conduct voluntary?
- If so, did he have the necessary criminal capacity at the time?
- If so, did he have the necessary intention to commit murder?

The court held further that the state had not proved beyond reasonable doubt that when Arnold shot and killed his wife, he was acting *consciously* and not *subconsciously*. It held further that even if one assumed that he had been acting consciously, the state had failed to prove beyond reasonable doubt that he had had the necessary criminal capacity at the time. He was acquitted outright.[14]

In 1987, the defence of lack of criminal capacity due to severe emotional stress or distress came before the AD for the first time in *S v Campher*.[15]

S v Campher

Mrs Campher was an abused wife who shot and killed her husband. They had been married for about nine months and Mr Campher had abused his wife, emotionally and physically, from the start. For instance, he assaulted her in the presence of her nine-year-old daughter, he belittled her

10 *S v Van Vuuren* 1983 (1) SA 12 (A).

11 *S v Van Vuuren* at 17F–H. Note, however, that the AD rejected the accused's evidence that he was so drunk and had been so severely provoked that he did not know what he was doing when he shot and killed the deceased.

12 *S v Arnold* supra (facts discussed previously in section 3.3).

13 *S v Arnold* supra at 263C.

14 What was not really considered by the court was the fact that Arnold's conduct immediately before and after the event was focused and goal directed. He never explained how he came to reload the gun or why he did not disable it after the first accidental shot was fired. In light of what the courts have held in this regard in later decisions, it seems likely that Arnold's case was wrongly decided on the facts.

15 *S v Campher* 1987 (1) SA 940 (A).

religion, he was highly authoritarian and regarded her children by a previous relationship as an encumbrance. He seems to have been mentally unbalanced.[16]

His hobby was to keep doves; he was obsessed with them. He forced Mrs Campher to clean out their cage with a vacuum cleaner. On the day in question, he made Mrs Campher help him fix the door of the dovecote. He insulted her. She went inside and fetched a loaded gun. He then went into the house and dragged her back outside to the dovecote (with the gun) and made her hold a lock against the door so that he could drill a hole through it. Because she was so tired, she could not hold the lock steady and the hole he drilled was crooked. He ordered her to get down on her knees and pray for the hole to become straight. While she was kneeling down, with Mr Campher standing over her, she shot and killed him with the gun she was holding.

Mrs Campher was tried for murder and raised the defence that she lacked criminal capacity, not because she was unable to appreciate that it was wrong to kill her husband, but because she was unable, at the time, to act in accordance with that appreciation. No psychiatric evidence was led at the trial to support this claim. Mrs Campher's own evidence was that at the time she shot him, she no longer saw her husband as a person, but as a monster whom she wanted to destroy.

The trial court convicted her of murder, saying that despite her emotional stress and the provocation she had received, she had consciously yielded to the impulse to kill her husband. She therefore had the necessary criminal capacity plus intention to kill. However, because of extenuating circumstances, she was not given the death penalty, but sentenced to 10 years imprisonment, half of which was suspended.

She appealed to the AD against her conviction. Three judges heard the appeal and came to different conclusions - both on the law and on the facts:

- *On the law*, two of the judges (Viljoen and Boshoff) held that in principle, severe emotional stress could exclude criminal capacity and thus lead to a complete acquittal, that is, they confirmed what the High Court had said in *Arnold*. One judge (Jacobs) held that lack of criminal capacity was a defence only when it resulted from mental illness or intellectual disability.
- *On the facts*, only one judge (Viljoen) held that Mrs Campher had lacked criminal capacity. Judge Boshoff held that he could not make such a finding because there was no psychiatric evidence to support it. Judge Jacobs held that because Mrs Campher was not suffering from any mental illness or intellectual disability, she therefore had criminal capacity. Accordingly, by a majority of two to one, Mrs Campher's conviction and sentence were confirmed.

The next attempt to raise severe emotional stress as a defence before the AD was in *S v Laubscher*[17] in 1988.

S v Laubscher

Laubscher's defence was that his conduct was the result of a temporary total psychological breakdown or disintegration of his personality. Consequently, his conduct was involuntary and he was therefore not criminally responsible. This defence failed because according to Laubscher's own version of events, his behaviour immediately before, during and immediately after the shooting was goal directed and purposeful, which is not consistent with automatic behaviour.

The court also found that he had powers of discernment (insight) and restraint (self-control), so he did not lack criminal capacity. It found, rather, that he had *diminished responsibility*. He was convicted and his conviction was confirmed by the AD. However, because of his diminished responsibility, he did not receive the death penalty. Instead, he was sentenced to an effective three

16 At times he saw himself as Jesus, at other times as Hitler, and he was terrified of spirits.

17 *S v Laubscher* 1988 (1) SA 163 (A) (facts discussed previously in section 3.3).

years' imprisonment. However, for the first time, the AD accepted unanimously that, *in principle*, an accused's criminal capacity could be excluded by non-pathological factors of a temporary nature, as opposed to a mental illness, thus coining the term 'temporary non-pathological criminal incapacity' (TNPCI).

Note that Laubscher's defence was that his conduct was involuntary and that he was accordingly not criminally accountable, that is, he lacked criminal capacity. There was therefore no attempt on his part to distinguish between the defences of *sane automatism* and the newly coined defence of TNPCI. The AD did not attempt to draw any such distinction either. On the contrary, it appears to have equated the two defences although the two terms are hardly synonymous. Sane automatism is a defence that excludes the element of unlawful conduct (*actus reus*), whereas the TNPCI suggests a defence aimed at excluding the element of criminal capacity.

In 1990, the defence of TNPCI was raised before the AD in *S v Wiid*.[18]

S v Wiid

Mrs Wiid shot and killed her husband after enduring a long period of abuse and emotional distress. Immediately before the shooting, the deceased had assaulted her severely enough to break her nose, some teeth and her glasses. She was also taking prescription drugs at the time, had not eaten at all that day and had consumed a small quantity of alcohol. After the shooting, she appeared confused and disorientated and remembered nothing of the incident – her first act was to ask what she had done. She was tried for murder in the Durban and Coast Local Division of the High Court and raised the defence of TNPCI. The trial court did not regard her as a credible witness and rejected her defence. She was convicted of murder. On appeal, the AD found her version was reasonably possibly true: it referred to the fact that she was confused and disorientated after the event and did not seem to know what she had done. It also referred to the fact that she might well have been suffering from concussion as a result of the earlier assault. It concluded that there was a reasonable doubt as to whether she had acted voluntarily, but that even if she had, there was also room for doubt as to whether she had acted with the requisite criminal capacity. Her appeal therefore succeeded and she was acquitted outright.

Wiid confirmed that the three-stage enquiry, as set out in *S v Arnold*, is the correct approach. It also made it clear that in such a case (unlike the position where the accused raises the defence of pathological criminal incapacity), the state bears the onus of proof at all three stages of the enquiry.

However, as in *Arnold*, what the AD did not do was to make a definite finding as to whether Mrs Wiid's conduct had been involuntary (a case of sane automatism) or whether she had merely lacked criminal capacity. From the evidence on record,[19] it seems more likely to have been the former. Thus, Mrs Wiid's defence was essentially no different from the defence raised in cases such as *R v Dhlamini*, *R v Mkize*, *S v Viljoen* and *S v Stellmacher*.[20] Accordingly, although *Wiid* has generally been regarded as a victory for the defence of TNPCI, this is probably misleading.[21]

18 *S v Wiid* 1990 (1) SACR 561 (A).

19 Apart from Mrs Wiid's emotional distress, there were definite physical factors that accounted for her state of mind, namely the medication she had been taking, lack of food, consumption of alcohol and, most importantly, the possibility of concussion. Our courts have never been reluctant to accept a defence of sane automatism where it is attributable to clearly identified physical factors.

20 See section 3.3 for a discussion of these cases: *R v Dhlamini* 1955 (1) SA 120 (T); *R v Mkize* 1959 (2) SA 260 (N); *S v Viljoen* 1992 (1) SACR 601 (T); and *S v Stellmacher* 1983 (2) SA 181 (SWA).

21 Note that *Wiid* does not represent a victory for the defence of *psychogenic* sane automatism either since there were definite physical factors that played a role in her mental state. These factors undoubtedly weighed as heavily with the court, if not more so, than her emotional distress.

After the apparent success of the defence of TNPCI in *Wiid*, the AD (and subsequently the Supreme Court of Appeal (SCA)) was inundated with cases involving the defence of TNPCI or psychogenic sane automatism, which naturally presented a more attractive option for an accused than the defence of temporary insanity with all its attendant disadvantages. In none of these cases did the defence succeed.[22] Through them, however, the AD was able to develop and refine its approach to the defence. In so doing, the following guidelines were laid down:

- When an accused raises the defence of TNPCI or psychogenic sane automatism, the state bears the onus of proving that he had criminal capacity at the relevant time.
- In discharging this onus, the state is assisted by the natural inference that in the absence of exceptional circumstances, a sane person who engages in conduct that would ordinarily give rise to criminal liability, does so consciously and voluntarily.
- Although the accused does not bear the onus of proof, he must nevertheless place sufficient evidence before the court to cast reasonable doubt as to his criminal capacity.
- The defence will not be lightly accepted, nor will a court simply accept the accused's own word that he lost the capacity for self-control. Therefore, evidence in support of the defence will be carefully scrutinised.
- While expert evidence may assist the court,[23] it is for the court itself to decide the question of the accused's criminal capacity having regard to all the facts and circumstances of the case, including the nature of the accused's actions during the relevant period.
- Incapacity should not be confused with mere loss of temper. True cases of TNPCI or sane automatism are rare, and the same facts that an accused may advance to support his case that he was acting involuntarily, such as severe provocation, could often point, just as easily, towards a deliberate act of retaliation.
- Psychogenic automatism should also not be confused with psychogenic amnesia: the subconscious repression of an unacceptable memory.

However, in none of these cases did the AD specifically consider the relationship, or the distinction if any, between the defences of psychogenic sane automatism and TNPCI. Often, they were simply assumed to be the same thing.

Although the defence of TNPCI or psychogenic sane automatism did not succeed again in the AD, there were two High Court cases (*S v Nursingh* and *S v Moses*) in which the defence did succeed and which, because of the facts of each case, caused great concern in legal circles. These were true cases of alleged TNPCI and not psychogenic sane automatism as the defence did not argue that the accused had acted unconsciously and thus involuntarily. The accused conceded that they had been conscious of their actions and knew that they were wrong, but claimed that they were simply unable to control their behaviour (the second leg of the capacity enquiry).[24]

---

22 See, for example, *S v Kensley* 1995 (1) SACR 646 (A); *S v Cunningham* 1996 (1) SACR 631 (A); *S v Henry* 1999 (1) SACR 13 (SCA); *S v Kok* 2001 (2) SACR 106 (SCA).

23 In cases dealing with abnormal psychology (mental illness), a court is heavily reliant on expert evidence. However, where the defence is TNPCI or psychogenic sane automatism, a court is less reliant on expert evidence because in cases of normal psychology, a court itself is in a position to judge whether an adequate defence has been made out.

24 The first of these cases to be reported was that of *S v Nursingh* 1995 (2) SACR 331 (D). Nursingh, a young medical student, shot and killed his mother and grandparents one evening at their home. He fired off 10 rounds with a 9 mm pistol. All of the shots hit one or other of the deceased.

At his trial for murder, he raised the defence of TNPCI, saying that he had acted in a 'red rage', which the experts who testified on his behalf referred to as an 'emotional storm' at 336F. Evidence was led that he had a history of intolerable conflict with his mother, as well as probable sexual abuse at her hands. He had poor control. Expert evidence was led on his behalf to the effect that, given Nursingh's emotional vulnerability, the events of the evening in question

These controversial High Court cases were followed by the SCA judgment in *S v Eadie*,[25] the most extensive and authoritative case on the subject.[26]

S v Eadie

Eadie was charged with murder after he attacked and clubbed a fellow motorist to death in an apparent case of road rage. Like Nursingh, Eadie adduced expert evidence to support his claim that he had acted in a state of 'altered consciousness', in which he had been aware of his actions, but was incapable of controlling himself.[27] The psychiatrist who testified on his behalf referred to this as a 'dissociative' state.[28]

However, the trial court found that Eadie had acted in a focused and goal-directed manner when he killed the deceased. It also took into account Eadie's attempt, immediately afterwards, to conceal his involvement in the incident. It concluded that Eadie had not lost his capacity for self-control - he had simply lost his temper. Eadie was accordingly convicted of murder.

Eadie appealed to the SCA, arguing that the trial court had confused his defence (TNPCI) with the defence of psychogenic sane automatism. Eadie argued that the trial court had wrongly applied the requirements for the defence of sane automatism, whereas his defence was actually something entirely different. Therefore, for the first time, the SCA was obliged to consider the relationship and distinction, if any, between the two defences.

In so doing, the SCA reviewed the cases dealing with the defences of TNPCI and sane automatism, and concluded that the two defences are one and the same thing.[29] The SCA thus rejected the notion that a person may act voluntarily, that is, with conscious control of his bodily

---

had triggered a state of 'altered consciousness' in which he experienced a separation of the emotion and the intellect at 331G–H. In killing the deceased, he had acted with no more intellect than 'a dog biting in a moment of response to provocation' at 333D.

The state did not lead any expert evidence to gainsay the evidence of the defence experts. The trial court accepted Nursingh's defence and he was acquitted outright.

After *Nursingh*, many leading academics, such as professors Burchell and Milton, expressed concern that a person could accurately shoot and kill three people, yet escape all liability. The question was asked whether Nursingh had suffered any more abuse, or had been under any more stress or provocation than, say, Mrs Campher, who had been convicted.

Nursingh was followed shortly by a case that caused even greater consternation, namely that of *S v Moses* 1996 (1) SACR 701 (C). Moses, aged 24, attacked and killed his gay lover after they had just had unprotected penetrative sex for the first time and the deceased had revealed to Moses that he was HIV-positive. Moses first picked up an ornament in the bedroom and hit the deceased on the head with it, but the ornament broke. He then ran to the lounge and fetched another, heavier ornament and hit the deceased twice on the head. He then ran to the kitchen and fetched a small knife, which he used to stab the deceased. He then went back to the kitchen and returned with a large knife, which he used to cut the deceased's throat and wrists, killing him.

At his trial, Moses testified that he was conscious of what he was doing, but he was so angry that he could not control himself. A clinical psychologist, Dr Yodaiken, and a psychiatrist, Dr Gittleson, testified on his behalf that Moses had a history of poor control (impulsive behaviour) and was susceptible to outbursts of anger. He had come from a dysfunctional family and was sexually abused by his father. When he killed the deceased, he was acting in 'an annihilatory rage', in which he was unable to control his behaviour. Dr Jedaar, a state psychiatrist, testified on behalf of the state that 'a person can never lose control except in a state of sane automatism' at 711B–C.

The court, however, accepted the evidence for the defence and acquitted Moses outright. Despite Moses' tragic circumstances, it is clear from the nature of his fatal assault on the deceased that his actions were focused and goal directed; he had simply lost his temper. The decision in the case was criticised for sending out the message that as long as a person is angry enough, he can commit murder and get away with it.

25 *S v Eadie* 2002 (3) SA 719 (SCA).

26 For commentary and analyses, see Snyman CR 'The tension between legal theory and policy considerations in the general principles of criminal law' in Burchell JM and Erasmus A (eds) *Criminal Justice in a New Society: Essays in Honour of Solly Leeman* (2003) 1; Burchell JM *Principles of Criminal Law* 5 ed (2016) 329–332; Hoctor *A peregrination through the law of provocation* 153–155 and 160.

27 *S v Eadie* supra at 17.

28 *S v Eadie* supra at 17. This psychiatrist was the same Dr Jedaar who had earlier testified in *S v Moses* supra that a person can never lose control except in a state of automatism.

29 *S v Eadie* supra at 57.

movements, but nevertheless be unable to control his behaviour (the second part of the capacity enquiry): 'It must now be clearly understood that an accused can only lack self-control when he is acting in a state of automatism'.[30] With these words, the SCA effectively put an end to TNPCI as a defence in its own right, separate and distinct from that of sane automatism.[31]

18.3 Questions arising from the judgment in *S v Eadie*

Although the judgment in *Eadie* was clearly intended to settle the law on TNPCI once and for all, it has provoked more comment and debate than all its predecessors together. Discussion has revolved chiefly around two issues.

The first issue is the construction to be placed on the dictum: 'It must now be clearly understood that an accused can only lack self-control when he is acting in a state of automatism'.[32] The question arises as to what exactly this statement represents. Is it a statement of fact or a statement of law? It appears to be a simple statement of fact, but if so, it can hardly be necessary for it to be 'clearly understood' since findings of fact do not set a precedent for future cases. It must therefore be assumed that the statement was intended to be a statement of law. Even so, its implications are unclear. It surely cannot have been intended to apply to all cases since it has long been accepted that young children and mentally ill or intellectually disabled persons can be quite capable of controlling their bodily movements, and yet be incapable of controlling their behaviour. This, after all, is a characteristic feature of immature age, as well as certain forms of mental illness. The same could also apply to persons who are so intoxicated that their conative functions have temporarily disintegrated. Therefore, the only logical construction to be placed on the statement is that it must be read in the context of the defence of TNPCI.

In essence, what the SCA appears to be saying is that whatever medical experts may say to the contrary, the law is simply not prepared to accept that a relatively sane and sober adult, who is able to control his bodily movements, is not also capable of controlling his behaviour.[33] This reinforces the earlier dictum that TNPCI and sane automatism are one and the same thing,[34] and puts an end to the possibility of TNPCI being regarded as a defence in its own right.

The second issue is the construction to be placed on the dictum in italics in the following passage:

> **Part of the problem appears to me to be a too-ready acceptance of the accused's *ipse dixit* concerning his state of mind. *It appears to me to be justified to test the accused's evidence about his state of mind, not only against his prior and subsequent conduct but also against the court's experience of human behaviour and social interaction.* Critics may describe this as principle yielding to policy.[35] In my view it is an acceptable method for testing the veracity of an accused's evidence about his state of mind and as a necessary brake to prevent unwarranted extensions of the defence.[36] (Emphasis added)**

30 *S v Eadie* supra at 70.

31 Since, by his own admission, Eadie had not been acting in a state of automatism, his appeal was dismissed and his conviction upheld.

32 *S v Eadie* supra at 70.

33 This is also Snyman's interpretation. He refers to it as the policy approach to provocation, as opposed to the theoretical approach, which is based on pure legal principle. Snyman 'The tension between legal theory and policy considerations in the general principles of criminal law' 15.

34 *S v Eadie* supra at 57.

35 See the corrigenda 2002 (2) *SACR* (September) page xii.

36 *S v Eadie* supra at 64.

The issue here is whether, through this dictum, the SCA has introduced, or intended to introduce, a normative (objective) element into the test for determining loss of self-control in cases that deal with the defence of TNPCI or sane automatism.[37] If so, it would constitute a significant, and possibly objectionable, deviation from established principle since the test for criminal capacity in our law has always been a wholly subjective enquiry.

A less controversial and more likely interpretation is that the SCA was simply laying down guidelines for courts to use when evaluating the evidence in such cases, holding that to assess the accused's credibility, a court may take judicial cognisance of normal human behaviour and social interaction. It is a perfectly common and unremarkable practice for courts to lay down evidential guidelines of this nature. The latter would no doubt be the obvious interpretation had it not been for the addition of the sentence '[c]ritics may describe this as principle yielding to policy'. If the court was simply stating a rule of evidence, there would be no question of principle yielding to policy. Rules of evidence do not alter the principles of substantive law. Even so, the observation is unlikely to have resulted in much serious interest, had it not been for the fact that the English law defence of provocation, as encapsulated in section 141 of the Transkei Penal Code, also contained objective elements (see above).

Academic commentators have therefore been on the alert for indications that courts may seek to introduce a similarly objective element into the present defence of TNPCI or psychogenic sane automatism. Thus, for example, Louw interpreted Navsa JA's dictum as explicitly introducing an objective element into the enquiry, harking back to the time when the English law defence of provocation formed part of our law.[38] Snyman considers the passage from the judgment nonsensical,[39] but argues in any event for the adoption of an objective (normative) approach to loss of control in such cases (his so-called policy approach).[40]

The correct interpretation of the passage is probably the most likely one, namely that the SCA was simply stating a rule of evidence, indicating that in such cases, courts are not confined to the evidence placed before them, but are permitted to take judicial cognisance of normal human nature and behaviour. The addition of the confusing comment '[c]ritics may describe this as principle yielding to policy' is unfortunate, but probably meaningless. Therefore, in short, there is no need to construe this passage as an attempt to introduce a normative element into the enquiry. It does not, however, detract from the significance of the previous dictum, which, as Snyman correctly points out, does indeed indicate the adoption of a policy-orientated and thus normative approach.

DISCUSSION

No provocation defence in South Africa. What about domestic abuse and reactions to it?

As we know, provocation is not a defence in South Africa. Arguing for the abolishment of provocation as a defence in English law, Jeremy Horder noted that it is one thing to 'feel great anger at great provocation; but quite another (ethical) thing to experience and express that anger in retaliatory form'.[41] But sometimes provocation and abuse can be persistent, making life a living hell for the victim.

37 See Snyman 'The tension between legal theory and policy considerations in the general principles of criminal law'; Snyman *Criminal Law* 161–163.

38 Louw in Kaliski SZ (ed) *Psycholegal Assessment in South Africa* (2006).

39 Snyman *Criminal Law* 161–163.

40 Snyman 'The tension between legal theory and policy considerations in the general principles of criminal law' 15.

41 Horder J *Provocation and Responsibility* (1992) 197. Reprinted by permission of Oxford University Press. (URL http://www.oup.com<http://www.oup.com)

If someone's life or safety is threatened, the appropriate defence would normally be private defence (self-defence). Domestic abuse often does not reach the threshold that would make reliance on private defence appropriate, but it is also clear that such instances of persistent abuse, where the victims are most often vulnerable women and children, call for careful consideration of potential defences where the victims respond with violence.[42] Burchell suggests that it is an open question whether 'the criminal law will treat cases of domestic abuse resulting in severe emotional stress in the same way as *Eadie*-type provocation'. He submits that 'there are strong reasons to distinguish domestic abuse cases from provocation cases' and, furthermore, that 'the effects of the *Eadie* judgment should not be interpreted as extending beyond a narrow conception of provocation'.[43]

Since provocation is clearly not available as a defence in South African criminal law, and since there is a great need to respond to the real problem of domestic abuse in an ethical and appropriate way, the correct approach is not to resurrect the provocation defence for this purpose, but rather to consider the four legal responses to domestic abuse as identified by Burchell:[44]

- *First*, the phenomenon of domestic abuse, and the so-called battered woman/person syndrome, must be acknowledged and evidence in this regard should be admissible in criminal cases.[45]
- *Second*, as already pointed out, in certain cases of domestic abuse, self-defence against the abuse will be the appropriate defence. Burchell correctly points out that an expanded notion of self-defence, thus providing for inevitable abuse and not just imminent attacks, would need to be considered.
- *Third*, the evidence in certain cases of domestic abuse could be viewed as support for a defence of lack of capacity or, in appropriate cases, putative private defence. As Burchell points out, both lack of capacity and putative private defence have strong subjective bases, thus catering for the particular circumstances of each case.
- *Fourth*, a statutory remedy in the form of protection orders issued under the Domestic Violence Act 116 of 1998 could be of some assistance.

THIS CHAPTER IN ESSENCE

1. Provocation is not a defence or even a partial defence in South African law, but merely a factor that a court must take into account, along with all the other evidence, in determining whether the accused acted voluntarily, and had the necessary criminal capacity and fault for the crime concerned. In most cases, it will merely be a mitigating factor to be taken into account on sentence.
2. However, it may happen that a person who has been subjected to emotional abuse, humiliation and/or provocation over a prolonged period of time, may experience a temporary mental malfunction, in which he loses the ability to control his conduct according to his conscious will. If so, he could raise the defence of psychogenic sane automatism or TNPCI. Despite the fact that these defences appear to be aimed at excluding different elements of criminal liability, they are regarded as synonymous.

42 For statistics and analysis, see Vetten L 'Domestic violence in South Africa' Institute for Security Studies *Policy Brief* 71 (November 2014).

43 Burchell *Principles of Criminal Law* 332.

44 Burchell *Principles of Criminal Law* 333–337.

45 See, for instance, the evidence admitted in *S v Ferreira and others* 2004 (2) SACR 454 (SCA).

3. Pursuant to *Eadie*, however, it is clear that it will not avail an accused to argue that he acted voluntarily (he was able to control his bodily movements), but was merely unable to control his behaviour (he lacked criminal capacity).[46] This will not be accepted by courts. Therefore, for an accused to escape liability, he would have to present sufficient evidence to show that he acted involuntarily. It follows, however, that where a person acts in a state of automatism, his conscious mind is not functioning at all and criminal capacity would therefore also be excluded.
4. Where an accused raises this defence, the onus remains on the state to disprove it. However, the state is assisted by the natural inference that in the absence of exceptional circumstances, a sane person who engages in conduct that would ordinarily give rise to criminal liability, does so both consciously and voluntarily. Although the accused does not bear the onus of proof, he nevertheless attracts a fairly heavy evidentiary burden.
5. Furthermore, a court will not merely accept the accused's own word that he was unable to control himself. A court will consider all the events leading up to, during and after the event to see whether they are consistent with the accused's claim that he was acting unconsciously and thus involuntarily. In particular, a court will be careful not to mistake mere loss of temper for TNPCI or sane automatism.
6. Where the defence is one of mental illness or intellectual disability, that is, in cases dealing with abnormal psychology, a court will rely heavily on expert psychiatric evidence. However, where the defence is TNPCI or psychogenic sane automatism, a court is less reliant on expert evidence because in cases of normal psychology, a court itself is in a position to judge whether an adequate defence has been made.
7. In so doing, a court will test the evidence of the accused and his experts against its own experience of normal adult behaviour and social interaction. Whether this is simply a rule of evidence, or whether it implies that a normative (objective) element to the enquiry exists, remains a matter of conjecture.

46 Lack of criminal capacity would also naturally exclude *dolus* since without criminal capacity, a person is unable to form a criminal intent.

Chapter 19

Intention

CHAPTER OBJECTIVES

The objectives of this chapter are to:

- introduce the concept of fault (*mens rea*)
- identify the two principal forms of fault in our law
- explain the concept of *dolus*
- distinguish between *dolus* and motive, and *dolus* and premeditation
- identify and define the three different forms of *dolus*
- explain and apply the requirements for *dolus eventualis*
- explain and illustrate the process of inferential reasoning that is commonly used to establish *dolus eventualis*.

19.1 The concept of fault (*mens rea*)

We have dealt with the first two elements of criminal liability: unlawful conduct and criminal capacity. We now deal with the final element of liability: fault.[1]

The idea that criminal liability rests not only on the offender's outward conduct, but also on his mental guilt was an established principle of Roman law by the second century AD. Mental guilt is also called the wicked or guilty mind, or *mens rea*, to use the established, but imperfect, legal term.[2] Roman law recognised and distinguished between two forms of *mens rea*: *dolus* and *culpa*.

The concept of *mens rea* was unknown in early Germanic law, which based liability purely on the accused's conduct. Although the offender's state of mind was not entirely irrelevant, it was only taken into account to the extent that it was translated into overt conduct. Thus, for example, murder was defined as the killing of a person *followed by concealment of the corpse*, while theft required a *secret* carrying away of the goods.[3] The clandestine nature of the acts in each case was significant since this was regarded as ruling out the possibility that the offender had acted from an innocent motive. There was, however, never an enquiry into the offender's actual intentions – the enquiry was concerned only with outward appearances.[4]

Accordingly, when Germanic law replaced Roman law as the preferred system of law throughout Western Europe, the concept of *mens rea* was largely forgotten. It was only reintroduced during the Middle Ages as a result of the influence of Christian doctrine concerning the nature of sin.[5] From these teachings, the idea developed that punishment should be imposed only for acts that were committed with *mens rea* – an idea that gained currency in both English and Continental legal systems.

In 1797, the prominent English jurist, Edward Coke, coined the Latin maxim *actus non facit reum, nisi mens sit rea*,[6] meaning 'an unlawful act does not make a person guilty unless the mind is also guilty'. Alternatively, as it is often more succinctly expressed, 'there is no criminal liability without fault'.

By the 19th century, English and Continental jurists had adopted the view, derived from Roman law, that fault could take one of two possible forms: *intentional wrongdoing*, which corresponded with the Roman law concept of *dolus*, or *negligence*, which corresponded with the Roman law concept of *culpa*.

The general rule was that because of the gravity of the criminal sanction, *dolus* was a prerequisite for criminal liability. *Culpa* would suffice for civil liability.[7] Even so, because of the obvious difficulties associated with having to establish and prove the accused's state of mind at the time that he conducted himself unlawfully, English law developed a number

1 See, in general, Burchell JM *South African Criminal Law and Procedure Vol I: General Principles of Criminal Law* 4 ed (2011) 353–359.

2 The terms 'fault' and '*mens rea*' are often used interchangeably in literature and in the law reports. Some authors prefer the term 'fault', for example Burchell *South African Criminal Law and Procedure Vol I* 353–356, while others avoid using the term '*mens rea*' in favour of the term 'culpability' – see Snyman CR *Criminal Law* 6 ed (2014) 146.

3 Von Bar CL et al *A History of Continental Criminal Law* (1916) 70.

4 Von Bar *A History of Continental Criminal Law* 70.

5 See section 14.1.

6 Justinian I and Thomas JAC *The Institutes of Justinian: Text Translation and Commentary Part II* (1797 edition) Chapter 1 folio 10.

7 The notable exception, of course, is the crime of culpable homicide. The negligent killing of a person is considered sufficiently serious in itself to warrant recourse to the criminal sanction. See further, Chapter 27.

of rules and presumptions to assist the Crown in discharging its onus of proof.[8] For a long time, there was a presumption that every person intends the natural and probable consequences of his conduct even if those consequences were not actually intended or foreseen.[9] There was also a rule that where a person intentionally embarks on a course of unlawful conduct, he will be at fault, and thus liable, for *all* the consequences resulting from that course of conduct, including those consequences that were not actually intended or foreseen, or even reasonably foreseeable.[10] Another presumption was that everyone knows the law, so a person could not escape liability on the basis of his actual ignorance or mistake of law, hence the maxim, *ignorantia juris neminem excusat* (ignorance of the law is no excuse).[11]

These rules and presumptions found their way into South African law and applied for a number of years. However, during the 1940s and 1950s, there began a determined move towards the subjectivisation of *dolus*, that is, towards basing guilt on the actual state of mind of the accused at the time that he conducted himself unlawfully. In the process, the various presumptions that detracted from this approach were steadily eradicated, although they have not always disappeared without leaving a shadow.

In principle, our law now takes the view that as a general rule, fault is required for every crime. In addition, the onus lies with the state to prove that the accused possessed the necessary form of fault in respect of each and every element of that particular crime.[12]

19.2 Forms of fault

As in Roman law, fault in South African law may take two principal forms: intention (*dolus*) and negligence (*culpa*). In accordance with the rule that *dolus* is the norm in criminal matters, all common law crimes require fault in this form. The exceptions are culpable homicide and contempt of court when committed by a newspaper editor publishing matter that is *sub judice*.[13] In both these cases, *culpa* will suffice.

In the case of statutory offences, the form of fault required will depend on the intention of the legislature when it created the offence in question. Indeed, there is a presumption of statutory interpretation that the legislature intended fault (*dolus* or *culpa*) as an element or requirement of criminal liability in terms of the relevant statute.[14] In addition, the legislature, if it sees fit, can impose strict or no-fault liability.[15]

We now turn to a detailed consideration of the two principal forms of fault in our law: *dolus* and *culpa*. We will begin with *dolus*.

8 A presumption is a legal fiction, that is, a certain fact deemed to be true even though it may not actually be true. Note that these presumptions did not apply in Roman and Roman-Dutch law, which took a subjective view of *dolus*.

9 See, for example, *R v Jolly and others* 1923 AD 176. This presumption was challenged in *R v Valachia and another* 1945 AD 826 at 831, but even so, persisted for a few years after.

10 This was known as the *versari in re illicita* rule. It will be discussed in more detail in section 22.2.2.

11 This presumption endured until 1977 when the Appellate Division (AD) held in *S v De Blom* 1977 (3) SA 513 (A) that it no longer applied.

12 See the opinion by O'Regan J in *S v Coetzee and others* 1997 (3) SA 527 (CC) at 176. For a discussion of the case, see Kemp GP 'Die grondwetlikheid van statutêre vermoedens' (1998) 9(1) *SLR* 106–114.

13 See *S v Harber and another* 1988 (3) SA 396 (A); Snyman *Criminal Law* 326–327.

14 Burchell *South African Criminal Law and Procedure Vol I* 353, 404–406 and 448.

15 We will discuss fault in statutory offences in Chapter 22.

19.3 *Dolus* (intent)

19.3.1 The concept of *dolus*

It is important to appreciate from the outset that although we commonly use the English term 'intention' (or more accurately, *criminal* intention) as a convenient substitute for the Latin term *dolus*, it is not an exact translation. Firstly, 'intention' in the legal sense does not mean that the accused must have actually meant, wanted or aimed to commit the crime in question. An accused's criminal intention would also encompass his conscious acceptance of such risks of unlawful conduct as he foresaw occurring while he was pursuing some other aim or object, whether lawful or unlawful. Secondly, the term *dolus* denotes conscious wrongdoing. It therefore implies not merely the intention to perform the unlawful conduct comprising the *actus reus*, but also to do so while knowing that such conduct is or may be a crime.[16] A person who is completely unaware of the unlawfulness of his conduct cannot, therefore, be said to have *dolus*.[17]

It is also important to distinguish between *dolus* and motive on the one hand, and between *dolus* and premeditation on the other. *Motive* means the underlying reason for the accused's unlawful conduct. It must not be confused with the intention to conduct oneself unlawfully. Thus, for example, in *S v Hartmann*, the accused's *motive* was to end his father's suffering.[18] His *intention*, however, was to kill him unlawfully. He was therefore guilty of murder. This is not to say that motive is never relevant in criminal proceedings. The motive with which a particular accused acted may affect his *moral blameworthiness* and may thus act as a mitigating or aggravating factor in relation to the sentence. Furthermore, the state can rely on evidence that a particular accused had a particular motive to commit the crime in question[19] to assist it to build up a circumstantial case against the accused. Some statutory crimes, for instance the crime of terrorism, require the state to prove that a particular act was committed not only with the required *mens rea*, but also for a particular purpose, for instance the advancement of an individual or collective political, religious, ideological or philosophical motive, objective, cause or undertaking.[20]

Premeditation means the decision *in advance* to commit a particular crime. *Dolus* can be formed at the instant of committing the crime and does not imply or necessitate any degree of forethought or planning on the part of the accused. However, as with motive, premeditation (or lack thereof) will generally affect the accused's *moral blameworthiness* and may thus act as a mitigating or aggravating factor in relation to the sentence. Thus, for example, the Criminal Law Amendment Act 105 of 1997 provides for a mandatory sentence of life imprisonment in cases of premeditated murder.[21]

---

16 For a discussion of so-called 'colourless intention' (intention in the ordinary sense of the word) and *dolus* or 'coloured intention' (intention in the ordinary sense in addition to knowledge of unlawfulness and knowledge of the elements of the crime), see Snyman *Criminal Law* 176–177.

17 In *S v Ntuli* 1975 (1) SA 429 (A) at 436, the AD defined *dolus* as the intention to conduct an unlawful act. See also *S v Dougherty* 2003 (2) SACR 36 (W) for a discussion on the meaning of *dolus*.

18 *S v Hartmann* 1975 (3) SA 532 (C).

19 See, for instance, *R v Kumalo and Nkosi* 1918 AD 500 at 504; *S v Sithole* 1980 (4) SA 148 (D) at 150. On the evidentiary value of motive in criminal trials, see Schwikkard PJ and Van der Merwe SE *Principles of Evidence* 4 ed (2016) 56–60.

20 S 1(1)(xxv)(*c*) of the Protection of Constitutional Democracy Against Terrorist and Related Activities Act 33 of 2004; and see further the discussion on motive in the context of the crime of terrorism in Chapter 49.

21 S 51 read with Schedule 2, Part I of the Criminal Law Amendment Act 105 of 1997. See also *S v Alam* 2006 (2) SACR 613 (Ck) at 18.

19.3.2 Forms of *dolus*

Where *dolus* is required for the commission of a particular crime, the accused must have had *dolus* in one or other of the recognised forms in respect of each and every definitional element of that crime, at the time that he was engaging in the unlawful conduct. South African law recognises three different types[22] or forms of *dolus*:

1. ***Dolus directus*** or direct intention means *actual intention* in the ordinary, everyday sense of the word, namely that the commission of the crime in question was the accused's actual aim and objective. For example, X, a landlord, sets fire to his block of flats to claim the insurance money. Here, X's objective (to burn down the flats) and his legal intention (to commit arson) coincide exactly.
2. ***Dolus indirectus*** or indirect intention refers to the situation in which the commission of the crime in question was *not* the accused's actual aim or objective, but he nevertheless foresaw it as an inevitable and certain, or virtually certain consequence of achieving that objective and persisted anyway. For example, X sets fire to his block of flats to claim the insurance money, knowing full well that there are people inside who will inevitably be burned to death.[23] It is not his main aim to kill anybody, but he foresees the deaths of the occupants as a necessary and certain, or virtually certain, consequence of achieving his objective. Here, X's objective (to burn down the flats) and his legal intention (to kill the occupants) do not coincide, but it will not avail him to argue that because he did not actually wish or desire to kill anyone, he did not intend to commit murder. He had intention in the form of *dolus indirectus*.
3. ***Dolus eventualis*** refers to the situation in which the commission of the crime in question was not the accused's actual aim or objective, but he nevertheless foresaw it as a *possible* consequence of achieving that objective and persisted anyway. For example, X sets fire to his block of flats to claim the insurance money. He does not know for a fact that there are people inside who will be burned to death. However, he foresees the possibility (the risk) that there *might* be people in the building and that they *might possibly* die in the fire, and he nevertheless continues with his action regardless of this possible consequence (he takes the risk). Once again, X's objective and his legal intention do not coincide, but once again, it will not avail him to argue that he did not intend to commit murder. He had intention in the form of *dolus eventualis*.

It is important to note that the law does not, as a rule, distinguish between the three forms of *dolus* for purposes of determining criminal liability. Where the crime is one that requires

---

22 International criminal law also recognises a form of intent known as ***dolus specialis*** (special intention), which is an aggravated criminal intention. See Werle G and Jessberger F *Principles of International Criminal Law* 3 ed (2014) 177. This form of intention is especially relevant for the purposes of the crime of genocide where the accused must have the 'intent to destroy, in whole or in part, a national, ethnical, racial or religious group'. Thus, the accused must first have the intent (*dolus directus* or *indirectus*), for instance to kill or to cause serious bodily or mental harm to an individual or multiple individuals (the underlying acts). In addition, the accused must have the intent (*dolus specialis*) to target these individuals, not as human beings, 'but only as a member of the persecuted group'. See the discussion of *Jorgic* (30 April 1999) before the German Federal Court of Justice (1999) in Cassese A *International Criminal Law* (2003) 103. The International Criminal Tribunal for Rwanda (ICTR), in the historic *Akayesu* case (ICTR *Prosecutor v Jean-Paul Akayesu* (trial judgment) ICTR-96-4-T September 1998) held at 498 as follows:

> **Genocide is distinct from other crimes inasmuch as it embodies a special intent or *dolus specialis*. Special intent of a crime is the specific intention, required as a constitutive element of the crime, which demands that the perpetrator clearly seeks to produce the act charged. Thus, the special intent in the crime of genocide lies in 'the intent to destroy, in whole or in part, a national, ethnical, racial or religious group, as such'.**

23 Compare with the facts in *R v Kewelram* 1922 AD 213.

fault in the form of *dolus*, then any one of the three forms of *dolus* will suffice.[24] It is also possible for the accused to have different forms of *dolus* in respect of different elements of the crime in question.

However, the distinction between the different forms of *dolus* is not entirely without significance in that a person who commits a crime with *dolus eventualis* will generally be regarded as less morally blameworthy than one who commits a crime with *dolus directus* or *dolus indirectus*. Hence, this is a factor that a court would take into account in relation to the sentence.

The first two types of *dolus* are straightforward and need no further elucidation, but the concept of *dolus eventualis* has given rise to more debate in our law and hence requires more detailed discussion.

19.3.3 Dolus eventualis

19.3.3.1 Background to the concept of *dolus eventualis*

The law is understandably reluctant to allow individuals to escape responsibility for the natural and probable consequences of their conduct. As mentioned previously, there was, in fact, a presumption in our law to the effect that every person intends the natural and probable consequences of his conduct.[25] This presumption was inherited from English law and was not part of Roman-Dutch law. In Roman-Dutch law, intention was seen as a purely subjective concept; that is, it was concerned with what was actually in the accused's mind at the time of the unlawful conduct.

During the purist movement, which gained momentum when the National Party came to power in 1948, and which continued well into the 1970s and 1980s, courts made a conscious effort to return to the so-called 'pure' Roman-Dutch law principles and to eradicate the influence of English law. Among other things, this involved a return to a purely subjective approach to *dolus*. Accordingly, in a line of cases that began with *R v Valachia* in 1945,[26] the abovementioned presumption was steadily abandoned and the courts began to rely instead on the Roman-Dutch law concept of *dolus eventualis*.[27]

Thus, instead of presuming that the accused intended the natural and probable consequences of his conduct, courts adopted the approach that if the accused had foreseen a particular consequence as a possible outcome of his conduct, this would be sufficient to constitute intention. In other words, to prove *dolus*, it was not necessary for the state to prove that the accused had actually meant, aimed or desired to produce the consequence in question or that he had foreseen it as a necessary and inevitable outcome of his conduct. To determine whether the accused had foreseen the consequence as a possible outcome, a court could resort to inferential reasoning. Clearly, the more likely or obvious the consequence, the easier it would be for a court to draw the inference that the accused must indeed have foreseen it. The use of inferential reasoning in such cases is discussed more fully below.

---

24 It is, however, always open to the legislature, when creating a statutory offence, to prescribe that only one of the higher forms of *dolus* will suffice.

25 See, for example, *R v Jolly and others* supra.

26 *R v Valachia and another* supra at 831.

27 For an account of the historical development of *dolus eventualis*, see Hoctor S 'The concept of *dolus eventualis* in South African law: An historical perspective' (2008) 14(2) *Fundamina* 14. See also Paizes A '*Dolus eventualis* reconsidered' (1988) 105(4) *SALJ* 636.

19.3.3.2 The requirements for *dolus eventualis*

Dolus eventualis exists where the accused subjectively foresees the possibility (a risk) of conducting himself unlawfully,[28] but nevertheless proceeds with his intended course of conduct, that is, he 'reconciles himself' to the possibility, he 'takes [that possibility] into the bargain' or is 'reckless'[29] as to whether or not it materialises. In the case of crimes that involve positive conduct, pure omissions and states of affairs, the test for *dolus eventualis* can be framed as follows:

- Did the accused *subjectively foresee* the *possibility* of committing the unlawful act or omission, or of being in an unlawful state of affairs, as the case may be? (This part of the enquiry is sometimes referred to as the *cognitive* component of the enquiry.[30])
- And if so, did the accused *accept that possibility* into the bargain? (This part of the enquiry is sometimes referred to as the *conative, volitional* or *voluntative* component of the enquiry.[31])

In the case of a consequence crime such as murder, the accused must have subjectively foreseen the possibility of causing the actual consequence in question, that is, the *death* of the deceased and not merely injury short of death. At the same time, the accused must *also* have foreseen the possibility of causing that consequence in substantially the same manner as he did in fact cause it to occur. He must also have foreseen the possibility of causing that consequence to the particular victim or object in question, or someone/something in the same position, class or category.[32] Intention to kill one person is no substitute for intention to kill the person who actually died.[33]

Thus, the cognitive part of the enquiry for *dolus eventualis* in the case of murder is slightly more complex and can be framed as follows:

- Did the accused *subjectively foresee* the possibility of:
    - killing the deceased or someone in the same position, class or category
    - in substantially the *same manner* as he did in fact kill him?
- The conative part of the enquiry remains the same, namely:
    - did the accused accept the foreseen possibility into the bargain?

19.3.3.2.1 Subjective foresight

Since the test for *dolus* in our law is now wholly subjective, it is clear that what is required is *actual foresight* on the part of the accused; that is, the accused must have personally foreseen (predicted) the possibility of committing the unlawful act or omission, being in the unlawful state of affairs, or causing the unlawful consequence, as the case may be. Thus, what the accused ought to have foreseen, or what a reasonable person in the accused's position would have foreseen, does not enter the question.[34]

But how does a court know what a particular accused foresaw? What if the accused does not admit, for example, that he foresaw the possibility of the deceased's death occurring as

28 That is, committing an unlawful act or omission, being in an unlawful state of affairs, or causing an unlawful consequence as the case may be.

29 *S v Ngubane* 1985 (3) SA 677 (A) at 685.

30 For the meaning of the term 'cognitive' see section 14.3. It is important, however, not to confuse foresight with insight, which forms part of the criminal capacity enquiry.

31 For the meaning of the term 'conative', see section 14.3.

32 This is sometimes referred to as concrete intention. It will be considered in section 24.5 in the discussion on *aberratio ictus*.

33 See *S v Mavhungu* 1981 (1) SA 56 (A).

34 *R v Nsele* 1955 (2) SA 145 (A).

a result of his conduct? In such cases, foresight may be proved by inferential reasoning.[35] A court will consider all the facts and circumstances that must have been known to the accused at the relevant time, together with the way in which the accused acted with that knowledge. The court may then draw the inference that the accused *must* have foreseen the possibility in question and that therefore, by necessary inference, the accused *did in fact* foresee that possibility.[36] As the Supreme Court of Appeal (SCA) explained in *S v Humphreys*:

> **[T]he process of inferential reasoning may start out from the premise that, in accordance with common human experience, the possibility of the consequences that ensued would have been obvious to any person of normal intelligence. The next logical step would then be to ask whether, in the light of all the facts and circumstances of this case, there is any reason to think that the appellant would not have shared this foresight, derived from common human experience, with other members of the general population.**[37]

However, the Appellate Division (AD) and SCA have also frequently warned against being too ready to make the leap of logic from what an accused must have foreseen to what the accused did in fact foresee.[38] In ***S v Mini***, the AD explained the court's duty, when applying inferential reasoning, in the following terms:

> **[A] trier of fact should try mentally to project himself into the position of that accused at that time. He must of course be on guard against the insidious subconscious influence of *ex post facto* knowledge.**[39]

19.3.3.2.2 Degree of risk foreseen – real or remote?

The question has arisen as to whether it is necessary for the accused to have foreseen the unlawful conduct as a real possibility (something with a realistic chance of occurring) or whether foresight of any possibility, however remote, will suffice. In the earliest cases, it was held that the possibility must have been foreseen as *likely* to materialise. 'Likely' implies a degree of probability. However, in *R v Horn*, the AD held that all that was required was foresight of the *possibility* of the consequence occurring.[40] Even so, the debate continued for some years,[41] with judges of the AD wavering between different positions.

In *S v Mini*, Holmes JA, in his minority judgment, referred to a 'possibility, even if slight, of death resulting'.[42] He reiterated this approach in his minority judgment in *S v De Bruyn*,

---

35 An inference is a conclusion. In *S v Sigwahla* 1967 (4) SA 566 (A) at 570D-E, the AD held that:

> **[s]ubjective foresight, like any other factual issue, may be proved by inference. To constitute proof beyond reasonable doubt the inference must be the only one which can reasonably be drawn. It cannot be so drawn if there is a reasonable possibility that subjectively the accused did not foresee, even if he ought reasonably to have done so, and even if he probably did do so.**

36 See, for example, *R v Nsele* supra; *S v Nhlapo and another* 1981 (2) SA 744 (A); *S v Shaik and others* 1983 (4) SA 57 (A). See also *S v Lungile and another* 1999 (2) SACR 597 (SCA), previously discussed in section 6.4.2, for a case with facts and reasoning similar to those in *S v Nhlapo*.

37 *S v Humphreys* 2013 (2) SACR 1 (SCA) at 13. We discuss the facts of this case in section 19.3.3.2.4.

38 See, for example, *S v Du Preez* 1972 (4) SA 584 (A); *S v Mamba en 'n ander* 1990 (1) SACR 227 (A); *S v Maritz* 1996 (1) SACR 405 (A).

39 *S v Mini* 1963 (3) SA 188 (A) at 196E.

40 *R v Horn* 1958 (3) SA 457 (A).

41 The debate was fuelled by academics who argued that the possibility ought to have been foreseen as a real or substantial possibility, otherwise the threshold for *dolus eventualis* would be set lower than that for *culpa*, which requires reasonable foreseeability (Burchell EM, Milton JRL and Burchell JM *South African Criminal Law and Procedure Vol I* 2 ed (1983) 147). See Burchell JM *Principles of Criminal Law* 5 ed (2016) 373–378, 380–385 for an assessment of *dolus eventualis* and the concept of conscious negligence.

42 *S v Mini* supra at 191F.

where he held that *dolus eventualis* is 'foresight of a possibility, however remote'.[43] He also held that the 'proximity or remoteness of the foreseen possibility ... is irrelevant to the verdict'.[44] In *S v Shaik,*[45] the AD held that it did not matter how remote the possibility was, as long as the accused foresaw it; the remoteness of the possibility may make it difficult for a court to draw the inference that the accused actually foresaw it, but once that inference is properly drawn, it will not help the accused to argue that the possibility was only foreseen as unlikely, highly improbable or remote.

In *S v Ngubane,*[46] the AD took a new approach. It held that although it does not matter to the foresight (cognitive) element whether the possibility was foreseen as real or remote, it may become relevant when determining whether the accused accepted that possibility into the bargain, that is, the conative part of the enquiry. In *S v Beukes*, however, the AD pointed out that cases have hardly ever turned on whether the accused 'accepted the possibility into the bargain'.[47] It held, therefore, that *dolus eventualis* would normally only be present where the accused foresaw the possibility as a *reasonable* one.

The approach in *S v Beukes* was subsequently followed in Namibia in the case of *S v Van Wyk,*[48] but South African courts have not been as quick to follow suit. Thus, for example, in *S v Sethoga*, the AD referred to foresight of 'a possibility, however remote'.[49] However, more recently in *S v Cameron,*[50] as well as *Dlamini and another v The State,*[51] but without discussing the point at all, the SCA defined *dolus eventualis* as foresight of a 'reasonable possibility'. In *Dlamini*, the SCA cited *Van Wyk* as authority rather than *Beukes*. In *Cameron*, no authority was cited.[52]

In *S v Makgatho*, the SCA held (also citing *Van Wyk*) that 'it must be shown that a "real" – as opposed to a remote – possibility of that consequence resulting was foreseen'.[53] Given the need for legal clarity, it is to be hoped that this dictum will finally settle the question.[54] If so, the adoption of the term 'real' rather than 'reasonable' is to be welcomed since it will avoid the possibility of an objective element insinuating itself into the enquiry.[55]

---

43 *S v De Bruyn en 'n ander* 1968 (4) SA 498 (A) at 510F–G.
44 *S v De Bruyn en 'n ander* supra at 511H.
45 *S v Shaik and others* supra.
46 *S v Ngubane* supra.
47 *S v Beukes en 'n ander* 1988 (1) SA 511 (A) at 522C–E.
48 See *S v Van Wyk* 1992 (1) SACR 147 (NmS).
49 *S v Sethoga and others* 1990 (1) SA 270 (A) at 275–276.
50 *S v Cameron* 2005 (2) SACR 179 (SCA) at 11.
51 *S v Dlamini and another* (175/01) [2006] ZASCA 164 (26 September 2006) at 11.
52 It should be pointed out, however, that in neither of these cases did liability turn on the degree of risk foreseen by the accused so the relevant dicta must presumably be regarded as obiter and hence of persuasive value only.
53 *S v Makgatho* 2013 (2) SACR 13 (SCA) at 9. See also Burchell *Principles of Criminal Law* 366.
54 In *Director of Public Prosecutions, Gauteng v Pistorius* 2016 (2) SA 317 (SCA), the SCA held (at para 26) that

> **a person's intention in the form of *dolus eventualis* arises if the perpetrator foresees the risk of death occurring, but nevertheless continues to act *appreciating that death might well occur*, therefore "gambling" as it were with the life of the person against whom the act is directed ... Terminology aside, it is necessary to stress that the wrongdoer does not have to foresee death as a probable consequence of his or her actions. It is sufficient that the possibility of death is foreseen which, coupled with a disregard of that consequence, is sufficient to constitute the necessary criminal intent'. (Emphasis added)**

Although the SCA did not speak of a 'real' possibility in this case, its use of the expression 'appreciating that death might well occur' lends support to the view that the possibility must have been foreseen as one with a real chance of occurring and not merely as a remote, theoretical or statistical possibility.
55 In the previous edition of this book, the authors pointed out that the term 'reasonable' in criminal law invariably suggests an objective standard, most usually the standard of the reasonable person. Unless the term 'reasonable' were given something other than its usual legal meaning, which would inevitably lead to confusion, this would mean introducing an objective element into what is intended to be a purely subjective enquiry. This problem could be circumvented, however, by avoiding the term 'reasonable' and instead requiring foresight of a 'real', 'substantial' or 'concrete' risk.

19.3.3.2.3 Foresight of the causal sequence (consequence crimes only)

For many years, it appeared to be settled law that as long as the consequence was foreseen, for example death in the case of murder, then this would be sufficient to establish *dolus eventualis*. In other words, it was not necessary for the accused to have foreseen the manner in which the consequence came about. Where the consequence occurred in an unusual or unexpected manner, the case would rather turn on the question of legal causation, that is, whether there was a *novus actus interveniens* breaking the chain of causation.

However, in 1989, in *S v Goosen*,[56] the AD adopted a new approach influenced by German law. This was that there is no *dolus eventualis* if the consequence occurs in a manner that differs markedly or substantially from what the accused foresaw happening.

S v Goosen

Goosen, a person of markedly low intelligence, took part in a robbery, in the course of which the victim was shot and killed. The band of robbers followed the deceased from work and stopped him on the road. One of them, Mazibuko, stood in front of the car with a firearm, which he aimed at the deceased, while another robber struck the deceased on the jaw, possibly knocking him out. As a result, the deceased's car lurched or rolled forward towards Mazibuko. This caused Mazibuko to pull the trigger involuntarily, killing the deceased. Goosen pleaded guilty to murder on the advice of his counsel. He was convicted and sentenced to death. Meanwhile, Mazibuko had pleaded not guilty to murder on the basis that he had killed the deceased involuntarily. He was convicted of culpable homicide.

Goosen then brought an appeal on the grounds that he had been improperly advised by his counsel and that this had resulted in a miscarriage of justice. On appeal, the AD held that it was satisfied that Goosen had foreseen the possibility of the deliberate shooting of the deceased. It held further that another individual may also have foreseen the possibility of the firearm going off by accident, but it was not satisfied beyond reasonable doubt that Goosen, because of his low intelligence, had subjectively foreseen this latter possibility as well. The AD held that because Goosen might not have foreseen the death of the deceased occurring *in substantially the same manner as it did in fact occur*, he did not have *dolus eventualis* in respect of murder. His conviction was altered to one of culpable homicide.

The approach in *S v Goosen* was subsequently followed in *S v Mitchell and another*.[57] However, the decision in *Goosen* has not received unqualified approval. Snyman's view is that *Goosen* was wrongly decided, because a mistake as to the causal sequence is not a material (essential) mistake and should therefore not serve to exonerate the accused. He is also concerned that the new requirement is vague because the AD did not specify what it meant by 'markedly' different.[58]

However, although *Goosen* attracted a great deal of comment, it has not had quite the impact that may at first have been feared. For example, in *S v Lungile*,[59] although the deceased's death was caused in a somewhat unusual manner, the SCA had no difficulty in drawing the inference that the accused must in fact have foreseen this particular manner of

56 *S v Goosen* 1989 (4) SA 1013 (A). See Burchell *Principles of Criminal Law* 366–373 for a detailed discussion and critique of this case.
57 *S v Mitchell and another* 1992 (1) SACR 17 (A).
58 Snyman *Criminal Law* 191–192.
59 *S v Lungile and another* supra (previously discussed in section 6.4.2).

death among other possibilities.[60] We may therefore conclude that the need to prove foresight of the causal sequence is unlikely to pose a serious hurdle for the state in cases where the accused are persons of normal intelligence and life experience. It is only likely to be of assistance in cases where the consequence occurs in a truly freakish manner, or where the accused is not a person of normal intelligence and/or life experience.

19.3.3.2.4 Reconciling oneself to the possibility

Opinion has long been divided as to precisely what is required by the conative (or volitional) component of the enquiry. The central question is whether it is sufficient if, with the necessary subjective foresight of the possibility, the accused simply persisted in his intended course of conduct (took a conscious risk), or whether something more is required and, if so, what.[61] This part of the enquiry has often been described as reconciling oneself to the possibility, accepting the possibility into the bargain, consenting to it, or recklessness or indifference as to whether it materialises.[62] Those who advocate the approach that *dolus eventualis* requires something more than mere conscious risk taking argue that this additional subjective mental element is necessary to distinguish *dolus eventualis* from conscious or advertent negligence (*luxuria*).[63]

Until recently, the debate was largely one of academic interest. In *S v Beukes*, Van Heerden JA pointed out that there had been no reported case in which an accused, who had subjectively foreseen a particular risk, had nevertheless escaped liability on the grounds that he had not been indifferent towards its materialisation.[64] Cases invariably turned on whether there had been subjective foresight of the risk in the first place. Because of this, some commentators have questioned whether the so-called conative leg of the test adds any real value to the enquiry, or whether it should not rather be abandoned in favour of the simple requirement that the necessary subjective foresight must have existed contemporaneously with the unlawful conduct.[65]

To explain this point, suppose that X is assaulting Y and, during the course of the assault, X foresees the possibility that Y might die as a result. If X continues his assault, he can be said to have accepted the possibility of Y's death into the bargain, that is, he has reconciled himself to the possibility of causing Y's death and/or he is reckless or indifferent as to whether or not this possibility materialises. If, however, X stops his assault at the moment when he foresees the possibility of causing Y's death, then he cannot be said to have reconciled himself to that possibility.[66]

---

60 The deceased was shot and killed, not by one of the robbers, but by a police officer who intervened in an attempt to stop the robbery.

61 See *S v Beukes* supra at 522B–G. See also Whiting R 'Thoughts on *dolus eventualis*' (1988) 1(3) *SACJ* 440; Paizes '*Dolus eventualis* reconsidered' 636.

62 In *S v Ngubane* supra at 685, Jansen JA explained this part of the enquiry as follows:

> **[T]he agent (the perpetrator) 'consents' to the consequence foreseen as a possibility, he 'reconciles himself' to it, he 'takes it into the bargain' ... Our cases often speak of the agent being 'reckless' of that consequence, but in this context it means consenting, reconciling or taking into the bargain ... and not the 'recklessness' of the Anglo-American systems nor an aggravated degree of negligence. It is the particular, subjective, volitional mental state in regard to the foreseen possibility which characterises *dolus eventualis* and which is absent in *luxuria*.**

63 See Jansen JA's dictum in *S v Ngubane* supra; also Carstens P 'Revisiting the relationship between *dolus eventualis* and *luxuria* in the context of vehicular collisions causing the death of fellow passengers and/or pedestrians: *S v Humphreys* 2013 (2) SACR 1 (SCA)' (2013) 26(1) *SACJ* 67 at 68.

64 *S v Beukes en 'n ander* supra at 522.

65 See, for example, Smith PT 'Recklessness in *dolus eventualis*' (1979) 96(1) *SALJ* 81 at 92–93 and Paizes '*Dolus eventualis* reconsidered' 636.

66 Smith 'Recklessness in *dolus eventualis*' 92–93.

Note further that X will not be liable for Y's death if Y happens to die as a result of injuries sustained *before* X foresaw the possibility of causing Y's death. This is because of the fundamental requirement that for liability to arise, fault and unlawful conduct must be contemporaneous. In other words, they must exist simultaneously.[67] Thus, if there is *unlawful conduct without fault*, for example because the accused has not yet foreseen the possibility of causing the unlawful consequence, then there is no criminal liability. Equally, if there is *fault without unlawful conduct*, for example because the accused desists from his unlawful conduct as soon as he foresees the possibility of causing the unlawful consequence, then there is also no criminal liability.[68]

Despite the logic of this argument, Van Heerden JA in *Beukes* highlighted a particular situation where he thought that the conative component of the enquiry may indeed be relevant. This is where the accused foresees an unlawful consequence as a possibility before he proceeds with his course of conduct, but is convinced that he will be able to prevent it from materialising by taking particular precautions or by exercising particular care or skill. In such cases, it could be said that the accused did not reconcile himself to the possibility or accept it into the bargain. Van Heerden JA conceded, however, that in such cases, it could equally well be said that the accused did not subjectively foresee the consequence as one with a reasonable possibility of materialising in the circumstances.[69]

In *S v Maritz*, Van den Heever JA endorsed the idea that a person does not accept the risk of an unlawful consequence where he is convinced, albeit mistakenly, that he can prevent it from occurring.[70] Nevertheless, once again the accused's liability did not turn on this point as the court ultimately found that Maritz had lacked subjective foresight of the possibility of causing the deceased's death and had merely been negligent in that regard.[71] The question arose again directly, however, in the case of *S v Humphreys*.[72]

S v Humphreys

Humphreys was charged with 10 counts of murder and four counts of attempted murder after he drove his minibus taxi laden with schoolchildren in front of an oncoming train at a level crossing, causing a fatal collision. When he approached the crossing, the warning lights signalling the train's approach were flashing and the boom-gate was down, blocking the left-hand lane. There was already a queue of cars ahead of him, waiting for the train to pass. Despite these warning signs,

---

67 This is known as the contemporaneity rule. We will discuss it in more detail in Chapter 21.

68 Smith 'Recklessness in *dolus eventualis*' 92–93.

69 *S v Beukes* supra at 522E.

70 *S v Maritz* supra. The facts of this case were that in the course of a murder investigation, Maritz, a police officer, had tied a suspect to the front of his Nyala armoured vehicle with an 8 m long rope and had made him run in front of the vehicle while Maritz drove behind. The rope became entangled in the wheels of the Nyala and the suspect was dragged underneath and run over before Maritz was able to stop. The trial court found Maritz guilty of murder on the basis of *dolus eventualis*.

On appeal, the AD found that the trial court had been wrong to reject Maritz's evidence that he did not know his actions might lead to the deceased's death. It highlighted certain objective factors that supported Maritz's evidence, for example the fact that none of Maritz's colleagues, who were also present, warned or tried to stop him. The vehicle also had good brakes, was not travelling fast when the incident occurred, and Maritz was a proficient driver. The AD also found that Maritz's exclamation of shock after he ran over the deceased, and the fact that he was extremely shocked when the incident was reported, indicated that he had not reconciled himself with the possible consequences of his actions. The AD thus found that the trial court had fallen into the trap of too readily proceeding from what Maritz ought to have foreseen to what he must have foreseen and from there to what he by necessary inference in fact foresaw. His conviction was altered to one of culpable homicide.

71 For an analysis of the Maritz judgment, see Boister N 'General principles of liability: *Dolus eventualis*' (1996) 9(2) *SACJ* 226.

72 *S v Humphreys* supra.

he pulled into the right-hand lane, overtook the stationary vehicles and entered the crossing, still travelling in the right-hand lane and bypassing the boom-gate. The approaching train struck the minibus, killing 10 children and injuring four others. Humphreys was injured, but survived.

At his trial, two of his surviving passengers gave evidence that he had successfully completed the same manoeuvre on two previous occasions. The trial court found that he had *dolus eventualis* in respect of the deaths of his passengers and convicted him accordingly. On appeal, however, the SCA found that while Humphreys must have foreseen the possibility of the fatal collision, it was not satisfied that he had reconciled himself to such a consequence:

> **The true enquiry under this rubric is whether the appellant took the consequences that he foresaw into the bargain; whether it can be inferred that it was immaterial to him whether these consequences would flow from his actions. Conversely stated, the principle is that if it can reasonably be inferred that the appellant may have thought that the possible collision he subjectively foresaw would not actually occur, the second element of *dolus eventualis* would not have been established.**[73]

The court held that for Humphreys to reconcile himself to the deaths of his passengers, he would also have had to reconcile himself to the possibility of his own death, but there was no evidence that it was immaterial to him whether he lived or died. It concluded that although he foresaw the possibility of the collision, he thought that it would not happen. He took a risk that he thought would not materialise. This belief was supported by the fact that he had completed the same manoeuvre previously without mishap. His convictions were consequently set aside and replaced with 10 convictions of culpable homicide.

The SCA's decision in *Humphreys* met with widespread criticism from many leading commentators.[74] The essence of much of this criticism is that the court confused the conative leg of the enquiry for *dolus eventualis* with the cognitive leg (the enquiry for subjective foresight). We would agree. When the court held that Humphreys did not reconcile himself to the deaths of his passengers because he 'took a risk which he thought would not materialise',[75] this (as Van Heerden JA had pointed out years before in *Beukes*) was tantamount to saying that he did not subjectively foresee the fatal consequence as one with a *real* possibility of materialising in the circumstances.[76] The proper finding should then have been that the *cognitive* element of the enquiry had not been satisfied. It stands to reason, of course, that a person cannot accept or reconcile himself to a risk that he believes will not actually materialise.[77] Thus, if the *cognitive* element of the enquiry fails, the *conative* element must necessarily fail as well. Despite these criticisms, however, it seems that the SCA has chosen to abide by the approach adopted in *Humphreys:*

73 *S v Humphreys* at 17.

74 See, for example, Van der Merwe S and Paizes A '*Dolus eventualis* revisited: *S v Humphreys* 2013 (2) SACR 1 (SCA)' (2013) 1 *CJR* 6; Hoctor S 'Death on the roads and *dolus eventualis*: *S v Humphreys* 2013 (2) SACR 1 (SCA)' (2013) 26(1) *SACJ* 75; Watney M 'Moord en strafbare manslag by padsterftes *S v Humphreys* 2013 2 SASV 1 (HHA)' (2013) 4 *TSAR* 770; Van der Merwe HJ '"One moment of extreme irresponsibility": Notes and comments on *Humphreys v S* and the volitional component of *dolus eventualis* in the context of dangerous or irresponsible driving' *Law, Democracy and Development* (2013) 17(1) 64; Paizes A '*Dolus eventualis* again' (2014) 1 *CJR* 11; Burchell *Principles of Criminal Law* 375-377. For an opposing view, however, see Snyman *Criminal Law* 182-183.

75 *S v Humphreys* at 18.

76 The requirement that the possibility must have been foreseen as a real one was articulated by the SCA only a few days later in *S v Makgatho* supra.

77 See Boister's analysis of the judgment in *Maritz* supra, Boister N 'General principles of liability' 228.

S v Tonkin

In *S v Tonkin*,[78] the appellant had been convicted of malicious injury to property in the magistrates' court for breaking a glass pane in the door of a police charge office by striking it with the palm of his hand. His defence was that he had struck the glass pane in order to open the door. He was not aware that the door could not swing open because it was latched and that there was a possibility that the glass would break instead. The magistrate found that the appellant had known that the glass could break, 'nevertheless he proceeded and he reconciled himself with that fact and the [appellant], on his own version, had the necessary *dolus eventualis* in breaking the window-pane'.[79] The High Court subsequently refused him leave to appeal against his conviction. In considering his appeal against this refusal, the SCA held that the magistrate had not applied the correct test for the conative element of *dolus eventualis*. Citing *Humphreys*, it held that 'reconciliation ... involves more than the perpetrator merely proceeding with his or her proposed conduct, despite the subjective appreciation of the consequences that ensue. If the perpetrator genuinely believed - despite the unreasonableness of that belief - that the foreseen consequences would not materialise, the element of reconciliation cannot be said to be present ...'[80] The SCA held that it could be argued that, even if the appellant had foreseen the possibility that the glass could break, he thought it would not actually happen because the door would give way. He was accordingly granted leave to appeal.

S v Ndlanzi

In *S v Ndlanzi*,[81] the appellant was convicted of murder and various other charges in the regional magistrates' court. While driving a taxi in an urban area during peak-hour traffic, he mounted the pavement, collided with a dustbin and a newspaper stall and knocked over the deceased, who was walking on the pavement. After he had also collided with a stop sign, he then reversed his vehicle over the deceased and left the scene. At his trial, he testified that when he drove onto the pavement, he had not seen the deceased, only a newspaper stall and a pole, which he thought he could avoid. He was not even aware that he had collided with the deceased. This was not disputed. On appeal, the SCA applied the approach taken in *S v Humphreys*. It held that 'any person with a modicum of intelligence would have appreciated that driving a motor vehicle onto a pavement in the prevailing circumstances ... raised the possibility that a collision with a pedestrian would occur ... [and that] any right-minded person would have foreseen the possibility of the death of a pedestrian'. It concluded that there was no basis to find 'that the appellant did not possess the requisite subjective intent [foresight] in accordance with this standard'.[82] The SCA however went on to hold that, although the appellant subjectively foresaw the possibility of a fatal collision with a pedestrian, he did not think such a possibility would materialise. The second part of *dolus eventualis* was accordingly not satisfied. The appellant was thus acquitted of murder and convicted of culpable homicide instead.[83]

Although it is to be expected that the correct enquiry for the conative element of the *dolus eventualis* enquiry will remain the subject of academic debate for some time to come,[84] what

78 *S v Tonkin* 2014 (1) SACR 583 (SCA).
79 *S v Tonkin* supra at para 10.
80 *S v Tonkin* supra at paras 11 and 12.
81 *S v Ndlanzi* 2014 (2) SACR 256 (SCA).
82 *S v Ndlanzi* supra at paras 35–36.
83 For a criticism of this judgment, see Paizes A '*Dolus eventualis* again' (2014) 1 *CJR* 11.
84 See Paizes A '*Dolus eventualis* again' supra; Burchell *Principles of Criminal Law* 375–377. See also the dissenting judgment of Willis JA in *S v Van Schalkwyk* 2016 (2) SACR 334 (SCA) at paras 27–34 together with Paizes' and Hoctor's commentaries on this judgment (Paizes A '*Dolus eventualis*: Two more decisions by the Supreme Court of Appeal' (2016) 1 *CJR* 7; Hoctor S 'General principles and specific offences' (2016) 29(3) *SACJ* 339 at 345).

does emerge clearly from these recent judgments is that where the accused subjectively believed that there was no real prospect of the risk materialising, then, no matter how unrealistic his belief, he has not satisfied the requirements for *dolus eventualis* as a whole. At most, he will be adjudged negligent.

DISCUSSION

Should there be a more nuanced approach towards *dolus eventualis*?

Despite criticism of the decision in *Humphreys*, the fact remains that courts are generally reluctant to convict of murder in cases of vehicular homicide.[85] Writing in 1988, Professor Whiting thought that such a verdict, even if strictly warranted by the facts, would be offensive to our sense of justice.[86] He suggested that the decision as to whether a particular accused satisfied the requirements for *dolus eventualis* could be affected by a variety of factors, one being the type of activity involved. Certain types of activity are tolerated and even encouraged because of their importance to society, although they involve some risk of injury and even death. Driving is one such activity; mining another. The social utility (or otherwise) of the activity in which an accused was engaged is a factor that may legitimately be taken into account when deciding whether he was negligent. Does it also influence a court (*de facto*, if not *de jure*) in deciding whether he had *dolus eventualis*?

It is instructive to compare the verdict in *Humphreys* with the verdict in *S v Qeqe*[87] where the accused was convicted of murder after he collided with three children while driving recklessly to evade arrest. Might the verdict have been different if he had been going about his lawful business instead of evading arrest? And might the verdict in *Humphreys* have been different if, instead of transporting children to school, Humphreys had been transporting a large quantity of dagga? Would the existence of such an unwritten rule help to explain the alacrity with which the courts find subjective foresight in respect of murder when people are killed in the course of robberies and house-breakings? And should such a rule perhaps be articulated as a principle of law? Should the law in fact take a more nuanced approach towards defining the requirements for *dolus eventualis*[88] so as to take account of the type of activity involved? Or would this merely be tantamount to applying the now-defunct doctrine of *versari in re illicita* in a new guise?[89]

19.4 *Dolus indeterminatus* and *dolus generalis*

A discussion of *dolus* would be incomplete without a reference to the term *dolus indeterminatus* or, as it is also known, *dolus generalis*.[90] These terms are sometimes used to describe an accused's intention in cases where he did not have a specific victim in mind, but

85 In addition to *Humphreys* and *Ndlanzi* supra, see *S v Maarohanye and another* 2015 (2) SA 73 (GJ).

86 Whiting 'Thoughts on *dolus eventualis*'. Professor Whiting was, of course, writing at a time before the road accident death rate had reached the levels of carnage experienced today.

87 *S v Qeqe* 2012 (2) SACR 41 (ECG).

88 Further in this regard, see Paizes '*Dolus eventualis* revisited: *S v Humphreys* 2013 (2) SACR 1 (SCA)' and '*Dolus eventualis*: Two more decisions by the Supreme Court of Appeal' (2016) 1 *CJR* 7. See also the dissenting judgment of Willis JA in *S v Van Schalkwyk* 2016 (2) SACR 334 (SCA) at para 34.

89 For a discussion of the *versari in re illicita* doctrine, see section 22.2.2 below.

90 Snyman *Criminal Law* 196–197.

merely intended to injure or kill any one or more members of a particular class or category of persons.

For example, suppose that X places a bomb on a bus, knowing or foreseeing that there will be passengers on board when it explodes. X does not know who will be on the bus, nor can he know which of them will be injured or die in the resulting explosion. It could be any of them or even all of them. In a case like this, X can be said to have had *dolus indeterminatus* (or *dolus generalis)* in respect of the deaths and injuries of whichever of the bus passengers does happen to die or be injured in the explosion.[91]

Similarly, in cases where the accused caused a shooting affray in which persons have been killed, courts have spoken of the accused as having had *dolus indeterminatus* in respect of the deaths of the victims, in the sense that although they did not intend to kill anyone specific, they must have foreseen the possibility that anyone in the vicinity or present at the scene could be killed in the crossfire.[92]

Dolus indeterminatus and *dolus generalis* are not additional forms of *dolus*, over and above *dolus directus, dolus indirectus* and *dolus eventualis* (as previously defined and explained). They are merely convenient terms for indicating that the accused had *dolus*, but without having a specific victim in mind. They do not replace the need for the state to prove the normal requirements of *dolus* for the crime concerned.

For an accused to be liable, he would still require *dolus* in one or other of the three recognised forms. He would also still require concrete intention in the sense that, although he may not have had a specific person or figure in mind as the intended or potential victim, he must nevertheless have foreseen the possibility of killing someone in the same position, class or category as the person(s) who did in fact die; for example, passengers on the bus, persons present at the scene, or persons in the vicinity of the shootout.[93] Where, however, the deceased was *not* someone in the same position, class or category as the foreseen victim(s), concrete intention would be lacking and the accused would not be liable. Thus, to use the previous example of the bomb on the bus, if X happened to use an explosive that was far more powerful than he had realised, so that the resulting explosion killed and injured not only passengers on the bus, but also motorists and pedestrians some distance away, X could argue that he did not have *dolus* in respect of the deaths and injuries of these *additional* persons, because they were not members of the same class or category as the foreseen victims. On this basis, he would escape liability for these additional crimes.

Having considered *dolus*, we will now deal with the second form of fault in our law: *culpa* or negligence. It will be seen that *culpa* is a very different form of fault from *dolus* since it is determined by means of an objective standard, namely the standard of the reasonable person.

---

91 Compare with the facts in *R v Jolly* supra.

92 See, for instance, *S v Nkombani and another* 1963 (4) SA 877 (A); *S v Nhlapo and another* 1981 (2) SA 744 (A); *S v Lungile and another* supra. Note, however, that the term was incorrectly used in *Director of Public Prosecutions, Gauteng v Pistorius* supra at para 31, where the court held that a person acts with *dolus indeterminatus* where his intention is directed at a person or persons of unknown *identity*. It is correct that an accused need not know the identity of his intended or possible victim(s) in order to have *dolus*, but where the accused *did* have a specific target in mind, as in this case (the person in the toilet cubicle) he is directing his intention at a *determinate* victim, not an *indeterminate* one. See further, Hoctor S 'General principles and specific offences' (2016) 29(1) *SACJ* 54 at 56.

93 *S v Mavhungu* supra.

THIS CHAPTER IN ESSENCE

1. The general rule is that criminal liability will not arise in the absence of fault (*mens rea*). The maxim *actus non facit reum nisi mens sit rea* applies. South African law recognises two forms of fault:
   1.1 *Dolus* (criminal intent)
   1.2 *Culpa* (negligence)
2. *Dolus* is the form of fault normally required in criminal matters. It denotes conscious wrongdoing. It therefore implies not merely the intention to perform the *actus reus*, but to do so while knowing that such conduct is, or may be, a crime. It is a wholly subjective concept, determined according to what was actually in the accused's mind at the time of the unlawful conduct. This is normally determined by inferential reasoning (logical deduction) taking all the facts of the case into account.
3. *Dolus* may take three possible forms:
   3.1 *Dolus directus* (direct or actual intention)
   3.2 *Dolus indirectus* (indirect intention, which requires subjective foresight of the certainty or virtual certainty of conducting oneself unlawfully)
   3.3 *Dolus eventualis* (which requires subjective foresight of the mere possibility (the risk) of conducting oneself unlawfully, together with the acceptance of that risk)
4. Any of these three forms of *dolus* will usually be sufficient for a crime that requires fault in the form of *dolus*.
5. Liability is therefore not limited to cases in which the accused actually meant to commit the crime in question. It also extends to cases in which the accused knew very well that he would be committing a crime although without actually wanting to do so. It extends even further to cases in which the accused foresaw the mere possibility (the risk) that he might be committing a crime, yet nevertheless took that risk.
6. In international criminal law, a form of *dolus* is recognised, known as *dolus specialis* (specific, aggravated intent), in particular for the crime of genocide.

Chapter 20

Negligence

CHAPTER OBJECTIVES

The objectives of this chapter are to:

- explain the concept of *culpa*
- explain the concept of the reasonable person
- explain and apply the test for *culpa*
- highlight the distinction between *culpa* and *dolus eventualis*.

20.1 The concept of *culpa*

Although *dolus* is the normal form of fault required for criminal liability, there are instances where *culpa* (negligence) will suffice.[1] One such instance is the crime of culpable homicide. Another is contempt of court when committed by a newspaper editor publishing comment on a matter that is *sub judice* (still under judicial consideration).[2] In addition, however, there are numerous instances in which the legislature has created statutory offences where *culpa* will be a sufficient form of fault.[3]

Culpa may arise in two possible situations:

1. The accused did not subjectively foresee the possibility of conducting himself unlawfully, but *ought to have foreseen* it because a reasonable person in the same position as the accused would have foreseen that possibility.
2. The accused did foresee the possibility of conducting himself unlawfully, but simply *failed to take the steps* that a reasonable person in the same position would have taken to prevent the possibility from materialising.[4]

Whereas the enquiry for *dolus* is concerned with the accused's actual state of mind at the time when he committed the unlawful conduct and is a subjective concept, the enquiry for *culpa* is concerned with whether the accused's foresight and conduct measure up to a certain standard imposed by law, namely the standard of foresight and conduct expected of the reasonable person. It is thus both an objective and a normative concept.[5]

20.2 Who is the reasonable person?

The reasonable person is a fictitious person, who represents a norm (a standard) against which we can measure the foresight and conduct of the accused to determine whether he was negligent. In short, the reasonable person is an *ideal*. Neethling et al describe him as 'the legal personification of those qualities which the community expects from its members'.[6]

Roman law used the terms '*bonus paterfamilias*' and '*diligens paterfamilias*' to describe this same concept.[7] The term 'reasonable man' was originally used in English law. In South African law, the term 'reasonable person' is certainly more in line with the constitutional ethos of non-sexism.[8]

Because the reasonable person is an ideal, his characteristics and attributes cannot be discovered by empirical means, nor can they be proved in court by means of evidence. They are questions of law and are therefore determined by the judge or magistrate. The reasonable person is therefore not simply the same as the average person.

---

1 See, in general, Snyman CR *Criminal Law* 6 ed (2014) 204–216; Burchell JM *Principles of Criminal Law* 5 ed (2016) 416–436.

2 See *S v Harber and another* 1988 (3) SA 396 (A). Burchell however considers this decision questionable in view of the SCA's ruling in *S v Hoho* 2009 (1) SACR 276 (SCA) 289f–h on the form of fault required for criminal defamation by the media (see Burchell *Principles of Criminal Law* 874).

3 We will discuss fault in statutory offences in Chapter 22.

4 This second form of negligence is sometimes referred to as conscious (or advertent) negligence. See Burchell *Principles of Criminal Law* 373.

5 *Culpa* is an *objective* concept in that it is determined without reference to the accused's subjective state of mind. It is also a *normative* concept in that it is concerned with establishing the standard of conduct against which the conduct of the accused is measured. A norm is a standard.

6 Neethling J, Potgieter JM and Visser PJ *Law of Delict* 2 ed (1994) 124–126.

7 The good or diligent/conscientious head of the household (literally: father of the family).

8 See also comments by Snyman *Criminal Law* 210.

Nevertheless, we cannot allow our ideal (the reasonable person) to stray too far from reality (the average person), or we would set an impossibly high standard. Our courts have therefore been at pains over the years to emphasise that the reasonable person is not a paragon of perfection, but simply an ordinary person using his powers of reason and common sense. To cite Van Den Heever JA in the frequently quoted passage from the delictual case of *Herschel v Mrupe*:

> **The [reasonable person] is not that of a timorous faintheart always in trepidation lest he or others suffer some injury; on the contrary, he ventures out into the world, engages in affairs and takes reasonable chances.**[9]

20.3 Individualising the standard

An important question that arises is whether the concept of the reasonable person (and hence the test for negligence) is a strictly objective one, that is, a single standard applicable to everyone, or whether it is subjectivised (or at least individualised) by taking account of the personal attributes and characteristics of the accused in any given case. This question has been vigorously debated over the years. One particular case that fuelled the debate was that of *R v Mbombela*.[10]

R v Mbombela

Mbombela was a rural youth of 18–20 years old, and somewhat below normal intelligence. On the day in question, he was at his home and the eldest person present. The children playing in the homestead saw something in a supposedly empty hut that had 'two small feet'. They thought it might be a *tokoloshe*[11] and in fear ran to fetch Mbombela. Mbombela brought a hatchet (small axe) and attacked this being without looking at it properly. Then he dragged it out of the hut and found that he had killed his nine-year-old nephew. When he was tried for murder, he raised the defence that he had not known that he was killing a human being, that is, he lacked *dolus* in respect of murder. The trial court rejected this defence because it found that his mistake was not a reasonable one and he was convicted of murder.

Mbombela appealed to the Appellate Division (AD) with specific reference to the question of whether there was only one type of reasonable person or whether allowance should be made for the fact that the accused had a different system of beliefs. On appeal, the AD held that there is only one type of reasonable person, thus 'the accused's race, idiosyncrasies, superstitions and level of intelligence do not enter the question'.[12] The AD, however, found that the accused did not have *dolus* in respect of murder, that is, it correctly applied a *subjective* test for his mistake and altered his conviction to one of culpable homicide. He was sentenced to 12 months' hard labour.

Mbombela highlights the difficulties inherent in applying a rigidly objective test for negligence, especially in a highly diverse society like South Africa's. Because of this case, many leading academics (and from time to time the courts) took the view that a strictly

9 *Herschel v Mrupe* 1954 (3) SA 464 (A) at 490E–F. See also the equally well-known dictum of Holmes JA in *S v Burger* 1975 (4) SA 877 (A) at 879D:

> **One does not expect of a *diligens paterfamilias* any extremes of Solomonic wisdom, prophetic foresight, chameleonic caution, headlong haste, nervous timidity, or the trained reflexes of a racing driver. In short, a *diligens paterfamilias* treads life's pathway with moderation and prudent common sense.**

10 *R v Mbombela* 1933 AD 269.

11 A mythical character in traditional folklore.

12 *R v Mbombela* supra at 269.

objective test is unduly harsh in that it unfairly penalises those who, through no fault of their own, are ignorant, inexperienced and/or lacking in intelligence, and it makes no allowance for personal or cultural differences and idiosyncrasies.[13]

South African courts eventually moved away from their original rigid approach. While the test for negligence is still an objective one, it is now individualised to the extent that the hypothetical reasonable person is placed *in the same circumstances* as the accused and imbued with the same knowledge, characteristics and experience. The major decision heralding this development was that of the AD in *S v Van As*.[14]

S v Van As

Van As slapped the deceased on his cheek. The deceased, who was very fat, lost his balance, fell over backwards and struck his head on the floor. He lost consciousness and died. Van As was initially convicted of culpable homicide, but the AD altered his conviction to common assault on appeal. It held that a reasonable man in the position of the accused would not have foreseen the possibility of death resulting from such a minor assault. It held further that the reasonable man is viewed both objectively and subjectively because he represents a particular group or type of persons who are in the same circumstances as the accused and who have the same capacity for knowledge. Thus, it is only if the accused failed to foresee what other persons *in that group* could and would have foreseen, that his failure to foresee will be regarded as negligent.

The approach in *Van As* was subsequently applied and amplified in yet another *tokoloshe* case – that of *S v Ngema*.[15]

S v Ngema

Ngema arrived home after a hard day's work, somewhat drunk, and went to his hut. The deceased, a two-year-old child, accompanied him. Ngema fell asleep and, while he was sleeping, the deceased climbed onto his lap. Ngema then dreamed that he was being throttled by a *tokoloshe*. He woke up, grabbed a cane knife that he had with him and hacked the child to death. He was charged with murder and, like Mbombela, raised the defence that he did not have the necessary *dolus* for murder as he did not know that he was killing a human being.

The court accepted this defence, albeit somewhat reluctantly. Having found that Ngema was not guilty of murder, it then had to consider whether he was guilty of culpable homicide. In so doing, it had to consider the standard against which Ngema's conduct should be tested. It held that the test for negligence in our law is still objective, but it should be applied according to the standard of the reasonable person of the same background, educational level, culture, sex and race as the accused. It held further that a belief in the *tokoloshe* is not uncommon among persons like Ngema and that this was thus a factor that the court could take into account. It found, however,

13 See remarks by Hefer JA in *S v Melk* 1988 (4) SA 561 (A) at 578F–G. See also the discussion of the dilemma in Burchell JM *South African Criminal Law and Procedure Vol I: General Principles of Criminal Law* 4 ed (2011) 434–438. Burchell's suggestion is that value judgments concerning the impact of subjective factors, such as superstition, culture, education and so on, must play a role somewhere in determining criminal liability. The author argues that it does not matter whether this value judgment is exercised as part of the criminal capacity enquiry or as part of the negligence enquiry. Burchell (at 438) favours the approach in terms of which the individualisation is achieved 'within the already partially subjective, preliminary inquiry into capacity'. Furthermore, the capacity criterion 'has the advantage of starting from a subjective test which can accommodate objective aspects as compared with the negligence criterion which starts from an objective assessment and can include some subjective aspects'.

14 *S v Van As* 1976 (2) SA 921 (A).

15 *S v Ngema* 1992 (2) SACR 651 (D).

that Ngema's conduct in warding off the perceived danger in the way he did was unreasonable in that he knew that the deceased had gone into the hut with him and he should have been more careful. Ngema was convicted of culpable homicide.

Note, however, that the test remains a *normative* one. It is therefore individualised only to the extent of taking legitimate personal qualities and characteristics into account. Thus, it would not avail an accused to argue that special allowance should be made for him on account of being a habitual drunkard, an indoctrinated racist[16] or a career criminal. These would not be regarded as legitimate qualities or characteristics.

DISCUSSION

The test for negligence in a diverse and complex society: Individualising, relativism and the objective standard

How should we view the test for negligence in a culturally and socio-economically diverse society like South Africa? Should we (and can we) entrust the determination of reasonableness to a judiciary that many view as still untransformed and not representative of the views and values of the majority of South Africans? In light of these questions, do you think the factors listed in *Ngema* are sufficient? The question is whether we should add other factors to the list. Ultimately, if factors become highly individualised, we may well ask whether the test for negligence is still objective.

20.3.1 Special skill or expertise

Individualising the test does not always work in the accused's favour. It has long been accepted that where the accused is a person who, by virtue of the task that he undertakes, is expected to have a particular skill, knowledge or expertise that the ordinary person does not have, for example, a motorist, doctor or engineer, then he will be tested against the standard of the reasonable person with that particular skill, knowledge or expertise.[17] The principle does not apply only to individuals who are qualified in the mainstream professions.[18] Note also that motorists are expected to display skill in driving and a high degree of care towards persons that may be injured or killed as a result of their driving.[19]

20.3.2 Children

There is no special test for negligence in the case of children. Allowances are made for the frailties of youth in the test for criminal capacity, but once it is established that the child had criminal capacity, the test for negligence is an objective one, based on the standard of the ordinary reasonable person.[20]

16 On reasonableness in a diverse society like South Africa, see Heyns C '"Reasonableness" in a divided society' (1990) 107(2) *SALJ* 279.

17 See, for example, *S v Mkwetshana* 1965 (2) SA 493 (N); *S v Kramer and another* 1987 (1) SA 887 (W).

18 See, for example, *S v Mahlalela* 1966 (1) SA 226 (A). Mahlalela was a herbalist who gave a young girl a brew of poisonous herbs. The girl died. The court held that although a normal reasonable person may not have known of the fatal properties of the herbs, extra knowledge had to be attributed to Mahlalela because of his profession and thus a higher standard of care was expected of him. He was convicted of culpable homicide.

19 *S v Mkwanazi* 1967 (2) SA 593 (N).

20 *Weber v Santam Versekeringsmaatskappy BPK* 1983 (1) SA 381 (A) at 400 A; *Eskom Holdings Ltd v Hendricks* 2005 (5) SA 503 (SCA) paras 15–17; *S v TS* 2015 (1) SACR 489 (WCC) paras 19–27.

20.4 The requirements for *culpa*

20.4.1 Reasonably foreseeable possibility

The first part of the enquiry is whether a reasonable person in the same circumstances as the accused, that is, with same background, knowledge, experience, culture, skill and so on, would have foreseen the possibility of committing the unlawful act, making the unlawful omission, being in the unlawful state of affairs, or causing the unlawful consequence as the case may be, and including the unlawfulness of that act, omission, state of affairs or consequence. If so, the possibility was reasonably foreseeable.

When dealing with culpable homicide, it is not sufficient that the reasonable person would merely have foreseen harm coming to the victim; it is the possibility of death that must have been reasonably foreseeable.[21] Burchell argues, on the basis of the AD's decision in *S v Goosen*,[22] that where the foreseeable manner of death occurring is substantially different from the actual manner in which it does occur, then the accused will not have been negligent.[23] In support of his argument, he cites *S v Bochris Investments*.[24]

S v Bochris Investments

Bochris Investments, the owner of a pleasure resort, together with its manager, were convicted of culpable homicide in a regional court after a young boy drowned in the resort's swimming pool. The boy had dived to the bottom of the pool and placed his bottom against the opening of the outlet pipe where the pressure of the water forced it into the pipe so that he could not escape.

On appeal, the AD held that the reasonable person would not have foreseen the freakish combination of circumstances that occurred, nor appreciated the way in which an accident of that kind could happen. Without such an appreciation, the possibility of death could not reasonably have been foreseen.

20.4.2 Duty to guard against the possibility materialising

It is not enough for the state to prove that a reasonable person would have foreseen the possibility of committing the unlawful act or omission, of being in the unlawful state of affairs, or causing the unlawful consequence. It must also prove that a reasonable person in the same circumstances as the accused would have taken steps to guard against that unlawful act, omission, state of affairs or consequence to prevent it from occurring.[25]

In delictual cases, this particular requirement is often placed in issue because delict spans a wider range of wrongdoing. In criminal cases, because the reasonable person would

21 See, for example, *S v Bernardus* 1965 (3) SA 287 (A). Bernardus threw a knobkierrie at the deceased from a distance of 9-11 paces. The stick had a pointed end and, by sheer chance, the point pierced the deceased's skull and killed him. The trial court convicted Bernardus of culpable homicide.

However, the matter was taken on appeal on a question of law, namely: 'Is a person guilty of culpable homicide where he unlawfully assaults another and in so doing causes his death, but under circumstances where he could not have reasonably foreseen the death?' The Appellate Division (AD) per Steyn CJ held that death must be foreseeable, not merely bodily injury short of death. However, Holmes JA, who delivered a minority judgment, pointed out that where a reasonable person would foresee the possibility of causing serious injury, the reasonable person would also then foresee 'the possibility of death hovering in attendance' (because the two go together) (at 307A). The AD found that Bernardus ought to have foreseen the possibility of killing the deceased anyway. His conviction was upheld. See also *S v Van As* supra; *S v Van Der Mescht* 1962 (1) SA 521 (A) (discussed in section 22.2.2 below).

22 *S v Goosen* 1989 (4) SA 1013 (A) (discussed above in section 19.3.3.2.3).

23 Burchell *Principles of Criminal Law* 423.

24 *S v Bochris Investments (Pty) Ltd and another* 1988 (1) SA 861 (A).

25 Burchell *South African Criminal Law and Procedure Vol I* 431; Snyman *Criminal Law* 212–213.

realise that he could very well be committing a crime if he does not take steps to guard against the possibility, the reasonable person would normally be expected to take such steps. The reasonable person is always a law-abiding person.

Generally speaking, the greater the risk is of the possibility coming to pass, and the greater the harm or danger inherent in that possibility, the greater is the duty placed on a person to prevent the possibility from materialising. Thus, if the foreseeable possibility of harm is very remote and/or the potential harm is very slight, the reasonable person might not be expected to take any steps to guard against it at all. Figure 20.1 depicts this relationship.

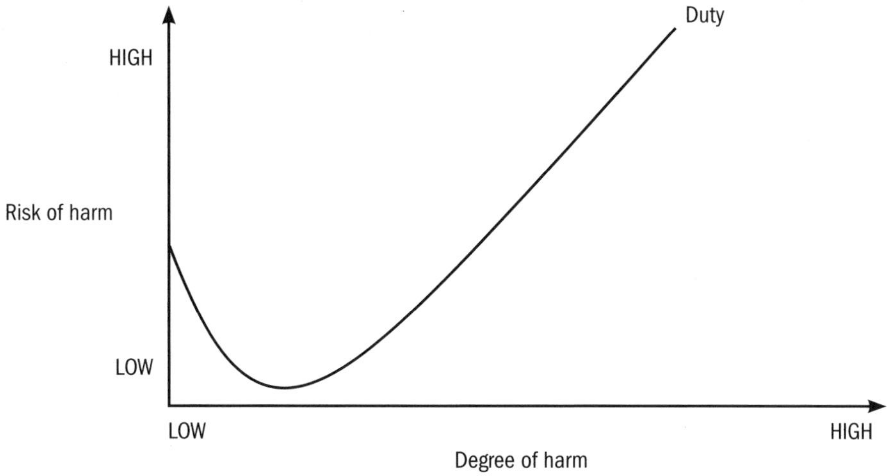

Figure 20.1 *Duty to guard against the possibility of harm materialising*

By the same token, the reasonable person who is involved in some urgent or important action of great social utility, for example an ambulance driver rushing a seriously ill or injured person to hospital, might well be expected to take more risks than normal,[26] such as exceeding the speed limit or going through red traffic lights.[27]

20.4.3 Failure to take reasonable steps

The last part of the enquiry is whether the accused failed to take the steps that a reasonable person in the same circumstances would have taken to prevent the possibility materialising.[28] This raises the question of what lengths the accused should have gone to in order to prevent the possibility from coming to pass.

---

26 See Burchell *Principles of Criminal Law* 423.

27 See, for example, *S v Mkwanazi* supra. Mkwanazi was driving a bus on the main road between Durban and Umlazi when he came across an abandoned car blocking his lane. He could not get around it without crossing the solid white barrier line down the centre of the road, but there was a bend in the road and he could not see whether there was any oncoming traffic. He stopped behind the car and hooted twice, then pulled out onto the wrong side of the road. A car travelling in the opposite direction came round the bend at that moment and collided with the bus, with the result that a passenger in the car was killed. Mkwanazi was convicted of culpable homicide and appealed to the High Court.

On appeal, the court held that if a driver of a vehicle is faced with the decision of whether to take a course that involves some potential risk to himself and to other users of the road, or to suffer delay that could be prejudicial to his passengers, he might be justified in taking the risk if it is very slight or remote, and if the alternative to taking it could have serious results. However, he would not be justified in taking the risk where the risk is very real and the alternative would have no such results. The court held that Mkwanazi had had other options open to him and that, in the circumstances, he should not have taken the risk that he took. His conviction was upheld.

28 Burchell *Principles of Criminal Law* 434.

Clearly, a person is not required to take steps that were impossible for him to take at the time, nor is he required to take steps that were so costly or inconvenient that a reasonable person in the same position would not have taken them. Once again, the answer will depend very much on what is at stake. If, for example, a person's life is at stake, then the accused is expected to go to far greater lengths than if he was merely facing conviction for some minor offence.

It may be that the accused did take *some* steps. The question is then whether they were sufficient according to the standards of the reasonable person.[29] In *S v Mkwanazi*,[30] for example, the accused did take some steps to prevent an accident by hooting twice before proceeding, but the court found that this was not enough. Similarly in *S v Maritz*,[31] the accused did take some precautions to avoid running over the deceased by driving slowly and carefully, but once again they were not enough. He was found to have been negligent and was accordingly convicted of culpable homicide.

20.5 Degrees of negligence

In the law of delict, the contributory negligence of the victim and other persons is taken into account when determining the extent of the defendant's liability to pay damages. In criminal law, however, no distinction is made between degrees of negligence for purposes of establishing liability. Thus, even if the accused is only slightly negligent, he has the required form of fault and he will be liable accordingly. However, where the accused's negligence is only very slight, a court would take this into account in mitigation of sentence.

20.6 The relationship between intention and negligence

Are *dolus* and *culpa* mutually exclusive?[32] For example, if X kills someone unlawfully and the state charges him with culpable homicide rather than murder, but the evidence shows that he actually foresaw the possibility of causing the deceased's death and accepted this possibility into the bargain, does this mean that he cannot now be found guilty of culpable homicide as charged?

Until *S v Ngubane*,[33] this was a highly contested issue. The dispute arose largely out of some earlier definitions of negligence, which regarded it simply as a *failure to foresee* what the reasonable person would have foreseen.[34] Obviously, a person cannot both foresee and at the same time also fail to foresee. In *S v Ngubane*, the AD decided the issue, albeit controversially, at least from a theoretical perspective.[35] It held (per Jansen JA) that negligence does not necessarily require an absence of subjective foresight (a failure to foresee). It merely requires that the accused's conduct does not measure up to the standards of the reasonable person. It held further that a person who intentionally and unlawfully kills another *always* falls short of the standards of the reasonable person. Thus, the existence of *dolus*, in one or another of the accepted forms, does not exclude *culpa*.

---

29 See *Kruger v Coetzee* 1966 (2) SA 428 (A).

30 *S v Mkwanazi* supra.

31 *S v Maritz* 1996 (1) SACR 405 (A).

32 See also Snyman *Criminal Law* 214–215.

33 *S v Ngubane* 1985 (3) SA 677 (A).

34 In other words, they disregarded the second and third steps in the enquiry.

35 For criticism of the judgment by the AD, see Snyman *Criminal Law* 214 fn 242.

20.7 *Culpa* compared with *dolus eventualis*

Table 20.1 Comparing culpa *with* dolus eventualis

***Culpa* (negligence)**	***Dolus eventualis* (foresight of a possibility)**
The possibility must have been reasonably foreseeable	The possibility must have been subjectively foreseen
An objective/normative enquiry established by using the reasonable person test: *'should/ought to have foreseen'*	A subjective enquiry established by inferential reasoning: *'must have foreseen, therefore did in fact foresee'*
The possibility must have been foreseen as reasonably likely to occur	Foresight of a real possibility
Failure to take reasonable steps to prevent the possibility from materialising	Reconciliation with the possibility; persistence in the conduct, with the necessary subjective foresight

THIS CHAPTER IN ESSENCE

1. *Culpa* (negligence), unlike *dolus*, is both an objective and a normative concept. It is concerned with whether the accused's foresight and conduct measure up to a certain standard imposed by law, namely the standard of the reasonable person in the same circumstances as the accused and with the same capacity for knowledge.
2. Although the standard is an objective one, and is therefore determined without reference to the accused's actual state of mind, it is individualised according to the accused's background, educational level, culture, sex and race.
3. Where the accused is a person who, by virtue of the task that he undertakes, is expected to have a particular skill, knowledge or expertise that the ordinary person does not have (for example, a motorist, doctor or engineer), then he will be tested against the standard of the reasonable person with that particular skill, knowledge or expertise.
4. *Culpa* is established by means of a three-stage enquiry:
   - 4.1 Would the reasonable person, in the same circumstances as the accused, have foreseen the reasonable possibility of conducting himself unlawfully?
   - 4.2 Would the reasonable person, in the same circumstances as the accused, have taken steps to prevent that possibility from materialising?
   - 4.3 Did the accused fail to take the steps that he should reasonably have taken to prevent that possibility from materialising?
5. If the answer to all three questions is 'yes', the accused is considered to have been negligent.
6. Although *culpa* and *dolus* are fundamentally different concepts, they are not mutually exclusive.
7. Accordingly, the mere fact that the accused is found to have had *dolus* at the time of the unlawful conduct does not mean that he cannot now be convicted of a crime for which *culpa* is the required form of fault. A person who intentionally engages in unlawful conduct will always fall short of the standard of the reasonable person.

Chapter 21

The contemporaneity rule

CHAPTER OBJECTIVES

The objectives of this chapter are to:
- explain the contemporaneity rule
- show how courts have approached the contemporaneity rule in the so-called 'cadaver disposal' cases
- extract and explain the relevant principles.

21.1 The contemporaneity rule

It is a fundamental principle of South African criminal law that where fault, whether in the form of *dolus* or *culpa*, is required for the commission of a particular crime, then in order for criminal liability to arise, the accused must have had the required form of fault at precisely the same time as he was engaging in the unlawful conduct. In addition, the accused must have had criminal capacity, because without criminal capacity a person cannot form an intention or be negligent. In other words, for criminal liability to arise, all three elements of liability must be present and they must be *contemporaneous* – they must exist at one and the same time. This is known as the **contemporaneity rule.**[1]

For example, X plans to murder her husband Y tonight by drowning him in his bath. However, on her return home, she accidentally runs Y over and kills him while she is driving her car into the yard. X will not be guilty of murder because she did not have the necessary intention to kill Y at the time that she actually caused his death, not even if she later expresses her joy or satisfaction at the fact that she has done so. She may of course be guilty of culpable homicide if she drove negligently, but it is X's state of mind *at the time* that she caused Y's death that is the point of the enquiry.

What, however, is the position if, in the above example, X proceeds with her plan to drown Y in the bath? She pushes him under the water and holds him there until she thinks he is dead. She then decides to dispose of Y's body by driving it to a deserted spot and setting fire to the car with the body in it to make it look as though Y died by accident. But, unbeknown to her, Y is still alive when she sets fire to the car and so Y actually dies in the

1 Burchell JM *Principles of Criminal Law* 5 ed (2016) 445–446; Snyman CR *Criminal Law* 6 ed (2014) 148–149.

fire. Will X be guilty of murder in these circumstances even though she did not intend to kill Y at the time that she actually caused his death?

It could be argued that on a strict application of the contemporaneity rule, X should escape liability for murder in this case because her initial unlawful assault, although accompanied by the intention to kill, was not the actual cause of death, while her subsequent killing of the deceased was not accompanied by any form of intention because she mistakenly believed that the deceased was already dead. However, for policy reasons, our courts have been understandably reluctant to acquit an accused in such circumstances.[2]

21.2 Problems in establishing contemporaneity

The contemporaneity rule has come under discussion in a number of problematic cases in which the accused has committed what he mistakenly believed to be a fatal assault with the necessary intention to kill, whether in the form of *dolus directus* or *dolus eventualis*, but actually caused the death of the deceased by his subsequent act of concealing or disposing of the supposed remains.[3] This problem came before the Appellate Division (AD) in *S v Masilela and others*.[4]

S v Masilela and others

Masilela and his co-accused wanted to rob the deceased. During the course of the robbery, they decided to kill him as well. They assaulted the deceased by hitting him over the head and throttling him with a tie. This did not kill the deceased, but only rendered him unconscious. They left the deceased on a bed while they ransacked the house. Then, believing the deceased to be dead, they set fire to the bed and left. According to the postmortem report, the cause of the deceased's death was carbon monoxide poisoning from the smoke created by the fire. He was obviously still alive when the bed was set on fire. The trial Court convicted them all of murder, but reserved a question of law for decision by the AD, namely whether they were indeed guilty of murder.

The AD held that the deceased's initial injuries, which were administered with the intention to kill, were 'a directly contributory cause' of his death from carbon monoxide poisoning.[5] It rejected the contention that the accused's intention to kill fell away once they believed the deceased was dead. They were therefore guilty of murder even though there was no premeditated plan to kill and the killing was improvised during the course of the robbery.

Note, however, that the decision in *Masilela* predated *S v Goosen*, in which the AD decided that a mistake as to the causal sequence will exclude *dolus eventualis*.[6] In *Goosen*, the AD referred to its earlier decision in *Masilela*.[7] It held that in *Masilela*, the court was dealing with a mistake in respect of the *precise* manner of death. Furthermore, it was dealing with a case in which the accused actually desired the death of the deceased (the accused had *dolus directus* in respect of murder), but were simply mistaken as to which of a number of their acts was the actual cause of death. Accordingly, the AD held that *Masilela* was no authority for the proposition that mistake as to the causal sequence can *never* be a valid defence in our law.

2 See *S v Masilela and another* 1968 (2) SA 558 (A). Applied in *S v Kruger en andere* 1987 (4) SA 326 (T). See also *S v Daniels en 'n ander* 1983 (3) SA 275 (A); *S v Goosen* 1989 (4) SA 1013 (A).

3 See *R v Shorty and others* 1950 SR 280; *Thabo Meli and others v The Queen* [1954] 1 WLR 228; *R v Chiswibo* 1961 (2) SA 714 (FC).

4 *S v Masilela* supra.

5 *S v Masilela* supra at 571F–G.

6 *S v Goosen* supra.

7 *S v Goosen* supra at 1022–1023.

Thus, in *Goosen*, the AD drew a clear distinction between cases in which the accused had *dolus directus* in respect of the death of the deceased and those in which he merely foresaw the possibility of causing death. It held that in cases in which the accused has *dolus directus* in respect of killing the deceased, he will be liable for murder even if death occurs in a manner different from what the accused actually intended. It is only in cases where the state is relying on *dolus eventualis* that the accused's mistake as to the causal sequence will be a defence.

On the question of whether the accused's act of disposal of the supposed remains will be regarded as a *novus actus interveniens*, the Zimbabwean case of *S v Mtombeni*[8] is relevant.

S v Mtombeni

Mtombeni and an accomplice planned to steal from the house where the deceased worked. They spent the evening in her company, then got up and strangled her with a belt. Believing she was dead, they left her on a bed while removing valuables from the house. Mtombeni later returned to the house and set fire to it. The postmortem revealed that the deceased had not died from strangulation, but from suffocation due to smoke inhalation. Mtombeni was convicted of murder and appealed to the Zimbabwean Supreme Court.

On appeal, the Supreme Court confirmed that he had been rightly convicted. It held that where there is a preconceived plan to murder and then dispose of the body or conceal the crime, there is no question that the act of disposal should be regarded as a *novus actus interveniens*, provided that the two acts are so closely connected in time and method of performance that they constitute a single transaction. It held further that the initial unlawful assault, which was accompanied by *dolus*, was a *sine qua non* of the deceased's death, and the act of disposal did not constitute a break in the chain of causation. Accordingly, it found that Mtombeni had had the intention to kill at the time that he caused the deceased's death and he was therefore liable for murder.

In the most recently reported case in which a similar situation arose, namely *S v Nair and another*,[9] the AD did not consider the implications of the contemporaneity rule at all. However, in this case, there was insufficient evidence that the accused had genuinely believed that the deceased was dead when they put him into the water. Thus, regardless of their actual intention at the time of the initial assault, the court concluded that they had *dolus eventualis* in respect of his death at whichever time and in whichever manner they believed they might cause it.

THIS CHAPTER IN ESSENCE

1. To summarise, it appears that the correct approach in such cases is to determine at the outset what form of intention the accused had in respect of the murder at the time of his initial unlawful assault.
   1.1 Where the accused had *dolus directus* (actual intention to kill the deceased) at the time of the initial assault, then it makes no difference that the deceased did not die in the course of that assault, but in the course of the accused's subsequent attempt to dispose of the 'body'. The accused will still be guilty of murder for the following reasons:
      (a) The accused's attempt to dispose of the supposed remains will not rank as a *novus actus interveniens* because it is not an abnormal intervening act or event that occurred independently of the initial assault by the accused. All the events are therefore regarded as a single, unbroken transaction.

8 *S v Mtombeni* 1993 (1) SACR 591 (ZS).
9 *S v Nair and another* 1993 (1) SACR 451 (A).

(b) For *dolus directus*, it does not matter if the intended manner of death differs from the actual manner of death (*S v Masilela* and *S v Goosen*).

(c) The causing of the death was therefore accompanied by the requisite *dolus*.

1.2 The same rule would presumably apply where the accused had *dolus indirectus* (foresight of a certainty) because it does not appear that foresight of the causal sequence is a requirement for this form of *dolus*.

1.3 Where, however, the accused did not actually intend to kill the deceased at the time of the initial assault, but merely foresaw the *possibility* of doing so, then, if the deceased did not die in substantially the same manner as that foreseen by the accused, he will not be guilty of murder (*S v Goosen*). The contemporaneity rule would not be satisfied nor would the requirements for *dolus eventualis* be established. At most, the accused would be guilty of attempted murder or culpable homicide.

2. Therefore, the fundamental principle appears to be that a mistake as to the causal sequence will be a defence only when the state is relying on *dolus eventualis*. It will not afford a defence when the state is able to prove *dolus directus*.

Chapter 22

Fault in statutory offences, and strict and vicarious liability

CHAPTER OBJECTIVES

The objectives of this chapter are to:

- explain how the form of fault is determined in statutory offences
- explain the rules of interpretation that apply and the factors to be taken into account when the intention of the legislature cannot be clearly ascertained from the wording of the relevant section
- explain the concepts of strict and no-fault liability
- explain the now defunct *versari in re illicita* rule
- explain the concept of vicarious liability
- explain the extent to which vicarious liability applies in the case of corporate entities.

22.1 Fault in statutory offences

As we have seen, there are two main forms of fault in South African criminal law, namely intent (*dolus*) and negligence (*culpa*). How, then, do we determine which form of fault is required for a particular offence?

In the case of common law crimes, the required form of fault is invariably a definitional element of the crime. We have pointed out that there are only two common law crimes for which *culpa* is a sufficient form of fault: culpable homicide and contempt of court when committed by a newspaper editor publishing matter on a subject that is *sub judice*. *Dolus* is therefore the norm in terms of common law crimes and any of the three accepted forms of *dolus* will suffice.

In statutory offences, the position is more complex, because when the legislature creates a statutory offence, it can provide for any form of fault that it considers appropriate to attain the object of the legislation. Here, the legislature has three main options:

1. It can provide that *dolus* is required.
2. It can provide that *culpa* will suffice.
3. It can provide that fault does not need to be proved at all (true strict or no-fault liability), or does not need to be proved in respect of certain elements of the *actus reus* (partial strict liability).

In addition, where the legislature has provided that *dolus* is required, it may provide that only one of the higher forms of *dolus* will suffice, for example *dolus specialis* for the crime of genocide under the Implementation of the Rome Statute of the International Criminal Court Act 27 of 2002.[1] Sometimes the wording of a legislative provision is not explicit in terms of the form of intent that is required. It then becomes necessary to use the interpretative tools discussed below. An example is the crime of 'dealing in any dependence-producing substance or any dangerous dependence-producing substance or any undesirable dependence-producing substance'.[2] On the face of it, the *mens rea* requirement refers to specific knowledge regarding the nature of the drug(s) in question, combined with the further intention to deal in the drug(s). However, the specific nature of the language does not imply a requirement of *dolus directus* or some or other of the higher forms of *dolus*. Courts have interpreted this provision to include *dolus eventualis*.[3]

The form of fault required for the commission of a particular statutory offence, and indeed whether fault is required at all, therefore depends on the intention of the legislature as evidenced in the first instance by the wording of the relevant section. The legislature will almost never use the terms '*dolus*' and '*culpa*' as such, so it is necessary to use the methods discussed below to determine the intention of the legislature.

22.1.1 The wording of the section

Where the intention of the legislature is clear from the wording of the relevant section, then this will be decisive. Thus, for example, the use of words such as 'intentional' or 'intentionally' and 'negligent' or 'negligently' make it abundantly clear that fault is required in the form of *dolus* and *culpa* respectively.[4] When the statute uses words such as 'maliciously', 'knowingly', 'corruptly' or 'fraudulently', this is usually taken as indicating that *dolus* is required. However, the absence of such words does not always indicate that *culpa* will be sufficient or that the offence is one for which fault is not required at all.

22.1.2 Secondary rules of interpretation

Where the intention of the legislature is not clear from the wording of the relevant section, it becomes necessary to look to the so-called secondary rules of interpretation. There are two longstanding rules of interpretation that assist in criminal cases: presumption of fault and fault means *dolus*.

---

1 See Part 1 of Schedule 1 of the Act.

2 S 5(*a*) and s 5(*b*) read with s 13(*e*) and s 13(*f*) of the Drugs and Drug Trafficking Act 140 of 1992.

3 See, for instance, *S v Muholi* (450/05) [2006] ZASCA 38; [2006] SCA 44 (RSA) (28 March 2006) at 13.

4 Fortunately, because of the current trend in favour of plain language drafting, the use of such explicit terminology is becoming more common. However, in the case of some older statutes and those that are less well drafted, the required form of fault is not always spelt out as clearly.

22.1.2.1 Presumption of fault

The general rule, *actus non facit reum nisi mens sit rea* (there is no criminal liability without fault), applies as much to statutory offences as to common law crimes. Accordingly, in interpreting a statutory offence, it is presumed that some degree of fault is required, that is, either *dolus* or *culpa*, unless there are 'clear and convincing indications to the contrary'.[5] To put it differently, there is a presumption against no-fault liability.[6]

22.1.2.2 Fault means *dolus*

Where fault is required, it is further presumed, unless there are clear indications to the contrary, that the required form of fault is *dolus* rather than *culpa*. In other words, *dolus* is the presumed norm in criminal matters.[7]

The abovementioned presumptions refer to the absence of 'clear indications to the contrary'. What, then, are these contrary indications? Essentially they are the following:

- The language or context of the injunction or prohibition, that is, the way in which the offence is framed, may indicate that *culpa* will suffice, or that this is a case of no-fault liability.
- The scope and object of the legislation may indicate likewise. Thus, for example, where the purpose of the legislation is to penalise reckless, careless or negligent behaviour, this would tend to indicate that *culpa* will suffice. Similarly, where non-compliance with the statute would result in a great risk of serious harm or danger to human life, this would also tend to indicate that *dolus* may be dispensed with in favour of *culpa*, and it may even indicate that the legislature intended strict or no-fault liability.[8] Typical examples here would be road traffic legislation; legislation dealing with the preparation, storage and distribution of food and drugs; and legislation concerning occupational health and safety. The nature and extent of the prescribed penalty may indicate the form of fault that is required. The more severe the prescribed punishment is, the higher the form of fault normally required for the commission of the offence, that is, *dolus* as opposed to *culpa*.
- Considerations that relate to difficulty of proof may indicate a lower form of fault. For example, in cases where offenders would easily be able to escape liability merely by raising lack of *dolus* as a defence, thus frustrating the purpose of the legislation, this would tend to indicate that the legislature did not intend the state to have to prove *dolus* and that *culpa* was therefore the intended form of fault. It may even indicate that the legislature intended strict or no-fault liability.
- Conversely, considerations of reasonableness may indicate a higher form of fault. The legislature is always presumed to intend to act reasonably. Thus, for example, if applying fault in the form of *culpa* or no-fault liability would result in undue hardship to the ordinary person in the street, this would tend to indicate that this was *not* what the legislature intended. However, where the legislation is aimed at controlling the conduct of a specific sector of individuals who choose to engage in a particular form of enterprise, or pursue a particular course of conduct which might pose a danger to the public, then it would not be unreasonable to impose a higher standard of care upon them.[9]

---

5 *S v Arenstein* 1964 (1) SA 361 (A) at 365B–D.

6 See, for example, *S v Arenstein* supra; *Amalgamated Beverage Industries Natal (Pty) Ltd v City Council of Durban* 1994 (1) SACR 373 (A); *S v De Blom* 1977 (3) SA 513 (A) at 532B–C.

7 See, for example, *S v Naidoo* 1974 (4) SA 574 (N); *S v Magidson* 1984 (3) SA 825 (T) at 829; *S v Van Zyl* 2000 (1) SACR 259 (C).

8 See the discussion in this regard in *ABI Natal (Pty) Ltd v City Council of Durban* supra.

9 See, for example, *S v Naidoo* supra. See also Burchell JM *Principles of Criminal Law* 5 ed (2016) 397 and Snyman CR *Criminal Law* 6 ed (2014) 240–241.

None of the above indications will be decisive in and of itself. Each is merely a factor that a court must weigh up and balance against the other factors when determining the intention of the legislature.[10]

22.2 Liability without fault

22.2.1 Statutory provisions

We have explained that when creating a statutory offence, it is open to the legislature to provide for liability without fault or for so-called strict liability[11] if it so chooses. Such provisions would naturally have to meet the requirements of constitutionality,[12] but it does not appear that the mere lack of a fault requirement would automatically render such a provision unconstitutional.[13]

South African law does not appear to distinguish between **strict liability** and **no-fault liability.**[14] The two terms tend to be used interchangeably by courts to describe a situation in which liability for the offence in question is based on unlawful conduct *plus* criminal capacity. However, fault is not an element of the offence at all (**true strict liability**), or is not required in respect of a particular element (or elements) of the *actus reus* (**partial strict liability**). This means that the accused would not be able to rely on lack of fault as a defence. However, he could still raise the defence that his conduct was involuntary or that it was justified in the circumstances, and he could also raise lack of criminal capacity.

There is another option, namely **absolute liability**, which is, fortunately, unknown in South African law.[15] It describes the situation in which, apart from dispensing with the normal fault and criminal capacity requirements, the legislature makes it unnecessary even for all

10 See, for example, the court's approach in *ABI Natal (Pty) Ltd v City Council of Durban* supra. *ABI Natal (Pty) Ltd* was convicted in the magistrates' court of contravening by-law 18(*c*) of the Food By-Laws of the City of Durban (causing or permitting the distribution of contaminated food) after a bee was discovered in a bottle of its mineral water. On appeal, the Appellate Division (AD) held:

> **Arising from the *nulla poena sine culpa* principle [no punishment without fault] of the common law there is, as James JP indicated in *Ismail and another v Durban Corporation* 1971 (2) SA 606 (N) at 607E, 'a strong current of judicial opinion ... against finding anyone guilty of an unlawful act unless that act is accompanied by *mens rea*'.**

However, it is generally accepted by courts that the legislature may dispense with the requirement of *mens rea* and the only question in any given case is, therefore, whether it has in fact done so. The answer is to be found in the intention of the legislature. Sometimes its intention is expressed precisely and in clear language, but often it is not. The approach in such cases was described as follows in *S v Arenstein* supra at 365C–D:

> **The general rule is that *actus non facit reum nisi mens sit rea* [an act does not make a defendant guilty without a guilty mind], and that in construing statutory prohibitions or injunctions, the Legislature is presumed, in the absence of clear and convincing indications to the contrary, not to have intended innocent violations thereof to be punishable ... Indications to the contrary may be found in the language or the context of the prohibition or injunction, the scope and object of the statute, the nature and extent of the penalty, and the ease with which the prohibition or injunction could be evaded if reliance could be placed on the absence of *mens rea* ...**

After considering and weighing up the abovementioned factors in relation to the relevant by-law, the AD concluded that fault in the form of *culpa* was required for the commission of the offence.

11 Burchell JM *South African Criminal Law and Procedure Vol I: General Principles of Criminal Law* 4 ed (2011) 447–453.

12 In other words, they would need to comply with the provisions of s 36 of the Constitution of the Republic of South Africa, 1996, the so-called limitations clause. On the face of it, strict liability violates the fair trial rights of the accused in that the state does not have to prove the element of fault.

13 *S v Magagula* 2001 (2) SACR 123 (T) at 49, but see, however, the obiter dictum of O'Regan J in *S v Coetzee and others* 1997 (1) SACR 379 (CC) at 442H–I. See also Burchell *South African Criminal Law and Procedure Vol I* 453.

14 See the use of the term in *ABI Natal (Pty) Ltd v City Council of Durban* supra.

15 Burchell *South African Criminal Law and Procedure Vol I* 453.

the normal requirements of unlawful conduct to be met. Thus, for example, an accused would be unable to rely on the involuntariness of his conduct, or on any of the justification defences.

Even though the legislature may provide for strict liability when creating statutory offences, it is an expedient that has fallen out of favour in recent years.[16] Furthermore, courts have relied increasingly on the presumption against no-fault liability (as described above) when interpreting the requirements of statutory offences. In cases where this may mean that offenders could easily frustrate the objects of the legislation by relying on lack of subjective fault (*dolus*) as a defence, courts have generally been able to resolve the problem by lowering the form of fault to *culpa* and/or by requiring the accused to bear the onus of proving lack of fault.[17] The net result is that it is doubtful whether there are any remaining instances of true strict liability on the statute books.

As far as the common law is concerned, there is no longer any provision in our law for liability without fault.

22.2.2 The common law and the now defunct *versari in re illicita* rule[18]

In introducing the concept of fault, we explained that at one time, there was a common law rule, the ***versari in re illicita*** rule, that when a person engaged in an illegal activity, he would be held criminally liable for all the consequences that he caused in the course of that activity, regardless of whether those consequences were intended, foreseen or even foreseeable. This was an old doctrine of both Roman-Dutch and English law that South African law followed for many years. It is, however, clearly inconsistent with the principle *actus non facit reum nisi mens sit rea* (no liability without fault). With the trend towards the subjectivisation of fault during the 1950s and 1960s, the doctrine was reconsidered and eliminated from the law.[19]

However, where two or more persons join together to commit a crime such as robbery, taking lethal weapons with them, courts will readily infer that each of them must have foreseen, and therefore did in fact foresee, the possibility that the victim may offer resistance,

16 Thus, for example, although s 175 of the former Liquor Act 27 of 1989 and s 50(5) of the former Sea Fisheries Act 12 of 1988 provided for partial strict liability, the relevant provisions were not retained in their modern counterparts. See further, Snyman CR *Criminal Law* 6 ed (2014) 237.

17 See, for example, *S v Elkon* 1981 (4) SA 62 (T). Bear in mind, however, that reversing the onus of proof will not always pass constitutional muster these days, as shown in *S v Coetzee and others* supra. See also commentary by Kemp GP '*Die grondwetlikheid van statutêre vermoedens*' 1998 9(1) *Stell LR* 106–114.

18 The full maxim reads, *versari in re illicita omnia imputantur quae sequuntur ex delicto* (to one who is involved in an unlawful activity must be imputed all the consequences of his unlawful act).

19 Two important cases that lent impetus to this process were *S v Van Der Mescht* 1962 (1) SA 521 (A) and *S v Bernardus* 1965 (3) SA 287 (A).

In *S v Van Der Mescht*, Van der Mescht and Groesbeek had illegally come into possession of unwrought gold in amalgam form, an offence under mining rights legislation. They melted the amalgam on a stove to extract the gold. The melted amalgam gave off a poisonous gas, which killed Groesbeek and four children who were sleeping in the house at the time. The trial court convicted Van der Mescht of culpable homicide.

On appeal, the AD held that a reasonable person in Van der Mescht's position, with no particular knowledge or expertise in metallurgy, would not have known that the melted amalgam would give off poisonous gas. Therefore, Van der Mescht had not been negligent. It held further that the mere fact that he was involved in an illegal activity at the time did not make him guilty of culpable homicide in the absence of fault on his part. His conviction was set aside.

In *S v Bernardus*, the accused threw a knobkierie at the deceased. His conduct (assault) was thus *prima facie* unlawful. The AD had to consider whether he should be convicted of culpable homicide on the basis that he was involved in an illegal activity when he caused the deceased's death. It held that the *versari in re illicita* rule is in direct conflict with one of the fundamental principles of South African criminal law, namely no liability without fault. It held further that the mere intention to commit an assault is not a substitute for *dolus* or *culpa* in respect of causing the death of the deceased. The AD found, however, that Bernardus had in fact been negligent in respect of the deceased's death and confirmed his conviction for culpable homicide.

The AD's ruling in *S v Bernardus* officially put an end to the *versari in re illicita* rule in our law, but a last vestige of the doctrine is sometimes evident in the way in which the courts apply the requirements for *dolus eventualis* in cases that involve common purpose.

that the weapons may be used to overcome such resistance, that other armed persons may come to their assistance, and that anyone in the vicinity, even a person other than one of the intended victims, may be killed as a result. Each of the accused will therefore be liable not only for robbery, but also for murder, or at least culpable homicide, if someone is in fact killed in the course of the robbery.[20] The alacrity with which courts will infer subjective foresight in such cases sometimes comes very close to the *versari* rule in disguise.

22.3 Vicarious liability

Strict liability and **vicarious liability** may at first glance seem to be the same, but they are distinct concepts.[21] The former is based on the conduct of the accused personally, whereas the latter concerns the liability of an accused for the acts of another person. Strict liability crimes also do not establish vicarious liability by necessary implication.[22]

According to the principle of vicarious liability, an employer or principal will be jointly liable for damages caused by the wrongful and negligent conduct of his employee or agent, that is, his representative, acting in the course and scope of his employment, or his authority as agent. In such cases, the employer's or principal's liability is based on the conduct and fault of the employee or agent, not on his own conduct and/or fault. Therefore, it will not avail him to argue that he was in no way negligent in his management or control of his employee or agent.

Vicarious liability is not a principle of South African criminal law. Burchell correctly states that it is a 'fundamental negation of the principle that criminal liability is based on individual fault (*mens rea*)', more so than even the concept of strict liability.[23] It is a principle more suited to the law of delict. However, it is open to the legislature to provide for vicarious criminal liability in specific instances, should it choose to do so.

DISCUSSION

Vicarious liability as dubious criminalisation strategy: the risk of over-criminalisation

We submit that vicarious liability does not belong in modern South African criminal law. There are instances where the legislature has imposed such liability, either expressly[24] or by necessary implication. One fairly far-reaching instance is in section 332(1) of the Criminal Procedure Act 51 of 1977 in relation to corporate entities, which is explored further in the next chapter.[25] Legislatures often justify forms of vicarious liability in the context of public welfare legislation. The rationale is offered that vicarious liability ensures that 'the implementation of public welfare legislation is not hindered by employers who evade their duties and responsibilities by hiding behind the wrongs of commission and omission of their employees'.[26] Given the vast extent of public welfare legislation,[27] one can see the risk of over-criminalisation, which is also not good public policy.

20 See, for example, *S v Nhlapo and another* 1981 (2) SA 744 (A) and *S v Lungile and another* 1999 (2) SACR 597 (SCA) (discussed in section 19.3.3).
21 Burchell *South African Criminal Law and Procedure Vol I* 460.
22 *Hoosain NO v Johannesburg City Council* 1948 (1) SA 564 (T).
23 Burchell *South African Criminal Law and Procedure Vol I* 460.
24 See, for example, s 24(1) of the Drugs and Drug Trafficking Act.
25 See also the discussion in Chapter 23.
26 Burchell *Principles of Criminal Law* 449–450.
27 For an overview and discussion of the most important public welfare legislation, see Milton JRL, Cowling MG and Hoctor SV (eds) *South African Criminal Law and Procedure* (Statutory Offences) Vol III 2 ed (1988) (revision service 27, 2017).

THIS CHAPTER IN ESSENCE

1. In this chapter, we have considered how fault is determined in statutory offences and the various rules of interpretation that apply in such cases.
2. We have also considered various forms of liability without fault, for example strict liability and vicarious liability.
3. Because of historical and constitutional reasons, these forms of liability without fault are no longer part of South African criminal law.
4. Any temptation to return to liability without fault via statutory provisions should be resisted or, at the very least, carefully scrutinised in light of the Constitution, in particular the right to a fair trial, which includes the principle that the state must prove all the elements of a crime, including the element of *mens rea* or fault.

Chapter 23

Corporate criminal liability

CHAPTER OBJECTIVES

The objectives of this chapter are to:
- give an overview of historical, comparative and international positions regarding the notion of corporate criminal liability
- discuss the essential components of corporate criminal liability in South African law with particular reference to section 332 of the Criminal Procedure Act 51 of 1977.

23.1 Historical, comparative and international perspectives

The cornerstone of criminal law is the notion of individual criminal liability. This means that a person who commits a crime is generally, and with a number of exceptions as explained elsewhere in this work, held criminally responsible for his deeds. But what about non-human entities recognised by the law as 'persons' with their own autonomous identities - so-called juristic persons (legal persons) or corporations?[1] Can they also commit crimes and, if so, should they be held criminally liable like human (natural) persons? The practical and legal reality is that a juristic person can be the 'bearer of rights and duties, without having a physical or visible body or a mind'.[2] Flowing from this is the practical reality that juristic persons can act and their actions have consequences in real life. Unfortunately, these consequences are sometimes criminal in nature.

1 Juristic persons have autonomous existence in law. In other words, they exist independently from the natural persons or other entities that form their members, for instance the shareholders in a company. This principle is well established in South African law. See *Salomon v A Salomon & Co Ltd* [1897] AC 22; *Dadoo Ltd and others v Krugersdorp Municipal Council* 1920 AD 530, and more recently, *Airport Cold Storage (Pty) Ltd v Ebrahim and others* 2008 (2) SA 303 (C). S 19(1) of the Companies Act 71of 2008 confirms the common law position: 'From the date and time that the incorporation of a company is registered, ... the company - (*a*) is a juristic person ...'. On the nature and consequences of legal personality, see, in general, Davis D and Cassim F (eds) *Companies and Other Business Structures in South Africa* 2 ed (2011) 23–27.

2 Snyman CR *Criminal Law* 6 ed (2014) 245.

The notion of individual criminal liability assumes *personal culpability* as we have seen in the previous chapters.[3] However, this does not mean that all legal systems or the evolving system of international criminal law recognises corporate criminal liability as a natural and logical extension of the notion of individual criminal liability.[4]

Historically, English common law recognised criminal liability of corporations via the notion of vicarious liability. Before the adoption of the predecessors of the current Criminal Procedure Act 51 of 1977 (first in 1917 and later 1939[5]), South African courts followed the English common law approach.[6] The current position regarding criminal liability of juristic persons in South Africa is provided for in section 332 of the Criminal Procedure Act, which is discussed below.

The seemingly uncontroversial notion that corporations can be held criminally liable in South Africa masks a rather ambivalent history, at least in terms of the doctrinal and academic support.[7] De Wet, for instance, did not support the notion of corporate criminal liability. His opposition to this form of criminal liability was informed by the fact that he could not find support for this form of liability in the old Roman-Dutch authorities. In addition, De Wet put the emphasis on the *personal* nature of criminal liability. Consequently, an abstract entity like a corporation could not fulfil the requirements necessary for culpability.[8] This view is not shared by other prominent South African authors such as Snyman and Burchell.[9]

Unlike English common law, which has recognised corporate criminal liability since at least the early 19th century,[10] continental European legal systems were much more reluctant to accept this form of criminal liability.[11] German legal doctrine, under the influence of writers such as Von Feuerbach and Von Savigny, resisted the expansion of criminal liability to include juristic persons.[12] Presently, the German Criminal Code provides for the liability of certain administrators and officers of companies.[13] However, there is certainly no general principle of corporate criminal liability. As a general rule, only natural persons over the age of 14 years can be held criminally liable under German law.[14] Other continental European

3 See, for instance, the following paragraph from a judgment by the International Criminal Tribunal for the Former Yugoslavia (ICTY) in ICTY *Prosecutor v Dusko Tadić* (appeal judgment) IT-94-1-A July 1999 at 186:

> **The basic assumption must be that in international law as much as in national systems, the foundation of criminal responsibility is the principle of personal culpability: nobody may be held criminally responsible for acts or transactions in which he has not personally engaged or in some other way participated (*nulla poena sine culpa*).**

4 See, in general, Stessens G 'Corporate criminal liability: A comparative perspective' (1994) 43(3) *ICLQ* 493; Stoitchkova D *Towards Corporate Liability in International Criminal Law* (2010) 113–121; Wagner M 'Corporate criminal liability: National and international responses' 25(2) *CLB* (1999) 600–608, on the historical origins and current position of corporate criminal liability in selected common law and civil law jurisdictions.

5 Act 31 of 1917 and Act 23 of 1939.

6 See, for instance, *R v Dundee Coal Mining Co* (1904) 25 NLR 23.

7 Kemp G 'Toerekening, sanksionering en strafregtelike aanspreeklikheid van regspersone in Suid-Afrikaanse perspektief' in Faure M and Neethling J (eds) *Aansprakelijkheid, risico en onderneming: Europese en Zuid-Afrikaanse perspectieven* (2003) 163–171.

8 See De Wet JC and Swanepoel HL *Strafreg* 4 ed (1985) 53–62.

9 See Snyman *Criminal Law* 245–246 and Burchell J *Principles of Criminal Law* 5 ed (2016) 458–470.

10 Kemp 'Toerekening, sanksionering en strafregtelike aanspreeklikheid van regspersone' 164.

11 See, in general, Adam S, Colette-Basecqz N and Nihoul M (eds) *Corporate Criminal Liability in Europe* (2008).

12 Kemp 'Toerekening, sanksionering en strafregtelike aanspreeklikheid van regspersone' 164.

13 S 14 of the German Criminal Code.

14 S 19 of the German Criminal Code. See, in general, Bohlander M *Principles of German Criminal Law* (2009) 23.

countries, such as France,[15] the Netherlands[16] and Belgium,[17] do recognise corporate criminal liability.[18] At a regional level, there is also growing pressure from the European Union on member states to sanction juristic persons preferably via criminal law or, if this is not possible, then by means of administrative sanctions.[19]

Many national legal systems influenced by Western legal thought, either in the Anglo-American common law tradition or those influenced by continental European systems, recognise corporate criminal liability in some form or another, often based on some form of vicarious liability. Examples of such states are the US, Canada, Israel, Australia and Switzerland.[20] Some systems use legal presumptions to make it easier to allocate corporate criminal responsibility. Japan, for instance, adopted a legal framework that provides for a rebuttable presumption of corporate liability in situations where corporations are involved in criminal conduct.[21]

Corporate criminal liability in international criminal law is still under-developed.[22] Indeed, arguably the most important instrument for purposes of international criminal law, the Rome Statute of the International Criminal Court, 1998, does not provide for criminal liability of juristic persons. Article 25(1) of the Rome Statute, which deals with individual criminal responsibility, provides that the International Criminal Court 'shall have jurisdiction over natural persons'. Further, a person who commits a crime within the jurisdiction of the International Criminal Court (genocide, war crimes, crimes against humanity and the crime of aggression) 'shall be individually responsible and liable for punishment'.[23] This notion of criminal responsibility under international criminal law is perhaps unrealistically restrictive given the role of organisations, including corporations, in mass human rights violations and crimes of international concern such as crimes against humanity and genocide.[24]

23.2 Corporate criminal liability in South Africa

We pointed out above that before the adoption of relevant statutory provisions on the subject, South African courts initially followed the English common law approach to criminal liability of juristic persons. At present, the criminal liability of juristic persons is dealt with in terms of section 332 of the Criminal Procedure Act.[25]

---

15 Since 1994. Corporate criminal liability in France is still limited in scope. For commentary, see Elliott C 'France' in Reed A and Bohlander M *Participation in Crime: Domestic and Comparative Perspectives* (2013) 286–289.

16 Since 1976.

17 Since 1999. For commentary, see Van den Wyngaert C, Vandromme S and De Smet B *Strafrecht en Strafprocesrecht in Hoofdlijnen* 9 ed Boek 1 (2015) 123–139.

18 Kemp 'Toerekening, sanksionering en strafregtelike aanspreeklikheid van regspersone' 164.

19 Van den Wyngaert, Vandromme and De Smet *Strafrecht en Strafprocesrecht* 123.

20 Stoitchkova *Towards Corporate Liability in International Criminal Law* 113–118.

21 See the citation in Heine G 'New developments in corporate criminal liability in Europe: Can Europeans learn from the American experience or vice versa?' *St. Louis-Warsaw Transatlantic LJ* (1998) 173 at 182.

22 For a critical assessment, see Stoitchkova *Towards Corporate Liability in International Criminal Law*.

23 Art 25(2) of the Rome Statute of the International Criminal Court, 1998.

24 See also submissions by Stoitchkova *Towards corporate liability in international criminal law* 167–190.

25 For a brief discussion, see Snyman *Criminal Law* 246–248. For a more comprehensive and critical discussion, see Burchell *Principles of Criminal Law* 464-468. See further, Du Toit et al *Commentary on the Criminal Procedure Act* (revision service 54, 2015) 33-3–33-8.

23.2.1 Section 332 of the Criminal Procedure Act 51 of 1977

Section 332(1) of the Criminal Procedure Act provides, in essence, that where a director[26] or employee[27] of a corporate body (that is, an incorporated entity, not other affiliations or entities like trusts created by notarial deed)[28] commits a crime in the exercise of his powers or the performance of his duties (that is, in his official capacity), or instructs or permits someone else to do so, the corporate body will be liable for that crime. This is because the official acts of the directors or employees are deemed to be the acts of the corporate entity.[29] Section 332(2) provides further that, in such cases, the fault of the director or employee will be imputed (attributed) to the corporate body as well.[30] The practical result is that corporations can commit virtually any crime where *dolus*, *culpa* or even strict liability is applicable.[31] It is doubtful, however, that corporations can commit crimes such as rape and compelled rape. This is not a doctrinal issue, but rather a question of the particular nature and elements of the crime.[32]

Conversely, section 332(5) used to provide that a director or employee of a corporate body would be liable for a crime committed by the corporate body, unless he could prove that he did not take part in the commission of the crime and could not have prevented it. This provision, read together with the previous ones, meant in effect that one director or employee of a corporate body could be held liable for crimes committed by another director or employee in his official capacity. However, section 332(5) was declared unconstitutional in *S v Coetzee*[33] on the grounds that by placing the onus of proof on the accused, it offended unreasonably and unjustifiably against the presumption of innocence. Therefore, as matters stand at present, it is only the corporate entity that can be held liable for crimes committed by its directors or employees. The other directors and employees cannot also be held liable, unless they actively associated themselves with the commission of the crime.

Section 332(7) contains a presumption in respect of unincorporated associations, such as partnerships and clubs, in terms similar to those used in section 332(5). The constitutional validity of this section has not yet been challenged, but it would no doubt be found unconstitutional too for the same reasons as in *S v Coetzee*.[34]

---

26 See also s 332(10) and *S v Marks* 1965 (3) SA 834 (W) for the extended meaning of 'director'.

27 The term 'servant' is not defined in s 332, but it is generally understood to mean any individual regularly employed by the company, 'whether by contract or otherwise'. See Du Toit et al *Commentary on the Criminal Procedure Act* (revision service 59, 2017) 33-8.

28 *S v Peer* 1968 (4) SA 460 (N).

29 *S v SA Metal & Machinery Co (Pty) Ltd* 2010 (2) SACR 413 (SCA). The position seems to be that a company cannot be convicted when the employee on whose conduct the prosecution relied was acquitted. The elements of the crime are attributed to the company via the employee or director acting and thinking on behalf of the company. The Supreme Court of Appeal (SCA) (at 16) also confirmed that corporate entities are equally entitled to the right to a fair trial provided for in s 35 of the Constitution of the Republic of South Africa, 1996.

30 Strictly speaking, this means that it is not a case of true vicarious liability since the corporate entity is *deemed* to have fault. In true vicarious liability, the employer/principal does not require fault at all.

31 See, for instance, *S v Joseph Mtshumayeli (PVT) Ltd* 1971 (1) SA 33 (RA); *Ex parte Minister van Justisie: In re S v Suid-Afrikaanse Uitsaaikorporasie* 1992 (4) SA 804 (A); *S v Dersley* 1997 (2) SACR 253 (Ck). See also Rycroft A 'Corporate homicide' (2004) 17(2) *SACJ* 141–157.

32 See also the discussion in Burchell *Principles of Criminal Law* 466.

33 *S v Coetzee and others* 1997 (3) SA 527 (CC). For a discussion of the case, see Kemp GP 'Die grondwetlikheid van statutêre vermoedens' (1998) 9(1) *Stell LR* 106.

34 Burchell *Principles of Criminal Law* 468.

DISCUSSION **Criminal liability of 'morally blameless corporations'**

Given the present legal position in South Africa, is it indeed desirable to punish juristic persons, such as companies, on the basis of section 332(1), which creates 'an irrebuttable deeming provision'?[35] Does this 'irrebuttable deeming provision' violate the presumption of innocence (section 35 of the Constitution) in that the *company* as a juristic person can raise no defence once section 332(1) has been triggered?

The problem is that the company can be convicted of a crime essentially committed by another person, for example a director, when the company in actual fact did not participate in the criminal activity. Section 332(1) of the Criminal Procedure Act can be attacked on constitutional grounds because (1) the company may not have participated in the crime, (2) the company may have had no knowledge of the crime, (3) the company may have taken reasonable steps to prevent the crime, and (4) the company may not reasonably have been able to prevent the crime.

In terms of the effect of section 332(1) of assigning blame to a 'morally blameless person' (the company), some argue that one should rather investigate what the company actually intended (via the 'controlling mind' - presumably the board of directors). This will be in line with the confirmation in *Burg Trailers SA (Pty) Ltd and another v ABSA Bank Ltd and others* that a 'single juristic entity' (the company) 'could only have had one intention'.[36]

However, it is also necessary to consider the enormous socio-economic impact of corporate entities and the very real presence that they have in the daily lives of people. There seems to be a clear policy rationale for the principle that corporate entities must be held accountable, especially in the context of clear or implied legal duties.[37] There are also international and comparative examples that show a greater willingness to hold corporate entities criminally liable.[38]

THIS CHAPTER IN ESSENCE

1. In this chapter, we have discussed the essential elements of corporate criminal liability in South African criminal law. This discussion must be considered against the historical, comparative and international background.
2. In modern South African criminal law, the criminal liability of juristic persons is governed by the Criminal Procedure Act. However, prior to the current statutory framework, the notion of corporate criminal liability was established under South African common law, mainly under the influence of English law. Comparative and international law show that the notion of corporate criminal liability is not universally accepted. The idea that a juristic person can think or can have the necessary *mens rea* is still dogmatically controversial in some jurisdictions.

35 Van Eeden H, Hopkins K and Adendorff C 'Criminal liability of morally blameless corporations' (Sept 2011) *De Rebus* 27 at 29.

36 *Burg Trailers SA (Pty) Ltd and another v ABSA Bank Ltd and others* 2004 (1) SA 284 (SCA) at 7.

37 For an interesting proposition, see Van der Bijl C 'Corporate "assault": Bullying and the aegis of criminal law (part 1)' (2014) 3 *TSAR* 482–495; (part 2) (2014) 4 *TSAR* 760–775.

38 See further, Borg-Jorgensen V and Van der Linde KE 'Corporate criminal liability in South Africa: time for change? (Part 1)' 2011 (3) *TSAR* 452; (Part 2) 2011 (4) *TSAR* 684.

3. Because of the scope of corporate activity in modern society, the notion of corporate criminal liability seems to be progressively accepted in jurisdictions that previously did not accept this as part of their criminal law. The notion is also a point of debate in international criminal law.

Chapter 24

Defences excluding fault

CHAPTER OBJECTIVES

The objectives of this chapter are to:
- define the term 'mistake'
- distinguish between a mistake and an accident
- distinguish between a mistake of fact and a mistake of law
- explain the requirements for a mistake of fact or law to exclude *dolus*
- explain the requirements for a mistake of fact or law to exclude *culpa*
- explain what is meant by putative justification
- identify situations where the various forms of putative justification would be the appropriate defence
- identify the circumstances in which youth, mental illness or intellectual disability, intoxication, and severe emotional distress will exclude *dolus* without also excluding criminal capacity.

24.1 Introduction: Correspondence of fault and conduct

Having considered the forms of fault in South African law and their various requirements, we now turn to consider the defences that an accused may raise in order to exclude the element of fault.

Where fault is a requirement of a particular crime, as it normally is, fault and conduct must *correspond*. This means that the accused must have the required form of fault in respect of *each and every essential element* of the *actus reus* at the time when he conducts himself unlawfully. If he does not have the required form of fault in respect of each and every essential element of the *actus reus*, then he will not be criminally liable.

To illustrate, murder is defined as the *intentional unlawful killing of another person*. The essential elements of the *actus reus* for murder are, therefore, the (1) unlawful (2) killing (3) of another person, while the *mens rea* for murder consists of the intention to do *all three* of these things. Thus, to be liable for murder, the accused must not only have *done* all three things, but he must also have *intended* to do them. That is, he must have intended to *kill* (not merely injure); he must have intended to kill another *living human being* (not, for example, an animal or a *tokoloshe*);[1] and he must have intended to do so *unlawfully* (not in the mistaken belief that his conduct was legally justified).[2] If he lacked the intention to do any one of these things, then he lacked the intention to commit *murder* and he cannot be held liable for this crime.

It is evident, therefore, that certain types of mistake or ignorance will constitute a valid defence in our law, excluding the element of fault.

24.2 The defence of mistake or ignorance

At the outset, it is important to distinguish between the terms 'mistake' and 'accident'. In common parlance, they are often used interchangeably and incorrectly, as in 'I answered the wrong question by accident', or 'I missed the target and shot the deceased by mistake'. The terms have different and distinct meanings. This distinction is important in law:

- A *mistake (error)* means a misapprehension, an erroneous or incorrect impression or state of mind, possibly leading to inappropriate action being taken.[3]
- An *accident (casus)* means a chance occurrence, an unintended or unforeseen physical event in which something goes unexpectedly wrong.

Thus, an accused's statement, 'I killed the deceased by mistake' has a very different meaning in law from 'I killed the deceased by accident'. The first statement denotes that the accused was mistaken *in his mind* about some aspect of the situation in which he acted, implying that if he had known the truth, he would have acted differently. The second statement denotes that the killing was the result of *external* events unfolding in a way other than the accused intended, desired or foresaw. In both cases, the accused may well escape liability for murder, but different principles will apply.

However, our law does not distinguish between mistake and ignorance (lack of knowledge). It takes the view that if a person is mistaken about something, then he is ignorant of the true position. Ignorance and mistake are therefore treated the same in our law. For present purposes, we will deal principally with mistake in the true sense: an erroneous state of mind on the part of the accused or ignorance of the true position. On the question of accident, however, see section 24.5 below on *aberratio ictus*.

1 See, for example, *S v Ngema* 1992 (2) SACR 651 (D) (discussed previously in section 20.3 above).
2 Putative justification is discussed further in section 24.3 below.
3 It is also necessary to distinguish between a *mistake* and a *delusion* or a *hallucination*. A mistake is the product of *rational* thought (see *S v De Oliveira* 1993 (2) SACR 59 (A) at 65D; *Director of Public Prosecutions, Gauteng v Pistorius* 2016 (2) SA 317 (SCA) para 53), whereas delusions and hallucinations are products of a *disordered* mind, due to mental illness or intoxication, where a person cannot perceive reality as it actually exists. In such a case, the appropriate defence would be lack of criminal capacity, not mistake of fact.

The fundamental rule is that a person who is genuinely unaware of the fact that he is, or may possibly be, committing a crime, cannot be said to have criminal intention. *Dolus* denotes conscious wrongdoing or, as the Appellate Division (AD) put it in *S v Ntuli*, '*dolus* consists of an intention to do an unlawful act'.[4]

South African law has traditionally distinguished between two main types of mistake or ignorance: mistake or ignorance of *fact*, and mistake or ignorance of *law*.[5] Until the AD's decision in *S v De Blom*,[6] only a mistake of fact would be a valid defence, not a mistake of law. Now, they are both valid defences to crimes that require fault, although we will discuss them separately for purposes of convenience and because there are still slight differences in the approach to each.

24.2.1 Mistake or ignorance of fact excluding *dolus*

To exclude *dolus* and thus absolve the accused from liability for a crime requiring this form of fault, for example, murder, theft or rape, the accused's mistake or ignorance need only meet two requirements, namely that it must be both *genuine* and *essential*:

- *Genuine*: This simply means that the mistake or ignorance must be *bona fide*, that is, not feigned or pretended. It does not mean that the mistake need also be a reasonable one.[7] However, if the accused suspects that he may be mistaken and proceeds regardless, or deliberately refrains from making enquiries as to the true position, he will be found to have had *dolus* in the form of *dolus eventualis*.
- *Essential*: This means that the mistake or ignorance must concern some essential element of the *actus reus* of the alleged crime. The essential elements of a crime are the elements contained in the definition of the crime, as illustrated above.[8]

It is important to note that a mistake or ignorance concerning a non-essential feature of the crime (something that is not contained in the definition of the crime) will *not* be sufficient to exclude *dolus* in respect of that crime and will therefore not constitute a valid defence. Thus, for example, if A kills B, mistaking him for his enemy C, A will still be liable for murder because he intended to kill a specific person (B) unlawfully and did so. He therefore had intention in respect of all the essential elements of murder. His mistake as to B's identity does not concern one of the essential elements of murder and will therefore not exonerate him.[9]

Similarly, if A steals a valuable necklace from B, believing it to be cheap costume jewelry, A would still be liable for the theft of the necklace. His mistake about its value does not concern an essential element of the crime of theft. It would be different, however, if (hypothetically) we were to redefine theft as 'the intentional unlawful taking of another

4 *S v Ntuli* 1975 (1) SA 429 (A) at 436F. See also *S v Dougherty* 2003 (2) SACR 36 (W).

5 For mistake or ignorance of the law affecting knowledge of unlawfulness, see, in general, Burchell *Principles of Criminal Law* 390–395; Snyman *Criminal Law* 199–204.

6 *S v De Blom* 1977 (3) SA 513 (A).

7 Because *dolus* is tested *subjectively*, the standards of the reasonable person do not enter the enquiry. Note, however, that where the accused's mistake was grossly unreasonable, a court will be unlikely to accept that it was *genuine*. See, for example, *S v Nel and another* 1980 (4) SA 28 (E); *S v Reabow* 2007 (2) SACR 292 (E); *Director of Public Prosecutions, Gauteng v Pistorius* supra at para 53.

8 See the example, given above, setting out the essential (definitional) elements of the crime of murder.

9 A good 'rule of thumb' test is to ask whether, if the facts had actually been as the accused believed them to be, this would have been sufficient to make the accused completely innocent of the crime (see the old English cases of *R v Prince* (1875) 13 Cox CC 138 at 156 and *R v Tolson* (1889) 23 QB 168 at 181). A *non*-essential mistake may, however, lead to a *further* mistake, which *is* essential. Thus, a mistake of identity, which is non-essential in itself, may lead to the accused believing that he is about to be attacked and is therefore justified in defending himself when this was not in fact the case. See, for example, *S v Naidoo* 1997 (1) SACR 62 (T), discussed below (see also the discussion on this point in *Director of Public Prosecutions, Gauteng v Pistorius* supra at paras 30–32).

person's *valuable* property'. In this case, the value of the stolen property would be an essential (definitional) element of the crime of theft and a mistake in this regard would be an essential mistake.[10]

24.2.2 Mistake or ignorance of fact excluding *culpa*

To exclude *culpa* and thus absolve the accused from a crime requiring this form of fault, for example culpable homicide, then not only must that mistake or ignorance have been genuine and essential as above, but there are two further requirements that must be met: the mistake or ignorance must have been reasonable and the accused must have acted reasonably in light of his mistake:

- *Reasonable mistake or ignorance*: The test is whether a reasonable person in the same position as the accused would also have had the same erroneous impression or would also have been ignorant in the same respect.
- *Reasonable conduct*: The question here is whether the accused acted reasonably in light of his mistake. In other words, the accused is still required to act as a reasonable person would have acted with the same subjective state of mind, that is, in the circumstances *as perceived* by him.[11]

If these two further requirements are not met, the accused will be adjudged negligent and he will be liable if the crime is one for which *culpa* is a sufficient form of fault.[12]

24.3 Putative justification defences

Bearing the above requirements in mind, there is a group of defences that require special mention, namely the defences of putative[13] private defence of person or property, putative necessity, putative impossibility, putative obedience to superior orders, putative public authority, putative consent, and so forth. For ease of reference, we will refer to them collectively as **putative justification.**[14] These defences are simply a convenient way of referring to a particular kind of *mistake of fact.*

It may happen that a person makes a mistake of fact, which leads him to believe that his conduct is justified and therefore lawful,[15] whereas this is not in fact the case. An example of this is where the accused genuinely believed that he was justified in using force to defend himself against an unlawful attack by another person, even though:

- the attack had not yet begun and was not imminent; or
- the attack was already over; or
- there was never any actual unlawful attack or threat of such attack; or
- there was an actual attack, but it was not as serious as the accused thought, so that the force or means used by the accused were in fact excessive in the circumstances.

We have explained previously that, in such a case, the accused cannot rely on the defence of private defence, because he does not meet the requirements for that defence tested

10 See *R v Prince* (1875) 13 Cox CC 138 at 156 and *R v Tolson* (1889) 23 QB 168 at 181, mentioned above.

11 These two requirements are nothing more than an abbreviated version of the three-stage test for negligence as discussed in section 20.4.

12 See, for example, *S v Ngema* supra (discussed in section 20.3); *S v Naidoo* supra.

13 'Putative' means supposed, thought or believed.

14 Note, however, that there is no *general* ground of justification in South African criminal law. When raising such a defence, therefore, it is necessary to specify the ground of justification upon which the accused believed he was acting at the time.

15 On the basis of one of the justification defences discussed above under 'Defences excluding unlawfulness'.

objectively, that is, from an external point of view, according to the actual facts of the case.[16] The same applies in cases where the accused genuinely believed that he was acting in a situation of necessity, impossibility, in obedience to superior orders, with public authority, or with the complainant's consent, whereas this was not in fact the case.

Unlike the case where there is actual justification for the accused's conduct, the accused's mistaken belief that he is acting lawfully can never render his conduct lawful. However, such a mistake will exclude *dolus* in relation to an essential element of the crime, namely the intention to perform the relevant act *unlawfully*.[17] In this case, the appropriate defence for the accused to raise would be one of the putative justification defences. These defences are tested according to the requirements for mistake of fact, as set out and explained above. The significance of the distinction between actual justification and putative justification is summed up in this passage from *S v De Oliveira*:

> **A person who acts in private defence acts lawfully, provided his conduct satisfies the requirements laid down for such a defence and does not exceed its limits ... In putative private defence it is not lawfulness that is in issue but culpability [i.e. fault]. If an accused honestly believes his life or property to be in danger, but objectively viewed they are not, the defensive steps he takes cannot constitute private defence. If in those circumstances he kills someone his conduct is unlawful. His erroneous belief that his life or property was in danger may well (depending upon the precise circumstances) exclude *dolus*, in which case liability for the person's death based on intention will also be excluded; at worst for him he can then be convicted of culpable homicide.**[18]

In the above situation, the accused will only be liable for culpable homicide if the state proves that he was negligent. If, however, (1) the accused's mistaken belief was a reasonable one, and (2) the accused acted reasonably in light of that mistake, then *culpa* would also be excluded and the accused would be completely exonerated.[19]

---

16 See section 7.3.

17 The unlawfulness of the prohibited conduct is an essential element of every offence and *dolus* requires *knowledge of unlawfulness*.

18 *S v De Oliveira* 1993 (2) SACR 59 (A) at 63H–64A. See also *Director of Public Prosecutions, Gauteng v Pistorius* supra at para 52.

19 See, for example, the accused in *S v Sataardien* 1998 (1) SACR 637 (C). See further, *S v Naidoo* supra. Naidoo, aged 19 years, was in the kitchen of his home with his mother and sister late at night after a gathering at his family home. He heard someone rattling the security door. Naidoo called out three times asking who was there, but got no answer. He was frightened because there had been previous attempted burglaries at the house and his car had been broken into. He got his gun, went to the kitchen door and opened it slightly. He could not see who was outside. He heard another rattle at the gate and let off a shot, aiming at head height. He then heard someone screaming, saying, 'It's daddy.' He went outside and found to his shock and horror that he had shot his father in the head. He was charged with his father's murder. He tried to raise the defence of self-defence, but, because he was not actually under attack, this defence could not succeed.

The court then had to decide whether he was conscious of the unlawfulness of his conduct at the time of the shooting. It held that Naidoo had genuinely believed that he was under attack. He therefore had no intention in respect of the unlawfulness of his conduct and hence no *dolus*. He could not be found guilty of murder. The court also found that his mistake was a reasonable one in the circumstances, but held that a reasonable person in the same circumstances would not have simply shot to kill – he had had other options, for example to fire a warning shot, or to slam and lock the door and wait for further developments. The court therefore found that he was negligent and convicted him of culpable homicide.

Note that the principles applied in *Naidoo* are essentially no different from those that were applied in *S v Ngema* supra, where the court found that Ngema's mistaken belief that he was being attacked by a *tokoloshe* was reasonable for a person in the same circumstances (or at least not unreasonable), but that he *acted* unreasonably because he knew that the two-year-old deceased had entered the hut with him and he should have taken more care to avoid killing the child.

The same principles will apply, *mutatis mutandis*, to cases of putative private defence of property, putative necessity, putative impossibility, putative obedience to superior orders, putative disciplinary chastisement, putative public authority and putative consent.[20]

24.4 Mistake or ignorance of the law

Until 1977, under South African law, everyone was presumed to know the law. Ignorance of the law and mistake of the law were therefore no excuse: *ignorantia juris neminem excusat*. The logic behind this presumption was that if mistake and ignorance of the law were allowed as a defence, people might deliberately refrain from making enquiries as to their legal duties. Also, there would be great practical difficulties for the state in proving what the accused did and did not know.[21]

During the 1960s and 1970s, this presumption attracted a great deal of criticism in academic circles, for example from professors Van der Vyfer, Van Rooyen and De Wet.[22] The essence of this criticism was that *dolus* – intention to commit an unlawful act – requires that the accused knew, or at the very least foresaw, the possibility that he was conducting himself unlawfully. Clearly, a person cannot act with a guilty mind[23] if he has no idea that he is breaking the law. The principle that ignorance of the law is no excuse was therefore clearly at variance with the trend towards the subjectivisation of *dolus*. At the same time, there was an appreciation that with the proliferation of statute law in modern times and the consequent increase in the number of statutory offences, it is no longer realistic (if it ever was) to expect every person to know every law and criminal provision. The turning point came with the AD decision in *S v De Blom*.[24]

---

20 See Burchell JM *Principles of Criminal Law* 5 ed (2016) 411–415 for examples of situations where these defences would be appropriate.

21 Burchell JM *South African Criminal Law and Procedure Vol I: General Principles of Criminal Law* 4 ed (2011) 394–395 on the traditional arguments for the *ignorantia juris* rule.

22 Van der Vyver JD 'Wederregtelikheidsbewussyn by strafregtelike aanspreeklikheid' (1967) 30 *TSAR* 271; Van Rooyen JCW 'Regsdwaling en dolus in die strafreg' (1974) 37 *TSAR* 35; De Wet JC and Swanepoel HL *Strafreg* 3 ed (1975) 148–149. Professor De Wet viewed the fiction that everybody is assumed to know the law as 'grotesque' (at 149), and further (at 149):

> ***Die punt is egter dat mens die dader die verwyt dat hy opsetlik gehandel het, nie kan maak nie, tensy hy ook bewus was van die ongeoorloofdheid van sy optrede. By misdade waarby opset vereis word, moet regsonkunde en regsdwaling steeds verskoningsgrond wees, omdat dolus of opset ontbreek, mits die dwaling wesenlik is.* [The point is that one cannot hold the perpetrator accountable for his intentional actions unless he had knowledge of the unlawfulness of his conduct. In the context of crimes of intent, ignorance of the law and mistake of law should still be regarded as excuses, because dolus or intent is missing, if it is a material mistake of law.]**

Thus, a clear preference for the theoretically correct position (also under influence of continental European thought) that knowledge of unlawfulness (*wederregtelikheidsbewussyn*) constitutes an essential element of intent. The Anglo-American fiction that everybody is presumed to know the law is therefore not only unrealistic, but also in conflict with criminal law theory.

23 The so-called coloured intent, referred to in section 19.3.1.

24 *S v De Blom* supra. For mostly positive discussions of the judgment, see Stassen JC '*S v De Blom* 1977 3 SA 513 (A)' (1977) 3 *TSAR* 259; Labuschagne JMT 'Vonnisbesprekings *S v De Blom* 1977 (3) SA 513 (A)' (1978) 11 *De Jure* 386. For more general discussions of the law post-*De Blom*, see Leistner M 'Bewys van wederregtelikheidsbewussyn: De Blom en daarna' (1982) 15 *De Jure* 34. For a more critical (negative) assessment of the impact of *De Blom*, see Snyman CR *Criminal Law* 6 ed (2014) 201–204. For a positive assessment of *De Blom*, see Burchell *South African Criminal Law and Procedure Vol I* 400–403. The author submits that the *De Blom* rule works well in practice and is consistent with South African criminal law theory (at 403).

S v De Blom

Mrs De Blom was charged with two counts of contravening the Exchange Control Act and Regulations by taking money and jewellery out of the country without the necessary permission, an offence for which *dolus* is the required form of fault. She claimed that she had not known it was an offence to do this. The trial court applied the rule that ignorance of the law is no excuse and convicted her on both counts.

Mrs De Blom appealed to the AD. The court (per Rumpff CJ) considered the background to the rule that ignorance of the law is no excuse as well as the various criticisms levelled against this rule, and held that knowledge of unlawfulness is required for *dolus*. It found that the fact that Mrs De Blom had concealed the money in a hidden compartment in her suitcase indicated, despite her denial, that she had known it was unlawful to take it out. Her conviction was upheld on this count.

As far as the jewellery was concerned, however, the AD accepted her explanation that she liked to wear a lot of jewellery, and that she had taken it out to wear and return. She was acquitted on this count. In the course of his judgment, Rumpff CJ made the further point (obiter) that a person who works in a particular sphere of activity has a duty to know the law relating to that activity, for example a builder ought to know the building regulations. If he does not, he will be negligent[25] and can therefore be held liable for an offence requiring this form of fault.

24.4.1 Mistake or ignorance of the law excluding *dolus*

As a result of the decision in *S v De Blom*, it is now well established in our law that a genuine mistake or ignorance of the law will afford a valid defence to a crime for which *dolus* is required. However, in order to attract liability, an accused does not have to know precisely which law he is contravening or what its exact provisions are, merely that he is or may possibly be breaking the law.[26]

For this reason, it will be difficult for an accused of normal intelligence and life experience to rely on the defence of mistake or ignorance of the law when his conduct was *malum in se* (inherently bad and immoral) because the court will not lightly accept that the accused did not foresee at least a possibility that there may be a law aimed at penalising such conduct. Since South African common law crimes, for instance murder, theft and robbery, generally involve conduct that is *malum in se*, it will be difficult for an accused to escape liability for such a crime on the basis of his alleged mistake or ignorance of the law.

24.4.2 Mistake or ignorance of the law excluding *culpa*

24.4.2.1 Rumpff's obiter dictum

In the case of crimes for which *culpa* is a sufficient form of fault, the exception referred to in Rumpff CJ's obiter dictum has since been applied in numerous cases that involve statutory offences. An early case was that of *S v Bailey*.[27]

S v Bailey

Bailey was a medical doctor who was charged with failing to render certain statutorily required information concerning his practice. He initially relied on his right to privacy, which the court found was not a valid defence to the charge. He then tried to raise the defence that he was ignorant of

25 *S v De Blom* supra 531–532.

26 See *S v Magidson* 1984 (3) SA 825 (T); *S v Hlomza* 1987 (1) SA 25 (A) at 32.

27 *S v Bailey* 1981 (4) SA 187 (N).

the relevant statute. The court found, however, that he had been negligent in failing to acquaint himself with the correct legal position, for example he had not sought legal advice and that he therefore had fault in the form of *culpa*. Finding further that *culpa* was a sufficient form of fault for the offence in question, Bailey was found liable.

However, note that in its original formulation, Rumpff CJ's obiter dictum referred to a person who *works in a particular sphere of activity*. The scope of the exception has, however, since been extended considerably to the point where it may now be regarded as the rule rather than the exception.[28] The scope of the exception is now so wide that in the case of offences where *culpa* is a sufficient degree of fault, it will be extremely difficult for an accused to escape liability on the basis of his actual ignorance or mistake of law. It seems that whenever a person embarks on any activity, however brief, he has a duty to take reasonable steps to ascertain the applicable law so that he does not contravene it. If he does not do so, he will be regarded as having been negligent.

24.4.2.2 Obtaining legal advice

Since the accused's duty is to take reasonable steps to ascertain the applicable law, what is the position where the accused obtains legal advice and relies on it (believes it and acts on it), but the advice turns out to be wrong?

In *S v Longdistance (Natal) Pty Ltd*,[29] the AD held that legal advice has 'no magic which justifies the recipient in jettisoning his common sense'. Clearly, therefore, an accused cannot take shelter behind the mere fact that he was relying on legal advice when he broke the law. However, in *S v Claasens*,[30] the court amplified the legal position. It held that a person is entitled to rely on legal advice unless there are indications that the advice is *unreliable*, for example where the advice is patently absurd or the lawyer is clearly out of his depth.

Thus even where a person obtains and relies on legal advice, he will still be considered negligent if such reliance was unreasonable; that is, if a reasonable person in the same circumstances would not have believed and acted on that same advice, but would have sought further and better advice.

Table 24.1 When is the defence of ignorance of the law likely to succeed?

	Common law crimes	**Statutory offences**
Crimes requiring *dolus*	The defence is not likely to succeed. The conduct in such crimes is usually inherently bad, so a court will probably infer that the accused must have foreseen at least a possibility that the conduct was unlawful.	The defence could well succeed, especially if the offence is not well known.
Crimes requiring *culpa*	The defence is not likely to succeed. The accused has a duty to take reasonable steps to ascertain the relevant law before acting. Failure to do so constitutes negligence in itself.	The defence is not likely to succeed. The accused has a duty to take reasonable steps to ascertain the relevant law before acting. Failure to do so constitutes negligence in itself.

28 See *S v Du Toit* 1981 (2) SA 33 (C); *S v Evans* 1982 (4) SA 346 (C).
29 *S v Longdistance (Natal) (Pty) Ltd and others* 1990 (2) SA 277 (A) at 283I.
30 *S v Claasens* 1992 (2) SACR 434 (T).

24.5 *Aberratio ictus* (going astray of the blow) and concrete intention

We have pointed out that it is necessary to distinguish between a mistake and an accident. What, then, is the position with regard to accidental unlawful conduct? The answer, simply, is that there is no specific set of rules that relate to accidents. The accused's liability will be determined according to the normal principles of criminal law, in particular:

- whether his conduct was voluntary in the first instance, and
- whether, despite the unexpected turn of events, he had the necessary form of fault (*dolus* or *culpa*) for the crime in question.

One situation that has received particular attention is that of *aberratio ictus* or the going astray of the blow.[31] This term is used to describe the situation in which force or violence (a blow) that is meant for a particular person accidentally goes astray and injures or kills the wrong person. For example, suppose that A shoots at B, aiming to kill him, but misses and instead the bullet strikes and kills C, standing in the background. Would A be liable for C's murder in these circumstances?

Older authorities took the view that because A had the intention to kill a person (B), it did not matter that it was C who died instead of B. A had the necessary intention to commit murder and would be liable accordingly.[32] This was sometimes referred to as *transferred intention*, in the sense that A's intention to kill B was regarded as having been transferred to C. The principle involved was commonly referred to as the *aberratio ictus* rule.

However, the current position in South African law is that intention to kill one person is no substitute for intention to kill the person who actually died.[33] In other words, the accused must have had a specific individual, figure, class or category of person in mind as the potential victim, even if he did not know his actual identity.[34] This form of intention is sometimes referred to as *concrete intention*.

Therefore, faced with a situation of *aberratio ictus*, the court will enquire whether, despite the fact that A did not have *dolus directus* in respect of C's death, he nevertheless had *dolus* in one of the other accepted forms - *dolus indirectus* or, as is more likely, *dolus eventualis*. In other words, did A foresee the possibility that he may cause the death of C or someone in the same position, class or category as C,[35] in substantially the same manner as he did in fact cause it, and did he accept that possibility into the bargain?[36] If the answer is 'no', then A cannot be held liable for murder. However, he will not necessarily escape liability altogether, as the court will then proceed to consider whether he was negligent in respect of C's death and, if so, he will be liable for culpable homicide.

---

31 See Snyman *Criminal Law* 193–196; Burchell *Principles of Criminal Law* 401–404.

32 See, for example, *R v Kuzwayo* 1949 (3) SA 761 (A); *R v Koza* 1949 (4) SA 555 (A).

33 *S v Mavhungu* 1981 (1) SA 56 (A). See also the earlier cases of *S v Mtshiza* 1970 (3) SA 747 (A); *S v Tissen* 1979 (4) SA 293 (T); *S v Raisa* 1979 (4) SA 541 (O).

34 It has previously been explained that mistaken identity is not a defence on a charge of murder.

35 In other words, *dolus indeterminatus* or *dolus generalis*.

36 See, for example, *S v Nkombani and another* 1963 (4) SA 877 (A).

24.6 Other defences excluding *dolus*: Youth, mental illness or intellectual disability, intoxication and severe emotional distress

Youth, mental illness or intellectual disability, intoxication, and severe emotional stress or distress all impair a person's cognitive functions to some extent. As already discussed, in their more extreme forms, youth, mental illness or intellectual disability, intoxication and severe emotional distress may exclude criminal capacity, and may thus be raised as a defence to exclude this element of liability. In their less extreme forms, they will not exclude criminal capacity, but they may result in the accused not knowing or foreseeing the unlawfulness of his conduct, or not having subjective foresight of the possible consequences of that conduct. If this is the case, the accused will simply lack the necessary intention to commit the crime concerned (*dolus*).

To illustrate this point, consider the case of *S v Chretien*.[37] Chretien was not so drunk that he lacked criminal capacity, but, due to his mild intoxication, the court was unable to draw the inference that he must have foreseen (and therefore did in fact foresee) the possibility that he might collide with the persons in the road, thereby injuring or even killing them. He escaped liability because the state was unable to prove that he had *dolus* in any of the recognised forms.

By the same token, in *S v Goosen*, the accused's intelligence was not so low that he could be said to suffer from an intellectual disability.[38] He clearly had criminal capacity. However, because of his low intelligence, the court was unable to draw the inference that he must have foreseen the possibility that the deceased might be killed by accident in the course of the robbery. Like Chretien, Goosen escaped liability because the state was unable to prove that he had *dolus*.

On the effect of severe emotional distress, for example, the AD held in *S v Bailey*: 'It is conceivable that the accused can become so terrified that he cannot foresee the consequences of his conduct or foresee that what he is doing is unlawful.'[39]

Note that these defences will not assist an accused where there is ample evidence of *dolus directus*, but they may do so where the state is relying on *dolus eventualis*, or where the accused raises the defence of mistake of fact or law. Furthermore, these defences will seldom be sufficient to exclude *culpa* and are thus unlikely to assist an accused where the crime is one that requires this form of fault, such as culpable homicide.

THIS CHAPTER IN ESSENCE

1. Where an accused is required to have fault for the commission of a crime, as is usually the case, he must have the required form of fault in respect of each and every essential element of the *actus reus* at the time that he committed it. If he does not, then he cannot be held liable.
2. Accordingly, where an accused was genuinely mistaken or ignorant concerning an essential element of the crime, including the unlawfulness of the relevant conduct, then he does not have the necessary intention (*dolus*) to commit that crime. Therefore, if the crime is one that requires *dolus*, the accused will escape liability for it.

37 *S v Chretien* 1981 (1) SA 1097 (A).
38 *S v Goosen* 1989 (4) SA 1013 (A).
39 *S v Bailey* 1982 (3) SA 772 (A) at 796C (own translation).

3. Where the crime is one that requires *culpa*, the accused will escape liability as long as his genuine and essential mistake or ignorance was also reasonable, and as long as the accused acted as a reasonable person would have done in the same circumstances and with the same subjective state of mind.
4. It may happen that a person makes a mistake of fact, which leads him to believe that his conduct is justified and therefore lawful, whereas this is not in fact the case. An example of this would be where the accused genuinely believed that he was justified in using force to defend himself against an unlawful attack even though one or more of the requirements for private defence of person had not been met. In this case, the appropriate defence for the accused to raise would be one of putative private defence. The various putative justification defences are simply a particular type of mistake of fact.
5. Our law currently recognises that fault may also be excluded by mistake or ignorance of the law. The old maxim that ignorance of the law is not a defence no longer applies.
6. However, where an accused relies on the defence of mistake or ignorance of law in a case where *culpa* is the required form of fault for the crime concerned, this defence is unlikely to succeed because the law takes the view that whenever a person embarks on any activity, however brief, he has a duty to take reasonable steps to ascertain the applicable law. If he does not, he will be regarded as negligent.
7. A mistake must be distinguished from an accident. There is no particular set of rules that relate to accidental conduct. The accused's liability will be determined according to the normal principles of criminal law, in particular:
   7.1 whether his conduct was voluntary in the first instance
   7.2 whether, despite the unexpected turn of events, he nevertheless had the necessary form of fault for the crime in question.

Chapter 25

Participants in crime

CHAPTER OBJECTIVES

The objectives of this chapter are to:

- identify and distinguish between the three main categories of participants in crime
- define the terms 'perpetrator' and 'co-perpetrator'
- explain the common purpose rule with particular reference to:
  - the basis of common purpose liability

  - what is meant by conduct falling within the scope of a common purpose
  - the requirements for association in a common purpose
  - the requirements for effective dissociation from a common purpose
- explain the nature of accomplice liability and the requirements for liability as an accomplice
- explain the requirements for liability as an accessory after the fact.

25.1 Introduction

We have now completed our discussion of the three principal elements of criminal liability together with the defences that can be raised in respect of each element. There are, however, certain further general principles of liability that need to be investigated before this section of the book can be regarded as complete. The first of these principles is a discussion of the different ways in which a person may incur criminal liability other than by committing the crime himself.

As explained in the introductory section, the principle of personal responsibility, which is fundamental to South African criminal law, implies that as a general rule, a person may only be punished for his *own* criminal conduct. However, like most modern legal systems,[1] South African law also takes the view that a person who *actively associates* with the commission of a crime by another person must share in the responsibility for that crime. It would be contrary to the interests of society and justice for liability to be limited solely to the person who actually executed the crime.[2] Therefore, this chapter is concerned with the questions of how and to what extent the law attributes criminal liability to a person who associates himself with the commission of a crime by another person.[3]

25.2 Historical perspective

Roman-Dutch law dealt with such questions by applying the principle of mandate (or quasi-mandate), as expressed in the maxim, *qui facit per alium facit per se* (he who acts through another, acts through himself).[4] Thus, where one person orchestrated the commission of a crime by another person, the former would be liable for the crime as fully and effectively as if he had committed it himself.

Although the Roman-Dutch law principle also forms part of South African law, the major source of influence was English law, which, by the early part of the 19th century, had developed a complex and sophisticated set of rules and distinctions. For purposes of determining liability in respect of all serious crimes (felonies),[5] English law recognised, and distinguished between, four categories or degrees of participation in crime:

1. *Principals in the first degree*: The person who actually committed the crime, whether acting alone or together with others

---

1 For comparative discussions, see Reed A and Bohlander M (eds) *Participation in Crime: Domestic and Comparative Perspectives* (2013).

2 See also the rationale put forward for the notion of corporate criminal liability, discussed in Chapter 23.

3 See, in general, Burchell JM *South African Criminal Law and Procedure Vol I: General Principles of Criminal Law* 4 ed (2011) 485–534; Burchell JM *Principles of Criminal Law* 5 ed (2016) 473–523; Snyman CR *Criminal Law* 6 ed (2014) 249–274.

4 This principle forms the basis of the law of agency.

5 The rules were simplified in the case of less serious crimes (misdemeanours). South African law does not distinguish between felonies and misdemeanours, so the distinction is irrelevant for present purposes.

2. *Principals in the second degree*: The person who did not commit the crime, but who either conspired towards or was present during its commission[6] and actively aided, abetted or encouraged the actual perpetrator[7]
3. *Accessories before the fact (also known as principles in the third degree)*: A person who procured the commission of a crime or provided advice or encouragement towards its commission before the event (the 'fact'), but who was not present when it was committed
4. *Accessories after the fact*: A person who was not involved with the commission of the crime, but who assisted a criminal to evade justice after the crime had been committed[8]

To determine the liability of persons falling into the first two categories, English law developed a rule known as the **doctrine of common purpose**. According to this rule, where a number of persons acted together to commit a crime, every act performed by each of them in pursuance of the crime was regarded as an act by all of them and they would therefore all be equally liable for that act.[9] The rule applied both in cases where the participants were co-principals in the first degree and where they were principals in the first degree and principals in the second degree.[10]

South Africa adopted the common purpose rule from English law and initially also adopted the English terminology and distinction between the four categories of participants.[11] The way in which the common purpose rule was subsequently developed and applied in South African law, however, soon led to the distinction between the first three categories of participants disappearing. The reasoning was that *anyone* who intentionally conspired with, or actively assisted another person to commit a crime, whether during its commission or beforehand, and whether present at the scene or not, was an *equal* partner in the commission of that crime – a ***socius criminis*** or **partner in crime**. All such persons, therefore, came to be regarded simply as co-perpetrators.[12] The only distinction that was preserved was that of the accessory after the fact.

Thus, for many years, South African law distinguished between only two categories of participants:

1. *Socii criminis (partners in crime)*: These were the people who participated in the commission of the crime at any time before its final completion. They were all considered equally liable for the crime itself, together with the person who committed the deed.

---

6 'Presence' was given a fairly broad interpretation. Thus, it could include a person who was outside the house where the crime was being committed as long as he was near enough to assist, for example by giving warning; Smith JC and Hogan B *Criminal Law* (1965) 70.

7 A principal in the second degree was liable for the same crime as the principal in the first degree.

8 Williams GL *Criminal Law: The General Part* 2 ed (1961) 346–415; Smith and Hogan *Criminal Law* 68–86.

9 See, for example, *R v Macklin, Murphy and others* (1838) 2 Lewin 225; 168 ER 1136 A. See generally, Rabie MA 'The doctrine of common purpose in criminal law' (1971) 88(3) *SALJ* 334.

10 Its application is well illustrated in the early case of *R v Swindall and Osborne* (1846) 2 Car & Kir 230; (1846) 175 ER 95. Swindall and Osborne were cart drivers, who challenged each other to a cart race on a public road. During the race, one of them ran over an elderly man and killed him. It was not known which of them had actually caused the death, but the court held that since both of them were driving furiously and urging each other on in the race, it was immaterial which of them had actually run over the deceased. They were both convicted of manslaughter.

11 The first case in which the common purpose rule was expressly applied was the delictual case of *McKenzie v Van der Merwe* 1917 AD 41. An early criminal case was that of *R v Garnsworthy and others* 1923 WLD 17 (Special Criminal Court). See Rabie MA 'The doctrine of common purpose in criminal law' 230 for a more detailed account of the adoption of the common purpose rule.

12 English law used the term 'principal' to denote the person who was liable for the crime itself (i.e the 'direct perpetrator'). South African law has opted for the term 'perpetrator' instead. For more on the English law, see Sullivan B in Reed and Bohlander *Participation in Crime* 32–34.

2. *Accessories after the fact*: These were the people who assisted the perpetrators only after the commission of the crime was complete. They were not liable for the crime itself but were liable for the lesser offence of being an accessory after the fact to that crime – a separate and distinct offence, which usually attracted a lesser punishment.

However, since 1980, pursuant to the decision of the Appellate Division (AD) in *S v Williams*,[13] South African law has once again drawn a distinction between liability as a co-perpetrator and liability of a more accessorial nature (this distinction will be discussed in more detail below). Accordingly, South African law currently recognises and distinguishes between three main categories of participants:

1. Perpetrators/co-perpetrators
2. Accomplices
3. Accessories after the fact

We will show below how, in adopting this taxonomy, South African law has not simply returned to the original English law position.

25.3 Perpetrators

25.3.1 Categories of perpetrators

Burchell explains that there are three categories of persons who will be regarded as perpetrators:[14]

- *Those who personally commit the* actus reus, *either acting alone or together with other persons*: For example, X breaks into a house and steals the television set, or X and Y both break into a house and together carry off the television set.
- *Those who get some innocent or unwitting agent to commit the crime on their behalf*: For example, X breaks the window of a house and instructs his six-year-old child to enter the house and steal.
- *Those who form a common purpose to commit the crime with someone else who actually executes the crime*: For example, X asks Y, an adult, to break into a house and steal, or X keeps watch for Y while Y does so.

Perpetrators in the first category are clearly liable in their own right. Perpetrators in the second category will also be liable on the basis of the maxim, *qui facit per alium facit per se*.[15] In this case, the perpetrator alone will be liable, but not the innocent or unwitting agent, because the latter lacks the requirement of fault or, as in the example, may even lack criminal capacity. In the case of perpetrators in the third category, both participants will be equally liable based on the common purpose rule. We will discuss this rule and its requirements in more detail below.

---

13 *S v Williams en 'n ander* 1980 (1) SA 60 (A).

14 Burchell *Principles of Criminal Law* 475.

15 'He who acts through another (is considered) to act himself', from the Latin *qui facit per alium facit per se*, formulated in Bonifatius VIII Regulae iuris 88, in *Corpus Iuris Canonici* (see translation in Hiemstra VG and Gonin HL *Trilingual Legal Dictionary* 3 ed (1992) 266).

25.3.2 The common purpose rule

The **common purpose rule** holds that where two or more people associate together to commit a crime, each of them will be liable for the criminal conduct of the other(s) that falls within the scope of their common purpose.[16] They will be regarded as **co-perpetrators**.

Their *actus reus* in such a case consists of their act of *associating together* with a common purpose to commit the crime,[17] which is ultimately committed by one of them.[18] In other words, the common purpose rule absolves the state from having to prove all the usual requirements of unlawful conduct on the part of each of the participants.

In the case of consequence crimes, such as murder, it is not necessary for the state to prove that each participant contributed towards causing the prohibited consequence, or even identify the participant who actually caused the consequence. All the state needs to prove is that the consequence was caused by *one or other* of the participants and that the rest shared a common purpose with him to commit the crime. As a matter of policy, the conduct of each perpetrator is **imputed** (attributed) to all the others.[19]

The common purpose rule only dispenses with the need for the state to prove unlawful conduct in the usual form. Each participant is still required to have the necessary criminal capacity and form of fault for the crime in question. Therefore, each participant's liability must still be determined individually, according to his own criminal capacity and fault at the time of the act of association.[20]

Note also that the common purpose rule does not apply to all crimes. Certain crimes can only be committed *personally*, for example rape,[21] perjury and bigamy as well as offences that relate to acts that require a personal permit or licence, for example driving offences, or which can be performed only by a person of a particular status, such as a prisoner or an insolvent.[22] A person will only be guilty of one of these crimes if he personally commits the *actus reus*. Thus, for example, paying someone else to commit perjury does not make a person guilty of perjury. However, as discussed further on, it will make that person an *accomplice* to perjury.[23]

Let us now examine the critical concepts involved in the common purpose rule.

25.3.2.1 What is meant by conduct falling within the scope of the common purpose?

A person will only be liable for the criminal conduct of a co-perpetrator if the conduct in question formed part of their shared plan, intention or design. However, it is essential to appreciate that the scope of a common purpose is not limited to the criminal conduct that

16 For present purposes, 'common' means shared. 'Purpose' simply means a plan, design or intention.

17 *S v Thebus and another* 2003 (2) SACR 319 (CC) at 43.

18 The common purpose rule can therefore be regarded as adding a further form of unlawful conduct.

19 See, for example, *R v Morela* 1947 (3) SA 147 (A); *R v Sikepe and others* 1946 AD 745; *S v Madlala* 1969 (2) SA 637 (A) at 640F–H. Subsequently, this principle was discussed and reaffirmed in *S v Safatsa and others* 1988 (1) SA 868 (A) and *S v Thebus* supra.

20 This means that different parties to the same common purpose may be liable for different crimes, depending on what they knew and foresaw as possible in the circumstances or, in the case of culpable homicide, what they ought reasonably to have foreseen. Thus, for example, where A, B and C share a common purpose to assault X and X dies as a result of the assault, A will be guilty of murder if he subjectively foresaw the possibility of causing X's death; B will be guilty of culpable homicide if he did not subjectively foresee that possibility, but a reasonable person in the same circumstances would have done so; and C will be guilty of assault if he had neither subjective foresight nor negligence in respect of X's death, but merely foresaw the possibility of injury.

21 This was the position regarding common law rape. It is not entirely clear whether it still applies to rape as defined in the present Criminal Law (Sexual Offences and Related Matters) Amendment Act 32 of 2007. See further, Chapter 28.

22 *S v Kimberley and another* 2004 (2) SACR 38 (E) at 42H–43E.

23 *S v Saffier* 2003 (2) SACR 141 (SE).

the participants actually intended, that is, conduct in respect of which they had *dolus directus*. It *also* includes criminal conduct which they subjectively foresaw they might possibly commit while pursuing their actual aim and object, that is, conduct in respect of which they had *dolus eventualis*.[24] As explained previously, the existence of *dolus eventualis* is commonly established by inferential reasoning.[25]

Thus, for example, suppose that X and Y set out to commit a crime such as housebreaking, but X murders somebody in the course of committing that crime. Y is not only jointly liable with X for the housebreaking, but he is also liable for the murder if he subjectively foresaw the killing of the deceased as a possibility when he and X embarked on the housebreaking, even though it was not part of their actual plan or intention.

25.3.2.2 How does a common purpose arise?

A common purpose may arise in two possible ways:

1. *By prior conspiracy (agreement) to commit the crime in question*: For example, X and Y (or X, Y and Z) agree in advance to commit a particular crime, which implies a bilateral or multilateral act of association.[26]
2. *By conduct (active association)*: For example, X notices Y (or Y and Z) committing a crime and simply joins in. This is a unilateral act of association.[27] This form of association is most commonly found in cases of mob violence.

In the first scenario, for X and Y to be liable as co-perpetrators, it is not necessary for both of them to be present at the scene of the crime when it is committed. It is enough if they were both involved in the initial conspiracy.[28] Note, however, that conspiracy requires agreement – that is, consensus – between the parties. Where they are still deliberating or negotiating there is no conspiracy yet.[29]

In the second scenario, X must obviously be present at, or near enough to, the scene of the crime for him to join in with the commission of the crime. However, this alone is not enough. Merely being present at the scene of a crime, and even performing an act that might *appear* to coincide with the conduct of the actual perpetrator, is not sufficient to constitute a common purpose.[30]

For common purpose to arise, there are four further requirements:

1. The participant in question (X) must have been aware that the crime was being, or was about to be, committed.
2. He must have intended to form a common purpose with those who were actually committing it.

---

24 Where the crime is one that requires *culpa*, then it would also include conduct that was *reasonably foreseeable* in pursuit of the common design (see further below).

25 See section 19.3.3.2.1. See further the following cases: *S v Nselezz*1955 (2) SA 145 (A); *S v Nhlapo and another* 1981 (2) SA 744 (A); *S v Shaik and others* 1983 (4) SA 57 (A); *S v Lungile and another* 1999 (2) SACR 597 (SCA); *S v Goosen* 1989 (4) SA 1013 (A); *S v Mitchell and another* 1992 (1) SACR 17 (A).

26 For a full discussion of what is meant by 'conspiracy', see Chapter 26.

27 See Whiting R 'Joining in' (1986) 103(1) *SALJ* 38.

28 *R v Bergstedt* 1955 (4) SA 186 (A); *R v Kgolane and others* 1960 PH H110 AD; *S v Nkombani and another* 1963 (4) SA 877 (A); *R v Njenje and others* 1966 (1) SA 369 (SRA); *S v Yelani* 1989 (2) SA 43 (A).

29 See, for example, the facts in *S v Dewnath* (269/13) [2014] ZASCA 57 (17 April 2014); 2014 JDR 0804 (SCA) (unreported); and see further, section 26.4.2.1. It is however not necessary for the state to produce direct evidence of the existence of a conspiracy. Proof can be by way of inference (*R v Itumeling* 1932 OPD 10, 12).

30 See, for example, *S v Mbambo and another* 1965 (2) SA 845 (A) and the majority judgment in *S v Daniels en n ander* 1983 (3) SA 275 (A), cases referred to previously in section 6.3.

3. He must have manifested (shown) this intention by performing some positive act of association with the conduct of the others.[31]
4. He must have had the necessary *mens rea* in respect of the particular crime, whether *dolus directus, dolus eventualis*[32] or *culpa*.[33]

25.3.2.3 Act of association (active association)

A person cannot become a party to a common purpose merely by being present at the scene of the crime and doing nothing to prevent it – not even where the person had a legal duty to prevent the commission of the crime, as in the case of a police officer.[34] Therefore, for a common purpose to arise, the accused must have performed some *positive* act to show his intention of associating with the commission of the crime.[35]

Where the accused was under a duty to prevent the commission of the crime, then he may well attract liability based on his unlawful omission. If so, he will be liable in his own right, that is, as a perpetrator in the first category and not based on the common purpose rule. In this case, the state is not absolved from the need to prove causation on the part of the accused in question.

There is no closed list of what type of conduct will be regarded as sufficient for active association. Merely lending moral support to the actual perpetrator, for example by uttering verbal encouragement,[36] keeping watch or standing guard,[37] or standing by ready to lend assistance if required,[38] has been regarded as sufficient to constitute an overt act of association in various reported cases. In the unreported case of *S v Dewnath*, however, the SCA emphasised that the 'most critical requirement' of active association is necessary to curb the scope of liability:[39]

> **Current jurisprudence, premised on a proper application of *S v Mgedezi & others*, makes it clear that (i) there must be a close proximity in fact between the conduct considered to be active association and the result; and (ii) such active association must be significant and not a limited participation removed from the actual execution of the crime.**

The court went on to hold that the accused's mere knowledge and/or approval of his parents' plan to have the deceased murdered was not sufficient to constitute active association with the murder.[40]

---

31 *S v Gxabhu and others* Case CC 129/07 (High Court, Eastern Cape); [2012] JOL 28578 (ECM) at 10.

32 *S v Dube and others* 2010 (1) SACR 65 (KZP).

33 See *S v Mgedezi and others* 1989 (1) SA 687 (A). *Mgedezi* tends to suggest that these requirements apply only to cases of spontaneous association, but in fact they apply equally to all cases that involve common purpose. It is just that they are more or less self-evident in cases where there is a prior conspiracy.

34 This is a rule inherited from English law – *R v Atkinson* (1869) 11 Cox CC 330. See also the discussions on this point in *R v Chenjere* 1960 (1) SA 473 (FC) and *S v A en 'n ander* 1993 (1) SACR 600 (A), cases discussed previously in section 4.2. Note that the same does not apply in the case of accomplice liability – see section 25.4.

35 Earlier authorities spoke explicitly of an '*act of* association', adopting the terminology used by the court in *S v Mgedezi* supra. This term has been abandoned in more recent times in favour of the broader, vaguer and less satisfactory term 'active association' used in *S v Safatsa* supra and subsequently adopted by the Constitutional Court in *S v Thebus* supra. This, in our view, is an unfortunate development, since it leads to lack of clarity and confusion. Burchell is of the view that the term 'active association' is so vague that it might in fact offend against the principle of legality (Burchell *Principles of Criminal Law* 488). Whatever the merits of this argument, we would prefer a return to the original term 'act of association'.

36 See, for example, the conduct of the fourth accused in *S v Safatsa* supra, discussed below.

37 See, for example, the conduct of the first appellant in *S v Thebus and another* 2003 (2) SACR 319 (CC); 2003 (6) SA 505 (CC).

38 *R v Mbande and others* 1933 AD 382; *R v Tapeson* 1965 (2) SA 761 (SRA).

39 *S v Dewnath* supra at para 15a.

40 *S v Dewnath* supra at para 16.

25.3.2.4 When must the act of association take place?

The rule is that a person will only be liable for a crime on the basis of common purpose if he was a party to a common purpose to commit that crime at the time that it was committed.[41] This implies that the act of association must have taken place at some time *before* the commission of the crime, and the accused must *still* be a party to the common purpose at the time of its commission. In other words, he must not have withdrawn.[42]

Merely sharing in the proceeds of a crime after the event is not sufficient to render a person party to a common purpose to commit that crime. A person cannot become liable for a criminal act by subsequent ratification.[43] Thus, for liability to arise, the accused must have been party to the common purpose at the time that the crime was committed.[44]

What, however, is the position where the accused *joins in*[45] with a common purpose to commit a consequence crime, such as murder, only after the fatal blow has already been delivered by someone else, but before the victim dies? Will the accused be liable for murder in such a case? For some time, our law was not clear on this point.

This question came before the AD in *S v Khoza*.[46] This case mainly concerns accomplice liability, but Judge Corbett, in his minority judgment, considered the question in relation to the doctrine of common purpose. He held that as a rule, the accused must have acceded to the common purpose before the causal act was committed.[47] Two other judges agreed with Judge Corbett, but two dissented. These judges took the view that the crime of murder is only complete when the victim dies. Thus, if the accused joined in at any time before the victim died, he would be liable either as a co-perpetrator or as an accomplice.[48]

In *S v Motaung*,[49] the question came before the AD once again. This time, it brought legal certainty regarding the question of 'joining in' cases by holding unanimously that the question had to be decided with reference to established legal principle, namely the contemporaneity rule. Accordingly, it held that where the accused only acceded to the common purpose after the deceased had already received the fatal injury and the accused did nothing to expedite (hasten) the deceased's death, he could not be found guilty of murder, but only of attempted murder.

25.3.2.5 Liability for additional crimes (apparent change of purpose)

X and Y set out with a common purpose to commit a particular crime. In the process, X decides on his own initiative to commit some additional crime. Is Y also liable for this additional crime?[50] Under the now defunct *versari in re illicta* rule,[51] the answer would invariably have been 'yes'. However, the question must now be decided according to the above principles.

Firstly, a court will consider whether the additional crime was in fact conduct falling within the scope of X and Y's *original* common purpose. The court will do this by using inferential reasoning to determine whether Y had *dolus eventualis* in respect of the additional

41 This is simply an application of the contemporaneity rule.
42 Withdrawal from a common purpose is discussed in section 25.3.2.6.
43 See *S v Chimbamba and another* 1977 (4) SA 803 (RA).
44 This is merely an application of the contemporaneity rule.
45 See Snyman *Criminal Law* 264–265.
46 *S v Khoza* 1982 (3) SA 1019 (A).
47 *S v Khoza* supra at 1036.
48 The dissenting view was subsequently followed by Thirion J in *S v Dlamini and others* 1984 (3) SA 360 (N).
49 *S v Motaung and others* 1990 (4) SA 485 (A).
50 Some authorities refer to such additional crimes as 'collateral' crimes.
51 This is the doctrine that held that a person could be held criminally liable for all the consequences tainted by the original criminal conduct. This doctrine no longer applies in South African criminal law. See also section 22.2.2.

crime at the time that he associated with X. If not, then Y cannot be held liable for the additional crime, unless he associated himself with X's purpose to commit that crime once he became aware of such purpose. In other words, for Y to be liable, he must have either (1) entered into a fresh conspiracy (agreement) with X to commit the additional crime, or he must have (2) actively associated himself with X's commission of the additional crime.[52]

This illustrates the fact that a common purpose may develop, evolve or mutate over time. As long as the accused in question had become party to a common purpose to commit the crime in question at the time that it was committed, he will be liable for it.

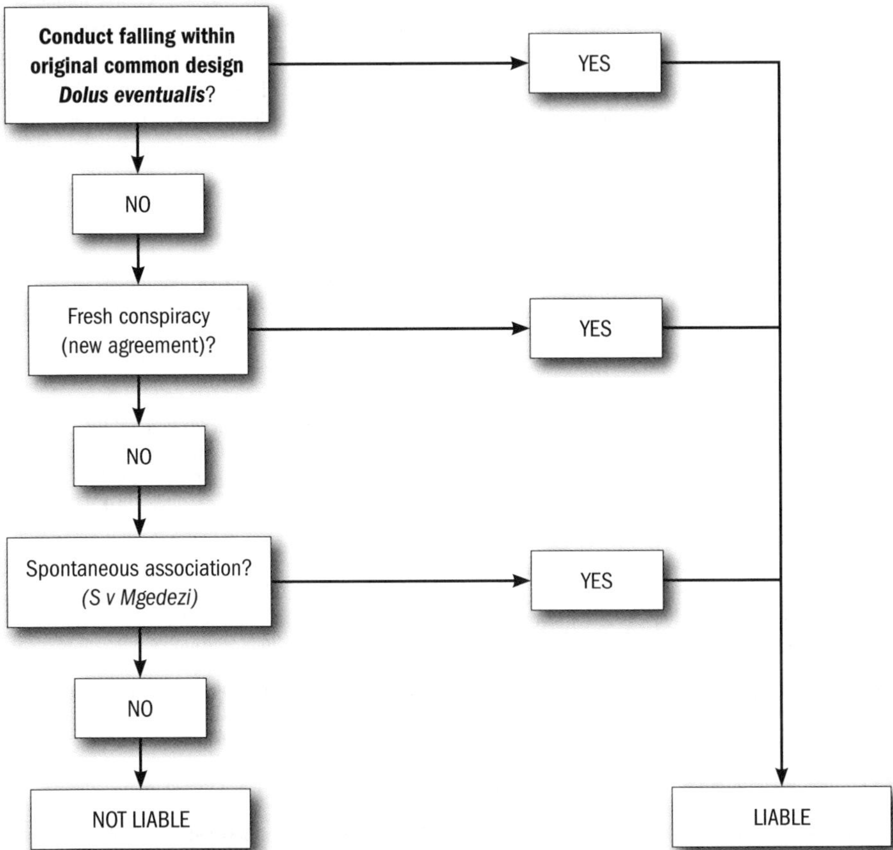

Figure 25.1 *Liability for additional crimes*

25.3.2.6 Dissociation from a common purpose

What is the position where an existing party to a common purpose changes his mind and decides to withdraw? Will he still be liable for the criminal acts of his former partners in crime? Our law takes the view that a party to a common purpose can withdraw from a common purpose and he will not be liable for anything done after his withdrawal by his former partners in crime.[53] However, the law also lays down certain requirements in this regard.

52 In which case, he must satisfy the five requirements set out in *S v Mgedezi* supra.

53 He will still be liable for any criminal conduct committed *before* his withdrawal while he was still party to the common purpose.

Firstly, and most importantly, a mere change of mind, according to the accused's own evidence, is not enough. The accused needs to have performed some overt act to demonstrate that he had changed his intention and was withdrawing from the common purpose. Exactly what form this act should take will depend to a great extent on how he acceded to the common purpose in the first place.

As a rule, the law adopts a more relaxed approach in cases where there was an association by mere conduct (active association or joining in) as opposed to a prior conspiracy. In the case of association by mere conduct, it will usually be sufficient if the accused simply desists from his active participation in the crime, for example by leaving the scene before the unlawful conduct takes place (or, in the case of murder, before the fatal assault takes place).[54]

In cases where there was a prior conspiracy to commit the crime in question, the law requires something more from the party seeking to withdraw. How much more will depend on the extent of that party's participation and on how far the participants have progressed towards achieving their common purpose. In some cases, the party seeking to withdraw may be required to undo whatever he has done towards the commission of the crime and/or take other steps to prevent its commission or completion.[55]

---

54 See, for example, the judgment of the AD in *S v Singo* 1993 (1) SACR 226 (A). Singo joined in with a mob that was stoning an old woman to death for allegedly bewitching a young girl. After throwing two stones at the deceased, Singo was himself injured and left to return home. The trial court found it possible that the fatal injuries were inflicted only after Singo had left but convicted him of the murder anyway because it did not accept his leaving the scene as sufficient evidence of his change of intention. He appealed.

The AD distinguished between the present case and cases where there is an express agreement or conspiracy. It held that where the common purpose is manifested purely by the accused's conduct of joining in, along with his intention to commit the crime in question together with the other participants, then his liability will continue only for so long as his intention and conduct *both* continue. Thus, where the accused desists from active participation and/or abandons his intention to commit the crime, he is not liable for any acts committed by the other participants afterwards. It held further that when Singo left the scene, he was ending his active participation and was probably also abandoning his intention to kill the deceased. Either way, he was no longer a party to the common purpose to commit murder. The conviction of murder was set aside and substituted with a conviction of attempted murder.

55 See *S v Nduli and others* 1993 (2) SACR 501 (A). Nduli and two others conspired to commit a robbery at a petrol station in Reservoir Hills, Durban. Nduli's role was to stand guard outside the premises, armed with a firearm. The other two would enter the premises and carry out the robbery. The getaway car was driven by Malinga, who turned state witness. Malinga stopped at the petrol station and the three of them got out. Nduli then went back to Malinga and borrowed R2,00 from him, complaining that the job was too heavy for him. He then took up a position about 40 paces from the entrance to the building, near a bus stop. The other two went into the petrol station building and carried out the robbery, in the course of which the owner was stabbed and shot to death. The two then ran out of the building with a bag of money, pursued by the deceased's son who chased them in a car, firing shots. At this point, a bus pulled up and Nduli got onto it, using the R2,00 he had borrowed as bus fare. He returned to their rendezvous point where he was later joined by Malinga. The second and third accused had meanwhile run off in the direction of the Umgeni River, which they attempted to cross on foot. One of them, who had the bag with the money, was swept away by the current. He was rescued by the police and arrested. The other escaped and joined Nduli and Malinga at the rendezvous point where they shared out the proceeds: R530,00.

At the trial, Nduli tried to claim that he had dissociated himself from the conspiracy at the point when he borrowed the R2,00 from Malinga. The court rejected this argument and convicted him of murder and robbery. He appealed against his convictions.

On appeal, the AD had to consider whether Nduli had in fact dissociated himself from the conspiracy at the time that he claimed. It held (at 504) that dissociation consists of some form of *conduct* by a collaborator with the intention of discontinuing his collaboration. The more advanced the accused's participation in the commission of the crime is, the more pertinent and pronounced his conduct will have to be to convince a court, after the event, that he genuinely meant to dissociate himself from it at the time. At the very least, the accused must give timeous and unequivocal notice to his co-conspirators of his withdrawal from the common purpose, accompanied by appropriate conduct. Where possible, he should also attempt to frustrate the commission of the crime and/or nullify the effect of his contribution thus far.

The AD held further (at 506) that evidence of how the accused behaved after the event can serve as an indication of his state of mind at the time. The AD went on to find that Nduli's complaint and act of borrowing the R2,00 to catch the bus was not an unequivocal indication of a decision to withdraw from the robbery before the event. His conduct afterwards – meeting up with the other participants – also indicated that he had still been a willing participant at the time of the murder. His convictions were confirmed. See also *S v Nzo and another* 1990 (3) SA 1 (A); *S v Lungile* supra; *S v Musingadi and others* 2005 (1) SACR 395 (SCA).

However, there is no set of hard and fast rules. In each case, it is a question of fact and evidence.[56] A court will have little sympathy for an accused who claims that he was too scared of his fellow conspirators to perform the required overt act of dissociation.[57]

25.3.2.7 Can a person be liable for culpable homicide based on common purpose?

The term 'common purpose' means a purpose that is shared *consciously* by all the co-perpetrators. Because of this, the question has arisen as to whether it is possible for a co-perpetrator to be convicted of culpable homicide, a crime that requires negligence rather than intention, on the basis of common purpose.

Some doubt was raised in this regard in *S v Coetzee*.[58] However, the AD has since answered the question in the affirmative in *S v Nkwenja and another*.[59] Nkwenja and his co-accused decided to rob the occupants of a motor car. They each opened one of its doors and assaulted the occupants. One of the occupants died as a result of a subdural haematoma. The deceased's external injuries were relatively slight, however, so the court could not conclude that either of the accused had subjectively foreseen the possibility of causing the deceased's death through their assault. The court convicted them both of culpable homicide on the basis that it was reasonably foreseeable that the violence they had used could result in death. This conviction was confirmed by the AD when the matter was taken on appeal.

25.3.2.8 Common purpose: Consequence crimes and circumstance crimes

In the preceding paragraphs, we have for the most part focused on common purpose in the context of *consequence crimes* such as murder. The position with respect to *circumstance crimes*, such as possession, was described by the Supreme Court of Appeal in *S v Ramoba*[60] as follows:

> **The principles of joint possession in relation to the crime of unlawful possession of firearms in instances of robbery committed by a group of people, as in this case, are trite. They were aptly explained by Marais J in *S v Nkosi* who, after finding in that case that there was actual physical possession (*corpus*) of the three guns by the three robbers individually, stated that the only question to be decided was whether there was the necessary mental intention or animus to render their physical possession of the guns, possession by the group as a whole. The learned judge then said that the question of whether the group (and hence the appellant) possessed the guns had to be decided with reference to the issue of whether the state had established, on the facts from which it could be inferred by a court, firstly, that the group had the intention (*animus*) to exercise possession of the guns through the actual detentor and secondly, the actual detentors had the intention to hold the guns on behalf of the group.**[61]

From the above, it is clear that for purposes of circumstance crimes, a court will have to first find that there is evidence from which it can be inferred that an accused person had the intent to effect, for instance, the possession through the perpetrators who actually had the

---

56 *S v Musingadi* supra at paras 34–39.
57 See, for example, *S v Lungile* supra.
58 *S v Coetzee en 'n ander* 1974 (3) SA 571 (T).
59 *S v Nkwenja en 'n ander* 1985 (2) SA 560 (A). See also, for example, *S v Goosen* supra; *S v Kwadi* 1989 (3) SA 524 (NC).
60 *S v Ramoba* 2017 (2) SACR 353 (SCA).
61 *S v Ramoba* at 11.

relevant items in their possession or, alternatively, that those perpetrators had the intent to hold the items on behalf of all of the co-accused. For instance, in an armed robbery scenario, a court should not assume that an accused who associated himself with the robbery in a common purpose scenario, also had the intent to unlawfully possess firearms jointly with the co-perpetrators who were in actual possession of the firearms. The unlawful possession of firearms and ammunition is a distinct crime and can be charged separately from the charge of robbery, and an accused can under those circumstances be convicted for robbery with aggravating circumstances *and* unlawful possession of firearms and ammunition, if the requirements as articulated by the SCA in *S v Ramoba* are met. This approach to common purpose in the context of circumstance crimes was also confirmed and applied by the Constitutional Court in *S v Makhubela*.[62]

25.3.2.9 Criticisms of the doctrine of common purpose

Although it is generally accepted that the law needs a mechanism for attributing some form of liability to individuals who commit crimes in concert, the common purpose doctrine, as it is applied in our law, is not without its critics. Criticism has been aimed, inter alia, at the issues discussed below:

- It is not necessary for the state to show that the accused's conduct contributed in any way towards the commission of the crime. This is regarded by some as an unwarranted lowering of the threshold for criminal liability, especially since (as will be shown below) a causal connection *is* required for liability as an accomplice.[63]
- Consequently, liability for a serious crime, such as murder, can arise from a relatively trivial act of association that in no way contributed towards the death of the deceased, or encouraged or facilitated the commission of the crime.[64]
- The scope of a common purpose includes not only conduct that the accused actually agreed upon or intended, but also conduct in respect of which they had *dolus eventualis*. Bear in mind that in our law, subjective foresight of even the remotest possibility has in the past been regarded as sufficient for this form of *dolus*.[65]
- The fact that in cases involving common purpose, the process of inferential reasoning applied by courts to determine the existence of *dolus eventualis* is sometimes so robust that it amounts to the now defunct *versari in re illicita* rule in disguise.
- The fact that an accused seeking to establish withdrawal from a common purpose attracts an evidential burden so heavy that it virtually amounts to a reversal of the normal onus of proof.[66]
- The fact that, when meting out sentence in such cases, courts seldom draw a sufficient distinction between the individual participants based on their actual role in and contribution towards the commission of the crime.[67]

---

62 *S v Makhubela and another* 2017 (2) SACR 665 (CC) at 57.

63 See *S v Safatsa* supra and the discussion on this point in *S v Thebus* supra.

64 See, for example, the conduct of the fourth accused in *S v Safatsa* supra (discussed below). The situation is undoubtedly exacerbated by the fact that, unlike English and American law, South African law does not distinguish between different degrees of intentional unlawful killing – murder is simply murder.

65 See, for example, *S v De Bruyn en 'n ander* 1968 (4) SA 498 (A); *S v Shaik* supra; *S v Ngubane* 1985 (3) SA 677 (A). However, compare with the English law approach, which requires that the commission of the crime in question must have been foreseen as a real or substantial risk – see *R v Rook* [1993] 2 All ER 955.

66 See, for example, *S v Nduli* supra at 504E: 'The more advanced an accused person's participation in the commission of the crime, the more pertinent and pronounced his conduct will have to be *to convince a court*, after the event, that he genuinely meant to dissociate himself from it at the time'. (Emphasis added)

67 See also Burchell *Principles of Criminal Law* 485–491.

The result is that a number of commentators and judges[68] believe that the common purpose rule in our law has been so extended that it now spreads the scope of liability too widely.[69] One notorious case that gave rise to a considerable amount of criticism in this regard was that of *S v Safatsa* – the trial of the so-called Sharpeville Six.[70]

S v Safatsa

On 3 September 1984, the deputy mayor of Lekoa, Mr Dlamini, was murdered by a mob outside his house in Sharpeville, near Vereeniging. Firstly, a mob of about 100 people attacked his house, throwing stones. The police arrived and dispersed the mob. The police tried to convince the deputy mayor to leave, but he refused. After the police had left, the mob reconvened and started throwing stones and petrol bombs. The house was set alight. The deputy mayor appeared at the door with a gun and fired a shot. This angered the mob further. As he fled, he was caught by some members of the mob who disarmed him of his pistol. Stones were then thrown at him and some members of the mob bashed him on the head with stones. Unconscious, he was put on top of his car, which by then had been set alight, but he kept falling off. Eventually, petrol was poured over him and he was set alight. He burnt to death. The postmortem showed that he would have died of the head wounds, even if he had not been burnt, and vice versa.

Eight members of the mob were identified and tried for his murder. Two of them (the fifth and sixth accused) were acquitted and six were convicted. The two who were acquitted escaped liability on the basis that there was only evidence that they were part of the mob that had stoned the house at the beginning. There was no evidence that they were still part of the mob when it decided to kill Mr Dlamini. Regarding the other six, the trial court found that each of them had the intention to kill the deceased and had actively associated themselves with the conduct of the mob, which was directed at killing the deceased:

- The first accused had grabbed the deceased, wrestled with him for the gun and thrown the first stone, which struck him down.
- The second accused had thrown a stone that struck the deceased.
- The third accused was found almost two months later in possession of the deceased's gun. The court concluded that he must have wrestled it from the deceased.
- The fourth accused, a young woman, had shouted to the crowd to kill the deceased and, when another woman tried to intercede for the deceased, she slapped her.
- The seventh and eighth accused had both made petrol bombs and helped to set the house and car alight.

They were convicted of murder and sentenced to death. They appealed against their convictions and sentences. One of their grounds of appeal was that the state had not proved beyond a reasonable doubt that there was a causal connection between the conduct of each of the accused and the death of the deceased. In support of this contention, they relied on the cases of *S v Maxaba* and *S v Thomo*.[71]

The AD reviewed the evidence and confirmed that the trial court had been correct in finding that each of the six accused:

- shared a common purpose to kill the deceased with the mob as a whole
- by their conduct, actively associated themselves with the achieving of that common purpose
- had the necessary intention to commit murder.

68 See the reasoning in *S v Mzwempi* 2011 (2) SACR 237 (ECM). This judgment favours a more restricted approach to common purpose.

69 See, for example, Steyn JA's dissenting judgment in *S v Nzo* supra at 14–16.

70 *S v Safatsa* supra. For a criticism of this case, see Cameron E 'Inferential reasoning and extenuation in the case of the Sharpeville Six' (1988) 1(2) *SACJ* 243.

71 S *v Maxaba en andere* 1981 (1) SA 1148 (A); *S v Thomo and others* 1969 (1) SA 385 (A).

On the question of causation, the AD reviewed the case law and held that the decision in *Maxaba* was based on an incorrect interpretation of *S v Williams*,[72] and that in *Thomo*, it was never intended that there had to be a causal connection between the conduct of each participant and the death of the deceased. That being the case, there was no reason to depart from the well-established principle that proof of causation is not required in cases where the state relies on common purpose. Their convictions and sentences were confirmed.

Given the controversial application of the common purpose doctrine in South African criminal law and the problematic political-legal context[73] in which it developed,[74] as illustrated by cases such as *Safatsa* and *Nzo*,[75] it came as no surprise that the doctrine eventually received constitutional scrutiny.[76] The constitutionality of the common purpose doctrine was challenged in the Constitutional Court in *S v Thebus*.[77] The appellants argued that the doctrine of common purpose was unconstitutional on the grounds that:

- by failing to distinguish between individual participants, it de-individualised and dehumanised them, thus infringing their fundamental right to dignity
- it based liability on the most tenuous link with individual conduct, thus violating the right not to be deprived of freedom arbitrarily
- it reduced the requirements of proof for certain elements of a crime to suit the convenience of the state, thus violating the presumption of innocence.

After considering these arguments, however, the Constitutional Court (per Moseneke J) found that they were without merit and held that the doctrine was not unconstitutional:

> **Common purpose does not amount to an arbitrary deprivation of freedom. The doctrine is rationally connected to the legitimate objective of limiting and controlling joint criminal enterprise. It serves vital purposes in our criminal justice system. Absent the rule of common purpose, all but actual perpetrators of a crime and their accomplices will be beyond the reach of our criminal justice system, despite their unlawful and intentional participation in the commission of the crime. Such an outcome would not accord with the considerable societal distaste for crimes by common design. Group, organised or collaborative misdeeds strike more harshly at the fabric of society and the rights of victims than crimes perpetrated by individuals. Effective prosecution of crime is a legitimate, 'pressing social need'. The need for 'a strong deterrent to violent crime' is well acknowledged because 'widespread violent crime is deeply destructive of the fabric of our society'. There is a real and pressing social concern about the high levels of crime. In practice, joint criminal conduct often poses peculiar difficulties of proof of the result of the conduct of each accused, a problem which hardly arises in the case of an individual accused person. Thus there is no objection to this norm of culpability even though it bypasses the requirement of causation.**[78]

72 *S v Williams* supra (discussed in section 25.4.1).

73 For a popular account of one of the famous apartheid era common purpose trials, see Durbach A *Upington: A Story of Trials and Reconciliation* (1999).

74 Cameron 'Inferential reasoning and extenuation in the case of the Sharpeville Six'.

75 For a thorough analysis of the facts and findings in *S v Nzo* supra, see Burchell *Principles of Criminal Law* 480–482. See also Burchell J 'Criminal law: *S v Nzo* 1990 (3) SA 1 (A) Common purpose liability' (1990) 3 *SACJ* 345.

76 For a synthesis of the controversies surrounding the common purpose cases (the older cases such as *Safatsa* and *Nzo*) as well as the Constitutional Court judgment in *Thebus*, see Burchell *South African Criminal Law and Procedure Vol I* 495–502; Burchell *Principles of Criminal Law* 479–493.

77 *S v Thebus and another* 2003 (2) SACR 319 (CC); 2003 (6) SA 505 (CC).

78 *S v Thebus* supra at 40.

25.3.2.10 Digression: Common purpose and the international criminal law doctrine of joint criminal enterprise (JCE)

In *S v Thebus*, discussed above, Moseneke J reasoned that the common purpose doctrine is not unconstitutional since it is 'rationally connected to the legitimate objective of limiting and controlling *joint criminal enterprise*'.[79] The term 'joint criminal enterprise' is not generally used in South African criminal law literature or jurisprudence. The doctrine of participation in a joint criminal enterprise (in short, joint criminal enterprise doctrine or JCE) plays an important role in international criminal law, especially with reference to crimes such as genocide and crimes against humanity.[80] These crimes are seldom, if ever, committed by a lone individual acting on his own. It is almost always (and due to the nature of the crimes, inevitably) committed by individuals acting in concert and as part of a common plan or design. We will discuss the specific elements of these crimes in Part Four of the book. For present purposes, it is necessary to draw attention to the different elements or components of JCE and to distinguish this doctrine from the doctrine of common purpose, which was considered in *S v Thebus*, and which survived constitutional scrutiny, as was pointed out above.

The doctrine of JCE is recognised and applied in the case law of international criminal tribunals.[81] The International Criminal Tribunal for the Former Yugoslavia (ICTY), especially, played an important role in developing the doctrine of JCE.[82] The general position regarding criminal liability based on JCE was formulated in *Prosecutor v Vasiljević* as follows: '[A]ll of the participants in a joint criminal enterprise are equally guilty of the committed crime regardless of the part played by each in its commission'.[83]

There are three forms of JCE:[84]

1. The basic form 'applies whenever several persons agree to commit a crime and execute it, with corresponding intent according to their common design'.[85] This basic form of JCE is perhaps closest to the South African understanding of the doctrine of common purpose, although there is not a perfect overlap.
2. The second form of JCE stems from the so-called 'concentration camp cases'. The focus here is on participation in a structure or system aimed at the ill treatment of people and for committing crimes under international law, such as crimes against humanity. The key element for individual criminal liability is the subjective element. Thus, the 'perpetrator must be aware of the character of the system and act with intent to further the system of mistreatment'.[86]
3. The third and more problematic form of JCE is where a participant in a JCE commits 'excesses that go beyond the framework of the common plan'.[87] The question is then whether the other participants in the common plan should be held liable for the excessive

---

79 *S v Thebus* supra. (Emphasis added)

80 Van Sliedregt E 'Joint criminal enterprise as a pathway to convicting individuals for genocide' (2007) 5(1) *JICJ* 184; Haan V 'The development of the concept of joint criminal enterprise at the International Criminal Tribunal for the Former Yugoslavia' (2005) 5(2) *Int'l Crim L Rev* 167.

81 Such as the International Criminal Tribunal for the Former Yugoslavia (ICTY), the International Criminal Tribunal for Rwanda (ICTR) and the Special Court for Sierra Leone (SCSL).

82 It was first applied in ICTY *Prosecutor v Dusko Tadić* (appeal judgment) IT-94-1-A July 1999 (see para 194 *et seq*). In *ICTY Prosecutor v Prlic and others* (appeal judgment) IT-04-74-A, 29 November 2017, in its final decision, the Appeals Chamber confirmed (at para 591) that JCE, including in the extended form, was firmly established under customary international law. The Appeals Chamber thus upheld its previous expositions and application of the JCE.

83 *Prosecutor v Vasiljevic* Case No IT-98-32-T, T Ch 11, 29 November 2002, para 67.

84 See, in general, Werle G and Jessberger F *Principles of International Criminal Law* 3 ed (2014) 200–207.

85 Werle and Jessberger *Principles of International Criminal Law* 202–203.

86 Werle and Jessberger *Principles of International Criminal Law* 203. See also *Prosecutor v Dusko Tadić* supra at paras 202 and 220.

87 Werle and Jessberger *Principles of International Criminal Law* 203.

> acts of the first participant. Remarkably, international jurisprudence suggests that each participant in the JCE can be held responsible even for the excesses that went beyond the original plan or framework of the common plan if the consequences of the acts were *natural and foreseeable*, and if the participants *willingly took the risk* of their occurrence. In terms of the element of *mens rea*, this means 'a person can be found guilty as a perpetrator of genocide, even if that person him or herself lacked the (specific) genocidal intent'.[88]

Commentators suggest that the provision on JCE in the Rome Statute of the International Criminal Court, 1998,[89] is somewhat stricter than the jurisprudence of the other tribunals discussed above. Under the Rome Statute, an *essential contribution* (in other words, more than 'mere participation', 'any contribution' or 'active association') is required for JCE. Werle and Jessberger describe a contribution as essential 'if the other perpetrators could not execute the common plan without it'.[90] The more restrictive approach to the objective and subjective components of JCE under the Rome Statute seems to be dogmatically sound and in line with fairness in criminal justice.

DISCUSSION

Critical assessment of the common purpose doctrine: A comparative perspective

The scope and application of the common purpose doctrine (or extended common purpose as it is known in some jurisdictions) is not only controversial in South Africa, but also in other countries where it is applied. In a minority opinion in the Australian case of *Clayton v The Queen*, the view was expressed that the present law of extended common purpose[91] liability is 'unjust, overbroad and anomalous. It should be re-expressed to narrow its ambit'.[92] The minority opinion further identified certain anomalies in the application of the doctrine of extended common purpose:

> **If a *principal* offender were to kill the victim, foreseeing only the possibility (rather than the probability) that his or her actions would cause death or grievous bodily harm, that person would not be guilty of murder. Yet a *secondary* offender with a common purpose could, on the current law, be found guilty of murder of the same victim on the basis of extended common purpose liability if the jury were convinced that he or she had foreseen the possibility that one of the group of offenders might, with intent, cause grievous bodily harm and if, in the result, one of the group does indeed kill the victim with the intention to cause such grievous bodily**

88 Werle and Jessberger *Principles of International Criminal Law* 203. Compare also the discussion of *dolus specialis* in Chapter 19.

89 Art 25(3)(*a*) of the Rome Statute of the International Criminal Court, 1998, provides as follows:

> **In accordance with this Statute, a person shall be criminally responsible and liable for punishment for a crime within the jurisdiction of the Court if that person: (*a*) Commits such a crime, whether as an individual, *jointly with another* or through another person, regardless of whether that other person is criminally responsible. (Emphasis added)**

The third alternative mentioned in art 25(3)(*a*) (commission through another person) is the so-called 'perpetrator by means'.

90 Werle and Jessberger *Principles of International Criminal Law* 205–206.

91 That is where A and B agree to commit a crime and, while carrying out the agreement, one of them (A) incidentally commits some other crime as well. B is then implicated as an accessory, provided he foresaw its commission as a possible outcome of the common purpose.

92 *Clayton v The Queen* (2006) 231 ALR 500 at 98. For a summary and discussion, see Arenson KJ, Bagaric M and Gillies P *Australian Criminal Law in the Common Law Jurisdictions: Cases and Materials* 3 ed (2011) 609–616.

> harm. On the face of things, the secondary offender's moral blameworthiness in such a case is significantly less than that of the principal offender. Yet (particularly in separate trials) it is quite possible, on current legal doctrine, that the secondary offender might be convicted of murder whilst the principal offender is acquitted, or convicted of a lesser offence.[93]

It is worthwhile to compare this minority opinion from an Australian case with the legal position in South Africa post-*Thebus*.

25.4 Accomplices

As previously explained, the English law distinction between principals in the first and second degrees, and accessories before the fact, fell away in South African law because of the way in which the common purpose rule was developed and applied. However, in *S v Williams*,[94] the AD saw fit to distinguish once again between liability as a co-perpetrator (*socius criminis*) and liability of a more accessorial nature.

S v Williams

Williams and his three co-accused were members of the notorious 'Hard Livings' gang, operating on the Cape Flats. On the day in question, they were travelling together on a train. There was no evidence that they started out with a common purpose to commit any crime. At a certain point, three of the accused attacked and killed another passenger. The first accused stabbed him with a knife and then the second accused grabbed him by the neck and pulled him along the coach. While he was holding him, the third accused stabbed the deceased with a bottleneck. The fourth accused remained totally passive and did nothing.

The trial court convicted the first and third accused of murder as co-perpetrators, and the second and fourth accused as accomplices to murder. The second and fourth accused appealed against their convictions. The AD (per Joubert JA) distinguished between co-perpetrators and accomplices (*mededaders* and *medepligtiges*) in the following terms:

> An accomplice's liability is accessory in nature so that there can be no question of an accomplice without a perpetrator or co-perpetrator who commits the crime. A perpetrator complies with all the requirements of the definition of the relevant crime. Where co-perpetrators commit the crime in concert, each co-perpetrator complies with the requirements of the definition of the relevant crime. On the other hand, an accomplice is not a perpetrator or co-perpetrator, since he lacks the *actus reus* of the perpetrator. An accomplice associates himself wittingly with the commission of the crime ... in that he knowingly affords the perpetrator or co-perpetrator the opportunity, the means or the information which furthers the commission of the crime ... [A]ccording to general principles there must be a causal connection between the accomplice's assistance and the commission of the crime by the perpetrator ...[95]

The AD then proceeded to confirm the second accused's conviction as an accomplice but acquitted the fourth accused because he had done nothing whatsoever to associate himself with the conduct of the other accused.

93 *Clayton v The Queen* supra at 100–101.
94 *S v Williams* supra.
95 *S v Williams* supra at para 63A–F; Burchell's translation in Burchell *Principles of Criminal Law* 505.

25.4.1 Discussion of *S v Williams*

It is evident, from the passage cited above, that Joubert JA was seeking to revive the old English law distinction between principals in the first degree (the actual perpetrator or co-perpetrators) and secondary participants, namely those persons whose liability was founded on their complicity with the actual perpetrator (principals in the second degree and accessories before the fact). It is also evident that he was seeking to introduce an additional requirement for liability as a secondary participant, which is now termed an *accomplice*,[96] namely that there must be a causal connection between the conduct of the accomplice and the commission of the crime by the actual perpetrator. This clearly represented a significant departure from established law, which regarded proof of causation as unnecessary in cases where the state is able to rely on common purpose.[97]

The following year, in *S v Maxaba*, the AD (per Viljoen JA) interpreted its earlier decision in ***Williams*** as meaning that the state must indeed prove a causal connection, both to establish liability for murder as a co-perpetrator and to establish liability as an accomplice to murder.[98] However, this interpretation was not permitted to stand. Presumably believing that it had gone too far in its decisions in *Williams and Maxaba*, the AD (per Botha AJA) attempted to rectify matters in *S v Khoza*:

> **Generally, I should make it clear that I do not accept that it was intended in *Williams'* case to supplant, qualify, or detract from, the substance of the practice of the Courts in relation to common purpose in previous cases decided over a period of many years.**[99]

Since accused persons continued to argue the point in subsequent cases, Botha JA, delivering the AD's judgment in *S v Safatsa*, made it abundantly clear that ***Williams*** had not altered the established law relating to the common purpose rule and its implications:

> **In my view the Court in *Williams'* case did not intend to supplant, qualify, or detract from the substance of the practice of the Courts in relation to common purpose. I expressed this view in *Khoza's* case *supra* at 1054C. It has turned out to be correct, having regard to the manner in which cases of common purpose have continued to be dealt with in the decisions of this Court subsequent to *Williams'* case, as mentioned above ... *For practical purposes, in applying the law relating to cases of common purpose, the judgment in Williams' case can safely be left out of consideration altogether.***[100]

After criticising Viljoen JA's interpretation of *Williams* in *S v Maxaba*, Botha JA went on to hold that the judgment in *Maxaba* could safely be ignored in the future treatment of common purpose cases insofar as it relates to the question of causation.[101]

Against the above background, let us now consider what is required for accomplice liability, bearing in mind that it is necessary to piece these requirements together from a number of sources, some of them contradictory.

96 The Afrikaans term '*medepligtige*' was used in the judgment. The term 'accomplice' has been adopted as its English equivalent.

97 See Chapter 6.

98 *S v Maxaba* supra at 1155F–G and 1156H–1157A.

99 *S v Khoza* supra at 1054C.

100 *S v Safatsa* supra at 898F–I. (Emphasis added)

101 *S v Safatsa* supra at 898J–900A.

25.4.2 What is an accomplice?

An **accomplice** is a person who intentionally furthers or assists in the commission of a crime at any time before or during its commission, but who is someone *other than* a perpetrator or a co-perpetrator.[102] To ascertain whether a particular person was an accomplice to a crime, it is therefore necessary, in the first instance, to use a process of elimination. We must first ascertain whether he was a perpetrator or co-perpetrator by applying the definitions set out above.[103] If so, he cannot also be an accomplice.[104] Only if he is not a perpetrator or co-perpetrator do we then proceed to enquire whether the person concerned was an accomplice, by applying the further requirements set out below.

It is clear, therefore, that whatever the AD may have intended in *S v Williams*, an accomplice is not merely another term for the English law concepts of principal in the second degree and/or accessory before the fact, although there are certain residual resemblances. English law drew a technical distinction between these categories of participants and principals in the first degree *despite* the common purpose rule. South African law does not.

25.4.3 Requirements for accomplice liability

25.4.3.1 Unlawful conduct

The *actus reus* of an accomplice consists of *furthering or assisting in the commission of a crime*, for example by supplying the perpetrator with the means, opportunity, information or advice to help him commit the crime.[105] There must therefore be a *causal relationship* between the conduct of the accomplice and the unlawful conduct of the perpetrator.[106] This is not in the sense that the crime could not have been committed at all if it had not been for the conduct of the accomplice, but in the sense that the accomplice must in some way have facilitated the commission of the crime and made it easier for the actual perpetrator to commit the crime.[107] This means that the assistance rendered must have taken some practical form. In this respect, liability as an accomplice differs from liability on the basis of common purpose, which does not require any type of causal connection between the conduct of a secondary party and the commission of the crime by the actual perpetrator.

It does not matter whether the actual perpetrator was aware of the assistance that he received, or the identity of the person from whom he received it.[108] The accomplice's assistance need not take the form of positive conduct. It can take the form of an omission[109]

102 See, in general, Snyman *Criminal Law* 265–270; Burchell *South African Criminal Law and Procedure Vol I* 515–522; Burchell *Principles of Criminal Law* 505–506. See also *S v Msomi* 2010 (2) SACR 173 (KZP) for a discussion of the distinction between perpetrators and accomplices.

103 See section 25.3.

104 Note that the liability of the second accused in *S v Williams* was not correctly decided according to this rule. The second accused acceded by conduct to a common purpose to murder the deceased, thus rendering himself liable as a co-perpetrator. He could not, therefore, also have been an accomplice to murder according to our present understanding of this form of participation. See RC Whiting's commentary on this point in 'Principals and accessories in crime' (1980) 97(2) *SALJ* 199.

105 Snyman *Criminal Law* 267–268.

106 *S v Khoza* supra.

107 Snyman *Criminal Law* 267.

108 Burchell *Principles of Criminal Law* 510.

109 See, for example, *S v Mahlangu en andere* 1995 (2) SACR 425 (T). Mahlangu carried out a robbery at a garage where the second and third accused were employed. Mahlangu alleged that the second and third accused were integrally involved in planning and executing the robbery. The trial court agreed with this and convicted them of the robbery on the basis of common purpose, but it held (obiter) that even if they had merely been passive bystanders, as employees they were in a position of trust. They therefore had a duty to warn their employer of the intended robbery, which they knew about. Because their inaction was a breach of this duty, they could equally have been held liable as accomplices to Mahlangu. See also the AD's dicta in *S v Williams* supra at 63H and *S v A en 'n ander* 1993 (1) SACR 600 (A) at 606H.

if there was a legal duty on the accused in question to prevent the commission of the crime.[110]

Lastly, note that although (as previously explained) there are certain crimes to which the common purpose rule does not apply because a person can only become liable by personally satisfying all the requirements of liability, a person who furthers or assists the commission of such a crime can nevertheless be held liable as an accomplice to that crime.[111] Thus, for example, a person who lends his car to an unlicensed person to drive, could be found guilty of being an accomplice to the offence of driving without a valid licence.

25.4.3.2 Fault

The accused must have intended to further or assist the commission of a crime committed by someone else. *Dolus eventualis* is sufficient for this purpose, but mere negligence is not because this would cast the net of criminal liability too widely.

According to English law, concrete intention is not required for accomplice liability. Thus, for example, where X supplies Y with the means to commit one or more of a range of possible crimes, such as robbery, murder or burglary, X renders himself liable as an accomplice to Y's crime, even though he may not know exactly which crime Y proposes to commit, or the identity of its target. It is enough if X knew or foresaw that he was assisting Y to commit one or more of a range of possible crimes, which includes the *type of crime* that Y did in fact commit.[112] Although the question has not been decided by South African courts, it is likely that they would take the same approach.

DISCUSSION

Can victims of crime be accomplices to their own harm?

An interesting and morally complex question is whether a victim of crime can, under certain conditions, be treated as an accomplice to his or her own harm. The issue can be discussed with reference to the example of sadomasochism. Dennis Baker discussed the following example:

> **If X, a sadomasochist, consents to Y (who is also a sadomasochist) poking her eyes out, she has not only used herself as a mere means, but also allowed Y to use (wrong and harm) her to a grave degree. Y has used X as a mere means and is criminally liable for wrongfully harming her without excuse or justification. In effect sadomasochists and gladiators wrong not only themselves, but each other ... Masochism is not a mere case of self-harm and we do not criminalise the consenter. Instead it is the actions of the harm-doer that are criminalized ... The degree of moral wrongdoing involved in serious self-harm and serious harm to others is equal, but self-wrongs are not criminalizable because they do not wrong or harm others.[113]**

110 In this respect, too, liability as an accomplice differs from liability on the basis of common purpose. It is a rule derived from the English law relating to principals in the second degree, which has survived in South African law. See Williams *Criminal Law: The General Part* 360.

111 This, too, is a surviving application of the English law relating to the liability of secondary participants. See Williams *Criminal Law: The General Part* 349 *et seq.*

112 *R v Bainbridge* [1959] 3 All ER 200; *R v Jogee* [2016] UKSC 8; *Ruddock v The Queen* [2016] UKPC 7 at para 14–15. See Smith JC and Hogan B *Criminal Law* (1965) 74–75; Burchell *Principles of Criminal Law* 501.

113 Baker DJ *The Right not to be Criminalized: Demarcating Criminal Law's Authority* (2011) 184–185.

In reaction to Baker's discussion of the sadomasochism example, Jonathan Herring pointed out that if the masochist (Y) is punished for harming the 'victim' (X) and that the harm in question is a recognised legal wrong, 'Why should the "victim" not be liable as an accomplice to the wrong the principal (Y) has done'?[114] Herring argued further that the fact that the law normally does not punish self-harm is beside the point if the focus is on the accessorial argument. 'We are punishing X not for harming himself, but encouraging someone to harm another.'[115]

Of course, in a discussion like this, one must also take into account the element of *consent* that was discussed in Chapter 12. Assuming consent is not an issue, the question of whether a victim of crime can be regarded as an accomplice, based on accessorial contribution, seems to present a number of moral and dogmatic issues.

25.4.4 How can a person become an accomplice without becoming a co-perpetrator?

It is evident that in most cases, it will be impossible for a person to perform any act aimed at furthering or assisting the commission of a crime without becoming party to a common purpose with the actual perpetrator and thereby becoming a co-perpetrator himself. In this case, by definition, he cannot also be an accomplice. How, then, can a person become an accomplice, properly speaking? Essentially, there are three possibilities:

1. The assistance takes the form of an omission in breach of a duty to prevent the commission of the crime in question (as in *S v Mahlangu*). As previously discussed, a person cannot become party to a common purpose by mere omission, but he can certainly become an accomplice.
2. The assistance is rendered in the commission of a crime that can only be committed personally by the actual perpetrator, such as perjury, bigamy, driving offences, and so forth.[116] In this case, the only form of liability that can attach to the person who assists is that of accomplice.
3. A third possibility, although the position is not entirely clear, is that liability as an accomplice might conceivably also arise in the case where the accused in question lacked concrete intention, in the sense that while he provided the means to commit the crime, he did not know or foresee what crime the perpetrator actually intended to commit.

Therefore, accomplice liability spans a narrow range of conduct. In the vast majority of cases, a person who intentionally furthers or assists in the commission of a crime will be a co-perpetrator.

114 Herring J in Reed and Bohlander *Participation in Crime* 90.

115 Herring in Reed and Bohlander 90.

116 See, for example, *R v Shikuri* 1939 AD 225, *S v Saffier* 2003 (2) SACR 141 (SE); *S v Kimberley and another* 2004 (2) SACR 38 (E).

25.5 Accessories after the fact

An accessory after the fact is a person who intentionally associates himself with the crime only *after* its commission is complete, and who helps the perpetrator or an accomplice to evade justice. Examples include concealing the commission of the crime; concealing, falsifying or disposing of evidence; or harbouring the perpetrator or accomplice.[117]

Once again, being an accessory after the fact to a crime is regarded as a crime in its own right. In terms of section 257 of the Criminal Procedure Act 51 of 1977, it is a competent verdict on any charge.[118]

According to *S v Nooroodien*, an accessory after the fact is '[a] person who (1) unlawfully and (2) intentionally (3) assists a perpetrator or an accomplice (4) after the commission of a crime/offence (5) to avoid liability for his/her criminal act (6) with the object of defeating or interfering with the administration of justice'.[119]

As in the case of accomplices, intention includes *dolus eventualis*, but mere negligence will not be sufficient for liability as an accessory after the fact.

The act of assistance can take the form of an omission if it is in breach of a duty to act and if it is done with the necessary object of assisting the perpetrator to evade justice.[120] The following passage from the headnote to *S v Nooroodien* puts it well:

> **With reference to the position of someone who fails to report a crime, it is clear that such failure *per se* does not constitute that person an accessory after the fact. It is a failure to report the offence, *coupled* with other circumstances of the accused's conduct which constitutes an association with the crime whereby material assistance is rendered to the principal offender. Thus, where a member of the public witnesses the commission of an offence, but calmly goes about his business, he does not incur accessorial liability. The position is different, however, if he is questioned by the police, and denies that he saw the offence being committed. The question then arises whether he suppressed his knowledge of the offence with the intention of assisting the offender to evade justice. If the answer to that question is affirmative, such a person is guilty as an accessory after the fact.**[121]

As a matter of principle, a person cannot be an accessory after the fact to his own crime. This gives rise to a problem in cases where a number of people are charged with a crime, such as murder, but the state is unable to prove which of them killed the deceased, nor can it prove that there was a common purpose between them to kill the deceased. All that can be established beyond reasonable doubt is that one or more of them committed the murder and that the others are assisting him to evade justice by refusing to identify the actual perpetrator. On a strict application of the above principle, none of the accused could then be convicted of being accessories after the fact to murder since it is reasonably possible that any of them may have committed the murder themselves.

117 See, for instance, *S v Terblanche* 2011 (1) SACR 77 (ECG) – accessory after the fact in a murder case.

118 The common law crime of accessory after the fact has been largely eclipsed by the statutory offence of defeating or obstructing the course of justice.

119 *S v Nooroodien en andere* 1998 (2) SACR 510 (NC) at 526E–F (translated from the Afrikaans).

120 See, for example, *S v Barnes and another* 1990 (2) SACR 485 (N) (discussed in section 4.2.3.1) and *S v Phallo and others* 1999 (2) SACR 558 (SCA). But compare these cases with *S v Williams* supra.

121 *S v Nooroodien* supra.

In *R v Gani*,[122] the AD (per Schreiner JA) addressed this problem by holding that those who had not committed the murder themselves were clearly guilty of the crime of being accessories after the fact to the murder. Those who had committed the murder themselves were in turn associating themselves with the crime committed by the former, and were therefore liable for it as co-perpetrators on the basis of the common purpose rule. All the accused were accordingly convicted of being accessories after the fact to murder.

Despite criticism of this approach, it has since been followed in a number of cases, including *S v Phallo*.[123] In this case, the Supreme Court of Appeal (SCA) held that in a case where there are several accused who have tried to cover up a crime, such as murder, which may have been committed by only one of them, the accused persons, other than the actual murderer, commit the crime of being accessories after the fact to the murderer's crime when, for instance, they hide the body. This crime is their own distinct crime and is not part of the crime committed by the murderer. If then, the actual murderer acts in concert with them, he is participating in their distinct crime of being accessories after the fact to murder as their accomplice. In such a case, all the accused can therefore be convicted as accessories after the fact to murder.

Having considered the different categories of participants recognised in our law, we will in the next chapter discuss the last of the general principles of liability, namely the extent to which liability may arise out of a crime that is incomplete, or inchoate, to use the preferred legal term.

THIS CHAPTER IN ESSENCE

1. South African law currently recognises and distinguishes between three different categories of participants in crime:
   1.1 Perpetrators and co-perpetrators
   1.2 Accomplices
   1.3 Accessories after the fact
2. A perpetrator is a person who:
   2.1 personally fulfils all three elements of criminal liability
   2.2 has the necessary criminal capacity and fault, and orchestrates the commission of the crime by an innocent or unwitting agent
   2.3 has the necessary criminal capacity and fault, and forms a common purpose to commit the crime with the person who actually committed it.
3. The common purpose rule holds that where two or more people associate together to commit a crime, they will each be liable for the criminal conduct of the others that falls within the scope of their common purpose. They will be regarded as co-perpetrators. Their *actus reus* consists of their act of associating together with a common purpose to commit the crime, which was ultimately committed by one of them. As a matter of policy, the conduct of each perpetrator is imputed to all the others.
4. In the case of consequence crimes, it is not necessary for the state to prove that each participant contributed in any way towards causing the prohibited consequence, or even who actually caused it, as long as it can prove that the consequence was caused by one or other of them and that the rest shared a common purpose to commit the crime at the time of the causal act. A common purpose can be formed through conspiracy (agreement) or by spontaneous association (conduct), but cannot arise from mere omission. Positive conduct is required.

122 *R v Gani and others* 1957 (2) SA 212 (A).
123 *S v Phallo* supra.

5. An accomplice is a person who intentionally furthers or assists in the commission of a crime at any time before or during its commission, but who is someone other than a perpetrator or a co-perpetrator. To ascertain whether a person was an accomplice to a crime, it is therefore necessary, in the first instance, to ascertain whether he was a perpetrator or co-perpetrator. If so, he cannot also be an accomplice. Only if he is not a perpetrator or co-perpetrator, do we then proceed to enquire whether the person concerned was an accomplice.
6. An accessory after the fact is a person who intentionally associates himself with the crime only *after* its commission is complete, and who helps the perpetrator or accomplice evade justice. Examples include concealing the commission of the crime, concealing or disposing of evidence, or harbouring the perpetrator or accomplice. A person cannot be an accessory after the fact to his own crime.

Chapter 26

Incomplete crimes

CHAPTER OBJECTIVES

The objectives of this chapter are to:
- distinguish between complete and incomplete attempts
- distinguish between attempts and acts of mere preparation
- explain the principles relating to liability for an attempt to commit a crime
- explain the principles relating to attempts to commit the impossible
- define the term 'incitement'
- explain the principles relating to liability for incitement to commit a crime
- define the term 'conspiracy'
- explain the principles relating to liability for conspiracy to commit a crime.

26.1 Introduction

One of the principal elements of criminal liability is unlawful conduct of some kind. Society does not demand that a person should be punished for merely harbouring the intention to commit a crime – no one is punished for their intentions alone.

Thus, if X *plans* to murder someone, but stops short of putting his plan into action, there will be no unlawful conduct and thus no crime for which X can be held liable. At this stage of the enquiry, we can rightly ask why[1] the criminal justice system should concern itself 'with punishing conduct that does not apparently cause any direct harm to an individual or society generally'.[2] An exclusively *subjective approach* to culpability would lead to the conclusion that criminal law punishes the guilty intent. The fact that, for whatever reason, the plan did not materialise should, in principle, make no difference to the individual's culpability. Such a subjectivist approach seems to focus on the irrelevance, from a moral point of view, between the person who forms a criminal intent to do something but does not succeed in doing it, and the person who succeeds in implementing his criminal plan.[3]

It is clear, however, that modern criminal law does not follow this exclusively subjective approach to criminal attempts. Something more is needed for criminal liability. As Duff puts it, '[we] cannot give a purely subjectivist account of what it is to act, since action must be understood as an engagement with and in our shared material and social world'. Furthermore, '[t]he character of the blame that the wrongdoer deserves depends crucially on the *actual impact* of his/her action on the world'.[4] This approach is known as the *objectivist approach* to culpability for attempts.

Thus, what is the legal position if X intends to murder someone, plans the murder, gathers the means for its commission and starts to put his plan into effect, but then gets cold feet or is interrupted, and does not see it through? Or, perhaps X tries to shoot Y but misses. Under certain circumstances, X's conduct thus far will be unlawful per se. Depending on what he has done, he may be liable for attempted murder, conspiracy to commit murder or possibly incitement to commit murder. An attempt to commit a crime, conspiracy to commit a crime and incitement to commit a crime are all regarded as discrete crimes. In effect, therefore, they constitute additional forms of unlawful conduct. We will consider each of these forms of liability in turn.

26.2 Attempts

While Roman law apparently did not punish attempts to commit crime,[5] Roman-Dutch law certainly regarded attempts as punishable.[6] Modern South African law also punishes attempts. An attempt to commit a common law crime, such as murder, is punishable in terms of the common law. However, attempts to commit statutory crimes are punishable in terms

1 On the rationale for criminalising attempt, conspiracy and incitement, see Snyman CR *Criminal Law* 6 ed (2014) 275. The author bases the rationale for punishing anticipatory conduct on the so-called 'relative theories of punishment' (especially the preventive and reformative theories). See also reasons identified by Burchell JM *Principles of Criminal Law* 5 ed (2016) 527–530.

2 Burchell JM *South African Criminal Law and Procedure Vol I: General Principles of Criminal Law* 4 ed (2011) 537.

3 See Stuart D 'The *actus reus* in attempts' (1970) *Crim LR* 505; Duff RA 'Subjectivism, objectivism and criminal attempts' in Simester AP and Smith ATH (eds) *Harm and Culpability* (1996) 19–44. For a South African perspective, see De Wet JC and Swanepoel HL *Strafreg* 3 ed (1975) 159–160.

4 Duff 'Subjectivism, objectivism and criminal attempts' 39 (emphasis added). Reprinted by permission of Oxford University Press. (URL www.oup.com<http://www.oup.com)

5 For instance, D.47.2.21.7–9.

6 Burchell *South African Criminal Law and Procedure Vol I* 540.

of section 18(1) of the Riotous Assemblies Act 17 of 1956.[7] This section provides that any person:

> **... who attempts to commit any offence against a statute or a statutory regulation shall be guilty of an offence and, if no punishment is expressly provided thereby for such an attempt, be liable on conviction to the punishment to which a person convicted of actually committing *that* offence would be liable.**

Snyman submits that this provision also includes attempts to commit offences contained in provincial statutory provisions and municipal by-laws.[8]

South African criminal law distinguishes between two types of attempts to commit a crime: completed attempts and incomplete attempts.[9]

26.2.1 Completed attempts

Completed attempt is the term used to describe a situation in which the would-be perpetrator has done everything that he set out to do, but merely failed to achieve his purpose, either through lack of skill, sheer accident or for some other reason. For example, X shoots at Y intending to kill him, but misses or only injures him.

This type of attempt is generally not too difficult for the state to prove. The only likely area of difficulty is establishing the intention with which the accused acted, for example that he intended to kill the complainant rather than merely injure or frighten him. As in the case of completed crimes, however, intention can be established by circumstantial evidence and inferential reasoning. Thus, for example, an attack with a lethal weapon would generally be interpreted as a case of attempted murder rather than assault.

26.2.2 Incomplete attempts

Incomplete attempt is the term used to describe a situation in which the would-be perpetrator starts to commit the crime but is interrupted by some external agency and does not see it through. For example, X accosts Y with the intention of robbing him, but a police officer arrives on the scene and X runs away empty-handed.

This type of attempt can be more problematic, because it is often difficult to tell when the accused has passed beyond the stage of merely preparing to commit the crime and has started to commit it. The general rule is that *mere acts of preparation* are not punishable by law. A person will be punished only if he has gone *beyond* the preparation stage and has embarked on the commission of the crime, that is, if he has *commenced the consummation of the crime*. Once this stage is reached, the accused can no longer withdraw from the attempt and he will be liable accordingly.[10]

26.2.3 Commencement of the consummation of the crime

The expression 'commencement of the consummation of the crime' has been interpreted to mean 'the beginning of the final series of acts which complete the crime'.[11] The test for

7 See, in general, on common law attempts and attempts in terms of the Riotous Assemblies Act 17 of 1956, Snyman *Criminal Law* 276; Burchell *South African Criminal Law and Procedure Vol I* 540; De Wet and Swanepoel *Strafreg* 168.

8 Snyman *Criminal Law* 276 fn 2.

9 *R v Schoombie* 1945 AD 541.

10 For comments on the difficult line between mere preparation and attempt, see Simester and Smith (eds) *Harm and Culpability* (1996) 10–11.

11 *Hicks v Commonwealth* (19 Am State Rep 891).

commencement of the consummation of the crime was originally formulated in American law and adopted into South African law in the early case of *R v Sharpe.*[12]

R v Sharpe

Sharpe threatened to shoot a man called Smith. He then left, fetched a loaded gun and returned to look for Smith. He was, however, arrested before he could find him. He was convicted of attempted assault and appealed to the Transvaal Supreme Court. On appeal, the court (per Innes CJ) referred to Roman-Dutch, English and American authority and held that an attempt implies two things:

- The intention to commit the crime
- An overt act directed towards carrying out that intention

Mere acts of preparation, although done with criminal intent, do not amount to attempts to commit a crime and are not punishable. It held further that the acts conducted by Sharpe were mere acts of preparation and did not amount to an attempt. If, however, Sharpe had found Smith, his preparation would have been complete and any further steps taken by him towards accomplishing the crime would have amounted to an attempt.

The commencement of the consummation test was subsequently endorsed and applied by the Appellate Division (AD) in the case of *R v Nlhovo.*[13]

R v Nlhovo

Nlhovo wanted to kill a man called Jacob. He gave a young boy, Nhlana, some poison and told him to put it into Jacob's food, saying it was medicine. Nhlana did not do so but handed the poison over to Jacob. Nlhovo was subsequently convicted of attempted murder. He appealed.

The AD held that an attempt to commit a crime is made up of two elements:

- The intention to commit the crime
- A direct but ineffectual (unsuccessful) act done towards its commission. This act must reach far enough towards the accomplishment of the desired result so as to amount to the commencement of the consummation of the crime

While there is a distinction between acts that are immediately connected with the fulfillment of a crime and those that are only remotely connected with its fulfillment, there is difficulty in deciding where to draw the line. The AD found that Nlhovo's act of procuring the poison was merely an act of preparation and did not amount to attempted murder.

It then had to decide whether his act of giving the poison to Nhlana, with the instruction to put it in Jacob's food, took matters any further. The AD held that because, according to his own evidence, Nhlana never intended to carry out Nlhovo's instruction, his involvement took matters no further. It concluded, therefore, that Nlhovo's conduct did not amount to attempted murder. The court added, rather illogically, that if Nhlana had gone ahead and put the poison in Jacob's food as instructed, then Nlhovo would indeed have been guilty of attempted murder.[14]

---

12 *R v Sharpe* 1903 TS 868.

13 *R v Nlhovo* 1921 AD 485.

14 This is bizarre reasoning because it means, in effect, that Nlhovo's liability was assessed not on the basis of his own conduct and fault, but according to that of Nhlana. This is entirely contrary to established principle. We should perhaps remember, however, that the law on the subject was still largely undeveloped and it is unlikely that a court would come to the same conclusion today. See, for example, the court's decision in *S v Mlambo* 1986 (4) SA 34 (E).

The difficulty with the commencement of the consummation test is that it is extremely vague and provides a court with little in the way of practical guidance as to whether the accused has passed the stage of preparation and has actually embarked on the commission of the crime. Therefore, over the years, courts have attempted to amplify and clarify the enquiry, although without a great deal of success. A case in point was that of *R v Schoombie*.[15]

R v Schoombie

Schoombie wanted to burn down a shop, so he went there one night with a can of petrol and a tin of flammable material. He put the tin against the door and poured petrol into it and around it so that the petrol ran under the door. Before he could light it, he was interrupted by the arrival of a police officer. He was convicted of attempted arson and appealed. His argument was that he had not yet actually embarked on the commission of the crime – he was still merely preparing to commit it.

On a point of law reserved for its decision, the AD distinguished between complete and incomplete attempts. The present case obviously fell into the second category. It referred to the dictum in *Nlhovo* on the commencement of the consummation of the crime. It held that in the case of interrupted crimes, an attempt to commit the crime is proved when a court is satisfied beyond a reasonable doubt that the perpetrator (1) intended to commit the crime and (2) had at least carried his purpose through to the stage where he was commencing the consummation of the crime. The time at which the commencement of the consummation of the crime begins will vary with the nature of the crime and the facts of each case, but the following general considerations will apply:

- Once a wrongdoer has finally made up his mind to commit a crime and has taken steps to carry out that decision, the exact moment at which he is interrupted should not be the sole factor in determining his guilt.
- As long as his acts have reached the stage where a court can properly infer that he had finally made up his mind to commit the crime, he should be held liable for attempt.
- Commencement of the consummation includes conducting acts that would constitute a continuous operation, unbroken by intervals of time that may give an opportunity for reconsideration.
- The AD held that the placing of the tin and the pouring of the petrol were acts that formed part of *one continuous operation* of setting the shop on fire and were not mere acts of preparation. Schoombie was therefore rightly convicted of attempted arson.

In *R v Katz*,[16] the court considered the earlier authorities and concluded that in each case, a court has to make a value judgment of a practical nature, based on all the available facts, similar to the judgment that a court has to make in other areas of law where the court has to decide questions of proximity and remoteness:

> **After full consideration of the authorities one is left with the conclusion that a value judgment of a practical nature is to be brought to bear upon each set of facts as it arises for consideration – a judgment similar to what is called for in other spheres of law governed by notions of proximity and remoteness, as for example the determination of the limits to which damages caused by delict or breach of contract are legally recoverable, or of the 'real' cause of injury or loss in a case of contributory negligence, or of the 'proximate' cause of a transaction in respect of which agent's**

15 *R v Schoombie* supra.
16 *R v Katz* 1959 (3) SA 408 (C).

> **commission is claimed, or even of a question whether an errant servant was or was not acting within the scope of his employment. In all these cases the human mind grapples in vain with an endeavour to find a formula, test or criterion readily applicable to every case that arises; and those that are devised are continually grafted with exceptions and qualifications or completely revised. The 'uncertain and wavering line' is drawn 'as best we can' (*Feldman (Pty.) Ltd v Mall*, 1945 AD 733 at p. 750). In the guiding considerations one finds the same kind of conceptions and even of expressions: 'the natural course of events'; 'proximate in time' is not necessarily 'proximate in law' etc. and experience in all these spheres appears to dictate caution as to the over-ready, rule-of-thumb application of any single expression or consideration. The overriding endeavour must needs be to assign to every constituent part of a particular situation such weight as common sense dictates, and then to decide whether the whole thereof can in a fair and practical sense be said to be too remote to fall within the requisite realm of legal cognizance.**[17]

From the above cases, we can conclude that in drawing the line between acts of mere preparation and conduct that amounts to an attempt to commit a crime, the court is essentially required to make a *value judgement* based on the nature of the crime and the facts of the case.[18] In general, the enquiry is a proximity enquiry, that is, the court has to decide whether the accused has gone far enough towards realising his intention to commit the crime. To put it another way, acts that are considered too remote from the accused's intentions being realised will not be regarded as attempts, but as acts of mere preparation. There is no hard and fast test for proximity, but the court will have regard for factors such as the following:

- The outcome, in the natural course of events, had the accused not been interrupted
- The accused's proximity to the commission of the crime in terms of both time and space
- The extent to which the accused still had control over the train of events that he was busy putting into motion (and could thus stop or reverse)
- The point at which the court can properly infer, from the accused's actions, that he intended (1) to go through with the commission of the crime and (2) to commit the crime in question as opposed to some lesser offence or even some innocent act

26.2.4 Change of mind

What is the position where a person attempts to commit a crime (that is, his conduct goes beyond the stage of mere preparation), but then changes his mind and decides not to proceed? The rule is that once the accused's conduct has reached the stage where it amounts to an attempt, the fact that he, of his own volition, decides not to proceed makes no difference to his liability for attempt. However, in an appropriate case, it may be regarded as a mitigating factor. This is because an attempt to commit a crime is a crime in itself. Thus, once the accused has committed it, he cannot reverse or undo his liability. The leading case on this point is *S v Hlatwayo*.[19]

---

17 *R v Katz* supra at 422H–423C.

18 In *S v Mekula* 2012 (2) SACR 521 (ECG), the accused concealed a bottle of whisky under his clothes before he left the liquor store. Before he could leave the store, he was spotted by a security guard on duty. The accused then tried to put the bottle back on the shelf, but in this process, he broke the bottle. On review, the magistrates' court verdict of theft was changed to one of attempted theft.

19 *R v Hlatwayo and another* 1933 TPD 441.

S v Hlatwayo

Ms Hlatwayo was a domestic worker who decided to poison her employers by putting caustic soda into the porridge she was cooking for them. Another employee saw her and threatened to inform on her. Ms Hlatwayo then threw out the poisoned porridge. She was convicted of attempted murder and the matter was taken on review to the High Court.

The High Court confirmed her conviction, saying that her conduct in putting the poison into the porridge, which she knew was going to be eaten by the members of the household, had gone beyond an act of mere preparation. It amounted to an attempt to commit murder. The fact that she thereafter voluntarily desisted from completing her criminal purpose did not exonerate her from liability for attempted murder.

26.2.5 The fault element

The *mens rea* required for an attempt to commit a crime is the intention to commit the crime itself. This means that the accused must have had *dolus* in respect of the principal crime. Consequently, it is not possible to attempt to commit a crime for which *culpa* (negligence) alone is required. A person cannot attempt to be negligent. Thus, for example, a person cannot be guilty of attempted culpable homicide[20] or attempted negligent driving. However, *dolus eventualis* in respect of the principal crime is sufficient.[21]

26.2.6 Attempts to commit the impossible

What is the position where a person attempts to commit a crime that is impossible to commit? For example, what is X's liability if he attempts to kill someone who is already dead or attempts to steal an item that turns out to be his own property?[22] South African criminal law in this regard distinguishes between two types of impossibility: physical impossibility and legal impossibility.

Under the first category fall crimes that are physically impossible to commit. Examples include attempting to murder a person who is already dead[23] or who has already received the fatal injury, or attempting to rape a dead person.[24] In such cases, the law takes a *subjective* view. For example, if the accused subjectively intended to commit murder, and always provided that his conduct had passed the stage of mere preparation, then he will be guilty of an attempt to commit the intended crime.[25]

---

20 *S v Ntanzi* 1981 (4) SA 477 (N).

21 See, for example, *S v Nango* 1990 (2) SACR 450 (A). Nango was a member of a group of men who attacked a group of policemen who had come to carry out an arrest. After one of the policemen had been knocked down, Nango approached him with a raised axe as though he was going to chop him. The policeman then drew his firearm and shot Nango. Nango was charged with and convicted of attempted murder. He appealed.

On appeal, the court held that Nango's conduct had gone beyond an act of preparation to an act of consummation. Regarding the nature of Nango's intention, the court held that the only reasonable inference to be drawn from his conduct was that he foresaw the possibility of the death of the policeman if he chopped him with the axe and he was reckless as to the consequences. Accordingly, Nango had attempted to assault the policeman with intent (in the form of *dolus eventualis*) to kill him and he had been rightly convicted of attempted murder. See also the earlier AD case *R v Huebsch* 1953 (2) SA 561(A) and see *S v Phiri* 2014 (1) SACR 211 (GNP), in which the North Gauteng Provincial Division of the High Court upheld the conviction for attempted murder of an HIV/AIDS counsellor, who was himself HIV-positive and who had unprotected sex with the complainant, whom he knew to be HIV-negative. In upholding the accused's conviction, the High Court confirmed that he had had the necessary intention to kill in the form of *dolus eventualis*.

22 For an example, see *R v Huebsch* supra.

23 See, for example, *S v Ndlovu* 1984 (3) SA 23 (A).

24 See, for example, *S v W* 1976 (1) SA 1 (A).

25 In *R v Davies and another* 1956 (3) SA 52 (A), the Appellate Division (AD) settled this issue. See further, Snyman *Criminal Law* 282, who advocates a move away from a consistent application of the strictly subjective approach.

The second category of crimes that are legally impossible to commit can give rise to the following scenarios:

- *The situation where a person commits an act that he believes to be a crime whereas there is no such crime in our law*: For example, X commits or attempts to commit adultery, believing it to be a crime, whereas adultery is no longer a crime in our law. In such a case, X will not be guilty of attempted adultery. Intent to commit a putative crime will not constitute an attempt to commit a crime in South African criminal law.[26] To be guilty of an attempt to commit a crime, therefore, the intended conduct must first be defined as a crime according to our law.
- *The situation where a person commits or attempts to commit an act that is defined as a crime in our law, but which is not in fact a crime because of the particular circumstances of the case*: For example, X goes to her friend's house and takes an umbrella that she sees lying in his hall with the intention of stealing it. However, it turns out to be her own umbrella that she left there some time ago and forgot about. Since the law says that, as a rule, one cannot steal one's own property, X cannot be convicted of the theft of the umbrella. However, in these circumstances, she can be convicted of attempted theft. The principle that applies in such cases is exactly the same as in the case of crimes that are physically impossible to commit, that is, the court applies a subjective test.

26.2.7 Crimes that are not possible to attempt

There are some crimes that do not allow for attempts either on the basis of logic or because of the way in which they are defined - one either commits the crime itself or no crime at all. A typical example is a crime of pure omission, for example failing to render one's tax return timeously. A person either renders the return in time or he does not. There is no scope for an attempt. Do not assume, however, that this applies to all crimes of omission. Thus, for example, if a parent fails to provide his child with food or medical care while foreseeing the possibility that this failure could result in the child's death, this would amount to attempted murder.

Another category of crimes that are logically not possible to attempt, are crimes for which *culpa* is the required form of fault, such as culpable homicide and negligent driving. This is because negligence can be judged only once the accused's conduct is complete and a court can then determine whether that conduct measured up to the standard of the reasonable person.

In addition to the above, certain offences are framed in terms that make committing any act to further an objective an act of committing the crime itself, for example treason. Treason is defined as the unlawful commission of any overt act of hostile intent by a person owing allegiance to a state, that is, the intention to overthrow, threaten or damage the state by unconstitutional means. Any overt act that shows the existence of a hostile intent is sufficient for treason. Hence, it is impossible to commit an act that would amount to attempted treason without committing treason itself.[27]

---

26 *R v Davies* supra 64; Snyman *Criminal Law* 282–283. See further, *S v Palmos* 1979 (2) SA 82 (A); Burchell *South African Criminal Law and Procedure Vol I* 572–575.

27 Burchell *South African Criminal Law and Procedure Vol I* 575–576.

26.3 Incitement

26.3.1 Definition

At common law, **incitement** means encouraging or prompting another person to commit a crime. Incitement is itself a crime even if nothing comes of the incitement.[28] Based on the judgment in *S v Nkosiyana*,[29] incitement is defined as 'unlawfully making a communication to another with the intention of influencing him/her to commit a crime'.[30]

Incitement to commit a crime is also a statutory offence in terms of section 18(2)(*b*) of the Riotous Assemblies Act. It provides as follows:

> **(2) Any person who:**
> **(*a*) ...**
> **(*b*) incites, instigates, commands, or procures any other person to commit any offence, whether at common law or against a statute or statutory regulation, shall be guilty of an offence and liable on conviction to the punishment to which a person convicted of actually committing that offence would be liable.**

26.3.2 Requirements

26.3.2.1 *Actus reus*

The *actus reus* for incitement consists of the accused making a communication to the incitee. It is not necessary for the initial communication to have come from the accused. It may be that the incitee himself first suggested the commission of the crime to the accused. However, if the incitee took all the initiative and the accused merely fell in with his suggestions, then the accused will not be guilty of incitement.

The communication must have reached the mind of the incitee, that is, it must actually have come to his attention. For example, if X writes a letter to Y, suggesting that Y should commit a crime, but the letter goes astray in the mail, X has not committed incitement. The communication must also have been one that was calculated to influence the incitee *knowingly* to commit a crime. Thus, a communication aimed at getting the recipient to perform some criminal act by misleading him into believing that it is an innocent act is not incitement.

It is not necessary for the incitee to have been influenced into acting on the communication. The crime is complete once the necessary communication reaches the attention of the incitee.[31]

26.3.2.2 *Mens rea*

The accused must have intended that:

- his communication would reach the mind of the incitee
- it would influence the incitee to commit the envisaged crime.[32]

---

28 *R v Nlhovo* supra.

29 *S v Nkosiyana and another* 1966 (4) SA 655 (A).

30 Compare the adaptation of the definition in *Nkosiyana* by Burchell *South African Criminal Law and Procedure Vol I* 541. See the definition formulated by Holmes JA in *S v Nkosiyana* supra at 658H: 'An inciter is one who reaches and seeks to influence the mind of another to the commission of a crime.'

31 See Burchell *South African Criminal Law and Procedure Vol I* 541–543. See further, *S v Nkosiyana* supra at 658–659; *S v Dreyer* 1967 (4) SA 614 (E) at 621.

32 Burchell *South African Criminal Law and Procedure Vol I* 543.

The accused's intention need not take the form of *dolus directus*: *dolus indirectus* and *dolus eventualis* will be sufficient. For example, in *R v Segale and others*,[33] the accused were charged with inciting municipal workers to stay away from work (an illegal stay-away). The court held that the accused must have known that their communication would inevitably reach the minds of the workers and that they must therefore have intended it to reach them.

Burchell[34] argues that, logically, the same must also apply to *dolus eventualis*, that is, the situation where the accused foresaw the possibility that his communication would reach and influence the mind of the incitee and proceeded anyway. *Culpa*, however, is not a sufficient form of fault as this would spread the net of criminal liability too widely.

26.4 Conspiracy

26.4.1 Definition

Conspiracy to commit a crime is defined as two or more persons agreeing to (***a***) commit; or (***b***) assist in; or (***c***) procure the commission of a crime.[35] The crime of conspiracy in South African criminal law is criminalised in terms of section 18(2)(*a*) of the Riotous Assemblies Act.[36]

With reference to the crime of conspiracy in South Africa, Burchell noted that the prosecution of criminal conspiracy 'has not been frequently resorted to, probably because the common-purpose rule has served as a far more vigorous sanction against group criminal activity'.[37]

26.4.2 Requirements

26.4.2.1 *Actus reus*

The *actus reus* in this case consists of two or more persons reaching an agreement regarding the commission of a crime. This must be a genuine agreement, although it need not be expressed in words. The agreement could also be tacit (by conduct), but there must be a 'meeting of the minds' (consensus) between the parties to the conspiracy.[38]

If the parties are still negotiating or deliberating, or if one of the parties is only feigning agreement, there is no conspiracy.[39] It follows that a conspiracy must take place between two or more persons, although it is not necessary for the state to charge all of them.

---

33 *R v Segale and others* 1960 (1) SA 721 (A).

34 Burchell *South African Criminal Law and Procedure Vol I* 543–547.

35 For a comparable definition, see Burchell *South African Criminal Law and Procedure Vol I* 551. See also Snyman *Criminal Law* 286–289 for a brief discussion of the statutory offence.

36 *S v Agliotti* 2011 (2) SACR 437 (GSJ) at 9. The court held that s 18(2)(*a*) does not differentiate between a successful conspiracy (that is, one followed by the actual commission of the offence) and one not followed by any further steps towards the commission of the crime.

37 Burchell *South African Criminal Law and Procedure Vol I* 550.

38 *S v Libazi and another* 2010 (2) SACR 233 (SCA).

39 See, for example, *R v Harris* (1927) 48 NLR 330. Harris, a detective sergeant in the CID, suggested to Lockwood, a public prosecutor, that they should solicit bribes from accused persons in return for withdrawing the charges against them. Lockwood pretended to agree to this in order to trap Harris into going ahead with his scheme. Harris was subsequently charged with and convicted of corruption. He appealed. On appeal, the court held that because Lockwood was only pretending to agree, there was no genuine conspiracy between Harris and Lockwood. Harris was, however, found guilty of attempted conspiracy to commit the crime of corruption.

Just as a person can be an accomplice to a crime that is impossible for one to commit as a co-perpetrator, for example rape, perjury and bigamy, so can a person also be guilty of conspiracy to commit such a crime.

26.4.2.2 *Mens rea*

The fault element for conspiracy consists of the intention that the agreement between the parties should result in the commission of a crime either by one of them or by someone else.[40] Although our courts have not been called on to decide the question, it is more than likely that *dolus eventualis* will suffice for this purpose, although *culpa* would not.

26.4.3 Conspiracy concluded in South Africa, but the crime completed in a foreign country

Where two or more persons reached an agreement in South Africa to commit a crime subsequently committed in a foreign country, the state will be able to charge the conspirators under section 18(2)(*a*) of the Riotous Assemblies Act. Indeed, the actualisation of the plan (whether in South Africa or abroad) is not necessary for a conviction under section (18(2)(*a*). Conspiracy is an offence 'whether it is implemented or not'.[41]

In *S v Frederiksen*,[42] the accused was charged that he unlawfully and intentionally conspired with a number of individuals to kill a certain woman. It was common cause that the woman was subsequently killed in Lesotho. While South Africa does not have extraterritorial jurisdiction over the crime of murder, the court agreed with the prosecution that the accused in this matter could be charged with conspiracy under section 18(2)(*a*) of the Riotous Assemblies Act. Even if the woman was not killed as planned, the conspiracy charge would still have been possible.

DISCUSSION

Is conspiracy liability a better alternative to the problematic common purpose doctrine?

Burchell raised the point that *conspiracy* might be a better alternative to the common purpose doctrine, which seems to be doctrinally problematic and constitutionally dubious. The author further notes that in South Africa, 'the prosecution of criminal conspiracy has not been frequently resorted to, probably because the common-purpose rule has served as a far more vigorous sanction against group criminal activity'.[43] It logically follows that if conspiracy is going to get more attention from prosecutors as a vehicle to prosecute multiple persons involved in crime, then it may give rise to the same questions and doctrinal issues that have put the common purpose doctrine in the constitutional and doctrinal spotlight.

40 Burchell *South African Criminal Law and Procedure Vol I* 553; Snyman *Criminal Law* 289.
41 *S v Basson* 2007 (1) SACR 566 (CC) at 209.
42 *S v Frederiksen* 2017 JDR 1654 (FB).
43 Burchell *South African Criminal Law and Procedure Vol I* 550.

26.5 Incitement and conspiracy to commit crimes that are not capable of commission

Unlike cases of attempts to commit the impossible, our courts have tended to take an objective approach towards incitement and conspiracy to commit crimes that are incapable of commission, regardless of the reason for the impossibility.[44] Burchell argues that the considerations and principles that are involved are essentially the same as in cases of attempts to commit the impossible. The approach should therefore be the same, that is, essentially a subjective one, based on whether the accused believed that the principal offence was a crime.[45] However, so far, the authorities, although far from conclusive, have not taken the same view.

THIS CHAPTER IN ESSENCE

1. A person cannot be punished for merely planning to commit a crime or for merely preparing to do so. Criminal liability requires unlawful conduct of some kind. Where, however, a person goes beyond the stage of merely planning or preparing to commit a crime, and takes active steps to bring about its commission, then depending on the steps he has taken towards the commission of the crime, they may amount to unlawful conduct in their own right.
2. Thus, attempting to commit a crime, conspiring to commit a crime and inciting another person to commit a crime are all regarded as crimes in their own right, regardless of the fact that the intended crime was never actually committed.
   2.1 An attempt to commit a crime consists of the intention to commit the crime itself, coupled with a direct but unsuccessful act performed towards its commission. The act must be more than one of mere preparation; it must go far enough towards the commission of the crime to amount to the commencement of the consummation of the crime.
   2.2 A conspiracy to commit a crime consists of two or more persons agreeing to commit a crime, assisting in the commission of a crime, or procuring the commission of a crime, with the intention that their agreement should result in the commission of that crime.
3. Incitement to commit a crime consists of unlawfully making a communication to another person with the intention of influencing that person to commit knowingly a crime.

44 See, for example, *R v Wolff* 1930 TPD 821.

45 Burchell *Principles of Criminal Law* 537 and 545.

PART THREE

Specific crimes

SECTION 1 CRIMES AGAINST HUMAN LIFE, THE PERSON AND THE FAMILY

SECTION 2 PROPERTY CRIMES

SECTION 3 CRIMES AGAINST THE COMMUNITY

SECTION 4 CRIMES AGAINST THE STATE AND ADMINISTRATION OF JUSTICE

SECTION 5 ORGANISED AND COMMERCIAL CRIME

Chapter 27

Crimes against human life and the person

CHAPTER OBJECTIVES

The objectives of this chapter are to:

- give an overview of the underlying reasons for the criminalisation of the crimes in this chapter
- identify and discuss the elements of the crime of murder
- identify and discuss the elements of the crime of attempted murder
- identify and discuss the elements of the crime of culpable homicide
- identify and discuss the elements of infanticide and neonaticide (as forms of murder)
- identify and discuss the most important crimes under the Choice on Termination of Pregnancy Act 92 of 1996
- identify and discuss the elements of the crime of common assault
- identify and discuss the elements of the crime of assault with intent to do grievous bodily harm
- identify and discuss the elements of the crime of kidnapping
- identify and discuss the elements of the crime of *crimen iniuria*
- identify and discuss the elements of criminal defamation
- illustrate the relationship between the Protection from Harassment Act 17 of 2011 and some of the crimes against the person discussed in this chapter.

27.1 General introduction

Human life and physical integrity are legal interests protected by criminal law. The sanctity of the legal interest in life is reflected by the fact that it is protected against all harmful conduct.[1]

Indigenous legal systems in South Africa recognised homicide (the killing of fellow human beings) as a wrong. However, there was not always a clear differentiation between *criminal* and *civil* wrongs.[2] Anthropologists and legal historians have identified some

1 Skeen A st Q and Hoctor S 'Criminal law' in Joubert WA and Faris JA (eds) *Law of South Africa Encyclopaedia* (*LAWSA*) 2 ed (2011) Vol 6 at para 11.

2 Labuschagne JMT and Van den Heever JA 'Die oorsprong van en die onderskeid tussen die fenomene misdaad en delik in primigene regstelsels' (1991) *Obiter* 80.

instances approximating *criminal* liability for the deliberate or negligent killing of another person. The deliberate or negligent killing of another person (*palao*) was punishable by death under the law of the Northern Sotho people of South Africa.[3] While the Tembu people did not differentiate between murder and culpable homicide, the killing of another person was nevertheless treated as a crime. This crime was not against the victim but rather against the tribal chief, to whom all his subjects 'belonged'.[4] The Ndebele people differentiated between deliberate homicide (*ukubulala ngabomu*) and negligent homicide (*ukubulala ngokunganaki*). Both forms of conduct were regarded as crimes and were punishable with death in the case of deliberate homicide and more lenient forms of punishment (such as fines or corporal punishments) for negligent homicide.[5] In the most general sense one can say that the protected interest underlying homicide offences in the indigenous legal systems of South Africa was that of the collective or the tribal chief, rather than the life of the individual victim per se. Unpacking these collective/tribal interests, the legal anthropologists Labuschagne and Van den Heever conclude that the protected interests underlying homicide offences in indigenous systems were: bio-arithmetical (loss in human numbers); socio-psychological (loss of social and emotional support and interaction); and economic (loss of labour and/or potential *lobolo*[6]).[7]

Modern South African law, as influenced by Roman-Dutch and English law, puts the emphasis on the protection of individual human life as the interest underlying the criminalisation of homicide offences. The value of individual human life is protected in section 11 of the Constitution of the Republic of South Africa, 1996, which provides that everyone has the right to life. The generally unqualified nature of the right has been used to emphasise its strong protection in South African constitutional law.[8] The scope of such protection is somewhat blurred at either extremity of life, namely birth and death. This is partly due to some jurisprudential uncertainty as to when life begins and ends. To what extent does a pregnant woman have freedom and control over her body? Under what circumstances may a medical practitioner withdraw artificial life support to a patient who is brain dead?[9]

Closely associated with the right to life is the right to human dignity, as emphasised by O'Regan J in *S v Makwanyane*, where she stated:

> **... the right to life ... incorporates the right to dignity. So, the rights to human dignity and life are entwined. The right to life is more than existence, it is a right to be treated as a human being with dignity: without dignity, human life is substantially diminished. Without life, there cannot be dignity.**[10]

3 Labuschagne JMT and Van den Heever JA 'Liability arising from the killing of a fellow human being in South African indigenous law' (1995) 28 *Comp & Int'l LJ S Afr* 422 at 423.

4 Labuschagne and Van den Heever 'Liability arising from the killing of a fellow human being in South African indigenous law' 426.

5 Labuschagne and Van den Heever 'Liability arising from the killing of a fellow human being in South African indigenous law' 427.

6 A traditional form of dowry payable to the family of the bride-to-be.

7 Labuschagne and Van den Heever 'Liability arising from the killing of a fellow human being in South African indigenous law' 430.

8 *S v Makwanyane and another* 1995 (3) SA 391 (CC). For commentary on the significance of the judgment for South African jurisprudence and human rights discourse, see Currie I and De Waal J *The Bill of Rights Handbook* 6 ed (2013) 258–268.

9 See also the discussion on the euthanasia debate in section 27.2.3.3.

10 *S v Makwanyane* supra at 326–327.

However, as in the case of any right, the right to life is not absolute. It is permissible, for example, to kill in self-defence[11] or to kill while making an arrest under certain circumstances.[12] The precise ambit of the rights to life, physical integrity, freedom and security of the person, and dignity are measured against crimes against a person, which offer a qualified protection to such rights. The sanctity of a person's physical integrity has been protected by laws concerning the safety, health and well-being of a person's body. It is complemented by our society's protection of personality interests such as dignity, reputation and privacy.

Part of the legacy that modern South African law inherited from Roman law includes the recognition of personality interests, which were identified as *iniuria(e)/injuria(e)*. The legal recognition of *iniuria* afforded remedies to those who were harmed physically through their reputation or their *dignitas.* The oldest criminal *iniuria* is that of physical harm or injury to the human body. It is called **assault** in South African criminal law.

The *corpus* (physical form) of a person is at the heart of a human being's bodily integrity and personality interests. Violations of a person's *corpus* may cause injury and, if sufficiently severe, even death. Society's respect for the sanctity of a person's *corpus* is reflected in our criminal law through the prohibition and punishment of unlawful applications (and threats of application) of force to another human being.

Violations of a person's *dignitas* are punishable in South African law as *crimen iniuria.* South African law also allows for prosecution of **criminal defamation**. The legal interests underlying these two crimes are a person's dignity and reputation.

27.2 Murder

27.2.1 A brief history

Under Roman and Roman-Dutch law, a distinction was drawn between the murder of a close relative, parent and infants on the one hand, and the murder of persons falling outside these categories on the other.[13] No such distinction exists in modern South African law except that **infanticide**[14] is recognised as a separate form of murder.

27.2.2 Definition

Murder is the intentional unlawful killing of another human being.[15]

27.2.3 Elements

The elements of murder are:

- causing the death of another human being
- intent
- unlawfulness.

27.2.3.1 Causing death

X must *cause* the death of Y. Although suicide is not a crime, if X assists Y to commit suicide, X may be convicted of murder where it can be proved that X had unlawfully caused Y's death

11 See Chapter 7.
12 See s 49 of the Criminal Procedure Act 51 of 1977.
13 *LAWSA* 6 at para 237.
14 See the discussion in section 27.5.1.
15 *S v Ntuli* 1975 (1) SA 429 (A); Burchell JM *Principles of Criminal Law* 5 ed (2016) 577; Snyman CR *Criminal Law* 6 ed (2014) 437.

in accordance with the requirements of causation.[16] Thus, where X agrees to help Y to commit suicide, X may be convicted of murder, despite Y carrying out the final act of committing suicide.[17] The legal consequences of so-called 'assisted suicide' and 'euthanasia', two distinct but obviously related concepts,[18] will be discussed in more detail below.

In determining criminal responsibility, there is a factual enquiry followed by a decision on legal liability. Where X deliberately inflicts an intrinsically fatal wound, it is irrelevant whether others failed to intervene to save the deceased. Such a failure does not diminish the legal culpability of X.[19]

S v Tembani

In *S v Tembani*, Cameron JA considered 'whether an assailant who inflicts a wound which without treatment would be fatal, but which is readily treatable, can escape liability for the victim's death because the medical treatment in fact received is substandard and negligent'.[20] After being shot by the accused, the deceased was admitted to hospital on the night of the shooting where she died 14 days later of septicaemia. The court found that those who treated the deceased were negligent.

In establishing causation, a two-stage process is involved:

- There is factual enquiry as to whether the accused in fact caused the death of the deceased. The wounds inflicted by the accused were intrinsically fatal.
- Legal policy is considered. Is the infliction of the wounds sufficiently closely linked to death to merit liability?

The court found that the accused remains accountable for his actions even in circumstances where the deceased had been negligently treated unless the victim had recovered to the extent that at the time of the treatment, the original injury no longer posed a danger to life. Cameron JA relied on two primary reasons to support this approach. Firstly, the moral culpability of a person who inflicts an intrinsically fatal injury on another is not diminished by the subsequent negligence of those who treat the injury. Secondly, it would be wrong for the accused to assume that the victim would receive adequate medical treatment in a country where improper medical treatment is not extraordinary. An accused would not escape liability even where the treatment of the victim was grossly negligent, provided that those responsible for the treatment did not act in bad faith.

27.2.3.2 Causing the death of another human being

X must kill a living human being.[21] For the crime of murder, the meaning of 'a living human being' is paramount. At present, the general view is that 'a living human being is a person who has been born alive and who is still alive when the fatal conduct occurs'.[22] This question of fact is determined based on medico-legal evidence.[23] The forms of murder known as infanticide and **neonaticide** are considered below. For present purposes, it is necessary to

16 See the discussion of the relevant principles in *Ex parte Die Minister van Justisie: In re S v Grotjohn* 1970 (2) SA 355 (A) at 365G–H.

17 *Ex parte Die Minister van Justisie: In re S v Grotjohn* supra.

18 See remarks by Kgomo J in *S v Agliotti* 2011 (2) SACR 437 (GSJ) at 12. See also *Minister of Justice and others v Estate Stransham-Ford* 2017 (3) SA 152 (SCA) and the discussion in section 12.3.

19 *S v Tembani* 2007 (1) SACR 355 (SCA).

20 *S v Tembani* supra at 357F–G.

21 See also the discussion on termination of pregnancy in section 27.6.

22 Burchell *Principles of Criminal Law* 580.

23 Du Toit et al *Commentary on the Criminal Procedure Act* (revision service 50, 2015) 24-114–24-114A.

point out that the question of 'live birth' is provided for by statute. Section 239(1) of the Criminal Procedure Act provides as follows:

> **At criminal proceedings at which an accused is charged with the killing of a newly-born child, such child shall be deemed to have been born alive if the child is proved to have breathed, whether or not the child had an independent circulation, and it shall not be necessary to prove that such child was, at the time of its death, entirely separated from the body of its mother.**

If the accused attacked someone with the intention of killing him, but the person was already dead, the accused will be charged with attempted murder since he did not, in fact, kill another living human being.[24]

27.2.3.3 Unlawfulness

The killing must be unlawful.[25]

DISCUSSION **Suicide, assisted suicide and the euthanasia debate**

In *S v Agliotti*,[26] the court touched on one of the most controversial debates in law and ethics: assisted suicide and euthanasia. The court (per Kgomo J) made it clear that the two concepts may be related, but euthanasia is not the same as assisted suicide. Euthanasia normally takes place in a medical context; assisted suicide could occur in any given place or context.

The solution is not a piecemeal approach through the courts, but rather via statutory reform. Legislation about active voluntary euthanasia should give effect to the ethical and legal principles highlighted in case law and in relevant literature.[27] In 2015, the debate gained further momentum with the decision of the North Gauteng High Court in *Stransham-Ford v Minister of Justice and Correctional Services*.[28]

Stransham-Ford v Minister of Justice and Correctional Services

In this matter, the court (per Fabricius J) considered an urgent application by the applicant, who at the time had terminal stage four cancer. The application was for a declaration that the applicant may request a medical practitioner to end his (the applicant's) life ('physician assisted euthanasia', or PAE), or to enable the applicant to end his own life by the administration or provision of some or other lethal agent ('physician assisted suicide', or PAS). Furthermore, the applicant requested the court to declare that the medical practitioner who would administer or provide the lethal agent to the applicant should not be held accountable and should be free from any civil, criminal or disciplinary liability that may otherwise arise from the administration or provision of the lethal agent to the applicant. The court was requested to develop, to the extent required, the common law by

24 *S v Ndlovu* 1984 (3) SA 23 (A). See also the discussion in section 27.3.

25 See chapters 3–13.

26 *S v Agliotti* supra.

27 See further, Larsen JV 'Active euthanasia – potential abuse in South Africa: Correspondence' (2011) 101(4) *SAMJ* 211; Malherbe R and Venter R 'Die reg op lewe, die waarde van menslike lewe en die eutanasie-vraagstuk' (2011) 3 *TSAR* 466; Burchell J *South African Criminal Law and Procedure Vol 1: General Principles of Criminal Law* 4 ed (2011) 219–226 (for a discussion of euthanasia in the context of consent). See also Bateman C 'Euthanasia in SA – sacrificing one to render many vulnerable?' *SAMJ* 105 (10) (2015) 801.

28 *Stransham-Ford v Minister of Justice and Correctional Services and others* 2015 (4) SA 50 (GP).

declaring the requested assisted suicide or euthanasia to be lawful and constitutional in the particular circumstances of this matter.

Judge Fabricius was correct to observe that the issues of PAE and PAS are complex in nature.[29] The court considered the facts and circumstances of the matter, comparative law, the recommendations of the SALRC (Project 86) and relevant legal principles, notably various fundamental rights, including human dignity and freedom to bodily and psychological integrity. It concluded that the applicant should be granted his request. The applicant was thus granted the right to be assisted by a qualified medical doctor, 'who is willing to do so, to end his life, either by administration of a lethal agent or by providing the applicant with the necessary lethal agent to administer himself'.[30]

Importantly, the judge also made an order regarding the implications of this ruling for the common law crimes of murder and culpable homicide. The judge declared as follows:

> **The common law crimes of murder or culpable homicide in the context of assisted suicide by medical practitioners, insofar as they provide for an absolute prohibition, unjustifiably limit the Applicant's constitutional rights to human dignity, ... and freedom to bodily and psychological integrity ..., and to that extent are declared to be overbroad and in conflict with the said provisions of the Bill of Rights.**[31]

The Supreme Court of Appeal in *Minister of Justice and Correctional Services v Estate Stransham-Ford* set the order by the High Court aside.[32] First, the SCA reasoned that the applicant had died before the order had been made and the High Court was consequently not competent to grant the order. Second, in terms of the merits of PAE and PAS and the impact on the crimes of murder and culpable homicide, the SCA considered the various avenues available to medical practitioners in dealing with terminally ill patients. The SCA noted that *passive euthanasia* is lawful in South Africa, even if accompanied by palliative treatment that has the secondary effect of hastening the patient's death.[33] In contrast, PAE amounts to murder according to current South African criminal law. For such conduct to be legalised, the law would require considerable development.[34] PAS, on the other hand, is different. In terms of current South African criminal law, PAS is not unlawful per se, but should be evaluated on a case-by-case basis.[35] If a development of the common law was required in relation to PAS, a court would then have to decide whether that development should take the form of a 'different view of causation, or of intention (*mens rea*), or of unlawfulness.'[36] The SCA noted that the 'possibility of a special defence for medical practitioners or carers would arise and have to be explored.'[37] Unfortunately, the SCA did not benefit from any reasoning by the High Court with regard to the development of PAS in terms of causation, intent or unlawfulness. The SCA was also not presented with arguments in this regard, and the SCA noted the 'complete absence of evidence on these issues'.[38]

Given the complexities of both PAE and PAS, as well as the far-reaching consequences of developing the common law crimes of murder and culpable homicide, the SCA's view that the

---

29 *Stransham-Ford v Minister of Justice* supra at 1.
30 *Stransham-Ford v Minister of Justice* supra at 45.
31 *Stransham-Ford v Minister of Justice* supra at 45.
32 *Minister of Justice and others v Estate Stransham-Ford* 2017 (3) SA 152 (SCA).
33 *Estate Stransham-Ford* (SCA) supra at 30–34.
34 *Estate Stransham-Ford* (SCA) supra at 36–40.
35 *Estate Stransham-Ford* (SCA) supra at 55 and 56.
36 *Estate Stransham-Ford* (SCA) supra at 56.
37 *Estate Stransham-Ford* (SCA) supra at 56.
38 *Estate Stransham-Ford* (SCA) supra at 56.

reform of homicide offences in light of developing views on PAS and PAE should be left to parliament, is supported.[39] The SCA (per Wallis JA) stated:

> [The High Court] was wrong to hold that the common-law crimes of murder and culpable homicide needed to be or should be developed to accommodate PAE and PAS ... When an appropriate case comes before our courts the common law will no doubt evolve in the light of the considerations outlined there and the developments in other countries. It is of course possible that Parliament will, as has occurred in other countries, intervene and pass legislation on the topic. That would be welcome if only because it would give effect to the proper role of Parliament in a society where the doctrine of the separation of powers has application. Lobby groups could then make their voices heard and a proper debate and process of reflection could occur. In general, whilst recognising the role that the Constitution confers upon the courts, it is desirable in my opinion that issues engaging profound moral questions beyond the remit of judges to determine, should be decided by the representatives of the people of the country as a whole.[40]

27.2.3.4 Intent

Intention (*dolus*) is necessary for the crime of murder.[41] Motive is irrelevant. Negligence is insufficient for a conviction of murder. While it may be difficult to lead direct evidence as to the subjective state of mind of the accused at the time of the assault, this may be established by drawing inferences from circumstances of the assault, the nature of the weapon used and the extent of the injuries inflicted. This is not a piecemeal exercise. A holistic approach is required when attempting to establish the subjective state of mind of the accused.[42]

DISCUSSION

The divide between life and death, and the question of passive euthanasia

In murder, the accused must cause the victim's death. Traditionally, the point of death was established when the heart stopped beating. However, this does not cater for the situation where the heart continues to beat with the assistance of a machine in a patient who has suffered irreversible brain damage.[43] Thirion J considered this issue in *Clarke v Hurst NO and others*.[44] The applicant's wife applied to be appointed *curatrix personae* with the power to discontinue certain life-sustaining procedures in respect of her husband who was in an irreversible vegetative state. The judge held that:

> ... judged by society's legal convictions, the feeding of the patient does not serve the purpose of supporting human life as it is commonly known and the applicant, if appointed as *curatrix*, would act reasonably and would be justified in discontinuing the artificial feeding and would therefore not be acting wrongfully if she were to do so.[45]

Although the uncoupling of a ventilator in these circumstances may accelerate the moment of death, this simple factual causation is insufficient to attract legal liability. Ultimately, the *curatrix* is obliged to act in the best interests of the patient. Can it be said that she did so by discontinuing the artificial life support?

39 See critical comments by Jordaan L 'Recent cases' 1 *SACJ* (2017) 74–80.
40 *Estate Stransham-Ford (SCA)* supra at 101.
41 *S v Agliotti* supra at 10.
42 *S v Van Aardt* 2009 (1) SACR 648 (SCA).
43 Burchell *Principles of Criminal Law* 578–579.
44 *Clarke v Hurst NO and others* 1992 (2) SACR 676 (D).
45 *Clarke v Hurst* supra at 702E–F.

27.3 Attempted murder

Where the accused intended to kill another living human being, but was unsuccessful, for example because he missed the shot, the victim did not die from the wounds or because of inadequate means, he can be found guilty of the separate crime of attempted murder. As pointed out above, where the accused thought he had killed another living human being but the person was already dead, he can still be guilty of the crime of attempted murder. The emphasis for criminal liability is thus on the subjective state of mind of the accused.[46]

In *S v Nyalungu*,[47] the court held that the principles of common law were sufficiently wide to justify a conviction of attempted murder and rape where the accused, being fully aware of his HIV status, raped the complainant without using any protective measures. The court went on to hold that it was irrelevant whether the complainant underwent a test for HIV. It was sufficient to prove that the accused had acted with the intention of bringing about a result. The fact that the result did not eventuate does not detract from returning an attempted murder verdict.

The court in *S v Phiri*[48] followed this approach to attempted murder where an HIV-positive person has unprotected sex with an HIV-negative person and where that partner would not know about the HIV status of the accused. Significantly, the court in *Phiri* took judicial notice of the fact that there is 'at present no cure for HIV/AIDS'.[49]

27.4 Culpable homicide

27.4.1 A brief history

Although the distinction between murder and culpable homicide was unknown in Roman and Germanic law, the Commentators did regard negligent and intentional homicide as different but both punishable forms of conduct.[50] The distinction has been recognised in South African law consistently since the early 19th century.[51]

27.4.2 Definition

X commits **culpable homicide** where he unlawfully and negligently causes the death of another human being.[52]

27.4.3 Elements

The four elements of culpable homicide are:

1. causing death
2. causing the death of another human being
3. unlawfulness
4. negligence.

46 *R v Davies and another* 1956 (3) SA 52 (A); *S v Ngcamu and another* 2011 (1) SACR 1 (SCA).
47 *S v Nyalungu* 2013 (2) SACR 99 (T). See also *S v Ndlanzi* 2014 (2) SACR 256 (SCA).
48 *S v Phiri* 2014 (1) SACR 211 (GNP).
49 *S v Phiri* supra at 9.
50 Burchell *Principles of Criminal Law* 583.
51 *LAWSA* 6 at para 243.
52 *S v Burger* 1975 (4) SA 877 (A); Snyman *Criminal Law* 442; Burchell *Principles of Criminal Law* 584.

27.4.3.1 Elements 1–3

The first three elements of culpable homicide are the same as those for murder.[53]

27.4.3.2 Negligence

It is this requirement of negligence that distinguishes culpable homicide from murder. The test for negligence is an objective one where the conduct of X is measured against that of a reasonable person.[54] This objective test should, of course, still be analysed contextually, for instance in the context of medical care.[55]

Sometimes the division between murder and culpable homicide is difficult to draw in the context of *dolus eventualis*. This is a type of intent required for murder in circumstances where the accused foresaw the possibility of death and reconciled himself with that possibility.[56] This aspect was considered in *S v Humphreys*[57] where the driver of a vehicle ignored signals when entering a boom-controlled level crossing while a train was approaching. The resultant accident cost the lives of 10 passengers. In setting aside the murder conviction and substituting it with one of culpable homicide, the Supreme Court of Appeal (SCA) held that, as it had not been established that the appellant had reconciled himself with the possibility of death, *dolus eventualis* had not been proved.

27.5 Infanticide and neonaticide

27.5.1 Infanticide

27.5.1.1 A brief history

In Roman-Dutch law, infanticide was referred to as *crimen expositionis infantis.*[58] It comprised abandoning a child with the expectation that it would die, and this attracted the death penalty. It also included the less serious offence of abandoning a child in a place where it was likely to be fostered, which carried a more lenient penalty.[59] The former is recognised as a separate crime in South Africa.[60] The latter is a statutory offence under the Child Care Act 74 of 1983.

27.5.1.2 Definition

Infanticide is the killing of a new-born child.

27.5.1.3 Elements

The elements of infanticide are the same as those for murder as the intentional killing of an infant amounts to murder.[61]

---

53 See section 27.2.
54 See Chapter 20.
55 See *S v van Heerden and another* 2010 (1) SACR 529 (ECP) on culpable homicide in the context of medical negligence.
56 A *novus actus interveniens* can affect the foreseeability of an eventuality. See *S v De Jager and others* 2016 (2) SACR 716 (ECG) at 12–13.
57 *S v Humphreys* 2013 (2) SACR 1 (SCA).
58 See Van der Westhuizen C 'An historical overview of infanticide in South Africa' (2009) 15(2) *Fundamina* 174.
59 Burchell *Principles of Criminal Law* 582.
60 *R v Adams* (1903) 20 SC 556; *S v Jokasi* 1987 (1) SA 431 (ZS). See also Snyman *Criminal Law* 444–445.
61 Burchell *Principles of Criminal Law* 582.

27.5.2 Neonaticide

27.5.2.1 A brief history

Neonaticide has yet to establish itself as a separate crime in South Africa. However, the crime has attracted attention, particularly in the context of doctors not treating severely disabled infants at the request of the parents, thereby allowing the infant to die from its disability.

27.5.2.2 Definition

Neonaticide is the killing of an infant within 24 hours of its birth.[62]

27.5.2.3 Elements

Other than the timing of the killing, the elements for neonaticide are the same as those for infanticide, subject to the comments below on intent and unlawfulness.

27.5.2.3.1 Intent

The accused must intend to kill the newborn child. Reference has been made to a neonaticide syndrome,[63] which impacts on the capacity and mental state of the accused (in this context, the mother of the baby). Evidence of this syndrome could be admissible when challenging the guilt of the accused on the merits of the case or in mitigation.[64]

27.5.2.3.2 Unlawfulness

Where neonaticide may be regarded as an act of mercy in terms of the quality of life that a severely disabled child would have to endure, it is arguable that death in these circumstances would not attract criminal liability in the eyes of the community.[65]

27.5.3 Digression: Causing the death of an unborn child (other than in cases of abortion)

Does the shooting of a pregnant mother, thus causing the death of the unborn child, amount to murder? This was a question considered in *S v Mshumpa*[66] where the accused shot a pregnant woman.

> ***S v Mshumpa***
>
> At the time of the shooting, the mother was in her 38th week of pregnancy. Medical examinations prior to the shooting confirmed that the foetus was healthy. Because of the shooting, the unborn child was killed. Froneman J had to decide whether the common law definition of murder ought to be extended to cover the facts before him. In declining to develop the common law, the judge stated that:
>
> > **... such a development of the common law of crimes must be done incrementally and cautiously in accordance with the dictates of the Constitution ...; that the development should not have**

62 Burchell *Principles of Criminal Law* 583 fn 40 who refers to commentary by Fazio CA and Comito JL 'Rethinking the tough sentencing of teenage neonaticide offenders in the United States' (1999) 67(6) *Fordham Law Review* 3109. For comments on the determination of live birth, see Le Roux-Kemp A and Wilkinson J 'A novel application of the hydrostatic test in determining live (non)-birth' (2012) 25(2) *SACJ* 271–285.

63 Colloquially also known as post-natal depression.

64 Burchell *Principles of Criminal Law* 583 n 40.

65 Burchell *Principles of Criminal Law* 583, where the author submits that similar reasoning has been used in *Clarke v Hurst NO and others* 1992 (4) SA 630 (D), which dealt with the issue in the context of a form of euthanasia.

66 *S v Mshumpa and another* 2008 (1) SACR 126 E.

> **retrospective effect, dealing with the past, because that would offend the principle of legality, but that it is competent to effect the development prospectively, to operate only in future ...**[67]

> On this basis, the accused could not be convicted retrospectively of murder as it would offend the principle of legality. Froneman J further declined to extend the definition of murder prospectively. The Constitution does not protect the rights of an unborn child. The assault on an unborn child is primarily an assault on the mother, which is adequately catered for under common law. The full nature of the assault may properly be considered at the stage of sentence. If the definition of murder were to be extended, this is best left to the legislature.

The development of the common law definition of murder is probably not the appropriate route to go. Unlike the development of the common law definition of the crime of rape by the Constitutional Court,[68] the development of the common law definition of murder to include the unborn is arguably a step too far. There is simply not enough in the Constitution and other relevant legal principles to work with to develop the common law also to include the unborn in the element of person or human being. However, given the moral outrage over cases such as *Mshumpa*, it is *certainly the political and moral duty of the legislature to debate and consider seriously the possibility of creating a statutory offence of feticide.*[69] One commentator proposed the following working definition for a statutory crime of feticide: feticide is '[t]he unlawful and intentional or negligent causing of the death of an unborn by a third party and without the consent of the pregnant woman bearing the unborn'.[70]

27.6 Termination of pregnancy

27.6.1 A brief history

The emotionally charged and morally complex topic of abortion is to a significant extent decriminalised in South Africa. In Roman law and Roman-Dutch law, it was criminalised as a separate crime.[71] It was essentially criminalised under South African law, but a gradual process of decriminalisation led to the current dispensation, discussed below.

After an investigation into abortion, the Abortion and Sterilisation Act 2 of 1975 was passed, which prescribed restrictive conditions under which abortion could be performed. This Act was subsequently repealed by the Choice on Termination of Pregnancy Act 92 of 1996 (the Act), which significantly widens the circumstances under which an abortion may be performed lawfully.[72] The focus now falls on the woman concerned and her medical practitioner.

---

67 *S v Mshumpa* at 150IJ–151A relying on *Masiya v Director of Public Prosecutions, Pretoria and another (Centre for Applied Legal Studies and another, amici curiae)* 2007 (2) SACR 435 (CC).

68 *Masiya v DPP, Pretoria* supra.

69 For a useful analysis, see Du Plessis GA 'Feticide: Creating a statutory crime in South African law' (2013) 24(1) *SLR* 73–92.

70 Du Plessis 'Feticide: Creating a statutory crime in South African law' supra 91. Reprinted by permission of © Juta & Company Ltd.

71 See De Wet JC and Swanepoel HL *Strafreg* (1949) 192–194 for a discussion of the historical roots of the crime of abortion under Roman law, Roman-Dutch law and South African law.

72 For a critique of the Act (notably from a legality point of view) see Van Oosten F 'The Choice on Termination of Pregnancy Act: Some comments' (1999) 116(1) *SALJ* 60 at 72–76.

27.6.2 What constitutes the offence of termination of pregnancy?

The Choice on Termination of Pregnancy Act provides for several offences. Section 10(1) provides for a number of offences, collectively known as unlawful termination of pregnancy:

> **(1) Any person who—**
>
> **(*a*) is not a medical practitioner, or a registered midwife or registered nurse who has completed the prescribed training course, and who performs the termination of a pregnancy referred to in section 2(1)(*a*);**
>
> **(*b*) is not a medical practitioner and who performs the termination of a pregnancy referred to in section 2(1)(*b*) or (*c*);**
>
> **(*c*) prevents the lawful termination of a pregnancy or obstructs access to a facility for the termination of a pregnancy; or**
>
> **(*d*) terminates a pregnancy or allows the termination of a pregnancy at a facility not approved in terms of section 3(1) or not contemplated in section 3(3)(*a*),**
>
> **shall be guilty of an offence and liable on conviction to a fine or to imprisonment for a period not exceeding 10 years.**[73]

27.6.3 Elements

The elements of the termination of pregnancy or abortion are:

- unlawfulness
- termination of a pregnancy
- termination not by a medical practitioner, or registered midwife or registered nurse who has completed the prescribed training course (depending on the gestation period in question)
- fault.[74]

27.6.3.1 Unlawfulness

According to Burchell, the defence of necessity, which is available where an abortion is performed to save the life of a mother, is also relevant in the context of the statutory offence under consideration.[75]

The pregnancy may be terminated only with the informed consent of the woman unless she is not able to give such consent.[76] The conditions under which the pregnancy may be terminated differ according to the stage of pregnancy at the time of the termination.[77] Note that the consent of the mother only (of any age) is required. The consent of the biological father of the unborn child, the husband, the parents or guardian where the pregnant woman is a minor is not required, although minors are to be counselled to consult relevant individuals such as parents, the father of the unborn child, and so on. However, no one can veto the mother's informed decision to terminate the pregnancy.

73 When indicting under the Choice on Termination of Pregnancy Act 92 of 1996, care should be taken to assess correctly the gestation period to bring the charge(s) under the correct section(s) of the Act. See *S v Dembe* 2010 (1) SACR 360 (NCK).

74 Burchell *Principles of Criminal Law* 573.

75 Burchell *Principles of Criminal Law* 573.

76 *Christian Lawyers Association v National Minister of Health and others* 2004 (10) BCLR 1086 (T) at 1092.

77 S 2 of the Choice on Termination of Pregnancy Act.

For present purposes, three different stages of the pregnancy are relevant.[78] Any prosecution for crimes under the Choice on Termination of Pregnancy Act must be based on acts that occurred during the relevant periods discussed below:[79]

- *The first 12 weeks*: The pregnancy may be terminated by a medical practitioner registered in terms of the relevant legislation[80] at the request of the mother. During this period, a registered midwife or registered nurse who has completed the prescribed training course,[81] may also terminate the pregnancy on request of the mother. This is the only period during which a person other than a registered medical practitioner may terminate the pregnancy.
- *The 13th to (and including) the 20th week*: Termination of pregnancy during this period, characterised by the development of brain activity in the foetus, is conditional on certain therapeutic,[82] eugenic[83] and humanitarian[84] considerations that the medical practitioner must take into account after consultation with the pregnant woman.
- *After 20 weeks*: During this period, a medical practitioner may only terminate the pregnancy after consultation with another medical practitioner or a registered midwife, and only because in their opinions, the woman's life would be in danger or because the prognosis for the foetus would be that of 'severe malformation'.[85]

27.6.3.2 Termination of a pregnancy

Termination of a pregnancy is defined in the Act as the medical or surgical separation and expulsion of the contents of the pregnant uterus.

27.6.3.3 Fault

Regarding the question of fault, Burchell states:

> **On general principles the fault element of the crime consists in the intention to perform an abortion unlawfully. Thus the abortionist must know or foresee that the woman is pregnant and intend to bring about the termination of the pregnancy. The abortionist must also know or foresee that the termination is unlawful.**[86]

If, for example, the abortionist believes in good faith that the foetus is no longer alive, then the fault element will be missing.

27.6.4 Other crimes related to the termination of pregnancy

Given the controversial nature of termination of pregnancy and the potential for unlawful reactions against this dispensation, the legislature has provided for certain statutory crimes:

- Section 10(1)(*c*) of the Act provides that any person who *prevents the lawful termination* of a pregnancy, commits a crime.

---

78 See the discussion in Burchell *Principles of Criminal Law* 574–575.
79 See observations by Majiedt J in *S v Dembe* supra.
80 Health Professions Act 56 of 1974.
81 Nursing Act 50 of 1978.
82 S 2(1)(*b*)(i) of the Act. Typical therapeutic considerations include the woman's physical and mental health.
83 S 2(1)(*b*)(ii) of the Act. Here, the relevant consideration is the physical and mental prognosis for the foetus. If there is a substantial risk of severe physical or mental abnormality, the medical practitioner may terminate the pregnancy after consultation with the mother.
84 Various considerations are relevant here, for instance where the pregnancy is the result of rape or incest, or where the socio-economic conditions of the mother would justify the termination of the pregnancy.
85 See ss 2(1)(*c*)(i) and 2(1)(*c*)(ii) of the Act.
86 Burchell *Principles of Criminal Law* 575.

- The above section further provides that any person who *obstructs access to a facility* for the termination of pregnancies, commits a crime.
- Section 10(1)(*d*) provides that it is a criminal offence to terminate a pregnancy or allow the termination of a pregnancy at a facility that is not approved for these purposes under the Act.

27.7 Common assault

27.7.1 A brief history

Bodily aggressions were recognised under Roman law as a form of *iniuria* directed at the *corpus* of the victim. Serious bodily aggressions were subject to civil and criminal sanctions. Roman law recognised that punishable bodily aggressions included direct and indirect applications of force. The recognised forms of indirect force included the administration of a toxic substance and inspiring apprehension of physical aggression against a complainant.[87]

Roman-Dutch law accepted that physical aggression was not unlawful if it was conducted in terms of consent, self-defence or legitimate authority. Further, Roman-Dutch law also advocated the punishment of inspiring apprehension of an immediate assault.

English law differentiated between the crime of assault and the crime of battery.[88] English law defined assault as an unlawful and intentional act that induces another person to anticipate that immediate personal violence will be applied to his body. English law considered conditional threats as unlawful assaults whenever they imposed an unlawful restraint against the complainant. English law punished the unlawful and intentional application of force as the crime of battery. The complainant did not need to be aware of the application of force when it was applied. The accused remained liable for battery regardless of whether the accused's conduct resulted in an injury.

English law has been seminal in the development of the South African crime of common assault. However, South African law does not differentiate between the English crimes of assault and battery. In the South African context, they have been fused together to form the one crime of common assault. In this regard, the South African approach has more in common with the Roman law approach.[89]

27.7.2 Definition

Common assault is defined as the unlawful and intentional application of force to the complainant, or inspiring a belief of imminent use of force against the complainant.

27.7.3 Elements

The essential elements of common assault are:

- unlawfulness
- intent
- applying force or inspiring the apprehension of force.

87 See the *lex Cornelia de injuriis* after it had been extended by a *utilis actio*, and D 47.10.

88 Schreiner J in *R v Sibanyone* 1940 JS 40 (T) at 257.

89 For a brief historical overview, see also Snyman *Criminal Law* 447–448; Burchell *Principles of Criminal Law* 591–594.

27.7.3.1 Unlawfulness

The defences that are most commonly associated with this offence include authority, private defence, necessity, consent and the *de minimis* rule.[90]

The defence of authority can take one of two forms: lawful arrest or moderate private disciplinary chastisement. Originally, court authority legitimised corporal punishment. However, the practice has subsequently been abolished.[91] Further, employers may not corporally punish their employees.[92]

Private defence and necessity are valid where the accused behaved reasonably.[93] However, the accused must not use more force than is reasonably necessary to avoid the harm posed by a legitimate threat.

Public policy or *boni mores* determine whether consent legalises an act that would otherwise be unlawful. Consent legalises the conduct that is objectively unlikely to cause more than minor injury. Further, the law recognises that there is an implied consent to contact, which is customary in everyday usage.

The *de minimis* rule applies to appropriate cases of assault. It provides that completely trivial assaults are not punishable by law. However, a mere touching may be more than a trivial case, as in the example of a sexual assault.

27.7.3.2 Intent

The state is obliged to prove that the accused intended to assault the complainant. This is a subjective enquiry. Where there was no force, but the state can prove that the accused nevertheless intended to intimidate and frighten the complainant, it will be sufficient for purposes of common assault.[94]

27.7.3.3 Application of force or inspiring apprehension of force

27.7.3.3.1 Application of force

The application of force may be direct or indirect. The accused directly applies force where he applies physical force by using his own body against the body of the victim. The application of force is indirect where the accused uses an instrument or other strategy to apply force to a part of the victim's body. In the case of *R v Jolly*, the court confirmed that indirect application of force is as reprehensible as direct application of force because the harm visited on the victim is identical.[95]

There is also an indirect application of force by the accused if another person applies force on the victim as a result of instructions from the accused. This principle was illustrated in the case of *S v A*, where a police officer was found guilty of assault after he used threats to compel the victim to masturbate.[96]

---

90 For more detail, see chapters 7–13.

91 *S v Williams and others* 1995 (3) SA 632 (CC).

92 *S v Collett* 1978 (3) SA 206 (RA).

93 If the accused had exceeded the limits of private defence through excessive force and was charged with assault with the intent to do grievous bodily harm, then the charge may be reduced to common assault.

94 Burchell *Principles of Criminal Law* 599.

95 *R v Jolly and others* 1923 AD 176. In this case, the appellants caused a train to be derailed by removing fishplates hours before a train passed over that portion of the line. The derailment amounted to an indirect application of force by the appellants on the passengers. The victims were traumatised in the same manner as if they had been attacked directly by the accused.

96 *S v A en 'n ander* 1993 (1) SACR 600 (A).

If the accused has a duty to protect a victim, and he intentionally fails to intervene when the victim is being assaulted by another, he will also be liable for the assault.

The case of *S v Marx* illustrates that there is also an indirect application of force if the accused administers a substance that causes the drinker bodily harm.[97] The force may be applied internally or externally. The offending substance could be poison, drugs, alcohol or urine. There is an overlap between the crime of assault and the substantive crime of administering poison or another noxious substance. However, the crime of administering poisonous or noxious substances also overlaps with murder when the poisoning results in death. The accused would remain liable for assault even if the substance were not poisonous.

In *S v Marx*, the court held that the mere discomfort caused by the fraudulently induced ingestion of a purgative should suffice. In *S v A*, the court accepted that the ingestion of urine amounted to an assault.[98] The qualification of bodily harm is not given a particularly narrow meaning. It is irrelevant whether the victim consumed the substance voluntarily or whether the consumption was fraudulently induced. However, where there is no harm or discomfort caused, there is no application of force. If the harm or discomfort is only trivial, the *de minimis* rule can be applied to remove the taint of unlawfulness.

The concept of 'application of force' does not need to be qualified by a specific degree of violence. The slightest touch may be sufficient to sustain liability for assault. For example, unlawfully and intentionally spilling a drink on another person is an assault subject, again, to the *de minimis* rule.

The force must be applied to the physical person of the victim. The use of force on a person's clothes is an assault if it involves the use of force on his body or if it induces a fear of aggression on his body.

27.7.3.3.2 Inspiring apprehension of force

This type of assault may be committed through words, acts or gestures that have the effect of creating, in the mind of the victim, the apprehension that he is about to suffer an attack on his person. The threat must be directed at the physical body of the victim. Certain conduct, for example pointing a firearm or something likely to be believed to be a firearm, can also constitute a statutory crime.[99] Threats of an attack on property will not amount to an assault by inspiration of fear.

Words alone are sufficient to satisfy this requirement. Originally, the inspiration of fear could only come from acts or gestures. In the past, the words had to be accompanied by some type of application of force before they could sustain liability and English law did not consider words alone to amount to assault.[100] South African law followed a similar approach in cases such as *R v Umfaan* where the court held that there cannot be an assault by 'mere

---

97 *S v Marx* 1962 (1) SA 848 (N). The accused gave two children aged five and seven years of age three glasses of wine each and the children became intoxicated. The youngest child was unable to walk and was semiconscious. The accused was convicted of common assault.

98 *S v A en 'n ander* 1993 (1) SACR 600 (A).

99S 120(6) of the Firearms Control Act 60 of 2000 provides as follows:

> **It is an offence to point - (*a*) any firearm, an antique firearm or an airgun, whether or not it is loaded or capable of being discharged, at any other person, without good reason to do so; or (*b*) anything which is likely to lead a person to believe that it is a firearm, an antique firearm or an airgun at any other person, without good reason to do so.**

This statutory crime is a crime of intent. See *S v Hodgkinson* 2010 (2) SACR 511 (GNP).

100 It was based on authority from *R v Meade and Belt* (1823) 1 Lew CC 184: 'no words or singing are equivalent to an assault'.

words'.[101] Fortunately, the law has evolved to reflect accurately that an assault can be made through words alone.

The relevant consideration relates to the impression that is created in the mind of the victim. It is not necessary for the victim to experience fear. The test is whether the threatened party subjectively believes that the conduct of the accused will immediately cause some sort of contact with his body. It becomes irrelevant whether the threatened party subsequently experienced fear.

Once a court is satisfied that the victim subjectively believed that the application of force was imminent, the court assesses the subsequent requirements objectively. In *R v Sibanyone*, Schreiner J held that:

> **... there must have been a threat of immediate personal violence in circumstances that lead the person threatened reasonably to believe that the other intends and has the power immediately to carry out the threat.**[102]

This dictum illustrates the three core requirements for a threat to qualify as a form of common assault: imminent harm, present ability to carry out the threat and a reasonable apprehension of harm.

The first requirement is that the accused must be threatening to inflict *imminent harm*. The harm must be immediate and not at a future time. For example, in *R v Sibanyone*, the accused was eventually acquitted on appeal because he was threatening to inflict harm at a future time, not at the time that he made the threat. The accused was not threatening to inflict immediate violence on the victim.

There was a stage where there was controversy about whether a conditional threat would amount to an assault by inspiring fear. One of the arguments provided that in such scenarios, the harm could be confirmed to be imminent only if a specified condition was met. The controversy was eventually settled in *S v Miya* where the court held that the mere fact that the threat is conditional does not protect the accused from liability.[103] The court held that where the accused makes a threat, which he is legally entitled to impose as a condition, then the conduct of the accused is lawful. For example, there is nothing criminal when a person threatens to use a reasonable degree of force to defend himself or his property where the rights relating to either are threatened.

The second requirement (present ability) has been attributed to the dictum from the English case of *Stephens v Myers* where the court held that there must, in all cases, be the means of carrying the threat into effect.[104] If it is not possible to carry the threat out, then it does not qualify as something that deserves a criminal sanction. Besides this fact, if it did not seem possible that the harm could be inflicted immediately, then the victim should not have perceived the threat as reasonable. There are some English academics who have

101 *R v Umfaan* 1908 TS 62 at 64.

102 *R v Sibanyone* 1940 JS 40 (T) at 41. In this case, the accused advanced towards the complainant with his finger pointed at her while he threatened her. He said he was going away to see someone, and if the complainant did not drive her family from the property, he would come back and kill them.

103 In *S v Miya and others* 1966 (4) SA 274 (N), the three accused picked up stones and threatened to throw them at the complainant. The court observed that the threat was conditional. The harm would only ensue if the complainant advanced against the accused persons. The court held that the condition that was attached to the threat was for acting in private defence. Further, the court observed that the accused lacked *mens rea*. The intention of the accused was self-defence, not an unlawful attack. The court set aside the conviction against the accused because the requirements for assault through inspiration of fear had not been satisfied.

104 *Stephens v Myers* (1830) 4 CAR & P 349 at 350. In this case, the accused was convicted of assault after he used threatening words and was advancing with clenched fists towards the chairman, but was stopped before he could reach him.

suggested that the impossibility of carrying the threat out is irrelevant because the accused's liability hinges on whether fear is inspired. South African law takes a different approach to English law because the liability of the accused does not exclusively hinge on whether the victim was afraid or not.

The final feature of a prohibited threat focuses on the reasonableness of apprehension. This is an objective qualification because the perceptions of the victim must be compared to the perceptions of a reasonable person. In principle, there is no assault if the apprehension was unreasonable.

27.7.4 Some general comments

There is a definite overlap between the crime of common assault and the crime of administering poisonous or noxious substances. The only real difference lies in the fact that the accused would be liable for assault by administering a substance that is *contra bonos mores*, even if such a substance were not poisonous. However, in such a case, the accused would not be liable for the crime of administering poisonous or noxious substances. Thus, the crime of common assault can always accommodate the liability of an accused who administers poisonous or noxious substances. If the substance causes the death of the victim, the accused would be liable for murder. Therefore, the offensive conduct can be easily accommodated without having to refer to the crime of administering poisonous or noxious substances. As a result, leading academics have argued that the crime of administering poisonous or noxious substances should be abrogated by disuse.[105] Prosecutions for the crime are rare.[106]

It is also controversial to enquire whether the victim had an objectively reasonable apprehension of harm. Many academics focus on the example of an accused who targets a victim who is vulnerable to anticipating an objectively unreasonable threat as subjectively reasonable. It seems absurd to require that there must be a reasonable apprehension of harm for sustaining liability for an assault. The harm perpetrated against the victim remains reprehensible even though the anticipation of harm is objectively unreasonable.

27.8 Assault with intent to do grievous bodily harm

27.8.1 A brief history

Assault with the intent to commit another crime was a subspecies of the crimes confined to the genus of assault. These forms of assault are substantive offences and not aggravated forms of assault. The development of these crimes was in response to English law nomenclature and practice.[107] Examples of these crimes include assault with the intent to rape, murder or rob, and do grievous bodily harm. This approach contradicts the Roman and Roman-Dutch approaches that basically considered them to be aggravated forms of common assault. One of the criticisms of these substantive crimes was that there was a distinct overlap between such crimes and the attempts to commit the crimes preceded by the assaults.

105 Including Burchell *Principles of Criminal Law* 602.

106 Snyman *Criminal Law* 444.

107 *Matzukis v The King* 1940 SR 76 at 78–79.

The substantive crime of assault with the intent to do grievous bodily harm deserves special attention because the others all require proof of liability for common assault and the intention to commit the respective crime. The requirements for common assault have already been discussed in the preceding portion of this chapter.

27.8.2 Definition

Assault with the intention to do grievous bodily harm is defined as the application of force to the complainant with the intention to cause serious bodily harm.

27.8.3 Elements

The essential elements for assault with intent to do grievous bodily harm are:
- assault
- intent
- grievous bodily harm.

27.8.3.1 Assault

Conduct that amounts to common assault satisfies the requirements of the first element of this crime. This form of assault implies the use of actual force.

27.8.3.2 Intent

It is not required that the victim should suffer from actual grievous bodily harm. It is enough that the accused intended to inflict such harm.[108] The intention to commit grievous bodily harm is normally established by inference from objective facts, including the type of wounds inflicted or weapons used.

27.8.3.3 Grievous bodily harm

The qualification of grievous bodily harm is not easy to define. Section 150 of the Transkei Penal Code[109] listed the types of injuries that would amount to grievous bodily harm as including emasculation, permanent loss of sight or hearing, privation of any member or joint, loss of the use of a limb or organ, disfiguration of the head or face, fracture or dislocation of a bone, and any hurt that endangers life or causes the sufferer to be (or at least within the space of 20 days) in severe bodily pain or unable to follow his ordinary pursuits.

However, the provisions of the Transkei Penal Code are not a safe yardstick for qualifying grievous bodily harm.[110] In *R v Edwards*, the court preferred to consider grievous bodily harm 'such as to seriously interfere with health'.[111]

In *S v Mbelu*, Miller J pointed out that:

> **... however one expresses it, it is at least clear that there must be an intent to do more than inflict the casual and comparatively insignificant and superficial injuries which would ordinarily follow upon assault. There must be an intent to injure and to injure in a serious respect.**[112]

108 *R v Zondi* 1930 TPD 107.
109 Which was repealed through the provisions of s 3 of Proc 30 of 1951.
110 *R v Edwards* 1957 R & N 107 at 109–110.
111 *R v Edwards* supra at 109.
112 *S v Mbelu* 1966 (1) PH H176 (N) at 178. See also *S v Dipholo* 1983 (4) SA 757 (T) at 760.

27.9 Kidnapping

27.9.1 A brief history

Roman law punished kidnapping, detaining, concealing or selling a free(d) man or child, and the theft of slaves.[113] The crime was intended to protect the liberty of free men and partly to deter the deprivation of certain types of property.

Roman-Dutch law punished the crime under the name of *plagium*. Roman-Dutch law did not impose an obligation that the deprivation of liberty had to last for longer than a very short period.

English law had three separate crimes to house what is accommodated by the single crime of kidnapping in South African law. English law punished child stealing,[114] false imprisonment[115] and kidnapping.[116]

In South Africa, kidnapping was punished as early as 1823. The South African version of the crime protects the interests of *personal liberty* and the *parental control over minors*.[117]

Freedom and security of the person is a fundamental right in South Africa.[118] This human right underscores the rationale for the criminalisation of kidnapping as an outrage on the freedom of a person and an individual's human dignity.

27.9.2 Definition

The crime of **kidnapping** is defined as unlawfully and intentionally depriving a person of liberty of movement and/or his custodians of control.

27.9.3 Elements

The essential elements of kidnapping are:

- unlawfulness
- deprivation of liberty/custody
- depriving a person
- intent.

27.9.3.1 Unlawfulness

Valid justifications for depriving a person of his liberty include court or statutory authority, necessity, consent[119] of the person removed[120] and the other ordinary incidents of parental power. A parent cannot kidnap his own child even if the parent does not have legal custody over the child. However, a parent who violates the custody order may be liable for being in contempt of court.

113 See the *lex Fabia de Plagiariis* as it was dealt with in D 48.15.

114 As it is defined in s 56 of the Offences Against the Person Act of 1861. It did not require an intention to deprive permanently the parent/guardian/other person of having lawful care for a child below the age of 14.

115 This involves restraining the victim's freedom of movement from a particular place.

116 This English common law crime is an aggravated form of false imprisonment. It is complete when the victim is carried away against his will.

117 Snyman *Criminal Law* 471–474 classifies the crime as a 'crime against freedom of movement'. Burchell *Principles of Criminal Law* 659–661 classifies kidnapping as a crime against the person.

118 S 12 of the Constitution.

119 See *S v Burger and others* 2010 (2) SACR 1 (SCA). It is submitted that the SCA in this case gave too little weight to the possibility that the consent obtained was not the result of free will, but rather the coarse and 'overbearing' conduct of the police, who were convicted in the trial Court on a charge of kidnapping.

120 Unless the person is a child. In such cases, it is the lawful custodian's consent that is necessary.

27.9.3.2 Deprivation of liberty/custody

Deprivation of liberty usually occurs in the context of an application of force. However, the use of force is not a necessary feature for all deprivations. Depriving a person of his liberty includes physically carrying a person off to a separate location, imprisoning or concealing a person, or luring the victim away by fraudulent means. Any act that causes the prohibited deprivation of liberty of the victim is sufficient to found liability. The duration of deprivation is irrelevant.[121]

27.9.3.3 Depriving a person

Any natural person may be a victim of kidnapping.

27.9.3.4 Intent

The accused must have actual or legal intention to deprive a person of liberty or the relevant custodian of control. The accused must at least know or be able to foresee that the victim (or parent/custodian) has not consented. Motive is irrelevant.

27.10 *Crimen iniuria*

27.10.1 A brief history

Roman law punished, as an *iniuria*, any unlawful act conducted with the intention of impairing the *dignitas* of another. The wrong consisted of an unjustifiable outrage, insult or wanton interference with the personality rights of another. This included any unlawful act that showed contempt for the lawful personality interests of the victim or was intended to lower the victim in the estimation of others. Examples of the offensive violation of *dignitas* under Roman law included immoral solicitation that impaired the modesty of a woman, the abduction of an attendant or slave of a citizen, persistent following, abusive and unflattering remarks, ridiculing another person, violations of domestic peace and privacy (such as when a home is unlawfully entered), and conduct such as where X threw stones at the statue of Y's father. The crime also included cases of *iniuria per consequentias* where, because of his relationship with the person insulted, Y himself has an action.

If the complainant was not originally offended by what had been done, he could not later complain about it. This principle is based on the premise that the *dignitas* of the complainant was not impaired at the time of his being aware of the accused's conduct. The complainant need not know of the accused at the time of his conduct. However, the complainant must feel offended at the moment of becoming aware of the conduct.

Roman-Dutch law recognised that only serious violations were subject to prosecution. It also recognised the *boni mores* as a general principle for the application and development of the law. English law did not recognise the substantive crime of *crimen iniuria.*

The South African common law has followed the approach based on the Roman and Roman-Dutch jurisprudence.[122] However, courts have emphasised that what may have been punishable under Roman law is not necessarily punishable under our common law. Prosecutions for *crimen iniuria* flourished in the context of sexual activity. There was an overlap between *crimen iniuria* and the conduct that failed to amount to indecent assault.

---

121 In *S v Mellors* 1990 (1) SACR 347 (W), the court held that the deprivation which lasted two-and-a-half hours was sufficient.

122 See Snyman *Criminal Law* 461–467; Burchell *Principles of Criminal Law* 648–658.

Only serious violations of *dignitas* are punishable. The seriousness of the violation is subject to the *boni mores*. However, in *R v Nyandora*, Hopely J commented as follows:

> **Personally, I think that the somewhat recently resuscitated crime of criminal *injuria* should be resorted to as seldom as possible, because of its vagueness, and because it would be hard to get juries and magistrates to grasp all that it implies.**[123]

Crimen iniuria is different to criminal defamation. There may be an overlap where the act impairs both *dignitas* and *fama*. However, a case of *crimen iniuria* may not amount to criminal defamation where there is no publication. The accused would remain liable for *crimen iniuria* even if he only communicated the insult to the complainant.[124]

27.10.2 Definition

Crimen iniuria is defined as unlawfully, intentionally and seriously impairing the *dignitas* of another person.

27.10.3 Elements

The essential elements of *crimen iniuria* are:

- unlawfulness
- impairment
- *dignitas*
- intent.

27.10.3.1 Unlawfulness

Unlawfulness may be disproved in appropriate circumstances by consent,[125] necessity,[126] private defence,[127] statutory authority and conduct that is condoned as objectively reasonable when the *boni mores* are considered.[128]

27.10.3.2 Impairment

The accused's conduct must impair the *dignitas* of the victim. In *De Lange v Costa*, the Appellate Division (AD) explained that the test for impairing the *dignitas* of the victim comprises two questions that must be answered positively for the court to be satisfied that the victim's *dignitas* has been impaired:

1. Was the plaintiff's self-esteem subjectively offended?
2. Would a person of ordinary sensibilities regard the conduct as objectively offensive?[129]

There is an exception to having to answer the first question with a positive answer. It is not necessary for the state to prove that the victim's *dignitas* was subjectively impaired in cases

---

123 *R v Nyandora* 1917 SR 1 at 2.

124 *R v Chipo and others* 1953 (3) SA 602 (SR) at 614.

125 In *R v Heyneke and Heyneke* 1959 (2) PH H185 (OPA), the defence of consent failed because although the complainants had consented to the overseas publication of photographs of themselves in the nude, they had not consented to the conduct of the accused, which was to sell the pictures locally.

126 Compare the cases of *S v I and another* 1976 (1) SA 781 (RA) with *S v A and another* 1971 (2) SA 293 (T) for the defence of necessity against a charge of *crimen iniuria*. In both cases, the accused persons were private detectives who had been hired by clients to spy on the victims. The defence of necessity worked for one private detective and not the other.

127 *S v Ndlangisa* 1969 (4) SA 324 (E); *R v Van Vuuren and another* 1961 (3) SA 305 (E).

128 In *De Lange v Costa* 1989 (2) SA 857 (A) at 862, the court confirmed that the law does not punish conduct that is objectively reasonable. See also *R v Chipo* supra.

129 *De Lange v Costa* supra at 862.

that involve children and people who suffer from mental illness because such categories of persons may be incapable of understanding the communication.[130]

There is another *possible* exception in the context of peeping toms (voyeurs). In *R v Holliday*,[131] the court found the accused guilty, even though the victim was not actually aware of the conduct at the time of the incident.

Courts have accepted that there are various ways to impair the *dignitas* of another person. Some of the circumstances that the courts have found offensive include public or private indecent exposure,[132] peeping toms,[133] making sexual overtures or suggestions that invite sexual impropriety,[134] indecent assault,[135] vulgar abuse,[136] racist abuse,[137] insults[138] and humiliation,[139] inducing engagement or intercourse by fraud,[140] and invasion of privacy.[141]

The offensive conduct may take the form of words alone (written or oral), acts or gestures alone, or a combination of words and conduct. No publication is necessary to sustain liability for *crimen iniuria*.

---

130 *R v Holliday* 1927 CPD 395 at 401.

131 *R v Holliday* supra.

132 *R v Kobi* 1912 TPD 1106 at 1108.

133 *R v Holliday* supra.

134 *S v K* 1975 (3) SA 446 (N); *R v E* 1954 (4) SA 501 (SR). In *S v Van Ieperen* 2017 (1) SACR 226 (WCC), the appellant, an attorney, made unwanted and sexually charged comments, telling the complainant (a fellow attorney) that he wanted to 'smack her bum'; that 'she wore sexy shoes' and that 'she needs a man'. The court concluded (at 34) that the 'offending words collectively, used in the context where both the appellant and the complainant are attorneys present in a courtroom where other colleagues and members of the public were present, had the effect of humiliating and belittling the complainant'.

135 *R v S* 1948 (4) SA 419 (GW). On the relationship between *crimen iniuria* and sexual offences, see Watney, M '*Crimen iniuria*: Its role vis-à-vis sexual offences legislation' (2017) 2 *TSAR* 405.

136 *R v Dibden* 1967 (1) PH H137 (RA).

137 In 2017, defendant Vicky Momberg was convicted of *crimen iniuria* in the Randburg magistrates' court. Momberg was charged with *crimen iniuria* because she used a certain racist word a total of 48 times during interactions with black police officers. In March 2018, Momberg was sentenced to an effective two years in prison, an unprecedented sentence for verbal abuse. Since the verdict and sentence were handed down by a magistrates' court (as opposed to a High Court), it is not appropriate to speak of a 'precedent-setting judgment'. Nevertheless, the decision confirms the growing sense that South African criminal law needs to give effect to the fight against racism and the need to protect the dignity of all people. The content and future development of *crimen iniuria* as a crime under South African law must be seen in this light. At the time of writing, it was not clear whether Momberg was going to appeal the sentence. Whether prison sentences for aggravated forms of *crimen iniuria* (especially where there is an element of racism) will become the new norm is yet to be determined. Public reaction to the sentence was predictably divided, but there seems to be a measure of support from civil society, political parties, and members of the public for the notion that cases such as Momberg's deserve harsh punishment. For more on this case and the debates surrounding the magistrates' court's decision, see 'The murky case of Vicky Momberg and *crimen injuria*' 29 March 2018, available at http://www.witsjusticeproject.co.za/news-and-insights-category/the-murky-case-of-vicki-momberg-and-crimen-injuria; 'Analysis: Why the Vicky Momberg racism sentence deserves scrutiny' 29 March 2018, available at https://www.dailymaverick.co.za/article/2018-03-29-analysis-why-the-vicki-momberg-racism-sentence-deserves-scrutiny/#.WsVHvn9x2JA; and 'IJR welcomes the sentencing of Vicky Momberg noting that more needs to be done to #RootOutRacism' 29 March 2018, available at https://www.ijr.org.za/2018/03/29/ijr-welcomes-the-sentencing-of-vicki-momberg-noting-that-more-needs-to-be-done-to-rootoutracism/.

138 *R v Walton* 1958 (3) SA 693 (SR); *S v M* 1979 (2) SA 25 (A); *S v Bugwandeen* 1987 (1) SA 787 (N); *S v Steenberg* 1999 (1) SACR 594 (N).

139 *R v Sethuntsa* 1945 EDL 128; *S v Brereton* 1971 (1) SA 489 (RA).

140 *R v Youngleson* (11) 1948 (1) SA 822 (W) at 826; *R v Howard* (1917) 38 NPD 192. These cases should be compared with the decision in *R v Henning* 1933 (2) PH H209 (TPD) where a married man escaped liability despite seducing and impregnating a girl he had misrepresented himself to when he promised to marry her if she became pregnant.

141 *S v A and another* 1971 (2) SA 293 (T).

Only cases of serious impairment of the *dignitas* of another are subject to being punished as *crimen iniuria*.[142] In *R v Walton*, the court held that 'in the ordinary hurly-burly of everyday life a man must be expected to endure minor or trivial insults to his dignity'.[143]

Establishing whether there is a serious impairment depends on the contemporary *boni mores*. In *R v Fuleza*, the AD held that it may be difficult to draw a line to apply the limitation as a legal principle between cases that are serious and those that are not.[144]

The enquiry in each case is unique to that case. 'It is not greatly furthered by reference to the individual circumstances of other cases, save that some assistance may be obtained from them [regarding] the factors [that] a court should [take into account] in determining whether there has been an impairment of a person's dignity.'[145] Further, the *boni mores* may have changed to condone behaviour that was previously considered taboo or vice versa. In addition, some of the decisions may offer misleading guidance. For instance, insulting a police officer was considered to be *crimen iniuria* in *S v Momberg*.[146] However, insulting a policewoman by calling her a 'bitch' may be lawful (*S v Sharp*).[147] This anomaly is particularly confusing because the *boni mores* are often quoted as favouring liability in cases involving conduct that tends to victimise women.[148] However, bear in mind that the court in *Sharp* also found the accused's conviction to be fallible on the ground that the prosecution had failed to adduce evidence to suggest that the *dignitas* of the complainant had been subjectively impaired.[149]

Note that words that are deemed sufficiently offensive can form the basis for a civil claim for damages in terms of the law of delict and the same words can form the basis for a criminal case of *crimen iniuria*. However, there is some authority that supports the argument that the essential difference between the civil action and the crime of *crimen iniuria* involves a threshold of seriousness: 'Every insult to dignity which is serious enough to found a civil action will not necessarily be serious enough to warrant criminal prosecution'.[150]

27.10.3.3 *Dignitas*

Dignitas has been broadly defined as a person's right to self-respect, mental tranquillity and privacy. The Romans considered it to be a violation of the respect due to a free person (not of the physical integrity of a person). Melius de Villiers is accredited with the popular definition that describes *dignitas* as '[t]hat valued and serene condition in [a citizen's] social or individual life which is violated when [a person] is either publicly or privately, subjected by another to offensive and degrading treatment, or when he is exposed to ill-will; ridicule; disesteem or contempt.'[151]

---

142 *R v Umfaan* 1908 TS 62; *R v Kobi* supra at 1109; *R v Howard* supra at 196–197; *R v Dibden* supra; *R v Olakawu* 1958 (2) SA 357 (C) at 359; *S v Jana* 1981 (1) SA 671 (T).

143 *R v Walton* supra at 695G. See also *S v S* 1964 (3) SA 319 (T) at 322H. Marais J remarked that 'not every insulting word can be made the subject of a criminal charge. Chaos in the courts would otherwise result. It is only when the welfare of society and good order generally demand some criminal sanction that the State would and should interfere'.

144 *R v Fuleza* 1951 (1) SA 519 (A) at 532D–533A. See also *R v Olakawu* supra at 359D–F where Van Winsen J, who was dealing with the issue of determining whether the impairment was serious, stated that no general principles can profitably be devised as to what conduct that is calculated to impair the dignity of persons living in our society merits punishment.

145 *R v Olakawu* supra at 359D–F.

146 *S v Momberg* 1970 (2) SA 68 (C).

147 *S v Sharp* 2002 (1) SACR 360 (Ck).

148 *R v Van Meer* 1923 OPD 77 at 80; *R v Muller* 1938 OPD 141 at 143; *R v Walton* supra at 695–696.

149 *S v Sharp* supra.

150 *Ryan v Petrus* 2010 (1) SACR 274 (ECG) at 281F (referring to *R v Walton* supra).

151 As it was quoted in *R v Holliday* 1927 CPD 395 at 401.

It is easy for people to be misled into thinking that *dignitas* only refers to the dignity of a person. This is not true.[152] Although the concept of *dignitas* does include a person's right to dignity, *dignitas* also includes other personality rights. *Dignitas* is a general concept that covers all personality rights other than reputation or the bodily integrity of the victim.

The purpose of the crime is to protect every person's right to be free from insults, degrading behaviour, offensive or humiliating treatment, and invasions of privacy.

27.10.3.4 Intent

The state must prove that the accused had actual or legal intention for each element of the crime. The accused must know or at least foresee that his conduct will unlawfully impair the victim's *dignitas*. For example, in *R v Koza*, the accused was acquitted because he had *accidentally* exposed himself during a state of intoxication.[153] Motive is irrelevant if the accused at least has fault in the form of *dolus eventualis*.

27.10.4 Some general comments

One of the reasons why the accused was acquitted in *S v Sharp*[154] was the fact that there was no allegation that the complainant subjectively felt that her *dignitas* had been impaired. However, the rigid application of this old principle seems to ignore the fact that it completely overlooks the state's interest in the offensive conduct. If the state, on behalf of society, does not have an interest worth protecting, then the conduct should not be criminal because it is not of public interest. However, if the conduct is of public interest, then it should be punished, regardless of whether the victim was also subjectively offended by the offensive conduct.

The test for establishing whether the *dignitas* of the victim has been seriously impaired is vague. In *Bugwandeen*, the court held as follows:

> **The test requiring the *injuria* to be 'serious' in so far as it can be called a test at all is so nebulous as to lead to arbitrariness in its application. While *injuria* of a trivial nature should not engage the attention of the courts (they can be excluded on the principle *de minimis non curat lex*), any real and substantial impairment of a person's *dignitas* should merit punishment, irrespective of whether it is of such a nature that it should be punished in the interests of the State – unless under 'interest of the State' is understood in this regard, that interest which the State generally has in safeguarding the right of the individual to the tranquil enjoyment of his rights of personality, self-respect, privacy and mental tranquillity.**[155]

27.11 Criminal defamation

27.11.1 A brief history

Originally, Roman law did not punish defamation as a substantive crime. Defamation was punishable as an *iniuria*,[156] whether it was written or spoken.[157] The law required proof of publication of the defamatory matter. The law also required proof of *animus iniuriandi*,

152 *R v Holliday* supra at 400. See Burchell J 'Protecting dignity under common law and the Constitution: The significance of *crimen iniuria* in South African criminal law' (2014) 27(3) *SACJ* 250–271.

153 *R v Koza* 1958 (2) PH H218 (SR).

154 *S v Sharp* supra.

155 *S v Bugwandeen* supra at 796A–B.

156 D 47.10.

157 D 47.10 and C 9.36.

which was tested subjectively. The offender had to appreciate that his conduct may injure the victim's reputation.[158] The publication had to be unlawful. The publication was not considered unlawful if it was executed in terms of private or public authority, or if the published material was the truth (even if it was not for a public benefit).

Roman-Dutch law has always regarded defamation as a criminal offence, but it was still considered to be a form of *iniuria*. Roman-Dutch law no longer accepted truth as a defence excluding unlawfulness. The publication had to be for the public benefit.[159] Other defences that could exclude the unlawfulness of the publication included authority (privilege), consent and self-defence. Fault was required in the form of *animus iniuriandi*. Roman-Dutch law also required proof that the accused was aware that there was no justification for publishing the defamatory material. Roman-Dutch law punished any publication whether it was written, spoken or made through conduct that impaired the reputation of another private individual or public official.

English law did not punish slander (verbal defamation), but it did punish libel (defamation in writing) at common law and in terms of legislation such as the Libel Act of 1843. English law imposed criminal liability for libel because publication to the person defamed amounted to a violation of the preservation of the public peace.[160] The libel had to cause a breach of the peace or seriously affect the reputation of the person defamed. The unlawful character of the libel could be excluded by the justifications of public benefit, privilege, fair comment and truth. Intention or recklessness was required as the *mens rea* for the crime.

In *R v Harrison and Dryburgh*,[161] Innes CJ referred to cases where defamatory libel was prosecuted as an *iniuria* in the early occupation of the Cape by the British (1810) and, most notably, during the time when the Dutch East India Company was the most dominant European influence in the Cape. Many of these proceedings involved complaints by naval officers.[162]

Once the British occupation was well established in the Cape, the early tendency to indict for *iniuria* was replaced by the tendency to indict *eo nomine* for criminal libel or defamation. South African practice would eventually create crimes that would focus on specific aspects of what was originally punished as *iniuria*:

- Violations of bodily integrity were punished as assault.
- Violations of *dignitas* were punished as *crimen iniuria*.
- Violations of reputation (*fama*) became punishable as criminal defamation.

The case of *R v Houghton and Wright*[163] was the first occasion where there was an indictment based on the charge of libel on a private person. The court justified the conviction on the ground that Roman-Dutch law recognised the crime of libel on a private individual.[164] That position was reinforced with the advent of the Cape Libel Act 46 of 1882, which punished the publication of defamatory libel.[165]

158 According to D 47.10, *injuriam nemo facit nisi qui scit se injuriam facere.*

159 Voet 47.10.9.

160 *R v Adams* (1888) 22 QBD 66.

161 *R v Harrison and Dryburgh* 1922 AD 320 at 334–336.

162 See *R v Fuleza* supra.

163 *R v Houghton and Wright* (1881–1882) 2 EDC 35.

164 *R v Houghton and Wright* supra at 40.

165 The courts have considered this Act to be the codification of *crimen iniuriae litteris* in cases including *R v Ginsberg* 1934 CPD 166 and *R v Fuleza* supra.

The Transvaal courts accepted that ordinary slander and serious defamation were both criminal.[166] Since then, the South African common law has punished both slander and libel under the rubric of criminal defamation.[167]

There may be overlaps between the crimes of criminal defamation and *crimen iniuria* in cases where the conduct of the accused impairs both the *fama* and the *dignitas* of the complainant.

27.11.2 Definition

Criminal defamation is defined as unlawful and intentional publication of matter that tends to injure the reputation of another.[168]

27.11.3 Elements

The essential elements of criminal defamation are:
- unlawfulness
- publication
- defamatory matter
- intent.

27.11.3.1 Unlawfulness

General defences excluding unlawfulness have been recognised to include consent[169] and private defence.[170] Truth will also exclude liability if the publication is also for the public benefit. The defence of truth is not limited to cases that involve the literal truth in every detail. Truth will be available as a defence in cases where there is substantial truth in the material allegations.[171] Partial truths have been recognised to mitigate the sentence.[172]

Whether the truthful publication is for public benefit depends on factors including the position occupied by the victim, the content of the statement and 'the time, the manner and the occasion of the publication'.[173] Everyone who plays a public part in public affairs is deemed and taken to submit to criticism for such participation.[174] However, the manner of publication may nevertheless justify a conviction.[175] The public benefit does apply to cases other than those involving public bodies and their representatives. There may be a public interest present in the case of publications regarding any natural private person.[176] This principle applies in cases that involve a private person who has recently committed offences against the law or society. It is considered in the public interest for those who are dealing with the guilty individual to be informed of the true character of the guilty individual.[177]

166 *R v Japel* 1906 TS 108.

167 The position only became uniform in the national common law once the provisions of the Cape Libel Act 46 of 1882 were repealed by the Pre-Union Statute Law Revision Act 43 of 1977.

168 *S v Hoho* 2009 (1) SACR 276 (SCA) at 23.

169 *Jordaan v Delarey* 1958 (1) SA 638 (W) at 639.

170 *Rhodes University College v Field* 1947 (3) SA 437 (A) at 463–464.

171 *Johnson v Rand Daily Mail* 1928 AD 190 at 205–206.

172 *R v Shaw and Fennell* (1883–1884) 3 EDC 323 at 328–329.

173 *Patterson v Engelenburg and Wallach's Ltd* 1917 TPD 350 at 361.

174 *R v Shaw and Fennell* supra at 325.

175 In *R v Shaw and Fennell* supra at 330, the court held that regardless of the truth about the publication made in reference to the Dean of Grahamstown, it was not for the public benefit to publish the comments in the manner used by the accused persons. The court objected to the publication of the comments in a scurrilous paper, which is 'in itself a public scandal and offence'.

176 In *Graham v Kerr* (1891–1892) 9 SC 185 at 187, it was recognised that the public interest 'would suffer rather than benefit from any unnecessary reviving of forgotten scandals'.

177 *Graham v Kerr* supra at 187.

The right to free speech is the foundation of the defence of fair comment.[178] The limits of the right have mostly been identified in civil cases[179] because of the shortage of common law examples.[180] This justification is only available if three conditions are met: the publication must be such that a reasonable person would regard it as a comment and not as a statement of fact;[181] the comment must be *bona fide*, fair and relevant to the facts commented on;[182] and the facts commented on must be true and must be matters of public interest.[183]

The law relating to the defence of privilege has been most significantly developed through civil cases, but there have been common law cases that have recognised the justification of privilege.[184] The accused does not bear an onus of proving privilege because such onus is on the state.[185] There are forms of privilege, such as parliamentary privilege, which protect speech, even if it is *mala fide.* However, most forms of privilege are forfeited where the accused acts *mala fide.*[186] Forms of qualified privilege may fall into one of the following categories: privileged reports;[187] statements made in judicial and quasi-judicial proceedings;[188] and statements made in the maintenance, protection or discharge of a duty.[189]

The historical development of the crime of defamation suggests that harm that is not considered serious is not punishable as a crime. It is not based on a legal principle, but on the reality that prosecutors do not prosecute cases where the defamation is not serious.

27.11.3.2 Publication

The defamatory material must be communicated to a person other than the complainant.[190] This is a consequence of the fact that defamation is a wrong against *fama* and not *dignitas.* A defamatory matter is published from the moment it is communicated to any person other than the complainant.[191] There is no publication in situations if the person receiving the communication of defamatory material does not appreciate the defamatory significance.[192]

27.11.3.3 Defamatory matter

The publication must be such that a reasonable person would understand that it referred to the complainant.[193] The defamatory matter may be in the form of words (written or spoken), acts[194] or omissions.[195] The matter is considered to be defamatory if it tends to 'expose any

178 *Crawford v Albu* 1917 AD 102 at 114; *Kemsley v Foot* [1951] 1 ALL ER 331 (CA) at 338.

179 See, for example, *Coetzee v Union Periodicals Ltd and others* 1931 WLD 37.

180 One such example was *S v Modus Publications (Private) Ltd and another* 1998 (2) SACR 151 (ZS) at 154.

181 *Crawford v Albu* supra at 105; *Pearce v Argus Printing and Publishing Co Ltd* 1943 CPD 137 at 144; *SA Associated Newspapers Ltd and another v Yutar* 1969 (2) SA 442 (A) at 454.

182 *Crawford v Albu* supra at 114–115.

183 *Crawford v Albu* supra at 114.

184 *R v Japel* supra at 111; *R v Masoja and Mtelo* 1930 SR 167 at 171; *R v Ginsberg* supra at 176–181; *R v Dewberry* 1935 EDL 97 at 100–105.

185 *S v Marangarire* 1977 (4) SA 237 (R) at 239.

186 *R v Ginsberg* supra at 178–181; *R v Dewberry* supra at 103–105.

187 *Van Leggelo v Argus Printing and Publishing Co Ltd* 1935 TPD 230; *Benson v Robinson & Co (Pty) Ltd and another* 1967 (1) SA 420 (A).

188 *Gluckman v Schneider* 1936 AD 151; *Basner v Trigger* 1946 AD 83; *SA Associated Newspapers Ltd and another v Yutar* supra.

189 *Ehmke v Grunewald* 1921 AD 575; *De Waal v Ziervogel* 1938 AD 112; *Molepo v Achterberg* 1943 AD 85; *Rhodes University College v Field* supra; *Jordaan v Van Biljon* 1962 (1) SA 286 (A).

190 *R v McIver* 1929 TPD 574 at 577–578; *R v Mabona* 1935 TPD 407; *Sutter v Brown* 1926 AD 155; *S v Gibson NO and others* 1979 (4) SA 115 (D) at 141–142.

191 *R v Shaw and Fennell* supra at 324.

192 *Sutter v Brown* supra at 164; *R v Mabona* supra; *Vermaak v Van der Merwe* 1981 (3) SA 78 (N).

193 *S v Gibson NO and others* supra at 142–145; *Young v Kemsley and others* 1940 AD 258 at 281.

194 *Tolley v JS Fry and Sons Ltd* [1931] AC 333 (HL).

195 *Byrne v Deane* [1937] 1 KB 818 (CA), [1937] 2 ALL ER 204 (CA).

person to hatred, contempt or ridicule',[196] and lowers the esteem of the complainant in the eyes of a reasonable person. The test is objective. Mere vulgar abuse does not tend to lower the esteem of the complainant in the eyes of ordinary reasonable members of society and is therefore not defamatory.[197]

27.11.3.4 Intent

The term '*animus iniuriandi*' specifically refers to the intention to defame. In criminal law, it is tested subjectively. Motive is irrelevant. The accused has the prohibited intention if he knows or at least foresees the possibility that he is publishing unlawful defamatory material against the complainant.[198] Negligence is insufficient for criminal liability. A bona fide mistake should entitle the accused to an acquittal.

27.11.4 Some general comments

The influence of English law has created similarities between the delict of defamation and the crime of defamation. However, there remain certain fundamental differences between the delict and the crime. One such fundamental difference is the fact that there is a delictual presumption of *mens rea* in cases involving the publication of defamatory material. There is no similar presumption in the context of the crime of defamation. This difference is justified because of the different policy considerations that apply in civil cases and criminal cases. A presumption of this nature would be inappropriate in criminal law because of considerations including the right to a fair trial and the right to be presumed innocent. In criminal law, the onus of proof is always on the state. Presumptions that tend to shift the onus of proof are unwelcome in the context of criminal law. In criminal cases, the state bears the onus of proving intention, at least in the form of *dolus eventualis*, without having the benefit of relying on a presumption of *mens rea*.

27.11.5 Has the crime of criminal defamation been repealed through disuse by silent consent of the whole community?

In *S v Hoho*, the SCA considered the question of whether the crime of defamation is still extant or whether it has been abrogated by disuse. Streicher JA formulated the issue as follows:

> **The doctrine that law may be abrogated by disuse is well established in our law. The basis of the doctrine is the tacit repeal 'through disuse by silent consent of the whole community'. It is therefore necessary to consider whether it can be said that the South African community tacitly consented that defamation should no longer constitute a criminal offence.**[199]

Although a quantitative approach (number of complaints, prosecutions, and so on) seems like the obvious way to determine whether the 'South African community tacitly consented that defamation should no longer constitute a criminal offence', Streicher JA considered the test to be more nuanced. While the number of prosecutions and convictions for criminal defamation are relevant indicators,[200] the SCA held that criminal defamation has not been repealed as a crime by silent consent of the whole community.

---

196 *R v Shaw and Fennell* supra at 324.
197 *R v Walton* supra at 696; *Wood NO and another v Branson* 1952 (3) SA 369 (T); *Brenner v Botha* 1956 (3) SA 257 (T).
198 *Iniuriam nemo facit nisi qui scit se iniuriam facere.* See *Maisel v Van Naeren* 1960 (4) SA 836 (C) at 840E–F.
199 *S v Hoho* supra at 9.
200 *S v Hoho* supra at 9 and 11.

27.11.6 Constitutionality of the crime of defamation

We pointed out above that freedom of speech is the foundation of the defence of fair comment in the context of criminal defamation. Thus, we can ask whether the crime of defamation should still exist in a constitutional democracy like South Africa.[201] One argument is that civil law already provides for an adequate course of action in cases of defamation. It can be argued that the common law crime of defamation constitutes unnecessary criminalisation of speech.

The SCA rejects this argument, having determined that the common law crime of criminal defamation is not incompatible with the Constitution.[202] The court reasoned that a limitation on freedom of expression 'can be consistent with the Constitution only if it can be said that "an appropriate balance is struck between the protection of freedom of expression on the one hand, and the value of human dignity on the other"'[203] Thus, the court held that the criminalisation of defamation constitutes a reasonable and not too drastic limitation on the right to freedom of expression. Furthermore, the court added the following additional reason for the criminalisation of defamation:

> **There have been cases in the past where complainants required the State to prosecute for defamation and there may well be such cases in the future. It is true that there is a civil remedy available for defamation but there is also a civil remedy available for common assault, yet nobody would suggest that there is for that reason no need for the crime of common assault. There is ... no reason why the State should oblige and prosecute in the case of a complaint in respect of an injury to a person's physical integrity, but not in the case of a complaint in respect of an injury to reputation, which may have more serious and lasting effects than a physical assault.**[204]

27.12 The Protection from Harassment Act 17 of 2011

The Protection from Harassment Act 17 of 2011 entered into force on 27 April 2013. The Act mainly provides for civil remedies against harassment and is aimed at the protection of individual security, privacy and dignity. Section 2 of the Act provides for the application of a protection order by a complainant in a case of harassment.

The Protection from Harassment Act recognises the overlap between the interests protected by the Act, and the interests protected by crimes such as *crimen iniuria*, assault, trespass, extortion or any other crime which affects the person or property of the complainant. Section 2(2)(*b*) of the Act provides that an unrepresented complainant in a harassment matter must be informed by the clerk of the court of the right also to lodge a criminal complaint against the respondent. Typically, this could involve complaints of *crimen iniuria*, assault, trespassing and so on.

---

201 See s 16 of the Constitution, which protects freedom of expression; *Khumalo and others v Holomisa* 2002 (5) SA 401 (CC). See also Hoctor S 'The crime of defamation – still defensible in a modern constitutional democracy?' (2013) 34(1) *Obiter* 125–135. In neighbouring Lesotho, that country's Constitutional Court considered the constitutionality of criminal defamation. In *Basildon Peta v Minister of Law, Constitutional Affairs and Human Rights CC11/2016*, 18 May 2018 (Constitutional Court of Lesotho), sections 104, 102 and 101 of the Penal Code Act 6 of 2010 were declared to be inconsistent with the Constitution of the Kingdom of Lesotho, 1993. It was held (at para 24) that criminal defamation constitutes an undesirable criminalisation of speech; a violation of freedom of expression under s 14 of the Constitution of Lesotho; and that the crime is also overbroad and generally vague. The court noted that 'civil remedies for reputational encroachment are more suited to redressing such reputational harm' (at para 24).

202 *S v Hoho* supra, particularly at 31 and 33.

203 *S v Hoho* supra at 31.

204 *S v Hoho* supra at 35.

THIS CHAPTER IN ESSENCE

1. The crimes in this chapter cover a number of fundamental protected interests. Indeed, we can argue that the interest of human life must be the most important interest protected by law because without human life, law as we know it is meaningless.
2. The crimes of murder, attempted murder and culpable homicide are therefore well established and, at least as far as the rationale for the criminalisation is concerned, not controversial.
3. The crimes of assault and assault with intent to do grievous bodily harm also protect a fundamental interest, namely bodily integrity. It is hard to imagine a legal system that would not protect this legal interest by means of criminal law. The same applies to a crime such as kidnapping, which concerns the legal interest of freedom of the person and freedom of movement.
4. The law does not only protect a person's bodily integrity, but also other aspects of personhood, namely a person's sense of dignity, good name and reputation. The criminalisation of *crimen iniuria* and criminal defamation seek to protect these interests although the constitutionality and rationale of a crime such as criminal defamation seems to be less obvious than some of the other crimes in this chapter.
5. Perhaps the most controversial aspect of this chapter concerns the basic question: when does human life start? Because of this morally complex issue, the group of crimes, in terms of the Choice on Termination of Pregnancy Act, sit rather uncomfortably in a chapter that deals with crimes against human life. At the same time, the fact that some forms of abortion still attract criminal sanction can perhaps be viewed as confirmation that this chapter is, after all, the right place to discuss these crimes.
6. Other, equally complex issues, such as assisted suicide and euthanasia, affect the contours of the age-old crimes of murder and culpable homicide.

Chapter 28

Sexual crimes

CHAPTER OBJECTIVES

The objectives of this chapter are to:

- provide a historical overview of the most important common law and statutory sexual crimes under South African criminal law
- systematically identify and discuss the elements of the crimes provided for in the Criminal Law (Sexual Offences and Related Matters) Amendment Act 32 of 2007, which is, to a significant degree, a consolidation of sexual crimes in South Africa.

28.1 Historical context

South African criminal law has punished participants in sexual relations where they offended the direct victim of the conduct[1] or family life.[2] Further, the common law also criminalised certain types of sexual relations because the impugned conduct was considered to offend morality. Not all crimes against morality were concerned with sexual relations. They also included crimes such as blasphemy,[3] violating a grave and violating a dead body.[4]

Criminal punishment for immoral sexual behaviour existed under Roman law.[5] However, the most serious form of sexual offence, which in modern criminal law is described as rape, did not have a name of its own. Under Roman law, it was a type of violent crime to force someone to have sexual intercourse. Sexual intercourse with underage girls was punished, even where the sexual intercourse was not coupled with violence.[6]

During the 16th century, there were a number of sexual offences, such as *fornicatio, adulterium, incestus, raptus* and *stuprum*. These offences were punished as separate forms of crimes against sexual morality.[7]

1 For example, rape, indecent assault and *crimen iniuria*.

2 For example, abduction, bigamy and incest.

3 In *R v Webb* 1934 AD 493 at 495, Wessels CJ answered the suggestion that the crime of blasphemy had been abrogated by stating 'there is nothing to justify that view'. Perhaps the learned judge would have reconsidered that position with the advent of the Constitution of the Republic of South Africa, 1996.

4 S 68(1)(*b*) of the Criminal Law (Sexual Offences and Related Matters) Amendment Act 32 of 2007 (the Sexual Offences Act) repeals the crime of violation of a corpse in so far that it relates to the commission of a sexual act with a corpse.

5 For an historical overview, see De Wet JC and Swanepoel HL *Strafreg* 3 ed (1975) 249.

6 D 48.19.38.3.

7 De Wet and Swanepoel *Strafreg* 249.

Western morality has been interpreted to be based on Christianity. Consequently, Western morality is said to have considered heterosexual intercourse between parties who were married to each other to be the only lawful form of sexual intercourse.[8] Sexual intercourse between unmarried persons was punishable as the crime of fornication as pointed out above with reference to the state of the law in Western Europe during the 16th century. Extramarital intercourse involving a married person who was not married to his or her sexual partner was also criminally punishable as the crime of adultery.

South African criminal law was inconsistent in its punishment of sexual immorality. Very few cases of adultery were punished. Gradually, the focus of criminal law deviated from fornication and adultery to other characteristics that rendered the sexual conduct to be objectionable. There was penalised conduct, which remains objectionable even under contemporary norms. Such conduct includes crimes such as bestiality, pedophilia and commercial sex. There were other sexual morality crimes, which were originally considered to be objectionable because of factors including the religion,[9] race[10] or gender[11] of the participants. The law also punished conduct that was considered to be sexually deviant from the legal sexual norms. Such conduct was punished as unnatural sexual offences.[12] Criminally deviant sexual conduct included transvestism[13] and peeping toms.[14]

The Criminal Law (Sexual Offences and Related Matters) Amendment Act 32 of 2007 (the Sexual Offences Act) can be described as a codification or at least a consolidation of sexual crimes under South African law.[15] However, the crime of bigamy is a morality crime that does not include sexual acts in the *actus reus.* Consequently, bigamy is not punished in terms of the Act. Nonetheless, bigamy is still punishable as a common law crime. The provisions of the Act define every other sexual crime.[16] The Act further provides that its objects also include repealing common law sexual crimes[17] and replacing them with expanded or extended statutory versions.[18] The discussions of the new statutory crimes, which were based on similar versions from the common law, will include a brief history of the common law equivalent version of the crime. For example, the discussion of the new statutory crime of sexual assault will be preceded by a discussion of the repealed common law crime of indecent assault.

The Act also introduces a number of new crimes that did not exist under the common law, such as compelled rape, compelled sexual assault and compelled self-sexual assault.

8 Brundage JA *Law, Sex and Christian Society in Medieval Europe* (1990).

9 Even Roman-Dutch law proscribed sexual relations between Christians and Jews under the crime of *stuprum qualificatum*. The crime also punished conduct including fornication with young girls, nuns, widows in mourning, guardians and their wards, and persons with intellectual disabilities. Voet 48.5.2; Carpzovious 69.37; Damhouder 96.10.

10 S 16 of the Immorality Act 23 of 1957 criminalised sexual relations between persons who were categorised as white and those who were categorised as non-white.

11 Homosexual intercourse between males was punishable as sodomy until the Constitutional Court abolished the crime in the case of *National Coalition for Gay and Lesbian Equality and another v Minister of Justice and others* 1999 (1) SA 6 (CC). However, lesbianism was not punished at common law.

12 *R v Gough and Narroway* 1926 CPD 159.

13 The Prohibition of Disguises Act 16 of 1969; *S v Kola* 1966 (4) SA 322 (A).

14 The Sexual Offences Act 23 of 1957; *R v Holliday* 1924 AD 250; *R v H and another* 1959 (4) SA 427 (A).

15 Snyman CR *Criminal Law* 6 ed (2014) 341.

16 S 2(*a*) of the Sexual Offences Act provides that one of the objects of the Act is to enact all matters that relate to sexual offences.

17 S 68(1)(*b*) of the Sexual Offences Act repeals the common law crimes of rape, indecent assault, incest, bestiality and violation of a corpse insofar as the last crime relates to the commission of a sexual act with a corpse.

18 S 2(*c*) of the Sexual Offences Act.

Crimes in this category do not have a history dating back to the Roman, Roman-Dutch or English law that forms part of the inherited jurisprudence of South African law.[19]

28.2 Incest

28.2.1 A brief history

Roman law had sources that sometimes indicated that there was confusion as to whether incest was punished only where marriage *simpliciter*[20] was present or whether proof of sexual intercourse was necessary.[21] However, the common feature among the texts was the fact that incest was punishable as an offence.[22] The offence was punishable when it was between persons who were prohibited to intermarry[23] because they were related to a prohibited degree as a result of affinity (marriage), consanguinity (blood relationship) or an adoptive relationship.[24]

Roman-Dutch law followed a similar approach to Roman law in the context of the crime of incest. One of the biggest similarities is the fact that they both focused on punishing only those persons who were prohibited to intermarry because of the degree of their family relationship. Roman-Dutch law was generally unambiguous on the fact that the prohibition applied specifically to sexual intercourse between persons who are prohibited to intermarry.[25]

English law started prohibiting incest only when the provisions of the Punishment of Incest Act of 1908 became law. However, the English approach punished only a limited degree of incest compared to what was recognised in Roman-Dutch law or South African law. South African law largely followed the Roman-Dutch approach.[26]

However, the provisions of the common law crime of incest have been repealed and replaced by the provisions of section 68(1)(*b*) of the Sexual Offences Act.[27]

28.2.2 Definition

Section 12(1) of the Sexual Offences Act defines **incest** as follows:

> **Persons who may not lawfully marry each other on account of consanguinity, affinity or an adoptive relationship and who unlawfully and intentionally engage in an act of sexual penetration with each other, are, despite their mutual consent to engage in such act, guilty of the offence of incest.**

---

19 Note that the Sexual Offences Act provides for a number of offences in chapters 2, 3 and 4, for example sexual assault, compelled sexual assault and compelled self-sexual assault, which do not contain any penalty clauses. This feature of the Act is in contrast with other provisions in the Act that do contain penalty clauses. The Criminal Law (Sexual Offences and Related Matters) Amendment Amendment Act 6 of 2012 was enacted to provide expressly that the imposition of penalties in respect of certain offences contained in the Sexual Offences Act is left to the discretion of the courts. Section 56A was thus inserted into the main Act and provides that a court 'shall, if- (a) that or another court has convicted a person of an offence in terms of this Act; and (b) a penalty is not prescribed in respect of that offence in terms of this Act or by any other Act, impose a sentence, as provided for in section 276 of the Criminal Procedure Act, 1977 (Act No 51 of 1977), which that court considers appropriate and which is within that court's penal jurisdiction.' For more on this, see Chapter 1 section 1.9.5.

20 D 23.2.39.1.

21 Inst 1.10.1.

22 D 23.2.39.1; D 48.5.7; D 48.18.4.

23 D 23.2.39.1.

24 D 45.1.35.1.

25 Matthaeus 48.3.6.1; Van der Keessel *Crim* 48.5.26.

26 South Africa was already punishing offenders as early as 1875, for example in the cases of *R v K* (1875) 5 Buch 98 and *R v Paterson* 1907 TS 619.

27 See Snyman *Criminal Law* 378–381; Burchell JM *Principles of Criminal Law* 5 ed (2016) 677–684.

28.2.3 Elements

The elements of incest are:

- unlawfulness
- intent
- an act of sexual penetration
- an act of sexual penetration between two people who may not lawfully marry each other because of consanguinity, affinity or an adoptive relationship.

28.2.3.1 Unlawfulness

The provisions of section 12(1) of the Sexual Offences Act make it abundantly clear that the mutual consent of the parties plays no role in absolving them of their liability. However, proof of compulsion has been accepted under the common law as excluding unlawfulness.[28]

Section 56(4) excludes the liability of the accused if two requirements are met.[29] Firstly, at the time when the act of sexual penetration was first committed, an accused person may escape liability if the accused was below the age of 18 years. Secondly, at the time when the act of sexual penetration was first committed, an accused person may escape liability if the other participant to the incestuous sexual penetration exercised power or authority over the accused who was younger than 18, or a relationship of trust existed between the accused and the other person.

28.2.3.2 Intent

The parties must intend to participate in conduct that involves sexual penetration with the knowledge that they are prohibited from intermarrying or participating in sexual penetration because of their relationship.[30] If there is reasonable doubt resulting from a mistake of fact about the prohibitive nature of the relationship, the accused lacks *mens rea*.[31]

28.2.3.3 Sexual penetration

The prohibited act consists of sexual penetration by any person with another person without his or her consent. Section 1(1) of the Sexual Offences Act defines 'sexual penetration' as including any act that causes penetration to any extent whatsoever[32] by:

> **(*a*) the genital organs of one person into or beyond the genital organs, anus, or mouth of another person;**
>
> **(*b*) any other part of the body of one person, or any object, including any part of the body of an animal, into or beyond the genital organs or anus of another person; or**
>
> **(*c*) the genital organs of an animal, into or beyond the mouth of another person.**[33]

---

28 *R v Bourne* (1952) 36 Cr App R 125.

29 S 56(4) provides as follows:

> **A person ('A') may not be convicted of an offence in terms of section 12 if, at the time when the act of sexual penetration was first committed –**
>
> **(*a*) A was below the age of 18 years; and**
>
> **(*b*) the other person ('B') exercised power or authority over A or a relationship of trust existed between A and B.**

30 *R v Pieterse* 1923 EDL 232.

31 *R v Pieterse* supra.

32 The common law also recognised any degree of penetration by a male's penis into a female's vagina as sufficient for liability. The emission of semen was irrelevant. See *R v Giles* 1926 WLD 211 at 211–213.

33 S 1 of the Sexual Offences Act further provides that the term 'sexually penetrates' has a corresponding meaning to the statutory definition of 'sexual penetration'.

Further, section 1 of the Act defines the term 'genital organs' as including the whole or part of the male or female genital organs, as well as surgically constructed or reconstructed genital organs.

The scope of the current definition of sexual penetration eclipses the scope of what was defined as sexual intercourse in the common law. For example, the common law did not recognise oral penetration as unlawful conduct for the purpose of the crime of incest.

28.2.3.4 People who may not intermarry[34]

The new statutory crime of incest is a codification of the common law crime of incest. Other than the inclusion of the other forms of sexual penetration, there is no material difference between the common law crime and the statutory crime. The general principles that relate to the prohibited degrees of relation are congruent between the previous common law crime and the new statutory crime.

Section 12(2) of the Sexual Offences Act provides that for the purpose of the statutory crime of incest:

> **(*a*) the prohibited degrees of consanguinity (blood relationship) are the following:**
> **(i) ascendants and descendents in the direct line; or**
> **(ii) collaterals, if either of them is related to their common ancestor in the first degree of descent;**
> **(*b*) the prohibited degrees of affinity are relations by marriage in the ascending and descending line; and**
> **(*c*) an adoptive relationship is the relationship of adoption as provided for in any other law.**

Consanguinity consists of a blood relationship or descent from a common ancestor.[35] The term 'ascendants' refers to parents[36] and grandparents who may not marry their descendants – their children or grandchildren – in the direct line. Collateral blood relations have a common ancestor in the first degree of descent (within one generation). Examples of collateral blood relations include siblings,[37] uncles and their nieces,[38] and aunts and their nephews. Under the common law crime, the prohibition against incest was as equally applicable to the cases of illegitimate offspring as it was to legitimate offspring.[39] Similarly, half-blood relatives were equally prohibited from participating in incestuous relationships.[40] Cousins were outside the common law prohibition for the same reasons they were not punishable under Roman law.[41] Presumably, courts will refer to the common law position for clarity whenever the statute is silent on an issue.

Examples that violate the prohibition on incest between relations by affinity[42] include those between a person and his or her (former) father-/mother-/daughter-/son-in-law or stepfather/-mother/-daughter/-son.

---

34 The prohibition against intermarriage must be on account of consanguinity, affinity or adoptive relationship. See *R v Delport* (1901) 18 SC 355; *R v Mulder and another* 1954 (1) SA 228 (E) at 229.

35 Maasdorp AFS and Hall CG *Institutes of South African Law Vol 1* 7 ed (1947) at 7.

36 *R v Piet Arends* (1890–1891) 8 SC 176; *R v Richards* (1908) 18 CTR 561; *R v Giles* supra; *R v Tom Koos* 1931 GWLD 1; *R v C and C* 1945 CPD 26; *S v A* 1962 (4) SA 679 (E); *S v D* 1972 (3) SA 202 (O); *S v M* 1999 (2) SACR 548 (SCA).

37 *R v Ball* [1911] AC 47; *R v Troskie* 1920 AD 466.

38 *R v M* 1957 (2) SA 73 (E).

39 *R v Piet Arends* supra; *R v Richards* supra.

40 *R v Mbanjwa* 1906 NHC 42; *R v Blaauw & Blaauw* 1934 SWA 3 at 5–6; *R v Botes and Botha* 1945 NPD 43.

41 Voet 23.2.31; Van der Linden 1.3.6.1; Grotius 1.5.7; *S v Shasha* 1996 (2) SACR 73 (Tk) at 75.

42 Voet 23.2.30; Grotius 1.5.10; Brouwer 2.15.2.

The common law crime of incest[43] and the provisions of section 20(4) of the Child Care Act 74 of 1983 prohibit an adoptive parent from marrying or experiencing sexual penetration with a child they have adopted. Strangely, there is no prohibition against marriage or sexual penetration between the adopted child and the siblings they accrued due to the adoption.

28.2.4 Some general comments

It is important to note that the introduction of the definition of sexual penetration has expanded the scope of persons who may perform incest in the sense that it is no longer restricted to what was traditionally defined as sexual intercourse. The provisions of the Act will now also prohibit homosexual activities between persons who are not allowed to marry because of consanguinity, affinity or adoption.

The crime only punishes sexual penetration. Even though it is more inclusive than the common law approach, which was exclusively limited to sexual intercourse as it was defined by the common law, the new crime does not go far enough. The new statutory crime does not include any crimes associated with sexual violations between people who may not intermarry.

Another interesting anomaly is the fact that the prohibition between relations by affinity does not apply to collaterals. It is an anomaly that cannot be explained by a principle of law or logic. It is purely a reflection of the moral code that created the crime of incest in the first place. In terms of the original common law position, a man could not marry or have sexual relations with blood relations of his dead wife that would have been prohibited if the relative were a man.[44] However, modern reflections of the current *boni mores*, such as the Marriage Act 25 of 1961, provide that a widower may marry his deceased or divorced wife's sister or any other relative who is not an ascendant or descendant of the deceased/divorced spouse.[45] Thus, people who were related collaterally by affinity could intermarry and have sexual intercourse without violating the prohibition against incest if the relevant spouse was deceased or divorced. There was a time when the common law accepted that the accused was guilty of incest if he had sexual intercourse with a woman who was related by collateral affinity while he was married to his wife.[46] However, the cases that came after 1931 suggested that such conduct was not incestuous.[47] Nonetheless, courts have accepted that it is not unlawful for a man to have sexual intercourse with or marry his brother's wife's sister.[48]

Another interesting feature of the common law prohibition between relations by affinity was the fact that it applied ad infinitum. Even if the marriage that created that relation was terminated by death or divorce, the prohibition would remain in force.[49] However, the prohibition applied only where one of the accused was a party to the original marriage that created the relationship by affinity.[50]

43 *S v M* 1968 (2) SA 617 (T) at 621.
44 Grotius 1.5.9; Van der Linden 1.3.6; *R v Paterson* supra; *R v Mulder* supra at 229A–B.
45 S 28 of the Marriage Act 25 of 1961.
46 *R v Abraham Mentoor* (1896–1897) 11 EDC 125; *R v Delport* supra.
47 *R v Van Wyk* 1931 TPD 41; *R v Botes and Botha* supra; *R v Mulder* supra.
48 *R v V* 1959 (3) SA 621 (T).
49 *R v Botes and Botha* supra; *R v Mulder* supra.
50 Voet 23.2.36.

28.3 Bestiality

28.3.1 A brief history

Roman-Dutch law punished all unnatural sexual conduct, including homosexuality and bestiality, under the title *venus monstrosa*.[51] *Venus monstrosa* constituted 'gratification of sexual lust in a manner contrary to the order of nature'.[52] Penetration *per anum* or *per vaginam* between human beings and animals were undisputed examples of *venus monstrosa*.[53] Proof of emission of semen was not necessary.[54] Under English law, the crimes of sodomy and bestiality were collectively called buggery.[55]

South African law eventually separated[56] the crimes of sodomy, bestiality and 'unnatural offences'.[57] Bestiality (*zoophilia*) was defined as unlawful and intentional sexual relations *per anum* or *per vaginam* by a person with an animal. Proof of penetration was required,[58] but not proof of semen emission. The provisions of the common law crime of bestiality have been repealed and replaced by the provisions of section 68(1)(*b*) of the Sexual Offences Act.[59]

28.3.2 Definition

Section 13 of the Sexual Offences Act defines **bestiality** as follows:

> **A person ('A') who unlawfully and intentionally commits an act—**
> **(*a*) which causes penetration to any extent whatsoever by the genital organs of—**
> **(i) A into or beyond the mouth, genital organs or anus of an animal; or**
> **(ii) an animal into or beyond the mouth, genital organs or anus of A; or**
> **(*b*) of masturbation of an animal, unless such act is committed for scientific reasons or breeding purposes, or of masturbation with an animal, is guilty of the offence of bestiality.**

28.3.3 Elements

The elements of bestiality are:

- unlawfulness
- intent
- an act that causes penetration by genital organs or masturbation of an animal
- an act by a person with an animal.

28.3.3.1 Unlawfulness

Proof of compulsion has been accepted under the common law as excluding unlawfulness.[60]

51 Carpzovius 69.9; *R v Gough and Narroway* supra at 161.
52 Carpzovius 69.9; *R v Gough and Narroway* supra at 161.
53 Voet 48.5.24; Van der Linden 2.7.7; Carpzovius 69; Matthaeus 48.3.6.8; Van der Keessel *Crim* 48.5.29.
54 Carpzovius 69.32.
55 *R v Bourne* (1952) 36 Cr App R 125.
56 *R v Gough and Narroway* supra at 161; *R v V* 1953 (3) SA 314 (A) at 321.
57 Unnatural offences consisted of a residual group of sexual acts that were prohibited by law. The sexual acts could be between persons or between a person and an animal. They included acts such as oral sex between males, but not where a female allowed insertion of a male penis into her mouth. See *R v K and F* 1932 EDL 71 at 73–74. It was never resolved whether lesbianism amounted to an unnatural offence under the common law. Luckily, the current legislative position does not prohibit private consensual behaviour between adults. This position is consistent with the standard set in the case of *National Coalition for Gay and Lesbian Equality v Minister of Justice* supra.
58 *R v Nkani* 1909 NHC 3; *R v Le Fleur* 1927 (1) PH H87 (CPD); *S v P* 1980 (3) SA 782 (NC).
59 Snyman *Criminal Law* 381–382.
60 *R v Bourne* supra. In this case, a man forced his wife to submit to penetration by a dog.

28.3.3.2 Intent

There must be proof of actual or legal intention by the accused. If the conduct occurs by mistake, the accused would not be liable for bestiality.[61]

28.3.3.3 An act that causes penetration by genital organs or masturbation of an animal

Section 13(*a*)(i) of the Sexual Offences Act proscribes any act that causes any penetration by the genital organs of the accused into or beyond the mouth, genital organs or anus of an animal. Section 13(*a*)(ii) proscribes any act that causes any penetration by the genital organs of the animal into or beyond the mouth, genital organs or anus of the accused. Section 13(*b*) proscribes any masturbation of or with an animal unless such act is committed for scientific reasons or breeding purposes. We submit that conduct committed for scientific reasons or breeding purposes should also escape criminal liability because the accused would lack the intention to act unlawfully.

28.3.3.4 An act by a person with an animal

The accused natural person may be a male or a female. The participating animal may be a male or female of its species. Any type of animal would qualify, provided that the penetration or masturbation was physically possible.[62]

28.3.4 Some general comments

Even though there have been suggestions to abrogate the crime of bestiality,[63] the crime remains in force and it has been judged to be constitutional because the *boni mores* consider the prohibited conduct to be reprehensible.[64]

DISCUSSION

Should bestiality remain a specific sexual crime?

The existence of the crime of bestiality in South African law was held to be compatible with the Constitution.[65] Snyman criticised the court's emphasis of the views of society on this matter, where it stated that bestiality is 'unnatural and contrary to good morals'.[66] The author points to the 'inconsistency in the way courts regard and listen to the views of society and 'community perceptions'. The author states:

> In dealing with other constitutional issues, such as the question whether the death sentence is constitutional, community perceptions are not allowed to cloud the issue by overruling what would otherwise be the meaning of a provision in the Constitution. There are arguments favouring the view that the crime's existence is unconstitutional. The crime is seldom committed, and almost always out of the sight of other people. The people who commit the deed are mostly people suffering from some psychological disability and who are in need of help. ...

61 *R v H* 1962 (1) SA 278 (SR).

62 In the case of *R v Brown* (1889) 24 QBD 357 (CCR), the accused was convicted of attempted bestiality because it was physically impossible to penetrate the fowl as he had intended.

63 Labuschagne JMT 'Dekriminalisasie van homo- en soofilie' (1986) 11(2) *Tydskrif vir Regswetenskap* 167; Snyman *Criminal Law* 381–382.

64 *S v M* 2004 (3) SA 680 (O). For support of the judgment, see Carnelley M and Hoctor S 'Bestiality: The paradox of the "paragon of animals"' (2004) 2 *Obiter* 506. For criticism, see Snyman *Criminal Law* 382.

65 *S v M* supra.

66 *S v M* supra at 15 (translated from the original Afrikaans).

> Inasmuch as there may possibly be injury to the animal, such causing of injury can be punished by using the criminal prohibitions dealing with cruelty to animals in the Animal Protection Act 71 of 1962. The court's argument that the animal cannot consent to the deed seems unrealistic, especially if one takes into consideration that millions of animals are slaughtered annually for human consumption, without noticeably affecting the community's perceptions relating to what conduct towards animals is acceptable.[67]

These observations by Snyman serve as a reminder, yet again, about the intricate relationship between law and morality, and about the delicate role of the convictions of the community in legal analysis.

28.4 Sexual acts with a corpse

28.4.1 A brief history

It appears that there was no specific criminal proscription under South African common law for people who were sexually gratified through sexual experiences with the dead, called necrophilia. It is doubtful that the conduct could have been punished as an unnatural offence because the corpse would not qualify as another person or animal.[68] The conduct may have been punishable as the common law crime of *spoliation* or *violation of a dead body*.[69] However, the *actus reus* contemplated for that crime was generally associated with the mutilation[70] of the corpse rather than sexual conduct. Courts have accepted that disrespectful physical *handling* of a corpse should be punished as a violation of the corpse.[71] The Sexual Offences Act repeals the crime of violation of a corpse insofar as it relates to the commission of a sexual act with a corpse.[72]

28.4.2 Definition

Section 14 of the Sexual Offences Act 32 of 2007 provides that a 'person who unlawfully and intentionally commits a sexual act with a human corpse, is guilty of the offence of committing a sexual act with a corpse'.[73]

28.4.3 Elements

The elements of necrophilia are:

- unlawfulness
- intent
- a sexual act
- a sexual act with a human corpse.

67 Snyman Criminal Law 382.
68 *R v Gough and Narroway* supra at 161.
69 The unlawful and intentional physical violation of a dead human body.
70 *R v Kunene and Mazibuko* 1918 JS 321 (NNHC); *R v Munyama* 1968 (3) SA 133 (RA) at 137.
71 *S v Misheck* 1972 (3) SA 131 (R).
72 S 68(1)(*b*) of the Sexual Offences Act.
73 See also Snyman *Criminal Law* 383.

28.4.3.1 Unlawfulness

The crime can be committed by a male or a female. The gender of the corpse is irrelevant. Proof of compulsion may exclude the unlawfulness of the conduct.

28.4.3.2 Intent

There must be proof of actual or legal intention by the accused. If the conduct occurs by mistake, then the accused would not be liable for the crime.

28.4.3.3 A sexual act

The term 'sexual act' is defined in section 1 of the Sexual Offences Act as meaning 'an act of sexual penetration or an act of sexual violation'. Section 1 of the Act also defines 'sexual penetration' as including any act that causes penetration to any extent whatsoever[74] by:[75]

> (*a*) **the genital organs of one person into or beyond the genital organs, anus, or mouth of another person;**
>
> (*b*) **any other part of the body of one person or, any object, including any part of the body of an animal, into or beyond the genital organs or anus of another person; or**
>
> (*c*) **the genital organs of an animal, into or beyond the mouth of another person.**

In the context of sexual penetration involving a corpse, the crime can occur only where the conduct of the accused causes any part of a corpse to penetrate the genital organs or anus of the accused. None of the other forms of sexual penetration will qualify because a corpse does not qualify as a person under South African law. Kissing a corpse on the lips would not fall within the definition of sexual violation because the mouth of the corpse would not qualify as the mouth of another person.[76] The legal status of being a person terminates on death for natural persons.[77]

Sexual violation[78] refers to cases not involving sexual penetration, such as:

---

74 The common law also recognised any degree of penetration by a male's penis into a female's vagina as sufficient for liability. The emission of semen was irrelevant. See *R v Giles* supra at 211–213.

75 Section 1 of the Sexual Offences Act further provides that the term 'sexually penetrates' has a corresponding meaning to the statutory definition of 'sexual penetration'.

76 For a contrary view, see Snyman *Criminal Law* 383.

77 Cronje DSP and Heaton J *Die Suid-Afrikaanse Personereg* 3 ed (2008) 31.

78 Sexual violation is broadly defined in s 1 as including any act that causes:

> (*a*) **direct or indirect contact between the**
>
> (i) **genital organs or anus of one person or, in the case of a female, her breasts, and any part of the body of another person or an animal, or any object, including any object resembling or representing the genital organs or anus of a person or an animal;**
>
> (ii) **mouth of one person and**
>
> (*aa*) **the genital organs or anus of another person or, in the case of a female, her breasts;**
>
> (*bb*) **the mouth of another person;**
>
> (*cc*) **any other part of the body of another person, other than the genital organs or anus of that person or, in the case of a female, her breasts, which could**
>
> (*aaa*) **be used in an act of sexual penetration;**
>
> (*bbb*) **cause sexual arousal or stimulation; or**
>
> (*ccc*) **be sexually aroused or stimulated thereby; or**
>
> (*dd*) **any object resembling the genital organs or anus of a person, and in the case of a female, her breasts, or an animal; or**
>
> (iii) **mouth of the complainant and the genital organs or anus of an animal;**
>
> (*b*) **the masturbation of one person by another person; or**
>
> (*c*) **the insertion of any object resembling or representing the genital organs of a person or animal, into or beyond the mouth of another person, but does not include an act of sexual penetration, and 'sexually violates' has a corresponding meaning.**

- direct or indirect contact involving genital organs and/or prohibited contact with the mouth of another person
- the masturbation of one person by another
- the insertion of any object resembling or representing the genital organs of a person or animal into or beyond the mouth of another person.

In terms of the sexual violation of a corpse, the crime occurs only where there is:
- direct or indirect contact between the genital organs (or female breasts) and the corpse
- direct or indirect contact between the mouth of the accused and any part of the corpse resembling the genital organs or anus of a person
- the insertion of any part of the corpse resembling or representing the genital organs of a person into or beyond the mouth of the accused.

28.4.3.4 A sexual act with a human corpse

The crime could be contemplated only in the context of the corpse being human.

28.4.4 Some general comments

The state has no interest worth protecting through this crime. It is purely a morality crime. However, the crime can be justified on the same grounds as the prohibition against bestiality.

28.5 Rape

28.5.1 A brief history

Roman law originally punished men who unlawfully deprived the patriarch's control over a woman who was in the patriarch's custody through the crime of *raptus*. The deprivation could occur by marrying the woman without the patriarch's consent or having sexual intercourse with her. Roman law also punished conduct that amounted to rape as a species of *stuprum* called *per vim stuprum*.[79] The conduct was also punished as an unlawful application of force under the *Lex Julia de vi publica*.[80] An interesting feature of Roman law was the fact that it proscribed violations perpetrated against males or females.[81] Roman law enforced the rule that boys under the age of 14 could not be held liable for rape.[82]

Roman-Dutch law restricted the proscription to forced violations against women.[83] The female victim was expected to make her case credible by demonstrating her lack of consent by crying out and immediately laying a complaint.[84] A husband could not be liable for raping his wife unless he was judicially separated from her.[85] Violations that took place by force were punishable by death.[86] If there was no force used, but the conduct was offensive because the victim lacked the capacity to consent,[87] or was a widow who was seduced during

79 D 48.5.30.9.

80 D 48.5.30; D 48.6.3.4.

81 D 48.5.30.9; D 48.6.3.4.

82 The rule was based on the premise that only men who had at least reached puberty can commit rape.

83 Voet 48.5.2; Van der Linden 2.7.4; Matthaeus 48.3.5.8.

84 Labuschagne JMT 'Die klagte by seksmisdade' (1978) 11 *De Jure* 18 at 19–20.

85 De Wet and Swanepoel *Strafreg* 263.

86 Voet 48.5.2; Van der Linden 2.7.4; Matthaeus 48.3.5.8.

87 Reasons including being a young girl; being asleep; being intoxicated; having a mental disorder; or being a prisoner, ward or pupil of the accused. Voet 48.5.2.

her mourning period,[88] the crime was punished with a punishment less severe than death. When a woman submitted to intercourse through fear, duress, fraud or unconsciousness, or where she was mentally impaired, it did not constitute rape but the lesser offence of *stuprum violentum*.[89]

English law followed the Roman law rule that boys below the age of 14 were irrebuttably presumed to be incapable of committing the crime of rape.[90] Liability could not be excluded by proof of whether the hymen was ruptured or whether there had been an emission of semen.[91] Only women could be victims of the crime and only men could be liable for the crime. However, women could be liable for aiding and abetting rape.[92]

English law originally enforced capital punishment against rapists who used force to achieve their purpose.[93] The original position of English law provided that where no force was used to induce sexual intercourse, the conduct was not punishable as rape.[94] Eventually, capital punishment was no longer applied to rape cases and gradually the law's attention focused on whether there was consent for the sexual intercourse.[95] Consequently, English law began to recognise unlawful instances other than those involving the use of force.

English law criminalised submission due to threats of force.[96] Fraudulent misrepresentations extinguished consent where they created *error in negotio*[97] or *error in personae*.[98] The victim was deemed to lack the capacity to consent if she was asleep,[99] severely intoxicated[100] or suffering from an intellectual disability.[101] English courts recognised that the youth of the victim may vitiate consent, but they did not see fit to impose a fixed age limit.[102]

English law did not recognise marital rape as a punishable offence even where force was used to induce sexual intercourse.[103] The conduct of the husband remained lawful even if he had a sexually transmitted infection.[104] A husband was only liable for raping his wife if there was a legally recognised agreement or decree of separation between the man and his wife.[105]

English law also required proof of fault in the form of intention. The accused would be acquitted if he could not at least foresee that the complainant was not consenting to the intercourse.

South African common law imported the English approach to the crime of rape by focusing on whether there had been legitimate consent to the sexual intercourse.[106] Consent

88 Voet 48.5.2.
89 *S v Ncanywa* 1992 (2) SA 182 (Ck) at 185.
90 *R v Brimilow* (1840) 2 Mood 122; *R v Groombridge* (1836) 7 C & P 582; *R v Waite* [1892] 2 QB 600.
91 *R v Russen* (1777) 1 East PC 438; *R v Lines* (1844) 1 Car & Kir 393.
92 *R v Ram and Ram* (1893) 17 Cox CC 609.
93 The 1285 Statute of Westminster II 13 Edw 1 c 34.
94 Koh KL 'Consent and responsibility in sexual offences' (1968) *Crim LR* 81 at 88–89.
95 *R v Camplin* 169 ER 163; *R v Fletcher* (1859) 28 LJMC 85.
96 *R v Day* (1841) 9 Car & P 722.
97 *R v Flattery* (1877) 2 QBD 410; *R v Williams* [1923] 1 KB 340.
98 *R v Dee* (1884) 15 Cox CC 579.
99 *R v Mayers* (1872) 12 Cox CC 311; *R v Young* (1878) 14 Cox CC 114.
100 *R v Camplin* supra; *R v Fletcher* (1859) Bell CC 63.
101 *R v Pressy* (1867) 10 Cox CC 635.
102 *R v Harling* [1938] 1 ALL ER 307.
103 *R v Clarence* (1888) 22 QBD 23 at 37, 46 and 51; *R v Clarke* [1949] 2 ALL ER 448.
104 *R v Clarence* supra.
105 *R v Clarke* supra; *R v Miller* [1954] 2 QB 282.
106 *R v Kalil Katib* 1904 ORC 1.

had to be given before penetration took place, but it could not be withdrawn once the act had begun.[107]

South African law accepted that consent could be vitiated using force.[108] Physical resistance has always been accepted to be the best proof of absent consent. The consent could be given expressly or impliedly. However, mere submission could not amount to consent.[109] Duress was considered to vitiate consent where the aggressor was in a position of absolute power over the victim. If the accused intentionally used the complainant's legitimate fear to induce submission to sexual intercourse, the accused would be liable for rape.[110]

South African common law accepted that a woman would lack the capacity to consent if she was asleep (unconscious),[111] under hypnosis,[112] severely intoxicated[113] or suffering from an intellectual disability.[114] South African law also accepted that misrepresentations by the accused, or mistakes made by the victim, amounting to *error in negotio* or *error in personae* vitiated the reality of consent.[115]

South African law also imported the English (or Roman) rule that males under 14 years of age were incapable of committing rape.[116] The presumption that males younger than 14 years could not be liable for rape was eventually repealed by the provisions of section 1 of the Law of Evidence and Criminal Procedure Amendment Act 103 of 1987.

The South African customary norms[117] and the Western norms imported through English law favoured the rule against criminalising marital rape.[118] In *R v Gumede*, the court held that the husband could escape liability for the charge of rape, but (anomalously) that he would be liable for the competent verdict of indecent assault.[119] The rule against punishing marital rape was eventually repealed with section 5 of the Prevention of Family Violence Act 133 of 1993. The provisions of section 56(1) of the Sexual Offences Act ensure that no accused may rely on a marital or other relationship to legitimise his belief in being entitled to induce submission to sexual intercourse.

South African law was like English law in the sense that it accepted that the youth of the victim could vitiate consent. However, South African law differed from the English approach as it created an irrebuttable presumption that girls younger than 12 years of age could not consent.[120]

Originally, South African law allowed evidence to be admitted that related to the complainant's sexual history as a means of discrediting her version of the events. That position was amended by the provisions of section 227 of the Criminal Procedure Act 51 of

107 *R v Handcock* 1925 OPD 147.

108 Labuschagne JMT 'Die klagte by seksmisdade' supra.

109 *R v Swiggelaar* 1950 (1) PH H61 (AD) at 110–111; *S v S* 1971 (2) SA 591 (A) at 596–597. However, if the victim was overwhelmed by her own passions, which resulted from consensual stimulation, she is not a victim of rape. *R v M* 1953 (4) SA 393 (A) at 398.

110 *S v Volschenk* 1968 (2) PH H283 (DCLD); *S v S* 1971 (2) SA 591 (A).

111 *R v C* 1952 (4) SA 117 (O) at 120.

112 *R v K* 1958 (3) SA 420 (A) at 421.

113 *R v K* 1958 (3) SA 420 (A) at 421–426.

114 *R v Kalil Katib* supra; *R v Ryperd Boesman* 1942 (1) PH H63 (HCSWA); *R v S* 1951 (3) SA 209 (C); *R v K* 1951 (4) SA 49 (O).

115 *R v Aaron* 1913 NHC 86; *R v Mahomed Rahanan* 1929 SR 17; *R v Williams* 1931 (1) PH H38 (E); *R v C* 1952 (4) SA 117 (O); *R v K* 1966 (1) SA 366 (RAD).

116 *S v Jeremy* (1895) 12 *Cape LJ* 251 (O); *R v M and others* 1949 (4) SA 831 (A).

117 *R v Mane* 1948 (1) SA 196 (E).

118 *R v Mosago and another* 1935 AD 32 at 34; *R v Gumede* 1946 (1) PH H68 (NPD).

119 *R v Gumede* supra.

120 See *R v Z* 1960 (1) SA 739 (A); *R v S* 1951 (3) SA 209 (C); *R v M and another* 1950 (4) SA 101 (T); *R v K* 1951 (4) SA 49 (O); *R v Socout Ally* 1907 TS 336 where the rule was applied to cases of indecent assault.

1977. Evidence of the complainant's sexual history is only admissible if a court allows it to be admitted on the ground that such evidence is relevant.[121] The application of the cautionary rule in rape cases was also criticised for stereotyping rape victims as being unreliable. The application of the cautionary rule was eventually abolished for sexual offence cases.[122]

South African law maintained the limited definition of sexual intercourse to the penetration *per vaginam* by the natural penis of the accused until the case of *Masiya v Director of Public Prosecutions*[123] was decided in 2007. The Constitutional Court extended the common law definition of rape to include non-consensual anal penetration of females.[124]

However, the common law crime of rape was in desperate need of reform. It was limited to instances where women were the victims and males were the aggressors. This was largely due to the limited definition of sexual intercourse, which precluded males from being victims and excluded other forms of non-consensual sexual penetration.

There were also questionable limitations on circumstances where consent was vitiated. A classic example of such a limitation comes from the requirement that the accused must exercise absolute power over the victim before the use of such power would be considered as duress. The common law did not recognise a threat of loss of employment as sufficient duress to vitiate consent.[125] Fraudulent misrepresentations that did not amount to *error in negotio/personae* were not sufficient to justify a conviction for rape, but they were sufficient to justify a conviction for *crimen iniuria*.[126] Another questionable limitation came in the form of the arbitrary presumption that only girls below the age of 12 years were irrebuttably presumed to be incapable of consenting. Boys were irrebuttably presumed to be incapable of consenting to sex only if they were under the age of seven years. A problematic limitation for the common law was the fact that it did not have a suitable crime for punishing cases of compelled rape.

Legislative reform of South African common law started in 1996 when the South African Law Reform Commission (SALRC)[127] initially investigated sexual offences relating to children. It eventually expanded the investigation into sexual offences generally.[128] The first draft of the bill was tabled as the Criminal Law (Sexual Offences) Amendment Bill of 2003.[129] The bill was then revised and transformed into the Draft Criminal Law (Sexual Offences) Amendment Bill of 2004.[130] The 2004 bill was also revised and tabled for the second time before Parliament in October 2006[131] in the form of the Criminal Law (Sexual Offences and Related Matters) Amendment Bill of 2006.[132] The definition of sexual penetration proposed

121 S 227(2) of the Criminal Procedure Act 51 of 1977.

122 *S v Jackson* 1998 (2) SA 984 (SCA).

123 *Masiya v Director of Public Prosecutions, Pretoria and another (Centre for Applied Legal Studies and another as amici curiae)* 2007 (5) SA 30 (CC).

124 *Masiya v DPP* supra at 45 in the judgment of Justice Nkabinde on behalf of the majority of the court. For critical discussions of this case, see Hoctor S 'Specific crimes' (2007) 20(1) *SACJ* 78; Snyman CR 'Extending the scope of rape: A dangerous precedent' (2007) 124(4) *SALJ* 677; Phelps K 'A dangerous precedent indeed: A response to CR Snyman's note on Masiya' (2008) 125(4) *SALJ* 648; Kemp GP 'Supreme crimes and outrageous acts: Criminalisation and the legality principle – A South African and international perspective' (2010) Stellenbosch University.

125 *S v S* 1971 (2) SA 591 (A).

126 *R v Youngleson* (11) 1948 (1) SA 822 (W).

127 Formerly referred to as the South African Law Commission.

128 South African Law Commission *Sexual Offences Against Children Project 108 Issue Paper 10* (1997); South African Law Commission *Report on Sexual Offences Project 107* (2002).

129 Bill [B50-2003].

130 Presented to the Justice Portfolio Committee on 24 February 2004.

131 On 10 October 2006.

132 Bill [B03-2006].

by the SALRC finally replaced the common law concept of sexual intercourse with the advent of the Criminal Law (Sexual Offences and Related Matters) Amendment Act 32 of 2007.

The objects of the Act include replacing common law crimes, such as rape, with statutory crimes[133] that have an expanded ambit compared to their common law counterparts.[134] Section 68(1)(*b*) of the Sexual Offences Act repeals the common law crime of rape.[135] The new expanded version of the crime is defined in section 3 of the Act.[136]

28.5.2 Definition

Section 3 of the Sexual Offences Act defines **rape** as follows:

> **Any person ('A') who unlawfully and intentionally commits an act of sexual penetration with a complainant ('B'), without the consent of B, is guilty of the offence of rape.**[137]

28.5.3 Elements

The elements of rape are:

- unlawfulness
- intent
- sexual penetration
- the complainant.

28.5.3.1 Unlawfulness

The crime can be committed by a male or a female as section 3 provides that any natural person[138] may be the perpetrator of the crime. Proof of compulsion may exclude the unlawfulness of the conduct. The only other defence that will exclude unlawfulness is consent. Section 1(2) of the Sexual Offences Act specifically provides a definition of consent for the purposes of the crime of rape: '"consent" means voluntary or uncoerced agreement'.[139]

Further, section 1(3) of the Act identifies the circumstances where any alleged consent by the complainant is presumed to lack the requirements of consent as it is defined in section 1(2) of the Act.[140]

---

133 This has procedural implications. See, for instance, *S v Pietersen* [2010] JOL 24862 (ECG) where the court noted that the accused should have been charged with the statutory crime and not the common law crime of rape.

134 S 2(*c*) of the Sexual Offences Act.

135 The fact that the common law crime of rape is repealed does not preclude prosecutions for common law rape committed *before* 16 December 2007 when the relevant sections of the Sexual Offences Act came into operation. See the judgment by the Constitutional Court in *S v Acting Regional Magistrate, Boksburg and another* (2011) 1 SACR 256 GSJ at 19.

136 For some practical insight on the implications of the legislative reform, see Moreland S 'Talking about rape – and why it matters: Adjudicating rape in the Western Cape High Court' (2014) 47 *SACQ* 5–15.

137 For commentary, see Burchell *Principles of Criminal Law* 610–626; Snyman *Criminal Law* 343–358.

138 Burchell *South African Criminal Law and Procedure Vol I* 477 notes that juristic persons (such as corporations) can be guilty of rape as an *accomplice*, for instance by creating or allowing a work environment that facilitates sexual assault.

139 For critical comments, see L du Toit 'From consent to coercive circumstances: Rape law reform on trial' (2012) 28 (3) *SAJHR* 380.

140 Section 1(3) reads as follows:

> **Circumstances in subsection (2) in respect of which a person ('B') (the complainant) does not voluntarily or without coercion agree to an act of sexual penetration, as contemplated in sections 3 and 4, or an act of sexual violation as contemplated in sections 5(1), 6 and 7 or any other act as contemplated in sections 8(1), 8(2), 8(3), 9, 10, 12, 17(1), 17(2), 17(3)(*a*), 19, 20(1), 21(1), 21(2), 21(3) and 22 include, but are not limited to, the following:**
>
> **(*a*) Where B (the complainant) submits or is subjected to such a sexual act as a result of—**
>
> **(i) the use of force or intimidation by A (the accused person) against B, C (a third person) or D (another person) or against the property of B, C or D; or**
>
> **(ii) a threat of harm by A against B, C or D or against the property of B, C or D;**

The circumstances identified in section 1(3)(*a*) relate to circumstances in which the complainant submits because of the use of force, intimidation or threats of harm against the complainant, another person, the property of the complainant or another person. In many ways, the provisions of section 1(3)(*a*) reflect the *ratio* from the case of *R v Swiggelaar*.[141] However, the statutory approach goes well beyond the scope of common law. Common law generally applied to cases where the threat was aimed at the victim directly. The provisions of section 1(3)(*a*) also recognise any harm waged against any other person or property as sufficient to vitiate the reality of the consent of the complainant.

There is no qualification for the type of harm that may vitiate the legitimacy of the consent. Courts must determine whether the threats need to be of immediate harm or whether threats of future harm will suffice. Courts will have to determine whether the threat would still exclude consent if it created a reasonable apprehension of future harm. Such a threat would not amount to common assault by inspiration of fear, but it may be sufficient to exclude consent. The Sexual Offences Act is also silent on whether the complainant should have a reasonable apprehension of harm. Courts will have to decide whether the apprehension of harm must be subjectively or objectively reasonable, or even whether it has to be both subjectively and objectively reasonable.

There is also no qualification for the type of property that may be worthy of inducing the victim to submit. There is no indication as to whether the property needs to be corporeal or incorporeal, or whether it must have patrimonial or non-patrimonial value. The provisions of section 1(3)(*a*) are silent as to whether the value of the property is a material consideration or even whether the value is assessed objectively or subjectively.

Section 1(3)(*b*) relates to cases where the legitimacy of consent is vitiated by the abuse of power or authority. Common law had also recognised these circumstances as excluding the legitimacy of the consent. However, common law limited itself to circumstances where the accused extorted the sexual conduct as a result of a fear of the absolute power or authority of the accused.[142] Common law excluded the threat of loss of employment from the context where the consent would be illegitimate.[143] Courts still retain the discretion to interpret purposively section 1(3)(*b*) to include any abuse of authority or retain the limitation on circumstances where the victim is physically unable to escape the intentions of the accused. Courts may also have to decide whether the alleged authority of the accused was subjectively and/or objectively reasonably capable of inducing the complainant to submit.

(*b*) where there is an abuse of power or authority by A to the extent that B is inhibited from indicating his or her unwillingness or resistance to the sexual act, or unwillingness to participate in such a sexual act;

(*c*) where the sexual act is committed under false pretences or by fraudulent means, including where B is led to believe by A that–

(i) B is committing such a sexual act with a particular person who is in fact a different person; or

(ii) such a sexual act is something other than that act; or

(*d*) where B is incapable in law of appreciating the nature of the sexual act, including where B is, at the time of the commission of such sexual act—

(i) asleep;

(ii) unconscious;

(iii) in an altered state of consciousness, including under the influence of any medicine, drug, alcohol or other substance, to the extent that B's consciousness or judgement is adversely affected;

(iv) a child below the age of 12 years; or

(v) a person who is mentally disabled.

141 *R v Swiggelaar* supra.

142 *S v Volschenk* supra; *S v S* 1971 (2) SA 591 (A).

143 *S v Volschenk* supra; *S v S* supra.

The provisions of section 1(3)(*c*) refer to cases, including misrepresentations by the accused or a mistake induced by the accused, amounting to *error in negotio*[144] or *error in personae*[145] that would vitiate consent. This approach is consistent with the approach of common law.[146] However, the provisions of section 1(3)(*c*) recognise circumstances involving false pretences beyond *error in negotio/personae* without identifying the criteria for other fraudulent circumstances that would vitiate the reality of consent. Traditionally, common law did not recognise misrepresentations of attributes of the accused or the consequences of the intercourse as vitiating the consent. It will be interesting to observe whether courts will dogmatically stick to common law standards or whether they will extend the traditional limitations. It is possible to argue in favour of considering any material misrepresentation as vitiating consent. However, for such arguments, it would be necessary to know whether the misrepresentation was subjectively or objectively material. The problem with using an objective qualification is that it has the potential to undermine the intimate nature of the violation.

The provisions of section 1(3)(*d*) refer to circumstances in which the complainant lacks the capacity to appreciate the nature of the sexual act at the time when the act took place. Such circumstances include those where the complainant is asleep,[147] unconscious,[148] in an altered state of consciousness, including intoxication, to the extent that the cognitive functions are adversely affected,[149] a child below the age of 12 years[150] and a person who is mentally disabled.[151] The circumstances identified in section 1(3)(*d*) are consistent with common law categories for persons who lack the capacity to give legitimate consent. The only notable difference is that the Sexual Offences Act extends the presumption of a 12-year-old girl's incapacity to give valid consent to apply to children of either gender. The presumption is reinforced through the provisions of section 57(1) of the Sexual Offences Act.[152]

28.5.3.2 Intent

The intention of the accused must be to cause sexual penetration unlawfully. The accused would lack intention if there was a legitimate mistake in causing the sexual penetration.[153] The mistake usually refers to whether there was legitimate consent to sexual penetration. The accused must at least have foreseen the possibility that the complainant had not consented and yet proceeded with the sexual penetration regardless.[154]

---

144 S 1(3)(*c*)(ii) of the Sexual Offences Act.

145 S 1(3)(*c*)(i) of the Sexual Offences Act.

146 *R v Aaron* supra; *R v Mahomed Rahanan* supra; *R v Williams* supra; *R v C* 1952 (4) SA 117 (O); *R v K* 1966 (1) SA 366 (SRA).

147 S 1(3)(*d*)(i) of the Sexual Offences Act.

148 S 1(3)(*d*)(ii) of the Sexual Offences Act.

149 S 1(3)(*d*)(iii) of the Sexual Offences Act.

150 S 1(3)(*d*)(iv) of the Sexual Offences Act.

151 S 1(3)(*d*)(v) of the Sexual Offences Act. Further, s 57(2) of the Sexual Offences Act provides that 'notwithstanding anything to the contrary in any law contained, a person who is mentally disabled is incapable of consenting to a sexual act'. See also *S v Chinridze* 2015 (1) SACR 364 (GP).

152 S 57(1) of the Sexual Offences Act provides that 'notwithstanding anything to the contrary in any law contained, a male or female person under the age of 12 years is incapable of consenting to a sexual act'.

153 *R v H* 1962 (1) SA 278 (SR).

154 *R v K* 1958 (3) SA 420 (A) at 421–423; *R v Z* 1960 (1) SA 739 (A) at 743 and 745.

28.5.3.3 Sexual penetration

Section 1 of the Sexual Offences Act defines 'sexual penetration' as including any act that causes penetration to any extent whatsoever[155] by:[156]

> **(*a*) the genital organs of one person into or beyond the genital organs, anus, or mouth of another person;**
>
> **(*b*) any other part of the body of one person or, any object, including any part of the body of an animal, into or beyond the genital organs or anus of another person; or**
>
> **(*c*) the genital organs of an animal, into or beyond the mouth of another person.**

A significant feature of the definition of sexual penetration is that it relates to an act that 'causes penetration'. This is significant because it does not restrict the gender of the accused. This means that a woman may be liable for rape if she causes the penetration of her genital organs by the genital organs of a male victim. Similarly, a woman may be liable for rape if she causes the penetration of another woman's genital organs by using any other part of her body or any object. This is a monumental departure from the previous common law position. Further, the Act defines the term 'genital organs' as including the whole or part of the male or female genital organs, as well as surgically constructed or reconstructed genital organs.[157]

The scope of the current definition of sexual penetration eclipses the scope of what was defined as sexual intercourse in common law. For example, common law did not even recognise oral penetration as part of the *actus reus* for the crime of rape.

Conduct that precedes the act of sexual penetration can form the basis for a charge of attempted rape. In *S v Silo*[158] the court held that the pushing of the complainant onto a bed in her flat by the appellant (who had said that he wanted to have sex with her), the slapping of the complainant in the face, the instruction by the appellant that the complainant remove her gown and underwear, and the attempt by the appellant to fetch a knife to threaten and restrain even further the complainant, are indeed acts in the commencement of the crime of rape. Based on these facts, the court held:

> **An assault, therefore, on a victim before a rape takes place is considered an act of consummation and would constitute attempted rape, if it is clear that the perpetrator inflicted such assault, with the intention to rape, in order to restrain or overcome the resistance of a victim. Much more than that happened in this case.**[159]

The court in *Silo* thus dismissed the appeal against the conviction of attempted rape in contravention of s 55 of the Sexual Offences Act.

28.5.3.4 Complainant

Section 1 of the Sexual Offences Act defines the term 'complainant' as meaning the alleged victim (any person) of a sexual offence.

---

155 Common law also recognised any degree of penetration by a male's penis into a female's vagina as sufficient for liability. The emission of semen was irrelevant. See *R v Giles* 1926 WLD 211 at 211–213.

156 S 1 of the Sexual Offences Act further provides that the term 'sexually penetrates' has a corresponding meaning to the statutory definition of 'sexual penetration'.

157 S 1 of the Sexual Offences Act.

158 *S v Silo* 2016 (2) SACR 259 (WCC).

159 *S v Silo* supra at 25.

28.5.4 Some general comments

The English law rule, established in *R v Clarence*,[160] legitimised the reluctance of South African law to recognise the failure to disclose the possibility of a sexually transmitted infection as vitiating consent. The legislature flirted with the idea of introducing such conduct as vitiating consent. The argument for considering such a failure to disclose the possibility of infection is that it is a material fact for the victim to give legitimate consent.[161] However, the objections were persuasive for abandoning the legislative proposal. They considered that the provisions would unfairly stigmatise those living with HIV.

Nonetheless, the content of section 1(3)(*c*) allows courts to recognise material fraudulent non-disclosures as vitiating the legitimacy of the consent. The provisions of section 1(3)(*c*) provide that consent may be vitiated by fraudulent circumstances *including* those that induce *error in negotio/personae*. The provisions of section 1(3)(*c*) thus afford courts the discretion of recognising other circumstances in which false pretences exclude consent. It may be possible for courts to recognise the failure to disclose the possibility of passing on a sexually transmitted infection as a material and fraudulent non-disclosure in circumstances where the accused ought to disclose such information. The only concern associated with this approach is that the accused may escape liability if he was ignorant of the presence of the infection. It would thus encourage people to avoid getting tested for sexually transmitted infections because knowledge of their status could expose them to liability for an offence.

The South African law approach of considering children younger than 12 years of age to be incapable of giving legitimate consent is subject to questioning. The age of 12 was arbitrarily selected and has only been justified on the ground of public policy. Extending the rule to cover both genders does not detract from the arbitrary nature of selecting 12 years to be the defining age at which a child may consent to sexual activity. It takes no consideration of whether there is any legitimate difference in *intellectus* or *judicium* of children between the ages of 10 and 13 years. The provisions in Chapter 3 of the Sexual Offences Act offer more clarity on dealing with sexual crimes against children. The arbitrary rule for children under 12 years of age should have more legitimate considerations that must justify why 13-year-old children should not be given the benefit of an irrebuttable presumption of incapacity to consent. Reliance on the Roman law excuse of requiring a child to have at least reached puberty does not offer any support for the age of 12 years. Roman, Roman-Dutch, English and South African law (initially) strictly maintained the rule of a boy younger than 14 years of age being unable to commit rape. Lowering the age to 12 years in the name of equality does not sufficiently address the problem created by the arbitrary selection of the age of 12.

Originally, common law would not accept a threat of loss of employment to be severe enough to vitiate consent.[162] However, it will be interesting to observe whether courts will eventually overcome this limitation by relying on the provisions of section 1(3)(*b*) of the Sexual Offences Act and recognising it as an abuse of power that is capable of vitiating the legitimacy of consent. This would be consistent with one of the objects of the Act, which is to replace common law crimes, such as rape, with statutory crimes that have an expanded ambit compared to their common law counterparts.[163]

If the accused was under the mistaken but honest belief that he was entitled to compel the complainant to submit to intercourse, the accused lacks *mens rea*. This principle may

160 *R v Clarence* (1888) 22 QBD 23.

161 See also Snyman *Criminal Law* 366–367.

162 *S v Volschenk* supra; *S v S* 1971 (2) SA 591 (A).

163 S 2(*c*) of the Sexual Offences Act.

have been raised in cases involving marital rape. There have also been cases where accused persons were under the mistaken belief that their conduct was justified by custom.[164] One of the mistakes that courts recognised was the thinking that custom would legitimise the reprehensible conduct.[165] The provisions of section 56(1) of the Sexual Offences Act ensure that no accused person may rely on a marital or other relationship to justify rape.

28.6 Compelled rape

28.6.1 A brief history

Under South African common law, necessity (compulsion) excluded the unlawful nature of a case of rape. However, the person who had unlawfully compelled others to participate in an act of sexual intercourse was liable for rape. The accused had to be the man who had vaginally penetrated the victim with his penis. The person who was responsible for causing the unlawful intercourse was liable for assault with intent to do grievous bodily harm or at least extortion. Fortunately, the introduction of the Sexual Offences Act heralded the creation of the new offence of compelled rape.[166]

28.6.2 Definition

Section 4 of the Sexual Offences Act defines **compelled rape** as follows:

> **Any person ('A') who unlawfully and intentionally compels a third person ('C'), without the consent of C, to commit an act of sexual penetration with a complainant ('B'), without the consent of B, is guilty of the offence of compelled rape.**

28.6.3 Elements

The elements of compelled rape are:

- unlawfulness
- intent
- compelling a third person
- sexual penetration
- the complainant.

28.6.3.1 Unlawfulness

The crime can be committed by a male or a female as section 4 provides that any natural person may be the perpetrator of the crime. Proof of compulsion on the part of the accused may exclude the unlawfulness of his conduct.

The accused would apparently escape liability if the participants of the sexual penetration act had consented to his use of compulsion to induce sexual penetration between the participants.

For the crime defined in section 4 of the Act, consent is defined by the provisions of section 1(2). Consent for the statutory crime of compelled rape is absent in the context of the circumstances identified in section 1(3) of the Act. The contents of sections 1(2) and 1(3) have already been discussed under the element of unlawfulness in the crime of rape.

---

164 *R v Mane* supra; *R v Nqawuzana* 1912 NHC 5; *R v Nomandindi Mcunu* 1912 NHC 7.

165 *R v Mane* supra at 199.

166 For commentary, see Snyman *Criminal Law* 358–360; Burchell *Principles of Criminal Law* 617–618.

28.6.3.2 Intent

The intention of the accused must be to compel unlawfully a third person and the complainant to engage in sexual penetration. The state bears the onus of proving that the accused had actual or legal intention. The state must prove that the accused intended to compel the third person to penetrate sexually the complainant, knowing or foreseeing that neither the complainant nor the third person had legitimately consented, and yet carried on regardless.

28.6.3.3 Compelling a third person

The term 'third person' describes a person other than the accused or the complainant. The conduct of the third person must meet the requirements for the justification of necessity as proof that he was acting out of compulsion. Thus, the accused must have been threatening a worthy legal interest,[167] posing a threat that had either commenced or was imminent or posing a threat that was not due to the complicit conduct of the third person. Further, the conduct of the third person must have been necessary and reasonable under the circumstances. Courts examine these factors objectively.

28.6.3.4 Sexual penetration

The meaning of the term 'sexual penetration' for the purpose of the Sexual Offences Act has already been discussed under the corresponding element for the crime of rape. The accused must be responsible for causing the sexual penetration to occur. The sexual penetration must take place between the third person and the complainant. The accused has to be both the factual and legal cause of the sexual penetration before he is liable for the crime defined in section 4 of the Act.

28.6.3.5 The complainant

The meaning of the term 'complainant' for the purpose of the Act has already been discussed under the corresponding element for the crime of rape.

28.7 Sexual assault

28.7.1 A brief history

South African common law was inspired by the English approach of criminalising indecent assault.[168] South African common law punished indecent assault as an independent substantive crime.[169] Legislative recognition of the substantive crime of indecent assault was illustrated through instruments including the Criminal Procedure and Evidence Act 31 of 1917.[170] This legislative trend was reinforced through the current Criminal Procedure Act 51 of 1977.[171]

---

167 Worthy legal interests have generally been accepted to include life, bodily integrity and property. A person may invoke the defence of necessity to protect the worthy legal interests of another. Purely economic interests cannot be used to invoke the defence of necessity. See *R v Canestra* 1951 (2) SA 317 (A).

168 For example, s 52 of the English statute called the Offences Against the Person Act of 1861 (24 & 25 Vict C 100).

169 *R v August* (1887–1888) 5 SC 216; *R v Usigutshwana* (1896) 17 NLR 112; *R v Socout Ally* supra; *R v Petersen* 1910 TS 859; *R v Sideropoulos* 1910 CPD 15; *R v Abrahams* 1918 CPD 590; *R v Jacob* 1920 SWA 9; *R v Taylor* 1927 CPD 16.

170 For example, s 233 recognised indecent assault as a competent verdict in appropriate cases.

171 For example, ss 261, 266, 268 and 269 repealed of the Criminal Procedure Act.

Indecent assault was defined under common law as an assault that is itself indecent in character.[172] The crime had two basic elements: an assault and an indecent character. The onus was on the state to prove that the accused intended to assault the victim unlawfully and to assault the victim indecently.[173]

The unlawfulness of the conduct could be excluded only by legitimate consent from the victim. Girls below the age of 12 years and boys under the age of seven years were irrebuttably presumed to lack the capacity to give valid consent.[174] There was no presumption protecting a husband against a charge of indecently assaulting his wife.[175] However, courts retained the discretion of not recognising consent as a defence in circumstances that offended public policy.[176] Consent could also be vitiated by youth[177] or duress.[178]

Mere touching was sufficient to amount to using force.[179] Originally, in *R v Abrahams*, the court held that the indecent assault could be recognised only in the context of an indecent application of actual physical force.[180] The court held that threats were insufficient for liability for indecent assault.[181] Nor was it sufficient that the accused had touched himself indecently.[182] However, subsequent cases accepted that an assault could be recognised as indecent through an assault by inspiration of fear.[183]

The *locus classicus* for this crime has been *R v Abrahams*,[184] which has been consistently followed by the courts.[185] The *ratio decidendi* from the majority decision in *Abrahams* emphasises the importance of contact with the private parts of the victim for the contact to qualify as indecent.[186] It was enough for the victim to experience force indirectly through clothing in cases where the accused was making direct contact with the clothing of the victim.[187] The accused would remain liable even if his hand was rebuffed while it was en route to the victim's private parts.[188] English law has held that a mere invitation to engage in an indecent act would not amount to an assault by inspiration of fear because it would not arouse the impression that the victim would be overwhelmed by force.[189]

In *Abrahams*, the dissenting judgment was written by Searle J.[190] The dissenting judgment was ready to accept that indecent language that took the form of common assault by inspiration of fear should be punished as indecent assault. Searle J held that it was sufficient

---

172 *R v Abrahams* supra.
173 *S v Muvhaki* 1985 (4) SA 317 (ZH) at 319.
174 *R v Socout Ally* supra; *R v Sideropoulos* supra; *R v Sagaye* 1932 NPD 236.
175 *R v Gumede* supra.
176 English law recognised this principle in the case of *R v Donovan* [1934] 2 KB 498. South African common law followed the same principle in cases such as *R v McCoy* 1953 (2) SA 4 (SR); *S v Sikunyana and others* 1961 (3) SA 549 (E); *S v D* 1963 (3) SA 263 (E); *S v Kock* 2003 (2) SACR 5 (SCA).
177 *S v Marx* 1962 (1) SA 848 (N); *R v Phiri* 1963 R & N 395 (SR).
178 *R v McCoy* supra.
179 *R v M* 1961 (2) SA 60 (O) at 61–63.
180 *R v Abrahams* supra at 593.
181 *R v Abrahams* supra.
182 *R v Abrahams* supra.
183 For example, in *R v Z* 1957 (2) PH H240 (NPD) at 434, Broome JP upheld a conviction for indecent assault by deciding that a verbal threat would amount to indecent assault where it was aimed at the private parts of the victim (even if it was through the victim's clothing). See also *S v Kock* supra at 9.
184 *R v Abrahams* supra.
185 For example, *R v Hart* 1931 OPD 102; *R v Herbst* 1942 AD 434; *R v Jeremiah* 1947 (2) SA 938 (SR); *R v Motsoakoe and another* 1952 (1) PH H26 (OPD).
186 *R v Abrahams* supra at 593.
187 *R v Curtis* 1926 CPD 385 at 389–390; *R v M* 1947 (4) SA 489 (N) at 490.
188 *R v Curtis* supra; *R v Barden* 1942 JS 117 (T).
189 *R v Burrows* [1952] 1 ALL ER 58; *Fairclough v Whipp* [1951] 2 ALL ER 834.
190 *R v Abrahams* supra at 597–598.

for the state to prove that the indecency was so closely connected to the physical violence that it formed a material part of the offensive conduct. The learned judge did concede that proof of actual indecent physical handling is more readily admissible and persuasive. However, Searle J maintained that where there is sufficient proof of indecency connected to the conduct of the accused, he should not escape by merely relying on the absence of actual physical handling.

The dissenting judgment from *Abrahams* found favour with Ackermann J in *S v F*.[191] Ackermann J had convincing arguments for criminalising touching that was not directed at the private parts of the victim. Ackermann J advocated focusing on whether it was the intention of the accused to touch the victim indecently and whether that intention was communicated to the victim. Further, Ackermann J held that this intention could be communicated by words, conduct or implication. Based on the reasoning of Ackermann J, the accused would be liable for indecent assault if the state could prove beyond reasonable doubt that the accused communicated to the victim that he was obtaining sexual gratification or was enjoying the stimulation, and that this was his intention.

The approach advocated by Ackermann J received support among legal academics.[192] However, courts preferred the approach advocated in the majority decision in *Abrahams*.[193] The crime of indecent assault was eventually repealed by the provisions of section 68(1)(*b*) of the Sexual Offences Act. The crime of indecent assault has been replaced with the new statutory crime of sexual assault, defined in section 5 of the Sexual Offences Act. A notable feature of section 5 is that it defines two separate, but related crimes. One common feature between the crime created by section 5(1) and the crime created by section 5(2) is the element of sexual violation. Otherwise, each crime has its own distinct *actus reus* and its own distinctive requirements for proof of *mens rea*.[194]

The legislature essentially resolved the conflict between the approach favoured by the majority decision in *R v Abrahams* and the approach favoured in *S v F*, and the dissenting judgment in *R v Abrahams*. The simple solution was to create two separate forms of the crime of sexual assault:

- Section 5(1) favours the approach advocated by the majority decision in *R v Abrahams* in the sense that it relates to an application of force that causes a sexual violation.
- Section 5(2) favours the approach advocated by Ackermann J and Searle J. Section 5(2) criminalises inspiring a belief that the complainant will be sexually violated.

28.7.2 Definition

Section 5 of the Sexual Offences Act defines **sexual assault** as follows:

> **(1) A person ('A') who unlawfully and intentionally sexually violates a complainant ('B'), without the consent of B, is guilty of the offence of sexual assault.**
>
> **(2) A person ('A') who unlawfully and intentionally inspires the belief in a complainant ('B') that B will be sexually violated, is guilty of the offence of sexual assault.**

191 *S v F en 'n ander* 1982 (2) SA 580 (T).
192 See, for instance, Snyman *Criminal Law* (2002) 437.
193 The SCA applied the approach advocated by the majority decision in *R v Abrahams* in *S v Kock* supra.
194 Snyman *Criminal Law* 360–368; Burchell *Principles of Criminal Law* 602–609.

28.7.3 Elements of sexual assault as defined in section 5(1)

The elements of sexual assault as defined in section 5(1) are:

- unlawfulness
- intent
- an act of sexual violation
- the complainant.

28.7.3.1 Unlawfulness

The crime can be committed by a natural person who is either a male or a female. Proof of compulsion may exclude the unlawfulness of the conduct.

For the crime defined in section 5(1) of the Sexual Offences Act, consent is defined by the provisions of section 1(2). Consent for the statutory crime of compelled rape is absent in the context of the circumstances identified in section 1(3) of the Act. The contents of sections 1(2) and 1(3) have already been discussed under the element of unlawfulness in the crime of rape.

28.7.3.2 Intent

The intention of the accused must be to cause sexual violation unlawfully without the consent of the complainant. He would lack intention if there was a legitimate mistake in causing the sexual violation. The mistake may refer to whether there was legitimate consent to sexual violation. The accused must at least foresee the possibility that the complainant is not consenting and proceed with the sexual violation regardless.

The state bears the onus of proving that the accused had actual or legal intention to perpetrate the conduct. The state must prove that the accused intended to apply force unlawfully to violate the complainant sexually without the consent of the complainant. The accused must at least know or foresee that using force will sexually violate the complainant and know or foresee that the complainant had not legitimately consented, and yet proceeded with the sexual violation regardless.

28.7.3.3 Sexual violation

Sexual violation[195] refers to cases that do not involve sexual penetration. The statutory definition of sexual violation includes direct or indirect contact between the genital organs

---

195 'Sexual violation' is broadly defined in s 1 as including any act that causes:

(*a*) direct or indirect contact between the

(i) genital organs or anus of one person or, in the case of a female, her breasts, and any part of the body of another person or an animal, or any object, including any object resembling or representing the genital organs or anus of a person or an animal;

(ii) mouth of one person and

(*aa*) the genital organs or anus of another person or, in the case of a female, her breasts;

(*bb*) the mouth of another person;

(*cc*) any other part of the body of another person, other than the genital organs or anus of that person or, in the case of a female, her breasts, which could

(*aaa*) be used in an act of sexual penetration;

(*bbb*) cause sexual arousal or stimulation; or

(*ccc*) be sexually aroused or stimulated thereby; or

(*dd*) any object resembling the genital organs or anus of a person, and in the case of a female, her breasts, or an animal; or

(iii) the mouth of the complainant and the genital organs or anus of an animal;

(*b*) the masturbation of one person by another person; or

(*c*) the insertion of any object resembling or representing the genital organs of a person or animal, into or beyond the mouth of another person, but does not include an act of sexual penetration, and 'sexually violates' has a corresponding meaning.

(or anus of another person or a female's breasts) and any other object or part of the body of another person. Essentially, sexual violation refers to prohibited forms of sexual conduct that do not amount to sexual penetration.

The definition of sexual violation also includes direct or indirect contact between the mouth of a person and:

- the mouth of another person
- any object resembling the genital organs (or anus of another person or a female's breasts) of another person
- any part of another person's body that can be used for sexual penetration, stimulation or arousal
- the mouth of the complainant and the genital organs (or anus) of an animal without causing sexual penetration.

Sexual violation also includes the masturbation of one person by another person, or the insertion of any object resembling or representing the genital organs of a person or animal into or beyond the mouth of another person.

28.7.3.4 The complainant

The meaning of the term 'complainant' for the purpose of the Sexual Offences Act has already been discussed under the corresponding element for the crime of rape.

28.7.4 Elements of sexual assault as defined in section 5(2)

The elements of sexual assault as defined in section 5(2) are:

- unlawfulness
- intent
- inspiring a belief
- an act of sexual violation
- the complainant.

28.7.4.1 Unlawfulness

The crime can be committed by a male or a female as section 5(2) provides that any natural person may be the perpetrator of the crime. Proof of compulsion on the part of the accused may exclude the unlawfulness of his conduct.

One of the most interesting features about the crime created by section 5(2) of the Sexual Offences Act is that consent is not available as a justification for the accused's conduct. The definition of the crime of section 5(2) does not include content that recognises consent as a means of justifying the conduct of the accused. Further, section 1(2) does not include section 5(2) as a crime where the statutory definition of consent can be used.[196] This feature is particularly interesting because section 5(2) becomes the first sexual crime that cannot be justified by the consent of the victim.

28.7.4.2 Intent

The intention of the accused must be to inspire unlawfully a belief that the complainant will be sexually violated. The accused would lack intention if there was a legitimate mistake in inspiring this belief. The mistake on the part of the accused must refer to his perception of

196 S 1(2) indicates that the definition of consent can only be used for the purposes of ss 3, 4, 5(1), 6, 7, 8(1), 8(2), 8(3), 9, 10, 12, 17(1), 17(2), 17(3)(*a*), 19, 20(1), 21(1), 21(2), 21(3) and 22.

the lawfulness of his conduct. The accused must at least foresee the possibility that his conduct is unlawful and yet proceed with the sexual violation regardless. This creates a unique problem for the crime defined in section 5(2). Typically, the lawfulness of a sexual crime is determined by referring to the consent of the complainant. Since consent is not available as a justification for the conduct impugned in section 5(2), it is not clear when the accused may be under the impression that he is acting lawfully when he inspires the belief that the complainant will be sexually violated.

The state bears the onus of proving that the accused had actual or legal intention to perpetrate the conduct. It must prove that the accused intended to inspire a belief unlawfully that the complainant will be sexually violated. The accused must at least know or foresee that he is unlawfully inspiring this belief, and yet proceed with the sexual violation regardless.

28.7.4.3 Inspiring a belief

Common law requirements for an assault by inspiring belief appear to be apposite in the context of the crime of sexual violation. The three core requirements for an assault by inspiring fear have been identified as imminent harm, present ability to carry out the threat and a reasonable apprehension of harm.[197]

28.7.4.4 Sexual violation

The meaning of 'sexual violation' for the purpose of the Sexual Offences Act has already been discussed under the corresponding element for the crime defined in section 5(1) of the Act.

28.7.4.5 The complainant

The meaning of 'complainant' for the purpose of the Act has already been discussed under the corresponding element for the crime of rape.

28.7.5 Some general comments

Many eminent jurists have favoured the approach advocated by Searle J in his dissenting judgment in *R v Abrahams*.[198] One of the most notable supporters of this approach is Ackermann J in *S v F*.[199] We submit that the argument advocated by Searle J is correct in principle and logic. However, the judge did also concede that proving the liability of the accused beyond reasonable doubt is easier in cases where there is actual physical handling. Trying to prove a case for liability beyond reasonable doubt, based purely on the impression of a victim, which can only be proved by the victim's *ipse dixit*, should be a daunting challenge for any prosecutor. It stands to reason that proving liability beyond reasonable doubt is therefore an extreme disadvantage for the prosecution.

If the crime created by section 5(2) only punishes threats of an imminent sexual violation, it would ignore victims who suffered from an inspiration that they will be intentionally and unlawfully sexually violated solely on the ground that the accused was threatening to perpetrate the act at a later stage. This consequence is based on a principle that is consistent with the common law crime of sexual assault. However, it is questionable whether this is consistent with the intention of the legislature when they omitted any reference to an

197 In *R v Sibanyone* 1940 JS 40 (T), the accused advanced towards the complainant with his finger pointed at her while he threatened her. He said he was going away to see someone and if the complainant did not drive her family from the property, he would come back and kill them.

198 *R v Abrahams* supra at 597–598.

199 *S v F en 'n ander* 1982 (2) SA 580 (T).

imminent sexual violation in the definition in section 5(2). Perhaps the legislature intended to extend the scope of the crime to prohibit any threat to inspire unlawfully and intentionally a belief that the complainant will be sexually violated by the accused. Perhaps this is the reason why the legislature defined the crime as such. However, courts will decide whether it is necessary for the threat to refer to imminent harm.

There is an overlap between this crime and the common law crime of *crimen iniuria*, which has not been repealed by the provisions of section 68(1)(*b*) of the Sexual Offences Act.[200] The crime of *crimen iniuria* punishes invitations to engage in sexual impropriety,[201] and abusive or degrading conduct or communications.[202] One notable advantage for the crime of *crimen iniuria* is that it does not have a requirement for the threatened harm to occur immediately. *Crimen iniuria* has been a competent verdict for cases that involve indecent behaviour.[203]

28.8 Compelled sexual assault

28.8.1 Definition

Section 6 of the Sexual Offences Act defines 'compelled sexual assault' as follows:[204]

> **A person ('A') who unlawfully and intentionally compels a third person ('C'), without the consent of C, to commit an act of sexual violation with a complainant ('B'), without the consent of B, is guilty of the offence of compelled sexual assault.**

28.8.2 Elements

The elements of compelled sexual assault are:

- unlawfulness
- intent
- compelling a third person
- sexual violation
- the complainant.

28.8.2.1 Unlawfulness

The crime can be committed by a male or a female as section 6 provides that any natural person may be the perpetrator of the crime. Proof of compulsion on the part of the accused may exclude the unlawfulness of his conduct.

The accused would apparently escape liability if the participants of the act of sexual violation had consented to his use of compulsion to induce sexual violation between the participants. For the crime defined in section 6 of the Sexual Offences Act, consent is defined by the provisions of section 1(2). Consent for the statutory crime of compelled sexual assault is absent in the context of the circumstances identified in section 1(3) of the Act. The contents of sections 1(2) and 1(3) have already been discussed under the element of unlawfulness in the crime of rape.

---

200 For commentary, see Watney, M '*Crimen iniuria*: Its role vis-à-vis sexual-offences legislation' (2017) 2 *TSAR* 405.

201 *R v E* 1954 (4) SA 501 (SR); *S v K* 1975 (3) SA 446 (N).

202 *R v Walton* 1958 (3) SA 693 (SR); *R v Dibden* 1967 (1) PH H137 (RAD); *S v Brereton* 1971 (1) SA 489 (RA).

203 *R v X and Y* 1938 EDL 30; *R v Youngleson* supra; *R v S* 1948 (4) SA 419 (GW). See also *S v Ieperen* 2017 (1) SACR 226 (WCC).

204 For commentary, see Snyman *Criminal Law* 368–369.

28.8.2.2 Intent

The intention of the accused must be to compel unlawfully a third person and the complainant to engage in sexual violation. The state bears the onus of proving that the accused had actual or legal intention to perpetrate the conduct. The state must prove that the accused intended to compel the third person to perform an act of sexual violation with the complainant knowing or foreseeing that neither the complainant nor the third person had legitimately consented, and yet carried on regardless.

28.8.2.3 Compelling a third person

The term 'third person' refers to a person other than the accused or the complainant. The conduct of the third person must meet the requirements for the justification of necessity as proof that the third person was acting out of compulsion. Thus, the accused must have been threatening a worthy legal interest,[205] posing a threat that had either commenced or was imminent, or posing a threat that was not due to the complicit conduct of the third person. Further, the conduct of the third person must have been necessary and reasonable under the circumstances. Courts examine these factors objectively.

28.8.2.4 Sexual violation

The statutory meaning of 'sexual violation' has already been discussed under the corresponding element for the crime of sexual assault.

28.8.2.5 The complainant

The meaning of the term 'complainant' for the purpose of the Act has already been discussed under the corresponding element for the crime of rape.

28.8.3 Some general comments

There is an overlap between this crime and the common law crime of *crimen iniuria,*[206] which has not been repealed by the provisions of section 68(1)(*b*) of the Sexual Offences Act. The crime of *crimen iniuria* punishes abusive or degrading conduct or communications.[207] For example, a farmer was held liable for *crimen iniuria* after he compelled women to strip and walk before farm labourers after he had caught the women stealing maize.[208]

28.9 Compelled self-sexual assault

28.9.1 Definition

Section 7 of the Sexual Offences Act defines 'compelled self-sexual assault' as follows:

> **A person ('A') who unlawfully and intentionally compels a complainant ('B'), without the consent of B, to—**
>
> **(*a*) engage in—**
>
> **(i) masturbation;**

---

205 Worthy legal interests have been generally accepted to include life, bodily integrity and property. A person may invoke the defence of necessity for protecting the worthy legal interests of another. Purely economic interests cannot be used to invoke the defence of necessity. *R v Canestra* supra.

206 See also section 27.10.

207 *R v Walton* supra; *R v Dibden* supra; *S v Brereton* supra.

208 *S v Brereton* supra.

(ii) **any form of arousal or stimulation of a sexual nature of the female breasts; or**

(iii) **sexually suggestive or lewd acts, with B himself or herself;**

(*b*) **engage in any act which has or may have the effect of sexually arousing or sexually degrading B; or**

(*c*) **cause B to penetrate in any manner whatsoever his or her own genital organs or anus, is guilty of the offence of compelled self-sexual assault.**

28.9.2 Elements

The elements of compelled self-sexual assault are:

- unlawfulness
- intent
- the complainant
- compelling the complainant
- engaging in conduct set out in section 7.

28.9.2.1 Unlawfulness

The crime can be committed by a male or a female as section 7 provides that any natural person may be the perpetrator of the crime. For the crime defined in section 7 of the Sexual Offences Act, consent is defined by the provisions of section 1(2). Consent for the statutory crime of compelled self-sexual assault is absent in the context of the circumstances identified in section 1(3) of the Act. The contents of sections 1(2) and 1(3) have already been discussed under the element of unlawfulness in the crime of rape.

28.9.2.2 Intent

The intention of the accused must be to compel unlawfully the complainant to engage in conduct set out in section 7 of the Sexual Offences Act. The state bears the onus of proving that the accused had actual or legal intention to perpetrate the conduct. The state must prove that the accused intended to compel the complainant to perform an act listed in section 7, knowing or foreseeing that the complainant had not legitimately consented, and yet carried on regardless.

28.9.2.3 The complainant

The meaning of the term 'complainant' for the purpose of the Act has already been discussed under the corresponding element for the crime of rape.

28.9.2.4 Compelling the complainant

The conduct of the complainant must meet the requirements for the justification of necessity as proof that the complainant was acting out of compulsion. Thus, the accused must have been threatening a worthy legal interest,[209] posing a threat that had either commenced or was imminent or posing a threat that was not due to the complicit conduct of the complainant. Further, the conduct of the complainant must have been necessary and reasonable under the circumstances. Courts examine these factors objectively.

---

209 Worthy legal interests have been generally accepted to include life, bodily integrity and property. A person may invoke the defence of necessity for protecting the worthy legal interests of another. Purely economic interests cannot be used to invoke the defence of necessity. *R v Canestra* supra.

28.9.2.5 Engaging in conduct set out in section 7

Section 7 proscribes conduct in three categories.[210] The categories are not mutually exclusive. The prohibited conduct includes conduct that involves penetration of genital organs[211] or the anus of a person, but the prohibition extends beyond acts of penetration.

The first category of prohibited conduct relates to cases where the complainant is compelled to engage in conduct including lewd or sexually suggestive acts, self-masturbation, or any sexual arousal or stimulation of a female's breasts.[212]

The second category is a general prohibition against any conduct that compels a complainant to engage in conduct that has the effect of sexually arousing or degrading the complainant.

The last category prohibits any conduct that compels the complainant to penetrate the complainant's own genital organs or anus. There is no limitation on what the complainant may be forced to use to complete the penetration. The prohibition applies to the use of any object that the complainant may be compelled to use for completing the penetration of the complainant's genital organs or anus.

28.9.3 Some general comments

The second category of prohibited conduct listed in section 7 of the Sexual Offences Act is very general. The Act clearly prohibits conduct that sexually arouses or degrades the complainant. It is not clear what the consequence would be if the accused intended to induce sexual arousal, but the complainant is not actually aroused. In principle, the accused should escape liability if his conduct did not achieve the intended arousal.

The conduct of the accused may perhaps still be punished if it is sexually suggestive or lewd. However, section 7 does not offer guidance as to which conduct will then amount to sexually suggestive or lewd acts. We submit that this is a highly subjective qualification, which may be difficult to prove objectively beyond reasonable doubt.

Further, section 7 does not indicate whose perceptions will be referred to for qualifying the conduct as degrading, lewd or sexually suggestive. The Act does not indicate whether it should be the victim who finds the conduct degrading or whether the conduct should be objectively qualified as degrading. What would be the consequence if the victim subjectively found the conduct to be degrading but the court does not consider it to be?

There is an overlap between this crime and the common law crime of *crimen iniuria*, which has not been repealed by the provisions of section 68(1)(*b*) of the Sexual Offences Act. The crime of *crimen iniuria* also punishes abusive or degrading conduct or communication.[213]

---

210 S 7 of the Sexual Offences Act lists the following prohibited conduct:

(*a*) engage in—

(i) masturbation;

(ii) any form of arousal or stimulation of a sexual nature of the female breasts; or

(iii) sexually suggestive or lewd acts, with B himself or herself;

(*b*) engage in any act which has or may have the effect of sexually arousing or sexually degrading B; or

(*c*) cause B to penetrate in any manner whatsoever his or her own genital organs or anus.

211 As they are defined in s 1 of the Sexual Offences Act.

212 In cases where the complainant is a female.

213 *R v Walton* supra; *R v Dibden* supra; *S v Brereton* supra.

28.10 Compelled witnessing of sexual offences (adults)

28.10.1 A brief history

Various forms of immoral conduct, including public indecency, were punished under Roman-Dutch law as *crimina extraordinaria*.[214] English law also punished indecent exposure,[215] and indecent or obscene exhibitions.[216]

South African law was confirmed to punish the crime of public indecency in *R v Marais*[217] for reasons including the fact that the crime had been punished by the Cape Court and under English law. The crime was originally defined as 'such conduct in public as from its very nature must tend to the depravement of the morals of others'.[218] In *S v F*, the court defined the crime as unlawfully, intentionally and publicly committing an act that tends to deprave the morals of others or which outrages the public's sense of decency and propriety.[219] It was not necessary for the conduct of the accused to occur in a public place. All that was required was for the accused's conduct to be audible or visible to members of the public, regardless of whether they were in a public[220] or a private place.[221] Even if the act took place in a public place, it would not amount to public indecency if it was improbable that members of the public were aware of it.[222] Fornication was held to be an act that could qualify as public indecency.[223]

The provisions of section 8 of the Sexual Offences Act codify and clearly define those elements of public indecency that are infringed when a person older than 18 years of age is exposed to self-masturbation or a sexual offence or act against his will. The other significant difference between the crime proscribed in section 8 and the common law crime of public indecency refers to the publicity of the offensive conduct. The crime created by section 8 has no requirement for the indecent conduct to take place publicly.[224]

28.10.2 Definition

Section 8 of the Sexual Offences Act defines 'compelled witnessing of sexual offences' as follows:

> **(1) A person ('A') who unlawfully and intentionally, whether for the sexual gratification of A or of a third person ('C') or not, compels or causes a complainant 18 years or older ('B'), without the consent of B, to be in the presence of or watch A or C while he, she or they commit a sexual offence, is guilty of the offence of compelling or causing a person 18 years or older to witness a sexual offence.**
>
> **(2) A person ('A') who unlawfully and intentionally, whether for the sexual gratification of A or of a third person ('C') or not, compels or causes a complainant 18 years or older ('B'), without the consent of B, to be in the presence of or watch –**
>
> **(*a*) A while he or she engages in a sexual act with C or another person ('D'); or**
>
> **(*b*) C while he or she engages in a sexual act with D, is guilty of the offence of compelling or causing a person 18 years or older to witness a sexual act.**

214 Voet D 47.11.2.

215 *R v Sedley* (1663) 1 Keb 620.

216 *R v Grey* (1864) 4 F & F 73; *R v Sanders* (1875) 1 QBD 15.

217 *R v Marais* (1888–1889) 6 SC 367.

218 *R v Marais* supra at 368.

219 *S v F* 1977 (2) SA 1 (T) at 4.

220 *R v Marais* supra; *R v B* 1955 (3) SA 494 (D).

221 *R v B* 1955 (3) SA 494 (D).

222 *R v Arends* 1946 NPD 441.

223 *R v Arends* supra; *R v B and C* 1949 (2) SA 582 (T), 1949 (2) PH H205 (AD).

224 See further, Burchell *Principles of Criminal Law* 633-634; Snyman *Criminal Law* 371–372.

(3) **A person ('A') who unlawfully and intentionally, whether for the sexual gratification of A or of a third person ('C') or not, compels or causes a complainant 18 years or older ('B'), without the consent of B, to be in the presence of or watch A or C while he or she engages in an act of self-masturbation, is guilty of the offence of compelling or causing a person 18 years or older to witness self-masturbation.**

28.10.3 Elements

The elements of compelled witnessing of sexual offences (adults) are:

- unlawfulness
- intent
- the complainant
- compelling a complainant 18 years of age or older
- being in the presence of or watching self-masturbation or a sexual offence/act.

28.10.3.1 Unlawfulness

The crime can be committed by a male or a female as section 8 of the Sexual Offences Act provides that any natural person may be the perpetrator of the crime. Proof of compulsion on the part of the accused may exclude the unlawfulness of his conduct.

The accused would escape liability if the complainant had consented to the accused's use of compulsion to induce conduct identified in section 8.

For the crime defined in section 8 of the Act, consent is defined by the provisions of section 1(2). Consent for the statutory crime of being compelled to watch or be in the presence of self-masturbation or sexual offences/acts is absent in the context of the circumstances identified in section 1(3) of the Act. The contents of sections 1(2) and 1(3) have already been discussed under the element of unlawfulness in the crime of rape.

28.10.3.2 Intent

The intention of the accused must be to compel unlawfully the complainant to be in the presence of or watch self-masturbation or a sexual offence/act. The state bears the onus of proving that the accused had actual or legal intention to perpetrate the conduct. The state must prove that the accused intended to compel the complainant to be in the presence of or watch self-masturbation or a sexual offence/act, knowing or foreseeing that the complainant had not legitimately consented, and yet carried on regardless.

28.10.3.3 The complainant

The meaning of the term 'complainant' for the purpose of the Act has already been discussed under the corresponding element for the crime of rape. In the context of the crime in section 8 of the Sexual Offences Act, the complainant must be 18 years of age or older.

28.10.3.4 Compelling the complainant

The conduct of the complainant must meet the requirements for the justification of necessity as proof that the complainant was acting out of compulsion. Thus, the accused must have been threatening a worthy legal interest,[225] posing a threat that had either commenced or

225 Worthy legal interests have been generally accepted to include life, bodily integrity or property. A person may invoke the defence of necessity for protecting the worthy legal interests of another. Purely economic interests cannot be used to invoke the defence of necessity. *R v Canestra* supra.

was imminent or posing a threat that was not due to the complicit conduct of the complainant. Further, the conduct of the complainant must have been necessary and reasonable under the circumstances. Courts examine these factors objectively.

28.10.3.5 Being in the presence of or watching self-masturbation or a sexual offence/act

Section 1 of the Sexual Offences Act defines a sexual offence as any offence in terms of chapters 2, 3 and 4, and sections 10, 55 and 71(1), (2) and (6) of the Act. Thus, compelling the complainant to witness an intentional and unlawful criminal act defined in the listed provisions in the definition of a sexual offence, is criminalised by the provisions of section 8(1) of the Sexual Offences Act.

Section 1 of the Sexual Offences Act defines a sexual act as an act of sexual penetration or an act of sexual violation as they are defined in section 1 of the Act. The meaning of the terms 'sexual penetration' and 'sexual violation' for the purpose of the Act have already been discussed under the corresponding elements for the crimes of rape and sexual assault as defined in section 5(1). Section 8(2) prohibits the non-consensual live exposure of a complainant older than 18 years of age to sexual acts between persons other than the complainant.

One of the significant differences between the conduct proscribed by sections 8(1) and 8(2) is the issue of consent. Section 8(1) generally prohibits conduct where the necessary consent is missing or impossible to apply as a defence. Section 8(2) prohibits conduct that the participants of the sexual act may be performing consensually with the other participants. The sexual act itself may be lawful. It is the exposure to the non-consenting complainant who is older than 18 years of age that criminalises the conduct.

Compelling the complainant to watch or be in the presence of the accused or another person who self-masturbates, falls within the ambit of the conduct prohibited by section 8(3).

28.10.4 Some general comments

The common law crime of public indecency has not been repealed by the provisions of section 68(1)(*b*) of the Sexual Offences Act. If the facts of the case allow for an overlap, the prosecution retains the discretion to indict the accused either under the provisions of the Sexual Offences Act or the common law crime. The common law crime of public indecency is competent for indictment where the conduct of the accused occurs publicly, and objectively tends to deprave or outrage the public norms of decency.

The statutory crime created by section 8 of the Sexual Offences Act also overlaps with the crime of *crimen iniuria* where there is an impairment of *dignitas*. The common law crime of *crimen iniuria* has not been repealed by the provisions of section 68(1)(*b*) of the Sexual Offences Act.

28.11 Flashing to adults

28.11.1 A brief history

Under Roman law, various forms of immoral conduct, including public indecency, were punished as *crimina extraordinaria*.[226] English law also punished indecent exposure.[227]

226 Voet D 47.11.2.

227 *R v Sedley* supra.

Section 19(*b*) of the Sexual Offences Act 23 of 1957 criminalised the conduct of any person who intentionally and openly exhibited himself in an indecent dress or manner at any door or window, or within the view of any public street or place to which the public have access. The crime consisted of consciously displaying the body to expose it to the public. The unlawfulness of the conduct could be excluded by the locality of the behaviour. For example, exposure such as a woman exposing her breasts may be unlawful in a public office, but it may not be indecent in a place such as a beach.[228] The crime is now provided for in the Sexual Offences Act.[229]

28.11.2 Definition

Section 9 of the Sexual Offences Act defines 'flashing' as follows:

> **A person ('A') who unlawfully and intentionally, whether for the sexual gratification of A or of a third person ('C') or not, exposes or displays or causes the exposure or display of the genital organs, anus or female breasts of A or C to a complainant 18 years or older ('B'), without the consent of B, is guilty of the offence of exposing or displaying or causing the exposure or display of genital organs, anus or female breasts to a person 18 years or older.**

28.11.3 Elements

The elements of flashing to adults are:

- unlawfulness
- intent
- the complainant
- exposure or display of a designated body part.

28.11.3.1 Unlawfulness

The crime can be committed by a male or a female as section 9 of the Sexual Offences Act provides that any natural person may be the perpetrator of the crime. Proof of necessity or compulsion on the part of the accused may exclude the unlawfulness of his conduct. The conduct of the accused must meet the requirements for the justification of necessity. Thus, the accused would have to have been experiencing a threat to a worthy legal interest, posing as a threat that had either commenced or was imminent, and a threat that was not due to his complicit conduct. Further, the conduct of the accused must have been necessary and reasonable under the circumstances. Courts examine these factors objectively.

The accused would escape liability if the complainant had consented to the conduct of the accused. For the crime defined in section 9 of the Act, 'consent' is defined by the provisions of section 1(2). Consent for the statutory crime of being compelled to watch or be in the presence of self-masturbation or sexual offences/acts is absent in the context of the circumstances identified in section 1(3) of the Act. The contents of sections 1(2) and 1(3) have already been discussed under the element of unlawfulness in the crime of rape.

Further, the location of the exposure may also exclude the unlawfulness of the display. For example, topless sunbathing may be lawful at a beach.[230] Section 56(8) provides that a person may not be convicted of an offence in terms of section 9 if he commits such act in compliance with, and in the interest of, a legitimate cultural practice. For example, it should

228 *S v C* 1978 (3) SA 978 (N) at 981; *S v K* 1983 (1) SA 65 (C); *S v NDLELA S* 1987 (1) PH H31 (NPD).
229 Snyman *Criminal Law* 372–373; Burchell *Principles of Criminal Law* 634.
230 *S v C* 1978 (3) SA 978 (N) at 981; *S v K* 1983 (1) SA 65 (C); *S v S* 1987 (1) PH H31 (N).

not be unlawful for witnesses at functions, such as a traditional Zulu reed dance, to be exposed to the bare breasts of the maidens.

28.11.3.2 Intent

The intention of the accused must be to expose/display unlawfully a designated body part to the complainant. The state bears the onus of proving that the accused had actual or legal intention to perpetrate the conduct. The state must prove that the accused intended to expose/display a designated body part to the complainant, knowing or foreseeing that the complainant had not legitimately consented, and yet carried on regardless.

28.11.3.3 The complainant

The meaning of the term 'complainant' for the purpose of the Sexual Offences Act has already been discussed under the corresponding element for the crime of rape. In the context of the crime in section 9 of the Act, the complainant must be 18 years of age or older.

28.11.3.4 Exposure or display of a designated body part

The conduct of the accused may be punished for violating the provisions of section 9 only where he was responsible for exposing or displaying the genital organs, anus or female breasts of a person other than the complainant, to the complainant.

28.11.4 Some general comments

There is an overlap between the crime punished by the provisions of section 9 of the Sexual Offences Act and *crimen iniuria*. The common law crime of *crimen iniuria* has not been repealed by the provisions of section 68(1)(*b*) of the Sexual Offences Act. The crime of *crimen iniuria* also punishes acts of indecent exposure.[231]

28.12 Exposure of child pornography to persons 18 years of age or older

28.12.1 Definition

Section 10 of the Sexual Offences Act defines 'exposure of child pornography' as follows:[232]

> **A person ('A') who unlawfully and intentionally, whether for the sexual gratification of A or of a third person ('C') or not, exposes or displays or causes the exposure or display of child pornography to a complainant 18 years or older ('B'), with or without the consent of B, is guilty of the offence of exposing or displaying or causing the exposure or display of child pornography to a person 18 years or older.**

28.12.2 Elements

The elements of exposure of child pornography (to persons 18 years of age or older) are:
- unlawfulness
- intent
- the complainant
- exposure or display of child pornography.

231 *R v Kobi* 1912 TPD 1106; *R v Holliday* 1927 CPD 395.

232 See also Snyman *Criminal Law* 373.

28.12.2.1 Unlawfulness

The crime can be committed by a male or a female as section 10 of the Sexual Offences Act provides that any natural person may be the perpetrator of the crime. Proof of necessity or compulsion on the part of the accused may exclude the unlawfulness of his conduct. The conduct of the accused must meet the requirements for the justification of necessity. Thus, the accused would have to have experienced a threat to a worthy legal interest, posing as a threat that had either commenced or was imminent, and a threat that was not due to his complicit conduct. Further, the conduct of the accused must have been necessary and reasonable under the circumstances. Courts examine these factors objectively.

The accused would escape liability if the complainant had consented to the accused's conduct. For the crime defined in section 10 of the Act, consent is defined by the provisions of section 1(2). Consent for the statutory crime of being compelled to watch or be in the presence of self-masturbation or sexual offences/acts is absent in the context of the circumstances identified in section 1(3) of the Act. The contents of sections 1(2) and 1(3) have already been discussed under the element of unlawfulness in the crime of rape.

28.12.2.2 Intent

The intention of the accused must be to expose/display unlawfully child pornography to the complainant. The state bears the onus of proving that the accused had actual or legal intention to perpetrate the conduct. The state must prove that the accused intended to expose/display child pornography to the complainant, knowing or foreseeing that the complainant had not legitimately consented, and yet carrying on regardless.

28.12.2.3 The complainant

The meaning of the term 'complainant' for the purpose of the Act has already been discussed under the corresponding element for the crime of rape. In the context of the crime in section 10 of the Sexual Offences Act, the complainant must be 18 years of age or older.

28.12.2.4 Exposure or display of child pornography

The accused's conduct may be punished only if it violates the provisions of section 10 where the accused was responsible for exposing or displaying child pornography to the complainant. It is irrelevant if the actual display/exposure was perpetrated by another person. The person who was responsible for causing the exposure/display to the complainant remains liable for the violation against the complainant.

Section 1 of the Sexual Offences Act defines 'child pornography' as meaning:

> **any image, however created, or any description or presentation of a person, real or simulated, who is, or who is depicted or described or presented as being, under the age of 18 years, of an explicit or sexual nature, whether such image or description or presentation is intended to stimulate erotic or aesthetic feelings or not, including any such image or description of such person—**
>
> **(*a*) engaged in an act that constitutes a sexual offence;**
> **(*b*) engaged in an act of sexual penetration;**
> **(*c*) engaged in an act of sexual violation;**
> **(*d*) engaged in an act of self-masturbation;**
> **(*e*) displaying the genital organs of such person in a state of arousal or stimulation;**
> **(*f*) unduly displaying the genital organs or anus of such person;**
> **(*g*) displaying any form of stimulation of a sexual nature of such person's breasts;**

(*h*) engaged in sexually suggestive or lewd acts;
(*i*) engaged in or as the subject of sadistic or masochistic acts of a sexual nature;
(*j*) engaged in any conduct or activity characteristically associated with sexual intercourse;
(*k*) showing or describing such person—
 (i) participating in, or assisting or facilitating another person to participate in; or
 (ii) being in the presence of another person who commits or in any other manner being involved in, any act contemplated in paragraphs (*a*) to (*j*); or
(*l*) showing or describing the body, or parts of the body, of such person in a manner or in circumstances which, within the context, violate or offend the sexual integrity or dignity of that person or any category of persons under 18 or is capable of being used for the purposes of violating or offending the sexual integrity or dignity of that person, any person or group or categories of persons.

28.12.3 Some general comments

The possession, making and distribution of child pornography are already criminalised by section 27 of the Films and Publications Act 65 of 1996. This crime simply criminalises the non-consensual exposure/display of child pornography. It does not criminalise the conduct where a person is a consenting viewer. This does not make sense because the accused would be guilty of being in possession of the offensive material and liable in terms of section 27 of the Films and Publications Act. Perhaps a consenting viewer should be charged as an accomplice to the crime.

28.13 Engaging sexual services

28.13.1 A brief history

The new statutory crime created by the provisions of section 11 of the Sexual Offences Act is highly innovative. Its closest predecessor was the crime that was punished by the provisions of section 20 of the Sexual Offences Act 23 of 1957. The conduct that was criminalised by the provisions of section 20 of this Act referred to 'persons living on earnings of prostitution or committing or assisting in commission of indecent acts'.[233]

In *S v H*,[234] after considering the pre-Union legal position, the Appellate Division (AD) confirmed that section 20 of the Sexual Offences Act 23 of 1957 did not apply to the prostitute. Thereafter, the legislature created section 20(1)(aA), which was inserted into the Act by

233 Section 20 of the Sexual Offences Act 23 of 1957 originally provided:

20. Persons living on earnings of prostitution or committing or assisting in commission of indecent acts –
 (1) Any person who:
  (*a*) knowingly lives wholly or in part on the earnings of prostitution; or
  (*b*) in public commits any act of indecency with another person; or
  (*c*) in public or in private in any way assists in bringing about, or receives any consideration for, the commission by any person of any act of indecency with another person, shall be guilty of an offence.
 (2) If it is made to appear to a magistrate by information on oath that there is reason to suspect that any house is used by a female for purposes of prostitution and that any person residing in or frequenting the house is living wholly or in part on the earnings of the prostitute, the magistrate may issue a warrant authorizing any police officer not below the rank of sergeant to enter and search the house and to arrest that person.

234 *S v H* 1988 (3) SA 545 (A), which confirmed the decision in *S v H* 1986 (4) SA 1095 (T).

section 7(*a*) of the Immorality Amendment Act 2 of 1988. The provisions of section 20(1)(aA) made it an offence for 'any person to have unlawful carnal intercourse, or commit an act of indecency, with any other person for reward'. A notable difference between the provisions of section 20(1)(aA) and the new crime is that section 20(1)(aA) targeted the person providing the sexual services, whereas the new crime targets the person providing the reward/benefit in exchange for the sexual services.

In *S v C*,[235] Van Dijkhorst J expressed his concern about the ambit of the crime that had been created by section 20(1)(aA) of the Sexual Offences Act 23 of 1957. Judge Van Dijkhorst was convinced that the provisions of section 20(1)(aA) criminalised more than just prostitution. Van Dijkhorst J was convinced that the crime included 'the novice as well as the hardened street-walker' in its scope.[236]

When the Transvaal Provincial Division (now the North Gauteng High Court) had to hear the case of *S v Jordan and others*,[237] the court also concluded that the reach of section 20(1)(aA) of the Sexual Offences Act 23 of 1957 was excessive. Judge Spoelstra held:

> **In principle there is no difference between a prostitute who receives money for her favours and her sister who receives, for rendering a similar service, a benefit or reward of a different kind, such as a paid-for weekend, a free holiday, board and lodging for a shorter or longer period, a night at the opera, or any other form of quid pro quo.**[238]

Since the Transvaal Provincial Division had declared a portion of national legislation invalid, the Constitutional Court had to confirm the order of invalidity. The majority of the Constitutional Court declined to confirm the order of invalidity because they were convinced that a proper interpretation of the section would survive a constitutional challenge.

The majority of the Constitutional Court[239] concluded that the provisions of section 20(1)(aA) are 'directed at the prostitute only and not the customer'.[240] The majority decision stressed that 'the purpose of section 20(1)(aA) is to prohibit commercial sex, not to protect the person who pays for sexual favours'.[241]

The minority decision[242] confirmed that it has generally been accepted in our law that 'section 20(1)(aA) criminalises only the conduct of the prostitute and not that of the client'.[243] The minority also held as follows:

> **It should be recalled that until 1988 the law in South Africa, like that in many other Commonwealth countries, such as the United Kingdom, India, Australia and Canada, did not penalise prostitution as such, but only activities associated with it, such as pimping, soliciting and brothel-keeping. Clearly, in 1988 the legislature intended to criminalise the conduct of the prostitute. Had it, however, intended to penalise the conduct of patronising a prostitute as well, it could have done so in appropriate language.**[244]

235 *S v C* 1992 (1) SACR 174 (W).
236 *S v C* 1992 (1) SACR 174 (W) at 176 F–G.
237 *S v Jordan and others* 2001 (10) BCLR 1055 (T).
238 *S v Jordan* supra at 1058.
239 Chaskalson CJ, Kriegler, Madala JJ, Du Plessis and Skweyiya AJJ concurred in the judgment of Ngcobo J in *S v Jordan and others (Sex Workers Education and Advocacy Task Force and others as Amici Curiae)* 2002 (6) SA 642 (CC).
240 *Jordan* (CC) supra at 8.
241 *Jordan* (CC) supra at 12 and 15.
242 Langa DCJ, Ackermann and Goldstone JJ concurred in the judgment of O'Regan and Sachs JJ in *Jordan* (CC) supra.
243 *Jordan* (CC) supra at 41.
244 *Jordan* (CC) supra at 44.

To decide whether the provisions of section 20(1)(aA) are 'reasonably capable of being read so as to cover only commercial sex, that is, sex where the body is made available for sexual stimulation on a paid basis',[245] the court relied on contextual pointers to reach its conclusion. For example, it relied on the heading of a section for the interpretation of the section. The Constitutional Court had followed an identical approach in *President of the Republic of South Africa and another v Hugo*.[246] The minority decision relied on the heading of section 20 to conclude that section 20(1)(aA) applies only to the context of commercial sex (or prostitution).[247] 'However, it does not criminalise sexual intercourse between consenting adults which does not constitute prostitution or commercial sex.'[248]

28.13.2 Definition

Section 11 of the Sexual Offences Act defines 'engaging sexual services' as follows:[249]

> **A person ('A') who unlawfully and intentionally engages the services of a person 18 years or older ('B'), for financial or other reward, favour or compensation to B or to a third person ('C')—**
> **(*a*) for the purpose of engaging in a sexual act with B, irrespective of whether the sexual act is committed or not; or**
> **(*b*) by committing a sexual act with B,**
> **is guilty of the offence of engaging the sexual services of a person 18 years or older.**

28.13.3 Elements

The elements of engaging sexual services are:

- unlawfulness
- intent
- engaging the services of a person 18 years of age or older
- a benefit to any person
- the purpose of engaging in a sexual act or committing a sexual act with the person whose services were engaged.

28.13.3.1 Unlawfulness

The crime can be committed by a male or a female as section 11 of the Sexual Offences Act provides that any natural person may be the perpetrator of the crime. Proof of necessity or compulsion on the part of the accused may exclude the unlawfulness of the accused's conduct. The accused's conduct must meet the requirements for the justification of necessity. Thus, the accused would have to have been experiencing a threat to a worthy legal interest, posing as a threat that had either commenced or was imminent, and a threat that was not due to the complicit conduct of the accused. Further, the accused's conduct must have been necessary and reasonable under the circumstances. Courts examine these factors objectively.

28.13.3.2 Intent

The intention of the accused must be to engage unlawfully the services of a person 18 years of age or older for a benefit to any person, for engaging in a sexual act or committing a sexual

245 *Jordan* (CC) supra at 48.
246 *President of the Republic of South Africa and another v Hugo* 1997 (4) SA 1 (CC); 1997 (6) BCLR 708 (CC) at 12.
247 *Jordan* (CC) supra at 49–50.
248 *Jordan* (CC) supra at 50.
249 See also Snyman *Criminal Law* 373–377; Burchell *Principles of Criminal Law* 634–635.

act with the person whose services were engaged. The state bears the onus of proving that the accused had actual or legal intention to perpetrate the conduct.

28.13.3.3 Engaging the services of a person 18 years of age or older

The act of engaging with another party suggests reaching an agreement. The nature of the prohibited conduct suggests a quid pro quo agreement for engaging in a sexual act or committing a sexual act in exchange for a benefit to another person.

28.13.3.4 A benefit to any person

Section 11 provides that the benefit may take the form of a financial or other reward, favour or compensation. It may be corporeal or incorporeal. It may be proprietary or non-proprietary. The benefit must be due to the person whose services were engaged or any other person.

28.13.3.5 For the purpose of engaging/participating in a sexual act

Section 11 the Sexual Offences Act criminalises the conduct of the accused from the moment the agreement is completed, regardless of whether the sexual act takes place.

Section 1 of the Sexual Offences Act defines a 'sexual act' as an act of 'sexual penetration' or an act of 'sexual violation' as they are defined in section 1 of the Act. The meaning of the terms 'sexual penetration' and 'sexual violation' for the purpose of the Act have already been discussed under the corresponding elements for the crimes of rape and sexual assault as they are defined in section 5(1).

28.13.4 Some general comments

The accused would be liable for violating the prohibition in section 11 regardless of whether the sexual act occurs or not. It seems redundant to criminalise the conduct of the accused again if the act does occur. This fact may be relevant for sentencing, but it makes no difference to the liability of the accused.

The fact that any benefit in any form may be sufficient to justify liability should be cause for concern. The Constitutional Court has already declared that the crime can only be justified in the context of commercial sex work. However, the fact that the legislature wanted to criminalise the exchange of *any* benefit as part of an agreement for engaging in a sexual act, suggests that the legislature may have intended to extend the scope of liability beyond the scope of commercial sex work. However, courts are unlikely to punish conduct beyond the scope of commercial sex work because of the Constitutional Court's decision in *Jordan*.[250]

28.14 Statutory rape

28.14.1 A brief history

Sexual abuse and indecency against a person who is legally classified as a youth have been punished through common and statutory law. The most notable offences in this category include acts of indecency by a male with an under-aged male, acts of indecency by a female with an under-aged female, and immoral or indecent acts with under-aged persons.

Section 14(1)(*b*) of the Sexual Offences Act 23 of 1957 prohibited males from committing or attempting to commit an immoral or indecent act with a boy who was younger than

250 *S v Jordan* supra. See section 28.13.1.

19 years of age. Consent by the male who was younger than 19 years could not exclude the liability of the accused.

Homosexual acts between consenting women were not criminalised until 1988. The advent of the Immorality Amendment Act 2 of 1988 necessitated the insertion of section 14(3)(*b*) in the Sexual Offences Act 23 of 1957. Consequently, it became a criminal act for a female to commit or attempt to commit an immoral or indecent act with a girl who was younger than 19 years of age.

Note that neither section 14(1)(*b*) nor section 14(3)(*b*) prescribed an age for the offender. Therefore, offenders could also be younger than 19 years of age. However, if both participants were over the age of 19 years, then no crime was committed.[251] This feature of the crimes in sections 14(1)(*b*) and 14(3)(*b*) emphasised that the crime proscribed the sexual exploitation of children rather than prohibiting homosexual activity.

Section 14 of the Sexual Offences Act 23 of 1957 also criminalised sexual intercourse with children under the age of 16 years. In addition, section 14 identified defences that would exclude the unlawfulness of the accused's conduct. Such defences included situations in which the child was a prostitute and the accused was a first-time offender who was younger than 21 years of age. Another defence was that the accused had been deceived by the child (or the person who had custody over the child) into believing that the child was over the age of 16 years.

The SALRC recommended the repeal of section 14 and its replacement with provisions that would criminalise all forms of sexual exploitation of children.[252]

The provisions of the Sexual Offences Act 23 of 1957 have now been replaced by the provisions in Chapter 3 of the Sexual Offences Act 32 of 2007.[253] The latter Act defines criminal behaviour in the context of:

> **... consensual sexual acts with certain children; sexual exploitation and sexual grooming of children, exposure or display of or causing exposure or display of child pornography or pornography to children and using children for pornographic purposes or benefiting from child pornography; compelling or causing children to witness sexual offences, sexual acts or self-masturbation and exposure or display of or causing exposure or display of genital organs, anus or female breasts ('flashing') to children.**

28.14.2 Definition

In the case of *Teddy Bear Clinic for Abused Children and another v Minister of Justice and Constitutional Development and another* (the *Teddy Bear* case),[254] the Constitutional Court found that sections 15 and 16 of the Sexual Offences Act are unconstitutional insofar as they criminalise sexual conduct between adolescents. Both sections have consequently been amended by the Criminal Law (Sexual Offences and Related Matters) Amendment Act Amendment Act 5 of 2015.[255]

251 Especially once the crime of sodomy was repealed in *National Coalition for Gay and Lesbian Equality v Minister of Justice* supra.

252 South African Law Commission *Sexual Offences: The Substantive Law Project 107* Discussion Paper 85 (1999); *Project 107 Process and Procedure* Discussion Paper 102 (2002); *Project 107 Sexual Offences Report* (2002).

253 For commentary, see Snyman *Criminal Law* 383–390.

254 *Teddy Bear Clinic for Abused Children and another v Minister of Justice and Constitutional Development and another* 2014 (2) SA 168 (CC).

255 *GG* 38977, GN 593, 7 July 2015.

The Preamble to the Amendment Act 5 of 2015 notes that the primary objective of sections 15 and 16 of the Act, namely to protect children who are 12 years or older but under the age of 16 years, from adult sexual predators remains unaffected by the Constitutional Court judgment and consequently also does not lower the age of consent in respect of sexual acts to 12 years.

The amended section 15(1) of the Sexual Offences Act defines 'statutory rape' as follows:

> (1) **A person ('A') who commits an act of sexual penetration with a child ('B') who is 12 years of age or older but under the age of 16 years is, despite the consent of B to the commission of such an act, guilty of the offence of having committed an act of consensual sexual penetration with a child, unless A, at the time of the alleged commission of such an act, was—**
>
> (*a*) **12 years of age or older but under the age of 16 years; or**
>
> (*b*) **either 16 or 17 years of age and the age difference between A and B was not more than two years.**

28.14.3 Elements

The elements of statutory rape are:

- unlawfulness
- fault
- sexual penetration
- the child.

28.14.3.1 Unlawfulness

Originally, the crime could be committed by a male or a female who was older than 12 years as section 15 provided that any natural person may be the perpetrator of the crime. However, this changed when the Constitutional Court decided the *Teddy Bear* case.[256] In the *Teddy Bear* case, the Constitutional Court interrogated the constitutional validity of criminalising consensual sexual acts between adolescents. The court relied on identifying children younger than 16 as adolescents as a means of differentiating them from other children who are younger than 18.[257] The court concluded that it is unconstitutional to criminalise consensual acts of sexual penetration performed by adolescents with other adolescents. Thus, the crime cannot be perpetrated by children who are younger than 16 years old when they engage in sexual penetration with other children who are younger than 16 years old.[258]

The Amendment Act 5 of 2015 further gives effect to the decriminalisation of consensual adolescent sexual relationships by providing that if a child of 16 or 17 years of age commits an act of sexual penetration with a child younger than 16 years, but where the age difference between the two is not more than two years, such a child does not commit the crime of statutory rape.

The *Teddy Bear* case and the subsequent adoption of the Amendment Act 5 of 2015 effectively decriminalises consensual adolescent sexual penetration.[259] This development in criminal law does not mean that the state encourages adolescents to engage prematurely

256 *Teddy Bear Clinic v Minister of Justice* supra.
257 *Teddy Bear Clinic v Minister of Justice* supra at 11.
258 *Teddy Bear Clinic v Minister of Justice* supra at 117.
259 See also comments by Burchell *Principles of Criminal Law* 632.

in consensual sexual conduct.[260] It also does not affect the criminalisation of sexual penetration with children under the age of 12.[261]

A person younger than the age of 12 years is irrebuttably presumed to be incapable of consenting to a sexual act.[262] The irrebuttable presumption applies regardless of the gender of the person under the age of 12.[263]

Section 56(2)(*a*) excludes the unlawful nature of the accused's conduct where the child deceived him into believing that the child was at least 16 years old at the time of the alleged commission of the offence. Further, section 56(2)(*a*) requires the accused to have a reasonable belief that the child was at least 16 years old.[264] Section 56(3) provides that the provisions of section 56(2)(*a*) do not apply to cases in which the accused person is related to the child within the prohibited incest degrees of blood, affinity or adoptive relationship.[265]

28.14.3.2 Fault

The intention of the accused must be to cause unlawfully sexual penetration. The accused would lack intention if there was a legitimate mistake in causing the sexual penetration.[266] The mistake may refer to the age of the child. The accused must know or at least foresee the possibility that the complainant is not consenting, and yet proceed with the sexual penetration regardless.[267]

The provisions of section 56(2)(*a*) require the accused to have a reasonable belief that the child was at least 16 years old.[268] Where the accused had an unreasonable or negligent belief that the child was at least 16 years old, he would be liable for contravening section 15(1) of the Sexual Offences Act. *Culpa* is sufficient for proving the liability of an accused charged with contravening the prohibition in section 15(1) of the Sexual Offences Act.[269]

28.14.3.3 Sexual penetration

The meaning of 'sexual penetration' for the purpose of the Act has already been discussed under the corresponding element for the crime of rape.

28.14.3.4 The child

Section 1 of the Sexual Offences Act has been amended by the Amendment Act 5 of 2015 and now defines 'child' and 'children' as follows:

> **"child" means a person under the age of 18 years and "children" has a corresponding meaning.**

260 See the Preamble to the Amendment Act 5 of 2015.

261 See the Preamble to the Amendment Act 5 of 2015.

262 S 57(1) of the Sexual Offences Act provides: 'Notwithstanding anything to the contrary in any law contained, a male or female person under the age of 12 years is incapable of consenting to a sexual act'.

263 S 57(1) of the Sexual Offences Act. See also s 1(3)(*d*)(iv) of the Sexual Offences Act.

264 S 56(2)(*a*) of the Sexual Offences Act provides that whenever an accused person is charged with an offence under:

> **... section 15 or 16, it is, subject to subsection (3), a valid defence to such a charge to contend that the child deceived the accused person into believing that he or she was 16 years or older at the time of the alleged commission of the offence and the accused person reasonably believed that the child was 16 years or older.**

265 S 56(3) of the Sexual Offences Act.

266 *R v H* 1962 (1) SA 278 (SR).

267 *R v K* 1958 (3) SA 420 (A) at 421–423; *R v Z* 1960 (1) SA 739 (A) at 743 and 745.

268 S 56(2)(*a*) of the Sexual Offences Act provides that whenever an accused person is charged with an offence under:

> **... section 15 or 16, it is, subject to subsection (3), a valid defence to such a charge to contend that the child deceived the accused person into believing that he or she was 16 years or older at the time of the alleged commission of the offence and the accused person reasonably believed that the child was 16 years or older.**

269 For a contrary view, see Snyman *Criminal Law* 386–387.

28.14.4 Some general comments

In the *Teddy Bear* case, the Constitutional Court determined that the prosecution regime for statutory rape under section 15 of the Sexual Offences Act was irrational and that it also exacerbated the harm done to the children.[270] In essence, the previous section 15(2) provided that the prosecution of statutory rape cases under section 15 had to be authorised in writing by the National Director of Public Prosecutions (NDPP). Further, if the NDPP authorised the prosecution of one participating child in the rape, the other child also had to be charged under section 15(1).

The prosecutorial regime under section 15(2) has been amended by the Amendment Act 5 of 2015. Section 15(2) now provides as follows:

> **(2) (*a*) The institution of a prosecution for an offence referred to in subsection (1) must be authorised in writing by the Director of Public Prosecutions if A was either 16 or 17 years of age at the time of the alleged commission of the offence and the age difference between A and B was more than two years.**
>
> **(*b*) The Director of Public Prosecutions concerned may delegate his or her power to decide whether a prosecution in terms of this section should be instituted or not.**

28.15 Statutory sexual assault

28.15.1 Definition

The judgment of the Constitutional Court in the *Teddy Bear* case prompted the amendment of section 16 of the Sexual Offences Act.[271] The amended section 16(1) defines the crime of 'statutory sexual assault' as follows:

> **(1) A person ('A') who commits an act of sexual violation with a child ('B') who is 12 years of age or older but under the age of 16 years is, despite the consent of B to the commission of such an act, guilty of the offence of having committed an act of consensual sexual violation of a child, unless A, at the time of the alleged commission of such an act, was—**
>
> **(*a*) 12 years of age or older but under the age of 16 years; or**
>
> **(*b*) either 16 or 17 years of age and the age difference between A and B was not more than two years.**

28.15.2 Elements

The elements of statutory sexual assault are:

- unlawfulness
- fault
- sexual violation
- the child.

270 *Teddy Bear Clinic v Minister of Justice* supra at 77.

271 See the Amendment Act 5 of 2015. See also, in general, *Teddy Bear Clinic v Minister of Justice* supra.

28.15.2.1 Unlawfulness

A person younger than the age of 12 years is irrebuttably presumed to be incapable of consenting to a sexual act.[272] The irrebuttable presumption applies regardless of the gender of the person.[273] Section 16(1) criminalises consensual sexual violation of a minor. The provisions of section 16(1) clearly provide that a child's consent does not exclude the unlawfulness of the conduct. On the contrary, it fulfils an element of the crime of consensual sexual violation of a child. Non-consensual sexual violation is punished as sexual assault as it is defined in section 5(1).

Originally, the crime could be committed by any male or a female older than 12 years as section 16(1) provided that any natural person may be the perpetrator of the crime. However, this changed when the Constitutional Court decided the *Teddy Bear* case. In the *Teddy Bear* case, the Constitutional Court interrogated the constitutional validity of criminalising consensual sexual acts between adolescents. The court relied on identifying children younger than 16 as adolescents as a means of differentiating them from other children who are younger than 18.[274] The court concluded that it is unconstitutional to criminalise consensual acts of sexual violation performed by adolescents with other adolescents. The crime cannot be perpetrated by children who are younger than 16 years old when they engage in consensual sexual acts other than sexual penetration. Both children must be 12 years of age or older, but under the age of 16. If one of the children engaging in the consensual sexual activity is either 16 or 17 years of age and the age difference between the children is not more than two years, the conduct will be lawful.

Thus, consensual mutual masturbation, kissing or touching of genital organs, or any other sexual act other than sexual penetration between two consenting adolescents is lawful. We noted above under statutory rape (28.14.3.1) that the decriminalisation of consensual sexual conduct in the case of adolescents does not mean that the state encourages premature sexual activities. The same is true for consensual sexual behaviour in the context of the decriminalisation of statutory sexual assault as described above. The conduct of adult sexual predators towards children is obviously still criminalised regardless of consent.[275]

Section 56(2)(*a*) excludes the unlawful nature of the accused's conduct where the child deceived him into believing that the child was at least 16 years old at the time of the alleged commission of the offence. Further, section 56(2)(*a*) requires the accused to have a reasonable belief that the child was at least 16 years old.[276] Section 56(3) provides that the provisions of section 56(2)(*a*) do not apply to cases where the accused person is related to the child within the prohibited incest degrees of blood, affinity or adoptive relationship.[277]

Further, the now repealed section 56(2)(*b*) provided that it was a valid defence for a child charged with contravening section 16(1) to contend that both the accused persons were children and the age difference between them was not more than two years at the time of

---

272 S 57(1) of the Sexual Offences Act provides: 'Notwithstanding anything to the contrary in any law contained, a male or female person under the age of 12 years is incapable of consenting to a sexual act.'

273 S 57(1) of the Sexual Offences Act. See also s 1(3)(*d*)(iv) of the Act.

274 *Teddy Bear Clinic v Minister of Justice* supra at 11.

275 See also *Teddy Bear Clinic v Minister of Justice* supra at 117; Preamble to the Amendment Act 5 of 2015. For a definition of 'sexual violation', see s 1 of the Sexual Offences Act 2007, and the discussion under section 28.7.3.3.

276 S 56(2)(*a*) of the Sexual Offences Act provides that whenever an accused person is charged with an offence under:

> **... section 15 or 16, it is, subject to subsection (3), a valid defence to such a charge to contend that the child deceived the accused person into believing that he or she was 16 years or older at the time of the alleged commission of the offence and the accused person reasonably believed that the child was 16 years or older.**

277 S 56(3) of the Sexual Offences Act.

the alleged commission of the offence.[278] In the *Teddy Bear* case the court described this defence as the 'close-in-age defence'.[279] Given the amended definition of statutory sexual assault, the defence provided for in section 56(2)(*b*) became redundant. This section was consequently deleted by Amendment Act 5 of 2015.

28.15.2.2 Fault

The intention of the accused must be to cause sexual penetration unlawfully. The accused would lack intention if there was a legitimate mistake in causing the sexual violation.[280] The mistake may refer to the age of the child.

The provisions of section 56(2)(*a*) require the accused to have a reasonable belief that the child was at least 16 years old.[281] This provision suggests that where the accused had an unreasonable or negligent belief that the child was at least 16 years old, he would be liable for contravening section 16(1) of the Sexual Offences Act. Thus, *culpa* is sufficient for proving the liability of an accused charged with contravening the prohibition in section 16(1) of the Sexual Offences Act.[282]

28.15.2.3 Sexual violation

The meaning of 'sexual violation' for the purpose of the Act has already been discussed under the corresponding element for the crime of sexual assault as it is defined in section 5(1).

28.15.2.4 The child

For the definition of 'child' and 'children', see section 28.14.3.4.

28.15.3 Some general comments

The institution of a prosecution for statutory sexual assault must be authorised in writing by the relevant Director of Public Prosecutions if the accused was either 16 or 17 years of age at the time of the alleged commission of the offence and the age difference between the accused and the child complainant was more than two years. The DPP concerned may delegate his power to decide whether a prosecution under section 16 of the Sexual Offences Act should be instituted or not.[283]

---

278 S 56(2)(*b*) of the Sexual Offences Act provided that whenever an accused person is charged with an offence under 'section 16, it is a valid defence to such a charge to contend that both the accused persons were children and the age difference between them was not more than two years at the time of the alleged commission of the offence'. This subsection was deleted by s 9 of Act 5 of 2015.

279 *Teddy Bear Clinic v Minister of Justice* supra at 24. See also Mahery P 'Reporting sexual offences involving child patients: What is the current law following the Constitutional Court judgment?' (2014) 7(1) *South African Journal of Bioethics and Law* 26–29.

280 *R v H* 1962 (1) SA 278 (SR).

281 S 56(2)(*a*) of the Sexual Offences Act provides that whenever an accused person is charged with an offence under:

> **... section 15 or 16, it is, subject to subsection (3), a valid defence to such a charge to contend that the child deceived the accused person into believing that he or she was 16 years or older at the time of the alleged commission of the offence and the accused person reasonably believed that the child was 16 years or older.**

282 See also Snyman *Criminal Law* 387–388.

283 S 16(2) of the Sexual Offences Act, 2007, was amended by the Amendment Act of 2015.

28.16 Sexual exploitation of children

28.16.1 Definition

Section 17 of the Sexual Offences Act provides as follows:[284]

> (1) A person ('A') who unlawfully and intentionally engages the services of a child complainant ('B'), with or without the consent of B, for financial or other reward, favour or compensation to B or to a third person ('C')—
> (*a*) for the purpose of engaging in a sexual act with B, irrespective of whether the sexual act is committed or not; or
> (*b*) by committing a sexual act with B, is, in addition to any other offence which he or she may be convicted of, guilty of the offence of sexual exploitation of a child.
>
> (2) A person ('A') who unlawfully and intentionally offers the services of a child complainant ('B') to a third person ('C'), with or without the consent of B, for financial or other reward, favour or compensation to A, B or to another person ('D')—
> (*a*) for purposes of the commission of a sexual act with B by C;
> (*b*) by inviting, persuading or inducing B to allow C to commit a sexual act with B;
> (*c*) by participating in, being involved in, promoting, encouraging or facilitating the commission of a sexual act with B by C;
> (*d*) by making available, offering or engaging B for purposes of the commission of a sexual act with B by C; or
> (*e*) by detaining B, whether under threat, force, coercion, deception, abuse of power or authority, for purposes of the commission of a sexual act with B by C, is guilty of an offence of being involved in the sexual exploitation of a child.
>
> (3) A person ('A') who—
> (*a*) intentionally allows or knowingly permits the commission of a sexual act by a third person ('C') with a child complainant ('B'), with or without the consent of B, while being a primary care-giver defined in section 1 of the Social Assistance Act, 2004 (Act No. 13 of 2004), parent or guardian of B; or
> (*b*) owns, leases, rents, manages, occupies or has control of any movable or immovable property and intentionally allows or knowingly permits such movable or immovable property to be used for purposes of the commission of a sexual act with B by C, with or without the consent of B, is guilty of the offence of furthering the sexual exploitation of a child.
>
> (4) A person ('A') who intentionally receives financial or other reward, favour or compensation from the commission of a sexual act with a child complainant ('B'), with or without the consent of B, by a third person ('C'), is guilty of an offence of benefiting from the sexual exploitation of a child.
>
> (5) A person ('A') who intentionally lives wholly or in part on rewards, favours or compensation for the commission of a sexual act with a child complainant ('B'), with or without the consent of B, by a third person ('C'), is guilty of an offence of living from the earnings of the sexual exploitation of a child.

284 See also Snyman *Criminal Law* 388–389.

(6) A person ('A'), including a juristic person, who—

(*a*) makes or organises any travel arrangements for or on behalf of a third person ('C'), whether that other person is resident within or outside the borders of the Republic, with the intention of facilitating the commission of any sexual act with a child complainant ('B'), with or without the consent of B, irrespective of whether that act is committed or not; or

(*b*) prints or publishes, in any manner, any information that is intended to promote or facilitate conduct that would constitute a sexual act with B, is guilty of an offence of promoting child sex tours.

28.16.2 Elements

The elements of sexual exploitation of children are:

- unlawfulness
- intent
- the child
- a sexual act
- exploitation.

28.16.2.1 Unlawfulness

A person younger than the age of 12 years is irrebuttably presumed to be incapable of consenting to a sexual act.[285] The irrebuttable presumption applies regardless of the gender of the person under the age of 12.[286] Section 56(5)[287] excludes the unlawful nature of the conduct relating to sections 17(4) or (5) where the accused is a child[288] and not a person contemplated by the provisions of sections 17(1) and 17(2).[289]

28.16.2.2 Intent

The accused's intention must be to exploit the child unlawfully sexually. Proof of actual or legal intention is sufficient to prove liability.

28.16.2.3 The child

For the definition of 'child' and 'children', see section 28.14.3.4.

28.16.2.4 A sexual act

All the offences created by the provisions of section 17 refer to sexual acts. Section 1 of the Sexual Offences Act defines a 'sexual act' as an act of 'sexual penetration' or an act of 'sexual violation' as they are defined in section 1 of the Act. The meanings of the terms 'sexual penetration' and 'sexual violation' for the purpose of the Act have already been discussed under the corresponding elements for the crimes of rape and sexual assault as it is defined in section 5(1).

---

285 S 57(1) of the Sexual Offences Act provides: 'Notwithstanding anything to the contrary in any law contained, a male or female person under the age of 12 years is incapable of consenting to a sexual act'.

286 S 57(1) of the Sexual Offences Act. See also s 1(3)(*d*)(iv) of the Act.

287 S 56(5) of the Sexual Offences Act provides:

> **A person may not be convicted of an offence in terms of section 17(4) or (5) or section 23(4) or (5) or section 54, if that person is –**
>
> **(*a*) a child; and**
>
> **(*b*) not a person contemplated in section 17(1) and (2) or 23(1) and (2), as the case may be.**

288 S 56(5)(*a*) of the Sexual Offences Act.

289 S 56(5)(*b*) of the Sexual Offences Act.

28.16.2.5 Exploitation

Section 17 identifies a number of prohibited forms of exploitation. Section 17(1) of the Sexual Offences Act prohibits engaging a child's services for a benefit to any person for the purpose of engaging in a sexual act or committing a sexual act with the child whose services were engaged. This offence is called *sexual exploitation of a child.*

Section 17(2) deals with the offence of *being involved in the sexual exploitation of a child.* It prohibits natural persons from offering the services of a child complainant to another person for a financial or other reward, favour or compensation to any person for the purpose of committing a sexual act between the child and another person by:

- inviting, persuading or inducing the child to allow another person to commit a sexual act with the child, by participating in, being involved in, promoting, encouraging or facilitating the commission of a sexual act with the child by another person
- making available, offering or engaging the child for the purposes of the commission of a sexual act with the child by another
- detaining the child by duress, abuse of power or deception for commission of a sexual act with the child by another person.

Section 17(3) identifies two forms of exploitation. The first form criminalises primary care-givers[290] (parents or guardians of a child) who allow or knowingly permit the commission of a sexual act between a child in their care and another person.[291] The second form criminalises the conduct of persons who intentionally allow or knowingly permit the use of property for committing a sexual act with a child by another.[292] The property may be movable or immovable. The property must be corporeal and capable of being used for committing a sexual act with a child by another person. The accused must have a legal interest in the property in the form of ownership, lease, rental agreement, management, occupation or control. This offence is called *furthering the sexual exploitation of a child.*

Section 17(4) criminalises any person who benefits from the commission of a sexual act with a child. The benefit may be in the form of a financial or other reward, favour or compensation. The benefit may be corporeal or incorporeal. It may be proprietary or non-proprietary. This offence is called *benefiting from the sexual exploitation of a child.*

Section 17(5) creates a crime that criminalises any person who lives wholly or in part on rewards, favours or compensation from the commission of sexual acts with a child by another person. This offence is called *living from the earnings of the sexual exploitation of a child.*

Section 17(6) relates to forms of the offence called *promoting child sex tours.* This section applies to any natural person and also includes a juristic person as a possible perpetrator. The first form of this crime refers to making or organising any travel arrangements for or on behalf of another person with the intention of facilitating the commission of a sexual act with a child.[293] The crime is completed regardless of whether the sexual act occurs. The second form of this offence refers to printing or publishing any information that is intended to promote or facilitate a sexual act with a child.[294]

290 As defined in s 1 of the Social Assistance Act 13 of 2004.
291 S 17(3)(*a*) of the Sexual Offences Act.
292 S 17(3)(*b*) of the Sexual Offences Act.
293 S 17(6)(*a*) of the Sexual Offences Act.
294 S 17(6)(*b*) of the Sexual Offences Act.

28.16.3 Some general comments

The crime created by the provisions of section 17(3)(*a*) has the potential to attract controversy when it comes to cultural and religious practices that arrange marriages for children younger than 16 years of age. If such marriages include a recognition of sexual acts being a feature of a typical marriage, then this may attract liability relating to the provisions of section 17(3)(*a*) of the Sexual Offences Act. The legal defence of compliance with and in the interest of a legitimate cultural practice is recognised only in the context of the crimes in sections 9 and 22 of the Sexual Offences Act.

28.17 Sexual grooming of children

28.17.1 Definition

Section 18 of the Sexual Offences Act provides as follows:[295]

> **(1) A person ('A') who—**
> > **(*a*) manufactures, produces, possesses, distributes or facilitates the manufacture, production or distribution of an article, which is exclusively intended to facilitate the commission of a sexual act with or by a child ('B');**
> > **(*b*) manufactures, produces, possesses, distributes or facilitates the manufacture, production or distribution of a publication or film that promotes or is intended to be used in the commission of a sexual act with or by 'B';**
> > **(*c*) supplies, exposes or displays to a third person ('C')—**
> > > **(i) an article which is intended to be used in the performance of a sexual act;**
> > > **(ii) child pornography or pornography; or**
> > > **(iii) a publication or film, with the intention to encourage, enable, instruct or persuade C to perform a sexual act with B; or**
> >
> > **(*d*) arranges or facilitates a meeting or communication between C and B by any means from, to or in any part of the world, with the intention that C will perform a sexual act with B, is guilty of the offence of promoting the sexual grooming of a child.**
>
> **(2) A person ('A') who—**
> > **(*a*) supplies, exposes or displays to a child complainant ('B')—**
> > > **(i) an article which is intended to be used in the performance of a sexual act;**
> > > **(ii) child pornography or pornography; or**
> > > **(iii) a publication or film, with the intention to encourage, enable, instruct or persuade B to perform a sexual act;**
> >
> > **(*b*) commits any act with or in the presence of B or who describes the commission of any act to or in the presence of B with the intention to encourage or persuade B or to diminish or reduce any resistance or unwillingness on the part of B to—**
> > > **(i) perform a sexual act with A or a third person ('C');**
> > > **(ii) perform an act of self-masturbation in the presence of A or C or while A or C is watching;**

295 See also Snyman *Criminal Law* 389; Burchell *Principles of Criminal Law* 635–638.

(iii) be in the presence of or watch A or C while A or C performs a sexual act or an act of self-masturbation;

(iv) be exposed to child pornography or pornography;

(v) be used for pornographic purposes as contemplated in section 20(1); or

(vi) expose his or her body, or parts of his or her body to A or C in a manner or in circumstances which violate or offend the sexual integrity or dignity of B;

(*c*) arranges or facilitates a meeting or communication with B by any means from, to or in any part of the world, with the intention that A will commit a sexual act with B;

(*d*) having met or communicated with B by any means from, to or in any part of the world, invites, persuades, seduces, induces, entices or coerces B—

(i) to travel to any part of the world in order to meet A with the intention to commit a sexual act with B; or

(ii) during such meeting or communication or any subsequent meeting or communication to—

(*aa*) commit a sexual act with A;

(*bb*) discuss, explain or describe the commission of a sexual act; or

(*cc*) provide A, by means of any form of communication including electronic communication, with any image, publication, depiction, description or sequence of child pornography of B himself or herself or any other person; or

(*e*) having met or communicated with B by any means from, to or in any part of the world, intentionally travels to meet or meets B with the intention of committing a sexual act with B, is guilty of the offence of sexual grooming of a child.

28.17.2 A general comment

The decision by the Supreme Court of Appeal in *S v SM*[296] was handed down before the entry into force of section 18 of the Sexual Offences Act. However, the remarks by the SCA about the meaning of sexual grooming can be useful to give meaning to the statutory term currently in use. The SCA stated as follows:

> **It is accepted that sexual grooming consists of the perpetrator of the subsequent sexual abuse utilising and manipulating a position of authority over the victim and the victim's environment in a manner which opens the victim up to the intended abuse itself.**

The crime often occurs in the context of unequal power relationships, or in relationships where there is a high risk of abuse of trust. The relationship between a teacher and a learner at school is one such risk area.

296 *S v SM* 2013 (2) SACR 111 (SCA).

S v RC

In *S v RC*[297] the appellant appealed against his conviction and sentence under section 18 of the Sexual Offences Act. The complainant in this case was a 13-year-old girl. She was a pupil at a school where the 33-year-old appellant was a teacher. The charge of sexual grooming was based on the allegation that the appellant had described various forms of oral sex to the complainant with the intention of encouraging or persuading her to perform, or to diminish resistance on her part to the performance of a sexual act with him. The appellant argued that the state failed to establish that the conduct had been performed with the intention of encouraging or persuading the complainant to perform, or to diminish or reduce any resistance or unwillingness in that regard on her part. During trial the complainant testified that the appellant had asked her whether she understood the meaning of certain sexual terms which were part of the vernacular. The appellant admitted that the exchanges were graphic in nature, but he contended that the subjects arose and were canvassed because of an enquiry in each instance by the complainant. The appellant admitted that he was not qualified to provide sex education or guidance in life issues. The complainant testified that, a few weeks after the graphic exchanges between the appellant and the complainant, during an extra lesson in school, the appellant placed his knee between her thighs. She was wearing her school skirt and after a while he mouthed words at her telling her to open her legs a little wider. He then removed his knee and moved himself forward so that his chest touched the edge of the table top and placed his hands or a hand under the desk and under her skirt and commenced caressing the complainant's inner mid-thigh. The appellant contended that this was a complete fabrication. The trial court however accepted the complainant's version of events, thus confirming the trial court's factual findings.

The important remaining question was that of intent. The court noted that section 18(2)(*b*) of the Sexual Offences Act struck at two forms of adult misconduct. First, there is conduct with the intention to 'encourage or persuade' a child to perform a sexual act and, second, conduct with the intention to 'diminish or reduce any resistance or unwillingness' on the part of the child to engage in a sexual act. In terms of defences excluding intent, the court held that it might very well be an acceptable defence to say that 'I would not have done it' and therefore lacked intention. However, the same cannot be said with respect to the second form of intent. Indeed, *manipulation* of a child's sexual psyche by an adult for his or her own amusement or sexual diversion is harmful conduct which may have far-reaching consequences for the child, even if the adult had no intention of ultimately performing any overt sexual act with the child.[298] Regarding the accused's subjective knowledge and foresight, the court held as follows:

> **The appellant must have understood that, within the framework of the relationship that had developed between him and the complainant, a private and intimate explanation in full detail of the type of sexual activities he explained to her would have the effect of reducing her inhibitions and of diminishing a 13-year-old girl's natural resistance or unwillingness to indulge in a sexual act with the person with whom such intimacies were shared. The episode of touching which followed a little later removes any residual reasonable doubt as to whether the appellant's intention fell within the section under which he was charged.**[299]

The conviction under section 18 of the Sexual Offences Act was thus confirmed.

297 *S v RC* 2016 (1) SACR 34 (KZP).

298 *S v RC* supra at 55.

299 *S v RC* supra at 56.

28.18 Exposure of children to pornography

28.18.1 Definition

Section 19 of the Sexual Offences Act provides as follows:[300]

> **A person ('A') who unlawfully and intentionally exposes or displays or causes the exposure or display of—**
>
> **(*a*) any image, publication, depiction, description or sequence of child pornography or pornography;**
>
> **(*b*) any image, publication, depiction, description or sequence containing a visual presentation, description or representation of a sexual nature of a child, which may be disturbing or harmful to, or age-inappropriate for children, as contemplated in the Films and Publications Act, 1996 (Act No. 65 of 1996), or in terms of any other legislation; or**
>
> **(*c*) any image, publication, depiction, description or sequence containing a visual presentation, description or representation of pornography or an act of an explicit sexual nature of a person 18 years or older, which may be disturbing or harmful to, or age-inappropriate, for children, as contemplated in the Films and Publications Act, 1996, or in terms of any other law, to a child ('B'), with or without the consent of B, is guilty of the offence of exposing or displaying or causing the exposure or display of child pornography or pornography to a child.**

28.18.2 Elements

The elements of the exposure of children to pornography are:

- unlawfulness
- intent
- the child
- exposure or display of pornography or child pornography.

28.18.2.1 Unlawfulness

The crime can be committed by a male or a female as section 19 of the Sexual Offences Act provides that any natural person may be the perpetrator of the crime. Proof of necessity or compulsion on the part of the accused may exclude the unlawfulness of the accused's conduct. The accused's conduct must meet the requirements for the justification of necessity. Thus, the accused would have to have been experiencing a threat to a worthy legal interest, posed by a threat that had either commenced or was imminent, and a threat that was not due to the complicit conduct of the accused. Further, the accused's conduct must have been necessary and reasonable under the circumstances. Courts examine these factors objectively.

28.18.2.2 Intent

The accused's intention must be to unlawfully expose, display or cause the exposure or display of child pornography or pornography to a child. Proof of actual or legal intention is sufficient to prove liability.

300 See also Snyman *Criminal Law* 389.

28.18.2.3 The child

For the definition of 'child' and 'children', see section 28.14.3.4.

28.18.2.4 Exposure or display of child pornography

The accused's conduct may be punishable only if he violated the provisions of section 19 where the accused was responsible for exposing or displaying pornography or child pornography to the child. It is irrelevant if the actual display or exposure was perpetrated by another person. The person who was responsible for causing the exposure or display to the child remains liable for the violation against the child. The definition of 'child pornography' in the context of this crime is the same as the definition used in the crime created by the provisions of section 10 of the Sexual Offences Act. This is not accidental as both crimes are based on the definition of 'child pornography' in section 1 of the Act.

Section 1 of the Sexual Offences Act defines 'pornography' as:

> **any image, however created, or any description of a person, real or simulated, who is 18 years or older, of an explicit or sexual nature that is intended to stimulate erotic feelings, including any such image or description of such person—**
>
> **(*a*) engaged in an act that constitutes a sexual offence;**
> **(*b*) engaged in an act of sexual penetration;**
> **(*c*) engaged in an act of sexual violation;**
> **(*d*) engaged in an act of self-masturbation;**
> **(*e*) displaying the genital organs of such person in a state of arousal or stimulation;**
> **(*f*) unduly displaying the genital organs or anus of such person;**
> **(*g*) displaying any form of stimulation of a sexual nature of the female breasts;**
> **(*h*) engaged in sexually suggestive or lewd acts;**
> **(*i*) engaged in or as the subject of sadistic or masochistic acts of a sexual nature;**
> **(*j*) engaged in any conduct or activity characteristically associated with sexual intercourse; or**
> **(*k*) showing or describing the body, or parts of the body, of that person in a manner or in circumstances which, within the context, violate or offend the sexual integrity or dignity of that person or any other person or is capable of being used for the purposes of violating or offending the sexual integrity or dignity of that person or any other person.**

Section 19(1)(*a*) generally criminalises the conduct of unlawfully exposing or displaying (or causing the display or exposure) of child pornography or pornography. Section 19(1)(*b*) essentially prohibits the display or exposure of material depicting children that may not amount to child pornography but is offensive to the standards of the Films and Publications Act. Section 19(1)(*c*) prohibits the display or exposure of material depicting children that amounts to pornography and is offensive to the standards of the Films and Publications Act.

28.19 Using a child or benefiting from child pornography

28.19.1 Definition

Section 20 of the Sexual Offences Act provides as follows:[301]

> **(1) A person ('A') who unlawfully and intentionally uses a child complainant ('B'), with or without the consent of B, whether for financial or other reward, favour or compensation to B or to a third person ('C') or not—**
> **(*a*) for purposes of creating, making or producing;**
> **(*b*) by creating, making or producing; or**
> **(*c*) in any manner assisting to create, make or produce, any image, publication, depiction, description or sequence in any manner whatsoever of child pornography, is guilty of the offence of using a child for child pornography.**
>
> **(2) Any person who knowingly and intentionally in any manner whatsoever gains financially from, or receives any favour, benefit, reward, compensation or any other advantage, as the result of the commission of any act contemplated in subsection (1), is guilty of the offence of benefiting from child pornography.**

28.19.2 Some general comments

It is not a valid defence to a charge of using a child for child pornography for a visual representation that the accused believed that a performer in the representation that is alleged to constitute child pornography was (or was depicted as) 18 years or older unless the accused took all necessary steps to ascertain the age of that person. The accused must also have taken all reasonable steps to ensure that where the person was 18 years or older, the representation did not depict that person as being under the age of 18 years.

Section 56(6) of the Sexual Offences Act provides that it is not a valid defence to a charge under section 20(1) in respect of a visual representation that:

> **(*a*) the accused person believed that a person shown in the representation that is alleged to constitute child pornography, was or was depicted as being 18 years or older unless the accused took all reasonable steps to ascertain the age of that person; and**
> **(*b*) took all reasonable steps to ensure that, where the person was 18 years or older, the representation did not depict that person as being under the age of 18 years.**

28.20 Compelled witnessing of sexual offences (children)

The nature of the conduct proscribed by the provisions of section 21 of the Sexual Offences Act is analogous to the provisions of section 8 of the Act. There are only two significant differences between the two sections. The first difference is that the provisions of section 21 apply only to the context where the complainants are children (persons younger than 18 years of age).[302]

---

301 See Snyman *Criminal Law* 389–390.

302 *S v MD and another* 2017 (1) SACR 268 (ECB). The complainant, a 10-year-old child, was allegedly forced to witness or be in the presence of her parents, while they were engaging in a sexual act. The parents were charged under s 21(2)(*a*) of the Sexual Offences Act. The court held (at 70) that the accused 'must have consciously and deliberately created circumstances that conduce to a child witnessing the sexual activity being engaged in ... [and] the perpetrators must be conscious of the fact that the child is watching them engage in sex'. The court was unable to find beyond reasonable doubt that the accused in this case acted with the necessary intent. Both accused were thus acquitted on the charge under s 21(2)(*a*).

The provisions of section 8 apply to persons older than 18 years of age. The second difference is that the consent of the person who is older than 18 years would exclude the liability of the accused. However, the consent of the child will not exclude the unlawful nature of the accused's conduct.[303]

28.21 Flashing to children

The nature of the conduct proscribed by the provisions of section 22 of the Sexual Offences Act is analogous to the provisions of section 9 of the Act. There are only two significant differences between the two sections. The first difference is that the provisions of section 22 apply only to the context where the complainants are children (persons younger than 18 years of age). The provisions of section 9 apply to persons older than 18 years. The second difference is that the consent of the person who is older than 18 years would exclude the liability of the accused. However, the consent of the child will not exclude the unlawful nature of the accused's conduct.

28.22 Sexual exploitation of mentally disabled persons

Ever since 1977, there has been legislative recognition that there are mental conditions that vitiate the legal recognition of a person's participation in an act. This recognition was the result of the work concluded by the Commission chaired by Rumpff J.[304] These conditions affect a person's capacity for insight[305] and/or self-control.[306] A person with a mental illness or intellectual disability has a reduced capacity to participate in a manner that is given legal recognition.

Section 1 of the Sexual Offences Act defines a 'person who is mentally disabled' as:

> **[A] person affected by any mental disability, including any disorder or disability of the mind, to the extent that he or she, at the time of the alleged commission of the offence in question, was—**
>
> **(*a*) unable to appreciate the nature and reasonably foreseeable consequences of a sexual act;**
>
> **(*b*) able to appreciate the nature and reasonably foreseeable consequences of such an act, but unable to act in accordance with that appreciation;**
>
> **(*c*) unable to resist the commission of any such act; or**
>
> **(*d*) unable to communicate his or her unwillingness to participate in any such act.**

People who are mentally disabled are particularly vulnerable to being exploited by offenders who want to take advantage of their reduced capacity for insight and/or self-control. The categories identified in the Sexual Offences Act also explicitly include people who are unable to resist or communicate their unwillingness as a result of their disability.[307]

---

303 See also Snyman *Criminal Law* 390.

304 Report of the Commission of Inquiry into the Responsibility of Mentally Deranged Persons and Related Matters R.P. 69/1967, under the chairmanship of Mr Justice F. Rumpff, Judge of Appeal.

305 This refers to a person's cognitive functions. These functions relate to a person's ability to assimilate, recall, organise and process information in a logical manner. See, generally, Chapter 14.

306 This refers to a person's conative functions. They relate to a person's capacity to act voluntarily. See, generally, Chapter 14.

307 Snyman *Criminal Law* 390–392; Burchell *Principles of Criminal Law* 635–638. See also *S v Chinridze* 2015 (1) SACR 364 (GP).

In *S v Prins*[308] the court considered whether a 19-year-old woman with an apparent intellectual disability, could lawfully give consent to sexual intercourse. A report by a psychologist was submitted to the trial court. The report indicated that the complainant had an IQ range of between 50 and 69, which put her in the category of 'mild intellectual disability'. Although the complainant did receive sex education at school, and had a general anatomical awareness, she was clearly sexually inexperienced and had no comprehension of sexually transmitted illnesses and the risk of pregnancy because of intercourse. The trial court held that the complainant was unable to give lawful consent to sexual intercourse. On appeal, it was held that the concept 'person who is mentally disabled' means that such an individual must suffer from a disability or disorder which precluded the victim from being able to appreciate one or more of the consequences set out in s1 of the Act (quoted above). The court in *Prins* held that the complainant had suffered from a mental disability with the consequence that she was 'unable to appreciate both the nature and reasonably foreseeable consequences of participating in an act of sexual intercourse'.[309] The conviction for rape was upheld.

The nature of the conduct proscribed by the provisions of section 23 of the Sexual Offences Act is analogous to the provisions of section 17 of the Act. There is only one significant difference between the two sections. The difference is that the provisions of section 17 apply only to the context where the complainants are children (persons younger than 18 years of age). The provisions of section 23 may apply to persons older than 18 years.

28.23 Sexual grooming of mentally disabled persons

The nature of the conduct proscribed by the provisions of section 24 of the Sexual Offences Act is analogous to the provisions of section 18 of the Act. There is only one significant difference between the two sections. The difference is that the provisions of section 18 apply only to the context where the complainants are children (persons younger than 18 years of age). The provisions of section 24 may apply to persons older than 18 years.

28.24 Exposure of mentally disabled persons to pornography

The nature of the conduct proscribed by the provisions of section 25 of the Sexual Offences Act is analogous to the provisions of section 19 of the Act. There is only one significant difference between the two sections: the provisions of section 19 apply only to the context where the complainants are children (persons younger than 18 years of age); the provisions of section 25 may apply to persons older than 18 years.

28.25 Benefiting from mentally disabled persons for pornographic purposes

The nature of the conduct proscribed by the provisions of section 26 of the Sexual Offences Act is analogous to the provisions of section 20 of the Act. There is only one significant difference between the two sections: the provisions of section 20 apply only to the context where the complainants are children (persons younger than 18 years of age); the provisions of section 26 may apply to persons older than 18 years.

308 *S v Prins* 2017 (1) SACR 20 (WCC).

309 *S v Prins* supra at 22–23.

THIS CHAPTER IN ESSENCE

1. The crimes provided for in the Sexual Offences Act can be regarded as a consolidation of sexual crimes in South African criminal law.
2. The Act also creates crimes not previously criminalised in South African law.
3. Although this statutory framework can indeed be described as a consolidation of sexual crimes, note that there are common law crimes, such as *crimen iniuria* (discussed in Chapter 27), that are also relevant in the context of a discussion of criminal conduct of a sexual nature.

Chapter 29

Bigamy

CHAPTER OBJECTIVES

The objectives of this chapter are to:
- provide a brief historical overview of the crime of bigamy
- identify and discuss the elements of the crime of bigamy
- critically consider the rationale for the criminalisation of bigamy in a pluralistic, liberal society such as South Africa.

29.1 Historical context

There is no clear evidence of a free-standing substantive crime of bigamy under Roman law, but it was punished in one form or another.[1] There is evidence to suggest that it may have been punished as a form of *stuprum*[2] or **adultery**.[3] The unmarried party to the second marriage would escape liability if he were ignorant of the continuation of the first marriage.[4] This is proof of a *mens rea* requirement in the Roman law conception of the crime.

Roman-Dutch law seems to have been conflicted on several issues relating to understanding the crime of bigamy. Some sources suggest that there was an additional requirement for proof of sexual intercourse between the parties of the second marriage before the accused were susceptible to liability.[5] This approach to defining marriage includes the idea of consummating the marriage as a formality, which renders the marriage voidable

1 Inst 1.10.7. See also De Wet JC and Swanepoel HL *Strafreg* 4 ed (1985) 276.
2 C 9.9.18.
3 Nov 117.11.
4 C 9.9.18.
5 Van der Keessel *Crim* 48.5.6.

in innocent circumstances. Other sources suggested that the accused were liable from the moment the proposal of marriage was accepted.[6] There is evidence to suggest that the dominant view was that mere engagement was insufficient for liability, while proof of an unconsummated marriage was sufficient for liability. Proof of sexual intercourse served only as aggravating circumstances in sentencing.[7] A mistaken belief in the termination of the first marriage was sufficient to exclude *mens rea*.[8]

The provisions of section 57 of the Offences Against the Person Act of 1861 are a classic illustration of the English law approach to the crime of bigamy. The provisions of the section punished any married person who married another during the subsistence of the first marriage. The English law approach also required proof of *mens rea*. The state satisfied the onus of proof with evidence of an intention to enter into a second marriage. An accused person lacked *mens rea* if there was proof of a reasonable and bona fide belief that the first spouse was dead[9] or the first marriage was void.[10] English law did not condone a reasonable and bona fide mistaken belief that the first marriage had been terminated by divorce as excluding *mens rea*.[11]

South African courts have favoured the English law approach to punishing bigamy.[12] However, there are some fundamental differences between the two legal systems. One of the most significant differences relates to the English approach of excluding *mens rea* with a reasonable and bona fide belief. The English approach is objective and is not consistent with the subjective approach that is synonymous with the South African requirements for proof of *mens rea*.

The purpose for maintaining the crime of bigamy has been based on what was described by Cockburn CJ:

> **It involves an outrage on public decency and morals, and creates a public scandal by the prostitution of a solemn ceremony, which the law allows to be applied only to a legitimate union, to a marriage at best colourable and fictitious, which may be made and too often is made, the means of the most cruel and wicked deception.**[13]

This premise has been the justification for considering bigamy to be a crime against the community and the family.[14] The public nature of the scandalous prostitution of a solemn ceremony makes it an offence against the community. The cruel deception is perpetrated against the parties of the legitimate marriage and the purported marriage.

29.2 Definition

The definition of the crime of **bigamy** is unlawfully and intentionally entering into what purports to be a lawful marriage ceremony with one person, while at the same time being lawfully married to another.[15]

---

6 De Groot *Inl* 1.5.2.
7 Matthaeus 48.3.1.13.
8 Van der Keessel *Crim* 48.5.6.
9 *R v Tolson* (1889) 23 QBD 168.
10 *R v King* [1963] 3 ALL ER 561.
11 *R v Wheat and Stocks* [1921] 2 KB 119.
12 *R v Mdiya Lutuli* (1902) 23 NLR 253 at 255; *R v McIntyre* 1904 TS 804 at 808; *R v Jacobs* 1926 OPD 184 at 186.
13 *R v Allen* (1872) LR 1 CCR 367 at 374–375.
14 The longstanding acceptance of this premise is illustrated by early sources such as Matthaeus 48.3.1.13.
15 See also Snyman CR *Criminal Law* 6 ed (2014) 393; Burchell JM *Principles of Criminal Law* 5 ed (2016) 673.

29.3 Elements

The essential elements of bigamy are:
- unlawfulness
- intent
- a subsisting lawful first marriage
- a purported lawful second marriage.

29.3.1 Unlawfulness

The only defence that has been accepted to exclude unlawfulness is compulsion (necessity).[16] Proof of necessity or compulsion on the part of the accused may exclude the unlawfulness of the accused's conduct. The accused's conduct must meet the requirements for the justification of necessity. Thus, the accused would have to have experienced a threat to a worthy legal interest, posed by a threat that had either commenced or was imminent, and a threat that was not due to the complicit conduct of the accused. Further, the accused's conduct must have been necessary and reasonable under the circumstances. Courts examine these factors objectively.

29.3.2 Intent

The state must prove beyond reasonable doubt that the accused had fault in the form of *dolus* at the time of entering into what purported to be a lawful second marriage ceremony. At that time, the accused must have known or been able to foresee that he was still party to a subsisting marriage. The accused lacks *mens rea* if he has a bona fide belief that the first marriage was null and void *ab initio*,[17] or *was* terminated by divorce[18] or the death of the other spouse.

Further, the accused must know or be able to foresee that he is entering into what purports to be a lawful second marriage. There have been instances where marriages have been set aside because of *error in negotio*[19] where foreigners were unaware that they were participating in a marriage ceremony conducted in English.

29.3.3 A subsisting lawful first marriage

There must be proof of an existing monogamous marriage that is recognised by the state as a valid marriage.[20] There will be no liability in cases where the first marriage was null and void *ab initio*,[21] or terminated because of divorce or death of a participating spouse before the accused entered into what purports to be a lawful marriage ceremony.

29.3.4 A purported lawful second marriage

The accused must enter into what purports to be a lawful marriage ceremony with one person while being lawfully married to another.[22] It does not matter whether the purported marriage is void or voidable for any other reason other than it is bigamous.[23]

---

16 *Smith v Smith* 1948 (4) SA 61 (N).

17 *R v King* supra.

18 English law did not accept a mistaken belief that the first marriage was terminated by divorce as evidenced in cases including *R v Lees* 1927 EDL 314. Fortunately, South African law does not suffer from the same handicap.

19 *Benjamin v Salkinder and another* (1908) 25 SC 512; *Kanatopsky v Kanatopsky* 1935 EDL 308.

20 *R v McIntyre* supra at 808.

21 The marriages must have been void and not merely voidable. Void marriages cannot sustain liability for the accused. However, a voidable first marriage is sufficient to satisfy the requirement of a valid first marriage. Voidable marriages remain valid marriages until they are officially annulled.

22 *R v Brawn* (1843) 1 Car & Kir 144; *R v Allen* supra; *R v Mdiya Lutuli* supra; *R v Jacobs* supra.

23 *R v Brawn* supra; *R v Allen* supra.

29.4 Some general comments

There is a superficial overlap between this crime and the crime of fraud. However, if the parties misrepresent themselves in their marriage vows, this is not punishable as fraud. In many related instances, the prejudice is considered to be too trivial, remote or fanciful to warrant liability. If they lie about their marital status, they will be guilty of bigamy.

Mistakes of law[24] or fact have the capacity to exclude *mens rea.* A person who is under the impression that it is lawful to enter into the second marriage should escape liability. An example is where an immigrant comes from a background where polygamy is legitimate. The same should hold true for a person who enters into a marriage with the expectation that it is a legitimate customary practice. The mistake must be bona fide and reasonable to exonerate the accused. A court needs to use a degree of additional caution when assessing the reasonableness of the mistake. The enquiry must avoid resembling a test for *culpa.*

Zimbabwean courts were prepared to recognise indigenous, customary, polygamous marriages as satisfying the requirements of a valid first marriage at a time when the South African courts did not.[25] Purporting to enter into a second marriage with another party through authorised marriage officers was recognised as bigamy.[26]

Polygamous marriages were originally not recognised in South African law for the purpose of bigamy. Customary marriages were not recognised under South African law as lawful marriages because of what has been acknowledged to be discriminatory public policies. The principle was stated as regardless of whether the polygamous marriage was the first marriage or the second purported ceremony, the law did not recognise polygamous marriages as valid marriages.[27]

This anomaly was controversial. A question that arose was related to cases where the traditional marriages were the second marriages. The question raised was whether a traditional marriage ceremony qualifies as being part of the prohibited *actus reus*. It is difficult to explain how a traditional marriage ceremony would amount to a purported lawful second marriage if it were not carried out in the manner that the law recognised as characteristic of a valid marriage. For example, as in *R v Jacobs*, a second marriage that was conducted by a person who was not a legitimate marriage officer would not qualify.[28] In principle, a polygamous marriage should not qualify as a second marriage because it would not purport to create a legally binding arrangement.

However, there has been some relief to the legal confusion associated with customary marriages. All existing and future customary marriages were given recognition in South African law with the provisions of section 2(3) of the Recognition of Customary Marriages Act 120 of 1998.[29] The only limitation imposed on traditional polygamous marriages is a requirement that the participants must apply for a court order to approve a written agreement on the future matrimonial property system.[30]

Section 3(2) of the Customary Marriages Act prohibits spouses who are party to a customary marriage from entering into civil marriages with other people. Section 10(4) prohibits spouses who are party to a civil marriage from entering into customary marriages.

---

24 *S v De Blom* 1977 (3) SA 513 (A).
25 *R v Tshipa* 1958 (2) SA 384 (SR) at 390.
26 *R v Kaodza* 1912 SR 6; *R v M'Gedesa* 1917 SR 37.
27 *R v Zonyane* 1912 EDL 361.
28 *R v Jacobs* supra. The principle was also recognised in *R v Allen* supra.
29 On 15 November 2000.
30 S 7(6) of the Recognition of Customary Marriages Act 120 of 1998.

Thus, it is clear that the legislature intended to recognise polygamous marriages, but only in the context of customary or traditional marriages. Civil marriages are still limited to being officially monogamous. It is interesting to note that the law will not criminalise the presence of a *de facto* additional spouse who enjoys the full benefits and duties of marriage, but will criminalise a *de jure* spouse even where they have no benefit of marriage from their *de jure* spouse.

Does the accused escape liability if the second purported wife and the legitimate wife know about and support the second marriage? There may be no offence relating to the deception of anyone. However, the *prejudice* created by the prostitution of a solemn ceremony may be sufficient to punish the accused. If the parties to the marriage all participated with full awareness of the role of the other parties, then they may all be liable, at least as accomplices.

If the accused was a serial divorcé with an abundance of ex-spouses, why would he be considered to be respectful of the sanctity attached to the solemn ceremony? Perhaps the law merely reflects our society's position that there is no criminal significance for respecting the sanctity of marriage and the vows made in respect of that marriage. However, the law protects the sanctity of the process of legally recognising a marriage. If a party misrepresents himself by suggesting that he is unmarried, he will be criminally liable. However, if a party misrepresents himself by promising to be faithful to his spouse for the rest of their married lives, such conduct is currently considered to be outside the realm of criminal liability.[31] Criminal consequences only attach to circumstances that involve an authorised state official who participates in a defective process. Any breach of promise made in terms of the vows themselves is no longer subject to criminal punishment.[32]

DISCUSSION

Personal liberty, privacy and morality (and the views of society)

JS Mill was of the firm belief that the use of public power against a member of society should only be relevant in circumstances where it is necessary to prevent prejudice to other members of society.[33] The criminalisation of bigamy remains anathematic to the approach advocated by Mill because of the use of public power in a circumstance where the prejudice to other members of society is at least questionable, if not remote, farfetched or negligible.

There is a point where respect for a free person's autonomy is beyond public scrutiny. There is a degree of prejudice that is worthy of criminal attention. There is also a degree of respect that must be given to the privacy of how married couples choose to manage their marriage(s) as with the rest of their private lives.[34] Public/private morality and the law, as well as the convictions of society, seem to be a recurring theme of special relevance for criminal law.

The criminalisation of bigamy seems to rest on more than just private morality or personal choice. To the extent that third parties (or society at large) is made to believe that a couple is lawfully married (while they are not), all sorts of consequences can flow from such a wrong belief, hence the continued justification for the existence of this crime.

31 Adultery is no longer recognised as a crime in South Africa. See *Fitzgerald v Green* 1911 EDL 432 and, most notably, *Fitzgerald v Green and others* 1914 AD 88.

32 Adultery was subject to penal sanctions in medieval Europe. See Brundage JA *Law, Sex and Christian Society in Medieval Europe* (1990) 518–519.

33 Mill JS *On Liberty* 2 ed (1859).

34 Report of the Wolfenden Committee on Homosexual Offences and Prostitution (1957) Cmnd 247 at Section 61.

THIS CHAPTER IN ESSENCE

1. The rationale for the criminalisation of human conduct is not always clear or self-evident. It is also not always easy to classify crimes, for instance as a crime against the family, and so on.
2. This chapter shows that the criminalisation of bigamy remains based on society's moral interest in the protection of the institution of marriage.
3. However, as we suggested in the discussion box above, in a liberal and pluralistic society, the protected interest of the institution of marriage may be regarded as more fluid and not entirely self-evident.

Chapter 30

Abduction

CHAPTER OBJECTIVES

The objectives of this chapter are to:

- provide a brief historical overview of the common law crime of abduction
- identify and discuss the elements of the crime of abduction
- evaluate the rationale for this crime with reference to the Constitution and statutory frameworks aimed at protecting vulnerable persons.

30.1 Historical context

Roman law under Justinian was particularly harsh in punishing perpetrators of the crime of *raptus*. This crime consisted of removing, whether by violence or consent, a woman of any marital status to marry or have sexual intercourse with her. The interests protected included those of the victim as well as her guardians or relatives. However, the law tended to focus on the rights of the parent/guardian because both parties to the abduction were liable to be executed. The rights protected included the right of the parent/guardian to consent to marriage. The right to kill an abductor caught *in flagrante delicto* was given to the woman's father, blood relative, husband, tutor, patron and owner in the case of a slave. If the woman agreed to the marriage against the wishes of her parents, her abductor's property was forfeit to her parents.

In Germanic law, the parent/guardian had a direct pecuniary interest in every woman under his authority and protection. Forcibly abducting women was a recognised mode of securing marriage. However, the *parental power* formed a part of the estate of the parent/guardian and could be sold like any other portion of the estate. Ordinarily, parental power was sold as any ordinary chattel (personal property/goods) during a valid marriage with proper consent. It would be illegally lost where there was a clandestine marriage without the consent of the parent/guardian. The crime was thus a species of theft despite the woman's consent.

Roman-Dutch law also considered abduction, normally with violence as an element, to be an infringement of the paternal power or guardianship.[1] Some of the old Dutch jurists were ready to accept that the crime of *raptus* included the abduction of minor girls or boys from their lawful guardians to marry or have sexual intercourse with the minor without the guardians' consent. Circumstances that mitigated punishment included those where the woman was a harlot (unless reformed), the accused had previously seduced the woman, the woman was the man's fiancée, the woman consented, marriage followed, and where the woman was still a virgin.

The English law approach was originally best illustrated by sections 17–21 of the Sexual Offences Act of 1956. Four of these sections create crimes that involve taking a girl from her parent/guardian's possession. Some of the offences focus on a sexual motive while one is for proprietary gain. The crime created by section 20 simply criminalised the taking of an unmarried girl under the age of 16 years. These crimes do not really correspond with the South African version of the crime.

South African law recognised the crime of abduction from an early stage. Reported cases can, at the very least, be traced back to 1880. The approach in South African law was based on the Roman-Dutch approach, which provided that the crime was evident despite the absence or presence of consent, or whether the purpose was marriage or intercourse. There was a need to distinguish the crime from seduction, which is not a crime. The distinction was based on the abductor's intention to take the complainant away from her custodian's control permanently or for a substantial period.

The protected interests primarily focus on the rights of the parent/guardian. Where the victim is no longer legally under the parent/guardian's authority, she cannot be abducted. However, she may be a victim of kidnapping if she was taken against her will. The crime of abduction primarily protects the interests of those whose consent is necessary for marriage. Therefore the minor's consent does not exclude the unlawfulness of the act. However, the older the minor is, the less severe the punishment is. Forcible abduction is also considered to be a wrong against the minor's interests.

There may be an overlap between kidnapping and abduction. If the minor did not give consent, there is an overlap between the two crimes. If the minor did consent, there may still be a case of abduction even if there may not be a case of kidnapping.

The fundamental difference between the crime of abduction and the crime of kidnapping relates to the interests which are protected through the crime. Kidnapping focuses on protecting the victim's liberty. The victim of kidnapping is the person who is taken against his will. Abduction differs from kidnapping because the real victim is not the person who is taken. The true victim of abduction is the parent of the child. The crime of abduction occurs when the parent is deprived of parental control over the child through the actions of another person.

---

1 For an overview of the Roman-Dutch authorities, see De Wet JC and Swanepoel HL *Strafreg* 4 ed (1985) 255–262.

30.2 Definition

Abduction is the 'unlawful taking of a minor out of the control of his or her custodian with the intention of enabling someone to marry or have sexual intercourse with that minor'.[2]

30.3 Elements

The essential elements of common law abduction are:

- unlawfulness
- taking
- taking a minor
- removal from the custodian's control
- intent.

30.3.1 Unlawfulness

The consent of the custodian is the best defence to exclude unlawfulness. The consent of both parents is required because this is the necessary consent for the minor to be married. The father may no longer overrule the mother. Where the parents are divorced, it is the consent of the custodian parent that is required. The consent of one parent will be sufficient if the other parent has passed away. Where both parents are dead, the consent of the de facto custodian suffices.

The consent may be given expressly or tacitly. Consent induced by duress or fraud is insufficient. The consent must be both for the physical removal of the minor and the purpose of the removal, whether it is marriage or sexual intercourse. A parent can give consent for the minor to marry. Parental consent to the removal of the minor, even for immoral purposes, is a valid defence. The parent's consent would exclude liability for abduction, but it would not exclude liability for rape.

Consent of the minor is irrelevant for abduction. Even if the minor solicited the abduction or induced the accused to take her away,[3] the minor's willingness to leave does not exclude liability. If the guardian consents but the minor does not, the crime may be assault or rape, but not abduction. Compulsion may also exclude the unlawfulness of the act.

A court order may legitimise taking the minor, but the idea of a court order obliging the minor to be taken away for marriage or for having sexual intercourse with another person is difficult to imagine.

30.3.2 Taking

Taking does not necessarily imply the use of force. The accused may complete taking the victim even if this occurs with her consent and cooperation. As previously mentioned, the minor's willingness to be with the abductor does not vitiate the unlawfulness of the conduct. Further, it does not detract from the fact that taking has been completed even if there was no force used to facilitate the taking.

The taking may be physical, which involves the abductor physically moving the minor from one place to another. In such instances, the accused provides the means for taking the minor out of parental control. The taking may also be constructive, for example where the accused does not actually take the minor away but persuades her to leave. In such instances,

2 Snyman, CR *Criminal Law* 6 ed (2014) 395; Burchell *Principles of Criminal Law* 5 ed (2016) 666.

3 *R v Kahn* 1928 CPD 328; *R v Ndlanavu and others* 1910 EDL 335.

the minor accompanies the abductor voluntarily. It follows that the minor need not actually leave with the accused when leaving the parental control. It is sufficient if she leaves voluntarily after arranging to meet with the accused somewhere else. Another example is when the minor is already away from home and she is persuaded not to return.

It is not essential for the victim to be moved physically from one place to another. If the accused were to induce marriage to a minor at her parent's home but without their consent, this would be a case of taking and the accused would be liable for abduction.

The minor must be removed from the control of her custodians. This control is not limited to the time she is physically inside the home. Parental control remains in effect when the minor is away through persons who are *in loco parentis.*

The taking need not be for a permanent or an indefinite period. Taking for any substantial period will suffice. The test for abduction is whether the accused had the intention to take the complainant away from her custodian's control either permanently or for a substantial period.

There needs to be proof of a causal link between the conduct of the accused and the removal of the minor from the control of the custodians. Where the accused played a passive role, providing neither the physical means of leaving nor inducement to do so, he does not commit abduction. For example, an accused person cannot be liable for abduction for taking the minor to live with him after she removed herself from control.[4]

There may be cases where the custodians have completely relinquished control over the minor. An example is when a minor has left home and the parents neither know nor care about the minor's whereabouts. In such cases, abduction is not possible because there is no parental control that is being infringed.

30.3.3 Taking a minor

The common law originally provided that the person who was taken out of parental control must be a minor. The abducted person may be male or female. The common law standard relating to minority was based on the idea that minority would terminate once a person reaches the age of 18 years (coming of age) or when the person marries.

Recent developments relating to various laws which apply to the concept of minority have made it necessary to consider relinquishing reliance on the term 'minor'. It has been argued that it is more accurate to describe the person who is taken as a 'child' instead of a minor. The Constitution clearly identifies that a 'child' is any person who is younger than 18 years old.

However, a challenge to relying on the term 'child' instead of the term 'minor' is the fact that the term 'child' does not distinguish between unmarried and married children. Children who are already married cannot be victims of abduction because they are not subject to parental control. The crime of abduction can be perpetrated only in the context of an unmarried child who is subject to parental control.

The fact that the victim is not a virgin or is a prostitute does not affect liability. It may, however, affect the sentencing.[5]

30.3.4 Removal from the custodian's control

The custodian's control must have been de facto in effect at the time of the taking. There is no abduction in cases where the victim has already escaped the custodian's control when

4 *R v Pearston* 1940 OPD 153; *R v Cornick* 1957 (2) PH K140 (CPD).

5 *R v Adams and Ibrahim* 1911 CPD 863 at 868–870; *R v Clark* 1914 TPD 50 at 54.

the accused exerts an influence over the minor.[6] It is enough that the minor should be in somebody's control. It is irrelevant who the de facto custodian was. It is important to determine who had control over the minor because otherwise there is no crime.

The custodian does not need to abandon control over the minor.[7] The minor is not free from parental control when the custodian has consented to the minor's visit or stay with someone. The person who is entrusted with the care of the minor becomes *in loco parentis.*

The minor is also not free from parental control when she goes somewhere without intending to leave parental control. For example, when a minor goes to a party without permission from the custodian and decides to leave with the accused, the accused remains liable for abduction if the custodian's control was de facto in effect when he persuaded the minor to leave with him. However, if the girl left with the accused after she had independently decided to escape parental control, then the accused cannot be liable for abduction.

The deprivation of the custodian's control may be complete where the accused intends to marry the minor, even before the accused accomplishes that ambition. *R v Hanna*[8] is an excellent illustration of this principle.

R v Hanna

In this case, the minor girl was an 18-year-old living in her brother's house. The accused was her boyfriend. The girl claimed that she was pregnant by the accused, thereby inducing him to marry her. They went to the magistrate's office to get married. The magistrate refused to perform the marriage. The minor was returned to her brother's house within a few hours. The accused was originally convicted of abduction. His appeal against his conviction was dismissed. The court was unmoved by the plea from the accused that he planned to return the minor to her brother's home after he had married her. He was guilty of abduction even though the marriage never took place.

30.3.5 Intent

The *mens rea* for this crime can consist of *dolus directus, dolus indirectus* or *dolus eventualis.* There are two principal aspects to the intention for abduction:

- Intention about the essential elements of the offence
- A specific intent that someone shall marry or have sexual intercourse with the minor, and that the minor shall remain out of the *de facto* control for a substantial period

The prosecutor must prove that the accused knew, or at least foresaw as a possibility which he recklessly disregarded, that the abductee was a minor, the minor was in somebody's control and there was no consent to the taking. The accused must have intended to take the minor unlawfully.[9]

---

6 In *R v Pearston* supra, the minor girl wanted to escape parental custody. The accused did not further her cause by word or deed. The girl told the accused that she intended to walk to Pretoria. The accused tried to dissuade her and even tried to get the police to stop her. He eventually accompanied her because he did not want to allow an unescorted girl to walk the road at night. Once they had walked quite a distance, he secured a ride for her on a wagon. The court could not find a causal link between his assistance and her absconding.

7 In *R v Cornick* supra, a schoolgirl did not want to go home from school because she feared a thrashing from her mother. She persuaded the accused to allow her to stay at his house by threatening to commit suicide. It was held that the girl herself had left home and she had not been abducted or taken. The girl's parents did not have to abandon parental control before the court accepted that the girl was no longer under parental control when the accused allowed her to stay at his house. A similar line of reasoning was taken in *R v Pearston* supra.

8 *R v Hanna* 1937 TPD 236 at 237.

9 *R v Churchill* 1959 (2) SA 575 (A); *S v Sashi* 1976 (2) SA 446 (N).

The accused must know that the consent required is actual consent by the guardian. No accused can say that he thought that a custom could override the refusal of consent or override criminal law. In taking the minor from custodial control, the accused must have the specific intention that he or someone else will marry or have sexual intercourse with the minor. If the accused intends something else, even if it is of a sexual or indecent character, which excludes these objects, there is no abduction.

The prohibited intention must be operative at the time when the accused took the minor out of custodial control. It makes no difference that the accused considers his object to be conditional on receiving subsequent parental ratification. If the motive of the accused is innocent at the time in question, he will not be guilty of abduction if his altruism transforms into lust and he has intercourse with her after she has escaped from parental control. The minor is already out of the custodian's control by the time the accused exerts an influence.

S v Sashi[10]

The accused was a traditional healer who came to a kraal where the 17-year-old minor lived with her father. The accused lived at the kraal for some time with the minor and her father. On two occasions, the accused had travelled with the minor with the father's consent. On a third occasion, the accused and the minor did not return to the father's kraal. The accused and the minor began to live together as man and wife. The accused was originally convicted of abduction. However, the conviction and sentence were set aside on review. There was nothing in the evidence to show that the appellant had the intention of marrying or having intercourse with the minor at the time that he took her away from her kraal.

Mere seduction is not abduction.[11] It becomes abduction only if the accused intends to keep the minor away permanently or for a substantial period.[12] The courts have not been exact in defining how much time should be considered a substantial period.[13] However, a whole night has been previously accepted as a substantial period.[14] An intention of permanent or substantial deprivation may be proved directly.[15] The period for which the minor is kept away is relevant to showing the state of mind of the accused.[16] If the accused only intends to have intercourse with the minor before returning the minor home a few hours later, it would be seduction (and possibly rape), but not abduction.

However, if the accused intends to marry the minor, it does not matter if he does not want her to be away from home for a substantial period.[17] The underlying principle seems to be that the accused intends to invade the custodian's control. The former minor's now majority status would terminate the custodian's control over the minor. It is irrelevant that no one married or had intercourse with the minor. All that is relevant is whether the accused intended intercourse or marriage to follow the taking.[18]

10 *S v Sashi* supra.
11 *R v Hanna* supra.
12 *R v Adams and Ibrahim* supra at 867; *R v Ismail* 1943 CPD 418 at 421; *R v Hlapo* 1944 OPD 166 at 168; *R v Hanna* supra at 239; *S v Killian* 1977 (2) SA 31(C) at 35–36.
13 *R v Ismail* supra at 421.
14 *R v Kahn* supra at 333; *R v Hanna* supra at 239.
15 *R v Hanna* supra at 239.
16 *R v Hanna* supra at 239.
17 *R v Hanna* supra 236.
18 *R v Hanna* supra.

30.4 Some general comments

The position adopted in *R v Hanna* may be too extreme. The fact that there was no actual removal from parental control should have been taken into consideration. At best, there was only an attempt to remove the minor from parental control. This case may have been best described as attempted abduction. The accused's liability for the crime is also controversial because it was the minor who induced the accused to marry her. We submit that the accused may have been acting under compulsion when he submitted to his girlfriend's pressure and this should have excluded the unlawfulness of his conduct.

However, the court was clear in holding that it did not consider the consent of the minor, or the fact that she had induced the accused, to be a valid defence. The court considered the accused to be liable from the moment he intended to marry the minor. This position seems extreme because it raises the question of when the conduct of the accused would be an attempted abduction only rather than the completed crime.

The crime protects the factual exercise of control over the minor and the custodian's consent to marriage. The crime can now be committed in the context of male or female victims. However, it is restricted to the context of unmarried minors. Legislative versions of the crime have complemented and supplemented the common law crime throughout the history of the South African common law crime.

The legislative interventions were enacted as part of a legislative scheme to suppress child prostitution. Examples of such legislative interventions can be seen in the provisions of sections 12 and 13 of the Sexual Offences Act 23 of 1957. The most recent legislative interventions have been created through the provisions of the Criminal Law (Sexual Offences and Related Matters) Amendment Act 32 of 2007 (Sexual Offences Act).

The introduction of legislation, such as the Sexual Offences Act, accommodates the shortcomings of the common law crime of abduction. One such classic shortcoming is that the crime of abduction can be committed only in the context of people who want to take the minor for marriage or sexual intercourse. The common law definition of sexual intercourse was originally limited to the penetration of the female genital organ by a male genital organ. It was only in 2007 that anal penetration of a female was considered to be sexual intercourse.[19]

Anal penetration of a male has never been accepted as sexual intercourse in the South African common law. The provisions of the Sexual Offences Act recognise anal and genital penetration to be part of the definition of sexual penetration. Therefore, a male minor who was taken out of custodial control for homosexual intercourse would not be a victim of abduction as it is defined in our common law. However, the provisions of the Sexual Offences Act are available to ensure that the perpetrators are now punished. The provisions that relate to human trafficking and child prostitution are available to accommodate the shortcomings of the common law.[20]

Further, the provisions of the legislation accommodate victims other than unmarried minors. The common law provisions are concerned only with the welfare of unmarried minors. If the minor was married or a person with full majority status, she could never be a victim of abduction. Now, any person who is unlawfully taken for purposes including sexual slavery may be prosecuted in terms of the legislative provisions.

19 *Masiya v Director of Public Prosecutions, Pretoria and another (Centre for Applied Legal Studies and another, amici curiae)* 2007 (5) SA 30 (CC); 2007 (2) SACR 435 (CC).

20 See Chapter 49.

30.5 The custom of *ukuthwala*

A special consideration in the context of South African customary law is the concept of *ukuthwala*.[21] This is a customary form of abduction that was recognised as legitimate modus of obtaining marriage. This custom was recognised as unlawful in *R v Sita*.[22]

In 2010, a 14-year-old girl from the village of eNgcobo, in the Eastern Cape, was kidnapped from her home and forced to marry her kidnapper, Mvumeleni Jezile, by her grandmother. The girl was subsequently raped and assaulted by her kidnapper, a 32-year-old man. When the girl managed to escape and return to her home, her family forced her to return to Mvumeleni Jezile.

Once the kidnapper was arrested and charged, he tried to justify his conduct by relying on the claim that he was practicing the custom of *ukuthwala intombi*, commonly referred to as *ukuthwala*. Mvumeleni Jezile claimed that he had facilitated a customary marriage to the girl through the custom of *ukuthwala*. One of the questions the court had to answer was whether *ukuthwala* could constitute a valid defence. The court rejected this aberrant form of *ukuthwala* as a valid defence.[23]

Taking girls for inducing a customary marriage is not unique to the case against Mvumeleni Jezile. The practice of *ukuthwala* is notoriously rife in many rural areas in South Africa. Unfortunately, most cases go unreported.

30.5.1 What is the custom of *ukuthwala*?

A customary marriage between spouses-to-be generally involves formal negotiations between their families. The father of the bride is the only party who is expected to consent to the marriage. The consent of the bride is preferred but it is not necessary. As a consequence, the father of the bride could arrange a marriage with a person whom the bride may not desire. The father could also refuse an offer for marriage from a suitor the bride favours. The father could refuse the offer for any reason including the suitor's inability to pay *lobola* or because he simply does not like the suitor. Some theorists believe that the practice of *ukuthwala* evolved as a means of circumventing the obligation to receive the father of the bride's consent.

There is evidence of a practice resembling the contemporary version of *ukuthwala* in the 19th century. Early colonial court records show evidence of customary marriages which were concluded without the consent of the father of the bride and/or the bride herself. The phrase *ukuthwala intombi* became synonymous with customary marriages which were concluded without the consent of the bride and/or the bride's father. However, the colonial records show that in most instances the bride was a willing accomplice of her husband.

In the original context of customary marriages preceded by *ukuthwala*, the practice was a means of forcing the bride's family to negotiate with the family of the man who had taken the prospective bride. The negotiation between the families is a feature which distinguishes *ukuthwala* and a form of kidnapping which was not tolerated by custom. The family initiating the *ukuthwala* custom would inform the prospective bride's family of their intentions and

21 A Nguni word, the English translation of which is 'to carry'. See also Olivier NJJ et al *Indigenous Law* (1995) 9–10; Bennett TW *Customary Law in South Africa* (2004) 212–213.

22 *R v Sita* 1954 (4) SA 20 (E). The accused abducted a 14-year-old girl. He claimed the abduction was in accordance with the custom of *ukuthwala*. The court, *a quo*, upheld the defence and acquitted the accused. On appeal, the verdict of the magistrate was set aside, and the case was remitted for further hearing. The court held that the requirement for consent cannot be overridden by custom. Custom would also not legitimise rape.

23 See *Jezile v S and others* (A 127/2014) [2015] ZAWCHC 31; 2015 (2) SACR 452 (WCC); 2016 (2) SA 62 (WCC); [2015] 3 All SA 201 (WCC) (23 March 2015).

the amount they were prepared to pay for *lobola*. There is evidence to suggest that the prospective spouses would not engage in sexual intercourse until the negotiations for the marriage had been concluded. The prospective bride would be in the care of the women of her prospective in-laws. If sexual intercourse did take place before the negotiations were concluded, then the prospective groom would also have to pay damages as well as paying the *lobola*.

A significant controversy which has brewed around the custom of *ukuthwala* is whether the practice condones the taking of girls as young as 12 years. The answer differs depending on the source of the answer. There are traditional leaders who take offence at the idea and there are communities and traditional leaders who are not as offended. Modern communities where the practice is prevalent generally accept that children can be targeted for *ukuthwala*. The controversy is exacerbated by the fact that the Constitution recognises and endorses customs which are based on the practices of modern communities. However, the Constitution also protects the best interests of children as being of paramount importance.

DISCUSSION

Does the crime of abduction provide sufficient protection against ***ukuthwala*****?**

The crime of abduction is relevant to the context of *ukuthwala*. Cultural critics of the custom of *ukuthwala* have criticised the fact that the custom focuses on the removal of the child from parental control and extinguishes the parent's role in consenting to their child's marriage. One of the main roles of the crime of abduction is the protection of the parent's right to decide who and when the child can marry, thus preserving parental control over the child. However, the crime of abduction does have its limitations in the context of *ukuthwala*.

The crime of abduction ignores the custom's impact on the girl who is taken. Critics of *ukuthwala* have voiced their objection to the fact that the custom perpetuates outdated notions of patriarchal power and cultural patriarchy. In the context of *ukuthwala*, the crime of abduction is subject to the same criticism.

The crime is only relevant when the girl is taken out of parental control by the abductor. If an underage girl unilaterally escapes from parental control, the person who takes her for marriage and/or rape is not liable for the crime of abduction. The damage to the health and well-being of the girl is not a relevant consideration for determining liability for abduction. The fact that the girl is cruelly robbed of her childhood is not a significant consequence to determine liability for abduction. The secondary victimisation to an underage girl who tries to escape from the perpetrators of *ukuthwala* also includes being shunned by her community, who consider the custom to be legitimate.

The harm to the girl is not an interest that is protected by the crime of abduction. In the context of *ukuthwala*, the crime of abduction is only relevant when it can preserve patriarchal power and cultural patriarchy. Fortunately, the shortcomings of the common law crime of abduction can be addressed by punishing *ukuthwala* as a form of human trafficking. Some suggest that 'a *bona fide* belief in the lawfulness of the *ukuthwala* custom might well exclude fault'.[24]

24 Burchell *Principles of Criminal Law* 672.

In *S v Jezile,*[25] the court rejected the notion that an aberrant form of *ukuthwala* could secure protection under South African law. This form of *ukuthwala* was thus rejected as a possible defence against charges of human trafficking and rape.[26]

30.5.2 Is *ukuthwala* a form of human trafficking?

The question of whether *ukuthwala* constitutes a form of human trafficking is further explored in Chapter 49.

THIS CHAPTER IN ESSENCE

1. The common law crime of abduction still exists in South African law as a crime against the family.
2. The crime of abduction must be viewed in the context of societal changes and changes in public morality. It must also be viewed in the context of statutory frameworks that deal with the protection of vulnerable persons such as children.
3. It is important to view the common law crime of abduction in the context of sexual crimes that are discussed in Chapter 28 as well as the crime of human trafficking discussed in Chapter 49.

25 *Jezile v S* supra.
26 *Jezile v S* supra 95.

Chapter 31

Theft

CHAPTER OBJECTIVES

The objectives of this chapter are to identify and discuss the elements of the most important common law and statutory forms of theft, namely:

- common law theft, including theft of money
- theft by false pretences
- possession of stolen property
- receiving stolen property
- unauthorised borrowing.

31.1 Theft

31.1.1 A brief history

A historical review of theft reveals that the law is generally against spoliation. The legal emphasis falls on a consensual transfer of property consistent with encouraging orderly economic activity. Theft is the antithesis of this. For this reason, it attracted criminal liability in early Roman law where theft was defined as 'the fraudulent handling of a thing with the intention of deriving a benefit, either from the thing itself, or from its use, or from its possession'.[1] Roman law required an act of theft, or *contrectatio*, which amounted to a physical handling of the property. This definition was generally endorsed in Holland and was accepted in South African law. English law exerted some influence via the Transkei Penal Code.[2]

1 This is a translation by Snyman of the Digest 47.2.1.3 as it appears in Burchell JM *Principles of Criminal Law* 5 ed (2016) 690 fn 9 and Snyman CR *Criminal Law* 6 ed (2014) 487 fn 56.

2 S 176 of the Transkei Penal Code.

31.1.2 Definition

X commits **theft** by unlawfully and intentionally taking the property of Y, which is capable of being stolen, without Y's consent, and appropriating it to himself, X.[3]

31.1.3 Elements

The elements of theft are:

- unlawfulness
- intent
- appropriation
- the property must be capable of being stolen.

31.1.3.1 Unlawfulness

Unlawfulness may be negated by Y consenting to the removal of the property by X. Other circumstances negating unlawfulness include *negotiorum gestio*[4] and the application of the *de minimis* rule.[5]

31.1.3.2 Intent

This element excludes the consideration of motive and negligence. The state is not required to prove that the removal of an article was for gain.[6] Nor is it possible to commit theft negligently. The intention must relate to each element of theft.

As to *unlawfulness*, X must be aware that Y has not consented to the removal of his property.[7] Further, where X is under the misapprehension that he is entitled to remove the property as a matter of right, X does not commit theft.[8]

As to *appropriation*, X must intend to appropriate property. This involves an *intention to deprive permanently the owner of his benefit of ownership of the article.* X must intend to make the article his own.[9] The temporary retention of property, removed by X from Y, with the intention to return it, does not amount to theft. Theft does not include the unauthorised borrowing of property. In *R v Sibiya*,[10] the appellant and another, employed at a garage, took a car parked at the garage for a joy ride. At all material times they intended to return the car, but during their journey, the appellant's companion crashed the car in a donga at the side of the road. Both were still at the scene of the accident when the police arrived. In allowing the appeal and setting the conviction aside, Schreiner ACJ came to the following conclusion:

> **The law requires for the crime of theft, not only that the thing should have been taken without belief that the owner ... had consented ... to the taking, but also that the taker should have intended to terminate the owner's enjoyment of his rights, or, in other words, to deprive him of the whole benefit of his ownership.**[11]

---

3 *R v Jona* 1961(2) SA 301 (W). See Snyman *Criminal Law* 475; Burchell *Principles of Criminal Law* 689.

4 This occurs where X intervenes in the affairs of Y without the consent of Y by, for example, removing Y's property from Y's burning house while Y is away.

5 *De minimis non curat lex.* The law does not concern itself with trivialities where, for example, the property concerned is of little value. See *S v Kgogong* 1980 (3) SA 600 (A). See also Chapter 13.

6 *R v Kinsella* 1961 (3) SA 519 (C).

7 *S v Speedy* 1985 (2) SA 782 (A).

8 *R v De Ruiter* 1957 (3) SA 361 (A).

9 See *Riba v S* [2010] 1 All SA 331 (SCA) where the accused, a police officer, failed to enter stolen goods in a police register. The court held that the conduct of the accused and his co-accused strongly indicated intent to appropriate the goods in question. The court rejected the explanations for the late entry into the relevant register (SAP 13) of the complainant's goods that were seized earlier.

10 *R v Sibiya* 1955 (4) SA 247 (A).

11 *R v Sibiya* supra at 257C.

As to the *property being capable of being stolen*, the distinction between a fungible thing (a thing consumed by use) and a non-fungible one is important. When X removes a fungible thing and consumes it, theft has taken place even if he intended to replace it at a later stage. Alternatively, the unauthorised borrowing of a non-fungible thing does not amount to theft.[12]

31.1.3.3 Appropriation

South African law has adopted the Roman law element of *contrectatio*, which requires the assumption of control by X of Y's property. However, control may be assumed without the actual removal or carrying away of the article.[13] A school of thought contends that the Roman law of *contrectatio* ought to be replaced with the more flexible concept of appropriation. This concept focuses on an assumption of rights of ownership by X to the detriment of Y who has been deprived of his proprietary rights.[14]

In this regard, Snyman argues persuasively that the Roman law element of handling property, *contrectatio*, does not suit current mercantile requirements.[15] The author prefers the use of the more adaptable concept of appropriation as adopted by our courts. Appropriation comprises the deprivation of a person's property and the concomitant ostensible exercise of ownership[16] of the property by the appropriator. This envisages negative and positive components that comprise appropriation. If either is missing, the appropriation requirement has not been met. This leads the author to the following conclusion:

> **The view held in some earlier cases that for theft to be committed it is sufficient that there be an assumption of control, *even if Y was not deprived of his property*, is incorrect. If this is all that is required to constitute an act of theft, it would be impossible to distinguish between attempted and completed theft.**[17]

31.1.3.4 The property must be capable of being stolen

To the extent that theft involves the taking of property, it must be physically capable of being moved. This requirement *excludes* the following from the ambit of theft:

- *Immovables*: Immovables include, for example, buildings, farmland, and so on.
- *Incorporeals*: These are things that cannot be perceived by the senses, such as rights and duties, as opposed to corporeals, such as a book or a car, which can. Only corporeal, movable things can be stolen.[18] This restriction poses something of a dilemma for current banking practices as succinctly illustrated by Burchell:

> **Thus the proposition that theft can only be committed in respect of corporeal property implies that a person who dishonestly credits his account and debits**

12 Skeen A st Q and Hoctor S 'Criminal law' in Joubert WA and Faris JA (eds) *Law of South Africa Encyclopaedia* (*LAWSA*) 2 ed (2007) Vol 6 at para 291.

13 Burchell *Principles of Criminal Law* 693 illustrates this by referring to a theft being committed in a self-service store without the thief having removed the property from the store. See *S v Dlamini* 1984 (3) SA 196 (N).

14 Burchell *Principles of Criminal Law* 695–700; Snyman *Criminal Law* 478–481.

15 Snyman *Criminal Law* 478–481.

16 See also *Riba v S* supra.

17 Snyman *Criminal Law* 479 (emphasis in the original). See also *S v Nkosi* 2012 (1) SACR 87 (GNP) where the court at 90H cautioned against applying the shoplifting principle slavishly 'to all other cases where a determination has to be made between completed and attempted theft'. The court was critical of this principle as enunciated in *S v Ncube en 'n ander* 1998 (1) SACR 174 (T) which held that a person is guilty of theft when he hides an item intending to steal it from a self-service store but is prevented from carrying out his intention through the intervention of security officers. The shoplifting principle was also not followed in *S v Mekula* 2012 (2) SACR 521 (ECG) which dealt with an interrupted removal of an article from a store.

18 *R v Cheeseborough and another* 1948 (3) SA 756 (T).

another's account with a sum of money does not commit theft because there has been no physical handling of corporeal notes or coins.[19]

Theft of money, as a form of the common law crime, is discussed further below. This dilemma relates to the broader question of the development of the common law to reflect current realities. It is also not always clear whether courts develop new general principles. Referring to *S v Graham*,[20] where the court accepted that an entry in books of account amounted to theft of money, Burchell submits that it is unclear 'whether this practice is merely an exception to the general rule demanded by the realities of modern financial transactions or *whether it represents a general principle that incorporeal things are capable of being stolen*'.[21]

- *Res extra commercium*: Property that falls outside the commercial sphere is incapable of being stolen. This includes *res communes* (things common to all, such as air and the sea),[22] *res derelictae* (abandoned property)[23] and *res nullius* (property belonging to nobody, such as wild animals or birds).[24] In *S v Mostert*, the Supreme Court of Appeal (SCA) expressed the *prima facie* view that water could not be stolen from a river.[25] This approach was based on the view in Roman law that public water, running in a river, was *res communes*.[26] The court held further that this view was not altered by 1998 legislation, which placed water resources under the trusteeship of the state.[27] This aspect alone does not mean that water is capable of being owned and therefore susceptible to be stolen under the common law.[28]
- *Res sua*: As theft involves the appropriation of property belonging to another, an owner cannot steal his own property.[29]

DISCUSSION

Theft of electricity and the development of the common law

In *S v Mintoor*,[30] the court considered the scope and content of the common law crime of theft and held that, because of its nature, electricity cannot be stolen for purposes of common law theft. This decision was criticised and ultimately not followed in *S v Ndebele and others*.[31] In *Ndebele*, the court again examined the true nature of electricity and concluded that it is indeed something that can be stolen. It appears that some policy considerations, as well as scientific insights, were also at play:

> **[If] electricity is not capable of being stolen, then anyone would be entitled without permission of the owner to attach a load to his batteries and deplete the**

19 Burchell *Principles of Criminal Law* 696.
20 *S v Graham* 1975 (3) SA 569 (A).
21 Burchell *Principles of Criminal Law* 697 (emphasis added). See also *S v Harper and another* 1981 (2) SA 638 (D) where the court held that shares, as opposed to share certificates, could be stolen. Compare also *S v Mintoor* 1996 (1) SACR 514 (C) where the court held that electricity could not be stolen. For a contrary view regarding the theft of electricity, see *S v Ndebele and others* 2012 (1) SACR 245 (GSJ). See also the discussion box under 31.1.3.4.
22 *R v Laubscher* 1948 (2) SA 793 (C).
23 *S v Cele* 1993 (2) SACR 52 (N).
24 *S v Mnomiya* 1970 (1) SA 66 (N).
25 See the opinion of Leach AJA in *S v Mostert and another* 2010 (1) SACR 223 (SCA) at 23.
26 Justinian *Institutes* 2.1.1.
27 National Water Act 36 of 1998.
28 It is, however, an offence to use water other than as prescribed in s 151 of the National Water Act.
29 *R v Janoo* 1959 (3) SA 107 (A). This proposition is qualified by the principle of the law governing the theft of money discussed below.
30 *S v Mintoor* supra.
31 *S v Ndebele and others* supra.

> energy within them, thereby rendering the batteries useless. Yet nothing will have been stolen. Nothing physically has been taken from the battery; however, its characteristics have changed. It appears to me that modern-day society has already advanced and accepted that there can be theft of this nature.[32]

Both *Mintoor* and *Ndebele* show how courts grapple with the scope and content of a common law crime such as theft, and how this crime should be applied, and perhaps developed, to keep it relevant in terms of the changing nature of property and things that are capable of being stolen. Some commentators disagree with the view that the common law crime of theft should be developed like this. Snyman submits that the decision in *Mintoor* 'is to be preferred' and that electricity should not be regarded 'as a thing capable of being stolen'. According to Snyman, such a development of the common law would offend the legality principle.[33]

31.1.4 A continuing crime: Substantive and procedural implications

The common law crime of theft continues to be committed for as long as the thief remains in possession of the stolen property.[34] This has two consequences:

1. A person may be convicted of theft if he steals property at a place outside the jurisdiction of a court on the basis that he is found in possession of the stolen property in the court's jurisdiction.[35]
2. A person who assists a thief still in possession of the stolen property after its removal is not an accessory after the fact. He is guilty of theft since it is a continuing crime.[36]

31.1.5 Digression: The theft of credit and the unauthorised appropriation of trust funds

In modern commercial life, money in the form of cash (notes and coins) is, of course, still used, but it is money in the form of credit that is really the motor of the economy. Snyman points out that the theft of credit was unknown in common law but was later developed and accepted by courts in South Africa as a form of theft.[37]

Theft of money, or its value, requires special attention as we indicated above. Money in the form of coins or notes constitutes corporeal property capable of being stolen. Theft of the *value* of money is distinguishable.

Where X hands over cash to Y, Y will normally acquire ownership of the money. However, if X hands over the money to Y with an instruction that Y is to deal with the money in a particular way, what is the position if Y acts in breach of the mandate? In these circumstances, courts have held that Y's breach amounts to theft of the money.[38]

The focal point is the *value of the money* as opposed to the physical coins or notes. The identity of the true owner of the money is no longer decisive in determining liability for theft. This involves a radical departure from the requirements for theft as it involves the theft of

---

32 *S v Ndebele* supra at 256G–H.

33 Snyman *Criminal Law* 482–483.

34 *S v Kruger en andere* 1989 (1) SA 785 (A). Snyman *Criminal Law* 500–501; Burchell *Principles of Criminal Law* 703.

35 *S v Kruger* supra at 793.

36 *S v Naryan* 1998 (2) SACR 345 (W); Snyman *Criminal Law* 500–501.

37 For a detailed discussion of the theft of credit and the unauthorised appropriation of trust funds, see Snyman *Criminal Law* 493–500.

38 *R v Manuel* 1953 (4) SA 523 (A); *R v Scoulides* 1956 (2) SA 388 (A); *S v Kotze* 1965 (1) SA 118 (A).

incorporeal property and flies in the face of the rule that a person cannot steal his own property.[39] From this, it follows that although no physical cash exchanges hands, it is now possible to steal credit by, for example, transferring funds from one account to another without the requisite authority.[40]

For instance, where the accused obtains the complainant's credit card and the PIN number, and uses this card to withdraw money, he could, in principle, be charged with the crime of theft.[41] However, it is more likely that the accused in this scenario will be charged with fraud since he misrepresented himself to the bank as the lawful owner and user of the credit card.

Similar principles apply to trust funds in circumstances where X entrusts money to Y to be dealt with in accordance with certain instructions. If Y acts contrary to his mandate, he is, in principle, guilty of theft.[42] There are two possible defences that the accused could raise in the context of unauthorised appropriation or use of trust funds. For instance, Y, a widower, entrusts an amount of money to X, her attorney, to invest in a retirement housing development. However, X instead uses the money to finance his own overseas vacation. The defences are as follows:

- *The first possible defence*: If X, the attorney, has at the time when he used the money for a different purpose a liquid fund that could cover the amount entrusted to him by Y, then X would not be guilty of theft. Typically, a liquid fund in this scenario could be an overdraft facility at a bank. Assets in the form of real estate would not qualify as liquid funds. The rationale underlying this defence is the proposition that a trust is essentially the absence of risk.[43] If the trustee can immediately replace funds entrusted to him by other and equal funds, then there is no risk and hence there is also no crime of theft.[44] Note that in this scenario, even if X's conduct is not regarded as theft because of the availability of an equal liquid fund, his conduct as an attorney may still be considered to constitute unethical behaviour.
- *The second possible defence*: In the scenario above, there is clearly a trust relationship in the traditional sense of the word - Y entrusted funds to X to deal with according to instructions. Say, however, the relationship between X and Y is that of a debtor and creditor where Y lends money to X to finance a new car or an overseas vacation. If X then spends the money on something else, he, X, does not commit theft.[45]

31.1.6 Acquiring effective control over the property

Where X handles property but Y remains in a position to exercise control over the property, this may constitute an *attempt* at theft as opposed to theft. For example, a verdict of attempted theft is normally returned where X is apprehended in the process of tampering with a motor vehicle before being able to drive it away.[46]

However, case law is unclear where X is arrested in the process of removing goods from an area where they are normally kept. Thus, where X is arrested by a security guard at a gate after being found in possession of copper wire that he was in the process of removing from

39 See also *S v Oosthuizen* 2014 (1) SACR 192 (ECG).
40 Burchell *Principles of Criminal Law* 706–707.
41 Snyman *Criminal Law* 494.
42 *S v Gathercole* 1964 (1) SA 21 (A).
43 See *Incorporated Law Society, Transvaal v Visse and others* (1) *Incorporated Law Society, Transvaal v Viljoen and others* (2) 1958 (4) SA 115 (T) at 118.
44 Snyman *Criminal Law* 497.
45 Snyman *Criminal Law* 497–498.
46 *R v Brand* 1960 (3) SA 637 (A).

the premises of Y, he is convicted of theft.[47] It has been submitted that the correct verdict is attempted theft as Y was not deprived of control of the wire.[48]

Shoplifting cases in self-service stores provide a similar scenario. For example, X removes an item from a shelf and is apprehended before passing through the till point, or, having second thoughts, replaces the item on the shelf before leaving the shop. Courts have been equivocal in this regard. Some have returned a verdict of attempted theft and others of theft.[49] It is a factual enquiry as to the precise point in time when X acquires control and Y loses control as both cannot compete for control over the same item simultaneously. The issue of control aside, it may be preferable to allow X to pass the pay point without paying and to effect an arrest outside the premises to avoid the difficulty of being met with the defence that there was no intention to steal.

31.2 Embezzlement

31.2.1 Definition

X commits **embezzlement**, also known as '"theft by conversion", if he appropriates another's (Y's) property *which is already in his (X's) possession*'.[50]

31.2.2 Elements

Note that embezzlement and the general common law crime of theft share the same elements of *unlawfulness*, *property* and *intention*. Given the definition of the crime provided above, the distinguishing element is that of *appropriation*.

31.2.2.1 Appropriation

Since X is already in possession of Y's property, the question is whether X exercised rights over the property as if he was the owner of it and with the necessary intent to appropriate it.[51] In principle, it does not matter how X came to be in possession of the property.[52] Examples of appropriation include the following:

- Y entrusted X to look after and care for Y's property.
- Y's prized cattle walked onto X's farm.
- X, an employee, takes money for his own use from the petty cash box of the company for which he works. X is responsible for the administration of the petty cash box of the company.

The assumption is, of course, that X came into possession of the property lawfully. If he came into possession of the property unlawfully, the appropriate form of theft would not be embezzlement, but perhaps one of the other forms of theft. It is also clear from the examples

47 *R v Banda* 1953 (2) SA 781 (N).

48 *LAWSA* 6 at para 298.

49 See the authorities referred to in *LAWSA* 6 at para 2, including *S v Mqabuzana* 1976 (1) SA 212 (E) where a verdict of attempted theft was returned, and *S v Dlamini* supra where it was held that unlawful appropriation of goods may occur before the accused passed the till. In *S v Mekula* supra, the review court changed the verdict of theft to one of attempted theft. In this case, the accused concealed a bottle of whisky under his clothes before he left the liquor store. He was spotted by a security guard before he could leave the store and, in his attempt to put the bottle back, he broke it.

50 Snyman *Criminal Law* 490.

51 See, in general, the approach in *S v Boesak* 2000 (3) SA 381 (SCA).

52 Snyman *Criminal Law* 491.

above that appropriation in cases of embezzlement often occurs in the context of trust relationships.

31.3 Theft by false pretences

31.3.1 A brief history

No reference to this offence can be found in Roman-Dutch law, but it appears to have been introduced by the Cape courts in the 19th century.[53]

31.3.2 Definition

For example, X commits theft by false pretences when X unlawfully, and with the intent to steal, induces Y by means of a misrepresentation to hand over property to X, which is capable of being stolen.[54]

31.3.3 Elements

The elements of theft by false pretences are:

- theft
- misrepresentation.

31.3.3.1 Theft

All the elements discussed under theft are equally applicable to theft by false pretences.

31.3.3.2 Misrepresentation

The elements of misrepresentation are the same as those as discussed under fraud.[55]

31.3.4 Some general comments

The precise reason for separately classifying theft by false pretences is unclear. As theft by false pretences incorporates the two crimes of theft and fraud, Snyman questions whether it is necessary to have a separate offence styled theft by false pretences.[56]

A factual example of the offence is where X falsely represents to Y that he qualifies for a free service to his motor vehicle. Acting on the strength of this misrepresentation, Y hands over the keys to the vehicle to X who then appropriates it. A theft has been committed as the consent obtained by X from Y is vitiated by fraud, and consent acquired fraudulently does not amount to a valid consent in law.[57]

While it is theoretically questionable whether a theft has been committed where Y voluntarily hands over the property to X, the offence of theft by false pretences is now firmly established in our law.[58] A fraud has been committed: the misrepresentation made by X and acted on by Y.[59] However, the crime of theft by false pretences is only complete on appropriation of the property pursuant to the misrepresentation.[60]

---

53 Snyman *Criminal Law* 535.
54 Snyman *Criminal Law* 535–537.
55 See Chapter 35.
56 Snyman *Criminal Law* at 536–537.
57 *Ex Parte Minister of Justice: In re R v Gesa, R v De Jongh* 1959 (1) SA 234 (A).
58 *R v Mofoking* 1939 OPD 117.
59 *S v Nkomo* 1975 (3) SA 598 (N).
60 *R v Davies* 1928 AD 165.

31.4 Possession of stolen property

31.4.1 A brief history

The creation of this statutory offence in 1955 arose from the difficulty of proving for the common law crime of possession that the person found in possession of stolen property knew that it was stolen and the impossibility of proving theft where the identity of the person from whom the property was stolen is unknown.[61]

31.4.2 Definition

Section 36 of the General Law Amendment Act 62 of 1955 defines the crime of being in possession of stolen property as follows:

> **Any person who is found in possession of any goods, other than stock or produce as defined in *section thirteen* of the Stock Theft Act, 1923 (Act No. 26 of 1923), in regard to which there is a reasonable suspicion that they have been stolen and is unable to give a satisfactory account of such possession, shall be guilty of an offence and liable on conviction to the penalties which may be imposed on a conviction of theft.**

31.4.3 Elements

The elements of the section 36 offence of being in possession of stolen property are:

- goods as referred to in section 36
- goods found in the possession of a person
- a reasonable suspicion that the goods have been stolen
- the person found in possession of the goods must be unable to give a satisfactory explanation of the possession.

31.4.3.1 Goods referred to in section 36

The reference to goods relates to property capable of being stolen[62] except for unidentifiable money. Were it not for this exception, those involved in the exchange of money on an extensive commercial basis would attract an intolerable onus.[63]

31.4.3.2 Goods found in possession of a person

The suspect must have personal and direct control over the goods[64] at the time the goods are found by the police.[65] The physical possession of the goods by the suspect is decisive. It is irrelevant as to whether the suspect is holding the goods as an agent on behalf of someone else.[66]

31.4.3.3 A reasonable suspicion that the goods have been stolen

The finder must harbour a reasonable suspicion that the goods have been stolen at the time that he finds the goods in the possession of the suspect.[67] The reasonableness of the suspicion must be objectively ascertainable.[68]

---

61 Snyman *Criminal Law* 515. See also Burchell *Principles of Criminal Law* 714.
62 See also *S v Furlong* 2012 (2) SACR 620 (SCA).
63 *R v Monyane en 'n ander* 1960 (3) SA 20 (T).
64 *S v Essack* 1963 (1) SA 922 (T).
65 *R v Hassen* 1956 (4) SA 41 (N).
66 *R v Tsotitsie and another* 1953 (1) SA 239 (T).
67 *S v Zuma* 1992 (2) SACR 488 (N).
68 *S v Khumalo* 1964 (1) SA 498 (N).

31.4.3.4 Inability to give a satisfactory explanation of the possession

The suspect must be unable to give a satisfactory account of his possession. The explanation need not be tendered at the time the goods were found. It is sufficient if it is given later.[69] The account must be satisfactory in the sense that it discloses the goods were not stolen. Alternatively, it shows that the suspect honestly believed that they were not stolen or that he was entitled to possess them.[70]

The accused's explanation of (or inability to explain) the possession of stolen goods can also be evaluated considering the 'doctrine of recent possession'. The content, limitations and application of this doctrine was considered by the Supreme Court of Appeal in *S v Mothwa*.[71]

S v Mothwa

The appellant was found in possession of a vehicle three days after it had been taken in a robbery. The appellant testified that he had been asked to take the car to Botswana by a certain individual. That person informed him that it belonged to his nephew and handed him the registration papers as well as what appeared to be an affidavit permitting him to drive the vehicle to Botswana. The registration details of the vehicle were changed after the robbery. For purposes of the appellant's explanation of his possession of the vehicle, the SCA considered the 'doctrine of recent possession'. The SCA described the application of the doctrine as follows:

> [It] permits the court to make the inference that the possessor of the property had knowledge that the property was obtained in the commission of an offence and in certain instances was also a party to the initial offence. The court must be satisfied that (a) the accused was found in possession of the property; and (b) the item was recently stolen. When considering whether to draw such an inference, the court must have regard to factors such as the length of time that passed between the possession and the actual offence, the rareness of the property, and the readiness with which the property can or is likely to pass to another person.
>
> There is no rule about what length of time qualifies as recent. It depends on the circumstances generally and, more particularly, on the nature of the property stolen. If the property stolen is commonplace the time might be very short as it is always easy to trade it. It can thus change hands easily and much more quickly. Property such as money and motor vehicles are easily circulated.
>
> Courts have repeatedly emphasised that the doctrine of recent possession must not be used to undermine the onus of proof which always remains with the state. It is not for the accused to rebut an inference of guilt by providing an explanation. All that the law requires is that, having been found in possession of property that has been recently stolen, he gives the court a reasonable explanation for such possession.[72]

31.4.4 Constitutionality of section 36

The Constitutional Court considered the constitutionality of section 36 in *Osman v Attorney-General, Transvaal*.[73] In this case, the appellants faced a charge under section 36 of being found in possession of tyres that were reasonably suspected to have been stolen and in respect of which they were allegedly unable to give a satisfactory account. In objecting to

69 *Osman and another v Attorney-General of Transvaal* 1998 (1) SACR 28 (T).
70 Snyman *Criminal Law* 518–519.
71 *S v Mothwa* 2016 (2) SACR 489 (SCA).
72 *S v Mothwa* at 8–10.
73 *Osman and another v Attorney-General, Transvaal* 1998 (2) SACR 493 (CC).

the charge, the appellants submitted that it conflicted with the interim Constitution[74] in two respects:

- Section 25(2)(*c*) affords an arrested person the right 'not to be compelled to make a confession or admission which could be used in evidence against him or her ...'.
- Section 25(3)(*c*) guarantees an accused person 'to be presumed innocent and to remain silent during plea proceedings or trial and not to testify during trial ...'.

The objection focused on the inability to give a satisfactory explanation, it being contended that an accused is pressurised to give an explanation that carries the attendant danger of a conviction should the accused fail to respond. As to the issue of compulsion, in finding section 36 to be compatible with the interim Constitution, Madala J held that section 36 does not compel a person to do anything. The choice is left to the individual to provide an explanation or remain silent. It is always open to such a person to proffer an explanation at the trial.

As to the issue of the presumption of innocence, Madala J emphasised that it was the inability, rather than the failure or refusal to give an explanation, that would trigger a conviction, provided that the other elements of the crime had been proved. The onus of proving its case beyond a reasonable doubt remained on the state. It had to prove each element of the offence, including persuading the court that the explanation tendered by the accused was unsatisfactory. Accordingly, the judge concluded that the presumption of innocence had not been impugned by section 36.

As to the issue of the right to silence, a person facing a charge under section 36 is in a position like any other accused in the sense that he can choose whether to tender an explanation or remain silent. Such a choice does not amount to a breach of the right to silence. In explaining this, Madala J said:

> **Our legal system is an adversarial one. Once the prosecution has produced evidence sufficient to establish a *prima facie* case, an accused who fails to produce evidence to rebut that case is at risk ... The fact that an accused has to make such an election is not a breach of the right to silence. If the right to silence were to be so interpreted, it would destroy the fundamental nature of our adversarial system of criminal justice.**[75]

31.4.5 What constitutes a satisfactory account?

In *S v Aube*, Whiting AJ focused on the requirement that a person is unable to give a satisfactory account of his possession by holding that:

> **... for an account to be satisfactory, it must be to the effect that the person *bona fide* believed his possession to be innocent ... However, it has been a somewhat controversial question whether this is sufficient or whether the person's belief must be not only *bona fide* or honest, but also reasonable.**[76]

The application of an objective test in circumstances normally associated with subjectivity in a criminal law context has attracted criticism. In dissenting from two Free State cases,[77] which required that the belief must be *bona fide* and reasonable, Whiting J preferred the

74 The Constitution of the Republic of South Africa Act 200 of 1993.
75 *Osman v Attorney-General, Transvaal* supra at 501A–C.
76 *S v Aube* 2007 (1) SACR 655 (W) at 657B–D.
77 *S v Mokoena* 1962 (2) PH H144 (O); *S v Nader* 1963 (1) SA 843 (O).

subjective approach. The language used in section 36 suggests dishonesty when compared to section 37, where the objective test, based in negligence, applies. He reasoned that if objectivity were to prevail under section 36, the legislature would have used language in section 36 that was like that of section 37. Further, the corresponding provision under the Stock Theft Act 57 of 1959, on which section 36 is based, simply requires a subjective test. The judge concluded as follows:

> **For an account to be satisfactory ..., it must be to the effect that the person concerned *bona fide* believed his possession to be innocent ..., but it will not matter that such belief is not also a reasonable one.**[78]

31.4.6 Confessions and admissions

In *S v Mahlasela*,[79] Magid J dealt with the questioning of an accused in terms of section 112(1)(*b*) of the Criminal Procedure Act 51 of 1977 who pleaded guilty to a charge under section 36. He referred to Snyman who submits that it is impossible in law for an accused to confess to a section 36 offence as the crime is only completed once the court finds that the accused is unable to give a satisfactory explanation.[80] A confession can only take place once the crime has been committed. Magid J held, however, that it is possible for an accused to make an *admission* in these circumstances. He went on to emphasise that it is insufficient to ask the accused what explanation he gave to the police. He should be asked 'whether he had *any other or amplified explanation* which he wanted to give in court'.[81]

31.5 Receiving stolen property

31.5.1 A brief history

The common law crime of receiving stolen property was amplified in 1955 by legislation, primarily because of the problem of proving that the receiver knew or foresaw that the goods were stolen.[82] The statutory offence of receiving stolen property will be considered below.

31.5.2 Definition

Section 37(1) of the General Law Amendment Act provides as follows:

> (*a*) **Any person who in any manner, otherwise than at a public sale, acquires or receives into his (or her) possession from any other person stolen goods, other than stock or produce as defined in *section 1* of the Stock Theft Act, 1959, without having reasonable cause for believing at the time of such acquisition or receipt that such goods are the property of the person from whom he or she receives them or that such person has been duly authorized by the owner thereof to deal with or to dispose of them, shall be guilty of an offence and liable on conviction to the penalties which may be imposed on a conviction of receiving stolen property knowing it to have been stolen except insofar as the imposition of any such penalty may be compulsory.**

78 *S v Aube* supra at 658D–E.
79 *S v Mahlasela* 2005 (1) SACR 269 (N).
80 Snyman *Criminal Law* 518.
81 *S v Mahlasela* supra at 271I. (Emphasis added)
82 Burchell *Principles of Criminal Law* 714.

(*b*) **In the absence of evidence to the contrary which raises a reasonable doubt, proof of such possession shall be sufficient evidence of the absence of reasonable cause.**

31.5.3 Elements

The elements of receiving stolen property referred to in section 37 are:

- possession
- a reasonable cause for believing.

31.5.3.1 Possession

The type of possession required is the same as that for section 36 considered earlier. It is unnecessary to show that a person possessed the property for his own use. It is sufficient if, for example, the person held the property as an agent on behalf of another.

31.5.3.2 Reasonable cause for believing

The requirement that a person must have reasonable cause for believing that he received the goods from the owner or an authorised person is objectively determined. A *bona fide* subjective belief is not a defence.[83] The belief must exist at the time that a person receives the goods. If the belief subsequently turns out to be misplaced, this change of mind does not support a conviction.[84]

31.5.4 Constitutionality of section 37

The original section 37 placed the onus on the receiver to prove that he had reasonable cause to believe that the giver of the goods was the owner or was authorised to dispose of them. The Constitutional Court considered the constitutionality of section 37 in *S v Manamela*[85] where the court reviewed this reverse onus against the right to a fair trial with reference to section 35(3)(*h*) of the Constitution.[86]

S v Manamela

The appellants were arrested while carrying boxes proved to have been stolen shortly before from a vehicle parked in the vicinity. They said that they had been asked to carry the boxes by a third party. They were allegedly unaware that the goods were stolen, believing at all material times that they belonged to the person who had asked them to carry the boxes. In rejecting their evidence that they had believed that the goods were not stolen, the appellants were convicted of contravening section 37. They were subsequently acquitted on appeal on grounds, inter alia, that the reverse onus was unconstitutional, an issue that the Constitutional Court was called on to confirm.

Section 37 places the onus on the accused to prove, on a balance of probabilities, that he believed the person from whom he received the goods was the owner or had authority to dispose of them, and that such a belief was reasonable. The court held that reversal of the onus

83 In questioning the propriety of this requirement, Snyman *Criminal Law* 521 states: It is a pity that the legislature prescribed an objective rather than a subjective test. The objective test does not accord with current views relating to intention and mistake in criminal law. A person can accordingly be convicted under the section even though he would not be guilty if he were charged with common-law receiving, since in the latter crime the test for determining the presence or absence of intention is subjective.

84 *S v Mkhize* 1980 (4) SA 36 (N).

85 *S v Manamela and another (Director-General of Justice Intervening)* 2000 (1) SACR 414 (CC). Pursuant to this judgment, s 37 was amended by s 2 of the Judicial Matters Amendment Act 62 of 2000 to bring it in line with the findings of the Constitutional Court.

86 The Constitution of the Republic of South Africa, 1996.

transgressed both the right to silence and the presumption of innocence. It could not find any circumstances justifying the restriction on the presumption of innocence, but it required the accused to furnish evidence as to the reasonableness of his belief.

The court ruled that the phrase 'proof of which shall be on such first-mentioned person' is invalid. It added the following sentence to the end of section 37(1)(*b*): 'In the absence of evidence to the contrary which raises a reasonable doubt, proof of such possession shall be sufficient evidence of the absence of reasonable cause.'

31.5.5 The Second-Hand Goods Act 6 of 2009

What to do about the theft of and trading in copper, cellphones and other goods? The legitimate trade in second-hand goods in South Africa is big business. Unfortunately, there also seems to be a big market for stolen goods in the second-hand goods economy. Legitimate trade in second-hand goods therefore involves all sorts of risks. Copper, other metals, cars, cellphones and other electronic products, to name but a few categories of products, are often stolen with the aim of selling them in the second-hand goods market. The legislature adopted the Second-Hand Goods Act 6 of 2009 to criminalise certain conduct and to regulate the second-hand goods market. It is submitted that the offences provided for in this Act form, together with the crimes relating to possessing and receiving stolen goods, a comprehensive framework aimed at combating receiving, possessing and trading in stolen goods.

Section 32 of the Act provides for a number of offences and penalties. The following offences are created:

- Failure to register as a dealer in terms of the Act
- Failure to apply for registration of all premises where a dealer intends to conduct business, including additional premises where second-hand goods are stored
- Furnishing false information in support of an application to register as a dealer
- Contravening or failing to apply the prescribed certificate or the conditions specified on such prescribed certificate by dealing in classes of goods other than those specified on the certificate of registration; conducting business from premises other than those specified on the certificate of registration; or conducting business in a manner other than specified on the certificate of registration
- Contravening or failing to comply with the provisions of section 8(1) or (4):

> **The holder of a certificate of registration must notify the National Commissioner [of the South African Police Service] in writing within 30 days if—**
> **(*a*) there is any change with regard to any information that was submitted in respect of the application for registration;**
> **(*b*) there is a change in the control or ownership of the dealer; or**
> **(*c*) there is any change that impacts on the ability of the dealer to meet all or any of the requirements for its registration in terms of the Act. Furthermore, upon receipt of an amended certificate, the dealer must immediately hand all previous certificates relating to the registration to the police official who is handing over the amended certificate.**

- Contravening or failing to comply with section 10(2) or (6):

> **If a dealer stops trading or is unable to carry on business in terms of the Act (or any other relevant law), such dealer must immediately notify the National Commissioner [of the South African Police Service]. Furthermore, a dealer whose registration has**

> **terminated must immediately (*a*) hand all certificates relating to the registration to the police official serving the notice [from the National Commissioner]; or (*b*) return all certificates to the National Commissioner in the event of termination (of registration) contemplated in terms of the Act.**

- Failure to renew registration as a dealer in terms of section 11
- Failure to surrender or transfer a certificate other than in the manner prescribed in section 12 of the Act
- Contravening or failing to comply with section 15, namely the proper and prominent display and maintenance of certificates
- Contravening or failing to comply with section 21(1), (3), (4), (5), (6) or (7), relating to proper record-keeping by dealers
- Contravening or failing to comply with section 22(1) or (3) relating to false information and stolen goods:

> **If a dealer suspects, or on reasonable grounds should suspect, that (*a*) any name, address or document furnished to the dealer is false; (*b*) goods or goods for pawn, as the case may be, offered to such a dealer are stolen goods; or (*c*) the appearance or aspects of an item offered to such dealer have been tampered with or there was an attempt to alter the appearance or aspects thereof in order to conceal the identity of the item, such dealer must immediately report the matter to a police official on duty at the police station in whose area the dealer carries on business.**

- Contravening or failing to comply with section 23 which provides for certain restrictions on dealers and pawnbrokers, including the prohibition to buy any pawn goods from persons under the age of 18
- Contravening or failing to comply with section 24(1), (3), (4) or (5) relating to dealing in second-hand motor vehicles
- Contravening or failing to comply with section 25(1), (4) or (5) relating to dealing in recycled controlled metals
- Contravening or failing to comply with section 26(1), (3), (4) or (5) relating to dealing in second-hand communication equipment
- Contravening or failing to comply with section 28 where dealers must submit to routine inspections of their premises by the police
- Contravening or failing to comply with section 37 which provides for defaced, lost or stolen certificates
- Contravening or failing to comply with section 43(1), (2) or (3) providing for certain transitional provisions, pertaining to persons who, immediately before the commencement of the Act, carried on business as a dealer and who must, within three months of the date of such commencement, apply for registration in terms of the Act

In terms of section 32(2), any person convicted of a contravention of or a failure to comply with any section mentioned in column 1 of Schedule 3 (basically the list of offences mentioned above), may be sentenced to a fine or to imprisonment for a period not exceeding the period mentioned in column 2 of Schedule 3, or to both a fine and such imprisonment.

31.6 Unauthorised borrowing

31.6.1 A brief history

After some doubt about whether the Roman law on unauthorised borrowing (*furtum usus*) was a common law crime in South Africa, the Appellate Division (AD) decided that it was not.[87] The legislature then made it a statutory offence in 1956.

31.6.2 Definition

Section 1(1) of the General Law Amendment Act 50 of 1956 provides as follows:

> **Any person who without a *bona fide* claim of right and without the consent of the owner or the person having the control thereof, removes any property from the control of the owner or such person with the intent to use it for his own purposes without the consent of the owner or any other person competent to give such consent, whether or not he intends throughout to return the property to the owner or person from whose control he removes it, shall, unless it is proved that such person, at the time of the removal, had reasonable grounds for believing that the owner or such other person would have consented to such use if he had known about it, be guilty of an offence and the court convicting him may impose upon him any penalty which may lawfully be imposed for theft.**

31.6.3 Elements

The elements of unauthorised borrowing are:

- removal of property
- without consent
- control
- fault.

31.6.3.1 Removal of property

The property must be removed from the control of another.[88] Other than fungible things, which are consumed by their use, property that is capable of being stolen falls within the ambit of section 1.[89]

31.6.3.2 Without consent

The removal must be unauthorised.[90] Absence of consent is the key element here. However, as pointed out by Snyman, section 1(1) does not simply provide for unlawfulness as absence of consent *generally*.[91] It requires a 'double absence' of consent. Thus, the accused contravenes section 1(1) only if he (1) *removes the property without the owner's consent* (2) to use it without the latter's consent.

Although it is assumed that consent or authorisation should be genuine and not based on fraud or a false pretence, the court in *S v Schwartz*[92] held that regardless of the fact that

87 *R v Sibiya* 1955 (4) SA 247 (A).
88 Burchell *Principles of Criminal Law* 716.
89 Burchell *Principles of Criminal Law* 716.
90 *S v Ngqaso* 1976 (2) PH H 142 (OKA).
91 Snyman *Criminal Law* 506.
92 *S v Schwartz* 1980 (4) SA 588 (T).

the accused had misled the owner of a car about the reason for borrowing the car, the owner's consent was nevertheless enough, and the accused did not contravene section 1(1). This decision has rightly been criticised as contrary to the intention of the legislature.[93]

31.6.3.3 Control

When a person gives property to another, this is inconsistent with the concept of removal from the control of another. This excludes from the ambit of the offence the extra-contractual use of property where a person exceeds his contractual rights in the use of property entrusted to him.[94]

Control means some form of detention. This is more than mere physical possession. It entails complete control with the right to use it. The nature of the control is established by considering the nature of the property and the circumstances surrounding its physical possession by a person other than the owner.

The thing must be removed from the control of the owner. The removal requirement precluded a conviction under section 1(1) where the owner had voluntarily handed control over to another. The focus falls on control as opposed to use. The extra-contractual use of a thing is not punished. However, in *S v Rheeder*,[95] the SCA has now criminalised extra-contractual use under certain circumstances.

S v Rheeder

The accused was a policeman in charge of the vehicle theft unit. He had limited control over stolen vehicles attached to the police. This control was confined to acting in a limited administrative capacity in that the recovered vehicles were placed in storage until retrieved by their owners. He used the vehicles for his personal use on occasions and then returned them to storage. The court found that his unauthorised removal of the vehicles from the police storage yard amounted to their *removal* from the said control and a contravention of section 1(1).

Burchell has criticised this judgment. The contrived interpretation of the word 'control' has been occasioned by the legislature's inability to draft section 1(1) properly to include extra-contractual use. This has the unfortunate result of the judiciary straying into the field of the legislature in its attempt to rescue the situation, thereby crossing the constitutional boundary that separates the legislative and judicial powers. He concludes, '[i]t is better for a court not to read into legislation what the Legislature perhaps wanted to say, but did not, and leave the option of change in the scope of criminality to the elected representatives of the people'.[96]

31.6.3.4 Fault

At the time of the removal of the property, the person responsible for its removal must be aware that the owner or person in control of the property has not consented to the removal.[97]

93 See Snyman *Criminal Law* 506.

94 Burchell *Principles of Criminal Law* 716 makes the following point: 'Instead of punishing unlawful *use* of another's property, the Legislature confused the issue by punishing *removal of property from the control of the owner*'. (Emphasis in the original)

95 *S v Rheeder* 2001 (1) SA 348 (SCA).

96 Burchell *Principles of Criminal Law* 719–720. For a brief analysis, see Snyman *Criminal Law* 505.

97 Burchell *Principles of Criminal Law* 720.

THIS CHAPTER IN ESSENCE

1. Theft (together with robbery, which is discussed in the next chapter) is perhaps the most common form of property crime.
2. Commercial needs, the changing nature of property and the resultant inadequacy of the common law crime of theft, as well as the difficulties involved in proving cases of theft, have resulted in some specific statutory interventions, including forms of theft or crimes against property in addition to the common law crime of theft.
3. Theft, in the form of theft by false pretences, overlaps with the common law crime of fraud, which is discussed in Chapter 35.
4. It is questionable whether the crime of theft by false pretences should coexist with the crime of fraud.

Chapter 32

Robbery

CHAPTER OBJECTIVES

The objectives of this chapter are to:
- identify the elements of the common law crime of robbery
- discuss the basic features of the crime of robbery where aggravating circumstances are present
- discuss the applicability of minimum sentences in the context of robbery with aggravating circumstances.

32.1 Robbery

32.1.1 A brief history

When compared to theft, the distinguishing feature of robbery is that robbery is theft accompanied by violence.[1] Some authors favour reference to the more fluid term 'force' rather than 'violence'.[2] Regarded under the common law as a form of theft, robbery is now classified as a separate common law crime.[3]

1 Skeen A st Q and Hoctor S 'Criminal law' in Joubert WA and Faris JA (eds) *Law of South Africa Encyclopaedia* (*LAWSA*) 2 ed (2007) Vol 6 at para 295.

2 Hoctor S 'Examining the expanding crime of robbery' (2012) 25(3) *SACJ* 361.

3 *LAWSA* 6 at para 296; Snyman CR *Criminal Law* 6 ed (2014) 508–512; Burchell JM *Principles of Criminal Law* 5 ed (2016) 721–729.

32.1.2 Definition

X commits **robbery** by stealing Y's property through the intentional use of violence, or threats of violence, to induce Y to submit to the theft.[4]

32.1.3 Elements

The elements of robbery are:

- theft
- actual or threatened violence, causally linked to the theft
- an intention to acquire the property by means of violence.

32.1.3.1 Theft

All the elements of theft also apply to robbery.[5] This is why the crime of theft is a competent verdict for purposes of a charge of robbery.[6] If the state cannot prove robbery, for instance the causal link between the violence and the taking of the property, but all the elements of theft are supported by the evidence, then the accused can be convicted of the crime of theft, even where theft was not listed as an alternative charge.[7]

32.1.3.2 Actual or threatened violence, causally linked to the theft

There must be a causal link between the violence or threat of violence and the taking of the property (theft).[8] Where X robs Y, X must use violence against Y to overcome Y's resistance when taking the property. A threat of violence that subjectively has the effect on Y's mind of negating Y's resistance is sufficient.[9] In the case of actual violence, it may be slight or severe, provided that it is directed at Y. Where it incapacitates Y by putting him out of action, a robbery has taken place, provided that X intended to steal property from him.[10]

As to causation, there must be a link between the violence and the theft in that X must obtain the property as a result of the violence. Usually, the violence will precede the theft. However, there may be circumstances where an assault, subsequent to the theft, is so closely connected that a robbery is found to have taken place.[11]

32.1.3.3 Intent

There must be an intention to acquire property by means of violence.[12]

32.1.4 Digression: Snatching

Consider the situation where X suddenly snatches Y's bag, Y being unable to resist because of the surprise nature of X's action. Originally, this did not constitute robbery because of the lack of actual violence and the concomitant intention to acquire property by means of violence. On this basis, only theft has been committed.[13]

---

4 *S v Benjamin en 'n ander* 1980 (1) SA 950 (A) at 958H; Burchell *Principles of Criminal Law* 721; Snyman *Criminal law* 508.

5 *S v Benjamin* supra at 958H.

6 S 260(*d*) of the Criminal Procedure Act 51 of 1977. See further, Du Toit E, De Jager FJ, Paizes A, Skeen A st Q and Van der Merwe S *Commentary on the Criminal Procedure Act* (revision service 52, 2014) 26-9.

7 See *S v Mia and another* 2009 (1) SACR 330 (SCA).

8 *S v Marais* 1969 (4) SA 532 (NC) at 533A.

9 *Ex parte Minister of Justice: In re R v Gesa, R v De Jongh* 1959 (1) SA 234 (A).

10 *S v L and another* 1982 (2) SA 768 (ZH).

11 See *S v Yolelo* 1981 (1) SA 1002 (A) at 1015 where X, having been found in Y's house in possession of Y's property, assaulted Y. X was convicted of robbery on the basis that there was a close association between the theft and the assault.

12 *LAWSA* 6 at para 299.

13 *S v Tladi* 1978 (2) SA 476 (O).

The approach of courts has now changed. X's conduct involves the intentional use of force by way of a sudden movement to break the hold that Y has on her bag. Even in the absence of resistance by Y, the bag-snatching constitutes robbery in that Y's hold on the bag was designed to protect it.[14] Thus, in *S v Salmans,*[15] the accused grabbed a cellphone from the hand of the complainant as she was about to put it to her ear. Foxcroft J held that:

> **... the physical grabbing of a bag or a cellphone out of a complainant's hand constitutes a physical intervention necessary for the dispossession, and whether one calls it force or violence, one has a physical act committed against the person of another. This ... complies with the definition of robbery.**[16]

However, contrast this with the case where X surreptitiously removes a protruding bag from the jacket pocket of Y without X using any violence towards Y. This amounts to theft only as the element of violence is missing.[17]

32.1.5 The property need not be on the victim's person or in his presence

X attacked Y and removed the keys to Y's shop which was 2 km away from the assault. After incapacitating Y by tying her to a lamp pole, he drove her car to the shop where he stole money and certain property. These facts supported a conviction of robbery despite the fact that the stolen items were neither on the person of Y nor were they in her presence.[18]

32.2 Robbery with aggravating circumstances

32.2.1 What constitutes aggravating circumstances?

In terms of section 1 of the Criminal Procedure Act 51 of 1977, aggravating circumstances in the context of robbery comprise:

- the wielding of a firearm or any other dangerous weapon[19]
- the infliction of grievous bodily harm
- a threat to inflict grievous bodily harm.

Those held liable under section 1 are 'the offender or an accomplice on the occasion when the offence is committed, whether before or during or after the commission of the offence ...'[20]

S v Masingili

In *S v Masingili,*[21] the court accepted that the accomplices were guilty of robbery. However, there was some doubt in the mind of the court whether the state had proved that they had *dolus* (intention) regarding the perpetuation of any aggravating circumstances. The court had to decide

14 *S v Sithole* 1981 (1) SA 1186 (N); *S v Witbooi* 1984 (1) SA 242 (C). See also Snyman *Criminal Law* 510–511; Burchell *Principles of Criminal Law* 727–728.

15 *S v Salmans* 2006 (1) SACR 333 (C).

16 *S v Salmans* supra at 340D.

17 *S v Gqalowe* 1992 (2) SACR 172 (E). In *S v M* 1996 (2) SACR 127 (T), X snatched a cellphone attached to Y's belt by a plastic clip. Since no violence was committed, theft, not robbery, was proved.

18 This was the finding in *Ex parte Minister van Justisie: In re S v Seekoei* 1984 (4) SA 690 (A), where the Appellate Division (AD) disagreed with the court *a quo* that the facts did not support a robbery conviction.

19 For instance, a knife (*S v Hlongwane* 2014 (2) SACR 397 (GP)) or a large stone (*S v Mdaka* 2014 (2) SACR 393 (KZP)).

20 For robbery with aggravating circumstances and the common purpose doctrine, see *Makhubela v S, Matjeke v S* (CCT216/15, CCT221/16) [2017] ZACC 36; 2017 (2) SACR 665 (CC); 2017 (12) BCLR 1510 (CC) (29 September 2017), available at http://www.saflii.org/za/cases/ZACC/2017/36.html.

21 *S v Masingili and others* 2013 (2) SACR 67 (WCC).

whether the reference to accomplice in the definition of aggravating circumstances creates strict liability (liability without fault) in respect of the offence of robbery with aggravating circumstances. If so, this may be unconstitutional.

One accomplice had acted as a scout by inspecting the premises where the robbery took place. The other accomplice drove the car which was used to transport the robbers to and from the scene. From an ordinary interpretation of the language used, the court concluded that, as strict liability was envisaged in the definition, this amounted to a breach of section 12(1)(*a*) of the Constitution which guarantees the right to freedom and security of the person.[22] In addition, the inclusion of accomplices in the definition contravened the presumption of innocence, thereby infringing the right to a fair trial as envisaged in section 35(3)(*h*) of the Constitution. To the extent that these aspects amounted to a limitation of these constitutional rights, this could not be justified under section 36 of the Constitution. There was no logical or practical reason for treating this type of offence differently. On this basis, the reference to accomplices was declared invalid.

The Constitutional Court did not confirm this approach when the state appealed against these findings.[23] It took the view that it was wrong to focus on the phrase 'or accomplice' in the legislation as this did not refer to the issue of intent. Nevertheless, the court went on to consider whether the Constitution required that the state had to prove that the accomplice had intended the commission of the aggravating circumstance before a person could be convicted of being an accomplice to robbery with aggravating circumstances. It was wrong to treat armed robbery as a separate crime. It is simply 'a form of robbery with more serious consequences for sentencing'.[24] The elements were the same for robbery. Intent regarding aggravating circumstances was not required for a conviction as such circumstances were relevant to sentence only in respect of an accused who has already been convicted of robbery with the requisite intent.

Without laying down any firm rules, the court held that in the absence of intent in relation to, for example, the use of a knife during the course of a robbery, this feature may amount to a mitigating factor resulting in a finding of substantial and compelling circumstances justifying a lighter sentence. On this basis, the court ruled that the presence of aggravating circumstances justified a harsher sentence than that appropriate for 'mere' robbery. This did not amount to an infringement of the constitutional rights in terms of section 12(1)(*a*) as it is not a constitutional requirement that an accused must have intended the specific circumstances associated with the robbery.

Nor was section 35(3)(*h*) of the Constitution breached. The state has to prove all the elements of robbery as well as the existence of aggravating circumstances, the latter having to be proved objectively.

For example, although a toy gun used in the course of a robbery does not amount to a firearm, having regard to the circumstances of the case, its use may amount to a threat to inflict serious bodily harm, thereby constituting an aggravating circumstance.[25] In *S v Mdaka*,[26] the appellant was at the time of the alleged robbery in possession of a large stone which he used to inflict and induce fear. On appeal, the court held the stone to be a dangerous weapon under the circumstances. The court concluded as follows:

> **It is clear on an analysis of the evidence that the appellant's conduct showed that he had used the stone to first assault the complainant in count 2 and later in counts 4 and 5 he used the stone in a manner wherein it was believed that he had a firearm.**

---

22 The Constitution of the Republic of South Africa, 1996.

23 *Minister of Justice and Constitutional Development and another v Masingili and another* 2014 (1) SACR 437 (CC).

24 *Minister of Justice v Masingili* at 448D.

25 *S v Anthony* 2002 (2) SACR 453 (C).

26 *S v Mdaka* supra.

They believed that it was an object that he could use to harm them if they did not co-operate. Pursuant to his threat, they handed him their belongings. In both counts they discovered only afterwards that in truth and in fact it was not a firearm but a large stone.

Given these circumstances I am satisfied that the learned magistrate was neither misdirected on the law nor on the facts when he convicted the appellant on counts 2, 4 and 5 of robbery with aggravating circumstances as intended in s 1 of the [Criminal Procedure] Act and not on robbery simpliciter.[27]

As to the meaning of aggravating circumstances, the Supreme Court of Appeal (SCA) has held as follows:

By virtue of the provisions of section 1 of the [Criminal Procedure] Act, once a common purpose on the part of the accused to rob was proved and the infliction of grievous bodily harm upon the victim was established, the offence of robbery with aggravating circumstances was proved against all three accused. In such a situation, if it is uncertain which of the parties, to the common purpose to rob, inflicted grievous bodily harm upon the victim, it matters not. It is not necessary to prove that this consequence was foreseen by the members to the common purpose to rob, provided that it is established that one or the other, or all of them, inflicted such harm.[28]

DISCUSSION

Another view: Armed robbery and robbery with aggravating circumstances as separate offences

The Constitutional Court's characterisation of robbery with aggravating circumstances as a *form* of robbery, rather than a separate crime, seems to be correct, in principle. However, it is important to note some of the criticism that was raised concerning the court's treatment of the substantive and procedural consequences flowing from the relevant legislation, namely section 1(1)(*b*) of the Criminal Procedure Act. Thus, the authors of *Commentary on the Criminal Procedure Act* observed as follows:

> It is true that [s 1(1)(*b*) of] the [Criminal Procedure] Act presents 'aggravating circumstances' in a way that suggests that they are an adjunct to the existing offence of robbery, and that no new, distinct offence is being created. But there can be no doubt that the cumulative effect of the legislation is to create a separate and significantly more serious 'criminal status', in terms of which more dire criminal consequences must be imposed upon an accused unless substantial and compelling circumstances exist which justify the imposition of a lesser sentence.[29]

And further:

> The significantly increased penal and social consequences to which an accused is exposed when aggravating circumstances are present do not, in our view, permit a court to place its trust in the legislature's apparent failure to identify armed

27 *S v Mdaka* supra at 7–8. (Emphasis added)

28 *S v Maselani and another* 2013(2) SACR 172 (SCA) at 175J–176A, relying on *S v Dhlamini and another* 1974 (1) SA 90 (A) at 94B–D.

29 Du Toit et al *Commentary on the Criminal Procedure Act* (revision service 59, 2017) def 4.

> **robbery formally as a separate offence. Arguments of this kind, although not uncommon in the pre-constitutional era, are insufficiently faithful to the spirit and thrust of the Constitution.**[30]

The authors of *Commentary* also warn against the Constitutional Court's approach in this case in terms of the *mens rea* element of robbery/armed robbery. The Constitutional Court noted that once an accused in a case such as *Masingili* 'actively and culpably chose to participate in an inherently violent unlawful activity', such an accused 'may be held accountable for this choice, even if she or he did not intend the exact circumstances that occurred, or method used'.[31] The authors of *Commentary* regarded the foregoing statement of the Constitutional Court to echo the now defunct doctrine of *versari in re illicita*. In terms of this doctrine, an accused could be held liable for unintended consequences of unlawful conduct. It is doubtful whether the Constitutional Court actually wanted to reintroduce the *versari* doctrine and the warning by the authors of *Commentary* is supported. The working of section 1(1)(*b*) of the Criminal Procedure Act cannot be such that in a factual scenario comparable to the *Masingili* case, an accused (an accomplice) is held criminally liable on any ground other than common purpose. The alternative construction of the section would be to create strict liability or a fallback on the defunct *versari* doctrine, which would not be constitutionally tenable.[32]

32.2.2 Minimum sentence

Section 51 of the Criminal Law Amendment Act 105 of 1997 prescribes mandatory periods of imprisonment for robbery where aggravating circumstances are found to be present.[33] The purpose is to deter those who may be disposed to committing this offence and to introduce an element of retribution.[34] The minimum period for a first offender is 15 years, for a second offender, 20 years, and for a third or subsequent offender, 25 years.

32.2.3 Discretion to impose a lesser sentence

Where it would be inequitable to impose the minimum sentence, a court is given a limited discretion under section 51(3)(*a*) of the Criminal Law Amendment Act to ameliorate the sentence if it finds 'substantial and compelling circumstances' that justify the imposition of a lesser sentence than the one prescribed.[35] Where, for example, the minimum sentence is disproportionate to the crime, having regard to the offender and the needs of society, a court may exercise its discretion in favour of the accused.[36]

---

30 Du Toit et al *Commentary on the Criminal Procedure Act* (revision service 59, 2017) def 4. (Emphasis in the original)

31 *Minister of Justice v Masingili* supra at 56.

32 For further critical comments on the Constitutional Court decision in *Masingili*, see Burchell *Principles of Criminal Law* 730–735.

33 In *S v Khoza and others* 2010 (2) SACR 207 (SCA), the SCA held that the prescribed minimum sentence was too lenient, considering the nature of the armed robbery and the related crimes.

34 *S v Montgomery* 2000 (2) SACR 318 (N) at 322H–I.

35 *S v Mambo and others* 2006 (2) SACR 563 (SCA).

36 *S v Malgas* 2001 (1) SACR 469 (SCA).

THIS CHAPTER IN ESSENCE

1. The crime of robbery (including the form of robbery known as robbery with aggravated circumstances) is a separate crime against property.
2. It has the same elements as the common law crime of theft, together with the key element of violence or threat of violence.
3. There must be a causal link between the violence or threat of violence and the taking of the property.
4. Because of the prevalence of violent crime in South Africa, robbery with aggravated circumstances is one of the crimes included in the statutory mandatory minimum sentencing framework.

Chapter 33

Housebreaking

CHAPTER OBJECTIVES

The objectives of this chapter are to identify and discuss the elements of the crime of housebreaking (with intent to commit a crime).

33.1 A brief history

Housebreaking with intent to commit a crime did not form part of Roman-Dutch law. The equivalent offence took the form of theft, with the act of housebreaking regarded as an aggravating feature. The focus fell on the theft as opposed to the housebreaking.

Under the influence of English law, the emphasis switched from theft to housebreaking, coupled with the intention to commit another crime. This resulted in the current crime of housebreaking with intent in South Africa today.[1]

33.2 Definition

X commits **housebreaking with intent to commit a crime** when he unlawfully and intentionally breaks and enters into a building with the intention to commit a crime.[2]

---

1 Skeen A st Q and Hoctor S 'Criminal law' in Joubert WA and Faris JA (eds) *Law of South Africa Encyclopaedia* (*LAWSA*) 2 ed (2007) Vol 6 at para 335; Snyman CR *Criminal Law* 6 ed (2014) 543–550; Burchell JM *Principles of Criminal Law* 5 ed (2016) 765–771.

2 *R v Badenhorst* 1960 (3) SA 563 (A). In *S v Maswetswa* 2014 (1) SACR 288 (GSJ), having regard to the provisions of s 51 of the Criminal Law Amendment Act 105 of 1997, it was considered advisable to separate the allegations of housebreaking with intent to commit an offence from a substantive charge of robbery where a minimum sentence is prescribed on conviction.

33.3 Elements

The elements of the crime of housebreaking with intent to commit a crime are:

- breaking
- entering
- a building
- unlawfulness
- intent.

33.3.1 Breaking

To constitute the element of breaking, it is not necessary for X to cause damage to the building concerned. It is sufficient if X opens a closed window or an unlocked door. Where X enters a building through an open window or an open door, the element of breaking is not met. Accordingly, there must be a removal of an impediment forming part of the building to gain access.[3]

S v Bhengu

In *S v Bhengu*,[4] the court noted that there was insufficient evidence to show that the two accused actually displaced anything in order to enter the cottage of the complainant. Although there was evidence of an unsuccessful attempt to break in, there was no evidence to show how they eventually got into the cottage. Given the vagueness of the facts, the court simply assumed that the accused and the co-accused entered the cottage through an open door, presumably left open by the complainant. The appropriate conviction was thus for attempted housebreaking with intent to steal (with aggravating circumstances).

S v Small

In *S v Small*,[5] the accused was convicted of housebreaking on the basis that he put his hands through an open window of the complainant's house, pushed a curtain aside and removed a speaker. Foxcroft J preferred the view that curtains do not form an obstruction nor can they be regarded as part of the building. On this basis, the action of the accused did not constitute a breaking in the sense that there was 'a removal or displacement of any obstacle which bars entry to the structure and which forms part of the structure itself'.[6]

33.3.2 Entering

The breaking must be accompanied by an entry. The entry element is satisfied where some part of X's body or instrument that he is using is inserted into the building, and which gives him the ability to exercise some control over the contents of the building.[7]

33.3.3 Building

The offence is not confined to immovable property in the form of buildings. It may also be committed in respect of structures habitable by humans or used for storing goods.[8]

---

3 *R v Mososa* 1931 CPD 348.
4 *S v Bhengu* 2011 (1) SACR 224 (KZP).
5 *S v Small* 2005 (2) SACR 300 (C).
6 *S v Small* supra at 302D
7 *R v Melville* 1959 (3) SA 544 (E).
8 *S v Ngobeza en 'n ander* 1992 1 SACR 610 (T).

The weight of authority suggests that if the structure is used to accommodate people, it may be movable or immovable, but if it is simply used to store goods, it must be immovable.[9]

For the purposes of this offence, a caravan may be regarded as a structure, even if broken into when it is unoccupied by people.[10] However, if it is simply used to store goods, then housebreaking is not committed.[11]

S v Mavungu

In *S v Mavungu*,[12] the court had to decide whether a person who had broken into a caravan could be convicted of housebreaking with the intent to contravene the Trespass Act 6 of 1959.[13] After endorsing the view that a caravan may constitute a structure that is ordinarily used for human habitation for supporting a conviction of housebreaking, Prinsloo J had to consider whether such action could amount to trespass, which requires the transgressor to enter or be in any building or part of a building. In finding that the Trespass Act had been contravened, he said to hold otherwise:

> ... could lead to the absurd result that one can break into a caravan (as long as nothing is damaged or stolen) and sleep there with impunity because it does not amount to trespassing, and house-breaking, in itself, is not a crime ...[14]

33.3.4 Unlawfulness

Unlawfulness is an element of the crime, so X will not be guilty of housebreaking if he enters with the consent of the building's owner where he acts out of *necessity* or in an official capacity.[15]

33.3.5 Intent

At the time of entering the building, X must intend to commit an offence, normally theft (or attempted theft),[16] but may be any offence including murder, rape, robbery or malicious injury to property. Housebreaking on its own does not amount to an offence.[17] If the state has difficulty in proving the precise nature of the intended offence, X may be charged with housebreaking with the intention of committing a crime unknown to the prosecutor.[18]

S v Slabb

In *S v Slabb*,[19] the accused had unlawfully entered the house of the complainant, but was disturbed before he could steal anything. The accused was convicted of housebreaking with intent to steal. When confirming the correctness of the verdict, Le Grange AJ dealt with the position where it is

9 See *S v Temmers* 1994 (1) SACR 357 (C), which dealt with the storage of goods. The court preferred the distinction based on the purpose of storage. If they were placed in a structure to safeguard them from the elements or theft, then housebreaking comes into play. However, this is not the case where the goods are in a structure for ease of storage or conveyance. On this basis, a crime cannot be committed where X forces open a suitcase to remove its contents. See also Snyman *Criminal Law* 546–547.

10 *S v Temmers* supra.

11 *S v Jecha and others* 1984 (1) SA 215 (ZH).

12 *S v Mavungu* 2009 (1) SACR 425 (T). For a discussion of this case, see Snyman CR 'Huisbraak ten opsigte van 'n karavaan - *S v Mavungu* 2009 (1) SASV 425 (T)' (2010) 73(1) *THRHR* 158.

13 S 1(1)(*b*) of the Trespass Act 6 of 1959.

14 *S v Mavungu* supra at 434 para 43.

15 *R v Melville* supra.

16 See, for instance, *S v Mzandi* 2011 (1) SACR 253 (WCC).

17 *R v Melville* supra.

18 S 95(12) of the Criminal Procedure Act 51 of 1977; Snyman *Criminal Law* 549–550.

19 *S v Slabb* 2007 (1) SACR 77 (C).

impossible to prove the crime that the accused intended to commit after unlawfully entering the premises as follows:

> There are numerous instances where perpetrators break into premises and commit heinous crimes. A common-sense approach is therefore called for in determining the intention of perpetrators when they face a charge of housebreaking with the intent to commit an offence unknown to the prosecution ... To view it any differently will in effect force the State to resort to trespass prosecutions, or to speculate in respect of some known offences, which may lead to questionable decisions. This would clearly place the prosecution in an untenable position and will make s 262 of the [Criminal Procedure] Act redundant.[20]

Where goods have been gathered in readiness for their removal from the premises, but not actually removed, a proper verdict would be housebreaking with intent to steal and attempted theft as the owner had not yet been deprived of his control of them.[21]

THIS CHAPTER IN ESSENCE

1. In South African criminal law, housebreaking with intent to commit a crime is criminalised with reference to two key elements: an act of housebreaking and intent to commit a crime. The crime can be any crime although in practice it is normally the crime of theft. The underlying protected interest is not the property (the building or premises) per se.
2. The crime of trespassing addresses the interests of privacy and property rights.
3. Housebreaking with intent to commit a crime is a separate crime that criminalises the preparatory and enabling conduct – the breaking in – in order to commit the primary crime such as theft.

20 *S v Slabb* supra at 81B–D.
21 *S v Mzandi* supra.

Chapter 34

Malicious damage to property and arson

CHAPTER OBJECTIVES

The objectives of this chapter are to:
- identify and discuss the elements of the crime of malicious damage to property
- identify and discuss the elements of the crime of arson
- highlight the principles applicable when an owner damages (through arson or otherwise) his own property.

34.1 Malicious damage to property

34.1.1 A brief history

The offence of malicious damage to property did not form part of either Roman or Roman-Dutch law. It was developed by courts, partially under the influence of English law, where it has become established as a separate offence.[1]

1 Skeen A st Q and Hoctor S 'Criminal law' in Joubert WA and Faris JA (eds) *Law of South Africa Encyclopaedia* (*LAWSA*) 2 ed (2007) Vol 6 at para 326; Snyman CR *Criminal Law* 6 ed (2014) 539–541; Burchell JM *Principles of Criminal Law* 5 ed (2016) 757–760.

34.1.2 Definition

X commits **malicious damage to property** where he unlawfully and intentionally damages the property of Y, or property belonging to himself in which Y has a substantial interest.[2]

34.1.3 Elements

The elements of malicious damage to property are:
- property
- damage
- unlawfulness
- intent.

34.1.3.1 Property

Movable or immovable corporeal property can be damaged. Usually, the damaged property will belong to a person other than the one inflicting the damage. However, this is not necessarily so.[3]

34.1.3.2 Damage

The concept of damage is wide ranging. The total or partial destruction of the property is not necessary. The property may remain intact. If the damage causes the complainant to spend money or use labour to neutralise the effect of the damage, for example painting over street names as a protest action, this is sufficient for a conviction. The work of graffiti artists on public or private property is another example.[4] However, the damage should not be too trifling, which brings the *de minimis* principle into operation.[5]

34.1.3.3 Unlawfulness

The accused may escape liability on a charge of malicious damage to property where he is entitled in law to act, where he acts out of necessity or where he does so with the consent of the owner. However, the force used should not be disproportionate to the circumstances.[6]

34.1.3.4 Intent

Despite the reference to the English law adjective of 'malicious' when proving intent, the state does not have to show that the accused acted with a motive indicative of spite or ill will as his motive is irrelevant. Intent in its standard form applies, namely it must be wrongful and intentional either as *dolus directus* or *dolus eventualis*.[7] Negligence is insufficient to secure a conviction.[8]

34.1.4 Digression: Damage to a person's own property

A person is generally free to treat his property as he pleases. However, where a complainant has a substantial interest in the property that the accused (the owner of the property) damages, the accused may be convicted of malicious damage to property. For example, X, unhappy with the faded tint on the windscreen of his car, hits the windscreen with a hammer

---

2 *S v Mnyandu* 1973 (4) SA 603 (N) at 606A.
3 See the digression below.
4 *R v Bowden en 'n ander* 1957 (3) SA 148 (T).
5 Burchell *Principles of Criminal Law* 759.
6 *R v Pope* 1953 (3) SA 890 (C).
7 *R v Shelembe* 1955 (4) SA 410 (N); *S v Mnyandu* supra.
8 *S v Kgware and another* 1977 (2) SA 454 (O).

in order to have it replaced under an insurance claim for a broken windscreen.[9] This scenario could, of course, depending on the facts, also give rise to a charge of fraud (in the form of insurance fraud). Burchell comments as follows:

> **His act would be fraud if and when he falsely reported the damage to the insurance company. But, if he has not so reported, can he be convicted of malicious injury to property? Somewhat illogically, it has been held that he can.[10]**

Perhaps a verdict of attempted fraud may be returned where the windscreen was broken with an intention to commit fraud, but, for some reason, no claim was filed.

34.2 Arson

34.2.1 A brief history

The crime of arson has its roots in the crimes of *incendium* in Roman law and *brandstichting* in Roman-Dutch law. It is regarded as a type of malicious damage to property.[11]

34.2.2 Definition

The crime of **arson** is committed where X unlawfully and intentionally sets fire to the immovable property of Y, or to the immovable property of X in which Z has an interest.

34.2.3 Elements

The elements of arson are:

- setting on fire
- immovable property
- unlawfulness
- intent.

34.2.3.1 Setting on fire

The crime is completed at the time when the property is set on fire.[12] Where the accused is involved at a preparatory stage prior to ignition, he may be convicted of attempted arson.[13]

34.2.3.2 Immovable property

Generally, the immovable property will belong to a person other than the arsonist. However, where a person sets fire to his own property in order to prosecute an insurance claim, he is guilty of arson.[14]

While it has been held that a husband married in community of property could not be convicted of arson by setting fire to property falling in the joint estate as he was part owner of the property,[15] the Appellate Division in *R v Mavros*[16] held that a person may be convicted

---

9 *S v Mnyandu* supra at 606A; *R v Mavros* 1921 AD 19 (a case where a person was convicted of arson by setting fire to his own property to benefit from an insurance claim). For a critical view, see Snyman *Criminal Law* 540.

10 Burchell *Principles of Criminal Law* 759 with reference to *R v Gervais* 1913 EDL 167.

11 Snyman *Criminal Law* 542; Burchell *Principles of Criminal Law* 761–764. See also Hoctor S 'The nature of the crime of arson in South African law' (2013) 19(2) *Fundamina* 321–332.

12 *R v Viljoen* 1941 AD 366 at 367.

13 *R v Schoombie* 1945 AD 541.

14 *R v Mavros* supra.

15 *R v Van Vliet* (1891–1892) 9 SC 273.

16 *R v Mavros* supra.

of arson by setting fire to his own property. Here, the accused had been convicted of arson in that he had set fire to his own store with intent to defraud an insurance company of the money for which it had insured the store. This conclusion was based on the concept of *brandstichting*, which was equated with arson. Burchell argues that this conduct could also attract a conviction of fraud.[17]

Other than a fraudulent context, the *Mavros* judgment has been relied on to support the view that arson is committed by a person who sets fire to his own property with the intention of harming another. For example, arson is committed where the owner, who has let his house to another, burns the house down to damage or destroy the movable property of the lessee.[18]

In *S v Dalindyebo*,[19] the Supreme Court of Appeal followed the approach in *Mavros* and held that the appellant, the paramount chief of the AbaThembu people in the Eastern Cape, was correctly convicted of arson in that he had set fire to the dwellings of three of his subjects (and tenants) to secure their eviction for having breached his rules. The dwellings were constructed on communal land controlled by the paramount chief. The SCA held that arson can be committed where a person sets fire to his own immovable property with the intention to prejudice the property interests of another. Even though the paramount chief of the AbaThembu can be regarded as the owner of the communal lands, this ownership is qualified by the legitimate interests of his subjects who live on the lands. Importantly, the SCA observed that even if the paramount chief were to be regarded as the unqualified owner of the lands on which the damaged or destroyed dwellings were built, a conviction of arson would still be possible if there was intent to injure the subjects. On the facts in *Dalindyebo* the SCA concluded that the appellant set fire to each of the complainants' homes 'with the intent to injure'.[20]

34.2.3.3 Unlawfulness

The defences discussed under malicious damage to property are equally applicable to arson.

34.2.3.4 Intent

There must be an intention, actual or constructive, to damage the property by setting fire to it and which results in loss to another.[21]

THIS CHAPTER IN ESSENCE

1. The crimes of malicious damage to property and arson are related but distinct.
2. The crimes affect both an owner's rights and his interests in his property.
3. The key difference between the two crimes is that malicious damage to property can be committed to movable or immovable property, while arson can only be committed to immovable property.
4. The crimes can, depending on the facts, also be committed by an owner against his own property, normally when a third party has an interest in the property as well.

17 Burchell *Principles of Criminal Law* 764 fn 30.
18 *S v Van Zyl* 1987 (1) SA 497 (O).
19 *S v Dalindyebo* 2016 (1) SACR 329 (SCA).
20 *S v Dalindyebo* supra at para 66.
21 *R v Shein* 1925 AD 6.

Chapter 35

Fraud

CHAPTER OBJECTIVES

The objectives of this chapter are to:
- identify and discuss the elements of the common law crime of fraud
- identify and discuss the elements of the common law crime of forgery
- identify and discuss the elements of the common law crime of uttering
- evaluate the constitutionality of some substantive and procedural issues in the context of the crime of fraud.

35.1 Fraud

35.1.1 A brief history

The Roman law crime of fraud was based on the crimes of *stellionatus* and various *crimina falsi*.[1] These crimes were subsequently merged into a single offence under the Roman-Dutch law crime of fraud, referred to as *falsitas*.[2] The unitary concept of fraud as a crime involving proprietary and non-proprietary interests, as well as real or potential prejudice, was accepted by the Appellate Division (AD), now the Supreme Court of Appeal (SCA), early in the 20th century.[3]

35.1.2 Definition

X commits **fraud** when he unlawfully and intentionally makes a misrepresentation to Y causing prejudice, potential or otherwise, to Y.[4]

35.1.3 Elements

The elements of fraud are:

- misrepresentation
- unlawfulness
- intent
- prejudice.

35.1.3.1 Misrepresentation

There must be a misrepresentation involving a distortion of the truth. This may take various forms. It may be expressed or implied.[5] For example, if the accused buys goods on credit from the complainant, the accused implicitly represents to the complainant that he, the accused, will pay for them at some future date and will be able to do so. If, at the material time, the accused harboured no such intention or belief, he misrepresents his state of mind to the complainant.[6]

The misrepresentation may take the form of a positive act or an omission. An omission arises where the accused is under a legal duty to disclose a fact, the non-disclosure of which may induce the complainant to act to his prejudice. The legal duty to disclose may also arise from legislation.[7] In *S v Heller*,[8] Trollip J articulated the legal principles with respect to fraud based on non-disclosure[9] as follows:

- A duty to disclose the particular fact must exist.

---

1 D 47.20.3.1; for example, D 48.10.8–9.

2 Snyman CR *Criminal Law* 6 ed (2014) 523.

3 See, for instance, *R v Dyonta and another* 1935 AD 52; *R v Kruse* 1946 AD 524; *R v Heyne and others* 1956 (3) SA 604 (A).

4 Snyman *Criminal Law* 523; Burchell JM *Principles of Criminal Law* 5 ed (2016) 742.

5 For an example of the behaviour that constitutes a fraudulent misrepresentation, see *S v Mdantile* 2011 (2) SACR 142 (FB), notably the court's reasoning at 33 and 38.

6 *R v Persotam* 1938 AD 92; R *v Latib* 1973 (3) SA 982 (A).

7 The example that appears in Skeen A st Q and Hoctor S 'Criminal law' in Joubert WA and Faris JA (eds) *Law of South Africa Encyclopaedia* (*LAWSA*) 2 ed (2007) Vol 6 at para 309 is where a director is obliged under s 234 of the previous Companies Act 61 of 1973 to disclose the nature of his interest in a contract concluded between the company and a third party. S 76(2)(*b*) of the Companies Act 71 of 2008 provides that directors must disclose information to the board that may affect the interests of the company. For more on the fiduciary duty, see *Cyber Scene Ltd and others v i-Kiosk Internet and Information (Pty) Ltd* 2000 (3) SA 806 (C).

8 *S v Heller and another* (2) 1964 (1) SA 524 (W).

9 See also *S v Gardener and another* 2011 (1) SACR 570 (SCA) where the Supreme Court of Appeal (SCA) applied the principles identified in *S v Heller* supra and *S v Malan* 2013 (2) SACR 655 (WCC) at 659–660.

- There must be a willful breach of this duty under such circumstances as to equate the non-disclosure with a representation of the non-existence of that fact.
- There must be an intention to defraud. This involves knowledge of the particular fact, awareness and appreciation of the existence of the duty to disclose, and deliberate refraining from disclosure in order to deceive and induce the representee to act to its prejudice or potential prejudice.
- Actual or potential prejudice of the representee must occur.

Alternatively, the accused may be under a duty to correct a misconception of the complainant where, in the normal course of events, the complainant would be misled if the accused failed to take corrective measures.[10]

S v Yengeni[11] further illustrates the duty to make a disclosure where a member of Parliament failed to disclose a gift in breach of the parliamentary code of conduct. Although a breach of the code per se did not amount to fraud, the court found that there was a legal obligation on the accused to speak. His failure to do so was intended to mislead Parliament. This amounted to fraud.

A misrepresentation is not confined to the past or present. It is sufficiently wide to embrace the future. If the accused promises the complainant that he will act in a certain way in the future, but at the time of making the promise he has no intention of keeping it, the accused has misrepresented his state of mind to the complainant. This situation arises in the field of negotiable instruments where the accused draws a cheque in favour of the complainant, at a time when the accused knows that there will be insufficient funds in his (the accused's) bank account to honour the cheque when it is presented for payment. By drawing the cheque, the accused implicitly represents to the payee, the complainant, that the cheque will be met on the due date.[12]

35.1.3.2 Unlawfulness

Theoretically, the usual defences, such as coercion considered in the context of the general principles of criminal law, will be available to the accused. However, it is no defence to allege that the complainant was aware of the falsity of the misrepresentation.[13]

35.1.3.3 Intent

The onus is on the state to prove that the accused intended to defraud. This is discharged directly where it proves that the accused was aware that his misrepresentation was false. It is not necessary for the state to allege and prove that the accused intended to defraud any particular person. It is, however, necessary to allege and prove that a more generic *somebody*[14] has been prejudiced or potentially prejudiced. Section 103 of the Criminal Procedure Act 51 of 1977 provides as follows:

> **In any charge in which it is necessary to allege that the accused performed an act with an intent to defraud, it shall be sufficient to allege and to prove that the accused**

10 See *R v Larkins* 1934 AD 91 where X, omitting to disclose to Y that he had ceded his salary to Z, informed Y that his salary would be deposited into X's bank account at the end of the month. Based on this information, Y lent money to X. The omission was considered fraudulent. See also *S v Yengeni* 2006 (1) SACR 405 (T).

11 *S v Yengeni* supra.

12 *S v MacDonald* 1982 (3) SA 220 (A).

13 *LAWSA* 6 at para 311; *S v Heller* supra.

14 *R v Jones and More* 1926 AD 350 at 354; Du Toit et al *Commentary on the Criminal Procedure Act* (revision service 54, 2015) 14-44–14-45.

> **performed the act with intent to defraud without alleging and proving that it was the intention of the accused to defraud any particular person, and such a charge need not mention the owner of any property involved or set forth the details of any deceit.**[15]

It is open for the state to prove intention in the form of *dolus eventualis*. This type of *dolus* is present where the accused makes a representation foreseeing the possibility that it may be false, but nevertheless goes ahead with it. The accused may be indifferent as to whether it is true or false. The reckless conduct of the accused in this regard satisfies the requirement of *dolus eventualis*.[16]

An intention to deceive should not be confused with an intention to defraud. *Prejudice* is the key to the distinction between each form of intent. Deception takes place when X attempts to persuade Y that something is true when it is in fact false. Fraud involves this deception but goes further. It includes an intention to induce Y to act to his *prejudice*.[17]

Once an intention to defraud has been proved, the actual motive behind the intent is irrelevant.[18]

35.1.3.4 Prejudice

The prejudice must be actual or potential.[19] While actual prejudice is clear, potential prejudice requires further explanation. The prejudice must not be too remote. There must be a reasonable possibility that the misrepresentation may prejudice another.[20] The emphasis falls on the potential nature of prejudice. It is irrelevant whether the complainant acted on the representation or whether the accused's deception was successful.[21] Nor does it matter whether the complainant was aware at any moment that the misrepresentation was false.[22] On this basis, the accused may be convicted of fraud where he is the target of a police trap. The fact that members of the trap were aware that the accused's misrepresentation was false is not a defence to a charge of fraud.[23]

The prejudice, whether actual or potential, need not be proprietary in nature. Writing an examination in the name of another candidate amounts to fraud in circumstances where the intention is to deceive the examiners as to the identity of the person who attempted the examination.[24] This approach was confirmed in the context of tender fraud where the appellants failed to disclose in a tender application their connection to the entity which had awarded the tender, in this case the Department of Education. It was argued on their behalf that the department had not suffered prejudice as it had paid moneys for services rendered. However, the court held that the non-disclosure was 'prejudicial to other tenderers, and the community at large, and frustrate[d] the state's efforts to eliminate the favouritism the "declaration of interest" seeks to combat'.[25]

The failure to allege prejudice in the indictment renders an indictment alleging fraud defective.[26]

---

15 Emphasis added. See further, *S v Avion Motor Enterprises (Pty) Ltd* 1978 (4) SA 692 (T) at 694B.
16 *Ex parte Lebowa Development Corporation Ltd* 1989 (3) SA 71 (T).
17 *S v Isaacs* 1968 (2) SA 187 (D).
18 *S v Shepard and others* 1967 (4) SA 170 (W).
19 *S v Kruger and another* 1961 (4) SA 816 (A); *S v Van Niekerk* 2014 JDR 2196 (KZP).
20 *S v Myeza* 1985 (4) SA 30 (T).
21 *S v Isaacs* supra.
22 *S v Campbell and others* 1991 (1) SACR 435 (Nm).
23 *S v Swarts en 'n ander* 1961 (4) SA 589 (GW).
24 *R v Thabeta and another* 1948 (3) SA 218 (T).
25 *S v Tshopo and others* 2013 (1) SACR 127 (FB) at 130B–C.
26 *Essop v S* [2014] 3 All SA 337 (KZP).

35.1.4 Digression: The crime of fraud and constitutional issues

35.1.4.1 Section 245 of the Criminal Procedure Act 51 of 1977: Presumption of false representation

Section 245 of the Criminal Procedure Act provides:

> **If at any criminal proceedings at which an accused is charged with an offence of which a false representation is an element, it is proved that the false representation was made by the accused, he shall be deemed, unless the contrary is proved, to have made such a representation knowing it to be false.**

Section 245 placed the onus on the accused to prove that on a balance of probabilities, he knew that the representation was false. Reversing the onus in these circumstances could result in a conviction on a charge of fraud where the accused is unable to discharge the onus placed on him 'despite the existence of a reasonable doubt as to his or her guilt'.[27]

Alive to this difficulty, the Constitutional Court declared section 245 unconstitutional and therefore invalid in *S v Coetzee.*[28] Under section 25(3)(*c*) of the interim Constitution[29] (the equivalent of section 35(3)(*h*) of the Constitution[30]), the accused has a right to be presumed innocent. An essential element of fraud is that the person making the false representation must be aware of its falsity. The effect of the presumption is that if an accused is proved to have made a representation, the presumption as to the requisite *mens rea* is triggered, thereby relieving the state of the onus to prove this aspect of its case.

The court, in *S v Coetzee*, had to decide whether this restriction on the presumption of innocence could be justified in terms of section 33(1) of the interim Constitution (the equivalent of the limitations clause, section 36 of the Constitution, 1996). This clause essentially provides that the restriction must be reasonable and justifiable in an open and democratic society. This enquiry involves balancing 'the pressing social need for the effective prosecution of crime ... against the rights that are guaranteed by the Constitution which puts a high premium on the values of freedom and equality'.[31]

On one side of the scale is the difficulty the state may experience in proving the state of mind of the accused who is, in any event, ideally placed to disclose why he made the representation. On the other side is 'the importance of the rights entrenched in s 25(3)(*c*) of the [interim] Constitution, which include the right to be presumed innocent, in an open and democratic society based on freedom and equality'.[32]

The court found that the scale tipped in favour of the accused's constitutional rights. It was not persuaded that any difficulty the state faced in discharging its onus outweighed the severe inroads made into the rights flowing from a presumption of innocence, which are regarded as fundamental in the new constitutional democracy.

---

27 *LAWSA* Vol 19(10) at para 309.
28 *S v Coetzee and others* 1997 (1) SACR 379 (CC).
29 Constitution of the Republic of South Africa Act 200 of 1993.
30 Constitution of the Republic of South Africa, 1996.
31 *S v Coetzee* supra per Langa J at 384B–C.
32 *S v Coetzee* supra at 384C–D.

DISCUSSION **Is there a need for a statutory presumption of false representation?**

Given the extent of commercial crime in South Africa, should there not be a presumption like that contained in the now invalid section 245 of the Criminal Procedure Act? One can look at other presumptions and how they are structured for guidance on constitutionality, for example in the context of corporate criminal liability or the National Road Traffic Act 93 of 1996. Another possibility might be to structure it along the lines of the presumptions contained in section 24 of the Prevention and Combating of Corrupt Activities Act 12 of 2004. The presumption should obviously not create a reverse onus but should rather assist the prosecution without unjustly infringing on the rights of accused persons, notably the presumption of innocence and the right to remain silent.

35.1.4.2 The constitutionality of potential prejudice

In *S v Friedman*,[33] the accused was charged with common law fraud. Before pleading, he objected to the charge on the basis that the definition of fraud was too wide with reference to the general nature of potential prejudice. Although the definition of fraud is broad, Cloete J did not consider it to be repugnant to the Constitution. He could 'find nothing objectionable in the approach which punished fraud not because of the actual harm which it causes, but because of the possibility of the harm or prejudice inherent in the misrepresentation'.[34] In this regard, he drew an analogy between the civil and criminal law. As to the former, redress is confined to actual prejudice suffered. As to the latter, he held that 'it is not the primary function of the criminal law to satisfy individuals who have been wronged but to punish people who have transgressed defined norms'.[35]

The wide scope of fraud, with reference to the requirement of prejudice, was confirmed in *S v Mngqibisa*.[36]

S v Mngqibisa

In this case, Y was an employee of company A that administered claims on behalf of insurance company Z, which insured X's motor vehicle. X falsely represented to Y that X was the driver of the vehicle at the time of an accident whereas, in truth, X's wife was the driver. As his wife was in possession of a learner driver's licence, an additional excess was payable. After this misrepresentation, X informed another employee of company A that his wife was in fact the driver of the vehicle at the material time. After a review of the prejudice element in fraud, Mlambo JA confirmed the approach by the AD in *R v Kruse* where it was held that:

> **... if the false representation is of such a nature as, in the ordinary course of things, to be likely to prejudice the complainant, the accused cannot successfully contend that the crime of fraud is not established because the Crown has failed to prove that the false representation induced the complainant to part with his property.**[37]

In finding that potential prejudice had occurred at the time of the misrepresentation, the court concluded that X had correctly been convicted of fraud. The fact that X had subsequently told the truth did not alter this position.

33 *S v Friedman* (1) 1996 (1) SACR 181 (W).
34 *S v Friedman* supra at 194H.
35 *S v Friedman* supra at 195B.
36 *S v Mngqibisa* 2008 (1) SACR 92 (SCA).
37 *R v Kruse* supra at 533–534.

The issue of potential prejudice also received the attention of the SCA in *S v Shaik*,[38] where the misrepresentation comprised the irregular writing-off of certain amounts in the books of a company. This involved potential prejudice to the probable readers of the financial statements concerned. The court relied[39] on *R v Heyne*,[40] which held that 'the false statement must be such as to involve some risk of harm, which need not be financial or proprietary, but must not be too remote or fanciful, to some person, not necessarily the person to whom it is addressed'. The court found that communication to another was sufficient to constitute fraud, even if that person may not have been prejudiced personally by the misrepresentation.[41]

35.2 Forgery and uttering

35.2.1 A brief history

Forgery per se did not form part of Roman law. The separate crimes of forgery and uttering were developed in South Africa under the influence of English law.[42]

35.2.2 Definition

X commits **forgery** where he unlawfully makes a false document with the intent to defraud the actual or potential prejudice of Y.[43]

35.2.3 Elements

The elements of forgery are:

- falsification of a document
- intent
- unlawfulness
- prejudice.

35.2.3.1 Falsification of a document

Forgery is a form of fraud, which includes all the elements of fraud. The difference is when the offence is complete. In the case of fraud, the misrepresentation by X must come to the notice of Y. This is not necessary for forgery. On falsification of the document, forgery is complete.[44] The presentation of the forged document to Y amounts to the separate offence of uttering.[45]

The document must contain more than untrue statements. The falsity element is satisfied when the document purports to be something other than it is, for example where it purports to have been drawn up by a person other than its author.[46]

While courts have not settled on a definition of what constitutes a document for the purposes of forgery, the weight of authority suggests that a broad interpretation will be

38 *S v Shaik and others* 2007 (1) SACR 247 (SCA).
39 *S v Shaik* supra at 302B.
40 *R v Heyne* supra at 622E–F.
41 See also *R v Jones and More* supra.
42 *R v Hymans* 1927 AD 35; *S v Banur Investments (Pty) Ltd en 'n ander* 1970 (3) SA 767 (A).
43 *LAWSA* 6 at para 321; Snyman *Criminal Law* 532; Burchell *Principles of Criminal Law* 754.
44 *R v Hymans* supra.
45 See section 35.2.4.
46 *R v Leballo* 1954 (2) SA 657 (O).

adopted.[47] Burchell, quoting Hunt, finds the following to be a satisfactory definition of a 'document':

> **[A document is] any writing in any form, on any material, which communicates to some person or persons a human statement, whether of fact or fiction.[48]**

35.2.3.2 Intent

This requirement is the same as that for fraud. There must be an intention to defraud as opposed to merely deceive.[49]

35.2.3.3 Unlawfulness

This requirement is the same as that for fraud.

35.2.3.4 Prejudice

This requirement is the same as that for fraud, except that potential prejudice may be inferred on completion of the forged document.[50] The prejudice may be potential or actual, patrimonial or non-patrimonial.[51]

35.2.4 Definition of uttering

X commits the crime of **uttering** a false document when he unlawfully, and with intent to defraud, presents a false document to Y, to Y's actual or potential prejudice.[52] X may or may not be the author of the false document.

35.2.5 Elements

The elements of uttering are exactly the same as those of forgery, except that the document must be *presented* to Y.[53] The document must be *communicated by X to Y* in some way with X holding out to Y that it is a genuine document.[54] If the attempt at communication fails, for example a posted false document does not reach Y, then the crime of attempted uttering has been committed. X is guilty of uttering even if Y is not misled by the false document.[55]

THIS CHAPTER IN ESSENCE

1. The crimes of fraud, forgery and uttering concern the crime of a misrepresentation on which persons act to their prejudice, including potential prejudice.
2. Ultimately, the criminalisation of fraud, forgery and uttering reflect the interest of society in honest commercial and economic interaction.

---

47 Snyman *Criminal Law* 533.
48 Hunt PMA *South African Criminal Law and Procedure Vol II: Common Law Crimes* 3 ed by Milton J (1996) Ch 35 IC2, quoted in Burchell *Principles of Criminal Law* 755. Reproduced with permission of The Licensor through PLSclear.
49 *S v Bell* 1963 (2) SA 335 (N).
50 *R v Hymans* supra.
51 See *R v Adams* 1948 (1) SA 1199 (N) for the limited scope to omit an allegation of prejudice from a charge of forgery.
52 *LAWSA* 6 at para 321; Snyman *Criminal Law* 535; Burchell *Principles of Criminal Law* 756.
53 Snyman *Criminal Law* 535.
54 *Kolia v R* 1937 NPD 105.
55 *R v Dyonta* supra.

Chapter 36

Corruption

CHAPTER OBJECTIVES

The objectives of this chapter are to:

- discuss the historical origins of the crime of corruption under South African law
- identify the underlying interests applicable to the crime of corruption
- identify and discuss the main elements of the unbundled crime of corruption provided for in the Prevention and Combating of Corrupt Activities Act 12 of 2004
- briefly discuss other relevant matters, such as extraterritorial jurisdiction, provided for in the Prevention and Combating of Corrupt Activities Act.

36.1 A brief history

The crime of **corruption** under South African law is an unbundled crime in terms of the Prevention and Combating of Corrupt Activities Act 12 of 2004 (the Corruption Act).[1] The crime is unbundled in the sense that there is not one single definition, but rather a general crime of corruption, complimented by various specific forms of corruption under the Act. This was not always the case. This unbundled crime, which we will discuss in more detail below, has its roots in the common law crime of bribery. In its most basic form, the crime of bribery involves a scenario in which the accused gives someone something (gratification) in return for a favour, for instance a government contract.[2]

However, the common law crime of bribery was rather narrow in its application since it could be committed only 'by or in respect of a state official'.[3] Due to this limitation in the common law, the legislature adopted the Prevention of Corruption Act 6 of 1958 to expand the net of criminal liability for corruption to include individuals in the private sector. Both the common law crime of bribery and the statutory forms criminalised under the Prevention of Corruption Act of 1958 were replaced by a more comprehensive criminalisation of corruption in terms of the Corruption Act 94 of 1992. However, unlike the 2004 Act, the 1992 Corruption Act contained only one broad and all-encompassing crime of corruption.[4]

36.2 The crime of corruption in criminological, transnational and international perspectives

The crimes that we discuss in this book are classified in terms of broad underlying interests, for example crimes against human life or crimes against property. This system of classification is not an exact science and it is particularly difficult to classify the crime of corruption in this way. In popular parlance, corruption, or corrupt behaviour, is often used synonymously with crime or criminal behaviour. Thus, we often hear people in conversation or in the media refer to a corrupt society when they mean a society struggling with high levels of crime. This chapter deals with corruption in the legal-technical sense rather than as shorthand for all sorts of criminality. However, the nature of corruption affects various interests as illustrated by the Preamble of the Corruption Act.[5]

The drafters further characterised the Corruption Act as an instrument that needs to help with preventing and combating corruption as a criminal phenomenon that affects *public and private spheres* of economic and political life. It is also a crime that can be *transnational* in nature, and it is often part of or linked to organised crime and money laundering. In this sense, we could classify corruption as a form of organised crime.[6] However, despite its transnational and organised crime connotations and contexts, corruption has, as its core, the *criminal phenomenon of bribery*. Of course, under the Corruption Act, the unbundled crime of corruption is also more than bribery under common law. Corruption can

1 See Burchell JM *Principles of Criminal Law* 5 ed (2016) 804–809; Snyman CR *Criminal Law* 6 ed (2014) 401.
2 *S v Gouws* 1975 (1) SA 1 (A).
3 Snyman *Criminal Law* 401–402.
4 Snyman *Criminal Law* 402; Preamble of the Corruption Act 94 of 1992.
5 The Preamble refers to interests such as 'the institutions and values of democracy and ethical values and morality', 'sustainable development', 'the rule of law', 'credibility of governments', 'democratic institutions' and 'national economies'. For background on the problem of corruption, also from an African perspective, see Palmer R 'Combating grand corruption in Africa' (2012), available at http://www.osisa.org/openspace/global/combating-grand-corruption-africa-robin-palmer.
6 See Part Three Section 5.

be committed by one individual (X bribing Y) or as part of complex transnational organised crime.

Indeed, the Corruption Act is in large part not only a response to the problem of corruption in South Africa, but also a confirmation of South Africa's international obligation to fight corruption. Various international and regional instruments call on states to criminalise and combat corruption.[7] Some of these instruments, notably the United Nations Convention against Transnational Organized Crime of 2000, the so-called Palermo Convention,[8] link the fight against corruption with the broader fight against transnational organised crime. South Africa's response,[9] in the form of the Corruption Act of 2004, certainly satisfies the main aims of the Palermo Convention in this regard. The Corruption Act also provides for extraterritorial jurisdiction over the crime of corruption.[10] This confirms the view that the legislature regards corruption also as a transnational criminal phenomenon that affects broader interests.

Considering the above discussion, we classify corruption as *primarily* a crime against the community and public welfare, while emphasising the *secondary* need also to study this crime in the context of organised crime and transnational crime.

36.3 The unbundled crime of corruption

We noted above that the crime of corruption in terms of the Corruption Act is an unbundled crime. The crime of corruption is divided into a *general crime of corruption,*[11] which resembles the common law crime of bribery, and *specific forms of corruption,* namely:

- corrupt activities relating to specific persons, for example corrupt activities relating to public officers[12]
- corrupt activities relating to receiving or offering unauthorised gratification, notably unauthorised gratification by or to a party to an employment relationship[13]
- corrupt activities relating to specific matters, for example in respect of corrupt activities relating to witnesses and evidentiary material during certain proceedings.[14]

The Corruption Act also contains certain miscellaneous crimes relating to possible conflicts of interest and other unacceptable conduct, for example interfering with, hindering or obstructing an investigation of an offence.[15] In addition, the Corruption Act provides for various forms of liability based on participation before and after the commission of the crime. Finally, it also provides for inchoate crimes, including incitement and conspiracy to commit the various forms of corruption in the Act.[16]

---

7 For example, the Southern African Development Community Protocol against Corruption 2001; the United Nations Convention against Transnational Organized Crime 2000; the United Nations Convention against Corruption 2003. See also De Sousa C 'Combatting corruption in the SADC' (2015) 551 *De Rebus* 12–13.

8 Kemp G 'The United Nations Convention Against Transnational Organized Crime: A milestone in international criminal law' (2001) 14(2) *SACJ* 152.

9 For a discussion of the legislative proposals preceding the adoption of the Corruption Act, see Kemp G 'The Prevention of Corruption Bill in international perspective' (2002) 23(1) *Obiter* 150.

10 See section 36.6.

11 Part 1 s 3 of the Corruption Act.

12 Part 2 of the Corruption Act.

13 Part 3 of the Corruption Act.

14 Part 4 of the Corruption Act.

15 Part 5 of the Corruption Act.

16 See ss 20 and 21 in Part 6 of the Corruption Act.

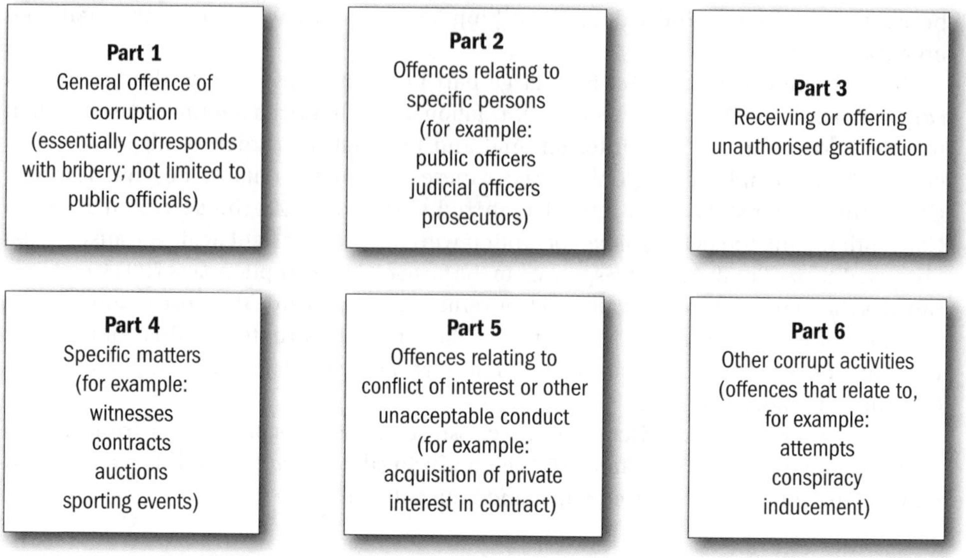

Figure 36.1 Prevention and Combating of Corrupt Activities Act 24 of 2004

36.3.1 The general crime of corruption

36.3.1.1 Definition

Section 3 of the Corruption Act provides for the general crime of corruption:

> **Any person who, directly or indirectly—**
>
> **(*a*) accepts or agrees or offers to *accept* any *gratification* from any other person, whether for the benefit of himself or herself or for the benefit of another person; or**
>
> **(*b*) *gives or agrees or offers to give* to any other person any gratification, whether for the benefit of that other person or for the benefit of another person, in order to act, personally or by influencing another person so to act, in a manner—**
>
> **(i) that amounts to the—**
>
> **(*aa*) illegal, dishonest, unauthorised, incomplete, or biased; or**
>
> **(*bb*) misuse or selling of information or material acquired in the course of the exercise, carrying out or performance of any powers, duties or functions arising out of a constitutional, statutory, contractual or any other legal obligation;**
>
> **(ii) that amounts to—**
>
> **(*aa*) the abuse of a position of authority;**
>
> **(*bb*) a breach of trust; or**
>
> **(*cc*) the violation of a legal duty or a set of rules,**
>
> **(iii) designed to achieve an unjustified result; or**
>
> **(iv) that amounts to any other unauthorised or improper inducement to do or not to do anything, is guilty of the offence of corruption.**

For this discussion, a number of words in the above extract from section 3 that defines corruption are in italics. These words are defined in the definitions and interpretation sections of the Act:[17]

- *Accept, including 'agree to accept' and 'offer to accept'*: To demand, ask for, seek, request, solicit, receive or obtain a gratification; to agree to commit the aforementioned acts; to offer to commit the aforementioned acts
- *Gratification*: This includes money in cash or otherwise; any donation, gift, loan, fee, reward, valuable security, property or interest in property of any description, whether movable or immovable, or any other similar advantage; the avoidance of a loss, liability, penalty, forfeiture, punishment or other disadvantage; any office, status, honour, employment, contract of employment or services, any agreement to give employment or render services in any capacity, and residential or holiday accommodation; any payment, release, discharge or liquidation of any loan, obligation or other liability whether in whole or in part; any forbearance to demand any money or money's worth or valuable thing; any other service, favour or advantage of any description including protection from any penalty or disability incurred or apprehended, or from any action or proceedings of a disciplinary, civil or criminal nature, whether already instituted or not, and includes the exercise or the forbearance from the exercise of any right or any official power or duty; any right or privilege; any real or pretended aid, vote, consent, influence or abstention from voting; and any valuable consideration or benefit of any kind including any discount, commission, rebate, bonus, deduction or percentage
- *Give or agree or offer to give*: To promise, lend, grant, confer or procure the gratification; to agree to lend, grant, confer or procure the gratification; to offer to lend, grant, confer or procure the gratification
- *Inducement*: Includes persuading, encouraging, coercing, intimidating, threatening or causing a person to do something

The statutory construction of the general crime of corruption seems complicated, but we can use the helpful, simplified definition by Snyman to explain the essence of this crime:

> **Anybody who (a) accepts any gratification from anybody else, or (b) gives any gratification to anybody else in order to influence the receiver to conduct herself in a way which amounts to the unlawful exercise of any duties, commits corruption.**[18]

36.3.1.2 Elements

The elements of the general crime of corruption are:

- the act of giving or receiving
- unlawfulness
- intent.

36.3.1.2.1 The act of giving or receiving

We explained this element above with reference to the element of gratification. Corruption can be committed by the giver or the recipient. This is also referred to as *active and passive corruption*.[19] It is not necessary for both parties to be prosecuted or convicted – if the state

17 Ss 1 and 2 respectively.
18 Snyman *Criminal Law* 403.
19 Snyman *Criminal Law* 403.

can prove active corruption, this will be enough to convict the giver of the gratification.[20] Conversely, if the state can only prove that someone (the recipient) received gratification with the necessary corrupt intent, such an accused's conviction will not depend on the conviction of the giver (active party).[21]

36.3.1.2.2 Unlawfulness

Although the Corruption Act does not expressly provide for the element of unlawfulness in the definition of corruption, Snyman correctly submits that we must read this element into the definition.[22] Indeed, this is a basic element of any crime under South African law. This element concerns the legal and moral convictions of the community. We submit that the *context* in which the alleged corruption occurred will be crucial, for instance, public versus private sector, or gratification (exchange of gifts) in the context of product marketing versus giving lavish gifts in the context of public sector tender processes. In one context, giving gifts, such as expensive liquor or clothing, may be perfectly acceptable as normal business practice, whereas in another context it may suggest an improper, corrupt relationship.[23]

DISCUSSION

'Systemic corruption', 'state capture' and 'grand corruption'

In late 2016, the Public Protector of South Africa published her report on how senior government officials, including at the highest levels of power, colluded with corrupt business and political entities to 'capture the state', that is, the systematic subjugation of state policies and resources to benefit a network of corrupt individuals.[24] 'State capture' is not a discrete crime in itself; the phenomenon can rather be described as a complex of crimes consisting mainly of corruption, fraud, theft, embezzlement, racketeering and money laundering, which are committed systematically and are often collectively described as 'grand corruption', which aims to 'distort policies or the central functioning of the state, enabling leaders to benefit at the expense of the public good'.[25]

The question, then, is whether it is necessary to criminalise 'grand corruption' as a discrete crime with its own elements, or whether the phenomenon can best be dealt with by means of diligent enforcement of existing laws against corruption, theft, fraud, organised crime, and so on. However, given the systemic nature and contextual elements of 'grand corruption', the more appropriate response may be to criminalise it as a discrete crime, analogous to the criminalisation of systemic and widespread human rights violations as crimes against humanity. The hearings and expected report of the Zondo Commission of Inquiry into State Capture, which was established by the state president in 2018 with the mandate to investigate the allegations of state capture mentioned in the Public Protector's report, will shed further light on the elements of the phenomenon of state capture/grand corruption. This will hopefully assist lawmakers to draft more appropriate legislation to deal with systemic or grand corruption.

20 *S v Shaik and others* 2007 (1) SA 240 (SCA).
21 See, for instance, *S v Selebi* 2012 (1) SACR 209 (SCA).
22 Snyman *Criminal Law* 410.
23 See the facts in *S v Shaik* supra and *S v Selebi* supra.
24 Public Protector South Africa, Report No 6 of 2016/17, *State of Capture*, available at http://saflii.org/images/329756472-State-of-Capture.pdf.
25 Transparency International Report, *The Anti-Corruption Plain Language Guide* (2009) 23, available at https://www.transparency.org/whatwedo/publication/the_anti_corruption_plain_language_guide.

36.3.1.2.3 Intent

Corruption is a crime of intent – negligence is not enough.[26] Section 2(1) of the Corruption Act provides for the various forms of knowledge of a fact. These different forms of knowledge correspond with the various forms of *dolus*, including *dolus eventualis*. It also provides for intentional omission, but not negligent omission.[27] The accused in the case of active corruption must have the necessary corrupt intent at the moment when he gives the gratification. In the case of passive corruption, the accused must have the necessary corrupt intent at the moment when he receives the gratification. The crime of corruption is often committed with reference to multiple acts that occur over an extended period of time,[28] for example the cultivation of a generally corrupt relationship. Intent, at least in the form of *dolus eventualis*, must be present during all material times.

36.3.2 Specific forms of corruption (other than the general crime of corruption)

As indicated above, the Corruption Act provides for a number of specific forms of corruption that cover a wide and diverse range of activities in the public[29] and private sectors. It is not possible to discuss all the different specific forms of corruption.[30] Corruption in respect of public officers is briefly discussed as an illustration of a specific form of corruption.

36.3.2.1 Corruption in respect of public officers

Section 4(1) of the Corruption Act provides as follows:

> (1) Any—
> (*a*) **public officer who, directly or indirectly, accepts or agrees or offers to accept any gratification from any other person, whether for the benefit of himself or herself or for the benefit of another person; or**
> (*b*) **person who, directly or indirectly, gives or agrees or offers to give any gratification to a public officer, whether for the benefit of that public officer or for the benefit of another person, in order to act, personally or by influencing another person so to act, in a manner—**
> (i) **that amounts to the—**
> (*aa*) **illegal, dishonest, unauthorised, incomplete, or biased; or**
> (*bb*) **misuse or selling of information or material acquired in the course of the, exercise, carrying out or performance of any powers, duties or functions arising out of a constitutional, statutory, contractual or any other legal obligation;**
> (ii) **that amounts to—**
> (*aa*) **the abuse of a position of authority;**
> (*bb*) **a breach of trust; or**
> (*cc*) **the violation of a legal duty or a set of rules;**
> (iii) **designed to achieve an unjustified result; or**
> (iv) **that amounts to any other unauthorised or improper inducement to do or not to do anything, is guilty of the offence of corrupt activities relating to public officers.**

26 Snyman *Criminal Law* 410–412.
27 Snyman *Criminal Law* 410–412.
28 *S v Shaik* supra; *S v Selebi* supra.
29 See also Mukadam S, Schulz-Herzenberg C and Felton J 'The effectiveness of financial disclosure regulations as an anti-corruption tool in local government' (2012) *Institute for Security Studies Papers* Issue 242.
30 For a brief overview of the specific forms of corruption, see Snyman *Criminal Law* 415–417.

S v Selebi[31]

In this case, the Supreme Court of Appeal (SCA) considered the application of section 4(1) of the Corruption Act. The prosecution's essential allegation was that the appellant, the former National Police Commissioner, received various gifts, mostly in the form of expensive clothing as well as money, from a businessman.[32] These gifts were allegedly intended to influence Commissioner Selebi in return for information and other favours. The court first had to establish whether the appellant had in fact received payments and gifts. Secondly, it had to determine whether the accused – the recipient or passive party – had provided any unlawful quid pro quo to the giver. The court also considered whether the appellant had received the gifts with the necessary corrupt intent.

To bring the accused within the ambit of section 4(1), the court accepted that the appellant was at all relevant times a public officer. As such, the appellant also received gifts in an unlawful way. The SCA identified the crucial elements as:

- acceptance
- gratification
- an influence to act in a certain way
- unlawfulness
- intent.[33]

The SCA held that the state had established beyond reasonable doubt that the gifts and payments were accepted by the appellant with the requisite corrupt intent.[34] While this would normally also fall under the rubric of the general crime of corruption, the accused's status as a senior public officer made it possible for the court to confirm his conviction under section 4(1) of the Corruption Act.

36.4 The rebuttable presumption of *mens rea* in section 24 of the Prevention and Combating of Corrupt Activities Act 12 of 2004

Section 24 of the Corruption Act provides for a rebuttable presumption of *mens rea*, which makes it potentially easier for the state to prove corrupt intent. This presumption relates to the crimes under parts 1 and 2 as well as section 21 of the Act. In *S v Selebi*, the SCA summarised, with reference to the crime contained in section 4 of the Corruption Act, the elements of the presumption in section 24 as follows:

> **Once the prosecution has proved that gratification (payment) was accepted or agreed:**
> - **and the state can show that despite having taken reasonable steps**
> - **the state was not able with reasonable certainty**
> - **to link the acceptance of the gratification**
> - **to a lawful authority or excuse on the part of the person charged**
> - **and in the absence of evidence to the contrary which raises reasonable doubt**
> - **it is sufficient evidence that the person charged accepted such gratification of that person**
> - **in order to act in a manner envisaged in the relevant criminalisation section in Part 1 or Part 2 of the Act.**[35]

31 *S v Selebi* supra.
32 Mr Glenn Agliotti, who was the focal point of criminal investigations.
33 *S v Selebi* supra at para 8.
34 *S v Selebi* supra at para 40.
35 *S v Selebi* supra at para 39.

The above elements do not constitute a reverse onus. Therefore, the state must still prove its case beyond reasonable doubt, but the rebuttable presumption in section 24 can help the state to establish more easily the necessary *mens rea*. The legislature was careful to avoid a possible constitutional attack based on earlier precedents where reverse onuses were found to be unconstitutional because they violated the presumption of innocence and the right to remain silent.[36]

36.5 The crime of failure to report corrupt conduct

The various crimes of corruption are often committed in political, official or business environments, far removed from public scrutiny or public knowledge. The legislature has therefore created a crime in section 34 of the Corruption Act, 'which consists in the failure by a person in a position of authority who knows or ought reasonably to have known that certain crimes created in the Act have been committed, to report the commission of such crimes to a police officer'.[37] Examples of persons in positions of authority can be found in section 34(4). They typically include persons in management positions. It is important to note that the crime in section 34 is not a crime of intent only, but that negligence will be enough to constitute culpability. Because of this, we can expect business managers and heads of state departments to be vigilant and to put systems in place to monitor possible corrupt behaviour by their employees.

36.6 The crime of corruption and extraterritorial jurisdiction

The reality of transnational corruption is not only rhetorically acknowledged in the Preamble of the Corruption Act, but also in terms of the jurisdictional reach of the Act.[38] Section 35 of the Act provides for extraterritorial jurisdiction over crimes provided for in the Act whenever these crimes are committed abroad. However, some jurisdictional links to South Africa are required, which could include the following:

- The accused must be a *citizen* of South Africa.
- The accused must *ordinarily be resident* in South Africa.
- The accused must have been *arrested* in South Africa.
- The accused must be a *company incorporated or registered* in South Africa (or be a body of persons in South Africa).

Thus, if a director of a company registered in South Africa bribed a government official at a meeting in London to obtain a contract on behalf of the company to deliver certain products to the government of the UK, a South African court will have jurisdiction over the matter.

36 S 35(3)(*h*) of the Constitution of the Republic of South Africa, 1996. See also *S v Coetzee and others* 1997 (3) SA 527 (CC). For a discussion of this case, see Kemp G 'Die grondwetlikheid van statutêre vermoedens' (1998) 9(1) *Stell L R* 106.

37 For a brief discussion, see Snyman *Criminal Law* 417.

38 See also Kemp 'The Prevention of Corruption Bill in international perspective'.

THIS CHAPTER IN ESSENCE

1. The unbundled statutory crime of corruption in terms of the Corruption Act is fairly sweeping in terms of jurisdictional reach (substantive and in terms of enforcement). It criminalises the general crime of corruption, which resembles the common law crime of bribery, and further provides for various specific forms of corruption and corruption-related crimes.
2. Importantly, the Act also provides for a duty to report corruption, for certain presumptions, as well as for extraterritorial jurisdiction over the various crimes in the Act.
3. These features of the Corruption Act can be seen as attempts to cast a wide net in the fight against corruption in South Africa and to give effect to South Africa's international obligations.

Chapter 37

Public violence

CHAPTER OBJECTIVES

The objectives of this chapter are to:

- give a brief historical background to the crime of public violence
- identify and discuss the main elements of the crime of public violence
- discuss some distinguishing features of the crime of public violence.

37.1 A brief history

As with terrorism,[1] the crime of public violence is not easily classified. On the face of it, the name of the crime suggests that it is a crime against public welfare. However, if the violence reaches certain levels or if the context suggests a broader aim to unsettle the functioning of the government, the crime may overlap with a crime such as sedition. In this case, it is then best classified as a crime against the state. However, we classify it primarily as a *crime against the community and public welfare*. It is essentially a serious disturbance of public peace and tranquility; this crime almost inevitably affects the rights of others.[2]

Historically, the crime of public violence has its roots in the Roman law concept of *vis publica*, and the Roman-Dutch distinction between public and private violence. South African law broadly followed Roman-Dutch law, but was influenced by English law. Our law thus requires that the crime of public violence can be committed only by multiple persons (more than two)[3] who act with a common purpose.[4]

1 See Chapter 49.

2 Snyman CR *Criminal Law* 6 ed (2014) 311; Burchell JM *Principles of Criminal Law* 5 ed (2016) 777.

3 The number of persons required for a conviction will depend on the circumstances of the case. *R v Cele and others* 1958 (1) SA 144 (N); *R v Nxumalo and others* 1960 (2) SA 442 (T).

4 Burchell *Principles of Criminal Law* 782.

37.2 Definition

Snyman defines **public violence** as 'the unlawful and intentional commission, together with a number of people, of an act or acts which assume serious dimensions and which are intended forcibly to disturb public peace and tranquility or to invade the rights of others'.[5]

37.3 Elements

The elements of public violence are:

- an act
- conducted by a number of people
- serious proportions (threshold of seriousness)
- unlawfulness
- the intention to:
  - disturb the peace and order by violent means
  - infringe on the rights of others.

37.4 *Mens rea* and a common purpose

Public violence is a crime of intent. The participants in the group must share a *common purpose* to commit the violent acts that are aimed at disturbing public peace and tranquility.[6]

S v Le Roux[7]

On the issue of common purpose, the Supreme Court of Appeal (SCA) in the case of *S v Le Roux* was required to consider whether the appellants had actively associated themselves with the unlawful acts of public violence perpetrated. The incident related to a brawl at a restaurant where a group of men assaulted patrons and damaged property. The trial court convicted the men of public violence.

On appeal, the appellants raised, among other issues, 'that the state had failed to adduce evidence linking them to any act of association in the commission of any transgression alleged to have been committed'.[8] The appellants, who were found not to have had any prior plan to be at the restaurant, were convicted by the trial court on the basis of being present at the scene and therefore having been complicit in the commission of transgressions by other members of the group.

The SCA held that liability purely on this basis was a misdirection.[9] The SCA held that if there was no prior plan to commit the offence of public violence, the conduct of each individual accused should be individually considered. It was not sufficient, as held by the trial court, to establish mere presence at the scene of the violence as a basis for complicity in the commission of transgressions by other members of the group.[10] The SCA then proceeded to examine the liability of each appellant based on the evidence available to it and, as a result, four of the seven appellants were successful in their appeal against conviction.

5 Snyman *Criminal Law* 311.
6 Snyman *Criminal Law* 311. See also Burchell *Principles of Criminal Law* 782.
7 *S v Le Roux and others* 2010 (2) SACR 11 (SCA).
8 *S v Le Roux* supra at 4.
9 *S v Le Roux* supra at 19.
10 *S v Le Roux* supra at 17.

37.5 Some general comments

The elements of the crime of public violence may overlap with other crimes such as assault, malicious injury to property, arson and robbery.

S v Whitehead and others[11]

The accused were convicted in a regional court of culpable homicide and public violence, and in the case of the seventh appellant, of assault with intent to do grievous bodily harm. The case, on appeal, considered whether the convictions of the offences of culpable homicide and public violence were a duplication of charges.

The SCA held that there was no infallible formula to determine whether there had been a duplication of convictions.[12] The various tests formulated by the courts were not rules of law nor were they exhaustive. They were simply useful practical guidelines, and if they failed to provide a satisfactory answer, the matter was correctly left to common sense, wisdom, experience and the sense of fairness of the court.

Also, when multiple convictions were contested, it was often submitted that they were premised on the *same set of facts*. This was the so-called *evidence test*, which enquired whether the evidence necessary to establish the commission of one offence involved proving the commission of another offence. The state would often be able to prove the crime of public violence without any reference to the negligent or other killing of any person. The opposite was also true - the offence of culpable homicide was capable of proof, independent of acts of public violence. The evidence of the general disturbance caused by the assailants to the public order would be sufficient to secure a conviction on the public violence charge, and the state was accordingly at liberty to continue to prove the offence of culpable homicide.[13]

The majority held that the conviction of the appellants on charges of public violence and of culpable homicide did not constitute a duplication of convictions. This conclusion was supported by both the evidence and intention tests, and prompted by common sense. The two offences in question had materially different elements, the result being that the state would be able to prove public violence without any reference to the negligent killing of a person. Conversely, the offence of culpable homicide was capable of proof, independent of acts of public violence.[14]

The distinguishing feature of the crime, apart from the fact that it must involve a number of people, is the fact that the violence or intended violence must 'assume serious or dangerous dimensions'.[15] Hence, it is more than a disturbance of the peace or a brawl in a public place.[16]

DISCUSSION **Violent protests, the protection of rights, and the future of the crime of public violence**

South Africa is a constitutional democracy and the right to peaceful protest is constitutionally enshrined. In a society with high levels of unemployment, socio-economic anxieties and dissatisfaction with poor or no service delivery, it is not

11 *S v Whitehead and others* 2008 (1) SACR 431 (SCA).
12 *S v Whitehead* supra at 34 and 35.
13 *S v Whitehead* supra at 39–41.
14 *S v Whitehead* supra at 39–43.
15 Snyman *Criminal Law* 313.
16 *S v Le Roux* supra at 14.

surprising that these high levels of dissatisfaction and disillusionment may from time to time boil over into violent protest action.

Khulekani Khumalo writes about this, and considers the past, present and future of the crime of public violence against the backdrop of social unrest in South Africa, and in particular the *#FeesMustFall* protests at South African universities. The author warns against the potential abuse of the criminal justice system by the ruling elites who may be tempted to stifle legitimate political opposition or legitimate public anger by prosecuting people unjustifiably for the crime of public violence. Having said that, the author concludes that far from being abused by government, the current reality is that there appears to be a 'lack of political will to pursue public violence cases'. This 'continued reluctance to prosecute public violence is becoming untenable as more people turn to the criminal law for the protection of their rights, pending effective political solutions to protests.' Ultimately, according to Khumalo, 'the continued failure of the crime [of public violence] to afford the requisite protection places it at risk of falling foul of the spirit, purport and objects of the Bill of Rights'.[17]

THIS CHAPTER IN ESSENCE

1. The crime of public violence, with its roots in Roman and Roman-Dutch law, has certain *qualitative* and *quantitative* features that distinguish it from other violent crimes:
   1.1 It must disturb the peace and tranquility through serious violence or threats of violence.
   1.2 Multiple persons, normally three or more, must participate in the violence and must share a common purpose.

17 Khumalo K 'Towards resuscitating the ailing public violence jurisprudence – lessons from history' (2017) 1 *SACJ* 23–37 at 37.

Chapter 38

Crimes against public morals

CHAPTER OBJECTIVES

The objectives of this chapter are to:
- discuss briefly the historical background to the common law crime of public indecency
- identify the main elements of the common law crime of public indecency
- critically discuss the rationale for the further criminalisation of the common law crime of public indecency in light of the adoption of the Criminal Law (Sexual Offences) Amendment Act 32 of 2007,[1] certain constitutional freedoms and the principle of legality
- discuss briefly the historical background and underlying protected interests of the common law crime of blasphemy
- consider critically the continued existence of the crime of blasphemy
- introduce the debate concerning the draft Prevention and Combating of Hate Crimes and Hate Speech Bill.

38.1 Public indecency

38.1.1 A brief history

The common law crime of public indecency was created by the courts in the Cape in the 19th century.[2] The common law crime of public indecency overlaps with conduct punishable under the new offences in sections 9 and 22 of the Criminal Law (Sexual Offences)

1 Discussed in Chapter 28.

2 *R v Marais* (1888–1889) 6 SC 367. See further, Snyman CR *Criminal Law* 6 ed (2014) 433; Burchell JM *Principles of Criminal Law* 5 ed (2016) 784–785.

Amendment Act 32 of 2007 (the Sexual Offences Act).[3] The common law offence of public indecency is not specifically repealed in section 68 of the Sexual Offences Act.

38.1.2 Definition

Public indecency is 'unlawfully, intentionally and publicly committing an act which tends to deprave the morals of others or which outrages the public sense of decency and propriety'.[4]

38.1.3 Some general comments

The adoption of the Sexual Offences Act can be regarded as a codification, or at least consolidation, of sexual crimes. This Act, together with the liberalisation of South African society and the impact of the Constitution of the Republic of South Africa, 1996, leave the continued existence of the common law crime of public indecency in doubt. The Constitution provides for the right to freedom of expression in section 16(1)(*c*): 'everyone has the right to freedom of expression, which includes – ... freedom of artistic creativity'. Behaviour that may have been classified as public indecency may now qualify as expression and as such may not be punishable.

The public, of course, have an interest in not being exposed to indecent behaviour and, therefore, the rights of the individual to freedom of expression may be limited in the public interest. This matter has thus far not been challenged on a constitutional basis. The test for indecency is objective in nature. In other words, it is irrelevant whether the conduct *in fact* depraves the morals of others.[5] We can therefore assume that the changing nature of the moral standards of the average, reasonable member of society in a multicultural society such as South Africa will make applying this common law crime even more difficult.

Because of the dynamic nature of public morality and the fact that this crime depends on the objective standard of the average, reasonable member of society, we agree with Snyman's observation that the vagueness of notions such as the 'public's sense of decency' may be incompatible with the principle of legality, notably the *ius certum* aspect thereof.[6]

38.2 Blasphemy

38.2.1 A brief history

The criminalisation of blasphemy has ancient origins. In South African common law, it was criminalised and accepted as a crime against the Christian God.[7] In a secular and liberal society under a constitution that protects freedom of speech and that prohibits unreasonable discrimination, the continued existence of this crime is debatable.[8]

38.2.2 Definition

Blasphemy is unlawfully, intentionally and publicly acting contemptuously towards God.[9]

3 See also Chapter 28.

4 *S v F* 1977 (2) SA 1 (T) at 4D as defined in Hunt PMA and Milton JRL *South African Criminal Law and Procedure Vol II* 3 ed (1996) 278; Snyman *Criminal Law* 433.

5 Snyman *Criminal Law* 434.

6 Snyman *Criminal Law* 434.

7 Burchell *Principles of Criminal Law* 790.

8 Snyman submitted in the third edition of *Criminal Law* that considering the Constitution, the crime of blasphemy 'has ceased to exist'. Indeed, the author no longer discusses the crime in the later editions (the latest being the sixth edition 2014) of *Criminal Law*.

9 Burchell *Principles of Criminal Law* 768.

38.2.3 Elements

The elements of blasphemy are:

- unlawfulness
- occurring in public
- contempt towards God
- intent.

38.2.4 Some general comments

Public morality and views regarding the limits to free speech are not static, as illustrated by public discourse and jurisprudence.

Van Loggerenberg and others v 94.7 Highveld Stereo[10]

In this case, the Broadcasting Complaints Tribunal considered a number of complaints relating to a radio broadcast that had included a joke containing a sexual innuendo and which referred in a frivolous manner to a central event in the Christian faith. A majority of the Tribunal found that although the sexual innuendo contained in the joke was objectionable, offensive and ill-conceived, it was not so repugnant as to amount to blasphemy. The joke did not amount to advocacy of hatred based on religion such as to constitute incitement to cause harm.

Islamic Unity Convention v Independent Broadcasting Authority and others[11]

In this case, the Constitutional Court held that the appropriate test in terms of the limitation to freedom of expression is contained in section 16(2) of the Constitution. Section 16 reads as follows:

(1) Everyone has the right to freedom of expression, which includes–
  (*a*) freedom of the press and other media;
  (*b*) freedom to receive or impart information or ideas;
  (*c*) freedom of artistic creativity;
  (*d*) academic freedom and freedom of scientific research.

(2) The right in subsection (1) does not extend to–
  (*a*) propaganda for war;
  (*b*) incitement of imminent violence; or
  (*c*) advocacy of hatred that is based on race, ethnicity, gender or religion, and that constitutes incitement to cause harm.

Following the Constitutional Court's decision, the Code of Conduct for Broadcasters was substantially amended, and the new Code came into operation on 7 March 2003. As a result, this Tribunal must now decide complaints, such as the example described above, in the light of the limitation to the right to freedom of expression as contained in section 16(2) of the Constitution. This is a strict test. The joke complained of would fail the test only if it amounted to the *advocacy of hatred based on religion* and, furthermore, that the words constituted *incitement to cause harm.*

The majority held the following:

- It is trite law that public policy is not a static phenomenon. What in the past was termed blasphemous, in present circumstances may not necessarily be so when regard is had to the public *mores* prevailing.

10 *Van Loggerenberg and others v 94.7 Highveld Stereo* 2004 (5) BCLR 561 (BCT).

11 *Islamic Unity Convention v Independent Broadcasting Authority and others* 2002 (5) BCLR 433 (CC).

- In *Stembridge v Stembridge*, the judge stated that a judge is concerned with the living present and not images of the past.[12]
- The Republic of South Africa is not inhabited only by Christians. It is inhabited by an amalgam of various cultures and religions, which all enjoy equal protection under the Constitution.
- It is the majority's view that the impugned joke in present-day South Africa cannot be said to be so beyond the pale that the joke would be regarded as blasphemous and constitute hate speech.
- The Tribunal finds that section 16 of the Constitution and the Broadcasting Code have not been contravened.

The common law crime of blasphemy is still a part of South African law as it has not been abolished by legislation or declared to be unconstitutional. However, there is uncertainty as to its scope. The basis of the crime is consideration for the religious feelings of a large section of the community, and thus the preservation of public peace and order rather than the protection of organised religion or religious dogma as such.[13] Whether this rationale for the continued existence of the crime is tenable in a secular society like South Africa is not obvious. At a minimum, it seems that the current content of the crime of blasphemy needs to be seriously debated and perhaps replaced by a more general crime of hate speech.[14]

DISCUSSION

Should blasphemy still be a crime?

In an article by Nazeem Goolam entitled 'The cartoon controversy: A note on freedom of expression, hate speech and blasphemy',[15] the author makes the following points:

- The right to freedom of expression is permitted if it does not encroach on the self-worth and dignity of a human being.
- Citing Burchell, the author points out that if the crime of blasphemy can be committed only in respect of the Christian God and religion, it is discriminatory because only those who attack Christian beliefs will be liable to prosecution while those who attack other religions will not.
- If this were the situation, then the crime of blasphemy would be unconstitutional, and cases of blasphemy would then be considered as incitement to religious hatred. The major advantage of this, Burchell argues, would be that the prohibition to incite religious hatred would apply to all religions equally.
- The Constitution provides that everyone has the right to equality, freedom of expression, and freedom of religion, belief and opinion.
- In conclusion, hate speech, hate propaganda and hate promotion in respect of any religion and the vilification of any religion will serve only to exacerbate tensions between different cultural and religious communities.

It is perhaps time to do away with this narrow and constitutionally problematic common law offence and to rather debate the merits of a broader approach to hate crimes and hate speech.

12 *Stembridge v Stembridge* [1998] 2 All SA 4 (D) at 14.

13 See also comments by Burchell *Principles of Criminal Law* 793.

14 See also comments by Burchell *Principles of Criminal Law* 793.

15 Goolam NMI 'The cartoon controversy: A note on freedom of expression, hate speech and blasphemy' (2006) 39(2) *CILSA* 333–350.

38.3 Towards the criminalisation of hate crimes and hate speech

Section 10 of the Promotion of Equality and Prevention of Unfair Discrimination Act 4 of 2000 prohibits hate speech or speech that is hurtful or harmful.[16] The current statutory and common law tools available to complainants in cases of hateful, harmful or defamatory speech must be evaluated in light of the constitutional protection of free speech, which is qualified in that the right to freedom of expression does not extend to propaganda for war, incitement of imminent violence or advocacy of hatred that is based on race, ethnicity, gender or religion, and that constitutes incitement to cause harm.[17] While the Constitution and the Promotion of Equality Act provide for a normative framework, it is clear that more clarity is needed for the norm against hate speech to have any meaningful role to play from a criminal law perspective.[18]

South Africa has a long and troubled history of colonialism, apartheid, racial oppression and institutionalised bigotry. The advent of the democratic constitutional order in 1994 did not bring an end to hate and bigotry, but it did bring into being a constitutional, legal and normative order which is premised on dignity, equality and freedom. The adoption of the Promotion of Equality Act in 2000 signaled a step towards the concretisation of the constitutional norms against hateful and harmful speech. There is, however, a need for a more comprehensive response against hate crimes and hate speech. The pervasiveness of xenophobia, racism, bigotry and homophobia demand a clear and decisive response; but without forfeiting the value of free speech in a democratic South Africa. To this end, the draft Prevention and Combating of Hate Crimes and Hate Speech Bill was published for commentary in 2016.[19] The draft bill aims, *inter alia*, to:

- give effect to South Africa's obligations in terms of the Constitution and international human rights instruments concerning racism, racial discrimination, xenophobia and related intolerance in accordance with international law obligations;
- provide for the offence of hate crimes and the offence of hate speech and the prosecution of persons who commit those crimes;
- provide for appropriate sentences that may be imposed on persons who commit hate crime and hate speech offences;
- provide for the prevention of hate crimes and hate speech;
- provide for the reporting on the implementation, application and administration of the Prevention and Combating of Hate Crimes and Hate Speech Act.

South Africa is a diverse society, with many different races, cultures, language groups, religions and belief systems still in the process of transforming from a divisive and oppressive past into a society based on the norms enshrined in the Constitution. It is important that

16 See further, Burchell *Principles of Criminal Law* 793.

17 Constitution of the Republic of South Africa, 1996, s 16(2). In *South African Human Rights Commission v Jonathan Dubula Qwelane* [EQ44/2009(EQ13/2012)] 18 Aug 2017 (available at http://www.justice.gov.za/legislation/hcbill/Judgment-20170818-Qwelane.pdf), the Equality Court, Gauteng Local Division, held that the hate speech provisions in the Equality Act, 2000, are compatible with the Constitution. The provisions do not unfairly curtail free speech. The applicant in the matter uttered statements in the media that were found to be derogatory to members of the LGBTI community, in that the applicant compared homosexual conduct to 'bestiality'. The Equality Court ordered that a copy of the findings be sent to the police for further investigation under s 21 of the Equality Act.

18 For comparative and constitutional perspectives, see Barries GN 'The divergent constitutional approach to hate speech in South Africa and the United States' (2013) 4 *TSAR 697*–707; Botha J and Govindjee A 'Regulating cases of extreme hate speech in South Africa: A suggested framework for a legislated criminal sanction' (2014) 27(2) *SACJ* 117–155.

19 *Government Gazette* No 40367, GenN 698, 24 October 2016, available at http://www.justice.gov.za/legislation/hcbill/2016-HateCrimes-HateSpeechBill.pdf.

legislation dealing with hate crimes and hate speech play a constructive role.[20] In our view, two principles should guide the eventual finalisation and adoption of the proposed Prevention and Combating of Hate Crimes and Hate Speech Bill: *first*, and self-evidently, the bill must be compatible with the Constitution which protects free speech as an important norm in a democratic society based on dignity, equality and freedom. *Second*, in line with the *ultima ratio* principle, criminalisation of conduct, including harmful conduct, should be the last resort. The principle of *ultima ratio* means, in short, that criminalisation should be reserved for those cases where other, less drastic, means (for instance through private law litigation, administrative sanctions or mediation/alternative dispute resolution) fail.[21]

Perhaps South Africa's post-apartheid history shows that a 'softer' approach to hate and bigotry does not have the desired effect. Rational, precise and constitutionally compliant criminalisation via the proposed Prevention and Combating of Hate Crimes and Hate Speech Bill may yet be the justified last resort to deal with hate and bigotry.[22]

THIS CHAPTER IN ESSENCE

1. The discussion in this chapter of the common law crime of public indecency must be read together with the relevant parts of Chapter 28 on sexual crimes.
2. Although the common law crime of public indecency has not been repealed by the Sexual Offences Act, its continued existence in a more liberal, multicultural South Africa is certainly debatable. The vagueness of the concept of public indecency also creates problems in terms of the principle of legality.
3. The continued existence of the common law crime of blasphemy is also debatable. In theory, if not in practice, it still exists as a separate crime under common law. A more appropriate vehicle to address the underlying interests of this crime is perhaps the possibility of criminalising hate speech in line with section 16 of the Constitution.
4. The debate concerning the draft Prevention and Combating of Hate Crimes and Hate Speech Bill is briefly introduced.

20 See comments by Naidoo K and Karels MG 'Prosecuting "hate": An overview of problem areas relating to hate crimes and challenges to criminal litigation' (2016) 41(1) *JJS* 65–82.

21 Jareborg N 'Criminalization as last resort (*Ultima Ratio*)' (2005) 2(2) *OSJCL* 521 at 525.

22 For detailed, critical reflections, see: Naidoo K 'The raison d'être of hate-crime laws' (2016) 29(2) *SACJ* 158; Naidoo K 'Are the perceived greater harms caused by hate crimes a plausible justification for the existence of hate-crime laws?' (2016) 27(3) *Stell L R* 634; Naidoo K 'Factors which influenced the enactment of hate-crime legislation in the United States of America: Quo vadis South Africa?' (2016) 4 *TSAR* 697; Naidoo K 'The shaping, enactment and interpretation of the first hate-crime law in the United Kingdom – An informative and illustrative lesson for South Africa' *PER/PELJ* (2017) 20 1–28, available at http://journals.assaf.org.za/per/article/view/1356.

Chapter 39

Drug offences

CHAPTER OBJECTIVES

The objectives of this chapter are to:

- discuss briefly the rationale for the criminalisation of illicit drug use and trading in illicit drugs
- discuss the crime of using or possessing prohibited substances
- discuss the crime of dealing in prohibited substances
- discuss developments surrounding the possible decriminalisation of the use of dagga.

39.1 General background

Human behaviour and perceptions can be altered or manipulated using chemical substances and stimulants.[1] Some of these chemicals can be used for medicinal or recreational purposes. However, dealing, using or possessing these substances may be a criminal offence because of their addictive or harmful consequences. Substances may be harmful because of their physical and psychological effects.[2] Although drug abuse often happens in private, the socio-economic impacts are such that this category of crimes can be described as crimes against the community and public welfare.

39.2 Drugs

39.2.1 A brief history

The South African national legislature began to criminalise the voluntary use of psychotropic substances through the provisions of section 10(1) of the Customs and Excise Duties Amendment Act 35 of 1922. The provisions of this legislation allowed for regulation by proclamation. The legislation regulated the import, transport, possession and sale of 'habit forming drugs'. The proscribed habit-forming drugs included cannabis, cocaine, heroin, morphine, opium and various other synthetic substances. The prohibition against habit-forming drugs was reinforced by the provisions of sections 61–72 of the Medical, Dental and Pharmacy Act 13 of 1928 and eventually by section 22A(10) of the Medicines and Related Substances Act 101 of 1965 (the Medicines Act).

The Abuse of Dependence-Producing Substances and Rehabilitation Centres Act 41 of 1971[3] created a number of new features that were not part of the scheme developed by the Medical, Dental and Pharmacy Act of 1928. Such features included the offence of failing (for certain persons) to report to the police any suspicion of contraventions of the Act in places of entertainment.[4] Another interesting feature of the Abuse of Dependence-Producing Substances Act included the forfeiture of the drugs concerned, vehicles, vessels, aircraft or receptacles, immovable property, and money standing to the credit of convicted persons in banks, building societies and other financial institutions on conviction under the Act.[5] The Act also had features that were intended to assist the state in securing convictions such as presumptions favouring the state[6] and far-reaching powers of investigation and interrogation.[7]

The Drugs and Drug Trafficking Act 140 of 1992 replaced and repealed the 1971 Abuse of Dependence-Producing Substances Act, and introduced new offences related to drug trafficking and money laundering. The state's powers for confiscating the proceeds of drug trafficking have been amplified by the provisions of the Prevention of Organised Crime Act 121 of 1998.

1 See also the general aims of the Prevention of and Treatment for Substance Abuse Act 70 of 2008. The Act entered into force on 31 March 2013. See Proc 8 in *GG* 36304 of 28 March 2013.

2 *Prince v President of The Law Society of The Cape of Good Hope and others* 2002 (3) BCLR 231 (CC) at 278; 2002 (1) SACR 431 (CC); 2002 (2) SA 794 (CC) at 252. See also Burchell JM *Principles of Criminal Law* 5 ed (2016) 821–822.

3 This statute came into force on 6 December 1971, by Proc R265, which was published in *GG* 3321, dated 3 December 1971.

4 S 6 of the Abuse of Dependence-Producing Substances and Rehabilitation Centres Act 41 of 1971.

5 S 8 of the Abuse of Dependence-Producing Substances Act.

6 S 10 of the Abuse of Dependence-Producing Substances Act.

7 Ss 11–13 of the Abuse of Dependence-Producing Substances Act.

It was necessary for the legislature to intervene by introducing the Drugs and Drug Trafficking Act because South Africa had been readmitted into the relevant United Nations structures after the end of apartheid. It was necessary to ensure that South African drug legislation was consistent with international obligations that the state had assumed by becoming a signatory to a number of conventions. The obligations originated from various conventions, including the Single Convention on Narcotic Drugs of 1961 as amended by the 1972 Protocol,[8] the Convention on Psychotropic Substances of 1971,[9] and the UN Convention Against Illicit Traffic in Narcotic Drugs and Psychotropic Substances of 1988.[10]

The possible decriminalisation of the private use of dagga, prompted by a decision by the High Court (discussed below under section 39.2.4) must be done with due regard to South Africa's international obligations. Indeed, the High Court in *Prince v Minister of Justice and Constitutional Development; Rubin v NDPP; Acton v NDPP*[11] (hereafter '*Acton et al*') noted that the 1988 UN Convention provides that the 'duty of a state party is to establish as a criminal offence under its domestic law the possession, purchase or cultivation of narcotic drugs or psychotropic substances for personal consumption, *subject to a state party's constitutional principles and the basic concepts of its legal system.*'[12] It can be argued that states have some leeway in how to deal with the problem of illicit drugs, and there is some scope to differentiate between drugs which can be regarded as dangerous ('particularly serious', in the words of the UN Drugs Convention) and others that are regarded as less dangerous (such as dagga, perhaps). State parties are invited to provide for alternatives to criminal punishment, including measures for the treatment, education, aftercare, rehabilitation or social reintegration of offenders.

The crimes that are of interest in this chapter are those related to the possession, use[13] and dealing[14] of prohibited drugs. Section 13 of the Drugs and Drug Trafficking Act provides that any person who contravenes the prohibitions against the use, possession or dealing of prohibited substances is guilty of an offence. Section 17 provides for the penalties for contravening the prohibitions against dealing, possessing or using prohibited substances. The Drugs and Drug Trafficking Act empowers magistrates' courts with the jurisdiction to impose any penalty mentioned in section 17, even though that penalty may exceed the punitive jurisdiction of a magistrate's court.[15] The legislature intended to punish dealing in prohibited substances with more severity than the crime of using or possessing a prohibited substance.[16]

8 Art 36(1)(*a*) of the Single Convention on Narcotic Drugs of 1961 (as amended by the 1972 Protocol) provides that the criminalisation of the listed forms of conduct must take place subject to each Party's constitutional limitations.

9 The 1971 Convention does not apply to cannabis (dagga).

10 Art 3(2) also provides that the criminalisation of the listed forms of conduct must take place subject to each party's constitutional limitations.

11 *Prince v Minister of Justice and Constitutional Development and Others; Rubin v National Director of Public Prosecutions and Others; Acton and Others v National Director of Public Prosecutions and Others* (4153/2012) [2017] ZAWCHC 30; [2017] 2 All SA 864 (WCC); 2017 (4) SA 299 (WCC) (31 March 2017), available at http://www.saflii.org/za/cases/ZAWCHC/2017/30.html.

12 *Acton et al* at para 119. (Emphasis added)

13 S 4 of the Drugs and Drug Trafficking Act. This section should be read with s 13(*c*) and 13(*d*) of the Act.

14 S 5 of the Drugs and Drug Trafficking Act. This section should be read with s 13(*e*) and 13(*f*) of the Act.

15 S 64(*a*) of the Drugs and Drug Trafficking Act.

16 *S v Solomon* 1986 (3) SA 705 (A) at 709.

39.2.2 Using or possessing prohibited substances

39.2.2.1 Definition

It is a crime for any person to be found using or in possession of any dependence-producing substance,[17] any dangerous dependence-producing substance or any undesirable dependence-producing substance.[18]

> **Section 4 of the Drugs and Drug Trafficking Act provides as follows:**
>
> **No person shall use or have in his possession—**
>
> **(*a*) any dependence-producing substance; or**
>
> **(*b*) any dangerous dependence-producing substance or any undesirable dependence-producing substance.**[19]

The provisions of section 4 thus create two crimes:[20]

1. Section 4(*a*) criminalises the unlawful and intentional use or possession of any dependence-producing substance.[21]

---

17 S 4(*a*) read with s 13(*c*) of the Drugs and Drug Trafficking Act.

18 S 4(*b*) read with s 13(*d*) of the Drugs and Drug Trafficking Act.

19 S 4(*b*) continues to list exceptions to the prohibition against use or possession by the accused as including circumstances where:

(i) he is a patient who has acquired or bought any such substance—

(*aa*) from a medical practitioner, dentist or practitioner acting in his professional capacity and in accordance with the requirements of the Medicines Act or any regulation made thereunder; or

(*bb*) from a pharmacist in terms of an oral instruction or a prescription in writing of such medical practitioner, dentist or practitioner, and uses that substance for medicinal purposes under the care or treatment of the said medical practitioner, dentist or practitioner;

(ii) he has acquired or bought any such substance for medicinal purposes—

(*aa*) from a medical practitioner, veterinarian, dentist or practitioner acting in his professional capacity and in accordance with the requirements of the Medicines Act or any regulation made thereunder;

(*bb*) from a pharmacist in terms of an oral instruction or a prescription in writing of such medical practitioner, veterinarian, dentist or practitioner; or

(*cc*) from a veterinary assistant or veterinary nurse in terms of a prescription in writing of such veterinarian, with the intent to administer that substance to a patient or animal under the care or treatment of the said medical practitioner, veterinarian, dentist or practitioner;

(iii) he is the Director-General: Welfare who has acquired or bought any such substance in accordance with the requirements of the Medicines Act or any regulation made thereunder;
[Sub-para. (iii) amended by s. 4 of Act 18 of 1996.]

20 **(iv) he, she or it is a patient, medical practitioner, veterinarian, dentist, practitioner, nurse, midwife, nursing assistant, pharmacist, veterinary assistant, veterinary nurse, manufacturer of, or wholesale dealer in, pharmaceutical products, importer or exporter, or any other person contemplated in the Medicines Act or any regulation made thereunder, who or which has acquired, bought, imported, cultivated, collected or manufactured, or uses or is in possession of, or intends to administer, supply, sell, transmit or export any such substance in accordance with the requirements or conditions of the said Act or regulation, or any permit issued to him, her or it under the said Act or regulation;**

(v) he is an employee of a pharmacist, manufacturer of, or wholesale dealer in, pharmaceutical products, importer or exporter who has acquired, bought, imported, cultivated, collected or manufactured, or uses or is in possession of, or intends to supply, sell, transmit or export any such substance in the course of his employment and in accordance with the requirements or conditions of the Medicines Act or any regulation made thereunder, or any permit issued to such pharmacist, manufacturer of, or wholesale dealer in, pharmaceutical products, importer or exporter under the said Act or regulation; or

(vi) he has otherwise come into possession of any such substance in a lawful manner.

See also Snyman CR *Criminal Law* 6 ed (2014) 420–423; Burchell *Principles of Criminal Law* 828–830.

21 S 1 defines the term 'dependence-producing substance' as meaning any substance or any plant from which a substance can be manufactured included in Part I of Schedule 2.

2. Section 4(*b*) criminalises the unlawful and intentional use or possession of any dangerous dependence-producing substance[22] or any undesirable dependence-producing substance.[23]

39.2.2.2 Elements

The elements of using or possessing a prohibited substance are:

- unlawfulness
- intent
- use or possession
- the prohibited substance.

39.2.2.2.1 Unlawfulness

Section 13 provides that it is unlawful to contravene the provisions of section 4(*a*)[24] and 4(*b*).[25] Proof of necessity[26] or compulsion may exclude the unlawfulness of the conduct. The provisions of section 4 allow for use or possession of designated substances in cases where the substances have been acquired by a patient,[27] a person who has acquired the substance for medicinal purposes,[28] the Director-General: Welfare[29] or an authorised person.[30]

A patient may lawfully acquire the designated substances when such acquisition is from a practitioner acting in accordance with the requirements of the Medicines Act or any regulation made thereunder.[31] A patient may also acquire the substances from a pharmacist who was acting under the oral instruction or written prescription from an authorised practitioner who is caring for the patient.[32]

A person may acquire the substance for medicinal purposes if the intention is to administer that substance to a patient or animal under the care or treatment of an authorised practitioner. A person may acquire the substance for medicinal purposes from a medical practitioner, veterinarian, dentist or practitioner acting in his professional capacity and in accordance with the requirements of the Medicines Act or any regulation made thereunder.[33] A person may also acquire the substance for medicinal purposes from a pharmacist in terms of an oral instruction or a written prescription from an authorised practitioner,[34] a veterinary assistant or veterinary nurse in terms of a written prescription from the relevant veterinarian.[35]

---

22 S 1 defines the term 'dangerous dependence-producing substance' as meaning any substance or any plant from which a substance can be manufactured included in Part II of Schedule 2.

23 S 1 defines the term 'undesirable dependence-producing substance' as meaning any substance or any plant from which a substance can be manufactured included in Part III of Schedule 2.

24 S 13(*c*) of the Drugs and Drug Trafficking Act.

25 S 13(*d*) of the Drugs and Drug Trafficking Act.

26 *S v Collett* 1991 (2) SA 854 (A).

27 S 4(*b*)(i) of the Drugs and Drug Trafficking Act.

28 S 4(*b*)(ii) of the Drugs and Drug Trafficking Act.

29 S 4(*b*)(iii) of the Drugs and Drug Trafficking Act. Further, the clause requires that the Director-General must come into possession of the substance in accordance with the requirements of the Medicines Act or any regulation made thereunder.

30 Ss 4(*b*)(iv)–(vi) of the Drugs and Drug Trafficking Act. The authorised persons are 'contemplated' in the Medicines Act or any regulation made thereunder, and they include any person who lawfully comes into possession of any such substance. This includes the people who come into possession for research or analytical purposes in terms of s 22A(10) of the Medicines Act read with Schedule 8 to the Medicines Act.

31 S 4(*b*)(i)(*aa*) of the Drugs and Drug Trafficking Act.

32 S 4(*b*)(i)(*bb*) of the Drugs and Drug Trafficking Act.

33 S 4(*b*)(ii)(*aa*) of the Drugs and Drug Trafficking Act.

34 S 4(*b*)(ii)(*bb*) of the Drugs and Drug Trafficking Act.

35 S 4(*b*)(ii)(*cc*) of the Drugs and Drug Trafficking Act.

39.2.2.2.2 Intent

The state bears the onus of proving that the accused had actual or legal intention to use or possess the prohibited substance unlawfully.

39.2.2.2.3 Use or possession

The word 'use' has synonyms that include words such as 'employ', 'draw on', 'exploit' and 'abuse'. In the context of the prohibited substances, the word 'use' relates to *any means employed to experience the psychotropic qualities of the substance.* The most notable means employed include injection, ingestion, smoking and inhalation.

Section 1 of the Drugs and Drug Trafficking Act defines the word 'possess' in relation to a drug as 'including to keep or to store the drug, or to have it in custody or under control or supervision'. This definition is almost identical to the one in the Abuse of Dependence-Producing Substances Act of 1971.[36] The only real difference is the fact that the definition in the 1971 Act expressly provided that the noun 'possession' was to have a corresponding meaning. This signifies the nature of the relationship between the drug and the person in possession thereof.[37]

The use of the word 'including' in the definition of the word 'possess' suggests that the meaning attributed to 'possession' is not the only meaning that the word can have in the Drugs and Drug Trafficking Act. The common law conception of 'possession' would thus be available to prove liability if the courts find it to be consistent with the purpose of the Act. This would make it possible to prove possession by applying rules relating to detention and *animus possidendi.*[38] Any meaning that is consistent with the intention of the legislature should therefore be available for defining the concept of possession.

The onus is on the state to prove beyond a reasonable doubt that the accused possessed the drug as the term is understood in terms of the Drugs and Drug Trafficking Act. The accused can also be held to be in possession of the drug if he occupies the land on which it was found and if the accused was aware of its existence because he is the person who is in control or has supervision over it.[39] An interesting phenomenon is the challenge posed by the situation in which a police officer arrests two people sitting at a table facing each other with drugs between them. If all the drugs belong to the first accused, and the second accused was merely assisting for the sole and private use of the first accused, then the second accused would not have been in possession of the drugs, and the converse would also be true.[40] If, however, the accused were joint owners or joint custodians, then each would have been in possession of the whole quantity of the drugs.[41]

Originally, the prosecutor was assisted by a legal presumption that inferred possession of a prohibited drug on the basis that it was found near to the accused.[42] Section 20 of the Drugs and Drug Trafficking Act originally provided as follows:

> **If in the prosecution of any person for an offence under this Act it is proved that any drug was found in the immediate vicinity of the accused, it shall be presumed, until the contrary is proved, that the accused was found in possession of such drug.**

---

36 *S v Skhosana* 1973 (1) SA 322 (O) at 330.

37 *S v Hendricks and another* [1976] 4 All SA 158 (C) at 161.

38 *R v Betelezie* 1941 TPD 191; *R v David* 1957 (2) SA 279 (SR); *S v Brick* 1973 (2) SA 571 (A); *S v Hanekom* 1979 (2) SA 1130 (C); *S v Cleminshaw* 1981 (3) SA 685 (C); *S v Young* 1983 (4) SA 120 (ZS); *S v Collet* supra; *S v Cameron* 2005 (2) SACR 179 (SCA).

39 *S v Guess* [1976] 4 All SA 534 (A) at 538.

40 *S v Hendricks* supra at 159.

41 *S v Mkize* 1975 (1) SA 517 (A) at 523.

42 *S v Majola* 1975 (2) SA 727 (A) at 731–732; *S v Mulligan and another* 1975 (2) SA 111 (N) at 114.

Once the presumption came into operation, it became incumbent on the accused to prove that he was not in possession on a balance of probabilities. A consequence of this presumption was the imposition of a reverse onus on the accused to do more than prove reasonable doubt to escape liability. The onus of proof shifted from the state and was placed squarely on the accused to prove his innocence.

In *S v Mello and another*,[43] the Constitutional Court found that the presumption contained in section 20 was unconstitutional. The court considered the presumption to be unjustifiable because it 'hits at the core of the right to be presumed innocent until proven guilty; a right which protects the basic values of justice in an open and democratic society based on freedom and equality'.[44] Consequently, section 20 of the Drugs and Drug Trafficking Act was declared unconstitutional and invalid. The state is now obliged to use regular legal means to prove that the accused was in possession of the offending substance without relying on a presumption.

39.2.2.3 Prohibited substance

Section 4 of the Drugs and Drug Trafficking Act proscribes the use or possession of any substance or any plant[45] from which a substance can be manufactured where such substance is listed in Schedule 2 of the Act. Section 63 allows the Minister of Justice to amend the contents of Schedule 2 by notice in the *Government Gazette* after consultation with the Minister of National Health.[46] The Minister of Justice may include,[47] delete[48] or otherwise amend the contents of the Schedule.[49] The Minister of Justice has exercised the discretion afforded by the Drugs and Drug Trafficking Act and occasionally amended the contents of Schedule 2.[50]

Schedule 2 of the Drugs and Drug Trafficking Act categorises prohibited substances into three groups:

1. Dependence-producing substances (Part I)
2. Dangerous dependence-producing substances (Part II)
3. Undesirable dependence-producing substances (Part III)

Part I of Schedule 2 identifies the prohibited dependence-producing substances. The list of prohibited dependence-producing substances includes barbiturates,[51] psychoactive substances,[52] certain stimulants with appetite suppressant qualities,[53] powerful sedatives with hypnotic and amnesic qualities,[54] and opioid analgesics.[55] Unless expressly excluded, all substances in Part I of Schedule 2 include the salts, esters, preparations and mixtures of the listed substances.

---

43 *S v Mello and another* 1998 (3) SA 712 (CC).
44 *S v Mello* supra at 717E.
45 S 1 of the Drugs and Drug Trafficking Act defines the word 'plant' as including any portion of a plant.
46 S 63 of the Drugs and Drug Trafficking Act.
47 S 63(*a*) of the Drugs and Drug Trafficking Act.
48 S 63(*b*) of the Drugs and Drug Trafficking Act.
49 S 63(*c*) of the Drugs and Drug Trafficking Act.
50 Examples of such amendments to Schedule 2 include the amendments by *GG* 17520 GN R1765 of 1 November 1996, *GG* 20194 GN R760 of 11 June 1999 and *GG* 22360 GN R521 of 15 June 2001.
51 Including amobarbital and butalbital.
52 Including cathine, which causes effects like those associated with amphetamines.
53 Including chlorphentermine and diethylpropion (amfepramone).
54 Including flunitrazepam (Rohypnol) and gluthethimide.
55 Including meptazinol and pentazocine.

Part II of Schedule 2 identifies the prohibited dangerous dependence-producing substances. The list of prohibited dangerous dependence-producing substances includes powerful analgesics;[56] chlorodyne (chloroform and morphine tincture); morphine; coca leaf and any salt, compound, derivative or preparation of coca leaf; ecgonine and the esters and derivatives that are convertible to ecgonine and cocaine; synthetic opioids;[57] opium and opiates and any salt, compound, derivative or preparation of opium or opiates; and opium poppy and poppy straw. Unless expressly excluded, all substances or plants in Part II of Schedule 2 include the isomers of the specified substances or plants; the esters and ethers of the specified substances or plants, and the isomers of such esters and ethers; the salts of the specified substances or plants of the isomers, esters, ethers and the isomers of such salts; and all preparations and mixtures of the specified substances or plants, and of the isomers, esters, ethers and salts.

Part III of Schedule 2 identifies the prohibited undesirable dependence-producing substances. The list of prohibited undesirable dependence-producing substances includes amphetamines;[58] powerful, naturally occurring hallucinogenics;[59] cannabis (dagga), the whole plant or any portion or product thereof;[60] a range of powerful psychoactive substances;[61] opioid analgesics;[62] and semi-synthetic opiates including heroin (diacetylmorphine) and methaqualone (including mandrax).[63] Unless expressly excluded, all substances or plants included Part III of Schedule 2 include the following: the isomers of the specified substances or plants; the esters and ethers of the specified substances or plants and the isomers of such esters and ethers; the salts of the specified substances or plants of the isomers and the esters, ethers and the isomers of such salts; and all preparations and mixtures of the specified substances or plants and of the isomers, esters, ethers and salts.

The penalty for using or being in possession of dependence-producing substances may be a fine that a court deems appropriate, imprisonment for a period not exceeding five years, or both a fine and imprisonment.[64] The penalty for contravening the provisions of section 4(*b*)

56 Including acetorphine, bezitramide and etonitazene.

57 Including acetylmethadol, alphacetylmethadol alphamethadol, alfentanil allylprodine, anileridine, benzethidine, benzylmorphine. butorphanol, clonitazene, codeine (methylmorphine), codoxime, dextromoramide, dextropropoxyphene, diampromide, dimenoxadol, dimethylthiambutene, drotebanol, hydroxypethidine, methadone, phenazocine, piritramide, racemorphan, sufentanil, thebaine and tilidine.

58 Including brolamfetamine, dexamphetamine, fenetylline, listed fentanyl-analogues, levamphetamine, levomethamphetamine, methamphetamine, methamphetamine racemate, 2-methoxy-4,5-methylenedioxyamphetamine (MMDA), 4-methyl-2,5-dimethoxyamphetamine (DOM) and the derivatives thereof, methylenedioxyamphetamine (MDA), N-ethyl-methylenedioxyamphetamine, N-hydroxy-methylenedioxyamphetamine, paramethoxyamphetamine (PMA) and 3,4,5-trimethoxy amphetamine (TMA).

59 Including bufotenine (N,N-dimethylserotonin), which comes from the skin of some psychoactive toads from the genus *Bufo*. The prohibited substance is also found in certain species of mushrooms and some plants. Harmine [7-methoxy-1-methyl-9H-pyrido (3,4-b)-indole] is another prohibited hallucinogenic substance that can be found in certain plants. Mescaline (3,4,5-trimethoxyphenethylamine) can be found in certain cacti and plants. It is the active hallucinogenic in peyote, which has been associated with Native American ceremonies. Psilocin (4-hydroxydimethyltryptamine) and psilocybin (4-phosphoryloxy-N,N-dimethyltryptamine) have been found in certain psychedelic mushrooms.

60 Including synthetic tetrahydrocannabinol, the synthetic cannabinoid nabilone and Parahexyl, the synthetic homologue of the active component in cannabis.

61 Including 4-bromo-2,5-dimethoxyphene-thylamine (2C-B) (Nexus), cathinone, diethyltryptamine [3-(2-(diethylamino)-ethyl)-indole], dimethyltryptamine [3-(2-(dimethylamino)-ethyl)-indole], gamma-hydroxybutyrate (GHB), which has also been associated with date rapes and doping in sports, harmaline (3,4-dihydroharmine), lysergide (lysergic acid diethylamide or LSD or Acid), methcathinone (2-(methylamino)-1-phenylpropan-1-one), phencyclidine (angel dust or PCP) and the congeners thereof, namely N-ethyl-1-phenylcyclohexylamine (PCE), 1-(1-phenylcyclohexyl) pyrrolidine (PHP or PCPY) and 1-[1-(2-thienyl) cyclohexyl] piperidine (TCP).

62 Including 1-methyl-4-phenyl-4-propionoxy-piperidine (MPPP); 1-methyl-4-phenyl-1,2,5,6-tetrahydropiperidine (MPTP); and 1-phenylethyl-4-phenyl-4-acetyloxy-piperidine (PEPAP).

63 Also including Isonox, Quaalude, or any other preparation containing methaqualone and known by any other trade name.

64 S 17(*b*) of the Drugs and Drug Trafficking Act.

may be a fine that the court deems appropriate, imprisonment for a period not exceeding 15 years, or both a fine and imprisonment.[65]

39.2.3 Dealing in prohibited substances

39.2.3.1 Definition

It is an offence to deal in any dependence-producing substance,[66] any dangerous dependence-producing substance or any undesirable dependence-producing substance.[67] Section 5 of the Drugs and Drug Trafficking Act provides as follows:

> **No person shall deal in—**
> **(*a*) any dependence-producing substance; or**
> **(*b*) any dangerous dependence-producing substance or any undesirable dependence-producing substance.**[68]

The provisions of section 5 create two offences:[69]

1. Section 5(*a*) criminalises the unlawful and intentional dealing in any dependence-producing substance.[70]
2. Section 5(*b*) criminalises the unlawful and intentional dealing in any dangerous dependence-producing substance[71] or any undesirable dependence-producing substance.[72]

---

65 S 17(*d*) of the Drugs and Drug Trafficking Act.

66 S 5(*a*) read with s 13(*e*) of the Drugs and Drug Trafficking Act.

67 S 5(*b*) read with s 13(*f*) of the Drugs and Drug Trafficking Act.

68 S 5(*b*) continues to list exceptions to the prohibition against dealing by the accused as including circumstances where:
> **(i) he has acquired or bought any such substance for medicinal purposes—**
> **(*aa*) from a medical practitioner, veterinarian, dentist or practitioner acting in his professional capacity and in accordance with the requirements of the Medicines Act or any regulation made thereunder;**
> **(*bb*) from a pharmacist in terms of an oral instruction or a prescription in writing of such medical practitioner, veterinarian, dentist or practitioner; or**
> **(*cc*) from a veterinary assistant or veterinary nurse in terms of a prescription in writing of such veterinarian, and administers that substance to a patient or animal under the care or treatment of the said medical practitioner, veterinarian, dentist or practitioner;**
> **(ii) he is the Director-General: Welfare who acquires, buys or sells any such substance in accordance with the requirements of the Medicines Act or any regulation made thereunder;**
> **[Sub-para. (ii) amended by Section 4 of Act 18 of 1996.]**
> **(iii) he, she or it is a medical practitioner, veterinarian, dentist, practitioner, nurse, midwife, nursing assistant, pharmacist, veterinary assistant, veterinary nurse, manufacturer of, or wholesale dealer in, pharmaceutical products, importer or exporter, or any other person contemplated in the Medicines Act or any regulation made thereunder, who or which prescribes, administers, acquires, buys, tranships, imports, cultivates, collects, manufactures, supplies, sells, transmits or exports any such substance in accordance with the requirements or conditions of the said Act or regulation, or any permit issued to him, her or it under the said Act or regulation; or**
> **(iv) he is an employee of a pharmacist, manufacturer of, or wholesale dealer in, pharmaceutical products, importer or exporter who acquires, buys, tranships, imports, cultivates, collects, manufactures, supplies, sells, transmits or exports any such substance in the course of his employment and in accordance with the requirements or conditions of the Medicines Act or any regulation made thereunder, or any permit issued to such pharmacist, manufacturer of, or wholesale dealer in, pharmaceutical products, importer or exporter under the said Act or regulation.**

69 Snyman *Criminal Law* 423–426; Burchell *Principles of Criminal Law* 823–828.

70 S 1 defines the term 'dependence-producing substance' as meaning any substance or any plant from which a substance can be manufactured included in Part I of Schedule 2.

71 S 1 defines the term 'dangerous dependence-producing substance' as meaning any substance or any plant from which a substance can be manufactured included in Part II of Schedule 2.

72 S 1 defines the term 'undesirable dependence-producing substance' as meaning any substance or any plant from which a substance can be manufactured included in Part III of Schedule 2.

39.2.3.2 Elements

The elements of dealing in prohibited substances are:

- unlawfulness
- intent[73]
- dealing
- the prohibited substance.

39.2.3.2.1 Unlawfulness

Section 13 of the Drugs and Drug Trafficking Act provides that it is unlawful to be in contravention of the provisions of section 5(*a*)[74] and 5(*b*).[75] Proof of compulsion may exclude the unlawfulness of the conduct. The provisions of section 5 allow for using or possessing designated substances in cases where the substances have been acquired by a person for medicinal purposes,[76] by the Director-General: Welfare[77] or by an authorised person.[78]

A person may acquire the substance for medicinal purposes to administer that substance to a patient or animal under the care or treatment of an authorised practitioner.[79] A person may acquire the substance for medicinal purposes from a medical practitioner, veterinarian, dentist or practitioner acting in his professional capacity and in accordance with the requirements of the Medicines Act or any regulation made thereunder.[80] A person may also acquire the substance for medicinal purposes from a pharmacist in terms of an oral instruction or a written prescription from an authorised practitioner,[81] or a veterinary assistant or veterinary nurse in terms of a written prescription from the relevant veterinarian.[82]

39.2.3.2.2 Intent

The state bears the onus of proving that the accused knew that the substance is proscribed as an illegal drug.[83] Further, the state must prove that the accused had actual or legal intention to deal unlawfully in the prohibited substance.[84] *Dolus eventualis* will be proved to be present where the accused foresees the possibility that the prohibited transaction of dealing might occur in substantially the same manner as that in which it actually does occur.

---

73 *S v Ngwenya* 1979 (2) SA 96 (A) at 100.

74 S 13(*e*) of the Drugs and Drug Trafficking Act. Section 17(*c*) of the Act provides that this offence is punishable by a fine that the court deems appropriate or imprisonment for a period not exceeding 10 years, or both a fine and imprisonment.

75 S 13(*f*) of the Drugs and Drug Trafficking Act. S 17(*e*) of the Act provides that this offence is punishable by imprisonment for a period not exceeding 25 years, or both imprisonment and a fine that a court may deem fit to impose. S 1 of the Act provides that an offence also falls within the definition of a 'drug offence' as it is understood in the Act.

76 S 5(*b*)(i) of the Drugs and Drug Trafficking Act.

77 S 5(*b*)(ii) of the Drugs and Drug Trafficking Act. Further, the clause requires that the Director-General must come into possession of the substance in accordance with the requirements of the Medicines Act or any regulation made thereunder.

78 S 5(*b*)(iii)–(iv) of the Drugs and Drug Trafficking Act. The authorised persons are 'contemplated' in the Medicines Act or any regulation made thereunder, and they include any person who is acting in the course and scope of their employment, and the attendant legal obligations.

79 S 5(*b*)(i) of the Drugs and Drug Trafficking Act.

80 S 5(*b*)(i)(*aa*) of the Drugs and Drug Trafficking Act.

81 S 5(*b*)(i)(*bb*) of the Drugs and Drug Trafficking Act.

82 S 5(*b*)(i)(*cc*) of the Drugs and Drug Trafficking Act.

83 *S v Hlomza* 1987 (1) SA 25 (A) at 31.

84 *S v Ngwenya* supra at 100.

39.2.3.2.3 Dealing

Section 1 of the Drugs and Drug Trafficking Act provides that the expression 'deal in', in relation to a drug, includes performing any act in connection with the trans-shipment, import, cultivation,[85] collection, manufacture,[86] supply, prescription, administration, sale, transmission or export of the drug. This definition is similar to the definition contained in section 1 of the Abuse of Dependence-Producing Substances Act.

Further, section 1 of the Drugs and Drug Trafficking Act also provides that the word 'sell', in relation to a drug, includes to offer, advertise, possess or expose the drug for sale, to dispose of it for consideration or otherwise, or to exchange it.[87] The word 'sale' ordinarily has a commercial connotation. However, the definition used in section 1 shows that 'sale' does not necessarily have to be a business transaction before it amounts to dealing in a prohibited substance.[88] Section 1 specifically provides that the word 'sell' includes transactions that are not for consideration or otherwise.

None of the acts listed in the definition of 'deal in' are limited to acts or transactions of a commercial nature.[89] The cultivation of prohibited plants falls within the ambit of dealing in drugs even if it is intended for the cultivator's own private use.[90] Introducing prohibited substances into the Republic, even if not intended for business purposes, constitutes dealing in drugs.[91]

There have been interesting explanations of the ambit of liability connected to the expression 'in connection with'. The legislature used that expression to link the 'sale' and 'supply' (as with each separately listed 'act') postulated in the definition related to 'deal in'. The legislature clearly intended using the expression to bring persons other than those directly involved in a prohibited transaction within its ambit. However, there are limits to the scope of the liability for acts 'in connection with' the acts listed in the definition of 'deal in'.

Originally, it was generally accepted that the accused was liable for dealing in the substance where he either purchased the drugs from another and resold it to a third person, or acted as an intermediary or broker in bringing about a sale between another and a third person.[92] The court would assume that in the legal sense, the drugs were 'sold' and 'supplied' once and for all when the drugs were bought and received on the purchaser's behalf.[93] The drug's subsequent delivery to the purchaser was not treated as either an integral part or a separate instance of such 'sale' or 'supply'.[94] The courts originally favoured the literal

85 *S v Guess* supra; *S v Kgupane en andere* 1975 (2) SA 73 (T). In *S v Mbatha* 2012 (2) SACR 551 (KZP), the majority of the court held that the wording of the Act clearly supports a conviction of dealing in dagga. 'Dealing' means more than commercial or transactional acts. It includes cultivation of dagga. In this instance, a fully grown dagga plant was found in the yard of the accused as well as a packet with dagga seeds alongside the house of the accused.

86 S 1 of the Drugs and Drug Trafficking Act defines the word 'manufacture', in relation to a substance, as including the preparing, extraction or production of the substance.

87 This definition is similar to the definition used in the Abuse of Dependence-Producing Substances Act. One of the minor differences relates to the fact that the definition from this Act further provided that the word 'sale' is said to have a corresponding meaning.

88 In *S v Majenge en 'n ander* 1978 (2) SA 661 (O) at 664, the court held that the legislative use of the word 'sale' refers to an activity and not necessarily to a completed transaction.

89 *S v Crawford and another* [1979] 1 All SA 395 (A) at 398.

90 *S v Kgupane* supra at 76.

91 *S v Crawford* supra at 398.

92 *S v Engelbrecht* 1975 (4) SA 909 (N) at 911; *S v Ngcube and another* 1976 (1) SA 341 (N), a judgment of the full bench.

93 *S v Engelbrecht* supra at 911.

94 *S v Engelbrecht* supra at 911. The *Engelbrecht* decision was followed in *S v Matamela* 1977 (1) SA 315 (T), *S v Gwabeni* 1977 (2) SA 27 (E) and *S v Rowles* 1977 (2) SA 440 (O). This approach was rejected in *S v Ntshingila* [1980] 2 All SA 318 (N) at 322.

interpretation to a degree where an accused who handed a dagga cigarette to another so that he could smoke it, was considered to be disposing of the drug in a manner that amounts to selling, and thus dealing in the drug.[95]

Further, a literal interpretation of the definition would mean that the purchase of a dagga cigarette is an 'act in connection with' its 'sale', and the acquisition of dagga is an 'act in connection with' its 'supply'. This would mean that a purchaser of the dagga cigarette would be liable as a dealer. Courts have considered this conclusion as doubtful,[96] inconceivable[97] and untenable.[98] The distinction between the serious crime of dealing in dagga and the lesser offence of possessing it would disappear if the literal interpretation was preferred.[99] Where the accused acquires the drug for personal consumption only, they should only be liable for the crime of possession or use.[100]

To seize on an 'act' that literally has some 'connection with' the 'sale' or 'supply' of a prohibited substance and declare it to be dealing is too simplistic for a final verdict, and not the end of the enquiry.[101] There is a distinction between the *verskaffingsaktiwiteite* (activities related to supply) and *verkrygingsaktiwiteite* (activities related to acquisition).[102] The proscription against dealing applies to the former alone and not to the latter at all.[103]

Before any 'act' can be classified for the definition's purposes as one 'in connection with' the 'sale' or 'supply' of drugs, the question that must be asked and answered in the affirmative is whether the act was connected with such 'sale' or 'supply' to a degree where it is distinct from and instead of the mere purchase or acquisition of the drugs.[104] The answer to this question can only be answered on a case by case basis on the particular facts of each case.[105] In appropriate cases, it is not difficult to distinguish between conduct related to the 'sale' or 'supply' of drugs and their purchase or acquisition for private use.[106] However, there are also occasions where courts will have nothing more to examine other than the type of role played by the accused in the context of an illegal transaction.[107] If an accused person is found to have been in possession of a large quantity of dagga, it may, depending on all the circumstances and in the absence of an explanation giving rise to a reasonable doubt, be sufficient circumstantial evidence of dealing, and a justification for imposing the higher penalties associated with being a drug dealer.[108]

In *Ntshingila*, the court held that the purchase or acquisition of dagga for personal use by the purchaser or acquirer does not amount to a proscribed form of dealing.[109] Conduct

95 *S v Nkosi and others* 1972 (2) SA 753 (T) at 759; *S v Gibson* 1974 (4) SA 478 (A) at 481–482. In *S v Joubert* 1976 (1) PH H91 (AA), the accused was found liable for dealing, even though the person who had received the dagga cigarette had not smoked it.

96 *S v Govender* 1976 (4) SA 949 (N).

97 *S v Majenge* supra; *S v Bester* 1977 (2) SA 141 (NC); *S v Morgan; S v Watson* 1979 (2) SA 609 (O).

98 *S v Ntshingila* supra at 321. Among the reasons cited by the court was that a literal interpretation would incorrectly render every possessor as a dealer. Only those who gain possession by stealing it or coming on it abandoned would escape liability for being dealers.

99 *S v Ntshingila* supra at 321.

100 *S v Solomon* supra. See also the discussion on the decriminalisation of the possession and use of dagga in a private dwelling, under 39.2.4 below.

101 *S v Ntshingila* supra.

102 *S v Morgan; S v Watson* supra; *S v Ntshingila* supra at 322; *S v Solomon* supra.

103 *S v Morgan; S v Watson* supra; *S v Ntshingila* supra at 322; *S v Solomon* supra.

104 *S v Ntshingila* supra at 322.

105 *S v Ntshingila* supra at 322.

106 *S v Ntshingila* supra at 322.

107 *S v Ntshingila* supra at 322.

108 *S v Bhulwana; S v Gwadiso* supra [1996] 1 All SA 11 (CC); 1996 (1) SA 388 (CC); (1995 (2) SACR 748 (CC); 1995 (12) BCLR 1579 (CC) at 19; *S v Sixaxeni* 1994 (3) SA 733 (C), 1994 (2) SACR 451 (C) at 455.

109 *S v Ntshingila* supra at 322; *S v Solomon* supra at 710.

that is subject to the proscription against dealing applies to the purchase or acquisition for the purpose of another sale.[110] Courts have accepted that the purchase of dagga on another's behalf cannot, on its own, be branded as an 'act in connection with' the dagga's 'sale' or 'supply'.[111] Where the accused acts as an agent for another, and purchases drugs for the other's personal use, he performs an act in connection with the acquisition of drugs and not an act relating to the supply or furnishing of drugs. Such persons cannot be liable as dealers. They may be liable for possession if they are found in that position. It was not the intention of the legislature to punish the acquisition of drugs for personal use as an act of dealing in the drugs.[112]

Presumptions that relate to be a drug dealer have been in force in South Africa since 1954.[113] Even the Abuse of Dependence-Producing Substances Act had the benefit of the egregious presumption for proving liability for the crime of being a dealer.[114] Section 21 of the Drugs and Drug Trafficking Act also provided the prosecution with the benefit of a number of excessive and harmful presumptions relating to be a drug dealer.

The most offensive feature of these presumptions was the fact that they created a *reverse onus* on the accused to prove that they were not dealers on a balance of probabilities. Failure to disprove an essential element of a criminal charge on a preponderance of probabilities would result in a conviction of the accused. This is an offensive consequence because South African criminal law has a founding principle that it is the prosecution that carries the burden of proving guilt beyond reasonable doubt. Presumptions that reverse the onus, incorrectly and unjustifiably place the onus on the accused. Further, presumptions of this nature are in breach of the constitutional right to be presumed innocent until proven guilty,[115] which is part of the accused's right to a fair trial.[116] This type of presumption created further prejudice for the accused because there are more substantial penalties for the offence of dealing than the offence of possession. Luckily, the unconstitutional nature of such provisions was exposed.[117]

The presumptions created by section 21(1)(*a*) applied where a person was charged with contravening the provisions of section 5(*b*) of the Drugs and Drug Trafficking Act. The accused would be presumed to be a dealer if he was found in possession of dagga exceeding 115 grams[118, 119] any dangerous dependence-producing substance in/on or within 100 metres

---

110 *S v Ntshingila* supra at 322.

111 *S v Morgan; S v Watson* supra.

112 *S v Solomon* supra at 710.

113 For example, the presumption relating to be a drug dealer by virtue of being in possession of dagga in excess of 115 grams was first introduced by s 31 of the Medical, Dental and Pharmacy Amendment Act 29 of 1954. It introduced the presumption as s 90*bis* of the Medical, Dental and Pharmacy Act 13 of 1928.

114 S 10(1) of the Abuse of Dependence-Producing Substances Act.

115 S 35(3)(*h*) of the Constitution of the Republic of South Africa, 1996.

116 S 35(3) of the Constitution.

117 *S v Zuma and others* 1995 (2) SA 642 (CC); 1995 (1) SACR 568 (CC); 1995 (4) BCLR 401(CC); *S v Bhulwana; S v Gwadiso* supra [1996] 1 All SA 11 (CC); 1996 (1) SA 388 (CC); 1995 (2) SACR 748 (CC); 1995 (12) BCLR 1579 (CC); *S v Mbatha; S v Prinsloo* 1996 (2) SA 464 (CC) (1996 (1) SACR 371 (CC); 1996 (3) BCLR 293 (CC); *S v Julies* 1996 (4) SA 313 (CC) 1996 (2) SACR 108 (CC); 1996 (7) BCLR 899 (CC); *S v Ntsele* 1997 (2) SACR 740 (CC) (1997 (11) BCLR 1543 (CC); *S v Mello* supra.

118 The quantity of 115 grams has remained relatively constant since the presumption was first introduced in 1954. Originally, it was expressed as four ounces by the Medical, Dental and Pharmacy Amendment Act of 1954. Four ounces is 113,4 grams. In *S v Bhulwana; S v Gwadiso* supra, the Constitutional Court accepted that the proscribed amount appears to be based on an arbitrary figure.

119 S 21(1)(*a*)(i) of the Drugs and Drug Trafficking Act. However, the state had first to prove that the accused was in possession of the drugs. The presumption of being a dealer could not operate where the proof of possession was itself based on a presumption. The possession must have been proved as a matter of fact. *S v Majola* supra at 735.

of the confines of a school,[120] or any undesirable dependence-producing substance other than dagga.[121]

Section 21(1)(*b*) provided that a person who was charged with the crime of contravening section 5(*b*) of the Drugs and Drug Trafficking Act by virtue of the fact that he cultivated prohibited plants, also had the onerous burden of trying to rebut the presumption he was a dealer[122] if it was proved that the accused was aware or could reasonably be expected to have been aware of the existence of the plants;[123] and the accused was the owner, occupier, manager or person in charge of the land.[124]

Section 21(1)(*c*) provided that people could be presumed to be dealers of any prohibited drug if it was proved that they conveyed any drug.[125] There was also a presumption created by section 21(1)(*d*),[126] which would apply if it was proved that any drug was found on/in any animal, vehicle, vessel or aircraft;[127] and the accused was on or in charge of, or that he accompanied, any such animal, vehicle, vessel or aircraft.[128]

The Constitutional Court invalidated the presumptions relating to being a dealer by virtue of being in possession of dagga in excess of 115 grams (section 21(1)(*a*)(i)),[129] any undesirable dependence-producing substance (section 21(1)(*a*)(iii))[130] or cultivating prohibited plants (section 21(1)(*b*)).[131] The presumptions relating to being a dealer by virtue of the provisions of sections 21(1)(*c*)[132] and (*d*) have also been declared unconstitutional.[133] The Constitutional Court has been consistently invalidating presumptions that create a reverse onus to a degree that they infringe on the right to be presumed innocent.[134] For an accused person to be convicted of dealing where a doubt exists as to liability for that offence is therefore an infringement of the presumption of innocence.[135]

39.2.3.2.4 Prohibited substance

Section 5 the Drugs and Drug Trafficking Act proscribes dealing in any substance or any plant from which a substance listed in Schedule 2 of the Act can be manufactured. The penalty for dealing in dependence-producing substances may be a fine that a court deems fit to impose, imprisonment for a period not exceeding 10 years, or both a fine and imprisonment.[136] The penalty for contravening the provisions of section 5(*b*) may be

---

120 S 21(1)(*a*)(ii) of the Drugs and Drug Trafficking Act. Further, the Act provides that 'school' means any educational institution, except a university, a college of education or a technikon, where full-time education, including pre-primary education, is provided to pupils; and 'school grounds', in relation to a school, means land, whether it is contiguous or not, buildings or accommodation, sporting or other facilities used for or in connection with the activities of the school.

121 S 21(1)(*a*)(iii) of the Drugs and Drug Trafficking Act.

122 S 21(1)(*b*) of the Drugs and Drug Trafficking Act.

123 S 21(1)(*b*)(i) of the Drugs and Drug Trafficking Act.

124 S 21(1)(*b*)(ii) of the Drugs and Drug Trafficking Act.

125 S 21(1)(*c*) of the Drugs and Drug Trafficking Act.

126 S 21(1)(*d*) of the Drugs and Drug Trafficking Act.

127 S 21(1)(*d*)(i) of the Drugs and Drug Trafficking Act.

128 S 21(1)(*d*)(ii) of the Drugs and Drug Trafficking Act.

129 *S v Bhulwana; S v Gwadiso* supra.

130 *S v Julies* supra at 899.

131 *S v Ntsele* supra.

132 S 21(1)(*c*) was also considered to be invalid by the Constitutional Court in *S v Manyonyo* 1999 (12) BCLR 1438 (CC).

133 *S v Mjezu* 1996 (2) SACR 594 (NC).

134 *S v Zuma* supra; *S v Bhulwana; S v Gwadiso* supra; *S v Mbatha; S v Prinsloo* supra; *S v Julies* supra; *S v Ntsele* supra; *S v Mello* supra; *S v Manyonyo* supra.

135 *S v Bhulwana; S v Gwadiso* supra at 18.

136 S 17(*c*) of the Drugs and Drug Trafficking Act.

imprisonment for a period not exceeding 25 years, or both imprisonment and a fine that a court may deem fit to impose.[137]

39.2.4 Towards the decriminalisation of the use of dagga?

In 2002, in the case of *Prince v President of the Law Society of the Cape of Good Hope*,[138] the Constitutional Court considered the constitutionality of section 4(*b*) of the Drugs and Drug Trafficking Act and section 22A of the Medicines and Related Substances Control Act. The applicant argued that the provisions against the use or possession of dagga conflicted with the constitutional right to freedom of religion. The Constitutional Court held that the general prohibition against possession or use of drugs is a reasonable and justifiable limitation on the freedom of religion.[139]

Dagga became criminalised around 1921 at a time 'when South African criminological thinking came to be obsessed with interracial sex, the provision of alcohol by whites to blacks and the reverse flow of dagga'.[140] It has been generally accepted that different groups of the South African population have different traditions and attitudes towards the use of dagga.[141] Even the Constitutional Court referred to the fact that:

> **it is general knowledge that some sections of the [African] population have been accustomed for hundreds of years to the use of dagga, both as an intoxicant and in the belief that it has medicinal properties, and do not regard it with the same moral repugnance as do other sections of the population.**[142]

Article 14(2) of the UN Convention against Illicit Traffic in Narcotic Drugs and Psychotropic Substances of 1988 provides that when state parties take measures to prevent illicit cultivation of plants containing prohibited substances, they must ensure that:

> **The measures adopted shall respect fundamental human rights and shall take due account of traditional licit uses, where there is historic evidence of such use.**[143]

While there is a legitimate public interest in the criminalisation of illicit drugs, Sachs J reasoned that a retreat on the criminalisation of private dagga use 'might make little if any difference to prosecution of the major battles against cartels importing heroin, cocaine and mandrax'.[144] The 'war on drugs' would be best served by focusing on 'manifestly harmful

---

137 S 17(*e*) of the Drugs and Drug Trafficking Act.

138 *Prince v President of the Law Society* supra.

139 *Prince v President of the Law Society* supra at 476.

140 *Prince v President of The Law Society* supra at fn 23 on 285 at para 153, where Sachs J was making a reference to Chanock M *The Making of South African Legal Culture 1902–1936: Fear, Favour and Prejudice* (2001) at 69 and 92–96.

141 *S v Nkosi* supra at 762. The court also made a reference to the work of Watt JM and Breyer-Brandwijk MG *The Medicinal and Poisonous Plants of Southern and Eastern Africa* (1962) at 35 which reads:

> **Cannabis sativa 1., Cannabis indica, Indian hemp, hemp, hashish, ganjah, dagga, Xhosa umya, Suto matakwane, matokwane, matekwane, mmoana, is smoked as an intoxicant among South African natives. The Fingoes use the leaves as a snake-bite remedy and the Xhosas as part of the treatment of bots in horses. The 'oil' from a dagga pipe has been used by European 'cancer curers' as an external application. In Southern Rhodesia, natives use the plant, among others, as a remedy for malaria, blackwater fever, blood-poisoning, anthrax and dysentery, and as a 'war medicine'. The Sotos administer the ground-up seeds with bread or mealiepap to children during weaning. Suto women smoke cannabis to stupefy themselves during childbirth.**

142 *Prince v President of The Law Society* supra at 285. Sachs J was making reference to the dictum from *S v Nkosi* supra at 762A.

143 Art 14 of The United Nations Convention against Illicit Traffic in Narcotic Drugs and Psychotropic Substances (1988) *United Nations Document* E/CONF.82.15 in force in late 1990.

144 *Prince v President of The Law Society* supra at 285.

drugs', which do not include dagga.[145] Sachs J described the threat posed by private use of dagga by the Rastafari as 'particularly harmless'.[146]

In addition to the constitutional issues raised in *Prince*, one can also point to other principles of criminal law to deal with the possession and use of dagga in a sensible way. Trivial cases of possession or use of dagga could be subject to the maxim *de minimis non curat lex*. The maxim may be applied in criminal cases where the whole matter is so trivial as not to be worthy of judicial attention.[147] In *Van der Merwe*, the court acquitted the accused who had been found in possession of a dagga plant that was in a can in his bedroom.[148] The court was not convinced that it was the intention of the legislature to convict as dealers, persons in the position of the accused.[149] In *Van Zyl*, the court was also of the opinion that participation of minor importance in producing and raising dagga plants should be disregarded as dealing by applying the maxim *de minimis non curat lex*.[150]

However, courts eventually started voicing a different opinion on the application of the maxim *de minimis non curat lex* to cases relating to possession of dagga or dagga plants. In *Kgupane*,[151] Bekker J questioned the correctness of the judgment of Addleson J in *Van der Merwe*.[152] Judge Bekker did not consider it appropriate to apply the maxim in the context of violations of the Abuse of Dependence-Producing Substances Act.

An interesting contribution to the controversy came from the judgment of Harcourt J in *Shangase*.[153] The decision of Harcourt J included an acknowledgment of the disturbing consequence of the operation of the Abuse of Dependence-Producing Substances Act, namely an increase in the convictions for possession of 'minute' quantities of dagga.[154] Nonetheless, Harcourt J did not want to give in to the temptation of applying the maxim *de minimis non curat lex*.[155] Judge Harcourt would not consider the harm caused by possession of minute quantities as 'so trifling a nature that the maxim can be properly applied by a court once a prosecution has been brought before it'.[156] However, the judge recommended that the prosecuting authorities may exercise the discretion vested in them to avoid bringing charges in cases involving minute quantities of dagga.[157]

The application of the *de minimis* maxim was also an issue in *S v Danster*.[158] The court referred to the judgment of Marais J in *S v Nkosi*[159] as support for its reasoning. The court noted that Marais J was ready to accept that a person who hands a dagga cigarette that he

---

145 *Prince v President of The Law Society* supra at 285.

146 *Prince v President of The Law Society* supra at 285.

147 *R v Dane* 1957 (2) SA 472 (N) at 473; *S v Bester* 1971 (4) SA 28 (T); *S v Van der Merwe* 1974 (4) SA 310 (E); *S v Van Zyl* 1975 (2) SA 489 (N).

148 *S v Van der Merwe* supra.

149 *S v Van der Merwe* supra.

150 *S v Van Zyl* supra at 492. In this case, the accused had been charged as a dealer. The accused had watered some dagga seeds, which had been supplied by his friends who were dagga smokers, that were in a flower pot in his room. The court accepted the accused's testimony that he only wanted to see what the plants would look like after germination. After the accused had seen the grown plants, he allegedly lost interest in them. On the accused's return from a vacation, he found that the plants had grown in his absence. The court accepted that other people must have been looking after the plants in his absence. However, the accused did nothing to destroy the plants.

151 *S v Kgupane* supra.

152 *S v Van der Merwe* supra.

153 *S v Shangase and others* 1972 (2) SA 410 (N).

154 *S v Shangase* supra at 425. In *S v Gibson* supra at 481–482, the Appellate Division (AD) considered the consequences to be 'tragic hardships'.

155 *S v Shangase* supra at 425.

156 *S v Shangase* supra at 425.

157 *S v Shangase* supra at 425.

158 *S v Danster* [1976] 3 All SA 408 (SWA) at 412.

159 *S v Nkosi* supra.

was smoking to a willing recipient who wanted to 'take a puff', was guilty of dealing in dagga.[160] The accused would remain liable for dealing despite the fact that his offence was trifling in comparison to a person who transported large amounts of dagga 'or a dealer who supplied heroin to a young person'.[161] In *S v Danster*, the court considered Judge Marais's example as proof of the fact that the courts could not simply dismiss cases involving minute quantities of dagga as trifling.[162]

However, the flaw of the relevant dictum from *S v Nkosi*[163] has already been attended to by the Supreme Court of Appeal.[164] A person who hands a dagga cigarette that he was smoking to a willing recipient will only be liable for dealing if it can be proved beyond reasonable doubt that it was an activity related to the supply/furnishing of dagga rather than the purchase or acquisition of the drugs.[165] Consequently, the argument relying on the dictum from *S v Nkosi*[166] should also be dismissed.

The argument advanced in *S v Danster* was also based on the proposition that the legislature had intended to punish even the most trifling examples of alleged dealing because of the harm attendant to offering a puff on a dagga cigarette.[167] The court cited the examples of children or rehabilitated drug addicts being offered a puff as a cause of the scourge that the legislature was trying to end.[168] The courts have considered this conclusion as doubtful,[169] inconceivable[170] and untenable.[171] Besides, the maxim might not apply in the examples cited in *Danster* because the harm attendant in such cases might not be trifling according to public perception. If the harm was trivial, it would not serve the interests of justice to insist on judicial attention. Even Harcourt J considered it best for the prosecutors to avoid pressing charges in cases where the matter was trivial.[172]

Following the decision by the Western Cape High Court in *Prince v Minister of Justice and Constitutional Development; Rubin v NDPP; Acton v NDPP*[173] (hereafter *'Acton et al'*), the debate on the continued criminalisation and prosecution of the private use of dagga (so-called 'recreational' use) shifted away from the 2002 Constitutional Court decision in *Prince*, where religious freedom was the main issue, and the marginal application of the *de minimis* principle, as referenced in the cases mentioned above, to a broader debate about the decriminalisation of the use of dagga in private.

The current South African legislative framework on the use of illicit drugs is in line with the prohibitionary approach to dagga and the use of dagga. Individuals are thus *discouraged* from using drugs (including dagga) and individuals are furthermore not 'trusted to exercise

160 *S v Nkosi* supra at 759. In *S v Danster* supra at 412, the court considered it to be irrelevant that the recipient took only one or two puffs of the dagga cigarette. The court considered the delivery of the cigarette to be worthy of punishment for dealing in dagga.

161 *S v Nkosi* supra at 759.

162 *S v Danster* supra at 412.

163 *S v Nkosi* supra.

164 *S v Solomon* supra. See also *S v Morgan; S v Watson* supra; *S v Ntshingila* supra.

165 *S v Ntshingila* supra at 322.

166 *S v Nkosi* supra.

167 *S v Danster* supra at 412.

168 *S v Danster* supra at 412.

169 *S v Govender* supra.

170 *S v Majenge* supra; *S v Bester* supra; *S v Morgan; S v Watson* supra.

171 *S v Ntshingila* supra at 321. Among the reasons cited by the court was that a literal interpretation would incorrectly render every possessor as a dealer. Only those who gained possession by stealing it or coming on it abandoned would escape liability for being dealers.

172 *S v Shangase* supra at 425.

173 *Prince v Minister of Justice and Constitutional Development; Rubin v NDPP; Acton v NDPP* [2017] ZAWCHC 30, 31 March 2017, available at http://www.saflii.org/za/cases/ZAWCHC/2017/30.html.

self-control or responsibility in the matter of drugs ... the individual becomes "an object to be regulated, conditioned, threatened, and institutionalized if necessary"'.[174] This is precisely what the current Drugs and Drug Trafficking Act purports to achieve.

In *Acton et al* the applicants sought a declaration that the relevant legislative provisions against the use of dagga and the possession, purchase and cultivation of dagga for personal or communal consumption to be invalid. The relevant legislative provisions which the applicants sought to be declared invalid were:

- sections 4(b) and 5(b) of the Drugs and Drug Trafficking Act (read with part 3 of Schedule 2 to the Act insofar as it relates to 'simple possession, cultivation, transportation and distribution of cannabis [dagga] for personal communal consumption');
- section 22A(10) of the Medicines and Related Substances Control Act 101 of 1965 (read with Schedule 7 of the Medicines Act insofar as it relates to consumption of dagga); and
- legislative provisions against the possession and use of dagga by adults.

The decision in *Acton et al* was informed by expert criminological and medical evidence, including the expert evidence provided by the *amici curiae*. Although most of the expert evidence focused on criminological, legal and medical issues, as opposed to broader cultural, historical and anthropological issues, the court should be commended for striving for an approach that ultimately led to the broadest possible analysis of the issues.[175]

The court was also presented with relevant official statistics, indicating the scope of drug-related offences in South Africa, such as the fact that in 2014/2015 the South African police made 251 944 arrests which were pursuant to drug-related crime. Indeed, drug related crime 'was responsible for more recorded charges than any other crime type beside a very broad category of "all theft not mentioned elsewhere".'[176] One of the experts, Professor Mark Shaw, submitted in his report that the police 'could free up significant resources if cannabis [dagga] related enforcement was not made a priority, was decriminalised or legalised'.[177]

The main question before the court, however, was not one of criminal justice policy, it was a constitutional issue, namely whether the prohibition of the use of dagga constitutes an unjustifiable limitation of the right to privacy, as provided for in section 14 of the Constitution, 1996.

The court noted that the right to privacy 'becomes more powerful and deserving of greater protection the more intimate the personal sphere of the life of a human being which comes into legal play'.[178] The right to privacy should not be analysed in isolation. There is, according to the court, 'a connection between an individual's right to privacy and the right to dignity which is protected in terms of s 10 of the Constitution'.[179] There is also a link between the right to privacy and the right to freedom; between privacy and the moral autonomy of citizens 'which is a central requirement of governance in a democracy'.[180] The court stated:

> **If privacy, considered to be analysed as a continuum of rights which starts with an inviolable inner core moving from the private to the public realm where privacy is only remotely implicated by interference, it must follow that those who wish to**

174 Lötter S 'The decriminalization of cannabis: Hallucination or reality?' (1999) 12(2) *SACJ* 184 at 185.
175 *Acton et al* at paras 126–129.
176 *Acton et al* at para 58.
177 *Acton et al* at para 58.
178 *Acton et al* at para 22.
179 *Acton et al* at para 23.
180 *Acton et al* at para 24.

> **partake of a small quantity of cannabis in the intimacy of their home do exercise a right to autonomy which, without clear justification, does not merit interference from the outside community or the State.**[181]

The court reached the same conclusion with regards to the cultivation of a dagga plant in the garden of a private home, 'if the plant was to be used exclusively for personal consumption'.[182] The court conceded that it is difficult to define 'small' in this context, but legislation needed to define quantities in the context of the regulation or criminalisation of dagga would at any rate have to pass constitutional muster in terms of a justifiable limitation of the right to privacy.[183]

Proceeding to the limitation argument, the court noted that the state needed to show a substantial state interest which justified the limitation. Historical, cultural, criminological, medical and legal comparative evidence were considered to be relevant by the court.[184] Considering all the relevant evidence, the court in *Acton et al* noted that, even if one assumes that the respondents are correct that the objectives of prevention of abuse, of negative and detrimental neurological effects on driving ability, and upon the cardiovascular and respiratory systems, are met by the relevant legislation (including the Drugs and Drug Trafficking Act), the state would still need to show 'why a less restrictive means to achieve the purpose does not exist'.[185] The court concluded that the evidence cannot be taken to 'justify the use of criminal law for the personal consumption of cannabis'.[186] The court held that the present criminalisation framework with respect to dagga did not employ the 'least restrictive means to deal with a social and health problem for which there [were] now a number of less restrictive options supported by a significant body of expertise'.[187] The court also alluded to the benefits of freeing up state resources in the event of decriminalisation of the use of dagga for private use.[188] Decriminalisation of dagga is indeed an important policy consideration, with the potential to contribute to a more effective criminal justice and penitentiary system (contributing, for instance, to less overcrowding in South African prisons).

The court in *Acton et al* made it clear that its decision on the invalidity of the criminalisation of the use of dagga in the privacy of one's home did not extend to children, as defined in South African law. In practical terms that means that the prohibition in terms of the Drugs and Drug Trafficking Act should still apply to persons under the age of 18. Indeed, the court took note of the 'prevalence of drug usage amongst minors and school going children'[189] to support its conclusion with respect to the continued criminalisation of the use of dagga by minors.[190]

The decision in *Acton et al* requires legislative reform. To this end, the court in *Acton et al* articulated important legal and constitutional principles that will serve parliament well in its legislative task. The court acknowledged the importance of the separation of powers and noted that it was not for the court 'to prescribe alternatives to decriminalisation of the

181 *Acton et al* at para 25.
182 *Acton et al* at para 26.
183 *Acton et al* at para 26.
184 *Acton et al* at paras 32–90
185 *Acton et al* at para 104.
186 *Acton et al* at para 106.
187 *Acton et al* at para 106.
188 *Acton et al* at para 106.
189 *Acton et al* at para 107.
190 *Acton et al* at para 107.

use of [dagga] for personal use and consumption'.[191] Indeed, it 'is for the legislature and the executive to decide on a suitable option or alternatives which can be made after these have been the subject of a deliberative process which is inherent in the idea of Parliament'.[192]

There is a risk of some confusion during the transitionary period after the decision in *Acton et al.* It is therefore important to understand that the decision is narrow in scope; it does not decriminalise dagga *carte blanche.* There will, however, for the interim, be practical consequences regarding the use of dagga in certain contexts. The declaration of invalidity is suspended for a realistic period to ensure Parliament may correct the defect. The court considered 24 months to be an appropriate period. Furthermore, for the interim period, the court ordered that prosecutions that fall within the legal provision declared to be unconstitutional should be stayed. The court ordered as follows:

> **1. The following provisions are declared inconsistent with the Constitution of the Republic of South Africa Act 108 of 1996 and invalid, only to the extent that they prohibit the use of cannabis by an adult in a private dwelling where the possession, purchase or cultivation of cannabis is for personal consumption by an adult:**
>
> **1.1 sections 4(b) and 5(b) of the Drugs and Drug Trafficking Act 140 of 1992 (the Drugs Act) read with Part III of Schedule 2 to the Drugs Act; and**
>
> **1.2 section 22A(9)(a)(i) of the Medicines and Related Substances Control Act 101 of 1965 (the Medicines Act) and s 22A(10) thereof read with schedule 7 of GN R509 of 2003 published in terms of s 22A(2) of the Medicines Act.**
>
> **2. This declaration of invalidity is suspended for a period of 24 months from the date of this judgment in order to allow Parliament to correct the defects as set out in this judgment.**
>
> **3. It is declared that until Parliament has made the amendments contemplated in paragraph 1 or the period of suspension has expired, it will be deemed to be a defence to a charge under a provision as set out in paragraph 1 of this order that the use, possession, purchase or cultivation of cannabis in a private dwelling is for the personal consumption of the adult accused'.**[193]

At the time of writing the legislative amendments were yet to be adopted by Parliament. For the time being, and in practical terms, the result of the decision in *Acton et al* is the moratorium on the prosecution for the possession and use of dagga by an adult in a private dwelling and where the possession, purchase or cultivation of dagga is for personal consumption by an adult. The progressive decision by the court in *Acton et al* clearly does not absolve parliament of its policy-making role. Indeed, the relevant law enforcement agencies, and the public at large, deserve clarity and a detailed legislative framework to find the right balance between the constitutional imperatives as highlighted by the court in *Acton et al,* on the one hand, and the legitimate expectations of a society which may still be skeptical about the decriminalisation of a substance such as dagga, on the other.

---

191 *Acton et al* at para 112.

192 *Acton et al* at para 112.

193 *Acton et al at* para 132.

DISCUSSION

Drugs, crime and punishment

The (de)criminalisation of the cultivation of dagga for private use[194] is subject to debate. The criminal justice approach to drug use, including dagga, traditionally imposes harsh sentences that may be too severe in the context of the harm that is posed by the conduct.[195]

The decision by the Western Cape High Court in *Prince, Rubin and Acton* (2017) further points to a potentially more liberal approach to the use of dagga in South Africa. It is, however, not the courts but Parliament that will have to give voice and structure to the normative and policy choices of the people of South Africa. It is suggested that the High Court's jurisprudence is a sensible and realistic starting point for an informed debate.[196]

THIS CHAPTER IN ESSENCE

1. The use of drugs in the generic sense of the word and stimulants such as caffeine, alcohol and tobacco, are not criminalised per se.
2. The examples of substance abuse that are highlighted in this chapter illustrate the rationale for the criminalisation of possession, use and dealing in certain drugs as crimes against the community and against public welfare.
3. It is also evident from the discussion that the *use* of these illicit drugs is normally viewed as a lesser crime than *trading* or *dealing* in these substances.
4. There is an ongoing debate about the decriminalisation of certain substances, notably dagga. Case law points to a more liberal approach, but the matter will have to be resolved by Parliament.

194 *S v Mbatha* supra. See also Stevens GP 'Dealing in drugs revisited: *S v Mbatha* 2012 (2) SACR 551 (KZP): Comments' (2014) 27(1) *SACJ* 37–47.

195 Compare the strict criminal justice approach with that of 'penal minimalism' or the notion that criminal law should be treated as a 'weapon of last resort in the government's regulatory armoury'. See Simester AP, Du Bois-Pedain A and Neumann U (eds) *Liberal Criminal Theory: Essays for Andreas von Hirsch* (2014) 339.

196 See also Fellingham RK, Dhai A, Guidozzi Y and Gardner J 'The "war on drugs" has failed: Is decriminalisation of drug use a solution to the problem in South Africa?' (2012) 5(2) *SAJBL* 78–82.

Chapter 40

Road traffic offences

CHAPTER OBJECTIVES

The objectives of this chapter are to discuss some of the most important crimes under the National Road Traffic Act 93 of 1996, namely:
- driving under the influence of alcohol or drugs
- driving with excessive alcohol in the blood
- negligent driving
- reckless driving
- speeding.

40.1 General background

The important role of road traffic in modern South African society cannot be overstated. It is impossible to imagine daily life and the economy functioning without road traffic. The use of public roads creates all sorts of risks. Indeed, individual drivers who act without regard for their fellow users of public roads not only cause great nuisance and unnecessary costs, but also commit crimes against the community and against public welfare. The National Road Traffic Act 93 of 1996, which deals comprehensively with aspects of road traffic, also provides for the criminalisation of certain reckless, negligent and unlawful behaviour.[1] Thus, the National Road Traffic Act 'requires drivers, while driving, to be sober and neither reckless nor negligent. These responsibilities are enforced by criminal sanctions'.[2]

1 For commentary on the National Road Traffic Act, see Hoctor SV *Cooper's Motor Law: Criminal Liability, Administrative Adjudication and Medico-legal Aspects* 2 ed (2008) Regular revisions.

2 Burchell JM *Principles of Criminal Law* 5 ed (2016) 810.

40.2 The main crimes under the National Road Traffic Act 93 of 1996

For purposes of this chapter, the following crimes, which correspond with the main risk areas in terms of the behaviour of drivers, are briefly discussed:

- Driving under the influence of alcohol or drugs
- Driving with excessive alcohol in the blood
- Negligent driving
- Reckless driving
- Speeding

Before we discuss the specific crimes, it is necessary to define briefly the terms 'driving', 'vehicle' and 'public road':

- *Driving*: The term 'driving' under the National Road Traffic Act has the ordinary meaning of driving, plus an extended meaning. Hence, in line with the ordinary (dictionary) meaning of driving, to drive means 'to urge forward and direct the course of an animal drawing a vehicle or ... a vehicle itself'.[3] In terms of the extended understanding of driving, it was held that a person steering a vehicle being towed can also be regarded as the driver of the vehicle.[4]
- *Vehicle*: In terms of the National Road Traffic Act, a vehicle is:

  > **a device designed or adapted mainly to travel on wheels or crawler tracks and includes such a device which is connected with a draw-bar to a breakdown vehicle and is used as part of the towing equipment of a breakdown vehicle to support any axle or all the axles of a motor vehicle which is being salvaged other than such a device which moves solely on rails.**[5]

  Apart from motor vehicles, pedal cycles/bicycles,[6] trailers,[7] carts drawn by animals[8] and even carts drawn by humans[9] qualify as vehicles for purposes of the National Road Traffic Act.
- *Public road*: The National Road Traffic Act defines a public road as:

  > **any road, street or thoroughfare or any other place (whether a thoroughfare or not) which is commonly used by the public or any section thereof or to which the public or any section thereof has a right of access, and includes—**
  >
  > **(*a*) the verge of any such road, street or thoroughfare**
  > **(*b*) any bridge, ferry or drift traversed by any such road, street or thoroughfare; and**
  > **(*c*) any other work or object forming part of or connected with or belonging to such road, street or thoroughfare.**[10]

---

3 *S v Van Rooyen* 1968 (1) SA 641 (T) at 643A; Hoctor *Cooper's Motor Law* B1-4.
4 *S v Ekstraal* 1981 (4) SA 406 (C).
5 S 1.
6 *S v Gertse* 1972 (3) SA 59 (C); *S v Tsiloane* 1977 (3) SA 336 (O).
7 *Santam Versekeringsmaatskappy Bpk v Kemp* 1971 (3) SA 305 (A).
8 *R v Khaname* 1959 (3) SA 925 (T); *S v Gertse* supra.
9 *R v Browns* (1893–1894) 8 EDC 151.
10 S 1.

The National Road Traffic Act furthermore provides for a presumption[11] that a road is a public road in the absence of evidence to the contrary. The words 'used by the public' normally mean 'used for driving a vehicle' on the said road, street, thoroughfare or place. It must be a street, thoroughfare or place '*commonly used by the public for driving vehicles*'. Therefore, there must normally be a '*right of access to drive* a vehicle on, or over, the [relevant] road, street, thoroughfare or place'.[12]

Table 40.1 The most important crimes in terms of the National Road Traffic Act 93 of 1996

Driving under the influence	Driving with excessive alcohol in the blood	Negligent or reckless driving	Speeding
• Intoxicating liquor • Drugs/narcotic effect • Under the influence • Medical evidence • Evidence of any witness (non-essential)	• Technical crime • More than 0,049 g alcohol per 100 ml of blood • Professional drivers: not more than 0,02 g per 100 ml • Medico-legal aspects are important • Chemical analysis	• Negligence *or* • recklessness ◆ without care ◆ indifference to danger, and so on	• General: ◆ 60 km (urban) ◆ 100 km (outside urban) ◆ 120 km (freeway) • Special for particular road • Limits for particular vehicles
Driving Vehicle Public road			

40.2.1 Driving under the influence of alcohol or drugs

Section 65(1) of the National Road Traffic Act states that:

> **no person shall on a public road—**
> **(*a*) drive a vehicle; or**
> **(*b*) occupy the driver's seat of a motor vehicle the engine of which is running, while under the influence of intoxicating liquor or a drug having a narcotic effect.**[13]

The elements of driving under the influence of alcohol or drugs are:
- driving
- vehicle
- public road
- under the influence
- fault.

To drive under the influence means that the 'skill and judgment normally required in the manipulation of a motor car is obviously diminished or impaired as a direct result of the consumption of alcohol'.[14] The same obviously applies to driving affected by the use of drugs.

11 S 69.
12 Hoctor *Cooper's Motor Law* B1-15.
13 For a detailed discussion, see Le Roux A 'Medico-legal aspects regarding drunk driving' (2007) 20(2) *SACJ* 220–242; Hoctor *Cooper's Motor Law* B11-36A and further.
14 *R v Lloyd* 1929 EDL 270 at 274.

This crime is not about the concentration of alcohol in the driver's blood; it is about the effect of the alcohol (or drug) consumption on a person's driving.[15]

The *mens rea* required can be in the form of *intention or negligence*.[16]

40.2.2 Driving with excessive alcohol in the blood

Section 65(2) of the National Road Traffic Act states that:

> **no person shall on a public road—**
>
> **(*a*) drive a vehicle; or**
>
> **(*b*) occupy the driver's seat of a motor vehicle the engine of which is running, while the concentration of alcohol in any specimen of blood taken from any part of his or her body is not less than 0,05 gram per 100 millilitres, or in the case of a professional driver referred to in section 32, not less than 0,02 gram per 100 millilitres.**

The elements of driving with excessive alcohol in the blood are:

- driving
- vehicle
- public road
- blood-alcohol level
- fault.

The state needs to prove the concentration of alcohol in the blood of the accused. This is done by first taking a specimen of blood and then tests need to show that the levels described in section 65(2) were present when the driver was driving the vehicle on a public road. *The offence is committed if the mass of alcohol exceeds 0,049 g per 100 ml of blood.*[17] A registered medical practitioner, including a registered nurse, may take a blood sample for the purpose of determining the level of alcohol. The blood analysis is done by a state laboratory 'or other recognised facility'.[18] Section 65(9) of the National Road Traffic Act requires the alleged offender to submit to the necessary medical tests.[19]

The *mens rea* required can be in the form of *intention or negligence*.[20]

40.2.3 Negligent or reckless driving

According to section 63(1) of the National Road Traffic Act, 'no person shall drive a vehicle on a public road recklessly or negligently'.

There are two separate offences in this section: negligent driving and reckless driving. The elements of negligent driving are:

- negligent
- driving
- vehicle
- public road
- fault.

---

15 Burchell *Principles of Criminal Law* 812.

16 *S v Els* 1972 (4) SA 696 (T); *S v Fouché* 1974 (1) SA 96 (A); *S v Hartyani* 1980 (3) SA 613 (T); Burchell *Principles of Criminal Law* 813.

17 Burchell *Principles of Criminal Law* 813. For the medico-legal aspects, see Le Roux 'Medico-legal aspects regarding drunk driving' supra.

18 S 37(2)(*a*) of the Criminal Procedure Act 51 of 1977; Le Roux 'Medico-legal aspects regarding drunk driving' supra 236.

19 See *S v Binta* 1993 (2) SACR 553 (C) on whether a refusal to supply a blood sample constitutes obstruction of justice. See also Le Roux 'Medico-legal aspects regarding drunk driving' supra 236–238.

20 Burchell *Principles of Criminal Law* 812.

The elements of reckless driving are:
- reckless
- driving
- vehicle
- public road.

Negligent driving concerns an objective test, namely:

> **whether a reasonable person, in the same circumstances, would have foreseen that a particular method of driving constituted a risk of harm to other persons using the road and would have guarded against that risk by desisting from driving in that manner or taking other appropriate avoiding action.**[21]

Reckless driving means to drive 'carelessly or thoughtlessly, rashly or inconsiderately, thereby creating a risk of harm to others'.[22] In legal terms, this means that recklessness can best be described as a serious form of negligence, that is, gross negligence. The test is still objective – a person 'who foresees a risk of harm but *unreasonably* concludes that the harm will not materialise can be found to have been grossly negligent'.[23] If the accused acted with intent (intentional reckless driving), it will also be an offence for purposes of section 63(1) of the Act.

40.2.4 Speeding

According to section 59(4) of the National Road Traffic Act, any person who drives a vehicle on a public road at a speed in excess of the speed limit commits an offence.

The elements of speeding are:
- unlawful
- driving
- vehicle
- public road
- speed limit.

This crime, arguably the most common of the crimes discussed here, concerns three types of speed limits:
1. A general speed limit[24]
2. A special speed limit determined for any particular road
3. A speed limit for particular vehicles[25]

There seems to be some academic and judicial agreement that this crime is one of strict liability. In other words, no fault is required.[26] From a dogmatic point of view, this seems to be illogical and perhaps unjust. We therefore agree with Burchell that fault in the form of *culpa* should be an element of the crime of speeding in terms of the National Road Traffic Act.[27]

---

21 Burchell *Principles of Criminal Law* 814. See also the exposition of the qualities of a reasonable person in *S v Burger* 1975 (4) SA 877 (A) at 879D–E.

22 Burchell *Principles of Criminal Law* 817.

23 Burchell *Principles of Criminal Law* 817; *S v Van Zyl* 1969 (1) SA 553 (A) at 557C–D.

24 At present: 60 km/h for urban areas, 100 km/h for public roads other than a freeway outside an urban area, and 120 km/h for freeways.

25 Burchell *Principles of Criminal Law* 818–820.

26 Burchell *Principles of Criminal Law* 820.

27 Burchell *Principles of Criminal Law* 820.

40.3 Some general comments

The two crimes, driving under the influence of alcohol and driving a motor vehicle while the concentration of alcohol in the blood is over the prescribed limit, are distinguished in terms of definition and in terms of punishment. The former is generally regarded as the more serious offence while the latter is regarded as being a technical offence. This distinction is also explained, in part at least, by the fact that the crime of driving under the influence requires proof of actual impairment of the accused's driving ability.[28]

THIS CHAPTER IN ESSENCE

1. The four categories of crimes in terms of the National Road Traffic Act discussed in this chapter concern particular risk areas, thus forming the underlying rationales for the criminalisation of the relevant conduct as crimes against the community and against public welfare.
2. Some of these offences - negligent or reckless driving, and driving under the influence of drugs or alcohol - primarily concern the application of general principles of criminal liability. The crime of driving a motor vehicle while the concentration of alcohol in the accused's blood is over the prescribed limit constitutes a technical offence. The various crimes of speeding constitute crimes of strict liability.

28 *S v Bagadi* 2008 (2) SACR 400 (T). For a discussion of the case, see Hoctor S 'Specific Crimes: Case review' (2009) 22(1) *SACJ* 88–94.

Chapter 41

Extortion

CHAPTER OBJECTIVES

The objectives of this chapter are to:

- describe briefly the historical, common law and statutory foundations of the crime of extortion
- identify and discuss the elements of the crime of extortion.

41.1 A brief history

The crime of extortion is committed when a person obtains an advantage from another person by subjecting the latter to pressure. This is called blackmail in common parlance. The crime of extortion has its origins in Roman and Roman-Dutch law (*concussio* or *knevelry*). Contrary to the suggestion of some old authorities, it is not necessary for the offender to represent that he is a public official.[1]

41.2 Definition

The offence of **extortion** is committed where the accused unlawfully and intentionally obtains some advantage, whether of a patrimonial nature or not, from the complainant by subjecting him to pressure that induces him to concede the advantage to the accused.[2]

1 Skeen A st Q and Hoctor S 'Criminal law' in Joubert WA and Faris JA (eds) *Law of South Africa Encyclopaedia* (*LAWSA*) 2 ed Vol 6 (replacement volume) (2007) at para 344; *R v G* 1938 AD 246; Snyman CR *Criminal Law* 6 ed (2014) 417–419; Burchell JM *Principles of Criminal Law* 5 ed (2016) 736–741.

2 *LAWSA* at para 344; s 1 of the General Law Amendment Act 139 of 1992; Snyman *Criminal Law* 418; Burchell *Principles of Criminal Law* 736.

41.3 The elements of extortion

The elements of extortion are:

- obtaining a benefit
- application of pressure
- unlawfulness
- intent.

41.3.1 Obtaining a benefit

The benefit or advantage obtained by the accused may be either patrimonial, for example money, or non-patrimonial, for example sexual favours.[3] The crime is only complete when the benefit is obtained by the accused. Prior to this event, only attempted extortion is possible.[4]

41.3.2 Application of pressure

The complainant must submit to the pressure exerted by the accused. The pressure may comprise intimidation in the form of threats to the complainant's physical integrity, or the threat may be directed towards a third party who may, for example, be a close relative of the complainant to put him under pressure.[5] There must be a causal connection between the pressure applied and the acquisition of the benefit. If the benefit is handed over by the complainant to the accused to trap the accused, then the offence of attempted extortion has been committed.[6]

41.3.3 Unlawfulness

Although the pressure applied must be done unlawfully, it is possible that the threat may be something that may be lawfully done. The *context* of the threat, coupled with the advantage sought, is critical. It is lawful for employees to embark on a strike to secure improved working conditions in terms of the law. Strike action will not amount to extortion. While it is lawful for a police officer to advise an arrested person that he will be prosecuted, such a reference becomes unlawful if the police officer couples it with an implied condition that the prosecution will proceed unless the person under arrest pays the officer a sum of money.[7]

41.3.4 Intent

The accused must intend his conduct to operate as a threat in the mind of the complainant. The accused must also know that the threat is illegal in the sense that he must be aware that he is disentitled to the extorted benefit.[8]

THIS CHAPTER IN ESSENCE

The crime of extortion, which covers patrimonial (monetary) as well as non-patrimonial advantages obtained through unlawful pressure, is a crime against the community and against public welfare in the sense that it distorts the social, official and commercial relationships between free people.

3 After some uncertainty in our case law on whether benefit included a non-patrimonial advantage, the Appellate Division in *Ex parte Minister van Justisie: In re S v J; S v Von Molendorff and another* 1989 (4) SA 1028 (A) concluded that it did not. However, the legislature removed any doubt by adopting s 1 of the General Law Amendment Act 139 of 1992, which makes provision for non-patrimonial advantage to be sufficient for a conviction in respect of extortion.

4 *S v Mtirara* 1962 (2) SA 266 (E).

5 *R v Lepheana* 1956 (1) SA 337 (A).

6 *R v Lutge* 1947 (2) SA 490 (N).

7 *S v Gokool* 1965 (3) SA 461 (N); Snyman *Criminal Law* 419; Burchell *Principles of Criminal Law* 738-740.

8 *S v Mtirara* supra; Snyman *Criminal Law* 419; Burchell *Principles of Criminal Law* 741.

Chapter 42

Crimes against the state

CHAPTER OBJECTIVES

The objectives of this chapter are to:

- discuss the elements of the common law crime of high treason
- discuss the elements of the common law crime of sedition.

42.1 High treason

42.1.1 A brief history

The crime against the state par excellence, today known as high treason, originated from the early Roman law crime of *perduellio*. In later Roman law, it became known as *crimen laesae maiestatis*. The essence of this somewhat vague crime was the impairment of the supreme power of the state or the emperor as embodiment of the state. These crimes were also known in Roman-Dutch law.[1] During the colonial period in South Africa, it was possible to argue that the South African state did not possess the necessary *maiestas* in the Roman and Roman-Dutch sense of the word because South Africa recognised a higher authority in its territory, namely the United Kingdom. In 1961, South Africa became an independent and sovereign republic and the element of *maiestas* was no longer required.[2] Today, South Africa is one sovereign, democratic state.[3]

1 Snyman CR *Criminal Law* 6 ed (2014) 301; Burchell JM *Principles of Criminal Law* 5 ed (2016) 838–849.
2 Snyman *Criminal Law* 301; Burchell *Principles of Criminal Law* 842.
3 S 1 of the Constitution of the Republic of South Africa, 1996.

42.1.2 Definition

The High Court in the most recent and high-profile treason case in the democratic era, the so-called *Boeremag Treason* trial,[4] constitutionalised the common law definition, thus preserving the crime under South African law, but with elements that are compatible with a supreme democratic Constitution, which is the legal and political foundation of the state. The definition, per Jordaan J in the *Boeremag Treason* trial, now reads:

> **The acts of treason should have been directed directly or indirectly at the Constitution or constitutional structures. It should have been alleged and proven by the prosecuting authority. The unlawfulness will stem from the fact that the intention was to replace the Constitution as such, in contravention of the provisions of the Constitution itself. The accused persons are however charged with an offence that obtained in the old dispensation in accordance with which parliament was sovereign, with a government that exercised that sovereignty.**[5]

Regarding the conduct that constitute acts of treason, the court in the *Boeremag* case noted the following elements:

> **High treason comprises unlawful conduct performed inside or outside the borders of the Republic by someone who owes allegiance to the Republic, with intent to—**
> **(*a*) overthrow the government of the Republic;**
> **(*b*) forcibly coerce the government to take any action or refrain from taking action;**
> **(*c*) violate, endanger or put at risk the continued existence, independence or safety of the Republic; or**
> **(*d*) alter the constitutional structure of the Republic.**[6]

42.1.3 The elements of high treason

42.1.3.1 Allegiance to the Republic

High treason can be committed only by persons owing allegiance to the Republic. This is still the case post-*Boeremag Treason* trial. Snyman points out that the category of persons owing allegiance is wider than the category of people who are citizens. Thus, people who owe allegiance include:

- citizens of the Republic
- persons who have sworn an oath of allegiance to South Africa[7]
- persons who are domiciled in South Africa
- persons who are resident in South Africa.[8]

---

4 *Visagie v S* (CC 91/03) [2012] ZAGPPHC (3 February 2012) North Gauteng High Court. The sheer volume of the decision by the High Court made it impractical for publication in the regular law reports. Burchell *Principles of Criminal Law* at 838, n 2, refers to the electronic version of the judgment, available on CD. The author analysed the judgment and used translations from the original Afrikaans.

5 Burchell *Principles of Criminal Law* 838, and the references to the *Boeremag Treason* judgment, n 3.

6 Burchell Principles of Criminal Law 838.

7 *Ex parte Schwietering* 1948 (3) SA 378 (O).

8 *S v Pastoors* [1986] 4 All SA 322 (W).

Burchell criticises the retention of *allegiance* as a foundational concept in treason law. The author states:

> **South African treason law in its present form is anachronistic and inappropriate for a modern popular democracy. This is primarily due to its reliance upon a concept of allegiance that is outdated and not compliant with modern conceptions of the relationship between the citizen and the state.[9]**

Foreign diplomats who are stationed in South Africa and are thus residing here obviously do not owe allegiance to South Africa.

42.1.3.2 Acts constituting high treason

It is not possible to compile a complete list of possible acts that would constitute high treason. Since allegiance to the Republic is the key element, any act, 'however innocent it may seem to be when viewed objectively, may constitute high treason if it is committed with the necessary hostile intent'.[10] Such acts can also overlap with other crimes such as public violence, sedition or terrorism. The determining factor, however, is the presence of *hostile intent*, which is more than just the subjective element of *mens rea*, but indeed part of the definitional elements of the crime.[11] Thus, an act of violence is not required; non-violent acts such as propaganda and the distribution of literature can also constitute acts of treason. These observations should also be read with what the High Court in the *Boeremag Treason* trial stated about conduct constituting treason (see section 42.1.2).

42.1.3.3 Intent

The form of *mens rea* required is generally known as hostile intent or *animus hostilis*. This means that the accused must have the intention to overthrow the state, or structures of the state,[12] or, in the post-*Boeremag Treason* trial understanding of high treason, the replacement of the Constitution or constitutional structures, in line with the definition as stated under section 42.1.2.

42.1.3.4 Acts of treason in times of peace and war

The crime of high treason can be committed in times of peace and in times of war. In case of the latter, the acts are associated with external threats to the Republic, but linked to the state of war. During peacetime, the existence of the state can also be threatened, for instance by internal uprisings or a plot to conspire with external enemies not yet at war with the Republic to attack the Republic.[13]

42.1.3.5 Unlawfulness

The acts constituting treason must be unlawful. Thus, in a constitutional democracy such as South Africa, it is not treason to belong to the political opposition of the government or to work for the replacement of the government of the day by *constitutional means*.

---

9 Burchell Principles of Criminal Law 839.

10 Snyman *Criminal Law* 302–304. See also *S v Hogan* 1983 (2) SA 46 (W); *S v Banda and others* 1989 (4) SA 519 (BG).

11 Snyman *Criminal Law* 304.

12 Burchell *Principles of Criminal Law* 847–848; Snyman *Criminal Law* 302–305; *S v Zwane and others (3)* 1989 (3) SA 253 (W) at 258.

13 For a discussion, see Snyman *Criminal Law* 302–304.

DISCUSSION **Should high treason still be a crime?**

Since the advent of the democratic constitutional dispensation in South Africa, there has been only one trial that concerned the crime of treason. The so-called '*Boeremag*' case,[14] which has the distinction of being the longest running criminal case in South African history, concerned a plan and failed attempt by a number of individuals who belonged to the self-styled extremist group. They planned to overthrow the African National Congress government and to reinstate a new Boer-administered republic. The main charge was high treason. One of the accused pleaded guilty; the others were convicted after a protracted trial. The trial included an unsuccessful application by one of the accused that he was entitled to prisoner-of-war status under the Geneva Conventions of 1949 and under Additional Protocol I of 1977.[15]

The first post-apartheid treason trial left the common law crime of treason intact. The constitutionalised definition and elements of conduct were discussed above under sections 42.1.2 and 42.1.3. This does not mean the end of the debate about the continued criminalisation of treason in a constitutional democracy such as South Africa.[16]

Apart from the fact that at least some aspects of the crime of treason may be outdated, a further point of criticism is the relative vagueness of the crime. Snyman argues that this vagueness may violate the legality principle provided for in section 35 of the Constitution.[17]

42.2 Sedition

42.2.1 A brief history

In Roman law and Roman-Dutch law, **sedition** (public disturbance or '*oproer*') was regarded as a form of *crimen laesae maiestatis*. However, the old authorities were not always clear on the distinction between treason, public violence and what we would today call sedition.

In South African law, sedition is recognised as a separate crime against the state. It differs from high treason in the following ways:

- For sedition, an intention to resist or challenge the authority of the state is required (thus not the *animus hostilis* of high treason).
- Sedition can be committed only by a number of persons acting together (unlike treason, which can be committed by one person acting alone).
- For sedition, no allegiance to the Republic is required.[18]

In Chapter 37, the crime of public violence was discussed as a crime against the community and against public welfare. Sedition differs from public violence because it is aimed at the

14 For a useful timeline of the case, see http://www.sahistory.org.za/topic/boeremag-treason-trial-timeline.

15 *Pretorius v Die Staat en andere* 2010 JDR 1275 (GNP).

16 In 1992, shortly before the dawn of the new democratic constitutional dispensation, Prof JMT Labuschagne argued for the abolishment of the crime of treason; see Labuschagne JMT 'Menslike Outonomie en Staatlike Majestas: Opmerkinge oor die dekriminalisasie van hoogverraad' (1992) 5(2) *SACJ* 117. Many of the author's arguments remain valid and worthy of consideration in the democratic era.

17 Snyman *Criminal Law* 306–308.

18 See the discussion in Snyman *Criminal Law* 308–311; Burchell *Principles of Criminal Law* 850–853.

authority of the state, while public violence (as was pointed out in Chapter 37) primarily affects public peace and tranquillity.

42.2.2 Elements of sedition

Although there is case law to suggest that even two people acting together can be guilty of sedition,[19] it is perhaps more in line with the nature of sedition to require that *a number of people (more than two)* must act in concert to challenge the authority of the state.

The gathering of this group of people who are acting together 'must be accompanied by *violence or threats of violence*'.[20]

The group of people must *challenge the authority of the state*. This can take many forms, for example where a group of vigilantes sets up a so-called people's court, thus taking the law into their own hands and unlawfully punishing people for alleged crimes.[21]

The gathering, and the participation in the gathering, must be *unlawful*. The participants must have the *intent* to challenge the authority of the state.[22]

THIS CHAPTER IN ESSENCE

1. The common law crimes of high treason and sedition constitute crimes against the state.
2. High treason can be viewed as the more serious crime because it aims to overthrow unlawfully the state, including the government.
3. Sedition is not aimed at overthrowing the state, but it is aimed at the authority of the state.
4. The content and scope of these common law crimes do not always sit comfortably in an open and democratic state such as South Africa. The principle of 'allegiance to the state' is probably outdated and not compatible with the ethos of freedom of assembly and of political expression. The crimes of high treason and sedition should be narrowly construed in order to make them compatible with democratic constitutional norms.

19 *S v Twala and others* 1979 (3) SA 864 (T) at 869F.

20 Snyman *Criminal Law* 310. (Emphasis added). The author criticises a number of decisions that took the view that violence is not an element of sedition. The view of Snyman is supported, especially considering the constitutional values of freedom of assembly and freedom of speech on which the South African democratic order rests.

21 *S v Zwane* supra; Snyman *Criminal Law* 311.

22 Snyman *Criminal Law* 311; *R v Viljoen and others* 1923 AD 90 at 97; *S v Twala* supra at 869.

Chapter 43

Crimes against the administration of justice

CHAPTER OBJECTIVES

The objectives of this chapter are to:
- discuss briefly the rationale for the criminalisation of crimes against the administration of justice
- discuss the crime of defeating or obstructing the course of justice
- discuss the crime of contempt of court (*in facie curiae* and *ex facie curiae*)
- discuss the crime of common law perjury
- discuss the crime of making conflicting statements under different oaths (contravention of section 319(3) of the Criminal Procedure Act 56 of 1955)
- discuss the crime of making false statements in an affidavit (contravention of section 9 of the Justices of the Peace and Commissioners of Oaths Act 16 of 1963)
- discuss crimes relating to obstructing police in the performance of their duties.

43.1 General background

The need to criminalise conduct that undermines or interferes with the administration of justice should be obvious. If people can undermine or disrupt the proper functioning of the justice system with impunity, the whole system will collapse. The criminalisation of obstructing justice is regarded as one of the core strategies in terms of a proper domestic justice system. Together with the criminalisation of corruption, organised crime and money laundering, it is also one of the four key phenomena that need to be criminalised to combat effectively transnational organised crime.[1] To put it differently, crime thrives without a functioning justice system.

43.2 Defeating or obstructing the course of justice

The crime of **defeating or obstructing the course of justice** consists of *unlawfully* and *intentionally* engaging in conduct that *defeats or obstructs the course or administration of justice*.[2] The court in *S v Burger*[3] referred to the difference between defeating and obstructing the course of justice. To defeat the course of justice, the accused must in fact have defeated the course of justice, for instance where an innocent person has been convicted as the result of the actions of the accused.[4] Obstructing is something less and is conduct that could lead to the result of defeating the course of justice. It is important to note that these are not two distinct crimes: *it is a single crime of defeating or obstructing the course of justice*.[5]

The *course or administration of justice* means the process 'which is destined to eventuate in a court case between parties or between the state and its subjects'.[6] A court case in this context means civil or criminal proceedings, and not quasi-judicial or administrative proceedings.[7]

The accused must have the *intent* to interfere with judicial proceedings. Intent in the form of *dolus eventualis* will be enough. This occurs when the accused foresees the possibility that his conduct may adversely affect the proper administration of justice but continues with it regardless. The accused's *conduct* can take many forms, for example influencing or trying to influence a witness, fabricating evidence and hampering the investigation of a crime.[8] Depending on the particular facts and circumstances, such actions can overlap with crimes such as forgery, fraud, extortion and corruption.

1 Kemp GP 'The United Nations Convention Against Transnational Organized Crime: A milestone in international criminal law' (2001) 14(2) *SACJ* 152.
2 *S v Burger* 1975 2 SA 601 (C) at 611–612; Snyman CR *Criminal Law* 6 ed (2014) 327; Burchell JM *Principles of Criminal Law* 5 ed (2016) 858.
3 *S v Burger* supra at 612A.
4 Snyman *Criminal Law* 328. For a somewhat different approach to defeating the course of justice, see *S v DD* 2015 (1) SACR 165 (NCK). We submit that the court in this instance should have made a factual finding of obstruction of justice rather than one of defeating the ends of justice. In this case, the ends of justice were not in fact defeated since the real criminal was ultimately convicted.
5 Snyman *Criminal Law* 328; *S v Mdakani* 1964 (3) SA 311 (T) at 312H.
6 *S v Bazzard* 1992 (1) SACR 302 (NC) at 306E (translated from the Afrikaans); Snyman *Criminal Law* 330.
7 *R v Nhlapo* 1958 (3) SA 142 (T); Snyman *Criminal Law* 331.
8 See Snyman *Criminal Law* 328–330 for more examples.

DISCUSSION

Warning other motorists about a speed trap: Does this constitute obstruction of justice?

There are two seemingly conflicting judgments on this point. In *S v Naidoo*,[9] the court held that warning other motorists about the presence of a speed trap is interfering with the due administration of justice. However, in *S v Perera*,[10] the court held that the accused can only be guilty of obstructing or defeating the course of justice if he had reason to believe that the approaching vehicle exceeded the speed limit. If the accused driver is simply warning people in general about the presence of a speed trap, he is in effect warning other drivers to obey the law, which can hardly be a crime. This seems to be a fine line, but the common sense approach of the court in *Perera* is probably closer to the mark.

43.3 Contempt of court

In South African law, two basic forms of contempt of court are criminalised:

1. Contempt of court *in facie curiae*, that is, contempt in the court, or literally in the face of the court
2. Contempt of court *ex facie curiae*, or conduct outside the courtroom

The underlying rationale for the crime of contempt of court is to protect the dignity and institution of courts as well as the administration of justice.[11] If the dignity and stature of courts are not generally respected, the justice system will not be able to function and in the long run it will collapse. Another contextual consideration is that in terms of South Africa's constitutional order, the independence of courts is an important value. Courts should therefore not be influenced, or worse, intimidated into reaching certain decisions. The crime of contempt of court thus protects the dignity and effective and independent functioning of the courts as important organs of the justice system.

43.3.1 Contempt of court *in facie curiae*

Contempt of court *in facie curiae* is committed 'when a person who is inside the court insults the presiding judicial officer (judge or magistrate) or otherwise misbehaves in a manner calculated to violate the dignity of the court or judicial officer while the court is engaged in its proceedings'.[12] The accused must have the necessary intention to insult or to misbehave.[13]

***Lewis v S*[14]**

In this case, the appellant's cellphone rang in court and he answered it on his way out of court. He was charged with contempt of court. On conviction, he was sentenced to one month's imprisonment. The Supreme Court of Appeal (SCA), however, held that the accused did not have the intent to disrupt court proceedings.

9 *S v Naidoo* 1977 (2) SA 123 (N).
10 *S v Perera* 1978 (3) SA 523 (T).
11 *S v Thenga* 2012 (2) SACR 628 (NCK).
12 Snyman *Criminal Law* 317–318; Burchell *Principles of Criminal Law* 867.
13 *In re Clark* 1958 (3) SA 394 (A) at 400.
14 *Lewis v S* [2007] 3 All SA 477 (SCA).

The power of the court (per magistrate or judge) to act summarily against the accused is somewhat controversial. The controversy stems from the fact that the presiding judicial officer can act against the accused without having to wait for the accused to be investigated and then prosecuted for this crime by the prosecutor. In other words, the magistrate or judge is investigator, prosecutor and judge for purposes of this crime.

The High Court has the inherent common law power[15] to deal with matters of contempt of court *in facie curiae*, but magistrates' courts, as creatures of statute, derive their powers to deal with contempt of court *in facie curiae* from legislation.[16]

Since the presiding officer in matters of contempt of court *in facie curiae* is both prosecutor and judge, care should be taken to strike a balance between the need to protect the dignity of the court on the one hand and the rights of the accused on the other.

S v Mitchell[17]

In this case, the accused swore at the prosecutor and referred to the prosecutor in a derogatory manner. This occurred while the accused was in the well of the court having his fingerprints taken. The magistrate proceeded to warn the accused to stop and to apologise. The accused refused. In fact, the accused dared the magistrate to punish him. The magistrate informed the accused about the provisions of section 108 of the Magistrates' Courts Act. Again, the accused was adamant and dared the magistrate to punish him. The magistrate then proceeded to convict the accused of contempt of court and sentenced him to undergo six months' imprisonment. On appeal, the conviction was confirmed, but the sentence was reduced. The court, per Schoeman J, emphasised the fact that presiding officers, in this instance a magistrate, must always act to protect the rights of the accused.[18]

It is important to note that since the presiding officer is at once prosecutor and judge in cases of contempt of court *in facie curiae*, the accused must have the opportunity to explain to the presiding officer why he should not be convicted of contempt.[19] The practice and crime of contempt of court *in facie curiae* is compatible with the Constitution of the Republic of South Africa, 1996[20] despite the potential for the violation of an accused person's rights as illustrated by the judgment in *S v Mitchell* above.

43.3.2 Contempt of court *ex facie curiae*

The forms of **contempt of court *ex facie curiae*** are normally divided into two groups:

1. Conduct that refers to pending cases
2. Conduct that does not refer to pending cases[21]

Both forms of contempt can only be committed *intentionally*. However, where the accused is a newspaper editor who is charged with contempt of court *ex facie curiae* for the publication of commentary or a report concerning a pending case, in other words, a violation of the *sub judice* rule, *negligence* will be enough for a conviction.[22]

15 *In re Clark* supra.
16 S 108 of the Magistrates' Courts Act 32 of 1944.
17 *S v Mitchell* 2011 (2) SACR 182 (ECP).
18 *S v Mitchell* supra at 16.
19 *S v Nel* 1991 (1) SA 730 (A).
20 *S v Lavhengwa* 1996 (2) SACR 453 (W).
21 Snyman *Criminal Law* 320–322; Burchell *Principles of Criminal Law* 868–873.
22 *S v Harber and another* 1988 (3) SA 396 (A) at 418D–E.

43.3.2.1 Contempt of court *ex facie curiae* (pending cases)

Contempt of court *ex facie curiae* (pending cases) is often described as a violation of the so-called *sub judice* rule. This means that no one may publish anything about a pending case or comment on a case where the publication or commentary is potentially prejudicial to the outcome of the case.[23] A case is pending from the moment of its commencement by, for instance, summons or arrest, until it has been finally disposed of in the judicial process. The judicial process includes the judgment of the final possible appeal.[24] Of course, newspapers report about pending cases all the time, but the tone and aim of the reporting must be factual rather than in the form of commentary, which could potentially be regarded as prejudicial to the outcome of the case. The rationale here is clearly to protect the integrity of the legal process. If information regarding a case is published before it commences, it will not constitute contempt of court, but it may still be the crime of defeating or obstructing the course of justice.[25]

At first glance, the crime of contempt of court *ex facie curiae* (pending cases) and the strict application of the *sub judice* rule seem to conflict with section 16(1) of the Constitution, which protects the right to freedom of expression and the freedom of the media, as well as the right to receive or impart information. Rights are, of course, not absolute, and we agree with Snyman's submission that the existence of the crime of contempt of court *ex facie curiae* (pending cases) does serve an important purpose, namely to protect the dignity and integrity of legal processes.[26] Indeed, the fair trial rights of the accused are better protected by a court process that stands above the often emotional and unbalanced reporting and commentary in the media. This is not to say that the media does not have an important role to play. It should and must report and inform – this is the constitutional imperative in an open and democratic society. However, this right must be balanced against the other concerns mentioned above, notably the rights of the accused.

DISCUSSION

Courts and the media in the information age

In considering the extent to which the media should be allowed to cover and report on ongoing court cases, a good starting point is the observations by the SCA in *Midi Television (Pty) Limited v Director of Public Prosecutions (Western Cape)* with regard to the different rights and interests at stake:

> Where constitutional rights themselves have the potential to be mutually limiting – in that the full enjoyment of one necessarily curtails the full enjoyment of another and vice versa – a court must necessarily reconcile them. They cannot be reconciled by purporting to weigh the value of one right against the value of the other and then preferring the right that is considered to be more valued, and jettisoning the other, because all protected rights have equal value. They are rather to be reconciled by recognising a limitation upon the exercise of one right to the extent that it is necessary to do so in order to accommodate the exercise of the other (or in some cases, by recognising an appropriate limitation upon the

23 *S v Van Niekerk* 1972 (3) SA 711 (A); *S v Harber* supra.

24 Snyman *Criminal Law* 320–322.

25 See section 43.2 above. See also *Afrikaanse Pers-Publikasie (Edms) Bpk en 'n ander v Mbeki* 1964 (4) SA 618 (A) at 627.

26 See Snyman *Criminal Law* 321.

> **exercise of both rights) according to what is required by the particular circumstances and within the constraints that are imposed by s 36.[27]**

The SCA ultimately held that a *narrower* test to determine prejudice to the courts is compatible with the Constitution. An approach to prejudice that is too wide, that is, where it is immaterial whether potentially prejudicial statements attracted the attention of the court and whether the court was in fact influenced by the statement, unjustifiably limits the constitutional right to freedom of speech. In terms of the narrower, constitutionally compatible approach to contempt of court *ex facie curiae*, 'commentary will amount to contempt only if there is a demonstrable relationship between the publication of the words and the prejudice for the administration of justice'.[28]

Apart from the constitutional right to freedom of speech, it is also apparent that the rapidly changing media environment – including broadcasting and social media – further qualifies the old approach to the *sub judice* principle and the rules pertaining to contempt of court *ex facie curiae*. A case in point is the much publicised case of Oscar Pistorius, which received unprecedented national and international media attention. In *Multichoice (Pty) Limited and others v National Prosecuting Authority and another, In re S v Pistorius; Media 24 Limited and others v Director of Public Prosecutions North Gauteng and others*,[29] the High Court in Pretoria had to decide on an application by the electronic, broadcast and print media of South Africa to broadcast the entire criminal trial in the matter of *S v Pistorius*.[30] The court held that not only is it in line with the constitutional right to freedom of speech to allow the broadcasting of the entire criminal trial of Pistorius but it is also compatible with sections 34 and 35(3)(*c*) of the Constitution which require that legal proceedings, including criminal proceedings, be accountable, transparent and open to the public.[31]

43.3.2.2 Interference with witnesses or with the presiding officer

It is a crime to influence improperly, or attempt to influence, a judge, a magistrate, an assessor, a party to a case, a witness, a complainant, an accused, an interpreter or a legal representative in a case.[32] This form of contempt of court *ex facie curiae* may overlap with the crime of corruption, for example corruption relating to judicial officers,[33] members of the prosecuting authority[34] or witnesses and evidential material.[35]

43.3.2.3 Failure to appear in court (common law and statutory forms)

If a person who was summoned to appear in court, fails to do so intentionally and for no good reason, such an individual can be prosecuted for the crime of contempt of court

27 *Midi Television (Pty) Ltd t/a E-TV v Director of Public Prosecutions (Western Cape)* 2007 (5) SA 540 SCA at 9.

28 Snyman *Criminal Law* 321. The author also supports this narrower test.

29 *Multichoice (Pty) Limited and others v National Prosecuting Authority and another, In re S v Pistorius; Media 24 Limited and others v Director of Public Prosecutions North Gauteng and others* 2014 (1) SACR 589 (GP).

30 *S v Pistorius* (CC113/2013) [2014] ZAGPPHC 793 (12 September 2014).

31 For further comments on the effect of the media coverage of high-profile cases such as *S v Pistorius*, see Wardle B 'The *sub judice* rule and the Oscar Pistorius case: Will the crime of contempt of court *ex facie curiae* become abrogated by disuse?' (2014) 543 *De Rebus* 27–29.

32 *Attorney-General v Crockett* 1911 TPD 893 at 927; Snyman *Criminal Law* 322.

33 S 8 of the Prevention and Combating of Corrupt Activities Act 12 of 2004.

34 S 9 of the Prevention and Combating of Corrupt Activities Act.

35 S 11 of the Prevention and Combating of Corrupt Activities Act.

(*ex facie curiae*).[36] This common law position is supplemented with statutory provisions, such as sections 55 and 187–188 of the Criminal Procedure Act 51 of 1977 and section 5(2) of the Magistrates' Courts Act.

43.3.2.4 Scandalising the court

This form of contempt of court *ex facie curiae* can be committed without reference to any particular or pending case. Essentially, it concerns commentary, publications or verbal communications that 'are likely to bring judges, magistrates or the administration of justice through the courts generally into contempt'.[37] It is not a material element of the crime that the administration of justice was in fact brought into disrepute as a result of the commentary or publication.[38]

The crime of contempt of court *ex facie curiae* in the form of scandalising the court was held to be compatible with the Constitution in the much criticised[39] case of *S v Mamabolo*.[40] The Constitutional Court highlighted a number of constitutional and policy considerations in its decision that this form of contempt of court is, indeed, constitutional. As a matter of public policy, the court noted that courts can only function effectively if they have the trust and respect of the public.[41]

The Constitutional Court emphasised that the reason for the criminalisation of contempt of court is not to stifle debate or commentary on the merits of judgments nor is it to protect the private interests or reputation of individual members of the judiciary. The criminalisation of contempt of court aims to protect the legitimacy and integrity of the legal process, in particular the work of the courts.[42] The constitutionally protected right to freedom of speech and opinion is not an unqualified right that can trump other rights, for instance human dignity. These rights need to be balanced.[43]

The question whether any given accused person has committed the crime of contempt of court involves an objective test, namely whether there is a reasonable possibility that the accused's words or conduct might bring the administration of justice into disrepute.[44]

Even though the Constitutional Court held that the crime of contempt of court is not unconstitutional, the court also pointed out that the scope of the crime is limited to those instances where judicial integrity is *likely to be damaged* by the words or conduct of the accused.[45]

We agree with the gist of the criticism against the Constitutional Court judgment in *S v Mamabolo*. It is evident that in a constitutional democracy, there is also a need to subject the institution of the judiciary to criticism. This is entirely different from commenting on the merits of a particular pending case. The transformation of the judiciary and the justice system are important items on the public discourse agenda. The crime of scandalising the court is not only unrealistic in the information era but is arguably also an unnecessary impediment to free speech and is incompatible with South Africa's constitutional ethos.

---

36 Snyman *Criminal Law* 322.

37 Snyman *Criminal Law* 322–323; Burchell *Principles of Criminal Law* 870–873.

38 *S v Mamabolo (E TV and others intervening)* 2001 (1) SACR 686 (CC).

39 See Pantazis A 'Criminal law: Case law' (2001) *Ann Surv S African L* 685 at 689; Snyman *Criminal Law* 324; Burchell *Principles of Criminal Law* 872–873.

40 *S v Mamabolo* supra.

41 *S v Mamabolo* supra at 19.

42 *S v Mamabolo* supra at 18, 19, 24, 25, 32 and 45.

43 *S v Mamabolo* supra at 41.

44 *S v Mamabolo* supra at 43, 44 and 50.

45 *S v Mamabolo* supra at 45.

43.4 Perjury and related crimes

43.4.1 General background

Perjury is making a false statement under oath or affirmation in the course of a judicial proceeding. Perjury is a crime under South African common law. The common law crime is supplemented by a statutory crime, namely making conflicting statements under different oaths (contravention of section 319(3) of the Criminal Procedure Act 56 of 1955). It is also a crime to make a false statement in an affidavit (contravention of section 9 of the Justices of the Peace and Commissioners of Oaths Act 16 of 1963).

The rationale for the criminalisation of these offences concerns an important aspect of the justice system, namely that witnesses should tell the truth and nothing but the truth in court or in affidavits. Without this, the system will not be able to function effectively and with integrity.

43.4.2 Common law perjury

This crime (with its roots in Roman and Roman-Dutch law) 'consists in the unlawful and intentional making of a false statement in the course of a judicial proceeding by a person who has taken the oath or made an affirmation before, or who has been admonished by, somebody competent to administer or accept the oath, affirmation or admonition'.[46]

The requirements for perjury are as follows:

- *False statement*: For the purposes of this crime, a statement means a verbal statement or a statement in writing in the form of an affidavit.[47] Although the point has not been authoritatively decided in South Africa, it seems that the statement must be objectively false. This means that a witness who intends (subjectively, in other words) to tell a lie in court, but the statement in actual fact turns out to be true, commits not perjury, but perhaps the crime of attempted perjury, or defeating or obstructing the course of justice.[48] The state *does not need to prove that the false statement is material* to any issue to be decided by the court.[49]
- *Judicial proceeding*: The crime of perjury can only be committed *in the course of a judicial proceeding* (criminal or civil in nature). Thus, affidavits made to the police in the context of an investigation do not qualify as a 'statement made in the course of judicial proceedings'.[50]
- *Oath, affirmation, or admonition*: This requirement implies that any statements by a legal representative in court as part of legal argument, in other words, not testimony under oath, will be excluded from the ambit of the common law crime of perjury. It is important to note that witnesses must be sworn in or the affirmation must be accepted by a court official who is competent.[51]
- *Intention*: The accused must know, or at least foresee, the possibility that his statement may be false. Thus, *dolus eventualis* will be sufficient. It is also necessary to show that the

46 Snyman *Criminal Law* 332. For a somewhat different take on the common law crime of perjury, see the definition by Burchell *Principles of Criminal Law* 876: 'Perjury consists in the unlawful and intentional making, upon oath, affirmation or admonition and in the course of judicial proceedings before a competent tribunal, of a statement which the maker knows to be or foresees may be false'.

47 *R v Beukman* 1950 (4) SA 261 (O) at 264A.

48 Snyman *Criminal Law* 332–333.

49 S 101(1) of the Criminal Procedure Act 51 of 1977.

50 *S v Carse* 1967 (2) SA 659 (C) at 663–664; Snyman *Criminal Law* 333–334.

51 See, generally, ss 162–164 of the Criminal Procedure Act 51 of 1977.

accused knew that he was under oath, affirmation or admonition, and that the relevant statement was made in the course of judicial proceedings.[52]

43.4.3 Making conflicting statements under different oaths (contravention of section 319(3) of the Criminal Procedure Act 56 of 1955)

Section 319(3) of the Criminal Procedure Act 56 of 1955[53] provides as follows:

> **If a person has made any statement on oath whether orally or in writing, and he thereafter on another oath makes another statement as aforesaid, which is in conflict with such first-mentioned statement, he shall be guilty of an offence and may, on a charge alleging that he made the two conflicting statements, and upon proof of those two statements and without proof as to which of the said statements was false, be convicted of such offence and punished with the penalties prescribed by law for the crime of perjury, unless it is proved that when he made each statement he believed it to be true.**

Unlike common law perjury, this statutory form of perjury does not require that the statements be made during a judicial proceeding.[54] Although the conflicting nature of the two statements would normally be self-evident, the Appellate Division (now the SCA) further qualified this requirement and held that the two statements must be 'mutually destructive'.[55]

DISCUSSION **Another unconstitutional reverse onus in criminal law?**

Snyman argues that the onus on the accused in terms of this statutory form of perjury is probably unconstitutional.[56] With reference to section 35(3)(*h*) (the right to be presumed innocent) of the Constitution, the author submits that this section creates a reverse onus 'which is not reasonable and justifiable'.[57] Thus, Snyman argues that the normal position should apply here as well, namely that the state needs to prove intention. Consider also the text of section 319(3) in light of the following Constitutional Court judgments: *S v Zuma*, *S v Bhulwana*, *S v Mbatha*, *S v Julies*, *S v Coetzee* and *S v Ntsele*.[58]

43.4.4 Making false statements in an affidavit (contravention of section 9 of the Justices of the Peace and Commissioners of Oaths Act 16 of 1963)

Section 9 of the Justices of the Peace and Commissioners of Oaths Act 16 of 1963 provides that 'any person who, in an affidavit, affirmation or solemn or attested declaration, made before a person competent to administer an oath or affirmation or take the declaration in question, has made a false statement knowing it to be false, [commits] an offence'. The crime

52 Snyman *Criminal Law* 335.
53 Which was not repealed by the Criminal Procedure Act 51 of 1977.
54 Snyman *Criminal Law* 336.
55 *S v Ramdas* 1994 (2) SACR 37 (A) at 40D-E.
56 Snyman *Criminal Law* 337–338.
57 Snyman *Criminal Law* 337.
58 *S v Zuma and others* 1995 (1) SACR 568 (CC); *S v Bhulwana; S v Gwadiso* 1995 (2) SACR 748 (CC); *S v Mbatha; S v Prinsloo* 1996 (1) SACR 371 (CC); *S v Julies* 1996 (2) SACR 108 (CC); *S v Coetzee and others* 1997 (1) SACR 379 (CC); *S v Ntsele* 1997 (2) SACR 740 (CC).

is completed when the false statement is made in proceedings other than testimony under oath during court proceedings.[59] The statutory provision explicitly requires *mens rea* in the form of intent.[60]

43.5 Obstructing police in the performance of their duties

Crimes against the administration of justice do not only involve the courts and the functioning of the courts, but, importantly and crucially, also the work of the police.[61] Therefore, section 67(1) of the South African Police Service Act 68 of 1995 provides that any person who resists or willfully hinders or obstructs any member of the police service in the exercise of his powers or the performance of his duties or functions, commits an offence. Interference with a police officer's uniform or equipment also constitutes a criminal offence.[62] It is a criminal offence to impersonate a police official or to pretend to be a member of the South African Police Service.[63] A mere utterance or statement is not enough. The statement or uttering should be accompanied by conduct associated with police work.[64]

THIS CHAPTER IN ESSENCE

1. The various crimes against the administration of justice, discussed above, affect different aspects of the justice system. Thus, for instance, pre-trial aspects are covered by the crime of *obstructing police in the performance of their duties* as well as by the crime of *making false statements in an affidavit.*
2. The integrity of trial proceedings, as well as the dignity of the courts, is protected by crimes such as perjury, and the two forms of *contempt of court*: *in facie curiae* and *ex facie curiae*.

59 Snyman *Criminal Law* 338.
60 See also *S v Theron* 1968 (4) SA 61 (T) at 62.
61 See *S v Claasen* 1997 (1) SACR 675 (C). See also Joubert C *Applied Law for Police Officials* 4 ed (2013) 186.
62 *S v Mzamo* 1993 (2) SACR 97 (Ck).
63 S 68(1) of the South African Police Service Act 68 of 1995.
64 Joubert *Applied Law for Police Officials* 188; *S v Mpanza* 1974 (2) SA 298 (N).

Chapter 44

Crimes under the Companies Act 71 of 2008

CHAPTER OBJECTIVES

The objectives of this chapter are to:
- provide briefly some background to the criminalisation provisions contained in the Companies Act 71 of 2008
- discuss the crimes relating to breach of confidence
- discuss the crimes relating to false statements, reckless conduct and non-compliance
- discuss the crimes relating to hindering the administration of the Act
- discuss briefly other offences in the Companies Act.

44.1 General background

The Companies Act 71 of 2008 has repealed the Companies Act 61 of 1973. The repeal of the 1973 Companies Act has had a significant impact on the decriminalisation of company law. The 1973 Companies Act contained approximately 124 criminal offences in an Act with 443 sections.

The Department of Trade and Industry issued an explanatory memorandum in 2004 in respect of new companies legislation.[1] In the memorandum, the Department of Trade and Industry addressed, among other things, the decriminalisation of company law. The department stated that there should be a balance between civil, administrative and criminal sanctions in light of the fact that 'the existing Companies Act too readily invokes criminal

1 South African Company Law for the 21st Century: Guidelines for Corporate Law Reform. *GG* 26493, GenN 1183 of 23 June 2004

penalties, when civil or administrative remedies could be more appropriate'.[2] The department also stated that there were no effective mechanisms to enforce duties of directors except 'in regard to the more outrageous criminal offences'.[3] Under the heading 'Guidelines for New Company Law', the document states that 'the decriminalisation of company law is key to ensuring more effective and credible redress'.[4] The effect of these stated objectives is that the Companies Act 71 of 2008 contains only a handful of offences.

44.2 The crimes under the Companies Act 71 of 2008

The offences in the Companies Act are found not only in Chapter 9 of the Act, but also across other sections of the Act. The offences under Chapter 9 are breaches of confidence,[5] making false statements, reckless conduct and non-compliance,[6] and hindering the administration of the Act.[7]

44.2.1 Breach of confidence

The Companies Act criminalises the disclosure of confidential information concerning the affairs of any person obtained in carrying out any function in terms of the Act or because of initiating a complaint or participating in any proceedings in terms of the Act.[8] Certain exceptions are then provided.[9] No equivalent provision existed under the Companies Act 61 of 1973. The question, therefore, is what is *confidential information*?

Some guidance can be found in section 212 of the Act. Section 212 provides that when a person submits information to the Companies and Intellectual Property Commission, the Takeover Regulation Panel, the Companies Tribunal, the Financial Reporting Standards Council, or an investigator or inspector who has been appointed in terms of the Act, that person may claim that the information is confidential and provide reasons for the claim.[10] The penalty for contravening the breach of confidence provisions is a fine or imprisonment for a period not exceeding 10 years, or both a fine and imprisonment.[11] In the absence of an equivalent provision in the 1973 Act, it is not entirely clear what the aim is of criminalising the disclosure of confidential information.

44.2.2 False statements, reckless conduct and non-compliance

The Companies Act contains a handful of offences under the broad spectrum of false statements, reckless conduct and non-compliance.[12] It is an offence to be a party to the falsification of any accounting records of a company.[13] The phrase 'party to' has been judicially interpreted in the context of the reckless conduct of a company's business in terms of the 1973 Companies Act. Under that Act, a person who was party to the reckless conduct of the business of a company could be held personally liable for the debts of the company. It has been held that to be a party to the reckless conduct of a company's business does not

2 P 11 of the memorandum.
3 P 18 of the memorandum.
4 P 46 of the memorandum.
5 S 213 of the Companies Act.
6 S 214.
7 S 215.
8 Ss 213(1)(*a*) and 213(1)(*b*).
9 S 213(2).
10 Ss 212(1) and 212(2).
11 S 216(*a*).
12 S 214.
13 S 214(1)(*a*).

have to involve taking positive steps but includes supporting or concurring in the conduct of the business.[14] It is therefore arguable that any person who supports or concurs in the falsification of the accounting records could be guilty of an offence.

A person is also guilty of an offence if that person with a *fraudulent purpose, knowingly provides false or misleading information* in any circumstances in which the Companies Act requires such a person to provide information or to give notice to another person.[15] The term 'knowingly' is defined in the Act as follows:

> **[W]hen used with respect to a person, and in relation to a particular matter, means that the person either—**
> **(*a*) had actual knowledge of the matter; or**
> **(*b*) was in a position in which the person reasonably ought to have –**
> **(i) had actual knowledge;**
> **(ii) investigated the matter to an extent that would have provided the person with actual knowledge; or**
> **(iii) taken other measures which, if taken, would reasonably be expected to have provided the person with actual knowledge of the matter.**[16]

Should a person, for example a director, provide false information about a shareholders' meeting or provide incorrect information about the place of the meeting in the notice of the meeting to shareholders with a purpose to defraud them and knowing that the information was incorrect, this director could be guilty of an offence as envisaged by the Act.

A person is also guilty of an offence if he was knowingly party to an act or omission by a company that was calculated to defraud a creditor or employee of the company, or a holder of the company's securities, or with another fraudulent purpose.[17] In terms of section 22(1) of the 2008 Companies Act, prior to its amendment by the Companies Amendment Act 3 of 2011, a person was also guilty of an offence if he was party to carrying on a company's business in a reckless, grossly negligent manner with the intention to defraud or for a fraudulent purpose. If the company traded under insolvent circumstances, it could also have meant that an offence was committed. The final version of the Companies Act has, however, done away with the harsh punishment if section 22 is contravened. The reckless or grossly negligent conduct of business or trading under insolvent circumstances should not per se lead to a criminal sanction.

A person also commits an offence if he is party to the preparation, approval, dissemination or publication of a prospectus or a written statement contemplated in section 101 of the Act, and the prospectus or written statement contains an untrue statement.[18] Companies that offer their securities to the public, or shareholders of companies who offer their shares to the public, have to provide detailed information about the companies of which shares are being offered. This is to ensure that the investing public is protected against unscrupulous companies and/or existing holders of securities in a company. In the case of an initial public offering of securities or a primary offer for securities,[19] the company must include a registered prospectus with that offer. The content

---

14 *Howard v Herrigel and another NNO* 1991 (2) SA 660 (A) at 674H; *Philotex (Pty) Ltd and others v Snyman and others; Braitex (Pty) Ltd and others v Snyman and others* 1998 (2) SA 138 (SCA) at 143.

15 S 214(1)(*b*).

16 S 1.

17 S 214(1)(*c*).

18 S 214(1)(*d*).

19 The terms 'initial public offering' and 'primary offering' are defined in ss 95(1)(*e*) and 95(1)(*i*) of the Companies Act respectively.

of the prospectus is set out in section 100 of the Act. In the case of a secondary sale of securities to the public, that is, the sale of shares in a company by an existing shareholder, such offer must be accompanied by either a registered prospectus or a written statement. The written statement must satisfy certain requirements and has to include certain information.[20] As mentioned above, the purpose of the prospectus and written information is to enable a potential investor in the company or purchaser in the secondary market to make an informed decision.

Any untrue statements in the prospectus or written statement could lead to severe financial harm to a potential purchaser of securities. An 'untrue statement' is defined in the Act as '[including] a statement that is misleading in the form and context in which it is made, subject to subsections (3) and (4)'.[21] The Act then provides when a person is 'party to' the mischief envisaged in section 214(1)(*d*).[22] It would appear that 'party to' has a much narrower meaning in this subsection than in section 214(1)(*c*) should previous case law in respect of the term in a civil context still be applicable. The penalty for contravening section 214 (1) is imprisonment for a period not exceeding 10 years, a fine, or both imprisonment and a fine.[23]

Failure to comply with a compliance notice is also an offence.[24] The Companies and Intellectual Property Commission[25] and the Takeover Regulation Panel[26] have the power to issue compliance notices in cases where there has been non-compliance with the Act or where a person assented to, was implicated in, or benefited from contravening the Act.[27] When a compliance notice has been issued to a person, the person should, inter alia, cease his contravention of the Act.[28] A person to whom a compliance notice has been issued and who fails to comply with that notice could be punished with an administrative fine[29] or be referred to the National Prosecuting Authority for prosecution as an offence.[30]

The last offence under section 214 of the Act provides that if a person contravenes sections 99(1), (2), (3), (4), (5), (8) or (9), and that person is a director or prescribed officer

---

20 Ss 101(4)–(6).

21 S 95(1)(*p*). Ss 95(3) and 95(4) provide that:

> **(3) An untrue statement is regarded to have been included in a prospectus, written statement, or summary directing a person to either a prospectus or written statement, if it is contained in any report or memorandum—**
>
> **(*a*) that appears on the face of the prospectus, written statement, or summary; or**
>
> **(*b*) that is incorporated by reference within, or is attached to or accompanies, the prospectus, written statement or summary.**
>
> **(4) An omission from a prospectus or written statement of any matter that, in the context, is calculated to mislead by omission constitutes the making of an untrue statement in that prospectus or written statement, irrespective of whether this Act requires that matter to be included in the prospectus or written statement.**

22 S 214(2) provides:

> **For the purposes of subsection (1)(*d*) [...] a person is a party to the preparation of a document contemplated in that subsection if—**
>
> **(*a*) the document includes or is otherwise based on a scheme, structure or form of words or numbers devised, prepared or recommended by that person; and**
>
> **(*b*) the scheme, structure or form of words is of such a nature that the person knew, or ought reasonably to have known, that its inclusion or other use in connection with the preparation of the document would cause it to be false or misleading.**

23 S 216(*a*).

24 S 214(3).

25 Established in terms of s 185 of the Companies Act.

26 Established in terms of s 196 of the Companies Act.

27 S 171(1).

28 S 171(2) sets out the possible actions that a person to whom a compliance notice has been issued needs to take.

29 S 171(7)(*a*).

30 S 171(7)(*b*) read with s 214(3).

of the company who was knowingly party to the contravention, he is guilty of an offence and is liable for any losses sustained due to that contravention.[31] The meaning of the word 'knowingly' has already been discussed above. Section 99 of the Act deals with restrictions on offers of securities of companies to the public. The section deals mainly with protective measures for the public where companies intend to offer their securities to the public. The protective measures in section 99 essentially deal with the registered prospectus or documents required by the relevant exchange in the case of listed securities. The aim is to protect the investing public against unscrupulous companies (directors), and not only to provide for a civil remedy, but also a criminal penalty to discourage abuse in the issue of securities of a company to the public. A contravention of section 214(4) carries a penalty of a fine or a maximum imprisonment period of one year, or both a fine and imprisonment.[32]

44.2.3 Hindering the administration of the Companies Act

It is an offence to hinder, obstruct or attempt to influence improperly the Commission, the Panel, the Companies Tribunal, an inspector or investigator, or a court when any of these is exercising a power or performing a duty delegated, conferred or imposed by the Companies Act.[33] A person commits an offence who:

> **(*a*) does anything calculated to improperly influence—**
> > **(i) the Commission, the Panel, the Companies Tribunal, an inspector or investigator concerning any matter connected with an investigation; or**
> > **(ii) the Companies Tribunal in any matter before it;**
>
> **(*b*) anticipates any findings of the Commission, the Panel, the Companies Tribunal, an inspector or investigator in a way that is calculated to improperly influence the proceedings or findings;**
>
> **(*c*) does anything in connection with an investigation or hearing that would have been contempt of court if the proceedings had occurred in a court of law;**
>
> **(*d*) refuses to attend when summoned, or after attending, refuses to answer any question or produce any document as required by the summons, other than as contemplated in section 176(*a*);**
>
> **(*e*) knowingly provides false information to the Commission, the Panel, the Companies Tribunal, an inspector or investigator;**
>
> **(*f*) improperly frustrates or impedes the execution of a warrant to enter and search, or attempts to do so;**
>
> **(*g*) acts contrary to or in excess of a warrant to enter and search; and**
>
> **(*h*) without authority, but claiming to have authority in terms of section 177—**
> > **(i) enters or searches premises; or**
> > **(ii) attaches or removes an article or document.**[34]

A person who commits any of these offences risks being fined or imprisoned for a maximum period of one year, or both fined and imprisoned.[35]

31 S 214(4).
32 S 216(*b*).
33 S 215(1).
34 S 215(2).
35 S 216(*b*).

44.2.4 Other offences in the Companies Act

There are also other offences in the Companies Act apart from those listed in sections 214 and 215 as discussed above. The following offences carry a penalty of a fine or imprisonment of up to one year, or both a fine and imprisonment if a person is found guilty:[36]

- It is an offence for a company to fail to accommodate any reasonable request for access or to refuse access unreasonably to any record that a person has a right to inspect or copy in terms of section 26 or section 31 of the Act.[37]
- It is also an offence to impede, interfere with or attempt to frustrate the reasonable exercise by any person of the rights set out in sections 26 or 31.[38] Section 26 generally provides the right for persons who hold a beneficial interest in a company, or a person who is a member of a non-profit company, to have access to certain documentation of the company, for example the memorandum of incorporation and any amendments to it and any rules,[39] the reports to annual meetings and annual financial statements,[40] and the securities register of a profit company or the members' register of a non-profit company.[41] Section 26 also provides the right for other persons to have access to certain company documentation.[42] Section 31 of the Act deals with access to the financial statements of a company or access to related information of the company.
- It is an offence for a company, with the intention to deceive or mislead a person, to fail to keep accurate or complete accounting records or to keep records other than in the prescribed manner and form.[43]
- It is an offence for a company to falsify any of its accounting records or permit any person to do so.[44]
- It is an offence for any person to falsify a company's accounting records.[45]

DISCUSSION

Is there unnecessary overlap of crimes under the Companies Act and other common law and statutory crimes of general application?

We could ask whether many of the offences in terms of the Companies Act are required as they could be covered under other crimes, for instance fraud or forgery. By including these offences under the Act, the specific penalties imposed under the Act would, however, be applicable. Du Toit et al state as follows with reference to *S v Mostert and another*:[46] 'The mere fact that certain conduct might constitute a common-law offence as well as a statutory offence, does not mean that the prosecution is obliged to proceed in terms of the relevant statutory offence'.[47] In terms of criminal law policy, can the particularised (contextual) criminalisation of conduct, otherwise recognisable as existing common law and statutory crimes, really be justified? Was one of the aims of the Companies Act not decriminalisation?

36 S 216(*b*).
37 S 26(9)(*a*).
38 S 26(9)(*b*).
39 S 26(1)(*a*).
40 S 26(1)(*c*).
41 S 26(1)(*e*).
42 S 26(2).
43 S 28(3)(*a*)(i).
44 S 28(3)(*a*)(ii).
45 S 28(3)(*b*).
46 *S v Mostert and another* 2010 (1) SACR 223 (SCA) at 18 and 19.
47 Du Toit E et al *Commentary on the Criminal Procedure Act* (revision service 46, 2011) 1–4T.

Section 29 deals with financial statements and provides that, subject to section 214(2), a person is guilty of an offence if he is *party to the preparation, approval, dissemination or publication of*:

(6) ...

(*a*) any financial statements, including any annual financial statements contemplated in section 30, knowing that those statements—

(i) fail in a material way to comply with the requirements of subsection (1); or

(ii) are materially false or misleading, as contemplated in subsection (2); or

(*b*) a summary of any financial statements, knowing that—

(i) the statements that it summarises do not comply with the requirements of subsection (1), or are materially false or misleading, as contemplated in subsection (2); or

(ii) the summary does not comply with the requirements of subsection (3), or is materially false or misleading.[48]

Section 31 should be read with the provisions of section 26 as mentioned above. It provides that it is an offence for a company to fail to accommodate any reasonable request for access or to refuse access unreasonably to any record that a person has a right to inspect or copy in terms of section 31. It also provides that it is an offence to impede, interfere with or attempt to frustrate the reasonable exercise by any person of the rights set out in section 31.[49]

The Companies Act penalises the abuse of the company's name or registration number.[50] Section 32 in the Act provides that:

(1) A company or external company must—

(*a*) provide its full registered name or registration number to any person on demand; and

(*b*) not misstate its name or registration number in a manner likely to mislead or deceive any person.

(2) If the Commission has issued to a company a registration certificate with an interim name, as contemplated in section 14(2)(*b*), the company must use its interim name, until its name has been amended.

(3) A person must not—

(*a*) use the name or registration number of a company in a manner likely to convey an impression that the person is acting or communicating on behalf of that company, unless the company has authorised that person to do so; or

(*b*) use a form of name for any purpose if, in the circumstances, the use of that form of name is likely to convey a false impression that the name is the name of a company.

(4) Every company must have its name and registration number mentioned in legible characters in all notices and other official publications of the company, including such notices and publications in electronic format as contemplated in the Electronic Communications and Transactions Act, and in all bills of exchange, promissory notes, cheques and orders for money or goods and in all letters, delivery notes, invoices, receipts and letters of credit of the company.

48 S 29(6).

49 S 31(4).

50 S 32(5) provides that a contravention of subss (1), (2), (3) or (4) is an offence.

44.3 The continued application of offences under the Companies Act 61 of 1973

Although the Companies Act 71 of 2008 has repealed the Companies Act 61 of 1973, the Act does provide that Chapter 14 of the 1973 Act continues to apply with respect to the winding-up and liquidation of insolvent companies.[51] Certain sections of Chapter 14 of the 1973 Act are then excluded and therefore those excluded sections will not continue to apply.[52] There are approximately eight offences under Chapter 14 of the 1973 Act that have not been excluded. The question is whether these offences continue to apply because they have not been expressly excluded. The only conclusion we can draw is that they continue to exist. Should this be the case, is there a penalty for these offences? The 1973 Companies Act contained a penalties clause that penalised different offences with different penalties.[53] However, the penalties clause under the 1973 Act does not fall under Chapter 14 (it falls under Chapter 16) and has therefore been repealed. If these offences still exist, have they become obsolete due to the fact that the penalties clause has been repealed? We submit that the answer may be found in section 216(*b*) of the 2008 Act, which provides that any person convicted of an offence in terms of this Act is liable to a fine or to a maximum prison term of one year, or both a fine and imprisonment. The offences under Chapter 14 continue to apply and should therefore be interpreted to be offences in terms of *this* Act as envisaged in section 216(*b*) of the 2008 Act.

These offences include a failure by a director or secretary of a company in liquidation to notify the liquidator after the commencement of the liquidation process of any change in address.[54] A person who gives, agrees or offers to give to any member, creditor or contributory of a company any reward with a view to securing his own nomination or appointment, or to securing or preventing the nomination or appointment of any person as a company's liquidator shall be guilty of an offence.[55] Other offences would be those in terms of sections 357, 363, 414, 418(5), 421 and 424.

THIS CHAPTER IN ESSENCE

1. The Companies Act 71 of 2008, which replaced the old Act of 1973, purports to encourage business activity and entrepreneurship, while at the same time recognising the need for sufficient regulation 'to make a company and its office bearers accountable to relevant stakeholders'.[56]
2. The offences provided for in the Companies Act should be interpreted and applied against this background.
3. One should also not lose sight of the fact that companies and their directors can, in theory, commit virtually all the crimes discussed in this book.
4. The crimes in this chapter are thus specifically aimed at the optimal functioning of a company in the relevant commercial and regulatory context.

51 Item 9 of Schedule 5.

52 According to Item 9(2) of Schedule 5, ss 343, 344, 346 and 348–353 do not apply to the winding-up of a solvent company except to the extent necessary to give full effect to the provisions of Part G of Chapter 2.

53 S 441.

54 S 363A(2) of the Companies Act 61 of 1973.

55 S 365(1) of the Companies Act 61 of 1973.

56 S 7. See also Davis D and Cassim F (eds) *Companies and Other Business Structures in South Africa* 2 ed (2010) 5.

Chapter 45

Organised crime and money laundering

CHAPTER OBJECTIVES

The objectives of this chapter are to:

- describe briefly the phenomenon of organised crime
- discuss the crime of racketeering in terms of the Prevention of Organised Crime Act 121 of 1998
- discuss the crime of money laundering in terms of the Prevention of Organised Crime Act 121 of 1998
- discuss the crime of participating in criminal gang activities in terms of the Prevention of Organised Crime Act 121 of 1998
- describe briefly aspects of asset forfeiture and proceeds of crime.

45.1 General background

In general, organised crime can be described as 'systematic criminal activity of a serious nature committed by a structured group of individuals or corporate body in order to obtain, secure or retain, directly or indirectly, a financial or other material benefit'.[1] In *National Director of Public Prosecutions v Vermaak*, the Supreme Court of Appeal (SCA) described organised crime as 'offences that have organisational features of some kind that distinguish them from individual criminal wrongdoing'.[2]

The United Nations Convention Against Transnational Organized Crime (2000) calls on states party to the convention to criminalise certain conduct, including organised crime and offences relating to the proceeds of crime, notably money laundering.[3] During the last decade of the previous century, South Africa made great strides in terms of adopting legal frameworks aimed at transnational organised crime and money laundering.[4] As we pointed out in previous chapters, crimes such as corruption and crimes against the administration of justice often form part of vast transnational criminal phenomena that are best dealt with in terms of multidisciplinary and multi-effort approaches. Indeed, South African law has long recognised crimes such as theft, fraud, robbery, murder, intimidation, kidnapping and bribery, either in the form of common law crimes or in statutory form. However, none of these crimes *specifically* dealt with the often complex and transnational criminal phenomena underlying and sustaining crime in general and economic crime in particular.[5] It is also a mistake to view South African law in isolation. The fact that South Africa has crimes such as theft, fraud and receiving stolen property at common law and statutory law, does not in itself guarantee the effective prevention or prosecution of transnational organised crime and money laundering. International cooperation in criminal matters in the procedural sense is not enough. States also need to *harmonise their substantive criminal laws* (that is, the criminalisation provisions) to make cooperation even more effective.[6]

During the apartheid era, transnational organised crime was less of a concern than it is today. The relative isolation from the global community, the strict exchange control regime and draconian laws made South Africa an unattractive place for organised crime syndicates to ply their trade. However, the advent of democracy in 1994 and the reintegration of the country into the global arena, coupled with the accompanying political instability, a liberal constitution and relatively sophisticated financial infrastructure, led to a surge in organised crime. It soon became apparent that the existing laws, law enforcement agencies and traditional investigative techniques were inadequate to combat this phenomenon. This led

1 Goredema C (ed) 'Legislation in South Africa, Swaziland and Zimbabwe to combat organised crime' Monograph 56 Ch 3 (June 2001) *Organised Crime in Southern Africa: Assessing Legislation* Institute for Security Studies. Available at https://issafrica.org/research/monographs/monograph-56-organised-crime-in-southern-africa-assessing-legislation-edited-by-charles-goredema.

2 *National Director of Public Prosecutions v Vermaak* 2008 (1) SACR 157 (SCA) at 4.

3 For a discussion, see Kemp GP 'The United Nations Convention Against Transnational Organized Crime: A milestone in international criminal law' (2001) 14(2) *SACJ* 152.

4 See the discussion in section 45.4.

5 For an overview, see Burchell JM *Principles of Criminal Law* 5 ed (2016) 889–892.

6 For a comprehensive argument in support of this approach, see Stessens G *Money Laundering: A New International Law Enforcement Model* (2000).

to the creation of several new offences and the amendment of certain existing crimes to fight organised crime better.[7] The most important of these are discussed below.

DISCUSSION **The organised crime and money laundering nexus**

In terms of a rationale for the criminalisation of organised crime and money laundering, as well as the concomitant comprehensive frameworks to combat these phenomena, Guy Stessens proposed the following:

> Because the classic tools of the criminal law were perceived to have failed in the fight against organised crime, legislators - with those from the United States in the front rank - considered the confiscation of the proceeds of crime and the incrimination of money laundering as new, more effective tools for tackling the problem of organised crime. These instruments are part of a new strategy against organised crime which is aimed at the structures of organised crime, rather than at deterring individuals from taking part in organised crime. This strategy is directed at the crucial function of organised crime: making money. By taking away the proceeds from crime and by making it more difficult to launder its proceeds, law enforcement authorities not only take away the incentive for organised crime, but, more importantly, seek to disrupt the functioning of organised crime itself. Organised crime groups depend on cash and assets to function just as much as their legitimate counterparts do.[8]

Considering the crimes discussed in this chapter, as well as crimes discussed in earlier chapters, such as theft, fraud, robbery and corruption, does the rationale for the criminalisation of organised crime and money laundering make sense?

7 In addition to the new criminal offences created, South Africa also embraced asset forfeiture provisions aimed at taking the profit out of crime and hence striking at the heart of the main motive for the commission of organised crime. In addition to this, new law enforcement units and regulatory bodies were created to enforce the new laws, such as the Directorate of Special Operations (or Scorpions as they were colloquially known), the Asset Forfeiture Unit and the Financial Intelligence Centre. The Directorate of Special Operations, which functioned in the Department of Justice, was later abolished and essentially moved to the Department of Safety and Security where it became known as the Hawks (Directorate for Priority Crime Investigation). Many observers and non-governmental organisations, such as the Helen Suzman Foundation, regarded this as a mistake from a crime-fighting and constitutional perspective. The move was successfully challenged in the Constitutional Court. See *Glenister v President of the Republic of South Africa and others* 2011 (3) SA 347 (CC). Parliament was tasked with rectifying the situation by providing for more independence for the Hawks, which it did by subsequently amending the South African Police Service Act 68 of 1995. But this was, again, successfully challenged. In *Helen Suzman Foundation v President of the Republic of South Africa and others; In re Glenister v President of South Africa and others* (23874/2012, 23933/2012) [2013] ZAWCHC 189; [2014] 1 All SA 671 (WCC); 2014 (4) BCLR 481 (WCC) (13 December 2013), the Western Cape High Court declared certain provisions of the South African Police Service Amendment Act 10 of 2012 to be inconsistent with the Constitution of the Republic of South Africa, 1996 and invalid to the extent that they fail to secure an adequate degree of independence for the Directorate for Priority Crime Investigation (the Hawks). The matter again landed before the Constitutional Court for confirmation. In *Helen Suzman Foundation v President of the Republic of South Africa and others; Glenister v President of the Republic of South Africa and others* (CCT 07/14, CCT 09/14) [2014] ZACC 32; 2015 (1) BCLR 1 (CC); 2015 (2) SA 1 (CC) (27 November 2014), the majority of the Constitutional Court confirmed that certain defects in the SAPS Amendment Act, highlighted in the earlier *Glenister* judgment, have indeed not been cured. These defects included the following: the unconstitutionality of the provisions relating to the extension of tenure of the national head of the Hawks; the undue political interference in the operations of the Hawks through ministerial policy guidelines; and the untrammelled power of the Minister of Police to remove the head of the Hawks. The Constitutional Court did not declare the whole Act to be unconstitutional. Instead, the Constitutional Court severed the parts of the Act that were found to be inconsistent with the constitutional obligation to create an anti-corruption unit that enjoys adequate structural, institutional and operational independence.

8 Stessens *Money Laundering* 9–10.

45.2 South Africa's response to the phenomena of organised crime and money laundering

In response to high levels of crime and international obligations,[9] South Africa adopted a number of important pieces of legislation dealing with various aspects of organised crime. The most important of these are the Prevention of Organised Crime Act 121 of 1998 (POCA) and the Financial Intelligence Centre Act 38 of 2001 (FICA).[10] These statutes contain various criminalisation provisions as well as comprehensive enforcement and regulatory frameworks.

An important additional component of the statutory regime concerning organised criminality is, of course, the criminalisation of corruption (as discussed in Chapter 36). We noted that although corruption in terms of the Prevention and Combating of Corrupt Activities Act 12 of 2004 is normally classified as a crime against the community and public welfare, it is often part of or linked to organised criminality and can in that sense also be dealt with in the context of organised crime and money laundering. Indeed, because organised crime is an ongoing phenomenon, its success depends largely on the avoidance of detection and prosecution as well as circumventing measures put in place to combat it. Therefore, corruption is an essential tool in the arsenal of the organised crime syndicates.

It is beyond the scope of this book to deal with all the substantive and procedural aspects of the complex legislative frameworks provided for in POCA and FICA. Although POCA and FICA can be regarded as important legislative tools in the fight against organised crime and money laundering, it is important to note that, certainly in the case of POCA, the Act does not exclusively deal with organised crime. Thus, it also applies to cases of individual criminality where appropriate.[11]

45.3 The crime of racketeering

One of the difficulties in effectively combating organised crime is that criminal organisations are an adaptive species that are constantly seeking new and innovative ways to conduct their business and evade detection or prosecution. They are largely unencumbered by laws, rules or borders and can adapt to their changing environment far more quickly than their law enforcement counterparts.

Another difficulty is that the persons in charge of criminal syndicates are seldom directly involved in the crimes committed by the group. Like company CEOs, they often manage their 'businesses' from large villas or plush offices and issue instructions to their 'employees' to go out and commit whatever crimes might fund their organisation. The application of traditional law enforcement methods and criminal offences to such enterprises is typically ineffective. This is because the persons who are usually caught and prosecuted are lower ranking members of the syndicate who are quickly and easily replaced with minimal disruption to operations. The strict code of silence that usually exists in such enterprises,

9 See the Preamble of the Prevention of Organised Crime Act 121 of 1998 (POCA); *Mohunram and another v National Director of Public Prosecutions and another* (*Law Review Project as amicus curiae*) 2007 (2) SACR 145 (CC) at 144.

10 For commentary, see De Koker L *South African Money Laundering and Terror Financing Law* (2017); Kruger A *Organised Crime and Proceeds of Crime Law in South Africa* (2008).

11 *National Director of Public Prosecutions v Geyser and another* (160/07) [2008] ZASCA 15; [2008] 2 All SA 616 (SCA); 2008 (2) SACR 103 (SCA) (25 March 2008). In *Mohunram v NDPP* supra at 74 and 140, the Constitutional Court noted that it may be difficult in some cases to distinguish between organised crime and ordinary crimes.

often violently enforced, means that those arrested will seldom inform on or testify against their superiors.

To combat the growing phenomenon of organised crime better, the legislature looked to international and comparative responses to this problem and the statutory crime of **racketeering** was born. What follows is a systematic discussion of the most important aspects of this statutory offence.

Section 2(1) of POCA provides as follows:

> **2 Offences**
>
> **(1) Any person who—**
>
> **(*a*) (i) receives or retains any property derived, directly or indirectly, from a pattern of racketeering activity; and**
>
> **(ii) knows or ought reasonably to have known that such property is so derived; and**
>
> **(iii) uses or invests, directly or indirectly, any part of such property in acquisition of any interest in, or the establishment or operation or activities of, any enterprise;**
>
> **(*b*) (i) receives or retains any property, directly or indirectly, on behalf of any enterprise; and**
>
> **(ii) knows or ought reasonably to have known that such property derived or is derived from or through a pattern of racketeering activity;**
>
> **(*c*) (i) uses or invests any property, directly or indirectly, on behalf of any enterprise or in acquisition of any interest in, or the establishment or operation or activities of any enterprise; and**
>
> **(ii) knows or ought reasonably to have known that such property derived or is derived from or through a pattern of racketeering activity;**
>
> **(*d*) acquires or maintains, directly or indirectly, any interest in or control of any enterprise through a pattern of racketeering activity;**
>
> **(*e*) whilst managing or employed by or associated with any enterprise, conducts or participates in the conduct, directly or indirectly, of such enterprise's affairs through a pattern of racketeering activity;**
>
> **(*f*) manages the operation or activities of an enterprise and who knows or ought reasonably to have known that any person, whilst employed by or associated with that enterprise, conducts or participates in the conduct, directly or indirectly, of such enterprise's affairs through a pattern of racketeering activity; or**
>
> **(*g*) conspires or attempts to violate any of the provisions of paragraphs (*a*), (*b*), (*c*), (*d*), (*e*) or (*f*), within the Republic or elsewhere, shall be guilty of an offence.**

45.3.1 A brief introduction and overview

The offence of racketeering is an entirely new type of crime, hitherto unknown in South African law. It is specifically aimed at combating organised crime. The legislation is closely modelled on the United States (US) Racketeer Influenced and Corrupt Organizations Act[12]

12 18 US Code Ch 96, 1961, enacted 15 October 1970, particularly s 1962.

(RICO).[13] It represents a substantial departure from traditional concepts of individual and collective criminal liability in our law. It also imposes severe penalties commensurate with the seriousness with which this offence is regarded.[14]

To understand the crime of racketeering, it is first necessary to grasp the rationale behind it. It recognises that a criminal organisation can have a life of its own, distinct from its members. It has an ongoing existence, which is often greater than the sum of its parts and is capable of inflicting tremendous damage on society over an extended period.[15] Thus, a solution is required that can address the phenomenon of the criminal organisation and not just the individuals who comprise it. It acknowledges further that, in certain circumstances, merely having a relationship with or performing certain acts relating to such criminal enterprise is conduct worthy of criminal sanction, quite apart from any other crimes that may be committed in the process.[16]

Secondly, one must come to grips with the meaning of the terms 'enterprise'[17] and 'pattern of racketeering activities'.[18] Finally, one must understand the relationship between the accused, the enterprise and the pattern of racketeering activities, which is illustrated by Figure 45.1. These concepts are discussed further within the context of the various racketeering offences.

---

13 The close correlation between South African racketeering legislation and the US legislation has both advantages and disadvantages. On the positive side, a plethora of US jurisprudence exists that can assist in giving content to these provisions. On the negative side, however, the substantial differences between the respective legal systems mean that the US jurisprudence often does not translate well into South African domestic law. In particular, bear in mind that the US jurisprudence has been strongly shaped by the fact that in the US, unlike South Africa, RICO is also applicable to civil litigation. For a discussion of some of the leading US cases and literature as they pertain to the South African crime of racketeering, see Burchell *Principles of Criminal Law* 899 *et seq*.

14 S 3 provides for a sentence of up to R1 000 million (i.e. R1 billion) or life imprisonment.

15 See *S v De Vries and others* 2009 (1) SACR 613 (C).

16 Thus, an accused may be convicted both of the offence of racketeering *and* any number of underlying offences that are relied on by the prosecution to establish the criminal nature of the enterprise. Furthermore, the prosecution may rely on a previous conviction, or even an offence of which an accused has been previously acquitted, as a racketeering act to establish the requisite pattern of racketeering activity. See *S v De Vries and others* 2012 (1) SACR 186 (SCA); *S v Dos Santos and another* 2010 (2) SACR 382 (SCA).

17 S 1(1) of POCA defines an enterprise as including 'any individual, partnership, corporation, association, or other juristic person or legal entity, and any union or group of individuals associated in fact, although not a juristic person or legal entity'. In practice, however, it is difficult to conceive how an individual could be charged as an enterprise. It is hard to imagine, for instance, how one would establish, for the purposes of s 2(1)(*e*), that the accused 'manages, is employed by or associated with' an enterprise when they are one and the same person. In *Savoi and others v National Director of Public Prosecutions and another* 2014 (5) BCLR 606 (CC), the Constitutional Court dismissed a challenge to this definition on the grounds of alleged vagueness.

18 S 1(1) of POCA defines a pattern of racketeering activity as follows: 'means the planned, ongoing, continuous or repeated participation or involvement in any offence referred to in Schedule 1 and includes at least two offences referred to in Schedule 1, of which one of the offences occurred after the commencement of this Act and the last offence occurred within 10 years (excluding any period of imprisonment) after the commission of such prior offence referred to in Schedule 1'. Schedule 1 lists most serious crimes and includes the catch-all category of 'any offence the punishment wherefor may be a period of imprisonment exceeding one year without the option of a fine'. It also includes any conspiracy, incitement or attempt to commit any offence referred to in this Schedule.

In *Savoi v NDPP* supra, the Constitutional Court likewise dismissed a challenge to this definition on the grounds of alleged over-breadth. At 25 the court observed:

> **Criminal syndicates work in a complex web-like manner. They operate in different areas of economic activity; utilise different agents and organisations; and thereby commit various offences – some relatively minor at face value – over time, in complex combination. It is the diversity of criminal activity, situated in complex organisational structures, occurring over time, where the lines of authority are deliberately obscured, that renders legislation in the nature of POCA a necessity. The concept of a 'pattern of racketeering activity' is thus tailored to meet the multifarious ways in which organised crime manifests itself.**

In *S v Roberts and Others* 2013 (1) SACR 369 (ECP), the High Court rejected the notion that the reference to 'two offences' in the definition of 'pattern of racketeering activity' requires the state to prove two separate and disparate offences specified in Schedule 1 of POCA. Thus, multiple commissions of the same offence will suffice to establish a pattern of racketeering activity.

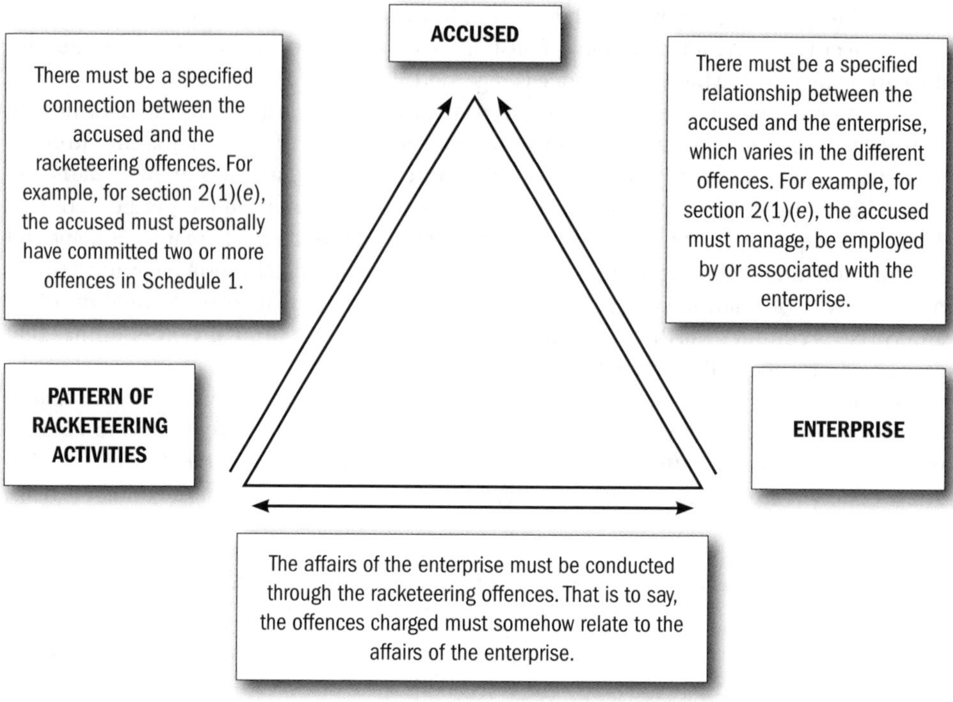

Figure 45.1 The crime of racketeering

Section 2 of POCA contains seven subsections and creates a number of different racketeering offences, which can be broadly grouped into three categories. The first three subsections[19] concern acts relating to property generated by the enterprise and may be broadly described as using or laundering the proceeds of racketeering. The next three subsections[20] concern participation in the enterprise and are the offences most likely to be encountered in practice. The last subsection[21] proscribes a conspiracy or attempt to commit any of the previous subsections.

Finally, racketeering legislation permits the prosecution to join, in a single case, a variety of charges and accused persons, connected by their relationship with the enterprise, in circumstances that may otherwise amount to an improper joinder.[22] This allows the court to see the big picture and to assess, in context, how a number of offences – that may in and of themselves be relatively minor – sustain a far more serious and persistent criminal phenomenon.[23] An additional tool placed at the prosecutor's disposal to place the big picture before the court is the relaxation of certain traditional evidentiary barriers, provided this does not render the trial unfair.[24]

19 S 2(1)(*a*)–(*c*) of POCA.

20 S 2(1)(*d*)–(*f*) of POCA.

21 S 2(1)(*g*) of POCA.

22 As to joinder of accused, see *S v Naidoo* 2009 (2) SACR 674 (GSJ).

23 See *Savoi v NDPP* supra and footnote 18 supra.

24 S 2(2) provides that a court may hear evidence, including evidence about hearsay, similar facts or previous convictions, relating to offences contemplated in s 2(1), notwithstanding that such evidence may otherwise be inadmissible, provided that such evidence would not render a trial unfair. In *Savoi v NDPP* supra, the Constitutional Court dismissed a challenge that s 2(2) per se limited an accused's right to a fair trial.

Due to the far-reaching implications of racketeering charges and the severity of the penalties, the legislature saw fit to require a degree of oversight over the application of this legislation. Section 2(4) provides that a person shall be charged with committing an offence contemplated in section 2(1) only if a prosecution is authorised in writing by the National Director.[25]

We will now define and discuss each of these racketeering offences, beginning with the participation sections, which are the most important in practice.

45.3.2 Participation offences

45.3.2.1 Section 2(1)(*f*) of POCA: Managing an enterprise

This section is aimed primarily at the head of the criminal syndicate although it can also apply to persons lower down in the hierarchy who perform a managerial function.[26] As will be seen, it is not necessary for the prosecution to prove that an accused charged under this section personally committed or even instructed the commission of any criminal offences, provided it can be proven that he had knowledge[27] of the fact that other persons employed by or associated with the syndicate were committing such offences or ought to have reasonably so known.[28]

The latter qualification introduces an objective element to the otherwise subjective requirement of knowledge. Thus, it would be sufficient for the prosecution to prove that a

25 As to the timing and content of the authorisation, see *National Director of Public Prosecutions v Moodley and others* 2009 (2) SA 588 (SCA); 2009 (1) SACR 461 (SCA) and *S v De Vries* (SCA) supra. In *Booysen v Acting National Director of Public Prosecutions and others* [2014] 2 All SA 391 (KZD), the court struck down a purported authorisation to prosecute under s 2(4) on the grounds that it was arbitrary and irrational, and hence did not conform with the principle of legality. Gorvin J held (at 22) that 'the information on which the NDPP relied to arrive at her decision must be rationally connected to the decision taken'. It remains to be seen whether this decision will find favour with other courts, particularly considering the specific exclusion of decisions to prosecute from review under the Promotion of Administrative Justice Act 3 of 2000 (PAJA). See also *National Director of Public Prosecutions v Zuma* 2009 (2) SA 277 (SCA); [2009] 2 All SA 243 (SCA).

26 Bear in mind that the US RICO Act does not have a corresponding provision to s 2(1)(*f*) of POCA. S 1962(*c*) of RICO is limited to persons 'employed by or associated with' the enterprise although this phrase would also encompass managers. US jurisprudence should accordingly be approached with some caution when interpreting this section.

27 The concept of knowledge is expanded by s 1(2) of POCA, which provides:

> **For purposes of this Act a person has knowledge of a fact if—**
> **(*a*) the person has actual knowledge of that fact; or**
> **(*b*) the court is satisfied that—**
> **(i) the person believes that there is a reasonable possibility of the existence of that fact; and**
> **(ii) he or she fails to obtain information to confirm the existence of that fact.**

28 This concept is further expanded by s 1(3) of POCA, which provides:

> **For the purposes of this Act a person ought reasonably to have known or suspected a fact if the conclusions that he or she ought to have reached are those which would have been reached by a reasonably diligent and vigilant person having both—**
> **(*a*) the general knowledge, skill, training and experience that may reasonably be expected of a person in his or her position; and**
> **(*b*) the general knowledge, skill, training and experience that he or she in fact has.**

In *Savoi v NDPP* supra, the Constitutional Court declined to confirm an order of the KwaZulu-Natal Provincial Division (*Savoi and others v National Director of Public Prosecutions and another* [2013] 3 All SA 548 (KZP)) declaring ss 2(1)(*a*)(ii), (*b*)(ii), (*c*)(ii) and (*f*) of POCA constitutionally invalid to the extent that they contain the words 'ought reasonably to have known'. The NPD reasoned, firstly, that these words expose an accused 'to conviction for an offence he had not committed' at 90 and 'the possibility of punishing an unintended, insensible or unconscious conduct' at 90; and secondly, these words are vague and unintelligible. The Constitutional Court disagreed. It found (at 87) that:

> **Nothing was placed before the High Court suggesting that the negligence standard was not suited to the offences concerned. Therefore, there are no grounds upon which we can conclude that the negligence standard provided for in section 2(1) is not constitutionally compliant.**

The court (at 91) also 'failed to see the unintelligibility [of the phrase] that the High Court saw' and found that there was nothing constitutionally objectionable with the formulation.

reasonable person in the position of the accused would have reached this conclusion. Furthermore, section 1(3) provides for an objective standard that is even higher than the normal negligence test by taking into account the knowledge, skill, training and experience *expected* of someone in the *accused's position*, as well as the accused's *actual* knowledge, skill, training and experience.[29]

The expanded meaning given to the requirement of knowledge by section 1(2) of POCA also prevents persons from turning a blind eye to the criminal activities of the enterprise they manage by criminalising a reckless failure to investigate a suspicion of racketeering offences.

45.3.2.1.1 Definition

This offence consists of managing the operations or activities of an enterprise while the accused knows or ought reasonably to have known that any person who is employed by or associated with that enterprise is conducting or participating in the conduct of such enterprise's affairs through a pattern of racketeering offences.

45.3.2.1.2 Essential elements

To prove a contravention of section 2(1)(*f*), the following elements must be proved:

- An enterprise[30] existed.
- The accused managed the operations or activities of the enterprise.
- Some person:[31]
  - was employed by or associated with the enterprise
  - conducted or participated in, directly or indirectly, the affairs of the enterprise
  - such conduct or participation took place through[32] a pattern of racketeering activity.[33]

The accused knew or ought reasonably to have known such persons were engaged in the conduct described above.

45.3.2.1.3 Some general comments

- *Enterprise*: The first important element is that of enterprise. As appears from the definition, an enterprise may take many forms.[34] It may consist of a formal legal entity, such as a company or close corporation. It may also take the shape of a formal organisation that does not necessarily have a separate legal persona, such as a business, guild or club. Usually, however, a criminal enterprise consists of what is known as an

29 See above.

30 See fn 17 above.

31 Some authorities suggest that this may either be the accused himself or another person. See Kruger *Organised Crime and Proceeds of Crime Law in South Africa* 15. However, if the person concerned is the accused himself, it is difficult to conceive how this section would differ from s 2(1)(*e*).

32 There must be a link between the offences committed as part of the pattern of racketeering activities alleged on one hand, and the affairs of the enterprise on the other. If the person committing the affairs was simply engaging in a frolic of his own, such conduct cannot be used to sustain a charge of racketeering. It is important, therefore, to try to link each offence relied on to the objectives of the enterprise. Typically, the main objectives of a criminal enterprise are to make a profit and to ensure its continued survival. Therefore, any offences committed to make money, cut expenses or protect the enterprise, and by extension its members, from detection, prosecution or competition would normally qualify.

33 That is to say (1) one or more of such persons committed at least two offences listed in Schedule 1, (2) one offence was committed after 21 January 1999, (3) another offence was committed within 10 years of the last offence and (4) the offences committed were part of a 'planned, ongoing, continuous or repeated' course of conduct.

34 See *S v Eyssen* 2009 (1) SACR 406 (SCA) at 6:

> **It is difficult to envisage a wider definition. A single person is covered. So, it seems is every other type of connection between persons known to the law or existing in fact; those which the legislature has not included specifically would be incorporated by the introductory word 'includes'.**

association-in-fact enterprise, comprising an informal group of individuals who associate with each other on an ongoing basis for the purpose of profiting from crime.[35] It is not required that the *sole* purpose of the enterprise, whatever its form, is the commission of crime. For instance, it is quite permissible to characterise as an enterprise a company that conducts a perfectly legitimate panel beating business during working hours but operates as a chop shop where stolen or hijacked vehicles are dismantled after hours.

- *Managed the operations or activities of the enterprise*: The term 'manage' is not defined and its ordinary meaning is to be applied.[36] The accused need not be the overall manager of the enterprise but must perform some sort of managerial function in the enterprise. In a formal organisation, such a manager would normally[37] be identifiable by the position he holds in the organisation and his duties. In an association-in-fact enterprise, evidence will have to be led that establishes that a person charged under this section had *de facto* authority to direct the activities of other members of the group.
- *Employed by or associated with*: These terms are also not defined, and regard must therefore be had to their ordinary meaning. In respect of a formal organisation, the 'employed by' requirement will usually be established by his or her position in the organisation. In an association-in-fact enterprise, it should be sufficient for the prosecution to prove that the person in question[38] performed some service for the enterprise and received some reward in return. We submit that it would be inappropriate to attempt to apply a formal requirement of employment as it is understood in labour law.

  The term 'associated with' is a wide one, which will have to be determined on the facts of each case. Again, with a formal enterprise, proof of association would normally not be too difficult. Thus, an accountant who audits the enterprise's books and assists in laundering the proceeds of its unlawful activities would be 'associated with' that enterprise.

  In an association-in-fact enterprise, proof of association would normally necessarily follow from proof of the enterprise since this necessarily requires proof of the association

35 In establishing whether the prosecution has proved the existence of an association-in-fact enterprise, factors such as the following will be relevant: the existence of an ascertainable structure and/or hierarchy, a common goal (for instance, the importation and sale of drugs for profit), the longevity of the enterprise, a degree of continuity in personnel and modus operandi. This is not to say, however, that changes in personnel or modus operandi will preclude the existence of an enterprise, as defined, although this may make the proof thereof more onerous. In US jurisprudence, the Supreme Court has ruled that the enterprise must be established separately from the pattern of racketeering activities. The existence of the enterprise may not therefore be inferred from its activities alone. However, in appropriate cases, the same evidence may be relied on to prove both elements. See *United States v Turkette* 452 U.S. 576 (1981). The SCA followed this approach in *S v Eyssen* supra at 6. In this instance, the court found (at 13) that the state had failed to establish the existence of an enterprise.

36 *S v Eyssen* supra at 5 relied on the *Concise Oxford Dictionary* edited by Pearshall 10 ed (2002) definition (reprinted by permission of Oxford University Press):

> **1 be in charge of, run; 2 supervise (staff); 3 be the manager of (a sports team or a performer). The mere fact that a person participated or was somehow connected with the operation or activities of an enterprise will not suffice. It must be proved that he managed, in the sense referred to above, the operation or activities of an enterprise.**

Note that it appears that the definition is not repeated in full. In the unreported CPD decision, the court stated as follows:

> **The state must prove that the accused managed the operation or activities of an enterprise. According to the Concise Oxford English Dictionary manage means '1 be in charge of; 2 supervise (staff); 3 be the manager of (a sports team or a performer); 4 administer and regulate (resources under one's control); 5 maintain control or influence over a (person or animal)'. The mere fact that a person participated or was somehow connected with the operation or activities of an enterprise, will not suffice. It must be proved that he managed, in the sense referred to above, the operation or activities of an enterprise.**

37 But not necessarily – it is conceivable that an ostensibly lower-ranking member of an organisation may hold authority over his notional superiors with respect to the criminal activities of the enterprise.

38 Either the accused himself in a s 2(1)(*e*) prosecution or another person employed by or associated with the enterprise in a prosecution under s 2(1)(*f*).

between the members of the enterprise. Furthermore, given that the state will also have to prove that the accused personally committed at least two or more racketeering acts in the course of conducting the affairs of the enterprise, this may in itself be sufficient to infer the necessary association.

- *Conducted, or participated in, directly or indirectly, the affairs of the enterprise*: This requirement has caused some difficulty in the US jurisprudence and has led to a number of conflicting decisions in the different circuits. The central issue of the debate revolved around whether this requirement limited liability only to persons who were part of the enterprise (and hence who participated in the 'operation or management' of the enterprise)[39] or whether persons outside the enterprise, but who associated themselves with the enterprise, were also covered. We submit that the US interpretation is unduly restrictive, resulting from the misapplication of the RICO legislation in civil cases. The words 'directly or indirectly' are clearly broad enough to encompass an outside associate of the enterprise who furthers the affairs of the enterprise through the commission of two or more racketeering acts.
- *Pattern of racketeering activity*: The definition of a pattern of racketeering activity is provided above. This requirement has been interpreted in the US jurisprudence as requiring *each person* in question to have personally[40] committed two or more racketeering acts.[41] This is also the way in which the legislation has been applied in South Africa to date by the prosecuting authority.[42] What remains to be emphasised, however, is that the conduct or participation by the person in question must be '*through*' a pattern[43] of racketeering activity.[44] This requires that there must be some relationship between the Schedule 1 offences committed and the affairs of the enterprise. A series of random offences, unrelated to the objectives of the enterprise, would not suffice.

39 The so-called 'Reves test', named after the 1993 US Supreme Court decision of *Reves v Ernst & Young* 494 U.S. 56 (1990), a civil RICO case in which the court adopted a restrictive interpretation.

40 This is not to say, however, that the accused must necessarily have *personally* committed the *actus reus*. We submit that legal responsibility for the offence will suffice. Thus, if the prosecution relies on a murder as a predicate offence, it would be sufficient to prove that the relevant accused had a common purpose to commit the murder even though another person may have inflicted the fatal wound.

41 Either the accused himself in a s 2(1)(*e*) prosecution or another person employed by or associated with the enterprise in a prosecution under s 2(1)(*f*). However, an important qualification to this rule exists in US jurisprudence, which is known as the 'Single Episode Rule', which states the following: when a single act or course of conduct may be charged as multiple offences or counts under the law governing those offences, it will be presumed that multiple racketeering acts may be charged corresponding to those multiple offences. The rationale behind this rule is that the requisite element of continuity would be satisfied in these circumstances. Thus, if this rule is to be applied by our courts, it would be permissible to charge the accused with, for instance, a single predicate offence of fraud committed over a period of time, but to rely on each misrepresentation as a separate racketeering act. An important exception to the single episode rule exists: when a single discrete short-lived course of conduct or act gives rise to multiple offences, those offences must be subpredicated and multiple racketeering acts may not be alleged. Thus, where a person sells cocaine, mandrax and dagga to a police trap in the course of one transaction, only one racketeering act may be alleged even though three separate Schedule 1 offences are committed. Similarly, this exception would apply where a person robs a bank using an unlicensed firearm and shoots a security guard in the process.

42 However, in the case of *Boekhout v S* case no SS134/06 dated 12/04/2010 Gauteng South High Court, Borchers J found that personal commission of two or more racketeering acts was not required by s 2(1)(*e*). The court held (at 26) that 'something less than guilt and conviction is required' and that '... involvement [in Schedule 1 offences] which falls short of actual participation, is also sufficient to satisfy the requirements of POCA'. This view was expressed obiter dicta, however. This interpretation is in conflict with the US jurisprudence and it remains to be seen whether it will find favour with other courts.

43 Having regard to the dictionary definition of 'pattern', the court held in *S v Eyssen* supra at 8 that 'neither unrelated instances of proscribed behaviour nor an accidental coincidence between them constitute a "pattern"...'.

44 This requirement has also given rise to considerable litigation in the US, but its meaning is now well established. Although the various circuits have developed different tests, all require that there must be a sufficient nexus between the pattern of racketeering activities and the affairs of the enterprise.

While the precise nature of this relationship has yet to be established in South African jurisprudence, we submit that this requirement will be satisfied where the offences in question were committed to advance the aims of the enterprise, such as making money, eliminating competition, protection from detection or prosecution, and the like.[45]

- *Knew or ought reasonably to have known*: The expanded definition of knowledge has already been discussed above. The question remains, however: what precisely is the accused required to have known? Is it necessary to prove knowledge of the actual individual offences committed or will it suffice to show a more general knowledge that certain types of offences are being committed in the course of conducting the enterprise's affairs? We submit that the latter interpretation is more consistent with the clear intention of the legislature to exclude willful blindness as a defence. It would, in most cases, be extremely difficult to prove that the manager bore specific knowledge of each racketeering act alleged.

45.3.2.2 Section 2(1)(e) of POCA: Conducting or participating in the conduct of an enterprise

This is the most important and most often used racketeering offence. It mirrors section 1962(*c*) of RICO almost word for word,[46] save that the US legislation does not include the word 'managing'.[47] Unlike section 2(1)(*f*), this section requires actual participation in the affairs of the organisation by committing two or more predicate offences listed in Schedule 1.[48]

45.3.2.2.1 Definition

This offence consists of conducting or participating in the conduct, directly or indirectly, of an enterprise's affairs through a pattern of racketeering activity, while managing, employed by or associated with such enterprise.

45.3.2.2.2 Essential elements

To prove a contravention of section 2(1)(*e*), the following elements must be proved:

- An enterprise existed.
- The accused managed, was employed by or was associated with the enterprise.
- The accused conducted or participated in the conduct, directly or indirectly, of the enterprise's affairs.

---

45 For instance, selling drugs for the benefit of the enterprise and laundering the proceeds of drug sales (Pietermaritzburg Regional Court case of *S v Ranjini Chetty and others* case no RC394/06 dated 8 July 2009, petition for leave to appeal refused by the NPD); robbery involving the hijacking of a truckload of cigarettes, which were sold for the profit of the enterprise (*S v De Vries* (SCA) supra); housebreaking and robbery (*S v Eyssen* supra) although in this case, the court held that the evidence was insufficient to establish that the offences that had been committed formed part of the operation or activities of the enterprise.

46 S 2(1)(*e*), however, omits the elements in the RICO section relating to 'interstate or foreign commerce' and 'the collection of unlawful debt'.

47 The inclusion of the word 'managing' in POCA may be significant, not only in introducing a different class of persons who may be prosecuted under this section, but also in interpreting the terms 'employed by' and especially 'associated with'. As discussed above, the US jurisprudence (in *Reves v Ernst & Young* supra and its progeny) has interpreted the terms 'associated with' as excluding outsiders to the enterprise unless they participated in the operation or management of the enterprise itself. Since management is now specifically included in the description of the offence, it may be argued that this is an indication that the legislature intended the term 'associated with' to be given its ordinary meaning and not to restrict it artificially to persons participating in the operations or management of the enterprise itself.

48 The question whether actual conviction for such offences is required or whether some other form of participation falling short of the actual commission of the offences in question will suffice was raised but not authoritatively decided in *Boekhout v S* supra.

Such conduct or participation was through a pattern of racketeering activity:

- The accused personally committed two or more offences listed in Schedule 1[49] while employed by or associated with the enterprise and:
  - (i) at least one offence was committed after 21 January 1999
  - (ii)another offence occurred within 10 years of the commission of the last offence.
- The committed offences were connected in that they were part of a planned, ongoing, continuous or repeated occurrence.[50]
- Some nexus exists between the offences committed and the affairs of the enterprise.[51]

45.3.2.2.3 Discussion

The relevant concepts have been dealt with above in the discussion of section 2(1)(*f*).

The difference and potential overlap between sections 2(1)(*e*) and 2(1)(*f*) is best illustrated with reference to a judgment concerning a so-called 'Ponzi' scheme.

S v Prinsloo

In *S v Prinsloo*[52] the Supreme Court of Appeal (SCA) considered two forms of racketeering: contravention of s 2(1)(*e*) and s 2(1)(*f*) of POCA, namely *conducting or participating in the conduct of an enterprise and managing an enterprise*. It should be noted that *Prinsloo* concerned a lengthy indictment of 218 683 charges, ranging from the charges under POCA to a number of other statutory offences and the common law crime of fraud.

The factual matrix, on which the indictment was based, was intricate and complex. In essence, it concerned a so-called 'Ponzi' scheme. The SCA referenced the etymology of the term, thus:

> **In 1919 Italian immigrant Charles Ponzi of Boston, Massachusetts, United States of America (US), devised a scheme by which he enticed some 11 000 Bostonians to invest approximately USD20 million with him, promising exceptionally high rates of return within a short period of time by purchasing international reply coupons from other countries and then redeeming them in the US for postage stamps. Initially he was able to pay these exorbitant returns to previous investors by simply drawing from the capital investments received from subsequent investors. However, seeing that the scheme was not based upon any viable underlying economic enterprise, it eventually had to collapse when no more investors could be persuaded to make further investments. Hence, schemes of this nature have, down the years, become known as Ponzi schemes.**[53]

In *Prinsloo*, a similar scheme was devised and effected from 1 March 1998 to 22 May 2002. Initially only the first appellant was involved, but she was later joined by the second to sixth appellants. During the four years, approximately R1,5 billion was invested in the fraudulent multiplication scheme and many investors ultimately lost all their money. The multiplication ('Ponzi') scheme and the resultant losses gave rise to the large number of charges against the appellants. It should be noted that much of the intricacies and details surrounding the structures that made

49 See above, however, regarding the US Single Episode Rule exception.

50 *S v Eyssen* supra.

51 There must be a link between the offences committed as part of the pattern of racketeering activities alleged on one hand, and the affairs of the enterprise on the other. If the person committing the affairs was simply engaging in a frolic of his own, such conduct cannot be used to sustain a charge of racketeering. It is important, therefore, to try to link each offence relied on to the objectives of the enterprise. Typically, the main objectives of a criminal enterprise are to make a profit and to ensure its continued survival. Therefore, any offences committed to make money, cut expenses or protect the enterprise (and by extension its members) from detection, prosecution or competition would normally qualify. See further, *S v Dos Santos* supra; *S v De Vries* (SCA) supra at 48.

52 *S v Prinsloo and others* 2016 (2) SACR 25 (SCA).

53 *S v Prinsloo* supra 1.

the scheme possible (various trusts, closed corporations and companies) were common cause. The remaining and fundamental questions, therefore, were, first, the role that each of the appellants played in these structures and, second, the knowledge that they had about the various activities.

Count 1 in *Prinsloo*, which was directed at the first accused only, was a charge formulated with reference to s 2(1)(*f*) of POCA. Count 2 was put to all the appellants, including the first appellant, and was formulated with reference to s 2(1)(*e*) of POCA. The SCA has had the opportunity to interrogate and explain the difference between the two racketeering offences in *S v Eyssen*,[54] which was decided in 2009. In this case, the court demarcated the two offences with reference to *conduct* and *knowledge*:

> The essence of the offence in ss (*e*) is that the accused must conduct (or participate in the conduct) of an enterprise's affairs. Actual participation is required (although it may be direct or indirect). In that respect the subsection differs from ss (*f*), the essence of which is that the accused must know (or ought reasonably to have known) that another person did so. Knowledge, not participation, is required. On the other hand, ss (*e*) is wider than ss (*f*) in that ss (*e*) covers a person who was managing, or employed by, or associated with the enterprise, whereas ss (*f*) is limited to a person who manages the operations or activities of an enterprise.[55]

Having considered the explanation of the differences between the two forms of racketeering in s 2(1)(*e*) and s 2(1)(*f*), the court in *Prinsloo* then turned to the meaning of two key concepts underlying these offences, namely 'manage' and 'enterprise'. While 'enterprise' is defined in POCA, 'manage' is not. The court therefore relied on the dictionary meaning of the concept: '1 [To] be in charge of; run. [Or] 2 Supervise staff. [Or] 3 [To] be the manager of a (sports team or a performer)'.[56] In terms of s 1 of POCA, '"enterprise" includes any individual, partnership, corporation, association, or other juristic person or legal entity, and any union or group of individuals associated in fact, although not a juristic person or legal entity'. With reference to the *dicta* in *Eyssen*, the SCA in *Prinsloo* noted how incredibly wide the definition of 'enterprise' is under POCA. Indeed, a 'single person, as well as every other type of connection between persons known to the law or existing in fact, is included'.[57] With reference to the statutory provisions, the *dicta* in *Eyssen* and the factual matrix in *Prinsloo*, the SCA stated the following regarding the first count of racketeering:

> [I]t is common cause that the first accused managed the operation or activities of the scheme. It was her brainchild and at all relevant times she was at the forefront of its day-to-day activities. The court a quo aptly described her as 'die dryfveer en moederbrein van die onderneming' ['the driving force and mother brain of the enterprise']. It was not disputed by her that the activities conducted through the various entities utilised by the scheme constituted an 'enterprise' as defined in s 1 of the POCA. The evidence showed that the accused were all consciously associated for the purpose of conducting the scheme for their common benefit. The first accused also did not seriously dispute the finding of the court a quo that a 'pattern of racketeering activities', as defined in s 1 of the POCA, had taken place in conducting the business of the scheme. As will become clear in due course, a multitude of offences referred to in [schedule] 1 of the POCA had been committed by the accused in conducting the scheme through its various entities, which offences had occurred prior to and after the commencement of the POCA, and within a 10-year period as prescribed by the POCA.[58]

54 *S v Eyssen* 2009 (1) SACR 406 (SCA).
55 *S v Eyssen* supra 5.
56 *S v Prinsloo* supra 46, quoting from the *Concise Oxford English Dictionary* 10 ed (2002) sv 'manage'.
57 *S v Prinsloo* supra 47.
58 *S v Prinsloo* supra 48.

The other important element that the state had to prove for a conviction of the first appellant on the first count of racketeering was the element of *mens rea*. Did she know or ought she reasonably to have known that a pattern of racketeering activity took place? In the trial court, and on appeal, counsel for the first appellant submitted that a contravention of s 2(1)(*f*) of POCA requires *mens rea* in the form of intent; negligence was not sufficient. This submission was rejected by the trial court. It was held that negligence is a sufficient form of *mens rea* for a contravention of the form of racketeering provided for in s 2(1)(*f*). It is important to note, however, that the trial court held, on the facts of the case that the first appellant had known, without any doubt, that the second to sixth appellants were in the service of the enterprise and that they had participated in the activities of the enterprise by way of the pattern of racketeering. The SCA therefore concluded that the trial court had correctly made a finding of *mens rea* in the form of intent on the part of the first appellant.[59] The SCA stated:

> In managing the affairs of the scheme by leading from the front, she had been fully aware that the affairs of the scheme had been conducted through a pattern of racketeering activity. Apart from common-law crimes such as theft and fraud having been committed in the furtherance of the business of the scheme, a multitude of statutory offences were also committed, and the excuse of the first accused, that she had not been aware of the unlawfulness of such conduct, does not only ring hollow, but was also correctly rejected as false beyond any reasonable doubt.[60]

The SCA furthermore confirmed that the wording of POCA (and in particular s 2(1)(*f*)) makes it clear that negligence is sufficient for a contravention of this subsection of s 2. This view is supported by s 1(3) of POCA.[61] The first appellant's conviction of count 1 (racketeering under s 2(1)(*f*) of POCA) was upheld by the Supreme Court of Appeal.

> The second count concerned the crime of racketeering under s 2(1)(e) of POCA - conducting or participating in the conduct of an enterprise. The state had to prove that, while managing the Ponzi scheme, the first appellant directly or indirectly participated in the conduct of the scheme's affairs through a pattern of racketeering activity. *Actual participation* (direct or indirect) is essential for purposes of s 2(1)(e), as opposed to *knowledge of the enterprise's activities*, which is the crux of the crime under s 2(1)(*f*).

The SCA found that an enterprise (the Ponzi scheme) existed in the case of *Prinsloo*. This scheme was managed and controlled by the first appellant, while conducting its affairs through a pattern of racketeering activity. The remaining question before the SCA was whether the first appellant participated in the scheme's affairs, and if so, to what degree. The SCA, in short, stated that the first appellant was indeed 'the heart and soul' of the business of the scheme and knowingly participated in contravening various statutory provisions and committing common law crimes. She was at the forefront of the Ponzi scheme at all relevant times.[62] The SCA held:

> To summarise, it is now well settled that the essence of the offence in terms of s 2(1)(*e*) of the POCA is participation through a pattern of racketeering activity, and not knowledge. Once it is

59 *S v Prinsloo* supra 50.

60 *S v Prinsloo* supra 50.

61 S 1(3) POCA provides as follows:

> For the purposes of this Act a person ought reasonably to have known or suspected a fact if the conclusions that he or she ought to have reached are those which would have been reached by a reasonably diligent and vigilant person having both—
> (*a*) the general knowledge, skill, training and experience that may reasonably be expected of a person in his or her position; and
> (*b*) the general knowledge, skill, training and experience that he or she in fact has.

62 *S v Prinsloo* supra 62.

> **proved that the accused has participated in the conduct of an enterprise's affairs through a pattern of racketeering activity, ie by committing two or more predicate offences listed in [schedule] 1 of the POCA, he or she is guilty of a contravention of s 2(1)(*e*) of the POCA. There is no need for a further inquiry, as suggested on behalf of the first accused, as to an additional *mens rea* requirement over and above the *mens rea* required by the predicate offences.**[63]

The SCA held that the state had proved, beyond reasonable doubt, the elements of the crime of racketeering under s 2(1)(*e*) of POCA. The appeal was dismissed.

It is noticeable that the majority of the SCA in *Prinsloo* confirmed the conviction of the first appellant on both counts under ss 2(1)(e) and 2(1)(*f*). Both counts were essentially based on the same facts. The majority of the SCA thus held that a conviction on both counts did not amount to a duplication of convictions.[64]

45.3.2.3 Section 2(1)(*d*) of POCA: Acquiring or maintaining an interest in or control of an enterprise

Section 2(1)(*d*) is seldom used in practice. This offence is aimed at preventing criminals or criminal organisations from taking over or controlling legitimate businesses through criminal means such as extortion, intimidation or some or other form of corruption, a practice that was not uncommon in the US in the heydays of organised crime.[65]

45.3.2.3.1 Definition

This offence consists of acquiring or maintaining, directly or indirectly, any interest in or control of any enterprise through a pattern of racketeering activity.

45.3.2.3.2 Essential elements

To prove a contravention of section 2(1)(*d*), the following elements must be proved:

- An enterprise existed.
- The accused has an interest in the enterprise.
- The accused acquired or maintained his interest in or control over the enterprise through a pattern of racketeering activity:
  - The accused personally committed two or more offences listed in Schedule 1:[66]
    - At least one offence was committed after 21 January 1999.
    - Another offence occurred within 10 years of the commission of the last offence.
  - The committed offences were connected in that they were part of a planned, ongoing, continuous or repeated occurrence.[67]
- Some nexus exists between the offences committed and the acquisition or maintenance of the accused's interest or control in the enterprise.

63 *S v Prinsloo* supra 64. As mentioned above, POCA is closely modelled on the United States (US) Racketeer Influenced and Corrupt Organizations Act (RICO). RICO has a provision similar to s 2(1)*(e)* of POCA. In a number of US cases, it was decided that no specific intent to engage in an unlawful pattern of racketeering prohibited by RICO is required. The *mens rea* underlying the predicate offences would be enough. See, for instance, *United States v Biasucci* 786 F 2d 504 (1986) (US Court of Appeals, Second Circuit) at para 8; *United States v Boylan* 620 F 2d 359 (1980) (US Court of Appeals, Second Circuit) at para 5; *United States v Scotto* 641 F 2d 47 (1980) (US Court of Appeals, Second Circuit) paras 4–6.

64 For the dissenting minority opinion, per Brand JA, see *S v Prinsloo* supra at 395.

65 For instance, so-called 'protection rackets' where criminal organisations extorted money from businesses for protection from the criminal organisations themselves. These rackets gave the crime of racketeering its name.

66 See, however, above remarks about the US Single Episode Rule exception.

67 *S v Eyssen* supra.

45.3.2.3.3 Discussion

Unlike sections 2(1)(*e*) and 2(1)(*f*) discussed above, in a prosecution under section 2(1)(*d*) of POCA, it is not necessary to prove that the *enterprise* or its members were committing crime. The emphasis, rather, is on the criminal manner in which the interest in the enterprise is *obtained or maintained*. Furthermore, the offence is not limited to organised criminal gangs. An individual accused who acquires or maintains an interest through such means may be charged under this section. Thus if X, through a series of acts of intimidation or extortion, induces Y to give him shares in Y's company, X will be guilty of a contravention of this section.

45.3.3 Property offences

These offences are aimed at persons who either benefit from the proceeds of a criminal enterprise, or who assist others by receiving or investing the proceeds of such enterprise on their behalf. They are once again modelled on provisions of the US RICO statute.[68]

Historically, in the US, these sections were enacted before there was any other legislation that specifically criminalised money laundering. These days, however, it would in most cases be easier to prosecute under the money laundering legislation (POCA and FICA)[69] than in terms of these racketeering property offences. As a result, the property offences of the RICO statute are not commonly used in the US, and they appear to have been grafted into POCA without too much regard for their effectiveness.

One of the reasons why a prosecution under sections 2(1)(*a*)-(*c*) is unattractive is that to obtain a conviction under these sections, it is first necessary to prove the existence of a section 2(1)(*e*) enterprise and then establish the additional elements relating to the receipt, retention, use or investment of the proceeds of such enterprise. Since section 2(1)(*e*) is already framed in such wide terms, it would normally be possible to secure a conviction under this section without proving the additional elements. Furthermore, since the wording of these sections overlaps substantially with the money laundering provisions in sections 4–6 of POCA,[70] these may be relied on as predicate offences to establish the pattern of racketeering offences necessary for a conviction under section 2(1)(*e*) or section 2(1)(*g*). However, the accused could just as well simply be charged for money laundering, which carried penalties not much less severe than racketeering.

45.3.3.1 Section 2(1)(*b*) of POCA: Receipt and use of property derived from a pattern of racketeering activity

This is the most basic of the property offences. It criminalises simply receiving or retaining property derived from a pattern of racketeering activities on behalf of an enterprise. Thus, for example, if a lawyer, X, receives the proceeds of the ongoing sale of drugs into his trust account on behalf of a drug-dealing enterprise and with the necessary *mens rea*, he will commit this offence. Similarly, if the prosecution believes that Y is the kingpin of a criminal enterprise, but is unable to establish that he actually managed it, he may be prosecuted under section 2(1)(*b*) if it can be proven that he was knowingly living off the proceeds of such an enterprise. As will be seen below, sections 2(1)(*a*) and 2(1)(*c*) require the prosecution to establish further elements relating to the manner in which such proceeds are used.

68 Ss 1962 (*a*) and (*b*) of RICO.

69 See the brief discussion of the main money laundering offence below in section 45.4.

70 See the discussion below in section 45.4.

45.3.3.1.1 Definition

This offence consists of receiving or retaining any property, directly or indirectly, on behalf of an enterprise by an accused who knows or ought reasonably to have known that such property derived or is derived from or through a pattern of racketeering activity.

45.3.3.1.2 Essential elements

To prove a contravention of section 2(1)(*b*), the following elements must be proved:

- An enterprise existed.
- A pattern of racketeering activity existed:
    - At least two or more offences listed in Schedule 1[71] were committed by some person or persons:
        - At least one offence was committed after 21 January 1999.
        - Another offence occurred within 10 years of the commission of the last offence.
    - The committed offences were connected in that they were part of a planned, ongoing, continuous or repeated occurrence.[72]
    - The accused received or retained property directly or indirectly.
    - The property was derived from or through a pattern of racketeering activity.
    - Such receipt or retention was on behalf of the enterprise.
    - The accused knew, or ought reasonably to have known,[73] that such property was derived from a pattern of racketeering activity.

45.3.3.1.3 Discussion

The relevant concepts have already been discussed in detail above.

45.3.3.2 Section 2(1)(*a*) of POCA: Use or investment of property derived from a pattern of racketeering activity

Section 2(1)(*a*) is aimed at combating the use of the proceeds of racketeering to acquire an interest in another legitimate enterprise. In addition to the receipt of the affected property with the requisite *mens rea*, the prosecution must also show that some portion of it was used to acquire an interest in another, usually legitimate, enterprise. Thus, if X were to use the proceeds acquired through conducting illegal gambling activities to acquire a stake in a legitimate casino, this offence would be committed.

45.3.3.2.1 Definition

This offence consists of receiving or retaining any property derived, directly or indirectly, from a pattern of racketeering activity while the accused knows or ought reasonably to have known that such property is so derived, and then using or investing, directly or indirectly, any part of such property in acquisition of any interest in, or the establishment or operation or activities of, any enterprise.

45.3.3.2.2 Essential elements

To prove a contravention of section 2(1)(*a*), the following elements must be proved:

- An enterprise existed.
- A pattern of racketeering activity existed:

71 See, however, remarks above regarding the US Single Episode Rule exception.

72 *S v Eyssen* supra.

73 The extended definition of knowledge as set out in ss 1(2) and 1(3) will apply. See the discussion above.

- At least two or more offences listed in Schedule 1[74] were committed by some person or persons:
  - At least one offence was committed after 21 January 1999.
  - Another offence occurred within 10 years of the commission of the last offence.
- The committed offences were connected in that they were part of a planned, ongoing, continuous or repeated occurrence.[75]
- The accused received or retained the property.
- Such property was derived, directly or indirectly, from a pattern of racketeering activity.
- The accused knew, or reasonably ought to have known, that such property was so derived.
- The accused used or invested any part of the property, directly or indirectly, in the acquisition of an interest in, or the establishment, operation or activities of any enterprise.

45.3.3.2.3 Discussion

The relevant concepts have already been discussed in detail above.

45.3.3.3 Section 2(1)(c) of POCA: Use or investment of property to acquire, establish or operate an enterprise

Section 2(1)(*c*) is aimed at combating laundering the proceeds of a criminal enterprise on the one hand and using the proceeds of racketeering to establish or operate any enterprise on the other. It would appear that one must distinguish between these two activities on the following basis: in the first instance, it would appear necessary to establish that a section 2(1)(*e*) type of enterprise existed that carries on its operations through a pattern of racketeering activities, and that the accused used or invested property derived from such criminal activities on behalf of the criminal enterprise.[76] In the second instance, the existence of a section 2(1)(*e*) type of enterprise need not be established. It will suffice to prove that property was derived from a pattern of racketeering activities, even if this is conducted by an individual, and that this property is then used to establish or maintain an enterprise, whether legitimate or not. Thus, where X, a drug dealer, uses the accumulated proceeds of his drug sales to set up a boutique for his daughter or to subsidise the running expenses thereof, he would commit this offence. Similarly, where an accountant, Y, uses such proceeds to set up a company on X's behalf, with the necessary *mens rea*, this offence is committed.[77]

45.3.3.3.1 Definition

This offence consists of using or investing any property, directly or indirectly, on behalf of any enterprise, or in the acquisition of any interest in, or the establishment or operation of any activities of any enterprise by an accused, who knows or ought reasonably to have known that such property was derived from a pattern of racketeering activity.

---

74 See the US Single Episode Rule exception.

75 *S v Eyssen* supra.

76 Bear in mind that such an enterprise may also have legitimate business, provided it can be established that at least some of its affairs were conducted through a pattern of racketeering activity.

77 However, in US jurisprudence, there are conflicting decisions regarding whether it is possible to charge a person under this section where he was not himself involved in the principal offence. As a matter of policy, indictment of such a person will not be approved unless he is also indicted for the underlying racketeering offence. No such policy, however, exists in South Africa, and there appears to be no reason why such a person could not be successfully prosecuted under this section.

45.3.3.3.2 Essential elements

To prove a contravention of section 2(1)(*c*), the following elements must be proved:

- An enterprise existed.
- A pattern of racketeering activity existed:
  - At least two or more offences listed in Schedule 1[78] were committed by some person or persons:
    - At least one offence was committed after 21 January 1999.
    - Another offence occurred within 10 years of the commission of the last offence.
  - The committed offences were connected in that they were part of a planned, ongoing, continuous or repeated occurrence.[79]
  - The property was derived from or through a pattern of racketeering activity.
  - The accused used or invested the property.
  - The accused did so, directly or indirectly:
    - on behalf of the enterprise OR
    - to acquire any interest in the enterprise OR
    - to establish the enterprise OR
    - for the operation or activities of the enterprise.
  - The accused knew, or ought reasonably to have known,[80] that such property was derived from or through a pattern of racketeering activity.

45.3.3.3.3 Discussion

The relevant concepts have already been discussed in detail above.

45.3.4 Conspiracy/attempt offence

45.3.4.1 Section 2(1)(*g*) of POCA: Conspiracy or attempt to commit racketeering

The final section 2(1)(*g*) makes it an offence to conspire or attempt to commit any of the preceding subsections. In doing so, it extends even further the ambit of sections such as 2(1)(*e*), which is already framed in extremely wide terms. Since conspiracy or attempt is most often alleged in relation to this section,[81] we will concentrate on this in the discussion that follows.

Section 2(1)(*g*) is once again based almost verbatim on section 1962(*d*) of the US RICO statute. Although it is a simply worded section, it has given rise to an enormous amount of litigation in the US. American cases on this issue must, however, be treated with circumspection because of the very different approach adopted to conspiracy prosecutions in that country.

Section 2(1)(*g*) criminalises an *agreement or attempt to commit racketeering*. In the context of section 2(1)(*e*), this would comprise an agreement or attempt to conduct or participate in the conduct of an enterprise's affairs through a pattern of racketeering activities. It is important to emphasise that the conspiracy or attempt must be aimed at the

78 See the US Single Episode Rule exception.

79 *S v Eyssen* supra.

80 The extended definition of knowledge as set out in ss 1(2) and 1(3) will apply. See the discussion above.

81 In the US, it is common to allege both ss 1962(*c*) and (*d*) violations as separate substantive charges, leading, in successful cases, to conviction on both counts and consecutive sentences. This is treated as an exception to the double jeopardy rule as this is regarded as statutorily authorised and consistent with congressional intent. See, for example, *United States v Pungitore* 910 F.2d 1084 1115–7 (3rd Circuit 1990). In South Africa, it is doubtful whether the courts would convict on both the charge of a s 2(1)(*g*) conspiracy as well as the completed offence in the absence of an explicit stipulation in the Act that provides for this.

commission of the relevant racketeering offence and *not* just one or more of the underlying Schedule 1 offences.[82] A section 2(1)(g) charge would normally be added where, for example, the prosecution was unable to prove that the conspirator personally committed two racketeering acts. So, for instance, if X joins a motorcycle gang that he knows is engaged in the business of smuggling drugs into the country but is arrested in possession of drugs on his first border crossing, it may be possible to secure a conviction under this section for conspiracy to violate section 2(1)(*e*) even though he has committed only one racketeering act.

To prove the alleged conspiracy or attempt, the normal elements would have to be established by the prosecution.[83]

DISCUSSION

The constitutionality of racketeering legislation

Racketeering legislation allows the conviction of an accused based on his relationship with a criminal enterprise even if he or she has not personally committed any predicated crimes. It also permits a court that is trying a racketeering case to hear evidence, including evidence with regard to hearsay, similar facts or previous convictions, notwithstanding that such evidence may otherwise be inadmissible, provided that such evidence would not render a trial unfair.[84] Furthermore, US jurisprudence and South African practice to date permits an accused to be convicted both of a racketeering offence under section 2 of POCA and the predicate offences on which the racketeering charge is based.

Consider the extent to which these provisions are consistent with the Bill of Rights. What rights are affected? Is the limitation of these rights reasonable and justifiable given the necessity to combat organised crime effectively?

45.4 Money laundering

45.4.1 A brief introduction and overview

The most important aim of organised crime and, for that matter, individual instances of crimes against property and commercial crime, is financial gain. Crimes such as theft, embezzlement, fraud, corruption and robbery, the predicate crimes, generate proceeds that the criminal would, obviously, want to enjoy at some stage. Thus, the 'ultimate goal of any money laundering operation is twofold: to conceal the predicate offences from which these proceeds are derived and to ensure that the criminals can "enjoy" their proceeds, by consuming or investing them in the legal economy'.[85]

82 Bear in mind that item 34 of Schedule 1 already includes any conspiracy, incitement or attempt to commit any of the foregoing offences as a racketeering act in its own right. Thus, if in a prosecution under s 2(1)(*e*), a manager, employee or associate of the enterprise is proved to have conspired in or attempted to commit two or more Schedule 1 offences, he may be convicted of the main offence.

83 See also Chapter 26.

84 S 2(2) of POCA.

85 Stessens *Money Laundering* 83. For a comparative perspective (South Africa and Germany), see Fernandez L and Heinrich B 'Die strafbarkeit des strafverteidigers wegen geldwäsche durch annahme des honorars nach Südafrikanischem und Deutschem recht' (2014) 126(2) *ZSTW* 382–445.

Money laundering as a criminal phenomenon is often described in terms of a process consisting of various stages as shown in Figure 45.2.[86] The South African Law Commission Project 104 on Money Laundering described the stages as follows:

- *Placement stage*: The proceeds are moved away from the place where they were obtained and placed in the financial system through financial institutions.
- *Layering stage*: The money, in the form of electronic funds, is distributed by layering transactions on top of others by means of, for example, electronic transfers, shield companies and false invoices. Because of such layered transactions, the laundered money becomes indistinguishable from legitimate money.
- *Integration stage*: The money is collected and made available under the guise of legitimate income.[87]

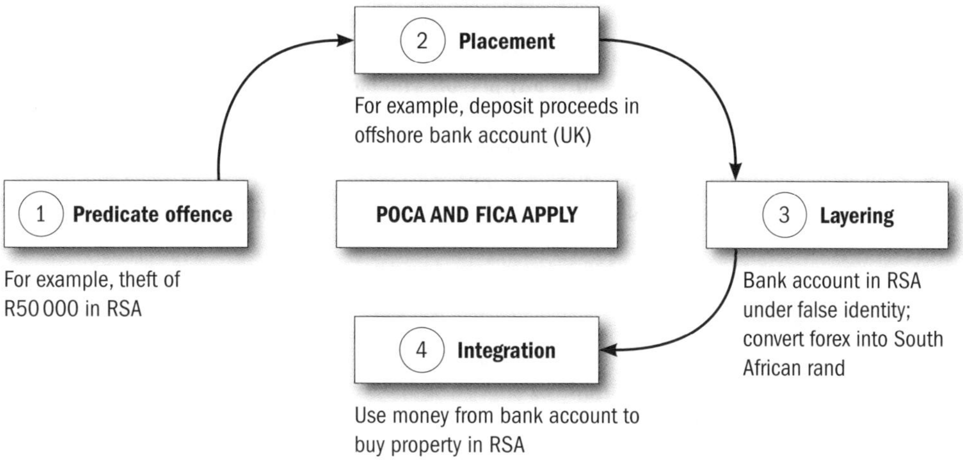

Figure 45.2 The basic process of money laundering

45.4.2 The various money laundering offences

The description of the process of money laundering in Figure 45.2 is not a legal-technical one, but is instead a useful way to illustrate the phenomenon. It is therefore necessary to turn to FICA and section 1 of POCA to find the definitions of the various *crimes* that are collectively known as money laundering. We can start with the definition of money laundering or money laundering activity provided for in section 1 of FICA:

> **'[M]oney laundering' or 'money laundering activity' means an activity which has or is likely to have the effect of concealing or disguising the nature, source, location, disposition or movement of the proceeds of unlawful activities or any interest which anyone has in such proceeds, and includes any activity which constitutes an offence in terms of section 64 of this Act [FICA] or section 4, 5 or 6 of the Prevention Act [POCA].**[88]

The four money laundering offences mentioned in the above definition are discussed below.

---

86 For a comprehensive discussion, see De Koker *South African Money Laundering and Terror Financing Law* (2017). See also Kruger *Organised Crime and Proceeds of Crime Law in South Africa* (2008); Burchell *Principles of Criminal Law* 911–923.

87 South African Law Commission Project 104 *Money Laundering and Related Matters* Report August 1996 at 2.

88 S 1 Financial Intelligence Centre Act 38 of 2001.

45.4.2.1 Section 4 of POCA: The offence of money laundering

Section 4 of POCA provides for the basic crime of money laundering:

> **Any person who knows or ought reasonably to have known that property is or forms part of the proceeds of unlawful activities and—**
>
> **(*a*) enters into any agreement or engages in any arrangement or transaction with anyone in connection with that property, whether such agreement, arrangement or transaction is legally enforceable or not; or**
>
> **(*b*) performs any other act in connection with such property, whether it is performed independently or in concert with any other person, which has or is likely to have the effect—**
>
> **(i) of concealing or disguising the nature, source, location, disposition or movement of the said property or the ownership thereof or any interest which anyone may have in respect thereof; or**
>
> **(ii) of enabling or assisting any person who has committed or commits an offence, whether in the Republic or elsewhere—**
>
> **(*aa*) to avoid prosecution; or**
>
> **(*bb*) to remove or diminish any property acquired directly, or indirectly, as a result of the commission of an offence, shall be guilty of an offence.**

45.4.2.1.1 Essential elements

To prove a contravention of section 4 of POCA, the following elements must be proved:

- The accused must know or ought reasonably to have known that property forms part of the proceeds of unlawful activities.
- The accused must enter into an agreement, arrangement or transaction, or perform any act in connection with the abovementioned property, which has or is likely to have a certain effect:
  - of concealing the nature of and dealings with the proceeds of crime OR
  - of assisting a person who committed a crime to avoid prosecution or to remove or diminish property acquired as a result of criminal activity.[89]

45.4.2.1.2 Some general comments

We pointed out above that one of the principal aims, often the only aim, of many criminal activities is financial gain. The crime of money laundering in terms of POCA concerns property that forms part of the *proceeds of unlawful activities*. The crime of money laundering involves not only money, but 'any property or any service, advantage, benefit or reward which was derived, received or retained, directly or indirectly, in the Republic or elsewhere ... in connection with or as a result of any unlawful activity carried on by any person, and includes any property representing property so derived'.[90] 'Property' is broadly defined as well, and includes, obviously, money, but also 'any other movable, immovable, corporeal or incorporeal thing and includes any rights, privileges, claims and securities and any interest

---

89 Kruger *Organised Crime and Proceeds of Crime Law in South Africa* 37; De Koker *South African Money Laundering and Terror Financing Law* Com 3-10-3-11.

90 S 1 of POCA. See, for instance, *S v De Vries* (SCA) supra at 56 where an accused was convicted under s 4 of POCA where he had used stolen cigarettes 'as part of his stock in trade as a wholesaler as if they were goods lawfully acquired, and thereby disguising or concealing the source, movement and ownership of the cigarettes and enabling and assisting the robbers to either avoid prosecution or to remove property acquired in the robberies'.

therein and all proceeds thereof'.[91] The predicate conduct ('*unlawful activity*') that generates the proceeds is also defined in broad terms, namely 'any conduct which constitutes a crime or which contravenes any law whether such conduct occurred before or after the commencement [of POCA] and whether such conduct occurred in the Republic or elsewhere'.[92]

In Figure 45.2, a simple money laundering scenario is illustrated. A thief stole R50 000 in South Africa and deposited the stolen money into a bank account in the UK. The scenario in Figure 45.2 goes further to illustrate the stages of layering and integration as well. If section 4 of POCA is applied to the scenario, the crime of money laundering has already been committed at Stage 2: Placement. The crime of money laundering can thus be committed by the perpetrator of the underlying unlawful activity himself, and he can be convicted of both the underlying activity, for instance theft, and the crime of money laundering. Although it may not always be possible in complex cases to distinguish between the predicate crime, for instance theft or fraud, and the laundering crime, in principle the predicate crime must have been completed[93] and the proceeds must have been 'derived, received or retained'.[94]

In *S v De Vries*, the appellant received a substantial quantity of stolen cigarettes. He knew the cigarettes were stolen, thus making himself guilty of the crime of theft (which is a continuing crime). The SCA held that by proceeding to use the cigarettes 'as part of his stock in trade as a wholesaler as if they were goods lawfully acquired, and thereby disguising or concealing the source, movement and ownership of the cigarettes and enabling and assisting the robbers to either avoid prosecution or to remove property acquired in the robberies, the appellant clearly made himself guilty of a contravention of [section 4 of POCA]'.[95]

The scope of the crime of money laundering provided for in section 4 of POCA covers virtually any type of economic activity involving financial and property transactions.[96]

S v Van der Linde

In *S v Van der Linde*[97] the accused was charged with numerous counts of fraud, one count of forgery, one count of uttering and a total of 63 counts of money laundering in contravention of s 4(*b*)(i) as read with ss 1 and 8 of POCA.

A fraudulent VAT scheme (masterminded by the accused) underpinned all the predicate charges (fraud, forgery and uttering). The court convicted the accused on the predicate charges, and the question then was whether he was also guilty of the secondary crime of money laundering. The factual basis for the charge of money laundering was rather simple: the deposit into an account of an entity of which the accused was the sole member. The deposits consisted of the proceeds of the fraudulent tax refunds. The legal question was whether a simple deposit into a bank account of the proceeds of crime is enough to constitute the crime of money laundering.

---

91 S 1 of POCA.

92 S 1 of POCA.

93 It is conceivable that a prosecutor will rely on the same evidence to prosecute the predicate crime, for instance theft, and the laundering crime. This means that prosecutions under POCA usually involve considerable overlap in evidence (predicate offence and the POCA offence). It was held in *S v Dos Santos* supra at 43 that such overlap 'does not in and of itself occasion an automatic invocation of an improper splitting of charges or duplication of convictions'. See also the decision by the SCA in *S v De Vries* (SCA) supra at 56.

94 De Koker *South African Money Laundering and Terror Financing Law* Com 3–8.

95 *S v De Vries* (SCA) supra at 56.

96 For examples, see *S v Gayadin* case no 41/900/01 (Regional Court, Durban); *S v Mei Ping Shen* case no 41/1745/02 (Regional Court, Johannesburg); *S v Moosagie and another* (CC 29/2010) [2012] ZAECPEHC 31 (17 May 2012); *S v De Vries* (SCA) supra. These examples include the use of offshore bank accounts, allowing one's bank account to be used for channelling the proceeds of crime, and receiving a share of profits derived from criminal activity.

97 *S v Van der Linde* 2016 (2) SACR 377 (GJ).

The court in *Van der Linde* defined money laundering as 'the process by which the proceeds of crime are converted into assets which appear to have a legitimate origin so that they can be retained permanently, or recycled into further criminal enterprises'.[98] The court proceeded to state the factual and legal positions, relevant for the money laundering charges, as follows:

> The accused is charged with s 4(*b*)(i) – concealing or disguising the nature and source of the funds which he knew to be from the proceeds of unlawful activities. Firstly, it must be shown that he knew or ought to have known that the property formed the proceeds of unlawful activities. The accused was the mastermind of the VAT fraud scheme and had such knowledge as required by s 4. It is common cause that the VAT refunds were the proceeds of crime. The accused initiated and managed the scheme, and as such, knew the refunds represented the proceeds of unlawful activities, namely fraud. In terms of s 4(*b*) he must perform – 'any other act in connection with such property, whether it is performed independently or in concert with another person'. The accused performed the following actions in connection with the proceeds of unlawful activities. He received 26 cheques in respect of the laundering counts 277–280, 283, 288 and 300–322. These proceeds were deposited into the accused's SPI Brokers bank account, of which he was the sole member. The cheque stubs in exh P [exhibit P] reflected the name of the accused as the beneficiary. All cheques drawn after June 2002 were issued after the death of the account holder, Mr Nkosi. The accused had access to all the proceeds for Andeltru, as he had Andeltru's blank, signed chequebook under his control. The state submits that the possession of the said chequebook warrants the inference of the accused having laundered the remaining funds and is thus guilty of counts 263–326.
>
> The final and crucial requirement of s 4(*b*)(i) is whether the accused's actions had the affect (sic) of concealing or disguising the nature, source, location or disposition of the funds. The state alleges that the cash cheques issued in respect of money-laundering counts 267–272, 274–278, 281–288, 290–295 and 300–301 once cashed, have the inherent effect of concealing property.'[99]

Having considered the wording of POCA, case law[100] and academic commentary,[101] the court concluded that 'in order to be found guilty of money-laundering, there must be a clear intention to hide or conceal what is often referred to as "hot" money'. This, according to the court, 'entails the laundering of the illegal funds to convert them into "clean" money, which the criminal can safely spend'.[102] Crucially, the court stated that for a charge under s 4(*b*)(i) to be successful, there has to be an element of concealment. Moreover, this element must either be proven by the state, or be inferred.[103] On this element, the court held as follows:

> In this matter, the moneys were merely divided and spent by the parties. On occasion, cheques were deposited into the SPI Brokers bank account. This was an entity wholly owned by the accused and no extensive investigation would have been required to trace the money. That this was a business belonging to the accused seemed to be well known by his staff at the accounting offices – Ms Gillian Venter certainly did not hesitate to explain that it was a labour-broking business of the accused, when asked if she knew anything about SPI Brokers. It seems that one of the weaknesses of the fraudulent VAT scheme was the ease with which the money trail could be followed. Almost immediately after the VAT refund was deposited into one of the bank accounts of the four entities,

98 *S v Van der Linde* supra 108.

99 *S v Van der Linde* supra 116-117.

100 Including: *S v De Vries and Others* 2012 (1) SACR 186 (SCA), *S v Prinsloo and Others* 2016 (2) SACR 25 (SCA), and *S v Moosagie and Another* (CC29/2010)[2012] ZAECPEHC (17 May 2012) at 31.

101 De Koker *South African Money Laundering and Terror Financing Law* (supra).

102 *S v Van der Linde* supra 124.

103 *S v Van der Linde* supra 124.

> **it was withdrawn in full and cashed, or deposited into the SPI Brokers bank account. There was no attempt whatsoever at concealment. There was no interruption in the flow of money, which may make it difficult for the authorities to investigate or trace. It is therefore my view that the accused cannot be found guilty of the money-laundering counts.**[104]

The court seems to have placed a lot of emphasis on the relative unsophisticated nature of the alleged money laundering scheme, which, in this instance, turned out to be no scheme at all. One can read this judgment to hold that a 'mere' deposit of proceeds of crime into a regular bank account does not constitute money laundering under s 4(*b*)(i) of POCA. An additional element of actual or attempted concealment of the criminal nature or source of the money is required. The court's conclusion in this matter was probably correct. Having said that, it should be noted that there is nothing in the wording of s 4(*b*)(i) that requires a certain threshold of sophistication. Indeed, an apparently simple, unsophisticated and seemingly 'innocent' series of bank deposits may very well be the best form of disguise. The test is clear: any act that *has or is likely* to have the *effect* of concealing or disguising the criminal nature or origins of money, can constitute an act of money laundering. It is not necessary for the State to prove that there was an attempt to construct an elaborate scheme to disguise the criminal origins of the money. Section 4(*b*)(i) requires that the accused (a) knew or reasonably ought to have known that the money was the proceeds of crime, and (b) performed *any other act* in connection with the money, which had or was likely to have the effect of concealing or disguising the criminal nature or origins of the money. It is submitted that 'any other act' could include a deposit into a regular bank account, if the effect (or *likely* effect) is that the bank may not detect the criminal origins of the money. The threshold is not that high, and the intention of the drafters of POCA should be kept in mind.[105]

45.4.2.2 Section 5 of POCA: The offence of assisting another to benefit from proceeds of unlawful activities

Section 5 of POCA provides for the crime of assisting another to benefit from proceeds of unlawful activities:

> **Any person who knows or ought reasonably to have known that another person has obtained the proceeds of unlawful activities, and who enters into any agreement with anyone or engages in any arrangement or transaction whereby—**
> **(*a*) the retention or the control by or on behalf of the said other person of the proceeds of unlawful activities is facilitated; or**
> **(*b*) the said proceeds of unlawful activities are used to make funds available to the said other person or to acquire property on his or her behalf or to benefit him or her in any other way, shall be guilty of an offence.**

45.4.2.2.1 Some general comments

Whereas the money laundering offence provided for in section 4 is primarily aimed at the perpetrator of the underlying predicate offence, for instance theft, the offence provided for in section 5 can only be committed by a *third party*. In other words, the offender is not the perpetrator of the predicate offence.[106] A typical scenario is the organised crime boss who

---

104 *S v Van der Linde* supra 125.

105 Preamble of POCA; *Mohunram and another v National Director of Public Prosecutions and another (Law Review Project as Amicus Curiae)* 2007 (2) SACR 145 (CC).

106 *S v Eyssen* case no CC 31/06 (CPD) unreported case 22 March 2007 at 105; Kruger *Organised Crime and Proceeds of Crime Law in South Africa* 40.

wants to launder large amounts of money and other proceeds of crime, and who uses financial or legal professionals to hide the proceeds. Friends and family members of the principal criminal are other categories of persons that could provide the type of assistance that is criminalised under section 5 of POCA.

By broadening the scope of money laundering offences to include the conduct of third parties, the legislature has provided for a potentially powerful tool in the hands of the prosecutor who can now also focus on the network of family and professionals who help with laundering the proceeds of crime generated by organised crime groups. The crime provided for in section 5 obviously creates risks for legal and financial services professionals. This in turn should make these professionals more vigilant, which is of course so intended by the legislature.[107]

45.4.2.3 Section 6 of POCA: The offence of acquisition, possession or use of proceeds of unlawful activities

Section 6 of POCA provides as follows:

> **Any person who—**
> **(*a*) acquires;**
> **(*b*) uses; or**
> **(*c*) has possession of, property and who knows or ought reasonably to have known that it is or forms part of the proceeds of unlawful activities of another person, shall be guilty of an offence.**

45.4.2.3.1 Some general comments

The offence in section 6, like the offence in section 5, can only be committed by a *third party*. In other words, the offender is not the principal perpetrator who generated the proceeds through the predicate offence. The rationale for this offence can arguably be compared with that of the statutory crimes of receiving and possessing stolen goods[108] – it broadens the scope of criminal liability and helps to cast the net wide to target the economic basis of organised criminality.

45.4.2.4 Section 64 of FICA: The structuring offence

Section 64 of FICA provides as follows:

> **Conducting transactions to avoid reporting duties.**
>
> **Any person who conducts, or causes to be conducted, two or more transactions with the purpose, in whole or in part, of avoiding giving rise to a reporting duty under this Act [FICA], is guilty of an offence.**

45.4.2.4.1 Some general comments

The offence provided for in section 64 of FICA complements the money laundering offences in POCA. It is primarily aimed at financial transactions that would normally attract unwanted attention from law enforcement agencies, or that are subject to the reporting duties provided for in FICA. Individuals who want to avoid the attention,[109] or who want to sidestep the

107 See comments by Dendy M 'Watching your back: A guide to Fica and Poca' (March 2006) *De Rebus* 33. See further, the discussion of the defence provided for in s 7A of POCA below.

108 See sections 31.4 and 31.5.

109 Compare, for instance, the facts in *S v Moosagie* supra.

reporting duties, often use a practice called *smurfing*. This practice is described by De Koker as follows:

> **Smurfing takes place where a transaction involving a large amount is structured and divided into a number of transactions involving smaller amounts to avoid being noticed. Smurfing is often rife in systems with cash threshold reporting obligations, but is not confined to such systems.**[110]

45.4.3 Section 7A of POCA: The reporting defence

Section 7A of POCA provides as follows:

> **(1) If a person is charged with committing an offence under section 2(1)(*a*) or (*b*), 4, 5, or 6, that person may raise as a defence the fact that he or she had reported a knowledge or suspicion in terms of section 29 of the Financial Intelligence Centre Act, 2001.**
>
> **(2) If a person who is an employee of an accountable institution as defined in the Financial Intelligence Centre Act, 2001, is charged with committing an offence under section 2(1)(*a*) or (*b*), 4,5 or 6, that person may also raise as a defence that fact that he or she had—**
>
> **(*a*) complied with the applicable obligations in terms of the internal rules relating to the reporting of information of the accountable institution; or**
>
> **(*b*) reported the matter to the person charged with the responsibility of ensuring compliance by the accountable institution with its duties under that Act; or**
>
> **(*c*) reported a suspicion to his or her superior, if any, if—**
>
> **(i) the accountable institution had not appointed such a person or established such rules;**
>
> **(ii) the accountable institution had not complied with its obligations in section 42(3) of that Act in respect of that person; or**
>
> **(iii) those rules were not applicable to that person.**

We pointed out above that the offences provided for in sections 5 and 6 of POCA create certain risks for third parties, including professionals such as lawyers and accountants, as well as financial officers of companies, among others. The defence provided for in section 7A of POCA can therefore be regarded as a necessary balance. Persons charged with the various money laundering offences (sections 4, 5 and 6 of POCA) as well as racketeering[111] and the FICA offences, can raise as a defence the fact that the knowledge or suspicion was indeed reported in terms of section 29 of FICA. The latter provides for the reporting of suspicious and unusual transactions relating to proceeds of unlawful activities or property that is connected to an offence relating to the financing of terrorist activities to the Financial Intelligence Centre.[112]

---

110 De Koker *South African Money Laundering and Terror Financing Law* Com 3-28(3).

111 But not all the racketeering offences. There is no reference to s 2(1)(*c*) of POCA. This is apparently a legislative oversight. See also comments by De Koker *South African Money Laundering and Terror Financing Law* Com 3-28(3).

112 Such reports can easily be made online at http://www.fic.gov.za.

45.4.4 Money laundering, *mens rea* and the meaning of knowledge of a fact

We noted in Chapter 22 that when the legislature creates a statutory offence, it can provide for any form of fault that it considers appropriate to attain the object of the legislation. The fault element for purposes of the money laundering offences under POCA and FICA must be understood with reference to section 1(2) of POCA and section 1(2) of FICA, which provide as follows:

> **For purposes of this Act a person has knowledge of a fact if—**
> **(*a*) the person has actual knowledge of that fact; or**
> **(*b*) the court is satisfied that—**
> **(i) the person believes that there is a reasonable possibility of the existence of that fact; and**
> **(ii) the person fails to obtain information to confirm or refute the existence of that fact.**

Section 1(3) of POCA and section 1(3) of FICA provide as follows:

> **For the purposes of this Act a person ought reasonably to have known or suspected a fact if the conclusions that he or she ought to have reached are those which would have been reached by a reasonably diligent and vigilant person having both—**
> **(*a*) the general knowledge, skill, training and experience that may reasonably be expected of a person in his or her position; and**
> **(*b*) the general knowledge, skill, training and experience that he or she in fact has.**

The above provisions do not create presumptions of intent or negligence, but they do make it easier, in theory at least, to prove knowledge of a fact. For instance, where section 5 of POCA provides that '[a]ny person who knows or ought reasonably to have known that another person has obtained the proceeds of unlawful activities', it is clear that sections 1(2) and 1(3) will make it easier to prove knowledge of the unlawful nature of the proceeds.

The *test for negligence* provided for in section 1(3) of POCA and FICA can best be described as an objective test with some subjective or individualised elements. A court will thus take into account the *expected* knowledge and skill of a person in the position of the accused, plus any *particular* knowledge and skill of the accused in question. In *Savoi v NDPP*,[113] the Constitutional Court declared, with reference to the racketeering offences in POCA, that there are no grounds on which it can be concluded that the negligence standard provided for in section 2(1) is not constitutionally compliant. We submit that the same holds true for negligence as a basis for liability for money laundering offences in POCA.

45.5 Participating in criminal gang activities

45.5.1 A brief introduction and overview

The social and criminological dynamics associated with gangs prompted the legislature to include the crime, or group of crimes, of *participating in criminal gang activities* in POCA. Indeed, in certain parts of South Africa, violent crime, sexual offences and drug-related offences can, to a large extent, be attributed to criminal gang activities.[114]

---

113 *Savoi v NDPP* supra. For further comments on the case, see De Koker *South African Money Laundering and Terror Financing Law* Com 3-19–3-24.

114 For more background, see Kruger *Organised Crime and Proceeds of Crime Law in South Africa* 54–55; Snyman CR *Criminal Law* 5 ed (2008) 441; Burchell *Principles of Criminal Law* 908–910.

45.5.2 The offences in section 9(1) of POCA

Section 9(1) of POCA provides as follows:

> **Any person who actively participates in or is a member of a criminal gang and who—**
> **(*a*) wilfully aids and abets any criminal activity committed for the benefit of, at the direction of, or in association with any criminal gang;**
> **(*b*) threatens to commit, bring about or perform any act of violence or any criminal activity by a criminal gang or with the assistance of a criminal gang; or**
> **(*c*) threatens any specific person or persons in general, with retaliation in any manner or by any means whatsoever, in response to any act or alleged act of violence, shall be guilty of an offence.**

45.5.3 The offences in section 9(2) of POCA

Section 9(2) of POCA provides as follows:

> **Any person who—**
> **(*a*) performs any act which is aimed at causing, bringing about, promoting or contributing towards a pattern of criminal gang activity;**
> **(*b*) incites, instigates, commands, aids, advises, encourages or procures any other person to commit, bring about, perform or participate in a pattern of criminal gang activity; or**
> **(*c*) intentionally causes, encourages, recruits, incites, instigates, commands, aids or advises another person to join a criminal gang, shall be guilty of an offence.**

45.5.4 Some general comments

Mere membership of a gang is not criminalised under South African law. Membership must be coupled with certain activities (section 9(1) of POCA). Section 9(2) criminalises conduct that contributes to a pattern of criminal gang activity.[115] Two concepts – *criminal gang* and *pattern of criminal gang activity* – are essential for the purposes of both sections 9(1) and 9(2):[116]

- *Criminal gang* includes any formal or informal ongoing organisation, association or group of three or more persons, which has as one of its activities the commission of one or more criminal offences, which has an identifiable name or identifying sign or symbol, and whose members individually or collectively engage in or have engaged in a pattern of criminal gang activity.

115 *S v Thomas* 2015 JDR 1932 (WCC). The case involved a line-up of 19 accused (facing 166 different charges). Sixteen of the accused were charged under POCA. The allegation was that the accused individuals belonged to the notorious Cape Town-based *28 Gang* and that they had participated in criminal gang-related offences. Furthermore, it was alleged that two of the other accused belonged to the *26 Gang* and one other accused to the *27 Gang*. They were also charged under POCA. Some of the alleged offences were committed by the members of the *26* and *27* gangs upon request of the leader of the *28 Gang*. The state called more than 160 witnesses to prove the various allegations. A number of the accused were convicted under s 9 of POCA. The leader of the *28 Gang* was also convicted under s 9. The leadership elements and command dynamics of the crime under s 9 were highlighted by the court.

It is not possible to summarise the facts of the case here. For present purposes it is important to note that this is one of the first significant judgments where a number of individuals were convicted not only of charges of racketeering but also the more problematic crime of gang-related offences in terms of s 9 of POCA

116 See definitions of these concepts in s 1 of POCA.

- *Pattern of criminal gang activity* includes the commission of two or more criminal offences referred to in Schedule 1:[117]

> **Provided that at least one of those offences occurred after the date of commencement of Chapter 4 [POCA] and the last of those offences occurred within three years after a prior offence and the offences were committed—**
> **(*a*) on separate occasions; or**
> **(*b*) on the same occasion, by two or more persons who are members of, or belong to, the same criminal gang.**

Snyman noted that the crimes created in section 9 cover, generally speaking, the same field as the rules of criminal law governing participation in crime, as well as the crimes of attempt, conspiracy and incitement.[118] However, he also points out that section 9(2)(*a*) is 'so widely defined that it may cover cases which do not amount to participation in crime or the commission of one of the anticipatory crimes'[119] (attempt, conspiracy and incitement).

Section 11 of POCA provides for some factors that a court *may* take into account in deciding whether a person is a member of a criminal gang:
- A person admits to criminal gang membership.
- A person is identified as a member of a criminal gang by a parent or guardian.
- A person resides in or frequents a particular criminal gang's area and adopts their style of dress, their use of hand signs, language or their tattoos, and associates with known members of a criminal gang.
- A person has been arrested more than once in the company of identified members of a criminal gang for offences which are consistent with usual criminal gang activities.
- A person is identified as a member of a criminal gang by physical evidence such as photographs or other documentation.

Section 11 also does not provide for any presumptions. The factors listed are discretionary factors – nothing more and nothing less.

DISCUSSION

Evaluating the criminalisation of gangsterism in South Africa

The legislative attempt to criminalise gangs and gangsterism in South Africa seems to be problematic at least in terms of criminal law theory as well as the practical choices for investigators, prosecutors and the courts. Burchell points out that section 9(1) of POCA 'appears to regulate conduct that coincides substantially with the common law concept of common purpose to commit offences'.[120] Indeed, some authors argue that it is more effective to rely on the common law principles, which are more adaptable to a variety of situations than to try and proscribe specific conduct in advance.[121]

However, one should not too readily discard the underlying rationale of the legislature's attempt to curb the real problems posed by criminal gangs, especially in

117 For instance, murder, rape, kidnapping, public violence, and so on.
118 Snyman *Criminal Law* 442.
119 Snyman *Criminal Law* 443.
120 Burchell *Principles of Criminal Law* 909.
121 Burchell *Principles of Criminal Law* 909.

poor and vulnerable communities. By giving the criminal behaviour a name and by providing certain statutory direction to the investigation and possible prosecution of criminal gang activities, the legislature has clearly attempted to give the police, the prosecutors and, ultimately, the courts more tools to work with.

As we have seen with racketeering and money laundering, there is an underlying rationale for POCA. Sometimes individuals commit a crime not in a strictly individual capacity, but as part of a bigger criminal scheme or organisation. Perhaps section 9 of POCA also tries to give meaning to that underlying rationale. It is, of course, debatable how effective it has been in terms of providing the criminal justice systems with tools to combat organised crime and criminal gangs, but the same can be asked of the common law crimes that still exist in South Africa.

45.6 Organised crime, proceeds and instrumentalities of crime, and asset forfeiture

Crime can be committed by natural persons and by corporations or legal entities. Although the commission of crime does not always involve property as instrumentalities, subjects or as proceeds,[122] it is safe to say that it would be hard to imagine crime as a sustainable venture without any property involved: the drug dealer using his house to manufacture illicit drugs; the bank robbers buying weapons with the stolen money to conduct the next robbery; the fraudster using her computer to create false financial products to lure innocent people to invest in such products.

Traditionally, law enforcement has focused on the prosecution of the individual accused persons with the courts imposing some form of punishment after conviction. The focus was, however, on the natural or legal entity guilty of the crime. Of course, part of the arsenal of sentencing options courts could impose has been forfeiture of the subject or instruments of the crime, for instance the illicit drugs or the equipment used to manufacture the drugs. This is known as *criminal forfeiture* since it is done after a guilty verdict and it is premised on the successful prosecution of the individual accused.

We will see below that POCA goes further than criminal forfeiture and introduced an enforcement regime known as *civil forfeiture* into the criminal justice system. While the traditional focus on the individual criminal is still there, a new front was opened, namely a focus on property associated with crime to put it in broad terms.[123]

While the focus of this chapter is a discussion of the three groups of crimes created by POCA (racketeering, money laundering and participation in criminal gang activities), it is appropriate to note briefly the important procedural regime created by POCA as part of a more comprehensive law enforcement strategy to combat crime in general[124] and organised

122 Sometimes referred to as *instrumentum sceleris, objectum sceleris* and *producta/fructa sceleris*. For more background, see Stessens *Money Laundering* 4.

123 See also observations by Ackermann J in *National Director of Public Prosecutions and another v Mohamed NO and others* 2002 (2) SACR 196 (CC) at 15–16.

124 It is important to note that POCA can also be applied to cases of individual criminal conduct. It is not a regime exclusively created for organised criminality, for instance in the form of racketeering or criminal gangs. See *NDPP v Geyser* supra; comments by Kruger *Organised Crime and Proceeds of Crime Law in South Africa* 6–7.

crime in particular. The focus on property as a strategy to combat crime involves the legal mechanism known as *asset forfeiture*. Burchell describes it thus:

> **Asset forfeiture involves procedures, invoked by the state, for the compulsory deprivation of the private property belonging to individuals (or corporations) that is derived from or linked to unlawful activities. The objective of the forfeiture is to remove the profit from crime.**[125]

The enforcement regime in POCA provides for two forms of asset forfeiture, namely criminal confiscation[126] and civil forfeiture.[127]

Criminal confiscation is premised on the conviction of an accused person. After conviction, the criminal court may enquire into any benefit derived from the relevant crime or from related criminal activity. If there is indeed evidence that the criminal acquired a benefit from the crime or related criminal activity, the court may also make an order for payment to the state of any appropriate amount in addition to any punishment that it is empowered to impose. An appropriate amount is normally the value of the proceeds of the crime or related criminal activity. In addition to the criminal confiscation orders provided for in Chapter 5 of POCA, a court can also impose a restraint order as an interim measure to secure the availability of assets for possible confiscation.[128] Criminal confiscation orders are also known as *in personam* orders since the focus is on the individual (guilty) criminal.[129]

Civil forfeiture, a practice well developed in the US,[130] focuses on the property and not the individual or corporate criminal.[131] It is therefore known as *in rem* forfeiture since the target is the property derived from criminal activities or property associated with criminal activities. It is not premised on a guilty verdict of an individual or corporate accused person. Indeed, not even a pending criminal charge against an individual or against a corporation is necessary for civil forfeiture in terms of Chapter 6 to become applicable.[132]

The regime provided for in Chapter 6 of POCA gives courts the power to grant temporary preservation of property orders on the basis of evidence that the relevant property is an instrumentality of an offence listed in Schedule 1 of POCA, or if the property is proceeds of criminal activities. In addition to the temporary preservation of property orders, Chapter 6 also provides for civil forfeiture orders. The latter action is civil (not criminal) in nature. The court must be satisfied that the relevant property is indeed an instrumentality of crime or the proceeds of criminal activities. A successful application for civil forfeiture means that the relevant property will be forfeited to the state. Of course, innocent owners or other affected persons have the necessary standing to go to court and to show that the property was acquired legally, and that they (the innocent owners or other affected persons) had no knowledge of the criminal origins of the property, or knowledge of the criminal conduct associated with the property.[133]

---

125 Burchell *Principles of Criminal Law* 924. See also Van der Walt AJ *Constitutional Property Law* (2005) 192–209 and the South African and foreign (especially American) cases discussed.

126 Ch 5 of POCA.

127 Ch 6 of POCA.

128 *National Director of Public Prosecutions v Rautenbach and others* 2005 (4) SA 603 (SCA) at 27.

129 Burchell *Principles of Criminal Law* 926; Van der Walt *Constitutional Property Law* 196.

130 See in general, SD Cassella *Asset Forfeiture Law in the United States* 2 ed (2013).

131 For more detail, see Burchell *Principles of Criminal Law* 928–936.

132 *National Director of Public Prosecutions v (1) RO Cook Properties (Pty) Ltd; (2) 37 Gillespie Street Durban (Pty) Ltd and another; (3) Seevnarayan* 2004 (8) BCLR 844 (SCA).

133 S 52 of POCA; *NDPP v (1) RO Cook Properties; (2) 37 Gillespie Street Durban; (3) Seevnarayan* supra.

THIS CHAPTER IN ESSENCE

1. The phenomenon of organised crime is complex and often difficult to define, and knows or respects no borders.
2. Various legislative frameworks in South Africa attempt to deal with this phenomenon by criminalising racketeering, money laundering and criminal gang activities.
3. While the primary objective of these statutes is to deal with organised criminality, it is the case that individuals (acting alone) can also be convicted of a crime such as money laundering.
4. The Prevention of Organised Crime Act 121 of 1998 (POCA) provides for various enforcement regimes - notably criminal and civil forfeiture - to combat crime in general and organised criminality in particular.

PART FOUR

International criminal law

Chapter 46

Introduction to international criminal law

CHAPTER OBJECTIVES

The objectives of this chapter are to:

- provide a working definition of the field of international criminal law
- give a historical overview of the development of international criminal law
- identify some key institutional and legal developments affecting modern international criminal law and South Africa's participation in the international criminal justice system.

46.1 Introduction: Defining international criminal law

The term '**international criminal law**' defies simple definition.[1] The matter is further complicated by the fact that the discipline is sometimes referred to under-inclusively as war crimes law, or over-inclusively as international criminal justice. Definitional challenges, it seems, are endemic to the discipline.

Most scholars define international criminal law *functionally*, that is, by what it does. For example, Cassese defines it as 'a body of international rules designed both to proscribe

1 In an influential essay entitled 'The problem of an international criminal law', written in the shadow of the Nuremberg and Tokyo Tribunals when the field was in its infancy, Schwarzenberger ascribed six possible meanings to the term before concluding that 'international criminal law in any true sense does not exist'. Whatever uncertainties may have existed then, the developments over the past 60 years mean that it can safely be said today that international criminal law exists. Definitional challenges, however, remain. See Schwarzenberger G 'The problem of an international criminal law' (1950) 3 *Current Legal Problems* 263 at 295, reprinted in Simpson GJ *War Crimes Law Vol 1* (2004) 5-38, 37. Although a single, universally acceptable definition of international criminal law is still contentious, there seems to be a movement away from the fragmented and descriptive approaches of earlier years towards a more coherent, material and integrative description of the subject area. For instance, international criminal law is no longer described simply as the awkward marriage between common law and civil law criminal justice systems, or in terms of the law and practice of international criminal tribunals, but rather in terms of a growing and operational global legal culture. For more on this, see Campbell K 'The making of global legal culture and international criminal law' 26 (2013) *LJIL* 155-172.

certain categories of conduct (war crimes, crimes against humanity, genocide, torture, aggression, terrorism) and to make those persons who engage in such conduct criminally liable'.[2] Similarly, Werle and Jessberger describe the field thus: 'International criminal law encompasses all norms that establish, exclude or otherwise regulate responsibility for crimes under international law'.[3] Bassiouni suggests that '[w]hat is contemporarily meant by [the term][4] is the application of the principle of accountability for certain international crimes, whether before an international or national judicial body'.[5]

Making international crimes the organising point of the field leads to complicating defining what international crimes are. A similar definitional challenge presents here. While all scholars agree that the core international crimes are genocide, crimes against humanity, war crimes and aggression, many would add terrorism, drug and narcotics trafficking, counterfeiting and piracy, among others, to the list of international crimes.[6] While all of these crimes are international, there is a difference between genocide and counterfeiting, for example. Here, a distinction can be drawn between international crimes and crimes under international law. What distinguishes the latter from the former category is that crimes under international law are 'crimes that involve direct individual responsibility under international law', namely war crimes, crimes against humanity, genocide and the crime of aggression.[7] International crimes, then, encompass a broader, looser category of crimes that may be considered international for one reason or another. For example, their effects may stretch across borders (drug trafficking) or they take place beyond the jurisdiction of a single state (piracy). The prosecution of crimes under international law is international criminal law in the strict sense.[8]

Other scholars approach the definition of international criminal law differently altogether. They conceptualise it with reference to its *place* within the international legal order – at the intersection of a number of subfields of international law, that is: international humanitarian law (IHL), international human rights law (IHRL) and general public international law.[9] In this regard, Van Schaak and Slye describe the field 'as a subset of public international law involving the use of criminal sanctions to enforce law that is *primarily*

2 Cassese A *International Criminal Law* 2 ed (2008) 3. By permission of Oxford University Press.

3 Werle G and Jessberger F *Principles of International Criminal Law* 3 ed (2014) 31. By permission of Oxford University Press.

4 Notably, Bassiouni uses the term 'international criminal justice'.

5 Bassiouni MC 'International criminal justice in historical perspective: The tension between states' interests and the pursuit of international justice' in Cassese A (ed-in-chief) *The Oxford Companion to International Criminal Justice* (2009) 131. By permission of Oxford University Press.

6 See, for example, Dugard J *International Law: A South African Perspective* 4 ed (2011) 157–169; Gaeta P 'International criminalization of prohibited conduct' in Cassese A (ed-in-chief) *The Oxford Companion to International Criminal Justice* (2009) 65; Schabas WA *Genocide in International Law: The Crime of Crimes* (2000) 26. Cassese is not alone in this respect; many scholars include torture and terrorism in the definition of international crimes. However, a number of factors counsel against adopting a more expansive definition of international crimes. Firstly, the four core crimes are undoubtedly crimes under customary international law, whereas there is lingering doubt about the customary character of other putative international crimes. Secondly, these four crimes are the crimes currently within the subject matter jurisdiction of the Rome Statute of the International Criminal Court 1998. Given that the implementing legislation for the Rome Statute (both present and future) of many states will form the basis of domestic prosecutions of international crimes, this selection of crimes by the drafters of the Rome Statute will undoubtedly influence and shape domestic prosecutions as well, not least in terms of their scope. For other crimes of international concern, mostly treaty-based crimes not under the jurisdiction of the ICC, see Chapter 49. By permission of Oxford University Press.

7 Werle and Jessberger *Principles of International Criminal Law* 31–33. Notably, Werle and Jessberger limit international criminal law to its international instantiations, whereas here we adopt a broader understanding of the field that includes domestic proceedings aimed at prosecuting crimes under international law.

8 It may be more accurately described as criminal international law.

9 Van Schaack B and Slye RC *Defining International Criminal Law* Santa Clara Univ. Legal Studies Research Paper No 07-32 (2007) 1, available at http://ssrn.com/abstract=1006089.

international in its origins. [They] thus define international criminal law as the body of law that assigns individual criminal responsibility for breaches of public international law'.[10]

However, to the extent that such definitions exclude from their remit the domestic prosecution of crimes under international law, they are excessively narrow. Domestic instantiations of international criminal law, as we will see, have not only been instrumental in the development of the field, but remain a key aspect of its enforcement.[11] Moreover, domestic prosecutions of crimes under international law cannot be separated from international law, which invariably instigates the domestic criminalisation of these offences, defines their contours, permits extraordinary exercises of jurisdiction by states for their prosecution, facilitates international cooperation to do so, and so on. Others approach international criminal law from its domestic antecedents: *internationalised* criminal law. As far as war crimes are concerned, this is certainly an accurate description of the evolution of these crimes. However, while their antecedents are domestic criminal law, war crimes have been criminal under international law since the turn of the 20th century at the very least.[12]

In this regard, Van Schaak and Slye note how situated such definitions tend to be:

> **Contemporary practitioners and scholars have entered the field from different origins, including domestic criminal law, international human rights law, and international humanitarian law. Their definition of the field is heavily influenced by their point of entry. So, domestic criminalists tend to build the field outward from a domestic law foundation to cover the transnational dimensions of domestic criminal law and the various ways that states endeavor, and are permitted, to extend their domestic penal law abroad ... Individuals who approach the field from the human rights tradition tend to focus on the prosecution of so-called 'atrocity crimes' – genocide, war crimes against civilians, and crimes against humanity ... Finally, individuals who approach international criminal law from the perspective of military justice are primarily interested in crimes committed in the context of armed conflict involving prohibited tactics of war and protected persons.**[13]

In the final analysis, there is no single, *correct* definition of international criminal law. As Cryer et al note:

> **Different meanings of international criminal law have their own utility for their different purposes and there is no reason to decide upon one meaning as the 'right' one. Nevertheless, it is advisable from the outset to be clear about the sense in which the term is used in any particular situation.**[14]

---

10 Van Schaack and Slye *Defining International Criminal Law* 1. The authors go on to note:

> **We recognize, however, that international criminal law is not purely a field of international law. Many substantive norms of international criminal law have been incorporated – with varying degrees of fealty to their international origins – into the domestic penal codes of the nations of the world.**

Available at SSRN: http://ssrn.com/abstract=1006089 or http:dx.doi.org/10.2139/ssrn.1006089. Reprinted by permission of Prof Beth van Schaack.

11 As Simpson notes:

> **It must surely now be legitimate to include extradition proceedings involving Senator Pinochet, the Belgium legislation criminalizing acts of genocide, wherever they happen to be committed, and the various legal instruments purporting to implement the new [ICC] statute into domestic law as part of any study of international criminal law. Purists may cavil but no comprehension of the field is possible without a study of a broad range of legal techniques and institutions.**

Simpson GJ *War Crimes Law Vol 1* xv.

12 See Chapter 47.

13 Van Schaack and Slye *Defining International Criminal Law* 1, available at http://ssrn.com/abstract=1006089 or http:dx.doi.org/10.2139/ssrn.1006089. Reprinted by permission of Prof Beth van Schaack.

14 Cryer et al *An Introduction to International Criminal Law and Procedure* 2.

With this in mind, for the purpose of this part of the book, international criminal law is defined as 'the prosecution of genocide, crimes against humanity, war crimes, and aggression by domestic and international courts'. This definition is both broader and narrower than some of those discussed above. It is broader in the sense that it covers the prosecution of these crimes by both international and domestic tribunals, and it is narrower in the sense that it focuses on four core crimes: war crimes, crimes against humanity, genocide and aggression.

46.2 Histories of international criminal law

46.2.1 The orthodox history of international criminal law

Given these debates on its definition, it is not surprising that the history of international criminal law is equally complex and contested.[15] Its reactionary nature, contested origins and lack of a unifying theory make a plain, linear rendition of its history difficult. Depending on how it is defined, it might reach back to antiquity or merely a decade prior to the formation of the ICC.

The approach of some international criminal law scholars - perhaps as an over-reaction to the perennial allegations of retrospectivity that plague the discipline - is to stretch the origins of the discipline as far back in time as possible. The usual suspect in this regard is the international prohibition on piracy, its offenders being the original *hostis humanis generis* (enemies of all mankind).[16] Another candidate for a clearly dated antecedent is the 19th century prohibition of slavery.[17] However, while international criminal law may be inspired by, or share an affinity with, these early injunctions in international law, the true beginnings of the current discipline lie in its more recent history.[18]

We suggest here that a more appropriate starting point for international criminal law - both substantively[19] and institutionally - is the Treaty of Versailles 1919.[20] In particular, articles 227–230 contained the first normative expression of modern-day international criminal law.[21] These articles called for the prosecution of Emperor William II of Hohenzollern 'for a supreme offence against international morality and the sanctity of treaties'. They proclaimed further 'the right of the Allied and Associated Powers to bring

---

15 At the risk of triteness, when mention is made here to the history of these crimes, reference is being made to their emergence as a matter of law, not of fact. Crimes that would meet the definition of war crimes, genocide and crimes against humanity have been perpetrated by mankind prior to and since recorded history.

16 Piracy was arguably the concern of the international community because of its transnational rather than its heinous nature, as many have argued. In fact, there are notable differences between the normative bases of piracy and the crimes of genocide, war crimes and crimes against humanity. As Simpson notes, 'Pirates were the enemies of empire or particular states, rather than humanity'. Simpson G *Law, War and Crime: War crimes trials and the reinvention of international law (2007)* 159–177.

17 See Van Schaack and Slye *A Concise History of International Criminal Law* 11.

18 See Schwarzenberger 'The problem of an international criminal law' 280–283.

19 An alternative modern antecedent for substantive international criminal law, and war crimes in particular, is the Protocol of the Brussels Conference 1874, which provided for 'the immediate punishment of ... persons who are guilty' of violations of the laws of war. The Protocol, however, never came into force. Van Schaack and Slye *A Concise History of International Criminal Law* 19.

20 Signed on 28 June 1919. See further, Simpson *Law, War and Crime* 40–41; Werle and Jessberger *Principles of International Criminal Law* 2–6; Van Schaack and Slye *A Concise History of International Criminal Law* 20–26.

21 Although war crimes were outlawed previously under customary IHL, the Treaty of Versailles was 'the first time, the idea of individual criminal responsibility under international law was explicitly recognised in an international treaty'. Werle and Jessberger *Principles of International Criminal Law* 4. For purely domestic prosecutions, see Van Schaack and Slye *A Concise History of International Criminal Law* 19.

before military tribunals persons accused of having committed acts in violation of the laws and customs of war'.[22] It also contained the first, subsequently aborted, attempt at a supranational institutional response to what would become international crimes. More specifically, article 227 called for the establishment of a 'special tribunal ... to try the accused' ... 'composed of five judges, one appointed by each of the following powers: namely, the United States of America, Great Britain, France, Italy and Japan'. It stated further that 'the tribunal will be guided by the highest motives of international policy, with a view to vindicating the solemn obligations of international undertakings and the validity of international morality'.[23] These provisions were, however, never used because the emperor found sanctuary in the Netherlands, which refused to extradite him for trial, and the contemplated trials of German war criminals were ultimately left to German domestic courts.[24]

What generally follows from Versailles, in any orthodox approach to the history of international criminal law, is a focus on the international, and predominantly institutional, developments.[25] For example, Werle and Jessberger refer to the Nuremberg tribunal, the ad hoc tribunals (International Criminal Tribunal for the Former Yugoslavia (ICTY) and the International Criminal Tribunal for Rwanda (ICTR)) and the permanent International Criminal Court (ICC) as the '[t]hree milestones [that] have marked the path of international criminal law'.[26]

The centrepiece of this orthodox history is the trial of defeated German and Japanese leaders in the aftermath of World War II at Nuremberg and Tokyo respectively. The Nuremberg Tribunal - established by Britain, France, the US and Russia under the London Agreement on 8 August 1945 - imposed international criminal responsibility on members of the Nazi High Command for violations of the laws of war, crimes against the peace and crimes against humanity.[27] In contrast, the approach and outcome of the Tokyo Tribunal,[28] which took place between 1946 and 1948, and was modelled on the Nuremberg Tribunal, are less respected and revered by international lawyers. This was especially due to the absence of appropriate legal standards, which makes its findings highly questionable.[29] This post-World War II period, according to Van Schaak and Slye, 'is nothing less than a watershed moment in the development' of the international criminal law field.[30] Similarly, Werle and Jessberger note that the Nuremberg trials 'can be considered the "birth certificate" of international criminal law'.[31]

Following a period of inactivity during the Cold War, the discipline was revitalised in the 1990s following the creation of the ICTY and the ICTR. If Nuremberg was an imperfect

---

22 Arts 227 and 228 of the Treaty of Versailles (1919).

23 Art 227 Treaty of Versailles (1919).

24 These trials took place in the German Supreme Court in Leipzig from 23 May to 16 July 1921 (hereinafter 'the Leipzig Trials'). See also art 230 of the Treaty of Sevres 1920 (with Turkey). Van Schaack and Slye *A Concise History of International Criminal Law* 25–26.

25 Note, for those who define international criminal law as a subset of international law, the exclusive focus on these international aspects is deliberate.

26 Werle and Jessberger *Principles of International Criminal Law* 2. By permission of Oxford University Press.

27 The tribunal indicted 24 German military and political leaders, 21 of whom were brought to trial. When its judgment was handed down on 30 September 1946, 12 defendants were sentenced to death, three to life imprisonment, four to extended prison sentences, and three were acquitted.

28 For a brief overview, see Comyns Carr AS 'The judgment of the International Military Tribunal for the Far East' (1948) 34 *Transactions of the Grotius Society* 141–151.

29 See Schwarzenberger 'The problem of an international criminal law' 289–290.

30 Van Schaack and Slye *A Concise History of International Criminal Law* 27.

31 Werle and Jessberger *Principles of International Criminal Law* 5.

beginning, then these UN-created tribunals were its redemption in the sense of being the first truly international institutions established to prosecute international crimes and its revival by precipitating a renaissance of international criminal law, which many had thought a dead letter.[32]

Brief mention must be made also of the hybrid tribunals established in Sierra Leone,[33] Cambodia,[34] Lebanon[35] and East Timor,[36] which lie 'in the intersection between national and international law'.[37] Unlike the ad hoc tribunals that were created by the UN Security Council, these courts are established by treaties, special agreements or under the domestic legal regimes. As Shraga notes:

> **While similar to the 'first generation' tribunals in their organizational structure, subject-matter jurisdiction and international legitimacy, mixed tribunals are distinguished from the former by their legal status, their mixed jurisdiction and composition and their funding mechanism.**[38]

For most international lawyers, these historical developments form the backdrop against which the ICC emerged in 1998. The faith and hope placed in the ICC by lawyers, academics and civil society cannot be overstated – it represents a turning point in international criminal law, both institutionally and normatively.[39] As Kress notes: 'With the birth of the ICC, the international community attempted to cut the cord that linked international criminal law to the criticisms that previously plagued it.'[40]

More recently the maturing ICC has faced criticism, especially from African states, for a perceived 'anti-African bias'. While African states represent a significant cohort in the ICC's Assembly of States Parties (ASP), the reality is that, at the time of writing, all active cases before the ICC were from Africa, even though Africa is not the only region of the world where mass atrocities occur. The reasons for this state of affairs are complex and contested and will not be explored here. Suffice to note that, as a result of the perceived anti-African bias, the institutional relationship between the ICC and the African Union (AU) has deteriorated quite

---

32 Van Schaack and Slye *A Concise History of International Criminal Law* 15.

33 The Special Court for Sierra Leone was established by the government of Sierra Leone and the UN (pursuant to Security Council resolution 1315 (2000) of 14 August 2000) to try those who bear the greatest responsibility for serious violations of international humanitarian law and Sierra Leonean law committed in the territory of Sierra Leone since 30 November 1996. On 26 April 2012, the Special Court convicted former Liberian president Charles Taylor on 11 counts of war crimes and crimes against humanity.

34 The extraordinary chambers in the courts of Cambodia were established pursuant to an agreement between the royal government of Cambodia and the UN to try senior members of the Khmer Rouge for serious violations of Cambodian penal law, international humanitarian law and custom, and violation of international conventions recognised by Cambodia, committed during the period between 17 April 1975 and 6 January 1979.

35 The special tribunal for Lebanon (STL) was established by an agreement between the UN and the Lebanese Republic (pursuant to Security Council Resolution 1664 (2006) of 29 March 2006) to try those responsible for the assassination of Rafic Hariri on 14 February 2005. The STL also has jurisdiction over a series of other attacks in Lebanon (between 1 October 2004 and 12 December 2005) if they are proven to be connected with the Hariri assassination. It is based in Leidschendam in the Netherlands.

36 The East Timor tribunal – officially the 'Special Panels of the Dili District Court' – was established in 2000 by the UN Transitional Administration in East Timor (UNTAET) to try cases of serious criminal offences, including murder, rape and torture, which took place in East Timor in 1999.

37 Shraga D 'Mixed or internationalized courts' in Cassese A *The Oxford Companion to International Criminal Justice* (2009) 424.

38 Shraga 'Mixed or internationalized courts' 424. By permission of Oxford University Press.

39 Kress C 'The International Criminal Court as a turning point in the history of international criminal justice' in Cassese A *The Oxford Companion to International Criminal Justice* (2009) 143–145.

40 Kress 'The International Criminal Court as a turning point in the history of international criminal justice' 143–145 at 143. By permission of Oxford University Press.

significantly. In 2017 the AU adopted a non-binding 'Withdrawal Strategy'.[41] A key part of the AU strategy is aimed at the reform of the international criminal justice system, including the ICC. An enhanced role for regional instruments and institutions dealing with international criminal law is envisaged.[42] If these reforms are not achieved, the AU Withdrawal Strategy 'aims to provide member states with a holistic approach, analysis and implications of initiating the withdrawal provision under the Rome Statute [of the ICC] in accordance with the constitutional provisions of individual African States Parties'.[43]

At present one African state party to the Rome Statute, Burundi, has registered its withdrawal from the ICC. Burundi's withdrawal took effect on 27 October 2017.[44] South Africa's governing party has also indicated its intention to withdraw from the ICC. The institutional and legal dynamics surrounding South Africa's possible withdrawal from the ICC are briefly discussed in section 46.3.

DISCUSSION **International criminal law and colonialism**

While African states were not engaged in the project's formative stages due to colonialism, Africa (and colonialism) was by no means absent from these moments. In fact, colonialism has made persistent and uncomfortable appearances from the project's outset, beginning with Justice Radhabinod Pal's fierce anti-colonial dissent at the International Military Tribunal for the Far East. Among other things, Justice Pal was concerned about the 'history of colonial domination by the Western powers', and questioned the 'moral authority of Great Britain, a colonial power, to pass judgement on the defeated colonial policies of Japan'.[45] The *unwritten* dissent at Nuremberg was not so much about the colonial past as it was about the colonial present.

The uncomfortable question of colonial crimes again emerged during the trials of World War II crimes in France four decades later.[46] Even today, claims continue to be brought – using the language of international crimes – by victims of colonial atrocities against the former colonial powers.[47]

---

41 AU Withdrawal Strategy 12 January 2017, available at https://www.hrw.org/sites/default/files/supporting_resources/icc_withdrawal_strategy_jan._2017.pdf.

42 Most notably the expansion of the jurisdiction of the African Court on Human and Peoples' Rights to also provide for criminal jurisdiction. The Malabo Protocol, adopted in 2014, provides for the amendment of the statute of the African Court of Justice and Human and Peoples' Rights. The court will thus have three chambers, including an 'International Criminal Law Section', with the jurisdiction to try individuals and corporations for crimes under international law, including the core crimes (genocide, crimes against humanity, war crimes and aggression) and other crimes of regional concern, such as corruption, unconstitutional change of government, trafficking in persons, piracy and terrorism. For a comprehensive commentary on the Malabo Protocol, see Werle G and Vormbaum M (eds) *The African Criminal Court – A Commentary on the Malabo Protocol* (2017).

43 AU Withdrawal Strategy para 9.

44 Detail on the situation and status of investigation in Burundi, as well as Burundi's withdrawal from the ICC, is available at https://www.icc-cpi.int/burundi.

45 See Gevers C 'International criminal law and individualism: An African perspective' in Schwöbel C (ed) *Critical Approaches to International Criminal Law: An Introduction* (2014) 225 and the authorities cited there.

46 For a further perspective, see Kaplan A 'On Alain Finkielkraut's "Remembering in Vain": The Klaus Barbie trial and crimes against humanity' (1992) 19(1) *Crit Inq* 70 at 79.

47 See further, Gevers C 'International criminal law and individualism: An African perspective' 221–245.

46.2.2 The hidden history of international criminal law

What is missing, however, in this historical version of the discipline up until the creation of the ICC is the formative influence of domestic law and prosecutions in the field's development: the so-called 'hidden history of international criminal law'.[48] Through an overemphasis on international developments – especially on Versailles, Nuremberg and Rome – as defining moments, insufficient attention has been paid to the important role that domestic prosecutions and developments have played, both in establishing the substantive norms of, and in enforcing, international criminal law. In contrast, these activities have sometimes been regarded as setbacks in the progression towards true international criminal law, that is, the prosecution of international crimes by international courts.[49]

Despite such negative attitudes, the fact remains that for much of the 20th century, international criminal law was primarily the concern of domestic courts.[50] In particular, in the absence of an international enforcement mechanism for international crimes, treaties for the suppression of such crimes were adopted in order to provide for the definitions of the crimes (financing of terrorism, human trafficking, money laundering, and so on) as well as for domestic criminalisation and prosecution of these crimes.[51] This has been termed *indirect enforcement* of international criminal law.[52] This was done primarily through domestic prosecution provisions in treaties.[53] Commentators have noted that international criminal tribunals, which now dominate the international criminal law landscape, could not have existed without domestic courts paving the way for greater accountability.[54] Even serious crimes of state or collective violence, affecting the international community as a whole (genocide, torture, apartheid, and so on) were defined in treaties which enjoined states to criminalise the relevant conduct and to prosecute the perpetrators at the domestic level, and to cooperate with other states in an effort to effectively punish and prevent these crimes effectively.[55]

In addition, to facilitate these national prosecutions, the customary rules of jurisdiction were modified to allow states to exercise jurisdiction over individuals accused of certain international crimes in situations where they would otherwise not have been able to do so. There were various examples of domestic prosecutions, with some being less successful than others.[56]

In terms of their relationship with international criminal law, these were not just incidental domestic prosecutions of international crimes, but rather they impacted on the substantive aspects of the field through the development of custom, both in terms of the existence and nature of particular crimes, and their general principles. There is unanimity among lawyers, academics and states that customary international law *directly* criminalises

48 Simpson *Law, War and Crime* 40.

49 See Chapter 48.

50 These crimes were international in the sense that they were of concern to the international community as a whole. The subject of treaties created legal obligations to prosecute them and allowed states to exercise extraordinary jurisdiction over those who transgressed them.

51 Cassese A et al *International Criminal Law* 3 ed (2013) 18–19.

52 Here, a distinction is drawn between the obligation to exercise jurisdiction over such crimes under international law contained in many treaties under the *aut dedere* principle (so-called indirect enforcement) and the actual criminalisation thereof under international law (direct enforcement).

53 Including *aut dedere aut judicare* (extradite or prosecute) provisions.

54 See, in general, Sikkink K *The Justice Cascade: How Human Rights Prosecutions Are Changing World Politics* (2011); Moyn S *Human Rights And The Uses Of History* 2 ed (2017) 78.

55 Cassese et al *International Criminal Law* 19.

56 For a discussion of some of the prominent domestic trials, see Cryer et al *An Introduction to International Criminal Law and Procedure* 37–90.

the core international crimes in the sense that international law imposes direct criminal sanctions on individuals without the intermediary of a state. However, how and when this came to be is contested.[57] What is clear is that the institutional high points mentioned above are not themselves sufficient indicators of states' practice and *opinio juris* to support a customary international law rule criminalising this conduct.[58]

The significance of domestic prosecutions is illustrated by the general principles relied on and developed further by the Nuremberg Tribunal. While it regarded itself as enforcing existing international law, these principles, in fact, must have originated from domestic antecedents.[59] As a result, a number of scholars look to more recent history for the time that crimes were criminalised internationally. For example, according to Gaeta, at the international level, the criminalisation of individual conduct is a recent phenomenon that evolved in the early 1990s only once the threat of criminal sanction existed in the form of the ad hoc tribunals and the ICC.[60] That said, the founding statutes of the ad hoc tribunals were worded in such a manner that they could not be interpreted as themselves forming custom. As Milanovic notes with regard to the ICTY: 'The UN Secretary General and the Security Council went [sic] to great pains to emphasise that by adopting the Statute ... the Council was not making any new law and that it would be applying pre-existing customary law'.[61]

Even the Rome Statute's substantive relationship with customary law is contentious. On one reading, the statute consolidated and codified a number of offences that already existed under customary international law[62] and imposed obligations on individuals directly. It has been argued that the Rome Statute is itself a substantive source of law, that is, that the adoption of the statute by 120 states (there are currently 123 state parties)[63] met the two requirements for the formation of customary international law. In other words, the statute does not merely collate existing international criminal law, it creates it as well.[64]

However, on another reading, the Rome Statute is merely jurisdictional: instead of directly binding individuals, it merely sets the limits of the ICC's subject matter jurisdiction.

---

57 The question of how and when international law criminalised these core crimes remains a relatively underexplored aspect of the discipline. It is not essential for the purposes of defining the field as the unifying aspect of international criminal law adopted here is the crimes themselves, not their source. See Jessberger F 'National legislation on international crimes' in Cassese A *The Oxford Companion to International Criminal Justice* (2009) 429. For more on the debate, see Erasmus MG and Kemp GP 'The application of international criminal law before domestic courts in the light of recent developments in international and constitutional law' (2002) 27 *SAYIL* 64–81; Ferdinandusse WN *Direct Application of International Criminal Law in National Courts* (2006).

58 See further, Milanovic M 'Is the Rome Statute binding on individuals? (and why we should care)'(2011) 9(1) *JICJ* 25–52.

59 Notably, at a meeting of the Allied Powers prior to the creation of the Nuremberg Tribunal, Sir David Maxwell Fyfe, the UK representative, noted: 'What we want to abolish at the trial is a discussion as to whether the acts are violations of international law or not. We declare what the international law is so that there won't be any discussion on whether it is international law or not.' United States, Dept of State. International Conference on Military Trials, London (1945, 1949) 99, quoted in Schwarzenberger 'The problem of an international criminal law' 290. See, however, Werle and Jessberger *Principles of International Criminal Law* 10.

60 Regarding criminalisation internationally, see Gaeta 'International criminalization of prohibited conduct' 65–68.

61 Milanovic 'Is the Rome Statute binding on individuals?' 29. Reprinted by permission of Oxford University Press.

62 Kress notes:

> **[T]he tradition of directly applying customary law by resting it on the mantel of broad jurisdictional phrases was replaced with an essentially code-based approach to criminal law. The ICCSt. [Rome Statute] codifies the applicable customary law in statutory definitions that are further specified in so-called Elements of Crimes.**

Kress 'The International Criminal Court as a turning point in the history of international criminal justice' 146. By permission of Oxford University Press.

63 For more detail, including ratification and implementation details, see https://asp.icc-cpi.int/en_menus/asp/states%20parties/Pages/the%20states%20parties%20to%20the%20rome%20statute.aspx.

64 See further, Milanovic 'Is the Rome Statute binding on individuals?'.

The crimes themselves therefore lie in another source of law, that is, pre-existing custom. As such, the significance of the *indirect enforcement* of international criminal law norms by domestic courts, together with relevant institutional milestones such as Versailles, Nuremberg and Rome, as evidence of both state practice and *opinio juris* in the formation of customary international criminal law, cannot be overstated.

International criminal justice, and the application and development of its principles, is not restricted to the domain of international institutions. Instead, international and national prosecutions should be considered to be formally distinct, yet *substantively intertwined* mechanisms in pursuit of a common goal: the enforcement of international criminal law.

In addition, there is arguably more to this hidden history of international criminal law than merely the under-appreciation of the role and influence of domestic courts just described. Simpson argues that not only is the domestic domain the arena in which many trials take place, but also that the field of international criminal law itself is constituted 'by this opposition or "movement between the domestic and the international"'.[65] By this, he means that even moments framed as 'international' have unmistakable domestic undertones or underpinnings. For example, the first modern international criminal law project – the Leipzig Trials – took place as a result of the failure of the Allies to give effect to the provisions of the Versailles Treaty regarding international prosecution.[66]

Even the internationalists' centrepiece of Nuremberg, with its international significance for many, was arguably 'more akin to municipal war crime trials'[67] than to an international court, with the Allies exercising a form of temporary sovereignty over defeated Germany.[68] Once again, this institutional moment was buttressed by domestic enforcement in the form of the Control Council Law Number 10 trials,[69] which 'were more numerous and represented a shift from the cooperative (albeit, limited) internationalism of the IMT to the local administration of justice ...'[70]

Finally, the ICC, which has no inherent jurisdiction, could be regarded as merely an aggregation of domestic jurisdiction in respect of international crimes, rather than as having proper international jurisdiction (with the exception of Security Council referrals). In summary, the history of international criminal law is 'a series of undulations between recourse to the administration of local justice and grand gestures towards the international rule of law'.[71]

---

65 Simpson *Law, War and Crime* 31.

66 As Van Schaack and Slye explain:

> **In the face of continued Allied equivocation over war crimes trials and fierce objections amongst the German public ..., Germany artfully proposed hosting domestic trials before the German Supreme Court in Leipzig. The Allies, desperate to salvage some vestige of the project, agreed.**

Van Schaack and Slye *A Concise History of International Criminal Law* 24–25. These trials, however, were not ideal. Only 12 of the over 800 accused were tried, with very few convictions.

67 Schwarzenberger notes:

> **As was pointed out in the Nuremberg Judgement, the signatories to the Charter of the Tribunal only did jointly what each of them, if in sole control of Germany, could have done alone ... For these very reasons, however, both these International Military Tribunals where in substance more akin to municipal war crime courts than to truly international tribunals.**

Schwarzenberger G 'The problem of an international criminal law' (1950) 3(1) *CLP* 263 at 290–291. By permission of University College London, Faculty of Laws.

68 Simpson *Law, War and Crime* 37.

69 Control Council Law No. 10, which came into force on 20 December 1945, was adopted to provide for the prosecution of lesser offences than those tried at the Nuremberg Tribunal. See Werle and Jessberger *Principles of International Criminal Law* 11–12.

70 Simpson *Law, War and Crime* 37–38.

71 Simpson *Law, War and Crime* 33.

46.3 South Africa and international criminal justice

South Africa's relationship with international criminal justice is, at best, complex. At the level of *principle*, South Africa has committed itself firmly to the ideal of international justice for human rights atrocities. Yet, its own transition to democracy in the 1990s involved the provision of amnesty to individuals who committed gross human rights violations, some of which may well amount to international crimes.[72] This was a clear exception to what was fast becoming *the* norm, if not a norm of international law, insofar as addressing such crimes: trial and punishment. When it comes to the *enforcement* of this principle, South Africa has 'flip-flopped' at both an international and domestic level. As one of the so-called 'Like Minded Group' of states, South Africa was a key participant in the drafting of the Rome Statute of the International Criminal Court and the establishment of the ICC.[73] Subsequently, however, South Africa has aligned itself with growing hostility towards the ICC on the African continent.

By 2016, in the aftermath of South Africa's failure to arrest President Omar Al-Bashir of Sudan (who is indicted by the ICC for war crimes, crimes against humanity and genocide) and to hand him over to the ICC for trial, it became clear that South Africa's relationship with the ICC has reached a critical low-point. While the Supreme Court of Appeal found that the South African government failed to uphold its constitutional and legal duties in the Al-Bashir-matter,[74] and the ICC itself found that South Africa, as a state party to the Rome Statute of the ICC, had failed to comply with its obligations under the Rome Statute by not executing the ICC's request for the arrest of President Al-Bashir and his surrender to the ICC,[75] at the political level the fate of South Africa's continued membership of the ICC seemed to have been sealed.[76]

In October 2016, the South African government deposited the Instrument of Withdrawal from the Rome Statute of the ICC,[77] which would trigger South Africa's official withdrawal from the ICC. However, this action by the South African government was found to be in violation of the Constitution. In *Democratic Alliance v Minister of International Relations*

72 Promotion of National Unity and Reconciliation Act 34 of 1995.

73 Washburn, J 'The negotiation of the Rome Statute for the International Criminal Court and international lawmaking in the 21st century' (1999) 11(2) *Pace Int'L L Rev* 361 at 368.

74 *Minister of Justice and Constitutional Development and others v Southern Africa Litigation Centre and others* 2016 (3) SA 317 (SCA). The SCA held, at 90, as follows:

> **There is no dispute that President Al Bashir is subject to the jurisdiction of the ICC and can be prosecuted by it for his alleged crimes. He has been stripped of any immunity when before the ICC. It is therefore important that the purpose of the Implementation Act is to provide a framework to ensure the effective implementation of the Rome Statute. It is to ensure that South Africa conforms with its obligations under the Rome Statute. In that regard there is no doubting its obligation to endeavor to bring President Al Bashir before the ICC for trial. The head-of-state immunity claimed for him is only a procedural bar to the enforcement of that obligation in this country. It is not an immunity that confers impunity for any wrongdoing on his part.**

75 *Prosecutor v Omar Hassan Ahmad Al-Bashir*, decision under article 87(7) of the Rome Statute on the non-compliance by South Africa with the request by the court for the arrest and surrender of Omar Al-Bashir, ICC-02/05-01/09, 6 July 2017.

76 For a critique of the South African government's decision to withdraw from the ICC, see Kemp, G 'South Africa's (possible) withdrawal from the ICC and the future of the criminalization and prosecution of crimes against humanity, war crimes and genocide under domestic law: A submission informed by historical, normative and policy considerations' (2017) 16(3) *Wash U Global Stud L Rev* 411.

77 The Instrument of Withdrawal, pursuant to a 127(1) of the Rome Statute of the ICC, was signed by the Minister of International Relations and Cooperation on 19 October 2016. See *Declaratory Statement by the Republic of South Africa on the Decision to Withdraw from the Rome Statute of the International Criminal Court*, C.N.786.2016.TREATIES-XVIII.10 (Depository Notification) (19 October 2016), available at https://treaties.un.org/doc/Publication/CN/2016/CN.786.2016-Eng.pdf.

and Cooperation[78] the court held that the Executive could not unilaterally, without parliamentary debate and approval, withdraw from the Rome Statute, which is a multilateral treaty. South Africa's attempted withdrawal from the ICC was stalled. In March 2017, the South African government delivered a notice of 'Withdrawal of Notification of Withdrawal' from the Rome Statute at the United Nations, thus signaling South Africa's continued membership of the ICC.[79]

At the governing ANC's national conference in December 2017, the political commitment to end South Africa's membership of the ICC was yet again renewed. Shortly thereafter, on 8 December 2017, the International Crimes Bill[80] was published by the Minister of Justice. This bill provides for the repeal of the Implementation of the Rome Statute of the International Criminal Court Act 27 of 2002. The substantive provisions of the bill will briefly be considered in Chapter 48, below. At the time of writing the International Crimes Bill was not yet adopted by parliament, and South Africa's withdrawal from the Rome Statute of the ICC was also not yet debated in parliament. It means that South Africa remains, for now, a member of the ICC.

In terms of the domestication of international criminal law, it should be noted that South Africa has adopted some of the most progressive legislation for the prosecution of international crimes by its courts.[81] However, in the so-called 'Zimbabwe Torture case', the relevant South African authorities dragged their feet in respect of the implementation of these laws (and then had those feet held to the fire by the courts for failing to do so).[82] All the while, during the course of this debacle, South Africa passed more implementing legislation regarding international crimes, notably the Implementation of the Geneva Conventions Act 8 of 2012 and the Prevention and Combating of Torture of Persons Act 13 of 2013. The prosecuting authority also successfully prosecuted its first universal jurisdiction case[83] (albeit related to terrorism[84]). What is more, this idiosyncratic approach to international criminal law is also reflected in the *substance* of its domestic implementing legislation, which is unclear and at times contradictory insofar as jurisdiction, definitions of crimes, modes of responsibility, immunity and the initiation of investigations are concerned.

While South Africa's implementation of international criminal law remains uneven and at times contradictory, what must be made clear at the outset of this section is that since 1994, South Africa has made considerable strides towards the creation of a legal framework for the domestic enforcement of international criminal law.

---

78 *Democratic Alliance v Minister of International Relations and Cooperation and Others (Council for the Advancement of the South African Constitution intervening)* 2017 (3) SA 212 (GP).

79 *South Africa: Withdrawal of Notification of Withdrawal*, 7 March 2017, C.N.121.2017.TREATIES-XVIII.10 (Depository Notification), available at https://treaties.un.org/doc/publication/CN.121.2017-Eng.pdf.

80 International Crimes Bill [B37-2017], *Government Gazette* No 41309, GenN 949, 8 December 2017.

81 See the Implementation of the Rome Statute of the International Criminal Court Act 27 of 2002 and the Implementation of the Geneva Conventions Act 8 of 2012.

82 See *Southern African Litigation Centre and Another v National Director of Public Prosecutions and Others* [2012] 3 All SA 198 (GNP); *National Commissioner of the South African Police Service and another v Southern African Human Rights Litigation Centre and another* 2014 (2) SA 42 (SCA); and *National Commissioner of Police v Southern African Human Rights Litigation Centre and Another* 2015 (1) SA 315 (CC).

83 See *S v Okah* 2015 (2) SACR 561 (GJ); on appeal: *S v Okah* 2017 (1) SACR 1 (SCA); on appeal to the Constitutional Court, *S v Okah* (CCT 315/16; CCT 193/17)[2018] ZACC 3 (23 February 2018). The case against Okah was brought under the Protection of Constitutional Democracy against Terrorist and Related Activities Act 33 of 2004 (which came into effect on 20 May 2005).

84 For a more comprehensive discussion, see Chapter 49.

DISCUSSION

The problematic internationalising impulse

Note that this tendency to emphasise the international aspects of the field is not just a historical preference or institutional bias. Rather, it is the normative choice on the part of many international lawyers driven by their conviction that international rather than domestic courts are the natural forum to prosecute crimes that '... disrupt the international legal order by threatening the "peace, security and well-being of the world".'[85] For those lawyers adopting such a viewpoint, national prosecutions are considered to be retrogressive setbacks.[86] The history of international criminal law on this reading is, therefore, one of progression away from the domestic and towards the international sphere,[87] with the ICC being regarded as the endpoint[88] for international criminal law.

Such an approach, with its internationalising impulse,[89] is problematic. Not only does it risk mischaracterising the history of international criminal law, but also blinding its followers to the flaws of previous institutional highpoints such as Nuremberg. More specifically, it risks misrepresenting the construction of the Rome system in at least two ways. Firstly, by creating the false impression that the domestic prosecution of such crimes is a new phenomenon, it downplays the responsibility of domestic courts, which is pivotal to the Rome Statute's principle of complementarity.[90] On this reading, there is the risk that complementarity is not regarded as an organising principle of the Rome system, but rather as an unfortunate concession to state sovereignty or as a practical compromise driven by scarce resources. Secondly, there is the risk that if too much weight is given to the ICC's function, which itself is not institutionally beyond reproach,[91] in the application and development of international criminal law, that any of its failings will be projected onto or assimilated within the discipline as a whole.[92]

---

85 Jessberger F 'International v national prosecution of international crimes' in Cassese A *The Oxford Companion to International Criminal Justice* (2009) 208. See, too, Simpson *Law, War and Crime* 30–53.

86 See Cassese A 'Reflections on international criminal justice' (1998) 61(1) *ModLRev* 1–10 at 1. For a conciliatory approach, see Alvarez 'Crimes of states/crimes of hate' 365. See, generally, Simpson *Law, War and Crime* Chapter 2. At 30, Simpson notes: 'This question of place has hovered over the war crimes field since its inception'.

87 Simpson notes:

> **For some international lawyers, these are not arbitrary historical tensions but rather a working through of the cosmopolitan trajectory. Domestic trials, court-martials, amnesties, or political settlements are viewed, quite often, as 'setbacks' for international justice ... The future is said to lie with international criminal courts and the supercession of the provincialism of domestic courts. The ICC itself, then, is not simply a high point of international criminal law but something of an endpoint, too (the domestic finally ceding to the international).**

Simpson *Law, War and Crime* 34.

88 Werle and Jessberger describe the ICC as 'the final milestone in the development of international criminal law'. Werle and Jessberger *Principles of International Criminal Law* 17.

89 Simpson *Law, War and Crime* 30.

90 The ICC will only be able to admit a case (where the other jurisdictional bases of nationality and territoriality are present) if the state party concerned is unwilling or unable to prosecute the offender nationally. See Preamble and art 17 of the Rome Statute.

91 See, generally, Megret F 'Three dangers for the International Criminal Court: A critical look at a consensual project' (2001) 12 *Finnish YBIL* 193 SSRN eLibrary. http://ssrn.com/abstract=1156086.

92 Simpson states:

> **International criminal law's most recent innovation, then, is simply a physical rehearsal of a movement between the domestic and the international that constitutes the field itself. The modalities of international justice involve a perpetual negotiation between the claims of the cosmopolitan and the needs of the local, the former constantly threatening to collapse into hegemony, the latter into parochialism ... This negotiation is the very stuff of international criminal law.**

Simpson *Law, War and Crime* 53.

THIS CHAPTER IN ESSENCE

1. International criminal law is a distinct field of study.
2. Some commentators classify it as part of public international law, while others view it as the international aspects of criminal law. Our approach is to treat it as distinct, but also as part of the South African criminal justice system.
3. Most of the crimes, notably the so-called core crimes under international law (as discussed in the next chapter), are also crimes under South African law. South Africa is also, by virtue of numerous international obligations, part of the system of international criminal justice briefly discussed in this chapter.

Chapter 47

The core international crimes

CHAPTER OBJECTIVES

The objectives of this chapter are to:
- identify and discuss the elements of the crime of genocide
- identify and discuss the elements of crimes against humanity
- identify and discuss the elements of war crimes
- identify and discuss the elements of the crime of aggression.

47.1 Introduction

Three of the core international crimes - genocide, crimes against humanity and war crimes - share a common structure in that they are made up of acts that when committed in conjunction with certain specified contextual elements, are elevated from the realm of ordinary to international criminal conduct. As discussed below, these contextual elements differ in substance and form between each of the three core crimes. An important distinction exists between war crimes and crimes against humanity, the contextual elements of which are material aspects of the crimes, and between war crimes and genocide for which the contextual element is either predominantly or wholly mental. In addition, we will discuss the fourth core crime, the pre-eminent crime against peace, namely the crime of aggression.

47.2 Genocide

47.2.1 Introduction

The practice of genocide is at least as old as recorded history. Numerous religious texts contain references, sometimes in disturbingly positive terms, to acts that would constitute genocide as it is understood today. The term 'genocide', however, is a more recent term. Raphael Lemkin, a prominent Polish lawyer, coined the term[1] when referring to the Nazi crimes of extermination committed against European Jews during World War II, although an earlier genocide had in fact occurred of up to one million Armenians living in Turkey at the start of World War I.[2] At the time, Lemkin defined genocide as 'actions aimed at the destruction of essential foundations of the life of a group and guided by a plan to annihilate the group'.[3]

Despite the classification and developing norms of an international crime of genocide, it was not prosecuted as such during the Nuremberg Tribunal. Instead, acts that would today be considered as genocide were prosecuted as the war crime of extermination and as the crime against humanity of persecution.[4] It was only after the Nuremberg Trials that the term 'genocide' became recognised as an international crime in its own right. In 1946, the United Nations (UN) General Assembly adopted Resolution 96(I), entitled The Crime of Genocide, which affirmed that 'genocide is a crime under international law which the civilized world condemns, and for the commission of which principals and accomplices - whether private

1 From the Latin *cide* (killing) and the Greek *genos* (tribe or race); Sands, P *East West Street: On the origins of Genocide and Crimes Against Humanity* (2016) 179.

2 The status of the Armenian genocide remains highly politicised and contested. Turkey continues to deny its occurrence and the US refuses to label the massacres 'genocide'. Some countries, such as France, have adopted legislation labelling it the 'Armenian genocide'. Werle and Jessberger *Principles of International Criminal Law* 289.

3 Werle and Jessberger *Principles of International Criminal Law* 292.

4 See (High Command Trial) *United States of America v Wilhelm von Leeb et al* US Military Tribunal (Nuremberg) Judgment of 27 October 1948.

individuals, public officials or statesmen, and whether the crime is committed on religious, racial, political or any other grounds – are punishable'.[5] It invited UN member states to 'enact the necessary legislation for the prevention and punishment of this crime'.[6]

This process culminated in the Convention for the Prevention and Punishment of the Crime of Genocide 1948[7] (Genocide Convention), the adopted definition of which formed the basis of article 6 of the Rome Statute 1998 (Rome Statute) on genocide. Despite the existence of state consensus as to its substantive terms and the need to prevent a reoccurrence of such atrocities,[8] the Genocide Convention was unable to prevent the occurrence of three probable genocides in more recent history:

1. The Rwandan genocide took place between April and July 1994, during which approximately 800 000 Tutsis and moderate Hutus were killed, and which led to the establishment of the International Criminal Tribunal for Rwanda (ICTR).
2. There were possible episodes of genocide following the collapse of the former Yugoslavia and during the resultant conflicts, for example the killing of 8 000 men and boys at Srebrenica in July 1995.[9] This led to the establishment of the International Criminal Tribunal for the Former Yugoslavia (ICTY).
3. The conflict that erupted in Darfur in 2004 has been characterised as genocide both politically and in a preliminary decision of the International Criminal Court (ICC) when it issued an arrest warrant for Sudanese President Omar Hassan Al-Bashir for his role in it.[10]

Certainly, any conviction of the crime of genocide carries with it significant gravitas as the crime of crimes. As the Appeals Chamber in *Krstic* opined:

> **Among the grievous crimes this Tribunal has the duty to punish, the crime of genocide is singled out for special condemnation and opprobrium. The crime is horrific in its scope; its perpetrators identify entire human groups for extinction. Those who devise and implement genocide seek to deprive humanity of the manifold richness its nationalities, races, ethnicities and religions provide. This is a crime against all of humankind, its harm being felt not only by the group targeted for destruction, but by all of humanity.**[11]

5 UN General Assembly Resolution 96(I) 11 December 1946 at 4. The Resolution defined genocide as follows at para 1:

> **Genocide is a denial of the right of existence of entire human groups, as homicide is the denial of the right to live of individual human beings; such denial of the right of existence shocks the conscience of mankind, results in great losses to humanity in the form of cultural and other contributions represented by these human groups, and is contrary to moral law and to the spirit and aims of the United Nations.**

6 UN General Assembly Resolution 96(I) 11 December 1946 at para 5.

7 Adopted on 9 December 1948 as General Assembly Resolution 260 A (III), and entered into force on 12 January 1951 once 20 states had ratified it. See article XIII of the Genocide Convention.

8 In 1951, the International Court of Justice (ICJ) declared that 'the principles underlying the Convention are principles which are recognized by civilized nations as binding on states, even without any conventional obligation'. Today, the prohibition on genocide is widely considered as a *jus cogens* norm of international law. See International Court of Justice Reservations to the Convention on the Prevention and Punishment of the Crime of Genocide Advisory Opinion of 28 May 1951 at 23.

9 See ICTY *Prosecutor v Vidoje Blagojevic and Dragan Jokic* (trial judgment) IT-02-60-T 17 January 2005 (*Blagojevic* trial), and ICTY *Prosecutor v Vidoje Blagojevic and Dragan Jokic* (appeal judgment) IT-02-60-A 9 May 2007 (*Blagojevic* appeal). See further, Gevers C and Du Plessis M 'Blagojevic and Jokic' in Sluiter G and Klip A (eds) *Annotated Leading Cases of International Criminal Tribunals* Student ed Vol XXVI (2011).

10 In ICC *Prosecutor v Omar Hassan Ahmad Al Bashir* ICC-02/05-01/09-94 July 2010 at 15–16 (second decision on the prosecution's application for a warrant of arrest), the ICC Pre-Trial Chamber 1 examined the alleged attacks on the targeted ethnic groups that affected hundreds of thousands of individuals in the Darfur region during a period of five years.

11 ICTY *Prosecutor v Radislav Krstic* (appeal judgment) IT-98-33-A April 2004 (*Krstic* appeal) at 36.

However, while it may be true politically that genocide is considered more serious than other crimes under international criminal law, none of the core crimes is more important or attracts more severe levels of punishment than another. As the Darfur Commission, aware of the political consequences of its finding that there was no genocidal policy on the part of the Sudanese Government in respect of Darfur, noted:

> **It is indisputable that genocide bears a special stigma, for it is aimed at the physical obliteration of human groups. However, one should not be blind to the fact that some categories of crimes against humanity may be similarly heinous and carry a similarly grave stigma. In fact, the Appeals Chamber of the ICTR reversed the view that genocide was the 'crime of crimes'. In *Kayishema* and *Ruyindana*, the accused alleged 'that the Trial Chamber erred in finding that genocide is the "crime of crimes" because there is no such hierarchical gradation of crimes'. The Appeals Chamber agreed: 'The Appeals Chamber remarks that there is no hierarchy of crimes under the Statute, and that all of the crimes specified therein are "serious violations of international humanitarian law", capable of attracting the same sentence.'**[12]

As Schabas suggests, this tendency to regard genocide as the crime of crimes may pass with time as other crimes, particularly persecution as a crime against humanity,[13] become part of popular political discourse.[14]

The exact contours of the crime of genocide remain contested by states and academics, as well as in the jurisprudence of international and domestic courts. There is disagreement also regarding how to structure a discussion of the crime of genocide. One approach is to separate the underlying acts of genocide and the protected groups (the material elements of genocide) from the special intent (the mental element of genocide). Another is to divide the crime into its objective elements (the underlying acts and protected groups) and its subjective elements (*mens rea* in respect of the underlying act and specific intent).[15] For the sake of consistency of approach with the other core crimes discussed here, the discussion is separated into the underlying acts of genocide, followed by consideration of its contextual elements. The contextual elements are made up of the protected groups, specific intent and the existence of a state policy as a possible additional element. The mental aspects are therefore considered in two places: first as part of the underlying act and then as the contextual element of specific intent.

47.2.2 Acts constituting genocide

The Genocide Convention lists five underlying acts of genocide that are repeated verbatim in article 6 of the Rome Statute of the ICC, and are accepted as part of customary international law:

1. Killing members of a protected group
2. Causing serious bodily or mental harm to members of a protected group

---

12 *Report of the International Commission of Inquiry on Darfur to the United Nations Secretary General: Pursuant to Security Council Resolution 1564 of 18 Sept 2004* Geneva 25 January 2005 at 506.

13 Persecution, as defined by art 7(1)(*h*) of the Rome Statute, is committed against 'any identifiable group or collectivity on political, racial, national, ethnic, cultural, religious, gender ... or other grounds that are universally recognized as impermissible under international law'.

14 Schabas WA *Genocide in International Law: The Crime of Crimes* 2 ed (2009) 119.

15 See Darfur Commission 490–491.

3. Deliberately inflicting conditions of life on a protected group calculated to bring about its physical destruction in whole or in part
4. Imposing measures intended to prevent births in a protected group
5. Forcibly transferring children of a protected group to another group[16]

47.2.2.1 Killing[17]

In *Akayesu*, the ICTR Trial Chamber noted that:

> **the term 'killing' used in the English version [of the Genocide Convention] is too general, since it could very well include both intentional and unintentional homicides, whereas the term '*meurtre*', used in the French version, is more precise. It is accepted that there is murder when death has been caused with the intention to do so ...[18]**

In contrast, according to the ICC Elements of Crimes, '[t]he term "killed" is interchangeable with the term "caused death"'.[19] Notably, the killing of a single person is sufficient for the purposes of this underlying act. Finally, for an act of killing to meet the requirements of an underlying act of genocide, the person killed must be a member of the protected group targeted for genocide.

47.2.2.2 Causing serious bodily or mental harm

In terms of the types of conduct that may fall in the category of serious harm, the ad hoc tribunals have found that this may include 'acts of torture, inhuman or degrading treatment, sexual violence including rape, interrogations combined with beatings, threats of death, and deportation'.[20] The ad hoc tribunals have held that while any harm caused need not be permanent or irremediable,[21] it must nevertheless 'resul[t] in a grave and long-term disadvantage to a person's ability to lead a normal and constructive life'[22] and constitute more than a minor or temporary impairment of mental faculties.[23]

47.2.2.3 Deliberately inflicting conditions of life calculated to bring about physical destruction

This underlying act was included in the Genocide Convention to cover acts that are intended to bring about the destruction of a group, or part thereof, indirectly or consequentially, and was influenced by various specific historical examples of such acts.[24] The approach of the

16 Although these are classified as acts of genocide, they include both their commission and omission. See, for example, section 47.2.2.3.

17 See further, Schabas *Genocide in International Law* 177–179.

18 ICTR *Prosecutor v Jean-Paul Akayesu* (trial judgment) ICTR-96-4-T September 1998 (*Akayesu* trial) at 500.

19 Art 6(*a*) fn 2 of the ICC Elements of Crimes.

20 ICTY *Prosecutor v Radislav Krstic* (trial judgment) IT-98-33-T August 2001 (*Krstic* trial) at 513. See also ICTR *Prosecutor v Georges Anderson Nderubumwe Rutaganda* (judgment and sentence) ICTR-96-3-T December 1999 (*Rutaganda* judgment and sentence) at 51.

21 ICTR *Prosecutor v Clément Kayishema and Obed Ruzindana* (trial judgment) ICTR-95-1-T May 1999 (*Kayishema* trial) at 108; *Akayesu* trial at 502; *Krstic* trial at 513.

22 *Krstic* trial at 513.

23 ICTR *Prosecutor v Laurent Semanza* (judgment and sentence) ICTR-97-20-T May 2003 (*Semanza* judgment and sentence) at 321–322. However, the International Law Commission (ILC) in its Draft Code of Crimes against the Peace and Security of Mankind with Commentaries 1996 at art 17 p 46 suggests a higher threshold, namely that '[t]he bodily harm or the mental harm inflicted on members of a group must be of such a serious nature as to threaten its destruction in whole or in part'.

24 During the debate leading up to its adoption, reference was made (by France) to the horrific conditions in the so-called ghettos during World War II.

ICTR, as reflected in *Akayesu*, has been that:

> **the expression, 'deliberately inflicting on the group conditions of life calculated to bring about its physical destruction in whole or in part', should be construed as the methods of destruction by which the perpetrator does not immediately kill the members of the group, but which, ultimately, seek their physical destruction.**[25]

In terms of the physical acts that may meet the requirements of this underlying act, the ICTR has held that the following acts do so: subjecting a group to a subsistence diet, systematic expulsion from homes, the reduction of essential medical services below minimum requirement,[26] rape, the starving of a group of people, and withholding sufficient living accommodation for a reasonable period.[27] To the extent that it satisfies the other requirements of genocide, this underlying act is also arguably the most appropriate to the extent that genocide can be committed by way of ethnic cleansing.[28]

47.2.2.4 Measures intended to prevent births

Although this underlying act was introduced against a specific historical backdrop, arguably such measures adopted 'need not be the classic action of sterilisation; separation of the sexes, prohibition of marriage and the like are measures equally restrictive and produce the same results'.[29] This raises the questions as to whether rape and other forms of sexual assault may also qualify as measures intended to prevent births.[30]

In *Bosnia*, Bosnia contended that 'rape and sexual violence against women led to physical trauma which interfered with victims' reproductive functions and, in some cases, resulted in infertility'.[31] Such infertility, as a physical consequence of such action, may well qualify under article 2(*d*) of the Geneva Convention. However, the other aspect of Bosnia's argument – that the psychological and social effects of rape and sexual violence would lead to a decline in births in such communities – is a much more remote causal connection in terms of qualifying as the underlying act of measures intended to prevent births. Ultimately, because the ICJ dismissed these arguments on factual rather than legal grounds due to insufficient evidence, they remain to be determined judicially.[32]

---

25 *Akayesu* trial at 505. Such an understanding of this underlying act is both unique and problematic in a number of respects. Although it is an underlying act – and part of the physical element or *actus reus* of genocide – it contains a mental aspect that overlaps considerably with the specific intent element of genocide, namely the requirement of the act being 'calculated to bring about physical destruction'. Therefore, unlike other underlying acts that may be satisfied by omissions, this one requires a deliberate calculation and mental intention to destroy the group. See Schabas *Genocide in International Law* 196.

26 *Akayesu* trial at 505–506.

27 *Kayishema* trial at 116.

28 The forcible transfer of members of a group, particularly when it involves the separation of family members, could also constitute genocide under subparagraph (*c*). See Werle and Jessberger *Principles of International Criminal Law* 318. Similarly, the ILC in its Report of the International Law Commission on the work of its 48th session (1996) at 46 considered that this underlying act covered deportation when carried out with the intent to 'destroy the group in whole or in part'. In addition, the practice of 'systematic expulsion from homes' was included in the ICC Elements of Crimes 3 under 'deliberately inflicting conditions of life calculated to bring about physical destruction'.

29 Robinson N *The Genocide Convention: A Commentary* (1960) 64.

30 Schabas *Genocide in International Law* 199.

31 ICJ *Application of the Convention on the Prevention and Punishment of the Crime of Genocide (Bosnia and Herzegovina v Serbia and Montenegro)* Judgment ICJ Reports 26 February 2007 at 356 (*Bosnia* judgment).

32 Schabas *Genocide in International Law* 199–200.

47.2.2.5 Forcibly transferring children from one group to another

Of the underlying acts of genocide, this is the most unclear and the least relied on. Schabas suggests that '[this provision] was added to the [Genocide] Convention almost as an afterthought with little substantive debate or consideration'.[33] The act of forcibly transferring children need not be done directly or even physically. This is reflected in the ICC Elements of Crimes, which states that:

> **[t]he term 'forcibly' is not restricted to physical force, but may include threat of force or coercion, such as that caused by fear of violence, duress, detention, psychological oppression or abuse of power, against such person or persons or another person, or by taking advantage of a coercive environment.[34]**

Further, in *Akayesu*, the ICTR Trial Chamber suggested that this provision included acts of threats or trauma, which by effect would lead to the forcible transfer of children from one group to another.[35] In terms of other qualifying criteria for this underlying act, it is also necessary that the act achieved its intended purpose of transferring children to another group,[36] and that the subjects of this act were children under the age of 18.[37]

47.2.3 The protected groups

Deciding which groups merit protection was by far the most controversial aspect of the drafting of the Genocide Convention, as much for the nature and contours of those groups included, as for those implicitly or explicitly excluded. Ultimately, the four groups protected were national, racial, ethnic and religious groups.[38] In terms of how these groups are established or defined, jurisprudence points to the existence of both subjective and objective elements for the identification of groups.[39] The subjective element is generally considered from the perspective of the perpetrator as it is the intent of the perpetrator that underpins the crime of genocide. However, in some cases, courts have considered whether the targeted individuals identified themselves as belonging to one of the protected groups. It appears that the emerging consensus is that both subjective and objective indicators are to be considered. In *Stakic*, the Appeals Chamber found that:

> **[c]ontrary to what the Prosecution argues, the *Krstic* and the *Rutaganda* trial judgments do not suggest that target groups may only be defined subjectively, by reference to the way the perpetrator stigmatises victims. The trial [chamber] in *Krstic* found only that 'stigmatization ... by the perpetrators' can be used as 'a criterion' when defining target groups – not that stigmatization can be used as the sole criterion. Similarly while the *Rutaganda* Trial Chamber found national, ethnic,**

---

33 Schabas *Genocide in International Law* 201.

34 Art 6(e)1 of the ICC Elements of Crimes. Also see Schabas *Genocide in International Law* 199–200.

35 *Akayesu* trial at 509; Schabas *Genocide in International Law* 199–201.

36 Schabas *Genocide in International Law* 202.

37 See art 6(e)6 of the ICC Elements of Crimes: 'The perpetrator knew, or should have known, that the person or persons were under the age of 18 years'.

38 The groups explicitly excluded from the protection of this crime during its drafting included political groups, ideological groups, linguistic groups and economic groups. Significantly, in *Akayesu* trial at 516, the ICTR Trial Chamber found that the protected groups were not limited to these four groups, but rather included 'any stable and permanent group'. This expansive construction of the term 'group' was initially followed in subsequent decisions of the ICTR. Furthermore, the Darfur Commission endorsed the *Akayesu* approach. However, this has been heavily and rightly criticised as judicial law making. Similarly, the push to include the concept of cultural genocide in the scope of this crime, which inclusion was rejected explicitly during the drafting of the Genocide Convention, has led some courts to adopt expansive interpretations of specific intent to include this crime in substance.

39 The group need not be a minority.

> **racial, and religious identity to be largely subjective concepts, suggesting that acts may constitute genocide so long as the perpetrator perceives the victim as belonging to the targeted national, ethnic, racial, or religious group, it also held that 'a subjective definition alone is not enough to determine victim groups, as provided for in the Genocide Convention'.**[40]

With this in mind, we will next examine the four protected groups - national, ethnic, racial and religious - in more detail. In doing so, it is important to keep in mind from the outset that often an overlap exists between these different categories of groups, both conceptually and in practice.

47.2.3.1 National groups

In *Akayesu*, the ICTR Trial Chamber defined a 'national group' as 'a collection of people who are perceived to share a legal bond based on common citizenship, coupled with reciprocity of rights and duties'.[41] Conversely, Schabas argues that national groups must be considered in the context within which the Genocide Convention was written and not defined by contemporary understandings of nationality that have evolved since then. Set within the context of 1948 and the writings of Raphael Lemkin, the term 'national group' dictates a large scope corresponding to the concept of 'minority' or 'national minority'. One that in reality is broad enough to encompass racial, ethnic and religious groups as well.[42]

47.2.3.2 Racial groups

The notion of 'race' is a controversial one. Although there was little debate over the inclusion of racial groups as a protected group in the Genocide Convention, reaching a universally or even widely accepted definition of what 'race' means has proved much more difficult. Reference to the International Convention on the Elimination of All Forms of Racial Discrimination 1965 is of little assistance in this regard as it defines 'racial discrimination' as 'any distinction, exclusion, restriction or preference based on race, colour, descent or national or ethnic origin'.[43] Again, this counsels against viewing these grounds as distinct, and rather - at least as national, racial and ethnic grounds are concerned - seeing them as Schabas suggested: as corner posts that delimit a general category of 'protected grounds'.[44]

47.2.3.3 Ethnic groups

Defining the term 'ethnic group' is similarly problematic. Consequently, Shaw argues that it is probably preferable to take the two concepts (race and ethnicity) together to cover relevant cases rather than attempting to distinguish between these so that unfortunate gaps appear.[45] The difficulties of delimiting the concept of ethnicity, and distinguishing it from that of race, were clearly evident in the debates in the ICTR regarding whether the Tutsi and Hutu groups were ethnic or racial. Finally, the ICTR decided, extraordinarily, to take judicial notice of the fact that both of these two groups, as well as the Twa, met the requirements of ethnic groups for the purposes of the Genocide Convention.[46]

---

40 ICTY *Prosecutor v Milomir Stakic* (appeal judgment) IT-97-24-A March 2006 (*Stakic* appeal) at 25.

41 *Akayesu* trial at 512.

42 Schabas *Genocide in International Law* at 134.

43 Art 1(1) of the International Convention on the Elimination of All Forms of Racial Discrimination 1965.

44 Schabas *Genocide in International Law* at 143.

45 Shaw MN *International Law* 6 ed (2008) 807.

46 Schabas *Genocide in International Law* 125.

47.2.3.4 Religious groups

The inclusion of religious groups was controversial due to the fact that individuals may join and leave such groups freely, unlike the other protected groups that are permanent or at least more stable. Unsurprisingly, the tendency has been to define religious groups broadly rather than narrowly to expand the scope of protection available under the Genocide Convention. Consequently, the concept has been interpreted to include even those who reject religious beliefs, that is, atheists.[47] One further point to note here is that due to the overlap that exists between religion and culture, this goes some way to affording protection for cultural genocide in practice, despite the fact that it has been rejected per se as a formal category to be protected under the Genocide Convention.

47.2.4 Specific intent (*dolus specialis*)

The requirement for intent to commit crimes of genocide exists at two levels. Firstly, each of the underlying acts must be committed with intent in the ordinary criminal law sense (*mens rea*).[48] Secondly, the perpetrator must possess the specific intent to destroy a protected group in whole or in part as the distinguishing element of genocide (*dolus specialis*). In this regard, the ICJ in *Bosnia* noted:

> **[Genocide] requires a further mental element. It requires the establishment of the 'intent to destroy, in whole or in part, ... [the protected] group, as such'. It is not enough to establish, for instance in terms of paragraph (*a*), that deliberate unlawful killings of members of the group have occurred. The additional intent must also be established, and is defined very precisely. It is often referred to as a special or specific intent or *dolus specialis*; ... It is not enough that the members of the group are targeted because they belong to that group, that is because the perpetrator has a discriminatory intent. Something more is required. The acts listed in Article II must be done with intent to destroy the group as such in whole or in part.**
>
> **The words 'as such' emphasize that intent to destroy the protected group.**[49]

This requirement of specific intent is subject to differing, contested interpretations by courts and academics alike. Chief among these controversies is 'the intent to destroy' element of

47 Lippman M 'The Convention on the Prevention and Punishment of the Crime of Genocide: Fifty years later' (1998) 15(2) *Ariz J Int'l & Comp L* 415 at 456. For an opposing view, see Werle and Jessberger *Principles of International Criminal Law* 299–300.

48 In this regard, certain underlying acts contain explicit mental considerations. As the ICJ noted in *Bosnia* at 186:

> **It is well established that the [underlying] acts ... themselves include mental elements. 'Killing' must be intentional, as must 'causing serious bodily or mental harm'. Mental elements are made explicit in paragraphs (*c*) and (*d*) of Article II by the words 'deliberately' and 'intended', quite apart from the implications of the words 'inflicting' and 'imposing'; and forcible transfer too requires deliberate intentional acts. The acts, in the words of the [International Law Commission], are by their very nature conscious, intentional or volitional acts.**

The ICJ cited the ICL's Commentary on article 17 of the Draft Code of Crimes against the Peace and Security of Mankind, ILC Report 1996, *Yearbook of the International Law Commission*, 1996, Vol II, Part Two, 46, para 15. In addition, at times the necessary intent for such acts is more than just volitional and requires the wilful seeking of a particular outcome, for example, 'deliberately inflicting on a protected group conditions of life calculated to bring about its physical destruction in whole or in part'. In such instances, the distinction between intention and motive, and between intent in respect of the underlying act (*mens rea*) and the broader requirement of specific intent, becomes blurred. See Schabas *Genocide in International Law* 176 and 263.

49 *Bosnia* at 187. In *Bosnia* at 189, the ICJ cautioned:

> **[S]pecific intent is ... to be distinguished from other reasons or motives the perpetrator may have. Great care must be taken in finding in the facts a sufficiently clear manifestation of that intent.**

specific intent. The central debate among lawyers and academics is whether the destruction contemplated in specific intent is limited to physical or biological destruction, or whether the intent to destroy can include the destruction of a group, as a group, through means other than physical or biological destruction of its constituents, such as displacement.

Despite the fact that 'the Genocide Convention, and customary international law in general, prohibit only the physical or biological destruction of a human group',[50] and that inclusion of the notion of cultural genocide was rejected, some judges and scholars have adopted formulations of the crime that seek to include the destruction of a group in non-physical and non-biological ways.[51] Notably, there are a number of reasons why this approach should be rejected.[52]

In addition, the requirement that the accused must have the intent to destroy a protected group 'in whole or in part ... as such' has also caused some controversy. While the concept of an intent to destroy the protected group as a whole is reasonably self-explanatory, some disagreement exists regarding the meaning of 'in part', specifically whether the subgroup (that is, the 'part' of the group) targeted is qualitatively or quantitatively relevant (or both).

Those who favour the *quantitative* construction of this element suggest that the 'part' should be substantial. The US, for example, suggests that the threshold for such a test is that 'a part of a group [is] of such numerical significance that the destruction or loss of that part would cause the destruction of the group as a viable entity within the nation of which such a group is part'.[53] This has been the approach adopted in the jurisprudence of the international tribunals.[54]

Others focus on the *qualitative* aspect of the targeted subgroup. As Schabas notes, under this construction, the 'part' targeted for destruction must be *significant* rather than substantial.[55] Such significance must be gauged in terms of the subgroup's importance to the continued survival of the group as a whole. The ILC has given several examples of what may constitute a significant 'part' of a group: 'political and administrative leaders, religious leaders, academics and intellectuals, business leaders, and others'.[56] Others have suggested that a group's law enforcement and military personnel may constitute a significant part of a group because neutralising them would render a group defenceless. Ultimately, the test of a subgroup's significance is 'whether the destruction of a social strata threatens the group's survival as a whole'.[57]

---

50 *Krstic* (appeal) at 25.

51 See the dissenting opinion of Judge Shahabuddeen in *Krstic* (appeal) at 50, where he notes:

> **It is the group which is protected. A group is constituted by characteristics – often intangible – binding together a collection of people as a social unit. If those characteristics have been destroyed in pursuance of the intent with which a listed act of a physical or biological nature was done, it is not convincing to say that the destruction, though effectively obliterating the group, is not genocide because the obliteration was not physical or biological.**

52 Firstly, the majority of the court in *Krstic* implicitly rejected Judge Shahabuddeen's hypothesis. Secondly, there is a compelling argument that the 'underlying act' and the 'intent with which it was done' cannot be separated as the learned Judge suggested because such an interpretation was implicitly rejected by the drafters of the Genocide Convention. On a more practical level, although the two elements are notionally distinct, they are often considered together. Therefore, the existence of the mental element, often, is inferred from the physical acts because it is seldom possible to prove specific intent by direct evidence.

53 Schabas *Genocide in International Law* 278.

54 Schabas *Genocide in International Law* 279.

55 Schabas *Genocide in International Law* 281–282.

56 Schabas *Genocide in International Law* 282.

57 Schabas *Genocide in International Law* 283.

A third approach, as illustrated by the ICJ's endorsement in *Bosnia*, is a mixed approach, with both quantitative and qualitative aspects:

> **In the first place, the intent must be to destroy at least a substantial part of the particular group. That is demanded by the very nature of the crime of genocide since the object and purpose of the convention as a whole is to prevent the intentional destruction of groups, [and] the part targeted must be significant enough to have an impact on the group as a whole.**[58]

A further construct is to consider the scope of destruction from a *geographical* perspective. Under this approach, the element of 'in whole or in part' becomes relative to the area concerned and not to the group generally. As the ICJ further noted in *Bosnia*: 'It is widely accepted that genocide may be found to have been committed when the intent is to destroy the group within a geographically limited area'.[59]

Ultimately, there is no unanimity in either national or international jurisprudence as to the correct approach to this sub-element of genocidal intent. Perhaps, therefore, the best approach is one that considers genocidal intent on a case-by-case basis, having regard to the quantitative, qualitative and possibly geographical aspects of the group targeted for destruction.

As far as establishing the existence of specific intent is concerned, in the absence of a public declaration of such specific intent or other documentary evidence, courts have inferred its existence from the context in which the crime took place. In *Jelisic*, the ICTY listed, 'the general context, the perpetration of other culpable acts systematically directed against the same group ..., the scale of atrocities committed, the systematic targeting of victims on account of their membership of a particular group, or the repetition of destructive and discriminatory acts' as the basis on which specific intent may be inferred.[60] This, however, does not mean that specific intent should be inferred lightly. Indeed, the ICTY Appeals Chamber counselled against this in *Krstic*, noting that '[g]enocide is one of the worst crimes known to humankind, and its gravity is reflected in the stringent requirement of specific intent. Convictions for genocide can be entered only where intent has been unequivocally established'.[61]

47.3 Crimes against humanity

47.3.1 Introduction

The term 'crimes against humanity' was first used in 1915 when France, Great Britain and Russia issued a joint condemnation of the atrocities committed against Armenians by Turkey.[62] Shortly thereafter, in 1919, the Commission on the Responsibility of the Authors of the War and on the Enforcement of Penalties – established by the Entente Powers after World War I – referred once again to 'violations of the laws of humanity' committed by the Central Powers. However, the notion was a political label rather than a legal classification.

58 *Bosnia* at 198.
59 *Bosnia* at 199.
60 ICTY *Prosecutor v Goran Jelisic* (appeal judgment) IT-95-10-A July 2001 at 47.
61 *Krstic* (appeal) at 134.
62 Werle and Jessberger *Principles of International Criminal Law* 329.

It was only after the end of World War II, in the face of having to respond to Nazi crimes, that the concept of crimes against humanity took on legal features and significance[63] primarily through its inclusion in the Nuremberg Charter[64] and its subsequent application to those responsible for these atrocities. However, its exact legal basis and contours were unclear.[65] This was done to cover the most heinous crimes committed by the Nazis, which war crimes law – as it stood then – did not address.

The Nuremberg Charter defines crimes against humanity as follows:

> **Murder, extermination, enslavement, deportation, and other inhumane acts committed against any civilian population, before or during the war, or persecutions on political, racial or religious grounds in execution of or in connection with any crime within the jurisdiction of the Tribunal, whether or not in violation of the domestic law of the country where perpetrated.**[66]

In terms of this basic definition, Cryer et al suggested that:

> **Three major features may be noted. First the reference to 'any' civilian population meant that even crimes committed against a country's own population were included ... Second, the requirement of connection to war crimes or the crime of aggression meant in effect that crimes against humanity could occur with some 'nexus' to armed conflict. Third, the reference to 'population' was understood to create some requirement of scale, but the precise threshold was specified neither in the Charter nor in the Nuremberg Judgement.**[67]

Following the Nuremberg and Tokyo Tribunals, Control Council Law No. 10,[68] which applied in occupied Germany and was aimed at the prosecution of war criminals other than those dealt with by the Nuremberg Tribunal, further developed the definition of crimes against humanity. It added rape, imprisonment and torture to the growing list of prohibited acts and, more importantly, removed the requirement that crimes against humanity be committed in connection with war crimes or an act of aggression.[69]

Although the UN General Assembly affirmed 'the principles of international law recognized by the [Nuremberg Charter] ... and the judgment of the Tribunal' and included the concept of crimes against humanity in its Resolution 95(1) (1946), it was the least developed of the Nuremberg crimes in the years to follow. Certain aspects of the crime, namely those concerned with persecutions on political, racial or religious grounds, were developed into the self-standing crime of genocide as described in the previous section. The only other significant international development for the following 40 years was the addition of apartheid as an underlying act by way of the Convention on the Suppression and Punishment of the Crime of Apartheid 1973.

---

63 Whether it was an international crime at the time of the IMT remains debatable.

64 Charter of the International Military Tribunal 8 August 1945.

65 The IMT argued that the crime already existed and was merely codified. On the IMT's lack of clarity regarding the demarcation of crimes against humanity vis-à-vis war crimes, see Cryer R, Friman H, Robinson D and Wilmshurst E *An Introduction to International Criminal Law and Procedure* (2007) 189.

66 Art 6(*c*) of the Nuremberg Charter.

67 Cryer et al *An Introduction to International Criminal Law and Procedure* 188.

68 Control Council Law No 10 Punishment of Persons Guilty of War Crimes, Crimes against Peace and against Humanity 20 December 1945.

69 Cryer et al *An Introduction to International Criminal Law and Procedure* 189.

It was not until the advent of the ad hoc tribunals in the 1990s that crimes against humanity were revived at the international level. Somewhat controversially at the time, article 5 of the ICTY Statute included reference to a jurisdictional link with an armed conflict as a necessary element of crimes against humanity. Similarly, article 3 of the ICTR Statute required that the attack must be committed against a civilian population on national, political, ethnic, racial or religious grounds to constitute a crime against humanity. The definition of crimes against humanity in article 7 of the Rome Statute removed these limiting factors - the link to an armed conflict (ICTY) and the discriminatory aspect of the attack (ICTR) - and defined crimes against humanity as 'the attack against a civilian population that is widespread or systematic'.[70] However, article 7(2)(*a*) of the Rome Statute did add an element, namely that the attack must be pursuant to a state or organisational policy. There is some debate as to whether the wording of article (7(2)(*a*) would include non-state actors (for example criminal gangs, terrorist groups, and so on) as potential perpetrators of crimes against humanity. A broad reading of 'organisational' supports the notion that non-state actors can also commit crimes against humanity. However, this view is generally not supported.[71]

In addition to the statutes of the ad hoc tribunals, the Rome Statute enumerated additional underlying acts of crimes against humanity: the forced transfer of populations, sexual slavery, enforced prostitution, forced pregnancy, enforced sterilisation, sexual violence, enforced disappearances and the crime of apartheid.

As noted previously, genocide, war crimes and crimes against humanity share a common structure: they consist of underlying acts and contextual elements. Given their common heritage, it is unsurprising that crimes against humanity, and genocide especially, are similar, both in structure and substance as the underlying acts overlap substantially.[72] However, an important difference exists between crimes against humanity and genocide in relation to their contextual aspects.[73]

47.3.2 Contextual elements

47.3.2.1 Attacks against civilians

The first contextual element of crimes against humanity requires that they involve an *attack against civilians*. This requirement has two sub-elements: firstly, the underlying acts must be committed in the context of an attack, and secondly, the attack must be directed against civilians. The former sub-element is rarely controversial because it is widely accepted that

70 Although the Pre-Trial Chambers of the ICC appear to have resurrected this element, noting in its decision authorising the investigation into the post-election violence (PEV) in Kenya (ICC-01/09-01/11-101 and ICC-01/09-02/11-96), 'The Chamber considers that the potential civilian victims of a crime under Article 7 of the Statute are groups distinguished by nationality, ethnicity or other distinguishing features'. See also ICC Pre-Trial Chamber II Decision Pursuant to Article 61(7)(*a*) and (*b*) of the Rome Statute on the Charges of the *Prosecutor v Jean-Pierre Bemba Gombo* ICC-01/05-01/08-424 at 76; Pre-Trial Chamber I Decision on the Confirmation of Charges ICC-01/04-01/07-717 at 399.

71 Bassiouni MC (ed) *The Legislative History of the International Criminal Court: Introduction, Analysis and Integrated Text Vol I* (2005) 151–152; Schabas, WA 'State policy as an element of international crimes' 98(3) (2008) *JCLC* 953 at 972–974.

72 Their common underlying acts include murder, torture, rape and sexual slavery. In addition, there are commonalities between war crimes and underlying acts of crimes against humanity as well.

73 For genocide, the underlying acts are accompanied by specific or genocidal intent whereas crimes against humanity are committed as part of a widespread or systematic attack directed against a civilian population pursuant to a state or organisational policy. In addition, to establish a crime against humanity, a nexus must exist between the underlying act (or specific crime) and the contextual elements, and such acts must be committed with knowledge of the attack. As with the case of genocide, it is this contextual aspect of crimes against humanity that elevate otherwise ordinary criminal acts to the level of international crimes.

the attack must be more than just a single, isolated act, and that it can take many different forms. In terms of the requirements of 'attack', article 7(2)(*a*) of the Rome Statute specifically requires 'the multiple commission of acts' against a civilian population for the threshold of crimes against humanity to be met, while the ICC Elements of Crimes clarifies that such acts 'need not constitute a military attack'.

The requirement that such an attack must be directed against civilians is the subject of some debate. Cryer et al suggest that '[t]he term "*civilian population*" connotes crimes directed against civilians rather than combatants'.[74] In contrast, Cassese argues that 'crimes against humanity need not be committed against civilians *per se*, and that members of the military can also be the victims of these crimes'.[75] One significant problem with this more expansive interpretative approach is that international humanitarian law (IHL) not only permits, but in fact facilitates widespread and systematic attacks, including killing, on members of the military under certain conditions in times of armed conflict.[76] The better approach is perhaps to interpret the 'civilian' aspect of 'civilian population' expansively so as to include mixed groups made up of both civilians and military personnel. The ICTY Trial Chamber took this approach in *Tadić* where it noted that the 'presence of certain non-civilians in [their vicinity] does not change the character of the population'.[77] Further, the term 'civilian' should be defined negatively, as is the approach in IHL, whereby all individuals who do not fall within its criteria for combatants are civilians.[78] This would include combatants who no longer take part in hostilities, who are rendered *hors de combat*, and who are prisoners of war.[79]

47.3.2.2 Widespread or systematic

The second contextual element requires that the attack is 'widespread or systematic'. The first thing to note about the contextual element of 'widespread or systematic' is that it must be considered disjunctively, namely that the attack may be either widespread or systematic, and need not be both.[80] With respect to the meaning of these terms, the Trial Chamber in *Akayesu* defined the concept of 'widespread' as 'massive, frequent, large scale action, carried out collectively with considerable seriousness and directed against a multiplicity of victims'.[81] As such an approach illustrates, the term 'widespread' is generally understood to refer to the scale of the attack. As with the quantitative aspect of genocide, there is no gold standard or numerical limit,[82] but rather what amounts to 'widespread' must be determined on a case-by-case basis.

However, while widespread typically refers to the cumulative effect of numerous inhumane acts, it could also be satisfied by a singular massive act of extraordinary magnitude.[83] Further clarification has been given by the ICC's Pre-Trial Chamber II in *Kenya*, where it noted that '[this] ... element refers to both the large-scale nature of the attack and

---

74 Cryer et al *An Introduction to International Criminal Law and Procedure* 192.

75 Cassese *International Criminal Law* 85.

76 Cryer et al *An Introduction to International Criminal Law and Procedure* 192.

77 ICTY *Prosecutor v Tadić* (Trial Chamber II) IT-94-1-T 7 May 1997 at 229 para 638.

78 Art 50 of the Protection of Victims of International Armed Conflicts 1977, called in short Additional Protocol I, an augmentation of the Geneva Conventions. See further, section 47.4.1.

79 See section 47.4.

80 *Akayesu* trial at 579.

81 *Akayesu* trial at 580.

82 Cryer et al *An Introduction to International Criminal Law and Procedure* 194.

83 Cryer et al *An Introduction to International Criminal Law and Procedure* 194–195.

the number of resultant victims. The assessment is neither exclusively quantitative nor geographical but must be carried out on the basis of the individual facts'.[84]

Conversely, 'systematic' refers to the nature of the attacks (not their scale) and 'the improbability of their random occurrence'.[85] In *Akayesu*, the Trial Chamber defined the concept of 'systematic' as 'thoroughly organised and following a regular pattern on the basis of a common policy involving substantial public or private resources'.[86] The ICTY's approach is more detailed, stating that 'systematicity' requires:

- a political objective or plan
- large-scale or continuous commission of crimes that are linked
- use of significant public or private resources
- the implication of high-level political and/or military authorities.[87]

47.3.2.3 Pursuant to a state or organisational policy

In contrast to the ICTY and ICTR, the Rome Statute's definition of crimes against humanity includes an additional contextual element, namely that the attack directed against a civilian population must be 'pursuant to or in furtherance of a state or organisational policy'.[88] As pointed out above under 47.3.1., there is some controversy about the scope of this requirement. There is also some debate about the basis of this requirement in customary international law.[89]

The *Kenya* cases before the ICC illustrate the shifting meaning of 'state or organisational policy' as contextual element of crimes against humanity under the Rome Statute of the ICC. The majority of the Pre-Trial Chamber of the ICC in the decision on the authorisation of an investigation into the situation in Kenya (the post-election violence cases) found that the ICC had jurisdiction over the violent events, because the crimes may have been committed pursuant to an organisational policy. The majority's understanding of 'state or organisational policy' in this context referred to any organisation (including political formations) which were capable of committing widespread or systematic attacks against a civilian population.[90] This understanding, as expressed by the majority of the judges in the Kenya cases, is evidently broader than the state-centred interpretation favoured by those who view article 7(2)(*a*) of the Rome Statute as limited to state policy or organisational policy linked to the state or state-like organs (thus excluding non-state actors). Cherif Bassiouni, who chaired the drafting committee at the Rome Diplomatic Conference where the ICC Statute was negotiated and drafted, also took the view that article 7 (crimes against humanity) should only apply to the state or bodies/organs within a state. Bassiouni was adamant that non-state

84 ICC Decision Pursuant to Article 15 of the Rome Statute on the Authorization of an Investigation into the Situation in the Republic of Kenya ICC-01/09 Pre-Trial Chamber II 31 March 2010 (*Kenya* pre-trial II) at 95.

85 ICC *Prosecutor v Germain Katanga and Mathieu Ngudjolo Chui* (decision on the confirmation of charges) ICC-01/04-01/07-717 Pre-Trial Chamber 1, 30 September 2008 at 394 fn 505.

86 *Akayesu* trial at 580.

87 ICTY *Prosecutor v Tihomir Blaskic* (trial judgment) IT-95-14-T March 2000 (*Blaskic* trial) at 203.

88 Art 7(2)(*a*) of the Rome Statute. According to the ICC Elements of Crimes art 7(3), 'It is understood that "policy to commit such attack" requires that the state or organization actively promote or encourage such an attack against a civilian population'.

89 Jalloh C 'What makes a crime against humanity a crime against humanity?' 28(2) (2013) *Am U Int'l L Rev* 381 at 402–408.

90 *Situation in the Republic of Kenya*, Case No ICC-01/09, Decision Pursuant to Article 15 of the Rome Statute on the Authorization of an Investigation into the Situation in the Republic of Kenya (31 March 2010), available at http://www.refworld.org/cases,ICC,4bc2fe372.html; *Situation in the Republic of Kenya*, Case No ICC-01/09-01/11, Decision on the Prosecutor's Application for Summons to Appear for William Samoei Ruto, Henry Kiprono Kosgey and Joshua Arap Sang (8 March 2011), available at https://www.icc-cpi.int/pages/record.aspx?uri=1037044; *Situation in the Republic of Kenya*, Case No ICC-01/09-02/11, Decision on the Prosecutor's Application for Summonses to Appear for Francis Kirimi Muthaura, Uhuru Muigai Kenyatta and Mohammed Hussein Ali (8 March 2011), available at https://www.icc-cpi.int/Pages/record.aspx?docNo=ICC-01/09-02/11-1.

actors like international terrorist organisations (such as al-Qaeda) or organised criminal groups (such as the Mafia) did not qualify for inclusion within the meaning of article 7 of the Rome Statute.[91]

The view of the majority[92] of the judges in the *Kenya* cases represent an evolving view of crimes against humanity and the notion that non-state actors can also commit these crimes. This view is the result of what some commentators see as a teleological reading of the Rome Statute. In terms of this approach the goal of the Rome Statute is to end impunity for gross human rights violations and other atrocity crimes, regardless of whether these crimes are committed by state or non-state actors[93] (including purely private organisations).[94]

47.3.3 Acts constituting crimes against humanity

The list of acts that constitute crimes against humanity (or prohibited acts) has developed and expanded over time, especially since the original five acts were enumerated in the Nuremberg Charter. Importantly, and in contrast with the underlying acts of genocide, the list of acts specified in article 7 of the Rome Statute is not closed due to inclusion of the catch-all phrase 'other inhumane acts'.

The list of acts that constitute crimes against humanity is too lengthy to explore fully here. It will suffice to make the following comments regarding the four most prevalent acts: murder, torture, persecution and sexual violence.

47.3.3.1 Murder

According to the ICC Elements of Crimes, murder encompasses the notions of 'killing' and 'causing death'.[95] Therefore, the underlying act of murder as a crime against humanity is the same as that of willful killing as a war crime and killing as an underlying act of genocide, the difference being the context within which these attacks take place.

Further guidance on the definition of murder for establishing a crime against humanity is given in *Akayesu* where the ICTR Trial Chamber defined it as 'the unlawful, intentional killing of a human being'.[96] More specifically, the Trial Chamber identified the elements of murder as:

> **the victim is dead; the death resulted from an unlawful act or omission of the accused or a subordinate; at the time of the killing, the accused or a subordinate had the intention to kill or inflict grievous bodily harm on the deceased, having known that such bodily harm was likely to cause the victim's death, and being reckless whether death ensues or not.**[97]

---

91 Bassiouni MC *The Legislative History of the International Criminal Court: Introduction, Analysis and Integrated Text Vol I* (2005) 151–152.

92 The minority opinion by Judge Kaul is more in line with the general academic interpretation of art 7(2(*a*), namely that crimes against humanity cannot be committed by non-state actors and other organisations outside state structures, because they lack the necessary structure and organisation. In terms of Judge Kaul's view, an organisation should at least have a fixed structure and hierarchy, with responsible command, before one can come to the conclusion that such an organisation is capable of 'organisational policy' as per art 7(2)(*a*) of the Rome Statute. See *Authorization of an Investigation (Kenya)* decision, supra, at para 51 (dissenting opinion of Judge Kaul).

93 See also *Prosecutor v Jean-Pierre Bemba Gombo*, Case No ICC-01/05-01/08-424, Decision Pursuant to Art. 61(7)(a) and (b) of the Rome Statute on the Confirmation of the Charges, 15 June 2009, available at https://www.icc-cpi.int/Pages/record.aspx?docNo=ICC-01/05-01/08-424. State or organisational policy requires that the crimes follow a 'regular pattern'.

94 Kress C 'On the outer limits of crimes against humanity: The concept of organization within the policy requirement: Some reflections on the March 2010 ICC Kenya Decision' (2010) 23(4) *LJIL* 855 at 861.

95 Art 7(1)(*a*) fn 7 Element 1 of the ICC Elements of Crimes.

96 *Akayesu* trial at 589.

97 *Akayesu* trial at 589.

47.3.3.2 Torture

The crime of torture is recognised universally as a violation of international law, which some argue should be viewed as a self-standing crime under international law.[98] Under the Rome Statute, however, only those acts of torture that occur in the context of crimes against humanity, genocide or war crimes, and which meet the requisite contextual requirements, may be prosecuted and punished. Further, although the definition of torture as an underlying act of a crime against humanity is substantially similar to the definition of torture under the Convention Against Torture and Other Cruel, Inhuman or Degrading Treatment or Punishment 1984[99] (CAT), there are notable differences. Under CAT, the conduct must be 'inflicted by or at the instigation of or with the consent or acquiescence of a public official or other person acting in an official capacity',[100] whereas under the Rome Statute, there is no corresponding requirement that torture must be committed by a public official or be linked to a public official.[101] However, the contextual requirements of a state or organisational policy may well indirectly revive the link between torture and public officials.

A further difference between torture under CAT and torture as a crime against humanity is that there is no requirement under the latter regime that the act must be carried out with a specific purpose.[102] It is worth noting, however, that the definition of torture as a war crime does include this requirement of purpose.[103] In terms of its scope, any 'pain or suffering arising only from, inherent in or incidental to, lawful sanctions' may not qualify as torture for establishing a crime against humanity,[104] but under certain conditions, rape may qualify as a form as torture.[105]

47.3.3.3 Sexual violence

Sexual violence, in the context of crimes against humanity, includes 'rape, sexual slavery, enforced prostitution, forced pregnancy, enforced sterilisation, or any other form of sexual violence of comparable gravity'.[106] As far as rape as a crime against humanity is concerned, the approach in *Akayesu* represents the *locus classicus*. In this case, the Trial Chamber found the following:

> **The Chamber considers that rape is a form of aggression and that the central elements of the crime of rape cannot be captured in a mechanical description of objects and body parts. The Convention against Torture and Other Cruel, Inhuman and Degrading Treatment or Punishment does not catalogue specific acts in its definition of torture, focusing rather on the conceptual frame work of state sanctioned violence. This approach is more useful in international law. Like torture, rape is used for such purposes as intimidation, degradation, humiliation,**

98 See the discussion of the crime of torture under South African law in Chapter 49.

99 Adopted by the UN General Assembly Resolution 39/46 in accordance with art 27(1) on 10 December 1984, and which came into force on 26 June 1987.

100 Art 1(1) of the Convention Against Torture and Other Cruel, Inhuman or Degrading Treatment or Punishment 1984 (CAT).

101 Although art 7(2)(*e*) of the Rome Statute does require that the victim must be 'in the custody or under the control of the accused'.

102 Art 7(1)(*f*) fn 14 of the ICC Elements of Crimes states: 'It is understood that no specific purpose need be proved for this crime'.

103 See further, ICC Elements of Crimes.

104 See art 7(2)(*e*) of the Rome Statute.

105 *Akayesu* trial at 597.

106 Art 7(1)(*g*) of the Rome Statute. See, in general, Bergsmo M, Butenschon Skre A and Wood EJ (eds) *Understanding and Proving International Sex Crimes* (2012).

> **discrimination, punishment, control or destruction of a person. Like torture, rape is a violation of personal dignity, and rape in fact constitutes torture when inflicted by or at the instigation of or with the consent or acquiescence of a public official or other person acting in an official capacity.**[107]

Sexual slavery is an aggravated form of enslavement, with an additional requirement that '[t]he perpetrator caused such person or persons to engage in one or more acts of a sexual nature'.[108]

Enforced prostitution takes place when a perpetrator:

> **[causes] one or more persons to engage in one or more acts of a sexual nature by force, or by threat of force or coercion, such as that caused by fear of violence, duress, detention, psychological oppression or abuse of power, against such person or persons or another person, or by taking advantage of a coercive environment or such person's or persons' incapacity to give genuine consent.**[109]

The sexual offence of forced pregnancy was controversial during the drafting stage of the Rome Statute. Nevertheless, the drafters agreed eventually on the following definition:

> **'Forced pregnancy' means the unlawful confinement of a woman forcibly made pregnant, with the intent of affecting the ethnic composition of any population or carrying out other grave violations of international law.**[110]

Enforced sterilisation as a crime against humanity - already included as an underlying act of genocide - is defined in the ICC Elements of Crimes as the deprivation of 'one or more persons of biological reproductive capacity'[111] that was 'neither justified by the medical or hospital treatment of the person or persons concerned nor carried out with their genuine consent'.[112] Finally, the Rome Statute contains a residual category of 'sexual violence' for conduct 'of a gravity comparable to the other offences in article 7, paragraph 1(g), of the Statute'.[113]

47.3.3.4 Persecution

The crime of persecution as a crime against humanity is complex both in its formulation and its relationship to the crime of genocide. As noted above, acts that do not meet the requirements of genocide in terms of specific intent, may well meet the requirements of persecution as a crime against humanity. In this regard, the ICTY has held as follows:

> **[T]he *mens rea* requirement for persecution is higher than for ordinary crimes against humanity, although lower than for genocide. In this context the Trial Chamber wishes to stress that persecution as a crime against humanity is an offence belonging to the same genus as genocide. Both persecution and genocide are crimes**

107 *Akayesu* trial at 597.

108 Art 7(1)(*g*)-2 Element 2 of the ICC Elements of Crimes.

109 Art 7(1)(*g*)-3 Element 1 of the ICC Elements of Crimes.

110 Art 7(2)(*f*) of the Rome Statute. Such interpretation, however, is subject to the caveat that it 'shall not in any way be interpreted as affecting national laws relating to pregnancy'.

111 Adding 'The deprivation is not intended to include birth-control measures which have a non-permanent effect in practice.' Art 7(1)(*g*)-5 fn 19 of the ICC Elements of Crimes.

112 Art 7(1)(*g*)-5 Element 2 of the ICC Elements of Crimes, further clarified at fn 20 that '"genuine consent" does not include consent obtained through deception'.

113 Art 7(1)(*g*)-6 Element 2 of the ICC Elements of Crimes.

> **perpetrated against persons that belong to a particular group and who are targeted because of such belonging. In both categories what matters is the intent to discriminate: to attack persons on account of their ethnic, racial, or religious characteristics (as well as, in the case of persecution, on account of their political affiliation). While in the case of persecution the discriminatory intent can take multifarious inhumane forms and manifest itself in a plurality of actions including murder, in the case of genocide that intent must be accompanied by the intention to destroy, in whole or in part, the group to which the victims of the genocide belong. Thus, it can be said that, from the viewpoint of *mens rea*, genocide is an extreme and most inhuman form of persecution. To put it differently, when persecution escalates to the extreme form of wilful and deliberate acts designed to destroy a group or part of a group, it can be held that such persecution amounts to genocide.**[114]

As far as the formulation of the crime of persecution is concerned, article 7(2)(*g*) of the Rome Statute defines it as the intentional and severe deprivation of fundamental rights contrary to international law by reason of the identity of the group or collectivity. This definition was developed from the earlier jurisprudence of the ad hoc tribunals.[115]

What remains controversial are the specific acts that may amount to *a severe deprivation of fundamental rights contrary to international law*.[116] Under article 7(1)(*h*), persecution must be connected to 'any act referred to in this paragraph or any crime within the jurisdiction of the Court'. What this means is that persecution will always be based on some other underlying act constituting a crime against humanity.

There is an additional requirement of establishing discriminatory intent on one or more of the accepted grounds. Article 7(2)(*g*) requires that any such persecution be on 'political, racial, national, ethnic, cultural, religious, gender' (that is, male or female) grounds. The inclusion of the phrase, 'or other grounds that are universally recognized as impermissible under international law', means that this list remains open-ended.

47.4 War crimes

47.4.1 Introduction

War crimes are unique in that they have emerged out of an older and more established body of international law: international humanitarian law (IHL). As a result, war crimes are the 'most codified'[117] branch of international criminal law. Nevertheless, it would be an over-simplification simply to consider international criminal law, in terms of war crimes, as the enforcement arm of IHL. While the two fields share common applications, they are by no means coextensive. Historically, although IHL has outlawed certain conduct in custom since time immemorial and in various treaties since the turn of the 20th century, it was only at a later date that violations of these rules attracted individual criminal responsibility under international law. Further, there are marked differences between the operating principles of the two systems.

---

114 ICTY *Prosecutor v Zoran Kupreški´c et al* (trial judgment) IT-95-16-T January 2000 (*Kupreški´c* trial) at 636.

115 Cryer et al *An Introduction to International Criminal Law and Procedure* 213.

116 Cryer *An Introduction to International Criminal Law and Procedure* 213.

117 Van Schaack B and Slye RC *A Concise History of International Criminal Law: Chapter 1 of Understanding International Criminal Law* Santa Clara University Legal Studies Research Paper No. 07-42 at 13.

A proper understanding of the evolution of war crimes requires a brief discussion of the history of IHL. Despite the belief of some that pre-modern wars were lawless, '[a]ncient societies had legal codes with humanitarian provisions similar to those found in the modern laws of war'.[118] Until the turn of the 20th century, the rules of war that would later form the basis of modern-day IHL were predominantly custom based.[119] The advent of legal positivism inspired the attempts to codify the hitherto unwritten war codes during the Hague Peace Conferences of 1899 and 1907.[120]

Following World War II, the most comprehensive codification of IHL took place in the form of the four Geneva Conventions in 1949,[121] which form the basis of modern IHL, and to a large extent, war crimes law.[122] To date, most states have ratified these Geneva Conventions and their provisions are largely considered to be part of customary international law. Although the primary focus of these conventions is on the detailed regulation of international armed conflicts, states did accept some degree, albeit minimal, of regulation of internal armed conflicts or, more appropriately, non-international armed conflicts, through the inclusion of article 3 common to all four Geneva Conventions.[123] The Geneva Conventions were augmented by two additional protocols in 1977: Protocol Additional to the Geneva Conventions of 12 August 1949 and relating to the Protection of Victims of International Armed Conflicts 1977 (Additional Protocol I); and Protocol Additional to the Geneva Conventions of 12 August 1949 and relating to the Protection of Victims of Non-International Armed Conflicts (Additional Protocol II). As with common article 3, the adoption of Additional Protocol II marked an important step towards the increased regulation of *non*-international armed conflicts.

The criminalisation of violations of IHL is a more recent development with important distinctions existing between international and non-international armed conflicts. With regard to *international armed conflicts* (IACs), the Treaty of Versailles 1919 contemplated the prosecution of war crimes and the IMTs prosecuted violations of the law of war. The Geneva Conventions put beyond any doubt the possibility of prosecuting such violations with the inclusion of its grave breaches regime. This regime not only considered certain grave breaches of IHL to be criminal in nature, but also placed an obligation on states to

118 Jochnick C and Normand R 'The legitimization of violence: A critical history of the laws of war' (1994) 35(1) *Harv Intl L J* 49 at 60. Moreover, despite claims of humanitarian antecedents in 'chivalric practices of Medieval Christian Europe', this period was characterised by practices that defy humanitarian considerations. Far from restraining the conduct of hostilities in the name of humanity and God, critical examination of these rules reveals their true purpose to have been 'to protect the lives and property of privileged knights and nobles, entitling them to plunder and kill peasant soldiers, non-Christians, enemies, and civilians of all religions and ethnicities' 60, 61. Reproduced with permission of NoDataAvailable in the format Republish in other published product via Copyright Clearance Center.

119 The exceptions to this being the 1863 Lieber Code, which regulated the American Civil War, and the 1856 Paris Declaration Respecting Maritime Law.

120 These culminated in agreement on the wording of a number of treaties governing the means and methods of warfare, the most notable being the fourth treaty: Respecting the Laws and Customs of War on Land (Hague IV) 1907, which codified a number of IHL rules in its annex. In addition, the preamble to the 1899 and 1907 Hague Conventions contained the Martens clause, the legal value and meaning of which remains contested, as does the humanitarian nature of these developments. For some, notwithstanding the promise of the golden age of legal positivism, these treaties reveal a remarkably consistent pattern of military necessity trumping putative humanitarian values with the scant limitations placed on the means of warfare generally related to obsolete practices or ones disfavoured by the great powers. For an historical and prognostic overview, see Werle and Jessberger *Principles of International Criminal Law* 392–399.

121 The four Geneva Conventions (August 12, 1949) are: Convention (I) for the Amelioration of the Condition of the Wounded and Sick in Armed Forces in the Field; Convention (II) for the Amelioration of the Condition of Wounded, Sick and Shipwrecked Members of Armed Forces at Sea; Convention (III) relative to the Treatment of Prisoners of War; and Convention (IV) relative to the Protection of Civilian Persons in Time of War.

122 Van Schaack and Slye *A Concise History of International Criminal Law* 17.

123 Up until this point, with the (possible) exception of the Lieber Code, IHL had been applied exclusively to international armed conflicts.

prosecute such breaches. In contrast, although Additional Protocol I was important for the development of IHL, its impact on the criminalisation of IHL violations was minimal. The development has been assisted greatly through the advent of the ad hoc tribunals, which have interpreted and applied them. The concept and content of such IHL violations were assisted further through their comprehensive cataloguing, or perhaps even their codification, during the drafting of the Rome Statute. Certainly, article 8 of the Rome Statute contains a comprehensive list of war crimes that may be committed during an international armed conflict.

As far as *non-international armed conflicts* (NIACs) are concerned, the criminalisation of IHL violations is less settled. Indeed, at the time of the Nuremberg Tribunal, '[b]ecause the entire concept of legal regulation of non-international armed conflict was in its infancy, it was not considered that there could be international criminal liability for violations of humanitarian law in non-international armed conflict'.[124] The imbalance between the attention given to the regulation of international compared with non-international armed conflicts is reflected in the fact that 'the 1949 Geneva Conventions and the 1977 Protocols contain close to 600 articles, of which only article 3 common to the 1949 Geneva Conventions and the 28 articles of Additional Protocol II apply to internal conflicts'.[125]

Much of this unevenness is attributable not only to the historically statist character of international law, but also because of the underpinning ethos of IHL, which relies on symmetry and reciprocity between states for its enforcement. Although Additional Protocol II elaborated on the laconic provisions of common article 3, it contained no provision for the criminalisation of breaches of such provisions.[126] As a result, the criminalisation of breaches of IHL applied to international armed conflicts only.[127]

Consequently, at the time of the ICTY's establishment, even the International Committee of the Red Cross (ICRC) acknowledged that 'according to humanitarian law as it stands today, the notion of war crimes is limited to situations of international armed conflict'.[128] Nevertheless, when the ICTR was created, article 4 of the ICTR Statute granted the tribunal jurisdiction over violations of common article 3 of the Geneva Conventions and Additional Protocol II.[129] The jurisprudence of the ad hoc tribunals has been instrumental in further developing war crimes under non-international armed conflicts. In particular, the Appeal Chamber's decision in *Tadić* is important in that it extended the applicability of war crimes to NIAC under the guise of customary international law.[130] What is more, the Appeal Chamber further affirmed the entailment of individual criminal responsibility when such customary norms were breached.[131]

124 First published in: Schabas WA 'Punishment of non-state actors in non-international armed conflict' (2003) 26(4) *Fordham Intl L J* 907 at 917.

125 Stewart JG 'Towards a single definition of armed conflict in international humanitarian law: A critique of internationalized armed conflict' (2003) 85 Issue 850 *IRRC* 313 at 320.

126 An option expressly rejected by the drafters. Schabas WA *Introduction to the International Criminal Court* (2001) 141.

127 See arts 146 and 147 of the 1949 Geneva Convention IV Relative to the Protection of Civilian Persons in Time of War.

128 See Werle and Jessberger *Principles of International Criminal Law* 406.

129 See further, Werle and Jessberger *Principles of International Criminal Law* 406–409.

130 ICTY *Prosecutor v Dusko Tadić* (decision on the defence motion for interlocutory appeal on jurisdiction) IT-94-1 October 1995 (*Tadić*). The Appeals Chamber noted at 127:

> **[I]t cannot be denied that customary rules have developed to govern internal strife. These rules ... cover such areas as protection of civilians from hostilities, in particular from indiscriminate attacks, protection of civilian objects, in particular cultural property, protection of all those who do not (or no longer) take active part in hostilities, as well as prohibition of means of warfare proscribed in international armed conflicts and ban of certain methods of conducting hostilities.**

131 For an overview of these developments, see Cryer et al *An Introduction to International Criminal Law and Procedure* 229–232.

The debate, however, has to a large extent been overtaken by the subsequent adoption of article 8 of the Rome Statute, which includes a comprehensive list of war crimes in both international and non-international armed conflicts.

47.4.2 The contextual element: An armed conflict

War crimes must be committed in the context of an armed conflict. In defining this term, the Appeals Chamber in *Tadić* stated that 'an armed conflict exists whenever there is a resort to armed force between states or protracted armed violence between governmental authorities and organised armed groups or between such groups within a state'.[132] While such a definition is of great assistance to the establishment of war crimes, no universally accepted definition of what constitutes an armed conflict exists. Rather, it depends on the nature of the conflict.

The Geneva Conventions define the term 'international armed conflict' as 'armed conflict ... between two or more of the High Contracting Parties, even if the state of war is not recognized by one of them'.[133] Further, the laws of international armed conflict apply 'to all cases of partial or total occupation of the territory of a High Contracting Party, even if the said occupation meets with no armed resistance'.[134] The concept was extended further by article 1(4) of Additional Protocol I, which refers to 'armed conflicts in which peoples are fighting against colonial domination and alien occupation and against racist regimes in the exercise of their right of self-determination'.

The term 'non-international armed conflict' is less settled. Common article 3 of the Geneva Conventions defines such conflicts as 'armed conflict not of an international character occurring in the territory of one of the High Contracting Parties'. In contrast, Additional Protocol II adopts a more detailed definition, which sets out four criteria for such a conflict: (1) it must take place in the territory of a high contracting party between its armed forces and dissident armed forces or other organised armed groups, which (2) are under responsible command, (3) exercise such control over a part of its territory as to enable them to carry out sustained and concerted military operations, and (4) implement Additional Protocol II.[135]

When the Rome Statute was drafted, there were thus two different definitions of non-international armed conflicts.[136] The drafters of the Rome Statute, presented with two possible definitions for NIAC, elected to formulate their own, namely 'armed conflicts that take place in the territory of a state when there is protracted armed conflict between governmental authorities and organized armed groups or between such groups'.[137]

The formulation adopted by the drafters of the Rome Statute was based on the definition of armed conflict adopted in *Tadić* and 'clarifies that the parties participating in the conflict must achieve a certain degree of organisation'.[138] In addition, the Rome Statute's definition of NIAC includes the requirement that it must be 'protracted'. In this sense, it may be considered

---

132 *Tadić* at 70.

133 See common art 2 of the Geneva Conventions.

134 Common art 2 of the Geneva Conventions.

135 Art 1(1) of Additional Protocol II.

136 Art 1(1) of Additional Protocol II expressly states that it 'develops and supplements [common Article 3] ... without modifying its existing conditions of applications'.

137 Art 8(2)(*f*) of the Rome Statute. Note that unlike the definition of IAC, this definition is not drawn from existing IHL treaties, but rather is a formulation introduced by the drafters of the Rome Statute. Such a definition is, nevertheless, reflective of the exclusion in Additional Protocol II of 'situations of internal disturbances and tensions, such as riots, isolated and sporadic acts of violence or other acts of a similar nature' from their definition of non-international armed conflict. See art 8(2)(*d*) of the Rome Statute.

138 Werle and Jessberger *Principles of International Criminal Law* 417.

broader than the definition in Additional Protocol II. Werle and Jessberger, however, suggest that this provision 'should not be understood as a purely temporal component'.[139] Furthermore, it has been suggested that this requirement for 'protracted armed conflict' must apply to both article 8(2)(*e*) and article 8(2)(*c*) to allow for a 'uniform definition of non-international armed conflict under the ICC statute'.[140]

47.4.3 Acts constituting war crimes

War crimes can be systematised in a number of ways. Here, four categories of war crimes will be considered: crimes against persons, crimes against property and other rights, prohibited methods of warfare, and prohibited means of warfare.[141]

47.4.3.1 Crimes against persons

War crimes against persons can be divided into:

- crimes against persons who by their nature cannot be targeted under IHL (that is, civilians)
- crimes against persons who are not absolutely protected as civilians, but who have gained protection by their conduct or incapacitation (*hors de combat*)
- crimes against persons who are lawful targets, for instance active soldiers participating in hostilities, but the nature of the act itself is unlawful (that is, crimes that involve mistreatment of some form or another).

Killing civilians[142] is a first order war crime. Any deadly attack against a civilian would be a breach of the fundamental principle of distinction and a violation of customary international law punishable as a war crime.[143] Furthermore, the prohibition on killing and murder applies not only to civilians, but to members of the armed forces who are not protected persons per se, but who have gained protective status by virtue of their surrender or incapacitation, for example through being wounded or rendered *hors de combat*.[144] Similarly, attacks on humanitarian personnel and peacekeepers would also amount to war crimes.[145]

The general position under IHL and international criminal law used to be that acts committed by members of armed forces against members of the *same side of the conflict*, were not criminalised under IHL or international criminal law (the conduct can, of course, violate relevant domestic criminal law). This position seems to be changing as a result of a broad and teleological reading of the war crimes provisions of the Rome Statute. In *Ntaganda*[146] the question was whether rape and sexual slavery committed by a combatant against an individual from the same side of the conflict would constitute a war crime. The Appeals Chamber of the ICC in *Ntaganda* held that the appropriate factor delineating ordinary crimes from war crimes is not whether the victims were fighting on the same side as the alleged perpetrators, but rather whether the conduct took place in the context of and

139 Werle and Jessberger *Principles of International Criminal Law* 418.

140 Werle and Jessberger *Principles of International Criminal Law* 419.

141 Werle and Jessberger *Principles of International Criminal Law* 410.

142 Called *wilful killing* in international armed conflicts and *murder* in non-international armed conflicts.

143 See art 8(2)(*a*)(i) and art 8(2)(*c*)(i) of the Rome Statute.

144 Art 8(2)(*c*) of the Rome Statute.

145 The Rome Statute criminalises '[i]ntentionally directing attacks against personnel ... involved in a humanitarian assistance or peacekeeping mission in accordance with the Charter of the United Nations, as long as they are entitled to the protection given to civilians ... under the international law of armed conflict ...', both in international (art 8(2)(*b*)(iii)) and non-international (art 8(2)(*e*)(iii)) armed conflict.

146 *Prosecutor v Bosco Ntaganda*, ICC Appeals Chamber, 15 June 2017, ICC-01/04-02/06 OA5, available at https://www.icc-cpi.int/CourtRecords/CR2017_03920.PDF.

was associated with an armed conflict of either international or non-international character.[147]

There are a number of war crimes that are criminalised, not on the basis of the object of the attack (for example, civilians and protected persons as discussed above), but rather on the basis of the nature of the conduct. In contrast to the former category, these offences that involve mistreatment may differ depending on the nature of the conflict.[148]

47.4.3.2 Crimes against property and other rights[149]

Certain offences committed against property may constitute war crimes as well. Some objects are protected because of their relationship to protected persons, such as civilians,[150] humanitarian personnel and peacekeepers,[151] and Red Cross officials.[152] Other objects are protected in their own right. For example, buildings dedicated to religion, education, art, science or charitable purposes, historic monuments, hospitals, and places where the sick and wounded are collected, have long since been protected under customary law.[153]

47.4.3.3 Prohibited methods of warfare[154]

Generally, in international armed conflicts, the use of military force is guided by two principles. Firstly, an attack must be directed at a *legitimate target*.[155] Secondly, even if the target is legitimate, the attack must be *proportional* to the intended military objective and must not cause excessive harm.[156] Violations of these guiding principles would amount to war crimes. The rules that govern targeting in non-international armed conflicts are far less developed.

In addition, a number of specific methods of warfare are prohibited as war crimes. These include the transfer by an occupying power of its civilians into the territory it occupies,[157]

---

147 *Ntaganda* at 68.

148 The following acts are prohibited regardless of the nature of the conflict: torture, mutilation, biological/medical/scientific experiments, inhumane or cruel treatment, sexual violence, humiliating and degrading treatment, slavery, punishment without regular trial, hostage taking, deportation or forcible transfer, and the use of child soldiers. In addition, the following acts are prohibited expressly in IAC only: causing suffering or injury to health, compelled service in military forces and operations of war, forced labour, unlawful confinement, delayed repatriation of prisoners of war and civilians, and the transfer of a party's own civilian population. Arguably, other forms of mistreatment, specifically the transfer into occupied territory of a party's own civilian population in NIAC, the forcible transfer of populations in NIAC and hostage taking, all fall more appropriately under the heading of 'methods of war' and are therefore discussed below. Another form of mistreatment, which exists uniquely as a war crime, is the act of conscripting or enlisting children under the age of 15 years into armed forces or groups, or using them to participate actively in hostilities, which is prohibited under art 8(2)(b)(xxvi) (IAC) and art 8(2)(e)(vii) (NIAC) of the Rome Statute.

149 Werle and Jessberger *Principles of International Criminal Law* 467–475.

150 For example, in international armed conflicts, the targeting of civilian objects (art 8(2)(*b*)(ii)) and '[a]ttacking or bombarding, by whatever means, towns, villages, dwellings or buildings which are undefended and which are not military objectives' (art 8(2)(*b*)(v)) are war crimes.

151 Similarly, the deliberate targeting of objects used for humanitarian assistance or peacekeeping missions under the UN Charter is prohibited regardless of the nature of the conflict under art 8(2)(*b*)(iii) (IAC) and art 8(2)(*e*)(iii) (NIAC) of the Rome Statute.

152 Directing attacks against buildings, material, medical units and transport, and personnel using the distinctive emblems of the Geneva Conventions in conformity with international law is prohibited by arts 8(2)(*b*)(xxiv) (IAC) and 8(2)(*e*)(ii) (NIAC) of the Rome Statute.

153 See art 8(2)(*b*)(ix) and art 8(2)(*e*)(iv) of the Rome Statute. See also *Prosecutor v Ahmad Al Faqi Al Mahdi*, ICC-01/12-01/15-171, Judgment and Sentence, 27 September 2016 Trial Chamber VIII Decision, available at https://www.icc-cpi.int/Pages/record.aspx?docNo=ICC-01/12-01/15-171.

154 Werle and Jessberger *Principles of International Criminal Law* 475–509.

155 Art 8(2)(*b*)(ii) of the Rome Statute.

156 See art 8(2)(*b*)(iv) and art 8(2)(*a*)(iv) of the Rome Statute.

157 Art 8(2)(*b*)(viii) of the Rome Statute.

the displacement of the civilian population,[158] starvation[159] and taking hostages.[160] Finally, there is the unique crime of perfidy – criminalised in international armed conflicts – which prohibits '[m]aking improper use of a flag of truce, the flag or the military insignia and uniform of the enemy or of the United Nations, as well as the distinctive emblems of the Geneva Conventions, resulting in death or serious personal injury'.[161]

47.4.3.4 Prohibited means of warfare[162]

Finally, IHL prohibits, and international criminal law criminalises, the use of certain weapons in armed conflicts. In *Tadić*, the Trial Chamber stated that:

> **[e]lementary considerations of humanity and common sense make it preposterous that the use by States of weapons prohibited in armed conflicts between themselves be allowed when States try to put down rebellion by their own nationals on their own territory. What is inhumane, and consequently proscribed, in international wars, cannot but be inhumane and inadmissible in civil strife.**[163]

However, the position of some states on the question of prohibiting certain weapons, irrespective of the nature of the conflict, still supports the distinction between international and non-international armed conflict.[164] At Rome, states were reticent to do away with the distinction between prohibited means in international and non-international armed conflict altogether. The main debate in this regard was the inclusion of nuclear weapons in the list of prohibited weapons. Ultimately, neither nuclear weapons nor chemical and biological weapons were included in the list of prohibited weapons in international armed conflict.

At the Kampala Review Conference of the Rome Statute in 2010, a resolution for the amendment of article 8 (war crimes) of the Rome Statute was adopted.[165] Article 8(2)(*e*) now provides for additional prohibited weapons in the context of *non-international* armed conflicts (the weapons were already prohibited with reference to *international* armed conflicts). The amendments were proposed and adopted in order to bring the Rome Statute in line with customary international law. The additional prohibitions in the context of non-international armed conflicts are: employing poison or poisoned weapons; employing asphyxiating, poisonous or other gases, and all analogous liquids, materials or devices; and,

---

158 Art 8(2)(*e*)(viii) of the Rome Statute specifies that ordering the displacement of the civilian population in IAC 'for reasons related to the conflict' is a war crime 'unless the security of the civilians involved or imperative military reasons' require such displacement.

159 Art 8(2)(*b*)(xxv) of the Rome Statute criminalises intentionally starving civilians as a method of warfare by depriving them of objects indispensable to their survival, including wilfully impeding relief supplies as provided for under the Geneva Conventions.

160 Taking hostages is prohibited in both international (art 8(2)(*a*)(viii)) and non-international (art 8(2)(*c*)(iii)) armed conflict. A number of other prohibited methods of warfare are specified under art 8 of the Rome Statute. One is the crime of killing or wounding treacherously, which is prosecutable in both IAC and NIAC under art 8(2)(*b*)(xi) and art 8(2)(*e*)(ix) respectively. Another is the crime of pillaging under art 8(2)(*b*)(xvi) (IAC) and art 8(2)(*e*)(v) (NIAC). Similarly, the crime of 'declaring that no quarter will be given' is included under art 8(2)(*b*)(xii) and art 8(2)(*e*)(x). Another significant prohibited method is the use of human shields. This is defined in art 8(2)(*b*)(xxiii) as 'utilizing the presence of a civilian or other protected person to render certain points, areas or military forces immune from military operations'. Perhaps somewhat surprisingly in the light of recent conflicts, this is an express war crime in IAC only.

161 Art 8(2)(*b*)(vii) of the Rome Statute.

162 Werle and Jessberger *Principles of International Criminal Law* 509–523.

163 *Tadić* at 45.

164 For example, in 1970, the General Assembly adopted Resolution 2677 (XXV), which called on 'all parties to any armed conflict to observe the rules laid down in the Hague Conventions'. However, in a number of subsequent resolutions, the General Assembly excised the word 'any' without explanation.

165 Resolution RC/Res.5, adopted at the 12th plenary meeting on 10 June 2010, Depository Notification C.N.651.2010 Treaties-6, 29 November 2010, available at https://treaties.un.org/doc/source/docs/RC-Res.5-ENG.pdf.

employing bullets which expand or flatten easily in the human body, such as bullets with a hard envelope which does not entirely cover the core or is pierced with incisions.

47.5 The crime of aggression[166]

Attempts to limit (and justify) recourse to war have preoccupied legal and political scholars since antiquity.[167] However, attempts to *criminalise* war of a certain nature are more recent.[168] The first such attempt was made after World War I with the victorious Allies' ultimately unsuccessful efforts to try Emperor Wilhelm II under the Treaty of Versailles. Thereafter, the abortive attempts of the League of Nations and the Kellogg-Briand pact to outlaw war were expressed in terms of state sanctions and not individual criminal responsibility.[169] Ultimately, the inter-war treaties failed to give legal substance to the burgeoning concept of aggression or accomplish their raison d'être: preventing the outbreak of a world war.

Following World War II, the international military tribunals for Germany and the Far East, and their various successors, represented a watershed moment in the criminalisation of aggression. Article 6 of the International Military Tribunal (IMT) Charter, established by the London Agreement,[170] granted the tribunal the power to 'try and punish persons who ... whether as individuals or as members of organizations' committed 'crimes against peace'.[171] Even then, however, in the face of broad political consensus, the legal character and content of aggression was contested by many.[172]

Following the failure of the League of Nations and the inter-war treaties to prevent the outbreak of World War II, the United Nations contains, as one of its founding precepts, the prohibition on the use of force by states (article 2(4)). Not content with merely outlawing the use of force (with limited exceptions) through the UN Charter, the Allies, and the US in particular,[173] set out to criminalise waging such wars by imposing individual criminal responsibility on those Nazi leaders responsible for breaching such norms and precipitating World War II.[174] Their resolve to do so was unwavering despite similar failed attempts made

166 See, in general, Kemp G *Individual Criminal Liability for the International Crime of Aggression* 2 ed (2016); Ambos K 'The crime of aggression after Kampala' (2010) 53 *GYIL* 463; Krzan B 'Frieden und gerechtigkeit nach der Kampala-Konferenz' (2010) 48(4) *Archiv des Völkerrechts* 467; McDougall C *The Crime of Aggression under the Rome Statute of the International Criminal Court* (2013); Werle and Jessberger *Principles of International Criminal Law* 529–556.

167 As evidenced by the writings of St Augustine, St Thomas Aquinas, Victoria and von Clausewitz. See Schuster M 'The Rome Statute and the crime of aggression: A Gordian knot in search of a sword' (2003) 14(1) *Crim L F* 1 2–3; O'Connell RL *Of Arms and Men: A History of War, Weapons, and Aggression* (1989).

168 Simpson GJ *Law, War and Crime: War Crimes Trials and the Reinvention of International Law* (2007) 142.

169 See further, Glennon MJ 'The blank-prose crime of aggression' (2010) 35(1) *Yale J Intl L* 71 at 74; Kemp *Individual Criminal Liability for the International Crime of Aggression* 79–81.

170 Signed by the Soviet Union, France, the United Kingdom and the United States of America on 8 August 1945.

171 The early formulation of what would come to be known as the crime of aggression.

172 Concerns over the legality of the prosecution of aggression under the *nullum crimen* principle are well rehearsed. See, for example, Dinstein Y *War, Aggression and Self-defence* 4 ed (2005) 119; Kemp *Individual Criminal Liability for the International Crime of Aggression* 84, 90–93. The Four Powers could not agree on a definition of aggression – deciding to outlaw the 'waging of a war of aggression, or a war in violation of international treaties, agreements or assurances'. See art 6(*a*) of the Charter of the International Military Tribunal.

173 For a historical overview of the legal and diplomatic efforts to criminalise aggression, see Kemp *Individual Criminal Liability for the International Crime of Aggression* 84–88.

174 Bass argues that notwithstanding the widely held belief that it was the crimes of the Holocaust that brought about the trials at Nuremberg, it was in fact primarily about punishing German aggression. He notes with regard to the US that 'the charges that were of the greatest interest to America were those that bore directly on America: the German instigation of World War II'. Bass GJ *Stay the Hand of Vengeance: The Politics of War Crimes Tribunals* (2000) at 148. Reproduced with permission of PRINCETON UNIVERSITY PRESS in the format Other Published Product via Copyright Clearance Center.

at trying Emperor Wilhelm in the aftermath of World War I.[175] To this end, on 8 August 1945, the Four Powers signed the London Charter,[176] establishing the International Military Tribunal (IMT) 'for the just and prompt trial and punishment of the major war criminals of the European Axis'.[177] The charter granted the Nuremberg Tribunal the power to 'try and punish persons who ... committed ... crimes against peace',[178] which were defined as the 'planning, preparation, initiation or waging of a war of aggression, or a war in violation of international treaties, agreements or assurances, or participation in a common plan or conspiracy for the accomplishment of any of the foregoing'.[179]

Undoubtedly, the crime of aggression was, in form and substance, the lynchpin of the prosecution of Nazi crimes at Nuremberg, as it was at the subsequent IMT for the Far East (the Tokyo Tribunal). From a legal perspective, although the Nuremberg Tribunal subject matter jurisdiction included crimes against humanity, it was only through the jurisdictional nexus to the *supreme crime* of aggression that the former could be punished.[180] Moreover, in passing judgment in the High Command case, the IMT held that 'to initiate a war of aggression ... is not only an international crime, it is the supreme international crime, differing only from other war crimes in that it contains within itself the accumulated evil of the whole'.[181]

However, the broad *political* consensus that prevailed among the world's most powerful nations at Nuremberg regarding the importance of punishing the crime of waging aggressive war, dissipated with the onset of the Cold War. Furthermore, the *legal* nexus between the crime *of war* and the prosecution of crimes committed *within war* (introduced to prevent inconvenient comparisons between Nazi atrocities and ongoing domestic depredations by the Fours Powers) did not prevail beyond Nuremberg. In the years that followed, international crimes were progressively delinked from war entirely, beginning almost immediately after Nuremberg by the Control Council Law No. 10, which governed the trial of lesser war criminals and which removed the *jurisdiction* connection between crimes against humanity and aggression.[182]

As a result, the development of the law governing international crimes over the proceeding 40 years was not mirrored by the development of the law relating to the crime of aggression. During this period, aggression was rendered a political epithet with subsequent endeavours to reach a substantive legal definition of aggression coming to very little.[183] This,

---

175 Thereafter, the abortive attempts of the League of Nations and the Kellogg-Briand pact to outlaw war were expressed in terms of state sanctions and not individual criminal responsibility.

176 Signed by the Soviet Union, France, the United Kingdom and the US on 8 August 1945.

177 Art 1 of the IMT Charter.

178 Art 6(*a*) of the IMT Charter.

179 Art 6(*a*) of the IMT Charter.

180 In terms of art 6(*c*) of the charter, crimes against humanity were defined as 'murder, extermination, enslavement, deportation, and other inhumane acts committed against any civilian population, before or during the war; or persecutions on political, racial or religious grounds in execution of or in connection with any crime within the jurisdiction of the Tribunal'.

181 IMT Nuremberg Trial Judgment (1946) IMT 171 at 186.

182 Art 11(1)(*c*) of the Control Council Law No. 10 defined crimes against humanity as 'atrocities and offences, including but not limited to murder, extermination, enslavement, deportation, imprisonment, torture, rape, or other inhumane acts committed against any civilian population, or persecutions on political, racial or religious grounds whether or not in violation of the domestic laws of the country where perpetrated'.

183 See, for example, the 1954 ILC Draft Code of Offences Against the Peace and Security of Mankind and General Assembly Resolution 3314 (1974) adopted to give guidance to the Security Council, but which made no mention of individual criminal responsibility for aggression. For an overview of the reasons for these shortcomings, see Cassese A 'On some problematical aspects of the crime of aggression' in Skouteris T and Vermeer-Kunzli A (eds) *The Protection of the Individual in International Law: Essays in Honour of John Dugard* (2007) 115–116.

in the words of one scholar, meant that '[t]he die had been cast in favour of politicization of aggression rather than juridicisation'.[184] Consequently, in the early 1990s, when international criminal law was awakened from its Cold War slumber and was put to use in the ICTR and ICTY (and the hybrid courts), states were little closer to an agreed definition of the 'supreme international crime' of aggression in order to assign individual criminal responsibility. Not surprisingly, neither one of those tribunals contained the crime of aggression, their creators limiting their scope to war crimes, genocide and crimes against humanity.

It was only the work of the ILC that 'seemed to promise the rehabilitation of the crime of aggression and the juridification of war'.[185] In its 1994 Draft Statute for an International Criminal Court, the ILC included the crime of aggression as one of the court's core crimes.[186] As a result, when delegates met in Rome in 1998 to draft what would become the Rome Statute of the International Criminal Court, there was renewed hope that it would include the crime of aggression. However, such hope soon faded following internecine disagreements over the role of the Security Council in the court's operation generally, and in the prosecution of aggression in particular. Some states, notably the US, objected to the inclusion of the crime in the final Rome Statute in any form. It was only at the insistence of the non-aligned movement and certain middle powers – notably Germany and Japan – that it was included.[187] The result was the codified impasse[188] contained in article 5(2) of the Rome Statute.[189]

Following the adoption of the Rome Statute, the final resolution of the 1998 Rome Conference instructed the PrepCom[190] to 'prepare proposals for a provision on aggression, including the definition and Elements of Crimes of aggression and the conditions under which the International Criminal Court shall exercise its jurisdiction with regard to this crime'. The PrepCom failed to make headway on the matter and, on its dissolution, the inaugural Assembly of states Parties established a Special Working Group on the Crime of Aggression (SWGCA), which started work in 2003.

From 2003 to 2010, much progress was made by the SWGCA. By February 2009, the SWGCA had agreed on a draft definition of amendments to the Rome Statute to allow for the prosecution of aggression.[191]At a conceptual level, there was unanimity on the fact that the prosecution of aggression consists of two components: the act of aggression and the

184 Bassiouni MC 'From Versailles to Rwanda in seventy-five years: The need to establish a permanent international criminal court' (1997) 10 *Harv Hum Rts J* at 9, original citation in Simpson *Law, War and Crime* 150.

185 Simpson *Law, War and Crime* 151.

186 Art 20 of the ILC's Draft Statute for an International Criminal Court with Commentaries (1994). The crime of aggression also featured in two concomitant drafting projects of the ILC, the Draft Code and the SR. See Simpson *Law, War and Crime* 151.

187 For a discussion of the drafting history of the Rome Statute with respect to the crime of aggression that resulted in the compromise text of art 5(2), see Kemp *Individual Criminal Liability for the International Crime of Aggression* 134–144.

188 It has more pejoratively been referred to as a 'Trojan Horse' and 'sleeper' provision. See Sadat LN and Carden SR 'The new International Criminal Court: An uneasy revolution' (2000) 88(3) *Georgetown L J* 381 at 436 and Schabas WA *An Introduction to the International Criminal Court* (2001) 26 respectively.

189 Art 5(2) of the Rome Statute states: 'The Court shall exercise jurisdiction over the crime of aggression once a provision is adopted in accordance with articles 121 and 123 defining the crime and setting out the conditions under which the Court shall exercise jurisdiction with respect to this crime. Such a provision shall be consistent with the relevant provisions of the Charter of the United Nations'.

190 The Preparatory Commission for the Establishment of an International Criminal Court, established by Resolution F of the Final Act of the United Nations Diplomatic Conference of Plenipotentiaries on the Establishment of an International Criminal Court. UN Doc A/CONF 183/10 8–9.

191 'Press Conference on Special Working Group on Crime of Aggression' UNDPI (2009) http://www.un.org/press/en/2009/090213_ICC.doc.htm (accessed 1 February 2010).

crime of aggression.[192] Further, there was growing consensus on the definition of the crime of aggression, which was based largely on General Assembly Resolution 3314 (1974).[193]

However, leading into Kampala there was no real indication that states were any closer to agreeing on the seminal issue that caused the crime's omission from the original text in Rome: the role of the Security Council in its prosecution. As a result, the SWGCA's working document leading into the Kampala Review Conference contained six alternative formulations of the jurisdictional trigger.[194]

Delegates at the Kampala Review Conference managed to reach agreement on the definition of the crime of aggression, with states' parties essentially adopting the definition that emerged from the SWGCA.[195] However, what came as a surprise to many observers was that notwithstanding the considerable outstanding disagreement on the jurisdictional trigger question beforehand, in the final hours of the Kampala Review Conference a comprehensive amendment to the Rome Statute – that included the jurisdictional trigger for its prosecution – was adopted by consensus.[196]

In terms of these amendments, the definition of aggression (article 8*bis*) is based on General Assembly 3314. It is made up of a number of specific acts of aggression (loosely considered uses of force by a state against the sovereignty, territorial integrity or political independence of another state), which, by their character, gravity and scale, constitute a manifest violation of the Charter of the United Nations (UN Charter). In terms of the definition, the crime of aggression is an act of commission (that is, planning, preparation, initiation or execution) by persons in a position effectively to exercise control over or to direct the political or military action of a state. In other words, it is a leadership crime,[197] distinguishable from other core crimes in this regard.

In December 2017, the ICC Assembly of States Parties (ASP) adopted a resolution which activates the jurisdiction of the ICC over the crime of aggression. The substantive basis for the ICC jurisdiction is the definition of the crime of aggression (article 8*bis*) as adopted at the Kampala Review Conference in 2010. The ASP resolution stipulates that the ICC will have jurisdiction over the crime of aggression as of 17 July 2018.[198]

---

192 The ILC noted this when drafting its 1996 Draft Code: 'Individual responsibility for such a crime is intrinsically and inextricably linked to the commission of aggression by a State'. *United Nations 1996 Yearbook of the International Law Commission* Vol III Part II 43. There is little support for the supposition that non-state entities can commit an act of aggression. See Cryer et al *An Introduction to International Criminal Law and Procedure* 272. However, see Stahn C 'International law at a crossroads? The impact of September 11' (2002) 62 *ZaöR V* 183 at 250 fn 330.

193 For detailed analysis, see Kemp *Individual Criminal Liability for the International Crime of Aggression* 114–120.

194 The first option states that in the absence of a Security Council (SC) determination that aggression has taken place, the prosecutor may not proceed with the investigation in respect of a crime of aggression. The second states that the prosecutor may not proceed with an investigation in the absence of an SC determination, 'unless the Security Council has ... requested the Prosecutor to proceed with the investigation in respect of a crime of aggression'. The third states that '[w]here no such determination is made within [6] months after' the prosecutor has notified the SC of his intention to investigate, he may proceed with the investigation in respect of a crime of aggression. The fourth allows the prosecution to proceed with an investigation after six months 'provided that the Pre-Trial Chamber has authorized the commencement of the investigation in respect of a crime of aggression in accordance with the procedure contained in article 15'. The fifth allows the prosecution to proceed with an investigation after six months 'provided that the General Assembly has determined that an act of aggression has been committed by the State referred to in article 8*bis*'. The sixth allows the prosecution to proceed with an investigation after six months 'provided that the International Court of Justice has determined that an act of aggression has been committed by the State referred to in article 8*bis*'.

195 For a detailed legislative history of the crime of aggression, including Resolution RC/Res 6 (11 June 2010) adopted at the Kampala Review Conference, see Barriga S and Kress C (eds) *The Travaux Préparatoires of the Crime of Aggression* (2012).

196 See Resolution RC/Res 6 The Crime of Aggression: Annex I Amendments to the Rome Statute of the International Criminal Court on the Crime of Aggression, available at https://treaties.un.org/doc/source/docs/RC-Res.6-ENG.pdf.

197 Kemp *Individual Criminal Liability for the International Crime of Aggression* 180.

198 Resolution ICC-ASP/16/Res.5, 14 December 2017, available at https://asp.icc-cpi.int/iccdocs/asp_docs/Resolutions/ASP16/ICC-ASP-16-Res5-ENG.pdf.

As far as the jurisdictional regime is concerned, the amendment adopted at Kampala contained two different triggers. States and the ICC Prosecutor may trigger a prosecution of aggression under extremely limited circumstances (article 15*bis*), while the Security Council has a broad discretion to do so (article 15*ter*). In the case of state referrals or *proprio motu* investigations by the ICC Prosecutor, the ICC shall not exercise its jurisdiction regarding a crime of aggression when committed by a national or on the territory of a state party that has not ratified or accepted the aggression amendments to the Rome Statute.[199] This imbalanced regime for the prosecution of aggression is the result of the difficult compromises that were necessary to bring about the amendment. While their effect on the ultimate prosecution of the crime will only become evident in time, the codification of aggression was nevertheless a political victory for the states - many of which were from Africa - that had campaigned since 1998 for the inclusion of this crime in the ICC regime.

DISCUSSION

Should crimes such as terrorism and human trafficking also be treated as core international crimes?

Should other crimes of international concern, for example terrorism and human trafficking, also be classified as core crimes? Some of these crimes are dealt with in Chapter 49. Should these be included in the Rome Statute of the ICC?

There are different ways to look at this. One way is to look at the content of the crimes and to ask the fundamental question: does this crime or phenomenon affect the whole of humankind? Does it shock the conscience of the world? Is it subject to the jurisdiction of an international criminal tribunal? Another way is perhaps more quantitative: how many states recognise the crime as a crime under domestic criminal law? A crime such as aggression certainly affects the whole of humankind; it is fundamentally in violation of the international order. However, it took many decades to come up with a relatively acceptable definition and enforcement regime. The path to the status of core international crime is not always obvious or easy.

THIS CHAPTER IN ESSENCE

1. The core crimes under international law - genocide, crimes against humanity, war crimes, and the crime of aggression - are well established and criminalised in terms of various international instruments, notably the Rome Statute of the International Criminal Court.
2. It is an open-ended question whether more crimes should be added to the list of core crimes under international law.

199 Par 2, Resolution ICC-ASP/16/Res.5.

Chapter 48

The prosecution of international crimes

CHAPTER OBJECTIVES

The objectives of this chapter are to:

- explain briefly the principle of complementarity and the domestic prosecution of international crimes
- discuss the legal framework for the prosecution of the core international crimes before South African courts
- describe and discuss the basic structure and powers of the International Criminal Court (ICC) as well as the basic features of the cooperation regime between the ICC and states.

48.1 Introduction

This chapter will consider the prosecution of genocide, crimes against humanity and war crimes by both domestic and international courts and tribunals. We begin by discussing the relationship between domestic and international prosecutions, both historically and under the principle of complementarity of the Rome Statute of the International Criminal Court (Rome Statute). We then consider the legal regimes available under South African law for the prosecution of such crimes: the Implementation of the Rome Statute of the International Criminal Court Act 27 of 2002 (the ICC Act), the Implementation of the Geneva Conventions Act 8 of 2012 (Geneva Conventions Act) and section 232 of the Constitution of the Republic of South Africa, 1996. Thereafter, we consider the prosecution of these crimes by the International Criminal Court (ICC) in The Hague.

It is worth noting at the outset that when it comes to the prosecutions of these crimes, both international and domestic legal rules apply. International law is relevant not only to *international* prosecutions, but also to setting out the parameters under which states may exercise criminal jurisdiction over persons and crimes, particularly those crimes that take place outside the territory of the concerned state.[1] Similarly, domestic law not only sets out the legal regime for the prosecution of such crimes in a particular state,[2] but also sets out the framework for such states to cooperate with the ICC in the collection of evidence, arrest of suspects, and so on.

48.2 The International Criminal Court, the principle of complementarity and the domestic prosecution of international crimes

International crimes are prosecuted in both international and domestic courts. However, as noted above, there is a tendency to downplay the domestic aspects of international criminal law both in terms of its history and its enforcement.[3] Historically, domestic prosecutions have featured prominently in the development of international criminal law. As a matter of record, for every international moment (Versailles, Nuremberg), there was a domestic counterpart (Leipzig, Control Council Law No. 10 trials).[4] Some may view these domestic prosecutions as necessary setbacks in the progression towards true international criminal law where international crimes are prosecuted by international courts. In substance, however, the very principles relied on and enforced by international courts were often domestic in origin. While the internationalists' centrepiece – the Nuremberg Tribunal – regarded itself as enforcing existing international law, many of these principles necessarily originated from domestic antecedents.[5] In fact, domestic prosecutions of international crimes have impacted on the substantive aspects of the field through the development of

1 In addition, international law regulates the cooperation among states in the suppression of such crimes.

2 This separation between international and domestic legal rules that apply to the prosecution of international crimes is particularly important in dualist countries such as South Africa.

3 For an overview, see Werle G and Jessberger F *Principles of International Criminal Law* 3 ed (2014) 128–151.

4 See Simpson's discussion on the hidden history of international criminal law in Simpson GJ *Law, War and Crime: War Crimes Trials and the Reinvention of International Law* (2007) 40.

5 Notably, at a meeting of the Allied Powers prior to the creation of the Nuremberg Tribunal, Sir David Maxwell Fyfe, the UK representative, noted: 'What we want to abolish at the trial is a discussion as to whether the acts are violations of international law or not. We declare what the international law is so that there won't be any discussion on whether it is international law or not'. United States Department of State International Conference on Military Trials London (1945, 1949) 19, quoted in Schwarzenberger G 'The problem of an international criminal law' (1950) 3(1) *Current Legal Problems* 263 at 290.

custom both in terms of general principles and, more importantly, the international *criminalisation* of conduct itself.

As far as enforcement is concerned, for a long time the *enforcement* of international criminal law was left to domestic courts.[6] This was done primarily through treaty provisions calling for domestic prosecutions of international crimes.[7] The introduction of the ICC in 1998 did nothing to change this. On the contrary, in addition to creating a permanent international institution, the Rome Statute *institutionalised* the role of domestic courts in the enforcement of international criminal law through the *principle of complementarity*.[8] In fact, unlike the ad hoc Tribunals, it created a preference for domestic proceedings through this principle. The Constitutional Court has explicitly endorsed this division of labour as noted in *S v Basson*:

> **[The] recognition of the principle of individual responsibility for atrocities in war as violations of the law of nations occurred during an early and relatively immature stage of the development of international law generally. ... The recent establishment of the International Criminal Court represents the culmination of a centuries-old process of developing international humanitarian law. *It in no way deprives national courts of responsibility for trying cases involving breaches of such law which are properly brought before them in terms of national law.*[9] (Emphasis added)**

As a result, since 1998 a number of states have adopted legislation to allow for the prosecution of core international crimes in domestic courts, thereby giving effect to the principle of complementarity. In Africa, South Africa, Kenya, Uganda, Burkina Faso and Senegal have all done so either through specialised Acts of Parliament or through amendments to their criminal codes, with a number of other countries currently in the process of doing the same. To facilitate these national prosecutions, international law has evolved to allow states to exercise universal jurisdiction over individuals accused of international crimes. The African Union (AU) adopted a Model Law on Universal Jurisdiction which is designed to allow African states 'to overcome the constraints in exercising the principle of universal jurisdiction'.[10]

6 In the absence of an international enforcement mechanism for international crimes, 'the international community ... [resorted] to the traditional institutional framework of specific treaties or treaty rules aimed at imposing on states a duty to criminalise the prohibited conducts, and organising judicial cooperation for their repression'. In this way, 'international law was used as a tool for the coordination of the exercise of criminal jurisdiction by states'. Gaeta P 'International criminalization of prohibited conduct' in Cassese A (ed-in-chief) *The Oxford Companion to International Criminal Justice* (2009) 64. By permission of Oxford University Press.

7 See art VI of the Convention on the Prevention and Punishment of the Crime of Genocide 1948 (Genocide Convention); art 49 of Convention I for the Amelioration of the Condition of the Wounded and Sick in Armed Forces in the Field (Geneva Convention I); art 50 of Convention II for the Amelioration of the Condition of Wounded, Sick and Shipwrecked Members of Armed Forces at Sea (Geneva Convention II); art 129 of Convention III relative to the Treatment of Prisoners of War (Geneva Convention III) and art 146 of Convention IV relative to the Protection of Civilian Persons in Time of War (Geneva Convention IV) (all 12 August 1949). Further, art 85(1) of the Protocol Additional to the Geneva Conventions of 12 August 1949 and relating to the Protection of Victims of International Armed Conflicts 1977 (Additional Protocol I) incorporates this provision by reference. These provisions in effect place an obligation on states parties to prosecute or extradite offenders who commit grave breaches.

8 Under the Rome Statute, the ICC will only be able to admit a case before it (where the other jurisdictional bases of nationality and territoriality are present) if the state party concerned is unwilling or unable to prosecute the offender nationally. See Preamble and art 17 of the Rome Statute. This principle is discussed further below in section 48.4.4.2.

9 *S v Basson* (CCT30/03A) [2005] ZACC 10; 2005 (12) BCLR 1192 (CC); 2007 (3) SA 582 (CC) (9 September 2005) (*S v Basson* CC 2) at 172.

10 Meeting of Government Experts and Ministers of Justice/Attorneys General AU Press Release Number 037/2012 'The African Union has a clear and unequivocal mandate to fight impunity' 14 May 2012 Assembly of the African Union, Eleventh Ordinary Session, 30 June to 1 July, Egypt 15 May 2012 Assembly of the African Union, Eleventh Ordinary Session, 30 June to 1 July, Egypt 15 May 2012. Decision on the Report of the Commission on the Abuse of the Principle of Universal Jurisdiction June 30–July 1 2008 Doc Assembly/ AU/14 (XI) Assembly/AU/Dec 199(XI). See also Jalloh C 'Universal jurisdiction, universal prescription? A preliminary assessment of the African Union perspective on universal jurisdiction' (2010) 21(1) *Criminal Law Forum* 1.

In summary, international criminal justice and the application and development of its principles should not be understood as being restricted to the domain of international institutions. Instead, international and national prosecutions, rather than being regarded as alternatives, should be considered to be formally distinct, yet substantively intertwined mechanisms in pursuit of a common goal: the enforcement of international criminal law.

48.3 Prosecuting the core international crimes under South African law

There are four separate regimes available for prosecuting the most serious crimes under international law in South Africa. The first and most comprehensive is the statutory regime provided for by the Implementation of the Rome Statute of the International Criminal Court Act 27 of 2002 (the ICC Act). The second is the Implementation of the Geneva Conventions Act 8 of 2012 (the Geneva Conventions Act). This Act makes certain breaches of the Geneva Conventions offences under South African law (i.e. war crimes). Thirdly, it is also possible for common law prosecutions to be brought under section 232 of the Constitution, which incorporates customary international law into South African common law.[11] Finally, the criminalisation and prosecution of torture as a crime under international law and South African law will be considered in Chapter 49 ('Other crimes of international concern').

48.3.1 The ICC Act 27 of 2002

In 2002, South Africa adopted the Implementation of the Rome Statute of the International Criminal Court Act 27 of 2002 to give effect to its obligations under the Rome Statute.[12] In addition to establishing a comprehensive cooperative scheme for South Africa with regard to the ICC, the ICC Act provides the basis for the national prosecution of genocide, crimes against humanity and war crimes before a South African court, thereby giving effect to the principle of complementarity.[13] The Preamble to the ICC Act speaks of South Africa's commitment to bring 'persons who commit such atrocities to justice ... in a court of law of the Republic in terms of its domestic laws where possible'. Further, section 3(*d*) of the ICC Act defines as one of its objects the enabling 'as far as possible and in accordance with the principle of complementarity ..., the national prosecuting authority of the Republic to prosecute and the High Courts of the Republic to adjudicate in cases brought against any person accused of having committed a crime in the Republic and beyond the borders of the Republic in certain circumstances'. The Preamble to the ICC Act also records that the obligation imposed on South African authorities under the Act is to '[bring] persons who commit such atrocities to justice, either in a court of law of the Republic in terms of its domestic laws where possible, pursuant to its international obligations to do so when the Republic became party to the Rome Statute of the International Criminal Court'.

To this end, section 4(1) of the ICC Act provides that '[d]espite anything to the contrary in any other law of the Republic, any person who commits a [international] crime, is guilty of an offence'. Further, the Rome Statute's definitions of the core crimes were incorporated

11 S 232 of the Constitution states: 'Customary international law is law in the Republic unless it is inconsistent with the Constitution or an Act of Parliament'. For commentary on the possibilities presented by this constitutional provision, see Erasmus MG and Kemp G 'The application of international criminal law before domestic courts in the light of recent developments in international and constitutional law' (2002) 27 *SAYIL* 64–81.

12 South Africa signed the Rome Statute on 17 July 1998. Ratified on 27 November 2000.

13 See the Preamble of the ICC Act and art 17 of the Rome Statute.

directly into South African law through a schedule appended to the Act.[14] Under the ICC Act, there are four grounds on which jurisdiction may be exercised over international crimes by South African courts: territorial jurisdiction, nationality, active personality and universal jurisdiction. Notably, nationality and active personality jurisdiction may be founded on citizenship or if the person concerned, either the perpetrator or the victim respectively, is 'ordinarily resident in the Republic'.[15]

As far as universal jurisdiction under the ICC Act is concerned, section 4(3)(*c*) states:

> **(3) In order to secure the jurisdiction of a South African court for purposes of this Chapter, any person who commits [an ICC] crime ... outside the territory of the Republic, is deemed to have committed that crime within the territory of the Republic if—**
>
> ...
>
> **(*c*) that person, after the commission of the crime, is present in the territory of the Republic.**

This section has led some to conclude that South Africa has adopted a so-called 'conditional' or 'limited' form of universal jurisdiction. The better view, however, is that section 4(3) merely confirms the territorial limits of South Africa's *enforcement* jurisdiction[16] and recognises that under South African law, the courts cannot hold trials in absentia. However, the *prescriptive* (criminalisation) jurisdiction of South African law over such crimes is universal in the fullest sense and is not conditional on the presence of the accused in the Republic after the commission of the crime.[17] As discussed below, the Constitutional Court in 2014 considered the proper interpretation of section 4(3) of the ICC Act. However, its findings focused on the issue of whether the presence of a suspect was a requirement *for the initiation of an investigation* under the ICC Act.[18]

As far as immunities are concerned, section 4(2)(*a*) of the ICC Act provides that notwithstanding:

> **[A]ny other law to the contrary, including customary and conventional international law, the fact that a person ... is or was a head of State or government, a member of a government or parliament, an elected representative or a government official ... is neither—**

---

14 While the ICC Act incorporates the definitions of these crimes into South African domestic law, neither the ICC Act nor Schedule 1 refers specifically to the ICC Elements of Crimes. There is nothing, however, that prevents a South African court from having regard to these were it to be involved in the domestic prosecution of an ICC offence.

15 Ss 4(3)(*b*) and (*d*) of the ICC Act respectively.

16 See O'Keefe R 'Universal jurisdiction: Clarifying the basic concept' (2004) 2(3) *JICJ* 735.

17 This must be so for a number of reasons, including (1) if it were not, it would create an absurd situation where a crime was inserted into South Africa's criminal law when the accused appeared, and then deleted therefrom should he leave the Republic, and (2) were the crime only prescribed at the time of the accused's entry into the Republic, it would violate the principle of legality in that it would amount to a retroactive application of criminal law. This would not only offend South Africa's international human rights obligations, but also violate the s 35(3)(*l*) of the Constitution, which contains a prohibition on retroactive application of criminal law.

18 The Constitutional Court upheld the decision of the Supreme Court of Appeal (SCA) to the effect that 'the SAPS are empowered to investigate the alleged offences *irrespective of whether or not the alleged perpetrators are present in South Africa*'. See *National Commissioner of the South African Police Service v Southern African Human Rights Litigation Centre and Another* (CCT 02/14) [2014] ZACC 30; 2015 (1) SA 315 (CC); 2015 (1) SACR 255 (CC); 2014 (12) BCLR 1428 (CC) (30 October 2014) at 17 and *National Commissioner of the South African Police Service v Southern African Human Rights Litigation Centre* (485/2012) [2013] ZASCA 168; 2014 (2) SA 42 (SCA); [2014] 1 All SA 435 (SCA) (27 November 2013) at 3.2.1. This was an appeal from the decision of the North Gauteng High Court to set aside the decision of the SAPS (and the NPA) not to open an investigation into crimes against humanity on the basis that *inter alia* the SAPS incorrectly concluded that they could not open an investigation without a suspect being present in the Republic. See the discussion below at section 48.3.4.

(i) **a defence to a crime; nor**

(ii) **a ground for any possible reduction of sentence once a person has been convicted of a crime.**

Many commentators have interpreted this provision as removing personal immunity before South African courts. Dugard and Abraham argue that section 4(2)(*a*) of the ICC Act represents a choice by the legislature not to follow the 'unfortunate' *Arrest Warrant* decision, 'of which it must have been aware'.[19] While section 232 of the Constitution makes customary international law part of South African law, it does so only to the extent that it is not 'inconsistent with the Constitution or *an Act of Parliament*'. Therefore, if the ICC Act is interpreted as removing immunity *ratione personae*, then it would do so notwithstanding the customary international law obligations on South Africa to observe it.[20]

However, in the alternative, one could argue that section 4(2)(*a*) is modelled on article 27(1) of the Rome Statute, which deals with the irrelevance of official capacity as a defence or as a ground for the reduction of sentence, rather than article 27(2), which deals with personal immunity.[21] If this is the case, then section 4(2)(*a*) of the ICC Act effectively removes *functional* immunity of persons, but leaves *personal* immunity intact.[22] One argument that may be raised in favour of the interpretation of this section adopted here is based on the interpretive presumption contained in section 233 of the Constitution, which states: 'When interpreting any legislation, every court must prefer any reasonable interpretation of the legislation that is consistent with international law over any alternative interpretation that is inconsistent with international law'.

Finally, the ICC Act sets out a special procedure for the prosecution of international crimes under its auspices that differs in some respects from ordinary prosecutions. Firstly, it provides that '[n]o prosecution may be instituted against a person accused of having committed a[n] [international] crime without the consent of the National Director [of Public Prosecutions (NDPP)]'.[23] If the NDPP declines to prosecute a person under the ICC Act, the Director-General for Justice and Constitutional Development must be provided with full reasons for that decision because he or she is then obliged to forward the decision, together with the reasons, to the Registrar of the ICC in The Hague. Secondly, the ICC Act requires that an appropriate, specialised High Court must be designated to hear cases brought under the Act. The ICC Act does not, however, provide any specific trial procedure or punishment regime for domestic courts, so it can be assumed that the regular trial procedure for a criminal trial will be followed and that the court will be empowered to pass any of the sentences regularly imposed.

---

19 See Dugard JC and Abraham G 'Public international law' (2002) *Annual Survey of South African Law* 140 at 166. The *Arrest Warrant* decision is a reference to the decision by the ICJ in the case concerning the Arrest Warrant of 11 April 2000. See ICJ *Case Concerning the Arrest Warrant of 11 April 2000* (*Democratic Republic of the Congo v Belgium*) (2002) 41(3) *International Legal Materials* 536.

20 In *Minister of Justice and Constitutional Development and others v Southern Africa Litigation Centre and others* 2016 (3) SA 317 (SCA) the court (at para 103) expressed the view that South Africa's Implementation of the Rome Statute of the ICC Act, 2002, was adopted on the basis that 'all forms of immunity, including head-of-state immunity, would not constitute a bar to the prosecution of international crimes in this country or to South Africa cooperating with the ICC by way of the arrest and surrender of persons charged with such crimes before the ICC, where an arrest warrant had been issued and a request for cooperation made'.

21 Art 27(2) states: 'Immunities or special procedural rules which may attach to the official capacity of a person, whether under national or international law, shall not bar the Court from exercising its jurisdiction over such a person'.

22 See further, Gevers C 'Immunity and the implementation legislation of South Africa, Kenya and Uganda" in Ambos K and Maunganidze OA (eds) *Power and Prosecution: Challenges and Opportunities for International Criminal Justice in Sub-Saharan Africa* (2012) 85–118.

23 S 5(1) of the ICC Act.

DISCUSSION

South Africa's (possible) withdrawal from the ICC, the incorporation of international crimes under domestic law, and the future of international criminal law in this country

It was noted in Chapter 46 that South Africa attempted to withdraw from the ICC in 2016.[24] That attempt was thwarted, mainly on procedural grounds, by the High Court in *Democratic Alliance v Minister of International Relations and Cooperation and others*.[25] However, at the national conference of the ANC which was held in December 2017, the governing party confirmed the political commitment to withdraw South Africa from the ICC. The Minister of Justice and Correctional Services subsequently published a bill, the International Crimes Bill [B37-2017],[26] which aims to repeal the Implementation of the Rome Statute of the International Criminal Court Act 27 of 2002; to criminalise conduct constituting international crimes; to regulate immunity from the prosecution of international crimes; to grant extra-territorial jurisdiction to the courts in respect of international crimes; to amend the Prevention and Combating of Torture of Persons Act, 2013, so as to confirm immunity for certain persons from prosecution in respect of the crime of torture; and to provide for cooperation with entities in respect of international crimes.

At the time of writing the International Crimes Bill was not yet debated in Parliament. On the assumption that this bill, or a version of it, will eventually be adopted, it is worth it to note a few aspects provided for in the bill.

The International Crimes Bill criminalises three of the core crimes under international law for prosecution in South African courts, namely genocide, crimes against humanity and war crimes. The definitions of the crimes as contained in the bill appear to be substantially the same as the ICC definitions of the crimes. There is no provision in the bill on the crime of aggression. The bill further provides that South African courts will have extra-territorial jurisdiction to hear an international crime committed outside the territory of South Africa. The bill also provides for the extradition of persons to foreign states for purposes of the prosecution of international crimes.

The big difference between the Implementation Act, 2002, and the International Crimes Bill is that the bill does not provide for a bilateral institutional and cooperation relationship between South Africa and the ICC. Instead, the bill provides for a more general framework for South Africa to surrender persons to 'entities'. According to the definitions clause in the bill, an 'entity' means 'the International Criminal Court, any international organisation, international tribunal, international court, or similar international body which has jurisdiction in respect of an international crime'. The bill thus leaves open the possibility for South Africa to cooperate with the ICC, but this modality would not be the mandatory cooperation regime provided for under the Rome Statute and the Implementation Act, 2002.

The controversial issue of immunities is also addressed in the International Crimes Bill. The bill provides that it does not apply to persons who are immune from the criminal jurisdiction of the courts of South Africa in accordance with customary

24 For a critical assessment, see Kemp G 'South Africa's (possible) withdrawal from the ICC and the future of the criminalization and prosecution of crimes against humanity, war crimes and genocide under domestic law: A submission informed by historical, normative and policy considerations' 16(3) *Wash U Global Stud L Rev* 411 (2017), available at https://openscholarship.wustl.edu/cgi/viewcontent.cgi?article=1624&context=law_globalstudies.

25 *Democratic Alliance v Minister of International Relations and Cooperation and Others (Council for the Advancement of the South African Constitution intervening)* 2017 (3) SA 212 (GP).

26 International Crimes Bill [B37-2017], available at http://www.justice.gov.za/legislation/bills/2017-b37-ICBill.pdf.

international law or as provided for in the Diplomatic Immunities and Privileges Act 37 of 2001. This means that the bill will not apply to visiting heads of state, thus avoiding a future incident like the Omar Al-Bashir debacle of 2015. South Africa will no longer be obliged to arrest and surrender visiting heads of state who are accused of international crimes, a significant departure from current law and jurisprudence.

48.3.2 The Geneva Conventions Act 8 of 2012

In 2012, South Africa finally implemented the 1949 Geneva Conventions[27] (60 years after it acceded to them) through the Implementation of the Geneva Conventions Act 8 of 2012.[28] According to its Preamble, the Act's purpose is twofold: (1) to enact the Geneva Conventions and Protocols additional to those Conventions into law; and (2) to ensure the prevention and punishment of grave breaches and other breaches of the Conventions and Protocols. The first aim is accomplished by annexing the Conventions in full to the Act and providing that '[s]ubject to the Constitution and this Act, the Conventions have the force of law in the Republic'.[29] The second purpose is accomplished by creating a war crimes regime for prosecuting breaches of the Geneva Conventions in South African courts.

In effect, the Geneva Conventions Act criminalises two categories of offences: grave breaches and other offences. The former category is made up of the first-order war crimes contained in the 1949 Geneva Conventions and its 1977 Additional Protocol I.[30] Notably, these crimes can only be committed in an *international armed conflict* between two states.[31]

In addition, the Geneva Conventions Act criminalises the contravention of any *other* provision not covered by the grave breaches regime.[32] This catch-all category of offences opens up the possibility of a second set of war crimes being prosecuted under this Act: war crimes committed in *non-international armed conflict*.[33] This is so because included in this catch-all category of offences would be common article 3, which covers violations committed in 'armed conflicts not of an international character'[34] as well as similar provisions in Additional Protocol II.

---

27 South Africa acceded to the four 1949 Geneva Conventions in 1952, and the 1977 Additional Protocols on 21 November 1995. For a discussion of South Africa's reasons for not implementing the Conventions sooner, see generally Gevers C, Du Plessis M and Wallis A 'Sixty years in the making. Better late than never? The implementation of the Geneva Conventions Act' (2012) *AYIHL* 185–200.

28 For an overview, see Gevers et al 'Geneva Conventions Act' 185–200.

29 S 4(1) of the Geneva Conventions Act.

30 According to ss 5(2)(*a*)–(*e*) of the Geneva Conventions Act, 'a grave breach' means a breach referred to in art 50 of Convention I, art 51 of Convention II, art 130 of Convention III, art 147 of Convention IV or art 11 or 85 of Protocol I. Notably, when Additional Protocol I was drafted, it was decided that breaches of its provisions would not attract criminal liability.

31 Or foreign occupation. See common art 2 of the 1949 Geneva Conventions and art 1 of Additional Protocol I (8 June 1977, 1125 UNTS 3).

32 The Act states at s 5(3) that '[a]ny person who within the Republic contravenes or fails to comply with a provision of the Conventions not covered by subsection (2), is guilty of an offence'.

33 During the Portfolio Committee hearing into the bill, submissions were made in favour of extending the grave breaches regime to *non-international armed conflicts* as well. Although the committee appeared supportive of these submissions, it ultimately declined to amend the bill accordingly.

34 In the *Nicaragua* case the ICJ held as follows:

> **Article 3 which is common to all four Geneva Conventions of 12 August 1949 defines certain rules to be applied in the armed conflicts of a non-international character. There is no doubt that, in the event of international armed conflicts, these rules also constitute a minimum yardstick, in addition to the more elaborate rules which are also to apply to international conflicts; and they are rules which, in the Court's opinion, reflect what the Court in 1949 called 'elementary considerations of humanity'.**

ICJ *Case Concerning Military and Paramilitary Activities in and against Nicaragua (Nicaragua v United States)* (merits, judgment) ICJ Reports (1986) 114 at para 218.

Notably, the Geneva Conventions Act provides for differing jurisdictional regimes for these two categories of offences. Grave breaches are subject to universal jurisdiction – they can be prosecuted by South African courts regardless of where they are committed.[35] In contrast, other offences under the Geneva Conventions Act, including non-international war crimes, are not subject to universal jurisdiction. These offences are subject to the traditional jurisdictional bases of territoriality[36] and nationality,[37] but not passive personality jurisdiction (that is, based on the victim's nationality).

Another notable feature of the Geneva Conventions Act is the enigmatic section 7(4), which states:[38] 'Nothing in this Act must be construed as precluding the prosecution of any person accused of having committed a breach under customary international law before this Act took effect'. While welcome in principle, the operation of this provision is potentially confusing: it confirms that prosecutions can take place in respect of crimes committed *before* the Act came into force, but it does not give any indication how this might take place. One possible avenue would be to interpret section 7(4) of the Act as a retroactivity clause that provides for the retroactive application of the Act until the point at which the breach in question became a breach under customary international law. This interpretation is supported by its reference to a *breach* of customary international law, a term that is peculiar to the Geneva Conventions. However, given the general interpretive presumption against retrospective application, such a provision would likely be formulated in express positive terms rather than defensively as section 7(4) is. Furthermore, this section differs considerably from the examples of such retroactive application provisions given during the public hearings on the Act – in particular those of Canada and the UK – which the drafters were open to follow. Another alternative interpretation of section 7(4) is that this provision recognises that South African courts are empowered to prosecute customary international law crimes without implementing legislation under customary international law.

The Geneva Conventions Act also introduces specialised modes of liability for international crimes.[39] Firstly, section 5 of the Act provides for responsibility by way of *direct perpetration* of breaches of the Convention. Secondly, section 6 of the Act incorporates the doctrine of command responsibility into South African law. This section provides that a 'military superior officer'[40] is guilty of an offence if (1) forces under his or her effective command, authority and control (2) commit a grave breach or an ordinary breach,[41] (3) the superior knew, or in the circumstances ought reasonably to have known, that his subordinates were committing such a breach,[42] and (4) failed to take the necessary steps to

35 S 5(1) of the Geneva Conventions Act states: 'Any person who, *whether within or outside the Republic*, commits a grave breach of the Conventions, is guilty of an offence'.

36 S 5(3) of the Geneva Conventions Act states: 'Any person who *within the Republic* contravenes or fails to comply with a provision of the Conventions not covered by subsection (2), is guilty of an offence'.

37 S 5(4) of the Geneva Conventions Act states: 'Any *citizen of the Republic who outside the Republic contravenes* or fails to comply with a provision of the Conventions not covered by subsection (2), is guilty of an offence'. The Act does not, *contra* the ICC Act, extend its nationality jurisdiction to persons ordinarily resident in the Republic. See s 4(3)(*b*) of the ICC Act.

38 During the public hearings on the Geneva Conventions Act, submissions were made to the Portfolio Committee on Defence and Military Veterans proposing that the Act specifically provide for retrospective application of its provisions. They recommended that South Africa follow the Canadian approach and leave the date of application to be determined by a court. The committee rejected this approach and appears to have inserted s 7(4) instead.

39 In this respect, the Geneva Conventions Act goes further than the ICC Act, but not as far as the Rome Statute itself.

40 The term 'military superior officer' includes a military superior officer and a person holding a superior civil position. See ss 6(4)(*a*) and (*b*) of the Geneva Conventions Act.

41 S 6(1)(*a*) of the Geneva Conventions Act.

42 S 6(1)(*b*) of the Geneva Conventions Act.

prevent and/or punish said breach.[43] Section 6(1)(*c*) further specifies that the failure to take necessary steps means failure to 'exercise effective command, authority and control over the forces',[44] 'take all necessary and reasonable measures within his or her power to prevent or repress the commission of any breach or offence',[45] or 'submit the commission of the breach or offence ... to the competent authorities for investigation and prosecution'.[46]

However, noticeably absent from its modes of liability provisions are forms of *indirect participation or accessorial liability*, such as aiding and abetting or procuring the commission of an offence, notwithstanding the fact that such liability has been accepted as part of international law since the trial at Nuremberg.[47] More recently, the principles of accessorial liability for international crimes were codified in the Rome Statute.[48] The omission of certain modes of liability from the Geneva Conventions Act is clumsy but not fatal as the Act empowers courts to consider and apply international law (both conventional and customary) and comparable foreign law. This should lead to the incorporation of further international modes of liability as required.[49]

48.3.3 Common law prosecutions

In addition to these legislative avenues, the potential exists for the prosecution of international crimes through the *direct* application of customary international law by South African courts. In this regard, section 232 of the Constitution states: 'Customary international law is law in the Republic unless it is inconsistent with the Constitution or an Act of Parliament'. As customary international law itself criminalises certain conduct, this raises

---

43 S 6(1)(*c*) of the Geneva Conventions Act.

44 S 6(1)(*c*)(i) of the Geneva Conventions Act.

45 S 6(1)(*c*)(ii) of the Geneva Conventions Act.

46 S 6(1)(*c*)(iii) of the Geneva Conventions Act.

47 As Cassel notes:

> **Since Nuremberg there has been no question that accomplices, including those who aid and abet crimes, are responsible under international criminal law. The Nuremberg Charter imposed individual responsibility on 'accomplices participating in the formulation or execution of a common plan or conspiracy to commit' a crime enumerated within the Charter. Although the Nuremberg Tribunal limited application of this provision to crimes against peace and did not apply it to other crimes, the International Law Commission ('ILC') of the United Nations in 1950 articulated Nuremberg Principle VII as follows: 'Complicity in the commission of a crime against peace, a war crime, or a crime against humanity ... is a crime under international law.'**

Cassel D 'Corporate aiding and abetting of human rights violations: Confusion in the courts' (2008) 6(2) *JHR* 304 at 307.

48 Arts 25(3)(*c*) and (*d*). A number of other international instruments also criminalise the conduct of a person who contributes to the commission of a crime. See art 7(1) of the Statute for the International Tribunal for the Prosecution of Persons Responsible for Serious Violations of International Humanitarian Law Committed in the Territory of the Former Yugoslavia since 1991 (ICTY Statute); art 6(1) of the Statute of the International Tribunal for Rwanda (ICTR Statute); art 4 of the United Nations Convention Against Torture and Other Cruel, Inhuman or Degrading Treatment or Punishment (CAT); art III(*b*) of the International Convention on the Suppression and Punishment of the Crime of Apartheid; art 6 of the Supplementary Convention on the Abolition of Slavery, the Slave Trade and Institutions and Practices Similar to Slavery; art III(*e*) of the Genocide Convention.

49 S 3 of the Geneva Conventions Act provides as follows:

> **In addition to the Constitution and the law, any court in the Republic hearing any matter arising from the application of this Act must also consider and, where appropriate, may apply—**
> **(*a*) conventional international law;**
> **(*b*) customary international law; and**
> **(*c*) comparable foreign law.**

This provision - including following submissions by civil society - is modelled on s 2 of the ICC Act. This raises broader issues of whether South African courts could extend the Act's criminal scope by interpretation using this provision, taking into account subsequent developments in international law. The Geneva Conventions came into force 62 years ago. They have thus been frequently interpreted and applied by both domestic and international courts and over time have developed considerably. Those developments could be a useful source of legal rules and principles for consideration and application by a South African court seized with a case under the Geneva Conventions Act.

the possibility of bringing prosecutions in South African courts by the *direct* application of customary international law without requiring a statutory criminal framework such as the ICC Act or the Geneva Conventions Act.

In *S v Basson*, the Constitutional Court recognised this potential, although it ultimately left the question open, noting as follows:

> **For the purposes of this case it is not necessary to enter into controversies surrounding the existence of universal jurisdiction for crimes against humanity and war crimes, and a concomitant duty to prosecute. *We have not found it necessary to consider whether customary international law could be used either as the basis in itself for a prosecution under the common law*, or, alternatively, as an aid to the interpretation of section 18(2)(*a*) of the Riotous Assemblies Act.[50] (Emphasis added)**

However, in *National Commissioner of the SAPS v SA Human Rights Litigation Centre*, the Constitutional Court explicitly endorsed the direct application of customary international law through section 232 of the Constitution, noting as follows:

> **Along with torture, the international crimes of piracy, slave-trading, war crimes, crimes against humanity, genocide and apartheid require states, even in the absence of binding international treaty law, to suppress such conduct because 'all states have an interest as they violate values that constitute the foundation of the world public order'. *Torture, whether on the scale of crimes against humanity or not, is a crime in South Africa in terms of section 232 of the Constitution because the customary international law prohibition against torture has the status of a peremptory norm.*[51] (Emphasis added)**

Furthermore, as noted above, it is possible to interpret section 7(4) of the Geneva Conventions Act as implicitly recognising the *direct* application of customary international (criminal) law by South African courts. A plain reading of the text of section 7(4), which refers to the '*prosecution of any person accused of having committed a breach under customary international law*', supports this interpretation.

The direct application of the common law in this manner is novel and will no doubt be controversial. As such, it is unlikely that it will be employed when there are statutory alternatives available such as the ICC Act and the Geneva Conventions Act. However, there are circumstances where those avenues will not be available. For one, prosecutions could be brought in respect of all customary international law crimes, including the crime of aggression which is not prosecutable under the existing statutory framework.[52] Furthermore, in a South African context, given the suggestion in *S v Basson* that both war crimes and crimes against humanity were committed under apartheid, but these crimes cannot be prosecuted under the Rome Statute Act which only applies prospectively from 2002, this

50 *S v Basson* supra at 172 fn 147. See also the separate opinion of Sachs J at 113 *et seq*.

51 *National Commissioner of the SAPS v SA Human Rights Litigation Centre* (CC) supra at 37. The court went on to extend this finding to crimes against humanity generally, finding at 39: 'In effect, torture is criminalised in South Africa under section 232 of the Constitution and the Torture Act *whilst torture on the scale of crimes against humanity is criminalised under section 232 of the Constitution*, the Torture Act and the ICC Act' (emphasis added). For torture as a discrete crime under South African statutory law, see also the discussion in Chapter 49.

52 There is no indication that South Africa intends to ratify the Kampala Resolution on the Crime of Aggression, discussed in Chapter 47. Indeed, considering South Africa's stated intention to withdraw from the ICC, it remains to be seen if South Africa will provide for any statutory criminalisation of the crime of aggression under South African law. The International Crimes Bill which was published in December 2017 does not provide for the crime of aggression. See also the discussion under section 48.3.1.

possibility arises for prosecuting such crimes by *direct* application of customary international criminal law.[53]

Finally, the *direct* application of customary international (criminal) law raises concerns in terms of the principle of legality as well as the retroactive application of law. However, provided that the offences in question were, at the time of their commission, unlawful under international law, their prosecution will not offend section 35(3)(*l*) of the Constitution. This is because the International Covenant on Civil and Political Rights 1966 (ICCPR), to which South Africa is a party, recognises the non-retroactivity of criminal law *in general*, but states as follows:

> **Nothing in this article shall prejudice the trial and punishment of any person for any act or omission which, at the time when it was committed, was criminal according to the general principles of law recognized by the community of nations.**[54]

The difficulty with this avenue is that it places the additional burden on those seeking prosecution to prove that the crimes in question were crimes under customary international law *at the relevant time*. Admittedly, this is no simple task. Crimes against humanity were only comprehensively codified when the ICTY statute[55] was adopted. Similarly, although war crimes are the oldest regime of international crimes, until recently they could only be committed in *international* armed conflicts.

48.3.4 International criminal law in South African courts

As of yet, there have not been any prosecutions in South African courts of the crimes of genocide, crimes against humanity or war crimes (or aggression, for that matter). Nevertheless, South African courts have had occasion to consider these crimes, and the obligations that arise from their commission, on three occasions.

Azanian Peoples' Organization (AZAPO) and others v President of the Republic of South Africa and others[56]

The first such occasion arose shortly after the transition to democracy when a group of victims of apartheid era crimes challenged the Promotion of National Unity and Reconciliation Act 34 of 1995 (the TRC Act), which offered civil and criminal amnesty 'to persons who make full disclosure of all the relevant facts relating to acts associated with a political objective'.[57] One of the grounds of their challenge was that 'the state was obliged by international law to prosecute those responsible for gross human rights violations and that the provisions of [the TRC Act] ... which authorised amnesty for such offenders constituted a breach of international law'.[58]

---

53 At the very least the crimes against humanity of murder and persecution have been recognised as forming part of customary international law since the post-World War II Nuremberg and Tokyo trials. Furthermore, it is by now incontrovertible that the 1949 Geneva Conventions' grave breaches regime forms part of customary international law. See ICJ Legality of the Threat or Use of Nuclear Weapons (advisory opinion) ICJ Reports (1996) 257 at para 79, endorsed by the Constitutional Court in *S v Basson* supra at 171–174.

54 Art 15(2) of the ICCPR. Similarly, art 7(2) of the [European] Convention for the Protection of Human Rights and Fundamental Freedoms as amended by Protocols No 11 and No 14, also makes the prohibition on retrospectivity subject to the following proviso: 'This Article shall not prejudice the trial and punishment of any person for any act or omission which, at the time when it was committed, was criminal according to the general principles of law recognised by civilised nations'.

55 Art 5 of the Statute of the ICTY (1993) 32(4) *ILM* 1193.

56 *Azanian Peoples' Organization (AZAPO) and others v President of the Republic of South Africa and others* (CCT17/96) [1996] ZACC 16; 1996 (8) BCLR 1015; 1996 (4) SA 672 (25 July 1996) (*AZAPO*).

57 Preamble of the TRC Act.

58 *AZAPO* at 25.

The claim was not without merit. Certainly, the atrocities committed during apartheid – those subject to amnesty under the TRC Act – made good candidates for international crimes. The system of apartheid *itself* was classified as a crime against humanity under the 1973 International Convention on the Suppression and Punishment of the Crime of Apartheid.[59] In addition, many of the atrocities routinely committed under apartheid, such as murder, forced disappearances, forced removal and torture, are listed as underlying acts of crimes against humanity.[60] Furthermore, arguably the level of violence during apartheid, both in South Africa and other frontline states, at times could be classified as amounting to an armed conflict, be it international and/or non-international, making human rights violations committed during this period potential war crimes. What is more, the TRC Act's proffer of amnesty for such acts came at a time when there was a growing recognition that certain international crimes must *as a matter of international law* be punished by states.[61]

Nevertheless, the Constitutional Court in *AZAPO* ultimately rejected this challenge and ruled that the TRC Act was consistent with the Constitution. On the question of international crimes, the court found that the struggle against apartheid could not, at any point, be classified as an *international armed conflict*.[62] Similarly, the court found that it was doubtful whether Additional Protocol II to the Geneva Convention (relating to non-international armed conflicts) applied. Even if it did, 'it actually requires the authorities in power, after the end of hostilities, to grant amnesty to those previously engaged in the conflict'.[63]

The scant legal reasoning underpinning these conclusions, contained in a footnote, are far from unassailable.[64] Nevertheless, the upshot was that there was no armed conflict in South Africa and crimes committed during this period could not be considered war crimes. In a later decision, the Constitutional Court accepted that *at certain points* South Africa was engaged in an armed conflict and that war crimes were committed.[65] Remarkably, the court did not even address the question of crimes against humanity.

---

59 Art 1 of the International Convention on the Suppression and Punishment of the Crime of Apartheid 1973 states as follows:

> **The States Parties to the present Convention declare that apartheid is a crime against humanity and that inhuman acts resulting from the policies and practices of apartheid and similar policies and practices of racial segregation and discrimination, as defined in article II of the Convention, are crimes violating the principles of international law, in particular the purposes and principles of the Charter of the United Nations, and constituting a serious threat to international peace and security.**

60 It would be easy to show that these crimes met the contextual requirements of being widespread and/or systemic. See art 7 of the Rome Statute.

61 While the existence of a general customary international obligation to punish such crimes remains controversial, at the very least there are, and were at the time, treaty-based obligations to punish war crimes and genocide under certain conditions. All four of the Geneva Conventions 1949 contain a common article setting out an obligation either to prosecute individuals alleged to have committed or ordered the commission of war crimes regardless of their nationality or to 'hand such persons over for trial to another High Contracting Party concerned, provided such High Contracting Party has made out a *prima facie* case'. See art 49 of the Geneva Convention I; art 50 of the Geneva Convention II; art 129 of the Geneva Convention III; art 146 of the Geneva Convention IV. See also arts I, II, IV and VI of the Genocide Convention and the ICJ *Application of the Convention on the Prevention and Punishment of the Crime of Genocide (Bosnia and Herzegovina v Serbia and Montenegro)* Judgment ICJ Reports 2007 43 (*Bosnia* judgment).

62 *AZAPO* at fn 29: 'The Geneva Conventions of 1949 apply only to cases of "declared war or of any armed conflict which may arise between two or more of the High Contracting Parties". (No High Contracting Parties were involved in the South African conflict.)' It also summarily dismissed the argument that art 1(4) of Additional Protocol I cannot be used to escalate the conflict as that instrument 'was never signed or ratified by South Africa during the conflict and no such "declaration" was deposited with *that* Council by any of the parties to the conflict' (at fn 29).

63 *AZAPO* at fn 29. The court did not consider whether the conflict in South Africa fell within the definition of common art 3 of the 1949 Geneva Conventions.

64 See Dugard J 'Is the truth and reconciliation process compatible with international law? An unanswered question? *AZAPO v President of the Republic of South Africa* 1996' (1997) 13(2) *SAJHR* 258.

65 See the discussion of *S v Basson* supra below.

S v Basson[66]

The Constitutional Court again addressed the question of apartheid-era crimes during the trial of Wouter Basson, the head of the apartheid government's chemical weapons programme.[67] Basson was alleged to have participated in a number of acts that may amount to international crimes, including the mass murder of South West African Peoples Organization (SWAPO) detainees in Namibia and the assassination of members of SWAPO and the ANC in Namibia, Swaziland, Mozambique and London. For reasons that remain unclear, Basson was charged with ordinary offences under South African law and not international crimes.[68] However, the serious nature of his alleged conduct, and the possibility that it amounted to international crimes, became relevant to the proceedings before the Constitutional Court.

Following Basson's acquittal by the Cape High Court in April 2002 on all 67 charges,[69] the state appealed to the Supreme Court of Appeal (SCA), and then the Constitutional Court.[70] In the end, the state enjoyed some degree of success in the Constitutional Court, which dismissed the appeals related to bias and the admissibility of the bail record, but overturned the quashing of certain charges by the High Court.[71] However, the state declined to pursue these charges against Basson.[72]

The Basson trial represents an ignominious beginning to South Africa's domestic enforcement of international criminal law. Nevertheless, in its two decisions on the matter the Constitutional Court made important remarks regarding the prosecution of international crimes. In its first decision, the Constitutional Court remarked that '[i]t is ... clear that the practice of apartheid constituted crimes against humanity and some of the practices of the apartheid government constituted war crimes'.[73] What is more, the court accepted that 'international law obliges the state to punish crimes against humanity and war crimes'.[74] Then, in its second decision, the court found

---

66 *S v Basson* (CCT 30/03) [2004] ZACC 13; 2005 (1) SA 171 (CC); 2004 (6) BCLR 620 (CC) (10 March 2004) (*S v Basson* CC 1); *S v Basson* (CCT30/03A) [2005] ZACC 10; 2005 (12) BCLR 1192 (CC); 2007 (3) SA 582 (CC) (9 September 2005) (*S v Basson* CC 2).

67 In 1999, Basson was charged on all 67 counts, including 229 murders, conspiracy to murder, fraud totalling R36 million, and manufacturing, possessing and dealing in drugs.

68 With respect to the acts committed abroad, Basson was charged with conspiring in South Africa to commit such acts as South African courts were unable to exercise direct jurisdiction over such crimes otherwise. The situation would have been different had Basson been charged with international crimes that are subject to universal jurisdiction.

69 The trial was a fiasco from the outset. At the beginning of the trial, the presiding Judge quashed six charges of conspiring to commit serious crimes, mainly murder, beyond the borders of South Africa (in England, Mozambique, Swaziland and Namibia) on the basis that the provision on which they were based did not apply to offences committed outside the Republic. Then, three months into the trial, the state applied unsuccessfully for the recusal of the presiding officer, Judge Hartzenberg, on the grounds that he was biased and had prejudged important issues in the case. Remarkably, the judgment was not reported.

70 The SCA rejected the appeal outright on procedural grounds and so the state turned to the Constitutional Court on the basis that the matter raised constitutional issues. See *S v Basson* 2004 (1) SA 246 (SCA) and *S v Basson* CC 1.

71 See *S v Basson* CC 2 supra at 260.

72 According to the National Prosecuting Authority (NPA), the reason for not pursuing the charges was that they 'could be met by a defence of *autrefois acquit* because of the overlap between these charges and a charge on which Basson [was] ... tried for and acquitted'. Swart, M 'The Wouter Basson Prosecution: The closest South Africa came to Nuremberg?' 68 *Zaö R V* (2008) 209 at 212 fn 19. However, the Constitutional Court had already noted (*S v Basson* CC 2 supra at 256) that Basson would 'not be able to raise the plea of *autrefois acquit* [in respect of the quashed charges] as there was no acquittal on the merits in respect of the ... charges. The accused did not plead to these charges and was therefore never in jeopardy of conviction upon them'. See, however, para 169.

73 *S v Basson* CC 1 at 37.

74 *S v Basson* CC 1 at 37. These remarks, albeit obiter dictum, are difficult to reconcile with the finding in *AZAPO* that crimes committed under apartheid could not constitute war crimes as South Africa was not engaged in an international or non-international armed conflict. Nor does the court's acceptance that (i) apartheid was a crime against humanity, and (ii) South Africa is under an obligation to prosecute such crimes, sit well with its failure to even consider the question of crimes against humanity in *AZAPO*.

that the conduct Dr Basson had been accused of 'grossly transgressed even the most minimal standards of international humanitarian law'. In other words, it amounted to war crimes.[75]

It is difficult to reconcile the Constitutional Court's finding in *AZAPO* to the effect that the Geneva Conventions of 1949 and its Protocols did not apply to the conduct for which amnesty was being granted with its subsequent findings, on two occasions, that war crimes were committed during apartheid. It is also difficult to square the court's twin assertions in *Basson* that crimes against humanity were committed in South Africa during apartheid and that South Africa was under an *international obligation* to prosecute such crimes, with the failure of the court in *AZAPO* even to consider such crimes.[76]

National Commissioner of the South African Police Service v Southern African Human Rights Litigation Centre and another[77]

The third, and potentially most far-reaching, case concerning international criminal law was an administrative review of the decision by the National Prosecuting Authority (NPA), on the advice of the South African Police Service (SAPS), not to institute an investigation into crimes against humanity committed in Zimbabwe in 2007. The genesis of the case was a docket - the Zimbabwe Torture Docket - which was compiled by the Southern African Human Rights Litigation Centre (SAHRLC) and handed to the NPA in 2008. Based on the docket, the SAHRLC had requested the NPA to investigate and if necessary prosecute the perpetrators under the Rome Statute Act, using the principle of universal jurisdiction.[78] When the relevant authorities refused to open an investigation, the SAHRLC, with the Zimbabwe Exiles Forum, took the decision on review.[79]

The applicants were successful in the North Gauteng High Court,[80] and successfully defended that decision in the SCA.[81] As a result, the SAPS appealed the matter to the Constitutional Court. In October 2014 the Constitutional Court handed down its decision, finding that the SAPS were obliged - in terms of the Constitution, relevant legislation and international law - to investigate alleged crimes against humanity committed in Zimbabwe.[82]

The immediate issue to be determined, as the court put it, was 'whether, in the light of South Africa's international and domestic law obligations, the SAPS has a duty to investigate crimes against humanity committed beyond our borders', and if so 'under which circumstances is this duty

75 *S v Basson* CC 2 at 179. Although the court focused its attention mainly on the crimes committed against hundreds of SWAPO captives in Namibia, the court's findings cannot be limited to such crimes; Dr Basson was also charged with crimes committed against members of the ANC (and others) in South Africa and beyond.

76 Whether or not there is such an obligation, and its scope, remains contentious. The point is, though, that the court *itself* found such an obligation exists under international law in *Basson*.

77 *National Commissioner of The South African Police Service v Southern African Human Rights Litigation Centre and Another* (CCT 02/14) [2014] ZACC 30; 2015 (1) SA 315 (CC); 2015 (1) SACR 255 (CC); 2014 (12) BCLR 1428 (CC) (30 October 2014).

78 See s 4 of the Rome Statute Act.

79 The decision was challenged under the Promotion of Administrative Justice Act 3 of 2000 (PAJA) and the principle of legality.

80 See *Southern African Litigation Centre and Another v National Director of Public Prosecutions and Others* (77150/09) [2012] ZAGPPHC 61; 2012 (10) BCLR 1089 (GNP); [2012] 3 All SA 198 (GNP) (8 May 2012). For a discussion of the judgment, see Werle G and Bornkamm PC 'Torture in Zimbabwe under scrutiny in South Africa: The judgment of the North Gauteng High Court in *SALC v. National Director of Public Prosecutions*' (2013) 11(3) *JICJ* 659 and Gevers C '*Southern Africa Litigation Centre and Another v NDPP and Others:* Note' (2013) 130(2) *SALJ* 293.

81 *National Commissioner of the South African Police Service v Southern African Human Rights Litigation Centre* (485/2012) [2013] ZASCA 168; 2014 (2) SA 42 (SCA); [2014] 1 All SA 435 (SCA) (27 November 2013). For a discussion, see Woolaver H 'Prosecuting international crimes in South Africa: Interpreting the requirement of the accused's presence in South African territory under the implementation of the Rome Statute of the ICC Act' (2014) 131(2) *SALJ* 253.

82 *National Commissioner of the SAPS v SAHRLC* (CC) supra at 55.

triggered?'.[83] However, the decision was of vital importance to the prosecution of international crimes in South Africa generally, and the ICC Act's application in particular.

The court's key findings concern:

- jurisdiction in international law
- the 'presence requirement' under the ICC Act (and international law)
- the obligation to investigate international crimes.

The court began its discussion of jurisdiction in international law by distinguishing between three different forms of jurisdiction: *prescriptive, adjudicative and enforcement* jurisdiction. It placed investigations under the adjudicative category.[84] The court went on to find, in essence, that while *enforcement jurisdiction* 'is confined to the territory of the state seeking to invoke it', prescriptive and, in some circumstances, *adjudicative* jurisdiction can be applied universally, that is, outside the territory of the state.[85] The court proceeded to set out three general factors that should be observed 'in order for universal jurisdiction to comply with the dictates of international law':[86]

- The existence of a substantial and *bona fide* connection between the subject matter and the source of the jurisdiction
- The principle of non-intervention in the domestic or territorial jurisdiction of other states
- Elements of accommodation, mutuality and proportionality

The second key finding by the court concerns whether the presence of a suspect is required for an investigation into international crimes to commence. The SAPS had consistently argued that a suspect had to be present in the Republic for an investigation to commence under the ICC Act (section 4(3)(*c*))[87] and international law. In rejecting this argument, the court held that 'section 4(3) sets the jurisdictional limits of South African courts', but 'it is silent on the circumstances under which our country has the duty to investigate international crimes committed outside of our territory'.[88] Therefore, in light of this silence, the lack of consensus among international lawyers that *international law* requires presence (and some evidence that it does not),[89] the court concluded that:

> **the exercise of universal jurisdiction, for purposes of the investigation of an international crime committed outside our territory, may occur in the absence of a suspect without offending our Constitution or international law.[90]**

The court avoided directly interpreting the presence requirement (under section 4(3) or *perhaps* international law) by consigning it to the 'more advanced stage of criminal proceedings',[91] in other

83 *National Commissioner of the SAPS v SAHRLC* (CC) supra at 21. Notably, while the court set out the SAPS's grounds of appeal, it was not guided or bound by them.

84 *National Commissioner of the SAPS v SAHRLC* (CC) supra at 25.

85 *National Commissioner of the SAPS v SAHRLC* (CC) supra at 29.

86 *National Commissioner of the SAPS v SAHRLC* (CC) supra at 28.

87 S 4(3)(*c*) states: 'In order to secure the jurisdiction of a South African court for purposes of this Chapter, any person who commits [an ICC] crime ... outside the territory of the Republic, is deemed to have committed that crime within the territory of the Republic if ... *that person, after the commission of the crime, is present in the territory of the Republic*' (emphasis added)

88 *National Commissioner of the SAPS v SA Human Rights Litigation Centre* (CC) supra at 43.

89 The court cited a 2005 Resolution of the *Institut de Droit Internationale* and the Rome Statute's separation of the investigation and prosecution phases of criminal proceedings. See *National Commissioner of the SAPS v SAHRLC* (CC) at 46.

90 *National Commissioner of the SAPS v SAHRLC* (CC) supra at 47.

91 *National Commissioner of the SAPS v SAHRLC* (CC) supra at 47.

words, the prosecution or trial phase where a court is involved. However, we are left in the dark as to when this stage commences.

The final – and potentially most far-reaching – finding by the court concerned the 'duty on the SAPS to investigate international crimes'.[92] After considering the relevant provision of the Constitution,[93] the South African Police Service Act 68 of 1995,[94] the National Prosecuting Authority Act 32 of 1998[95] and the ICC Act, the court found that the SAPS does not only have the *power* to investigate alleged international crimes, it has a *duty* (or obligation) to do so.[96] In doing so, the court also relied on the existence of an 'international obligation to investigate international crimes'.[97] Furthermore, the court did not limit this obligation to crimes committed in South African territory. On the contrary, it held that not only is this obligation engaged in respect of crimes committed abroad, but also that it 'is most pressing in instances where those crimes are committed ... within the territory of countries that are not parties to the Rome Statute, because to do otherwise would permit impunity'.[98]

Having set out a broad obligation on states to prosecute such crimes, the court added that 'the universal jurisdiction to investigate international crimes is not absolute',[99] and proceeded to set out two limitations in this regard. The first limiting principle[100] is made up of two distinct principles: subsidiarity and non-intervention. The *principle of subsidiarity* 'requires that ordinarily there must be a *substantial and true connection between the subject-matter and the source of the jurisdiction*'.[101] In terms of the *principle of non-intervention*, 'investigating international crimes committed abroad is permissible only if the country with jurisdiction is unwilling or unable to prosecute and only if the investigation is confined to the territory of the investigating state'.[102]

The second limiting principle is *practicability*, which requires that a state 'consider whether embarking on an investigation into an international crime committed elsewhere is reasonable and practicable in the circumstances of each particular case'.[103] This, according to the court, requires considering inter alia:

- whether the investigation is likely to lead to a prosecution and accordingly whether the alleged perpetrators are likely to be present in South Africa on their own or through an extradition request
- the geographical proximity of South Africa to the place of the crime and the likelihood of the suspects being arrested for prosecution
- the prospects of gathering evidence which is needed to satisfy the elements of a crime
- the nature and the extent of the resources required for an effective investigation.[104]

---

92 It is worth noting that in its judgment, the court uses the terms 'duty' and 'obligation' interchangeably, which is somewhat confusing at times and not beyond reproach.

93 S 205.

94 Ss 16(1), 16(2)(*a*)(i), 17C(1) and 17D(1)(*a*).

95 Ss 13(1)(*c*), 24(3) and 24(7).

96 *National Commissioner of the SAPS v SAHRLC* (CC) supra at 55.

97 The question of whether an international obligation to prosecute international crimes under international law exists (and under what circumstances) is a matter of some debate among international lawyers. Previously in *S v Basson* CC 1 at 37, the Constitutional Court noted that 'international law obliges the state to punish crimes against humanity and war crimes', but this statement was not without qualification.

98 *National Commissioner of the SAPS v SAHRLC* (CC) supra at 32.

99 *National Commissioner of the SAPS v SAHRLC* (CC) supra at 61.

100 *National Commissioner of the SAPS v SAHRLC* (CC) supra at 61.

101 *National Commissioner of the SAPS v SAHRLC* (CC) supra at 61. (Emphasis added)

102 *National Commissioner of the SAPS v SAHRLC* (CC) supra at 61.

103 *National Commissioner of the SAPS v SAHRLC* (CC) supra at 63.

104 *National Commissioner of the SAPS v SAHRLC* (CC) supra at 64.

This, the court concluded, is ultimately a question of whether the SAPS acted *reasonably* in opening or declining to open an investigation.

The court proceeded to apply these principles to the facts of the case, and in particular the reasons given by the SAPS for not opening an investigation. In doing so, the court emphatically rejected the 'political effects' reason advanced by SAPS, noting as follows:

> **The cornerstone of the universality principle, in general, and the Rome Statute, in particular, is to hold torturers, genocidaires, pirates and their ilk, the so-called *hostis humani generis*, the enemy of all humankind, accountable for their crimes, wherever they may have committed them or wherever they may be domiciled. *An approach like the one adopted by the SAPS in the present case undermines that very cornerstone. Political inter-state tensions are, in most instances, virtually unavoidable as far as the application of universality, the Rome Statute and, in the present instance, the ICC Act is concerned.*[105]**

Having done so, the court concluded that the SCA decision was correct and that 'on the facts of this case the torture allegations must be investigated by the SAPS'.[106] The Constitutional Court added that South Africa 'must take up [its] rightful place in the community of nations with its concomitant obligations', lest it becomes 'a safe haven for those who commit crimes against humanity'.[107]

48.4 The International Criminal Court

48.4.1 A brief history

The revolutionary institution[108] that is the ICC is the culmination of efforts that began well over a century ago. In 1872, Gustave Moynier, one of the founders of the International Committee of the Red Cross (ICRC), proposed the establishment of an international tribunal to punish violations of the 1864 Geneva Convention.[109] Following World War II and the subsequent trials of Nazi and Japanese war criminals, the project was invigorated. An initial draft of the 1948 Genocide Convention included a proposal for a permanent or ad hoc international court to punish crimes of genocide although neither was included in the final version.[110] However, on the same day that the Genocide Convention was adopted, the UN General Assembly passed a resolution calling on the International Law Commission (ILC) to 'study the desirability and possibility of establishing an international judicial organ for the trial of persons charged with genocide or other crimes'.[111] The ILC's work stalled in 1954, primarily as a consequence of difficulties with the question of defining aggression.[112]

In 1983, the ILC took up the issue again on its own accord when the General Assembly invited it to continue its work on the Draft Code of Offences Against the Peace and Security of Mankind, which had stalled in 1954.[113] Then in 1989, the General Assembly formally asked

105 *National Commissioner of the SAPS v SAHRLC* (CC) supra at 74. (Emphasis added)

106 *National Commissioner of the SAPS v SAHRLC* (CC) supra at 80.

107 *National Commissioner of the SAPS v SAHRLC* (CC) supra at 80.

108 Cassese A 'The Statute of the International Criminal Court: Some preliminary reflections' (1999) 10(1) *EJIL* 144.

109 Moynier G 'Note sur la création d'une institution judiciaire internationale propre à prévenir et à réprimer les infractions à la Convention de Genève' (1872) 3(11) *Bulletin International des Sociétés de Secours aux Militaires Blessés* Comité International at 122. See further, Hall CK 'The first proposal for a permanent International Criminal Court' (1998) 38(322) *IRRC* 57.

110 Schabas WA *The International Criminal Court: A Commentary on the Rome Statute* 2 ed (2016) 7.

111 General Assembly Resolution 260 (III)B.

112 Schabas *The International Criminal Court* 9.

113 Schabas *The International Criminal Court* 10.

the ILC to return to the issue, following a proposal by Trinidad and Tobago relating to 'illicit trafficking in narcotic drugs across national frontiers and other transnational criminal activities'.[114]

While the ILC was working on this proposal during the early 1990s, another development took place that would significantly influence the establishment of a permanent international criminal court: the establishment of the ad hoc tribunals for the former Yugoslavia (ICTY) and Rwanda (ICTR) by the Security Council.

In 1994, the ILC completed a draft of what would become the Rome Statute.[115] In response, the General Assembly first established an ad hoc committee, then later a preparatory committee for establishing an international criminal court[116] to make comments and refine the text.[117] Finally, the General Assembly decided that a diplomatic conference would be held in Rome, Italy, from 15 June to 17 July 1998, to establish the International Criminal Court.

As a result of these marathon efforts, on 17 July 1998, at the UN Diplomatic Conference of Plenipotentiaries on the Establishment of a Permanent International Criminal Court in Rome, 120 states adopted the Rome Statute of the International Criminal Court.[118] The Rome Statute empowers the ICC to prosecute the crimes of genocide, crimes against humanity, war crimes and the crime of aggression. According to the Preamble of the Rome Statute, its purpose is, inter alia, to 'establish an independent permanent International Criminal Court ..., with jurisdiction over the most serious crimes of concern to the international community as a whole' to 'put an end to impunity for the perpetrators of these crimes and thus to contribute to the prevention of such crimes'.[119]

48.4.2 Overview of the Rome Statute

The Rome Statute performs two distinct roles. The first is to set out the structure, powers and functions of the ICC in prosecuting the crimes of genocide, crimes against humanity, war crimes and aggression. The second is to set out a cooperation regime for state parties to assist the court in fulfilling this mandate. In addition, the statute provides for financial and administrative matters.

Before performing these roles, the ICC will need to consider briefly the basic organising principle of the Rome Statute system: complementarity. In terms of the principle of complementarity - referred to in articles 1 and 17, as well as in the Preamble of the Rome Statute - the ICC will only be able to admit a case before it (where the other jurisdictional bases of nationality and territoriality are present) if the state party concerned is unwilling or unable to prosecute the offender nationally.

This principle of complementarity is novel. It effectively affords state parties primary jurisdiction over international crimes committed in their jurisdiction. It is the reverse of the ad hoc tribunals for Yugoslavia and Rwanda, which enjoyed primacy over national legal systems.

The effect of this principle is not to allow states to frustrate the prosecution of individuals by using their primary jurisdiction as a shield. Article 17(2) expressly prevents such a

---

114 General Assembly Resolution 44/39. See Schabas *The International Criminal Court* 12.

115 Schabas *The International Criminal Court* 18–19.

116 See General Assembly 50/46.

117 Schabas *The International Criminal Court* 19–21.

118 Rome Statute of the International Criminal Court (1998) UN Doc.A/CONF.183/9, United Nations: Rome Statute of the International Criminal Court *International Legal Materials* (1998) 37(5) at 999. Seven voted against the final text with 21 abstentions.

119 Preamble of the Rome Statute.

scenario and obliges state parties to prosecute offenders or surrender them to the ICC so that it may do so. In terms of this principle, the ICC will only be able to try cases if the state party concerned is unwilling or unable to prosecute the offender nationally. This 'coercion' of state parties is one of many positive knock-on effects of this principle.[120]

However, more than being a mere presumption in favour of local prosecutions, the principle ensures that the ICC operates as a buttress in support of the criminal justice systems of state parties at a national level and as part of a broader system of international criminal justice. The principle proceeds from the belief that national courts should be the first to act. Aside from assuaging the concerns of states over the usurpation of sovereignty, the principle serves more noble ends such as the need for full victim participation, the practicality of local prosecutions and the very real limitations of a court with *potentially* universal jurisdiction. As such, when a state expresses a desire to undertake its own proceedings nationally, it should not be dismissed lightly.

48.4.3 The structure of the International Criminal Court

Under article 34 of the Rome Statute, the ICC is composed of four organs: the Presidency, Judges' Chambers, the Office of the Prosecutor (OTP), the Registry, and also the Assembly of States Parties (ASP) which, while not an organ of the ICC, is a key part of its structure.[121]

The *Presidency* consists of the president of the court with his first and second vice-presidents. The Presidency is primarily responsible for the proper administration of the ICC and various other functions conferred on it by the Rome Statute. This role, however, does not include the administration of the OTP, which is reserved for the prosecutor under article 42. The president, first vice-president and second vice-president, who are elected by an absolute majority of the judges of the ICC, serve for a term of three years or until the end of their respective terms of office as judges, whichever expires earlier, and are eligible for re-election once. Unlike the other judges, those who are elected to the Presidency serve on a full-time basis as soon as they are elected.

The *Judges' Chambers* are divided into three divisions: an Appeals Division, a Trial Division and a Pre-Trial Division. The Appeals Division is composed of the president and four other judges who sit as a single Appeals Chamber. The Trial Division is composed of not less than six judges, three of whom make up each Pre-Trial Chamber. The Pre-Trial Division consists of not less than six judges. Although three judges sit on each Pre-Trial Chamber, certain functions of this division are carried out by a single judge in relation to the states concerned and various procedural aspects (for example, the disclosure of evidence prior to trial) under the rules of procedure and evidence.

The ICC has 18 full-time judges who are nominated and elected under a complex procedure set out in article 36. Briefly, the Assembly of States Parties (ASP) elects the judges by secret ballot from candidates nominated by states parties to the Rome Statute, and who are not necessarily nationals of a nominating state. There are two lists: one comprises individuals with 'established competence in criminal law and procedure'[122] while the other details candidates with 'established competence in relevant areas of international law'.[123] Judges must be 'persons of high moral character, impartiality and integrity who possess the qualifications required in their respective states for appointment to the highest judicial offices'.[124]

120 See Sarooshi D 'The Statute of the International Criminal Court' (1999) 48(2) *ICLQ* 387.

121 For an overview, see O'Shea A 'The Statute of the International Criminal Court' (1999) 116(2) *SALJ* 243–261.

122 Art 36(3)(*b*)(i) of the Rome Statute.

123 Art 36(3)(*b*)(ii) of the Rome Statute.

124 Art 36(3)(*a*) of the Rome Statute.

Furthermore, in selecting judges, states must consider the need for representation of the principal legal systems of the world, equitable geographical representation, and a fair representation of female and male judges. Judicial terms are for nine years and, ordinarily, judges are not eligible for re-election. However, a judge assigned to a Trial or Appeals Chamber 'shall continue in office to complete any trial or appeal the hearing of which has already commenced before that Chamber'.[125] Judges assigned to the Appeals Division 'serve in that division for their entire term of office',[126] while judges assigned to the Trial and Pre-Trial Divisions shall serve in those divisions for a period of three years, and thereafter until the completion of any case the hearing of which has already commenced in the division concerned. Finally, no two judges may be nationals of the same state.

Once elected, judges are assigned to a division 'based on the nature of the functions to be performed by each division, and the qualifications and experience of the judges elected to the Court, in such a way that each division shall contain an appropriate combination of expertise in criminal law and procedure and in international law'.[127] Article 52 mandates judges to adopted regulations of the court 'necessary for its routine functioning'.[128] Article 41 sets out the procedure for excusing and disqualifying judges.

The *Office of the Prosecutor* (OTP) is a separate organ of the ICC. Headed by the prosecutor, it is responsible for receiving referrals and any substantiated information on crimes falling within the jurisdiction of the court, for examining them, and for conducting investigations and prosecutions before the court. The prosecutor and deputy prosecutor, who must be of different nationalities, are elected by secret ballot by the ASP for a non-renewable nine-year term. Both must be persons of high moral character, be highly competent, and have extensive practical experience in the prosecution or trial of criminal cases. To guarantee its independence, the prosecutor has full authority over the management and administration of the OTP, including the staff, facilities and other resources thereof. The issue of the independence of the prosecutor and the OTP was raised recently in the context of the introduction of an Independent Oversight Mechanism (IOM) by the ASP. In 2011, the ASP elected its second prosecutor, Fatou Bensouda, who is both the first female to hold the office as well as the first African.

The *Registry* is responsible for the 'non-judicial aspects of the administration and servicing of the Court'.[129] It is headed by the registrar, who falls under the authority of the president of the court. The registrar is elected by secret ballot by the judges of the court for a term of office of five years, which is renewable once. One of the key functions of the registrar is the establishment of a Victims and Witnesses Unit in the Registry.

The *Assembly of States Parties* (ASP) is not an organ of the ICC, yet is a key part of its structure. The numerous tasks assigned to the ASP under the statute can be divided into three categories: administrative, legislative and operational.

The *administrative functions* of the ASP are mostly set out in article 112, and include providing management oversight to the presidency, the prosecutor and the registrar regarding the administration of the court; considering reports and activities of the bureau and taking appropriate action with regard to them; budgetary matters; and the inspection, evaluation, and investigation of the court to enhance its efficiency and economy. The ASP is also responsible for a host of other administrative tasks under the statute. The ASP's administrative

125 Art 36(10) of the Rome Statute.
126 Art 39(3)(*b*) of the Rome Statute.
127 Art 39(1) of the Rome Statute.
128 Art 52(1) of the Rome Statute.
129 Art 43(1) of the Rome Statute.

role is relatively uncontroversial in theory although its functions have turned out to be less so in practice. In pursuance of its administrative functions, the ASP established the IOM.

The ASP's *legislative functions* are both specific and general. The ASP was assigned specific legislative tasks that could not be completed during the Rome Conference.[130] The *operational role* of the ASP is its most controversial one. Notwithstanding the court's independence, the statute provides for some limited role for the ASP in the operation of the court.

48.4.4 The power and functions of the International Criminal Court

48.4.4.1 Introduction

The powers and functions of the court are set, first and foremost, by the jurisdictional regime set out in the Rome Statute. This regime sets the limits of the court's power to investigate, arrest, try and sentence persons for genocide, crimes against humanity, war crimes and aggression. The crime of aggression has its own jurisdictional regime because of the complex compromises negotiated at the Kampala Review Conference of 2010 and the Resolution on the Crime of Aggression adopted at the ASP of December 2017.[131]

Just because a crime falls within the jurisdiction of the court, it does not mean the Court can pursue it; rather the court's powers are further limited by the admissibility requirements of the statute.

48.4.4.2 The jurisdiction of the International Criminal Court

The term 'jurisdiction' is used with imprecision in the Rome Statute to cover different conceptions of the term without always distinguishing between them. The predominant focus here is on the court's jurisdiction in the sense of its power to exercise prescriptive criminal jurisdiction over individuals in respect of specified international crimes. The court's jurisdiction is, for the most part, delimited by the Rome Statute.

The issue of the court's jurisdiction was one of the most divisive ones considered during the Rome Conference, and remains contentious to this day. The sticking points on jurisdiction were under what conditions prosecutions would be initiated (and therefore jurisdiction exercised), and what the basis of such jurisdiction would be. With reference to this former issue, in one camp were like-minded countries that argued for a progressive prosecutorial regime whereby the prosecutor could undertake ***proprio motu*** **prosecutions.** In the other camp were UN Security Council veto-bearing states, especially China and the US, that sought, somewhat predictably, a court that would be subject to Security Council control.

130 In this sense, it was the successor to the conference, reflected within art 112(2)(*a*), which states that the ASP is to '[c]onsider and adopt, as appropriate, recommendations of the Preparatory Commission', thereby progressing and where possible concluding certain unfinished business (including defining aggression). Other day-to-day legislative functions are assigned to the ASP. In addition to these, the ASP has a general legislative authority that reflects the fact that the Rome Statute is a treaty and, as such, may be subject to amendment and modification by its states parties. In this regard, arts 121–125 set out the procedures to be followed for amending the statute and establish the ASP as the forum for the adoption of amendments.

131 The rather narrow basis for the ICC's jurisdiction over the crime of aggression can be found in para 2 of the Resolution on the Crime of Aggression, ICC-ASP/16/24, 14 December 2017: the ASP confirms that, 'in accordance with the Rome Statute, the amendments to the Statute regarding the crime of aggression adopted at the Kampala Review Conference enter into force for those states parties which have accepted the amendments one year after the deposit of their instruments of ratification or acceptance and that in the case of a state referral or *proprio motu* investigation the Court shall not exercise its jurisdiction regarding a crime of aggression when committed by a national or on the territory of a state Party that has not ratified or accepted these amendments'.

This matter overlapped with the second issue of controversy, namely the basis on which the court would exercise jurisdiction. Some states, notably Germany, pushed for automatic, universal jurisdiction, whereas others sought to limit the court's jurisdiction to those states (and their nationals) who sign up to the Rome Statute. The result of these negotiations was a primarily consent-based jurisdictional regime - including options of both permanent and ad hoc consent to jurisdiction by states - with a special referral power for the Security Council, but with some limitations on how jurisdiction can be triggered.

48.4.4.2.1 The four bases of jurisdiction

There are four possible bases on which the court can exercise jurisdiction over war crimes, genocide, crimes against humanity and the crime of aggression (jurisdiction over the latter being further qualified in terms of the Resolution on the Crime of Aggression adopted in December 2017):[132]

1. The territorial jurisdiction over states parties (jurisdiction *rationae loci*)
2. Personal jurisdiction over nationals of states parties (jurisdiction *rationae personae*)
3. Ad hoc consent-based jurisdiction in respect of non-states parties
4. Conferred jurisdiction by the Security Council

The first two bases mimic the domestic bases of jurisdiction by the same name, as adopted and applied by the ICC:[133]

- *Territorial jurisdiction*: Under article 12(2)(*a*), the court may exercise its jurisdiction if '[t]he State on the territory of which the conduct in question occurred or, if the crime was committed on board a vessel or aircraft, the state of registration of that vessel or aircraft' is a party to the Rome Statute. In effect, this gives the ICC territorial jurisdiction over the core crimes committed in states parties to the Rome Statute.
- *National jurisdiction*: Similarly, under article 12(2)(*b*), the court may exercise its jurisdiction if '[t]he State of which the person accused of the crime is a national', is a state party. In effect, this gives the ICC personal jurisdiction over all such nationals, which gives the ICC jurisdiction over all core crimes committed by *nationals* of states parties to the Rome Statute.

The other two jurisdictional bases - ad hoc consent-based and Security Council-conferred jurisdiction - are unique to international law and, in the case of jurisdiction conferred by the Security Council, unique to the Rome Statute:

- *Ad hoc referrals by non-states Parties*: Article 12 of the Rome Statute also makes provision for a non-state party to accept the exercise of the court's jurisdiction over a crime in the subject-matter jurisdiction of the court that either took place on the territory of that state or else was committed by one of its nationals.[134] In such circumstances, article 12(3) provides that when a non-state party accepts the court's jurisdiction, it must do so by lodging a declaration to this effect with the registrar. Further, under this provision, the

132 The crime of aggression functions under a unique jurisdictional regime. See also observations in Chapter 47.

133 Some argue that these are 'assigned' by states parties to the ICC when states ratify the Rome Statute, but conceiving them in this way is not unproblematic.

134 The origins of this provision lie in the discussions of an opt-in jurisdictional system during the drafting of the Rome Statute. Although the system ultimately was not adopted, it is still available in respect of states not party to the statute. Difficulties of retrospectivity emerge within the context of this provision because arguably the jurisdiction of the court over such a crime is applied retrospectively from the date on which the declaration was made.

accepting state must cooperate with the court 'without any delay or exception in accordance with Part 9' of the Rome Statute.

- *Security Council referrals*: Under article 13(*b*), the UN Security Council can refer 'a situation in which one or more [core] ... crimes appears to have been committed' to the court for investigation and possible prosecution.[135] This referral power potentially has far-reaching implications for many states, particularly for the court's detractors. In particular, through this provision, the court's jurisdictional reach may extend to the territory and nationals of every state in the world, whether they are a party to the Rome Statute or not.[136] This extraordinary and unsurprisingly controversial jurisdiction stems from the binding nature of Chapter VII Security Council resolutions on all UN member states.[137] Article 13(*b*) is especially important in relation to intra-state conflicts that involve non-states parties, such as Sudan, because without it, such states, even if directly or indirectly involved in the alleged atrocities committed, would be beyond the jurisdictional reach of the ICC.[138]

There are a number of different ways in which jurisdiction is triggered.[139] In the case of the court's permanent jurisdiction – territorial and nationality – the exercise of such jurisdiction may be triggered either by the referral of a situation by a state party under article 14, or a *proprio motu* investigation by the prosecutor under article 15.

The *state referral mechanism* allows states parties to refer 'a situation in which one or more crimes within the jurisdiction of the Court appear to have been committed' to the prosecutor so that he may 'investigate the situation for the purpose of determining whether one or more specific persons should be charged with the commission of such crimes'.[140] State referrals may be made where any of the core crimes (1) occur on the territory of the referring state(s), or (2) are committed by its nationals, to the ICC prosecutor for investigation and possible prosecution.[141] Furthermore, the ICC shall not exercise its jurisdiction regarding a crime of aggression when committed by a national or on the territory of a state party that has not ratified or accepted the amendments to the Rome Statute as contained in the Kampala Resolution on the Crime of Aggression.

Alternatively, the exercise of the court's permanent jurisdiction over states parties may be triggered by the prosecutor's *proprio motu* under article 15. This provision empowers the prosecutor to initiate an investigation – and trigger the exercise of jurisdiction – on his own

---

135 For the referral to be lawful, it must be exercised in accordance with Chapter VII, that is, the situation referred to the court must constitute a 'threat to peace and security' in the international community as understood with respect to article 39 of the UN Charter. When the Rome Statute was drafted, and even after it came into force, such Security Council referrals were considered to be unlikely, especially given the initial negative responses to the court by some P5 states, specifically the US and China. However, to date, the Security Council already has used this article on two occasions, once in respect of Darfur by way of Resolution 1593, and more recently in respect of Libya by way of Resolution 1970.

136 Sadat LN and Carden SR 'The new International Criminal Court: An uneasy revolution' (2000) 88(3) *Geo L J* 381; Bourgon S 'Jurisdiction ratione temporis' in Cassese A et al (eds) *The Rome Statute of the International Criminal Court: A Commentary Vol I* (2002) 556.

137 Art 25 of the UN Charter.

138 On the relationship between the ICC and the UN generally, see Sadat LN *The International Criminal Court and the Transformation of International Law: Justice for the New Millennium* (2002) 78–81.

139 From the outset, it is necessary to distinguish between the bases on which the Court may exercise jurisdiction, and the conditions that trigger the court's exercise of them. Although these two are conceptually distinct, in practice this distinction is blurred when the court exercises jurisdiction on the basis of an article 13(*b*) referral by the Security Council.

140 Art 14(1) of the Rome Statute.

141 During the drafting of the Rome Statute, it was not anticipated that this jurisdictional trigger would be used by states parties to refer themselves to the court. In practice, however, it has been used twice already and, until recently, was the single most common jurisdictional trigger.

accord 'on the basis of information on crimes within the jurisdiction of the Court'.[142] The exercise of this power – which as noted above was controversial in Rome in 1998 and remains so – is not unfettered. Rather, the prosecutor must first obtain authorisation from the Pre-Trial Chamber before he can proceed with an investigation. The Pre-Trial Chamber will only sanction such an investigation if it concludes that 'there is a reasonable basis to proceed with an investigation, and that the case appears to fall within the jurisdiction of the Court'.[143] As with state referrals, in the case of a *proprio motu* investigation, the ICC shall not exercise its jurisdiction regarding a crime of aggression when committed by a national or on the territory of a state party that has not ratified or accepted the relevant amendments to the Rome Statute, adopted at the Kampala Review Conference.

As far as *ad hoc* referrals by a non-state party are concerned, the prosecutor has taken the position that under such circumstances, jurisdiction must still be triggered in one of the above ways, that is, by a state party referral or by the prosecutor's exercise of his *proprio motu* power.

The situation is different regarding the exercise of extraordinary jurisdiction following a Security Council referral under article 13(*b*). This will generally, although not necessarily, involve the exercise of jurisdiction in circumstances where the court will not otherwise have jurisdiction, that is, over non-states parties. In such circumstances, no further jurisdictional trigger is required; article 13(*b*) both founds and triggers jurisdiction in such instances.

48.4.4.2.2 Subject matter jurisdiction (*ratione materiae*)

For the court to exercise jurisdiction over a crime, it must also fall within its subject matter jurisdiction. Article 5(1) sets out the four core crimes that come within the ICC's jurisdiction. Importantly, article 5(2) qualifies the court's jurisdiction in respect of the crime of aggression by stating that the court 'shall exercise jurisdiction over the crime of aggression once a provision is adopted in accordance with articles 121 and 123 defining the crime and setting out the conditions under which the Court shall exercise jurisdiction with respect to this crime', with the added proviso that '[s]uch a provision shall be consistent with the relevant provisions of the Charter of the United Nations'. Article 8*bis* (definition of aggression) and articles 15*bis* and 15*ter* (jurisdictional aspects) were adopted at the First Review Conference of the Rome Statute in Kampala, Uganda.[144] The ICC's jurisdiction over the crime of aggression is activated as of 17 July 2018.[145]

48.4.4.2.3 Temporal jurisdiction (*ratione temporis*)

Finally, the court's jurisdiction is limited temporally in two respects. Firstly, under article 11(1), the court itself has jurisdiction only with respect to crimes committed after 1 July 2002 (or, in the case of the crime of aggression, 17 July 2018). This is a general temporal limitation

142 Art 15(1). Art 15(2) adds:

> **The Prosecutor shall analyse the seriousness of the information received. For this purpose, he or she may seek additional information from States, organs of the United Nations, intergovernmental or non-governmental organizations, or other reliable sources that he or she deems appropriate, and may receive written or oral testimony at the seat of the Court.**

143 Arts 15(3) and 15(4) of the Rome Statute. The Prosecutor exercised this power for the first time in respect of the post-electoral violence that occurred in Kenya (a state Party) in 2007, after receiving the authorisation of the Pre-Trial Chamber in March 2009. ICC Decision Pursuant to Article 15 of the Rome Statute on the Authorization of an Investigation into the Situation in the Republic of Kenya ICC-01/09-19 Pre-Trial Chamber II 31 March 2010 (*Kenya* pre-trial II).

144 See Chapter 47 above.

145 Para 1, Resolution on the Activation of the jurisdiction of the ICC over the crime of aggression, ICC-ASP/16/24, 14 December 2017.

on the court's jurisdiction, based on the *nullum crimen, nulla poena sine lege* principle discussed above.

Secondly, article 11(2) limits its temporal jurisdiction in respect of those states that ratified the statute after 1 July 2002. It states that 'the Court may exercise its jurisdiction only with respect to crimes committed after the entry into force of this Statute for that State'. An exception is created in circumstances where the state concerned has made a declaration to the registrar under article 12(3), accepting the court's jurisdiction, subject to the potential difficulty of retrospectivity.

48.4.4.3 The admissibility requirements of the Rome Statute

Jurisdiction is delimited by admissibility. Just because the court has jurisdiction over a situation on one of the bases discussed above in respect of a crime that satisfies the subject matter jurisdiction of the court, it does not necessarily mean the court will find a case admissible. The issue of admissibility is conceptually and procedurally different from that of jurisdiction. Despite this, and due to the manner in which the Rome Statute is set out, they are often confused and conflated.

Procedurally, admissibility differs from jurisdiction in that there are two different stages at which it may be challenged under the Rome Statute: at the preliminary stage under article 18 in respect of a situation, and thereafter under article 19 in respect of a specific case. Notably, these procedures also differ in substance and not only when they are brought.

Preliminary challenges to admissibility under article 18 may be brought by any state that 'would normally exercise jurisdiction over the crimes concerned'. In this regard, once the prosecutor has determined that there is a reasonable basis to initiate an investigation, either after a state referral or based on his *proprio motu* power, article 18 requires him to notify all states parties and any other states with jurisdiction over a particular case before beginning an investigation.[146] Such notification is important due to the principle of complementarity. Such states can, in effect, render the situation inadmissible before the ICC by informing the prosecutor, within one month of receipt of the notification, 'that it is investigating or has investigated its nationals or others within its jurisdiction with respect to criminal acts which may constitute crimes referred to in article 5 and which relate to the information provided in the notification to States'.[147] This deferral is subject to periodic review in case there is 'a significant change of circumstances based on the state's unwillingness or inability genuinely to carry out the investigation'.[148] Article 18 excludes explicitly any investigations by the prosecutor pursuant to Security Council referrals under this provision, which arguably extends also to non-states parties referrals, although the text here is ambiguous.

Admissibility can also be raised under article 19 in respect of specific cases, even if it was raised unsuccessfully under article 18, where there are 'additional significant facts or [a] significant change of circumstances'.[149] The procedure for challenging admissibility under article 19 is substantially the same as for challenging jurisdiction (discussed above), save that the court need not consider it, that is, it is permissive, not mandatory. As with challenges to jurisdiction, under article 19 admissibility may be challenged by a person against whom

146 Art 18(1) of the Rome Statute.

147 Art 18(2). The article goes on to state: 'At the request of that State, the Prosecutor shall defer to the State's investigation of those persons unless the Pre-Trial Chamber, on the application of the Prosecutor, decides to authorize the investigation'.

148 See arts 18(3)–(6) and Rules 52–57.

149 Art 18(7) of the Rome Statute.

a warrant of arrest or summons to appear has been issued or against whom charges have been confirmed, or by any state(s) ordinarily with jurisdiction over the case 'on the ground that it is investigating or prosecuting the case or has investigated or prosecuted [it]'.[150]

Similarly, admissibility challenges normally may be brought only once, and must be before or at the commencement of the trial phase. Only in exceptional circumstances will they be allowed after the commencement of a trial, or subsequently with the leave of the court, but only if 'based ... on article 17, paragraph 1 (*c*)'.[151]

Additionally, the prosecutor may 'seek a ruling' on the question of admissibility.[152] Finally, article 19(10) provides that '[i]f the Court has decided that a case is inadmissible under article 17, the Prosecutor may submit a request for a review of the decision when he or she is fully satisfied that new facts have arisen which negate the basis on which the case had previously been found inadmissible under article 17'. To this extent, the issue of admissibility may be the subject of ongoing review and assessment.

There are three grounds on which an admissibility challenge can be raised:

1. A challenge may be raised based on the principle of complementarity.[153] If a case already being investigated or prosecuted by a state is brought before the ICC under article 17, it 'shall determine that [such] a case is inadmissible',[154] notwithstanding the fact that the court may otherwise have jurisdiction in respect of the case. There are, however, two exceptions to this general rule. The court will not make a finding of inadmissibility if the state concerned is either unwilling or unable to carry out genuinely the investigation or prosecution. The principle applies equally in respect of any decision reached by a state not to proceed with a prosecution after investigating the matter. Here, the court still may declare such a case to be inadmissible if it believes that such a decision resulted from the state's unwillingness or inability genuinely to prosecute the case.[155]
2. Under article 17(1)(*d*), the court is required to rule that a case is inadmissible where it 'is *not of sufficient gravity* to justify further action by the Court'. In its March 2010 decision authorising the prosecutor's Kenya investigation, the Pre-Trial Chamber considered gravity 'against the backdrop of the likely set of cases or "potential case(s)" that would arise from investigating the situation'[156] because at that stage there were no 'concrete' cases presented by the prosecutor. According to the chamber, this consideration of gravity at this stage involves an examination of '(i) whether the persons or groups of persons that are likely to be the object of an investigation include those who may bear the greatest responsibility for the alleged crimes committed; and (ii) the gravity of the crimes allegedly committed within the incidents, which are likely to be the object of an investigation'.[157]
3. The third and final ground on which admissibility may be challenged is on the grounds of *non bis in idem* (in Anglo-American systems known as double jeopardy). In this regard, article 17(1)(*c*) states that the court shall determine a case to be inadmissible if '[t]he

150 Arts 19(2)(*b*) and (*c*) of the Rome Statute.

151 Art 19(4) of the Rome Statute.

152 Art 19(3) of the Rome Statute.

153 For a comprehensive analysis of this principle, see Kleffner JK *Complementarity in the Rome Statute and National Criminal Jurisdictions* (2008).

154 Art 17(1) of the Rome Statute.

155 Art 17(1)(*b*) of the Rome Statute.

156 *Kenya* pre-trial II at 58.

157 *Kenya* pre-trial II at 188. The Pre-Trial Chamber went on to find that, on the evidence presented, the gravity threshold had been met.

person concerned has already been tried for conduct which is the subject of the complaint, and a trial by the Court is not permitted under [article 20(3)]'. This ground differs from the others as it can only be raised in respect of a case, not a situation generally.

48.4.5 State cooperation with the International Criminal Court[158]

48.4.5.1 Introduction

The second broad purpose of the Rome Statute was to set out the regime for state cooperation with the court. In this regard, states that have ratified the Rome Statute are obliged to cooperate with the court in the arrest and surrender of suspects, investigation of crimes and other forms, as required by Part 9 of the statute.[159]

The issue of state cooperation was a controversial one when the court's statute was drafted in Rome in 1998. The final text strikes a delicate balance that both recognises the constraints of the court as a treaty-based mechanism, unlike the ICTY and ICTR,[160] and also creates a progressive cooperation regime that enables the court to operate effectively. The resultant cooperation regime, contained in Part 9 of the Rome Statute, is a hybrid between a horizontal model and a vertical model of cooperation. The horizontal model involves the relatively weaker form of inter-state cooperation while the vertical model is used to describe the more robust system of cooperation between the ad hoc tribunals and states – the 'supra-state model'.[161] As a result, aside from the general obligation created by article 86 of the statute for states to 'cooperate fully with the Court', the question of whether or not the court can *compel* cooperation cannot be answered generally, but rather must be determined with reference to the specific form of cooperation involved and its corresponding provision.

48.4.5.2 Cooperation in arrest and surrender

The Rome Statute empowers the Pre-Trial Chamber, on the application of the prosecutor, to issue a warrant of arrest for a person if there are reasonable grounds to believe that he has committed a crime within the jurisdiction of the court and his arrest appears necessary in the circumstances.[162] Such arrest will necessarily have to be effected by states.[163] However, the issuance of an arrest warrant alone appears to be insufficient to place an obligation on

---

158 For cooperation between South Africa and the ICC, see, in general, 'International and transnational criminal procedure' in Du Toit et al *Commentary on the Criminal Procedure Act* (revision service 59, 2017) Supplementary Volume, Appendix B, Part 4.

159 Although only states parties are obliged to cooperate under the Rome Statute (the situation might be different in respect of Security Council referrals under article 13(*b*)), the cooperation regime does not exclude voluntary cooperation from non-states parties.

160 In *Tadić*, the ICTY discussed the nature of the Security Council's Chapter VII power and stated that:

> **[t]hese powers are coercive vis-à-vis the culprit State or entity. But they are also mandatory vis-à-vis the other Member States, who are under an obligation to cooperate with the Organization (Article 2, paragraph 5, Articles 25, 48) and with one another (Articles 49), in the implementation of the action or measures decided by the Security Council.**

ICTY *Prosecutor v Dusko Tadić* (decision on the defence motion for interlocutory appeal on jurisdiction) IT-94-1 October 1995 at 31.

161 This classification was noted by the ICTY Appeals Chamber in ICTY *Prosecutor v Tihomir Blaskic* (appeals judgment) IT-95-14-A July 2004 (*Blaskic* appeal) and further developed by Cassese. It has been generally accepted by other scholars since. See Cassese 'The Statute of the International Criminal Court' at 164–165. See further, Swart B 'General problems' in Cassese A et al (eds) *The Rome Statute of the International Criminal Court: A Commentary* Vol II (2002) 1589 at 1590 and 1594–1598.

162 See art 58 of the Rome Statute.

163 See also *Southern Africa Litigation Centre v Minister of Justice and Constitutional Development and Others* (27740/2015) [2015] ZAGPPHC 402; 2016 (1) SACR 161 (GP); 2015 (5) SA 1 (GP); [2015] 3 All SA 505 (GP); 2015 (9) BCLR 1108 (GP) (24 June 2015) and the discussion of South Africa and international criminal law in section 46.3.

states in respect of arrest and surrender. Rather, on a literal interpretation, the statute appears to require a further request for cooperation to be made by the court under articles 89 and 91 in addition to the warrant.[164] Nevertheless, the court appears to have glossed over this anomaly in practice by treating it as a mere formality and ordering the registrar to communicate such requests to all states parties, as well as certain other states, without further consideration. To this end, when it issued both arrest warrants for President Al-Bashir of Sudan, the Pre-Trial Chamber directed the registrar to transmit article 89 requests to 'competent Sudanese authorities ..., to all States Parties to the Statute and all the United Nations Security Council members that are not States Parties to the Statute'.[165] The registrar promptly did so on both occasions.[166] While this approach eliminates the clumsy two-stage process in the statute in substance, its legality is not unassailable.[167]

Aside from the general obligation to 'cooperate fully' with the court contained in article 86, article 59(1) enjoins '[a] State Party which has received a request for provisional arrest or for arrest and surrender [to] ... immediately take steps to arrest the person in question in accordance with its laws and the provisions of Part 9.' Further, article 89(1) states, in relevant part, that 'States Parties shall, in accordance with the provisions of this Part and the procedure under their national law, comply with requests for arrest and surrender'.[168] Further, in terms of rule 184 of the court's Rules of Procedure and Evidence, states parties are under a positive obligation to 'immediately inform the Registrar when the person sought by the Court is available for surrender'.

Crucially, the obligation to cooperate in respect of arrest and surrender is not subject to the same exceptions as other forms of cooperation.[169] The provisions of the statute

---

164 Art 91(2) sets out modalities for 'a request for the arrest and surrender of a person for whom a warrant of arrest has been issued by the Pre-Trial Chamber under Article 58 ...' Moreover, under art 58(5): 'On the basis of the warrant of arrest, the Court may request the provisional arrest or the arrest and surrender of the person under Part 9'.

165 See ICC *Prosecutor v Omar Hassan Ahmad Al Bashir ('Omar Al Bashir')* Request for Arrest and Surrender for Omar Hassan Ahmad Al Bashir to the Republic of Indonesia ICC-02/05-01/09-94 at 28/30.

166 See Supplementary request to all states parties to the rome statute for the arrest and surrender of Omar Hassan Ahmad al Bashir ICC-02/05-01/0 (21 July 2010); ICC *The Prosecutor v Omar Hassan Ahmad Al Bashir* ('Omar Al Bashir'), Registrar, Request to the Republic of Sudan for the arrest and surrender of Omar Al Bashir No. ICC-02/05-01/09-5, 5 March 2009; Request to all states parties to the Rome Statute for the arrest and surrender of Omar Al Bashir, No. ICC-02/05-01/09-7, 6 March 2009; Request to all United Nations Security Council members that are not states parties to the Rome Statute for the arrest and surrender of Omar Al Bashir, No. ICC-02/05-01/09-8, 6 March 2009. See also No. ICC-02/05-01/09-96; No. ICC-02/05-01/09-97; No. ICC-02/05-01/09-98; No. ICC-02/05-01/09-99; No. ICC-02/05-01/09-100; No. ICC-02/05-01/09-101, 21 July 2010.

167 Although rule 176(2) of the court's Rules of Procedure and Evidence authorises the registrar to 'transmit the requests for cooperation made by the Chambers and ... receive the responses, information and documents from requested States', it is not at all clear that such requests can be made en masse as they were in the case of Al-Bashir. On the contrary, the wording on art 89 – 'The Court may transmit a request for the arrest and surrender of a person ... to any State on the territory of which that person may be found' – suggests that such request should be made in respect of specific states where the presence of an accused is proved or anticipated. Notably, Pre-Trial Chamber I in its decision of 27 August 2010 only mentioned article 87 in its discussion of Kenya's obligation to cooperate in respect of Al-Bashir, and not articles 89 or 91. That decision noted: 'The Republic of Kenya has a clear obligation to cooperate with the Court in relation to the enforcement of such warrants of arrest, which stems both from the United Nations Security Council Resolution 1593(2005) ..., and from Article 87 of the Statute of the Court, to which the Republic of Kenya is a State Party' at 3/4.

168 The full text of this article reads:

> **The Court may transmit a request for the arrest and surrender of a person, together with the material supporting the request outlined in article 91, to any State on the territory of which that person may be found and shall request the cooperation of that State in the arrest and surrender of such a person. States Parties shall, in accordance with the provisions of this Part and the procedure under their national law, comply with requests for arrest and surrender.**

169 These include art 93(3) (if execution of a cooperation measure clashes with a 'fundamental legal principle of general application'), art 72 read with art 93(4) (national security exception in respect of documents) and 'with respect to a request by the Court for a type of assistance which is not specified under article 93(1)(*a*)–(*k*), the obligation is limited to assistance "which is not prohibited by the law of the requested State" (art 93(1)(l))'.

concerning surrender of persons differ from those governing other forms of cooperation that contain grounds for the denial of a request. The fact that such exceptions were not made applicable to the surrender of persons indicates the drafters' approach to this important aspect of the court's functioning.[170] As far as action available to the court for non-compliance, the statute provides that:

> **[w]here a State Party fails to comply with a request to cooperate by the Court contrary to the provisions of this Statute, thereby preventing the Court from exercising its functions and powers under this Statute, the Court may make a finding to that effect and refer the matter to the Assembly of States Parties or, where the Security Council referred the matter to the Court, to the Security Council.**[171]

To facilitate the cooperation of states, the Rome Statute requires states parties to 'ensure that there are procedures available under their national law for all of the forms of cooperation which are specified under [the Rome Statute]'.[172] To this end, South Africa's ICC Act contains a number of provisions that relate to cooperation with the ICC. As far as the execution of ICC arrest warrants is concerned, section 8 of the ICC Act states that when South Africa receives a request from the ICC for the arrest and surrender of a person for whom the ICC has issued a warrant of arrest, it must refer the request to the Director-General of Justice and Constitutional Development together with the necessary documentation to satisfy a local court that there are sufficient grounds for the surrender of the person to the ICC in The Hague.[173] The director-general must then forward the request (along with the necessary documentation) to a magistrate who must endorse the ICC's warrant of arrest for execution in any part of the Republic.[174]

Following the arrest of the suspect, a magistrate must make a committal order to effect his surrender to the ICC. Before doing so, the magistrate must be satisfied that (1) the person before the court is the individual named in the warrant,[175] (2) the person has been arrested in accordance with the procedures set down by domestic law,[176] and (3) the person's rights, as contemplated in the Bill of Rights, have been respected.[177]

The surrender of an individual to the ICC should not be regarded as the same as extradition to a foreign state. There are important differences between the two processes. For instance, the ICC Act does not mention double criminality, 'nor does it refer to the

170 There is, of course, the well-known general exception to the state cooperation regime contained in Part 9, the exact nature of which has become perhaps the most controversial aspect of the Rome Statute: this is article 98, which deals with immunities (including head of state immunity). South Africa was the first state party to the Rome Statute to seek from the ICC a final legal determination on the extent of its obligations to execute a request for the arrest and surrender of a sitting head of state, namely President Al-Bashir of Sudan. That legal determination was done by Pre-Trial Chamber II, ICC Decision under article 87(7) of the Rome Statute on the non-compliance by South Africa with the request by the court for the arrest and surrender of Omar Al-Bashir, ICC-02/05-01/09, 6 July 2017. Although South Africa was found to be in violation of its obligations under the Rome Statute, the ICC opted not to impose any formal sanctions.

171 Art 87(7) of the Rome Statute.

172 Art 88 of the Rome Statute.

173 S 8(1) of the ICC Act.

174 S 8(2) of the ICC Act. S 9 details the second scenario (an arrest in terms of a warrant issued by the National Director of Prosecutions). In this situation, the Director-General of Justice and Constitutional Development is mandated to receive a request from the ICC for the provisional arrest of a person who is suspected or accused of having committed a core crime, or who has been convicted by the ICC. The director-general is then obliged under the ICC Act to immediately forward the request immediately to the National Director of Public Prosecutions, who must then apply for the warrant before a magistrate. See s 9(1) of the ICC Act.

175 S 10(1)(*a*) of the ICC Act.

176 S 10(1)(*b*) of the ICC Act.

177 S 10(1)(*c*) of the ICC Act.

requirement (in the context of extradition) that a *prima facie* case be shown against the individual sought'.[178]

South Africa's failure in 2015 to arrest President Omar Al-Bashir of Sudan, who is indicted by the ICC for war crimes, crimes against humanity and genocide, prompted hearings and court decisions at the national and international levels. At the national level the Supreme Court of Appeal (SCA) considered South Africa's constitutional, statutory and international treaty obligations. In *Minister of Justice and Constitutional Development v Southern Africa Litigation Centre*[179] the SCA stated as follows:

> **South Africa is bound by its obligations under the Rome Statute. It is obliged to cooperate with the ICC and to arrest and surrender to the court persons in respect of whom the ICC has issued an arrest warrant and a request for assistance. To this end [South Africa] passed the Implementation Act. The relationship between that Act and the head-of-state immunity conferred by customary international law and [the Diplomatic Immunities and Privileges Act] lies at the heart of this case. But the starting point is not immediately with these, but with the Constitution.**[180]

While the SCA conceded that there is at present under customary international law no 'international crimes exception' to the immunity of visiting heads of state, the SCA noted that the Rome Statute of the ICC was fully incorporated into South African law via section 231 of the Constitution and the Implementation of the Rome Statute of the ICC Act, 2002. As such, the issue of immunity of visiting heads of state cannot be considered in light of customary international law only. Indeed, the Constitution and statutory law demand an evaluation of the South African authorities' compliance with the full spectrum of *domestic law*, first and foremost. While customary international law and the Diplomatic Immunities and Privileges Act govern the question of head-of-state immunity, the Implementation Act 'excludes such immunity in relation to international crimes and the obligations of South Africa to the ICC'.[181] According to the SCA, the South African authorities violated domestic law, notably the Implementation Act, as well as the Constitution and South Africa's treaty obligations under the Rome Statute, when they failed to arrest President Al-Bashir during his visit to South Africa in 2015 and surrender him to the ICC. With its adoption of the Implementation Act, South Africa has made a deliberate and progressive choice to do away with immunity as a bar to the prosecution of the core international crimes or to cooperate with the ICC by way of the arrest and surrender of persons charged with such crimes before the ICC.[182]

Pre-Trial Chamber II of the ICC, in the matter of South Africa's failure to arrest and surrender Al-Bashir (*ICC South Africa Decision*),[183] the majority of the judges held that article 98(1) of the Rome Statute, which provides for adherence to head-of-state immunity of a non-state party such as Sudan, did not apply in the matter of the ICC's request for South Africa to arrest Al-Bashir of Sudan and to surrender him to the ICC. The reason for that

178 Du Toit et al *Commentary on the Criminal Procedure Act* (revision service 59, 2017) at App B62. For a more detailed discussion, see Du Plessis M 'South Africa's implementation of the ICC Statute: An African example' (2007) 5(2) *JICJ* 460–479, particularly at 468.

179 *Minister of Justice and Constitutional Development and others v Southern Africa Litigation Centre and others* 2016 (3) SA 317 (SCA).

180 *Minister of Justice and Constitutional Development v Southern Africa Litigation Centre* at 61.

181 *Minister of Justice and Constitutional Development v Southern Africa Litigation Centre* at 102.

182 *Minister of Justice and Constitutional Development v Southern Africa Litigation Centre* at 103.

183 Decision under art 87(7) of the Rome Statute on the non-compliance by South Africa with the request by the court for the arrest and surrender of Omar Al-Bashir, ICC-02/05-01/09-302, Pre-Trial Chamber II, 6 July 2017, available at https://www.icc-cpi.int/CourtRecords/CR2017_04402.PDF.

finding is that Sudan, a member of the UN, had rights and duties under Security Council Resolution 1593 which referred the situation in Sudan to the ICC in the first place. As such, Sudan should be treated as a state party to the Rome Statute and head-of-state immunity should be no bar to cooperation with the ICC. It is worth noting that Pre-Trial Chamber II of the ICC came to the same conclusion regarding the Kingdom of Jordan's failure to arrest and surrender Al-Bashir to the ICC.[184]

The approach of the SCA in the Al-Bashir matter is not an outlier on the African continent. In *Attorney General v The Kenya Section of International Commission of Jurists*[185] the Court of Appeal in Nairobi, Kenya, had to decide whether the government of Kenya was obliged to arrest President Al-Bashir of Sudan and surrender him to the ICC. The court noted that, despite the existence of ICC warrants for the arrest of Al-Bashir, Kenya, a state party to the Rome Statute who has implemented this treaty via domestic law, had failed to arrest Al-Bashir, on several occasions, while he was visiting Kenya. With reference to the decision of South Africa's Supreme Court of Appeal as well as the decision by ICC Pre-Trial Chamber II in the *South Africa Decision*, the Kenya Court of Appeal stated that President Al-Bashir was not protected by head-of-state immunity with regards to the execution of the relevant ICC arrest warrants, and that the government of Kenya had a legal duty to execute the warrants and to surrender Al-Bashir to the ICC.[186]

48.4.5.3 Other forms of cooperation under the Rome Statute

Article 93 of the Rome Statute requires states parties to provide 'other forms of cooperation' to the court in relation to its investigations or prosecutions of crimes within its jurisdiction. This includes:

- identifying and determining the whereabouts of persons or the location of items
- taking evidence, including testimony under oath, and producing evidence, including expert opinions and reports necessary to the court
- questioning any person being investigated or prosecuted
- serving documents, including judicial documents
- facilitating the voluntary appearance of persons as witnesses or experts before the court
- examining places or sites, including the exhumation and examination of grave sites
- executing searches and seizures
- protecting victims and witnesses, and preserving evidence
- identification, tracing and freezing or seizure of proceeds, property and assets, and instrumentalities of crimes for the purpose of eventual forfeiture.

Pursuant to article 88, Part 2 of South Africa's ICC Act sets out a variety of circumstances in which the 'relevant competent authorities in the Republic' must 'cooperate with, and render assistance to, the Court in relation to investigations and prosecutions'.[187] In addition, section 6 of the ICC Act provides the president with the power to declare any place in the

---

184 Decision under art 87(7) of the Rome Statute on the non-compliance by Jordan with the request by the court for the arrest and surrender of Omar Al-Bashir, ICC-02/05-01/09, Pre-Trial Chamber II, 11 December 2017, available at https://www.icc-cpi.int/CourtRecords/CR2017_07156.PDF. Jordan took the decision on appeal. See Hashemite Kingdom of Jordan's appeal against the Decision under article 87(7) of the Rome Statute on the non-compliance by Jordan with the request by the court for the arrest and surrender of Omar Al-Bashir, 12 March 2018 (ICC-02/05-01/09-326). At the time of writing, the outcome of the appeal was not yet known.

185 *Attorney General and others v The Kenya Section of International Commission of Jurists*, case numbers 105 of 2012 and 274 of 2011 consolidated, 16 February 2018.

186 *Attorney General (Kenya)* supra at 54 and 58.

187 See s 14 of the ICC Act.

Republic to be the seat of the ICC at the request of the ICC and by proclamation in the *Government Gazette*.[188] Finally, the statute provides for state cooperation in the enforcement of sentences.[189]

THIS CHAPTER IN ESSENCE

1. The enforcement of international criminal law essentially rests on two pillars: prosecution of crimes under international law before (1) domestic courts, and (2) international courts and tribunals.
2. The enforcement system of international criminal law is akin to a web with intricate and complex legal (and political) threads that are interconnected with one aim in mind, namely to end impunity for the worst crimes under international law.

188 S 6 of the ICC Act. Should such a declaration be made, the ICC Act sets out a variety of privileges and immunities for the court. First, the court is accorded such rights and privileges of a South African court of law in the Republic as may be necessary to enable it to perform its functions. See s 7 of the ICC Act.

189 Art 103(1)(*a*) of the Rome Statute states that 'a sentence of imprisonment shall be served in a State designated by the Court from a list of States which have indicated to the Court their willingness to accept sentenced persons'. See further, arts 103–106. See also Kress C and Sluiter G 'Imprisonment' in Cassese A, Gaeta P and Jones JRWD (eds) *The Rome Statute of the International Criminal Court: A Commentary* Vol II (2002) 1757–1821.

Chapter 49

Other crimes of international concern

CHAPTER OBJECTIVES

The objectives of this chapter are to:
- introduce the concept of crimes of international concern (other than the core crimes)
- discuss the crime of torture in terms of the Prevention and Combating of Torture of Persons Act 13 of 2013
- discuss the crime of terrorism in terms of the Protection of Constitutional Democracy against Terrorist and Related Activities Act 33 of 2004
- discuss the crime of human trafficking (and related crimes) in terms of the Prevention and Combating of Trafficking in Persons Act 7 of 2013.

49.1 Introduction

Chapter 47 dealt with the most important crimes under international law, also known as the core crimes. The prosecution of these crimes at the international and the national levels is dealt with in Chapter 48. There are crimes of international concern that are not yet classified as core crimes. We noted in Chapter 46 that international crimes (other than the core crimes) encompass a broader, looser category of crimes that may be considered international for one reason or another. For example, the effects of these crimes stretch across borders, or they take place beyond the jurisdiction of a single state, or they affect interests and values protected by international or regional[1] legal instruments.

In this chapter, the focus falls on some of these important crimes of international concern. This is not an exhaustive discussion of all crimes of international concern. The choice falls on three important treaty-based crimes that are also criminalised under South African law, thus giving effect to South Africa's international obligations.

The crimes discussed in the present chapter do not yet fall under the jurisdiction of the International Criminal Court (ICC) or any other international criminal tribunal. Torture as a crime against humanity falls under the jurisdiction of the ICC, but not torture as a discrete crime as illustrated below. Neither terrorism nor human trafficking falls under the jurisdiction of the ICC. In the absence of the ICC or other international or regional tribunals having jurisdiction over these crimes of international concern, the task falls on states to provide for substantive and enforcement jurisdiction under domestic law, and to provide for the necessary international cooperation and mutual legal assistance mechanisms in order to prevent and punish these crimes.

49.2 Torture

49.2.1 Historical, constitutional and international context

In general terms, torture can be defined as 'bodily or mental suffering inflicted for a purpose'.[2] Torture is, unfortunately, a practice as old as humanity itself.[3] It has been recorded in ancient civilizations, often as a form of punishment or as a method of obtaining information or evidence. The range of gruesome methods always had one thing in common: severe physical and/or mental suffering inflicted on a victim.[4] Torture practices are still prevalent today.[5]

Section 12(1)(*d*) of the Constitution of the Republic of South Africa, 1996, provides that everyone has the right to freedom and security of the person, which includes the *right not*

1 For instance, the Protocol on Amendments to the Protocol on the Statute of the African Court of Justice and Human Rights, adopted at the 25th Ordinary Session of the AU's Assembly of Heads of State and Governments, Malabo, Equatorial Guinea, 27 June 2014 (Malabo Protocol), provides for the creation of a criminal chamber in the African Court of Justice. This regional criminal court will have jurisdiction over the core crimes (genocide, crimes against humanity, war crimes and aggression), plus other crimes of international and regional concern, namely: the crime of unconstitutional change of government; piracy; terrorism; mercenarism; corruption; money laundering; trafficking in persons; trafficking in drugs; trafficking in hazardous wastes; and illicit exploitation of natural resources. For more detail and analysis, see Werle, G and Vormbaum, M (eds) *The African Criminal Court – A Commentary on the Malabo Protocol* (2017).

2 Derby DH 'Torture' in Bassiouni MC *International Criminal Law Vol I* 2 ed (1999) 706.

3 For various essays on the phenomenon of torture and strategies to end the practice, see Dunér B (ed) *An End to Torture: Strategies for its Eradication* (1998).

4 For a comprehensive historical account, see Scott, GR *The History of Torture Throughout the Ages* (1954).

5 For country reports, see the annual reporting by NGO's such as Amnesty International, available at https://www.amnesty.org/en/countries/.

to be tortured in any way. Section 12(1)(*e*) furthermore provides that individuals have the *right not to be treated or punished in a cruel, inhuman or degrading way*. South Africa is also a state party[6] to the United Nations (UN) Convention against Torture and Other Cruel, Inhuman or Degrading Treatment or Punishment 1984 (CAT).[7] The human rights expressed in section 12(1) of the Constitution do not provide a legal basis to *prosecute* anyone for the crime of torture. South Africa has, however, an obligation in terms of the CAT to criminalise torture and related crimes. To give effect to the above constitutional and international norms and obligations, Parliament adopted the Prevention and Combating of Torture of Persons Act 13 of 2013 (the Torture Act), which entered into force on 29 July 2013.[8]

It is important to note that torture as a crime can also constitute *a crime under international law* as incorporated and provided for in the Implementation of the Rome Statute of the International Criminal Court Act 27 of 2002 (the ICC Act), which we discussed in Chapter 47 of this book. If torture is committed in a certain *context*, for instance during an *armed conflict* or as part of *widespread or systematic human rights violations*, it could be a crime under international law, distinct from the crime of torture as defined in the CAT.[9]

The aim of the Torture Act is to provide, inter alia, for those instances of torture that would not necessarily be covered by the ICC Act. In other words, the Torture Act provides for torture not occurring during an armed conflict or in the context of crimes against humanity, but as a single, perhaps isolated, act by or on behalf of a public official.[10] The Act also provides for extraterritorial jurisdiction over the crime of torture. This means that a South African court will have jurisdiction over the crime regardless of the fact that it was committed outside the territory of the Republic.[11]

49.2.2 The crime of torture under the Prevention and Combating of Torture of Persons Act 13 of 2013

Section 3 of the Torture Act provides for the definition[12] of torture:

> **For the purposes of this Act, 'torture' means any act by which severe pain or suffering, whether physical or mental, is intentionally inflicted on a person—**
>
> **(*a*) for such purposes as to—**
>
> **(i) obtain information or a confession from him or her or any other person;**
>
> **(ii) punish him or her for an act he or she or any other person has committed, is suspected of having committed or is planning to commit; or**
>
> **(iii) intimidate or coerce him or her or any other person to do, or to refrain from doing, anything; or**

---

6 South Africa ratified the Convention on 10 December 1998.

7 United Nations: Draft Convention against Torture and Other Cruel, Inhuman or Degrading Treatment or Punishment *International Legal Materials* (1984) 23(5) at 1027 with changes in United Nations Convention Against Torture is opened for signature *International Legal Materials* (1985) 24(2) at 535. For background, see Lippman, M 'The development and drafting of the United Nations Convention Against Torture and Other Cruel, Inhuman or Degrading Treatment or Punishment' (1994) 17(2) *Boston College International & Comparative Law Review* 275.

8 *Government Gazette* 36716, GN 545, 29 July 2013.

9 *National Commissioner of The South African Police Service v Southern African Human Rights Litigation Centre and Another* (CCT 02/14) [2014] ZACC 30; 2015 (1) SA 315 (CC); 2015 (1) SACR 255 (CC); 2014 (12) BCLR 1428 (CC) (30 October 2014). See also Chapter 48.

10 For more on torture as a discrete crime under international law, see Cassese A *International Criminal Law* (2003) 117–119.

11 See s 6 of the Torture Act.

12 This definition is essentially the same as the definition of torture in the CAT.

> **(*b*) for any reason based on discrimination of any kind,**
> **when such pain or suffering is inflicted by or at the instigation of, or with the consent or acquiescence of a public official or other person acting in an official capacity, but does not include pain or suffering arising only from, inherent in or incidental to lawful sanctions.**

Section 4 of the Torture Act provides for individual criminal liability for the crime of torture:

> **(1) Any person who—**
> **(*a*) commits torture;**
> **(*b*) attempts to commit torture; or**
> **(*c*) incites, instigates, commands or procures any person to commit torture,**
> **is guilty of the offence of torture and is on conviction liable to imprisonment, including imprisonment for life.**
> **(2) Any person who participates in torture, or who conspires with a public official to aid or procure the commission of or to commit torture, is guilty of the offence of torture and is on conviction liable to imprisonment, including imprisonment for life.**
> **(3) Despite any other law to the contrary, including customary international law, the fact that an accused person—**
> **(*a*) is or was a head of state or government, a member of a government or parliament, an elected representative or a government official; or**
> **(*b*) was under a legal obligation to obey a manifestly unlawful order of a government or superior,**
> **is neither a defence to a charge of committing an offence referred to in this section, nor a ground for any possible reduction of sentence, once that person has been convicted of such offence.**
> **(4) No exceptional circumstances whatsoever, including but not limited to, a state of war, threat of war, internal political instability, national security or any state of emergency may be invoked as a justification for torture.**
> **(5) No one shall be punished for disobeying an order to commit torture.**

49.2.3 Some general comments

The Torture Act adds to an arsenal of international and domestic legal instruments aimed at preventing and punishing the practice of torture. This crime is more than a serious assault on the human body and mind; it offends against the sense of moral decency of the whole of humankind.[13]

Where a *private individual* kidnaps and seriously assaults another person over a long period of time for his own perverse motives, this does not constitute the crime of torture. The involvement of a *public official*, in some way or another, is required for the crime of torture. The same acts of assault, committed by a private individual for his own private motives, may constitute the crime of assault, assault with intent to do grievous bodily harm, attempted murder, or kidnapping and assault with intent to do grievous bodily harm, depending, of course, on the particular facts.

13 Court of Appeals for the Second Circuit Decision in *Filartiga v Peña-Irala*, 630 F.2d 876 (2d Cir. 1980) (30 June 1980) 19 *ILM* (1980) 19(4) 966.

DISCUSSION **Can the torture of persons ever be justified?**

Section 4(4) of the Torture Act provides that '[n]o exceptional circumstances whatsoever, including but not limited to, a state of war, threat of war, internal political instability, national security or any state of emergency may be invoked as a justification for torture'. Suppose the police have a suspect in custody who has planted a bomb somewhere in a big shopping mall. The suspect refuses to answer any questions about the location of the bomb. If the bomb were to explode, up to 2 000 people may die or be seriously injured. There is no time left to evacuate the people or to look for the bomb. Would section 4(4) of the Act apply in a scenario like this? Could torture ever be justified? Is the definition of torture (section 3 of the Act) so vague that a public official may be able to find a way to interrogate a suspect without falling foul of the Torture Act?[14]

In *Gäfgen v Germany*,[15] the European Court of Human Rights considered the ambit of article 3 (prohibition of torture) of the [European] Convention for the Protection of Human Rights and Fundamental Freedoms. Magnus Gäfgen, a resident of the German city of Frankfurt am Main, kidnapped and killed the young son of a banker. He pretended that the young boy was still alive to extract a ransom from the parents. He was ultimately arrested and detained by the police, who were at the time still under the impression that the boy was alive. The deputy chief of the Frankfurt police department threatened Gäfgen with torture in the hope that he would disclose the location of the boy. Gäfgen ultimately did disclose the location of the boy's body. Gäfgen asserted that he was the victim of torture.

When the matter eventually came before the Grand Chamber of the European Court of Human Rights, a majority of the judges agreed that he was, indeed, a victim of torture because the prohibition of torture under article 3 of the European Convention does not provide for any exemptions, even where the life of another is at stake. The court also decided that evidence obtained as a result of torture or a threat of torture should, in principle, be excluded from any subsequent criminal trial. Cases such as *Gäfgen* present a host of moral and legal dilemmas, but the wording of section 4(4) of the Torture Act is unambiguous and a South African court will probably follow the strict approach applied by the European Court of Human Rights in the *Gäfgen* case.

Section 4 expressly provides for the non-applicability of head-of-state or head-of-government immunity. These forms of immunity will not be available as defences to sitting or former heads of state or heads of government charged under the Torture Act for the crime of torture. This is an important feature of the Act and in line with modern international criminal law, which seeks to end impunity for crimes under international law, including torture.

14 For a view in support of the argument that, under certain circumstances, torture could be justified, see Anderson, B (Dec 2014) 'Yes, torture can be justified. Here's why' *The Spectator*, available at http://blogs.spectator.co.uk/coffeehouse/2014/12/there-are-certain-times-when-torture-can-be-justified/.

15 For an argument that torture can never be justified, see *Gäfgen v Germany* (App. 22978/05) 1 June 2010 (ECHR). For a comment, see Ast S 'The *Gäfgen* judgment of the European Court of Human Rights: On the consequences of the threat of torture for criminal proceedings' (2010) 11(12) *GLJ* 1393.

49.2.4 Extraterritorial jurisdiction over the crime of torture

Another important feature of the Torture Act, which also underscores South Africa's international obligations, is the provision on extraterritorial jurisdiction. This is in line with the international movement to end impunity for torture and to ensure that individuals guilty of torture are held accountable regardless of where in the world they are. The Torture Act provides for extraterritorial jurisdiction in line with the enforcement regime known as *aut dedere aut judicare* (extradite or prosecute).[16] Section 6 of the Act provides as follows:

> **(1) A court of the Republic has jurisdiction in respect of an act committed outside the Republic which would have constituted an offence under section 4(1) or (2) had it been committed in the Republic, regardless of whether or not the act constitutes an offence at the place of its commission, if the accused person—**
> **(*a*) is a citizen of the Republic;**
> **(*b*) is ordinarily resident in the Republic;**
> **(*c*) is, after the commission of the offence, present in the territory of the Republic, or in its territorial waters or on board a ship, vessel, off-shore installation, a fixed platform or aircraft registered or required to be registered in the Republic and that person is not extradited pursuant to Article 8 of the Convention; or**
> **(*d*) has committed the offence against a South African citizen or against a person who is ordinarily resident in the Republic.**
>
> **(2) If an accused person is alleged to have committed an offence contemplated in section 4(1) or (2) outside the territory of the Republic, prosecution for the offence may only be instituted against such person on the written authority of the National Director of Public Prosecutions contemplated in section 179(1)(*a*) of the Constitution, who must also designate the court in which the prosecution must be conducted.**

The Torture Act represents a concretisation of a constitutional norm and an incorporation into South African criminal law of an important international legal framework aimed at the prevention and eradication of the practice of torture.

49.3 Terrorism

49.3.1 Introduction: The phenomenon of terrorism

Acts of terrorism affect protected interests such as human life, the person and property. The crime of terrorism can therefore be classified as a crime against the community and public welfare. In many ways, it can be described as *the* crime against the community. Historical and comparative accounts of terrorism may suggest that the phenomenon shares a fundamental characteristic with the crime of treason, namely that it is also a crime against the state. However, it is more accurate to describe terrorism as a crime against the community because of the following characteristics:

---

16 For more on the theoretical basis of the notion of *aut dedere aut judicare*, see Sunga LS *The Emerging System of International Criminal Law: Developments in Codification and Implementation* (1997) 254–256.

- *Depersonalisation of the victim*:[17] An individual or group of individuals are attacked, intimidated or persecuted, not for their possessions, gender or other personal or monetary reasons, but to attain a political, religious or ideological purpose. The victim 'is simply an anonymous and expendable tool' for achieving the terrorist's aim.[18]
- *Random acts*: The primary acts, for instance murder, bombing, public violence and intimidation, are normally random, but in line with the political, religious or ideological motive referred to above.
- *An attack on the community and on public welfare*: The general thrust of the definition of terrorist activity provided for in the Protection of Constitutional Democracy Against Terrorist and Related Activities Act 33 of 2004 (the Terrorism Act), discussed below, underscores the view that terrorism is essentially, although not exclusively, an attack on the community and on public welfare.

In this book, we group terrorism together with other crimes of international concern[19] mainly because of the reality of international terrorism as a phenomenon as well as the fact that South Africa's antiterrorism legislation emphasises the international and regional efforts to combat terrorism. Indeed, in its Preamble, the Terrorism Act refers to various international and regional instruments, such as the International Convention for the Suppression of Terrorist Bombings 1997, the International Convention on the Suppression of the Financing of Terrorism 1999, and the African Unity Convention on the Prevention and Combating of Terrorism 1999. The Constitutional Court has also made it clear that South African courts have extra-territorial jurisdiction over acts of terrorism committed abroad.[20]

The focus in this chapter is on terrorism as a crime under South African law, but with due regard for the fact that it is also a crime of growing international and regional concern. The international phenomenon of terrorism has received considerable political and legal attention during the first decade of the 21st century, no doubt because of the terrorist attacks on New York and Washington DC in the US on 11 September 2001.

The concept of terrorism is still controversial, and clichés such as 'one man's terrorist is another man's freedom fighter' illustrate its complexity. *Motive* forms an important element in the crime of terrorism, thus adding to the moral ambiguity which sometimes surrounds the phenomenon and the crime of terrorism. If certain criteria are met, acts committed as part of legitimate struggles in the furtherance of the right to national liberation, self-determination and independence against colonialism are exempted from the definition of terrorism.[21]

Terrorism is a crime in South Africa in terms of the Terrorism Act. In its Preamble, this statute recognises the various considerations, contexts and protected interests, some of which we referred to above. For instance, the Preamble of the Terrorism Act refers to

17 The phrase was coined by the French academic and international criminal law specialist Professor M Delmas-Marty. See Cassese *International Criminal Law* 125.

18 See Cassese *International Criminal Law* 125.

19 Multiple UN resolutions on terrorism, various international treaties as well as state practice and *opinio juris* underscore the international character of the crime of terrorism. Indeed, one can point to an emerging customary rule of international law regarding the international crime of terrorism, at least in time of peace. See *Interlocutory Decision on the Applicable Law: Terrorism, Conspiracy, Homicide, Perpetration, Cumulative Charging*, Appeals Chamber of the Special Tribunal for Lebanon, Case No STL-11-01/1, 16 February 2011, at para 85, available at https://www.stl-tsl.org/en/the-cases/stl-11-01/main/filings/orders-and-decisions/appeals-chamber/534-f0936.

20 *S v Okah* (CCT 315/16; CCT 193/17) [2018] ZACC 3, (23 February 2018), available at http://www.saflii.org/za/cases/ZACC/2018/3.html.

21 S 1(4) Protection of Constitutional Democracy against Terrorist and Related Activities Act 33 of 2004.

protected interests such as South Africa's constitutional democracy 'where fundamental human rights, such as the right to life and free political activity, are constitutionally enshrined'. The Act refers to the motive of terrorism discussed above, namely to 'achieve political and other aims in a violent or otherwise unconstitutional manner, and thereby undermine democratic rights and values and the Constitution'. The Preamble also emphasises the international and regional efforts to combat terrorism.

49.3.2 The crime of terrorism in terms of the Protection of Constitutional Democracy Against Terrorist and Related Activities Act 33 of 2004

The Terrorism Act is a comprehensive and complex statute that provides for various substantive and procedural aspects. The aim of this discussion is not to analyse all aspects of the Act, but rather to identify and discuss briefly the main elements of the crime of terrorism under South African law. Chapter 2 of the Terrorism Act provides for 'the offence of terrorism', 'convention offences' (offences under international conventions) and 'other offences', for example harbouring or concealing persons committing certain offences.

49.3.2.1 The relevant statutory provisions

Section 2 of the Terrorism Act provides as follows:

> **Offence of terrorism.**
> **Any person who engages in a terrorist activity is guilty of the offence of terrorism.**

Section 3 of the Terrorism Act provides as follows:

> **Offences associated or connected with terrorist activities.**
> **(1) Any person who—**
> **(*a*) does anything which will, or is likely to, enhance the ability of any entity to engage in a terrorist activity, including to provide or offering to provide a skill or an expertise;**
> **(*b*) enters or remains in any country; or**
> **(*c*) makes himself or herself available, for the benefit of, at the direction of, or in association with any entity engaging in a terrorist activity, and who knows or ought reasonably to have known or suspected, that such act was done for the purpose of enhancing the ability of such entity to engage in a terrorist activity, is guilty of the offence associated with a terrorist activity.**
> **(2) Any person who—**
> **(*a*) provides or offers to provide any weapon to any other person for use by or for the benefit of an entity;**
> **(*b*) solicits support for or gives support to an entity;**
> **(*c*) provides, receives or participates in training or instruction, or recruits an entity to receive training or instruction;**
> **(*d*) recruits any entity;**
> **(*e*) collects or makes a document; or**
> **(*f*) possesses a thing; connected with the engagement in a terrorist activity, and who knows or ought reasonably to have known or suspected that such weapons, soliciting, training, recruitment, document or thing is so connected, is guilty of an offence connected with terrorist activities.**

It is clear from the above that the crimes under sections 2 and 3 have as a common material element, the concept of 'terrorist activity'. This element is defined in section 1(1)(xxv) of the Terrorism Act as follows:

(*a*) any act committed in or outside the Republic, which—
- **(i) involves the systematic, repeated or arbitrary use of violence by any means or method;**
- **(ii) involves the systematic, repeated or arbitrary release into the environment or any part of it or distributing or exposing the public or any part of it to—**
  - **(*aa*) any dangerous, hazardous, radioactive or harmful substance or organism;**
  - **(*bb*) any toxic chemical; or**
  - **(*cc*) any microbial or other biological agent or toxin;**
- **(iii) endangers the life, or violates the physical integrity or physical freedom of, or causes serious bodily injury to or the death of, any person, or any number of persons;**
- **(iv) causes serious risk to the health or safety of the public or any segment of the public;**
- **(v) causes the destruction of or substantial damage to any property, natural resource, or the environmental or cultural heritage, whether public or private;**
- **(vi) is designed or calculated to cause serious interference with or serious disruption of an essential service, facility or system, or the delivery of any such service, facility or system, whether public or private, including, but not limited to—**
  - **(*aa*) a system used for, or by, an electronic system, including an information system;**
  - **(*bb*) a telecommunication service or system;**
  - **(*cc*) a banking or financial service or financial system;**
  - **(*dd*) a system used for the delivery of essential government services;**
  - **(*ee*) a system used for, or by, an essential public utility or transport provider;**
  - **(*ff*) an essential infrastructure facility; or**
  - **(*gg*) any essential emergency services, such as police, medical or civil defence services;**
- **(vii) causes any major economic loss or extensive destabilisation of an economic system or substantial devastation of the national economy of a country; or**
- **(viii) creates a serious public emergency situation or a general insurrection in the Republic, whether the harm contemplated in paragraphs (*a*)(i) to (vii) is or may be suffered in or outside the Republic, and whether the activity referred to in subparagraphs (ii) to (viii) was committed by way of any means or method; and**

(*b*) which is intended, or by its nature and context, can reasonably be regarded as being intended, in whole or in part, directly or indirectly, to -
- **(i) threaten the unity and territorial integrity of the Republic;**

> (ii) **intimidate, or to induce or cause feelings of insecurity within, the public, or a segment of the public, with regard to its security, including its economic security, or to induce, cause or spread feelings of terror, fear or panic in a civilian population; or**
>
> (iii) **unduly compel, intimidate, force, coerce, induce or cause a person, a government, the general public or a segment of the public, or a domestic or an international organisation or body or intergovernmental organisation or body, to do or to abstain or refrain from doing any act, or to adopt or abandon a particular standpoint, or to act in accordance with certain principles, whether the public or the person, government, body, or organization or institution referred to in subparagraphs (ii) or (iii), as the case may be, is inside or outside the Republic; and**
>
> (*c*) **which is committed, directly or indirectly, in whole or in part, for the purpose of the advancement of an individual or collective political, religious, ideological or philosophical motive, objective, cause or undertaking.**

A key part of the structure of the crime of terrorism is the concept of 'specified offence', which is defined in section 1 of the Terrorism Act as follows:

> **'specified offence', with reference to section 4, 14 (in so far as It relates to section 4), and 23, means—**
>
> (*a*) **the offence of terrorism referred to in section 2, an offence associated or connected with terrorist activities referred to in section 3, a Convention offence, or an offence referred to in section 13 or 14 (in so far as it relates to the aforementioned sections); or**
>
> (*b*) **any activity outside the Republic which constitutes an offence under the law of another state and which would have constituted an offence referred to in paragraph (*a*), had that activity taken place in the Republic;**

The above quoted provisions of the Terrorism Act constitute the structural components of the complex crime of terrorism under South African law. These components, taken together, form the definition and elements of the crime of terrorism.

49.3.2.2 The components of the statutory definition of the crime of terrorism

The statutory structure of the crime of terrorism under South Africa law, as set out above, is complex and potentially wide in scope. Although legitimate protest action and practices, such as strike action by collectivities such as labour unions, are not criminalised under the Terrorism Act,[22] the definition of terrorist activity is still comprehensive (some would argue too vague - see the discussion below). It has correctly been suggested that courts should limit the application of the definition to 'clear cases'.[23]

There are three components to the crime of terrorism:

1. Specified offence
2. Offence of terrorism
3. Terrorist activity

22 See also commentary by De Koker L *South African Money Laundering and Terror Financing Law* (revision service 18, 2017) Com 4-6.

23 Kruger A *Organised Crime and Proceeds of Crime Law in South Africa* (2008) 129.

In *S v Okah*[24] the Constitutional Court formulated a very helpful compacted description of the three components mentioned above. The court stated:

> **[the] definition of 'specified offence' is closely integrated with the offence of terrorism that lies at the heart of the entire legislative scheme. Indeed, the definition reads: 'specified offence ... means the offence of terrorism referred to in section 2'. Section 2 provides that 'any person who engages in a terrorist activity is guilty of the offence of terrorism'. Terrorist activity is, in turn, widely defined in section 1. In compacted form, it includes any act committed 'in or outside the Republic' that creates specified deleterious effects; is intended to cause certain effects; and is committed 'for the purpose of the advancement of an individual or collective political, religious, ideological or philosophical motive, objective, cause or undertaking'.**[25]

It is important to treat the above described components as 'a carefully interconnected web', because the crime of terrorism (section 2) and the definition of terrorist activity (section 1) are linked to the very important conferral of extra-territorial jurisdiction for South African courts over the crime of terrorism. If any of these components - including the concept of 'specified offence' - is delinked from the statutory structure of the crime of terrorism, it will have the result of unraveling the entire legislative scheme to define terrorism and to provide the courts with the necessary jurisdiction, including extra-territorial jurisdiction.[26]

49.3.2.3 The required *mens rea*

A person who commits terrorist activities in or outside South Africa which is *intended*, or by its nature and context, can *reasonably be regarded as being intended*, to threaten the unity and territorial integrity of South Africa, intimidate or terrorise the public or a segment of the public, or unduly compel, force or coerce a person, an organisation, a government or the general public, whether the public, the person, the organisation or the government is inside or outside South Africa, and which is committed directly or indirectly for the *purpose* of the advancement of an individual or collective political, religious, ideological or philosophical motive, objective, cause or undertaking, will be guilty of the crime of terrorism.[27]

Motive is conceptually different from *intent*. On a charge of murder, for instance, the prosecutor must prove that X intended to kill Y. It is not necessary to prove *why* X killed Y. However, motive plays an important role in terrorism cases, since motive is what distinguishes a terrorist activity from other criminal activities, such as arson, intimidation or public violence. In a terrorism case the perpetrator must have acted for a 'political, religious, ideological or philosophical motive, objective, cause or undertaking' in order to be culpable.

49.3.2.4 The section 1(4) exemptions

Section 1(4) of the Terrorism Act exempts certain conduct from the definition of terrorism. Certain criteria must all be met, namely:

- the act must have taken place within the context of a 'struggle waged by peoples';

---

24 *S v Okah* (CCT 315/16; CCT 193/17) [2018] ZACC 3, (23 February 2018), available at http://www.saflii.org/za/cases/ZACC/2018/3.html.

25 *S v Okah* supra at 32.

26 *S v Okah* supra at 33.

27 Terrorism Act s 1 (xxv).

- the above-mentioned struggle must be 'in the exercise or furtherance of their legitimate right to national liberation, self-determination and independence against colonialism, or occupation or aggression or domination by alien or foreign forces'; and
- the act must be taken 'in accordance with the principles of international law, especially international humanitarian law'.

An individual accused of terrorism under the Terrorism Act must provide evidential material to support all the above mentioned criteria. It is submitted here that a court cannot simply take judicial notice of the existence of a national liberation struggle or an anti-colonial struggle or a struggle against aggressive occupation. Enough factual material and contextual evidence must be made available to the court which has to make the determination that all the criteria under section 1(4) were met. The third criterion, namely that the act must be taken 'in accordance with the principles of international law, especially international humanitarian law', needs further explanation.

The body of law known as international humanitarian law ('IHL') normally applies to international or non-international armed conflicts. This classification thus excludes acts of public violence or public disturbances which do not reach the threshold or characteristics of an international or non-international armed conflict from the ambit of IHL. Article 1(4) of the First Additional Protocol to the Geneva Conventions, 1977,[28] however provides that an 'international armed conflict' includes 'armed conflicts in which peoples are fighting against colonial domination and alien occupation and against racist regimes in the exercise of their right to self-determination'. The correct reading of the criteria under section 1(4) of the Terrorism Act is that the norms of IHL will apply in any situation in which the first two criteria under section 1(4) of the Act have been met.[29] For instance, the bombing of civilian targets, or where bombings or acts of violence are grossly indiscriminate, will be acts in violation of IHL and thus not be regarded as exemptions for purposes of section 1(4) of the Act.[30]

49.3.2.5 Harbouring or concealing a person committing terrorist crimes, and the duty to report the presence of a person suspected of intending to commit or having committed a terrorist crime

Section 11 of the Terrorism Act provides for the criminalisation of *harbouring or concealing* any person who is suspected of committing a terrorist crime or who is likely to commit such a crime. Section 12 of the Act provides for a *duty to report* the presence of a person suspected of intending to commit or having committed a terrorist crime. Failure to report this to the police is a crime.[31]

49.3.2.6 Extraterritorial jurisdiction over the crime of terrorism

Section 15 of the Terrorism Act provides in detail for jurisdiction, including *extra-territorial jurisdiction*, over the various crimes under the Act. This jurisdictional regime is clearly aimed at providing South African authorities and courts with the necessary legal tools to combat terrorism effectively, whether domestic or international. In *S v Okah*, the Supreme Court of

28 Additional Protocols to the Geneva Conventions, 1977, available at https://www.icrc.org/eng/assets/files/other/icrc_002_0321.pdf.

29 *S v Okah* supra at 48 fn 73.

30 *S v Okah* supra at 50–52.

31 See *S v Bogaards* (864/2010) [2011] ZASCA 196; [2012] 1 All SA 376 (SCA) (21 November 2011) for an interpretation of ss 11 and 12 of the Terrorism Act.

Appeal[32] mistakenly held that extra-territorial jurisdiction under section 15 is limited to the offence of *financing* of terrorism. This mistake was rectified by the Constitutional Court in *S v Okah*[33] and it was held that the courts should not, 'through a narrow interpretation of section 15(1), mistakenly perpetuate an historical disinclination to extra-territoriality'.[34]

Section 15(1) of the Terrorism Act confers jurisdiction over 'specified offences', a term defined in section 1(1) of the Act. Furthermore, section 15(2) of the Act provides that any conduct alleged to constitute an offence committed by a person not contemplated by section 15(1) may nonetheless be brought to justice in South African courts so long as there is a particular connection between the conduct or person and South Africa.

DISCUSSION

Criminalisation, stigmatisation, protected interests and the principle of legality

One can argue that the crime of terrorism unnecessarily duplicates other crimes such as assault, public violence, malicious damage to property, intimidation, murder, sedition and treason. The element of *motive* is the key distinguishing element, but is it enough? Take a look at the core content of some of these crimes and compare it with the core content of terrorism as discussed above. Are there any other interests protected by the criminalisation of terrorism that are not covered by *other* common law and statutory crimes? Does the exemption provided for in section 1(4) of the Terrorism Act help or hinder a proper understanding of the interests protected by the criminalisation of terrorism under South African law?

The **principle of legality** requires that laws should be clear and intelligible to all who are subject to them and to all who must enforce them. A vague law prevents persons from understanding what conduct places them at risk of criminal sanction while simultaneously subjecting them to the subjective and arbitrary discretion of law enforcement officers. Over-broad laws also offend the principle of legality because they reach beyond their presumed purpose, attracting harsh penalties for conduct that ordinary criminal laws are better suited to address. This is especially true of laws with extra-territorial reach.[35]

49.4 Human trafficking

49.4.1 The phenomenon of human trafficking

The phenomenon of human trafficking is often compared to the practice of slavery.[36] While these phenomena are different in terms of scope and means applied, both ancient slavery and modern human trafficking share one element: exploitation of humans.[37] The international community took note. In 2001 the UN adopted the Convention against Transnational

32 *S v Okah* 2017 (1) SACR 1 (SCA).

33 *S v Okah* (CC) supra at 18–43.

34 *S v Okah* (CC) supra at 43.

35 For further critical reflections on the criminalisation of terrorism, see Seto, TP 'The morality of terrorism' 35(4) (2002) *Loy L A L Rev* 1227.

36 Kreston SS 'Human trafficking legislation in South Africa: Consent, coercion and consequences' (2014) 27(1) *SACJ* 20. See also in general, Brysk A and Choi-Fitzpatrick A (eds) *From Human Trafficking to Human Rights: Reframing Contemporary Slavery* (2012).

37 Kreston 'Human trafficking legislation in South Africa' 21.

Organized Crime (the Palermo Convention).[38] In addition to the main instrument, the UN General Assembly also adopted two supplementing protocols, namely the Protocol to Prevent, Suppress and Punish Trafficking in Persons, Especially Women and Children, and the Protocol against the Smuggling of Migrants by Land, Sea and Air. Article 3 of the Protocol on Trafficking in Persons defines trafficking as follows:

> **The recruitment, transportation, transfer, harbouring or receipt of persons, by means of the threat or use of force or other forms of coercion, of abduction, of fraud, of deception, of the abuse of power or of a position of vulnerability or of the giving or receiving of payments or benefits to achieve the consent of a person having control over another person, for the purpose of exploitation. Exploitation shall include, at a minimum, the exploitation of the prostitution of others or other forms of sexual exploitation, forced labour or services, slavery or practices similar to slavery, servitude or the removal of organs.**

Since the adoption of the UN instruments there has been a growing awareness, both internationally and nationally, of the extent of human trafficking. Various civil society and governmental initiatives are aimed at creating further awareness and are also aimed at preventative measures.[39]

Against the above background, we will now turn to a brief discussion of the most important elements of human trafficking in terms of the UN instrument. Thereafter, we will discuss the South African legislative frameworks to combat human trafficking.

49.4.2 The notion of human trafficking under the UN Protocol

We pointed out above that the UN General Assembly adopted two protocols to supplement the Convention against Transnational Organized Crime.[40] The Protocol on Human Trafficking should therefore not be viewed as a discrete model law on domestic and international forms of human trafficking, but rather as a framework on a phenomenon with a particular link with transnational organised crime. However, as Kreston correctly points out, the elements of human trafficking as identified in the Protocol on Human Trafficking are a good starting point for a discussion on human trafficking, and in particular a discussion on national legislative responses to the phenomenon of human trafficking.[41]

In a globalised world where the mobility of people is almost taken for granted, the Protocol on Human Trafficking aims to address the issue of 'consent' as a key element of trafficking. The methods identified in article 3 of the protocol, for instance the use of force, threats or other forms of coercion, and abduction, impact on consent. The position of children is specifically provided for. The protocol states that the recruitment, transportation, transfer, harbouring or receipt of a child for the *purposes of exploitation* shall be considered 'trafficking in persons' even if this does not involve any of the means mentioned above, for instance threats or other forms of coercion. The question of consent is thus 'irrelevant when it is a child who is trafficked'.[42]

38 United Nations General Assembly Doc A/RES/55/25. For a discussion, see Kemp G 'The United Nations Convention Against Transnational Organized Crime: A milestone in international criminal law' (2001) 14(2) *SACJ* 152–167.

39 See the discussion by Manyathi-Jele N 'Analysis of the human trafficking awareness index report' (June 2015) *De Rebus* 9-11.

40 For signature and ratification status of these instruments, see http://www.unodc.org/unodc/en/treaties/CTOC/signatures.html, and https://treaties.un.org/pages/ViewDetails.aspx?src=TREATY&mtdsg_no=XVIII-12-a&chapter=18&clang=_en#EndDec.

41 Kreston 'Human trafficking legislation in South Africa' 21.

42 Kreston 'Human trafficking legislation in South Africa' 22.

49.4.3 Human trafficking under South African law

The Prevention and Combating of Trafficking in Persons Act 7 of 2013 (the Trafficking in Persons Act) was promulgated on 29 July 2013.[43] The Act, with the exception of sections 15, 16 and 31(2)(*b*)(ii), entered into force on 9 August 2015.[44] The UN Protocol on Human Trafficking discussed above and a number of other international instruments place obligations on South Africa to provide for effective mechanisms to combat human trafficking. The Act also seeks to give effect to the greater and better protection of the rights of individuals, especially vulnerable persons such as women and children. In this regard, constitutional rights such as the right to human dignity, equality, the right to freedom and security of the person, the right not to be treated in a cruel, inhuman or degrading way, the right not to be subjected to slavery, servitude or forced labour, and the right of children to be protected from maltreatment, neglect, abuse or degradation, play an important role.[45]

The Trafficking in Persons Act fills important *lacunae* in criminal law (common law and statutory law) in terms of the criminalisation of human trafficking.[46] The Act repeals or amends a number of statutes. For present purposes, it is important to note that whereas the Criminal Law (Sexual Offences and Related Matters) Amendment Act 32 of 2007 (the Sexual Offences Act) served as an interim legislative vehicle for the criminalisation of *trafficking in persons for sexual purposes*, that function has now been taken over by the Trafficking in Persons Act. This Act deals with various forms of trafficking in persons *including* trafficking in persons which was committed for sexual purposes.

Chapter 2 of the Trafficking in Persons Act provides for a number of offences. The key offence is, of course, *trafficking in persons*. Section 4 of the Act provides as follows:

> **(1) Any person who delivers, recruits, transports, transfers, harbours, sells, exchanges, leases or receives another person within or across the borders of the Republic, by means of—**
>
> **(*a*) a threat of harm;**
> **(*b*) the threat or use of force or other forms of coercion;**
> **(*c*) the abuse of vulnerability;**
> **(*d*) fraud;**
> **(*e*) deception;**
> **(*f*) abduction;**
> **(*g*) kidnapping;**
> **(*h*) the abuse of power;**
> **(*i*) the direct or indirect giving or receiving of payments or benefits to obtain the consent of a person having control or authority over another person; or**
> **(*j*) the direct or indirect giving or receiving of payments, compensation, rewards, benefits or any other advantage,**
>
> **aimed at either the person or an immediate family member of that person or any other person in close relationship to that person, for the purpose of any form or manner of exploitation, is guilty of the offence of trafficking in persons.**

---

43 *Government Gazette* 36715, GN 544, 29 July 2013. For a comparative discussion of the Act, see Iroanya RO 'Human trafficking with specific reference to South African and Mozambican counter-trafficking legislation' (2014) 27(2) *Acta Crim* 102–115; see also Kreston 'Human trafficking legislation in South Africa'.

44 *GG* 39078, Notice Number R 32, 7 August 2015.

45 Goliath P 'Protecting victims of human trafficking – Is South Africa doing enough?' (2016) 562 *De Rebus* 22.

46 For an international and comparative perspective, see Kruger B 'Towards a sharp prosecution sword to combat human trafficking: Comparing the new South African counter-trafficking law with international prosecution standards' (2016) 49(1) *CILSA* 53.

(2) Any person who—

(*a*) adopts a child, facilitated or secured through legal or illegal means; or

(*b*) concludes a forced marriage with another person,

within or across the borders of the Republic, for the purpose of the exploitation of that child or other person in any form or manner, is guilty of an offence.

S v Dos Santos

In *S v Dos Santos*[47] the accused was prosecuted under the Criminal Law (Sexual Offences and Related Matters) Amendment Act 32 of 2007, on three counts of trafficking in persons. It is submitted that for purposes of the current understanding of the crime of human trafficking under the Trafficking in Persons Act one can note the factual elements of human trafficking as identified by the court in *Dos Santos*. The salient facts of the case are as follows: the accused, a 28-year-old Mozambican national, met the three complainants on the beach near Maputo in Mozambique, where the complainants worked as prostitutes. The appellant, who owned a hair salon in Pretoria, regularly commuted between Pretoria and Maputo. The accused agreed to take the complainants to Pretoria and to accommodate them as prostitutes. The accused asked a friend of hers to transport the complainants to Pretoria. The complainants initially resided with the accused in her flat in Pretoria. Since the flat was very small, the accused decided to rent a house for the complainants a short distance from her flat. A brothel was kept at that house. It is at that house that the accused and the complainants were taken into custody. The accused was charged with human trafficking in the regional court, where she was also convicted. She appealed to the High Court. With reference to the elements of human trafficking, the High Court noted the following:[48]

- The accused, who secured the presence of the complainants in South Africa, kept them and harboured them under threat of prosecution as illegal immigrants.
- The complainants, desperate and of tender age, were vulnerable and exploited by the accused for they had no permission to be in South Africa.
- The complainants were forced, against their will, to perform sexual acts (sometimes as many as eight times per day) on the instructions of the accused.
- The complainants were under constant threat, lived in fear and were subjected to treatment that the court described as 'inhumane'.
- The accused acted 'out of pure greed'.

Apart from the elements noted above, the court also took into account the fact that the crimes were committed as part of an elaborate and organised criminal enterprise. First, the complainants were lured from Mozambique; they were made to believe that they would enjoy a better life in South Africa. Second, the court noted that there existed an illicit infrastructure to transport the young females across the international border under escort. Third, and most worryingly, the transport of the complainants across the international border occurred with the involvement of corrupt government officials.[49] The High Court ultimately dismissed the appeal and imposed a sentence of life imprisonment on the accused for her convictions on the charges of human trafficking.[50]

47 *S v Dos Santos* 2018 (1) SACR 20 (GP).

48 *Dos Santos* at 9.

49 *Dos Santos* at 11.

50 *Dos Santos* at 13.

A factual scenario as set out in the *Dos Santos* case is a good illustration of the phenomenon of human trafficking, which is often accompanied by elements of organised criminality, abuse of process and corruption. Chapter 2 of the Trafficking in Persons Act therefore provides for the following *additional* crimes:

- Debt bondage – involuntary status or condition that arises from a pledge by a person of, for instance, his or her personal services[51]
- Possession, destruction, confiscation, concealment of or tampering with documents (such as passports or identification documents) of a victim of trafficking[52]
- Using or benefiting from the services of victims of trafficking[53]
- Facilitating trafficking in persons, for instance leases or subleases of any room, house or building for facilitating trafficking in persons[54]
- Certain conduct of carriers transporting victims of trafficking[55]
- Attempt, incitement and conspiracy to commit trafficking in persons[56]

DISCUSSION

Human (child) trafficking and sexual exploitation

In addition to the legal frameworks provided by the Children's Act 38 of 2005 and the Sexual Offences Act, it is clear that South Africa needs specific legislation dealing with *the problem of human (child) trafficking in a more general sense (that is, not focused on the sexual exploitation aspect only)*. The Trafficking in Persons Act aims to address this concern. The question is whether the legislative measures will satisfy the obligation contained in the Protocol on Human Trafficking.

Prior to the advent of the Children's Act, abduction was the only available mechanism for prosecuting cases of human trafficking involving children. Cases of *ukuthwala*[57] would not even qualify as cases of abduction in instances where discontented parents of the girl who had been taken dropped charges and preferred to accept compensatory damages from a traditional court instead. The harm done to the girl was irrelevant until the introduction of the crime of human trafficking.

The domestic criminalisation of human trafficking was necessitated when South Africa became a signatory to the Protocol on Human Trafficking. The obligation arising from the protocol forced the country to consider the interests of the victims of human trafficking. This necessitated the creation of a crime that went beyond what was available through the crime of abduction. The idea of domestic legislation which would criminalise human trafficking began to take shape through legislation such as the Children's Act[58] and the Sexual Offences Act.[59]

Section 71(1) of the Sexual Offences Act was effectively used to prosecute and convict Mvumeleni Jezile when he kidnapped a 14-year-old girl in 2010 under the

51 S 5 of the Trafficking in Persons Act.
52 S 6 of the Trafficking in Persons Act.
53 S 7 of the Trafficking in Persons Act.
54 S 8 of the Trafficking in Persons Act.
55 S 9 of the Trafficking in Persons Act.
56 S 10 of the Trafficking in Persons Act.
57 See also the discussion in Chapter 30 above.
58 Ch 18 (ss 281 to 291, now repealed) of the Children's Act contained the provisions relating to criminalising trafficking in children.
59 Part 6 in Ch 7 (now repealed) of the Sexual Offences Act contained the transitional provisions relating to trafficking in persons for sexual purposes.

pretext of the *ukuthwala* custom.[60] However, the provisions of the Sexual Offences Act were always intended to operate on a transitional basis. There were still gaps which necessitated the creation of the Trafficking in Persons Act. The latest legislative incarnation which criminalises human trafficking is intended to be a more effective and comprehensive mechanism to stop human trafficking, prosecute traffickers and, most importantly, protect trafficking victims. It completely shifts the focus from the issue of parental control and directs it to the people who were directly involved in the act of trafficking, namely the accused and the victim.

Section 4(2)(*b*) of the Trafficking in Persons Act specifically provides that any person who concludes a forced marriage with another person for the purpose of the exploitation of that other person is guilty of the offence of trafficking in persons. As a consequence, the practice of *ukuthwala* falls squarely within the definition of human trafficking. Therefore, an accused person cannot legitimately rely on practising the custom of *ukuthwala* to escape liability against a charge of contravening section 4(2)(*b*) of the Trafficking in Persons Act.

49.4.4 Human trafficking and extra-territorial jurisdiction

Since trafficking in persons is primarily, but by no means exclusively, a transnational offence, it comes as no surprise that the Trafficking in Persons Act provides for extraterritorial jurisdiction. Section 12 of the Act provides as follows:

> **(1) A court of the Republic has jurisdiction in respect of an act committed outside the Republic which would have constituted an offence under this Chapter had it been committed in the Republic, regardless of whether or not the act constitutes an offence at the place of its commission, if the person to be charged—**
>
> **(*a*) is a citizen of the Republic;**
>
> **(*b*) is ordinarily resident in the Republic;**
>
> **(*c*) has committed the offence against a citizen of the Republic or a person who is ordinarily resident in the Republic;**
>
> **(*d*) is, after the commission of the offence, present in the territory of the Republic, or in its territorial waters or on board a ship, vessel, off-shore installation, a fixed platform or aircraft registered or required to be registered in the Republic;**
>
> **(*e*) is, for any reason, not extradited by the Republic or if there is no application to extradite that person; or**
>
> **(*f*) is a juristic person or a partnership registered in terms of any law in the Republic.**
>
> **(2) Only a High Court has jurisdiction in respect of a person referred to in subsection (1)(*d*).**
>
> **(3) A person who commits an offence referred to in subsection (1) is liable on conviction to the penalty prescribed for that offence.**
>
> **(4) (*a*) Subject to paragraph (*b*), the National Director of Public Prosecutions must, in writing, designate an appropriate court in which to conduct a prosecution against any person accused of having committed an offence**

60 *S v Jezile* 2016 (2) SA 62 (WCC).

under this Chapter in a country outside the Republic as provided for in subsection (1).

(*b*) For the purposes of determining the jurisdiction of a court to try the offence, the offence is deemed to have been committed—

(i) at the place where the accused person is ordinarily resident; or

(ii) at the accused person's principal place of business.

(5) The institution of a prosecution in terms of this section must be authorised in writing by the National Director of Public Prosecutions.

The Convention Against Transnational Organized Crime and the additional protocols thereto require of states parties to (1) criminalise the relevant crimes, notably organised crime, money laundering, corruption and human trafficking, and (2) to provide for extraterritorial jurisdiction over these crimes. The scope of section 12 of the Trafficking in Persons Act satisfies the required extraterritoriality provided for in the UN instruments.

THIS CHAPTER IN ESSENCE

1. Phenomena such as terrorism, torture and human trafficking affect more than just the jurisdiction in which the acts occur. Often, phenomena like these affect persons and interests across international borders. Such offences may be viewed as serious enough for the international community to require states to provide for the offences under domestic law as well as to provide for extraterritorial jurisdiction.
2. To illustrate the international community's concern with certain criminal behaviour, three treaty-based crimes are addressed in this chapter, namely torture, terrorism and human trafficking. The three crimes are not the only treaty-based crimes, but are illustrative of crimes of international concern that have not yet reached the threshold of core crimes under international law (discussed in Chapter 47).
3. In the absence of an international criminal tribunal with jurisdiction over the three crimes discussed in this chapter, it is essential for states to provide for the crimes under domestic law.

Annexure 1

How to answer problem-type questions

Problem-type questions in tests and examinations try, to some extent, to replicate legal problems as they occur in real life. These problems are typically presented as case studies with questions to be answered by the student. In summary, the seven-step methodology for answering these questions is as follows:

Reading and analysing the problem:

Step 1: Separate the *facts* of the case study from the sentence (or sentences) that contain the questions to be answered (circle with a pen).

Step 2: Extract the *questions* to be answered from the sentence(s), and number these questions in sequence (1, 2, 3, and so on).

Step 3: Circle the *instructional word* (advise, discuss, explain, criticise, etc.) in each listed question to remind yourself what information the examiner requires.

Writing your answer:

Step 4: *Issues*: In the first paragraph, state the questions isolated in step 2 above as the issues arising from the problem given.

Step 5: *Legal test*: In the second paragraph and subparagraphs, and dealing with each issue in turn, state the legal test governing each issue identified in step 4. (This may require a discussion of conflicting cases if the legal test is not clear cut.)

Step 6: *Apply the legal test to given facts*: In the third paragraph, and dealing with each issue in turn, apply the legal test to the given facts of the case. (Remember to comply with your instructions as per step 3; for example, do not 'discuss' if you were instructed to 'criticise'.)

Step 7: *Conclusion*: State your conclusion. This is the answer to the question(s) isolated in step 4.

We will now demonstrate this seven-step approach with reference to a sample criminal law examination question.

QUESTION 1

Abel is a 36-year-old businessman who lives in a house with two friends, Ben and Clara. On 1 April, he is due to catch a flight abroad, but oversleeps. In his panic, he shouts to his housemates Ben and Clara as he rushes to leave for the airport: 'I am going to have to drive like a maniac to get there on time!' He then throws his suitcase into his car and drives off at a great speed, overtaking slow-moving traffic and occasionally also overtaking on blind rises. At a blind rise near to the airport, he misjudges and collides head-on with a car being driven by Daniel. Daniel is badly injured in the collision, but his injuries, although serious, are not immediately life-threatening. Abel is protected by his car's airbag and is not hurt. Within a short time, an ambulance arrives and two paramedics, Eric and Fred, stabilise Daniel, put him into the ambulance and drive him to the hospital. When they arrive at the hospital, Eric and Fred put Daniel onto a stretcher to carry him into the hospital. As they are busy carrying him, Eric slips and drops the stretcher, and Daniel falls head-first onto the tarmac. Daniel's neck is broken in the fall, killing him instantly.

Is Abel likely to be convicted of murder or culpable homicide on this evidence?
Discuss. [10 marks]

Now apply the seven steps

Reading and analysing the problem:

Step 1: The first paragraph above contains the facts (case study), and the last sentence: 'Is Abel likely to be convicted of murder or culpable homicide on this evidence? Discuss.' contains the questions to be answered.

Step 2: The questions to be answered (extracted from this sentence) are:
1. Is Abel likely to be convicted of murder on this evidence?
2. Is Abel likely to be convicted of culpable homicide on this evidence?

Step 3: The answer requires a *discussion* of the two questions identified: the legal requirements of murder and culpable homicide, as well as the likely outcome on the given facts.

Writing your answer:

Step 4: The issues arising from this problem are whether, on the given facts, the legal requirements for a conviction of murder or culpable homicide appear to have been satisfied.

Step 5: The legal test for a conviction of murder is proof beyond a reasonable doubt of the following elements:
1. That Abel acted *unlawfully*
2. That Abel *intended* to kill Daniel
3. That Abel *caused* Daniel's death
4. That Daniel was a *human being*

The same legal test applies for culpable homicide, except that the second element requires proof that Abel *negligently* killed Daniel.

Step 6: On the given facts, it is not in dispute that the deceased, Daniel, was a human being (element 4), or that Abel acted unlawfully (element 1). The only issues that remain in dispute are:
- whether Abel acted *intentionally or negligently* (element 2)
- whether Abel *caused* Daniel's death (element 3).

On the given evidence, it is clear that Abel had no direct intention to cause anybody's death: he was in a hurry to get to the airport, and this resulted in him taking chances that a reasonable person in these circumstances would not have taken. He therefore drove negligently (*S v Goosen* 1989 (4) SA 1013 (A)).

Although it is arguable that Abel had intention in the form of *dolus eventualis,* this enquiry is not needed on the facts. In any event, a possible inference of intention does not preclude a finding of negligence (*S v Ngubane* 1985 (3) SA 677 (A)).

The causation requirement (element 3) is more problematic. On the facts, the injuries caused to Daniel in the collision were not life-threatening, and he died as a result of Eric dropping the stretcher. The dropping of the stretcher serves as a *novus actus interveniens,* which breaks the chain of legal causation, as it complies with the three requirements set out in *S v Lungile* 1999 (2) SACR 597 (SCA):

- The dropping of the stretcher occurred after the collision and immediately before Daniel broke his neck.
- The dropping of the stretcher was an unlikely event in the circumstances as paramedics seldom drop their patients causing their deaths.
- The dropping of the stretcher was sufficiently disconnected from Abel's initial conduct in causing the collision.

Therefore, Abel did not legally cause Daniel's death.

Step 7: In conclusion, although the collision with Daniel's car was as a result of Abel's negligence, Abel did not *cause* Daniel's death and he can therefore not be convicted of culpable homicide. (He could still, however, be charged with and convicted of reckless or negligent driving.)

If, however, the court could be persuaded that Abel had acted intentionally (on the basis of *dolus eventualis*), the failure to prove causation would nevertheless preclude a conviction of murder. He could be convicted of the competent verdict of attempted murder in the circumstances.

Bibliography

Books

Adam S, Colette-Basecqz N and Nihoul M (eds) (2008) *Corporate Criminal Liability in Europe* Bruxelles: La Charte

Alvarez JE (2009) 'Alternatives to international criminal justice' in Cassese A (ed-in-chief) *The Oxford Companion to International Criminal Justice* Oxford: Oxford University Press

Ambos K (2011) 'Defences in international criminal law' in B Brown (ed) *Research Handbook on International Criminal Law* Cheltenham: Edward Elgar

Ambos K and Maunganidze OA (eds) (2012) *Power and Prosecution: Challenges and Opportunities for International Criminal Justice in SubSaharan Africa* Portland: Hart

Aquinas T (2002) *The Treatise on Human Nature*: *Summa Theologica* Pars 1 and *Summa Contra Gentiles* reprinted ed (1975) Indianapolis: Hackett Pub Co

Arenson KJ, Bagaric M and Gillies P (2011) *Australian Criminal Laws in the Common Law Jurisdictions: Cases and Materials* 3 ed South Melbourne, Vic.: Oxford University Press

Ashworth A (1981) 'The elasticity of *mens rea*' in CFH Tapper (ed) *Crime, Proof and Punishment: Essays in Memory of Sir Rupert Cross* London: Butterworths

Ashworth A (2009) *Principles of Criminal Law* 6 ed Oxford, New York: Oxford University Press

Baker DJ (2011) *The Right Not to be Criminalized: Demarcating Criminal Law's Authority* Burlington, VT: Ashgate

Barriga S and Kress C (eds) (2012) *The Travaux Préparatoires of the Crime of Aggression* Cambridge, New York: Cambridge University Press

Bass GJ (2002) *Stay the Hand of Vengeance: The Politics of War Crimes Tribunals* Princeton, Oxford: Princeton University Press

Bassiouni MC (2009) 'International criminal justice in historical perspective: The tension between States' interests and the pursuit of international justice' in A Cassese (ed-in-chief) *The Oxford Companion to International Criminal Justice* Oxford: Oxford University Press

Bassiouni MC (1999) *International Criminal Law Vol I* 2 ed New York: Transnational

Bassiouni MC (ed) (2005) *The Legislative History of the International Criminal Court: Introduction, Analysis and Integrated Text Vol I* Leiden: Brill-Nijhoff

Bennett TW (2004) *Customary Law in South Africa* Cape Town: Juta

Bennett TW and Strug J (2013) *Introduction to International Law* Cape Town: Juta

Boberg PQR (1984) *The Law of Delict Vol I: Aquilian Liability* Cape Town: Juta

Bohlander M (2012) *Principles of German Criminal Law* Oxford, Portland, OR: Hart

Bourgon S (2002) 'Jurisdiction ratione loci' in A Cassese et al (eds) *The Rome Statute of the International Criminal Court: A Commentary* Oxford, New York: Oxford University Press

Brown BS (ed) (2011) *Research Handbook on International Criminal Law* Cheltenham; Northampton, MA: Edward Elgar

Brundage JA (1990) *Law, Sex and Christian Society in Medieval Europe* Chicago: University of Chicago Press

Brysk A and Choi-Fitzpatrick A (eds) (2012) *From Human Trafficking to Human Rights: Reframing Contemporary Slavery* Philadelphia: University of Pennsylvania Press

Burchell JM (2011) *South African Criminal Law and Procedure Vol 1: General Principles of Criminal Law* 4 ed Cape Town: Juta Law

Burchell JM (2016) *Principles of Criminal Law* 5 ed Cape Town: Juta

Burchell JM and Erasmus A (eds) (2003) *Criminal Justice in a New Society: Essays in Honour of Solly Leeman* Cape Town: Juta

Burchell JM and Milton J (2007) *Cases and Materials on Criminal Law* 3 ed Cape Town: Juta

Burchell EM, Milton JRL and Burchell JM (1983) *South African Criminal Law and Procedure Vol I* 2 ed Cape Town: Juta

Carstens A and Grebe H (eds) (2001) *Taallandskap: Huldigingsbundel vir Christo van Rensburg Pont* Pretoria: Van Schaik

Cassese A (2003) *International Criminal Law* Oxford, New York: Oxford University Press

Cassese A (2007) 'On some problematical aspects of the crime of aggression' in T Skouteris and A Vermeer-Kunzli (eds) *The Protection of the Individual in International Law: Essays in Honour of John Dugard* Cambridge: Cambridge University Press

Cassese A (2008) *International Criminal Law* Oxford, New York: Oxford University Press

Cassese A (ed-in-chief) (2009) *The Oxford Companion to International Criminal Justice* Oxford: Oxford University Press

Cassese A and Gaeta P (2013) *International Criminal Law* 3 ed Oxford: Oxford University Press

Cassese A et al (eds) (2002) *The Rome Statute of the International Criminal Court: A Commentary Vol 1* Oxford, New York: Oxford University Press

Cassese A et al (eds) (2002) *The Rome Statute of the International Criminal Court: A Commentary Vol 2* Oxford, New York: Oxford University Press

Cassese A, Gaeta P, Baig L, Fan M, Gosnell C & Whiting A (2013) *International Criminal Law* 3 ed (2013) Oxford: Oxford University Press

Concise Oxford English Dictionary (2002) 10th ed (edited by Pearsall) Oxford: Oxford University Press

Cronje DSP and Heaton J (2008) *Die Suid-Afrikaanse Personereg* 3 ed Durban: LexisNexis

Cryer R, Friman H, Robinson D and Wilmshurst E (2007) *An Introduction to International Criminal Law and Procedure* Cambridge: Cambridge University Press

Currie I and De Waal J (2013) *The Bill of Rights Handbook* 6 ed Cape Town: Juta

Davis D and Cassim F (eds) (2011) *Companies and Other Business Structures in South Africa* 2 ed Cape Town: Oxford University Press

De Koker L (1999) *KPMG Money Laundering Control Service Vol 1* (revision service 2007) Durban: LexisNexis Butterworths

De Koker L (1999) *South African Money Laundering and Terror Financing Law* (loose-leaf updated regularly) Durban: LexisNexis

Derby DH (1999) 'Torture' in MC Bassiouni *International Criminal Law Vol I* 2 ed New York: Transnational

Derrett JDM (1998) *Law and Morality* Pilkington Press

De Wet JC and Swanepoel HL (1949) *Strafreg* Durban: Butterworths

De Wet JC and Swanepoel HL (1960) *Die Suid-Afrikaanse Strafreg* 2 ed Durban: Butterworths

De Wet JC and Swanepoel HL (1975) *Strafreg* 3 ed Durban: Butterworths

De Wet JC and Swanepoel HL (1985) *Strafreg* 4 ed Durban: Butterworths

Duff RA (1996) 'Subjectivism, objectivism and criminal attempts' in AP Simester and ATH Smith (eds) *Harm and Culpability* Oxford: Clarendon Press

Dugard J with contributions by Bethlehem D, Du Plessis M and Katz A (2005) *International Law: A South African Perspective* 3 ed Cape Town: Juta

Dugard J (2011) *International Law: A South African Perspective* 4 ed Cape Town: Juta

Dunér B (ed) (1998) *An End to Torture: Strategies for its Eradication* London, New York: Zed Books

Du Plessis J and Lubbe G (eds) (2013) *A Man of Principle: The Life and Legacy of JC de Wet* Cape Town: Juta

Durbach A (1999) *Upington: A Story of Trials and Reconciliation* St Leonards, NSW: Allen and Unwin

Du Toit E et al (1987) *Commentary on the Criminal Procedure Act* Appendix B 'International and Transnational Criminal Procedure' (revision service 59, 2017)

Elliott C (2013) 'France' in A Reed and M Bohlander *Participation in Crime: Domestic and Comparative Perspectives* Farnham: Ashgate

Evans EP (1906) *The Criminal Prosecution and Capital Punishment of Animals* London: W Heineman

Faure MG and Neethling J (eds) (2003) *Aansprakelijkheid, Risico en Onderneming: Europese en Zuid-Afrikaanse Perspectieven* Antwerpen: Intersentia

Ferdinandusse WN (2006) *Direct Application of International Criminal Law in National Courts* The Hague: TMC Asser Press

Feuerbach PJA (1801) *Lehrbuch des Gemeinen in Deutschland Gültigen Peinlichen Rechts* Giessen: Georg Friedrich Heyer

Gaeta P (2009) 'International criminalization of prohibited conduct' in A Cassese (ed-in-chief) *The Oxford Companion to International Criminal Justice* Oxford: Oxford University Press

Gevers C (2012) 'Immunity and the implementation legislation of South Africa, Uganda and Kenya' in K Ambos and OA Maunganidze (eds) *Power and Prosecution: Challenges and Opportunities for International Criminal Justice in SubSaharan Africa* Portland, OR: Hart

Gevers C (2014) 'International criminal law and individualism: An African perspective' in C Schwobel (ed) *Critical Approaches to International Criminal Law: An Introduction* Milton Park, Abingdon, Oxon; New York, NY: Routledge, Taylor and Francis Group

Gevers C and Du Plessis M (2011) 'Blagojevic and Jokic' in G Sluiter and A Klip (eds) *Annotated Leading Cases of International Criminal Tribunals* student ed Vol XXIV Antwerpen: Intersentia

Gordon GH (1978) *The Criminal Law of Scotland* 2 ed Edinburgh: Scottish Universities Law Institute

Gross H (1979) *A Theory of Criminal Justice* New York: Oxford University Press; Solna, Sweden: Stockholm International Peace Research Institute

Hahlo HR and Kahn E (1973) *The South African Legal System and Its Background* Cape Town: Juta

Hart HLA and Honoré AM (1959) *Causation in the Law* Oxford: Clarendon Press

Hart HLA and Honoré T (1985) *Causation in the Law* 2 ed Oxford: Clarendon Press

Herring J (2013) 'Victims as defendants: When victims participate in crimes against themselves' in A Reed and M Bohlander (eds) *Participation in Crime: Domestic Comparative and International Perspectives* Farnham, Surrey: Ashgate

Hiemstra VG and Gonin HL (1992) *Trilingual Legal Dictionary* 3ed Cape Town: Juta

Hiemstra VG and Kruger A (2008) *Hiemstra's Criminal Procedure* 6 ed (regular updates) Durban: LexisNexis

Hoctor SV (2008) 'A peregrination through the law of provocation' in JJ Joubert (ed) *Essays in Honour of CR Snyman/Huldigingsbundel vir CR Snyman* Pretoria: University of South Africa

Hoctor SV and Cooper WE (2008) *Cooper's Motor Law. Criminal Liability, Administrative Adjudication and Medico-Legal Aspects* 2 ed (loose-leaf) Cape Town: Juta

Horder J (1992) *Provocation and Responsibility* Oxford, England: Oxford University Press

Hunt PMA and Milton JRL (1996) *South African Criminal Law and Procedure: Common Law Crimes* 3 ed Kenwyn: Juta

Jessberger F (2009) 'National legislation on international crimes' in A Cassese (ed-in-chief) *The Oxford Companion to International Criminal Justice* Oxford: Oxford University Press

Jörg N, Kelk C and Klip AH (2012) *Strafrecht Met Mate* 2 ed Alphen aan den Rijn: Tjeenk Willink

Joubert C (2013) *Applied Law for Police Officials* 4 ed Claremont: Juta

Joubert JJ (ed) (2008) *Essays in Honour of CR Snyman/Huldigingsbundel vir CR Snyman* Pretoria: University of South Africa

Joubert JJ (ed) et al (2017) *Criminal Procedure Handbook* 12 ed Cape Town: Juta

Joubert WA and Faris JA (eds) (2011) *Law of South Africa* (*LAWSA*) 2 ed vol 6 Durban: LexisNexis

Joyner K (ed) (2010) *Aspects of Forensic Medicine: An Introduction for Healthcare Professionals* Cape Town: Juta

Justinian I and Thomas JAC (1797) *The Institutes of Justinian: Text, Translation and Commentary Part II* Reprinted in 1975 Oxford : North-Holland

Kaliski S (ed) (2006) *Psycholegal Assessment in South Africa* Cape Town; New York: Oxford University Press

Kemp G (2003) 'Toerekening, sanksionering en strafregtelike aanspreeklikheid van regspersone in Suid-Afrikaanse perspektief' in MG Faure and J Neethling (eds) *Aansprakelijkheid, Risico en Onderneming: Europese en Zuid-Afrikaanse Perspectieven* Antwerpen: Intersentia

Kemp G (2013) 'Nullum crimen sine lege: Hoe staan dit nou in ons reg? in J Du Plessis and G Lubbe (eds) *A Man of Principle: The Life and Legacy of JC De Wet* Cape Town: Juta

Kemp G (2016) *Individual Criminal Liability for the International Crime of Aggression* 2ed Cambridge: Intersentia/Cambridge University Press

Kidd M and Hoctor S (eds) (2012) *Stella Juris: Celebrating 100 Years of Teaching Law in Pietermaritzburg* Cape Town: Juta

Kleffner JK (2008) *Complementarity in the Rome Statute and National Criminal Jurisdictions* Oxford, New York: Oxford University Press

Knoops GJ (2008) *Defenses in Contemporary International Criminal Law* 2 ed Leiden: Koninklijke Brill NV

Kress C (2009) 'The International Criminal Court as a turning point in the history of international criminal justice' in A Cassese (ed-in-chief) *The Oxford Companion to International Criminal Justice* Oxford: Oxford University Press

Kress C and Sluiter G (2002) 'Imprisonment' in A Cassese, P Gaeta and JRWD Jones (eds) *The Rome Statute of the International Criminal Court: A Commentary Vol II* Oxford, New York: Oxford University Press

Kruger A (1980) *Mental Health Law in South Africa* Durban: Butterworths

Kruger A (2008) *Organised Crime and Proceeds of Crime Law in South Africa* Durban: LexisNexis

Landman AA and Landman WJ (2014) *A Practitioner's Guide to the Mental Health Care Act* Cape Town: Juta

Le Roux-Kemp A (2011) *Law, Power and the Doctor-Patient Relationship* Saarbrücken: VDM Publishing House

Loubser M and Midgley R (eds) (2012) *The Law of Delict in South Africa* 2 ed Cape Town; Oxford: Oxford University Press

Louw R (2006) 'Principles of criminal law: Pathological and non-pathological criminal incapacity' in S Kalisky (ed) *Psycholegal Assessment in South Africa* Cape Town; New York: Oxford University Press

Maasdorp AFS and Hall CF (1947) *Maasdorp's Institutes of South African Law Vol 1* 7 ed Cape Town: Juta

Matthaeus A (1994) *De Criminibus, On Crimes: A Commentary on Books XLVII and XLVIII of the Digest* Cape Town: Juta

McDougall C (2013) *The Crime of Aggression Under the Rome Statute of the International Criminal Court* Cambridge: Cambridge University Press

Meiring, J (ed) (2017) *South Africa's Constitution at Twenty-One* Cape Town: Penguin Random House

Mill JS (1859) *On Liberty* 2 ed Todmorden, UK: JW Parker and Sons

Milton JRL, Cowling MG and Hoctor SV (eds) (1988) *South African Criminal Law and Procedure* (Statutory Offences) Vol III 2 ed (revision service 27, 2017)

Moorman J and Van Hasselt JJ (1770) *Verhandelinge over de Misdaden en der Selver Straffen* 2 ed Arnhem: Jakob Nyhoff

Moyn S (2017) *Human Rights And The Uses Of History* 2 ed New York: Verso

Neethling J and Potgieter JM (2010) *Neethling-Potgieter-Visser Law of Delict* 6 ed Durban: Butterworths

Neethling J, Potgieter JM and Visser PJ (1994) *Law of Delict* 2 ed Durban: Butterworths

O'Connell RL (1989) *Of Arms and Men: A History of War, Weapons, and Aggression* New York: Oxford University Press

Olivier NJJ et al (1995) *Indigenous Law* Durban: Butterworths

Ormerod DC (2011) *Smith and Hogan's Criminal Law* 13 ed Oxford, New York: Oxford University Press

Osiel MJ (1999) *Obeying Orders: Atrocity, Military Discipline and the Law of War* New Brunswick, NJ: Transaction

Packer HL (1968) *The Limits of the Criminal Sanction* Stanford, Calif.: Stanford University Press

Rabie MA, Strauss SA and Mare MC (1994) *Punishment: An Introduction to Principles* 5 ed Cape Town: Lex Patria

Reed A and Bohlander M (eds) (2013) *Participation in Crime: Domestic Comparative and International Perspectives* Farnham, Surrey: Ashgate

Robinson D (2010) 'The two liberalisms of international criminal law' in C Stahn and L Van den Herik (eds) *Future Perspectives on International Criminal Justice* The Hague: TMC Asser Press

Robinson N (1960) *The Genocide Convention: A Commentary* Institute of Jewish Affairs, World Jewish Congress

Roederer C and Moellendorf D (2004) *Jurisprudence* Cape Town: Juta

Sadat LN (2002) *The International Criminal Court and the Transformation of International Law: Justice for the New Millennium* Ardsley, NY: Transnational

Sands, P (2016) *East West Street: On the origins of Genocide and Crimes Against Humanity*

Schabas WA (2001) *An Introduction to the International Criminal Court* Cambridge; New York: Cambridge University Press

Schabas WA (2009) *Genocide in International Law: The Crime of Crimes* 2 ed Cambridge; New York: Cambridge University Press

Schabas WA (2016) *The International Criminal Court: A Commentary on the Rome Statute* Oxford, New York: Oxford University Press

Schärf, W and Nina, D (eds) (2001) *The Other Law: Non-state ordering in South Africa*

Schmidt E (1995) *Einfuhrung in die Geschichte der Deutschen Strafrechtspflege* Göttingen: Vandenhoeck and Ruprecht

Schwikkard PJ and Van der Merwe SE (2009) *Principles of Evidence* 3 ed Wetton: Juta

Schwikkard PJ and Van der Merwe SE (2016) *Principles of Evidence* 4 ed Wetton: Juta

Schwobel C (ed) (2014) *Critical Approaches to International Criminal Law: An Introduction* Milton Park, Abingdon, Oxon; New York, NY: Routledge, Taylor and Francis Group

Scott, GR (1954) *The History of Torture Throughout the Ages* London: Torchstream Books

Shaw MN (2008) *International Law* 6 ed Cambridge; New York: Cambridge University Press

Shraga D (2009) 'Mixed or internationalized courts' in A Cassese (ed-in-chief) *The Oxford Companion to International Criminal Justice* Oxford: Oxford University Press

Sikkink K (2011) *The Justice Cascade: How Human Rights Prosecutions Are Changing World Politics* New York: WW Norton & Co.

Simester AP, Du Bois-Pedain, A and Neumann, U (eds) (2014) *Liberal Criminal Theory: Essays for Andreas von Hirsch* Oxford: Hart

Simester AP and Smith ATH (eds) (1995) *Harm and Culpability* Oxford: Clarendon Press

Simpson GJ (2004) *War Crimes Law Vol 1* Burlington, VT: Ashgate/Dartmouth

Simpson GJ (2007) *Law, War and Crime: War Crimes Trials and the Reinvention of International Law* Cambridge: Polity

Skeen A st Q and Hoctor S (2011) 'Criminal law' in Joubert WA and Faris JA (eds) *Law of South Africa Encyclopaedia* (*LAWSA*) 2 ed vol 6 Durban: LexisNexis

Skouter T and Vermeer-Kunzli A (eds) (2007) *The Protection of the Individual in International Law: Essays in Honour of John Dugard* Cambridge: Cambridge University Press

Smith JC and Hogan B (1965) *Criminal Law* New York, NY: Oxford University Press

Snyman CR (1981) *Strafreg* Durban: Butterworths

Snyman CR (2003) 'The tension between legal theory and policy considerations in the general principles of criminal law' in J Burchell and A Erasmus (eds) *Criminal Justice in a New Society: Essays in Honour of Solly Leeman* Cape Town: Juta

Snyman CR (2014) *Criminal Law* 6 ed Durban: LexisNexis

Stahn C and Van den Herik L (eds) (2010) *Future Perspectives on International Criminal Justice* The Hague: TMC Asser Press

Stessens G (2000) *Money Laundering: A New International Law Enforcement Model* Cambridge; New York: Cambridge University Press

Stoitchkova D (2010) *Towards Corporate Liability in International Criminal Law* Portland, OR: Intersentia

Strydom, H et al (2016) *International Law*

Sunga LS (1997) *The Emerging System of International Criminal Law: Developments in Codification and Implementation* The Hague: Kluwer Law International

Swart B (2002) 'General problems' in A Cassese et al (eds) *The Rome Statute of the International Criminal Court: A Commentary* Oxford, New York: Oxford University Press

Tapper CFH (ed) (1981) *Crime, Proof and Punishment: Essays in Memory of Sir Rupert Cross* London: Butterworths

Terblanche SS (2007) *Guide to Sentencing in South Africa* 2 ed Durban: Butterworths

Terblanche SS (2016) *A Guide to Sentencing in South Africa* 3 ed Durban: Butterworths

Tredoux C et al (2005) *Psychology and Law* Cape Town: Juta

Van den Wyngaert C (2011) *Strafrecht en Strafprocesrecht* 8 ed Antwerpen, Apeldoorn: Maklu

Van den Wyngaert C and Vandromme S (2014) *Strafrecht en Strafprocesrecht in Hoofdlijnen: Boek 1: Strafrecht* 9 ed

Van den Wyngaert C, Van Dromme S and De Smet B (2014) *Strafrecht en Strafprocesrecht (in Hoofdlijnen)* 9 ed Belgium: Makla

Van der Berg J (2012) *Bail: A Practitioner's Guide* 3 ed Cape Town: Juta

Van der Walt AJ (2005) *Constitutional Property Law* Cape Town: Juta

Van Schaak B and Slye RC (2007) *A Concise History of International Criminal Law: Chapter 1 of Understanding International Criminal Law* Santa Clara University Legal Studies Research Paper No. 07–42, 11

Van Sliedregt E (2012) *Individual Criminal Responsibility in International Law* Oxford; New York: Oxford University Press

Von Bar CL et al (1916) *Geschichte des Deutschen Strafrechts / A History of Continental Criminal Law* (translated by TS Bell et al) Boston: Little Brown

Vormbaum T and Bohlander M (eds) (2013) *A Modern History of German Criminal Law* (translated by M Hiley) Berlin: Springer

Watt JM and Breyer-Brandwijk MG (1962) *The Medicinal and Poisonous Plants of Southern and Eastern Africa* 2 ed Edinburgh: Livingstone

Werle G and Jessberger F (2014) *Principles of International Criminal Law* 3 ed Oxford: Oxford University Press

Werle G and Vormbaum M (eds) (2017) *The African Criminal Court – A Commentary on the Malabo Protocol*

Williams GL (1961) *Criminal Law: The General Part* 2 ed London: Stevens

Zeffert DT and Paizes AP (2017) *The South African Law of Evidence* 3 ed Durban: LexisNexis

Journal articles

Ally D and Viljoen F (2003) Homicide in defence of property in an age of constitutionalism *SACJ* 16(2):121

Alvarez JE (1999) Crimes of states/crimes of hate: Lessons from Rwanda *Yale J Intl L* 24(2):365

Ambos K (2010) The crime of aggression after Kampala *GYIL* 53:463

Archbishop Desmond Tutu, quoted in Roche, D (2002) Restorative justice and the Regulatory state in South African townships *Brit J Crim* 42(3):514, at 520

Ast S (2010) The *Gäfgen* judgment of the European Court of Human Rights: On the consequences of the threat of torture for criminal proceedings *GLJ* 11:1393

Barries GN (2013) The divergent constitutional approach to hate speech in South Africa and the United States *TSAR* 4:697–707

Bassiouni MC (1997) From Versailles to Rwanda in seventy-five years: The need to establish a permanent international criminal court *Harv Hum Rts* J 10:9

Bateman C (2015) Euthanasia in SA – sacrificing one to render many vulnerable? *SAMJ* 105(10):801

Benatar SR (1992) Dying and 'euthanasia' *SAMJ* 82(1):35

Berger MA and Solan LM (2008) The uneasy relationship between science and law: An essay and introduction *Brook L Rev* 73(3):847

Berman PS (1994) Rats, pigs and statues on trial: The creation of cultural narratives in the prosecution of animals and inanimate objects *NYU L Rev* 69(2):288

Blackbeard M (1996) Epilepsy and criminal liability *SACJ* 9(2):191

Boister N (1993) Causation at the death? *Clarke v Hurst* 1992 (2) SA 676 (D) *THRHR* 56:516

Boister N (1993) General principles of liability: *Dolus Eventualis SACJ* 9(2):226

Borg-Jorgensen V and Van der Linde KE (2011) Corporate criminal liability in South Africa: time for change? (Part 1) *TSAR* (3):452; (Part 2) *TSAR* (4):684

Botha J and Govindjee A (2014) Regulating cases of extreme hate speech in South Africa: A suggested framework for a legislated criminal sanction *SACJ* 27(2):117–155

Burchell J (1990) Criminal law: *S v Nzo* (1990) 3 SA 1 (A) common purpose liability *SACJ* 3:345

Burchell J (2014) Protecting dignity under common law and the Constitution: The significance of *crimen iniuria* in South African criminal law *SACJ* 27(3):250–271

Cameron E (1988) Inferential reasoning and extenuation in the case of the Sharpeville Six *SACJ* 1(2):243

Campbell K (2013) The making of global legal culture and international criminal law *LJIL* 26:155–172

Carnelly M and Hoctor S (2004) Bestiality: The paradox of the 'paragon of animals' *Obiter* 2:506

Carstens P (2013) Revisiting the relationship between *dolus eventualis* and *luxuria* in the context of vehicular collisions causing the death of fellow passengers and/or pedestrians: *S v Humphreys* 2013 (2) SACR 1 (SCA) *SACJ* 26(1):67

Cartwright R (2004) Sleepwalking violence: A sleep disorder, a legal dilemma, and a psychological challenge *Am J Psychiatry* 16(7):1149

Cassel D (2008) Corporate aiding and abetting of human rights violations: Confusion in the courts *JHR* 6(2):304

Cassese A (1998) Reflections on international criminal justice *Mod L Rev* 61(1):1

Cassese A (1999) The Statute of the International Criminal Court: Some preliminary reflections *EJIL* 10(1):144

Christie, GC (1991) Current trends in the American law of punitive damages *Anglo-Am L Rev* 20(3):349

Convention against Torture and Other Cruel, Inhuman or Degrading Treatment or Punishment (Draft Convention) (1984) *ILM* 23(5):1027 with changes in (1985) *ILM* 24(2):535

Cornell, D and Van Marle, K (2005) Exploring ubuntu: Tentative reflections *Afr Hum Rts L J* 5(2):195, at 205–206

Crotty HD (1924) The history of insanity as a defence to crime in English criminal law *Cal L Rev* 12(2):105

Dendy M (2006) Watching your back: A guide to Fica and Poca *De Rebus* 33

Dörfling DF (1993) Eutanasie: Die reg van die curator personae om verdere behandeling van 'n pasient te verbied: 'n Nuwe regverdigingsgrond in die Suid-Afrikaanse reg *TSAR* 2:345

Dugard J (1996) Is the truth and reconciliation process compatible with international law: An unanswered question *Azapo v President of the Republic of South Africa SAJHR* 13(2):258

Dugard J and Abraham G (2002) Public international law *Ann Surv S African L* 140

Du Plessis A (2004) When can I fire? Use of lethal force to defend property *SACQ* 8:1 available online at: https://journals.assaf.org.za/sacq/article/view/1038

Du Plessis GA (2013) Feticide: Creating a statutory crime in South African law *Stell LR* 24(1):73

Du Plessis M (2007) South Africa's implementation of the ICC Statute: An African example *JICJ 5(2)*:460

Du Toit L (2012) From consent to coercive circumstances: Rape law reform on trial *SAJHR* 28(3):380

Eisenstat, S (2004) 'Revenge, justice and law: Recognizing the victim's desire for vengeance as a justification for punishment' 50(4) *Wayne L. Rev* 1115

Erasmus MG and Kemp G (2002) The application of international criminal law before domestic courts in the light of recent developments in international and constitutional law *SAYIL* 27:64

Fazio CA and Comito JL (1999) Rethinking the tough sentencing of teenage neonaticide offenders in the United States *Fordham L Rev* 67(6):3109

Fellingham R, Guidozzi Y and Gardner J (2012) The 'war on drugs' has failed: Is decriminalisation of drug use a solution to the problem in South Africa? *SAJBL* 5(2):78

Fernandez L and Heinrich B (2014) Die strafbarkeit des strafverteidigers wegen geldwäsche durch annahme des honorars nach Südafrikanischem und Deutschem recht *ZStW* 126(2):382

Gevers C (2013) *Southern African Litigation Centre and Another v NDPP and Others:* Note *SALJ* 130(2):293

Gevers C, Du Plessis M and Wallis A (2012) Sixty years in the making. Better late than never? The implementation of the Geneva Conventions Act *AYIHL* 185

Glennon MJ (2010) The blank-prose crime of aggression *Yale J Intl L* 35(1):71

Goliath, P (2016) Protecting victims of human trafficking – Is South Africa doing enough? *De Rebus* 562:22

Goolam MI (2006) The cartoon controversy: A note on freedom of expression, hate speech and blasphemy *CILSA 39(2)*:333

Goredema C (2001) Legislation in South Africa, Swaziland and Zimbabwe to combat organised crime *Monograph* 56

Haan V (2005) The development of the concept of joint criminal enterprise at the International Criminal Tribunal for the former Yugoslavia *Int'l Crim L Rev* 5(2):167

Hall CK (1998) The first proposal for a permanent international criminal court *IRRC* 322:57

Hardisty JH (1973) Mental illness: A legal fiction *Wash L Rev* 48:735

Heine G (1998) New developments in Europe: Can Europeans learn from the American experience or vice versa? *St Louis-Warsaw Transatlantic Law Journal* 173

Heyns C (1990) Reasonableness in a divided society *SALJ* 107(2):279

Hoctor S (2004) Dignity, criminal law and the Bill of Rights *SALJ* 121(2):304

Hoctor S (2007) Recent cases: Specific crimes *SACJ* 20(1):78

Hoctor S (2008) The concept of *dolus eventualis* in South African law: An historical perspective *Fundamina* 14(2):14

Hoctor S (2009) Specific crimes: Case review *SACJ* 22(1):88

Hoctor S (2012) Examining the expanding crime of robbery *SACJ* 25(3):361

Hoctor S (2013) Death on the roads and *dolus eventualis*: *S v Humphreys* 2013 (2) SACR 1 (SCA) *SACJ* 26(1):75

Hoctor S (2013) The crime of defamation: Still defensible in a modern constitutional democracy? *Obiter* 34(1):125

Hoctor S (2013) The nature of the crime of arson in South African law *Fundamina* 19(2):321

Hoctor S (2016) General principles and specific offences *SACJ* 29(1):54

Hoctor S (2016) General principles and specific offences *SACJ* 29(3):339

Hoctor, SV (2006) Comparing criminal law rules: A role for customary law concepts?' *Fundamina* 12(1):168

Hoexter C (1989) The administration of justice, defence, indemnities and standing *SACJ* 2(3):346

Iroanya RO (2014) Human trafficking with specific reference to South African and Mozambican counter-trafficking legislation *Acta Crim* 27(2):102

Jalloh C (2009) Universal jurisdiction, universal prescription? A preliminary assessment of the African Union perspective on universal jurisdiction *Crim L F* 21:1

Jalloh, C (2013) What makes a crime against humanity a crime against humanity? *Am U Int'l L Rev* 28(2):381

Jareborg N (2005) Criminalization as last resort (*Ultima Ratio*) *OSJCL* 2(2):521

Jochnik C and Normand R (1994) The legitimization of violence: A critical history of the laws of war *Harv Intl L J* 35(1):49

Jordaan L (2017) Recent cases *SACJ* 1:74–80

Joubert AF, Verschoor T and Van Rensburg PHJJ (1997) Epilepsy and the law *Med & L* 16(4):769

Kaime, T (2009) The African Children's Charter: Does it represent a relevant vision of childhood and children's rights? *CLRJ* 29:11–29

Kaplan A (1992) On Alain Finkielkraut's 'Remembering in vain': The Klaus Barbie trial and crimes against humanity *Crit Inq* 19(1):70

Kemp GP (1998) Die grondwetlikheid van statutêre vermoedens *Stell LR* 9(1):106

Kemp GP (2001) The United Nations Convention Against Transnational Organized Crime: A milestone in international criminal law *SACJ* 14(2):152

Kemp GP (2002) The Prevention of Corruption Bill in international perspective *Obiter* 23(1):150

Kemp, G (2017) South Africa's (possible) withdrawal from the ICC and the future of the criminalization and prosecution of crimes against humanity, war crimes and genocide under domestic law: A submission informed by historical, normative and policy considerations *Wash U Global Stud L Rev* 16(3):411

Koh KL (1968) Consent and sexual offences *Crim L R* 81

Krause S (2012) Killing in defence of property: A constitutional approach *TSAR* 3:469

Kress, C (2010) On the outer limits of crimes against humanity: The concept of organization within the policy requirement: Some reflections on the March 2010 ICC Kenya Decision *LJIL* 23(4):855

Kreston SS (2014) Human trafficking legislation in South Africa: Consent, coercion and consequences *SACJ* 27(1):20

Kruger, B (2016) Towards a sharp prosecution sword to combat human trafficking: Comparing the new South African counter-trafficking law with international prosecution standards *CILSA* 49(1):53

Krzan B (2010) Frieden und gerechtigkeit nach der Kampala-Konferenz *AVR* 467

Khumalo K (2017) Towards resuscitating the ailing public violence jurisprudence – lessons from history *SACJ* 1:23–37

Labuschagne JMT (1978) Die klagte by seksmisdade *De Jure* 11:18

Labuschagne JMT (1986) Dekriminalisasie van homo- en soofilie *TRW* 11(2):167

Labuschagne JMT (1988) Dekriminalisasie van eutanasie *THRHR* 51:167

Labuschagne JMT (1992) Menslike outonomie en staatlike majestas: Opmerkinge oor die dekriminalisasie van hoogverraad *SACJ* 5(2):117

Labuschagne JMT and Van den Heever JA (1991) Die oorsprong van en die onderskeid tussen die fenomene misdaad en delik in primigene regstelsels *Obiter* 80

Labuschagne JMA and Van den Heever JA (1995) Liability arising from the killing of a fellow human being in South African indigenous law *Comp & Int'l LJ S Afr* 28:422

Lagodny O (1999) Human dignity and its impact on German substantive criminal law and criminal procedure *Is L R* 33(3):575

Larsen JV (2011) Active euthanasia – potential abuse in South Africa: Correspondence *SAMJ* 101(4):214

Le Grange, L (2016) 'Decolonising the university curriculum' *SAJHE* 30(2):1, at 3, available at http://dx.doi.org/10.20853/30-2-709

Le Roux A (2007) Medico-legal aspects regarding drunk driving *SACJ* 20(2):220

Le Roux J (2010) Private defence: Strict conditions to be satisfied – *Govender v Minister of Safety and Security* 2009 (2) SACR 87 (N) *THRHR* 73(2):328

Le Roux J and Nel PW (2010) 'n Kritiese perspektief op die rol van amnesie by die vasstelling van strafregtelike aanspreeklikheid *De Jure* 43(1):20

Le Roux J and Stevens GP (2012) Pathological criminal incapacity and the conceptual interface between law and medicine *SACJ* 25(1):44, at 48

Le Roux-Kemp A and Horne CS (2011) An analysis of the wording, interpretation and development of the provisions dealing with the use of lethal force in effecting an arrest in South African criminal procedure *SACJ* 24(3):266

Le Roux-Kemp A and Wilkinson J (2012) Novel application of the hydrostatic test in determining live (non)-birth *SACJ* 25(2):271

Lippman, M (1994) The development and drafting of the United Nations Convention Against Torture and Other Cruel, Inhuman or Degrading Treatment or Punishment 17(2) *BC Int'l & Comp L Rev* 17(2):275

Lippman M (1998) The Convention on the Prevention and Punishment of the Crime of Genocide: Fifty years later *Ariz J Int'l & Comp L* 15(2):415

Logan, A (2010) 'Women and the provision of criminal justice advice: Lessons from England and Wales 1944–1964' *Brit J of Crim* 50(6):1077

Lötter, S (1999) The decriminalization of cannabis: Hallucination or reality? *SACJ* 12(2):184

Malherbe R and Venter R (2011) Die reg op lewe, die waarde van menslike lewe en die eutanasie-vraagstuk *TSAR* 3:466

Manyathi-Jele N (2015) Analysis of the human trafficking awareness index report *De Rebus* 9–11

Matua M (1997) Never again: Questioning the Yugoslav and Rwanda Tribunals *Temple Intl Comp L J* 11:167

McQuoid-Mason D (2005) Pacemakers and 'living wills': Does turning down a pacemaker to allow death with dignity constitute murder? *SACJ* 18(1):24

Megret F (2001) Three dangers for the International Criminal Court: A critical look at a consensual project *Finnish Y B I L* 12:193

Milanovic M (2011) Is the Rome Statute binding on individuals? (and why we should care) *JICJ* 9(1):25

Milton JRL (1968) Killing in defence of property: An historical footnote *SALJ* 85(3):327

Morris HF (1974) A history of the adoption of codes of criminal law and procedure in British colonial Africa 1876–1935 *J Afr L* 18(1):6

Moynier G (1872) Note sur la création d'une institution judiciaire internationale propre à prévenir et à réprimer les infractions à la Convention de Genève *Bulletin International des Sociétés de Secours aux Militaires Blessés* 3(11):122

'NADEL discuss decolonisation of the law at AGM' *De Rebus*, 1 May 2017, available at http://www.derebus.org.za/nadel-discuss-decolonisation-law-agm/

Naidoo K and Karels MG (2016) Prosecuting 'hate': An overview of problem areas relating to hate crimes and challenges to criminal litigation *JJS* 41(1):65–82

Naylor, B and Saunders, B (2009) Whose rights? Children, parents and discipline *Alt L J* 34(2):80–85

O'Keefe R (2004) Universal jurisdiction: Clarifying the basic concept *JICJ* 2(3):735

O'Shea A (1999) The Statute of the International Criminal Court *SALJ* 116(2):243

Paizes A (1988) *Dolus eventualis* reconsidered *SALJ* 105(4):636

Paizes A (1988) Intoxication through the looking glass *SALJ* 105(4):776

Paizes A (2013) *Dolus eventualis* revisited: *S v Humphreys* 2013 (2) SACR 1 (SCA) *CJR* 1:6

Paizes A (2014) *Dolus eventualis* again *CJR* 1:11

Paizes A (2014) Factual causation: Which 'conditio' must be 'sine qua non?' A critical discussion of the decision in *Lee v Minister for Correctional Services SALJ* 131(3):500

Paizes A (2016) *Dolus eventualis*: Two more decisions by the Supreme Court of Appeal *CJR* 1:7

Palmer R (2012) Combating grand corruption: Should it be an international crime? *OSISA* 2:30

Pantazis A (2001) Criminal law: Case law *Ann Surv S African L* 689

Phelps K (2008) A dangerous precedent indeed: A response to CR Snyman's note on Masiya *SALJ* 125(4):648;

Price A (2014) Factual causation after Lee *SALJ* 131(3):491

Rabie MA (1976) Die strafteorieë: 'n Oorsig *Crime, Punishment and Correction 2:33*

Rabie MA (1971) The doctrine of common purpose in criminal law *SALJ* 88(1):334

Report of the Secretary-General Pursuant to Paragraph 2 of Security Council Resolution 808 (1993) UN SC Doc S/25704 (1993) *ILM* 32:1163

Robinson D (2008) The identity crisis of international criminal law *LJIL* 21(4):925

Roche, D (2002) Restorative justice and the Regulatory state in South African townships *Brit J Crim* 42(3):514

Roy, A (2018) 'Postcolonial theory and law: A critical introduction' *Adel L Rev* 29(2):315

Sadat LN and Carden SR (2000) The new International Criminal Court: An uneasy revolution *Geo L J* 88(3):381

Sarooshi D (1999) The Statute of the International Criminal Court *ICLQ* 48(2):387

Saunders BJ (2013) Ending the physical punishment of children by parents in the English-speaking world: The impact of language, tradition and law *Int'l J Child Rts* 21(2):278–304

Schabas WA (2002) Punishment of non-state actors in non-international armed conflict *Fordham Intl L J* 26(4):907

Schabas, WA (2008) State policy as an element of international crimes *JCLC* 98(3):953

Schuster M (2003) The Rome Statute and the crime of aggression: A Gordian knot in search of a sword *Criminal Law Forum* 14(1):1

Schwarzenberger G (1950) The problem of an international criminal law *Curr Legal Probs* 3(1):263

Seto, TP (2002) The morality of terrorism *Loy L A L Rev* 35(4):1227

Skelton A (2013) Proposals for the review of the minimum age of criminal responsibility *SACJ* 26(3):257

Slovenko R (1984) The meaning of mental illness in criminal responsibility *J Legal Med* 5(1):37

Sloth-Nielsen J and Gallinetti J (2011) 'Just say sorry?' *Ubuntu*, Africanisation and the child system in the Child Justice Act 75 of 2008 *PELJ* 14(4):63

Smith PT (1979) Recklessness in *dolus eventualis SALJ* 96(1):81

Snyman CR (2004) Private defence in criminal law: An unwarranted raising of the test of unreasonableness *THRHR* 67:325

Snyman CR (2007) Extending the scope of rape: A dangerous precedent *SALJ* 124(4):677

Snyman CR (2010) Huisbraak ten opsigte van 'n karavaan: *S v Mavungu* 2009 (1) SASV 425 (T) THRHR 73(1):158

Stahn C (2002) International law at a crossroads? The impact of September 11 *Zaö R B* 62:183

Stassen JC (1977) *S v De Blom* 1977 3 SA 513 (A) *TSAR* 3:259

Stessens G (1994) Corporate criminal liability: A comparative perspective *ICLQ* 43(3):493

Stevens GP (2014) Dealing in drugs revisited: *S v Mbatha* 2012 (2) SACR 551 (KZP): Comments *SACJ* 27(1):37

Stewart JG (2003) Towards a single definition of armed conflict in international humanitarian law: A critique of internationalized armed conflict *IRRC* 85:313

SA Strauss (1960) *Oorsaaklikheidsverband en daderskap: Moord sonder veroorsaking*? *THRHR* 23:95, 101–102

Strauss SA (1964) Bodily injury and the defence of consent *SALJ* 81(2):179

Strauss SA (1993) The right to die or passive euthanasia: One American and the other South African. Two important decisions *SACJ* 6:196

Stuart D (1970) The *actus reus* in attempts *Crim L R* 505

Taitz JL (1993) Euthanasia and the 'legal convictions of society' in a South African context *SALJ* 110:440

Tolmie J (2012) Consent to harmful assaults: The case for moving away from category based decision making *Crim L R* 656

United Nations (1984) Draft Convention against Torture and Other Cruel, Inhuman or Degrading Treatment or Punishment *ILM* 23(5)

United Nations (1985) United Nations Convention Against Torture is opened for signature *ILM* 24(2)

United Nations: Rome Statute of the International Criminal Court [adopted July 17, 1998]UN Doc No /A/CONF 183/9 *ILM* 37:999

United Nations: Secretary-General's Report (1993) Aspects of Establishing an International Tribunal for the Prosecution of Persons Responsible for Serious Violations of International Humanitarian Law Committed in the Territory of the Former Yugoslavia *ILM* 32:1163

Van den Heever P (1995) The patient's right to know: Informed consent in South African medical law *De Rebus* 53

Van der Bijl C (2014) Corporate 'assault': Bullying and the aegis of criminal law (Part 1) *TSAR* 3:482 (Part 2) *TSAR* 4:760

Van der Merwe DP (1980) Retribution in criminal law *Obiter* 43

Van der Merwe DP (1983) Die begrip verminderde toerekeningsvatbaarheid en die implementering daarvan *TRW* 8(2):172

Van der Merwe HJ (2013) 'One moment of extreme irresponsibility': Notes and comments on *Humphreys v S* and the volitional component of *dolus eventualis* in the context of dangerous or irresponsible driving *LDD* 17(1):64

Van der Merwe S and Paizes A (2013) *Dolus eventualis* revisited: *S v Humphreys* 2013 (2) SACR 1 (SCA) *CJR* 1:6

Van der Vyver JD (1967) Wederregtelikheidsbewussyn by strafregtelike aanspreeklikheid *TSAR 30:271*

Van der Walt T (2011) The use of force in effecting arrest in South Africa and the 2010 Bill: A step in the right direction? *PELJ* 14(1):138

Van der Westhuizen C (2009) An historical overview of infanticide in South Africa *Fundamina* 15(2):174

Van Drunen, D (2008) 'Natural law, the *lex talionis*, and the power of the sword' *Liberty U L Rev* 2(3):945

Van Eeden H, Hopkins K and Adendorff C (Sept 2011) Criminal liability of morally blameless corporations *De Rebus* 27

Van Oosten FFW (1980) S v Hibbert *1979 4 SA 717 (D) Aandadigheid aan selfmoord* 1980(1) *TSAR* 1:83

Van Oosten FFW (1985) Aandadigheid aan selfmoord in die Suid-Afrikaanse reg *TSAR* 2:189

Van Oosten FFW (1999) The Choice on Termination of Pregnancy Act: Some comments *SALJ* 116(1):60

Van Rooyen JCW (1974) Regsdwaling en *dolus* in die strafreg *THRHR* 37:35

Van Rooyen JH (1976) The psychopath in South African criminal and mental health law Part I *CILSA* 9(1):1

Van Sliedregt E (2007) Joint criminal enterprise as a pathway to convicting individuals for genocide *JICJ* 5(1):184

Vetten L (2014) Domestic violence in South Africa *Institute for Security Studies Policy Brief* 71

Wagner M (1999) Corporate criminal liability: National and international responses *CLB* 25(2):600–608

Walker S (2011) The requirements for criminal capacity in section 11(1) of the new Child Justice Act, 2008: A step in the wrong direction? *SACJ* 24(1):33

Walker S (2012) Determining reasonable force in cases of private defence: A comment on the approach in *S v Steyn* 2010 (1) SACR 411 (SCA) *SACJ* 25:84

Wardle B (2014) The *sub judice* rule and the Oscar Pistorius case: Will the crime of contempt of court *ex facie curiae* become abrogated by disuse? *De Rebus* 543:27

Washburn, J (1999) The negotiation of the Rome Statute for the International Criminal Court and international lawmaking in the 21st century *Pace Int'L L Rev* 11(2):361

Watney M (2013) Moord en strafbare manslag by padsterftes *S v Humphreys* 2013 2 SASV 1 (HHA) *TSAR* 4:770

Watney, M (2017) *Crimen iniuria*: Its role vis-à-vis sexual-offences legislation *TSAR* 2:405

Werle G and Bornkamm PC (2013) Torture in Zimbabwe under scrutiny in South Africa: The judgment of the North Gauteng High Court in *SALC v. National Director of Public Prosecutions JICJ* 11:659

Whiting RC (1971) The unwilling possessor of pornography *SALJ* 88(3):296

Whiting RC (1980) Principals and accessories in crime *SALJ* 97(2):199

Whiting RC (1986) Joining in *SALJ* 103(1):38

Whiting RC (1988) Thoughts on *dolus eventualis SACJ* 1(3):440

Woolaver H (2014) Prosecuting international crimes in South Africa: Interpreting the requirement of the accused's presence in South African territory under the implementation of the Rome Statute of the ICC Act *SALJ* 131(2):253.

Zimmermann H (1979) Self-determination, paternalism or human care? Suicide and criminal responsibility in South African and German law *TSAR* (3):183, at 189–190

Encyclopedias

Skeen A st Q and Hoctor S (2007) 'Criminal law' in WA Joubert and JA Faris (eds) *The Law of South Africa* 2 ed Vol 6 Durban: LexisNexis

Reports and theses

De Villiers DS (1988) *Die Strafregtelike Verantwoordelikheid van Kinders* (LLD Thesis, University of Pretoria)

Dörfling DF (1991) *'Genadedood' in die Strafreg: n Regsfilosofiese en Regsvergelykende Perspektief* (LLM Thesis, Rand Afrikaans University - now University of Johannesburg)

Kemp GP (2010) *Supreme Crimes and Outrageous Acts: Criminalisation and the Legality Principle: A South African and International Perspective* Stellenbosch University

Public Protector South Africa, Report No 6 of 2016/17, *State of Capture*, available at http://saflii.org/images/329756472-State-of-Capture.pdf

Report of the Commission of Inquiry into the Responsibility of Mentally Deranged Persons and Related Matters R.P. 69/1967

Report of the Secretary-General Pursuant to Paragraph 2 of Security Council Resolution 808 (1993) UN SC Doc S/25704

Report of the Wolfenden Committee on Homosexual Offences and Prostitution (4 Sept 1957) Cmnd 247 London: HMSO

Rumpff F (Chairman) (1967) *Report of the Commission of Inquiry into the Responsibility of Mentally Deranged Persons and Related Matters / Verslag van die Kommissie van Ondersoek na die Toerekeningsvatbaarheid van Geestelik Versteurde Persone en Aanverwante Aangeleenthede/Republiek van Suid-Afrika* Pretoria: Govt. Printer

Skelton A and Badenhorst C (2011) *The Criminal Capacity of Children in South Africa: International Developments and Considerations for Review* A Research Report Published by The Child Justice Alliance, The Children's Rights Project, Community Law Centre, University of the Western Cape

South African Law Commission (SALC) (1997) *Money laundering and Related Matters, Project 104* Pretoria: The Commission

South African Law Commission (SALC) (1997) *Sexual Offences Against Children, Project 108 Issue Paper 10* Pretoria: The Commission

South African Law Commission (SALC) (1998) *Report on Euthanasia and the Artificial Preservation of Life, Project 86* Pretoria: The Commission

South African Law Commission (SALC) (1999) *Sexual Offences: The Substantive Law Project 107* Discussion Paper 85 Pretoria: The Commission

South African Law Commission (SALC) (2002) *Project 107 Process and Procedure* Discussion Paper 102 Pretoria: The Commission

South African Law Commission (SALC) (2002) *Project 107 Sexual Offences Report* Pretoria: The Commission

South African Law Commission (SALC) (2002) *Sexual Offences Report, Project 107 Pretoria: SALC*

Transparency International Report (2009) *The Anti-Corruption Plain Language Guide* 23, available at https://www.transparency.org/whatwedo/publication/the_anti_corruption_plain_language_guide

US Department of Army *Pamphlet 27-161-2 II International Law, Applicable in Peace and War* (Oct. 23, 1962)

Van Rensburg ADJ (1970) *Juridiese Kousaliteit en Aspekte van Aanspreeklikheidsbeperking by die Onregmatige Daad* Thesis (LLD), University of South Africa

Internet sources

Additional Protocols to the Geneva Conventions, 1977, available at https://www.icrc.org/eng/assets/files/other/icrc_002_0321.pdf

Amnesty International, available at https://www.amnesty.org/en/countries/

Anderson, B (2014) Yes, torture can be justified. Here's why *The Spectator*, available at http://blogs.spectator.co.uk/coffeehouse/2014/12/there-are-certain-times-when-torture-can-be-justified/

Antisocial Personality, Sociopathy, and Psychopathy available at http://faculty.ncwc.edu/toconnor/428/428lect16.htm

AU Press Release Number 037/2012 'The African Union has a clear and unequivocal mandate to fight impunity' 15 May 2012. The Model Law is available at http://legal.au.int/en/sites/default/files/MODEL%20LAW%20FINAL-EN_0.pdf

AU Withdrawal Strategy 12 January 2017, available at https://www.hrw.org/sites/default/files/supporting_resources/icc_withdrawal_strategy_jan._2017.pdf

'*Boeremag*' case: For a useful timeline of the case, see http://www.sahistory.org.za/topic/boeremag-treason-trial-timeline

Burundi: detail on the situation and status of investigation as well as withdrawal from the ICC, available at https://www.icc-cpi.int/burundi

Chair in Customary Law at the University of Cape Town, available at https://africanlii.org/content/customary-law-bibliography

Decision under art 87(7) of the Rome Statute on the non-compliance by Jordan with the request by the court for the arrest and surrender of Omar Al-Bashir, ICC-02/05-01/09, Pre-Trial Chamber II, 11 December 2017, available at https://www.icc-cpi.int/CourtRecords/CR2017_07156.PDF

Decision under art 87(7) of the Rome Statute on the non-compliance by South Africa with the request by the court for the arrest and surrender of Omar Al-Bashir, ICC-02/05-01/09-302, Pre-Trial Chamber II, 6 July 2017, available at https://www.icc-cpi.int/CourtRecords/CR2017_04402.PDF

Declaratory Statement by the Republic of South Africa on the Decision to Withdraw from the Rome Statute of the International Criminal Court, C.N.786.2016.TREATIES-XVIII.10 (Depository Notification) (19 October 2016). Available at https://treaties.un.org/doc/Publication/CN/2016/CN.786.2016-Eng.pdf

Du Plessis A (2004) When can I fire? Use of lethal force to defend property *SA Crime Quarterly* 8:1 available at http://www.iss.org.za/pubs/CrimeQ/no.8/duPlessis.htm

Einolf CJ (2007) The fall and rise of torture: A comparative and historical analysis, available at http://www.social-sciences-and-humanities.com

Epilepsy: information available at ehealthMD.com website: http://www.ehealthmd.com/library/epilepsy/EPI_whatis.html

Financial Intelligence Centre, for the reporting of suspicious and unusual transactions relating to proceeds of unlawful activities or property that is connected to an offence relating to the financing of terrorist activities, available at http://www.fic.gov.za

Goredema C (ed) 'Legislation in South Africa, Swaziland and Zimbabwe to combat organised crime' Monograph 56 Ch 3 (June 2001) *Organised Crime in Southern Africa: Assessing Legislation* Institute for Security Studies. Available at https://issafrica.org/research/monographs/monograph-56-organised-crime-in-southern-africa-assessing-legislation-edited-by-charles-goredema

Government Gazette No 40367, GenN 698, 24 October 2016, available at http://www.justice.gov.za/legislation/hcbill/2016-HateCrimes-HateSpeechBill.pdf

Interlocutory Decision on the Applicable Law: Terrorism, Conspiracy, Homicide, Perpetration, Cumulative Charging, Appeals Chamber of the Special Tribunal for Lebanon, Case No STL-11-01/1, 16 February 2011, at par 85, available at https://www.stl-tsl.org/en/the-cases/stl-11-01/main/filings/orders-and-decisions/appeals-chamber/534-f0936

International Crimes Bill [B37-2017], available at http://www.justice.gov.za/legislation/bills/2017-b37-ICBill.pdf

International Law Commission *Draft Statute for an International Criminal Court with commentaries* 22 July 1994, available at http://www.refworld.org/docid/47fdfb40d.html

Judgment by the Landgericht Cologne, 7 May 2012, Docket No 151 Ns 169/11 – final. For a translation of the judgment and additional notes by A Aumüller and M Bohlander, see http://www.dur.ac.uk/ilm/news/itemno=14984

Kampala Review Conference (June 2010) managed to reach agreement on the definition of the crime of aggression, with states' parties essentially adopting the definition that emerged from the SWGCA. Ratified by at least 30 ICC States' Parties, available at https://treaties.un.org/Pages/ViewDetails.aspx?src=TREATY&mtdsg_no=XVIII-10-b&chapter=18&lang=en

Kemp G (2017) Grace Mugabe: Why diplomatic immunity isn't always an 'out of jail' ticket *The Conversation,* 21 August 2017, available at http://theconversation.com/grace-mugabe-why-diplomatic-immunity-isnt-always-an-out-of-jail-ticket-82721

Kenya: *Situation in the Republic of Kenya,* Case No ICC-01/09, Decision Pursuant to Article 15 of the Rome Statute on the Authorization of an Investigation into the Situation in the Republic of Kenya (31 March 2010), available at http://www.refworld.org/cases,ICC,4bc2fe372.html; *Situation in the Republic of Kenya,* Case No ICC-01/09-01/11, Decision on the Prosecutor's Application for Summons to Appear for William Samoei Ruto, Henry Kiprono Kosgey and Joshua Arap Sang (8 March 2011), available at https://www.icc-cpi.int/pages/record.aspx?uri=1037044; *Situation in the Republic of Kenya,* Case No ICC-01/09-02/11, Decision on the Prosecutor's Application for Summonses to Appear for Francis Kirimi Muthaura, Uhuru Muigai Kenyatta and Mohammed Hussein Ali (8 March 2011), available at https://www.icc-cpi.int/Pages/record.aspx?docNo=ICC-01/09-02/11-1

Le Grange, L (2016) 'Decolonising the university curriculum' *SAJHE* 30(2):1, at 3, available at http://dx.doi.org/10.20853/30-2-709

Megret F (2002) Three dangers for the International Criminal Court: A critical look at a consensual project 12 *Finnish Yearbook of International Law* 12, available at SSRN eLibrary http://ssrn.com/abstract=1156086

'NADEL discuss decolonisation of the law at AGM' *De Rebus,* 1 May 2017, available at http://www.derebus.org.za/nadel-discuss-decolonisation-law-agm/

Nomfundo M-J (June 2015) Analysis of the Human Trafficking Awareness Index Report *De Rebus* 553:9 Full Human Trafficking Awareness Index, available at http://www.lexisnexis.co.za/ruleoflaw

Organised crime in southern Africa: Assessing legislation Institute for Security Studies, available at http://www.social-sciences-and-humanities.com

Palmer R (2012) Combating grand corruption: Should it be an international crime? *Open Society Initiative for Southern Africa* 2:30, available at http://www.osisa.org/openspace/global/combating-grand-corruption-africa-robin-palmer

Practice of honour killings persists in tribal communities in many parts of the world to this day, available at http://www.amnestyusa.org/violence/honor-killings

Press Conference on Special Working Group on Crime of Aggression (UNDPI) (2009), available at http://www.icc4-cpi.int/NR/rdonlyres/9FCD3A51-6568-41DF-819F-5075C3857523/0/UNDOCPressConferenceonSWGCAENG.pdf

Prosecutor v Jean-Pierre Bemba Gombo, Case No ICC-01/05-01/08-424, Decision Pursuant to Art. 61(7)(a) and (b) of the Rome Statute on the Confirmation of the Charges, 15 June 2009, available at https://www.icc-cpi.int/Pages/record.aspx?docNo=ICC-01/05-01/08-424

Psychopaths versus sociopaths: what is the difference?, available at https://theconversation.com/psychopaths-versus-sociopaths-what-is-the-difference-45047

Public Protector South Africa, Report No 6 of 2016/17, State of Capture, available at http://saflii.org/images/329756472-State-of-Capture.pdf.

Resolution ICC-ASP/16/Res.5, 14 December 2017, available at https://asp.icc-cpi.int/iccdocs/asp_docs/Resolutions/ASP16/ICC-ASP-16-Res5-ENG.pdf

Resolution RC/Res.5, adopted at the 12th plenary meeting on 10 June 2010, Depository Notification C.N.651.2010 Treaties-6, 29 November 2010, available at https://treaties.un.org/doc/source/docs/RC-Res.5-ENG.pdf

Resolution RC/Res 6 The Crime of Aggression: Annex I Amendments to the Rome Statute of the International Criminal Court on the Crime of Aggression, available at https://treaties.un.org/doc/source/docs/RC-Res.6-ENG.pdf

Rome Statute: for more detail, including ratification and implementation, see https://asp.icc-cpi.int/en_menus/asp/states%20parties/Pages/the%20states%20parties%20to%20the%20rome%20statute.aspx

Sabbatini RME (1998) *The Psychopath's Brain*, available at http://www.cerebromente.org.br/n07/doencas/disease_i.htm.

Schrock K (2009) Should parents spank their kids? *Scientific American* 33 (Jan/Feb 2010), available at http://www.scientificamerican.com/article/to-spank-or-not-to-spank/

Skelton A and Badenhorst C (2011) The criminal capacity of children in South Africa: International developments and considerations for review published by the Child Justice Alliance, available at http://www.childjustice.org.za/publications/criminalcapacity_SA.pdf

Sleepwalking: information taken from health-cares.net, available at http://neurology.health-cares.net/sleepwalking-causes.php

Sodomy: colonial-era laws against sodomy, available online for a comparative overview: http://www.consultancyafrica.com/index.php?option=com_content&view=article&id=472:colonial-sodomy-homophobic-threat-within-common-law&catid=91:rights-in-focus&Itemid=296

South African Human Rights Commission v Jonathan Dubula Qwelane [EQ44/2009 (EQ13/2012)] 18 Aug 2017, available at http://www.justice.gov.za/legislation/hcbill/Judgment-20170818-Qwelane.pdf

South Africa: Withdrawal of Notification of Withdrawal, 7 March 2017, C.N.121.2017. TREATIES-XVIII.10 (Depository Notification), available at https://treaties.un.org/doc/publication/CN.121.2017-Eng.pdf

South Africa withdrawing from the ICC: Kemp, G 'South Africa's (possible) withdrawal from the ICC and the future of the criminalization and prosecution of crimes against humanity, war crimes and genocide under domestic law: A submission informed by historical, normative and policy considerations' 16(3) *Wash U Global Stud L Rev* 411 (2017), available at https://openscholarship.wustl.edu/cgi/viewcontent.cgi?article=1624&context=law_globalstudies

S v Okah (CCT 315/16; CCT 193/17)[2018] ZACC 3, (23 February 2018), available at http://www.saflii.org/za/cases/ZACC/2018/3.html

Torture: for a view in support of the argument that, under certain circumstances, torture could be justified, see: http://blogs.spectator.co.uk/coffeehouse/2014/12/there-are-certain-times-when-torture-can-be-justified/

Transparency International Report, *The Anti-Corruption Plain Language Guide* (2009) 23, available at https://www.transparency.org/whatwedo/publication/the_anti_corruption_plain_language_guide

UN General Assembly protocols to supplement the Convention against Transnational Organized Crime: for signature and ratification status of these instruments, see http://www.unodc.org/unodc/en/treaties/CTOC/signatures.html, and https://treaties.un.org/pages/ViewDetails.aspx?src=TREATY&mtdsg_no=XVIII-12-a&chapter=18&clang=_en#EndDec

Van Schaak B and Slye RC (2007) *A Concise History of International Criminal Law: Chapter 1 of Understanding International Criminal Law* Santa Clara University Legal Studies Research Paper No. 07-42, 11 available at http://ssrn.com/abstract=1016152

Vicky Momberg case: 'The murky case of Vicky Momberg and *crimen injuria*' 29 March 2018, available at http://www.witsjusticeproject.co.za/news-and-insights-category/the-murky-case-of-vicki-momberg-and-crimen-injuria; 'Analysis: Why the Vicky Momberg racism sentence deserves scrutiny' 29 March 2018, available at https://www.dailymaverick.co.za/article/2018-03-29-analysis-why-the-vicki-momberg-racism-sentence-deserves-scrutiny/#.WsVHvn9x2JA; and 'IJR welcomes the sentencing of Vicky Momberg noting that more needs to be done to #RootOutRacism' 29 March 2018, available at https://www.ijr.org.za/2018/03/29/ijr-welcomes-the-sentencing-of-vicki-momberg-noting-that-more-needs-to-be-done-to-rootoutracism/

Waterhouse S (2007) Status of corporal punishment in the South African Children's Amendment Bill law reform process *Article* 19(3):1, available at http://communitylawcentre.org.za/projects/childrens-rights

List of journal abbreviations

Afr Hum Rts L J African Human Rights Law Journal
Acta Crim Acta Criminologica
Adel L Rev Adelaide Law Review
AJ Acta Juridica
Alta L R Alberta Law Review
Alt L J Alternative Law Journal
Am J Psychiatry American Journal of Psychiatry
Anglo-Am L Rev Anglo-American Law Review
Ann Surv S African L Annual Survey of South African Law
AVR Archiv des Völkerrechts
AYIHL African Yearbook on International Humanitarian Law
BC Int'l & Comp L Rev Boston College International & Comparative Law Review
Brit J Crim British Journal of Criminology
Brook L Rev Brooklyn Law Review
Cal L Rev California Law Review
CILSA Comparative and International Law Journal of Southern Africa
CLRJ Children's Legal Rights Journal
CLB Commonwealth Law Bulletin
Crim L R Criminal Law Review
Crim L F Criminal Law Forum
Crit Inq Critical Inquiry
Curr Legal Probs Current Legal Problems
EJIL European Journal of International Law
Finnish YBIL Finnish Yearbook of International Law
Fordham Intl L J Fordham International Law Journal
Fordham L Rev Fordham Law Review
Geo L J Georgetown Law Journal
GLJ German Law Journal
GYIL German Yearbook of International Law
Harv Hum Rts J Harvard Human Rights Journal
Harv Intl L J Harvard International Law Journal
ICLQ International and Comparative Law Quarterly
ILM International Legal Materials
Int'l Crim L Rev International Criminal Law Review
Int'l J Child Rts International Journal of Children's Rights
IRRC International Review of the Red Cross
Is L R Israel Law Review
J Afr L Journal of African Law
JCLC Journal of Criminal Law & Criminology
JHR Northwestern University Journal of International Human Rights Law
JICJ Journal of International Criminal Justice
LDD Law, Democracy and Development
Liberty U L Rev Liberty University Law Review
LJIL Leiden Journal of International Law
Loy L A L Rev Loyola of Los Angeles Law Review
Med & L Medicine & Law
Mod L Rev Modern Law review
NYU L Rev New York University Law Review
OSISA Open Society Initiative for Southern Africa
PELJ/PER Potchefstroom Electronic Law Journal/ Potchefstroomse Elektroniese Regsblad
SACQ South African Crime Quarterly
SAJBL South African Journal of Bioethics and Law
SACJ South African Journal of Criminal Justice
SAJHR South African Journal on Human Rights
SAJP South African Journal of Psychiatry
SALJ South African Law Journal
SAMJ South African Medical Journal
SAJHE South African Journal of Higher Education
SAYIL South African Yearbook of International Law
St. Louis-Warsaw Transatlantic L J St Louis-Warsaw Transatlantic Law Journal
Stell L R Stellenbosch Law Review
Temple Intl Comp L J Temple International and Comparative Law Journal
THRHR Tydskrif vir Hedendaagse Romeins-Hollandse Reg
TRW Tydskrif vir Regswetenskap
TSAR Journal of South African Law/Tydskrif vir die Suid-Afrikaanse Reg
Wash U Global Stud L Rev Washington University Global Studies Law Review
Yale J Intl L Yale Journal of International Law
Zaö R B Zeitschrift für Ausländisches Öffenliches Recht und Völkerrecht
ZSTW Zeitschrift für die gesamte Strafrechtswissenschaft

Table of cases

D

E

F

G

H

I

J

K

O

P

R

S

South African legislation & policy documents

C

E

F

G

H

I

FOREIGN LEGISLATION

INTERNATIONAL INSTRUMENTS AND DOCUMENTS

Glossary

abduction unlawfully taking a minor out of the control of her custodian with the intention of enabling someone to marry or have sexual intercourse with her

aberratio ictus (Latin) going astray of the blow, for example where A aims to hit B, but hits C instead

absolute liability for criminal liability, the normal fault and capacity elements are dispensed with, together with the normal requirements for unlawful conduct

accessory after the fact a person who intentionally associates himself with the crime only after its commission is complete

accident (*casus*) a chance occurrence, an unintended or unforeseen physical event in which something goes wrong unexpectedly

accomplice a person who intentionally furthers or assists in the commission of a crime at any time before or during its commission, but who is someone other than a perpetrator or a co-perpetrator

actio libera in causa **rule** (Latin) lack of free will in committing a crime

actus reus the criminal act

ad (Latin) towards

adjectival law also called procedural law; the procedures to enforce legal claims in civil or criminal law; its two main branches are the law of civil procedure and the law of criminal procedure

adultery voluntary sexual intercourse between a married person and someone other than the lawful spouse

affective functions emotional responses

affidavit a written statement that is sworn to or affirmed before a person legally recognised as a Commissioner of Oaths; it is written evidence and, therefore, the law of evidence applies to it; it is the primary means of placing evidence before a court in application proceedings

appeal a procedure whereby a judgment of a lower court is considered by a higher court to establish whether the lower court reached an incorrect decision due to an error of fact or law

appeal court a term used to refer to any higher court that is legally entitled to hear an appeal from another court

appellant the party appealing a matter to a higher court

Appellate Division (AD) the previous term for the highest court of appeal in South Africa; it has now been replaced by the Supreme Court of Appeal (SCA)

application the term used for court proceedings brought by a notice of motion supported by affidavits; oral applications may also be made by counsel from the bar at court

a quo (Latin) from which; for example, the court *a quo* – the court from which the decision came

arson the unlawful and intentional setting on fire of immovable property

assault also called common assault; the unlawful and intentional application of force to another or inspiring the belief of imminent force

assault with intent to do grievous bodily harm an assault accompanied by the intention of inflicting serious injury

audi alteram partem (Latin) hear the other side; it is a principle of our law that courts will not generally grant an order without hearing the version of the party against whom the order is sought

aut dedere aut judicare (Latin) extradite or prosecute

automatism the state of a person who, though capable of action, is not conscious of what he is doing; unconscious involuntary action

bail an amount of money, determined by the court, which must be paid by the accused as security for his due appearance in court on the dates on which his case is due to proceed

bar the part of the courtroom from where legal representatives present and argue their cases; the term used for the professional voluntary society (the Society of Advocates) to which most practising advocates belong, hence 'member of the Bar', and the English term for advocate, namely barrister, for example in England and Wales

bestiality the crime committed by a human male or female who intentionally and unlawfully has sexual relations, or engages in masturbation, with an animal

bigamy unlawfully and intentionally entering into what purports to be a lawful marriage ceremony with one person while being lawfully married to another

blackout a period in which a person temporarily loses consciousness or memory; an alcohol-induced blackout is where an individual suffers from amnesia after consuming large amounts of alcohol

blasphemy unlawfully, intentionally and publically acting contemptuously towards God

bona fide (Latin) in good faith

bribery the offering, giving, receiving or soliciting of something of value for the purpose of influencing the action of an official in the discharge of his or her public or legal duties; the crime is now subsumed in the statutory crime of corruption

canon law the body of laws and regulations made or adopted by an ecclesiastical authority for the government of the Christian organisation and its members

causation connecting conduct with a resulting effect, usually an injury

charge sheet (in lower courts) or indictment (in the divisions of the High Court); contains the state's allegations against the accused in a criminal trial

charged with in criminal procedure, an accused is charged with a crime or crimes; the charge contains the essential allegation that the accused has committed a certain crime or crimes

Chief Justice the head of the judiciary; presides over the Constitutional Court

child any person under 18 years of age

circumstantial evidence (as opposed to direct evidence); evidence of other facts, from which the court is asked to infer (draw a conclusion as to) the accused's guilt

coerced forced to do something; also, to act under duress (see also 'compulsion')

coercion forcing another party using threats or intimidation to behave in a certain manner

cognitive functions brain processes whereby a person becomes aware of, perceives or comprehends things

common law the law of the land created by custom and judicial decisions, but excluding that created by legislation (statutory law)

common purpose rule where two or more people associate together to commit a crime, each of them will be liable for the criminal conduct of the other falling within the scope of their common purpose; they will be regarded as co-perpetrators

compelled rape when one person forces another to sexually penetrate someone else against his or her will

competent verdict where the state has failed to prove that the accused has committed the charged offence, the person may be found guilty of another offence if the evidence is sufficient to prove the accused's guilt on that offence, provided that it is a competent verdict for the charged offence, for example an accused person charged with robbery may be convicted of theft

complainant the party that makes a complaint about the commission of an alleged crime

completed attempt a situation in which the would-be perpetrator has done everything that he or she set out to do, but failed to achieve his or her purpose either through lack of skill, sheer accident or for some other reason

compulsion being forced to do something

conative functions the aspect of mental processes or behaviour directed towards action or change, and including impulse, desire, volition and striving

condonation where a court excuses non-compliance with the Rules of Court

consanguinity a blood relationship or descent from a common ancestor

consequence crimes crimes defined not in terms of what the accused did or failed to do, but in terms of the consequences that resulted from his conduct; sometimes referred to as materially defined crimes, for example murder

conspiracy two or more persons agreeing to (1) commit, (2) assist in or (3) procure the commission of a crime

Constitution the Constitution of the Republic of South Africa, 1996 is the supreme law of South Africa

contemporaneity rule the *actus reus* and *mens rea* must coincide, that is, exist at the same time

contempt of court (Latin *ex facie curiae*) contempt of court outside the courtroom

contempt of court (Latin *in facie curiae*) when a person who is inside the court insults the presiding judicial officer (judge or magistrate) or otherwise misbehaves in a manner calculated to violate the dignity of the court or judicial officer while the court is engaged in its proceedings

co-perpetrator a person who assists another in the commission of a crime

corruption to accept any gratification from anybody else, or to give any gratification to anybody else, in order to influence the receiver to conduct him- or herself in such a way that amounts to the unlawful exercise of any duties

count in criminal procedure, an accused is charged with one count or multiple counts of a specified crime (for instance, one count of murder; three counts of fraud)

crime established common law crimes or statutory offences

crimen iniuria (Latin) unlawfully, intentionally and seriously impairing the *dignitas* of another

crimes against humanity a term first used in 1915 with reference to atrocities committed by Turkey against Armenians; these crimes are now defined in article 7 of the Rome Statute of the International Criminal Court, 1998 (see also Implementation of the Rome Statute of the International Criminal Court Act 27 of 2002)

criminal defamation the unlawful and intentional publication of matter that tends to injure the reputation of another

criminal defamation unlawful and intentional publication of matter that tends to injure the reputation of another

criminal intent conscious wrongdoing; the intention to perform the unlawful conduct, while knowing that such conduct is or may be a crime

criminal law the study of the principles of law that apply to criminal liability and the legal elements that constitute crimes

criminal procedure the framework of laws and rules that govern the administration of justice in cases involving an individual who has been accused of a crime, beginning with the initial investigation of the crime and concluding either with an acquittal following a judgment of not guilty, or a conviction following a judgment of guilty

criminology the study of crime and criminal behaviour

culpa (Latin) negligence

culpable homicide the unlawful, negligent causing of the death of a human being

de jure (Latin) according to law (or, on a point of law), as opposed to de facto (in fact)

de lege (Latin) in accordance with the law

de minimis non curat lex (Latin) the law does not concern itself with trifles

de novo (Latin) to start anew or afresh

defeating or obstructing the course of justice unlawfully and intentionally engaging in conduct that defeats or obstructs the course or administration of justice

defendant the party that defends a civil action; there may be more than one defendant

delict a civil wrong giving rise to a civil claim

dignitas (Latin) a person's right to dignity, encompassing self-respect, mental tranquility and privacy

diminished responsibility a potential defence by excuse in which defendants argue that although they broke the law, they should not be held fully criminally liable for doing so as their mental functions were diminished or impaired; see section 78(7) of the Criminal Procedure Act 51 of 1977

direct evidence evidence given by a witness who testifies as to the accused's guilt on the basis of what he or she personally saw, heard or otherwise perceived with his or her own senses

doctrine of common purpose where two or more people associate together to commit a crime, each of them will be liable for the criminal conduct of the other that falls within the scope of their common purpose

dolus (Latin) intention

dolus directus (Latin) direct intention; actual intention in the ordinary, everyday sense of the word

dolus eventualis (Latin) a legal device for inferring intention where intention is denied by the perpetrator; in circumstances where the court is satisfied that any person in his position would have foreseen the consequences of his actions, yet he nevertheless persisted, he is deemed to have intended those consequences

dolus indirectus (Latin) indirect intention; the situation in which the commission of the crime in question was not the accused's actual aim or objective, but he nevertheless foresaw it as a certain or virtually certain consequence of achieving that objective and persisted anyway

driving under the influence of alcohol or drugs an offence in violation of section 65(1) of the National Road Traffic Act 93 of 1996

drug trafficking a global illicit trade involving the cultivation, manufacture, distribution and sale of substances that are subject to drug prohibition laws

duress actual compulsion or the threat of compulsion

embezzlement also known as theft by conversion; X appropriates Y's property which is already in X's lawful possession

emotional stress also called severe emotional stress; a condition that occurs when a person is under stress that affects their emotions; may lead to reliance on the defence of non-pathological criminal incapacity

English common law uncodified body of legal principles developed in England; characterised by the prominent role of judges and precedent

ex facie (Latin) on the face of it

extortion the accused unlawfully and intentionally obtains some advantage, whether of a patrimonial nature or not, from the complainant by subjecting him to pressure that induces him to concede the advantage to the accused

extraterritorial jurisdiction the legal ability of a state to exercise authority beyond its normal borders

fault (see also: *mens rea*) in addition to (human) conduct, fault, or mental guilt, is also required for criminal liability in modern criminal law

forgery and uttering forgery; where X unlawfully makes a false document with the intent to defraud Y to Y's actual or potential prejudice; X commits the crime of uttering a false document when he unlawfully, and with intent to defraud, presents a false document to Y, to Y's actual or potential prejudice

fraud X unlawfully and intentionally makes a misrepresentation to Y causing prejudice, potential or otherwise, to Y

genocide the systematic and widespread extermination or attempted extermination of an entire national, racial, religious or ethnic group; see also the definition in article 6 of the Rome Statute of the International Criminal Court, 1998

Government Gazette the official government publication in which legal information relating to various functions of the government, as well as other information of an official and legal nature, is published; for example, Bills of Parliament that are to become law and regulations passed by ministers in terms of various laws

high treason a common law crime where a person who owes allegiance to the Republic of South Africa unlawfully engages in conduct aimed at overthrowing the government, coercing the government by violence, endangering the security of the country, or changing the constitutional structure of the republic

homicide the killing of one human being by another human being

hostis humanis generis (Latin) enemies of all mankind; often used in the context of crimes under international law such as slavery and piracy

housebreaking with intent to commit a crime X unlawfully and intentionally breaks into and enters a building with the intention to commit a crime such as theft

human trafficking the recruitment, transportation, transfer, harbouring or receipt of persons, by means of threat or use of force or other forms of coercion, of abduction, of fraud, of deception, of the abuse of power or of a position of vulnerability or of the giving or receiving of payments or benefits to achieve the consent of a person having control over another person, for the purpose of exploitation

ICC International Criminal Court

ignorantia iuris neminem excusat (Latin) ignorance of the law is no excuse

imputed is assigned to someone

in absentia (Latin) in the absence of (where the person concerned is not physically present)

in camera (Latin) the exclusion of the public or non-essential persons from court; can also mean 'in chambers' in some jurisdictions

in casu (Latin) in this case or matter, or in this instance

in chambers in the judge's office (usually referring to decisions made by the judge outside the courtroom)

in limine (Latin) at the outset of the case

incest committed by persons who may not lawfully marry each other on account of consanguinity, affinity or an adoptive relationship and who unlawfully and intentionally engage in an act of sexual penetration with mutual consent

inchoate (incomplete) crimes certain attempts at committing a crime even though no actual harm eventuates

infanticide the killing of a newborn child

inter alia (Latin) among other things

international criminal law a body of laws, norms and rules governing international crimes, as well as rules addressing conflict and cooperation between national criminal-law systems

intoxication a state in which a person's normal capacity to act or reason is inhibited by alcohol or drugs

justification a reason acceptable to a court as to why the defendant did what he is charged with having done and, as a result, he will not be criminally liable for the crime; sometimes used as a synonym for a criminal 'defence'

kidnapping unlawfully and intentionally depriving a person of liberty of movement or his custodians of control over the person concerned

leave of the court with permission of the court

legality the legal ideal that requires all law to be clear, ascertainable and non-retrospective

legislation statutes passed by an elected body, such as the National Assembly; also called codified law

liability also: no-fault liability; liability for the offence in question is based on unlawful conduct and criminal capacity, but strict no form of fault is required (i.e. neither intent nor negligence)

major (person); this term should no longer be used as the Age of Majority Act 57 of 1972 has been repealed: a child is a person who is below 18 years of age, and an adult is a person 18 years or older

mala fide (Latin) in bad faith

mala in se (Latin) things bad or wrong in themselves; applied to acts that are wrong by their own nature, being contrary to the laws of morality

mala prohibita (Latin) offences that are wrong simply because there are formal, codified rules prohibiting them; as distinguished from *mala in se*, *mala prohibita* are acts that are wrong not in themselves, but by virtue that they have been prohibited by law

malicious damage to property the unlawful and intentional damage caused to the property of another

malum in se (Latin) singular form of mala in se

malum prohibitum (Latin) singular form of mala prohibita

mens rea (Latin) criminal intention

minor (person); this term should no longer be used as the Age of Majority Act 57 of 1972 has been repealed: a child is a person who is below 18 years of age, and an adult is a person 18 years or older

mistake (error); a misapprehension, an erroneous (incorrect) impression or state of mind, possibly leading to inappropriate action being taken

money laundering the process of taking the proceeds of criminal activity and making them appear legal; allows criminals to transform illegally obtained gain into seemingly legal funds

murder the unlawful and intentional killing of a human being

negligence (*culpa*) (Latin) a failure to exercise the standard of behaviour that would be expected from a reasonable person in the circumstances of the case; also called the reasonable person test

negligent driving an objective test, namely whether a reasonable person, in the same circumstances, would have foreseen that a particular method of driving constituted a risk of harm to other persons using the road and would have guarded against that risk by desisting from driving in that manner or taking other appropriate avoiding action

neonaticide the killing of an infant within 24 hours of its birth; has yet to establish itself as a separate crime in South Africa

no-fault liability also: strict liability; liability for the offence in question is based on unlawful conduct and criminal capacity, but no form of fault is required (i.e. neither intent nor negligence)

non-pathological criminal incapacity see temporary non-pathological criminal incapacity

novus actus interveniens (Latin) new intervening act which breaks the chain of causation

null and void *ab initio* (Latin) of no force or effect from the beginning

nullum crimen sine lege, nulla poena sine lege (the principle of legality) (Latin) no crime without a law; a criminal law principle that holds that a person cannot face criminal punishment except for an act that was criminalised by law before he performed the act

offence a crime created in terms of a statute

omission the failure to perform an act

onus of proof the onus placed on a party by law and which that party must overcome to succeed in the case at hand

organised crime transnational, national or local groupings of highly centralised enterprises run by criminals for the purpose of engaging in unlawful activity

partial strict liability fault is not required in respect of a particular element (or elements) of the conduct underlying the criminal offence

partner in crime also: socius criminis (Latin); a person who participates in the commission of a crime with another person; they are considered equally liable

per se (Latin) as such or by itself

perjury making a false statement under oath or affirmation; it is a common law crime and has a statutory counterpart; see section 319(3) of the Criminal Procedure Act 56 of 1955

plead to the charge, normally 'guilty' or 'not guilty' – other technical pleadings are also possible

pleading in criminal procedure, the accused enters a pleading (normally guilty or not guilty) after hearing the charge; in the case of a plea of not guilty, the pleading will normally also contain an explanation of the defence

premeditation deciding in advance to follow a certain course of action

principle of legality see *nullum crimen sine lege*

prior positive conduct a person who, through his positive conduct, creates a situation (and sets in motion a chain of events) that poses a potential danger to other persons, attracts a legal duty to prevent that danger from materialising and causing harm to others

private defence covers a fairly broad category of defences, namely self-defence, defence of other persons and defence of property; refers to a situation in which a private individual, as opposed to a police officer or other public official, uses force or violence to defend his legal interests or those of another person

pro deo (Latin) for God; indicates a situation where a legal representative appears on behalf of a party for a (usually reduced) fee that is paid by the State

***proprio motu* prosecutions** a technical term associated with the powers of the Prosecutor of the International Criminal Court; where the Prosecutor initiates a prosecution

prosecute to charge a person with a crime by means of criminal legal proceedings with the objective of obtaining a conviction

prostitution section 11 of the Criminal Law (Sexual Offences and Related Matters) Amendment Act 32 of 2007 provides that: 'A person ('A') who unlawfully and intentionally engages the services of a person 18 years or older ('B'), for financial or other reward, favour or compensation to B or to a third person ('C'), for the purpose of engaging in a sexual act with B, irrespective of whether the sexual act is committed or not; or by committing a sexual act with B, is guilty of engaging the sexual services of a person 18 years or older'

protective relationship when one person has a protective relationship with another, then the former attracts a legal duty to protect the latter from harm; such a relationship may arise by virtue of family ties, contractual undertaking, by law, or some other conduct whereby the accused assumes such a duty, even if only on a temporary basis

public indecency a common law crime consisting of unlawfully, intentionally and publicly committing an act that tends to deprave the morals of others or that outrages the public's sense of decency and propriety

public policy the broader context within which the law is interpreted; reflective of public interest, also used to justify law reform and the adoption of new laws

public violence the unlawful and intentional commission, together with a number of people, of any act or acts that assume serious dimensions and which are intended forcibly to disturb public peace and tranquility or to invade the rights of others

putative justification a species of mistake of fact; they include putative private defence of person or property, putative necessity, putative impossibility, putative obedience to superior orders, putative public authority, putative consent, and so forth

qui facit per alium facit per se (Latin) he who acts through another, acts through himself

racketeering criminal activity that is performed to benefit an organisation such as a crime syndicate; it originated with the criminal practice of demanding 'protection payments' from legitimate businesses by criminal organisations such as the Mafia, hence the reference to this type of behaviour as a racket; see section 2 of the Prevention of Organised Crime Act 121 of 1998

rape section 3 of the Criminal Law (Sexual Offences and Related Matters) Amendment Act 32 of 2007 provides that 'any person who unlawfully and intentionally commits an act of sexual penetration with a complainant, without the consent of B, is guilty of the offence of rape'

rebuttable presumption an assumption made by a court, one that may be taken to be true unless contested by persuasive evidence

reckless driving to drive carelessly or thoughtlessly, rashly or inconsiderately, thereby creating a risk of harm to others

res sua (Latin) one's own property

robbery X steals Y's property through the intentional use of violence, or threats of violence, to induce Y to submit to the theft

Roman-Dutch law a legal system based on Roman law as applied in the Netherlands in the 17th and 18th centuries, and transported to the Cape of Good Hope in 1652; the South African common law developed through an intermingling of Roman-Dutch and English law principles

Rome Statute the Rome Statute of the International Criminal Court 1998 the treaty that established the International Criminal Court (ICC)

sane automatism a state of mind (that may support the defence of non-pathological criminal incapacity) where the accused temporarily loses conscious control of his actions as a result of the combined effects of overwhelming psychological factors, such as severe provocation

sedition overt conduct, such as speech and organisation, that is deemed by the legal authority to tend towards insurrection against the established order; 'a number of people who unlawfully act in concert to challenge the authority of the State by using violence or threats of violence'

sexual acts with a corpse section 14 of the Criminal Law (Sexual Offences and Related Matters) Amendment Act 32 of 2007 provides that a 'person who unlawfully and intentionally commits a sexual act with a human corpse, is guilty of the offence of committing a sexual act with a corpse'

sexual assault section 5 of the Criminal Law (Sexual Offences and Related Matters) Amendment Act 32 of 2007 provides that: '(1) A person ('A') who unlawfully and intentionally sexually violates a complainant ('B'), without the consent of B, is guilty of the offence of sexual assault; (2) A person ('A') who unlawfully and intentionally inspires the belief in a complainant ('B') that B will be sexually violated, is guilty of the offence of sexual assault'

sexual penetration section 1 of the Criminal Law (Sexual Offences and Related Matters) Amendment Act 32 of 2007 defines sexual penetration as including any act that causes penetration to any extent whatsoever by: '(a) the genital organs of one person into or beyond the genital organs, anus, or mouth of another person; (b) any other part of the body of one person or, any object, including any part of the body of an animal, into or beyond the genital organs or anus of another person; or (c) the genital organs of an animal, into or beyond the mouth of another person'

sine qua non (Latin) without which not; a description of a requisite or condition that is indispensable; known as the 'but for' rule

socius criminis (Latin) a partner or accomplice in the commission of a crime

special verdict where a court pronounces the accused 'not guilty by reason of mental illness'

statutory rape consensual sexual penetration with someone who is a child, as defined in section 15(1) of the Criminal Law (Sexual Offences and Related Matters) Amendment Act 32 of 2007

sub judice (Latin) under judgment; a particular case or matter is currently under trial or being considered by a judge or court

suicide the act of intentionally causing one's own death

summons a document informing an individual to appear in court

temporary non-pathological criminal incapacity the temporary mental inability on the part of the perpetrator to appreciate the wrongfulness of the conduct or to act in accordance with this appreciation; it is due to factors that cannot be ascribed to a pathological condition or mental illness

termination of a pregnancy commonly known as abortion; defined in the Choice of Termination of Pregnancy Act 92 of 1996 as the medical or surgical separation and expulsion of the contents of the pregnant uterus

theft X unlawfully and intentionally takes the property of Y, which is capable of being stolen, without Y's consent, and without the intention of returning it

torture the practice or act of deliberately inflicting severe pain or suffering and possibly injury on a person, through physical or psychological means

trafficking in human beings the illegal trade of human beings for the purposes of commercial sexual exploitation or reproductive slavery, forced labour or a modern-day form of slavery

treaty a formal agreement between two or more states in reference to peace, alliance, commerce or other international relations

true strict liability fault is not an element of the criminal offence at all

ukuthwala a customary form of abduction that was recognised as a legitimate modus of obtaining marriage

unauthorised borrowing section 1(1) of the General Law Amendment Act 50 of 1956 provides: 'Any person without a bona fide claim of right and without the consent of the owner or the person having control thereof, removes any property from the control of the owner or such person with the intent to use it for his own purposes without the consent of the owner or any other person competent to give such consent, whether or not he intends throughout to return the property to the owner or the person from whose control he removes it, shall, unless it is proved that such person, at the time of the removal, had reasonable grounds for believing that the owner or such other person would have consented to such use if he had known about it, be guilty of an offence and the court convicting him may impose upon him any penalty which may lawfully be imposed for theft'

Uniform Rules also known as the Uniform Rules of Court; the uniform set of rules applicable to all the High Courts in South Africa; each High Court also has its own set of rules, which are much less detailed than the Uniform Rules, and which deal with procedures specific to that particular court

universal jurisdiction enables national courts to prosecute serious human rights violations that were committed anywhere in the world

unlawfulness conduct that is in contravention of the law, as described by statute, or by applying the 'legal convictions of the community' test

uttering where X unlawfully makes a false document with the intent to defraud Y to Y's actual or potential prejudice; X commits the crime of uttering a false document when he unlawfully, and with intent to defraud, presents a false document to Y, to Y's actual or potential prejudice

verdict a court pronounces the accused 'guilty' (convicts the accused), or 'not guilty' (acquits the accused)

***versari in re illicita* rule** (Latin) a common law rule that holds that where a person is engaged in an illegal activity, he would be held criminally liable for all the consequences that he caused in the course of that activity regardless of whether those consequences were intended, foreseen or even foreseeable; this rule is no longer part of South African law

vicarious liability an employer or principal will be jointly liable for damages caused by the wrongful and negligent conduct of his employee or agent, that is, his 'representative', acting in the course and scope of his employment, or his authority as agent; the test for the vicarious liability of state employees is whether they were 'acting within the scope of their authority as servants of the state'

void having no legal force or effect; not legally binding or enforceable

voluntary conduct conduct where the actions of the accused were controlled by his conscious will in the sense that the accused was physically able to direct them, prevent them or stop them if he had chosen to do so

voluntary intoxication the voluntary consumption of intoxicating liquor or substances

war crimes the Rome Statute of the International Criminal Court, 1998 defines war crimes as, inter alia, 'serious violations of the laws and customs applicable in international armed conflict' and 'serious violations of the laws and customs applicable in an armed conflict not of an international character'; see article 8 of the Rome Statute

Index

Page numbers in *italics* refer to figures, diagrams or tables.